Fundamentals of Business Law

Fourth Edition

Roger LeRoy Miller
Institute for University Studies
Arlington, Texas

Gaylord A. Jentz
Herbert D. Kelleher Professor in Business Law
MSIS Department
University of Texas at Austin

WEST

WEST EDUCATIONAL PUBLISHING
An International Thomson Publishing Company

Publisher/Team Director: Jack Calhoun
Acquisitions Editor: Rob Dewey
Development Editor: Jan Lamar
Production Editor: Bill Stryker
Marketing Manager: Mike Worls
Cover Design: Doug Abbott
Internal Design: Bill Stryker

Library of Congress Cataloging-in-Publication Data
Fundamentals of business law / Roger LeRoy Miller, Gaylord A. Jentz. — 4th ed.
    p.   cm.
    Includes bibliographic references and index.
    ISBN 0–538–88657–9 (softcover: alk. paper)
    1. Business law — United States — Cases. 2. Commercial law — United States.
I. Jentz, Gaylord A.   II. Title
KF889.M53   1998
346.7307 — dc21

                                                    98–13273
                                                    CIP

456789   65432109′

Printed in the United States of America
I(T)P®

International Thomson Publishing
West Educational Publishing is an ITP Company.
The ITP trademark is used under license.

Contents in Brief

Contents

Preface

Now, more than ever before, a fundamental knowledge of the tenets of business law is crucial for anyone contemplating work in the world of business. Consequently, we have written *Fundamentals of Business Law,* Fourth Edition, with this goal in mind: to present a clear and comprehensive treatment of what every student should know about commercial law. While some of this law may change, the fundamentals never do—and that's what students reading this text will acquire.

A Flexible Teaching/Learning Package

We realize that different people have different teaching philosophies and learning goals. We believe that the Fourth Edition of *Fundamentals of Business Law* and its extensive supplements offer business law instructors a flexible teaching/learning package. For example, although we have attempted to make the materials flow from chapter to chapter, most of the chapters are self-contained. In other words, generally, you can use the chapters in any order you wish.

Additionally, the extensive number of supplements accompanying *Fundamentals of Business Law* allows instructors to choose those supplements that will most effectively complement classroom instruction. These supplementary materials (including printed supplements, software, and videos) all contribute to the goal of making *Fundamentals of Business Law* a flexible teaching/learning package.

A Special Case Format

In each chapter, we present cases that have been selected to illustrate the principles of law discussed in the text. The cases are numbered sequentially for easy referencing in class discussions, homework assignments, and examinations. In choosing the cases to be included in this edition, our goal has been to achieve a balance between classic cases and very recent ones.

Each case is presented in a special format, which begins with the case title and citation. The full citation includes the name of the court deciding the case, the date of the case, and the major parallel reporters in which the case can be found. For federal court cases, the appropriate court seal is also presented. For state court cases, the seal of the state is presented.

For those instructors who like to see the entire set of court opinions for the cases presented in the text in summarized form, we have created a book, called *Case Printouts for Fundamentals of Business Law.* This supplement contains the output from WESTLAW (without headnotes) for virtually every case that is included in each chapter. If the instructor wishes, the full set of opinions may be copied and handed out to students.

Basic Case Format

- *Facts.*
- *Issue.*
- *Decision.*
- *Reason.*

For Critical Analysis

Each case in this edition of *Fundamentals of Business Law* concludes with a section entitled *For Critical Analysis.* This section consists of a question that requires the student to think critically about a particular issue raised by the case. The section addresses the AACSB's curriculum requirements by focusing on how particular aspects of the dispute or the court's decision relate to ethical, international, technological, cultural, or other types of issues. Each *For Critical Analysis* section has a subtitle indicating the type of issue to which the question relates. For example, in one case, the subtitle may be *Ethical Consideration*; in another, *Political Consideration*; and so on.

▌ Other Special Pedagogical Devices

We have included in *Fundamentals of Business Law* a number of additional pedagogical devices, including those discussed below.

Special Pedagogical Devices in Each Chapter

- Chapter Objectives
- Exhibits and forms (almost one hundred).

Chapter-Ending Pedagogy

- *Terms and Concepts* (with appropriate page references).
- *Chapter Summary* (in graphic format with page references).
- *For Review* (a series of brief review questions).
- *Questions and Case Problems* (including hypothetical and case problems; many of the case problems are based on very recent cases).
- A *Question of Ethics* and *Social Responsibility.*
- *Case Briefing Assignment.*

Unit-Ending Cumulative Questions

New to the Fourth Edition are unit-ending cumulative questions. These questions appear at the end of the *Questions and Case Problems* section in the final chapter of the unit. Each of these questions introduces a hypothetical business firm and then asks a series of questions about how the law applies to various actions taken by the firm. To answer the questions, the student must apply the laws discussed throughout the unit. Suggested answers to the unit-ending cumulative questions are included in the *Answers Manual.*

Accessing the Internet: Fundamentals of Business Law

We have included another special new feature in *Fundamentals of Business Law*, Fourth Edition, called Accessing the Internet: Fundamentals of Business Law. These features which appear at the ends of nearly all of the chapters, indicate how you and your students can access materials relating to chapter topics via the Internet. Specific Internet addresses and "navigational" instructions are included in these features.

▌ Guide to Personal Law

To make sure that your students get a sense of how the law can affect them on a personal level, we have developed a Guide to Personal Law, which is placed at the end of the book, just following Chapter 31. We view this handbook as a practical guide to an application of the law to personal, financial, business, and consumer problems.

▌ Appendices

Because the majority of students keep their business law text as a reference source, we have included at the end of the book the following full set of appendices:

A. How to Brief a Case and Selected Cases.
B. The Constitution of the United States
C. The Uniform Commercial Code (Excerpts—Article 1, Article 2, Article 2A, the Revised Articles 3 and 4, Article 4A, and Article 9).
D. Spanish Equivalents for Important Legal Terms in English.

▌ Supplemental Teaching Materials

This edition of *Fundamentals of Business Law* is accompanied by a vastly expanded number of teaching and learning supplements. Individually and in conjunction with a number of our colleagues, we have developed supplementary teaching materials that we believe are the best available today. The supplement package includes the following components.

Printed Supplements

- *Instructor's Manual.*
- *Study Guide.*
- A comprehensive *Test Bank.*
- *Answers Manual.*
- *Case Printouts*
- *Handbook on Critical Thinking and Writing*
- *West's Advanced Topics and Contemporary Issues, Second Edition.*
- *Unrevised Articles 3 and 4 of the Uniform Commercial Code.*
- *Transparency Acetates.*
- *Handbook of Selected Statutes.*
- Regional Reporters.

Software and Video Supplements

- Computerized Test Bank (WESTEST).
- Interactive Software—Contracts and Sales.
- "You Be the Judge" software.
- "The Legal Tutor on Contracts" software.
- "The Legal Tutor on Sales" software.
- Case-Problem Cases on Diskette.
- WESTLAW.
- West's Business Law and the Legal Environment Audiocassette Library.
- Videocassettes (including videos on specific legal applications).

▌ A Special Note to Users of the Third Edition

We thought that those of you who have been using *Fundamentals of Business Law* would like to know some of the major changes that have been made for the Fourth Edition. The book is basically the same, but we think that we have improved it greatly, thanks in part to the many letters, telephone calls, and reviews that we have received.

Organizational Changes

- Courts and court procedures are now presented in Chapter 2 instead of Chapter 3.
- The ethics chapter now appears as Chapter 3, concluding the first unit of the text.
- More separate units have been created for conceptual clarity. For example, torts and crimes are now covered in Unit Two. Sales and lease contracts now appear in a separate unit (Unit Four) from negotiable instruments (covered in Unit Five) and debtor-creditor relationships (covered in Unit Six).

New or Significantly Revised Chapters

- Chapter 1 (Sources of Business Law and the Global Legal Environment)—The material covered in this chapter has been revised and streamlined to make the text flow more smoothly. More coverage is given to classifications of law.
- Chapter 3 (Ethics and Social Responsibility)—This chapter, which appeared as Chapter 2 in the Third Edition, has been revised extensively. Many sections have been rewritten to reflect today's business environment and current ethical challenges. The discussion of corporate social responsibility is given a more real-world flavor by applying the concepts discussed to a hypothetical business firm. The section on measuring social responsibility has been completely rewritten to reflect today's increased emphasis on corporate process as an important "yardstick" for measuring corporate responsibility,
- Chapter 5 (Business Torts, Intellectual Property, and Cyberlaw)—This chapter includes greater coverage of electronic torts, including the electronic infringement of ownership rights in intellectual property (via the Internet, for example).
- Chapter 6 (Criminal Law)—This chapter now includes an exhibit showing the ways in which criminal law differs from civil law and a new section discussing the federal sentencing guidelines.
- Chapter 13 (The Formation of Sales and Lease Contracts)—This chapter now includes lease contracts and references to Article 2A of the Uniform Commercial Code (UCC). Additionally, a specific section has been added on the provisions of the

United Nations Convention on Contracts for the International Sale of Goods (CISG). The section compares the provisions of the UCC with those of the CISG with respect to specific requirements of sales contracts. The remaining chapters in the sales unit (Chapters 14 through 16) also include coverage of lease contracts.

• Chapter 15 (Performance and Breach of Sales and Lease Contracts)—This chapter has been reorganized to enhance readability. The remedies of the seller or lessor and the buyer or lessee are now grouped according to which party has possession of the goods at the time of the breach.

• Chapter 16 (Warranties and Product Liability)—This chapter includes more detail on actions in strict product liability.

• Chapter 17 (Negotiability, Transferability, and Liability)—This chapter and the subsequent chapter on negotiable instruments have been revised and rewritten as necessary so that the law discussed is based on the 1990 revision of Articles 3 and 4 of the UCC. Major differences between the revised and unrevised versions of these articles are indicated in footnotes.

• Chapter 19 (Checks and the Banking System)—This chapter now includes a discussion of the electronic check presentment and the electronic processing of checks.

• Chapter 20 (Creditors' Rights and Bankruptcy)—The section on bankruptcy has been revised to enhance understanding and to conform with the current Bankruptcy Code, as amended by the 1994 Bankruptcy Reform Act.

• Chapter 22 (Employment Law)—For the Fourth Edition we have added coverage of employment laws. Chapter 22 contains coverage of labor law, the Family and Medical Leave Act of 1993, and the major laws prohibiting employment discrimination.

• Chapter 23 (Sole Proprietorships, Partnerships, and Limited Liability Companies)—This chapter now includes sections on limited liability companies (LLCs) and limited liability partnerships (LLPs). Additionally, we have added footnote references to provisions of the Revised Uniform Partnership Act (RUPA) whenever the RUPA significantly changes or modifies an aspect of partnership law being discussed in the text.

• Chapter 25 (Corporate Directors, Officers, and Shareholders)—This chapter now contains a discussion of shareholder proposals in proxy materials.

• Chapter 27 (Investor Protection)—This chapter has been updated throughout, and the section on exemptions to registration requirements under the 1933 Securities Act has been rewritten to reflect current law. The chapter also looks at the current impact of the 1995 Private Securities Litigation Reform Act.

• Chapter 31 (Professional Liability)— For this edition, we have added a chapter on the liability of professionals, particularly accountants. This chapter covers common law grounds, as well as statutory bases, for accountants' liability.

What Else Is New?

In addition to the changes noted above, you will find a number of other new items or features in *Fundamentals of Business Law*, Fourth Edition, as listed below:

NEW FEATURES The following features are new to the Fourth Edition:

• *For Critical Analysis* questions concluding every case.
• Accessing the Internet: Fundamentals of Business Law.
• Unit-ending cumulative questions.

NEW EXHIBITS We have modified exhibits contained in the Third Edition of *Fundamentals of Business Law* whenever necessary to achieve greater clarity or accuracy. In addition, the following entirely new exhibits have been added for the Fourth Edition.

• The Legal Systems of Nations (Exhibit 1–1).
• Federal Courts and State Court Systems (Exhibit 2–2).
• Tort Lawsuit and Criminal Prosecution for the Same Act (Exhibit 4–1).
• Civil and Criminal Law Compared (Exhibit 6–1).
• The Check Collection Process (Exhibit 18–6).
• Terminology of Takeover Defenses (Exhibit 27–3).
• Exemptions under the 1933 Securities Act (Exhibit 27–1).
• A Sample Restricted Stock Certificate (Exhibit 27–2).
• A Sample Will (Exhibit 30–3).

NEW CASES AND CASE PROBLEMS There are approximately 100 new cases and 75 new case problems. Additionally, there are several new hypothetical questions, ethical questions, case briefing assignments, and questions "For Critical Analysis." Of course, all of the unit-ending hypothetical questions are new.

NEW APPENDIX MATERIAL

• Appendix C (The Uniform Commercial Code—Excerpts) now includes Article 2A on leases and the revised versions of Articles 3 and 4.

NEW SUPPLEMENTS

• *The Unrevised Articles 3 and 4 of the Uniform Commercial Code.*
• *Handbook of Selected Statutes.*

▌Acknowledgments

Kenneth Anderson
Mott Community College

Janie Blankenship
Del Mar College

Len Callahan
Embry-Riddle Aeronautical University

Philip E. De Marco
Mission College

Carol Docan
California State University, Northridge

James T. Foster
Florence Darlington Technical College

Frank Giesber
Texas Lutheran University

Thomas F. Goldman
Bucks County Community College

Daniel A. Levin
University of Colorado, Boulder

John F. Mastriani
El Paso Community College

Steven M. Platau
The University of Tampa

Lee Ruck
George Mason University

Alan L. Weldy
Goshen College

John O. Wheeler
University of Virginia

Paula York
Northern Maine Technical College

We wish to thank William Eric Hollowell for his masterful editing and proofing throughout all phases of this project. We, of course, must thank our editor, Rob Dewey. We also wish to thank Jan Lamar for supervising the development and production of many of the teaching supplements for this text. Additionally, we are indebted to Bill Stryker and Ann Rudrud for their superb production job. Finally, we wish to thank Suzanne Jasin and Roxy Lee for all of their efforts relating to the project.

If you have comments or criticism—whether you are a student or an instructor—we welcome them. We have been able to use your comments to improve this text, and wish to continue doing so for many years to come.

Roger LeRoy Miller
Gaylord A. Jentz

DEDICATION

To Paul Deakin,
Your hard work has paid off,
you deserve all of the success
that you're now receiving.
I hope to watch you play for
the next 50 years.

R.L.M.

I dedicate this edition to my wife, JoAnn;
my children, Kathy, Gary, Lori, and
Rory; and my grandchildren, Erin Marie,
Megan Kathleen, Eric Edward, Emily
Elizabeth, and Michelle Katherine.

G.A.J.

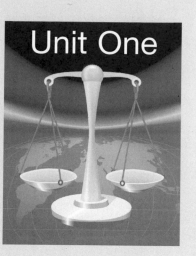

Unit One

The Legal Environment of Business

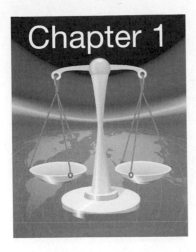

Chapter 1

Sources of Business Law and the Global Legal Environment

CHAPTER OBJECTIVES

After reading this chapter, you should be able to:

1. Explain what is generally meant by the term *law*.
2. Describe the origins and importance of the common *law* tradition.
3. Identify the four major sources of American law.
4. List some important classifications of law.
5. Distinguish between national law and international law.
6. Give some examples of how the Bill of Rights affects business.

Law is of interest to all persons, not just to lawyers. Those entering the world of business will find themselves subject to numerous laws and government regulations. A basic knowledge of these laws and regulations is beneficial—if not essential—to anyone contemplating a successful career in the business world of today.

In this introductory chapter, we first look at the nature of law and at some concepts that have significantly influenced how jurists and scholars view the nature and function of law. We then examine the common law tradition of the United States, as well as some of the major sources and classifications of American law. The chapter concludes with a discussion of the global legal environment, which frames many of today's business transactions.

▋ The Nature of Law

There have been and will continue to be different definitions of *law*. The Greek philosopher Aristotle

(384–322 B.C.E.) saw law as a "pledge that citizens of a state will do justice to one another." Aristotle's mentor, Plato (427–347 B.C.E.), believed that law was a form of social control. The Roman orator and politician Cicero (106–43 B.C.E.) contended that law was the agreement of reason and nature, the distinction between the just and the unjust. The British jurist Sir William Blackstone (1723–1780) described law as "a rule of civil conduct prescribed by the supreme power in a state, commanding what is right, and prohibiting what is wrong." In America, the eminent jurist Oliver Wendell Holmes, Jr. (1841–1935), contended that law was a set of rules that allowed one to predict how a court would resolve a particular dispute—"the prophecies of what the courts will do in fact, and nothing more pretentious, are what I mean by the law."

Although these definitions vary in their particulars, they all are based on the following general observation: **law** consists of enforceable rules governing relationships among individuals and between individuals and their society. In the study of law, often referred to as **jurisprudence**, this very broad statement concerning the nature of law is the point of departure for all legal scholars and philosophers.

▌ The Common Law Tradition

How jurists view the law is particularly important in a legal system in which judges play a paramount role, as they do in the American legal system. Because of our colonial heritage, much of American law is based on the English legal system. A knowledge of this tradition is necessary to an understanding of the nature of our legal system today.

Early English Courts of Law

In 1066, after the Normans conquered England, William the Conqueror and his successors began the process of unifying the country under their rule. One of the means they used to this end was the establishment of the king's courts, or *curiae regis*. Before the Norman Conquest, disputes had been settled according to the local legal customs and traditions in various regions of the country. The king's courts sought to establish a uniform set of rules for the country as a whole. What evolved in these courts was the beginning of the **common law**—a body of general rules that prescribed social conduct and that was applied throughout the entire English realm.

Courts developed the common law rules from the principles underlying judges' decisions in actual legal controversies. Judges attempted to be consistent, and whenever possible, they based their decisions on the principles suggested by earlier cases. They sought to decide similar cases in a similar way and considered new cases with care, because they knew that their decisions would make new law. Each interpretation became part of the law on the subject and served as a legal **precedent**—that is, a decision that furnished an example or authority for deciding subsequent cases involving similar legal principles or facts.

In the early years of the common law, there was no single place or publication in which court opinions, or written decisions, could be found. In the late thirteenth and early fourteenth centuries, however, portions of the more important decisions of each year were gathered together and recorded in *Year Books*. The *Year Books* were useful references for lawyers and judges. In the sixteenth century, the *Year Books* were discontinued, and other reports of cases became available. (How cases are reported, or published, in the United States today is discussed later in this chapter.)

Stare Decisis

The practice of deciding new cases with reference to former decisions, or precedents, eventually became a cornerstone of the English and American judicial systems. The practice forms a doctrine called *stare decisis*[1] ("to stand on decided cases"). Under this doctrine, judges are obligated to follow the precedents established within their jurisdictions. For example, if the Supreme Court of California (that state's highest court) has ruled in a certain way on an issue, that decision will control the outcome of future cases on that issue brought before the state courts in California. Similarly, a decision on a given issue by the United States Supreme Court (the nation's highest court) is binding on all inferior courts. Controlling precedents in a jurisdiction are referred to as **binding authorities,** as are statutes or other laws that must be followed.

The doctrine of *stare decisis* helps the courts to be more efficient, because if other courts have carefully reasoned through a similar case, their legal reasoning and opinions can serve as guides. *Stare decisis* also makes the law more stable and predictable. If the law on a given subject is well settled, someone bringing a case to court can usually rely on the court to make a decision based on what the law has been.

DEPARTURES FROM PRECEDENT Sometimes a court will depart from the rule of precedent if it decides that a given precedent should no longer be followed. If a court decides that a precedent is simply incorrect or that technological or social changes have rendered the precedent inapplicable, the court might rule contrary to the precedent.

Cases that overturn precedent often receive a great deal of publicity. In *Brown v. Board of*

---

1. Pronounced *ster*-ay dih-*si*-ses.

Education of Topeka,[2] for example, the United States Supreme Court expressly overturned precedent when it concluded that separate educational facilities for whites and blacks, which had been upheld as constitutional in numerous previous cases,[3] were inherently unequal. The Supreme Court's departure from precedent in *Brown* received a tremendous amount of publicity as people began to realize the ramifications of this change in the law.

WHEN THERE IS NO PRECEDENT Sometimes there is no precedent within a jurisdiction on which to base a decision, or there are conflicting precedents. A court then may look to precedents set in other jurisdictions for guidance. Such precedents, because they are not binding on the court, are referred to as **persuasive authorities.** A court may also consider a number of factors, including legal principles and policies underlying previous court decisions or existing statutes, fairness, social values and customs, public policy, and data and concepts drawn from the social sciences.

Which of these sources is chosen or receives the greatest emphasis will depend on the nature of the case being considered and the particular judge hearing the case. Although judges always strive to be free of subjectivity and personal bias in deciding cases, each judge has his or her own unique personality, set of values or philosophical leanings, and intellectual attributes—all of which necessarily frame the judicial decision-making process.

Equitable Remedies and Courts of Equity

In law, a **remedy** is the means given to a party to enforce a right or to compensate for the violation of a right. For example, suppose that Shem is injured because of Rowan's wrongdoing. A court may order Rowan to compensate Shem for the harm by paying Shem a certain amount of money.

In the early king's courts of England, the kinds of remedies that could be granted were severely restricted. If one person wronged another, the king's courts could award as compensation either

money or property, including land. These courts became known as *courts of law,* and the remedies were called *remedies at law.* Even though this system introduced uniformity in the settling of disputes, when plaintiffs wanted a remedy other than economic compensation, the courts of law could do nothing, so "no remedy, no right."

REMEDIES IN EQUITY Equity is that branch of unwritten law, founded in justice and fair dealing, that seeks to supply a fairer and more adequate remedy than any remedy available at law. In medieval England, when individuals could not obtain an adequate remedy in a court of law, they petitioned the king for relief. Most of these petitions were decided by an adviser to the king called the *chancellor.* The chancellor was said to be the "keeper of the king's conscience." When the chancellor thought that the claim was a fair one, new and unique remedies were granted. In this way, a new body of rules and remedies came into being, and eventually formal *chancery courts,* or *courts of equity,* were established. The remedies granted by these courts were called *remedies in equity.* Thus, two distinct court systems were created, each having a different set of judges and a different set of remedies.

Plaintiffs (those bringing lawsuits) had to specify whether they were bringing an "action at law" or an "action in equity," and they chose their courts accordingly. For example, a plaintiff might ask a court of equity to order a **defendant** (a person against whom a lawsuit is brought) to perform within the terms of a contract. A court of law could not issue such an order, because its remedies were limited to payment of money or property as compensation for damages. A court of equity, however, could issue a decree for *specific performance*—an order to perform what was promised. A court of equity could also issue an *injunction,* directing a party to do or refrain from doing a particular act. In certain cases, a court of equity could allow for the *rescission* (cancellation) of the contract so that the parties would be returned to the positions that they held prior to the contract's formation. Equitable remedies will be discussed in greater detail in Chapter 12.

THE MERGING OF LAW AND EQUITY Today, in most states, the courts of law and equity are merged, and thus the distinction between the two courts has largely disappeared. A plaintiff may now

---

2.   347 U.S. 483, 74 S.Ct. 686, 98 L.Ed. 873 (1954). (See the appendix at the end of this chapter for an explanation of how to read legal citations.)

3.   See *Plessy v. Ferguson,* 163 U.S. 537, 16 S.Ct. 1138, 41 L.Ed. 256 (1896).

request both legal and equitable remedies in the same action, and the trial court judge may grant either form—or both forms—of relief. The merging of law and equity, however, does not diminish the importance of distinguishing legal remedies from equitable remedies. To request the proper remedy, one must know what remedies are available for the specific kinds of harms suffered. Today, as a rule, courts will grant an equitable remedy only when the remedy at law (money damages) is inadequate.

▌Sources of American Law

There are numerous sources of American law. **Primary sources of law,** or sources that *establish* the law, include the following:

● The U.S. Constitution and the constitutions of the various states.
● Statutes, or laws, passed by Congress and by state legislatures.
● Regulations created by administrative agencies, such as the federal Food and Drug Administration.
● Case law (court decisions).

We describe each of these important primary sources of law in the following pages.

Secondary sources of law are books and articles that summarize and clarify the primary sources of law. Examples are legal encyclopedias, treatises, articles in law reviews published by law schools, or other legal journals. Courts often refer to secondary sources of law for guidance in interpreting and applying the primary sources of law discussed here.

Constitutional Law

The federal government and the states have separate written constitutions that set forth the general organization, powers, and limits of their respective governments. **Constitutional law** is the law as expressed in these constitutions.

The U.S. Constitution is the supreme law of the land. As such, it is the basis of all law in the United States. A law in violation of the Constitution, no matter what its source, will be declared unconstitutional and will not be enforced. Because of its paramount importance in the American legal system,

we discuss the Constitution at length later in this chapter and present the complete text of the U.S. Constitution in Appendix B.

The Tenth Amendment to the U.S. Constitution, which defines the powers and limitations of the federal government, reserves all powers not granted to the federal government to the states. Each state in the union has its own constitution. Unless they conflict with the U.S. Constitution or a federal law, state constitutions are supreme within their respective borders.

Statutory Law

Statutes enacted by legislative bodies at any level of government make up another source of law, which is generally referred to as **statutory law.**

FEDERAL STATUTES Federal statutes are laws that are enacted by the U.S. Congress. As mentioned, any law—including a federal statute—that violates the U.S. Constitution will be held unconstitutional.

Examples of federal statutes that affect business operations include laws regulating the purchase and sale of securities, or corporate stocks and bonds (discussed in Chapter 27); consumer protection statutes, and statutes prohibiting employment discrimination (discussed in Chapter 22). Whenever a particular statute is mentioned in this text, we usually provide a footnote showing its **citation** (a reference to a publication in which a legal authority—such as a statute or a court decision—or other source can be found). In the appendix following this chapter, we explain how you can use these citations to find statutory law.

STATE AND LOCAL STATUTES AND ORDINANCES State statutes are laws enacted by state legislatures. Any state law that conflicts with the U.S. Constitution, with federal laws enacted by Congress, or with the state's constitution will be deemed unconstitutional. Statutory law also includes the ordinances passed by cities and counties, none of which can violate the U.S. Constitution, the relevant state constitution, or federal or state laws.

Examples of state statutes include state criminal statutes (discussed in Chapter 6), state corporation statutes (discussed in Chapters 24 through 27), state deceptive trade practices acts, state laws governing wills and trusts (discussed in Chapter

30), and state versions of the Uniform Commercial Code (to be discussed shortly). Examples of local ordinances include zoning ordinances and local laws regulating housing construction and such things as the overall appearance of a community.

A federal statute, of course, applies to all states. A state statute, in contrast, applies only within the state's borders. State laws thus vary from state to state.

UNIFORM LAWS   The differences among state laws were particularly notable in the 1800s, when conflicting state statutes frequently made the rapidly developing trade and commerce among the states very difficult. To counter these problems, a group of legal scholars and lawyers formed the National Conference of Commissioners (NCC) on Uniform State Laws in 1892 to draft uniform statutes for adoption by the states. The NCC still exists today and continues to issue uniform statutes.

Adoption of a uniform law is a state matter, and a state may reject all or part of the statute or rewrite it as the state legislature wishes. Hence, even when a uniform law is said to have been adopted in many states, those states' laws may not be entirely "uniform." Once adopted by a state legislature, a uniform act becomes a part of the statutory law of that state.

The earliest uniform law, the Uniform Negotiable Instruments Law, was completed by 1896 and was adopted in every state by the early 1920s (although not all states used exactly the same wording). Over the following decades, other acts were drawn up in a similar manner. In all, over two hundred uniform acts have been issued by the NCC since its inception. The most ambitious uniform act of all, however, was the Uniform Commercial Code.

THE UNIFORM COMMERCIAL CODE (UCC)   The Uniform Commercial Code (UCC), which was created through the joint efforts of the NCC and the American Law Institute,[4] was first issued in 1952. The UCC has been adopted in all fifty states,[5] the District of Columbia, and the Virgin Islands. The UCC facilitates commerce among the states by providing a uniform, yet flexible, set of rules governing commercial transactions. The UCC assures businesspersons that their contracts, if validly entered into, normally will be enforced.

Because of its importance in the area of commercial law, we cite the UCC frequently in this text. We also present excerpts from the latest version of the UCC in Appendix C.

Administrative Law

An important source of American law consists of administrative law—the rules, orders, and decisions of administrative agencies. An administrative agency is a federal, state, or local government agency established to perform a specific function. Rules issued by various administrative agencies now affect virtually every aspect of a business's operation, including the firm's capital structure and financing, its hiring and firing procedures, its relations with employees and unions, and the way it manufactures and markets its products.

At the national level, numerous executive agencies exist within the cabinet departments of the executive branch. The Food and Drug Administration, for example, is within the Department of Health and Human Services. Executive agencies are subject to the authority of the president, who has the power to appoint and remove officers of federal agencies. There are also major independent regulatory agencies at the federal level, such as the Federal Trade Commission, the Securities and Exchange Commission, and the Federal Communications Commission. The president's power is less pronounced in regard to independent agencies, whose officers serve for fixed terms and cannot be removed without just cause.

There are administrative agencies at the state and local levels as well. Commonly, a state agency (such as a state pollution-control agency) is created as a parallel to a federal agency (such as the Environmental Protection Agency). Just as federal statutes take precedence over conflicting state statutes, so do federal agency regulations take precedence over conflicting state regulations. Because the rules of state and local agencies vary widely, we focus here exclusively on federal administrative law. Because Congress cannot possibly oversee the actual implementation of all the laws it enacts, it must delegate such tasks to others, partic-

---

4.   This institute was formed in the 1920s and consists of practicing attorneys, legal scholars, and judges.
5.   Louisiana has adopted only Articles 1, 3, 4, 5, 7, 8, and 9.

ularly when the issues relate to highly technical areas, such as air and water pollution. By delegating some of its constitutional authority to make and implement laws to agencies, Congress is able to monitor indirectly a particular area in which it has passed legislation without becoming bogged down in the many details relating to enforcement—details that are often best left to specialists.

Congress creates an administrative agency by enacting **enabling legislation**, which specifies the name, composition, purpose, and powers of the agency being created. For example, the Federal Trade Commission (FTC) was created in 1914 by the Federal Trade Commission Act.[6] This act prohibits unfair and deceptive trade practices. It also describes the procedures the agency must follow to charge persons or organizations with violations of the act, and it provides for judicial review (review by the courts) of agency orders. Other portions of the act grant the agency powers to "make rules and regulations for the purpose of carrying out the Act," to conduct investigations of business practices, to obtain reports from interstate corporations concerning their business practices, to investigate possible violations of the act, to publish findings of its investigations, and to recommend new legislation. The act also empowers the FTC to hold trial-like hearings and to **adjudicate** (resolve judicially) certain kinds of trade disputes that involve FTC regulations.

Note that the FTC's grant of power incorporates functions associated with the legislative branch of government (rulemaking), the executive branch (investigation and enforcement), and the judicial branch (adjudication). Taken together, these functions constitute what has been termed **administrative process,** which is the administration of law by administrative agencies.

Case Law and Common Law Doctrines

The body of law that was first developed in England and that is still used today in the United States consists of the rules of law announced in court decisions. These rules of law include interpretations of constitutional provisions, of statutes enacted by legislatures, and of regulations created by administrative agencies. Today, this body of law is referred to variously as the common law, judge-made law, or **case law.**

The common law—the doctrines and principles embodied in case law—governs all areas not covered by statutory law (or agency regulations issued to implement various statutes). In disputes concerning contracts for the sale of goods, for example, the Uniform Commercial Code (statutory law) applies instead of the common law of contracts. Similarly, in a dispute concerning a particular employment practice, if a statute regulates that practice, the statute will apply rather than the common law doctrine that applied prior to the enactment of the statute.

THE RELATIONSHIP BETWEEN THE COMMON LAW AND STATUTORY LAW The body of statutory law has expanded greatly since the beginning of this nation, and this expansion has resulted in a proportionate reduction in the scope and applicability of common law doctrines. Nonetheless, there is a significant overlap between statutory law and case law, and thus common law doctrines remain a significant source of legal authority.

For example, many statutes essentially codify existing common law rules, and thus the courts, in interpreting the statutes, often rely on the common law as a guide to what the legislators intended. Additionally, how the courts interpret a particular statute determines how that statute will be applied. If you wanted to learn about the coverage and applicability of a particular statute, for example, you would, of course, need to locate the statute and study it. You would also need to see how the courts in your jurisdiction have interpreted the statute—in other words, what precedents have been established in regard to that statute. Often, the applicability of a newly enacted statute does not become clear until a body of case law develops to clarify how, when, and to whom the statute applies.

RESTATEMENTS OF THE LAW The American Law Institute drafted and published compilations of the common law called Restatements of the Law, which generally summarize the common law rules followed by most states. There are Restatements of the Law in the areas of contracts, torts, agency, trusts, property, restitution, security, judgments, and conflict of laws. The Restatements, like other secondary sources of law, do not in themselves have the force of law but are an important source

---

6. 15 U.S.C. Sections 45–58.

of legal analysis and opinion on which judges often rely in making their decisions.

Many of the Restatements are now in their second or third editions. We refer to the Restatements frequently in subsequent chapters of this text, indicating in parentheses the edition to which we are referring. For example, we refer to the second edition of the *Restatement of the Law of Contracts* simply as the *Restatement (Second) of Contracts.*

▮ Classifications of Law

The huge body of the law may be broken down according to several classification systems. For example, one classification system divides law into **substantive law** (all laws that define, describe, regulate, and create legal rights and obligations) and **procedural law** (all laws that establish the methods of enforcing the rights established by substantive law).

Another classification system divides law into civil law and criminal law. **Civil law** spells out the rights and duties that exist between persons and between persons and their governments, and the relief available when a person's rights are violated. Contract law, for example, is part of civil law. The whole body of tort law (see Chapters 4 and 5), which deals with the infringement by one person on the legally recognized rights of another, is also an area of civil law. **Criminal law** has to do with a wrong committed against society for which society demands redress (see Chapter 6). Criminal acts are proscribed by local, state, or federal government statutes.

Other classification systems divide law into federal law and state law, private law (dealing with relationships between persons) and public law (addressing the relationship between persons and their government), and so on. One of the broadest classification systems divides law into national law and international law, a topic to which we now turn.

▮ National and International Law

Although the focus of this book is U.S. business law, increasingly businesspersons in this country are engaging in transactions that extend beyond our national borders. In these situations, the laws of other nations or the laws governing relationships among nations may come into play. For this reason, those who pursue a career in business today should have an understanding of the global legal environment.

We examine the laws governing international business transactions in later chapters (including parts of Chapters 13 through 15, which cover contracts for the sale of goods). It is worthwhile at this point, however, to summarize some important aspects of the international legal environment, because many of the topics covered in this text have international dimensions.

National Law

National law is the law of a particular nation, such as the United States or France. National law, of course, varies from country to country, because each country's law reflects the interests, customs, activities, and values that are unique to that nation's culture. Even though the laws and legal systems of various countries differ substantially, broad similarities do exist.

Basically, there are two legal systems in today's world. One of these systems is the common law system of England and the United States, which we have already discussed. The other system is based on Roman civil law, or "code law." The term *civil law,* as used here, refers not to civil as opposed to criminal law but to *codified* law—an ordered grouping of legal principles enacted into law by a legislature or governing body. In a **civil law system,** the primary source of law is a statutory code, and case precedents are not judicially binding, as they normally are in a common law system. Although judges in a civil law system commonly refer to previous decisions as sources of legal guidance, they are not bound by precedent; in other words, the doctrine of *stare decisis* does not apply.

Generally, those countries that were once colonies of Great Britain retained their English common law heritage after they achieved their independence. Similarly, the civil law system, which is followed in most of the continental European countries, was retained in the Latin American, African, and Asian countries that were once colonies of the continental European nations. Japan and South Africa also have civil law systems, and ingredients of the civil law system are found in the Islamic courts of predominantly Muslim countries. In the United States, the state of Louisiana, because of its historical ties to France, has in part a civil law system. The legal systems of Puerto Rico, Québec, and Scotland are similarly characterized as having elements of the civil law system.

International Law

International law can be defined as a body of written and unwritten laws observed by independent nations and governing the acts of individuals as well as governments. The key difference between national law and international law is the fact that national law can be enforced by government authorities. What government, though, can enforce international law? By definition, a *nation* is a sovereign entity, which means that there is no higher authority to which that nation must submit. If a nation violates an international law, the most that other countries or international organizations can do (if persuasive tactics fail) is resort to coercive actions against the violating nation. Coercive actions range from severance of diplomatic relations and boycotts to, at the last resort, war.

In essence, international law is the result of centuries-old attempts to reconcile the traditional need of each nation to be the final authority over its own affairs with the desire of nations to benefit economically from trade and harmonious relations with one another. Although no sovereign nation can be compelled to obey a law external to itself, nations can and do voluntarily agree to be governed in certain respects by international law for the purpose of facilitating international trade and commerce, as well as civilized discourse.

International law is an intermingling of rules and constraints derived from a variety of sources. The laws of individual nations are sources of international law, as are the customs that have evolved among nations in their relations with one another. Of increasing importance in regulating international activities, however, are treaties and international organizations.

TREATIES   A **treaty** is an agreement between two or more nations that creates rights and duties binding on the parties to the treaty, just as a private contract creates rights and duties binding on the parties to the contract. To give effect to a treaty, the supreme power of each nation that is a party to the treaty must ratify it. For example, the U.S. Constitution requires approval by two-thirds of the Senate before a treaty executed by the president will be binding on the U.S. government.

Bilateral agreements, as the term implies, occur when only two nations form an agreement that will govern their commercial exchanges or other relations with one another. Multilateral agreements are those formed by several nations. The European Union (EU), for example, which regulates commercial activities among its fifteen European member nations, is the result of a multilateral trade agreement. The North American Free Trade Agreement (NAFTA), which regulates trade among Canada, the United States, and Mexico, is another example of a multilateral trade agreement.

One treaty of particular significance to the international legal environment of business is the United Nations 1980 Convention on Contracts for the International Sale of Goods (CISG). Essentially, the CISG is to international sales transactions what the Uniform Commercial Code is to domestic sales transactions. The CISG governs the international sale of goods between firms or individuals located in different countries, providing that the countries involved have ratified the CISG. We examine the CISG and its provisions more closely in Chapters 13 through 15, in the context of the law governing the sale of goods.

INTERNATIONAL ORGANIZATIONS   International organizations and conferences also play an important role in the international legal arena. International organizations and conferences adopt resolutions, declarations, and other types of standards that often require a particular behavior of nations. The General Assembly of the United Nations, for example, has adopted numerous resolutions and declarations that embody principles of international law and has sponsored conferences that have led to the formation of international agreements. The United States is a member of more than one hundred multilateral and bilateral organizations, including at least twenty through the United Nations.

Commercial Contracts in an International Setting

Language and legal differences among nations can create special problems for parties to international contracts when disputes arise. It is possible to avoid these problems by including in a contract special provisions designating the official language of the contract, the legal forum (court or place) in which disputes under the contract will be settled, and the substantive law that will be applied in settling any disputes. Parties to international contracts should also indicate in their contracts what acts or events will excuse the parties from performance under the contract and whether disputes under the contract will be arbitrated or litigated.

CHOICE OF LANGUAGE A deal struck between a U.S. company and a company in another country normally involves two languages. The complex contractual terms involved may not be understood by one party in the other party's language. Typically, many phrases in one language are not readily translatable into another. To make sure that no disputes arise out of this language problem, an international sales contract should have a **choice-of-language clause** designating the official language by which the contract will be interpreted in the event of disagreement.

CHOICE OF FORUM When several countries are involved, litigation may be sought in courts in different nations. There are no universally accepted rules regarding the jurisdiction of a particular court over subject matter or parties to a dispute. Consequently, parties to an international transaction should always include in the contract a **forum-selection clause** indicating what court, jurisdiction, or tribunal will decide any disputes arising under the contract. It is especially important to indicate specifically what court will have jurisdiction. The forum does not necessarily have to be within the geographical boundaries of either of the parties' nations.

CHOICE OF LAW A contractual provision designating the applicable law—such as the law of Germany or England or California—is called a **choice-of-law clause.** Every international contract typically includes a choice-of-law clause. At common law (and in European civil law systems), parties are allowed to choose the law that will govern their contractual relationship provided that the law chosen is the law of a jurisdiction that has a sub-

stantial relationship to the parties and to the international business transaction.

Under Section 1–105 of the Uniform Commercial Code, parties may choose the law that will govern the contract as long as the choice is "reasonable." Article 6 of the United Nations Convention on Contracts for the International Sale of Goods (discussed in Chapter 13), however, imposes no limitation on the parties in their choice of what law will govern the contract. The 1986 Hague Convention on the Law Applicable to Contracts for the International Sale of Goods—often referred to as the Choice-of-Law Convention—allows unlimited autonomy in the choice of law. The Hague Convention indicates that whenever a choice of law is not specified in a contract, the governing law is that of the country in which the *seller's* place of business is located.

▌ Finding and Analyzing the Law

Laws pertaining to business consist of both statutory law and case law. The statutes, agency regulations, and case law referred to in this text establish the rights and duties of businesspersons engaged in various types of activities. The cases presented within the chapters provide you with concise, real-life illustrations of the interpretation and application of the law by the courts. Because of the importance of knowing how to find statutory and case law, we offer a brief introduction to how statutes and cases are published and to the legal "shorthand" employed in referencing these legal sources.

Finding Statutory and Administrative Law

When Congress passes laws, they are collected in a publication titled *United States Statutes at Large.* When state legislatures pass laws, they are collected in similar state publications. Most frequently, however, laws are referred to in their codified form—that is, the form in which they appear in the federal and state codes.

In these codes, laws are compiled by subject. The *United States Code* (U.S.C.) arranges all existing federal laws of a public and permanent nature by subject. Each of the fifty subjects into which the

U.S.C. arranges the laws is given a title and a title number. For example, laws relating to commerce and trade are collected in Title 15, which is titled "Commerce and Trade." Titles are subdivided by sections. A citation to the U.S.C. includes title and section numbers. Thus, a reference to "15 U.S.C. Section 1" means that the statute can be found in Section 1 of Title 15. ("Section" may also be designated by the symbol §, and "Sections" by §§.)

Sometimes a citation includes the abbreviation *et seq.*—as in "15 U.S.C. Sections 1 *et seq.*" The term is an abbreviated form of *et sequitur*, which in Latin means "and the following"; when used in a citation, it refers to sections that concern the same subject as the numbered section and follow it in sequence.

State codes follow the U.S.C. pattern of arranging law by subject. The state codes may be called codes, revisions, compilations, consolidations, general statutes, or statutes, depending on the preference of the states. In some codes, subjects are designated by number. In others, they are designated by name. For example, "13 Pennsylvania Consolidated Statutes Section 1101" means the statute can be found in Title 13, Section 1101, of the Pennsylvania code. "California Commercial Code Section 1101" means the statute can be found under the subject heading "Commercial Code" of the California code in Section 1101. Abbreviations may be used. For example, "13 Pennsylvania Consolidated Statutes Section 1101" may be abbreviated "13 Pa. C.S. § 1101," and "California Commercial Code Section 1101" may be abbreviated "Cal. Com. Code § 1101."

Rules and regulations adopted by federal administrative agencies are compiled in the *Code of Federal Regulations* (C.F.R.). Like the U.S.C., the C.F.R. is divided into fifty titles. Rules within each title are assigned section numbers. A full citation to the C.F.R. includes title and section numbers. For example, a reference to "17 C.F.R. Section 230.504" means that the rule can be found in Section 230.504 of Title 17.

Commercial publications of these laws and regulations are available and are widely used. For example, West Publishing Company publishes the *United States Code Annotated* (U.S.C.A.). The U.S.C.A. contains the complete text of laws included in the U.S.C., as well as notes of court decisions that interpret and apply specific sections of the statutes, plus the text of presidential proclama-

tions and executive orders. The U.S.C.A. also includes research aids, such as cross-references to related statutes, historical notes, and library references. A citation to the U.S.C.A. is similar to a citation to the U.S.C.: "15 U.S.C.A. Section 1."

Finding Case Law

Before discussing the case reporting system, we need to look briefly at the court system. As will be discussed in detail in Chapter 2, there are two types of courts in the United States, federal courts and state courts. Both the federal and state court systems consist of several levels, or tiers, of courts. *Trial courts*, in which evidence is presented and testimony given, are on the bottom tier (which also includes lower courts handling specialized issues). Decisions from a trial court can be appealed to a higher court, which commonly would be an intermediate *court of appeals*, or an *appellate court*. Appellate courts are known as *reviewing courts* because they do not hear evidence or testimony, as trial courts do; rather, an appellate court reviews all of the records relating to a case to determine whether the trial court's decision was correct. Decisions from these intermediate courts of appeals may be appealed to an even higher court, such as a state supreme court or the United States Supreme Court.

STATE COURT DECISIONS Most state trial court decisions are not published. Except in New York and a few other states that publish selected opinions of their trial courts, decisions from the state trial courts are merely filed in the office of the clerk of the court, where the decisions are available for public inspection. Written decisions of the appellate, or reviewing, courts, however, are published and distributed. The reported appellate decisions are published in volumes called *reports* or *reporters*, which are numbered consecutively. State appellate court decisions are found in the state reporters of that particular state.

Additionally, state court opinions appear in regional units of the *National Reporter System*, published by West Publishing Company. Most lawyers and libraries have the West reporters because they report cases more quickly and are distributed more widely than the state-published reports. In fact, many states have eliminated their own reporters in favor of West's National Reporter System. The National Reporter System divides the states into the following geographical areas: *Atlantic* (A. or A.2d), *South Eastern* (S.E. or S.E.2d), *South Western* (S.W. or S.W.2d), *North Western* (N.W. or N.W.2d), *North Eastern* (N.E. or N.E.2d), *Southern* (So. or So.2d), and *Pacific* (P. or P.2d). (The *2d* in the abbreviations refers to *Second Series.*) The states included in each of these regional divisions are indicated in Exhibit 1–1, which illustrates West's National Reporter System.

After appellate decisions have been published, they are normally referred to (cited) by the name of the case; the volume, name, and page number of the state's official reporter (if different from West's National Reporter System); the volume, unit, and page number of the *National Reporter*; and the volume, name, and page number of any other selected reporter. This information is included in the *citation*. (Citing a reporter by volume number, name, and page number, in that order, is common to all citations.) When more than one reporter is cited for the same case, each reference is called a *parallel citation*. For example, consider the following case: *Williams v. Garraghty*, 249 Va. 224, 455 S.E.2d 209 (1995). We see that the opinion in this case may be found in Volume 249 of the official *Virginia Reports*, on page 224. The parallel citation is to Volume 455 of the *South Eastern Reporter, Second Series*, page 209. In presenting appellate opinions in this text, in addition to the reporter, we give the name of the court hearing the case and the year of the court's decision.

A few of the states—including those with intermediate appellate courts, such as California, Illinois, and New York—have more than one reporter for opinions given by courts within their states. Sample citations from these courts, as well as others, are listed and explained in Exhibit 1–2.

FEDERAL COURT DECISIONS Federal district court decisions are published unofficially in West's *Federal Supplement* (F.Supp.), and opinions from the circuit courts of appeals (federal reviewing courts) are reported unofficially in West's *Federal Reporter* (F., F.2d, or F.3d). Cases concerning federal bankruptcy law are published unofficially in West's *Bankruptcy Reporter* (Bankr.). Opinions from the United States Supreme Court are reported in the *United States Reports* (U.S.), West's *Supreme Court Reporter* (S.Ct.), the *Lawyers'*

Edition of the Supreme Court Reports (L.Ed. or L.Ed.2d), and other publications.

The *United States Reports* is the official edition of all decisions of the United States Supreme Court for which there are written opinions. Published by the federal government, the series includes reports of Supreme Court cases dating from the August term of 1791, although originally many of the decisions were not reported in the early volumes.

West's *Supreme Court Reporter* is an unofficial edition dating from the Court's term in October 1882. Preceding each case report are a summary of the case and *headnotes* (brief editorial statements of the law involved in the case). The headnotes are given classification numbers that serve to cross-reference each headnote to other headnotes on similar points of law throughout the National Reporter System and other West publications. The numbers facilitate research of all relevant cases on a given point of law. This is important because, as may be evident from the discussion of *stare decisis* earlier in this chapter, a lawyer's goal in undertaking legal research is to find an authority that cannot be factually distinguished from his or her case.

The Lawyers Cooperative Publishing Company of Rochester, New York, publishes the *Lawyers' Edition of the Supreme Court Reports*, which is an unofficial edition of the entire series of the Supreme Court reports. The *Lawyers' Edition* contains many of the decisions not reported in the early official volumes. Additionally, among other editorial features, the *Lawyers' Edition*, in its second series, precedes the report of each case with a full summary, includes excerpts from the attorneys' notes on the cases, and discusses in detail selected cases of special interest to the legal profession.

Sample citations for federal court decisions are also listed and explained in Exhibit 1–2.

OLD CASE LAW On a few occasions, this text cites opinions from old, classic cases dating to the nineteenth century or earlier; some of these are from the English courts. The citations to these cases appear not to conform to the descriptions given above, because the reporters in which they were published have since been replaced. A sample citation for an English reporter is included in Exhibit 1–2. Whenever citations to old reporters are made in this text, the citations will be explained as they are presented.

♦ **Exhibit 1–1**
National Reporter System—Regional/Federal

Regional Reporters	Coverage Beginning	Coverage
Atlantic Reporter (A. or A.2d)	1885	Connecticut, Delaware, Maine, Maryland, New Hampshire, New Jersey, Pennsylvania, Rhode Island, Vermont, and District of Columbia.
North Eastern Reporter (N.E. or N.E.2d)	1885	Illinois, Indiana, Massachusetts, New York, and Ohio.
North Western Reporter (N.W. or N.W.2d)	1879	Iowa, Michigan, Minnesota, Nebraska, North Dakota, South Dakota, and Wisconsin.
Pacific Reporter (P. or P.2d)	1883	Alaska, Arizona, California, Colorado, Hawaii, Idaho, Kansas, Montana, Nevada, New Mexico, Oklahoma, Oregon, Utah, Washington, and Wyoming.
South Eastern Reporter (S.E. or S.E.2d)	1887	Georgia, North Carolina, South Carolina, Virginia, and West Virginia.
South Western Reporter (S.W. or S.W.2d)	1886	Arkansas, Kentucky, Missouri, Tennessee, and Texas.
Southern Reporter (So. or So.2d)	1887	Alabama, Florida, Louisiana, and Mississippi.

Federal Reporters		
Federal Reporter (F., F.2d, or F.3d)	1880	U.S. Circuit Court from 1880 to 1912; U.S. Commerce Court from 1911 to 1913; U.S. District Courts from 1880 to 1932; U.S. Court of Claims (now called U.S. Court of Federal Claims) from 1929 to 1932 and since 1960; U.S. Court of Appeals since 1891; U.S. Court of Customs and Patent Appeals since 1929; U.S. Emergency Court of Appeals since 1943.
Federal Supplement (F.Supp.)	1932	U.S. Court of Claims from 1932 to 1960; U.S. District Courts since 1932; and U.S. Customs Court since 1956.
Federal Rules Decisions (F.R.D.)	1939	U.S. District Courts involving the Federal Rules of Civil Procedure since 1939 and Federal Rules of Criminal Procedure since 1946.
Supreme Court Reporter (S.Ct.)	1882	U.S. Supreme Court since the October term of 1882.
Bankruptcy Reporter (Bankr.)	1980	Bankruptcy decisions of U.S. Bankruptcy Courts, U.S. District Courts, U.S. Courts of Appeals, and U.S. Supreme Court.
Military Justice Reporter (M.J.)	1978	U.S. Court of Military Appeals and Courts of Military Review for the Army, Navy, Air Force, and Coast Guard.

NATIONAL REPORTER SYSTEM MAP

□ Pacific
■ North Western
■ South Western
□ North Eastern
□ Atlantic
□ South Eastern
■ Southern

◆ **Exhibit 1–2**
How to Read Case Citations

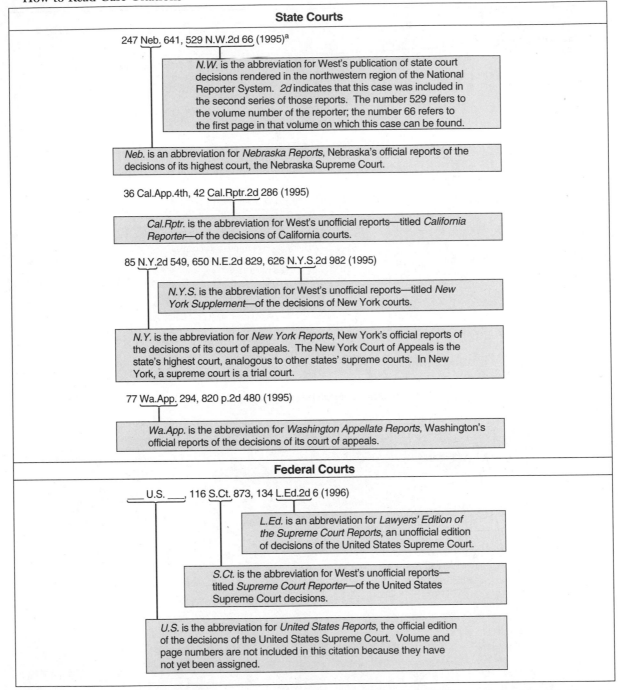

State Courts

247 Neb. 641, 529 N.W.2d 66 (1995)[a]

N.W. is the abbreviation for West's publication of state court decisions rendered in the northwestern region of the National Reporter System. *2d* indicates that this case was included in the second series of those reports. The number 529 refers to the volume number of the reporter; the number 66 refers to the first page in that volume on which this case can be found.

Neb. is an abbreviation for *Nebraska Reports*, Nebraska's official reports of the decisions of its highest court, the Nebraska Supreme Court.

36 Cal.App.4th, 42 Cal.Rptr.2d 286 (1995)

Cal.Rptr. is the abbreviation for West's unofficial reports—titled *California Reporter*—of the decisions of California courts.

85 N.Y.2d 549, 650 N.E.2d 829, 626 N.Y.S.2d 982 (1995)

N.Y.S. is the abbreviation for West's unofficial reports—titled *New York Supplement*—of the decisions of New York courts.

N.Y. is the abbreviation for *New York Reports*, New York's official reports of the decisions of its court of appeals. The New York Court of Appeals is the state's highest court, analogous to other states' supreme courts. In New York, a supreme court is a trial court.

77 Wa.App. 294, 820 p.2d 480 (1995)

Wa.App. is the abbreviation for *Washington Appellate Reports*, Washington's official reports of the decisions of its court of appeals.

Federal Courts

___ U.S. ___, 116 S.Ct. 873, 134 L.Ed.2d 6 (1996)

L.Ed. is an abbreviation for *Lawyers' Edition of the Supreme Court Reports*, an unofficial edition of decisions of the United States Supreme Court.

S.Ct. is the abbreviation for West's unofficial reports—titled *Supreme Court Reporter*—of the United States Supreme Court decisions.

U.S. is the abbreviation for *United States Reports*, the official edition of the decisions of the United States Supreme Court. Volume and page numbers are not included in this citation because they have not yet been assigned.

a. The Case names have been deleted from these citations to emphasize the publications. It should be kept in mind, however, that the name of a case is as important as the specific page numbers in the volumes in which it is found. If a citation is incorrect, the correct citation may be found in a publication's index of case names. The date of a case is also important because, in addition to providing a check on error in citations, the value of a recent case as an authority is likely to be greater than that of earlier cases.

♦ **Exhibit 1–2**
How to Read Case Citations—Continued

Federal Courts (continued)

74 F.3d 613 (5th Cir. 1996)

5th Cir. is an abbreviation denoting that this case was decided in the United States Court of Appeals for the Fifth Circuit.

912 F.Supp. 663 (E.D.N.Y. 1996)

E.D.N.Y. is abbreviation indicating that the United States District Court for the Eastern District of New York decided this case.

English Courts

9 Exch. 341, 156 Eng.Rep. 145 (1854)

Eng.Rep. is an abbreviation for *English Reports, Full Reprint,* a series of reports containing selected decisions made in English courts between 1378 and 1865.

Exch. is an abbreviation for *English Exchequer Reports*, which included the original reports of cases decided in England's Court of Exchequer.

Statutory and Other Citations

18 U.S.C. Section 1961(1)(A)

U.S.C. denotes *United States Code*, the codification of *United States Statutes at Large.* The number 18 refers to the statute's U.S.C. title number and 1961 to its section number within that title. The number 1 refers to a subsection within the section and the letter A to a subdivision within the subsection.

UCC 2–206(1)(b)

UCC is an abbreviation for *Uniform Commercial Code.* The first number 2 is a reference to an article of the UCC and 206 to a section within that article. The number 1 refers to a subsection within the section and the letter b to a subdivision within the subsection.

Restatement (Second) of Torts, Seciton 568

Restatement (Second) of Torts refers to the second edition of the American Law Institute's *Restatement of the Law of Torts.* The number 568 refers to a specific section.

17 C.F.R. Section 230.505

C.F.R. is an abbreviation for *Code of Federal Regulations*, a compilation of federal administrative regulations. The number 17 is a reference to the regulation's title number and 230.505 to a specific section within that title.

Reading and Understanding Case Law

Case law is critical to decision making in the business context because businesses must operate within the boundaries established by law. It is thus essential that businesspersons understand case law.

The cases in this text have been rewritten and condensed from the full text of the courts' opinions. For those wishing to review court cases for future research projects or to gain additional legal information, the following sections will provide useful insights into how to read and understand case law.

CASE TITLES AND TERMINOLOGY   The title of a case, such as *Adams v. Jones*, indicates the names of the parties to the lawsuit. The *v.* in the case title stands for *versus*, which means "against." In the trial court, Adams was the plaintiff—the person who filed the suit. Jones was the defendant. If the case is appealed, however, the appellate court will sometimes place the name of the party appealing the decision first, so that the case may be called *Jones v. Adams*. Because some reviewing courts retain the trial court order of names, it is often impossible to distinguish the plaintiff from the defendant in the title of a reported appellate court decision. You must carefully read the facts of each case to identify each party. Otherwise, the discussion by the appellate court will be difficult to understand.

The following terms and phrases are frequently encountered in court opinions and legal publications. Because it is important to understand what is meant by these terms and phrases, we define and discuss them here.

Plaintiffs and Defendants
As mentioned earlier in this chapter, the *plaintiff* in a lawsuit is the party that initiates the action. The *defendant* is the party against which a lawsuit is brought. Lawsuits frequently involve more than one plaintiff and/or defendant.

Appellants and Appellees
The *appellant* is the party that appeals a case to another court or jurisdiction from the court or jurisdiction in which the case was originally brought. Sometimes, an appellant that appeals a judgment is referred to as the *petitioner*. The *appellee* is the party against which the appeal is taken. Sometimes, the appellee is referred to as the *respondent*.

Judges and Justices
The terms *judge* and *justice* are usually synonymous and represent two designations given to judges in various courts. All members of the United States Supreme Court, for example, are referred to as justices. And justice is the formal title usually given to judges of appellate courts, although this is not always the case. In New York, a justice is a judge of the trial court (which is called the Supreme Court), and a member of the Court of Appeals (the state's highest court) is called a judge. The term *justice* is commonly abbreviated to J., and *justices* to JJ. A Supreme Court case might refer to Justice Kennedy as Kennedy, J., or to Chief Justice Rehnquist as Rehnquist, C.J.

Decisions and Opinions
Most decisions reached by reviewing, or appellate, courts are explained in written *opinions*. The opinion contains the court's reasons for its decision, the rules of law that apply, and the judgment.

There are four possible types of written opinions for any particular case decided by an appellate court. When all judges or justices unanimously agree on an opinion, the opinion is written for the entire court and can be deemed a *unanimous opinion*. When there is not a unanimous opinion, a *majority opinion* is written, outlining the views of the majority of the judges or justices deciding the case. Often, a judge or justice who feels strongly about making or emphasizing a point that was not made or emphasized in the unanimous or majority opinion will write a *concurring opinion*. That means the judge or justice agrees (concurs) with the judgment given in the unanimous or majority opinion but for different reasons. In other than unanimous opinions, a *dissenting opinion* is usually written by a judge or justice who does not agree with the majority. The dissenting opinion is important because it may form the basis of the arguments used years later in overruling the precedential majority opinion.

A Note on Abbreviations
In court opinions, as well as in other areas of this text, certain terms appearing in the names of firms or organizations will often be abbreviated. The terms *Company*, *Incorporated*, and *Limited*, for example, will frequently appear in their abbreviated forms as *Co.*, *Inc.*, and *Ltd.*, respectively, and *Brothers* is commonly abbreviated to *Bros.* Certain organizations and legislative acts are also frequently referred to by their initials or acronyms. In all such cases, to prevent confusion we will give the

complete name of the organization or act upon first mentioning it in a given section of the text.

A SAMPLE COURT CASE   Knowing how to read and analyze a court opinion is an essential step in undertaking accurate legal research. A further step involves "briefing" the case. Legal researchers routinely brief cases by summarizing and reducing the texts of the opinions to their essential elements. Instructions on how to brief a case and selected cases for briefing are given in Appendix A at the end of this text.

The cases contained within the chapters of this text have already been analyzed and briefed by the authors, and the essential aspects of each case are presented in a convenient format consisting of four basic sections: *Facts, Issue, Decision,* and *Reason.* This basic format is illustrated in the sample court case shown in Exhibit 1–3, which has also been annotated to illustrate the kind of information that is contained in each section. (Annotated excerpts from the actual court opinion for this case appear as the first case opinion in Appendix A in the back of this book.)

The Constitution As It Affects Business

We now turn to an examination of constitutional law. Constitutional law is all law that is based on the U.S. Constitution or the various state constitutions.

The U.S. Constitution, because it provides the legal basis for both state and federal (national) powers, is the supreme law in this country. Neither Congress nor any state may pass a law that conflicts with the Constitionl. Laws that govern business have their origin in the lawmaking authority granted by this document.

The Commerce Clause

Article I, Section 8, of the U.S. Constitution expressly permits Congress "[t]o regulate Commerce with foreign Nations, and among the several States, and with the Indian Tribes." This clause, referred to as the **commerce clause,** has had a greater impact on business than any other provision in the Constitution. This power was delegated to the federal government to ensure the uniformity of rules governing the movement of goods through the states.

For some time, the commerce power was interpreted as being limited to *interstate* commerce (commerce among the states) and not applicable to *intrastate* commerce (commerce within the states). In 1824, however, in *Gibbons v. Ogden,*[7] the United States Supreme Court held that commerce within states could also be regulated by the national government as long as the commerce concerned more than one state.

THE BREADTH OF THE COMMERCE CLAUSE   As a result of the decision in *Gibbons v. Ogden,* the commerce clause allowed the national government to exercise increasing authority over all areas of economic affairs throughout the land. In a 1942 case,[8] for example, the Court held that wheat production by an individual farmer intended wholly for consumption on his own farm was subject to federal regulation. The Court reasoned that the home consumption of wheat reduced the demand for wheat and thus could have a substantial effect on interstate commerce. In *McLain v. Real Estate Board of New Orleans, Inc.,* a 1980 case, the Supreme Court acknowledged that the commerce clause had "long been interpreted to extend beyond activities actually in interstate commerce to reach other activities, while wholly local in nature, which nevertheless substantially affect interstate commerce."[9]

In 1995, however, in *United States v. Lopez,*[10] the Supreme Court held—for the first time in sixty years—that there was a limit to the reach of the commerce clause. In the *Lopez* case, the Supreme Court concluded that Congress had exceeded its constitutional authority when it passed the Gun-Free School Zones Act in 1990. The Court stated that the act, which banned the possession of guns within one thousand feet of any school, was unconstitutional because it attempted to regulate an area that had "nothing to do with commerce, or any sort of economic enterprise." The Court held that activities regulated under the commerce clause, to be constitutional, must substantially affect interstate commerce.

---

7.   22 U.S. (9 Wheat.) 1, 6 L.Ed. 23 (1824).
8.   See *Wickard v. Filburn,* 317 U.S. 111, 63 S.Ct. 82, 87 L.Ed. 122 (1942).
9.   444 U.S. 232, 100 S.Ct. 502, 62 L.Ed.2d 441 (1980).
10.   514 U.S.549, 115 S.Ct. 1624, 131 L.Ed.2d 626 (1995).

♦ Exhibit 1-3
A Sample Court Case

1 — [**SUGGS v. SERVICEMASTER EDUCATION FOOD MANAGEMENT**
      [United States Court of Appeals,
2 — [Sixth Circuit, 1996.
3 — [72 F.3d 1228.

4 —   **FACTS**   Sharon Suggs had a B.S. degree in food and nutritional sciences. She operated a food ser-
      vice facility at Tennessee State University (TSU) for ServiceMaster Education Food Management.
      Ranked fifth among ServiceMaster's twelve area directors, Suggs received satisfactory ratings on per-
      formance and client satisfaction, as well as regular merit raises. Six months before ServiceMaster
      lost the TSU account, Suggs was terminated and replaced by a man. She filed a suit in a federal
      district court against ServiceMaster, alleging discrimination based on her gender in violation of
      Title VII of the Civil Rights Act of 1964. ServiceMaster claimed that Suggs was discharged for
      "client dissatisfaction, operational problems and failure to meet financial and budget commit-
      ments." The court awarded Suggs back pay and ordered that she be reinstated. ServiceMaster
      appealed.

5 — [**ISSUE**   Was Suggs's gender a determining factor in ServiceMaster's decision to fire her?

6 —   **DECISION**   Yes. The U.S. Court of Appeals for the Sixth Circuit affirmed this part of the lower
      court's decision.

7 —   **REASON**   The appellate court concluded "that ServiceMaster's stated reasons for terminating her
      employment were pretextual and that Suggs was actually terminated because she was a female.
      Suggs was qualified for the position she held. She was replaced by a man and was not offered
      another position with the company when she was removed from the TSU account and later termi-
      nated, although ServiceMaster had identified positions available at other locations. In contrast to
      ServiceMaster's treatment of Suggs, other directors in Suggs's area, who had been ranked below
      Suggs for profitability and client satisfaction, were offered transfers and relocations when their
      accounts were lost. Those directors were men."

8 —   **FOR CRITICAL ANALYSIS—Cultural Consideration:** *Why do some employers discriminate
      against employees on the basis of characteristics that have nothing to do with their jobs?*

The decision in the *Lopez* case was a close one (four of the nine justices dissented), and the extent to which the decision will curb the regulation of purely local business activities under the commerce clause is as yet unclear. It is notable that just a few days after the *Lopez* case was decided, the Supreme Court again declared that what appeared (to many) to be fundamentally local activities sufficiently affected interstate commerce to be subject to a federal statute. In *United States v. Robertson,*[11] the Court held that the activities of an Alaska gold miner involved interstate commerce because the

---

11.   514 U.S. 669, 115 S.Ct. 1732, 131 L.Ed.2d 714 (1995).

♦ **Exhibit 1–3**
  A Sample Court Case—Continued

Review of Sample Court Case

1.   The name of the case is *Suggs v. ServiceMaster Education Food Management.* Suggs is the plaintiff (appellee); ServiceMaster is the defendant (appellant).

2.   The court deciding this case was the U.S. Court of Appeals for the Sixth Circuit, a federal appellate court; the case was decided in 1996.

3.   This citation indicates that the case can be found in Volume 72 of West's *Federal Reporter, Third Series,* on page 1228.

4.   The *Facts* section identifies the parties to the action and describes the events leading up to the lawsuit, the allegations made by the plaintiff, the defendant's response to these allegations, and (because this case is an appellate court decision) the trial court's decision and the party appealing that decision.

5.   The *Issue* section presents the central issue (or issues) to be decided by the court. Cases frequently will involve more than one issue.

6.   The *Decision* section contains the court's decision on the issue or issues before the court. The decision reflects the opinion of the majority of the judges or justices hearing the case. Appellate courts frequently phrase their decisions in reference to the lower courts' decisions. That is, the appellate court may "affirm" the lower court's ruling or "reverse" it. In this particular case, the appellate court affirmed the lower court's judgment.

7.   The *Reason* section indicates what relevant laws and judicial principles were applied in forming the particular conclusion arrived at in the case at bar ("before the court"). In this case, the relevant statute was Title VII of the Civil Rights Act of 1964, which prohibits employment discrimination on the basis of race, color, national origin, religion, and gender. The appellate court concluded that ServiceMaster's treatment of Suggs constituted gender-based discrimination in violation of Title VII.

8.   The *For Critical Analysis—Cultural Consideration* section raises a question to be considered in relation to the case just presented. Here the question involves a "cultural" consideration. In other cases presented in this text, the "consideration" may involve a social, political, international, environmental, technological, or ethical consideration.

---

miner purchased some equipment and supplies in Los Angeles for use in his mining enterprise, recruited workers from outside Alaska, and took some gold (about 15 percent of the mine's output) out of state.

Today, at least theoretically, the power over commerce authorizes the national government to regulate every commercial enterprise in the United States. The breadth of the commerce clause permits the national government to legislate in areas in which there is no explicit grant of power to Congress. In the following case, a motel owner challenged the constitutionality of the Civil Rights Act of 1964, alleging that Congress lacked the authority to regulate what the motel owner claimed was "local" business.

CASE 1.1

Heart of Atlanta Motel v. United States

Supreme Court of the United
States, 1964.
379 U.S. 241,
85 S.Ct. 348,
13 L.Ed. 2d 258.

FACTS   The owner of the Heart of Atlanta Motel refused to rent rooms to African Americans in violation of the Civil Rights Act of 1964. The motel owner brought an action in a federal district court to have the act declared unconstitutional, alleging that Congress had exceeded its power to regulate commerce by enacting the act. The owner argued that his motel was not engaged in interstate commerce but was "of a purely local character." The motel, however, was accessible to state and interstate highways. The owner advertised nationally, maintained billboards throughout the state, and accepted convention trade from outside the state (75 percent of the guests were residents of other states). The court sustained the constutitionality of the act and enjoined (prohibited) the owner from discriminating on the basis of race. The owner appealed. The case ultimately went to the United States Supreme Court.

ISSUE   Did Congress exceed its constitutional power to regulate interstate commerce by enacting the Civil Rights Act of 1964?

DECISION   No. The United States Supreme Court upheld the constitutionality of the act.

REASON   The Court noted that the act was passed to correct "the deprivation of personal dignity" accompanying the denial of equal access to "public establishments." Testimony before Congress leading to the passage of the act indicated that African Americans in particular experienced substantial discrimination in attempting to secure lodging while traveling. This discrimination impeded interstate travel and thus impeded interstate commerce. As for the owner's argument that his motel was "of a purely local character," the Court said that even if this was true, "if it is interstate commerce that feels the pinch, it does not matter how local the operation that applies the squeeze." Therefore, under the commerce clause, "the power of Congress to promote interstate commerce also includes the power to regulate the local incidents thereof, including local activities."

FOR CRITICAL ANALYSIS—Political Consideration   *Suppose that only 5 percent of the motel's guests—or even 2 or 1 percent—were from out of state. In such a situation, would the Court still have been justified in regulating the motel's activities?*

THE REGULATORY POWERS OF THE STATES   A problem that frequently arises under the commerce clause concerns a state's ability to regulate matters within its own borders. The U.S. Constitution does not expressly exclude state regulation of commerce, and there is no doubt that states have a strong interest in regulating activities within their borders. As part of their inherent sovereignty, states possess **police powers.** The term does not relate solely to criminal law enforcement but also to the right of

state governments to regulate private activities to protect or promote the public order, health, safety, morals, and general welfare. Fire and building codes, antidiscrimination laws, parking regulations, zoning restrictions, licensing requirements, and thousands of other state statutes covering virtually every aspect of life have been enacted pursuant to a state's police powers.

When state regulations impinge on interstate commerce, courts must balance the state's interest in the merits and purposes of the regulation against the burden placed on interstate commerce. Generally, state laws enacted pursuant to a state's police powers carry a strong presumption of validity. If state laws substantially interfere with interstate commerce, however, they will be held to violate the commerce clause of the Constitution.

In *Raymond Motor Transportation, Inc. v. Rice*,[12] for example, the United States Supreme Court invalidated Wisconsin administrative regulations limiting the length of trucks traveling on its

---

12.   434 U.S. 429, 98 S.Ct. 787, 54 L.Ed.2d 664 (1978).

highways. The Court weighed the burden on interstate commerce against the benefits of the regulations and concluded that the challenged regulations "place a substantial burden on interstate commerce and they cannot be said to make more than the most speculative contribution to highway safety."

Because courts balance the interests involved, it is extremely difficult to predict the outcome in a particular case. The following case concerns an issue that has elicited much controversy in recent years: whether states have the power to discriminate against shipments of out-of-state waste to intrastate disposal facilities.

CASE 1.2

Oregon Waste Systems, Inc. v. Department of Environmental Quality of the State of Oregon

Supreme Court of the United States, 1994.
511 U.S. 93,
114 S.Ct. 1345,
128 L.Ed.2d 13.

FACTS Oregon Waste Systems, Inc., operates a waste-disposal facility in Gilliam County, Oregon. The facility receives waste from sources in Oregon and from sources outside the state. In 1989, Oregon imposed a fee ($.85 per ton) on all of the solid waste that such facilities receive from sources in Oregon and imposed a higher fee ($2.25 per ton) on solid waste generated outside the state. Oregon Waste, other operators of waste-disposal facilities in Oregon, and Gilliam County filed a suit against the state in an Oregon court, challenging the higher fee as a violation of, among other things, the commerce clause. The court upheld the higher fee, and the plaintiffs appealed. The Oregon Supreme Court affirmed the ruling. The plaintiffs appealed to the United States Supreme Court.

ISSUE Does the higher fee imposed by Oregon on solid waste generated outside the state violate the commerce clause?

DECISION Yes. The Supreme Court held that Oregon's treatment of out-of-state waste was invalid under the commerce clause.

REASON The Supreme Court pointed out that the first step in analyzing a law under the commerce clause is to determine whether it "regulates evenhandedly with only 'incidental effects' on interstate commerce." If a restriction is discriminatory—that is, if it favors in-state economic interests over their out-of-state counterparts—it is invalid. The Court concluded that Oregon's out-of-state fee was obviously discriminatory. It "subjects waste from other States to a fee almost three times greater than the * * * charge imposed on * * * in-state waste." The state argued, among other things, that the higher fee was necessary to make nonresidents pay their "fair share" of the costs imposed on Oregon by the disposal of their waste. The Court noted that the state was unable to specify what waste-disposal costs, in terms of taxes, residents paid that nonresidents did not. Besides, the Court pointed out, in-state shippers of out-of-state waste were charged the higher fee even though they paid all other Oregon taxes.

(Continued)

Case 1.2—Continued   **FOR CRITICAL ANALYSIS—Economic Consideration**   *In terms of the outcome in this case, would it have mattered if the fee for out-of-state waste was only, say, 10 cents per ton higher than the fee for in-state waste?*

The Bill of Rights

The importance of a written declaration of the rights of individuals eventually caused the first Congress of the United States to submit twelve amendments to the Constitution to the states for approval. The first ten of these amendments, commonly known as the **Bill of Rights,** were adopted in 1791 and embody a series of protections for the individual against various types of interference by the federal government.[13] Some constitutional protections apply to business entities as well. For example, corporations exist as separate legal entities, or *legal persons,* and enjoy many of the same rights and privileges as *natural persons* do.

Summarized here are the protections guaranteed by these ten amendments.[14] The due process clause of the Fourteenth Amendment, which we discuss later in this chapter, applies many of the rights guaranteed by these first ten amendments to the states.

1. The First Amendment guarantees the freedoms of religion, speech, and the press and the rights to assemble peaceably and to petition the government.
2. The Second Amendment guarantees the right to keep and bear arms.
3. The Third Amendment prohibits, in peacetime, the lodging of soldiers in any house without the owner's consent.
4. The Fourth Amendment prohibits unreasonable searches and seizures of persons or property.
5. The Fifth Amendment guarantees the rights to indictment by grand jury (see Chapter 6), to due process of law, and to fair payment when private property is taken for public use (see Chapter 29). The Fifth Amendment also prohibits compulsory self-incrimination and double jeopardy (trial for the same crime twice).
6. The Sixth Amendment guarantees the accused in a criminal case the right to a speedy and public trial by an impartial jury and with counsel. The accused has the right to cross-examine witnesses against him or her and to solicit testimony from witnesses in his or her favor.
7. The Seventh Amendment guarantees the right to a trial by jury in a civil case involving at least twenty dollars.[15]
8. The Eighth Amendment prohibits excessive bail and fines, as well as cruel and unusual punishment.
9. The Ninth Amendment establishes that the people have rights in addition to those specified in the Constitution.
10. The Tenth Amendment establishes that those powers neither delegated to the federal government nor denied to the states are reserved for the states.

The rights secured by the Bill of Rights are not absolute. Ultimately, it is the United States Supreme Court, as the interpreter of the Constitution, that both gives meaning to these constitutional rights and determines their boundaries.

FREEDOM OF SPEECH   In interpreting the meaning of the First Amendment's guarantee of free speech, the United States Supreme Court has made it clear that certain types of speech will not be protected. Speech that harms the good reputation of another, or defamatory speech (see Chapter 4), will not be protected under the First Amendment. Speech that violates criminal laws (such as

13. One of these proposed amendments was ratified 203 years later (in 1992) and became the Twenty-seventh Amendment to the Constitution. See Appendix B.
14. See the Constitution in Appendix B for the complete text of each amendment.
15. Twenty dollars was forty days' pay for the average person when the Bill of Rights was written.

threatening speech, pornography, and so on) is not constitutionally protected.

Other unprotected speech includes "fighting words," or words that are likely to incite others to respond violently, and obscene speech. Numerous state and federal statutes make it a crime to disseminate obscene materials. The United States Supreme Court has grappled from time to time with the problem of trying to establish an operationally effective definition of obscene speech, but frequently this determination is left to state and local authorities. Generally, obscenity is still a constitutionally unsettled area, whether it deals with speech, printed materials, or filmed materials. In the interest of protecting against the abuse of children, however, the Supreme Court has upheld state laws prohibiting the sale and possession of child pornography.[16] In the interest of protecting women against sexual harassment in the workplace, at least one court has banned lewd speech and pornographic pinups in the workplace.[17] In recent years, obscenity issues have also arisen in relation to television shows, movies, the lyrics and covers of music albums, and the content of monologues by "shock" comedians.

Political speech that otherwise would be within the protection of the First Amendment does not lose that protection simply because its source is a corporation. For example, in *First National Bank of Boston v. Bellotti*, national banking associations and business corporations sought United States Supreme Court review of a Massachusetts statute that prohibited corporations from making political contributions or expenditures that individuals were permitted to make. The Court ruled that the Massachusetts law was unconstitutional because it violated the right of corporations to freedom of speech.[18] Similarly, the Court has held that a law forbidding a corporation from using bill inserts to express its views on controversial issues also violates the First Amendment.[19]

Does a state law banning the distribution of anonymous political leaflets unconstitutionally restrain political speech? This question is at issue in the following case.

---

16. See *Osborne v. Ohio*, 495 U.S. 103, 110 S.Ct. 1691, 109 L.Ed.2d 98 (1990).
17. *Robinson v. Jacksonville Shipyards, Inc.*, 760 F.Supp. 1486 (M.D.Fla. 1991).

18. 435 U.S. 765, 98 S.Ct. 1407, 55 L.Ed.2d 707 (1978).
19. *Consolidated Edison Co. v. Public Service Commission*, 447 U.S. 530, 100 S.Ct. 2326, 65 L.Ed.2d 319 (1980).

CASE 1.3

McIntyre v. Ohio Elections Commission

Supreme Court of the United States, 1995.
514 U.S. 334,
115 S.Ct. 1511,
131 L.Ed.2d 426.

FACTS In April 1988, Margaret McIntyre distributed leaflets to persons attending public meetings at the Blendon Middle School in Westerville, Ohio. The leaflets expressed opposition to a proposed school tax. Some of the leaflets did not identify an author but only purported to express the views of "CONCERNED PARENTS AND TAX PAYERS." A school official filed a complaint with the Ohio Elections Commission under a state statute that prohibits the distribution of campaign literature that does not contain the name and address of the person or official issuing it. The commission imposed a fine of $100. McIntyre appealed to an Ohio state court, arguing that the statute was unconstitutional. The court agreed and dropped the fine. An Ohio appellate court reinstated the fine, and the Ohio Supreme Court affirmed. The state supreme court concluded that the statute was reasonable in light of the state's interests in providing voters with information and in preventing fraud. McIntyre appealed to the United States Supreme Court.

ISSUE Does a statute prohibiting the anonymous distribution of campaign literature violate the First Amendment?

DECISION Yes. The Supreme Court held that the First Amendment protects the freedom to publish anonymously. *(Continued)*

Case 1.3–Continued

REASON The Supreme Court declared that "handing out leaflets in the advocacy of a politically controversial viewpoint is the essence of First Amendment expression." Thus, Ohio's statute could be upheld "only if it is narrowly tailored to serve an overriding state interest." Ohio's interests in providing information and in preventing fraud were not enough to justify the statute's restraint on speech, the Court concluded. Providing information "does not justify a state requirement that a writer make statements or disclosures that she would otherwise omit. Moreover, in the case of a handbill written by a private citizen unknown to the [reader], the name and address of the author adds little, if anything, to the reader's ability to evaluate the document's message." Regarding the state's interest in preventing fraud, the Court pointed out that the statute covered all documents, regardless of whether they were fraudulent, false, or libelous. Besides, Ohio has other "detailed and specific" regulations covering false statements in political campaigns.

FOR CRITICAL ANALYSIS—Political Consideration *When the source of political speech is a corporation, should the corporation be required to identify itself? Would such a requirement be constitutional?*

FREEDOM OF RELIGION The First Amendment states that the government may neither establish any religion nor prohibit the free exercise of religious practices. The first part of this constitutional provision is referred to as the **establishment clause,** and the second part is known as the **free exercise clause.** Government action, both federal and state, must be consistent with this constitutional mandate.

Federal or state regulation that does not promote religion or place a significant burden on religion is constitutional even if it has some impact on religion. "Sunday closing laws," for example, make the performance of some commercial activities on Sunday illegal. These statutes, also known as "blue laws" (from the color of the paper on which an early Sunday law was written), have been upheld on the ground that it is a legitimate function of government to provide a day of rest. The United States Supreme Court has held that the closing laws, although originally of a religious character, have taken on the secular purpose of promoting the health and welfare of workers.[20] Even though closing laws admittedly make it easier for Christians to attend religious services, the Court has viewed this effect as an incidental, not a primary, purpose of Sunday closing laws.

The First Amendment does not require a complete separation of church and state. On the contrary, it affirmatively mandates *accommodation* of all religions and forbids hostility toward any.[21] The courts do not have an easy task in determining the extent to which governments can accommodate a religion without appearing to promote that religion and thus violate the establishment clause. For business firms, an important issue involves the accommodation that businesses must make for the religious beliefs of their employees. We examine this issue in Chapter 22, in the context of employment discrimination.

DUE PROCESS Both the Fifth and the Fourteenth Amendments provide that no person shall be deprived "of life, liberty, or property, without due process of law." The **due process**

---

20. *McGowan v. Maryland,* 366 U.S. 420, 81 S.Ct. 1101, 6 L.Ed.2d 393 (1961).

21. *Zorach v. Clauson,* 343 U.S. 306, 72 S.Ct. 679, 96 L.Ed. 954 (1952).

clause of these constitutional amendments has two aspects—procedural and substantive.

Procedural Due Process *Procedural* due process requires that any government decision to take life, liberty, or property must be made fairly. For example, fair procedures must be used in determining whether a person will be subjected to punishment or have some burden imposed on him or her. Fair procedure has been interpreted as requiring that the person have at least an opportunity to object to a proposed action before a fair, neutral decision maker (which need not be a judge). Thus, for example, if a driver's license is construed as a property interest, some sort of opportunity to object to its suspension or termination by the state must be provided.

Substantive Due Process *Substantive* due process focuses on the content, or substance, of legislation. If a law or other governmental action limits a *fundamental right*, it will be held to violate substantive due process unless it promotes a *compelling or overriding state interest.* Fundamental rights include interstate travel, privacy, voting, and all First Amendment rights. Compelling state interests could include, for example, the public's safety. Thus, laws designating speed limits may be upheld even though they affect interstate travel, if they are shown to reduce highway fatalities, because the state has a compelling interest in protecting the lives of its citizens.

In all other situations, a law or action does not violate substantive due process if it rationally relates to any legitimate governmental end. It is almost impossible for a law or action to fail the "rationality" test. Under this test, virtually any business regulation will be upheld as reasonable—the United States Supreme Court has sustained insurance regulations, price and wage controls, banking controls, and controls of unfair competition and trade practices against substantive due process challenges.

To illustrate, if a state legislature enacted a law imposing a fifteen-year term of imprisonment without a trial on all businesspersons who appeared in their own television commercials, the law would be unconstitutional on both substantive and procedural grounds. Substantive review would invalidate the legislation because it abridges freedom of speech. Procedurally, the law is unfair because it imposes the penalty without giving the accused a chance to defend his or her actions. The lack of procedural due process will cause a court to invalidate any statute or prior court decision. Similarly, a denial of substantive due process requires courts to overrule any state or federal law that violates the Constitution.

Constitutional Law in Cyberspace

The growing use of the Internet for both personal and business communications has created new legal challenges in virtually every area of the law, including many of the areas discussed in this text. Here we examine selected legal issues relating to constitutional law.

Regulating Online Obscenity

As discussed earlier in this chapter, obscene speech is not protected by the First Amendment. In 1996, in response to public concern over access to pornographic and obscene materials via the Internet, Congress enacted the Communications Decency Act (CDA). This act, which was part of the Telecommunications Act of 1996, made it a criminal offense to transmit "indecent" speech or images to minors (those under the age of eighteen) or to make such speech or images available online to minors. The act defined indecent speech as any communication that depicts or describes sexual or execretory activities or organs in a way that is "patently offensive," as measured by current community standards. Violators of the act could be fined up to $250,000 or imprisoned for up to two years.

A major legal issue raised by the language of the act was that there is no national standard by which to measure "indecent" or "patently offensive" speech. The CDA's definition of these terms followed the traditional practice of measuring obscenity by current community standards. Generally, the United States Supreme Court has held that in a legal action concerning obscene speech, the relevant standard is that of the community in which the information is accessed or the jury sits. With respect to Internet transmissions, however, obscene materials can be accessed by virtually anyone in any community in the United States (as well as globally). In effect, this means that any Internet transmission that is "patently offensive" by even the most restrictive community standards would be illegal under the CDA.

The American Civil Liberties Union (ACLU) and other organizations immediately challenged the constitutionality of the CDA in a lawsuit against the U.S. attorney general, Janet Reno, and the Justice Department. The plaintiffs alleged that the CDA's definition of indecency was unconstitutionally vague and subjected persons to criminal penalties without specifically identifying the crimes to which these penalties attach. In *American Civil Liberties Union v. Reno,*[22] a federal district court in Pennsylvania agreed with the plaintiffs and issued a temporary restraining order prohibiting the government from enforcing the section of the CDA pertaining to indecent materials. Shortly thereafter, another federal district court held that the act was unconstitutional because it was overbroad and impermissibly regulated constitutionally protected communications between adults.[23]

In 1997, the United States Supreme Court held that the CDA's provisions regarding "indecent" and "patently offensive" transmissions violated the First Amendment because of their "unprecedented" breadth: although the government has an interest in protecting children from potentially harmful materials, the CDA suppressed a large amount of speech that adults have a constitutional right to send and receive.[24]

Cryptography and Constitutional Protections

One of the foremost concerns of the business community today is the security of electronic proprietary and commercial information. To protect electronic data from being accessed by unauthorized persons, many companies use hardware or software with encryption capabilities. When data is *encrypted*, the access codes are scrambled to protect against unauthorized use. The widespread practice of encrypting data has created some interesting legal issues.

ENCRYPTED DATA AND CRIMINAL LAW One issue has to do with the Fourth Amendment protection against unreasonable searches and seizures. Suppose that law enforcement personnel obtain a search warrant to search an individual's office or home for certain information. If this information consists of encrypted data stored in a computer's hard drive or on external storage devices, how can it be accessed? A law enforcement agent might succeed in decrypting the data, but whether it would be lawful would depend on whether the information, once known, fell properly within the search warrant's description of the material to be searched and seized.

If law enforcement personnel could not "break" the code and decrypt the data, another issue would arise: Could the owner or possessor of the data be compelled to provide the encryption code? Under the Fifth Amendment, no person can be compelled to give evidence if that evidence would be self-incriminating. Traditionally, persons have been compelled to produce certain types of physical evidence, such as fingerprints, but whether a person can be compelled to use his or her *mind* to assist law enforcement personnel in obtaining incriminating evidence is not clear.

ENCRYPTION SOURCE CODES AND FREE SPEECH A constitutional issue that has recently come before the courts is whether computer source codes used in encryption software constitute "speech" protected by the First Amendment. The issue arose in the context of a controversy over government restrictions on the export of encryption software.

Under the International Traffic in Arms Regulations (ITAR),[25] administered by the U.S. Department of State, any firm that wishes to export encryption software or products containing encryption components must first obtain a license from the government to do so. In the past, it was difficult, if not impossible, to obtain such a license. In 1996, however, the government began to relax the regulations somewhat. Firms are now allowed to sell certain types of high-level encryption software for commercial purposes only. Software manufacturers complain that any restrictions unfairly place them at a disadvantage in the international mar-

---

22.   929 F.Supp. 824 (E.D.Pa. 1996).
23.   *Shea v. Reno,* 930 F.Supp. 916 (S.D.N.Y. 1996).
24.   *Reno v. American Civil Liberties Union,* ___U.S.___, 117 S.Ct. 2329, 138 L.Ed.2d 874 (1997).

---

25.   22 C.F.R. Sections 120–130.

ketplace. The government, however, contends that restrictions on the export of encryption software are necessary to prevent the software from falling into the hands of terrorists or others who could use it in ways that could threaten national security.

The constitutional issue currently before the courts is whether encryption software—more specif-ically, the source codes used to encrypt data—con-stitute speech. If so, then the government's regula-tion of this speech may be challenged on constitutional grounds. Whether cryptography qual-ifies as speech falling under the protection of the First Amendment is at issue in the following case.

CASE 1.4

Bernstein v. U.S. Department of State

United States District Court,
Northern District of
California, 1996.
922 F.Supp. 1426.

FACTS   As a graduate student at the University of California at Berkeley in the field of cryptography, Daniel Bernstein developed an encryption system he called "Snuffle." Bernstein asked the U.S. Department of State whether he needed a license to "export" Snuffle—that is, to teach and discuss its source code at conferences, in journals, and in online discussion groups. A license to disclose certain technical data to "foreign person[s]" is required under the Arms Export Control Act (AECA)[a] and the International Traffic in Arms Regulations (ITAR). The State Department said that Bernstein did need a license. Bernstein filed a suit in a federal district court against the State Department, contending in part that the AECA and the ITAR were uncon-stitutional as applied to Snuffle. He asked the court to, among other things, block their enforcement until his claim could be heard. The State Department filed a motion to dismiss, arguing in part that the Snuffle source code was not "speech" and thus was not protected by the First Amendment to the Constitution.

ISSUE   Is a cryptographic code speech protected by the First Amendment?

DECISION   Yes. The court held that the regulations were unconstitu-tional. The court denied the State Department's motion to dismiss and granted Bernstein's request to block their enforcement temporarily.

REASON   The court explained that "even if Snuffle source code, which is easily compiled into object code for the computer to read and easily used for encryption, is essentially functional, that does not remove it from the realm of speech. Instructions, do-it-yourself manuals, recipes, even technical information about hydrogen bomb construction, are often purely functional; they are also speech."

FOR CRITICAL ANALYSIS—Political Consideration   *If the court had ruled against Bernstein in this case, what effect might that have had on other software developers and exporters?*

a.   22 U.S.C. Section 2278.

Free Speech and Unwanted Electronic Mail

Many First Amendment cases involve the question of whether the government can prohibit persons from distributing political, religious, or other leaflets or printed materials in public forums. Nor-mally, any law that restricts or prohibits *speech* (that is, the political, religious, or other *message* com-municated in the leaflets or other printed materi-als) must relate to one of the categories of punishable speech (such as "fighting words," obscenity, defamation, and so on) or be justified by a *compelling state interest.*

Any law concerning speech-related conduct (that is, the distribution of leaflets or other printed materials) may reasonably restrict the time, place, or manner in which the conduct takes place. To be constitutional, however, the law must (1) be *content neutral,* (2) be *narrowly tailored* to serve a significant government interest, and (3) leave open sufficient *alternative channels of communication.* Recall that the Bill of Rights, including the First Amendment, protects persons from *government* actions, not actions undertaken by private parties. The rules just stated, however, apply even to certain privately owned facilities, such as shopping malls, because such areas are deemed to be community business centers and thus serve a public function.

ELECTRONIC LEAFLETS   What about the transmission of "electronic leaflets" over the Internet? Should the same principles apply? Is the transmission of such material—often referred to as "junk mail" or "spam"—over the Internet significantly different from the distribution of leaflets in a shopping mall or on a public street? This issue arose in a recent dispute between America Online (AOL), the well-known Internet service provider, and Cyber Promotions (CP). CP transmits electronic ads to thousands of e-mail addresses, including AOL subscribers. In response to complaints from its subscribers, AOL blocked all e-mail from CP. AOL also gathered all of CP's e-mail messages together and returned them to CP in an "e-mail bomb" that brought down the computer system of CP's Internet service provider. CP sued AOL, claiming, among other things, that its electronic messages were protected speech under the First Amendment.

AOL claimed that the First Amendment, which prohibits the government from restraining speech-related conduct, does not apply to AOL, which is a private company. Therefore, AOL can block e-mail transmissions directed to its subscribers without violating the First Amendment. CP contended that because the Internet was initially subsidized by the government, speech over the Internet should be constitutionally protected. In CP's suit against AOL, a federal district court declared that CP did not have a constitutional right, under the First Amendment, to send unsolicited e-mail advertisements to AOL subscribers and that AOL was entitled to block CP's attempts to do so.[26]

OTHER ISSUES   Some questions raised in this case relate to other areas of the law. For example, in regard to intellectual property law (discussed in Chapter 4), are the e-mail addresses of AOL's subscribers AOL's property, or are they more like the addresses in a telephone book, which anybody can access and use? Additionally, should the government regulate unwanted e-mail just as it does unwanted faxes? After all, recipients of ads and leaflets distributed through the mails or in shopping malls do not have to pay for those materials. In contrast, subscribers of online service providers, such as AOL, pay an hourly fee for the service, which shifts the cost of e-mail ads to the customer.

---

26. *Cyber Promotions, Inc. v. America Online, Inc.,* 948 F.Supp. 436 (E.D.Pa. 1966). Note that in a similar case brought against CP by CompuServe in 1997, a federal district court held that CP's sending unsolicited e-mail advertisements to CompuServe's proprietary network, after CompuServe had repeatedly demanded CP to cease transmitting such materials, was actionable as a trespass to personal property (a tort, or wrongful act, discussed in Chapter 4). See *CompuServe, Inc. v. Cyber Promotions, Inc.,* 962 F.Supp. 1015 (S.D. Ohio 1997).

▌ Terms and Concepts

adjudicate 7
administrative agency 6
administrative law 6
administrative process 7
Bill of Rights 22
binding authority 3

case law 7
choice-of-language clause 10
choice-of-law clause 10
citation 5
civil law 8
civil law system 8

commerce clause 17
common law 3
constitutional law 5
criminal law 8
defendant 4
due process clause 24

▮ Terms and Concepts (continued)

enabling legislation 7
establishment clause 24
executive agency 6
forum-selection clause 10
free exercise clause 24
independent regulatory
  agency 6
international law 9

jurisprudence 2
law 2
national law 8
persuasive authority 4
plaintiff 4
police powers 20
precedent 3
primary source of law 5

procedural law 8
remedy 4
secondary source of law 5
stare decisis 3
statutory law 5
substantive law 8
treaty 9

▮ Chapter Summary: Sources of Business Law and the Global Legal Environment

The Nature of Law *(See pages 2–3.)*	Law can be defined as a body of enforceable rules governing relationships among individuals and between individuals and their society.

The Common Law Tradition
(See pages 3–5.)
	1. *Common law*—Law that originated in medieval England with the creation of the king's courts, or *curia regis,* and the development of a body of rules that were common to (or applied throughout) the land.
	
	2. *Stare decisis*—A doctrine under which judges "stand on decided cases"—or follow the rule of precedent—in deciding cases. *Stare decisis* is the cornerstone of the common law tradition.
	
	3. *Remedies*—
	  a. Remedies at law—Money or something else of value.
	  b. Remedies in equity—Remedies that are granted when the remedies at law are unavailable or inadequate. Equitable remedies include specific performance, an injunction, and contract rescission (cancellation).

Sources of American Law *(See pages 5–8.)*	1. *Constitutional law*—The law as expressed in the U.S. Constitution and the various state constitutions. The U.S. Constitution is the supreme law of the land. State constitutions are supreme within state borders to the extent that they do not violate the U.S. Constitution or a federal law. 2. *Statutory law*—Laws or ordinances created by federal, state, and local legislatures and governing bodies. None of these laws can violate the U.S. Constitution or the relevant state constitutions. Uniform laws, when adopted by a state legislature, become statutory law in that state. 3. *Administrative law*—The rules, orders, and decisions of federal or state government administrative agencies. Federal administrative agencies are created by enabling legislation enacted by the U.S. Congress. Agency functions include rulemaking, investigation and enforcement, and adjudication. 4. *Case law and common law doctrines*—Judge-made law, including interpretations of constitutional provisions, of statutes enacted by legislatures, and of regulations created by administrative agencies. The common law—the doctrines and principles embodied in case law—governs all areas not covered by statutory law (or agency regulations issued to implement various statutes).
Classifications of Law *(See page 8.)*	The law may be broken down according to several classification systems, such as substantive or procedural law, civil or criminal law, federal or state law, and private or public law. <div align="right">*(Continued)*</div>

Chapter Summary: Sources of Business Law and the Global Legal Environment—Continued

National and International Law (*See pages 8–10.*)	1. *National law*—Most nations today have either a common law system or a civil law system: a. Common law system—See the summary of the common law tradition above. Generally, those countries that were once colonies of Great Britain retained their English common law heritage after they achieved their independence. Today, nations with common law systems include England, the United States, Ireland, Canada, Australia, New Zealand, and India. b. Civil law system—A legal system stemming from Roman "code law," in which the primary source of law is a statutory code—an ordered grouping of legal principles enacted into law by a legislature or governing body. Precedents are not binding in a civil law system. Most of the continental European countries have a civil law system, as do those African, Latin American, and Asian nations that were once colonies of those European countries. Japan and South Africa also have civil law systems. 2. *International law*—A body of written and unwritten laws observed by independent nations and governing the acts of individuals as well as governments. Sources of international law include national laws, customs, treaties, and international organizations and conferences.
The Constitution and American Business (*See pages 17–25.*)	1. *Commerce clause*—Expressly permits Congress to regulate commerce. That power authorizes the national government, at least theoretically, to regulate every commercial enterprise in the United States. Under their police powers, state governments may regulate private activities to protect or promote the public order, health, safety, morals, and general welfare. 2. *Bill of Rights*—The first ten amendments to the U.S. Constitution. They embody a series of protections for individuals—and in some cases, business entities—against various types of interference by the federal government. One of the freedoms guaranteed by the Bill of Rights that affects businesses is the freedom of speech guaranteed by the First Amendment. Also important are the protections of the Fifth and the Fourteenth Amendments, which provide that no person shall be deprived of "life, liberty, or property, without due process of law."

For Review

1. What is the common law tradition?
2. What is a precedent? When might a court depart from precedent?
3. What is the Uniform Commercial Code?

4. What is the difference between civil law and criminal law?
5. What is the Bill of Rights? What rights and liberties does this document establish?

Questions and Case Problems

1–1. Legal Systems. What are the key differences between a common law system and a civil law system?

Why do some countries have common law systems and others have civil law systems?

1–2. **Reading Citations.** Assume that you want to read the entire court opinion in the case of *White v. York International Corp.*, 45 F.3d 357 (10th Cir. 1995). The case deals with the question of whether an employer violated the Americans with Disabilities Act of 1990, a federal statute that prohibits discrimination against persons with disabilities. Read the section entitled "Finding Case Law" in this chapter, and then explain specifically where you would find the court's opinion.

1–3. **Sources of American Law.** This chapter discussed a number of sources of American law. Which source of law takes priority in the following situations, and why?

    (a) A federal statute conflicts with the U.S. Constitution.

    (b) A federal statute conflicts with a state constitution.

    (c) A state statute conflicts with the common law of that state.

    (d) A state constitutional amendment conflicts with the U.S. Constitution.

    (e) A federal administrative regulation conflicts with a state constitution.

1–4. *Stare Decisis.* In the text of this chapter, we stated that the doctrine of *stare decisis* "became a cornerstone of the English and American judicial systems." What does *stare decisis* mean, and why has this doctrine been so fundamental to the development of our legal tradition?

1–5. **Common Law versus Statutory Law.** Courts are able to overturn precedents and thus can change the common law. Should judges have the same authority to overrule statutory law? Explain.

1–6. **Binding versus Persuasive Authority.** A county court in Illinois is deciding a case involving an issue that has never been addressed before in that state's courts. The Iowa Supreme Court, however, recently decided a case involving a very similar fact pattern. Is the Illinois court obligated to follow the Iowa Supreme Court's decision on the issue? If the United States Supreme Court had decided a similar case, would that decision be binding on the Illinois court? Explain.

1–7. **Freedom of Speech.** The Allstate Insurance Co. agreed to refer its policyholders to members of the USA-GLAS Network for automobile glass repair and replacement. In response to the concerns of independent glass businesses over the loss of revenue caused by the arrangement, the South Dakota legislature passed a statute prohibiting an insurance company from requiring or recommending that a policyholder "use a particular company or location for the providing of automobile glass replacement or repair services or products." Allstate filed a suit against the state, challenging the validity of the statute as, among other things, an unconstitutional restriction on commercial speech. Will the court agree with Allstate? Why or why not? [*Allstate Insurance Co. v. State of South Dakota*, 871 F.Supp. 355 (D.S.D. 1994)]

1–8. **Commerce Clause.** South Dakota Disposal Systems, Inc. (SDDS), applied to the South Dakota Department of Water and Natural Resources (DWNR) for a permit to operate a solid-waste-disposal facility (Lonetree). It was estimated that 90 to 95 percent of the waste would come from out of state. The DWNR determined that Lonetree would be environmentally safe and issued a permit. Later, a public referendum was held. The state attorney general issued a pamphlet to accompany the referendum that urged the public to vote against "the out-of-state dump" because "South Dakota is not the nation's dumping grounds." SDDS filed a suit against the state, challenging the referendum as a violation of, among other things, the commerce clause. Was the referendum unconstitutional? Why or why not? [*SDDS, Inc. v. State of South Dakota*, 47 F.3d 263 (8th Cir. 1995)]

U.S. **2 F2d** **CASE BRIEFING ASSIGNMENT**
1–9. *Examine Case A.1* [Austin v. Berryman, 878 F.2d 786 (4th Cir. 1989)] *in Appendix A. The case has been excerpted there in great detail. Review and then brief the case, making sure that you include answers to the following questions in your brief.*

    1. Who were the plaintiff and defendant in this action?

    2. Why did Austin claim that she had been forced to leave her job?

    3. Why was Austin refused state unemployment benefits?

    4. Did the state's refusal to give Austin unemployment compensation violate her rights under the free exercise clause of the First Amendment?

    5. What logic or reasoning did the court employ in arriving at its conclusion?

▌Accessing the Internet: Fundamentals of Business Law

The Internet is a web of educational, corporate, and research computer networks around the world. The Internet has many uses, including transmitting weather reports, doing library searches, and finding addresses of university students and faculty thousands of miles away. On the Internet, you will find discussion groups, news groups, electronic publications, and electronic mail (E-mail), the most common use of the Internet.

Every site and every document on the Internet has a specific address described by uniform resource locators, known as URLs. You can think of URLs as the phone numbers of information on the Internet. A URL in effect tells computers where a particular site you wish to visit is located. It further tells the computer where the information at that site can be obtained. You have to type the URLs exactly as written: upper and lower case are important. Here are some useful Internet addresses for you to use now:

Legal Information Institute: **http://www.law.cornell.edu**

Virtual Law Library: **http://www.law.indiana.edu/**

Yahoo: **http://www.yahoo.com/Government/Law/**

You can also get updated information on legal sites on the Internet by contacting Nolo Press at

http://www.nolo.com

There are several other collections of law sites that you might want to access. The 'Lectric Law Library offers a large variety of legal information. Its Internet address on the Web is

http://www.lectlaw.com

FindLaw is a directory of law-related Web sites at

http://www.findlaw.com/

The Internet Law Library (sponsored by the U.S. House of Represntatives) offers links to federal and state legislative and regulatory materials, including the U.S. Code and the Code of Federal Regulations at

http:/www.house.gov/

The Library of Congress offers extensive links to state and federal government resources at

http://www.loc.gov/

The World Wide Web version of the Constitution provides hypertext links to amendments and other changes. Go to

http://www.law.cornell.edu/constitution/constitution.overview.html/

You can obtain all constitutional decisions of the United States Supreme Court by using a site developed by Cornell Law School at

http://www.law.cornell.edu/syllabi?constituional+unconstitutional

For information on the effect of new computer and communications technologies on the constitutional rights and liberties of Americans, go to the Center for Democracy and Technology at

http://www.cdt.org/

The Cyberspace Law Institute (CLI) also focuses on law and communications technology. According to the CLI, it is devoted to studying and helping to develop "the new forms of law and lawmaking required by the growth of global communications networks and online communities." By using the CLI site, you can find articles and information on such topics as privacy, flaming, obscenity, and other issues relating to constitutional law. Go to

http://www.cli.org

The constitutions of almost all of the states are now online. You can find them at

http:www.findlaw.com/llstategov/

If you would like to see constitutions of various other countries in the world, go to

http:www.eur.nl/iacl/const.html

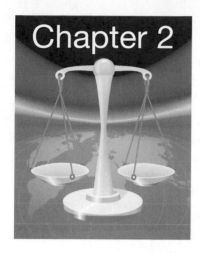

Chapter 2

Courts and Procedures

CHAPTER OBJECTIVES

After reading this chapter, you should be able to:

1. Explain the concepts of jurisdiction and venue.
2. State the requirements for federal jurisdiction.
3. Identify the basic components of the federal and state court systems.
4. Compare and contrast the functions of trial courts and appellate courts.
5. Discuss the various ways in which disputes can be resolved outside the court system.

Ultimately, we are all affected by what the courts say and do. This is particularly true in the business world—nearly every businessperson faces either a potential or an actual lawsuit at some time or another in his or her career. For this reason, anyone contemplating a career in business will benefit from an understanding of American court systems, including the mechanics of lawsuits.

In this chapter, after examining the judiciary's overall role in the American governmental scheme, we discuss some basic requirements that must be met before a party may bring a lawsuit before a particular court. We then look at the court systems of the United States in some detail and, to clarify judicial procedures, follow a hypothetical case through a state court system. Even though there are fifty-two court systems—one for each of the fifty states, one for the District of Columbia, plus a federal system—similarities abound. Keep in mind that the federal courts are not superior to the state courts; they are simply an independent system of courts, which derives its authority from Article III, Section 2, of the U.S. Constitution. The chapter concludes with an overview of some alternative methods of settling disputes.

The Judiciary's Role in American Government

As you learned in Chapter 1, the body of American law is vast and complex. It includes the federal and state constitutions, statutes passed by legislative bodies, administrative law, and the case decisions and legal principles that form the common law. These laws would be meaningless, however, without the courts to interpret and apply them. This is the essential role of the judiciary—the courts—in the American governmental system: to interpret and apply the law.

As the branch of government entrusted with interpreting the laws, the judiciary can decide, among other things, whether the laws or actions of the other two branches are constitutional. The process for making such a determination is known as **judicial review.** The power of judicial review enables the judicial branch to act as a check on the other two branches of government, in line with the checks and balances system established by the U.S. Constitution.

The power of judicial review is not mentioned in the Constitution, however. Rather, it was established by the United States Supreme Court's decision in *Marbury v. Madison.*[1] In that case, which was decided in 1803, the Supreme Court stated, "It is emphatically the province and duty of the Judicial Department to say what the law is. . . . If two laws conflict with each other, the courts must decide on the operation of each. . . . So if the law be in opposition to the Constitution . . . [t]he Court must determine which of these conflicting rules governs the case. This is the very essence of judicial duty." Since the *Marbury v. Madison* decision, the power of judicial review has remained unchallenged. Today, this power is exercised by both federal and state courts.

▌ Basic Judicial Requirements

Before a lawsuit can be brought before a court, certain requirements must first be met. These requirements relate to jurisdiction, venue, and standing to sue. We examine each of these important concepts here.

Jurisdiction

In Latin, *juris* means "law," and *diction* means "to speak." Thus, "the power to speak the law" is the literal meaning of the term **jurisdiction.** Before any court can hear a case, it must have jurisdiction over the person against whom the suit is brought or over the property involved in the suit. The court must also have jurisdiction over the subject matter.

JURISDICTION OVER PERSONS   Generally, a court can exercise personal jurisdiction (*in personam* jurisdiction) over residents of a certain geographi-

cal area. A state trial court, for example, normally has jurisdictional authority over residents of a particular area of the state, such as a county or district. A state's highest court (often called the state supreme court)[2] has jurisdictional authority over all residents within the state.

In some cases, under the authority of a state **long arm statute,** a court can exercise personal jurisdiction over nonresident defendants as well. Before a court can exercise jurisdiction over a nonresident under a long arm statute, though, it must be demonstrated that the nonresident had sufficient contacts, or *minimum contacts*, with the state to justify the jurisdiction.[3] For example, if an individual has committed a wrong within the state, such as causing an automobile injury or selling defective goods, a court can usually exercise jurisdiction even if the person causing the harm is located in another state. Similarly, a state may exercise personal jurisdiction over a nonresident defendant who is sued for breaching a contract that was formed within the state.

In regard to corporations,[4] the minimum-contacts requirement is usually met if the corporation does business within the state. Suppose that a corporation incorporated under the laws of Maine and headquartered in that state has a branch office or manufacturing plant in Georgia. Does this corporation have sufficient minimum contacts with the state of Georgia to allow a Georgia court to exercise jurisdiction over the Maine corporation? Yes, it does. If the Maine corporation advertises and sells its products in Georgia, those activities may also suffice to meet the minimum-contacts requirements. In the following case, the issue is whether an Italian corporation had sufficient minimum contacts with the state of Arizona to permit a suit against the corporation to be brought in an Arizona state court.

---

1. 5 U.S. (1 Cranch) 137, 2 L.Ed. 60 (1803).

---

2. As will be discussed shortly, a state's highest court is often referred to as the state supreme court, but there are exceptions. For example, in New York, the supreme court is a trial court.
3. The minimum-contacts standard was established in *International Shoe Co. v. State of Washington*, 326 U.S. 310, 66 S.Ct. 154, 90 L.Ed. 95 (1945).
4. In the eyes of the law, corporations are "legal persons" — entities that can sue and be sued. See Chapter 24.

CASE 2.1

A. Uberti and Co. v. Leonardo

Supreme Court of Arizona, 1995.
892 P.2d 1354.

FACTS Aldo Uberti and Company, an Italian corporation, manufactures a replica of the Peacemaker known as the Cattleman. Uberti sells its guns to a U.S. distributor for sale throughout the country. Henry Pacho, a resident of Arizona, bought one of the guns, wrapped it in a towel, and put it under the seat of his car. His two-year-old niece Corrina was helping to clean the car when the gun fell out of the towel, hit the pavement, and discharged. The bullet struck Corrina in the head and killed her. Corrina's parents filed a suit in an Arizona state court against Uberti, alleging that the company was liable for the "design, manufacture, sale, and distribution of a defective and unreasonably dangerous product." Uberti asked the court to dismiss the suit on the ground that the court did not have personal jurisdiction over Uberti. The court refused, and Uberti appealed. The appellate court reversed. Corrina's parents then appealed to the Supreme Court of Arizona.

ISSUE Does selling a product in the United States in general constitute sufficient "minimum contacts" with Arizona to allow that state's courts to exercise personal jurisdiction over the manufacturer of the product?

DECISION Yes. The Supreme Court of Arizona held that Uberti could be sued in an Arizona state court.

REASON The state supreme court concluded that "the gun, as a replica of an American frontier weapon, was originally and primarily designed and made for the American market." Uberti knew that its products, through its American distributor, "would flow into local markets across America." Corrina's parents did not have to show intent on Uberti's part to sell its guns in Arizona specifically. "An intent to sell across America is enough," concluded the court. If it were otherwise, "no individual state could assert jurisdiction" over Uberti, because Uberti "did not target a particular state or group of states but instead intended to sell its product to all of America. The argument turns common sense on its head. Holding that a defendant intending to sell its products to any and all citizens in the United States could not be held accountable in any jurisdiction where its products caused injury defies any sensible concept of due process."

FOR CRITICAL ANALYSIS—Ethical Consideration *The typical car dealership directs its sales efforts toward the local market in a single state. If a customer buys a car and drives it to another state, where a defect in the car causes an accident, is it fair to allow that state's courts to exercise personal jurisdiction over the dealership located in the other state?*

JURISDICTION OVER PROPERTY A court can also exercise jurisdiction over property that is located within its boundaries. This kind of jurisdiction is known as *in rem* jurisdiction, or "jurisdiction over the thing." For example, suppose that a dispute arises over the ownership of a boat in dry dock in Fort Lauderdale, Florida. The boat is owned by an Ohio resident, over whom a Florida court cannot normally exercise personal jurisdiction. The other party to the dispute is a resident of Nebraska. In this situation, a lawsuit concerning the boat could be brought in a Florida state court on the basis of the court's *in rem* jurisdiction.

JURISDICTION OVER SUBJECT MATTER Jurisdiction over subject matter is a limitation on the types of cases a court can hear. In both the federal and state court systems, there are courts of *general* (unlimited) *jurisdiction* and courts of *limited jurisdiction.* An example of a court of general jurisdiction is a state or federal trial court. An example of a state court of limited jurisdiction is a probate court. **Probate courts** are state courts that handle only matters relating to the transfer of a person's assets and obligations after that person's death, including matters relating to the custody and guardianship of children. An example of a federal court of limited subject-matter jurisdiction is a bankruptcy court. **Bankruptcy courts** handle only bankruptcy proceedings, which are governed by federal bankruptcy law (discussed in Chapter 20). In contrast, a court of general jurisdiction can decide virtually any type of case.

A court's jurisdiction over subject matter is usually defined in the statute or constitution creating the court. In both the federal and state court systems, a court's subject-matter jurisdiction can be limited not only by the subject of the lawsuit but also by the amount of money in controversy, by whether a case is a felony (a more serious type of crime) or a misdemeanor (a less serious type of crime), or by whether the proceeding is a trial or an appeal.

ORIGINAL AND APPELLATE JURISDICTION The distinction between courts of original jurisdiction and courts of appellate jurisdiction normally lies in whether the case is being heard for the first time. Courts having original jurisdiction are courts of the first instance, or trial courts—that is, courts in which lawsuits begin, trials take place, and evidence is presented. In the federal court system, the *district courts* are trial courts. In the various state court systems, the trial courts are known by various names, as will be discussed shortly.

The key point here is that normally, any court having original jurisdiction is known as a trial court. Courts having appellate jurisdiction act as reviewing courts, or appellate courts. In general, cases can be brought before appellate courts only on appeal from an order or a judgment of a trial court or other lower court.

JURISDICTION OF THE FEDERAL COURTS Because the federal government is a government of limited powers, the jurisdiction of the federal courts is limited. Article III of the U.S. Constitution establishes the boundaries of federal judicial power. Section 2 of Article III states that "[t]he judicial Power

shall extend to all Cases, in Law and Equity, arising under this Constitution, the Laws of the United States, and Treaties made, or which shall be made, under their Authority."

Whenever a plaintiff's cause of action is based, at least in part, on the U.S. Constitution, a treaty, or a federal law, then a **federal question** arises, and the case comes under the judicial power of the federal courts. Any lawsuit involving a federal question can originate in a federal court. People who claim that their constitutional rights have been violated can begin their suits in a federal court.

Federal district courts can also exercise original jurisdiction over cases involving **diversity of citizenship.** Such cases may arise between (1) citizens of different states, (2) a foreign country and citizens of a state or of different states, or (3) citizens of a state and citizens or subjects of a foreign country. The amount in controversy must be more than $75,000 before a federal court can take jurisdiction in such cases. For purposes of diversity jurisdiction, a corporation is a citizen of both the state in which it is incorporated and the state in which its principal place of business is located. A case involving diversity of citizenship can be filed in the appropriate federal district court, or, if the case starts in a state court, it can sometimes be transferred to a federal court. A large percentage of the cases filed in federal courts each year are based on diversity of citizenship.

Note that in a case based on a federal question, a federal court will apply federal law. In a case based on diversity of citizenship, however, a federal court will apply the relevant state law (which is often the law of the state in which the court sits).

EXCLUSIVE VERSUS CONCURRENT JURISDICTION When both federal and state courts have the power to hear a case, as is true in suits involving diversity of citizenship, **concurrent jurisdiction** exists. When cases can be tried only in federal courts or only in state courts, **exclusive jurisdiction** exists. Federal courts have exclusive jurisdiction in cases involving federal crimes, bankruptcy, patents, and copyrights; in suits against the United States; and in some areas of admiralty law (law governing transportation on the seas and ocean waters). States also have exclusive jurisdiction in certain subject matters—for example, in divorce and adoption. The concepts of concurrent and exclusive jurisdiction are illustrated in Exhibit 2–1.

Venue

Jurisdiction has to do with whether a court has authority to hear a case involving specific persons, property, or subject matter. **Venue**[5] is concerned with the most appropriate location for a trial. For example, two state courts (or two federal courts) may have the authority to exercise jurisdiction over a case, but it may be more appropriate or convenient to hear the case in one court than in the other.

Basically, the concept of venue reflects the policy that a court trying a suit should be in the geo-graphical neighborhood (usually the county) in which the incident leading to the lawsuit occurred or in which the parties involved in the lawsuit reside. Pretrial publicity or other factors, though, may require a change of venue to another community, especially in criminal cases in which the defendant's right to a fair and impartial jury has been impaired.

For example, in 1992, when four Los Angeles police officers accused of beating Rodney King were brought to trial, the attorneys defending the police officers requested a change of venue from

---

5.   Pronounced *ven*-yoo.

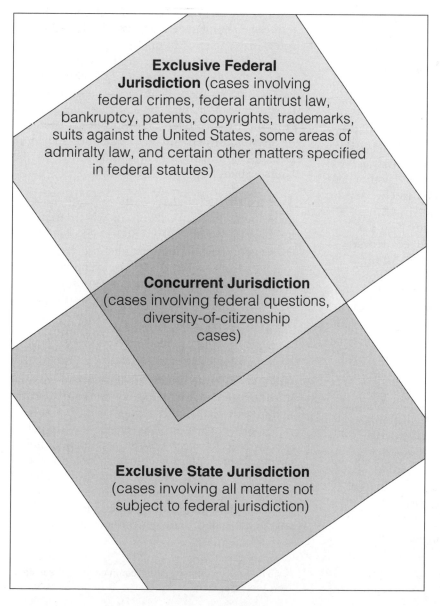

◆ **Exhibit 2–1**
Exclusive and
Concurrent Jurisdiction

Los Angeles to Simi Valley, California. The attorneys argued that to try the case in a Los Angeles court would jeopardize the defendants' right to a fair trial. The court agreed and granted the request. For similar reasons, a change of venue from Oklahoma City to Denver, Colorado, was ordered for the trial of Timothy McVeigh and Terry Nichols, who had been indicted in connection with the 1995 bombing of the Federal Building in Oklahoma City.

Standing to Sue

Before a person can bring a lawsuit before a court, the party must have **standing to sue,** or a sufficient "stake" in a matter to justify seeking relief through the court system. In other words, a party must have a legally protected and tangible interest at stake in the litigation in order to have standing. The party bringing the lawsuit must have suffered a harm, or been threatened a harm, by the action about which he or she complained. At times, a person will have standing to sue on behalf of another person. For example, suppose that a child suffered serious injuries as a result of a defectively manufactured toy. Because the child is a minor, a lawsuit could be brought on his or her behalf by another person, such as the child's parent or legal guardian.

Standing to sue also requires that the controversy at issue be a **justiciable**[6] **controversy**— a controversy that is real and substantial, as opposed to hypothetical or academic. For example, in the above example, the child's parent could not sue the toy manufacturer merely on the ground that the toy was defective. The issue would become justiciable only if the child had actually been injured due to the defect in the toy as marketed. In other words, the parent normally could not ask the court to determine, for example, what damages might be obtained *if* the child had been injured, because this would be merely a hypothetical question.

❚ The State and ❚ Federal Court Systems

As mentioned earlier in this chapter, each state has its own court system. Additionally, there is a system of federal courts. Although no state court system is the same, Exhibit 2–2 illustrates the basic organizational structure characteristic of the court systems in many states. The exhibit also shows how the federal court system is structured. We turn now to an examination of these court systems, beginning with the state courts.

State Court Systems

Typically a state court system will include several levels, or tiers, of courts. As indicated in Exhibit 2–2, state courts may include (1) trial courts of limited jurisdiction, (2) trial courts of general jurisdiction, (3) appellate courts, and (4) the state's highest court (often called the state supreme court). Judges in the state court system are usually elected by the voters for a specified term.

Generally, any person who is a party to a lawsuit has the opportunity to plead the case before a trial court and then, if he or she loses, before at least one level of appellate court. Finally, if a federal statute or federal constitutional issue is involved in the decision of the state supreme court, that decision may be further appealed to the United States Supreme Court.

TRIAL COURTS Trial courts are exactly what their name implies—courts in which trials are held and testimony taken. State trial courts have either general or limited jurisdiction. Trial courts that have general jurisdiction as to subject matter may be called county, district, superior, or circuit courts.[7] The jurisdiction of these courts is often determined by the size of the county in which the court sits. State trial courts of general jurisdiction have jurisdiction over a wide variety of subjects, including both civil disputes and criminal prosecutions. In some states, trial courts of general jurisdiction may hear appeals from courts of limited jurisdiction.

Some courts of limited jurisdiction are called special inferior trial courts or minor judiciary courts. **Small claims courts** are inferior trial courts that hear only civil cases involving claims of less than a certain amount, such as $2,500—the amount varies from state to state. Suits brought in small claims courts are generally conducted infor-

---

6.   Pronounced jus-*tish*-uh-bul.

7.   The name in Ohio is court of common pleas; the name in New York is supreme court.

♦ Exhibit 2–2
Federal Courts and State Court Systems

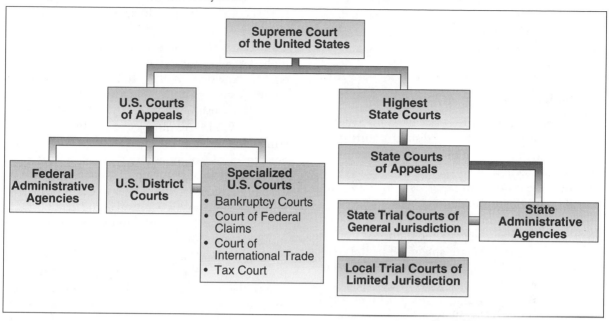

mally, and lawyers are not required. In a minority of states, lawyers are not even allowed to represent people in small claims courts for most purposes. Another example of an inferior trial court is a local municipal court that hears mainly traffic cases. Decisions of small claims courts and municipal courts may be appealed to a state trial court of general jurisdiction.

Other courts of limited jurisdiction as to subject matter include domestic relations courts, which handle only divorce actions and child custody cases, and probate courts, as mentioned earlier.

COURTS OF APPEALS   Every state has at least one court of appeals (appellate court, or reviewing court), which may be an intermediate appellate court or the state's highest court. About half of the states have intermediate appellate courts. Generally, courts of appeals do not conduct new trials, in which evidence is submitted to the court and witnesses are examined. Rather, an appellate court panel of three or more judges reviews the record of the case on appeal, which includes a transcript of the trial proceedings, and the panel determines whether the trial court committed an error.

Appellate courts look at *questions of law* (on which only a judge, not a jury, can rule) but usu-

ally defer to a trial court's findings on *questions of fact* (which may be decided by a judge or a jury based on evidence presented at trial). This is because the trial court judge and jury were in a better position to evaluate testimony—by directly observing witnesses' gestures, demeanor, and nonverbal behavior generally during the trial. At the appellate level, the judges review the written transcript of the trial, which does not include these nonverbal elements.

An appellate court will challenge a trial court's finding of fact only when the finding is clearly erroneous (that is, when it is contrary to the evidence presented at trial) or when there is no evidence to support the finding. For example, if a jury concluded that a manufacturer's product harmed the plaintiff but no evidence was submitted to the court to support that conclusion, the appellate court would hold that the trial court's decision was erroneous. The options exercised by appellate courts will be further discussed later in this chapter.

STATE SUPREME (HIGHEST) COURTS   The highest appellate court in a state is usually called the supreme court but may be called by some other name. For example, in both New York and Maryland, the highest state court is called the court of appeals. The decisions of each state's highest court on all questions of state law are final. Only when issues of federal law are involved can a decision made by a state's highest court be overruled by the United States Supreme Court.

The Federal Court System

The federal court system is basically a three-tiered model consisting of (1) U.S. district courts (trial courts of general jurisdiction) and various courts of limited jurisdiction, (2) U.S. courts of appeals (intermediate courts of appeals), and (3) the United States Supreme Court.

Unlike state court judges, who are usually elected, federal court judges—including the justices of the Supreme Court—are appointed by the president of the United States, subject to the approval of the U.S. Senate. All federal judges receive lifetime appointments (because under Article III they "hold their offices during Good Behavior").

U.S. DISTRICT COURTS At the federal level, the equivalent of a state trial court of general jurisdiction is the district court. There is at least one federal district court in every state. The number of judicial districts can vary over time, primarily owing to population changes and corresponding caseloads. Currently, there are ninety-six federal judicial districts.

U.S. district courts have original jurisdiction in federal matters. Federal cases typically originate in district courts. There are other trial courts with original, but special (or limited), jurisdiction, such as the federal bankruptcy courts and others shown in Exhibit 2–2.

U.S. COURTS OF APPEALS In the federal court system, there are thirteen U.S. courts of appeals—also referred to as U.S. circuit courts of appeals. The federal courts of appeals for twelve of the circuits hear appeals from the federal district courts located within their respective judicial circuits. The Court of Appeals for the Thirteenth Circuit, called the Federal Circuit, has national appellate jurisdiction over certain types of cases, such as cases involving patent law and cases in which the U.S. government is a defendant.

The decisions of the circuit courts of appeals are final in most cases, but appeal to the United States Supreme Court is possible. Exhibit 2–3 shows the geographical boundaries of U.S. circuit courts of appeals and the boundaries of the U.S. district courts within each circuit.

THE UNITED STATES SUPREME COURT The highest level of the three-tiered model of the federal court system is the United States Supreme Court. According to the language of Article III of the U.S. Constitution, there is only one national Supreme Court. All other courts in the federal system are considered "inferior." Congress is empowered to create other inferior courts as it deems necessary. The inferior courts that Congress has created include the second tier in our model—the U.S. courts of appeals—as well as the district courts and any other courts of limited, or specialized, jurisdiction.

The United States Supreme Court consists of nine justices. Although the United States Supreme Court has original, or trial, jurisdiction in rare instances (set forth in Article III, Section 2), most of its work is as an appeals court. The Supreme Court can review any case decided by any of the federal courts of appeals, and it also has appellate authority over some cases decided in the state courts.

To bring a case before the Supreme Court, a party requests the Court to issue a writ of *certiorari*. A **writ of *certiorari***[8] is an order issued by the Supreme Court to a lower court requiring the latter to send it the record of the case for review. The Court will not issue a writ unless at least four of the nine justices approve of it. This is called the **rule of four.** Whether the Court will issue a writ of *certiorari* is entirely within its discretion. The Court is not required to issue one, and most petitions for writs are denied. (Thousands of cases are filed with the Supreme Court each year, yet it hears, on average, less than one hundred of these cases.[9]) A denial is not a decision on the merits of a case, nor does it indicate agreement with the lower court's opinion. Furthermore, denial of the writ has no value as a precedent.

---

8. Pronounced sur-shee-uh-*rah*-ree.
9. From the mid-1950s through the early 1990s, the Supreme Court reviewed more cases per year than it has in the last few years. In the Court's 1982–1983 term, for example, the Court issued opinions in 151 cases. In contrast, only 77 cases were scheduled for review during the Court's 1995–1996 term.

♦ Exhibit 2–3
U.S. Courts of Appeals and U.S. District Courts

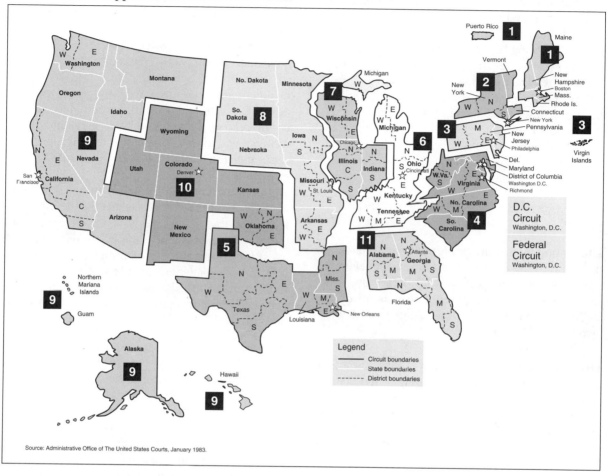

Source: Administrative Office of The United States Courts, January 1983.

Typically, the petitions granted by the Court involve cases that raise important constitutional questions or cases that conflict with other state or federal court decisions. Similarly, if federal appellate courts are rendering inconsistent opinions on an important issue, the Supreme Court may review the case and issue a decision to define the law on the matter.

Following a Case through the State Courts

To illustrate the procedures that would be followed in a civil lawsuit brought in a state court, we present a hypothetical case and follow it through the state court system. The case involves an automobile accident in which Kevin Anderson, driving a Mercedes, struck Lisa Marconi, driving a Ford Taurus. The accident occurred at the intersection of Wilshire Boulevard and Rodeo Drive in Beverly Hills, California. Marconi suffered personal injuries, incurring medical and hospital expenses as well as lost wages for four months. Anderson and Marconi are unable to agree on a settlement, and Marconi sues Anderson. Marconi is the plaintiff, and Anderson is the defendant. Both are represented by lawyers.

During each phase of the **litigation** (the process of working a lawsuit through the court system), Marconi and Anderson will be required to observe strict procedural requirements. A large body of law—procedural law—establishes the rules and standards for determining disputes in courts. Procedural rules are very complex, and they vary from court to court. There is a set of federal rules of procedure and various sets of rules for state courts. Additionally, the applicable procedures will depend on whether the case is a civil or criminal case. Generally, the Marconi-Anderson litigation will involve the procedures discussed in the following subsections. Keep in mind that attempts to settle the case may be ongoing throughout the trial. (For an extreme example of how legal fees can spiral during the litigation process, see this chapter's *Law in the Extreme.*)

The Pleadings

The complaint and answer (and the counterclaim and reply)—all of which are discussed below—taken together are called the **pleadings.** The pleadings inform each party of the claims of the other and specify the issues (disputed questions) involved in the case.

THE PLAINTIFF'S COMPLAINT Marconi's suit against Anderson commences when her lawyer files a **complaint** with the appropriate court. The complaint contains a statement alleging (asserting to the court, in a pleading) the facts necessary for the court to take jurisdiction, a brief summary of the facts necessary to show that the plaintiff is entitled to a remedy, and a statement of the remedy the plaintiff is seeking. Exhibit 2–4 illustrates how the complaint might read in the Marconi-Anderson case. Complaints may be lengthy or brief, depending on the complexity of the case.

After the complaint has been filed, the sheriff, a deputy of the county, or another *process server* (one who delivers a complaint and summons) serves a **summons** and a copy of the complaint on defendant Anderson. The summons notifies Anderson that he must file an answer to the complaint with both the court and the plaintiff's attorney within a specified time period (usually twenty to thirty days). The summons also informs Anderson that failure to answer will result in a **default judgment** for the plaintiff, meaning the plaintiff will be awarded the damages alleged in her complaint.

THE DEFENDANT'S ANSWER The defendant's **answer** either admits the statements or allegations set forth in the complaint or denies them and outlines any defenses that the defendant may have. If Anderson admits to all of Marconi's allegations in his answer, the court will enter a judgment for Marconi. If Anderson denies any of Marconi's allegations, the litigation will go forward.

Anderson can deny Marconi's allegations and set forth his own claim that Marconi was in fact negligent and therefore owes him money for damages to his Mercedes. This is appropriately called a **counterclaim.** If Anderson files a counterclaim, Marconi will have to answer it with a pleading, normally called a **reply,** which has the same characteristics as an answer.

Anderson can also admit the truth of Marconi's complaint but raise new facts that may result in dismissal of the action. This is called raising an *affirmative defense.* For example, Anderson could assert the running of the relevant statute of limitations (a state or federal statute that sets the maximum time period during which a certain action can be brought or rights enforced) as an affirmative defense.

MOTION TO DISMISS A **motion to dismiss** requests the court to dismiss the case for stated reasons. The motion to dismiss is often made by a defendant before filing an answer to the plaintiff's complaint. Grounds for dismissal of a case include improper delivery of the complaint and summons, improper venue, and the plaintiff's failure to state a claim for which a court could grant relief (a remedy). For example, if Marconi had suffered no injuries or losses as a result of Anderson's negligence, Anderson could move to have the case dismissed because Marconi had not stated a claim for which relief could be granted.

If the judge grants the motion to dismiss, the plaintiff generally is given time to file an amended complaint. If the judge denies the motion, the suit will go forward, and the defendant must then file an answer.

Note that if Marconi wishes to discontinue the suit because, for example, an out-of-court settlement has been reached, she can likewise move for dismissal. The court can also dismiss the case on its own motion.

Pretrial Motions

Either party may attempt to get the case dismissed before trial through the use of various pretrial

IN THE LOS ANGELES MUNICIPAL COURT
FOR THE LOS ANGELES JUDICIAL DISTRICT

CIVIL NO. 8–1026

Lisa Marconi
_____
        Plaintiff

        v.

                                                    COMPLAINT

Kevin Anderson
_____
        Defendant

    Comes now the plaintiff and for her cause of action against the defendant alleges and states as follows:

1. The jurisdiction of this court is based on Section 86 of the California Civil Code.
2. This action is between plaintiff, a California resident living at 1434 Palm Drive, Anaheim, California, and defendant, a California resident living at 6950 Garrison Avenue, Los Angeles, California.
3. On September 10, 1996, plaintiff, Lisa Marconi, was exercising good driving habits and reasonable care in driving her car through the intersection of Rodeo Drive and Wilshire Boulevard when defendant, Kevin Anderson, negligently drove his vehicle through a red light at the intersection and collided with plaintiff's vehicle. Defendant was negligent in the operation of the vehicle as to:

     a. Speed,
     b. Lookout,
     c. Management and control.

4. As a result of the collision plaintiff suffered severe physical injury that prevented her from working and property damage to her car. The costs she incurred included $10,000 in medical bills, $9,000 in lost wages, and $5,000 for automobile repairs.

WHEREFORE, plaintiff demands judgment against the defendant for the sum of $24,000 plus interest at the maximum legal rate and the costs of this action.

                    By _____
                    Roger Harrington
                    Attorney for the Plaintiff
                    800 Orange Avenue
                    Anaheim, CA 91426

motions. We have already mentioned the motion to dismiss. Two other important pretrial motions are the motion for judgment on the pleadings and the motion for summary judgment.

At the close of the pleadings, either party may make a **motion for judgment on the pleadings,** or on the merits of the case. The judge will grant the motion only when there is no dispute over the facts of the case and the only issue to be resolved is a question of law. In deciding on the motion, the judge may only consider the evidence contained in the pleadings.

In contrast, in a **motion for summary judgment,** the court may consider evidence outside the pleadings, such as sworn statements (affidavits) by parties or witnesses or other documents relating to the case. A motion for summary judgment can be made by either party. As with the motion for judgment on the pleadings, a motion for summary judgment will be granted only if there are no genuine questions of fact and the only question is a question of law.

Deciding whether a certain issue presents a question of fact or a question of law is not always easy, and judges sometimes disagree on whether summary judgment is appropriate in a given case. The following case illustrates this point.

CASE 2.2

Metzgar v. Playskool, Inc.
United States Court of Appeals,
Third Circuit, 1994.
30 F.3d 459.

FACTS   Ronald Metzgar placed his fifteen-month-old son Matthew, awake and healthy, in his playpen. Ronald left the room for five minutes and on his return found Matthew lifeless. A purple toy block had lodged in the boy's throat, choking him to death. Ronald called 911, but efforts to revive Matthew were to no avail. There was no warning of a choking hazard on the box containing the block. Matthew's parents sued Playskool, Inc., the manufacturer of the block, and others in a federal district court. They alleged, among other things, negligence[a] in failing to warn of the hazard of the block. Playskool filed a motion for summary judgment, arguing that the danger of a young child choking on a small block was obvious. The court entered a summary judgment in favor of Playskool. The parents appealed.

ISSUE   Is the question of the obviousness of the danger, in the context of a negligence claim, a question of fact for the jury to decide?

DECISION   Yes. The U.S. Court of Appeals for the Third Circuit held that the question of the obviousness in this case was not a proper subject for summary judgment and remanded the case for a trial.

REASON   The court explained that for purposes of the parents' claim, for a risk to be deemed obvious "there must be general consensus within the relevant community." Reasoned the court, "We cannot see how the purple Playskool block can be deemed as a matter of law an obvious safety hazard in the eyes of the relevant community, when Playskool itself believed the block was safe." The court pointed out that Matthew's parents did not believe the block posed an obvious threat and that Playskool did not offer any evidence to show the danger was obvious. The court concluded that "[u]nder a negligence theory, * * * the question of obviousness is more properly submitted to a jury than disposed on motion for summary judgment. The court's role in deciding a motion for summary judgment is merely to decide whether there is a genuine issue of material fact for trial." The lower court's dismissal of the parents' claim on the basis of a determination that the danger was obvious was "tantamount to holding that no reasonable jury could conclude otherwise. Based on the evidence of record, we cannot agree."

FOR CRITICAL ANALYSIS—Social Consideration   *When a case requires a determination of such matters as community standards, summary judgment is not considered appropriate. Such matters are given to juries to determine. Why?*

a.   *Negligence* is a failure to use the standard of care that a reasonable person would exercise in similar circumstances. See Chapter 4.

Discovery

Before a trial begins, each party can use a number of procedural devices to obtain information and gather evidence about the case from the other party or from third parties. The process of obtaining such information is known as **discovery.** Discovery includes gaining access to witnesses, documents, records, and other types of evidence.

The Federal Rules of Civil Procedure and similar rules in the states set forth the guidelines for discovery activity. The rules governing discovery are designed to make sure that a witness or a party is not unduly harassed, that privileged material (communications that need not be presented in court) is safeguarded, and that only matters relevant to the case at hand are discoverable.

Discovery prevents surprises at trial by giving parties access to evidence that might otherwise be hidden. This allows both parties to learn as much as they can about what to expect at a trial before they reach the courtroom. It also serves to narrow the issues so that trial time is spent on the main questions in the case. Currently, the trend is toward allowing more discovery and thus fewer surprises.[10]

DEPOSITIONS AND INTERROGATORIES Discovery can involve the use of depositions or interrogatories, or both. **Depositions** are sworn testimony by a party to the lawsuit or any witness. The person being deposed (the deponent) answers questions asked by the attorneys, and the questions and answers are recorded by an authorized court official and sworn to and signed by the deponent. (Occasionally, written depositions are taken when witnesses are unable to appear in person.) The answers given to depositions will, of course, help the attorneys prepare their cases. They can also be used in court to impeach (challenge the credibility of) a party or a witness who changes testimony at the trial. In addition, the answers given in a deposition can be used as testimony if the witness is not available at trial.

Interrogatories are written questions for which written answers are prepared and then signed under oath. The main difference between interrogatories and written depositions is that interrogatories are directed to a party to the lawsuit (the plaintiff or the defendant), not to a witness, and the party can prepare answers with the aid of an attorney. The scope of interrogatories is broader, because parties are obligated to answer questions, even if it means disclosing information from their records and files.

OTHER INFORMATION A party can serve a written request to the other party for an admission of the truth of matters relating to the trial. Any matter admitted under such a request is conclusively established for the trial. For example, Marconi can ask Anderson to admit that he was driving at a speed of forty-five miles an hour. A request for admission saves time at trial, because the parties will not have to spend time proving facts on which they already agree.

A party can also gain access to documents and other items not in his or her possession in order to inspect and examine them. Likewise, a party can gain "entry upon land" to inspect the premises. Anderson's attorney, for example, normally can gain permission to inspect and duplicate Marconi's car repair bills.

When the physical or mental condition of one party is in question, the opposing party can ask the court to order a physical or mental examination. If the court is willing to make the order, which it will do only if the need for the information outweighs the right to privacy of the person to be examined, the opposing party can obtain the results of the examination.

Pretrial Conference

Either party or the court can request a pretrial conference, or hearing. Usually, the hearing consists of an informal discussion between the judge and the opposing attorneys after discovery has taken place. The purpose of the hearing is to explore the possibility of a settlement without trial and, if this is not possible, to identify the matters that are in dispute and to plan the course of the trial.

Jury Selection

A trial can be held with or without a jury. If there is no jury, the judge determines the truth of the facts

---

10. This is particularly evident in the 1993 revision of the Federal Rules of Civil Procedure. The revised rules provide that each party must disclose to the other, on an ongoing basis, the types of evidence that will be presented at trial, the names of witnesses that may or will be called, and so on.

alleged in the case. The Seventh Amendment to the U.S. Constitution guarantees the right to a jury trial for cases in federal courts when the amount in controversy exceeds $20. Most states have similar guarantees in their own constitutions (although the threshold dollar amount is usually higher than $20). The right to a trial by jury does not have to be exercised, and many cases are tried without a jury. In most states and in federal courts, one of the parties must request a jury, or the right is presumed to be waived.

Before a jury trial commences, a jury must be selected. The jury-selection process is known as *voir dire*[11](a French phrase meaning "to speak the truth"). In most jurisdictions, the *voir dire* consists of oral questions that attorneys for the plaintiff and the defendant ask a group of prospective jurors (one at a time) to determine whether a potential jury member is biased or has any connection with a party to the action or with a prospective witness.

During *voir dire*, a party may challenge a certain number of prospective jurors *peremptorily*— that is, ask that an individual not be sworn in as a juror without providing any reason. Alternatively, a party may challenge a prospective juror *for cause*— that is, provide a reason why an individual should not be sworn in as a juror. If the judge grants the challenge, the individual is asked to step down. A prospective juror may not be excluded from the jury by the use of discriminatory challenges, however, such as those based on racial criteria[12] or gender.[13]

At the Trial

At the opening of the trial, the attorneys present their opening arguments, setting forth the facts that they expect to provide during the trial. Then the plaintiff's case is presented. In our hypothetical case, Marconi's lawyer would introduce evidence (relevant documents, exhibits, and the testimony of

witnesses) to support Marconi's position. The defendant has the opportunity to challenge any evidence introduced and to cross-examine any of the plaintiff's witnesses.

At the end of the plaintiff's case, the defendant's attorney has the opportunity to ask the judge to direct a verdict for the defendant on the ground that the plaintiff has presented no evidence that would justify the granting of the plaintiff's remedy. This is called a **motion for a directed verdict** (known in federal courts as a *motion for judgment as a matter of law*). If the motion is not granted (it seldom is), the defendant's attorney then presents the evidence and witnesses for the defendant's case. The plaintiff's attorney can challenge any evidence introduced and cross-examine the defendant's witnesses.

After the defense concludes its presentation, the attorneys present their closing arguments, each urging a verdict in favor of his or her client. The judge instructs the jury in the law that applies to the case (these instructions are often called *charges*), and the jury retires to the jury room to deliberate a verdict. In the Marconi-Anderson case, the jury will not only decide for the plaintiff or for the defendant but, if it finds for the plaintiff, will also decide on the amount of the **award** (the money to be paid to her).

Posttrial Motions

After the jury has rendered its verdict, either party may make a posttrial motion. If Marconi wins, and Anderson's attorney has previously moved for a directed verdict, Anderson's attorney may make a **motion for judgment n.o.v.** (from the Latin *non obstante veredicto*, which means "notwithstanding the verdict"—called a *motion for judgment as a matter of law* in the federal courts) in Anderson's favor on the ground that the jury verdict in favor of Marconi was unreasonable and erroneous. If the judge decides that the jury's verdict was reasonable in light of the evidence presented at trial, the motion will be denied. If the judge agrees with Anderson's attorney, then he or she will set the jury's verdict aside and enter a judgment in favor of Anderson.

Alternatively, Anderson could make a **motion for a new trial,** requesting the judge to set aside the adverse verdict and to hold a new trial. The motion will be granted if the judge is convinced, after look-

---

11.   Pronounced vwahr *deehr.*
12.   *Batson v. Kentucky,* 476 U.S. 79, 106 S.Ct. 1712, 90 L.Ed.2d 69 (1986).
13.   *J.E.B. v. Alabama ex rel. T.B.,* 511 U.S. 127, 114 S.Ct. 1419, 128 L.Ed.2d 89 (1994). (*Ex rel.* is Latin for *ex relatione.* The phrase refers to an action brought on behalf of the state, by the attorney general, at the instigation of an individual who has a private interest in the matter.)

ing at all the evidence, that the jury was in error but does not feel it is appropriate to grant judgment for the other side. A new trial may also be granted on the ground of newly discovered evidence, misconduct by the participants or the jury during the trial, or error by the judge.

The Appeal

Assume here that any posttrial motion is denied, and Anderson appeals the case. (If Marconi wins but receives a smaller money award than she sought, she can appeal also.) A notice of appeal must be filed with the clerk of the trial court within a prescribed time. Anderson now becomes the appellant, or petitioner, and Marconi becomes the appellee, or respondent.

FILING THE APPEAL Anderson's attorney files with the appellate court the record on appeal, which includes the pleadings, the trial transcript, the judge's ruling on motions made by the parties, and other trial-related documents. Anderson's attorney will also file with the reviewing court a condensation of the record, known as an abstract, which is filed with the reviewing court along with the brief. The **brief** is a formal legal document outlining the facts and issues of the case, the judge's rulings or jury's findings that should be reversed or modified, the applicable law, and arguments on Anderson's behalf (citing applicable statutes and relevant cases as precedents).

Marconi's attorney will file an answering brief. Anderson's attorney can file a reply to Marconi's brief, although it is not required. The reviewing court then considers the case.

APPELLATE REVIEW As mentioned earlier, a court of appeals does not hear evidence. Rather, it reviews the record for errors of law. Its decision concerning a case is based on the record on appeal, the abstracts, and the attorneys' briefs. The attorneys can present oral arguments, after which the case is taken under advisement. In general, appellate courts do not reverse findings of fact unless the findings are unsupported or contradicted by the evidence.

If the reviewing court believes that an error was committed during the trial or that the jury was improperly instructed, the judgment will be *reversed*. Sometimes the case will be *remanded*

(sent back to the court that originally heard the case) for a new trial. In most cases, the judgment of the lower court is *affirmed*, resulting in the enforcement of the court's judgment or decree.

If the reviewing court is an intermediate appellate court, the losing party normally may appeal to the state supreme court (the highest state court). Such a petition corresponds to a petition for a writ of *certiorari* in the United States Supreme Court. If the petition is granted, new briefs must be filed before the state supreme court, and the attorneys may be allowed or requested to present oral arguments. Like the intermediate appellate courts, the supreme court may reverse or affirm the appellate court's decision or remand the case. At this point, unless a federal question is at issue, the case has reached its end.

▌ Alternative Dispute Resolution

Because the number of court cases filling the **dockets** (court schedules listing the cases to be heard) grows every year and the cost of litigation continues to increase, more and more businesspersons, consumers, and others are turning to **alternative dispute resolution (ADR)** as an alternative to civil lawsuits.

Methods of ADR range from neighbors sitting down over a cup of coffee in an attempt to work out their differences to huge multinational corporations agreeing to resolve a dispute through a formal hearing before a panel of experts. The great advantage of ADR is its flexibility. Normally, the parties themselves can control how the dispute will be settled, what procedures will be used, and whether the decision reached (either by themselves or by a neutral third party) will be legally binding or nonbinding. Today, approximately 95 percent of cases are settled before trial through some form of ADR.

In the following sections, we look at some of the more commonly used methods of ADR. Keep in mind, though, that ADR is an ongoing experiment. In other words, new methods of ADR—or new combinations of existing methods—are continuously being devised and employed.

Negotiation

One of the simplest forms of ADR is **negotiation**, a process in which the parties attempt to settle their dispute informally, with or without attorneys to represent them. Attorneys frequently advise their clients to negotiate a settlement voluntarily before they proceed to trial.

Negotiation traditionally involves just the parties themselves and (typically) their attorneys. The attorneys, though, are advocates—they are obligated to put their clients' interests first. Often, parties find it helpful to have the opinion and guidance of a *neutral* (unbiased) third party when deciding whether or how to negotiate a settlement of their dispute. The methods of ADR discussed next all involve neutral third parties.

Mediation

In the **mediation** process, the parties themselves attempt to negotiate an agreement, but with the assistance of a neutral third party, a mediator. The mediator, who need not be a lawyer, usually charges a fee for his or her services (which can be split between the parties).

In mediation, the mediator talks with the parties and allows them to discuss their disagreement openly in a nonadversarial atmosphere. The mediator emphasizes points of agreement, helps the parties evaluate their positions, and proposes solutions. The mediator, however, does not make a decision on the matter being disputed.

Mediation is essentially a form of "assisted negotiation." So are mini-trials, early neutral case evaluations, and summary jury trials—in the sense that the neutral third party in these forms of ADR helps the parties themselves negotiate a settlement.

Mini-Trials

A **mini-trial** is a private proceeding in which each party's attorney briefly argues the party's case before the other party. Typically, a neutral third party, who acts as an adviser and an expert in the area being disputed, is also present. If the parties fail to reach an agreement, the adviser renders an opinion as to how a court would likely decide the issue. The proceeding assists the parties in determining whether they should settle their dispute or take it to court.

Early Neutral Case Evaluation

In **early neutral case evaluation**, the parties select a neutral third party (generally an expert in the

subject matter of the dispute) to evaluate their respective positions. The parties explain their positions to the case evaluator however they wish. There is no hearing and no discovery. The case evaluator then evaluates the strengths and weaknesses of the parties' positions, and this evaluation forms the basis for negotiating a settlement.

Summary Jury Trials

A form of ADR that has been successfully employed in the federal system is the **summary jury trial (SJT).** In an SJT, the litigants present their arguments and evidence, and the jury then renders a verdict. The jury's verdict is not binding, but it does act as a guide to both sides in reaching an agreement during the mandatory negotiations that immediately follow the trial. Because no witnesses are called, the SJT is much speedier than a regular trial, and frequently the parties are able to settle their dispute without resorting to an actual trial. If no settlement is reached, both sides have the right to a full trial later. Summary jury trials are now held by approximately sixty-five federal judges.

Arbitration

A more formal method of alternative dispute resolution is **arbitration,** in which an arbitrator (a neutral third party or a panel of experts) hears a dispute and renders a decision. The key difference between arbitration and the forms of ADR just discussed is that in arbitration, the third party's decision normally is legally binding on the parties.[14]

In some respects, formal arbitration resembles a trial, although usually the procedural rules are much less restrictive than those governing litigation. In the typical hearing format, the parties present opening arguments to the arbitrator and state what remedies should or should not be granted. Evidence is then presented, and witnesses may be

---

14. Depending on the parties' circumstances and preferences, the arbitrator's decision may also be nonbinding on the parties. In some situations, for example, the parties may remain free to reject the arbitrator's decision. Such nonbinding arbitration is more similar to mediation than to binding arbitration. Arbitration that is mandated by the courts (to be discussed shortly) is often not binding on the parties.

called and examined by both sides. The arbitrator then renders a decision, which is called an *award*.

An arbitrator's award is usually the final word on the matter. Although the parties may appeal an arbitrator's decision, a court's review of the decision will be much more restricted in scope than an appellate court's review of a trial court's decision. The general view is that because the parties were free to frame the issues and set the powers of the arbitrator at the outset, they cannot complain about the results. The award will only be set aside if the arbitrator's conduct or "bad faith" substantially prejudiced the rights of one of the parties, if the award violates an established public policy, or if the arbitrator exceeded his or her powers (arbitrated issues that the parties did not agree to submit to arbitration).

ARBITRATION CLAUSES AND STATUTES   Virtually any commercial matter can be submitted to arbitration. Frequently, parties include in an **arbitration clause** in a contract (a written agree-

ment—see Chapter 7) that any dispute that arises under the contract will be resolved through arbitration rather than through the court system. Parties can also agree to arbitrate a dispute after a dispute arises.

Most states have statutes (often based in part on the Uniform Arbitration Act of 1955) under which arbitration clauses will be enforced, and some state statutes compel arbitration of certain types of disputes, such as those involving public employees. At the federal level, the Federal Arbitration Act (FAA), enacted in 1925, enforces arbitration clauses in contracts involving maritime activity and interstate commerce. Because of the breadth of the commerce clause (see Chapter 1), arbitration agreements involving transactions only slightly connected to the flow of interstate commerce may fall under the FAA. In the following case, the United States Supreme Court considered whether the FAA applied to an arbitration agreement that, at the time of contracting, the parties did not expect to involve interstate commerce.

CASE 2.3

Allied-Bruce Terminix Companies, Inc. v. Dobson

Supreme Court of the United States, 1995.
513 U.S. 265,
115 S.Ct. 834,
130 L.Ed.2d 753.

FACTS   Steven Gwin signed a contract with Allied-Bruce Terminix Companies, Inc., a company with operations in many states, to protect his home from termite infestation. The contract specified that any dispute would be resolved by arbitration. After Gwin sold the home to Michael Dobson, the structure became infested with termites. Dobson filed a suit against Gwin and Allied-Bruce in an Alabama state court. Allied-Bruce asked the court to compel arbitration under the Federal Arbitration Act (FAA) section making enforceable a written arbitration provision in "a contract evidencing a transaction involving [interstate] commerce." The court refused to compel arbitration, concluding that at the time of contracting, the parties did not expect their contract to involve interstate commerce. Allied-Bruce appealed. The state supreme court affirmed, and the company appealed again—to the United States Supreme Court.

ISSUE   Is an arbitration clause enforceable under the FAA when the contract involves interstate commerce, even if the parties, at the time of contracting, did not expect it to involve interstate commerce?

DECISION   Yes. The Supreme Court held that the FAA is written broadly and extends to the limits of Congress's commerce clause power. The Supreme Court reversed the ruling of the state supreme court and remanded the case for further proceedings.

REASON   The Supreme Court acknowledged that the FAA applies only to an arbitration clause in "a contract evidencing a transaction involving commerce." The Court concluded, however, that "involving" means the

(Continued)

Case 2.3—Continued

same thing as "affecting," and "affecting interstate commerce" is the phrase that defines the extent of Congress's power under the commerce clause. The Court also concluded that "evidencing" requires only that a transaction in fact involve commerce. The Court reasoned that permitting parties to argue that they never expected a contract to involve interstate commerce would only lead to more lawsuits, which Congress had sought to avoid in designing the FAA.

FOR CRITICAL ANALYSIS—Ethical Consideration *The Federal Arbitration Act was enacted in 1925, when the commerce clause did not have the reach that it does today. Is it fair to expand the reach of the FAA with the expansion of the reach of the commerce clause?*

ARBITRABILITY The role of the courts in the arbitration process is limited. One important role is played at the prearbitration stage. When a dispute arises as to whether or not the parties have agreed in an arbitration clause to submit a particular matter to arbitration, one party may file suit to compel arbitration. The court before which the suit is brought will not decide the basic controversy but must decide the issue of *arbitrability*—that is, whether the matter is one that must be resolved through arbitration.

Even when a claim involves a violation of a statute passed to protect a certain class of people (such as investors), a court may determine that the parties must nonetheless abide by their agreement to arbitrate the dispute. Usually, a court will allow the claim to be arbitrated if the court, in interpreting the statute, can find no legislative intent to the contrary.[15] For example, in *Shearson/American Express,*

Inc. v. McMahon,[16] a case decided by the United States Supreme Court in 1987, customers of a brokerage firm alleged that the firm had engaged in fraudulent trading on their accounts in violation of two federal acts—the Racketeer Influenced and Corrupt Organizations Act (see Chapter 5) and the Securities Exchange Act of 1934 (see Chapter 27). When the customers sued the firm, the firm moved to compel arbitration of the claims in accordance with an arbitration clause in the contract. The Court found that when Congress enacted these federal acts, it did not intend to bar enforcement of all predispute arbitration agreements, and thus the claims were arbitrable.

Subsequent to the *Shearson* case, the Court faced a similar question: Should claims involving alleged violations of federal statutes protecting employees from employment discrimination also be arbitrable? The Court answered this question in the following landmark case.

---

15. This general principle for determining the arbitrability of such claims was recently confirmed by the United States Supreme Court in *First Options of Chicago, Inc. v. Kaplan,* 514 U.S. 938, 115 S.Ct. 1920, 131 L.Ed.2d 985 (1995).

16. 482 U.S. 220, 107 S.Ct. 2332, 96 L.Ed.2d 185 (1987).

CASE 2.4

Gilmer v. Interstate/Johnson Lane Corp.

Supreme Court of the United States, 1991.
500 U.S. 20,
111 S.Ct. 1647,
114 L.Ed.2d 26.

FACTS Interstate/Johnson Lane Corporation required some of its employees, including Robert Gilmer, to register as securities representatives with the New York Stock Exchange (NYSE). The registration application included an agreement to arbitrate when NYSE rules required it. One of the rules requires the arbitration of any controversy arising out of a registrant's termination of employment. Interstate terminated Gilmer's employment. Gilmer, who was sixty-two years old when he was terminated, filed a suit in a federal district court, alleg-

Case 2.4—Continued

ing that he had been discharged in violation of the Age Discrimination in Employment Act (ADEA) of 1967.[a] (This act prohibits employers from discriminating against older employees—see Chapter 33.) Interstate asked the court to order the arbitration of Gilmer's claim, according to the agreement in Gilmer's registration application with the NYSE. The court denied the employer's request, but on appeal, the appellate court ordered the arbitration. Gilmer appealed to the United States Supreme Court.

ISSUE   Can an age discrimination claim be subject to compulsory arbitration?

DECISION   Yes. The United States Supreme Court held that claims of age discrimination are arbitrable.

REASON   The Supreme Court pointed out that arbitration is favored under the Federal Arbitration Act (FAA). Thus, to avoid the enforcement of an arbitration clause governed by the FAA on the basis that a dispute concerns a particular statutory right, a party must show that Congress intended "to preclude a waiver of a judicial forum" (regular court). The Supreme Court could find nothing in the text, legislative history, or underlying purposes of the ADEA indicating a congressional intent to preclude enforcement of arbitration agreements. The Court thus affirmed the order of the court of appeals.

FOR CRITICAL ANALYSIS—Ethical Consideration   *The decision to compel arbitration may seem to contradict the public policy enunciated in such statutes as the ADEA. For what practical reason might courts favor the arbitration of disputes, even in the employment context?*

a.   29 U.S.C. Sections 621–634.

Providers of ADR Services

ADR services are provided both by government agencies and by private organizations. A major provider of ADR services is the American Arbitration Association (AAA). Most of the largest law firms in the nation are members of this nonprofit association. Founded in 1926, the AAA now settles nearly sixty thousand disputes a year in its numerous offices around the country. Cases brought before the AAA are heard by an expert or a panel of experts in the area relating to the dispute and are usually settled quickly. Generally, about half of the panel members are lawyers. To cover its costs, the AAA charges a fee, paid by the party filing the claim. In addition, each party to the dispute pays a specified amount for each hearing day, as well as a special additional fee in cases involving personal injuries or property loss.

Hundreds of for-profit firms around the country also provide dispute-resolution services. Typically, these firms hire retired judges to conduct arbitration hearings or otherwise assist parties in settling their disputes. The leading firm in this relatively new private system of justice is JAMS/Endispute, which is based in Santa Ana, California. Private ADR firms normally allow the parties to decide on the date of the hearing, the presiding judge, whether the judge's decision will be legally binding, and the site of the hearing—which may be a conference room, a law-school office, or a leased courtroom. The judges follow procedures similar to those of the federal courts and use similar rules. Usually, each party to the dispute pays a filing fee and a designated fee for a hearing session or conference.

ADR and the Courts

ADR clearly offers many advantages to disputing parties. It also provides the courts with a means of reducing the number of cases that go to trial. As early as the 1950s, some courts were experimenting with requiring those who filed suits to undergo arbitration before proceeding to trial.

COURT-RELATED ADR   Today, at least thirty-five states either require or encourage parties to undergo mediation or arbitration prior to trial. Courts in several federal districts require arbitration prior to trial in cases involving less than $100,000, and numerous other federal courts provide for voluntary arbitration. Generally, when a trial court refers cases for arbitration, the arbitrator's decision is not binding on the parties. If they do not agree to the arbitrator's decision, they can go forward with their lawsuit.

The types of court-related ADR programs in use vary widely. In some states, ADR is voluntary. For example, in Missouri, when a party files a lawsuit, he or she is advised of various ADR options and given the names of individuals and organizations that provide ADR services. In other states, such as Minnesota, parties are required to undertake ADR before they can have their case heard in court—as in the federal district courts mentioned above. Some programs refer cases for ADR based on the amount of the claims involved. Hawaii, for example, has a program of mandatory, nonbinding arbitration for disputes involving less than $150,000. Other programs refer cases for ADR according to their subject matter. ADR programs also vary in terms of the types of ADR offered.

Some states, such as Minnesota, offer a menu of options. Other states, including Florida (which has a statewide, comprehensive mediation program), offer only one alternative.

ADR programs are not limited to the trial courts. More than forty state appellate courts now also offer some form of ADR to help parties settle civil disputes prior to appellate review.

OTHER COURT-RELATED ALTERNATIVES   Today's courts are experimenting with a variety of other alternatives to speed up (and reduce the cost of) justice. These alternatives include summary procedures for commercial litigation, the appointment of special masters to assist judges in deciding complex issues, and permitting an expanded use of paralegals in the handling of routine legal matters.

Some states, including Arizona, California, and Florida, are even experimenting with a type of electronic court. Electronic kiosks (about the size of soda machines) have been installed in shopping malls and other convenient places to allow persons to obtain information, via a computerized system, about certain areas of the law. Arizona's "QuickCourt" system goes a step further. For example, a person who wants to obtain a divorce can go to a QuickCourt, key in the information requested by the computer, and receive a printout of the divorce petition and related forms that can then be filed with the court to initiate divorce proceedings.

▌Terms and Concepts

alternative dispute resolution
   (ADR) 47
answer 42
arbitration 48
arbitration clause 49
award 46
bankruptcy court 36
brief 47
complaint 42
concurrent jurisdiction 36
counterclaim 42
default judgment 42
depositions 45
discovery 45
diversity of citizenship 36
docket 47
early neutral case

evaluation 48
exclusive jurisdiction 36
federal question 36
interrogatories 45
judicial review 34
jurisdiction 34
justiciable controversy 38
litigation 41
long arm statute 34
mediation 48
mini-trial 48
motion for a directed
   verdict 46
motion for a new trial 46
motion for judgment *n.o.v.* 46
motion for judgment on
   the pleadings 43

motion for summary
   judgment 44
motion to dismiss 42
negotiation 47
pleadings 42
probate court 36
reply 42
rule of four 40
small claims court 38
standing to sue 38
summary jury trial (SJT) 48
summons 42
venue 37
voir dire 46
writ of *certiorari* 40

▌Chapter Summary: Courts and Procedures

The Judiciary's Role in American Government *(See pages 33–34.)*	The role of the judiciary—the courts—in the American governmental system is to interpret and apply the law. Through the process of judicial review—determining the constitutionality of laws—the judicial branch acts as a check on the executive and legislative branches of government. The power of judicial review was established by Chief Justice John Marshall in *Marbury v. Madison* (1803).

Basic Judicial Requirements *(See pages 34–38.)*	1. *Jurisdiction*—Before a court can hear a case, it must have jurisdiction over the person against whom the suit is brought or the property involved in the suit, as well as jurisdiction over the subject matter.
	  a. Limited versus general jurisdiction—Limited jurisdiction exists when a court is limited to a specific subject matter, such as probate or divorce. General jurisdiction exists when a court can hear any kind of case.
	  b. Original versus appellate jurisdiction—Original jurisdiction exists with courts that have authority to hear a case for the first time (trial courts). Appellate jurisdiction exists with courts of appeals, or reviewing courts; generally, appellate courts do not have original jurisdiction.
	  c. Federal jurisdiction—Arises (1) when a federal question is involved (when the plaintiff's cause of action is based, at least in part, on the U.S. Constitution, a treaty, or a federal law) or (2) when a case involves diversity of citizenship (citizens of different states, for example), and the amount in controversy exceeds $50,000.
	  d. Concurrent versus exclusive jurisdiction—Concurrent jurisdiction exists when two different courts have authority to hear the same case. Exclusive jurisdiction exists when only state courts or only federal courts have authority to hear a case.
	2. *Venue*—Venue has to do with the most appropriate location for a trial, which is usually the geographical area in which the event leading to the dispute took place or where the parties reside.
	3. *Standing to sue*—A requirement that a party must have a legally protected and tangible interest at stake sufficient to justify seeking relief through the court system. The controversy at issue must also be a justiciable controversy—one that is real and substantial, as opposed to hypothetical or academic.

The State and Federal Court Systems *(See pages 38–41.)*	1. *Trial courts*—Courts of original jurisdiction, in which legal actions are initiated.
	  a. State—Courts of general jurisdiction can hear any case; courts of limited jurisdiction include divorce courts, probate courts, traffic courts, small claims courts, etc.
	  b. Federal—The federal district court is the equivalent of the state trial court. Federal courts of limited jurisdiction include the U.S. Tax Court, the U.S. Bankruptcy Court, and the U.S. Court of Federal Claims.
	2. *Intermediate appellate courts*—Courts of appeals, or reviewing courts; generally without original jurisdiction. Many states have an intermediate appellate court; in the federal court system, the U.S. circuit courts of appeals are the intermediate appellate courts.
	3. *Supreme (highest) courts*—Each state has a supreme court, although it may be called by some other name, from which appeal to the United States Supreme Court is only possible if a federal question is involved. The United States Supreme Court is the highest court in the federal court system and the final arbiter of the Constitution and federal law.

Procedural Rules *(See pages 41–47.)*	Rules of procedure prescribe the way in which disputes are handled in the courts. Rules differ from court to court, and separate sets of rules exist for federal and state

(Continued)

▌Chapter Summary: Courts and Procedures—Continued

Procedural Rules — Continued	courts, as well as for criminal and civil cases. A sample civil court case in a state court would involve the following procedures:
	1. *The pleadings*—
	a. Complaint—Filed by the plaintiff with the court to initiate the lawsuit; served with a summons on the defendant.
	b. Answer—Admits or denies allegations made by the plaintiff; may assert a counterclaim or an affirmative defense.
	c. Motion to dismiss—A request to the court to dismiss the case for stated reasons, such as the plaintiff's failure to state a claim for which relief can be granted.
	2. *Pretrial motions (in addition to the motion to dismiss)*—
	a. Motion for judgment on the pleadings—May be made by either party; will be granted if the parties agree on the facts and the only question is how the law applies to the facts. The judge bases the decision solely on the pleadings.
	b. Motion for summary judgment—May be made by either party; will be granted if the parties agree on the facts. The judge applies the law in rendering a judgment. The judge can consider evidence outside the pleadings when evaluating the motion.
	3. *Discovery*—The process of gathering evidence concerning the case. Discovery involves *depositions* (sworn testimony by a party to the lawsuit or any witness), *interrogatories* (written questions and answers to these questions made by parties to the action with the aid of their attorneys), and various requests (for admissions, documents, medical examination, and so on).
	4. *Pretrial conference*—Either party or the court can request a pretrial conference to identify the matters in dispute after discovery has taken place and to plan the course of the trial.
	5. *Trial*—Following jury selection (*voir dire*), the trial begins with opening statements from both parties' attorneys. The following events then occur:
	a. The plaintiff's introduction of evidence (including the testimony of witnesses) supporting the plaintiff's position. The defendant's attorney can challenge evidence and cross-examine witnesses.
	b. The defendant's introduction of evidence (including the testimony of witnesses) supporting the defendant's position. The plaintiff's attorney can challenge evidence and cross-examine witnesses.
	c. Closing arguments by attorneys in favor of their respective clients, the judge's instructions to the jury, and the jury's verdict.
	6. *Posttrial motions*—
	a. Motion for judgment *n.o.v.* ("notwithstanding the verdict")—Will be granted if the judge is convinced that the jury was in error.
	b. Motion for a new trial—Will be granted if the judge is convinced that the jury was in error; can also be granted on the grounds of newly discovered evidence, misconduct by the participants during the trial, or error by the judge.
	7. *Appeal*—Either party can appeal the trial court's judgment to an appropriate court of appeals. After reviewing the record on appeal, the abstracts, and the attorneys' briefs, the appellate court holds a hearing and renders its opinion.
Alternative Dispute Resolution (ADR) *(See pages 47–52.)*	1. *Negotiation*—The parties come together, with or without attorneys to represent them, and try to reach a settlement without the involvement of a third party.
	2. *Mediation*—The parties themselves reach an agreement with the help of a neutral third party, called a mediator, who proposes solutions.
	3. *Mini-trial*—A private proceeding in which each party's attorney argues the party's case before the other party. Often, a neutral third party renders an opinion on how a court would likely decide the issue.

▌Chapter Summary: Courts and Procedures—Continued

Alternative Dispute Resolution (ADR) — Continued	4. *Early neutral case evaluation*—A private proceeding in which the parties argue their respective cases before a neutral third party, whose decision becomes the basis for negotiating a settlement.
	5. *Summary jury trial (SJT)*—A kind of trial employed by some federal courts in which litigants present their arguments and evidence and the jury renders a nonbinding verdict. The verdict guides the parties in reaching an agreement during the mandatory negotiations that immediately follow the trial.
	6. *Arbitration*—A more formal method of ADR in which the parties submit their dispute to a neutral third party, the arbitrator, who renders a decision. The decision may or may not be legally binding, depending on the circumstances.
	7. *Providers of ADR services*—The leading nonprofit provider of ADR services is the American Arbitration Association. Hundreds of for-profit firms also provide ADR services.
	8. *Court-related ADR*—Many state and federal courts now refer cases for some form of ADR prior to trial. In most cases, pretrial arbitration is nonbinding on the parties.

▌For Review

1. What is judicial review? How and when was the power of judicial review established?

2. Before a court can hear a case, it must have jurisdiction. Over what must it have jurisdiction? In what circumstances does a federal court have jurisdiction?

3. What is the difference between a trial court and an appellate court?

4. In a lawsuit, what are the pleadings? What is discovery?

5. Name five methods of alternative dispute resolution (ADR). What advantages does ADR offer to the parties?

▌Questions and Case Problems

2–1. Appellate Process. If a judge enters a judgment on the pleadings, the losing party can usually appeal but cannot present evidence to the appellate court. Does this seem fair? Explain.

2–2. Arbitration. In an arbitration proceeding, the arbitrator need not be a judge or even a lawyer. How, then, can the arbitrator's decision have the force of law and be binding on the parties involved?

2–3. Appellate Process. Sometimes on appeal there are questions concerning whether the facts presented in the trial court support the conclusion reached by the judge or the jury. An appellate court, however, nor-

mally defers to the trial court's decision with regard to the facts. Can you see any reason for this?

2–4. Jurisdiction. Marya Callais, a citizen of Florida, was walking near a busy street in Tallahassee one day when a large crate flew off a passing truck and hit her, resulting in numerous injuries to Callais. She incurred a great deal of pain and suffering plus numerous medical expenses, and she could not work for six months. She wishes to sue the trucking firm for $300,000 in damages. The firm's headquarters are in Georgia, although the company does business in Florida. In what court may Marya bring suit—a Florida state court, a Georgia state court, or a federal court? What factors might influence her decision?

2–5. Jurisdiction. Shem and Nadine Maslov, who live in Massachusetts, saw an advertisement in the *Boston Globe* for vacationers that was sponsored by a national hotel chain: "Stay in Maximum Inns' beachfront hotel in Puerto Rico for one week for only $400; continental breakfast included." The Maslovs decided to accept the offer and spent a week at the hotel. On the last day, Nadine fell on a wet floor in the hotel lobby and sustained multiple fractures to her left ankle and hip. Because of her injuries, which were subsequently complicated by infections, she was unable to work at her job as an airline flight attendant for ten months. The hotel chain does not do business in Massachusetts. If Nadine sues Maximum Inns in a Massachusetts state court, can the court exercise jurisdiction over Maximum Inns? What factors should the court consider in deciding this jurisdictional issue?

2–6. Arbitration. Gates worked for Arizona Brewing Co. A contract between Gates's employer and the union to which Gates belonged stated that the employer and the union were to try to settle their differences, but if the parties could not reach a settlement, the matter was to be decided by arbitration. Gates brought a lawsuit against his employer (instead of submitting the dispute to arbitration) to recover wages. The employer argued that Gates could not bring a lawsuit until after arbitration had occurred. Gates claimed that the arbitration clause was void under an Arizona arbitration statute, which stated that "this act shall not apply to collective [bargained] contracts between employers and . . . associations of employ[ees]." Must Gates undergo arbitration before bringing a lawsuit? Explain. [*Gates v. Arizona Brewing Co.*, 54 Ariz. 266, 95 P.2d 49 (1939)]

2–7. Arbitration. Phillip Beaudry, who suffered from mental illness, worked in the Department of Income Maintenance for the state of Connecticut. Beaudry was fired from his job when it was learned that he had misappropriated approximately $1,640 in state funds. Beaudry filed a complaint with his union, Council 4 of the American Federation of State, County, and Municipal Employees (AFSCME), and eventually the dispute was submitted to an arbitrator. The arbitrator concluded that Beaudry had been dismissed without "just cause," because Beaudry's acts were caused by his mental illness and "were not willful or volitional or within his capacity to control." Because Beaudry was disabled, the employer was required, under state law, to transfer him to a position that he was competent to hold. The arbitrator awarded Beaudry reinstatement, back pay, seniority, and other benefits. The state appealed the decision to a court. What public policies (general policies as established by statutes or other laws) must the court weigh in making its decision? How should the court rule? [*State v. Council 4, AFSCME*, 27 Conn.App. 635, 608 A.2d 718 (1992)]

2–8. Arbitration. Randall Fris worked as a seaman on an Exxon Shipping Co. oil tanker for eight years without incident. One night, he boarded the ship for duty while intoxicated, in violation of company policy. This policy also allowed Exxon to discharge employees who were intoxicated and thus unfit for work. Exxon discharged Fris. Under a contract with Fris's union, the discharge was submitted to arbitration. The arbitrators ordered Exxon to reinstate Fris on an oil tanker. Exxon filed a suit against the union, challenging the award as contrary to public policy, which opposes having intoxicated persons operate seagoing vessels. Can a court set aside an arbitration award on the ground that the award violates public policy? Should the court set aside the award in this case? Explain. [*Exxon Shipping Co. v. Exxon Seamen's Union*, 11 F.3d 1189 (3d Cir. 1993)]

2–9. Jurisdiction. Cal-Ban 3000 is a weight loss drug made by Health Care Products, Inc., a Florida corporation, and marketed through CKI Industries, another Florida corporation. Enticed by North Carolina newspaper ads for Cal-Ban, the wife of Douglas Tart bought the drug at Prescott's Pharmacies, Inc., in North Carolina for her husband. Within a week, Tart suffered a ruptured colon. Alleging that the injury was caused by Cal-Ban, Tart sued Prescott's Pharmacies, CKI, the officers and directors of Health Care, and others, in a North Carolina state court. CKI and the Health Care officers and directors argued that North Carolina did not have personal jurisdiction over them because CKI and Health Care were Florida corporations. How will the court hold? Why? [*Tart v. Prescott's Pharmacies, Inc.*, 118 N.C.App. 516, 456 S.E.2d 121 (1995)]

2–10. Procedure. Washoe Medical Center, Inc., admitted Shirley Swisher for the treatment of a fractured pelvis. During her stay, Swisher suffered a fatal fall from her hospital bed. Gerald Parodi, the administrator of her estate, and others, filed an action against Washoe in which they sought damages for the alleged lack of care in treating Swisher. During *voir dire*, when the plaintiffs' attorney returned a few minutes late from a break, the trial judge led the prospective jurors in a standing ovation. The judge joked with one of the prospective jurors, whom he had known in college, about the judge's fitness to serve as a judge and personally endorsed another prospective juror's business. After the trial, the jury returned a verdict in favor of Washoe. The plaintiffs appealed, arguing that the tone set by the judge during *voir dire* prejudiced their right to a fair trial. Should the appellate court agree? Why or why not? [*Parodi v. Washoe Medical Center, Inc.*, 111 Nev. 365, 892 P.2d 588 (1995)]

▌Accessing the Internet: Fundamentals of Business Law

You can obtain opinions from all of the U.S. Circuit Courts of Appeals from a site provided by the Villanova Center for Information Law and Policy. Go to

http://www.law.vill.edu/

For information on the justices of the United States Supreme Court, go to

http://oyez.nwu.edu/oyez.html

This site offers biographies of the justices, links to opinions they have authored, and, for justices who have served after 1920, video and audio materials. Oral arguments before the Supreme Court are also posted on this site. A planned addition to the site is a video tour of the Court.

Some federal district courts offer their opinions electronically through the federal judiciary's PACER (Public Access to Court Electronic Records) system. PACER costs 75 cents a minute, but for many it is well worth it. To access PACER, you have to register by calling 1-800-676-6856, Monday through Friday, between 8 A.M. and 5 P.M. You will receive a form that you can mail or fax in. You can sign up with as many federal courts as you wish, out of a total number of over two hundred courts.

Increasingly, decisions of the state courts are also becoming available online. You can search through the texts of state cases that are on the Internet, as well as federal cases and state and federal laws, by accessing WashLaw at

http://lawlib.wuacc.edu/washlaw/searchlaw.html

A preeminent resource on the Internet for information on alternative dispute resolution (ADR) is the American Arbitration Association (AAA), which you can locate at

http://www.adr.org

The AAA's site offers information on ADR in a number of areas, including labor relations, employment, commerce, the construction industry, and international disputes. The site provides the text of AAA rules, samples of several AAA forms, and some useful articles on ADR.

ConflictNet, which describes itself as "a network of people dedicated to promoting the constructive resolution of conflict," provides information on ADR as well as links to other ADR resources on the Internet. To reach this site, go to

http://www.igc.apc.org/conflictnet

You can find publications pertaining to ADR by accessing the Federal Judicial Center at

http://www.fjc.gov

A pilot project involving online dispute resolution is the Virtual Magistrate Project, which is sponsored by several ADR organizations, including the American Arbitration Association, the Villanova Center for Information Law and Policy, and the Cyberspace Law Institute. For information on this project, including its docket and decisions, go to

http://vmag.vcilp.org

You can read a transcript of the first online mediation conducted by the Online Ombuds Office, a project of the University of Massachusetts Department of Legal Studies, at

http://www.ombuds.org/narrativel.html

The dispute being mediated was between a Web site developer and a newspaper that claimed the developer was violating its copyright

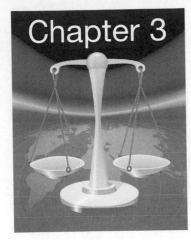

Chapter 3

Ethics and Social Responsibility

CHAPTER OBJECTIVES

After reading this chapter, you should be able to:

1. Define business ethics and its relationship to personal ethics.
2. Explain the relationship between the law and ethics.
3. Compare and contrast duty-based ethics and utilitarian ethics.
4. Identify the various groups to whom corporations are perceived to owe duties.
5. Discuss some of the difficulties involved in measuring corporate social responsibility.

Business and ethics have never been a truly happy couple. This is because business "must be in a sense selfish." After all, the primary reason for going into business is to make a profit. Throughout history, there has been an underlying tension between the pursuit of profits and the welfare of those groups (employees, consumers, suppliers, creditors, communities, and others) that are affected by this pursuit.

Business owners and managers traditionally have had to ensure that their profit-making activities did not exceed the ethical boundaries established by society. In the past, though, these boundaries were often regarded as being coterminous with the law—that is, if something was legal, it was ethical. Shady business dealings were regarded as "just business" more often than not. In the last few decades, however, the ethical boundaries within which business firms must operate have narrowed significantly. In the rights-conscious world of today, a business firm that decides it has no duties other than those prescribed by law may find it difficult to survive. If a firm's behavior is perceived as unethical—even though it may be legal—that firm may suffer negative publicity, boycotts, and lost profits.

In preparing for a career in business, you will find that a background in business ethics and a commitment to ethical behavior is just as important as a knowledge of the specific laws that you will read about in this text. In this chapter, we first examine the nature of business ethics and some of the sources of ethical standards that have guided others in their business decision making. We then look at some of the obstacles to ethical behavior faced by businesspersons. In the remaining pages of the chapter, which deals with corporate social responsibility, we explore the issue mentioned in the preceding paragraph: How can businesspersons act in an ethically responsible manner and at the same time make profits for their firms or their firms' owners?

The Nature of Business Ethics

To understand the nature of business ethics, we need to define what is meant by ethics generally. **Ethics** can be defined as the study of what constitutes right or wrong behavior. It is the branch of philosophy that focuses on morality and the way in which moral principles are applied to daily life. Ethics has to do with questions relating to the fairness, justness, rightness, or wrongness of an action. What is fair? What is just? What is the right thing to do in this situation?—these are essentially ethical questions.

Often, moral principles serve as the guiding force in an individual's personal ethical system. Although the terms *ethical* and *moral* are often used interchangeably, the terms refer to slightly different concepts. Whereas ethics has to do with the philosophical, rational basis for morality, morals are often defined as universal rules or guidelines (such as those rooted in religious precepts) that determine our actions and character.

Defining Business Ethics

Business ethics focuses on what constitutes ethical behavior in the world of business. Personal ethical standards, of course, play an important role in determining what is or is not ethical, or appropriate, business behavior. Business activities are just one part of the human enterprise, and the ethical standards that guide our behavior as, say, mothers, fathers, or students apply equally well to our activities as businesspersons. Businesspersons, though, often must address more complex ethical issues and conflicts in the workplace than they do in their personal lives—as you will learn in this chapter and throughout this book.

Business Ethics and the Law

Because the law reflects and codifies a society's ethical values, many of our ethical decisions are made for us—by our laws. Nevertheless, simply obeying the law does not fulfill all ethical obligations. In the interest of preserving personal freedom, as well as

for practical reasons, the law does not—and cannot—codify all ethical requirements. No law says, for example, that it is *illegal* to lie to one's family, but it may be *unethical* to do so. Likewise, in the business world, numerous actions might be unethical but not necessarily illegal. Even though it may be convenient for businesspersons to satisfy themselves by mere compliance with the law, such an approach may not always yield ethical outcomes.

In short, the law has its limits—it cannot make all our ethical decisions for us. When it does not, ethical standards must guide the decision-making process.

Sources of Ethical Standards

Religious and philosophical inquiry into the nature of "the good" is an age-old pursuit. Broadly speaking, though, ethical reasoning relating to business traditionally has been characterized by two fundamental approaches. One approach defines ethical behavior in terms of *duty*. The other approach determines what is ethical in terms of the *consequences*, or *outcome*, of any given action. We examine each of these approaches here.

Duty-Based Ethics

Is it wrong to cheat on an examination, if nobody will ever know that you cheated and if it helps you get into law school so that you can eventually volunteer your legal services to the poor and needy? Is it wrong to lie to your parents if the lie harms nobody but helps to keep family relations congenial? These kinds of ethical questions implicitly weigh the "end" of an action against the "means" used to attain that end. If you believe that you have an ethical *duty* not to lie or cheat, however, then lying and cheating can never be justified by the consequences, no matter how benevolent or desirable those consequences may be. Duty-based ethics may be based on religious precepts or philosophical reasoning.

RELIGION Duty-based ethical standards are often derived from moral principles rooted in religious sources. In the Judeo-Christian tradition, for example, the Ten Commandments of the Old Testament establish rules for moral action. Other religions have their own sources of revealed truth—such as the Koran in the Muslim world. Within the confines of their influence, moral principles are universal and *absolute*—they are not to be questioned. For example, consider one of the Ten Commandments: "Thou shalt not steal." This is an absolute mandate. Even a benevolent motive for stealing (such as Robin Hood's) cannot justify the act, because the act itself is inherently immoral and thus wrong. When an act is prohibited by religious teachings that serve as the foundation of a person's moral or ethical standards, the act is unethical for that person and should not be undertaken, regardless of its consequences.

Ethical standards based on religious teachings also may involve an element of *compassion*. Therefore, even though it might be profitable for a firm to lay off a less productive employee, if that employee were to find it difficult to find employment elsewhere and his or her family were to suffer as a result, this potential suffering would be given substantial weight by the decision makers. Compassionate treatment of others is also mandated—to a certain extent, at least—by the Golden Rule of the ancients ("Do unto others as you would have them do unto you"), which has been adopted by most religions.

KANTIAN PHILOSOPHY Ethical standards based on a concept of duty may also be derived solely from philosophical principles. Immanuel Kant (1724–1804), for example, identified some general guiding principles for moral behavior based on what he believed to be the fundamental nature of human beings. Kant held that it is rational to assume that human beings are qualitatively different from other physical objects occupying space. Persons are endowed with moral integrity and the capacity to reason and conduct their affairs rationally. Therefore, their thoughts and actions should be respected. When human beings are treated merely as a means to an end, they are being treated as the equivalent of objects and are being denied their basic humanity.

A central postulate in Kantian ethics is that individuals should evaluate their actions in light of the consequences that would follow if *everyone* in society acted in the same way. This **categorial imperative** can be applied to any action. For example, say that you are deciding whether to cheat on an examination. If you have adopted Kant's categorial imperative, you will decide not to cheat, because if everyone cheated, the examination would be meaningless.

Outcome-Based Ethics

"Thou shalt act so as to generate the greatest good for the greatest number." This is a paraphrase of the major premise of the utilitarian approach to ethics. **Utilitarianism** is a philosophical theory first developed by Jeremy Bentham (1748–1832) and then advanced, with some modifications, by John Stuart Mill (1806–1873)—both British philosophers. In contrast to duty-based ethics, utilitarianism is outcome oriented. It focuses on the consequences of an action, not on the nature of the action itself or on any set of preestablished moral values or religious beliefs.

Under a utilitarian model of ethics, an action is morally correct, or "right," when, among the people it affects, it produces the greatest amount of good for the greatest number. When an action affects the majority adversely, it is morally wrong. Applying the utilitarian theory thus requires (1) a determination of which individuals will be affected by the action in question; (2) a **cost-benefit analysis**—an assessment of the negative and positive effects of alternative actions on these individuals; and (3) a choice among alternative actions that will produce maximum societal utility (the greatest positive benefits for the greatest number of individuals).

Utilitarianism is often criticized because it tends to focus on society as a whole rather than on individual human rights. For example, from a utilitarian standpoint, it might be ethically acceptable to test drugs or medicines on human beings because presumably a majority of the population would benefit from the experiments. If, however, one accepts the principle that each individual has basic human rights (to life, freedom, and the pursuit of happiness), then an action that deprives an individual or group of individuals of these rights—even for the greater good of society—is ethically unacceptable. No amount of cost-benefit analysis can justify the action.

Applying Ethical Standards

Consider the following example: A corporation that markets baby formula in developing countries has learned that mothers in those countries often mix the formula with impure water, to make the formula go further. As a result, babies are suffering from malnutrition, diarrhea, and in some instances, even death. What is the corporation's ethical responsibility in this situation? Should it withdraw the product from those markets (and lose profits), or should it conduct a cost-benefit analysis and let the decision be guided by the results?

If the corporation's decision makers felt that they had an absolute duty not to harm others, then the only ethical response would be to withdraw the product from those markets. If the decision makers approached the problem from a utilitarian perspective, they would engage in a cost-benefit analysis. The cost of the action (the suffering and death of babies) would be weighed against its benefit (the availability of the formula to mothers). Having the formula available frees mothers from the task of breastfeeding and thus allows them to earn money to help raise their incomes and standards of living. The question in a utilitarian analysis would focus on whether the benefit outweighed the cost—not the inherent rightness or wrongness of the action.

In fact, this scenario is not hypothetical. In the 1970s, the Nestlé Company concluded, on the basis of a cost-benefit analysis, that it was ethically justified in continuing to market its baby formula in developing countries. Other companies marketing infant formula in those areas, however, reached a different decision: they pulled out of those markets. Nestlé was severely criticized for its behavior. The company's opponents were outraged, not because the formula had been marketed initially but because of Nestlé's decision to continue marketing the formula based on its cost-benefit analysis.

Obstacles to Ethical Business Behavior

People sometimes behave unethically in the business context, just as they do in their private lives. Some businesspersons knowingly engage in unethical behavior because they think that they can "get away with it"—that no one will ever learn of their unethical actions. Examples of this kind of unethical behavior include padding expense accounts, casting doubts on the integrity of a rival co-worker to gain a job promotion, stealing company supplies or equipment, and so on. Obviously, these acts are unethical, and many of them are illegal as well.

In other situations, businesspersons who would choose to act ethically may be deterred from doing so because of situational circumstances or external pressures. We look here at how both the corporate

environment and the conduct of management can sometimes act as deterrents to ethical behavior.

Ethics and the Corporate Environment

Some contend that the nature of the corporate structure itself acts as a deterrent to ethically responsible behavior. We examine the corporate structure in detail in Chapters 24 and 25. Briefly, a corporation is structured as follows: The owners of the corporation are the shareholders—those who purchase shares of stock in the company. The shareholders, however, do not run the corporation. Rather, they elect a board of directors and entrust those directors with the responsibility of directing and overseeing the corporate enterprise. The directors, in turn, hire officers and managers to handle the day-to-day business activities of the firm. A shareholder may also be a director, and a director may also be a corporate officer—the president or chief executive officer, for example.

ETHICS AND COLLECTIVE DECISION MAKING The corporate setting complicates ethical decision making because (normally) no one person makes a corporate decision. If you are an officer or manager of a large corporation, for example, you may find that the decision as to what is right or wrong for the corporation is not yours to make. Corporate officers and managers, of course, do make decisions that affect the corporation, and your input may weigh in the decision. The ultimate decision makers, however, are the members of the board of directors, who must make decisions as a group.

Collective decision making, because it places emphasis on consensus and unity of opinion, also tends to hinder individual ethical assertiveness. For example, suppose that a director has ethical misgivings about a planned corporate venture that promises to be highly profitable. If the other directors have no such misgivings, the director who does may be swayed by the enthusiasm of the others for the project and downplay his or her own criticisms.

DIMINISHED PERSONAL ACCOUNTABILITY To some extent, the corporate collectivity may shield corporate personnel from both personal exposure to the consequences of their decisions and personal accountability for those decisions. For example, suppose that a corporate board decides to market a new product that results in several consumers' deaths. Those who made the decision do not witness or deal directly with these consequences. Furthermore, just as normally no one individual is responsible for a corporate decision, so normally no one person is held accountable for the decision. (In recent years, however, the courts have been increasingly willing to look behind the "corporate veil" and hold individual corporate actors liable, or legally responsible, for actions resulting in harm to others—see Chapter 25.)

Ethics and Management

Much unethical business behavior occurs simply because it is not always clear what ethical standards and behaviors are appropriate or acceptable in a given context. Although most firms now issue ethical policies or codes of conduct, these policies and codes are not always effective in creating an ethical workplace. At times, this is because a firm's ethical policies are not communicated clearly to employees or do not bear on the real ethical issues confronting decision makers. Additionally, particularly in a large corporation, unethical behavior in one corporate department may simply escape the attention of those in control of the corporation or the corporate officials responsible for implementing and monitoring the company's ethics program.

Another deterrent to ethical behavior exists when corporate management, by its own conduct, indicates that ethical considerations take second place. If management makes no attempt to deter unethical behavior—through reprimands or employment terminations, for example—it will be clear to employees that management is not all that serious about ethics. Likewise, if a company doles out promotions or salary increases to those who obviously engage in unethical tactics to increase the firm's profits, then employees who do not resort to such tactics will be at a disadvantage. An employee in this situation may decide that because "everyone else does it," he or she might as well do so also.

Of course, an even stronger deterrent to ethical behavior occurs when employers engage in blatantly unethical or illegal conduct and expect their employees to do so as well. An employee in this situation faces two options, neither of which is satisfactory: participate in the conduct or "blow the whistle" on (inform authorities of) the employer's actions—and, of course, risk being fired. (See Chapter 22 for a more detailed discussion of "whistleblowing.")

▌Corporate Social Responsibility

We now return to the question posed in this chapter's introduction: How can businesspersons act in an ethically responsible manner and at the same time make profits for their firms or their firms' owners? This question is at the heart of the debate surrounding the concept of **corporate social responsibility**—the idea that corporations can and should act ethically and be accountable to society for their actions. No one contests the claim that corporations have duties to their shareholders, employers, and product users (consumers). Many of these duties are written into law—that is, they are *legal* duties. The question of corporate social responsibility concerns the extent to which a corporation has ethical duties to various groups in society that go beyond its legally prescribed duties.

To understand the debate over corporate social responsibility, consider a hypothetical firm: the Farthing Company. This firm markets its products, primarily paints and glues, throughout the world. The company is facing a financial crisis and must find a way to increase its profits if it is to survive. In so doing, however, Farthing will need to take into account the ethical ramifications of any decisions it makes. In the following pages, we examine some of the problematic aspects of a corporation's responsibilities in regard to shareholders, employees, consumers, the community, and society. As you will see, corporations like the Farthing Company face difficult conflicts in trying to be ethically responsible.

Duty to Shareholders

Corporate directors and officers have a duty to act in the shareholders' interest. Because of the nature of the relationship between corporate directors and officers and the shareholder-owners, the law holds directors and officers to a high standard of care in business decision making (see Chapter 25).

Traditionally, it was perceived that this duty to shareholders took precedence over all other corporate duties and that the primary goal of corporations should be profit maximization. Milton Friedman, the Nobel Prize–winning economist and a proponent of the profit-maximization view, saw "one and only one" social responsibility of a corporation: "to use its resources and engage in activities designed to increase its profits, so long as it stays within the rules of the game."[1] The "rules of the game" were the "basic rules of society, both those embodied in law and those embodied in ethical custom."[2]

Those who support the profit-maximization view of social responsibility contend that the duty to maximize profits must outweigh any other duty when duties conflict—to the extent, of course, that in maximizing shareholders' profits a firm does not violate the "basic rules of society." The question here is, What are these basic rules?

For example, suppose that our hypothetical firm, the Farthing Company, has suffered a setback because the U.S. government banned the sale of one of its paint thinners. The paint thinner, if allowed to touch the user's skin, can cause severe burns, and many consumers have complained of such injuries. The product is not banned in foreign markets, though, and thus Farthing faces an ethical question: Should it continue marketing the product in other countries? Certainly, it would benefit the shareholders to do so, but would such an action violate society's basic rules and ethical customs? Even if the action violated the ethical rules of even a small minority of Americans, that small minority, through activism and publicity, could harm Farthing's reputation as an ethically responsible corporation.

Duty to Employees

One of the primary concerns of every employer is the ability to control the workplace environment. After all, it is the employer who is responsible for making the business firm a success, and success requires qualified, competent, loyal employees and efficient operations. Employees, however, also

---

1. *Capitalism and Freedom* (Chicago: University of Chicago Press, 1962), p. 133.
2. Milton Friedman, "Does Business Have Social Responsibility?" *Bank Administration*, April 1971, pp. 13–14.

have concerns. They want to earn a fair wage; they want to work in an environment free of health-endangering hazards; they want to be treated fairly and equally by their employers; and increasingly in recent years, they want employers to respect their personal integrity and privacy rights.

By law, employers are required to provide a safe workplace, to pay a minimum wage, and to provide equal employment opportunities for all potential and existing employees. Does an employer also have ethical obligations to employees that go beyond these legal duties? Additionally, what if, in fulfillment of one ethical (or legal) obligation, another duty must be violated? We look here at some employment decisions facing employers in which various ethical or legal duties come into conflict. (See Chapter 22 for other ethical issues that arise in the employment context.)

EMPLOYMENT DISCRIMINATION As will be discussed in Chapter 22, federal laws require employers to offer equal employment opportunities to all job applicants and employees. These laws prohibit employers from discriminating against existing or potential employees on the basis of race, color, national origin, gender, religion, age, or disability. Many states have similar laws protecting employees. Sometimes, though, employers who are trying to fulfill a perceived ethical obligation to treat employees fairly and equally find themselves in a no-win situation.

The following case illustrates such a situation. Even though the employer went substantially beyond minimum legal compliance in attempting to provide a safe workplace for employees, the firm was nonetheless charged by some of its employees with having violated another ethical (and legal) duty—that of providing equal employment opportunities for women.

CASE 3.1

United Automobile Workers v. Johnson Controls, Inc.

Supreme Court of the United States, 1991.
499 U.S. 187,
111 S.Ct. 1196,
113 L.Ed.2d 158.

FACTS Johnson Controls, Inc., created its Battery Division in 1978. In 1982, as part of an ongoing attempt to reduce the health hazards that might result from lead exposure, Johnson adopted a "fetal protection policy," under which women of childbearing age were prohibited from working in the Battery Division. Johnson reached this decision after scientific studies indicated that a pregnant woman's exposure to high lead levels could harm the fetus. Employees and their union, United Automobile Workers, brought a suit in a federal

(Continued)

Case 3.1—Continued

court against Johnson, claiming that the fetal protection policy violated Title VII of the Civil Rights Act of 1964, which prohibits discrimination in employment on the basis of gender. The trial court held for Johnson, and the unions and employees appealed. The federal appellate court affirmed the trial court's ruling. The case was then appealed to the United States Supreme Court.

ISSUE   Did the fetal protection policy of Johnson Controls constitute illegal discrimination on the basis of gender?

DECISION   Yes. The Supreme Court reversed the judgment of the appellate court and remanded the case for further proceedings. The fetal protection policy was discriminatory in violation of Title VII of the Civil Rights Act of 1964 and the Pregnancy Discrimination Act of 1978.

REASON   The Court stated that employers may discriminate on the basis of "religion, sex, or national origin in those certain instances where religion, sex, or national origin is a bona fide occupational qualification [BFOQ][a] reasonably necessary to the normal operation of that particular business or enterprise." Therefore, the key issue to be decided was whether the BFOQ defense applied in this case. The Court held that it did not. In the eyes of the Court, neither gender nor pregnancy impaired an employee's ability to perform the job. In forming its decision, the Court looked to the Pregnancy Discrimination Act, an amendment to Title VII, which explicitly states that unless pregnant employees differ from others "in their ability or inability to work," they must be "treated the same" as other employees "for all employment-related purposes." The Court noted that "[f]ertile women, as far as [it] appears in the record, participate in the manufacture of batteries as efficiently as anyone else."

FOR CRITICAL ANALYSIS—Political Consideration   *The Court deemed it inappropriate for either the courts or employers "to decide whether a woman's reproductive role is more important to herself and her family than her economic role." Congress, by passing the Pregnancy Discrimination Act, "left this choice to the woman as hers to make." Should Congress have been more concerned about the rights of the unborn?*

a.   See Chapter 22 for a discussion of this defense to employment discrimination.

SEXUAL HARASSMENT VERSUS WRONGFUL DISCHARGE   Another conflict of duties that sometimes faces employers poises the choice of being sued for sexual harassment against the choice of being sued for wrongful discharge. Lawsuits for *sexual harassment* in the workplace (discussed in Chapter 22) have climbed dramatically in number in the past decade. So have suits for *wrongful discharge*—firing an employee without good cause or for discriminatory reasons (see Chapter 22). Suppose that an employee of the Farthing Company complains to her supervisor that a co-worker is sexually harassing her—physically touching her in objectionable ways, making lewd

comments about her and to her, and so on. The company immediately investigates the claim, and on finding that it is substantiated, promptly fires the harassing employee. The employee then sues the firm for wrongful discharge.

Can a court hold Farthing liable for wrongful discharge when, in firing the employee, the company was complying with a legal requirement? After all, federal law and the Equal Employment Opportunity Commission's guidelines require employers to take "immediate and appropriate corrective action" in response to an employee's complaint of sexual abuse. The answer to this question is that under some state laws and employment agreements, employers are prohibited from firing employees without a "just cause," and particular incidents of sexual harassment may or may not constitute just cause for firing the harasser.[3]

CORPORATE RESTRUCTURING AND EMPLOYEE WELFARE Suppose that our hypothetical firm, the Farthing Company, decided to reduce its costs by downsizing and restructuring its operations. Among other things, this would allow Farthing to cut back on its overhead by consolidating various supervisory and managerial positions. The question for Farthing is, Which employees should be retained and which should be let go? Should the firm retain its highly paid employees who have worked for—and received annual raises from—the firm for years? Alternatively, in the interests of cutting costs, should it retain (or hire) younger, less experienced persons at lower salaries?

The firm would not necessarily be acting illegally if it pursued the second option. Unless a fired employee can prove that the employer has breached an employment contract or violated the Age Discrimination in Employment Act (ADEA) of 1967, he or she will not have a cause of action

against the employer. The ADEA prohibits discrimination against workers forty years old and older on the basis of their age, but Farthing can always say that lack of performance or ability, not age, was the deciding factor. The question here is, Would such an action be ethical?

In deciding this issue, remember that Farthing must keep its eye on its profit margin. If it does not, the firm may fail, and the shareholders will lose their investments. Furthermore, why should the firm retain highly paid employees if it can obtain essentially the same work output for a lower price by retaining its less highly paid employees? Does Farthing owe an ethical duty to its employees who have served the firm loyally over a long period of time? Most people would say yes. Should this duty take precedence over Farthing's duty to the firm's owners to maintain or increase the profitability of the firm? Would your answer be the same if the firm faced imminent bankruptcy if it could not lower its operational costs? What if long-time employees were willing to take a slight reduction in pay to help the firm through its financial difficulties? What if they were not?

In the following case, an employer was confronted with a dwindling market and decreasing sales. The employer decided to reduce its costs of doing business by eliminating some of its obligations to its employees.

---

3. See, for example, *Chrysler Motors Corp. v. International Union, Allied Industrial Workers of America*, 959 F.2d 685 (7th Cir. 1992).

CASE 3.2

Varity Corp. v. Howe
Supreme Court of the United States, 1996.
516 U.S. 489,
116 S.Ct. 1065,
134 L.Ed.2d 130.

FACTS Varity Corporation manufactures and sells farm implements. In 1986, Varity set up a subsidiary, Massey Combines Corporation (MCC), to market its self-propelled combines and four-wheel-drive tractors. The sales of both products were at an all-time low. Varity convinced current and former employees who were, or had been, involved with the products to accept a transfer to MCC of their jobs and retirement benefit plans. Varity did not tell those employees that it expected MCC to fail. Within two years, MCC failed. Among other consequences, some retirees stopped receiving benefits. The retirees and other ex-employees sued Varity in a federal district court under the Employee Retirement Income Security Act of 1974 (ERISA).[a] They claimed that Varity owed them a fiduciary duty, which it had breached.[b] The court ruled in their favor, and the U.S. Court of Appeals for the Eighth Circuit affirmed the decision. Varity then appealed to the United States Supreme Court.

---

a. 29 U.S.C. Sections 1001–1461. See Chapter 22.
b. A *fiduciary* is a party who, because of something that he or she has undertaken to do, has a duty to act primarily for another's benefit.

(Continued)

Case 3.2—Continued

ISSUE Did Varity owe a fiduciary duty to its employees with respect to their retirement benefits? If so, did it violate that duty?

DECISION Yes, to both questions. The United States Supreme Court affirmed the decision of the lower court.

REASON The Supreme Court pointed out that under ERISA, a fiduciary is required to "discharge his [or her] duties with respect to a [retirement] plan solely in the interest of the participants and beneficiaries." It was on this statute that the Varity retirees based their suit. "To participate knowingly and significantly in deceiving a plan's beneficiaries in order to save the employer money at the beneficiaries' expense, is not to act "solely in the interest of the participants and beneficiaries." The Court stated that "[l]ying is inconsistent with the duty of loyalty owed by all fiduciaries."

FOR CRITICAL ANALYSIS—Ethical Consideration *Should a company continue to market a slow-selling line of products for the sole purpose of employing those who work on the products?*

Duty to Consumers

Clearly, a corporation has a duty to the users of its products. This is not just an ethical duty but a legal one as well—as you will read in later chapters of this book. The issue, with respect to corporate social responsibility, is the extent to which a corporation has an ethical duty *beyond* those duties mandated by law or when the corporation is uncertain that a legal duty exists. Often, the issue turns on how a firm (or the public or a court) answers the following question: At what point does corporate responsibility for the safety of consumers end and consumer responsibility begin?

PRODUCT MISUSE Suppose that the Farthing Company learns that one of its products—glue—was being inhaled by thousands of children in several Latin American countries. The health consequences of this misuse can include future kidney disease and brain damage. Consumer activists have launched a media campaign against Farthing, accusing it of being unethical by marketing its glue in those countries when such harms result. What is Farthing's responsibility in this situation? On the one hand, (1) it is not the company's fault that its product is being misused, (2) it has violated no legal duty, and (3) to cease selling the product in those areas would significantly cut into its profits. On the other hand, (1) suspending sales would reduce the suffering of children, and (2) if Farthing ignores the

public outcry, the continued adverse publicity could also cause the firm to lose sales—and thus profits. Farthing's solution will rest on the "ethical weight" it attaches to each of these factors.[4]

WHEN IS A RISK "OPEN AND OBVIOUS"? Whenever a corporation markets a product, the law imposes a duty on the firm to warn consumers, among other things, of the harms that can result from *foreseeable* misuses. When a risk is open and obvious, however, courts tend to hold that no warning is necessary. Sharp knives, for example, can obviously injure their users. Sometimes, a business firm has no way of predicting how a court might rule in deciding whether a particular risk is open and obvious or whether consumers should be warned of the risk. Courts normally decide the issue on a case-by-case basis, and courts often disagree on whether certain types of risks are open and obvious. The following case involves an allegation that an automobile manufacturer failed to warn consumers that seat belts would not necessarily protect them from injuries in head-on collisions.

---

4. When the H. B. Fuller Company faced this situation a few years ago, its solution was to suspend sales of its glues in some Latin American countries but not others. Fuller's critics contended that it should have suspended sales in all of the Latin American countries in which the product was being misused.

CASE 3.3

Mazda Motor of America, Inc. v. Rogowski

Court of Special Appeals of Maryland, 1995.
105 Md.App. 318,
659 A.2d 391.

FACTS Francis Rogowski fell asleep at the wheel of his Mazda pickup truck and collided head-on with a large tree. To recover for the cost of his injuries, Rogowski sued Mazda Motor of America, Inc., and others in a Maryland state court. Rogowski claimed, among other things, that Mazda should have warned him the seat belts would not protect him from all injuries if he were in an accident. The court agreed that Mazda was liable for failure to warn and awarded damages of $601,644 to Rogowski. Mazda appealed.

ISSUE Does an automobile manufacturer have a duty to warn the purchasers of its cars that seat belts cannot protect them from all injuries?

DECISION No. The Court of Special Appeals of Maryland held that the danger not warned about was clear and obvious, and it reversed and remanded the case to the lower court.

REASON The court reasoned that "there simply is no necessity to explain that which is obvious—that seat belts do not and cannot protect the occupants of the vehicle from injury no matter how severe the accident." The court also explained that "the giving of unnecessary warnings should be avoided because the presence of superfluous warnings seriously detracts from the efficacy [effectiveness] of warnings that are needed." The court believed that consumers, "[b]ombarded with nearly useless warnings about risks that rarely materialize[,]" might "give up on warnings altogether. And the few persons who might continue to take warnings seriously * * * would probably overreact, investing too heavily in their versions of 'safety.' Given these limits * * *, the optimal, rather than the highest, levels of risk information, measured both qualitatively and quantitatively, are what is called for."

FOR CRITICAL ANALYSIS—Social Consideration *If the notice Rogowski claimed should have been required in his case was required for every automobile manufacturer, presumably every motor vehicle owner's manual would say the same thing. What impact would this have on such a notice?*

Duty to the Community

In some circumstances, the community in which a business enterprise is located has a substantial stake in the firm. Assume, for example, that the Farthing Company employs two thousand workers at one of its plants. If the company decides that it would be profitable to close the plant or move it to another location, the employees—and the community—would suffer as a result. Today, to be considered socially responsible, a corporation must take both employees' needs and community needs into consideration when making such a decision.

Duty to Society

Perhaps the most disputed area in the controversy surrounding corporate social responsibility is the nature of a corporation's duty to society at large. Generally, the question turns less on whether corporations owe a duty to society than on how that duty can best be fulfilled.

PROFIT MAXIMIZATION Those who contend that corporations should first and foremost attend to the goal of profit maximization would argue that it is by generating profits that a firm can best contribute to society. Society benefits by profit-making activities, because profits can only be realized when a firm markets products or services that are desired by society. These products and services enhance the standard of living, and the profits accumulated by successful business firms generate national wealth. Our laws and court decisions promoting trade and commerce reflect the public policy that the fruits of commerce (income wealth) are desirable and good. Because our society values income wealth as an ethical goal, corporations, by contributing to income wealth, automatically are acting ethically.

Furthermore, profit maximization results in the efficient allocation of resources. Capital, labor, raw materials, and other resources are directed to the production of those goods and services most desired by society. If capital were directed toward a social goal instead of being reinvested in the corporation, the business operation would become less efficient. For example, if an automobile company contributes $1 million annually to the United Way, that contribution represents $1 million that is not reinvested in making better and safer cars.

Those arguing for profit maximization as a corporate goal also point out that it would be inappropriate to use the power of the corporate business world to fashion society's goals by promoting social causes. Determinations as to what exactly is in society's best interest are essentially political questions, and therefore the public, through the political process, should have a say in making those determinations. The legislature—not the corporate boardroom—is thus the appropriate forum for such decisions.

CRITICS OF PROFIT MAXIMIZATION Critics of the profit-maximization view believe that corporations should become actively engaged in seeking and furthering solutions to social problems. Because so much of the wealth and power of this country is controlled by business, business in turn has a responsibility to society to use that wealth and power in socially beneficial ways. Corporations should therefore promote human rights, strive for equal treatment of minorities and women in the workplace, take care to preserve the environment, and generally not profit from activities that society has deemed unethical. The critics also point out that it is ethically irresponsible to leave decisions concerning social welfare up to the government,

because many social needs are not being met sufficiently through the political process.

The Corporate Balancing Act

Today's corporate decision makers are, in a sense, poised on a fulcrum between profitability and ethical responsibility. If they emphasize profits at the expense of perceived ethical responsibilities, they may become the target of negative media exposure, consumer boycotts, and perhaps lawsuits. If they invest too heavily in good works or social causes, however, their profits may suffer. Striking the right balance on this fulcrum is not always easy, and usually some profits must be sacrificed in the process. Instead of *maximum profits*, many firms today aim for *optimum profits*—profits that can be realized while staying within legal and ethical limits.

Measuring Corporate Social Responsibility

Measuring corporate social responsibility is difficult because depending on whose yardstick one uses, the answer differs. Traditionally, corporate philanthropy has been used to measure social responsibility. Today, many feel that being ethically responsible involves much more than simply donating funds to charitable causes.

Corporate Philanthropy

Since the nineteenth century and the emergence of giant, wealthy business enterprises in America, corporations have generally contributed some of their shareholders' wealth to meet social needs. Frequently, corporations establish separate nonprofit foundations for this purpose. For example, Honda, Inc., created the American Honda Education Corporation, through which it donated $40 million over a ten-year period to launch and support the Eagle Rock School in Estes Park, Colorado. This school and educator training center gives preference to students who have not been able to succeed in the more rigid, highly structured public school systems. Today, virtually all major corporations routinely donate to hospitals, medical research, the arts, universities, and programs that benefit society.

A related yardstick for measuring corporate social responsibility is the specific causes to which a corporation contributes. One indication of this measure was evident in a worldwide poll conducted a few years ago. Pollsters found that two-thirds of the respondents would switch brands to a manufacturer that supported a social cause that they liked.[5]

Corporate Process

Increasingly, corporations are being judged less on the basis of their philanthropic activities than on their practices, or corporate process. Corporate process, in this sense, refers to how a corporation conducts its affairs at all levels of operation. Does it establish and effectively implement ethical policies and take those policies seriously? Does it deal ethically with its shareholders? Does it consider the needs of its employees—for day-care facilities or flexible working hours, for example? Does it promote equal opportunity in the workplace for women, minority groups, and persons with disabilities? Do the corporation's suppliers, particularly those from developing countries, protect the human rights of their employees (provide for safety in the workplace or pay a decent wage, for example)? Does the corporation investigate complaints about its products promptly and, if necessary, take action to improve them?

For many, the answers to these and similar questions are the key factors in determining whether a corporation is socially responsible. From this perspective, no matter how much a corporation may contribute to worthy causes, it will not be socially responsible if it fails to observe ethical standards in its day-to-day activities.

It Pays to Be Ethical

Most corporations today have learned that it pays to be ethically responsible—even if it means less profits in the short run (and it often does). Today's cor-

porations are subject to more intensive scrutiny—both by government agencies and the public—than they ever were in the past. If a corporation fails to conduct its operations ethically or respond quickly to an ethical crisis, its goodwill and reputation (and thus future profits) will likely suffer as a result.

There are other reasons as well for a corporation to behave ethically. Companies that demonstrate a commitment to ethical behavior—by implementing ethical programs, complying with environmental regulations, and promptly investigating product complaints, for example—often receive more lenient treatment from government agencies or the courts. Furthermore, by keeping their own houses in order, corporations may be able to avoid the necessity for the government to do so—through new laws or regulations.

Additionally, investors may shy away from a corporation's stock if the corporation is perceived to be socially irresponsible. Since the 1970s, certain investment funds have guaranteed to the purchasers of their shares that they will only invest in companies that are ethical. They did not invest in the Dow Chemical Company, for example, because it produced napalm that was used in the Vietnam War (1964–1975). They did not invest in corporations that had any dealings with South Africa because at that time, South Africa practiced *apartheid*, or complete separation of the races. Today, ethical funds base their investments on various ethical criteria. For example, some funds invest money only in corporations that are "environmentally kind."

▌Ethics in the Global Context

Given the varied cultures and religions of the world's nations, one might expect frequent conflicts in ethics between foreign and U.S. businesspersons. In fact, many of the most important ethical precepts are common to virtually all countries. Some important ethical differences do exist, however. In Islamic (Muslim) countries, for example, the consumption of alcohol and certain foods is forbidden by the Koran (the sayings of the prophet Mohammed, which lie at the heart of Islam and Islamic law). It would be thoughtless and imprudent to invite a Saudi Arabian business contact out for a drink.

5. Justin Martin, "Good Citizenship Is Good Business," *Fortune*, March 21, 1992, pp. 15–16.

The role played by women in other countries also may present some difficult ethical problems for firms doing business internationally. Equal employment opportunity is a fundamental public policy in the United States, and Title VII of the Civil Rights Act of 1964 prohibits discrimination against women in the employment context (see Chapter 22). Some other countries, however, largely reject any role for women professionals, which may cause difficulties for American women conducting business transactions in those countries.

Another ethical problem in international business dealings has to do with the legitimacy of certain side payments to government officials. In the United States, the majority of contracts are formed within the private sector. In many foreign countries, however, decisions on most major construction and manufacturing contracts are made by government officials because of extensive government regulation and control over trade and industry. Side payments to government officials in exchange for favorable business contracts are not unusual in such countries, nor are they considered to be unethical. In the past, U.S. corporations doing business in developing countries largely followed the dictum, "When in Rome, do as the Romans do."

In the 1970s, however, the U.S. press, and government officials as well, uncovered a number of business scandals involving large side payments by American corporations—such as Lockheed Aircraft—to foreign representatives for the purpose of securing advantageous international trade contracts. In response to this unethical behavior, Congress passed the Foreign Corrupt Practices Act (FCPA) in 1977, which prohibits American businesspersons from bribing foreign officials to secure advantageous contracts. The act has made it difficult for American companies to compete as effectively as they otherwise might in the global marketplace.

The Ever-Changing Ethical Landscape

Our sense of what is ethical—what is fair or just or right in a given situation—changes over time. Conduct that might have been considered ethical ten years ago might be considered unethical today. Indeed, most of the ethical and social issues discussed in this chapter and elsewhere in this text either did not exist or were of little public concern at the turn of the twentieth century and, in some cases, even as recently as a decade ago. Technological innovations, the communications revolution, pressing environmental problems, and social movements resulting in greater rights for minorities, women, and consumers have all dramatically changed the society in which we live and, consequently, the business and ethical landscape of America.

This changing ethical landscape is perhaps nowhere more evident than in the evolution of the concept of corporate social responsibility. Today's business manager must not only keep an eye on his or her firm's profit margins but also keep an "ear to the ground" to detect changing social perceptions of what constitutes ethical and socially responsible corporate behavior.

Terms and Concepts

business ethics 59	corporate social responsibility 62	ethics 59
categorical imperative 60	cost-benefit analysis 60	utilitarianism 60

Chapter Summary: Ethics and Social Responsibility

The Nature of Business Ethics *(See page 59.)*	Ethics can be defined as the study of what constitutes right or wrong behavior. Business ethics focuses on how moral and ethical principles are applied in the business context. The law reflects society's convictions on what constitutes right or wrong behavior. The law has its limits, though, and some actions may be legal yet not be ethical.

▌Chapter Summary: Ethics and Social Responsibility—Continued

Sources of Ethical Standards *(See pages 59–61.)*	1. *Duty-based ethics*—Ethics based on religious beliefs and philosophical reasoning, such as that of Immanuel Kant. 2. *Outcome-based ethics (utilitarianism)*—Ethics based on philosophical reasoning, such as that of John Stuart Mill.

Obstacles to Ethical Business Behavior *(See pages 61–62.)*	1. *The corporate structure—*
	   a. Collective decision making tends to deter individual ethical assertiveness.
	   b. The corporate structure tends to shield corporate actors from personal responsibility and accountability.
	
	 2. *Management—*
	   a. Uncertainty on the part of employees as to what kind of behavior is expected of them makes it difficult for them to behave ethically.
	   b. Unethical conduct by management shows employees that ethical behavior is not a priority.

Corporate Social Responsibility *(See pages 62–68.)*	Corporate social responsibility rests on the assumption that corporations should conduct their affairs in a socially responsible manner, but there is disagreement as to what constitutes socially responsible behavior. Corporations are perceived to hold duties to the following groups—duties that often come into conflict: 1. *Duty to shareholders*—Because the shareholders are the owners of the corporation, directors and officers have a duty to act in the shareholders' interest (maximize profits). 2. *Duty to employees*—Employers have numerous legal duties to employees, including providing employees with a safe workplace and refraining from discriminating against employees on the basis of race, color, national origin, gender, religion, age, or disability. These duties sometimes come into conflict. Many believe that employers hold ethical duties to their employees that go beyond those prescribed by law. 3. *Duty to consumers*—Corporate directors and officers have a legal duty to the users of their products. Most people feel that corporations also have an ethical duty that goes beyond what the law requires. Controversy exists over the point at which corporate responsibility for consumer safety ends and consumer responsibility begins. 4. *Duty to the community*—Most people hold that a corporation has a duty to the community in which it operates. The corporation should consider the needs of the community when making decisions that substantially affect the welfare of the community. 5. *Duty to society*—Most people hold that a corporation has a duty to society in general, but they differ in their ideas on how corporations can best fulfill this duty. One view is that corporations serve society's needs most effectively by maximizing profits because profits generally increase national wealth and social welfare. Another view holds that corporations, because they control so much of the country's wealth and power, should use their own wealth and power in socially beneficial ways and not engage in actions that society deems unethical.
The Corporate Balancing Act *(See page 68.)*	Today's corporate decision makers must balance profitability against ethical responsibility when making their decisions. Instead of maximum profits, corporations increasingly aim for optimum profits—the maximum profits that can be realized by the firm while pursuing actions that are not only legal and profitable but also ethical.
Measuring Corporate Social Responsibility *(See pages 68–69.)*	It is difficult to measure corporate social responsibility because different yardsticks are used. Traditionally, corporate philanthropy has been used as a means of measuring

(Continued)

▮ Chapter Summary: Ethics and Social Responsibility—Continued

Measuring Corporate Social Responsibility — Continued	corporate social responsibility. Increasingly, corporate process—how a corporation conducts its business on a day-to-day basis—is a key factor in determining whether a corporation is socially responsible.
Ethics in the Global Context (See pages 69–70.)	Despite the cultural and religious differences among nations, the most important ethical precepts are common to virtually all countries. Two notable differences relate to the role of women in society and the practice of giving side payments to foreign officials to secure favorable contracts. The Foreign Corrupt Practices Act (FCPA) of 1977, which prohibits the bribery of foreign officials through such side payments, put U.S. businesspersons at a relative disadvantage to businesspersons from other countries who are not subject to such laws.
The Ever-Changing Ethical Landscape (See page 70.)	What is considered ethical in a society may change over time as social customs change and new developments alter our social and business environment.

▮ For Review

1. What is ethics? What is business ethics? What are some sources of ethical standards?
2. What are some of the obstacles to ethical business behavior?
3. To what groups does a corporation owe duties? Why do these duties sometimes come into conflict?

4. What is the difference between maximum profits and optimum profits?
5. What are some of the yardsticks by which corporate social responsibility is measured?

▮ Questions and Case Problems

3–1. Business Ethics. Some business ethicists maintain that whereas personal ethics has to do with right or wrong behavior, business ethics is concerned with appropriate behavior. In other words, ethical behavior in business has less to do with moral principles than with what society deems to be appropriate behavior in the business context. Do you agree with this distinction? Do personal and business ethics ever overlap? Should personal ethics play any role in business ethical decision making?

3–2. Corporate Social Responsibility. Assume that you are a high-level manager for a shoe manufacturer. You know that your firm could increase its profit margin by producing shoes in Indonesia, where you could hire women for $40 a month to assemble them. You also know, however, that a competing shoe manufacturer recently was accused, by human rights advocates, of

engaging in exploitative labor practices because the manufacturer sold shoes made by Indonesian women for similarly low wages. You personally do not believe that paying $40 a month to Indonesian women is unethical, because you know that in that impoverished country, $40 a month is a better-than-average wage rate. Assuming that the decision is yours to make, should you have the shoes manufactured in Indonesia and make higher profits for your company? Should you instead avoid the risk of negative publicity and the consequences of that publicity for the firm's reputation and subsequent profits? Are there other alternatives? Discuss fully.

3–3. Corporate Social Responsibility. Do you agree with Milton Friedman's conclusion that there is "one and only one responsibility of business"—to increase its profits? If so, what arguments would you use in defending this statement? If not, what arguments would you raise against it?

3–4. Duty to Consumers. Two eight-year-old boys, Douglas Bratz and Bradley Baughn, were injured while riding a mini–trail bike manufactured by Honda Motor Co. Bratz, who was driving the bike while Baughn rode as a passenger behind him, ran three stop signs and then collided with a truck. Bratz did not see the truck because, at the time of the accident, he was looking behind him at a girl chasing them on another mini–trail bike. Bratz wore a helmet, but it flew off on impact because it was unfastened. Baughn was not wearing a helmet. The owner's manual for the mini–trail bike stated in bold print that the bike was intended for off-the-road use only and urged users to "Always Wear a Helmet." A prominent label on the bike itself also warned that the bike was for off-the-road use only and that it should not be used on public streets or highways. In addition, Bratz's father had repeatedly told the boy not to ride the bike in the street. The parents of the injured boys sued Honda, alleging that the mini–trail bike was unreasonably dangerous. Honda claimed it had sufficiently warned consumers of potential dangers that could result if the bike was not used as directed. Should Honda be held responsible for the boys' injuries? Why or why not? [*Baughn v. Honda Motor Co.*, 107 Wash.2d 127, 727 P.2d 655 (1986)]

3–5. Duty to Employees. In 1984, General Telephone Co. of Illinois, Inc. (GTE), for reasons of efficiency, decided to consolidate its nationwide operations and eliminate unnecessary job positions. One of the positions eliminated was held by John Burnell, a fifty-two-year-old employee who had worked for GTE for thirty-four years and had always received "above average" performance ratings. GTE offered Burnell the choice of either accepting another position within the firm at the same salary or accepting early retirement with a salary continuation for a certain period of time. Burnell did not want to retire, but he was afraid that if he did accept the other position and if the other position was later eliminated, he might not then have the choice of early retirement with the same separation benefit. Because he received no assurances that the other job would be secure in the future, he accepted the early-retirement alternative. Burnell later alleged that he had been "constructively discharged"—that is, that GTE had made his working conditions so intolerable that he was forced to resign. Had GTE constructively discharged Burnell? Can GTE's actions toward Burnell be justified from an ethical standpoint? Discuss. [*Burnell v. General Telephone Co. of Illinois, Inc.*, 181 Ill.App.3d 533, 536 N.E.2d 1387, 130 Ill.Dec. 176 (1989)]

3–6. Duty to Consumers. Beverly Landrine's infant daughter died after the baby swallowed a balloon while playing with a doll known as "Bubble Yum Baby."

When a balloon was inserted into the doll's mouth and the doll's arm was pumped, thereby inflating the balloon, the doll simulated the blowing of a bubble gum bubble. The balloon was made by Perfect Product Co. and distributed by Mego Corp. Landrine brought a suit against the manufacturer and distributor, alleging that the balloon was defectively made or inherently unsafe when used by children and that Perfect had failed to warn of the danger associated with the balloon's use. Discuss whether the producer and distributor of the balloon should be held liable for the harm caused by its product. [*Landrine v. Mego Corp.*, 95 A.D.2d 759, 464 N.Y.S.2d 516 (1983)]

3–7. Duty to Consumers. The Seven-Up Co., as part of a marketing scheme, placed two glass bottles of "Like" cola on the front entrance of the Gruenemeier residence. Russell Gruenemeier, a nine-year-old boy, began playing while holding one of the bottles. He tripped and fell, and the bottle broke, severely cutting his right eye and causing him to eventually lose his eyesight in the eye. Russell's mother brought an action against the Seven-Up Co. for damages, claiming that the cause of Russell's injury was Seven-Up's negligence. She claimed that the company was negligent because it placed potentially dangerous instrumentalities—glass bottles—within the reach of small children and that the firm should have used unbreakable bottles for its marketing scheme. Are glass bottles so potentially dangerous that the Seven-Up Co. should be held liable for the boy's harm? If you were the judge, how would you decide the issue? [*Gruenemeier v. Seven-Up Co.*, 229 Neb. 267, 426 N.W.2d 510 (1988)]

3–8. Duty to Consumers. The father of an eleven-year-old child sued the manufacturer of a jungle gym because the manufacturer had failed to warn users of the equipment that they might fall off the gym and get hurt, as the boy did in this case. The father also claimed that the jungle gym was unreasonably dangerous because, as his son began to fall and reached frantically for a bar to grasp, there was no bar within reach. The father based his argument in part on a previous case involving a plaintiff who was injured as a result of somersaulting off a trampoline. In that case [*Pell v. Victor J. Andrew High School*, 123 Ill.App.3d 423, 462 N.E.2d 858, 78 Ill.Dec. 739 (1984)], the court had held that the trampoline's manufacturer was liable for the plaintiff's injuries because it had failed to warn of the trampoline's propensity to cause severe spinal cord injuries if it was used for somersaulting. Should the court be convinced by the father's arguments? Why or why not? [*Cozzi v. North Palos Elementary School District No. 117*, 232 Ill.App.3d 379, 597 N.E.2d 683, 173 Ill.Dec. 709 (1992)]

3–9. Duty to Employees. Matt Theurer, an eighteen-year-old high school senior, worked part-time at a McDonald's restaurant in Oregon. Theurer volunteered to work an extra shift one day, in addition to his regular shifts (one preceding and one following the extra shift). After working about twelve hours during a twenty-four-hour period, Theurer told the manager that he was tired and asked to be excused from his next regularly scheduled shift so that he could rest. The manager agreed. While driving home from work, Theurer fell asleep at the wheel and crashed into a van driven by Frederic Faverty. Theurer died, and Faverty was severely injured. Faverty sued McDonald's, alleging, among other things, that McDonald's was negligent in permitting Theurer to drive a car when it should have known that Theurer was too tired to drive safely. Do employers have a duty to prevent fatigued employees from driving home from work? Should such a duty be imposed on them? How should the court decide this issue? How would you decide the issue if you were the judge? [*Faverty v. McDonald's Restaurants of Oregon, Inc.*, 133 Or.App. 514, 892 P.2d 703 (1994)]

**A QUESTION OF ETHICS
AND SOCIAL RESPONSIBILITY**

3–10. *Hazen Paper Co. manufactured paper and paperboard for use in such products as cosmetic wrap, lottery tickets, and pressure-sensitive items. Walter Biggins, a chemist hired by Hazen in 1977, developed a water-based paper coating that was both environmentally safe and of superior quality. By the mid-1980s, the company's sales had increased dramatically as a result of its extensive use of "Biggins Acrylic." Because of this, Biggins thought he deserved a substantial raise in salary, and from 1984 to 1986, Biggins's persistent requests for a raise became a bone of contention between him and his employers. Biggins ran a business on the side, which involved cleaning up hazardous wastes for various companies. Hazen told Biggins that unless he signed a "confidentiality agreement" promising to restrict his outside activities during the time he was employed by Hazen and for a limited time afterward, he would be fired. Biggins said he would sign the agreement only if Hazen raised his salary to $100,000. Hazen refused to do so, fired Biggins, and hired a younger man to replace him. At the time of his discharge in 1986, Biggins was sixty-two years old, had worked for the company nearly ten years, and was just a few weeks away from being entitled to pension rights worth about $93,000. In view of these circumstances, evaluate and answer the following questions. [Hazen Paper Co. v. Biggins, 507 U.S. 604, 113 S.Ct. 1701, 123 L.Ed.2d 338 (1993)]*

1. Did the company owe an ethical duty to Biggins to increase his salary, given the fact that its sales increased dramatically as a result of Biggins's efforts and ingenuity in developing the coating? If you were one of the company's executives, would you have raised Biggins's salary? Why or why not?

2. Generally, what public policies come into conflict in cases involving employers who, for reasons of cost and efficiency of operations, fire older, higher-paid workers and replace them with younger, lower-paid workers? If you were an employer facing the need to cut back on personnel to save costs, what would you do, and on what ethical premises would you justify your decision?

▌Unit One—Cumulative Hypothetical Problem

3–11. *Korman, Inc., a toy manufacturer, has its headquarters in Minneapolis, Minnesota. It markets its toys throughout the United States, as well as in overseas markets. Korman has recently placed on the market a new line of dolls with such irreverent names as "Harass Me," "Spit on Me," "Pull My Hair," "Watch Me Scream," "Cut Me Quick," and "Abuse Me, Please." The dolls are a success commercially and have netted Korman more profits than any of its other toys. Given these "facts," answer the following questions:*

1. Jan's Toy Mart, the California distributor of Korman toys, wants to sue Korman for allegedly breaching a contract. If Jan's Toy Mart brought its suit in a California state court, could that court exercise jurisdiction over Korman? Explain.

2. Suppose that in its contract with Korman, Jan's Toy Mart agreed to submit any dispute that arose between the two companies to binding arbitration. Following the arbitration hearing, the arbitrator concludes that Korman did not breach the contract. Jan's Toy Mart is unsatisfied with the arbitrator's award. Can Jan's Toy Mart appeal the arbitrator's decision to a court?

3. Parents and teachers claim that Korman's dolls encourage children to be violent and that it is unethical of Korman to continue marketing the dolls. Parent-teacher groups are organizing boycotts against Korman and the dolls and have launched a media campaign against the company. Recently, they picketed Korman's headquarters in Minneapolis, bearing such signs as "Korman Hates Kids" and "Watch Korman Scream." If you were a

Korman executive, would you recommend that the company cease manufacturing the toys? What factors would Korman's directors need to consider in making this decision?

4. Suppose that Korman does business only within the state of Minnesota. A Korman employee claims that the company has violated a federal employment law. Korman argues that it is not liable because the law applies only to employees of companies that are engaged in interstate commerce. What might a court decide? Discuss fully.

Accessing the Internet: Fundamentals of Business Law

The key to running an ethical business enterprise is effective and ethical management. A good source for information on management ethics is Academy of Management (AM) On-Line. AM can be accessed at

http://www.aom.pace.edu/

Mantis Consultants, Ltd., offers a number of services, including case studies, to help businesses better understand strategic management and the importance of management strategies in cultivating an ethical workplace. To access this company's home page, go to

http://northstar/bus/utk/edu/mgmtsci

The Foundation for Enterprise Development (FED) is an organization dedicated to fostering highly productive corporate cultures. FED provides practical guidelines on how companies can integrate employees into their business decision-making processes. To access FED's home page, go to

http://www.fed.org

A number of socially responsible corporations have taken up residence on the Internet. The Progressive Business Web Pages constitute a valuable source of information concerning these businesses, including information on environmentally conscious firms. To access these pages, go to

http://envirolink.org

For a wealth of information on philanthropic organizations in the United States, you can access the Internet Non-Profit Center, a project of the American Institute of Philanthropy, at

http://www.nonprofits.org/

Because of its extensive collection of information on corporations in the United States, Hoover's Online is an invaluable resource. For data on more than 1,500 corporations, access Hoover's Online at

http://www.hoovers.com

If you are interested in how another country views business ethics, you should explore Ethical Business, a site originating in Great Britain. You can find this site at

http://www.arq.co.uk/ethicalbusiness

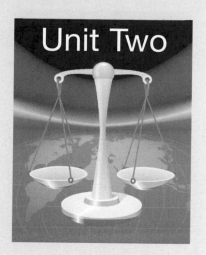

Unit Two

Torts and Crimes

▌Unit Contents

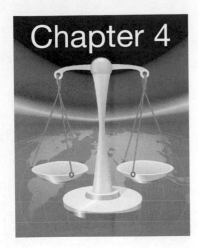

Chapter 4

Torts

CHAPTER OBJECTIVES

After reading this chapter, you should be able to:

1. Explain how torts and crimes differ.
2. State the purpose of tort law.
3. Identify some intentional torts against persons and property.
4. Name the four elements of negligence.
5. Define strict liability, and list some circumstances in which it will be applied.

Torts are wrongful actions.[1] Through tort law, society compensates those who have suffered injuries as a result of the wrongful conduct of others. Although some torts, such as assault and trespass, originated in the English common law, the field of tort law continues to expand as new ways to commit wrongs are discovered and new conceptions of what is right and wrong in a social or business context emerge.

Tort law covers a wide variety of injuries. Society recognizes an interest in personal physical safety, and tort law provides remedies for acts that cause physical injury or that interfere with physical security and freedom of movement. Society recognizes an interest in protecting personal property, and tort law provides remedies for acts that cause destruction or damage to property. Society also recognizes an interest in protecting certain intangible interests, such as personal privacy, family relations, reputation, and dignity, and tort law provides remedies for invasion of these protected interests.

Certain torts normally occur only in the business context. The important area of business torts will be treated in Chapter 6. In this chapter, we discuss torts that can occur in any context, including the business environment. In fact, as you will see in later chapters of this book, many of the lawsuits brought by or against business firms are based on the tort theories discussed in this chapter.

▮ The Basis of Tort Law

Two notions serve as the basis of all torts: wrongs and compensation. Tort law recognizes that some acts are wrong because they cause injuries to others. Of course, a tort is not the only type of wrong that exists in the law; crimes also involve wrongs. A crime, however, is an act so reprehensible that it is considered a wrong against the state or against society as a whole, as well as against the individual vic-

---

1. The term *tort* is French for "wrong."

tim. Therefore, the *state* prosecutes and punishes (through fines and/or imprisonment—and possibly death) persons who commit criminal acts. A tort action, in contrast, is a civil action in which one person brings a personal suit against another to obtain compensation (money **damages**) or other relief for the harm suffered.

Some torts, such as assault and battery (to be discussed shortly), provide a basis for a criminal prosecution as well as a tort action. For example, Joe is walking down the street, minding his own business, when suddenly a person attacks him. In the ensuing struggle, the attacker stabs Joe several times, seriously injuring Joe. A police officer restrains and arrests the wrongdoer. In this situation, the attacker may be subject both to criminal prosecution by the state and to a tort lawsuit brought by Joe. Exhibit 4–1 illustrates how the same wrongful act can result in both civil (tort) and criminal actions against the wrongdoer.

▌Intentional Torts against Persons

An **intentional tort,** as the term implies, requires *intent*. The **tortfeasor** (the one committing the tort) must intend to commit an act, the consequences of which interfere with the personal or business interests of another in a way not permitted by law. An evil or harmful motive is not required—in fact, the tortfeasor may even have a beneficial motive for committing what turns out to be a tortious act. In tort law, intent only means that the actor intended the consequences of his or her act or knew with substantial certainty that certain consequences would result from the act. The law generally assumes that individuals intend the *normal* consequences of their actions. Thus, forcefully pushing another—even if done in jest and without any evil motive—is an intentional tort (if injury results), because the object of a strong push can ordinarily be expected to go flying.

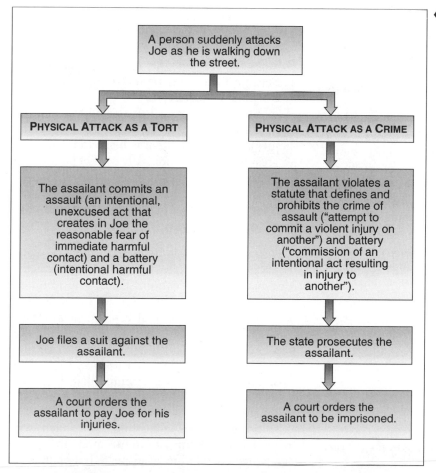

◆ Exhibit 4–1
Tort Lawsuit and Criminal Prosecution for the Same Act

This section discusses intentional torts against persons, including assault, battery, false imprisonment, infliction of emotional distress, defamation, invasion of privacy, and misrepresentation.

Assault and Battery

Any intentional, unexcused act that creates in another person a reasonable apprehension or fear of immediate harmful or offensive contact is an **assault**. Apprehension is not the same as fear. If a contact is such that a reasonable person would want to avoid it, and if there is a reasonable basis for believing that the contact will occur, then the plaintiff suffers apprehension whether or not he or she is afraid. The interest protected by tort law concerning assault is the freedom from having to expect harmful or offensive contact. The occurrence of apprehension is enough to justify compensation.

The *completion* of the act that caused the apprehension, if it results in harm to the plaintiff, is a **battery,** which is defined as an unexcused and harmful or offensive physical contact *intentionally* performed. For example, Ivan threatens Jean with a gun, then shoots her. The pointing of the gun at Jean is an assault; the firing of the gun (if the bullet hits Jean) is a battery. The interest protected by tort law concerning battery is the right to personal security and safety. The contact can be harmful, or it can be merely offensive (such as an unwelcome kiss). Physical injury need not occur. The contact can involve any part of the body or anything attached to it—for example, a hat or other item of clothing, a purse, or a chair or an automobile in which one is sitting. Whether the contact is offensive or not is determined by the *reasonable person standard.*[2] The contact can be made by the defendant or by some force the defendant sets in motion—for example, a rock thrown, food poisoned, or a stick swung.

COMPENSATION   With respect to battery, if the plaintiff shows that there was contact and the jury

agrees that the contact was offensive, the plaintiff has a right to compensation. There is no need to show that the defendant acted out of malice; the person could have just been joking or playing around. The underlying motive does not matter, only the intent to bring about the harmful or offensive contact to the plaintiff. In fact, proving a motive is never necessary (but is sometimes relevant). A plaintiff may be compensated for the emotional harm or loss of reputation resulting from a battery, as well as for physical harm.

DEFENSES TO ASSAULT AND BATTERY   A number of legally recognized **defenses** (reasons why plaintiffs should not obtain what they are seeking) can be raised by a defendant who is sued for assault or battery, or both:

1.   *Consent.* When a person consents to the act that damages him or her, there is generally no liability (legal responsibility) for the damage done.
2.   *Self-defense.* An individual who is defending his or her life or physical well-being can claim self-defense. In situations of both *real* and *apparent* danger, a person may use whatever force is *reasonably* necessary to prevent harmful contact.
3.   *Defense of others.* An individual can act in a reasonable manner to protect others who are in real or apparent danger.
4.   *Defense of property.* Reasonable force may be used in attempting to remove intruders from one's home, although force that is likely to cause death or great bodily injury normally cannot be used just to protect property.

False Imprisonment

False imprisonment is defined as the intentional confinement or restraint of another person's activities without justification. False imprisonment interferes with the freedom to move without restraint. The confinement can be accomplished through the use of physical barriers, physical restraint, or threats of physical force. Moral pressure or threats of future harm do not constitute false imprisonment. It is essential that the person being restrained not comply with the restraint willingly.

Businesspersons are often confronted with suits for false imprisonment after they have attempted to confine a suspected shoplifter for

---

2.   The reasonable person standard is an objective test of how a reasonable person would have acted under the same circumstances. See "The Duty of Care and Its Breach" later in this chapter.

questioning. Under the privilege to detain granted to merchants in some states, a merchant can use the defense of *probable cause* to justify delaying a suspected shoplifter. Probable cause exists when the evidence to support the belief that a person is guilty outweighs the evidence against that belief. The detention, however, must be conducted in a *reasonable* manner and for only a *reasonable* length of time.

Infliction of Emotional Distress

The tort of *infliction of emotional distress* can be defined as an intentional act that amounts to extreme and outrageous conduct resulting in severe emotional distress to another.[3] For example,

---

3. *Restatement (Second) of Torts*, Section 46, Comment d. The *Restatement (Second) of Torts* is a compilation of the law of torts by the American Law Institute.

a prankster telephones an individual and says that the individual's spouse has just been in a horrible accident. As a result, the individual suffers intense mental pain or anxiety. The caller's behavior is deemed to be extreme and outrageous conduct that exceeds the bounds of decency accepted by society and is therefore **actionable** (capable of serving as the ground for a lawsuit). Another example of this tort is "stalking" a person, thus causing that person to experience emotional distress from the fear of possible harm. Stalking is a crime, but courts in many states have concluded that it also constitutes the tort of intentional infliction of emotional distress.

Because infliction of emotional distress is a relatively new tort, it poses some problems. It is difficult to prove the existence of emotional suffering, so a few states require that the emotional disturbance be evidenced by some physical illness. In the following case, the court looks at some of the requirements that plaintiffs must meet in establishing an emotional distress claim.

CASE 4.1

Fudge v. Penthouse International, Ltd.
United States Court of Appeals, First Circuit, 1988.
840 F.2d 1012.

FACTS Leslie Fudge was a student at the Oakland Beach Elementary School in Warwick, Rhode Island. In the fall of 1985, because of apparent conflicts between some of the school's male and female students, the school's principal decided to segregate the sexes during recess periods. A Providence, Rhode Island, newspaper ran an item on the story, along with a photograph showing Leslie Fudge and other girls giving the thumbs-down sign to show their disapproval of the principal's decision. The story and the picture were eventually picked up by *Penthouse* magazine, which printed a one-paragraph story about the girls, along with a slightly cropped version of the photograph that had appeared in the Providence newspaper. The story was headlined "Little Amazons Attack Boys" and appeared in a section of the magazine entitled "Hard Times: A compendium of bizarre, idiotic, lurid, and ofttimes witless driblets of information culled from the nation's press." The brief item told how the Warwick school had segregated the sexes to protect the boys from the girls who "kick them in the shins, pull their hair, and kick them, well, in various painful places." Four of the girls in the picture and their parents brought an action in a federal district court against the owners of *Penthouse* magazine, Penthouse International, Ltd., alleging, among other things, that the publication of the photograph of the girls in a sexually explicit men's magazine constituted the intentional infliction of

(Continued)

Case 4.1—Continued

emotional distress. Penthouse moved for summary judgment, which the district court granted. The plaintiffs—the girls and their parents—appealed.

ISSUE   Does the publication of the photograph of the girls in *Penthouse* magazine constitute the tort of intentional infliction of emotional distress?

DECISION   No. The First Circuit Court of Appeals affirmed the district court's decision to grant Penthouse's motion for summary judgment.

REASON   Citing the *Restatement (Second) of Torts,* Section 46, Comment d, the court said that in emotional distress cases, "Liability has been found only where the conduct has been so outrageous in character, and so extreme in degree, as to go beyond all possible bounds of decency, and to be regarded as atrocious, and utterly intolerable in a civilized community." The court could find nothing in the plaintiffs' allegations that was "sufficiently extreme and outrageous to warrant the imposition of liability." There was nothing shocking about the photograph itself; what the plaintiffs objected to was the fact that it had been published in *Penthouse* magazine. The court stated, however, that "[m]agazines such as *Penthouse* are sufficiently a part of the contemporary scene that their reprinting of relatively innocuous news items or photographs that have already appeared in other media simply cannot be characterized as exceeding all possible bounds of decency, atrocious, or utterly intolerable in a civilized society."

FOR CRITICAL ANALYSIS—Social Consideration   *What would be the result for society if magazines such as* Penthouse *were held liable for any and all distress caused by the articles and photographs they publish?*

Defamation

Defamation of character involves wrongfully hurting a person's good reputation. The law has imposed a general duty on all persons to refrain from making false, defamatory statements about others. Breaching this duty orally involves the tort of **slander;** breaching it in writing involves the tort of **libel.** The tort of defamation also arises when a false statement is made about a person's product, business, or title to property. We deal with these torts in the following chapter.

The common law defines four types of false utterances that are considered torts *per se* (meaning no proof of injury or harm is required for these false utterances to be actionable):

1.   A statement that another has a loathsome communicable disease.

2.   A statement that another has committed improprieties while engaging in a profession or trade.

3.   A statement that another has committed or has been imprisoned for a serious crime.

4.   A statement that an unmarried woman is unchaste.

THE PUBLICATION REQUIREMENT   The basis of the tort of defamation is the publication of a statement or statements that hold an individual up to contempt, ridicule, or hatred. *Publication* here means that the defamatory statements are communicated to persons other than the defamed party. If Thompson writes Andrews a private letter accusing him of embezzling funds, the action does not constitute libel. If Peters calls Gordon dishonest, unattractive, and incompetent when no one else is around, the action does not constitute slander. In neither case was the message communicated to a third party.

The courts have generally held that even dictating a letter to a secretary constitutes publication, although the publication may be privileged (privileged communications will be discussed shortly). Moreover, if a third party overhears defamatory statements by chance, the courts usually hold that this also constitutes publication. Defamatory statements made via the Internet are also actionable. Note further that any individual who republishes or repeats defamatory statements is liable even if that person reveals the source of such statements.

The following case raises an interesting issue concerning the publication requirement: Can a plaintiff establish the publication of defamatory statements without the testimony of a third person regarding what he or she heard or understood?

CASE 4.2

Food Lion, Inc. v. Melton

Supreme Court of Virginia, 1995.
250 Va. 144,
458 S.E.2d 580.

FACTS In April 1991, after shopping at a Food Lion grocery store, sixty-eight-year-old Christine Melton was walking out of the store when a Food Lion security guard stopped her in the parking lot. The guard accused her of leaving with meat belonging to the store in her purse. According to Melton, the guard questioned her repeatedly, loudly, and in an accusatory manner, and "there were people stopping to listen and see what was going on." Finally, Melton allowed the guard to search her purse. No meat was found. Melton filed a suit against Food Lion in a Virginia state court, in part on the ground of defamation. Food Lion in effect denied that the incident ever happened. Melton was not able to identify any of the people who "stopped to listen" and could not offer proof as to what they heard. On the defamation claim, the court entered a judgment in favor of Food Lion, and Melton appealed to the Virginia Supreme Court.

ISSUE Does a party, to prove publication of defamatory remarks, have to present testimony from any third person?

DECISION No. The Virginia Supreme Court held that a party does not need to present testimony from any third person, or even to identify any such person, to prove publication. The court reversed the judgment of the lower court and remanded the case for a new trial.

REASON The court ruled that "a plaintiff may prove publication of defamatory remarks by * * * evidence that the remarks were heard by a third party who understood these remarks as referring to the plaintiff in a defamatory sense." The court noted that the security guard "made his accusations in a 'very loud tone' of voice" and "during this time, people * * * stopped 'to listen and see what was going on.' " The court concluded that this was enough "to permit a reasonable inference that the accuser's words were heard and understood by a third party as referring to Melton and as imputing the commission of a crime."

FOR CRITICAL ANALYSIS—Social Consideration *Under what circumstances should a court require testimony from third parties in order to prove that a statement was "published" for defamation purposes?*

DEFENSES AGAINST DEFAMATION Truth is normally an absolute defense against a defamation charge. In other words, if the defendant in a defamation suit can prove that his or her allegedly defamatory statements were true, the defendant will not be liable.

Another defense that is sometimes raised is that the statements were **privileged** communications, and thus the defendant is immune from liability. Privileged communications are of two types: absolute and qualified. Only in judicial proceedings and certain legislative proceedings is *absolute* privilege granted. For example, statements made by attorneys and judges during a trial are absolutely privileged. So are statements made by legislators during congressional floor debate, even if the legislators make such statements maliciously—that is, knowing them to be untrue. An absolute privilege is granted in these situations because judicial and legislative personnel deal with matters that are so much in the public interest that the parties involved should be able to speak out fully and freely without restriction.

In other situations, a person will not be liable for defamatory statements because he or she has a *qualified*, or conditional, privilege. For example, statements made in recommendation letters or in written evaluations of employees are qualifiedly privileged. Generally, if the communicated statements are made in good faith and the publication is limited to those who have a legitimate interest in the communication, the statements fall within the area of qualified privilege. The concept of conditional privilege rests on the common law assumption that in some situations, the right to know or speak is of equal importance with the right not to be defamed.

In general, false and defamatory statements that are made about *public figures* (those who exercise substantial governmental power and any persons in the public limelight) and that are published in the press are privileged if they are made without **actual malice.**[4] To be made with actual malice, a statement must be made *with either knowledge of falsity or a reckless disregard of the truth.* Statements made about public figures, especially when they are made via a public medium, are usually related to matters of general public interest; they are made about people who substantially affect all of us. Furthermore, public figures generally have some access to a public medium for answering disparaging (belittling, discrediting) falsehoods about themselves; private individuals do not. For these reasons, public figures have a greater burden of proof in defamation cases (they must prove actual malice) than do private individuals.

Invasion of Privacy

A person has a right to solitude and freedom from prying public eyes—in other words, to privacy. Four acts qualify as an invasion of that privacy:

1. The use of a person's name, picture, or other likeness for commercial purposes without permission. This tort, which is usually referred to as the tort of *appropriation*, will be examined in the next chapter.
2. Intrusion in an individual's affairs or seclusion in an area in which the person has a reasonable expectation of privacy.
3. Publication of information that places a person in a false light. This could be a story attributing to the person ideas not held or actions not taken by the person. (Publishing such a story could involve the tort of defamation as well.)
4. Public disclosure of private facts about an individual that an ordinary person would find objectionable.

Misrepresentation—Fraud (Deceit)

A misrepresentation leads another to believe in a condition that is different from the condition that actually exists. This is often accomplished through a false or incorrect statement. Misrepresentations may be innocently made by someone who is unaware of the existing facts, but the tort of **fraudulent misrepresentation,** or **fraud,** involves intentional deceit, usually for personal gain. The tort includes several elements:

1. Misrepresentation of facts or conditions with knowledge that they are false or with reckless disregard for the truth.
2. Intent to induce another to rely on the misrepresentation.

---

4. *New York Times Co. v. Sullivan,* 376 U.S. 254, 84 S.Ct. 710, 11 L.Ed.2d 686 (1964).

3. Justifiable reliance by the deceived party.
4. Damages suffered as a result of reliance.
5. Causal connection between the misrepresentation and the injury suffered.

For fraud to occur, more than mere **puffery**, or *seller's talk*, must be involved. Fraud exists only when a person represents as a fact something he or she knows is untrue. For example, it is fraud to claim that a roof does not leak when one knows it does. Facts are objectively ascertainable, whereas seller's talk is not. "I am the best accountant in town" is seller's talk. The speaker is not trying to represent something as fact, because the term *best* is a subjective, not an objective, term.[5]

Normally, the tort of misrepresentation or fraud occurs only when there is reliance upon a *statement of fact*. Sometimes, however, reliance on a *statement of opinion* may involve the tort of misrepresentation if the individual making the statement of opinion has a superior knowledge of the subject matter. For example, when a lawyer makes a statement of opinion about the law, a court would construe reliance on such a statement to be equivalent to reliance on a statement of fact. We examine fraudulent misrepresentation in further detail in Chapter 10, in the context of contract law.

Intentional Torts against Property

Intentional torts against property include trespass to land, trespass to personal property, and conversion. These torts are wrongful actions that interfere with individuals' legally recognized rights with regard to their land or personal property. The law distinguishes real property from personal property (see Chapters 28 and 29). *Real property* is land and things "permanently" attached to the land. *Personal property* consists of all other items, which are basically movable. Thus, a house and lot are real property, whereas the furniture inside a house is personal property. Money and securities are also personal property.

Trespass to Land

A **trespass to land** occurs whenever a person, without permission or legal authorization, enters onto, above, or below the surface of land that is owned by another; causes anything to enter onto the land; remains on the land; or permits anything to remain on it. Actual harm to the land is not an essential element of this tort, because the tort is designed to protect the right of an owner to exclusive possession of his or her property. Common types of trespass to land include walking or driving on the land, shooting a gun over the land, throwing rocks at a building that belongs to someone else, building a dam across a river and thus causing water to back up on someone else's land, and placing part of one's building on an adjoining landowner's property.

TRESPASS CRITERIA, RIGHTS, AND DUTIES Before a person can be a trespasser, the owner of the real property (or other person in actual and exclusive possession of the property) must establish that person as a trespasser. For example, "posted" trespass signs expressly establish as a trespasser a person who ignores these signs and enters onto the property. A guest in your home is not a trespasser—unless he or she has been asked to leave but refuses. Any person who enters onto your property to commit an illegal act (such as a thief entering a lumberyard at night to steal lumber) is established impliedly as a trespasser, without posted signs.

At common law, a trespasser is liable for damages caused to the property. In addition, a trespasser generally cannot hold the owner liable for injuries sustained on the premises. This common law rule is being abandoned in many jurisdictions in favor of a "reasonable duty of care" rule that varies depending on the status of the parties. For example, a landowner may have a duty to post a notice that the property is patrolled by guard dogs. Furthermore, under the "attractive nuisance" doctrine, children do not assume the risks of the premises if they are attracted to the premises by some object, such as a swimming pool, an abandoned building, or a sand pile. Trespassers normally can be removed from the premises through the use of reasonable force without the owner's being liable for assault and battery.

DEFENSES AGAINST TRESPASS TO LAND Trespass to land involves wrongful interference with

---

5. In contracts for the sale of goods, Article 2 of the Uniform Commercial Code distinguishes, for warranty purposes, between statements of opinion ("puffery") and statements of fact. See Chapter 16 for a further discussion of this issue.

another person's real property rights. If it can be shown that the trespass was warranted, however, as when a trespasser enters to assist someone in danger, a defense exists. Another defense is to show that the purported owner did not actually have the right to possess the land in question.

Trespass to Personal Property

Whenever any individual unlawfully harms the personal property of another or otherwise interferes with the personal property owner's right to exclusive possession and enjoyment of that property, **trespass to personal property**—also called *trespass to personalty*[6]—occurs. If a student takes another student's business law book as a practical joke and hides it so that the owner is unable to find it for several days prior to a final examination, the student has engaged in a trespass to personal property.

If it can be shown that trespass to personal property was warranted, then a complete defense exists. Most states, for example, allow automobile repair shops to hold a customer's car (under what is called an *artisan's lien,* discussed in Chapter 20) when the customer refuses to pay for repairs already completed.

Conversion

Whenever personal property is wrongfully taken from its rightful owner or possessor and placed in the service of another, the act of **conversion** occurs. Conversion is defined as any act depriving an owner of personal property without that owner's permission and without just cause. When conversion occurs, the lesser offense of trespass to personal property usually occurs as well. If the initial taking of the property was unlawful, there is trespass; retention of that property is conversion. If the initial taking of the property was permitted by the owner or for some other reason is not a trespass, failure to return it may still be conversion. Conversion is the civil side of crimes related to theft. A store clerk who steals merchandise from the store commits a crime and engages in the tort of conversion at the same time.

Even if a person mistakenly believed that he or she was entitled to the goods, a tort of conversion may occur. In other words, good intentions are not a defense against conversion; in fact, conversion can be an entirely innocent act. Someone who buys stolen goods, for example, commits the tort of conversion even if he or she does not know that the goods were stolen. If the true owner brings a tort action against the buyer, the buyer must either return the property to the owner or pay the owner the full value of the property, despite having already paid money to the thief.

A successful defense against the charge of conversion is that the purported owner does not in fact own the property or does not have a right to possess it that is superior to the right of the holder. Necessity is another possible defense against conversion. If Abrams takes Mendoza's cat, Abrams is guilty of conversion. If Mendoza sues Abrams, Abrams must return the cat or pay damages. If, however, the cat has rabies and Abrams took the cat to protect the public, Abrams has a valid defense—necessity (and perhaps even self-defense, if he can prove that he was in danger because of the cat).

▮ Unintentional Torts (Negligence)

The tort of **negligence** occurs when someone suffers injury because of another's failure to live up to a required *duty of care.* In contrast to intentional torts, in torts involving negligence, the tortfeasor neither wishes to bring about the consequences of the act nor believes that they will occur. The actor's conduct merely creates a *risk* of such consequences. If no risk is created, there is no negligence.

Many of the actions discussed in the section on intentional torts constitute negligence if the element of intent is missing. For example, if Juarez intentionally shoves Natsuyo, who falls and breaks an arm as a result, Juarez will have committed an intentional tort. If Juarez carelessly bumps into Natsuyo, however, and she falls and breaks an arm as a result, Juarez's action will constitute negligence. In either situation, Juarez has committed a tort.

In examining a question of negligence, one should ask four questions:

1.   Did the defendant owe a duty of care to the plaintiff?
2.   Did the defendant breach that duty?

---

6.   Pronounced *per*-sun-ul-tee.

3. Did the plaintiff suffer a legally recognizable injury as a result of the defendant's breach of the duty of care?

4. Did the defendant's breach cause the plaintiff's injury?

Each of these elements of neligence is discussed below.

The Duty of Care and Its Breach

The concept of a **duty of care** arises from the notion that if we are to live in society with other people, some actions can be tolerated and some cannot; some actions are right and some are wrong; and some actions are reasonable and some are not. The basic principle underlying the duty of care is that people are free to act as they please so long as their actions do not infringe on the interests of others.

When someone fails to comply with the duty of exercising reasonable care, a potentially tortious act may have been committed. Failure to live up to a standard of care may be an act (setting fire to a building) or an omission (neglecting to put out a campfire). It may be an intentional act, a careless act, or a carefully performed but nevertheless dangerous act that results in injury. Courts consider the nature of the act (whether it is outrageous or commonplace), the manner in which the act is performed (cautiously versus heedlessly), and the nature of the injury (whether it is serious or slight) in determining whether the duty of care has been breached.

THE REASONABLE PERSON STANDARD   Tort law measures duty by the **reasonable person standard.** In determining whether a duty of care has been breached, the courts ask how a reasonable person would have acted in the same circumstances. The reasonable person standard is said to be (though in an absolute sense it cannot be) objective. It is not necessarily how a particular person would act. It is society's judgment on how people *should* act. If the so-called reasonable person existed, he or she would be careful, conscientious, even tempered, and honest. This hypothetical reasonable person is frequently used by the courts in decisions relating to other areas of law as well.

That individuals are required to exercise a reasonable standard of care in their activities is a pervasive concept in business law, and many of the issues dealt with in subsequent chapters of this text have to do with this duty. What constitutes reasonable care varies, of course, with the circumstances.

DUTY OF LANDOWNERS   Landowners are expected to exercise reasonable care to protect from harm persons coming onto their property. As mentioned earlier, in some jurisdictions, landowners are held to owe a duty to protect even trespassers against certain risks. Landowners who rent or lease premises to tenants (see Chapter 29) are expected to exercise reasonable care to ensure that the tenants and their guests are not harmed in common areas, such as stairways, entryways, laundry rooms, and the like.

Retailers and other firms that explicitly or implicitly invite persons to come onto their premises are usually charged with a duty to exercise reasonable care to protect those persons, who are considered to be **business invitees.** For example, if you entered a supermarket, slipped on a wet floor, and sustained injuries as a result, the owner of the supermarket would be liable for damages if when you slipped there was no sign warning that the floor was wet. A court would hold that the business owner was negligent because the owner failed to exercise a reasonable degree of care in protecting the store's customers against foreseeable risks about which the owner knew or *should have known.* That a patron might slip on the wet floor and be injured as a result was a foreseeable risk, and the owner should have taken care to avoid this risk or to warn the customer of it. The landowner also has a duty to discover and remove any hidden dangers that might injure a customer or other invitee.

Some risks, of course, are so obvious that the owner need not warn of them. For example, a business owner does not need to warn customers to open a door before attempting to walk through it. Other risks, however, even though they may seem obvious to a business owner, may not be so in the eyes of another, such as a child. For example, a hardware store owner may not think it is necessary to warn customers that a stepladder leaning against the back wall of the store could fall down and harm them. It is possible, though, that a child could tip the ladder over and be hurt as a result and that the store could be held liable. In the following case, the court has to decide whether a supermarket owner should be held liable for a customer's injuries on the premises.

CASE 4.3

Dumont v. Shaw's Supermarkets, Inc.

Supreme Judicial Court of Maine, 1995.
664 A.2d 846.

FACTS   At Shaw's Supermarkets, Inc., chocolate-covered peanuts are sold in bulk with other unpackaged, unwrapped candy in bins next to the produce section. Shaw's is aware that self-serve, small, loose, slippery items create a hazard for customers, who may slip and fall if they step on them. Shaw's places mats next to some of the produce and in other locations, but Shaw's does not place mats on the floor next to the candy bins. While shopping at Shaw's, Shirley Dumont slipped on a chocolate-covered peanut, fell, and was injured. Dumont sued Shaw's in a Maine state court, alleging negligence. The court ruled that Dumont could recover only if she proved that Shaw's caused the candy to be on the floor, that Shaw's knew that the candy was on the floor, or that the candy was on the floor for such a length of time that Shaw's should have known it was there. Because Dumont proved none of these things, the court entered a judgment in favor of Shaw's. Dumont appealed to the state's highest court, the Supreme Judicial Court of Maine.

ISSUE   Is a store owner's awareness of the risk of a recurrent hazardous condition on the premises sufficient to hold the owner liable for a customer's injury that is caused by the condition?

DECISION   Yes. The Supreme Judicial Court of Maine held that it is not necessary to prove that the owner had actual notice of the specific condition giving rise to the injury. The court vacated (set aside) the lower court's judgment and remanded the case for further proceedings.

REASON   Dumont "presented evidence *   *   * that there existed a foreseeable risk of a recurrent condition and that Shaw's did not exercise reasonable care in failing to place mats next to the bulk candy display." The court emphasized that "Shaw's was aware that items with similar characteristics to the chocolate-covered peanuts created an increased hazard to customers and had placed mats on the floor to mitigate the risk." The court stated that "[i]n those circumstances, a store owner may be chargeable with constructive notice[a] of the existence of the specific condition." The court explained that "a store owner who is aware of the existence of a recurrent condition that poses a potential danger to invitees may not ignore that knowledge and fail reasonably to respond to the foreseeable danger of the likelihood of a recurrence of the condition."

FOR CRITICAL ANALYSIS—Social Consideration   *Does the principle applied in this case make a store owner the "absolute insurer" of the store's customers? In other words, is a store owner liable for injuries to customers on the premises even if the owner has taken precautions that are reasonably necessary to protect those customers?*

a.   Notice that is implied or imposed by law, as opposed to actual notice.

DUTY OF PROFESSIONALS   If an individual has knowledge, skill, or intelligence superior to that of an ordinary person, the individual's conduct must

be consistent with that status. Professionals—including doctors, dentists, psychiatrists, architects, engineers, accountants, lawyers, and others—are required to have a standard minimum level of special knowledge and ability. Therefore, in determining what constitutes reasonable care in cases involving professionals, their training and expertise is taken into account. In other words, an accountant cannot defend against a lawsuit for negligence by stating, "But I was not familiar with that principle of accounting."

If a professional violates his or her duty of care toward a client, the professional may be sued for **malpractice.** For example, a patient might sue a physician for *medical malpractice.* A client might sue an attorney for *legal malpractice.*

The Injury Requirement and Damages

For a tort to have been committed, the plaintiff must have suffered a *legally recognizable* injury. To recover damages (receive compensation), the plaintiff must have suffered some loss, harm, wrong, or invasion of a protected interest. Essentially, the purpose of tort law is to compensate for legally recognized injuries resulting from wrongful acts. If no harm or injury results from a given negligent action, there is nothing to compensate—and no tort exists. For example, if you carelessly bump into a passerby, who stumbles and falls as a result, you may be liable in tort if the passerby is injured in the fall. If the person is unharmed, however, there normally could be no suit for damages, because no injury was suffered. Although the passerby might be angry and suffer emotional distress, few courts recognize negligently inflicted emotional distress as a tort unless it results in some physical disturbance or dysfunction.

As already mentioned, the purpose of tort law is not to punish people for tortious acts but to compensate the injured parties for damages suffered. Occasionally, however, damages awarded in tort lawsuits include both **compensatory damages** (which are intended to reimburse a plaintiff for actual losses—to make the plaintiff whole) and **punitive damages** (which are intended to punish the wrongdoer and deter others from similar wrongdoing). Few negligent acts, however, are so reprehensible that punitive damages are available. Unlike in some other nations, in the United States the damages awarded do not depend on whether the tort was intentional or negligent.

Causation

Another element necessary to a tort is *causation.* If a person fails in a duty of care and someone suffers injury, the wrongful activity must have caused the harm for a tort to have been committed.

CAUSATION IN FACT AND PROXIMATE CAUSE   In deciding whether there is causation, the court must address two questions:

1.   *Is there causation in fact?* Did the injury occur because of the defendant's act, or would it have occurred anyway? If an injury would not have occurred without the defendant's act, then there is causation in fact. **Causation in fact** can usually be determined by the use of the *but for* test: "but for" the wrongful act, the injury would not have occurred. Theoretically, causation in fact is limitless. One could claim, for example, that "but for" the creation of the world, a particular injury would not have occurred. Thus, as a practical matter, the law has to establish limits, and it does so through the concept of proximate cause.
2.   *Was the act the proximate cause of the injury?* **Proximate cause,** or legal cause, exists when the connection between an act and an injury is strong enough to justify imposing liability. Consider an example. Ackerman carelessly leaves a campfire burning. The fire not only burns down the forest but also sets off an explosion in a nearby chemical plant that spills chemicals into a river, killing all the fish for a hundred miles downstream and ruining the economy of a tourist resort. Should Ackerman be liable to the resort owners? To the tourists whose vacations were ruined? These are questions of proximate cause that a court must decide.

FORESEEABILITY   The courts use *foreseeability* as the test for proximate cause. If the victim of the harm or the consequences of the harm done are unforeseeable, there is no proximate cause. It is difficult to predict when a court will say that something is foreseeable and when it will say that something is not. How far a court stretches foreseeability is determined in part by the extent to which the court is willing to stretch the defendant's duty of care. In the following case, the court considered whether, under the circumstances, the harm caused by arson is a reasonably foreseeable risk.

CASE 4.4

Addis v. Steele

Appeals Court of
Massachusetts, 1995.
38 Mass.App.Ct. 433,
648 N.E.2d 773.

FACTS On the morning of October 2, 1989, a fire started by an arsonist broke out in the Red Inn in Provincetown, Massachusetts. The inn had a smoke detector, sprinkler, and alarm system, which alerted the guests, but there were no emergency lights or clear exits. Attempting to escape, Deborah Addis and James Reed, guests at the inn, found the first-floor doors and windows locked. Ultimately, they forced open a second-floor window and jumped out. To recover for their injuries, they filed a suit in a Massachusetts state court against Tamerlane Corporation, which operated the inn under a lease, and others (including Duane Steele, who worked for the owner of the inn). Addis and Reed contended in part that Tamerlane was negligent. Tamerlane responded that harm caused by arson is not a reasonably foreseeable risk. The court entered a judgment against Tamerlane, and Tamerlane appealed. The appellate court affirmed the lower court's judgment. Tamerlane then appealed to a higher state court.

ISSUE Was the harm caused by the fire set by the arsonist a reasonably foreseeable risk?

DECISION Yes. The Appeals Court of Massachusetts affirmed the lower courts' judgments against Tamerlane.

REASON The court pointed out that "the possibility of fire was foreseen and guarded against with * * * smoke detector[s], sprinkler and alarm system[s]." Given the foreseeability of a fire, the court reasoned that Tamerlane should gain "no benefit from the fact that the fire was set." The court held that the duty to protect others against unreasonable risks of harm extends to risks arising from acts of third persons, "whether they be innocent, negligent, intentional, or even criminal." The court concluded that Tamerlane's "failure to provide adequate lighting and egress [exit] created a foreseeable risk that a fire, however started—innocently, negligently, or by a criminal act—would cause harm to its guests."

FOR CRITICAL ANALYSIS—Economic Consideration *Does a business always have a duty to protect its patrons from the harm caused by the criminal activity of third persons? In other words, is the harm caused by* all *crimes reasonably foreseeable under* all *circumstances? If not, under what circumstances is harm caused by crime foreseeable?*

SUPERSEDING INTERVENING FORCES An independent intervening force may break the connection between a wrongful act and an injury to another. If so, it acts as a *superseding cause*—that is, the intervening force or event sets aside, or replaces, the original wrongful act as the cause of the injury. For example, suppose that Derrick keeps a can of gasoline in the trunk of his car. The presence of the gasoline creates a foreseeable risk and is thus a negligent act. If Derrick's car skids

and crashes into a tree, causing the gasoline can to explode, Derrick would be liable for injuries sustained by passing pedestrians because of his negligence. If the explosion had been caused by lightning striking the car, however, the lightning would supersede Derrick's original negligence as a cause of the damage, because the lightning was not foreseeable.

In negligence cases, the negligent party will often attempt to show that some act has intervened after his or her action and that this second act was the proximate cause of injury. Typically, in cases in which an individual takes a defensive action, such as swerving to avoid an oncoming car, the original wrongdoer will not be relieved of liability even if the injury actually resulted from the attempt to escape harm. The same is true under the "danger invites rescue" doctrine. Under this doctrine, if Lemming commits an act that endangers Salter and Yokem sustains an injury trying to protect Salter, then Lemming will be liable for Yokem's injury, as well as for any injuries Salter may sustain. Rescuers can injure themselves, or the person rescued, or even a stranger, but the original wrongdoer will still be liable.

Defenses to Negligence

The basic defenses in negligence cases are (1) assumption of risk, (2) contributory negligence, and (3) comparative negligence.

ASSUMPTION OF RISK A plaintiff who voluntarily enters into a risky situation, knowing the risk involved, will not be allowed to recover. This is the defense of **assumption of risk.** The requirements of this defense are (1) knowledge of the risk and (2) voluntary assumption of the risk. For example, a driver entering a race knows there is a risk of

being killed or injured in a crash. The driver has assumed the risk of injury.

The risk can be assumed by express agreement, or the assumption of risk can be implied by the plaintiff's knowledge of the risk and subsequent conduct. Of course, the plaintiff does not assume a risk different from or greater than the risk normally carried by the activity. In our example, the race car driver assumes the risk of being injured in the race but not the risk that the banking in the curves of the racetrack will give way during the race because of a construction defect.

Risks are not deemed to be assumed in situations involving emergencies. Neither are they assumed when a statute protects a class of people from harm and a member of the class is injured by the harm. For example, employees are protected by statute from harmful working conditions and therefore do not assume the risks associated with the workplace. If an employee is injured, he or she will generally be compensated regardless of fault under state workers' compensation statutes (discussed in Chapter 22).

In the following case, the plaintiff suffered an injury to his pitching arm in a simulated baseball game during a tryout for a major league team. The issue before the court was whether the plaintiff had assumed the risk of the injury, thus precluding him from recovery.

CASE 4.5

Wattenbarger v. Cincinnati Reds, Inc.

California Court of Appeal, Third District, 1994.
28 Cal.App.4th 746,
33 Cal.Rptr.2d 732.

FACTS In June 1990, in Lodi, California, seventeen-year-old Jeffrey Wattenbarger tried out for the position of pitcher for the Cincinnati Reds. During the tryouts, Wattenbarger's shoulder popped. It occurred on his third pitch to a batter during a simulated game. He stepped off the mound and told the representatives of the Reds. Hearing no response, Wattenbarger stepped back onto the mound and threw another pitch. He immediately experienced severe pain. Later, it was discovered that a portion of the bone and tendons had pulled away sometime during Wattenbarger's pitching, and he underwent an operation on the arm. Seeking damages for the injury, Wattenbarger brought an action in a California state court against the Reds, claiming they had been negligent in allowing him to throw the fourth pitch. The Reds asserted, among other things, the defense of assumption of risk—that is, that Wattenbarger, by participating in the tryout, had assumed the risk of injury—and filed a motion for summary judgment. The court granted the motion, and Wattenbarger appealed to a state appellate court.

(Continued)

Case 4.5—Continued

ISSUE   By taking part in a sport, does an individual assume a risk of injury greater than the risks inherent in the sport?

DECISION   No. The California Court of Appeal held, among other things, that a participant does not assume a risk greater than the risks inherent in a sport. The court reversed the lower court's grant of summary judgment and remanded the case.

REASON   The court acknowledged that assumption of risk occurs when a person "voluntarily participates in a sporting event or activity involving certain inherent risks." The court stated that if Wattenbarger had stopped after his third pitch, "we would have no difficulty finding *   *   * assumption of risk a bar to recovery." The court explained, however, that the Reds "were not co-participants in the sport or activity but were instead in control of it." Thus, they owed a duty to the tryout participants "not to increase the risks inherent in the game of baseball." When Wattenbarger told them that his arm had popped, "he was seeking guidance as to how to proceed. Hearing nothing to countermand the original instruction *   *   *, [he] threw another pitch, thereby causing further injury."

FOR CRITICAL ANALYSIS—Cultural Consideration   *Baseball team managers are aware that young potential players, such as Wattenbarger, sometimes face significant cultural pressure to succeed in the sport. How does this knowledge affect baseball managers' duty of care during tryouts?*

CONTRIBUTORY NEGLIGENCE   All individuals are expected to exercise a reasonable degree of care in looking out for themselves. In a few jurisdictions, recovery for injury resulting from negligence is prevented if the plaintiff was also negligent (failed to exercise a reasonable degree of care). This is the defense of **contributory negligence.** Under the doctrine of contributory negligence, no matter how insignificant the plaintiff's negligence is relative to the defendant's negligence, the plaintiff will be precluded from recovering any damages.

An exception to the doctrine of contributory negligence may apply if the defendant failed to take advantage of an opportunity to avoid causing the damage. Under the "last clear chance" rule, the plaintiff may recover full damages despite his or her own negligence. For example, if Murphy walks across the street against the light, and Lewis, a motorist, sees her in time to avoid hitting her but hits her anyway, Lewis (the defendant) is not permitted to use Murphy's (the plaintiff's) prior negligence as a defense. The defendant negligently missed the opportunity to avoid injuring the plain-

tiff. In those states that have adopted the comparative negligence rule, discussed next, the last clear chance doctrine does not apply.

COMPARATIVE NEGLIGENCE   The majority of states now allow recovery based on the doctrine of **comparative negligence.** This doctrine enables both the plaintiff's and the defendant's negligence to be computed and the liability for damages distributed accordingly. Some jurisdictions have adopted a "pure" form of comparative negligence that allows the plaintiff to recover, even if the extent of his or her fault is greater than that of the defendant. For example, if the plaintiff was 80 percent at fault and the defendant 20 percent at fault, the plaintiff may recover 20 percent of his or her damages. Many states' comparative negligence statutes, however, contain a "50 percent" rule by which the plaintiff recovers nothing if he or she was more than 50 percent at fault. In the following case, the court had to determine the meaning of a particular state's comparative negligence statute.

Rodgers v. American Honda Motor Co.

United States Court of Appeals, First Circuit, 1995.
46 F.3d 1.

FACTS Brian Rodgers, an experienced all-terrain-vehicle (ATV) rider, helped a friend repair a three-wheel ATV. Without putting on a helmet, Rodgers gave the ATV a trial run. It flipped, and Rodgers struck his head, causing injuries to his brain. Rodgers's wife, Debra, and his other guardian filed a suit in a Maine state court against the American Honda Motor Company, the manufacturer of the ATV. During the trial, the plaintiffs asked the court to exclude testimony that Rodgers had not been wearing a helmet. The court ruled that the testimony was admissible, and the plaintiffs appealed to the U.S. Court of Appeals for the First Circuit.

ISSUE Does the doctrine of comparative negligence apply not only to fault for the cause of an accident but also to responsibility for the extent of any damage sustained?

DECISION Yes. The U.S. Court of Appeals for the First Circuit affirmed the ruling of the state court.

REASON Because the accident occurred in Maine, the appellate court reviewed the Maine statute that applied to the case. The statute provides that a reduction in the amount of a recovery is to be "just and equitable, having regard to the claimant's share in the responsibility for the damages * * * . If [a] claimant is found by the jury to be equally at fault, the claimant shall not recover." Noting that the last sentence was added later in the legislative process, the court read "at fault" to mean having "responsibility for the damage sustained." Thus, if a plaintiff was found to be at least equally responsible for the damage sustained, he or she could recover nothing. The court added that in this case, because "the uncontradicted evidence that plaintiff's failure to wear a helmet was responsible for essentially all the damage sustained, this reading of the statute is fatal to his case."

FOR CRITICAL ANALYSIS—International Consideration *When the plaintiff lives in one country and the defendant in another, and the respective countries use different formulas for measuring comparative negligence, which formula should be applied?*

Special Negligence Doctrines and Statutes

There are a number of special doctrines and statutes relating to negligence. We examine a few of them here.

RES IPSA LOQUITUR Generally, in lawsuits involving negligence, the plaintiff has the burden of proving that the defendant was negligent. In certain situations, when negligence is very difficult or impossible to prove, the courts may infer that negligence has occurred, in which case the burden of proof rests on the defendant—to prove he or she was *not* negligent. The inference of the defendant's negligence is known as the doctrine of **res ipsa loquitur,** which translates as "the facts speak for themselves." This doctrine is applied only when the event creating the damage or injury is one that ordinarily does not occur in the absence of negligence. *Res ipsa loquitur* has been applied to such events as trains derailing, wheels falling off moving vehicles, and bricks or windowpanes falling from a defendant's premises. For the doctrine to apply, the event must have been within the defendant's power to control, and it must not have been due to any voluntary action or contribution on the part of the plaintiff. Some courts will add still another condition—that the evidence available to explain the event be more accessible to the defendant than to the plaintiff.

NEGLIGENCE *PER SE*   Certain conduct, whether it consists of an action or a failure to act, may be treated as **negligence** *per se* ("in or of itself"). Negligence *per se* may occur if an individual violates a statute or an ordinance providing for a criminal penalty and that violation causes another to be injured. The injured person must prove (1) that the statute clearly sets out what standard of conduct is expected, when and where it is expected, and of whom it is expected; (2) that he or she is in the class intended to be protected by the statute; and (3) that the statute was designed to prevent the type of injury that he or she suffered. The standard of conduct required by the statute is the duty that the defendant owes to the plaintiff, and a violation of the statute is the breach of that duty.

For example, a statute may require a landowner to keep a building in a safe condition and may also subject the landowner to a criminal penalty, such as a fine, if the building is not kept safe. The statute is meant to protect those who are rightfully in the building. Thus, if the owner, without a sufficient excuse, violates the statute and a tenant is thereby injured, then a majority of courts will hold that the owner's unexcused violation of the statute conclusively establishes negligence—that is, that the owner's violation is negligence *per se*.

SPECIAL NEGLIGENCE STATUTES   A number of states have enacted statutes prescribing duties and responsibilities in certain circumstances, the violation of which will impose civil liability. For example, most states now have what are called **Good Samaritan statutes.** Under these statutes, persons who are aided voluntarily by others cannot turn around and sue the "Good Samaritans" for negligence. These laws were passed largely to protect physicians and medical personnel who voluntarily render their services in emergency situations to those in need, such as individuals hurt in car accidents.

Many states have also passed **dram shop acts,** under which a tavern owner or bartender may be held liable for injuries caused by a person who became intoxicated while drinking at the bar or who was already intoxicated when served by the bartender. In some states, statutes impose liability on *social hosts* (persons hosting parties) for injuries caused by guests who became intoxicated at the hosts' homes. Under these statutes, it is unnecessary to prove that the tavern owner, bartender, or social host was negligent.

▌ Strict Liability

Another category of torts is called **strict liability,** or *liability without fault.* Intentional torts and torts of negligence involve acts that depart from a reasonable standard of care and cause injuries. Under the doctrine of strict liability, liability for injury is imposed for reasons other than fault. Strict liability for damages proximately caused by an abnormally dangerous or exceptional activity is one application of this doctrine. Courts apply the doctrine of strict liability in such cases because of the extreme risk of the activity. For example, even if blasting with dynamite is performed with all reasonable care, there is still a risk of injury. Balancing that risk against the potential for harm, it is fair to ask the person engaged in the activity to pay for injury caused by that activity. Although there is no fault, there is still responsibility because of the dangerous nature of the undertaking.

There are other applications of the strict liability principle. Persons who keep dangerous animals, for example, are strictly liable for any harm inflicted by the animals. A significant application of strict liability is in the area of *product liability*— liability of manufacturers and sellers for harmful or defective products. Liability here is a matter of social policy and is based on two factors: (1) the manufacturing company can better bear the cost of injury, because it can spread the cost throughout society by increasing prices of goods and services, and (2) the m anufacturing company is making a profit from its activities and therefore should bear the cost of injury as an operating expense. We will discuss product liability in greater detail in Chapter 16.

In the following case, the issue before the court is whether a fumigation company should be held strictly liable for injuries caused by the Vikane gas that the company used during the fumigation of a condominium complex.

CASE 4.7
Old Island Fumigation, Inc. v. Barbee

District Court of Appeal of Florida,
Third District, 1992.
604 So.2d 1246.

FACTS Old Island Fumigation, Inc., fumigated Buildings A and B of a condominium complex. Residents in Buildings A and B were evacuated during the procedure, but occupants of Building C were not. Shortly after the fumigation, which involved the use of Vikane gas, several residents of Building C became ill and were treated for sulfuryl fluoride poisoning. Sulfuryl fluoride is the active ingredient of Vikane gas. Several months later, an architect discovered that the fire wall between Buildings B and C was defective and contained an open space measuring four feet by eighteen inches, through which the gas had entered Building C. The defect was visible only from within the crawl space, and thus it had been missed by various building inspectors, as well as by the fumigating company. Residents of Building C sued Old Island in a Florida state court, alleging that fumigation was an ultrahazardous activity and that Old Island was therefore strictly liable for their injuries. The company asserted that it should not be responsible for injuries caused by the negligence of others—the original architect and contractors for the condominiums, who had failed to note and repair the defect in the fire wall. The trial court granted the plaintiffs' motion for summary judgment against Old Island, and Old Island appealed.

ISSUE The issue in this case is twofold: (1) Is fumigation an ultrahazardous activity? (2) Even if fumigation is an ultrahazardous activity, can Old Island be held liable for damages when the negligence of others (including the building contractors) made the injuries possible?

DECISION Yes, to both questions. The Florida appellate court affirmed the trial court's judgment.

REASON Citing another case, the court stated that the factors to be considered in determining whether an activity is ultrahazardous are "whether [the] activity involves [a] high degree of risk of harm to property of others; whether [the] potential harm is likely to be great; whether [the] risk can be eliminated by [the] exercise of reasonable care; whether [the] activity is [a] matter of common usage; whether [the] activity is appropriate to [the] place where [the activity is] conducted [and] whether [the] activity has substantial value to [the] community." The court held that fumigation is an ultrahazardous activity because it "necessarily involves a risk of serious harm * * * which cannot be eliminated by the exercise of the utmost care, and is not a matter of common usage." Old Island was thus liable regardless of how careful it had been in fumigating the buildings. The court also emphasized that the fact that a third party had also been negligent did not relieve Old Island from liability for a hazard created by the company for its own profit.

FOR CRITICAL ANALYSIS—Social Consideration *Do you agree that business firms should bear the cost of injuries, even though the firms were not at fault, simply because the firms can spread the cost throughout society by increasing the prices of their goods or services?*

▌Terms and Concepts

▌Chapter Summary: Torts

Intentional Torts against Persons *(See pages 79–85.)*	1. *Assault and battery*—An assault is an unexcused and intentional act that causes another person to be apprehensive of immediate harm. A battery is an assault that results in physical contact. 2. *False imprisonment*—The intentional confinement or restraint of another person's movement without justification. 3. *Infliction of emotional distress*—An intentional act that amounts to extreme and outrageous conduct resulting in severe emotional distress to another. 4. *Defamation (libel or slander)*—A false statement of fact, not made under privilege, that is communicated to a third person and that causes damage to a person's reputation. For public figures, the plaintiff must also prove actual malice. 5. *Invasion of privacy*—The use of a person's name or likeness for commercial purposes without permission, wrongful intrusion into a person's private activities, publication of information that places a person in a false light, or disclosure of private facts that an ordinary person would find objectionable. 6. *Misrepresentation—fraud (deceit)*—A false representation made by one party, through misstatement of facts or through conduct, with the intention of deceiving another and on which the other reasonably relies to his or her detriment.
Intentional Torts against Property *(See pages 85–86.)*	1. *Trespass to land*—The invasion of another's real property without consent or privilege. Specific rights and duties apply once a person is expressly or impliedly established as a trespasser. 2. *Trespass to personal property*—Unlawfully damaging or interfering with the owner's right to use, possess, or enjoy his or her personal property. 3. *Conversion*—A wrongful act in which personal property is taken from its rightful owner or possessor and placed in the service of another.
Unintentional Torts—Negligence *(See pages 86–94.)*	1. *Negligence*—The careless performance of a legally required duty or the failure to perform a legally required act. Elements that must be proved are that a legal duty of care exists, that the defendant breached that duty, and that the breach caused damage or injury to another.

▌Chapter Summary: Torts—Continued

Unintentional Torts—Negligence Continued	2. *Defenses to negligence*—The basic defenses in negligence cases are (a) assumption of risk, (b) contributory negligence, and (c) comparative negligence.
	
	3. *Special negligence doctrines and statutes*—
	
	   a. *Res ipsa loquitur*—A doctrine under which a plaintiff need not prove negligence on the part of the defendant because "the facts speak for themselves." *Res ipsa loquitur* has been applied to such events as trains derailing, wheels falling off moving vehicles, and elevators falling.
	   b. Negligence *per se*—A type of negligence that may occur if a person violates a statute or an ordinance providing for a criminal penalty and the violation causes another to be injured.
	   c. Special negligence statutes—State statutes that prescribe duties and responsibilities in certain circumstances, the violation of which will impose civil liability. Dram shop acts and Good Samaritan statutes are examples of special negligence statutes.

Strict Liability (See pages 94–95.)	Under the doctrine of strict liability, a person may be held liable, regardless of the degree of care exercised, for damages or injuries caused by his or her product or activity. Strict liability includes liability for harms caused by abnormally dangerous activities, by wild animals, and by defective products (product liability).

▌For Review

1. What is the function of tort law?
2. What must a public figure prove to succeed in a defamation suit?
3. What are the four elements of negligence?
4. What defenses are available in an action for negligence?
5. What is strict liability? In what circumstances might this doctrine be applied?

▌Questions and Case Problems

4–1. Defenses to Negligence. Corinna was riding her bike on a city street. While she was riding, she frequently looked behind her to verify that the books that she had fastened to the rear part of her bike were still attached. On one occasion while she was looking behind her, she failed to notice a car that was entering an intersection just as she was crossing it. The car hit her, causing her to sustain numerous injuries. Three witnesses stated that the driver of the car had failed to stop at the stop sign before entering the intersection. Corinna sued the driver of the car for negligence. What defenses might the defendant driver raise in this lawsuit? Discuss fully.

4–2. Liability to Business Invitees. Kim went to Ling's Market to pick up a few items for dinner. It was a rainy, windy day, and the wind had blown water through the door of Ling's Market each time the door opened. As Kim entered through the door, she slipped and fell in the approximately one-half inch of rainwater that had accumulated on the floor. The manager knew of the weather conditions but had not posted any sign to warn customers of the water hazard. Kim injured her back as a result of the fall and sued Ling's for damages. Can Ling's be held liable for negligence in this situation? Discuss.

4–3. Negligence. In which of the following situations will the acting party be liable for the tort of negligence? Explain fully.

(a) Mary goes to the golf course on Sunday morning, eager to try out a new set of golf clubs she has just purchased. As she tees off on the first hole, the head of her club flies off and injures a nearby golfer.

(b) Mary's doctor gives her some pain medication and tells her not to drive after she takes it, as the medication induces drowsiness. In spite of the doctor's warning, Mary decides to drive to the store while on the medication. Owing to her lack of alertness, she fails to stop at a traffic light and crashes into another vehicle, in which a passenger is injured.

4–4. Causation. Ruth carelessly parks her car on a steep hill, leaving the car in neutral and failing to engage the parking brake. The car rolls down the hill, knocking down an electric line. The sparks from the broken line ignite a grass fire. The fire spreads until it reaches a barn one mile away. The barn houses dynamite, and the burning barn explodes, causing part of the roof to fall on and injure a passing motorist, Jim. Can Jim recover from Ruth? Why or why not?

4–5. Trespass to Land. During a severe snowstorm, Yoshiko parked his car in a privately owned parking lot. The car was later towed from the lot, and Yoshiko had to pay $100 to the towing company to recover his car. Yoshiko sued the owner of the parking lot, Icy Holdings, Inc., to get back the $100 he had paid. Icy Holdings claimed that notwithstanding the severe snowstorm, Yoshiko's parking of his car on its property constituted trespass, and therefore Icy Holdings did not act wrongfully in having the car towed off the lot. Discuss whether Yoshiko can recover his $100.

4–6. Tort Theories. The Yommers operated a gasoline station. In December 1967, the McKenzies, their neighbors, noticed a smell in their well water, which proved to be caused by gasoline in the water. McKenzie complained to the Yommers, who arranged to have one of their underground storage tanks replaced. Nevertheless, the McKenzies were unable to use their water for cooking or bathing until they had a filter and water softener installed. At the time of the trial, in December 1968, they were still bringing in drinking water from an outside source. The McKenzies sued the Yommers for damages. The Yommers claimed that the McKenzies had not proved that there was any intentional wrongdoing or negligence on the part of the Yommers, and therefore they should not be held liable. Under what theory might the McKenzies recover damages even in the absence of any negligence on the Yommers' part? Explain. [*Yommer v. McKenzie*, 255 Md. 220, 257 A.2d 138 (1969)]

4–7. Defenses to Negligence. George Giles was staying at a Detroit hotel owned by the Pick Hotels Corp. While a hotel employee was removing luggage from the back seat of Giles's car, Giles reached into the front seat to remove his briefcase. As he did so, he supported himself by placing his left hand on the center pillar to which the rear door was hinged, with his fingers in a position to be injured if the rear door was closed. The hotel employee closed the rear door, and a part of Giles's left index finger was amputated. Giles sued the hotel for damages. What defense or defenses against

negligence discussed in this chapter might relieve the hotel, partially or totally, from liability for Giles's injury? Explain fully. [*Giles v. Pick Hotels Corp.*, 232 F.2d 887 (6th Cir. 1956)]

4–8. Strict Liability. Danny and Marion Klein were injured when an aerial shell at a public fireworks exhibit went astray and exploded near them. They sued the Pyrodyne Corp., the pyrotechnic company that was hired to set up and discharge the fireworks, alleging, among other things, that the company should be strictly liable for damages caused by the fireworks display. Will the court agree with the Kleins? What factors will the court consider in making its decision? Discuss fully. [*Klein v. Pyrodyne Corp.*, 117 Wash.2d 1, 810 P.2d 917 (1991)]

4–9. Duty to Business Invitees. George Ward entered a K-Mart department store in Champaign, Illinois, through a service entrance near the home improvements department. After purchasing a large mirror, Ward left the store through the same door. On his way out the door, carrying the large mirror in front and somewhat to the side of him, he collided with a concrete pole located just outside the door about a foot and a half from the outside wall. The mirror broke, and the broken glass cut Ward's right cheek and eye, resulting in reduced vision in that eye. He later stated that he had not seen the pole, had not realized what was happening, and only knew that he felt "a bad pain, and then saw stars." Ward sued K-Mart Corp. for damages, alleging that the store was negligent. What was the nature of K-Mart's duty of care to Ward? Did it breach that duty by placing the concrete pole just outside the door? What factors should the court consider when deciding whether K-Mart should be held liable for Ward's injuries? Discuss fully. [*Ward v. K-Mart Corp.*, 136 Ill.2d 132, 554 N.E.2d 223, 143 Ill.Dec. 288 (1990)]

4–10. Duty of Care. As pedestrians exited at the close of an arts and crafts show, Jason Davis, an employee of the show's producer, stood near the exit. Suddenly and without warning, Davis turned around and collided with Yvonne Esposito, an eighty-year-old woman. Esposito was knocked to the ground, fracturing her hip. After hip-replacement surgery, she was left with a permanent physical impairment. Esposito filed a suit in a federal district court against Davis and others, alleging negligence. What are the factors that indicate whether or not Davis owed Esposito a duty of care? What do those factors indicate in these circumstances? [*Esposito v. Davis*, 47 F.3d 164 (5th Cir. 1995)]

4–11. Negligence *Per Se*. A North Carolina Department of Transportation regulation prohibits the placement of telephone booths within public rights of way. Despite this regulation, GTE South, Inc., placed a booth in the right of way near the intersection of

Hillsborough and Sparger Roads in Durham County. Laura Baldwin was using the booth when an accident at the intersection caused a dump truck to cross the right of way and smash into the booth. To recover for her injuries, Baldwin filed a suit in a North Carolina state court against GTE and others. Was Baldwin within the class of persons protected by the regulation? If so, did GTE's placement of the booth constitute negligence *per se*? [*Baldwin v. GTE South, Inc.*, 335 N.C. 544, 439 S.E.2d 108 (1995)]

CASE BRIEFING ASSIGNMENT

4–12. *Examine Case A.2 [Burlingham v. Mintz, 891 P.2d 527 (Mont. 1995)] in Appendix A. The case has been excerpted there in great detail. Review and then brief the case, making sure that you include answers to the following questions in your brief.*

1. Who were the plaintiff and defendant in this action?
2. Describe the events that led up to this lawsuit.
3. What was the central issue on appeal?
4. How did the state supreme court rule on this issue and dispose of the case?

▌Accessing the Internet: Fundamentals of Business Law

Within the legal interest group on the commercial service America Online, there is a subcategory on torts and contracts. If you subscribe to America Online, the key word is

LEGAL

Standards established by professional associations play an important role in determining the minimum standard of care expected of the members of those professions—and thus are an important factor in negligence cases. You can locate the professional standards for various professional organizations at the following Internet site:

http:www.lib.uwaterloo.ca/society/standards.html

Cornell Law School also provides business and professional codes for a number of states. To find these, go to

http://www.law.cornell.edu/statutes.html#state

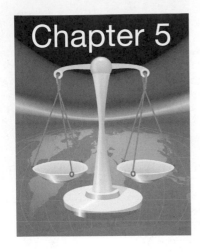

Chapter 5

Business Torts, Intellectual Property, and Cyberlaw

CHAPTER OBJECTIVES

After reading this chapter, you should be able to:

1. Explain the circumstances in which a party will be held liable for the tort of wrongful interference.
2. Indicate how the tort of appropriation occurs.
3. Summarize the laws protecting trademarks, patents, and copyrights.
4. Describe how trade secrets are protected by the law.
5. Point out how the Racketeer Influenced and Corrupt Organizations Act is applied in civil cases.

Our economic system of free enterprise is based on the ability of persons, acting either as individuals or as business firms, to compete freely for customers. Businesses may, generally speaking, engage in whatever is *reasonably* necessary to obtain a fair share of a market or to recapture a share that has been lost. They are not allowed to use the motive of complete elimination of competition to justify certain business activities, however. Those who enter into business should be acquainted with the point at which zealous competition might be construed by a court of law to cross over into tortious interference with the business rights of others.

Business torts are defined as wrongful interference with another's business rights. Included in business torts are such vaguely worded common law concepts as *unfair competition* and *interfering with the business relations of others*. Some torts that were discussed in the previous chapter, including defamation, also occur in the business context.

Of significant concern to businesspersons is the need to protect their rights in intellectual property. **Intellectual property** is any property resulting from intellectual, creative processes—the products of an individual's mind. Although it is an abstract term for an abstract concept, intellectual property is nonetheless wholly familiar to virtually everyone. The information contained in books and computer files is intellectual property. The software you use, the movies you see, and the music you listen to are all forms of intellectual property. In fact, in today's information age, it should come as no surprise that the value of the world's intellectual property now exceeds the value of physical property, such as machines and houses.

In this chapter, we examine business torts and the protection given to intellectual property rights under trademark, patent, copyright, and other laws. We also look at how the Racketeer Influenced and Corrupt Organizations Act (known more popularly as RICO) has been applied to fraudulent business activities.

Wrongful Interference

Business torts involving wrongful interference are generally divided into two categories: wrongful interference with a contractual relationship and wrongful interference with a business relationship.

Wrongful Interference with a Contractual Relationship

Tort law relating to *intentional interference with a contractual relationship* has expanded greatly in recent years. A landmark case involved an opera singer, Joanna Wagner, who was under contract to sing for a man named Lumley for a specified period of years.[1] A man named Gye, who knew of this contract, nonetheless "enticed" Wagner to refuse to carry out the agreement, and Wagner began to sing for Gye. Gye's action constituted a tort because it interfered with the contractual relationship between Wagner and Lumley. (Of course, Wagner's refusal to carry out the agreement also entitled Lumley to sue Wagner for breach of contract.)

Three elements are necessary for a wrongful interference with a contractual relationship to occur:

1. A valid, enforceable contract must exist between two parties.
2. A third party must *know* that this contract exists.
3. The third party must *intentionally* cause either of the two parties to break the contract.

The contract may be between a firm and its employees or a firm and its customers. Sometimes a competitor of a firm draws away one of the firm's key employees. If the original employer can show that the competitor induced the breach—that is, that the former employee would not otherwise have broken the contract—damages can be recovered from the competitor.

Wrongful Interference with a Business Relationship

Businesspersons devise countless schemes to attract customers, but they are forbidden by the courts to interfere unreasonably with another's business in their attempts to gain a share of the market. There is a difference between competition and **predatory behavior**—actions undertaken with the intention of unlawfully driving competitors completely out of the market.

The distinction usually depends on whether a business is attempting to attract customers in general or to solicit only those customers who have shown an interest in a similar product or service of a specific competitor. If a shopping center contains two shoe stores, an employee of Store A cannot be positioned at the entrance of Store B for the purpose of diverting customers to Store A. This type of activity constitutes the tort of wrongful interference with a business relationship, which is commonly considered to be an unfair trade practice. If this type of activity were permitted, Store A would reap the benefits of Store B's advertising.

Defenses to Wrongful Interference

A person will not be liable for the tort of wrongful interference with a contractual or business relationship if it can be shown that the interference was justified, or permissible. For example, bona fide competitive behavior is a permissible interference even if it results in the breaking of a contract. If Antonio's Meats advertises so effectively that it induces Alex's Restaurant Chain to break its contract with Alvarez Meat Company, Alvarez Meat Company will be unable to recover against Antonio's Meats on a wrongful interference theory. After all, the public policy that favors free competition in advertising outweighs any possible instability that such competitive activity might cause in contractual relations.

Wrongful Entry into Business

In a freely competitive society it is usually true that any person can enter into any business to compete for the customers of existing businesses. Two situations in which this notion of free competition does not hold, however, are (1) when entering into

---

1. *Lumley v. Gye*, 118 Eng.Rep. 749 (1853).

business is a violation of the law and (2) when competitive behavior is predatory.

Any business or profession not subject to regulatory agencies or occupational licensing standards is open to an individual. No one can open a business for the sole purpose of driving another firm out of business, however; such a motive is consid- ered to be predatory. What the courts consider normal competitive activity is not always easy to ascertain—where does the normal desire to compete and obtain profits end and the tortious action begin? The following landmark case illustrates how a Minnesota court grappled with the question of malicious injury to business.

CASE 5.1

Tuttle v. Buck

Supreme Court of
Minnesota, 1909.
107 Minn. 145,
119 N.W. 946.

FACTS The plaintiff, Edward Tuttle, a barber, filed suit in a Minnesota state court against the defendant, Cassius Buck, for malicious interference with his business. The plaintiff had owned and operated a barbershop for the past ten years and had been able to support himself and his family comfortably from the income of the business. The defendant was a banker in the same community. During the previous twelve months, the defendant had "maliciously" established a competitive barbershop, employed a barber to carry on the business, and used his personal influence to attract customers from the plaintiff's barbershop. Apparently, the defendant had circulated false and malicious reports and accusations about the plaintiff and had personally solicited, urged, threatened, and otherwise persuaded many of the plaintiff's patrons to stop using the plaintiff's services and to use the defendant's shop instead. The plaintiff charged that the defendant undertook this entire plan with the sole design of injuring the plaintiff and destroying his business, not to serve any legitimate business interest or to practice fair competition. The defendant filed a general demurrer, which the court did not grant.[a] The defendant appealed to the Supreme Court of Minnesota.

ISSUE Did the defendant's activities constitute malicious interference with the plaintiff's business?

DECISION Yes. The Supreme Court of Minnesota held that the defendant had maliciously interfered with the plaintiff's business.

REASON Based on the facts presented, the court determined that the defendant's sole purpose in establishing the competing barbershop was to deprive the plaintiff of his livelihood. The court was bound by precedent to preserve competition in the marketplace, but at the same time it was supposed to guard against abusive practices. When a person starts a competing business to drive a competitor out of business rather than to earn profits, that person is guilty of a tort and must answer for the harm done. "To call such conduct competition is a perversion of terms. It is simply the application of force without legal justification, which in its moral quality may be no better than highway robbery."

FOR CRITICAL ANALYSIS—International Consideration *The tort of wrongful entry into business may have made sense in nineteenth-century America—an era of mostly small businesses in small towns and rural areas. Does it have any relevance, however, to our time of multinational corporations and international competitors?*

a.   A *general demurrer* is an objection to a pleading that is the equivalent of a motion to dismiss for failure to state a claim on which relief may be granted.

▌Appropriation

The use by one person of another person's name, likeness, or other identifying characteristic, without permission and for the benefit of the user, constitutes the tort of **appropriation.** Under the law, an individual's right to privacy includes the right to the exclusive use of his or her identity. For example, in a case involving a Ford Motor Company television commercial in which a Bette Midler "sound-alike" sang a song that Midler had made famous, the court held that Ford "for their own profit in selling their product did appropriate part of her identity."[2]

A court ruled similarly in a case brought by Vanna White, the hostess of the popular television game show *Wheel of Fortune,* against Samsung Electronics America, Inc. Without White's permission, Samsung included in an advertisement for Samsung videocassette recorders (VCRs) a depiction of a robot dressed in a wig, gown, and jewelry, posed in a setting that resembled the *Wheel of Fortune* set, in a stance for which White is famous. The court held in White's favor, holding that the tort of appropriation does not require the use of a celebrity's name or likeness. The court stated that Samsung's robot ad left "little doubt" as to the identity of the celebrity whom the ad was meant to depict.[3]

Often, cases alleging appropriation require the courts to balance a celebrity's right to the exclusive use of his or her identity against the First Amendment right to freedom of speech. For example, in one case, a California newspaper reproduced in poster form various pages from its newspapers that contained a photograph and artist's rendition of Joe Montana, the well-known professional football player. In Montana's suit against the newspaper for the commercial misappropriation of his name, photograph, and likeness, however, the court held that the defendant newspaper's reproduction and sale of the posters was protected speech under the First Amendment.[4]

▌Defamation in the Business Context

As discussed in Chapter 4, the tort of defamation occurs when an individual makes a false statement that injures another's reputation. Defamation may take the form of libel (defamatory statements in written or printed form) or slander (defamatory statements made orally). Defamation becomes a business tort when the defamatory matter injures someone in a profession, business, or trade or when it adversely affects a business entity in its credit rating and other dealings.

Recently, questions have arisen about the potential liability of on-line computer information services, such as CompuServe and Prodigy, for defamatory statements made in sources included in their databases.

▌Disparagement of Property

Disparagement of property occurs when economically injurious falsehoods are made not about another's reputation but about another's product or property. Disparagement of property is a general term for torts that can be more specifically referred to as *slander of quality* or *slander of title.*

Slander of Quality

Publication of false information about another's product, alleging that it is not what its seller claims, constitutes the tort of **slander of quality**, or **trade libel.** The plaintiff must prove that actual damages proximately resulted from the slander of quality. In other words, the plaintiff must show not only that a third person refrained from dealing with the plaintiff because of the improper publication but also that there were associated damages. The economic calculation of such damages—they are, after all, conjectural—is often extremely difficult.

An improper publication may be both a slander of quality and a defamation. For example, a statement that disparages the quality of a product may also, by implication, disparage the character of the person who would sell such a product. In one case, for instance, claiming that a product that was marketed as a sleeping aid contained "habit-forming drugs" was held to constitute defamation.[5]

2. *Midler v. Ford Motor Co.,* 849 F.2d 460 (9th Cir. 1988).
3. *White v. Samsung Electronics America, Inc.,* 971 F.2d 1395 (9th Cir. 1992).
4. *Montana v. San Jose Mercury News, Inc.,* 34 Cal.App.4th, 40 Cal.Rptr.2d 639 (1995).

5. *Harwood Pharmacal Co. v. National Broadcasting Co.,* 9 N.Y.2d 460, 174 N.E.2d 602, 214 N.Y.S.2d 725 (1961).

Trademark law (to be discussed shortly) has, to some extent, made it easier for companies to sue other companies on the basis of purported false advertising. In the past, courts often ruled that companies could be liable for false advertising only when they misrepresented their own products. It mattered little what such companies claimed about their competitors' brands, particularly in so-called comparative advertisements. Today, false or misleading statements about another firm's products are actionable.

Slander of Title

When a publication denies or casts doubt on another's legal ownership of any property, and when this results in financial loss to that property's owner, the tort of **slander of title** may exist. Usually, this is an intentional tort in which someone knowingly publishes an untrue statement about property with the intent of discouraging a third person from dealing with the person slandered. For example, it would be difficult for a car dealer to attract customers after competitors published a notice that the dealer's stock consisted of stolen autos.

▌Intellectual Property Protection

The need to protect creative works was voiced by the framers of the U.S. Constitution over two hundred years ago: Article I, Section 8, of the Constitution authorized Congress "[t]o promote the Progress of Science and useful Arts, by securing for limited Times to Authors and Inventors the exclusive Right to their respective Writings and Discoveries." Laws protecting patents, trademarks, and copyrights are explicitly designed to protect and reward inventive and artistic creativity.

An understanding of intellectual property law is important because intellectual property has taken on increasing significance, not only in the United States but globally as well. Much of what is sold abroad, including popular American television series, computer programs, and videos, consists of intellectual property.

Trademarks and Related Property

A **trademark** is a distinctive mark, motto, device, or implement that a manufacturer stamps, prints, or otherwise affixes to the goods it produces so that they may be identified on the market and their origin vouched for. Statutory protection of trademarks and related property is provided at the federal level by the Lanham Trademark Act of 1946.[6] The Lanham Act was enacted in part to protect manufacturers from losing business to rival companies that used confusingly similar trademarks. The Lanham Act incorporates the common law of trademarks and provides remedies for owners of trademarks who wish to enforce their claims in federal court. Many states also have trademark statutes.

At common law, the person who used a symbol or mark to identify a business or product was protected in the use of that trademark. Clearly, if one used the trademark of another, it would lead consumers to believe that one's goods were made by the other. The law seeks to avoid this kind of confusion. In the following famous case concerning Coca-Cola, the defendants argued that the Coca-Cola trademark was entitled to no protection under the law, because the term did not accurately represent the product.

---

6.   15 U.S.C. Sections 1051–1128.

CASE 5.2

The Coca-Cola Co. v. Koke Co. of America

Supreme Court of the United States, 1920.
254 U.S. 143,
41 S.Ct. 113,
65 L.Ed. 189.

FACTS The Coca-Cola Company brought an action in a federal district court to enjoin other beverage companies from using the words "Koke" and "Dope" for the defendants' products. The defendants contended that the Coca-Cola trademark was a fraudulent representation and that Coca-Cola was therefore not entitled to any help from the courts. By use of the Coca-Cola name, the defendants alleged, the Coca-Cola Company represented that the beverage contained cocaine (from coca leaves). The district court granted the injunction, but the federal appellate court reversed. The Coca-Cola Company appealed to the United States Supreme Court.

Case 5.2—Continued

ISSUE Did the marketing of products called Koke and Dope by the Koke Company of America and other firms constitute an infringement on Coca-Cola's trademark?

DECISION Yes for Koke, but no for Dope. The Supreme Court enjoined the competing beverage companies from calling their products Koke, but the Court did not prevent them from calling their products Dope.

REASON The Court noted that, to be sure, prior to 1900 the Coca-Cola beverage had contained a small amount of cocaine, but this ingredient had been deleted from the formula by 1906 at the latest, and the Coca-Cola Company had advertised to the public that no cocaine was present in its drink. Coca-Cola was a widely popular drink "to be had at almost any soda fountain." Because of the public's widespread familiarity with Coca-Cola, the retention of the name of the beverage (referring to coca leaves and kola nuts) was not misleading: "Coca-Cola probably means to most persons the plaintiff's familiar product to be had everywhere rather than a compound of particular substances." The name Coke was found to be so common a term for the trademarked product Coca-Cola that the defendants' use of the similar-sounding Koke as a name for their beverages was disallowed. The Court could find no reason to restrain the defendants from using the name Dope, however.

FOR CRITICAL ANALYSIS—Social Consideration *How can a court determine when a particular nickname for a branded product has entered into common use?*

TRADEMARK REGISTRATION Trademarks may be registered with the state or with the federal government. To register for protection under federal trademark law, a person must file an application with the U.S. Patent and Trademark Office in Washington, D.C. Under current law, a mark can be registered (1) if it is currently in commerce or (2) if the applicant intends to put the mark into commerce within six months.

Under extenuating circumstances, the six-month period can be extended by thirty months, giving the applicant a total of three years from the date of notice of trademark approval to make use of the mark and file the required use statement. Registration is postponed until actual use of the mark. Nonetheless, during this waiting period, any applicant can legally protect his or her trademark against a third party who previously has neither used the mark nor filed an application for it. Registration is renewable between the fifth and sixth years after the initial registration and every twenty years thereafter.

Registration of a trademark with the U.S. Patent and Trademark Office gives notice on a nationwide basis that the trademark belongs exclusively to the registrant. The registrant is also allowed to use the symbol ® to indicate that the mark has been registered. Whenever that trademark is copied to a substantial degree or used in its entirety by another, intentionally or unintentionally, the trademark has been *infringed* (used without authorization). When a trademark has been infringed, the owner of the mark has a cause of action against the infringer. A person need not have registered a trademark in order to sue for trademark infringement, but registration does furnish proof of the date of inception of the trademark's use.

DISTINCTIVENESS OF MARK A central objective of the Lanham Act is to reduce the likelihood that registered marks will be so similar to one another that consumers cannot distinguish among them. The Lanham Act states, "No trademark by which the goods of the applicant may be distinguished from the goods of others shall be refused registration."[7] Only those trademarks that are deemed sufficiently distinctive from all competing trademarks will be protected, however. The trademarks must be sufficiently distinct to enable consumers to identify the manufacturer of the goods easily and to differentiate among competing products.

Strong Marks Fanciful, arbitrary, or suggestive trademarks are generally considered to be the most distinctive (strongest) trademarks, because they are normally taken from outside the context of the particular product and thus provide the best means of distinguishing one product from another.

Fanciful trademarks include invented words, such as "Xerox" for one manufacturer's copiers and "Kodak" for another company's photographic products. Arbitrary trademarks include actual words that have no literal connection to the product such as "English Leather" used as a name for an after-shave lotion (and not for leather processed in England).

-----

7.   15 U.S.C. Section 1052.

Suggestive trademarks are those that suggest something about a product without describing the product directly. For example, "Dairy Queen" suggests an association between its products and milk, but it does not directly describe ice cream.

Secondary Meaning Descriptive terms, geographical terms, and personal names are not inherently distinctive and do not receive protection under the law until they acquire a secondary meaning. A secondary meaning may arise when customers begin to associate a specific term or phrase, such as "London Fog," with specific trademarked items (coats with "London Fog" labels). Whether a secondary meaning becomes attached to a term or name usually depends on how extensively the product is advertised, the market for the product, the number of sales, and other factors. Once a secondary meaning is attached to a term or name, a trademark is considered distinctive and is protected.

An interesting issue in recent years has been whether a color can be trademarked on the basis that it has acquired a secondary meaning. In the following case, the United States Supreme Court addressed this issue.

CASE 5.3

Qualitex Co. v. Jacobson Products Co.
Supreme Court of the United States, 1995.
514 U.S. 159,
115 S.Ct. 1300,
131 L.Ed.2d 248.

FACTS   Since the 1950s, the Qualitex Company has manufactured Sun Glow press pads, which are used in dry cleaning and laundry establishments. The pads are a distinctive green-gold color. In 1989, the Jacobson Products Company began to sell its own press pads, which are a similar green-gold color. Qualitex brought an action against Jacobson in a federal district court, alleging, among other things, trademark infringement. The court entered a judgment in favor of Qualitex, and Jacobson appealed. The appellate court ruled in favor of Jacobson, and Qualitex appealed to the United States Supreme Court.

ISSUE   Can color alone serve as a trademark?

DECISION   Yes. The United States Supreme Court reversed the ruling of the appellate court and held that color alone can qualify for trademark protection.

REASON   The Supreme Court pointed out that under the Lanham Act, a trademark can consist of "any word, name, symbol, or device, or any combination thereof." The Court noted that the U.S. Patent and Trademark Office has registered, as trademarks, the shape of the Coca-Cola bottle, the sound of NBC's chimes, and the scent of sewing thread. A color may also serve as such a product "symbol," concluded the Court. Furthermore, a color can "identify and distinguish" a product "from those manufactured or sold by others," once customers associate the color with the

Case 5.3—Continued

product. The Court stated that the fact that there is a limited supply of colors does not justify prohibiting their use as trademarks.

FOR CRITICAL ANALYSIS—Technological Consideration *The Court pointed out that there is "no competitive need in the press pad industry for the green-gold color, since other colors are equally usable." If, however, a color were essential to a product's use or purpose, should that color be given trademark protection? Why or why not?*

Generic Terms Generic terms, such as *bicycle* or *computer*, receive no protection, even if they acquire secondary meanings. A particularly thorny problem arises when a trademark acquires generic use. For example, *aspirin* and *thermos* were originally trademarked products, but today the words are used generically. Other examples are *escalator*, *trampoline*, *raisin bran*, *dry ice*, *lanolin*, *linoleum*, *nylon*, and *corn flakes*. Even so, the courts will not allow another firm to use those marks in such a way as to deceive a potential consumer.

SERVICE, CERTIFICATION, AND COLLECTIVE MARKS

A **service mark** is similar to a trademark but is used to distinguish the services of one person or company from those of another. For example, each airline has a particular mark or symbol associated with its name. Titles and character names used in radio and television are frequently registered as service marks.

Other marks protected by law include certification marks and collective marks. A *certification mark* is used by one or more persons other than the owner to certify the region, materials, mode of manufacture, quality, or accuracy of the owner's goods or services. When used by members of a cooperative, association, or other organization, it is referred to as a *collective mark*. Examples of certification marks are the "Good Housekeeping Seal of Approval" and "UL Tested." Collective marks appear at the ends of the credits of movies to indicate the various associations and organizations that participated in the making of the movies. The union marks found on the tags of certain products are also collective marks.

TRADE NAMES Trademarks apply to *products*. The term **trade name** is used to indicate part or all of a business's name, whether the business is a sole proprietorship, a partnership, or a corporation. Generally, a trade name is directly related to a business and its goodwill. Trade names may be protected as trademarks if the trade name is the same as the company's trademarked product—for example, Coca-Cola. Unless also used as a trademark or service mark, a trade name cannot be registered with the federal government. Trade names are protected under the common law, however. As with trademarks, words must be unusual or fancifully used if they are to be protected as trade names. The word *Safeway*, for example, was held by the courts to be sufficiently fanciful to obtain protection as a trade name for a foodstore chain.[8]

Patents

A **patent** is a grant from the government that gives an inventor the exclusive right to make, use, and sell an invention for a period of twenty years from the date of filing the application for a patent. Patents for a fourteen-year period are given for designs, as opposed to inventions. For either a regular patent or a design patent, the applicant must demonstrate to the satisfaction of the U.S. Patent and Trademark Office that the invention, discovery, process, or design is genuine, novel, useful, and not obvious in light of current technology. A patent holder gives notice to all that an article or design is patented by placing on it the word "Patent" or "Pat." plus the patent number.

PATENT INFRINGEMENT If a firm makes, uses, or sells another's patented design, product, or process without the patent owner's permission, it commits the tort of patent infringement. Patent infringement may exist even though the patent owner has not put the patented product in commerce. Unlike in most other countries, in the United States patent protection is granted to the first person to invent a product, not to the first person to

---

8. *Safeway Stores v. Suburban Foods*, 130 F.Supp. 249 (E.D.Va. 1955).

file a patent application. In other words, if two individuals apply for patents, the one who prevails will be the person who first invented the product, not the first person to file for a patent on the product. Patent infringement may also occur even though not all features or parts of an invention are copied. (With respect to a patented process, however, all steps or their equivalent must be copied for infringement to exist.)

Often, litigation for patent infringement is so costly that the patent holder will instead offer to sell to the infringer a license to use the patented design, product, or process. Indeed, in many cases the costs of detection, prosecution, and monitoring are so high that patents are valueless to their owners; the owners cannot afford to protect them.

PATENTS FOR COMPUTER SOFTWARE   At one time, it was difficult for developers and manufacturers of software to obtain patent protection because many software products simply automate procedures that can be performed manually. In other words, the computer programs do not meet the "novel" and "not obvious" requirements previously mentioned. Also, the basis for software is often a mathematical equation or formula, which is not patentable. In 1981, the United States Supreme Court held that it is possible, however, to obtain a patent for a *process* that incorporates a computer program—providing, of course, that the process itself is patentable.[9] Subsequently, many patents have been issued for software-related inventions. Some critics believe that patents are being issued too readily for software that is not novel or that represents merely an obvious change of another's computer program. According to these critics, a proliferation of software patents will slow down the process of software innovation and application.

Another obstacle to obtaining patent protection for software is the procedure of obtaining patents. The process can be expensive and slow. The time element is a particularly important consideration for someone wishing to obtain a patent on software. In light of the rapid changes and improvements in computer technology, the delay could undercut the product's success in the marketplace.

Despite these difficulties, patent protection is used in the computer industry. If a patent is infringed, the patent holder may sue for an injunction, damages, and the destruction of all infringing copies, as well as attorneys' fees and court costs.

Copyrights

A **copyright** is an intangible property right granted by federal statute to the author or originator of certain literary or artistic productions. Currently, copyrights are governed by the Copyright Act of 1976,[10] as amended. Works created after January 1, 1978, are automatically given statutory copyright protection for the life of the author plus 70 years. For copyrights owned by publishing houses, the copyright expires 95 years from the date of publication or 120 years from the date of creation, whichever is first. For works by more than one author, the copyright expires 70 years after the death of the last surviving author.

Copyrights can be registered with the U.S. Copyright Office in Washington, D.C. A copyright owner no longer needs to place a © or "Copr." or "Copyright" on the work, however, to have the work protected against infringement. Chances are that if somebody created it, somebody owns it.

WHAT IS PROTECTED EXPRESSION?   Works that are copyrightable include books, records, films, artworks, architectural plans, menus, music videos, product packaging, and computer software. To obtain protection under the Copyright Act, a work must be original and fall into one of the following categories: (1) literary works; (2) musical works; (3) dramatic works; (4) pantomimes and choreographic works; (5) pictorial, graphic, and sculptural works; (6) films and other audiovisual works; and (7) sound recordings. To be protected, a work must be "fixed in a durable medium" from which it can be perceived, reproduced, or communicated. Protection is automatic. Registration is not required.

Section 102 of the Copyright Act specifically excludes copyright protection for any "idea, procedure, process, system, method of operation, concept, principle, or discovery, regardless of the form in which it is described, explained, illustrated, or embodied." Note that it is not possible to copyright an *idea*. The underlying ideas embodied in a work may be freely used by others. What is copyrightable is the particular way in which an idea is *expressed*. Whenever an idea and an expression are

9. *Diamond v. Diehr*, 450 U.S. 175, 101 S.Ct. 1048, 67 L.Ed.2d 155 (1981).

10. 17 U.S.C. Sections 101 *et seq.*

inseparable, the expression cannot be copyrighted. Generally, anything that is not an original expression will not qualify for copyright protection. Facts widely known to the public are not copyrightable. Page numbers are not copyrightable, because they follow a sequence known to everyone. Mathematical calculations are not copyrightable.

Compilations of facts, however, are copyrightable. Section 103 of the Copyright Act defines a compilation as "a work formed by the collection and assembling of preexisting materials of data that are selected, coordinated, or arranged in such a way that the resulting work as a whole constitutes an original work of authorship." The key requirement in the copyrightability of a compilation is originality. Thus, the White Pages of a telephone directory do not qualify for copyright protection when the information that makes up the directory (names, addresses, and telephone numbers) is not selected, coordinated, or arranged in an original way.[11] In one case, even the Yellow Pages of a telephone directory did not qualify for copyright protection.[12]

COPYRIGHT INFRINGEMENT Whenever the form or expression of an idea is copied, an infringement of copyright occurs. The reproduction does not have to be exactly the same as the original, nor does it have to reproduce the original in its entirety.

Penalties or remedies can be imposed on those who infringe copyrights. These range from actual damages (damages based on the actual harm caused to the copyright holder by the infringement) or statutory damages (damages provided for under the Copyright Act, not to exceed $100,000)

to criminal proceedings for willful violations (which may result in fines and/or imprisonment).

An exception to liability for copyright infringement is made under the "fair use" doctrine. In certain circumstances, a person or organization can reproduce copyrighted material without paying royalties (fees paid to the copyright holder for the privilege of reproducing the copyrighted material). Section 107 of the Copyright Act provides as follows:

> [T]he fair use of a copyrighted work, including such use by reproduction in copies or phonorecords or by any other means specified by [Section 106 of the Copyright Act,] for purposes such as criticism, comment, news reporting, teaching (including multiple copies for classroom use), scholarship, or research, is not an infringement of copyright. In determining whether the use made of a work in any particular case is a fair use the factors to be considered shall include—
> (1) the purpose and character of the use, including whether such use is of a commercial nature or is for nonprofit educational purposes;
> (2) the nature of the copyrighted work;
> (3) the amount and substantiality of the portion used in relation to the copyrighted work as a whole; and
> (4) the effect of the use upon the potential market for or value of the copyrighted work.

Because these guidelines are very broad, the courts determine whether a particular use is fair on a case-by-case basis. Thus, anyone reproducing copyrighted material may be subject to a violation.

A question that sometimes comes before the courts is whether a parody (satire) of a copyrighted work is a "fair use" of that work as a "criticism" or "comment" on the copyrighted version. At issue in the following case is whether a musical group's parody of another's copyrighted song constituted a fair use of the copyrighted music.

---

11. *Feist Publications, Inc. v. Rural Telephone Service Co.,* 499 U.S. 340, 111 S.Ct. 1282, 113 L.Ed.2d 358 (1991).
12. *Bellsouth Advertising & Publishing Corp. v. Donnelley Information Publishing, Inc.,* 999 F.2d 1436 (11th Cir. 1993).

CASE 5.4

Campbell v. Acuff-Rose Music, Inc.

Supreme Court of the United States, 1994.
510 U.S. 569,
114 S.Ct. 1164,
127 L.Ed.2d 500.

FACTS The song "Oh, Pretty Woman" was written in 1964 by Roy Orbison and William Dees. Their ownership rights in the song were transferred to Acuff-Rose Music, Inc. In 1989, the rap group 2 Live Crew parodied the song without Acuff-Rose's permission. In 1990, after about 250,000 copies of the parody version had been sold, Acuff-Rose sued 2 Live Crew and its record company in a federal district court, alleging copyright infringement. 2 Live Crew claimed that their parodic use of the original song fell within the "fair use" exception to the Copyright Act of 1976. 2 Live Crew contended that the parody

(Continued)

Case 5.4—Continued

commented on and satirized the original work, which is considered a fair use under the act in some circumstances. The district court found for 2 Live Crew, holding that the parody version was a fair use. Acuff-Rose appealed. The appellate court reversed, holding that 2 Live Crew's parody carried with it a presumption of unfair use because of its intrinsically commercial nature. 2 Live Crew appealed to the United States Supreme Court.

ISSUE   Could the parody version of "Oh, Pretty Woman" be considered a fair use of the original song under the Copyright Act of 1976?

DECISION   Yes. The Supreme Court reversed the appellate court's decision and remanded the case.

REASON   Section 107 of the Copyright Act sets forth a four-factor test to be used when determining whether the unauthorized use of another's copyrighted work is a "fair use." In regard to the first factor (the "purpose and character of the use, including whether such use is of a commercial nature"), the appellate court had held that the commercial nature of 2 Live Crew's parody rendered the group's use presumptively unfair. The Supreme Court, however, held that the transformative value of parody must also be considered. As to the second factor (the "nature of the copyrighted work"), the Supreme Court affirmed the lower courts' decision that the original version of "Oh, Pretty Woman" warranted copyright protection under the act. As to the third factor (the "amount and substantiality of the portion used in relation to the copyrighted work as a whole"), the appellate court held that 2 Live Crew's parody copied the heart, or essence, of the original work and therefore borrowed too much. The Supreme Court stated that a parody must necessarily "conjure up" enough of the original work for the audience to recognize the "critical wit" intended, and this may require copying the heart of the original version. Whether 2 Live Crew copied musical elements to a greater extent than necessary to accomplish this was an issue to be decided on remand. On the final factor (the "effect of the use upon the potential market for or value of the copyrighted work"), the Supreme Court held that because the original and parodic versions served different market functions, the parodic version would probably not affect the market for the original.

FOR CRITICAL ANALYSIS—Ethical Consideration   *Is it fair for one person to realize (sometimes substantial) profits by parodying another's copyrighted material?*

COPYRIGHT PROTECTION FOR COMPUTER SOFTWARE   In 1980, Congress passed the Computer Software Copyright Act, which amended the Copyright Act of 1976 to include computer programs in the list of creative works protected by federal copyright law. The 1980 statute, which classifies computer programs as "literary works," defines a computer program as a "set of statements or instructions to be used directly or indirectly in a computer in order to bring about a certain result."

Because of the unique nature of computer programs, the courts have had many problems in applying and interpreting the 1980 act. Traditionally, copyright protection was extended only to literary works that were perceptible to humans—that is, to things written or printed in intelligible notation. Computer programs, however, are expressed in a language "readable" by machines. Determining which elements of a computer program are protectable under copyright law and which are not has been a challenging task for the courts. We look below at the evolution of the case law on this issue.

Initial Decisions   In a series of cases decided in the 1980s, the courts held that copyright protection extended not only to those parts of a computer program that can be read by humans, such as the "high-level" language of a source code, but also to the binary-language object code of a computer program, which is readable only by the computer.[13] Additionally, such elements as the overall structure, sequence, and organization of a program were deemed copyrightable.[14]

"Look and Feel" Protection   By the early 1990s, the issue had evolved into whether the "look and feel"—the general appearance, command structure, video images, menus, windows, and other screen displays—of computer programs should also be protected by copyright. Although the courts have disagreed on this issue, the tendency has been to not extend copyright protection to "look and feel" aspects of computer programs. For example, in 1992, a federal district court held that the user interface of Apple's Macintosh computer is not protectable under a "look and feel" theory and that Apple's use of windows, icons, and menus, and generally the series of images that Apple calls a "desktop metaphor," are unprotectable "ideas."[15] Similarly, in 1995, the Court of Appeals for the First Circuit held that Lotus Development Corporation's menu command hierarchy for its Lotus 1-2-3 spreadsheet was not protectable under the Copyright Act. The court deemed that the menu command hierarchy was a "method of operation," and Section 102 of the Copyright Act specifically excludes methods of operation from

copyright protection.[16] The decision was affirmed by the United States Supreme Court in 1996.[17]

Trade Secrets

Some business processes and information that are not or cannot be patented, copyrighted, or trademarked are nevertheless protected against appropriation by a competitor as trade secrets. **Trade secrets** consist of customer lists, plans, research and development, pricing information, marketing techniques, production techniques, and generally anything that makes an individual company unique and that would have value to a competitor.

Virtually all law with respect to trade secrets is common law. Identical types of information reviewed by different courts in similar factual settings have been classified differently. In an effort to reduce the unpredictability of common law with respect to trade secrets, a model act, the Uniform Trade Secrets Act, was presented to the states in 1979 for adoption. Parts of it have been adopted in over twenty states. Typically, a state that has adopted parts of the act has adopted only those parts that encompass its own existing common law.

Unlike copyright and trademark protection, protection of trade secrets extends both to ideas and to their expression. (For this reason, and because a trade secret involves no registration or filing requirements, trade secret protection may be well suited for software.) Of course, the secret formula, method, or other information must be disclosed to some persons, particularly to key employees. Businesses generally attempt to protect their trade secrets by having all employees who use the process or information agree in their contracts never to divulge it.

Generally, the law protects an employer against a former employee's disclosure of trade secrets. The court in the following case considered whether an employer is entitled to protection against the *threat* of such a disclosure.

13. See *Stern Electronics, Inc. v. Kaufman*, 669 F.2d 852 (2d Cir. 1982); and *Apple Computer, Inc. v. Franklin Computer Corp.*, 714 F.2d 1240 (3d Cir. 1983).
14. *Whelan Associates, Inc. v. Jaslow Dental Laboratory, Inc.*, 797 F.2d 1222 (3d Cir. 1986).
15. *Apple Computer, Inc. v. Microsoft Corp.*, 799 F.Supp. 1006 (D.N.Cal. 1992). The district court's ruling was not overturned on appeal.
16. *Lotus Development Corp. v. Borland International, Inc.*, 49 F.3d 807 (1st Cir. 1995).
17. *Lotus Development Corp. v. Borland International, Inc.*, 516 U.S. 233, 116 S.Ct. 804, 113 L.Ed.2d 610 (1996). This issue may again come before the Supreme Court for decision, because in this case only eight justices heard the case, and there was a tied vote: four justices voted to affirm the decision, and four justices voted to reverse it. The effect of the tie was to affirm the lower court's decision.

CASE 5.5

Pepsico, Inc. v. Redmond

United States Court of Appeals, Seventh Circuit, 1995.
54 F.3d 1262.

FACTS William Redmond, as the general manager for PepsiCo, Inc., in California, had access to the company's inside information and trade secrets. In 1994, Redmond resigned to become chief operating officer for the Gatorade and Snapple Company, which makes and markets Gatorade and Snapple and is a subsidiary of the Quaker Oats Company. PepsiCo brought an action in a federal district court against Redmond and Quaker Oats, seeking to prevent Redmond from disclosing PepsiCo's secrets. The court ordered Redmond not to assume new duties that were likely to trigger disclosure of those secrets. Redmond appealed.

ISSUE Can a plaintiff obtain relief for trade secret misappropriation on showing that an ex-employee's new employment will inevitably lead him or her to rely on the plaintiff's trade secrets?

DECISION Yes. The U.S. Court of Appeals for the Seventh Circuit affirmed the order of the district court.

REASON The appellate court acknowledged that this was not a "traditional trade secret case." Under the applicable state statute, however, relief was available for the "actual or threatened" misappropriation of a trade secret. The court determined that Redmond inevitably would disclose PepsiCo's secrets in his new position with Quaker Oats. The court noted that Redmond had "extensive and intimate knowledge" of PepsiCo's goals for its sports and fruit drinks. Redmond and Quaker Oats conceded that the information Redmond obtained at PepsiCo could influence him. The court explained that "PepsiCo finds itself in the position of a coach, one of whose players has left, playbook in hand, to join the opposing team before the big game."

FOR CRITICAL ANALYSIS—Social Consideration *Does the ruling in this case mean that workers cannot pursue their livelihoods if they leave their jobs?*

Cyberlaw: Protecting Intellectual Property in Cyberspace

Not surprisingly, because of the unique nature of the Internet, its use creates unique legal questions and issues—particularly with respect to intellectual property rights. What exactly constitutes an infringing use of another's intellectual property rights in the online environment? How can the owners of intellectual property rights know when, and by whom, those rights are being infringed in this context? Should online service providers bear legal responsibility for infringing actions by users of their services? These are just a few of the questions raised by the presence of intellectual property in cyberspace.

The emerging body of law governing cyberspace is often referred to as *cyberlaw*. Here we look at cyberlaw as it applies to the types of intellectual property discussed in this chapter.

TRADEMARK PROTECTION ON THE INTERNET—DOMAIN NAMES One of the initial trademark issues involving intellectual property in cyberspace has been whether **domain names** (Internet addresses) should be treated as trademarks or simply as a means of access, similar to street addresses in the physical world. Increasingly, the courts are holding that the principles of trademark law should apply to domain names on the Internet. Before looking at trademark infringement and dilution issues, we need to briefly discuss some of the special characteristics of domain names and how they are registered.

Domain Names   A domain name consists of a series of "domains" separated by periods. A business's domain name typically consists of two domains. The top-level domain indicates the type of organization that is using the name—such as ".com" for a commercial entity (although noncommercial entities also use this name); ".net" for a network; ".edu" for an educational organization; or ".gov" for a government organization. The second-level domain usually consists of the name of the firm that maintains the site. Companies that do business on the Internet often use their names as domain names because this allows customers to access their sites without extensive searching. Consumers who want to locate those companies' World Wide Web sites also benefit from this practice.

Domain Name Registration   The entity responsible for registering domain names is Network Solutions, Inc. (NSI), which is funded by the U.S. National Science Foundation. NSI acts on behalf of the Internet Network Information Center (InterNIC), which, in turn, handles the daily administration of the domain name system in the United States. The top-level domains handled by the NSI apply worldwide. A new organization has developed an additional set of top-level domain names that may be in effect by the time you read this book.

Initially, domain names were handed out on a first-come, first-served basis, with few questions asked. Since 1995, however, the NSI has required any party seeking to register a domain name to state that the party's use of the name will not infringe on the intellectual property rights of any other party, that the party intends to use the name on "a regular basis on the Internet" (NSI may require a party that does not use the name for more than ninety days to relinquish the name), and that the party's use of the name will not be unlawful. If the party violates these representations made in the application, the NSI may cancel the domain name.

Trademark Infringement   One of the problems in applying trademark law to Internet domain names is that trademark law allows multiple parties to use the same mark—as long as the mark is used for different goods or services and will not cause customer confusion. On the Internet as it is cur-

rently structured, however, only one party can use a particular domain name, regardless of the type of goods or services offered. In other words, although two or more businesses can own the trademark Acme, only one business can operate on the Internet with the domain name "acme.com." Because of this restrictive feature of domain names, there is a question as to whether domain names should function as trademarks.

To date, the courts that have considered this question have held that the unauthorized use of another's mark in a domain name may constitute trademark infringement. In one case, for example, a publishing company, the Comp Examiner Agency (CEA), used "juris.com" as its domain name. Juris, Inc., contended that CEA's use of the domain name infringed on its trademark Juris, which it used in connection with software, because the use would likely cause customer confusion. The court agreed and granted an injunction against CEA's further use of the "juris.com" domain name.[18]

Trademark Dilution   Owners of famous trademarks also have succeeded in preventing others from using their marks as domain names under the Federal Trademark Dilution Act of 1995. For example, in one case, Hasbro, Inc., the maker of the famous children's board game Candy Land, sued a company that used the domain name "candyland.com." Hasbro contended that the company's commercial use of its mark diluted the mark's distinctiveness in violation of the federal dilution law. The court agreed and issued a preliminary injunction requiring the other party to relinquish the domain name.[19]

The 1995 act exempts from its coverage certain conduct, including noncommercial uses of marks. Thus, if a party registers another's famous mark as a domain name for a Web site that is not used for commercial purposes (to advertise or sell products and services), the owner of the famous mark will have no federal cause of action for trademark

18. *Comp Examiner Agency, Inc. v. Juris, Inc.* (C.D.Cal. 1996)[1996 WL 376600]. This decision, which is not reported in West's *Federal Supplement*, can be accessed by use of the WESTLAW (WL) citation.
19. *Hasbro, Inc. v. Internet Entertainment Group, Ltd.* (W.D.Wash. 1996) [1996 WL 84853]. This decision, which is not reported in West's *Federal Supplement*, can be accessed by use of the WESTLAW (WL) citation.

dilution. One of the significant questions concerning this exemption is whether "cybersquatting" constitutes a commercial use of a domain name. Cybersquatting occurs when a party registers another party's famous mark as a domain name and then holds the other party hostage—that is, the first party offers to forfeit its rights to the domain name to the owner of the famous mark in exchange for a sum of money. In the following case, the court addressed this issue.

CASE 5.6

Panavision International, L.P. v. Toeppen

United States District Court, Central District of California, 1996. 945 F.Supp. 1296.

FACTS Panavision International, Limited Partnership, is a supplier of photographic equipment. Panavision owns several famous trademarks, including Panavision, which it advertises to the public and to movie and television studios, networks, and production companies. Panavision's "Filmed with Panavision" credit appears at the end of many movies and television shows. Dennis Toeppen registered "panavision.com" as a domain name, precluding Panavision from using the name to identify its own Web site. Toeppen told Panavision that he would sell the name for $13,000. Panavision filed a suit in a federal district court against Toeppen, charging in part that he was in violation of the Federal Trademark Dilution Act of 1995.

ISSUE Does cybersquatting constitute a commercial use of a domain name?

DECISION Yes. The court ordered Toeppen to transfer the registration of "panavision.com" to Panavision.

REASON The court explained that "Toeppen has made a commercial use of the Panavision marks. Toeppen's 'business' is to register trademarks as domain names and then to sell the domain names to the trademarks' owners. * * * Toeppen's conduct, which prevented Panavision from using its marks in a new and important business medium, has diluted Panavision's marks within the meaning of the statute."

FOR CRITICAL ANALYSIS—Economic Consideration—What argument would you present to convince a court that cybersquatting does not constitute a commercial use of a domain name?

PATENTS FOR CYBERPRODUCTS   Almost every day, we hear of some innovation in communications technology, particularly Internet technology. It therefore is not surprising that new cyberproducts to meet the needs of Internet users and online service providers are being developed and patented at an unprecedented rate. Cyberproducts include data-compression software, encryption programs, software facilitating information linking and retrieval systems, and other forms of network software.

The problem faced by the developers of cyberproducts, who normally invest substantial time and money resources in the research and development of those products, is how to protect their exclusive rights to the use of the products.

A patent owner whose product is featured on the Internet may find it particularly difficult to prevent the unauthorized use of the patented property. For example, a video game maker might agree to provide part of a game on the Internet, through a third party's Web site, to give potential purchasers a sample of the product. How can the game maker prevent the third party from using, or letting others use, the product for other purposes (such as making and selling illegal copies of the game)?

Licensing the use of a product has proved to be one of the best ways to protect intellectual property on the Internet. In the context of a patent, a *license* is permission granted by the patent owner to another (the *licensee*) to make, sell, or use the patented item. Any license that a patent holder grants can be restricted to certain specified purposes and can be restricted to certain specified purposes and can be limited to the licensee only. Of course, because the Internet does not have any geographical boundaries, a licensing agreement should be made only in consideration of all U.S. foreign, and international laws. These same principles apply to the owners and licensees of other intellectual property, including copyrights and trademarks.

COPYRIGHTS IN CYBERSPACE Uploading, downloading, browsing—any of these activities conducted in cyberspace can infringe on a copyright owner's rights. The following subsections identify some of the many copyright issues that arise in cyberspace and discuss the liability of online providers for copyright infringement.

Online Issues The rights granted to copyright owners in the Copyright Act include the right to make copies of a copyrighted work, the right to publicly distribute those copies, and the right to perform or display copyrighted works. How those rights apply in cyberspace is still being debated.

A copyright owner might argue that the right to make copies of a work is infringed each time the work is stored in a computer's memory. Does software stored in a computer constitute a copy in this sense? A few courts have held that it does.[20] What about the digital storage of photographs, music, and other works? A few courts have held that these are also copies.[21]

Does the online transmission of a copyrighted work without permission violate the right to pub-

licly distribute the work? Some might claim that no right is violated because no physical copy is transferred. Others might argue that there is a violation if the recipient downloads what is transmitted to the hard disk drive of his or her computer.[22]

Some of the most controversial questions concern the right to perform copyrighted works. Does downloading a copy of a musical recording constitute a performance? What about playing it back after downloading? Questions also arise in relation to the right to publicly display a work. Is a work publicly displayed when it is visually browsed online? Most observers would agree that it is. Probably most would also agree that browsing is a "fair use," particularly if it is a noncommercial use and there is no downloading.

Online Liability One current controversy is whether online providers—including Internet access services, bulletin board service (BBS) operators, and others should be liable for the unauthorized copying, distribution, and performance or display of copyrighted work.

The most significant factor seems to be whether a provider is directly involved in the unauthorized use. An important case concerned the unauthorized uploading of literary works through an Internet access service.[23] The court held that the service was not liable for copyright infringement because, like a self-service photocopier, it only provided the system that permitted unauthorized copying.

In a second case, a BBS operator's customers uploaded and downloaded copyrighted photos, to and from the bulletin board, without the copyright owner's permission. The court held the operator liable for infringement of the owner's rights, in part because some of the photos were altered to include ads for the bulletin board.[24] In a third case, a bulletin board service encouraged its users to upload unauthorized copies of video game software. The court held the service liable because it knew that

---

20. See, for example, *MAI Systems Corp. v. Peak Computer, Inc.*, 991 F.2d 511 (9th Cir. 1993).
21. See, for example, *Religious Technology Center v. Netcom On-Line Communications Services, Inc.*, 907 F.Supp. 1361 (N.D.Cal. 1995).

22. See *Agee v. Paramount Communications, Inc.*, 59 F.3d 317 (2d Cir. 1995), for a further discussion of this issue. The court recommended that the Copyright Act be amended to answer the question.
23. *Religious Technology Center v. Netcom On-Line Communications Services, Inc.*, 907 F.Supp. 1361 (N.D.Cal. 1995).
24. *Playboy Enterprises, Inc. v. Frena*, 839 F.Supp. 1552 (M.D.Fla. 1993).

the copies were unauthorized and were being uploaded into its storage media.[25]

Many online providers believe that the Copyright Act needs to be amended to impose liability only when a provider knows that a use of its service is infringing on a copyright owner's rights and does nothing about it. Copyright owners favor imposing liability in *all* circumstances. The debate continues.

International Protection

For many years, the United States has been a party to various international agreements relating to intellectual property rights. For example, the Paris Convention of 1883, to which about ninety countries are signatory, allows parties in one country to file for patent and trademark protection in any of the other member countries.

International copyright agreements include the Berne Convention and the Universal Copyright Convention. Under the Berne Convention, if an American writes a book, his or her copyright in the book must be recognized by every country that has signed the convention. Also, if a citizen of a country that has not signed the convention first publishes a book in a country that has signed, all other countries that have signed the convention must recognize that author's copyright. Copyright notice is not needed to gain protection under the Berne Convention for works published after March 1, 1989.

These and other international agreements have given some protection to intellectual property on a worldwide level. None of them, however, has been as significant and far reaching in scope as the agreement on Trade-Related Aspects of Intellectual Property Rights, or, more simply, TRIPS. This agreement was signed by representatives from over one hundred nations in 1994, following the eighth and final round (called the "Uruguay Round") of negotiations among nations that were signatory to the General Agreement on Tariffs and Trade, or GATT.[26] The TRIPS agreement was one of several

documents that were annexed to the agreement creating the World Trade Organization, or WTO, which replaced GATT as of 1995—GATT no longer exists.

▍RICO

Increasingly in recent years, businesses have been sued for fraudulent or other tortious activities under the Racketeer Influenced and Corrupt Organizations Act.[27] The act, which is commonly known as RICO, was passed by Congress in 1970 as part of the Organized Crime Control Act. The purpose of the act was to curb the apparently increasing entry of organized crime into the legitimate business world.

Activities Prohibited by RICO

Under RICO, it is a federal crime (1) to use income obtained from racketeering activity to purchase any interest in an enterprise, (2) to acquire or maintain an interest in an enterprise through racketeering activity, (3) to conduct or participate in the affairs of an enterprise through racketeering activity, or (4) to conspire to do any of the preceding activities.

Racketeering activity is not a new type of substantive crime created by RICO; rather, RICO incorporates by reference twenty-six separate types of federal crimes and nine types of state felonies[28] and states that if a person commits two of these offenses, he or she is guilty of "racketeering activity." The act provides for both criminal liability (to be discussed in the following chapter) and civil liability.

Civil Liability under RICO

The penalties for violations of the RICO statute are harsh. In the event of a violation, the statute permits the government to seek civil penalties, including the divestiture of a defendant's interest in a business (called forfeiture—discussed in Chapter 6) or the dissolution of the business. Perhaps the most controversial aspect of RICO is that in some

---

25. *Sega Enterprises, Ltd. v. MAPHIA,* 857 F.Supp. 679 (N.D.Cal. 1994).
26. GATT had been originally negotiated in 1947 to minimize trade barriers among nations. Between 1947 and 1994, the GATT nations undertook seven more "rounds" of negotiations relating to tariffs and trade.

27. 18 U.S.C. Sections 1961–1968.
28. See 18 U.S.C. Section 1961(1)(A).

cases, private individuals are allowed to recover three times their actual losses (treble damages), plus attorneys' fees, for business injuries caused by a violation of the statute.

The broad language of RICO has allowed it to be applied in cases that have little or nothing to do with organized crime, and an aggressive prosecuting attorney may attempt to show that any business fraud constitutes "racketeering activity." In its 1985 decision in *Sedima, S.P.R.L. v. Imrex Co.*,[29] the United States Supreme Court interpreted RICO broadly and set a significant precedent for subsequent applications of the act. Plaintiffs have used

the RICO statute in numerous commercial fraud cases because of the inviting prospect of being awarded treble damages if they win. The most frequent targets of civil RICO lawsuits are insurance companies, employment agencies, commercial banks, and stockbrokerage firms.

One of the requirements of RICO is that there be more than one offense—there must be a "pattern of racketeering activity." What constitutes a "pattern" has been the subject of much litigation. Some courts have interpreted this to mean, in part, that there must be continued criminal activity. This is known as the "continuity" requirement. Part of this requirement is that the activity occur over a "substantial" period of time. The court in the following case considered whether "garden variety" fraud meets this requirement.

---

29.   473 U.S. 479, 105 S.Ct. 3275, 87 L.Ed.2d 346 (1985).

CASE 5.7

Tabas v. Tabas

United States Court of Appeals,
Third Circuit, 1995.
47 F.3d 1280.

FACTS   Charles and Daniel Tabas formed a partnership to conduct real estate and other business ventures. They agreed that if either partner died, the other would distribute the partnership income equally to himself and to the estate of the deceased partner. When Charles died, Daniel agreed to mail monthly partnership income checks to Charles's widow, Harriette. Daniel mailed monthly checks in the same amount to himself. In addition, Daniel drew a salary and paid a variety of personal expenses from partnership income. When Harriette and the executors of Charles's estate learned of Daniel's activities, they confronted him, and he agreed to dissolve the partnership and sell the assets. Continuing dissatisfaction with Daniel's conduct prompted Harriette and the executors (the plaintiffs) to file a suit in a federal district court against Daniel and others (the defendants), alleging, among other things, that acts of fraud over the previous three and a half years constituted violations of RICO. Daniel filed a motion for summary judgment, which the court granted. The court found no "continuity," reasoning that as soon as the partnership assets were sold, all of the alleged fraud would stop. The plaintiffs appealed to the U.S. Court of Appeals for the Third Circuit.

ISSUE   Did the allegations of fraud in the plaintiffs' complaint meet RICO's continuity requirement?

DECISION   Yes. The U.S. Court of Appeals for the Third Circuit reversed the district court's ruling and remanded the case for further proceedings.

REASON   The appellate court explained that "[e]ach time defendants misrepresented the business nature of an expense, made a questionable charge, or received compensation to which they were not entitled, they lessened the income available" to Charles's estate. The court noted that "these activities, which implemented defendants' purported scheme to

(Continued)

Case 5.7—Continued   defraud the Estate, lasted more than three and a half years." The court concluded that "a scheme lasting over three years extends over a 'substantial' period of time and therefore constitutes the type of 'long-term criminal conduct' that RICO was enacted to address." Thus, the court found that the plaintiffs "made a sufficient showing to survive summary judgment" on the continuity issue.

FOR CRITICAL ANALYSIS—Political Consideration *The United States Supreme Court has consistently struck down the efforts of lower courts to narrow the scope of RICO. Do you think that RICO is applied too broadly? If so, in light of the Supreme Court's decisions, who can narrow RICO's scope?*

▮ Terms and Concepts

appropriation 103	intellectual property 100	trade libel 103
business tort 100	patent 107	trade name 107
copyright 108	predatory behavior 101	trade secret 111
disparagement of	service mark 107	trademark 104
property 103	slander of quality 103	
domain name 112	slander of title 104	

▮ Chapter Summary: Business Torts, Intellectual Property, and Cyberlaw

Wrongful Interference *(See page 101.)*	1. *Wrongful interference with a contractual relationship*—The intentional interference with a valid, enforceable contract by a third party. 2. *Wrongful interference with a business relationship*—The unreasonable interference by one party with another's business relationship.
Wrongful Entry into Business *(See pages 101–102.)*	Entering into business in violation of the law or for the purpose of engaging in predatory behavior.
Appropriation *(See page 103.)*	The use by one person of another's name, likeness, or other identifying characteristic, without permission and for the benefit of the user.
Defamation in the Business Context *(See page 103.)*	A false statement that injures someone in a profession, business, or trade or that adversely affects a business entity in its credit rating and other dealings.
Disparagement of Property *(See pages 103–104.)*	Slanderous or libelous statements made about another's product or property; more specifically referred to as slander of quality (trade libel) or slander of title.
Intellectual Property Protection *(See pages 104–116.)*	1. *Trademark infringement and infringement of related property*—Occurs when one uses the protected trademark, service mark, or trade name of another without permission when marketing goods or services. 2. *Patent infringement*—Occurs when one uses or sells another's patented design, product, or process without the patent owner's permission. Computer software may be patented.

Chapter Summary: Business Torts, Intellectual Property, and Cyberlaw—Continued

Intellectual Property Protection Continued	3. *Copyright infringement*—Occurs whenever the form or expression of an idea is copied without the permission of the copyright holder. An exception applies if the copying is deemed a "fair use." The Computer Software Copyright Act of 1980 specifically includes software among the kinds of intellectual property covered by copyright law. 4. *Trade secrets*—Customer lists, plans, research and development, pricing information, and so on are protected under the common law and, in some states, under statutory law against misappropriation by competitors. 5. *International protection*—International protection for intellectual property exists under various international agreements. A landmark agreement is the 1994 agreement on Trade-Related Aspects of Intellectual Property Rights (TRIPS), which provides for the enforcement of intellectual property rights and the establishment of enforcement procedures in all countries signatory to the agreement.
RICO *(See pages 116–118.)*	The Racketeer Influenced and Corrupt Organizations Act (RICO) of 1970 makes it a federal crime (1) to use income obtained from racketeering activity to purchase any interest in an enterprise, (2) to acquire or maintain an interest in an enterprise through racketeering activity, (3) to conduct or participate in the affairs of an enterprise through racketeering activity, or (4) to conspire to do any of the preceding activities. The broad language of RICO has allowed it to be applied in cases that have little or nothing to do with organized crime.

For Review

1. What elements are necessary to establish the existence of wrongful interference with a contractual or business relationship?
2. What is the tort of appropriation? How might the tort of defamation occur in the business context?
3. What is intellectual property? How does the law protect intellectual property?
4. What is a trade secret? How are trade secrets protected by law?
5. What is RICO? What activities are prohibited by this act?

Questions and Case Problems

5–1. **Copyright Infringement.** In which of the following situations would a court likely hold Maruta liable for copyright infringement?
(a) At the library, Maruta photocopies ten pages from a scholarly journal relating to a topic on which she is writing a term paper.
(b) Maruta makes leather handbags and sells them in her small leather shop. She advertises her handbags as "Vutton handbags," hoping that customers might mistakenly assume that they were made by Vuitton, the well-known maker of high-quality luggage and handbags.
(c) Maruta owns a video store. She purchases the latest videos from various video manufacturers but buys only one copy of each video. Then, using blank videotapes, she makes copies to rent or sell to her customers.
(d) Maruta teaches Latin American history at a small university. She has a videocassette recorder (VCR) and frequently tapes television

programs relating to Latin America. She then takes the videos to her classroom so that her students can watch them.

5–2. Wrongful Interference. Jennings owns a bakery shop. He has been trying to obtain a long-term contract with the owner of Julie's Tea Salon for some time. Jennings starts a local advertising campaign on radio and television and in the newspaper. The campaign is so persuasive that Julie decides to break the contract she has had for some time with Orley's Bakery so that she can patronize Jennings's bakery. Is Jennings liable to Orley's Bakery for the tort of wrongful interference with a contractual relationship? Is Julie liable for this tort? For anything?

5–3. Patent Infringement. John and Andrew Doney invented a hard-bearing device for balancing rotors. Although they registered their invention with the U.S. Patent and Trademark Office, it was never used as an automobile wheel balancer. Some time later, Exetron Corp. produced an automobile wheel balancer that used a hard-bearing device with a support plate similar to that of the Doneys. Given the fact that the Doneys had not used their device for automobile wheel balancing, does Exetron's use of a similar hard-bearing device infringe upon the Doneys' patent?

5–4. Copyright Infringement. Max plots a new Batman adventure and carefully and skillfully imitates the art of DC Comics to create an authentic-looking Batman comic. Max is not affiliated with the owners of the copyright to Batman. Can Max publish the comic without infringing on the owners' copyright?

5–5. Business Tort Theories. After a careful study and analysis, Green Top Airlines decides to expand its operations into Harbor City. Green Top acquires the necessary regulatory authorizations and licenses, negotiates a lease at the airport terminal, and makes substantial capital expenditures renovating airport gates. Immediately thereafter, Red Stripe Airlines, Green Top's major competitor, also undertakes operations in Harbor City, even though (1) Harbor City is nowhere near any of Red Stripe's major existing routes and (2) Red Stripe will lose money by servicing Harbor City. Green Top claims that Red Stripe's entry into Harbor City constitutes a tort. Discuss fully Green Top's claim.

5–6. Copyright Infringement. West Publishing Co. brought a copyright infringement action against Mead Data Central, Inc., then the owner of LEXIS, a computer-assisted legal research system. At issue was a plan for a "star pagination" feature that Mead had developed for use on LEXIS. This feature would incorporate page numbers from West's case reporters into the opinions available on LEXIS and would allow LEXIS users to learn the precise page breaks in a West reporter without ever physically having to refer to a West volume. West claimed that Mead Data's proposed star pagination

system would constitute a copyright infringement of its reporting format. Mead Data contended that "mere page numbers" cannot be copyrighted. Can the use of page numbers, which cannot in themselves be copyrighted, fall under copyright protection in this case? If so, under what theory? [*West Publishing Co. v. Mead Data Central, Inc.*, 799 F.2d 1219 (8th Cir. 1986)]

5–7. Copyright Infringement. Jonathan Caven-Atack had been a member of the Church of Scientology for nine years when he decided that the church was a dangerous cult and its leader, L. Ron Hubbard, a vindictive and profoundly disturbed man. Caven-Atack spent the next several years investigating and then writing a book about Hubbard and the church. Caven-Atack's purpose was to expose what he believed was the pernicious nature of the church and the deceit upon which its teachings were based. Approximately 3 percent of Caven-Atack's book consisted of quotations from Hubbard's published works. When New Era Publications International, which held exclusive copyright rights in all of Hubbard's works, learned that the Carol Publishing Group planned to publish Caven-Atack's book, it sued Carol Publishing for copyright infringement. Carol Publishing claimed that Caven-Atack's use of Hubbard's works was a "fair use" of the copyrighted materials. What factors must the court consider in making its decision? How will the court likely decide the issue? [*New Era Publications International, ApS v. Carol Publishing Group*, 904 F.2d 152 (2d Cir. 1990)]

5–8. Trademark Infringement. In 1987, Quality Inns International, Inc., announced a new chain of economy hotels to be marketed under the name "McSleep Inns." McDonald's wrote Quality Inns a letter stating that the use of "McSleep Inns" infringed upon the McDonald's family of trademarks characterized by the prefix "Mc" attached to a generic term. Quality Inns claimed that "Mc" had come into generic use as a prefix, and therefore McDonald's had no trademark rights to the prefix itself. Quality Inns filed an action seeking a declaratory judgment from the court that the mark "McSleep Inns" did not infringe on McDonald's federally registered trademarks or common law rights to its marks and would not constitute an unfair trade practice. What factors must the court consider in deciding this issue? What will be the probable outcome of the case? Explain. [*Quality Inns International, Inc. v. McDonald's Corp.*, 695 F.Supp. 198 (D.Md. 1988)]

5–9. Wrongful Interference. Bombardier Capital, Inc., provides financing to boat and recreational vehicle dealers. Bombardier's credit policy requires dealers to forward immediately to Bombardier the proceeds of boat sales. When Howard Mulcahey, Bombardier's vice president of sales and marketing, learned that a dealer was not complying with this policy, he told Frank Chandler, Bombardier's credit director, of his concern. Before

Chandler could obtain the proceeds, Mulcahey falsely told Jacques Gingras, Bombardier's president, that Chandler was, among other things, trying to hide the problem. On the basis of Mulcahey's statements, Gingras fired Chandler and put Mulcahey in charge of the credit department. Under what business tort theory discussed in this chapter might Chandler recover damages from Mulcahey? Explain. [*Chandler v. Bombardier Capital, Inc.*, 44 F.3d 80 (2d Cir. 1994)]

5–10. RICO. During the 1980s, the Mutual Trading Corp. (MTC) bought and sold tires made by the Uniroyal Goodrich Tire Co. In the 1990s, Uniroyal discovered that MTC had perpetrated at least four separate schemes to swindle money from Uniroyal. As part of one scheme, for example, MTC had submitted fraudulent claims for reimbursement for amounts it had refunded to customers in Saudi Arabia. As part of another scheme, MTC had obtained from Uniroyal twice as much for its advertising costs in Nigeria as the parties had previously agreed. Uniroyal filed a suit against MTC and others in a federal district court, alleging, among other things, that these schemes violated RICO. MTC responded in part that the allegations depicted only a single scheme perpetrated on a single victim and that thus there was no "pattern of racketeering activity." What constitutes a "pattern" of activity to satisfy RICO? Is RICO satisfied in this case? [*Uniroyal Goodrich Tire Co. v. Mutual Trading Corp.*, 63 F.3d 516 (7th Cir. 1995)]

5–11. Trademark Infringement. CBS, Inc., owns and operates Television City, a television production facility in Los Angeles. Home to many television series, the name "Television City" is broadcast each week in connection with each show. CBS sells T-shirts, pins, watches, and so on emblazoned with "CBS Television City." CBS registered "Television City" with the U.S. Patent and Trademark Office as a service mark "for television production services." David and William Liederman wished to open a restaurant in New York City using the name "Television City." Besides food, the restaurant would sell television memorabilia such as T-shirts, sweatshirts, and posters. When CBS learned of the Liedermans' plans, it asked a federal district court to order them not to use "Television City" in connection with their restaurant. Does CBS's registration of "Television City" ensure its exclusive use in all markets and all products? If not, what factors might the court consider to determine whether the Liedermans can use "Television City" in connection with their restaurant? [*CBS, Inc. v. Liederman*, 866 F.Supp. 763 (S.D.N.Y. 1994)]

▌Accessing the Internet: Fundamentals of Business Law

Information on intellectual property law is available at the following site:
http://www.legal.net/intellct.htm
To perform patent searches and to access information on the patenting process, go to
http://sunsite.unc.edu/patents/intropat.html
You can find answers to frequently asked questions about patents at
http://www.sccsi.com/CaVinci/patentfaq.html
The U.S. Patent and Trademark Office provides online access to a broad range of U.S. and International trademark resources, including forms, links to relevant statutes, recent regulations, trademark registration forms, and links to international patent and trademark offices in such places as Japan, New Zealand, and Sweden. You can even order a trademark registration by e-mail using this site, which is located at
http://www.uspto.gov/
You can also access information on patent law at the following Internet site:
http://www.patents.com
An interesting Web site has recently been developed by three George Washington University lawyers in intellectual property law. The site offers information on trademarks and Internet domain names and examines some of the legal issues involved. The site includes background information on a number of well-known domain-name disputes, as well as links to other resources. You can access this site at
http://www.law.georgetown.edu/lc/

The Legal Information Institute at Cornell University's School of Law has developed a database containing United States Supreme Court decisions concerning intellectual property issues. You can find these decisions at

http:/www.law.cornell.edu/syllabi?copyright+patent+trademark

Another online magazine that deals, in part, with intellectual property issues is *Law Technology Product News.* The address for this publication is

http://www.ljextra.com/ltpn/

The Cyberspace Law Institute (CLI) offers articles and information on topics such as copyright infringement, privacy and trade secrets, trademarks, and domain names. Find this site at

http://www.cli.org

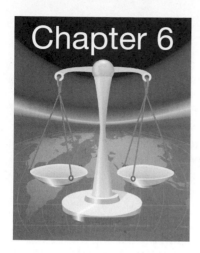

Chapter 6

Criminal Law

CHAPTER OBJECTIVES

After reading this chapter, you should be able to:

1. Explain the difference between criminal offenses and other types of wrongful conduct.
2. Indicate the essential elements of criminal liability.
3. Describe the constitutional safeguards that protect the rights of persons accused of crimes.
4. Identify and define the crimes that affect business.
5. Summarize the defenses to criminal liability.

Various sanctions are used to bring about a society in which individuals engaging in business can compete and flourish. These sanctions include damages for various types of tortious conduct (as discussed in the preceding chapters), damages for breach of contract (to be discussed in Chapter 12), and the equitable remedies discussed in Chapter 1. Additional sanctions are imposed under criminal law. Many statutes regulating business provide for criminal as well as civil sanctions. Therefore, criminal law joins civil law as an important element in the legal environment of business.

In this chapter, following a brief summary of the major differences between criminal and civil law, we look at how crimes are classified and what elements must be present for criminal liability to exist. We then examine criminal procedural law, which attempts to ensure that a criminal defendant's right to "due process of law" (see the above quotation) is enforced. In the remainder of the chapter, we focus on crimes affecting business and the defenses that can be raised to avoid liability for criminal actions.

▌Civil Law and Criminal Law

Civil law spells out the duties that exist between persons or between citizens and their governments, excluding the duty not to commit crimes. Contract law, for example, is part of civil law. The whole body of tort law, which deals with the infringement by one person on the legally recognized rights of another, is also an area of civil law. The right of people engaged in business to compete and flourish is sustained by the civil law, which imposes damages for various types of tortious conduct (as discussed in the preceding chapters) and damages for breach of contract (to be discussed in Chapter 12).

Criminal law, in contrast, has to do with crime. A **crime** can be defined as a wrong against society proclaimed in a statute and, if committed, punishable by society through fines and/or imprisonment—and, in some cases, death. Because crimes are *offenses against society as a whole*, they are prosecuted by a public official, not by victims. Exhibit 6–1 presents additional ways in which criminal and civil law differ.

▮ Classification of Crimes

Depending on their degree of seriousness, crimes are classified as felonies or misdemeanors. **Felonies** are serious crimes punishable by death or by imprisonment in a federal or state penitentiary for more than a year. The Model Penal Code[1] provides for four degrees of felony: (1) capital offenses, for which the maximum penalty is death; (2) first degree felonies, punishable by a maximum penalty of life imprisonment; (3) second degree felonies, punishable by a maximum of ten years' imprisonment; and (4) third degree felonies, punishable by a maximum of five years' imprisonment.

Under federal law and in most states, any crime that is not a felony is considered a **misdemeanor.** Misdemeanors are crimes punishable by a fine or by confinement for up to a year. If incarcerated (imprisoned), the guilty party goes to a local jail instead of a penitentiary. Disorderly conduct and trespass are common misdemeanors. Some states have different classes of misdemeanors. For example, in Illinois misdemeanors are either Class A (confinement for up to a year), Class B (not more than six months), or Class C (not more than thirty days). Whether a crime is a felony or a misde-

meanor can also determine whether the case is tried in a magistrate's court (for example, by a justice of the peace) or a general trial court.

In most jurisdictions, **petty offenses** are considered to be a subset of misdemeanors. Petty offenses are minor violations, such as violations of building codes. Even for petty offenses, however, a guilty party can be put in jail for a few days, fined, or both, depending on state law.

▮ Criminal Liability

Two elements must exist simultaneously for a person to be convicted of a crime: (1) the performance of a prohibited act and (2) a specified state of mind or intent on the part of the actor. Every criminal statute prohibits certain behavior. Most crimes require an act of *commission;* that is, a person must *do* something in order to be accused of a crime.[2] In some cases, an act of *omission* can be a crime, but only when a person has a legal duty to perform the omitted act. Failure to file a tax return is an example of an omission that is a crime.

The *guilty act* requirement is based on one of the premises of criminal law—that a person is punished for harm done to society. Thinking about killing someone or about stealing a car may be wrong, but the thoughts do no harm until they are translated into action. Of course, a person can be punished for attempting murder or robbery, but normally only if he or she took substantial steps toward the criminal objective.

---

1. The American Law Institute issued the Official Draft of the Model Penal Code in 1962. The Model Penal Code is not a uniform code. Uniformity of criminal law among the states is not as important as uniformity in other areas of the law. Types of crimes vary with local circumstances, and it is appropriate that punishments vary accordingly. The Model Penal Code contains four parts: (1) general provisions, (2) definitions of special crimes, (3) provisions concerning treatment and corrections, and (4) provisions on the organization of correction.

---

2. Called the *actus reus* (pronounced *ak*-tuhs *ray*-uhs), or "guilty act."

♦ Exhibit 6–1
Civil and Criminal Law Compared

ISSUE	CIVIL LAW	CRIMINAL LAW
Area of concern	Rights and duties between individuals	Offenses against society as a whole
Wrongful act	Harm to a person	Violation of a statute that prohibits some type of activity
Party who brings suit	Person who suffered harm	The state
Standard of proof	Preponderance of the evidence	Beyond a reasonable doubt
Remedy	Damages to compensate for the harm	Punishment (fine or imprisonment)

A wrongful mental state[3] is as necessary as a wrongful act in establishing criminal liability. What constitutes such a mental state varies according to the wrongful action. For murder, the act is

---

3. Called the *mens rea* (pronounced mehns *ray*-uh), or "evil intent."

the taking of a life, and the mental state is the intent to take life. For theft, the guilty act is the taking of another person's property, and the mental state involves both the knowledge that the property belongs to another and the intent to deprive the owner of it. Without the mental state required by law for a particular crime, there is no crime, as the following case illustrates.

CASE 6.1

Johnson v. State

Supreme Court of Florida, 1992.
597 So.2d 798.

FACTS Raymond Johnson allegedly snatched a purse left in an unattended car at a gas station. Because the purse contained both money and a firearm, among other items, the state trial court convicted and sentenced Johnson for burglary of a conveyance (vehicle), grand theft of property (cash and payroll checks), and grand theft of a firearm. On appeal, Johnson claimed that he could not be guilty of grand theft of a firearm because he did not know that the purse contained a firearm. In other words, intent to commit the latter crime was lacking, and therefore that crime had not been committed.

ISSUE Can Johnson be convicted and sentenced for the crime of grand theft of a firearm even though he did not know that the firearm was in the purse?

DECISION No. There can be only one conviction for grand theft in this case.

REASON The Supreme Court of Florida held that Johnson had committed the crime of theft and that it was grand theft because of the value of the property contained in the purse, including the value of the firearm. Only one crime of theft had occurred, however. The court stated that "a separate crime occurs only when there are separate distinct acts of seizing the property of another." In this case, the crime occurred "in one swift motion." Johnson saw the purse and snatched it without knowing what it contained: "there was one intent and one act[.]"

FOR CRITICAL ANALYSIS—Social Consideration *Why didn't the court conclude that because Johnson intended to steal the purse, he therefore intended to steal everything contained in the purse?*

▮ Procedure in Criminal Law

Criminal law brings the force of the state, with all its resources, to bear against the individual. Criminal procedures are designed to protect the constitutional rights of individuals and to prevent the arbitrary use of power on the part of the government.

Constitutional Safeguards

The U.S. Constitution provides specific safeguards for those accused of crimes. The United States Supreme Court has ruled that most of these safeguards apply not only in federal but also in state courts by virtue of the due process clause of the Fourteenth Amendment. These safeguards include the following:

1. The Fourth Amendment protection from unreasonable searches and seizures.
2. The Fourth Amendment requirement that no warrants for a search or an arrest can be issued without probable cause.
3. The Fifth Amendment requirement that no one can be deprived of "life, liberty, or property without due process of law."
4. The Fifth Amendment prohibition against **double jeopardy** (trying someone twice for the same criminal offense).[4]
5. The Fifth Amendment requirement that no person can be required to be a witness against (incriminate) himself or herself.
6. The Sixth Amendment guarantees of a speedy trial, a trial by jury, a public trial, the right to confront witnesses, and the right to a lawyer at various stages of criminal proceedings.
7. The Eighth Amendment prohibitions against excessive bail and fines and cruel and unusual punishment.

THE EXCLUSIONARY RULE   Under what is known as the **exclusionary rule,** all evidence obtained in violation of the constitutional rights spelled out in the Fourth, Fifth, and Sixth Amendments normally must be excluded, as well as all evidence derived from the illegally obtained evidence. Ille-

gally obtained evidence is known as the "fruit of the poisonous tree." For example, if a confession is obtained after an illegal arrest, the arrest would be "the poisonous tree," and the confession, if "tainted" by the arrest, would be the "fruit."

The purpose of the exclusionary rule is to deter police from conducting warrantless searches and other misconduct. The rule is sometimes criticized because it can lead to injustice. Many a defendant has "gotten off on a technicality" because law enforcement personnel failed to observe procedural requirements based on the above-mentioned constitutional amendments. Even though a defendant may be obviously guilty, if the evidence of that guilt is obtained improperly (without a valid search warrant, for example), it normally cannot be used against the defendant in court.

The courts, however, can exercise a certain amount of discretion in determining whether evidence is obtained improperly, thus balancing the scales somewhat. For example, in a 1995 case heard by the U.S. Court of Appeals for the Ninth Circuit, the judges had to decide whether evidence obtained from a legally conducted wiretap surveillance operation overseas violated the defendant's Fourth Amendment rights. If it did, the evidence would be inadmissible under the exclusionary rule. The court held that even though the wiretapping would have been illegal in the United States, the evidence legally obtained overseas was admissible. The court stated that the extent to which an American was protected from surveillance in another country is determined by the law of that country.[5]

The following case presents another interesting issue: Does the exclusionary rule require the suppression of evidence obtained during an arrest that was made on the basis of an erroneous computer record?

---

4. The prohibition against double jeopardy means that once a criminal defendant is acquitted (found "not guilty") or convicted of a particular crime, the government may not reindict the person and retry him or her for the same crime. The prohibition against double jeopardy does not preclude the crime victim from bringing a *civil* suit against the same person to recover damages. For example, a person found "not guilty" of assault and battery in a criminal case may be sued by the victim in a civil tort case for damages. Additionally, a state's prosecution of a crime will not prevent a separate federal prosecution of the same crime, and vice versa. For example, a defendant found "not guilty" of violating a federal law can be tried in a state court for the same act, if the act is defined as a crime under state law.

---

5. *United States v. Barona,* 56 F.3d 1087 (9th Cir. 1995).

CASE 6.2

Arizona v. Evans

Supreme Court of the United States, 1995.
514 U.S. 1,
115 S.Ct. 1185,
131 L.Ed.2d 34.

FACTS   During a routine traffic stop in Phoenix, Arizona, a police officer arrested Isaac Evans when the police computer indicated that there was an outstanding warrant for his arrest. In fact, the warrant had been quashed (voided) more than two weeks earlier, but court employees had wrongly failed to remove the warrant from the computer. The police searched Evans's car and discovered mar-

Case 6.1—Continued

ijuana. Evans was charged, in an Arizona state court, with possession of marijuana. He moved to suppress the evidence (marijuana), on the ground that the arrest was unlawful because the warrant had already been quashed. The court granted Evans's motion, but on appeal, the state appellate court reversed. The state supreme court vacated (set aside) the appellate court's ruling, and the case was appealed to the United States Supreme Court.

ISSUE   Is evidence admissible in a criminal trial if it was obtained during an arrest made on the basis of a computer record that was incorrect as a result of mistakes by court employees?

DECISION   Yes. The United States Supreme Court held that evidence seized in violation of the Fourth Amendment as a result of errors of court employees, causing an incorrect computer record, is admissible in a criminal trial. The Court reversed and remanded the case.

REASON   The Court explained that "the exclusionary rule was *   *   * designed as a means of deterring police misconduct, not mistakes by court employees." Evans offered no evidence that "court employees are inclined to ignore or subvert the Fourth Amendment or that lawlessness among these actors requires application of the extreme sanction of exclusion." In fact, the Court noted, this kind of mistake happens only once every three or four years. Additionally, the Court believed that application of the exclusionary rule in this case would not have "a significant effect on court employees responsible for informing police that a warrant has been quashed," because court employees "have no stake in the outcome of particular criminal prosecutions." Finally, application of the rule could not be expected to alter police officers' behavior. "There is no indication that the arresting officer was not acting *   *   * reasonably when he relied upon the police computer record."

FOR CRITICAL ANALYSIS—Social Consideration   *What if police department personnel (instead of court employees) had been responsible for the computer error? How would this circumstance affect the Court's reasoning?*

THE MIRANDA RULE   In *Miranda v. Arizona,*[6] the United States Supreme Court established the rule that individuals who are arrested must be informed of certain constitutional rights, including their right to remain silent and their right to counsel. If the arresting officers fail to inform a criminal suspect of these constitutional rights, any statements the suspect makes will not be admissible in court.

The Supreme Court and lower courts have enforced the *Miranda* rule hundreds of times since the *Miranda* decision. Over time, however, several

exceptions to the rule have been created. Congress in 1968 passed the Omnibus Crime Control and Safe Streets Act, which provided—among other things—that in federal cases a voluntary confession could be used in evidence even if the accused was not informed of his or her rights. The United States Supreme Court has carved out other exceptions. In 1984, for example, the Court recognized a "public safety" exception to the *Miranda* rule. The need to protect the public warranted the admissibility of statements made by the defendant (in this case, indicating where he placed the gun) as evidence in a trial, even when the defendant had not been informed of his *Miranda*

---

6.   384 U.S. 436, 86 S.Ct. 1602, 16 L.Ed.2d 694 (1966).

rights.[7] Today, juries can even accept confessions without being convinced of their voluntariness.

Criminal Process

As mentioned, a criminal prosecution differs significantly from a civil case in several respects. These differences reflect the desire to safeguard the rights of the individual against the state. Exhibit 6–2 summarizes the major steps in processing a criminal case. We discuss below in more detail three phases of the criminal process—arrest, indictment or information, and trial.

ARREST   Before a warrant for arrest can be issued, there must be probable cause for believing that the individual in question has committed a crime. *Probable cause* can be defined as a substantial likelihood that the person has committed or is about to commit a crime. Note that probable cause involves a likelihood, not just a possibility. Arrests may sometimes be made without a warrant if there is no time to get one, but the action of the arresting officer is still judged by the standard of probable cause.

INDICTMENT OR INFORMATION   Individuals must be formally charged with having committed specific crimes before they can be brought to trial. If issued by a grand jury, this charge is called an **indictment.**[8] A **grand jury** usually consists of a greater number of jurors than the ordinary trial jury. A grand jury does not determine the guilt or innocence of an accused party; rather, its function is to determine, after hearing the state's evidence, whether a reasonable basis (probable cause) exists for believing that a crime has been committed and whether a trial ought to be held.

Usually, grand juries are called in cases involving serious crimes, such as murder. For lesser crimes, an individual may be formally charged with a crime by what is called an **information,** or criminal complaint. An information will be issued by a magistrate (a public official vested with judicial authority) if the magistrate determines that

there is sufficient evidence to justify bringing the individual to trial.

TRIAL   At a criminal trial, the accused person does not have to prove anything; the entire burden of proof is on the prosecutor (the state). The prosecution must show that, based on all the evidence presented, the defendant's guilt is established **beyond a reasonable doubt.** If there is any reasonable doubt that a criminal defendant did not commit the crime with which he or she has been charged, then the verdict must be "not guilty." Note that giving a verdict of "not guilty" is not the same as stating that the defendant is innocent; it merely means that not enough evidence was properly presented to the court to prove guilt beyond all reasonable doubt.

The requirement that a defendant's guilt be proved beyond a reasonable doubt is a stricter standard of proof than the standard normally used in civil proceedings, in which a defendant's liability is usually decided based on a preponderance of the evidence. A *preponderance of the evidence* means that the evidence offered in support of a certain claim outweighs the evidence offered to negate the claim. The higher standard of proof in criminal cases reflects a fundamental social value—a belief that it is worse to convict an innocent individual than to let a guilty person go free.

Courts have complex rules about what types of evidence may be presented and how the evidence may be brought out in criminal cases, especially in jury trials. These rules are designed to ensure that evidence in trials is relevant, reliable, and not prejudicial against the defendant.

Federal Sentencing Guidelines

In 1984, Congress enacted the Sentencing Reform Act. This act created the U.S. Sentencing Commission, which was charged with the task of standardizing sentences for federal crimes. The commission fulfilled its task, and in 1987 its sentencing guidelines for all federal crimes became effective. The guidelines establish a range of possible penalties for each federal crime. Depending on the defendant's criminal record, the seriousness of the offense, and other factors specified in the guidelines, federal judges must select a sentence from within this range when sentencing criminal defendants.

---

7. *New York v. Quarles,* 467 U.S. 649, 104 S.Ct. 2626, 81 L.Ed.2d 550 (1984).
8. Pronounced in-*dyte*-ment.

♦ Exhibit 6–2
Major Steps in Processing a Criminal Case

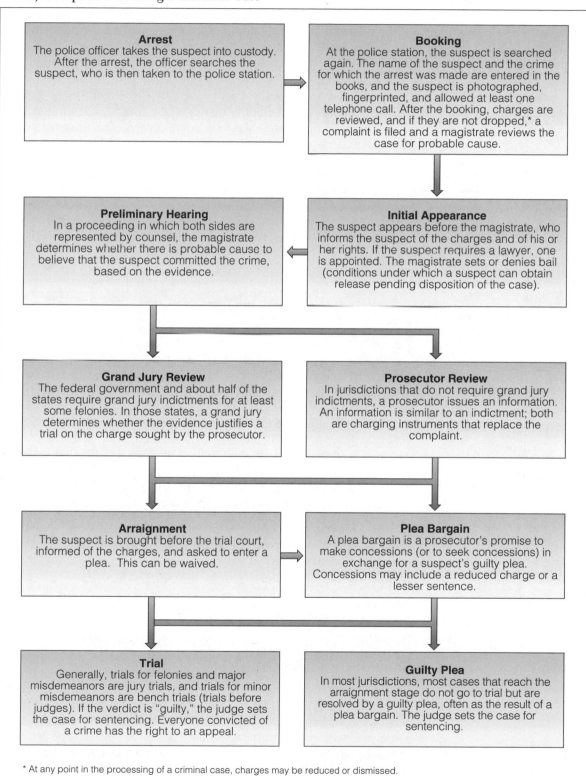

Arrest
The police officer takes the suspect into custody. After the arrest, the officer searches the suspect, who is then taken to the police station.

Booking
At the police station, the suspect is searched again. The name of the suspect and the crime for which the arrest was made are entered in the books, and the suspect is photographed, fingerprinted, and allowed at least one telephone call. After the booking, charges are reviewed, and if they are not dropped,* a complaint is filed and a magistrate reviews the case for probable cause.

Preliminary Hearing
In a proceeding in which both sides are represented by counsel, the magistrate determines whether there is probable cause to believe that the suspect committed the crime, based on the evidence.

Initial Appearance
The suspect appears before the magistrate, who informs the suspect of the charges and of his or her rights. If the suspect requires a lawyer, one is appointed. The magistrate sets or denies bail (conditions under which a suspect can obtain release pending disposition of the case).

Grand Jury Review
The federal government and about half of the states require grand jury indictments for at least some felonies. In those states, a grand jury determines whether the evidence justifies a trial on the charge sought by the prosecutor.

Prosecutor Review
In jurisdictions that do not require grand jury indictments, a prosecutor issues an information. An information is similar to an indictment; both are charging instruments that replace the complaint.

Arraignment
The suspect is brought before the trial court, informed of the charges, and asked to enter a plea. This can be waived.

Plea Bargain
A plea bargain is a prosecutor's promise to make concessions (or to seek concessions) in exchange for a suspect's guilty plea. Concessions may include a reduced charge or a lesser sentence.

Trial
Generally, trials for felonies and major misdemeanors are jury trials, and trials for minor misdemeanors are bench trials (trials before judges). If the verdict is "guilty," the judge sets the case for sentencing. Everyone convicted of a crime has the right to an appeal.

Guilty Plea
In most jurisdictions, most cases that reach the arraignment stage do not go to trial but are resolved by a guilty plea, often as the result of a plea bargain. The judge sets the case for sentencing.

* At any point in the processing of a criminal case, charges may be reduced or dismissed.

The commission also created specific guide

The commission also created specific guidelines for the punishment of crimes committed by corporate employees (white-collar crimes). These guidelines, which went into effect in 1991, established stiffer penalties for criminal violations of securities laws (see Chapter 27), antitrust laws, employment laws (see Chapter 22), mail and wire fraud, commercial bribery, and kickbacks and money laundering (all discussed later in this chapter). The guidelines allow federal judges to take into consideration a number of factors when selecting from the range of possible penalties for a specified crime. These factors include the defendant company's history of past violations, the extent of management's cooperation with federal investigators, and the extent to which the firm has undertaken specific programs and procedures to prevent criminal activities by its employees.

Criminal cases are sometimes appealed on the ground that the sentence imposed was too severe. In the following case, for example, the defendant, because of a check-kiting scheme, had been charged with bank fraud. Obtaining the property—including money—of a financial institution such as a bank is a federal crime. The issue before the appellate court is whether the defendant's sentence should be reduced in light of the fact that he immediately repaid the amount that he obtained through the fraudulent scheme.

CASE 6.3

United States v. Asher
United States Court of Appeals,
Seventh Circuit, 1995.
59 F.3d 622.

FACTS Asher Truck & Trailer, Inc., had facilities in Evansville, Indiana, and Mount Vernon, Illinois. Guy Asher, the company's owner and operator, kept separate bank accounts for the two facilities. When the business began to have cash flow problems, Asher began to write checks on the Evansville account and deposit them in the Mount Vernon account, and vice versa, knowing that the accounts on which the checks were drawn did not have sufficient funds to cover the checks. When the scheme was discovered, the Mount Vernon account was overdrawn by $160,000, which Asher promptly repaid. Asher was charged in a federal district court with bank fraud, and he pleaded guilty to the charge. Asher argued, however, that his sentence should be reduced because he had immediately repaid the bank. The court refused to reduce his sentence, and Asher appealed.

ISSUE For purposes of sentencing in bank fraud cases, should the amount of the loss be measured at the time the scheme is discovered or after a defendant has repaid the funds?

DECISION The U.S. Court of Appeals for the Seventh Circuit affirmed the district court's judgment that the amount of the loss should be measured at the time the scheme is discovered.

REASON The appellate court acknowledged that Asher's decision to repay the amount of the bank's loss when his scheme was uncovered "may indicate that he accepted responsibility for his fraudulent practices." The court pointed out, however, that "it does not indicate that his fraudulent practices created no loss to the bank." According to the court, the loss is the value of whatever is unlawfully taken. The argument that there was no loss to the bank because Asher promptly repaid the full amount "does not carry the day. *   *   * The mere fortuity that he had the financial resources available to him to repay the victim bank in full after his *   *   * scheme was discovered does not negate the fact that he engaged in fraudulent conduct which resulted in the loss of $160,000."

Case 6.3—Continued

FOR CRITICAL ANALYSIS—Economic Consideration *Do you think that the court's decision in this case will discourage criminals from repaying their victims?*

▮ Crimes Affecting Business

Many of the crimes that occur in the business context and that are discussed in the following pages are popularly referred to as **white-collar crimes.** Although there is no official definition of white-collar crime, the term is popularly used to mean an illegal act or series of acts committed by an individual or business entity using some nonviolent means to obtain a personal or business advantage. Usually, this kind of crime is committed in the course of a legitimate occupation. Corporate crimes, which are not treated here, also fall under the category of white-collar crimes. The liability of corporations and corporate personnel for criminal actions will be discussed in detail in Chapters 24 and 25.

Forgery

The fraudulent making or altering of any writing in a way that changes the legal rights and liabilities of another is **forgery.** If, without authorization, Severson signs Bennett's name to the back of a check made out to Bennett, Severson is committing forgery. Forgery also includes changing trademarks, falsifying public records, counterfeiting, and altering a legal document.

Robbery

At common law, **robbery** was defined as forcefully and unlawfully taking personal property of any value from another. The use of force or intimidation is usually necessary for an act of theft to be considered a robbery. Thus, picking pockets is not robbery, because the action is unknown to the victim. Typically, states have more severe penalties for *aggravated* robbery—robbery with the use of a deadly weapon.

Burglary

At common law, **burglary** was defined as breaking and entering the dwelling of another at night with the intent to commit a felony. Originally, the definition was aimed at protecting an individual's home and its occupants. Most state statutes have eliminated some of the requirements found in the common law definition. The time at which the breaking and entering occurs, for example, is usually immaterial. State statutes frequently omit the element of breaking, and some states do not require that the building be a dwelling. Aggravated burglary, which is defined as burglary with the use of a deadly weapon, burglary of a dwelling, or both, incurs a greater penalty.

Larceny

Any person who wrongfully or fraudulently takes and carries away another person's personal property is guilty of **larceny.** Larceny includes the fraudulent intent to deprive an owner permanently of property. Many business-related larcenies entail fraudulent conduct. Whereas robbery involves force or fear, larceny does not. Therefore, picking pockets is larceny, not robbery.

As society becomes more complex, the question often arises as to what is property. In most states, the definition of property that is subject to larceny statutes has expanded. Stealing computer programs may constitute larceny even though the "property" consists of magnetic impulses. Stealing computer time can also constitute larceny. So, too, can the theft of natural gas. Trade secrets can be subject to larceny statutes. Intercepting cellular phone calls to obtain another's phone card number—and then using that number to place long-distance calls, often overseas—is a form of property theft. These types of larceny are covered by "theft of services" statutes in many jurisdictions.

The common law distinction between grand and petit larceny depends on the value of the property taken. Many states have abolished this distinction, but in those that have not, grand larceny is a felony and petit larceny, a misdemeanor.

Obtaining Goods by False Pretenses

It is a criminal act to obtain goods by means of false pretenses—for example, buying groceries with a check, knowing that one has insufficient funds to cover it. Statutes dealing with such illegal activities vary widely from state to state.

Receiving Stolen Goods

It is a crime to receive stolen goods. The recipient of such goods need not know the true identity of the owner or the thief. All that is necessary is that the recipient knows or should have known that the goods are stolen, which implies an intent to deprive the owner of those goods.

Embezzlement

When a person entrusted with another person's property or money fraudulently appropriates it, **embezzlement** occurs. Typically, embezzlement involves an employee who steals money. Banks face this problem, and so do a number of businesses in which corporate officers or accountants

"jimmy" the books to cover up the fraudulent conversion of money for their own benefit. Embezzlement is not larceny, because the wrongdoer does not physically take the property from the possession of another, and it is not robbery, because force or fear is not used.

It does not matter whether the accused takes the money from the victim or from a third person. If, as the financial officer of a large corporation, Saunders pockets a certain number of checks from third parties that were given to her to deposit into the corporate account, she is embezzling.

Ordinarily, an embezzler who returns what has been taken will not be prosecuted, because the owner usually will not take the time to make a complaint, give depositions, and appear in court. That the accused intended eventually to return the embezzled property, however, does not constitute a sufficient defense to the crime of embezzlement. The role of intention in establishing whether embezzlement has occurred is emphasized in the following case.

CASE 6.4

United States v. Faulkner

United States Court of Appeals, Ninth Circuit, 1981. 638 F.2d 129.

FACTS Faulkner, a truck driver, was hauling a load of refrigerators from San Diego to New York for the trucking company that employed him. He departed from his assigned route and stopped in Las Vegas, where he attempted to display and sell some of the refrigerators to a firm. Although the refrigerators never left the truck, to display them he had to break the truck's seals, enter the cargo department, and open two refrigerator cartons. The store owner refused to purchase the appliances, and when Faulkner left the store, he was arrested. He was later convicted under federal law for the embezzlement of an interstate shipment. Faulkner appealed, claiming that there were no grounds for the charge, because he had never removed any equipment from the truck.

ISSUE Does the charge of embezzlement apply when the property has not been physically removed from the owner's possession?

DECISION Yes. The U.S. Court of Appeals for the Ninth Circuit affirmed the judgment of the lower court.

REASON The federal appellate court held that if a person has possession and control over the property of another and has the *intent* of converting the goods to his or her own use, then embezzlement occurs. By leaving his assigned route in order to sell the refrigerators and keep the proceeds, Faulkner exercised control over the property, with the intent to convert it to his own use.

Case 6.4—Continued   **FOR CRITICAL ANALYSIS—Social Consideration** *By definition, a crime involves both intent and a criminal act. What criminal act did Faulkner commit?*

Arson

The willful and malicious burning of a building (and in some states, personal property) owned by another is the crime of **arson**. At common law, arson applied only to burning down another person's house. The law was designed to protect human life. Today, arson statutes have been extended to cover the destruction of any building, regardless of ownership, by fire or explosion.

Every state has a special statute that covers a person's burning a building for the purpose of collecting insurance. If Smith owns an insured apartment building that is falling apart and sets fire to it himself or pays someone else to do so, he is guilty not only of arson but also of defrauding insurers, which is an attempted larceny. Of course, the insurer need not pay the claim when insurance fraud is proved.

Mail and Wire Fraud

One of the most potent weapons against white-collar criminals is the Mail Fraud Act of 1990.[9] Under this act, it is a federal crime to use the mails to defraud the public. Illegal use of the mails must involve (1) mailing or causing someone else to mail a writing—something written, printed, or photocopied—for the purpose of executing a scheme to defraud and (2) a contemplated or an organized scheme to defraud by false pretenses. If, for example, Johnson advertises by mail the sale of a cure for cancer that he knows to be fraudulent because it has no medical validity, he can be prosecuted for fraudulent use of the mails.

Federal law also makes it a crime to use wire, radio, or television transmissions to defraud.[10] Violators may be fined up to $1,000, imprisoned for up to five years, or both. If the violation affects a financial institution, the violator may be fined up to $1 million, imprisoned for up to thirty years, or both.

Computer Crime

The American Bar Association defines **computer crime** as any act that is directed against computers and computer parts, that uses computers as instruments of crime, or that involves computers and constitutes abuse. Frequently our laws are inadequate to deal with the various types of computer crimes that are committed. As mentioned earlier, larceny statutes were originally passed to prohibit the taking and carrying away of physical property belonging to another.

Computer crimes, however, such as those involving the theft of computer data or services, frequently do not require a physical "taking and carrying away" of another's property. Some states have expanded their definitions of property to allow computer crimes to fall within their larceny statutes, but in other states prosecutors have to rely on other criminal statutes. People committing computer crimes often receive lenient punishments, which has led lawmakers to put forth various proposals to deal with this type of crime.

A variety of different types of crime can be committed with or against computers. We look here at some of the ways in which computers have been involved in criminal activity, as well as at some of the difficulties involved in prosecuting computer crime.

FINANCIAL CRIMES   Many computer crimes fall into the broad category of financial crimes. In addition to using computers for information storage and retrieval, businesses commonly use computers to conduct financial transactions. This is equally true of the government, which handles virtually all of its transactions via computer. These circumstances provide opportunities for employees and others to commit crimes that can involve serious economic losses. For example, employees of accounting and computer departments can transfer monies among accounts with little effort and without the risk involved in transactions evidenced by paperwork. Thus, not only is the potential for crime in the area of financial transactions great, but also most monetary losses from computer crime are suffered in this area.

9.   18 U.S.C. Sections 1341–1342.
10.   18 U.S.C. Section 1343.

SOFTWARE PIRACY Given the expense of software, many individuals and businesses have been tempted to steal software by decoding and making unauthorized copies of software programs. Under most state laws, software piracy is classified as a crime. At the federal level, the traditional laws protecting intellectual property (such as patent and copyright laws) have been amended in the last decade or so to extend coverage to computer programs (see Chapter 5). In 1990, in an attempt to control further the unauthorized copying of computer programs, the federal government passed a law that prohibits, with some exceptions, the renting, leasing, or lending of computer software without the express permission of the copyright holder.

PROPERTY THEFT Computer crimes can also involve property theft. One type is the theft of computer equipment (hardware), which has become easier in recent years as computer components have become smaller and more readily transportable. Another type of property theft is the theft of computer-related property, which may involve taking goods that are controlled and accounted for by means of a computer application program. For example, an employee in a company's accounting department could manipulate inventory records to conceal unauthorized shipments of goods. The theft of computer equipment and the theft of goods with the aid of computers are subject to the same criminal and tort laws covering thefts of other physical property.

VANDALISM AND DESTRUCTIVE PROGRAMMING Another form of computer crime is the intentional destruction of computer hardware or software. In one instance, an individual erased a company's records merely by walking past computer storage banks with an electromagnet. Other destructive acts have required greater technical awareness and facility. A knowledgeable individual, such as an angry employee whose job has just been terminated, can do a considerable amount of damage to computer data and files. One ongoing problem for businesspersons and other computer users today is guarding against computer "viruses"—computer programs that are designed to rearrange, replace, or destroy data. This form of vandalism is difficult to combat because of the difficulty of locating and prosecuting those responsible for "unleashing" such programs.

THEFT OF DATA OR SERVICES Many people would agree that when an individual uses another's computer or computer information system without authorization, the individual is stealing. For example, an employee who used a computer system or data stored in a computer system for private gain and without the employer's authorization would likely be considered a thief, as would a politician who used a government computer to send out campaign brochures. Under an increasing number of revised criminal codes and broad judicial interpretations of existing statutes, the unauthorized use of computer data or services is considered larceny. The following case illustrates how one court interpreted a statute to cover the theft of computer time and storage.

CASE 6.5
United States v. Collins
United States Court of Appeals,
District of Columbia Circuit, 1995.
56 F.3d 1416.

FACTS Peter Collins worked for the U.S. Defense Intelligence Agency (DIA) and had access to the DIA's classified computer system. Collins was also involved in amateur ballroom dancing through the U.S. Amateur Ballroom Dance Association. Over a five-year period, Collins used the DIA's computer system to create hundreds of documents, including newsletters, mailing lists, and calendars, relating to his ballroom dance activities. Collins was subsequently prosecuted and convicted in a federal district court of, among other things, converting to his own use government computer time and storage. Collins appealed to the U.S. Court of Appeals for the District of Columbia Circuit. He argued in part that his conviction should be reversed on the ground that the statute under which he was convicted for the conversion of com-

Case 6.5—Continued

puter time and storage does not cover intangible property (property that, like computer data and services, does not have a physical existence).

ISSUE   Does the statute cover the theft of such intan-gible property as computer time and storage?

DECISION   Yes. The U.S. Court of Appeals for the District of Columbia Circuit affirmed the district court's judgment.

REASON   The U.S. Court of Appeals for the District of Columbia Circuit pointed out that the statute under which Collins was convicted provides for liability on the part of any person who "knowingly converts to his use or the use of another * * * any * * * thing of value of the United States or of any * * * agency thereof." The court emphasized that "Congress did not limit those things which could be converted to 'tangible property,' but rather any 'thing of value.'" The court explained that "Congress intended to enact a broad prohibition against the misappropriation of anything belonging to the national government, unrestrained by * * * fine and technical distinctions." This intent "clearly confirms" that the statute "covers the misappropriation of intangible property."

FOR CRITICAL ANALYSIS—Technological Consideration   *When computer time is stolen, it may never affect others' use of the computer. Why, then, is such an action prosecuted?*

PROSECUTING COMPUTER CRIME   In attempting to control computer crime, governments at both the federal and state levels have undertaken protective measures. The Counterfeit Access Device and Computer Fraud and Abuse Act of 1984, as amended, prohibits unauthorized access to certain types of information, such as restricted government information, information contained in a financial institution's financial records, and information contained in a consumer reporting agency's files on consumers. Penalties for violations include up to five years' imprisonment and a fine of up to $250,000 or twice the amount that was gained by the thief or lost by the victim as a result of the crime. Several states have also passed legislation specifically addressing the problem of computer crime.

One of the major problems in attempting to control computer crime is that it cannot be prosecuted if it is not reported. It seems clear to many people that the reason many computer crimes go unreported is because business firms are reluctant to disclose the vulnerability of their systems. Companies adversely affected by such crime do not want to publicize the fact, because they are afraid customers will doubt the accuracy and secu-

rity of computer-generated material. Cases involving computer crimes are thus often settled out of court to avoid publicity.

Bribery

Basically, three types of bribery are considered crimes: bribery of public officials, commercial bribery, and bribery of foreign officials.

BRIBERY OF PUBLIC OFFICIALS   The attempt to influence a public official to act in a way that serves a private interest is a crime. As an element of this crime, intent must be present and proved. The bribe can be anything the recipient considers to be valuable. It is important to realize that *the commission of the crime of bribery occurs when the bribe is offered.* The recipient does not have to agree to perform whatever action is desired by the person offering the bribe, nor does the recipient have to accept the bribe, for the crime of bribery to occur.

COMMERCIAL BRIBERY   Typically, people make commercial bribes to obtain proprietary information, cover up an inferior product, or secure new business. Industrial espionage sometimes involves commercial bribes. For example, a person in one firm may offer an employee in a competing firm some type of payoff in exchange for trade secrets and pricing schedules. So-called kickbacks or payoffs for special favors or serv-ices are a form of commercial bribery in some situations.

BRIBERY OF FOREIGN OFFICIALS   Bribing foreign officials to obtain favorable business contracts is a crime. The Foreign Corrupt Practices Act of 1977 was passed to curb the practice of bribery by American businesspersons in securing foreign contracts.

Bankruptcy Fraud

Today, federal bankruptcy law (see Chapter 20) allows individuals and businesses to be relieved of oppressive debt through bankruptcy proceedings. Numerous white-collar crimes may be committed during the many phases of a bankruptcy proceeding. A creditor, for example, may file a false claim against the debtor, which is a crime. Also, a debtor may fraudulently transfer assets to favored parties before or after the petition for bankruptcy is filed. For example, a company-owned automobile may be "sold" at a bargain price to a trusted friend or relative. Closely related to the crime of fraudulent transfer of property is the crime of fraudulent concealment of property, such as hiding gold coins.

Money Laundering

The profits from illegal activities amount to billions of dollars a year, particularly the profits from illegal drug transactions and, to a lesser extent, from racketeering, prostitution, and gambling. Under federal law, banks, savings and loan associations, and other financial institutions are required to report currency transactions of over $10,000. Consequently, those who engage in illegal activities face difficulties in placing their cash profits from illegal transactions.

As an alternative to simply placing cash from illegal transactions in bank deposits, wrongdoers and racketeers have invented ways to launder "dirty" money to make it "clean." This **money laundering** is done through legitimate businesses.

For example, a successful drug dealer might become a partner with a restaurateur. Little by little, the restaurant shows an increasing profit. As a shareholder or partner in the restaurant, the wrongdoer is able to report the "profits" of the restaurant as legitimate income on which federal and state taxes are paid. The wrongdoer can then spend those monies without worrying about whether his or her lifestyle exceeds the level possible with his or her reported income. The Federal Bureau of Investigation estimates that organized crime alone has invested tens of billions of dollars in as many as a hundred thousand business establishments in the United States for the purpose of money laundering.

Insider Trading

An individual who obtains "inside information" about the plans of large corporations can often make stock-trading profits by using such information to guide decisions relating to the purchase or sale of corporate securities. **Insider trading** is a violation of securities law and will be considered more fully in Chapter 27. At this point, it may be said that one who possesses inside information and who has a duty not to disclose it to outsiders may not profit from the purchase or sale of securities based on that information until the information is available to the public.

Criminal RICO Violations

The Racketeer Influenced and Corrupt Organizations Act (RICO) was passed in an attempt to prevent the use of legitimate business enterprises as shields for racketeering activity and to prohibit the purchase of any legitimate business interest with illegally obtained funds (see the discussion of RICO in Chapter 5).

Most of the criminal RICO offenses have little, if anything, to do with normal business activities, for they involve gambling, arson, and extortion. Securities fraud (involving the sale of stocks and bonds), as well as mail fraud, wire fraud, welfare fraud, embezzlement, and numerous other crimes defined by state or federal statutes, however, are also criminal RICO violations, and RICO has become an effective tool in attacking these white-collar crimes in recent years. Under criminal provisions of RICO, any individual found guilty of a violation is subject to a fine of up to $25,000 per violation, imprisonment for up to twenty years, or both.

▌ Defenses to Crimes

There are numerous defenses that the law deems sufficient to excuse a defendant's criminal behavior. Among the most important defenses to criminal liability are infancy, intoxication, insanity, mistake, consent, duress, justifiable use of force, entrapment, and the statute of limitations. Also, in some cases, defendants are given *immunity* and thus relieved, at least in part, of criminal liability for crimes they committed. We look at each of these defenses here.

Note that procedural violations (such as obtaining evidence without a valid search warrant) may operate as defenses also—because evidence obtained in violation of a defendant's constitutional rights may not be admitted in court. If the evidence is suppressed, then there may be no basis for prosecuting the defendant.

Infancy

The term *infant*, as used in the law, refers to any person who has not yet reached the age of majority (see Chapter 9). Exhibit 6–3 indicates the relationship between age and responsibility for criminal acts under the common law.

In all states, certain courts handle cases involving children who are alleged to have violated the law. In some states, juvenile courts handle children's cases exclusively. In most states, however, courts that handle children's cases also have jurisdiction over other matters, such as traffic offenses. Originally, juvenile court hearings were informal, and lawyers were rarely present. Since 1967, however, when the United States Supreme Court ordered that a child charged with delinquency must be allowed to consult with an attorney before being committed to a state institution,[11] juvenile court hearings have become more formal. In some states, a child will be treated as an adult and tried in a regular court if he or she is above a certain age (usually fourteen) and is guilty of a felony, such as rape or murder.

Intoxication

The law recognizes two types of intoxication, whether from drugs or from alcohol: *involuntary* and *voluntary*. Involuntary intoxication occurs when a person either is physically forced to ingest or inject an intoxicating substance or is unaware that a substance contains drugs or alcohol. Involuntary intoxication is a defense to a crime if its effect was to make a person incapable of understanding that the act committed was wrong or incapable of obeying the law.

Using voluntary drug or alcohol intoxication as a defense is based on the theory that extreme levels of intoxication may negate the state of mind that a crime requires. Many courts are reluctant to allow voluntary intoxication as a defense to a crime, however. After all, the defendant, by definition, voluntarily chose to put himself or herself into an intoxicated state. Voluntary intoxication as a defense may be effective in cases in which the defendant was *extremely* intoxicated when committing the wrong.

Insanity

Just as a child is often judged incapable of the state of mind required to commit a crime, so also may

---

11. *In re Gault*, 387 U.S.1, 87 S.Ct. 1428, 18 L.Ed.2d 527 (1967).

♦ **Exhibit 6–3**
  Responsibility of Infants for Criminal Acts under the Common Law

Age 0–7	Absolute presumption of incompetence.
Age 7–14	Presumption of incompetence, but government may oppose.
Age 14+	Presumption of competence, but infant may oppose.

be someone suffering from a mental illness. Thus, insanity may be a defense to a criminal charge. The courts have had difficulty deciding what the test for legal insanity should be, and psychiatrists as well as lawyers are critical of the tests used. Almost all federal courts and some states use the relatively liberal standard set forth in the Model Penal Code:

> A person is not responsible for criminal conduct if at the time of such conduct as a result of mental disease or defect he lacks substantial capacity either to appreciate the wrongfulness of his conduct or to conform his conduct to the requirements of the law.

Some states use the *M'Naghten* test,[12] under which a criminal defendant is not responsible if, at the time of the offense, he or she did not know the nature and quality of the act or did not know that the act was wrong. Other states use the irresistible-impulse test. A person operating under an irresistible impulse may know an act is wrong but cannot refrain from doing it.

Mistake

Everyone has heard the saying, "Ignorance of the law is no excuse." Ordinarily, ignorance of the law or a mistaken idea about what the law requires is not a valid defense. In some states, however, that rule has been modified. People who claim that they honestly did not know that they were breaking a law may have a valid defense if (1) the law was not published or reasonably made known to the public or (2) the people relied on an official statement of the law that was erroneous.

A *mistake of fact*, as opposed to a *mistake of law*, operates as a defense if it negates the mental state necessary to commit a crime. If, for example, Oliver Wheaton mistakenly walks off with Julie Tyson's briefcase because he thinks it is his, there is no theft. Theft requires knowledge that the property belongs to another.

Consent

What if a victim consents to a crime or even encourages the person intending a criminal act to commit it? The law allows **consent** as a defense if

the consent cancels the harm that the law is designed to prevent. In each case, the question is whether the law forbids an act that was committed against the victim's will or forbids the act without regard to the victim's wish. The law forbids murder, prostitution, and drug use whether the victim consents to it or not. Also, if the act causes harm to a third person who has not consented, there is no escape from criminal liability. Consent or forgiveness given after a crime has been committed is not really a defense, though it can affect the likelihood of prosecution. Consent operates as a defense most successfully in crimes against property.

Duress

Duress exists when the *wrongful threat* of one person induces another person to perform an act that he or she would not otherwise perform. In such a situation, duress is said to negate the mental state necessary to commit a crime. For duress to qualify as a defense, the following requirements must be met:

1. The threat must be of serious bodily harm or death.
2. The harm threatened must be greater than the harm caused by the crime.
3. The threat must be immediate and inescapable.
4. The defendant must have been involved in the situation through no fault of his or her own.

One crime that cannot be excused by duress is murder. It is difficult to justify taking a life even if one's own life is threatened.

Justifiable Use of Force

Probably the most well-known defense to criminal liability is **self-defense.** Other situations, however, also justify the use of force: the defense of one's dwelling, the defense of other property, and the prevention of a crime. In all of these situations, it is important to distinguish between the use of deadly and nondeadly force. Deadly force is likely to result in death or serious bodily harm. Nondeadly force is force that reasonably appears necessary to prevent the imminent use of criminal force.

Generally speaking, people can use the amount of nondeadly force that seems necessary to

---

12. A rule derived from *M'Naghten's Case,* 8 Eng.Rep. 718

protect themselves, their dwellings, or other property or to prevent the commission of a crime. Deadly force can be used in self-defense if there is a *reasonable belief* that imminent death or grievous bodily harm will otherwise result, if the attacker is using unlawful force (an example of lawful force is that exerted by a police officer), and if the defender has not initiated or provoked the attack. Deadly force normally can be used to defend a dwelling only if the unlawful entry is violent and the person believes deadly force is necessary to prevent imminent death or great bodily harm or—in some jurisdictions—if the person believes deadly force is necessary to prevent the commission of a felony (such as arson) in the dwelling.

Entrapment

Entrapment is a defense designed to prevent police officers or other government agents from encouraging crimes in order to apprehend persons wanted for criminal acts. In the typical entrapment case, an undercover agent *suggests* that a crime be committed and somehow pressures or induces an individual to commit it. The agent then arrests the individual for the crime.

For entrapment to be considered a defense, both the suggestion and the inducement must take place. The defense is intended not to prevent law enforcement agents from setting a trap for an unwary criminal but rather to prevent them from pushing the individual into it. The crucial issue is whether a person who committed a crime was predisposed to commit the crime or did so because the agent induced it.

An interesting variation of the entrapment defense is "sentencing entrapment." This occurs when undercover police officers induce a criminal suspect to commit a more serious crime than the crime contemplated by the suspect, thus causing the person, if convicted, to receive a harsher penalty under the federal sentencing guidelines discussed earlier. In the following case, the defendants claimed that they had been the victims of this form of entrapment.

CASE 6.6

United States v. Cannon

United States District Court,
District of North Dakota, 1995.
886 F.Supp. 705.

FACTS Keith and Stephanie Cannon sold crack cocaine to a deputy sheriff, who was operating undercover as a drug buyer. The Cannons asked the undercover officer to help them procure some handguns. He arranged for an agent of the BATF to pose as an illegal gun seller. The BATF agent, on his own initiative, brought a machine gun to the meeting with the Cannons. At that meeting, the Cannons again sold crack to the sheriff and bought three handguns from the agent. After the undercover officers exercised some persuasive sales tactics, the Cannons also bought the machine gun. They were promptly arrested and charged with using firearms during and in relation to drug trafficking. The Cannons were tried in a federal district court and convicted. Because one of the weapons was a machine gun, their convictions required minimum prison sentences of thirty years. At their sentencing hearing, the Cannons argued in part that they should receive a different minimum term (five years—the minimum mandatory sentence for the use of a firearm generally), on the ground of sentencing entrapment.

ISSUE Does the sale of an illegal machine gun by a government agent to drug traffickers constitute entrapment when the traffickers sought to buy only illegal handguns?

DECISION Yes. The federal district court ordered that the Cannons be sentenced as though no machine gun had been present during their offense.

(Continued)

Case 6.6—Continued

REASON   The court looked at all of the evidence, including video and audio recordings of the Cannons' transactions with the undercover officers, and read the trial transcripts, including the testimony of the BATF agent. The court reasoned, "based on all the evidence cognizable in imposing sentence," that "the defendants have met their burden of proving * * * that [they] were not predisposed to purchase a machine gun and that they were induced to do so by the government."

FOR CRITICAL ANALYSIS—Ethical Consideration   *Should there be any legal limits on the degree of temptation to which law enforcement officers can subject persons who are under investigation? Why or why not?*

Statute of Limitations

With some exceptions, such as for the crime of murder, statutes of limitations apply to crimes just as they do to civil wrongs. In other words, criminal cases must be prosecuted within a certain number of years. If a criminal action is brought after the statutory time period has expired, the accused person can raise the statute of limitations as a defense.

Immunity

At times, the state may wish to obtain information from a person accused of a crime. Accused persons are understandably reluctant to give information if it will be used to prosecute them, and they cannot be forced to do so. The privilege against self-incrimination is granted by the Fifth Amendment to the Constitution, which reads, in part, "nor shall [any person] be compelled in any criminal case to be a witness against himself." In cases in which the state wishes to obtain information from a person accused of a crime, the state can grant *immunity* from prosecution or agree to prosecute for a less serious offense in exchange for the information. Once immunity is given, the person can no longer refuse to testify on Fifth Amendment grounds, because he or she now has an absolute privilege against self-incrimination.

Often a grant of immunity from prosecution for a serious crime is part of the **plea bargaining** between the defendant and the prosecuting attorney. The defendant may be convicted of a lesser offense, while the state uses the defendant's testimony to prosecute accomplices for serious crimes carrying heavy penalties.

▌ Terms and Concepts

arson 133
beyond a reasonable
   doubt 128
burglary 131
computer crime 133
consent 138
crime 123
double jeopardy 126
duress 138

embezzlement 132
entrapment 139
exclusionary rule 126
felony 124
forgery 131
grand jury 128
indictment 128
information 128
insider trading 136

larceny 131
misdemeanor 124
money laundering 136
petty offense 124
plea bargaining 140
robbery 131
self-defense 138
white-collar crime 131

▌Chapter Summary: Criminal Law

Civil Law and Criminal Law *(See page 123.)*	1. *Civil law*—Spells out the duties that exist between persons or between citizens and their governments, excluding the duty not to commit crimes. In a civil case, damages are awarded to compensate those harmed by others' wrongful acts, or equitable remedies may be granted. 2. *Criminal law*—Has to do with crimes, which are defined as wrongs against society proclaimed in statutes and, if committed, punishable by society through fines and/or imprisonment—and, in some cases, death. Because crimes are *offenses against society as a whole*, they are prosecuted by a public official, not by victims. (See Exhibit 6–1 for a summary of how criminal and civil laws differ.)
Classification of Crimes *(See page 124.)*	1. *Felonies*—Serious crimes punishable by death or by imprisonment in a penitentiary for more than a year. 2. *Misdemeanors*—Under federal law and in most states, any crime that is not a felony.
Criminal Liability *(See pages 124–125.)*	1. *Guilty act*—In general, some form of harmful act must be committed for a crime to exist. 2. *Intent*—An intent to commit a crime, or a wrongful mental state, is required for a crime to exist.
Procedure in Criminal Law *(See pages 125–128.)*	1. *Constitutional safeguards*—The rights of accused persons are protected under the Constitution, particularly by the Fourth, Fifth, Sixth, and Eighth Amendments. Under the exclusionary rule, evidence obtained in violation of the constitutional rights of the accused will not be admissible in court. In *Miranda v. Arizona*, the United States Supreme Court ruled that individuals must be informed of their constitutional rights (such as their rights to counsel and to remain silent) on being taken into custody. 2. *Criminal process*—Procedures governing arrest, indictment, and trial for a crime are designed to safeguard the rights of the individual against the state. See Exhibit 6–2 for the steps involved in prosecuting a criminal case.
Federal Sentencing Guidelines *(See pages 128–131.)*	Guidelines established by the U.S. Sentencing Commission indicating a range of penalties for each federal crime; federal judges must abide by these guidelines when imposing sentences on those convicted of federal crimes.
Crimes Affecting Business *(See pages 131–137.)*	1. *Forgery*—The fraudulent making or altering of any writing in a way that changes the legal rights and liabilities of another. 2. *Robbery*—The forceful and unlawful taking of personal property of any value from another. 3. *Burglary*—At common law, defined as breaking and entering the dwelling of another at night with the intent to commit a felony. State statutes now vary in their definitions of burglary. 4. *Larceny*—The wrongful or fraudulent taking and carrying away of another's personal property with the intent to deprive the owner permanently of the property. 5. *Obtaining goods by false pretenses*—Such as cashing a check knowing that there are insufficient funds in the bank to cover it. 6. *Receiving stolen goods*—A crime if the recipient knew or should have known that the goods were stolen.

(Continued)

▌Chapter Summary: Criminal Law—Continued

Crimes Affecting Business—Continued	7. *Embezzlement*—The fraudulent appropriation of another person's property or money by a person to whom the property or money was entrusted.
	8. *Arson*—The willful and malicious burning of a building or (in some states) personal property owned by another.
	9. *Mail and wire fraud*—Using the mails, wires, radio, or television to defraud the public.
	10. *Computer crime*—Any act that is directed against computers and computer parts, that uses computers as instruments of crime, or that involves computers and constitutes abuse. Computer crime includes financial crimes that involve computers; theft of computer software, equipment, data, or services; and vandalism and destructive programming of computers.
	11. *Bribery*—Includes bribery of public officials, commercial bribery, and bribery of foreign officials. The crime of bribery is committed when the bribe is tendered.
	12. *Bankruptcy fraud*—Encompasses crimes committed in connection with bankruptcy proceedings, including false claims of creditors and fraudulent transfers of assets by debtors.
	13. *Money laundering*—Establishing legitimate enterprises through which "dirty" money (obtained through criminal activities) can be "laundered."
	14. *Insider trading*—The buying or selling of corporate securities by a person in possession of material nonpublic information in violation of securities laws.
	15. *Criminal RICO violations*—Include the use of legitimate business enterprises to shield racketeering activity, securities fraud, and mail fraud.
Defenses to Criminal Liability (*See pages 137–140.*)	1. *Infancy.* 5. *Consent.* 9. *Statute of limitations.* 2. *Intoxication.* 6. *Duress.* 10. *Immunity.* 3. *Insanity.* 7. *Justifiable use of force.* 4. *Mistake.* 8. *Entrapment.*

▌For Review

1. How are crimes distinguished from other wrongful acts?

2. What two elements must exist before a person can be held liable for a crime?

3. What constitutional safeguards exist to protect persons accused of crimes?

4. List and describe five crimes affecting business.

5. What defenses might be raised by criminal defendants to avoid liability for criminal acts?

▌Questions and Case Problems

6–1. Criminal versus Civil Trials. In criminal trials, the defendant must be proved guilty beyond a reasonable doubt, whereas in civil trials, the defendant need only be proved guilty by a preponderance of the evidence. Discuss why a higher standard of proof is required in criminal trials.

6–2. Types of Crimes. Determine from the facts below what type of crime has been committed in each situation.

(a) Carlos is walking through an amusement park when his wallet, with $2,000 in it, is "picked" from his pocket.

(b) Carlos walks into a camera shop. Without force and without the owner's noticing, Carlos walks out of the store with a camera.

6–3. Types of Crimes. The following situations are similar (all involve the theft of Makoto's television set), yet they represent three different crimes. Identify the three crimes, noting the differences among them.

(a) While passing Makoto's house one night, Sarah sees a portable television set left unattended on Makoto's lawn. Sarah takes the television set, carries it home, and tells everyone she owns it.

(b) While passing Makoto's house one night, Sarah sees Makoto outside with a portable television set. Holding Makoto at gunpoint, Sarah forces him to give up the set. Then Sarah runs away with it.

(c) While passing Makoto's house one night, Sarah sees a portable television set in a window. Sarah breaks the front-door lock, enters, and leaves with the set.

6–4. Types of Crimes. Which, if any, of the following crimes necessarily involve illegal activity on the part of more than one person?

(a) Bribery.
(b) Forgery.
(c) Embezzlement.
(d) Larceny.
(e) Receiving stolen property.

6–5. Double Jeopardy. Armington, while robbing a drugstore, shot and seriously injured a drugstore clerk, Jennings. Armington was subsequently convicted in a criminal trial of armed robbery and assault and battery. Jennings later brought a civil tort suit against Armington for damages. Armington contended that he could not be tried again for the same crime, as that would constitute double jeopardy, which is prohibited by the Fifth Amendment to the Constitution. Is Armington correct? Explain.

6–6. Receiving Stolen Property. Rafael stops Laura on a busy street and offers to sell her an expensive wristwatch for a fraction of its value. After some questioning by Laura, Rafael admits that the watch is stolen property, although he says he was not the thief. Laura pays for and receives the wristwatch. Has Laura committed any crime? Has Rafael? Explain.

6–7. Embezzlement. Slemmer, who had been a successful options trader, gave lectures to small groups about stock options. Several persons who attended his lectures decided to invest in stock options and have Slemmer advise them. They formed an investment club called Profit Design Group (PDG). Slemmer set up an account for PDG with a brokerage firm. Slemmer had control of the PDG account and could make decisions on which stock options to buy or sell. He was not authorized to withdraw money from the account for his own benefit. Nonetheless, he withdrew money from the

PDG account to make payments on real estate that he owned. Slemmer made false representations to the members of PDG, and he eventually lost all the money in their account. A jury found him guilty of first degree theft by embezzlement. Slemmer objected to the trial court's failure to instruct the jury that an intent to permanently deprive was an element of the crime charged. Is intent to permanently deprive another of property a required element for the crime of embezzlement? Explain. [*State v. Slemmer*, 48 Wash.App. 48, 738 P.2d 281 (1987)]

6–8. Self-Defense. Bernardy came to the defense of his friend Harrison in a fight with Wilson. Wilson started the fight, and after Harrison knocked Wilson down, Bernardy (who was wearing tennis shoes) kicked Wilson several times in the head. Bernardy stated that he did so because he believed an onlooker, Gowens, would join forces with Wilson against Harrison. Bernardy maintained that his use of force was justifiable because he was protecting another (Harrison) from injury. Discuss whether Bernardy's use of force to protect Harrison from harm was justified. [*State v. Bernardy*, 25 Wash.App. 146, 605 P.2d 791(1980)]

6–9. Criminal Liability. In January 1988, David Ludvigson was hired as chief executive officer of Leopard Enterprises, a group of companies that owned funeral homes and cemeteries in Iowa and sold "pre-need" funeral contracts. Under Iowa law, 80 percent of monies obtained under such a contract must be set aside in trust until the death of the person for whose benefit the funds were paid. Shortly after Ludvigson was hired, the firm began having financial difficulties. Ludvigson used money from these contracts to pay operating expenses until the company went bankrupt and was placed in receivership. Ludvigson was charged and found guilty on five counts of second degree theft stemming from the misappropriation of these funds. He appealed, alleging, among other things, that because none of the victims whose trust funds were used to cover operating expenses was denied services, no injury was done and thus no crime was committed. Will the court agree with Ludvigson? Explain. [*State v. Ludvigson*, 482 N.W.2d 419 (Iowa 1992)]

6–10. Defenses to Criminal Liability. The Child Protection Act of 1984 makes it a crime to receive knowingly through the mails sexually explicit depictions of children. After this act was passed, government agents found Keith Jacobson's name on a bookstore's mailing list. (Jacobson previously had ordered and received from a bookstore two *Bare Boys* magazines containing photographs of nude preteen and teenage boys.) To test Jacobson's willingness to break the law, government agencies sent mail to him, through five fictitious organizations and a bogus pen pal, over a period of two and a half years. Many of these "organizations" claimed that they had been founded to protect sexual freedom, freedom of choice, and so on. Jacobson eventually ordered a magazine. He testified at trial that he ordered the magazine because he was curious about "all the trouble and the hysteria over pornography and I wanted to see what the material was." When the magazine was delivered, he was arrested for violating the 1984 act. What defense discussed in this chapter might Jacobson raise to avoid criminal liability under the act? Explain fully. [*Jacobson v. United States*, 503 U.S. 540, 112 S.Ct. 1535, 118 L.Ed.2d 174 (1992)]

6–11. Entrapment. When Sharon Shepherd attempted to sell cocaine powder to an undercover law enforcement officer, the officer insisted that she first convert the powder to crack cocaine—which she did by "cooking" the powder in a microwave for a few minutes. The agent then purchased the cocaine in its converted state. The agent's purpose in requesting Shepherd to convert the powder to crack was to cause Shepherd to receive a more severe sentence. Under the federal sentencing guidelines, the mandatory sentence for the sale of crack cocaine is from 120 to 135 months in prison, whereas the sentence for the sale of cocaine powder is only 60 months. Was Shepherd a victim of "sentencing entrapment"? What factors should the court consider in deciding this issue? Discuss fully. [*United States v. Shepherd*, 857 F.Supp. 105 (D.C. 1994)]

▌Unit Two—Cumulative Hypothetical Problem

6–12. *CompTac, Inc., is one of the leading software manufacturers in the United States. The company invests millions of dollars in researching and developing new software applications and games that are sold worldwide. It also has a large service department and has taken great pains to offer its customers excellent support services. Recently, CompTac has been losing sales to a new competitor in the field, the Geminex Co. In view of these "facts," answer the following questions:*

1. Geminex has launched a new advertising campaign in which it compares its prices and support services to those offered by CompTac. The advertising campaign is so effective that many of CompTac's customers have switched to Geminex software and services. One of CompTac's most important customers, Allotran Corp., breached its contract with CompTac and started purchasing its software and services from Geminex instead. As a result of Allotran's breach of contract, CompTac stood to lose nearly $2 million in revenues. CompTac sues Geminex for wrongful interference with a contractual relationship. Will CompTac succeed in its suit? Why or why not?

2. In its advertising campaign against CompTac, Geminex claims that CompTac, instead of fully testing and debugging the computer programs before they are marketed, has its customers test the software. CompTac knows this is not true and that it is unfair of Geminex to make such a claim.

Could CompTac sue Geminex for the harm Geminex is causing to CompTac's reputation? If so, on what grounds? Explain.

3. CompTac has just developed a new software application that the company hopes will reap lucrative profits. It has taken the company two years and a substantial investment of money to create the program. CompTac learns that its competitor, Geminex, has already filed for a patent on a nearly identical program and has sold the software to many of its customers. CompTac learns from a reliable source that Geminex paid one of CompTac's employees a substantial sum of money to obtain a copy of the pro-gram. What legal recourse does CompTac have against Geminex? Discuss fully.

4. The head of CompTac's accounting department, Roy Olson, has to pay his daughter's college tuition within a week, or his daughter will not be able to continue taking classes. The payment due is over $20,000. Roy would be able to make the payment in two months, but cannot do so until then. The college refuses to wait that long. In desperation, Roy—through a fictitious bank account and some clever accounting—"borrows" funds from CompTac. Before Roy can pay back the borrowed funds, an auditor discovers what Roy did. CompTac's president alleges that Roy has "stolen" company funds and informs the police of the theft. Has Roy committed a crime? If so, what crime did he commit? Explain.

▌Accessing the Internet: Fundamentals of Business Law

A good starting place to find information on criminal law on the Internet is
http://www.fsu.edu/~crimdo/cj.html

This site, which is updated regularly, offers the most extensive collection of criminal law links on the Internet, including links to local, state, federal, and international resources, as well as to other crime-related Web sites.

Another site with a large number of links to crime-related topics is

http://dpa.state.ky.us:80/

If you are interested in looking at the text of the *U.S. Sentencing Guidelines Manual*, go to

http://www.ussc.gov

The Bureau of Justice Statistics in the U.S. Department of Justice offers an impressive collection of statistics on crime, including data on crimes and victims, drugs and crimes, criminal courts, criminal prosecution, sentencing, and corrections facilities. You can find this collection at

http://www.ojp.usdoj.gov/bjs

For information on criminal justice programs and initiatives, as well as other information on the criminal justice system, go to the U.S. Department of Justice's home page at

http://usdoj.gov

The Justice Information Center is an excellent source for information on criminal and juvenile justice throughout the world. To access this information, go to

http://www.ncjrs.org

The Federal Bureau of Investigation (FBI) offers abundant information and statistics on crime, including information concerning FBI investigations, international crime, wiretapping, electronic surveillance, and economic espionage. You can locate the FBI's home page at

http://www.fbi.gov

One of the goals of the National Institute of Justice, the research arm of the U.S. Department of Justice, is "to prevent and reduce crime and to improve the criminal justice system." To learn about the institute's research and its various projects (in such areas as community policing, violence against women, and drug courts), go to

http://www.ojp.usdoj.gov/nij

You can find information on the operations of the American Civil Liberties Union (ACLU) and obtain some information on the protection of constitutional rights within the criminal justice system at

http://www.aclu.org/issues/criminal/hmcj.html

If you would like to learn more about criminal procedures, the following site offers an "Anatomy of a Murder: A Trip through Our Nation's Legal Justice System":

http://tqd.advanced.org/2760

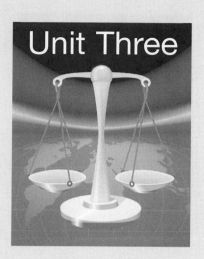

Unit Three

Contracts

▍Unit Contents

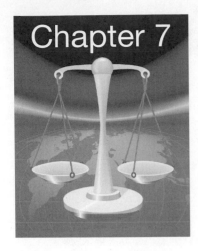

Chapter 7

Nature and Classification

CHAPTER OBJECTIVES

After reading this chapter, you should be able to:

1. Explain the function of contract law.
2. Define the term *contract,* and list the basic elements that are required for contract formation.
3. Discuss the objective theory of contracts.
4. Identify the various types of contracts.
5. Outline the rules that govern the courts' interpretation of contracts.

Keeping promises is important to a stable social order. Contract law deals with, among other things, the formation and keeping of promises. A **promise** is a declaration that something either will or will not happen in the future.

Like other types of law, contract law reflects our social values, interests, and expectations at a given point in time. It shows, for example, what kinds of promises our society thinks should be legally binding. It shows what excuses our society accepts for breaking such promises. Additionally, it shows what promises are considered to be contrary to public policy and therefore legally void. If a promise goes against the interests of society as a whole, it will be invalid. Also, if it was made by a child or a mentally incompetent person, or on the basis of false information, a question will arise as to whether the promise should be enforced. Resolving such questions is the essence of contract law.

In business law and the legal environment of business, questions and disputes concerning contracts arise daily. Although aspects of contract law

vary from state to state, much of it is based on the common law. In 1932, the American Law Institute compiled the *Restatement of the Law of Contracts.* This work is a nonstatutory, authoritative exposition of the present law on the subject of contracts and is presently in its second edition (although a third edition is in the process of being drafted). Throughout the following chapters on contracts, we will refer to the second edition of the *Restatement of the Law of Contracts* as simply the *Restatement (Second) of Contracts.*

The Uniform Commercial Code (UCC), which governs contracts and other transactions relating to the sale of goods, occasionally departs from common law contract rules. Generally, the different treatment of contracts falling under the UCC stems from the general policy of encouraging commerce. The ways in which the UCC changes common law contract rules will be discussed extensively in later chapters. In this unit covering the common law of contracts (Chapters 7 through 12), we only indicate briefly or in footnotes which common law rules have been altered by the UCC for sales contracts.

The Function of Contracts

No aspect of modern life is entirely free of contractual relationships. Indeed, even the ordinary consumer in his or her daily activities acquires rights and obligations based on contract law. You acquire rights and obligations, for example, when you borrow money to make a purchase or when you buy a house. Contract law is designed to provide stability and predictability for both buyers and sellers in the marketplace.

Contract law assures the parties to private agreements that the promises they make will be enforceable. Clearly, many promises are kept because of a moral obligation to do so or because keeping a promise is in the mutual self-interest of the parties involved, not because the **promisor** (the person making the promise) or the **promisee** (the person to whom the promise is made) is conscious of the rules of contract law. Nevertheless, the rules of contract law are often followed in business agreements to avoid potential problems.

By supplying procedures for enforcing private agreements, contract law provides an essential condition for the existence of a market economy. Without a legal framework of reasonably assured expectations within which to plan and venture, businesspersons would be able to rely only on the good faith of others. Duty and good faith are usually sufficient, but when dramatic price changes or adverse economic factors make it costly to comply with a promise, these elements may not be enough. Contract law is necessary to ensure compliance with a promise or to entitle the innocent party to some form of relief.

Definition of a Contract

A **contract** is an agreement that can be enforced in court. It is formed by two or more parties who agree to perform or to refrain from performing some act now or in the future. Generally, contract disputes arise when there is a promise of future performance. If the contractual promise is not fulfilled, the party who made it is subject to the sanctions of a court (see Chapter 12). That party may be required to pay money damages for failing to perform; in limited instances, the party may be required to perform the promised act.

In determining whether a contract has been formed, the element of intent is of prime importance. In contract law, intent is determined by what is referred to as the **objective theory of contracts,** not by the personal or subjective intent, or belief, of a party. The theory is that a party's intention to enter into a contract is judged by outward, objective facts as interpreted by a *reasonable* person, rather than by the party's own secret, subjective intentions. Objective facts include (1) what the party said when entering into the contract, (2) how the party acted or appeared, and (3) the circumstances surrounding the transaction. As will be discussed later in this chapter, in the section on express versus implied contracts, intent to form a contract may be manifested not only in words, oral or written, but also by conduct.

Requirements of a Contract

The following list describes the requirements of a contract. Each item will be explained more fully in the chapter indicated. Although we pair these requirements in subsequent chapters (for example, agreement and consideration are treated in Chapter 9), it is important to stress that each requirement is separate and independent. They are paired merely for reasons of space.

1. *Agreement.* An agreement includes an *offer* and an *acceptance.* One party must offer to enter into a legal agreement, and another party must accept the terms of the offer (Chapter 8).
2. *Consideration.* Any promises made by parties must be supported by legally sufficient and bargained-for *consideration* (something of value received or promised, to convince a person to make a deal) (Chapter 8).
3. *Contractual capacity.* Both parties entering into the contract must have the contractual *capacity* to do so; the law must recognize them as possessing characteristics that qualify them as competent parties (Chapter 9).

4. *Legality.* The contract's purpose must be to accomplish some goal that is *legal* and not against public policy (Chapter 9).

5. *Genuineness of assent.* The apparent consent of both parties must be *genuine* (Chapter 10).

6. *Form.* The contract must be in whatever *form* the law requires; for example, some contracts must be in writing to be enforceable (Chapter 10).

The first four items in this list are formally known as the *elements of a contract.* The last two are possible *defenses to the formation or the enforcement of a contract.*

Freedom of Contract and Freedom from Contract

As a general rule, the law recognizes everyone's ability to enter freely into contractual arrangements. This recognition is called *freedom of contract,* a freedom protected by the U.S. Constitution in Article I, Section 10. Because freedom of contract is a fundamental public policy of the United States, courts rarely interfere with contracts that have been voluntarily made.

Of course, as in other areas of the law, there are many exceptions to the general rule that contracts voluntarily negotiated will be enforced. For example, illegal bargains, agreements unreasonably in restraint of trade, and certain unfair contracts made between one party with a great amount of bargaining power and another with little power are generally not enforced. In addition, certain contracts with consumers, as well as certain clauses within those contracts, may not be enforceable if they are contrary to public policy, fairness, and justice (see Chapter 9 for a discussion of contracts contrary to public policy). These exceptions provide *freedom from contract* for persons who may have been forced into making contracts unfavorable to themselves.

Types of Contracts

There are numerous types of contracts. The categories into which contracts are placed involve legal distinctions as to formation, enforceability, or performance. The best method of explaining each type of contract is to compare one type with another.

Bilateral versus Unilateral Contracts

Every contract involves at least two parties. The **offeror** is the party making the offer. The **offeree** is the party to whom the offer is made. The offeror always promises to do or not to do something and thus is also a promisor. Whether the contract is classified as *unilateral* or *bilateral* depends on what the offeree must do to accept the offer and to bind the offeror to a contract.

BILATERAL CONTRACTS   If to accept the offer the offeree must only *promise* to perform, the contract is a **bilateral contract.** Hence, a bilateral contract is a "promise for a promise." An example of a bilateral contract is a contract in which one person agrees to buy another person's automobile for a specified price. No performance, such as the payment of money or delivery of goods, need take place for a bilateral contract to be formed. The contract comes into existence at the moment the promises are exchanged.

UNILATERAL CONTRACTS   If the offer is phrased so that the offeree can accept only by completing the contract performance, the contract is a **unilateral contract.** Hence, a unilateral contract is a "promise for an act."

A classic example of a unilateral contract is as follows: Joe says to Celia, "If you walk across the Brooklyn Bridge, I'll give you $10." Joe promises to pay only if Celia walks the entire span of the bridge. Only upon Celia's complete crossing does she fully accept Joe's offer to pay $10. If she chooses not to undertake the walk, there are no legal consequences. Contests, lotteries, and other prize-winning competitions are also examples of offers for unilateral contracts. If a person complies with the rules of the contest—such as by submitting the right lottery number at the right place and time—a unilateral contract is formed, binding the organization offering the prize to a contract to perform as promised in the offer.

REVOCATION OF OFFERS FOR UNILATERAL CONTRACTS   A problem arises in unilateral contracts when the promisor attempts to *revoke* (cancel) the offer after the promisee has begun performance but before the act has been completed. For example, suppose that Roberta offers to buy Ed's sailboat, moored in San Francisco, upon delivery of the boat to Roberta's dock in Newport Beach, three hundred miles south of San Francisco. Ed rigs the boat and sets sail. Shortly before his arrival at Newport Beach, Ed receives a radio message from Roberta withdrawing her offer. Roberta's offer is an offer for a unilateral contract, and only Ed's delivery of the sailboat at her dock is an acceptance.

In contract law, offers are normally *revocable* (capable of being taken back, or canceled) until accepted. Under the traditional view of unilateral contracts, Roberta's revocation would terminate the offer. Because of the harsh effect on the offeree of the revocation of an offer to form a unilateral contract, the modern-day view is that once performance has been substantially undertaken, the offeror cannot revoke the offer. Thus, in our example, even though Ed has not yet accepted the offer by complete performance, Roberta is prohibited from revoking it. Ed can deliver the boat and bind Roberta to the contract.

Express versus Implied Contracts

An **express contract** is one in which the terms of the agreement are fully and explicitly stated in words, oral or written. A signed lease for an apartment or a house is an express written contract. If a classmate calls you on the phone and agrees to buy your textbooks from last semester for $50, an express oral contract has been made.

A contract that is implied from the conduct of the parties is called an **implied-in-fact contract,** or an implied contract. This type of contract differs from an express contract in that the *conduct* of the parties, rather than their words, creates and defines the terms of the contract. For example, suppose that you need an accountant to fill out your tax return this year. You look through the Yellow Pages and find an accounting firm located in your neighborhood. You drop by the firm's office, explain your problem to an accountant, and learn what fees will be charged. The next day you return, giving the receptionist all of the necessary information and documents, such as canceled checks, W-2 forms, and so on. You say nothing expressly to the receptionist; rather, you walk out the door. In this situation, you have entered into an implied-in-fact

contract to pay the accountant the usual and reasonable fees for the accounting services. The contract is implied by your conduct. The accountant expects to be paid for completing your tax return. By bringing in the records the accountant will need to do the work, you have implied an intent to pay for the services.

The following three steps establish an implied-in-fact contract:

1. The plaintiff furnished some service or property.
2. The plaintiff expected to be paid for that service or property, and the defendant knew or should have known that payment was expected (by using the objective-theory-of-contracts test, discussed previously).
3. The defendant had a chance to reject the services or property and did not.

Quasi Contracts — Contracts Implied in Law

Quasi contracts, or contracts *implied in law*, are wholly different from actual contracts. Express contracts and implied-in-fact contracts are actual, or true, contracts. Quasi contracts, as the term suggests, are not true contracts. They do not arise from any agreement, express or implied, between the parties themselves. Rather, quasi contracts are fictional contracts imposed on parties by courts in the interests of fairness and justice. Quasi contracts are therefore equitable, rather than contractual, in nature. Usually, quasi contracts are imposed to avoid the *unjust enrichment* of one party at the expense of another.

For example, suppose that a vacationing doctor is driving down the highway and comes upon Emerson, who is lying unconscious on the side of the road. The doctor renders medical aid that saves Emerson's life. Although the injured, unconscious Emerson did not solicit the medical aid and was not aware that the aid had been rendered, Emerson received a valuable benefit, and the requirements for a quasi contract were fulfilled. In such a situation, the law will impose a quasi contract, and Emerson will have to pay the doctor for the reasonable value of the medical services rendered. The following case represents an example of circumstances in which unjust enrichment can occur.

CASE 7.1

ServiceMaster of St. Cloud v. GAB Business Services, Inc.

Court of Appeals of
Minnesota, 1995.
530 N.W.2d 558.

FACTS   Nancy Mollinedo's house was damaged in a fire. Her insurance company, Sentry Insurance, hired GAB Business Services, Inc., an independent insurance claims adjuster, to investigate the claim. GAB hired ServiceMaster of St. Cloud to repair the damage. While ServiceMaster worked on the house, Sentry decided to deny Mollinedo's claim on the ground that she deliberately set the fire. Sentry allowed the repairs to be continued, however, without informing either ServiceMaster or GAB that it would deny the claim. When the work was done, Sentry sent a check for the amount ServiceMaster charged for the work (a little more than $30,000) to the Federal Housing Administration (FHA), Mollinedo's mortgagee,[a] as required under the insurance policy's mortgagee clause. Sentry received in return a partial mortgage on the house. ServiceMaster received nothing. Subsequently, ServiceMaster filed a suit in a Minnesota state court against Sentry and GAB for, among other things, unjust enrichment. The court awarded damages to ServiceMaster. Sentry appealed.

ISSUE   Was Sentry unjustly enriched by the work performed by ServiceMaster?

DECISION   Yes. The Court of Appeals of Minnesota affirmed the award of the trial court.

REASON   The appellate court stated that "[t]o establish its unjust enrichment claim, ServiceMaster had to show that Sentry knowingly received something of value, while not being entitled to the benefit, and under circumstances that would make it unjust to permit its retention." Sentry argued in part that it did not receive a benefit but "suffered a loss because it had to pay out on the claim." ServiceMaster responded by pointing out that in return for Sentry's payment to the FHA, Sentry received a partial mortgage, which increased in value on completion of the repairs. ServiceMaster also argued that "Sentry allowed ServiceMaster to continue the repairs long after Sentry suspected that Mollinedo's claim would be denied." The trial court found these circumstances to be unjust. The appellate court concluded that "the trial court's findings * * * are not clearly erroneous."

FOR CRITICAL ANALYSIS—Ethical Consideration   *Is the mere fact that a person confers a benefit on another enough to require the other to pay? For example, a property owner who improves her property benefits her neighbors to some extent, but should she be entitled to payment from them?*

a.   A *mortgagee* is a creditor who takes an interest in a debtor's real property as security for the payment of a debt.

LIMITATIONS ON QUASI-CONTRACTUAL RECOVERY
Although quasi contracts exist to prevent unjust enrichment, situations exist in which the party who obtains a benefit will not be deemed to have been unjustly enriched by that benefit. Basically, the quasi-contractual principle cannot be invoked by the party who has conferred a benefit on someone else unnecessarily or as a result of misconduct or negligence.

Consider the following example. You take your car to the local car wash and ask to have it run through the washer and to have the gas tank filled.

While your car is being washed, you go to a nearby shopping center for two hours. In the meantime, one of the workers at the car wash has mistakenly believed that your car is the one that he is supposed to hand wax. When you come back, you are presented with a bill for a full tank of gas, a wash job, and a hand wax. Clearly, a benefit has been conferred on you, but this benefit has been conferred because of a mistake by the car wash employee. You have not been *unjustly* enriched under these circumstances. People cannot normally be forced to pay for benefits "thrust" upon them.

WHEN A CONTRACT ALREADY EXISTS   The doctrine of quasi contract generally cannot be used when an actual contract covers the area in contro-

versy. For example, Martinez contracts with Stevenson to deliver a furnace to a building project owned by Richards. Martinez delivers the furnace, but Stevenson never pays Martinez. Stevenson has been unjustly enriched in this situation, to be sure. Martinez, however, cannot collect from Richards in quasi contract, because Martinez had an existing contract with Stevenson. Martinez already has a remedy—he can sue for breach of contract to recover the price of the furnace from Stevenson. No quasi contract need be imposed by the court in this instance to achieve justice. In the following case, the issue concerned whether a party could recover in quasi contract even though an express contract covering the area in controversy already existed.

CASE 7.2

Industrial Lift Truck Service Corp. v. Mitsubishi International Corp.

Appellate Court of Illinois, First District, Fourth Division, 1982.
104 Ill.App.3d 357,
432 N.E.2d 999,
60 Ill.Dec. 100.

FACTS   In 1973 and again in 1976, an agreement was executed between Industrial Lift Truck Service Corporation (IL) and Mitsubishi International Corporation calling for IL to purchase forklift trucks from Mitsubishi and to use its best efforts to sell and service the trucks. The agreement also allowed Mitsubishi to terminate the agreement without just cause by giving ninety days' notice. From 1973 to 1977, IL allegedly became the nation's largest dealer of Mitsubishi forklift trucks. During this period, IL made design changes in the trucks to better suit the American market. Mitsubishi did not request these changes but later incorporated them into the trucks it sold to other dealers. In 1978, Mitsubishi terminated the agreement. IL sued Mitsubishi in an Illinois state court under quasi-contractual principles to recover the benefits conferred upon Mitsubishi by the design changes. The suit was dismissed, and IL appealed.

ISSUE   Could IL's quasi-contractual claim overcome the written contract attesting to the companies' relationship?

DECISION   No. The Illinois appellate court affirmed the lower court's dismissal, holding that the written contract between the parties defined their entire relationship.

REASON   The court reasoned that, in the absence of a valid amendment to the agreement, Mitsubishi had a right to assume that it did not have to compensate IL for any acts performed in relation to the subject matter of the contract except in accordance with the express provisions of the contract. The court characterized a contract implied in law (a quasi contract) as "fictitious and arising by implication of law wholly apart from the usual rules" of contract formation. At times, the court said, when one party confers a benefit on another party and the other party accepts the benefit, the law will impose a duty on the benefited party to pay for the

(Continued)

Case 7.2—Continued

services—provided that the benefit was not intended as a gift. When there is already a written contract concerning the same subject matter, however, the usual rule is that no quasi-contractual claim can arise. In this case, IL understood the terms of the existing contract, and it knew the risks involved in initiating the design changes it made. The court found that IL, by suing, attempted to unilaterally circumvent the contract into which it had freely entered. The contract controlled the relationship between the parties, and the suit had to be dismissed.

FOR CRITICAL ANALYSIS—Ethical Consideration *Is it fair, in a case such as the one presented above, for the court to hold that quasi-contractual recovery is unavailable if an existing contract covers the disputed area?*

Formal versus Informal Contracts

Formal contracts require a special form or method of creation (formation) to be enforceable. They include (1) contracts under seal, (2) recognizances, (3) negotiable instruments, and (4) letters of credit.[1] *Contracts under seal* are formalized writings with a special seal attached.[2] The significance of the seal has lessened, although about ten states require no consideration when a contract is under seal. A *recognizance* is an acknowledgment in court by a person that he or she will perform some specified obligation or pay a certain sum if he or she fails to perform. One form of recognizance is the surety bond.[3] Another is the personal recognizance bond used as bail in a criminal matter. As will be discussed at length in subsequent chapters, *negotiable instruments* include checks, notes, drafts, and certificates of deposit; *letters of credit* are agreements to pay contingent on the purchaser's receipt of invoices and bills of lading (documents evidencing receipt of, and title to, goods shipped).

Informal contracts (also called *simple contracts*) include all other contracts. No special form is required (except for certain types of contracts that must be in writing), as the contracts are usually based on their substance rather than on their form.

Executed versus Executory Contracts

Contracts are also classified according to their state of performance. A contract that has been fully performed on both sides is called an **executed contract.** A contract that has not been fully performed on either side is called an **executory contract.** If one party has fully performed but the other has not, the contract is said to be executed on the one side and executory on the other, but the contract is still classified as executory.

For example, assume that you agree to buy ten tons of coal from the Western Coal Company. Further assume that Western has delivered the coal to your steel mill, where it is now being burned. At this point, the contract is an executory contract—it is executed on the part of Western and executory on your part. After you pay Western for the coal, the contract will be executed on both sides.

Valid, Void, Voidable, and Unenforceable Contracts

A **valid contract** has the elements necessary for contract formation. Those elements consist of (1) an agreement (offer and an acceptance) (2) supported by legally sufficient consideration (3) for a legal purpose and (4) made by parties who have the legal capacity to enter into the contract. As mentioned, we will discuss each of these elements in the following chapters.

A **void contract** is no contract at all. The terms *void* and *contract* are contradictory. A void contract produces no legal obligations on the part of any of the parties. For example, a contract can be void because one of the parties was adjudged by a court to be legally insane (and thus lacked the legal

---

1. *Restatement (Second) of Contracts*, Section 6.
2. A seal may be actual (made of wax or some other durable substance), impressed on the paper, or indicated simply by the word *seal* or the letters *L.S.* at the end of the document. *L.S.* stands for *locus sigilli* and means "the place for the seal."
3. An obligation of a party guaranteeing that a second party will be paid if a third party does not perform.

capacity to enter into a contract) or because the purpose of the contract was illegal.

A **voidable contract** is a *valid* contract but one that can be avoided at the option of one or both of the parties. The party having the option can elect either to avoid any duty to perform or to *ratify* (make valid) the contract. If the contract is avoided, both parties are released from it. If it is ratified, both parties must fully perform their respective legal obligations.

As a general rule, contracts made by minors are voidable at the option of the minor (see Chapter 9). Contracts entered into under fraudulent conditions are voidable at the option of the defrauded party. In addition, contracts entered into under legally defined duress or undue influence are voidable (see Chapter 10).

An **unenforceable contract** is one that cannot be enforced because of certain legal defenses against it. It is not unenforceable because a party failed to satisfy a legal requirement of the contract; rather, it is a valid contract rendered unenforceable by some statute or law. For example, certain contracts must be in writing (see Chapter 10), and if they are not, they will not be enforceable except in certain exceptional circumstances.

▌ Interpretation of Contracts

Common law rules of contract interpretation have evolved over time to provide the courts with guidelines for determining the meaning of contracts.

The Plain Meaning Rule

When the writing is clear and unequivocal, a court will enforce it according to its plain terms (what is clearly stated in the contract), and there is no need for the court to interpret the language of the contract. The meaning of the terms must be determined from *the face of the instrument*—from the written document alone. This is sometimes referred to as the *plain meaning rule*. Under this rule, if a contract's words appear to be clear and unambiguous, a court cannot consider *extrinsic evidence*, which is any evidence not contained in the document itself. Admissibility of extrinsic evidence can significantly affect how a court may interpret ambiguous contractual provisions and thus the outcome of litigation.

Other Rules of Interpretation

When the writing contains ambiguous or unclear terms, a court will interpret the language to give effect to the parties' intent *as expressed in their contract*. This is the primary purpose of the rules of interpretation—to determine the parties' intent from the language used in their agreement and to give effect to that intent. A court normally will not make or remake a contract, nor will it normally interpret the language according to what the parties *claim* their intent was when they made it. The following rules are used by the courts in interpreting ambiguous contractual terms:

1. Insofar as possible, a reasonable, lawful, and effective meaning will be given to all of a contract's terms.
2. A contract will be interpreted as a whole; individual, specific clauses will be considered subordinate to the contract's general intent. All writings that are a part of the same transaction will be interpreted together.
3. Terms that were the subject of separate negotiation will be given greater consideration than standardized terms and terms that were not negotiated separately.
4. A word will be given its ordinary, commonly accepted meaning, and a technical word or term will be given its technical meaning, unless the parties clearly intended something else.
5. Specific and exact wording will be given greater consideration than general language.
6. Written or typewritten terms prevail over preprinted terms.
7. Because a contract should be drafted in clear and unambiguous language, a party who uses ambiguous expressions is held to be responsible for the ambiguities. Thus, when the language has more than one meaning, it will be interpreted against the party who drafted the contract.
8. Evidence of trade usage, prior dealing, and course of performance may be admitted to clarify the meaning of an ambiguously worded contract. (We define and discuss these terms in Chapter 13.) What each of the parties does pursuant to the contract will be interpreted as consistent with what the other does and with any relevant usage of trade and course of dealing or performance. Express terms (terms expressly stated in the contract) are given the greatest weight, followed by course of performance, course of dealing, and usage of trade—in that

order. When considering custom and usage, a court will look at the trade customs and usage common to the particular business or industry and to the locale in which the contract was made or is to be performed.

Plain Language Laws

To avoid disputes over contract interpretation, business managers should make sure that their intentions are clearly expressed in their contracts. A Harvard Law School study indicated that approximately one-fourth of all contract disputes resulted from poorly worded contracts.[4] Careful drafting of

contracts not only helps prevent potential disputes over the meaning of certain terms but also may be crucial if the firm brings or needs to defend against a lawsuit for breach of contract.

In the interests of helping consumers, as well as easing the work of the courts, the government has been active in the push for more clearly written legal contracts by enacting "plain language laws." These laws deal with private contracts in their entirety. Plain language laws attempt to reach a broad variety of consumer agreements relating to personal, family, and household matters, including residential leases.

---

4.   Rick Schmitt, "Law Schools, Firms Sending a Message: Polish Your Prose," *The Wall Street Journal*, August 28, 1995, p. B6.

▌ Terms and Concepts

bilateral contract 150
contract 149
executed contract 154
executory contract 154
express contract 151
formal contract 154
implied-in-fact contract 151

informal contract 154
objective theory of
    contracts 149
offeree 150
offeror 150
promise 148
promisee 149

promisor 149
quasi contract 151
unenforceable contract 155
unilateral contract 150
valid contract 154
void contract 154
voidable contract 155

▌ Chapter Summary: Nature and Classification

The Function of Contracts *(See page 149.)*	Contract law establishes what kinds of promises will be legally binding and supplies procedures for enforcing legally binding promises, or agreements.
Requirements of a Contract *(See pages 149–150.)*	1. *Elements of a valid contract*—Agreement, consideration, contractual capacity, and legality. 2. *Possible defenses to the enforcement of a contract*—Genuineness of assent and form.
Types of Contracts *(See pages 150–155.)*	1. *Bilateral*—A promise for a promise. 2. *Unilateral*—A promise for an act (acceptance is the completed—or substantial—performance of the act). 3. *Express*—Formed by words (oral, written, or a combination). 4. *Implied in fact*—Formed by the conduct of the parties. 5. *Quasi contract (contract implied in law)*—Imposed by law to prevent unjust enrichment.

▌ Chapter Summary: Nature and Classification—Continued

Types of Contracts—Continued	6. *Formal*—Requires a special form for creation. 7. *Informal*—Requires no special form for creation. 8. *Executed*—A fully performed contract. 9. *Executory*—A contract not yet fully performed. 10. *Valid*—The contract has the necessary contractual elements of offer and acceptance, consideration, parties with legal capacity, and having been made for a legal purpose. 11. *Void*—No contract exists, or there is a contract without legal obligations. 12. *Voidable*—One party has the option of avoiding or enforcing the contractual obligation. 13. *Unenforceable*—A contract exists, but it cannot be enforced because of a legal defense.
Interpretation of Contracts *(See pages 155–156.)*	When the terms of a contract are unambiguous, a court will enforce the contract according to its plain terms, the meaning of which must be determined from the written document alone. (Plain language laws enacted by the federal government and the majority of the states require contracts to be clearly written and easily understandable.) When the terms of a contract are ambiguous, the following rules are used by the courts in interpreting the terms: 1. A reasonable, lawful, and effective meaning will be given to all contract terms. 2. A contract will be interpreted as a whole, specific clauses will be considered subordinate to the contract's general intent, and all writings that are a part of the same transaction will be interpreted together. 3. Terms that were negotiated separately will be given greater consideration than standardized terms and terms not negotiated separately. 4. Words will be given their commonly accepted meanings and technical words their technical meanings, unless the parties clearly intended otherwise. 5. Specific wording will be given greater consideration than general language. 6. Written or typewritten terms prevail over preprinted terms. 7. A party who uses ambiguous expressions is held to be responsible for the ambiguities. 8. Evidence of prior dealing, course of performance, or usage of trade is admissible to clarify an ambiguously worded contract. In these circumstances, express terms are given the greatest weight, followed by course of performance, course of dealing, and usage of trade—in that order.

▌ For Review

1. What is a contract? What is the objective theory of contracts?

2. What are the four basic elements necessary to the formation of a valid contract?

3. What is the difference between an implied-in-fact contract and an implied-in-law contract (quasi contract)?

4. What is a void contract? How does it differ from a voidable contract? What is an unenforceable contract?

5. What rules guide the courts in interpreting contracts?

▌Questions and Case Problems

7–1. Express versus Implied Contracts. Suppose that McDougal, a local businessperson, is a good friend of Krunch, the owner of a local candy store. Every day at his lunch hour McDougal goes into Krunch's candy store and spends about five minutes looking at the candy. After examining Krunch's candy and talking with Krunch, McDougal usually buys one or two candy bars. One afternoon, McDougal goes into Krunch's candy shop, looks at the candy, and picks up a $1 candy bar. Seeing that Krunch is very busy, he waves the candy bar at Krunch without saying a word and walks out. Is there a contract? If so, classify it within the categories presented in this chapter.

7–2. Contractual Promises. Rosalie, a wealthy widow, invited an acquaintance, Jonathan, to her home for dinner. Jonathan accepted the offer and, eager to please her, spent lavishly in preparing for the evening. His purchases included a new blazer, new shoes, an expensive floral arrangement, and champagne. On the appointed evening, Jonathan arrived at Rosalie's house only to find that she had left for the evening. Jonathan wants to sue Rosalie to recover some of his expenses. Can he? Why or why not?

7–3. Contract Classification. Jennifer says to her neighbor, Gordon, "If you mow my lawn, I'll pay you $25." Gordon orally accepts her offer. Is there a contract? If so, is it a bilateral or a unilateral contract? What is the legal significance of the distinction?

7–4. Contract Classification. High-Flying Advertising, Inc., contracted with Big Burger Restaurants to fly an advertisement above the Connecticut beaches. The advertisement offered $5,000 to any person who could swim from the Connecticut beaches to Long Island across the Long Island Sound in less than a day. McElfresh saw the streamer and accepted the challenge. He started his marathon swim that same day at 10 A.M. After he had been swimming for four hours and was about halfway across the sound, McElfresh saw another plane pulling a streamer that read, "Big Burger revokes." Is there a contract between McElfresh and Big Burger? If there is a contract, what type(s) of contract is (are) formed?

7–5. Equitable Doctrines. Ashton Co., which was engaged in a construction project, leased a crane from Artukovich & Sons, Inc., and hired the Reliance Truck Co. to deliver the crane to the construction site. Reliance, while the crane was in its possession and without permission from either Ashton or Artukovich, used the crane to install a transformer for a utility company, which paid Reliance for the job. Reliance then delivered the crane to the Ashton construction site at the appointed time of delivery. When Artukovich learned of

the unauthorized use of the crane by Reliance, it sued Reliance for damages. What equitable doctrine could be used as a basis for awarding damages to Artukovich? [*Artukovich & Sons, Inc. v. Reliance Truck Co.*, 126 Ariz. 246, 614 P.2d 327 (1980)]

7–6. Bilateral versus Unilateral Contracts. William Greene began working for Grant Building, Inc., in 1959. Greene allegedly agreed to work at a pay rate below union scale in exchange for a promise that Grant would employ him "for life." In 1975, Oliver Realty, Inc., took over the management of Grant Building. Oliver Realty's president assured former Grant employees that existing employment contracts would be honored. During that same year, Greene explained the terms of his agreement to an Oliver Realty supervisor. The supervisor stated that he would look into the matter but never got back to Greene. After twenty-four years of service, Greene was fired by the new owners of the business. Greene sued Oliver Realty for breach of a unilateral contract. Discuss fully whether Greene and Oliver Realty had a unilateral contract. [*Greene v. Oliver Realty, Inc.*, 363 Pa.Super. 534, 526 A.2d 1192 (1987)]

7–7. Recovery for Services Rendered. Sosa Crisan, an eighty-seven-year-old widow, collapsed while shopping at a local grocery store. The Detroit police took her to the Detroit city hospital by ambulance. She was admitted to the hospital and remained there for fourteen days. Then she was transferred to another hospital, where she died some eleven months later. Crisan had never regained consciousness after her collapse at the grocery store. After she died, the city of Detroit sued her estate to recover the expenses of both the ambulance that took her to the Detroit city hospital and her Detroit city hospital stay. Is there a contract between Sosa Crisan and the Detroit city hospital? If so, how much can the hospital recover? [*In re Estate of Crisan*, 362 Mich. 569, 107 N.W.2d 907 (1961)]

7–8. Bilateral versus Unilateral Contracts. Nichols is the principal owner of Samuel Nichols, Inc., a real estate firm. Nichols signed an exclusive brokerage agreement with Molway to find a purchaser for Molway's property within ninety days. This type of agreement entitles the broker to a commission if the property is sold to any purchaser to whom the property is shown during the ninety-day period. Molway tried to cancel the brokerage agreement before the ninety-day term had expired. Nichols had already advertised the property, put up a "for sale" sign, and shown the property to prospective buyers. Molway claimed that the brokerage contract was unilateral and that she could cancel the contract at any time before Nichols found a buyer. Nichols claimed the contract was bilateral and that Molway's cancellation breached the contract. Discuss who should prevail at trial. [*Samuel Nichols, Inc. v. Molway*, 25 Mass.App. 913, 515 N.E.2d 598 (1987)]

7–9. Recovery for Services Rendered. Garris Briggs died on October 11, 1990, leaving $782 in unpaid medical bills. Following his death, insurance checks in the amount of $676.72, payable to Briggs, were sent to his widow, Beatrice Briggs. The Briggses had been living apart for the previous five years and during that time had not had any financial connections. Under state law, a surviving spouse, upon the execution of an affidavit (a statement signed under oath) before the appropriate county official, was entitled to all of the estate's assets without administration, and the assets of the estate up to $5,000 were free from all debts of the decedent (the person who died). Garris Briggs's estate was worth less than $5,000, so Beatrice Briggs signed the necessary affidavit, cashed the checks, and deposited the funds. The physicians who had provided medical services for Garris Briggs sued the widow in a New Jersey state court to recover the insurance proceeds. Should the physicians be able to recover the proceeds? If so, under what legal theory? Explain. [*Drs. Laves, Sarewitz and Walko v. Briggs*, 259 N.J.Super. 368, 613 A.2d 506 (1992)]

7–10. Recovery for Services Rendered. After Walter Washut had suffered a heart attack and could no longer take care of himself, he asked Eleanor Adkins, a friend who had previously refused Washut's proposal to marry him, to move to his ranch. For the next twelve years, Adkins lived with Washut, although she retained ownership of her own house and continued to work full-time at her job. Adkins took care of Washut's personal needs, cooked his meals, cleaned and maintained his house, cared for the livestock, and handled other matters for Washut. According to Adkins, Washut told her on numerous occasions that "everything would be taken care of" and that she would never have to leave the ranch. After Washut's death, Adkins sought to recover in quasi contract for the value of the services she had rendered to Washut. Adkins stated in her deposition that she performed the services because she loved Washut, not because she expected to be paid for them. What will the court decide, and why? [*Adkins v. Lawson*, 892 P.2d 128 (Wyo. 1995)]

▌Accessing the Internet: Fundamentals of Business Law

Within the legal interest group on the commercial service America Online, there is a subcategory on torts and contracts. If you subscribe to America Online, the key word is:

LEGAL

If you wish to partake in discussions of contract law and the teaching of contract law, you can peruse a news group about contracts, provided you subscribe to it. To subscribe by E-mail, contact

listserv@austin.onu.edu

Subject: **<anything>**

Message: **Subscribe Contracts <Your Name>**

The 'Lectric Law Library provides information on contract law, including a definition of a contract, the elements required for a contract, and so on. Go to

http://www.lectlaw.com

Then go to the Laypeople's Law Lounge, and scroll down to Contracts.

Findlaw's directory of law-related Web sites offers numerous links to aspects of contract law. Findlaw's URL is

http://findlaw.com/

Look in their index of legal subjects for Contracts, and you will find information ranging from a "Layman's Guide to Drafting and Signing Contracts" to contract law in cyberspace to sample contract forms.

The Law Office's URL is

http://www.thelawoffice.com/

Select the topic of Business Law from the USA Legal Topics list in the left-hand column. Go to Guide to Business Law and then to Contracts.

Law Guru, which allows you to access more than 160 legal search engines and indexes from a single location, can lead you to other sources on contract law. Go to

http:lawguru.com/lawlinks.html

Cornell University's School of Law provides links to online sources of law, including contract law, at

http://www.law.cornell.edu/topics/contracts.html

If you want to do further searching, try the Internet addresses provided in Chapter 1's *Accessing the Internet* feature for general sources of American law. Many of them include links to contract law sources. As mentioned in the *Accessing the Internet* section at the end of Chapter 3, decisions of the courts in several states are now online. Refer to that section for the URLs to use to access relevant sites.

Chapter 8

Agreement and Consideration

CHAPTER OBJECTIVES

After reading this chapter, you should be able to:

1. Identify the elements of contractual agreement.
2. State the requirements of an offer.
3. Describe how an offer can be accepted.
4. List and define the elements of consideration.
5. Explain the circumstances in which a promise will be enforced despite a lack of consideration.

In Chapter 7, we pointed out that promises and agreements, and the knowledge that certain of those promises and agreements will be legally enforced, are essential to civilized society. The homes we live in, the food we eat, the clothes we wear, the cars we drive, the books we read, the recordings we listen to—all of these have been purchased through contractual agreements that we have made with sellers. Contract law developed over time, through the common law tradition, to meet society's need to know with certainty the kinds of promises, or contracts, that will be enforced and the point at which a valid and binding contract is formed.

For a contract to be considered valid and enforceable, the requirements listed in Chapter 7 must be met. In this chapter, we look closely at two of these requirements, *agreement* and *consideration*.

▌Agreement

An essential element for contract formation is **agreement**—the parties must agree on the terms of

the contract. Ordinarily, agreement is evidenced by two events: an *offer* and an *acceptance*. One party offers a certain bargain to another party, who then accepts that bargain.

Because words often fail to convey the precise meaning intended, the law of contracts generally adheres to the *objective theory of contracts*, as discussed in Chapter 7. Under this theory, a party's words and conduct are held to mean whatever a reasonable person in the offeree's position would think they meant. The court will give words their usual meanings even if "it were proved by twenty bishops that [the] party . . . intended something else."[1]

---

1. Judge Learned Hand in *Hotchkiss v. National City Bank of New York*, 200 F. 287 (2d Cir. 1911), aff'd 231 U.S. 50, 34 S.Ct. 20, 58 L.Ed. 115 (1913). (The term *aff'd* is an abbreviation for *affirmed*; an appellate court can affirm a lower court's judgment, decree, or order, thereby declaring that it is valid and must stand as rendered.)

Requirements of the Offer

An **offer** is a promise or commitment to perform or refrain from performing some specified act in the future. As discussed in Chapter 7, the party making an offer is called the *offeror,* and the party to whom the offer is made is called the *offeree.*

Three elements are necessary for an offer to be effective:

1. There must be a *serious, objective intention* by the offeror.
2. The terms of the offer must be reasonably *certain,* or *definite,* so that the parties and the court can ascertain the terms of the contract.
3. The offer must be communicated to the offeree.

Once an effective offer has been made, the offeree has the power to accept the offer. If the offeree accepts, the offer is translated into an agreement (and into a contract, if other essential elements are present).

INTENTION   The first requirement for an effective offer to exist is a serious, objective intention on the part of the offeror. Intent is not determined by the *subjective* intentions, beliefs, or assumptions of the offeror. Rather, it is determined by what a reasonable person in the offeree's position would conclude the offeror's words and actions meant. Offers made in obvious anger, jest, or undue excitement do not meet the serious-and-objective-intent test. Because these offers are not effective, an offeree's acceptance does not create an agreement.

For example, you and three classmates ride to school each day in Julio's new automobile, which has a market value of $18,000. One cold morning the four of you get into the car, but Julio cannot get it started. He yells in anger, "I'll sell this car to anyone for $500!" You drop $500 in his lap. A reasonable person, taking into consideration Julio's frustration and the obvious difference in value between the car's market price and the purchase price, would declare that Julio's offer was not made with serious and objective intent and that you do not have an agreement. The concept of intention can be further explained by distinctions between offers and nonoffers.

Expressions of Opinion   An expression of opinion is not an offer. It does not evidence an inten-

tion to enter into a binding agreement. In *Hawkins v. McGee,*[2] for example, Hawkins took his son to McGee, a doctor, and asked McGee to operate on the son's hand. McGee said that the boy would be in the hospital three or four days and that the hand would *probably* heal a few days later. The son's hand did not heal for a month, but nonetheless the father did not win a suit for breach of contract. The court held that McGee did not make an offer to heal the son's hand in three or four days. He merely expressed an opinion as to when the hand would heal.

Statements of Intention   If Ari says "I *plan* to sell my stock in Novation, Inc., for $150 per share," a contract is not created if John "accepts" and tenders the $150 per share for the stock. Ari has merely expressed his intention to enter into a future contract for the sale of the stock. If John accepts and tenders the $150 per share, no contract is formed, because a reasonable person would conclude that Ari was only *thinking about* selling his stock, not promising to sell it.

Preliminary Negotiations   A request or invitation to negotiate is not an offer; it only expresses a willingness to discuss the possibility of entering into a contract. Examples are statements such as "Will you sell Forest Acres?" and "I wouldn't sell my car for less than $1,000." A reasonable person in the offeree's position would not conclude that such a statement evidenced an intention to enter into a binding obligation. Likewise, when the government and private firms need to have construction work done, contractors are invited to submit bids. The *invitation* to submit bids is not an offer, and a contractor does not bind the government or private firm by submitting a bid. (The bids that the contractors submit are offers, however, and the government or private firm can bind the contractor by accepting the bid.)

In the following case, the court addressed the question of whether a letter informing several people that a cottage was for sale was an offer or merely a preliminary negotiation.

---

2.   84 N.H. 114, 146 A. 641 (1929).

CASE 8.1

Mellen v. Johnson

Supreme Judicial Court
of Massachusetts, 1948.
322 Mass. 236,
76 N.E.2d 658.

FACTS Johnson, who owned a three-bedroom cottage in Nahant, Massachusetts, sent a letter to Mellen saying that he was putting the cottage on the market. Earlier, Mellen had expressed an interest in purchasing the cottage. The letter indicated that several other people, who had also expressed an interest in purchasing the property, were being informed by letter of its availability at the same time. Mellen, interpreting the letter as an offer, promptly accepted. Johnson sold the property to a higher bidder, and Mellen sued Johnson in a Massachusetts state court. The court found that the letter was an offer and ordered Johnson to convey the property to Mellen upon Mellen's payment of the purchase price. Johnson appealed.

ISSUE Was Johnson's letter to Mellen an offer?

DECISION No. The Supreme Judicial Court of Massachusetts (that state's highest court) reversed the lower court's decision. The letter did not constitute an offer.

REASON The court held that the letter merely expressed Johnson's desire to sell the property and thus was not an offer but instead an attempt to negotiate. Because the letter announced that Johnson was sending the same letter to other people, Mellen "could not reasonably understand this to be more than an attempt at negotiation. It was a mere request or suggestion that an offer be made to the defendant [Johnson]."

FOR CRITICAL ANALYSIS—Social Consideration *How can the kind of confusion that arose in this case be prevented? Is it enough to say to prospective purchasers that other parties have also been informed that certain property is for sale?*

Advertisements, Catalogues, and Circulars In general, mail-order catalogues, price lists, and circular letters (meant for the general public) are treated not as offers to contract but as invitations to negotiate.[3] Suppose that Tartop & Company advertises a used paving machine. The ad is mailed to hundreds of firms and reads, "Used Case Construction Co. paving machine. Builds curbs and finishes cement work all in one process. Price $11,250." If General Paving, Inc., calls Tartop and says, "We accept your offer," no contract is formed. A reasonable person must conclude that Tartop was not promising to sell the paving machine but rather was soliciting offers to purchase it, because the seller never has an unlimited supply of goods. If advertisements were offers, then everyone who

"accepted" after the retailer's supply was exhausted could sue for breach of contract.

Consider another example. You put an ad in the classified section of your local newspaper offering to sell your guitar for $75. Seven people call and "accept" your "offer" before you can remove the ad from the newspaper. If the ad were truly an offer, you would be bound by seven contracts to sell your guitar. Because *initial* advertisements are treated as *invitations* to make offers rather than offers, however, you would have seven offers to choose from, and you could accept the best one without incurring any liability for the six you rejected. On rare occasions, though, courts have construed advertisements to be offers because the ads contained such definite terms.

Price lists are another form of invitation to negotiate or trade. A seller's price list is not an offer to sell at that price; it merely invites the buyer to

---

3. *Restatement (Second) of Contracts,* Section 26, Comment b.

offer to buy at that price. In fact, the seller usually puts "prices subject to change" on the price list. Only in rare circumstances will a price quotation be construed as an offer.[4]

Auctions   In an auction, a seller "offers" goods for sale through an auctioneer. This is not, however, an offer for purposes of contract. The seller is really only expressing a willingness to sell. Unless the terms of the auction are explicitly stated to be *without reserve*, the seller (through the auctioneer) may withdraw the goods at any time before the auctioneer closes the sale by announcement or by fall of the hammer. The seller's right to withdraw the goods characterizes an auction *with reserve*; all auctions are assumed to be of this type unless a clear statement to the contrary is made.[5] At auctions without reserve, the goods cannot be withdrawn and must be sold to the highest bidder.

In an auction with reserve, there is no obligation to sell, and the seller may refuse the highest bid. The bidder is actually the offeror. Before the auctioneer strikes the hammer, which constitutes acceptance of the bid, a bidder may revoke his or her bid, or the auctioneer may reject that bid or all bids. Typically, an auctioneer will reject a bid that is below the price the seller is willing to accept. When the auctioneer accepts a higher bid, he or she rejects all previous bids. Because rejection terminates an offer (as will be pointed out later), those bids represent offers that have been terminated. Thus, if the highest bidder withdraws his or her bid before the hammer falls, none of the previous bids is reinstated. If the bid is not withdrawn or rejected, the contract is formed when the auctioneer announces, "Going once, going twice, sold!" (or something similar) and lets the hammer fall.

In auctions with reserve, the seller may reserve the right to confirm or reject the sale even after the "hammer has fallen." In this situation, the seller is obligated to notify those attending the auction that sales of goods made during the auction are not final until confirmed by the seller. The following case illustrates this point.

---

4.   See, for example, *Fairmount Glass Works v. Grunden-Martin Woodenware Co.*, 106 Ky. 659, 51 S.W. 196 (1899).
5.   See UCC 2–328.

CASE 8.2

Lawrence Paper Co. v. Rosen & Co.

United States Court of Appeals, Sixth Circuit, 1991.
939 F.2d 376.

FACTS   This dispute arose when some equipment, which had been used as security for a loan obtained by North Coast Corrugator Company from Ameritrust Company, was sold at auction to satisfy North Coast's debt to Ameritrust. Ameritrust Company employed Rosen & Company to conduct the sale. Included in Rosen's extensive advertisements of the sale was the announcement that the sale was subject to confirmation by Ameritrust. The auctioneer made a similar announcement at the time of the sale. Sixty bidders attended the auction. The auctioneer first offered the equipment in bulk, but only one bid—from Alpine Company for $50,000—was received. Then the equipment was offered piecemeal, and total bids of $139,000 were received. Two bids from Lawrence Paper Company and American Corrugated Machine Corporation (ACMC) were accepted, and both companies submitted checks for 25 percent of their bid totals, as requested. After the auction, Alpine offered $175,000 for the equipment, and Ameritrust sold the entire lot to Alpine. Lawrence and ACMC sued in a federal district court for breach of contract. The trial judge dismissed the suit, and the plaintiffs appealed.

ISSUE   Did contracts exist between Rosen and Lawrence and between Rosen and ACMC as a result of the auctioneer's acceptance of the two companies' bids?

Case 8.2—Continued

DECISION   No. The district court's decision was affirmed.

REASON   The district court judge had found that the auction was clearly "with reserve" and therefore there was "no acceptance of the bid, because the sale was not confirmed by the secured party." The appellate court agreed, concluding that "there was no binding contract and the sellers were free to accept the subsequent offer." The court stated that "where a sale is with reserve and subject to 'confirmation' by the seller, the bids are subject to rejection after the sale, even though accepted by the auctioneer."

FOR CRITICAL ANALYSIS—Ethical Consideration   *Are auctions with reserve unfair to the bidders, whose bids and partial payments toward the purchase prices of the items being sold may be freely ignored later by the seller?*

Agreements to Agree   Traditionally, agreements to agree—that is, agreements to agree to a material term of a contract at some future date—were not considered to be binding contracts. More recent cases illustrate the view that agreements to agree serve valid commercial purposes and often can be enforced if the parties clearly intended to be bound by the agreements. For example, suppose that Zahn Consulting leases office space from Leon Properties, Inc. Their lease agreement includes a clause permitting Zahn to extend the lease at an amount of rent to be agreed on when the lease is extended. Under the traditional rule, because the amount of rent was not specified in the lease clause itself, the clause would be too indefinite in its terms to be enforced. Under the modern view, a court could hold that the parties intended the future rent to be a reasonable amount and could enforce the clause.[6]

In other words, under the modern view, the emphasis is on the parties' intent rather than on form. For example, when the Pennzoil Company discussed with the Getty Oil Company the possible purchase of Getty's stock, a memorandum of agreement was drafted to reflect the terms of the conversations. After more negotiations over the price, both companies issued press releases announcing an agreement in principle on the terms of the memorandum. The next day, Texaco, Inc., offered to buy all Getty's stock at a higher price. The day after that, Getty's board of directors voted to accept Texaco's offer, and Texaco and Getty signed a merger agreement. When Pennzoil sued Texaco for tortious interference with its "contractual" relationship with Getty, a jury concluded that Getty and Pennzoil had intended to form a binding contract before Texaco made its offer, with only the details left to be worked out. Texaco was held liable for wrongfully interfering with this contract.[7]

DEFINITENESS   The second requirement for an effective offer involves the definiteness of its terms. An offer must have reasonably definite terms so that a court can determine if a breach has occurred and give an appropriate remedy.[8]

An offer may invite an acceptance to be worded in such specific terms that the contract is made definite. For example, suppose that Marcus Business Machines contacts your corporation and

---

6.   *Restatement (Second) of Contracts*, Section 33. See also UCC 2–204, 2–305.

7.   *Texaco, Inc. v. Pennzoil Co.*, 729 S.W.2d 768 (Tex.App—Houston [1st Dist.] 1987, writ ref'd n.r.e.). (Generally, a complete Texas court of appeals citation includes the writ-of-error history showing the Texas Supreme Court's disposition of the case. In this case, *writ ref'd n.r.e.* is an abbreviation for "writ refused, no reversible error," which means that Texas's highest court refused to grant the appellant's request to review the case, because the court did not consider there to be any reversible error.)

8.   *Restatement (Second) of Contracts*, Section 33. The UCC has relaxed the requirements regarding the definitiveness of terms in contracts for the sale of goods. See UCC 2–204(3).

offers to sell "from one to ten MacCool copying machines for $1,600 each; state number desired in acceptance." Your corporation agrees to buy two copiers. Because the quantity is specified in the acceptance, the terms are definite, and the contract is enforceable.

Definiteness is also required when a contract is modified. The terms of a contract as modified must be reasonably definite so that a court can determine if there has been a breach. The following case illustrates this point.

CASE 8.3
Ruud v. Great Plains Supply, Inc.
Supreme Court of
Minnesota, 1995.
526 N.W.2d 369.

FACTS   The corporate manual of Great Plains Supply, Inc., states that employees can be discharged at any time for any reason. This manual constitutes an employment contract between GPS and its employees. Kevin Ruud was a store manager for GPS. Before accepting an offer to transfer to an unprofitable store, he expressed worries about job security to Michael Wigley, GPS's owner, and Ronald Nelson, a GPS vice president. Wigley and Nelson each responded, "Good employees are taken care of." Ruud accepted the transfer, but when the store closed as he had feared, he was offered only lesser jobs at lower pay. Ruud quit his job and filed a suit in a Minnesota state court against GPS, Wigley, and Nelson for, among other things, breach of contract. Ruud alleged that their statements modified the terms of his contract with GPS to include permanent employment. The court dismissed the claims against Wigley and Nelson and granted GPS's motion for summary judgment. Ruud appealed, and the appellate court reversed the trial court's summary judgment on the issue. The case was then appealed to the state supreme court.

ISSUE   Were the statements of Wigley and Nelson sufficiently definite to modify the terms of Ruud's employment contract?

DECISION   No. The Supreme Court of Minnesota reinstated the order for summary judgment in favor of GPS.

REASON   The state supreme court interpreted the statements of Wigley and Nelson as "policy statements as to the general goodwill of the company toward Kevin Ruud and its other employees." Even if there was an intent to modify the terms of Ruud's contract, the court concluded that the statements were "so vague as to leave undeterminable the nature of that modification."

FOR CRITICAL ANALYSIS—Ethical Consideration   *Are there any circumstances under which an employer would intend to make a promise of permanent employment to any prospective or actual employee?*

COMMUNICATION   A third requirement for an effective offer is communication, resulting in the offeree's knowledge of the offer. Suppose that Tolson advertises a reward for the return of her lost cat. Dirlik, not knowing of the reward, finds the cat and returns it to Tolson. Ordinarily, Dirlik cannot recover the reward, because an essential element of a reward contract is that the one who claims the reward must have known it was offered. A few states would allow recovery of the reward, but not on contract principles—Dirlik would be allowed to recover on the basis that it would be unfair to deny him the reward just because he did not know about it. The following case is one of the classic reward suits in common law.

CASE 8.4

Glover v. Jewish War Veterans of the United States, Post No. 58

Municipal Court of Appeals for the District of Columbia, 1949. 68 A.2d 233.

FACTS The Jewish War Veterans of the United States placed in the newspaper an offer of a reward of $500 "to the person or persons furnishing information resulting in the apprehension and conviction of the persons guilty of the murder of Maurice L. Bernstein." Mary Glover gave police information that led to the arrest and conviction of the murderers, not knowing that a reward had been offered and not learning of it until the next day. In an action brought before a District of Columbia trial court, the court held that no contract existed because Mary Glover did not know about the reward at the time she gave the police the information. Glover appealed.

ISSUE Does a contract between Glover and the Jewish War Veterans exist, given the fact that Glover did not know of the reward when she delivered the requested information?

DECISION No. The appellate court affirmed the trial court's judgment. Glover's act did not constitute an acceptance, because she did not act in response to the offer.

REASON Glover was not entitled to the $500 reward because she was not aware of the nongovernmental offer when she gave the police the information. The *Restatement of the Law of Contracts* says: "It is impossible that there should be an acceptance unless the offeree knows of the existence of the offer."

FOR CRITICAL ANALYSIS—Political Consideration *With respect to awards offered by the government, should it be assumed by the government that members of the public have knowledge of government actions and that members of the public should receive government rewards without further proof of knowledge?*

Termination of the Offer

The communication of an effective offer to an offeree gives the offeree the power to transform the offer into a binding, legal obligation (a contract) by an acceptance. This power of acceptance, however, does not continue forever. It can be terminated by *action of the parties* or by *operation of law*.

TERMINATION BY ACTION OF THE PARTIES An offer can be terminated by the action of the parties in any of three ways: by revocation, by rejection, or by counteroffer.

Revocation of the Offer The offeror's act of withdrawing an offer is referred to as **revocation.** Unless an offer is irrevocable, the offeror usually can revoke the offer (even if he or she has promised to keep the offer open), as long as the revocation is

communicated to the offeree before the offeree accepts. Revocation may be accomplished by express repudiation of the offer (for example, with a statement such as "I withdraw my previous offer of October 17") or by performance of acts inconsistent with the existence of the offer, which are made known to the offeree.

For example, Geraldine offers to sell some land to Gary. A week passes, and Gary, who has not yet accepted the offer, learns from his friend Konstantine that Geraldine has in the meantime sold the property to Nunan. Gary's knowledge of Geraldine's sale of the land to Nunan, even though Gary learned of it through a third party, effectively revokes Geraldine's offer to sell the land to Gary. Geraldine's sale of the land to Nunan is inconsistent with the continued existence of the offer to Gary, and thus the offer to Gary is revoked.

The general rule followed by most states is that a revocation becomes effective when the offeree or offeree's agent (a person who acts on behalf of another) actually receives it. Therefore, a letter of revocation mailed on April 1 and delivered at the offeree's residence or place of business on April 3 becomes effective on April 3.

An offer made to the general public can be revoked in the same manner the offer was originally communicated. Suppose that a department store offers a $10,000 reward to anyone giving information leading to the apprehension of the persons who burglarized its downtown store. The offer is published in three local papers and four papers in neighboring communities. To revoke the offer, the store must publish the revocation in all seven papers for the same number of days it published the offer. The revocation is then accessible to the general public, and the offer is revoked even if some particular offeree does not know about it.

Irrevocable Offers   Although most offers are revocable, some can be made irrevocable. Increasingly, courts refuse to allow an offeror to revoke an offer when the offeree has changed position because of justifiable reliance on the offer (under the doctrine of detrimental reliance, or promissory estoppel, discussed later in the chapter). In some circumstances, "firm offers" made by merchants may also be considered irrevocable. We discuss these offers in Chapter 13.

Another form of irrevocable offer is an option contract. An **option contract** is created when an offeror promises to hold an offer open for a specified period of time in return for a payment (consideration) given by the offeree. An option contract takes away the offeror's power to revoke an offer for the period of time specified in the option. If no time is specified, then a reasonable period of time is implied. For example, suppose that you are in the business of writing movie scripts. Your agent contacts the head of development at New Line Cinema and offers to sell New Line your new movie script. New Line likes your script and agrees to pay you $5,000 for a six-month option. In this situation, you (through your agent) are the offeror, and New Line is the offeree. You cannot revoke your offer to sell New Line your script for the next six months. If after six months no contract has been formed, however, New Line loses the $5,000, and you are free to sell the script to another firm.

Option contracts are also frequently used in conjunction with the sale of real estate. For example, you might agree with a landowner to lease a home and include in the lease contract a clause stating that you will pay $2,000 for an option to purchase the home within a specified period of time. If you decide not to purchase the home after the specified period has lapsed, you forfeit the $2,000, and the landlord is free to sell the property to another buyer.

Rejection of the Offer by the Offeree   The offer may be rejected by the offeree, in which case the offer is terminated. Any subsequent attempt by the offeree to accept will be construed as a new offer, giving the original offeror (now the offeree) the power of acceptance. A rejection is ordinarily accomplished by words or by conduct evidencing an intent not to accept the offer.

As with revocation, rejection of an offer is effective only when it is actually received by the offeror or the offeror's agent. Suppose that Growgood Farms mails a letter to Campbell Soup Company offering to sell carrots at ten cents a pound. Campbell Soup Company could reject the offer by sending or faxing a letter to Growgood Farms expressly rejecting the offer, or by mailing the offer back to Growgood, evidencing an intent to reject it. Alternatively, Campbell could offer to buy the carrots at eight cents per pound (a counteroffer), necessarily rejecting the original offer.

Merely inquiring about the offer does not constitute rejection. For example, a friend offers to buy your CD-ROM library for $300. You respond, "Is this your best offer?" or "Will you pay me $375 for it?" A reasonable person would conclude that you did not reject the offer but merely made an inquiry for further consideration of the offer. You can still accept and bind your friend to the $300 purchase price. When the offeree merely inquires as to the firmness of the offer, there is no reason to presume that he or she intends to reject it.

Counteroffer by the Offeree   A **counteroffer** is a rejection of the original offer and the simultaneous making of a new offer. Suppose that Burke offers to sell his home to Lang for $170,000. Lang responds, "Your price is too high. I'll offer to purchase your house for $165,000." Lang's response is termed a counteroffer because it rejects Burke's offer to sell at $170,000 and creates a new offer by Lang to purchase the home at a price of $165,000.

At common law, the **mirror image rule** requires that the offeree's acceptance match the offeror's offer exactly. In other words, the terms of the acceptance must "mirror" those of the offer. If the acceptance materially changes or adds to the terms of the original offer, it will be considered not an acceptance but a counteroffer—which, of course, need not be accepted. The original offeror can, however, accept the terms of the counteroffer and create a valid contract.[9]

TERMINATION BY OPERATION OF LAW The offeree's power to transform an offer into a binding, legal obligation can be terminated by operation of the law if any of four conditions occur: lapse of time, destruction of the subject matter, death or incompetence of the offeror or offeree, or supervening illegality of the proposed contract.

Lapse of Time An offer terminates automatically by law when the period of time specified in the offer has passed. For example, Jane offers to sell her boat to Jonah if he accepts within twenty days. Jonah must accept within the twenty-day period, or the offer will lapse (terminate). The time period specified in an offer normally begins to run when the offer is actually received by the offeree, not when it is drawn up or sent. When the offer is delayed (through the misdelivery of mail, for example), the period begins to run from the date the offeree would have received the offer, but only if the offeree knows or should know that the offer is delayed.[10] For example, if Jane used improper postage when mailing the offer to Jonah, and Jonah knew about the improper mailing, the offer would lapse twenty days after the day Jonah would ordinarily have received the offer had Jane used proper postage.

If no time for acceptance is specified in the offer, the offer terminates at the end of a *reasonable* period of time. A reasonable period of time is determined by the subject matter of the contract, business and market conditions, and other relevant circumstances. An offer to sell farm produce, for example, will terminate sooner than an offer to sell farm equipment, because farm produce is perishable and subject to greater fluctuations in market value.

Destruction of the Subject Matter An offer is automatically terminated if the specific subject matter of the offer is destroyed before the offer is accepted. For example, if Bekins offers to sell his cow to Yatsen, but the cow dies before Yatsen can accept, the offer is automatically terminated.

Death or Incompetence of the Offeror or Offeree An offeree's power of acceptance is terminated when the offeror or offeree dies or is deprived of legal capacity to enter into the proposed contract, unless the offer is irrevocable.[11] An offer is personal to both parties and normally cannot pass to the decedent's heirs, guardian, or estate. This rule applies whether or not the one party had notice of the death or incompetence of the other party.

Supervening Illegality of the Proposed Contract A statute or court decision that makes an offer illegal will automatically terminate the offer. If Acme Finance Corporation offers to lend Jack $20,000 at 15 percent annually, and a state statute is enacted prohibiting loans at interest rates greater than 12 percent before Jack can accept, the offer is automatically terminated. (If the statute is enacted after Jack accepts the offer, a valid contract is formed, but the contract may still be unenforceable—see Chapter 9.)

Acceptance

An **acceptance** is a voluntary act by the offeree that shows assent, or agreement, to the terms of an offer. The offeree's act may consist of words or conduct. The acceptance must be unequivocal and must be communicated to the offeror.

WHO CAN ACCEPT? Generally, a third person cannot substitute for the offeree and effectively

---

9. The mirror image rule has been greatly modified in regard to contracts for the sale of goods. Section 2–207 of the UCC provides that a contract is formed if the offeree makes a definite expression of acceptance (such as signing the form in the appropriate location), even though the terms of the acceptance modify or add to the terms of the original offer (see Chapter 13).

10. *Restatement (Second) of Contracts*, Section 49.

---

11. *Restatement (Second) of Contracts*, Section 48. If the offer is irrevocable, it is not terminated when the offeror dies. Also, if the offer is such that it can be accepted by the performance of a series of acts, and those acts began before the offeror died, the offeree's power of acceptance is not terminated.

accept the offer. After all, the identity of the offeree is as much a condition of a bargaining offer as any other term contained therein. Thus, except in special circumstances, only the person to whom the offer is made or that person's agent can accept the offer and create a binding contract. For example, Lottie makes an offer to Paul. Paul is not interested, but Paul's friend José accepts the offer. No contract is formed.

UNEQUIVOCAL ACCEPTANCE To exercise the power of acceptance effectively, the offeree must accept unequivocally. This is the *mirror image rule* previously discussed. If the acceptance is subject to new conditions or if the terms of the acceptance materially change the original offer, the acceptance may be deemed a counteroffer that implicitly rejects the original offer.

Certain terms, when added to an acceptance, will not qualify the acceptance sufficiently to constitute rejection of the offer. Suppose that in response to a person offering to sell a painting by a

well-known artist, the offeree replies, "I accept; please send a written contract." The offeree is requesting a written contract but is not making it a condition for acceptance. Therefore, the acceptance is effective without the written contract. If the offeree replies, "I accept if you send a written contract," however, the acceptance is expressly conditioned on the request for a writing, and the statement is not an acceptance but a counteroffer. (Notice how important each word is!)[12]

The following case illustrates that the language in an offer or acceptance should be considered together. That is, a few unequivocal words or phrases should not be taken out of context and be given a meaning that they do not have.

---

12. As noted in footnote 9, in regard to sales contracts, the UCC provides that an acceptance may still be valid even if some terms are added. The new terms are simply treated as proposals for additions to the contract, or become part of the contract. See UCC 2–207(2).

CASE 8.5

Bourque v. Federal Deposit Insurance Corp.

United States Court of Appeals, First Circuit, 1994.
42 F.3d 704.

FACTS The Federal Deposit Insurance Corporation (FDIC) was selling all of the real estate owned by Newmark Investments, Inc. Raymond Bourque offered to buy a certain parcel of the property for $105,500. Curtis Cain, an FDIC account officer, responded in a letter to Bourque's attorney that "the FDIC is unable to accept Mr. Bourque's offer. FDIC's counteroffer is $130,000.00. All offers are subject to approval by the appropriate FDIC delegated authority." Bourque filled in an FDIC purchase-and-sale form to indicate a $130,000 selling price, signed it, and sent it to the FDIC. Elizabeth Carroll, another FDIC account officer, responded that the FDIC would not accept $130,000 for the property, but that Bourque could submit another offer. Bourque made no other offer, and the FDIC refused to sell the property to him. Bourque filed a suit in a federal district court against the FDIC and Newmark (the defendants) for breach of contract. The court issued a summary judgment in favor of the defendants. Bourque appealed to the U.S. Court of Appeals for the First Circuit.

ISSUE Can unequivocal language, such as the term *counteroffer* in Cain's letter to Bourque, be considered in isolation from other, qualifying language in the offer or acceptance?

DECISION No. The U.S. Court of Appeals for the First Circuit held that in the context of offers and acceptances, the qualifying language is likely to control. The court affirmed the district court's judgment.

REASON The appellate court stated that "[w]hen read as a whole, as it must be read," Cain's letter "sets forth with sufficient clarity that the recip-

Case 8.5—Continued

ient may 'accept' Cain's 'counteroffer' of $130,000, but only subject to final approval by the appropriate FDIC authority." In other words, Cain's response to Bourque's first offer was not itself an offer—even though Cain used the word "counteroffer." Instead, Cain was only inviting Bourque to make another offer. The court pointed out that Bourque made another offer, but the FDIC never accepted it, "so as a matter of law, no contract was ever formed between the parties."

FOR CRITICAL ANALYSIS—International Consideration   *If Cain had not used the word* counteroffer *in his letter, would Bourque have had any support for his argument that they had a contract? What are the implications of the importance of such terms in international deals, when more than one language is involved?*

SILENCE AS ACCEPTANCE   Ordinarily, silence cannot constitute acceptance, even if the offeror states, "By your silence and inaction, you will be deemed to have accepted this offer." This general rule applies because an offeree should not be put under a burden of liability to act affirmatively in order to reject an offer. No consideration—that is, nothing of value—has passed to the offeree to impose such a liability.

In some instances, however, the offeree does have a duty to speak, in which case his or her silence or inaction will operate as an acceptance. For example, silence may be an acceptance when an offeree takes the benefit of offered services even though he or she had an opportunity to reject them and knew that they were offered with the expectation of compensation. Suppose Jameson watches while a stranger mows her lawn, even though the stranger has not been asked to mow the lawn. Jameson knows the stranger expects to be paid and does nothing to stop him. Here, her silence constitutes an acceptance, and an implied-in-fact contract is created. She is bound to pay a reasonable value for the stranger's work. This rule normally applies only when the offeree has received a benefit from the goods or services.

Silence can also operate as acceptance when the offeree has had prior dealings with the offeror. If a merchant, for example, routinely receives shipments from a supplier and in the past has always notified the supplier of rejection of defective goods, then silence constitutes acceptance. Also, if a person solicits an offer specifying that certain terms and conditions are acceptable, and the offeror makes the offer in response to the solicitation, the offeree has a duty to reject—that is, a duty to tell the offeror that the offer is not acceptable. Failure to reject (silence) would operate as an acceptance.

COMMUNICATION OF ACCEPTANCE   Whether the offeror must be notified of the acceptance depends on the nature of the contract. In a bilateral contract, communication of acceptance is necessary, because acceptance is in the form of a promise (not performance), and the contract is formed when the promise is made (rather than when the act is performed). The offeree must communicate the acceptance to the offeror. Communication of acceptance is not necessary, however, if the offer dispenses with the requirement. Also, if the offer can be accepted by silence, no communication is necessary.[13]

Because in a unilateral contract the full performance of some act is called for, acceptance is usually evident, and notification is therefore unnecessary. Exceptions do exist, however. When the offeror requests notice of acceptance or has no adequate means of determining whether the requested act has been performed, or when the law requires such notice of acceptance, then notice is necessary.[14]

MODE AND TIMELINESS OF ACCEPTANCE   The general rule is that acceptance in a bilateral contract is timely if it is effected within the duration of

---

13.   Under the UCC, an order or other offer to buy goods that are to be promptly shipped may be treated as either a bilateral or a unilateral offer and can be accepted by a promise to ship or by actual shipment. See UCC 2–206 (1)(b).
14.   UCC 2–206(2).

the offer. Problems arise, however, when the parties involved are not dealing face to face. In such cases, the offeree may use an authorized mode of communication. Acceptance takes effect, thus completing formation of the contract, at the time the offeree sends the communication via the mode expressly or impliedly authorized by the offeror. This is the so-called **mailbox rule,** also called the "deposited acceptance rule," which the majority of courts uphold. Under this rule, if the authorized mode of communication is the mail, then an acceptance becomes valid when it is dispatched—not when it is received by the offeror. The mailbox rule was formed to prevent the confusion that arises when an offeror sends a letter of revocation but, before this letter is received by the offeree, the offeree sends a letter of acceptance. Thus, whereas a revocation becomes effective only when it is *received* by the offeree, an acceptance becomes effective upon *dispatch* (even if it is never received), providing that an *authorized* means of communication is used.

Authorized means can be either expressly authorized—that is, expressly stipulated in the offer—or impliedly authorized by facts or law.[15] When an offeror specifies how acceptance should be made (for example, by first-class mail or express delivery), *express authorization* is said to exist. Moreover, both the offeror and the offeree are bound in contract the moment that such means of acceptance are employed.

Most offerors do not specify expressly the means by which the offeree is to accept. Thus, the common law recognizes the following implied authorized means of acceptance:[16]

1.   The choice of a particular means by the offeror in making the offer implies that the offeree is authorized to use the *same* or a *faster* means for acceptance.
2.   When two parties are at a distance, *mailing* is impliedly authorized.

There are three basic exceptions to the rule that a contract is formed when acceptance is sent by authorized means:

1.   If the acceptance is not properly dispatched (if a letter is incorrectly addressed, for example, or is without the proper postage), in most states it will not be effective until it is received by the offeror.
2.   The offeror can specifically condition his or her offer upon the receipt of an acceptance by a certain time, in which case, to be effective, the acceptance must be received prior to the end of the time period.
3.   Sometimes an offeree sends a rejection first, then later changes his or her mind and sends an acceptance. Obviously, this chain of events could cause confusion and even detriment to the offeror, depending on whether the rejection or the acceptance arrived first. In such cases, the law cancels the rule of acceptance upon dispatch, and the first communication received by the offeror determines whether a contract is formed. If the rejection comes first, there is no contract.[17]

An acceptance given by means not expressly or impliedly authorized is not effective until it is received by the offeror.

Consideration and Its Requirements

In every legal system, some promises will be enforced, and some promises will not be enforced. The simple fact that a party has made a promise, then, does not mean the promise is enforceable. Under the common law, a primary basis for the enforcement of promises is consideration. **Consideration** is usually defined as the value given in return for a promise. We look here at the basic elements of consideration and then at some other contract doctrines relating to consideration.

---

15.   *Restatement (Second) of Contracts,* Section 30, provides that an offer invites acceptance "by any medium reasonable in the circumstances," unless the offer is specific about the means of acceptance. Under Section 65, a medium is reasonable if it is one used by the offeror or one customary in similar transactions, unless the offeree knows of circumstances that would argue against the reasonableness of a particular medium (the need for speed because of rapid price changes, for example).

16.   Note that under the UCC, acceptance of an offer for the sale of goods can be made by any medium that is *reasonable* under the circumstances. See UCC 2–206 (1)(a).

---

17.   *Restatement (Second) of Contracts,* Section 40.

Elements of Consideration

Often, consideration is broken down into two parts: (1) something of *legally sufficient value* must be given in exchange for the promise, and (2) there must be a *bargained-for* exchange.

LEGAL VALUE   The "something of legally sufficient value" may consist of (1) a promise to do something that one has no prior legal duty to do (to pay money on receipt of certain goods, for example), (2) the performance of an action that one is otherwise not obligated to undertake (such as providing accounting services), or (3) the refraining from an action that one has a legal right to undertake. Generally, to be legally sufficient, consideration must be either *detrimental to the promisee* or *beneficial to the promisor*. Note that legal detriment (creating, modifying, or giving up a legal right) is not the same as economic, or actual, detriment (paying money or suffering economic losses).

Consider the following example. Jerry says to his son, "When you finish painting the garage, I will pay you $100." Jerry's son paints the garage. The act of painting the garage is the consideration that creates Jerry's contractual obligation to pay his son $100. In this situation, the consideration is both detrimental to the promisee (the son) and beneficial to the promisor (Jerry). Jerry's garage was painted, and his son undertook an action that the son was not otherwise legally obligated to undertake.

BARGAINED-FOR EXCHANGE   The second element of consideration is that it must provide the basis for the bargain struck between the contracting parties. The consideration given by the promisor must induce the promisee to incur a legal detriment either now or in the future, and the detriment incurred must induce the promisor to make the promise. This element of bargained-for exchange distinguishes contracts from gifts.

For example, suppose that Jerry says to his son, "In consideration of the fact that you are not as wealthy as your brothers, I will pay you $500." This promise is not enforceable, because Jerry's son has not given any return consideration for the $500 promised.[18] The son (the promisee) incurs no legal detriment; he does not have to promise anything or

undertake (or refrain from undertaking) any action to receive the $500. Here, Jerry has simply stated his motive for giving his son a gift. The fact that the word *consideration* is used does not, alone, mean that consideration has been given.

Adequacy of Consideration

Legal sufficiency of consideration involves the requirement that consideration be something of value in the eyes of the law. Adequacy of consideration involves "how much" consideration is given. Essentially, adequacy of consideration concerns the fairness of the bargain. On the surface, fairness would appear to be an issue when the values of items exchanged are unequal. In general, however, courts do not question the adequacy of consideration if the consideration is legally sufficient. Under the doctrine of freedom of contract, parties are usually free to bargain as they wish. If people could sue merely because they had entered into an unwise contract, the courts would be overloaded with frivolous suits.

In extreme cases, however, a court of law may look to the amount or value (the adequacy) of the consideration, because apparently inadequate consideration can indicate that fraud, duress, or undue influence was involved or that a gift was made (if a father "sells" a $100,000 house to his daughter for only $1, for example). Additionally, in cases in which the consideration is grossly inadequate, the courts may declare the contract unenforceable on the ground that it is *unconscionable*[19]—that is, generally speaking, it is so one sided under the circumstances as to be overly unfair. (Unconscionability is discussed further in Chapter 9.)

Contracts That Lack Consideration

Sometimes, one of the parties (or both parties) to a contract may think that they have exchanged consideration when in fact they have not. Here we look at some situations in which the parties' promises or actions do not qualify as contractual consideration.

PREEXISTING DUTY   Under most circumstances, a promise to do what one already has a legal duty

---

18. See *Fink v. Cox*, 18 Johns. 145, 9 Am.Dec. 191 (N.Y. 1820).

19.   Pronounced un-*kon*-shun-uh-bul.

to do does not constitute legally sufficient consideration, because no legal detriment is incurred.[20] The preexisting legal duty may be imposed by law or may arise out of a previous contract. A sheriff, for example, cannot collect a reward for information leading to the capture of a criminal if the sheriff already has a legal duty to capture the criminal. Likewise, if a party is already bound by contract to perform a certain duty, that duty cannot serve as consideration for a second contract.

For example, suppose that Bauman-Bache, Inc., begins construction on a seven-story office building and after three months demands an extra $75,000 on its contract. If the extra $75,000 is not paid, it will stop working. The owner of the land, having no one else to complete construction, agrees to pay the extra $75,000. The agreement is not enforceable, because it is not supported by legally sufficient consideration; Bauman-Bache had a preexisting contractual duty to complete the building.

Unforeseen Difficulties   The rule regarding preexisting duty is meant to prevent extortion and the so-called holdup game. What happens, though, when an honest contractor, who has contracted with a landowner to build a house, runs into extraordinary difficulties that were totally unforeseen at the time the contract was formed? In the interests of fairness and equity, the courts sometimes allow exceptions to the preexisting duty rule. In the example just mentioned, if the landowner agrees to pay extra compensation to the contractor for overcoming the unforeseen difficulties, the court may refrain from applying the preexisting duty rule and enforce the agreement. When the "unforeseen difficulties" that give rise to a contract modification are the types of risks ordinarily assumed in business, however, the courts will usually assert the preexisting duty rule.[21]

Rescission and New Contract   The law recognizes that two parties can mutually agree to rescind their contract, at least to the extent that it is executory (still to be carried out). **Rescission**[22] is defined as the unmaking of a contract so as to return the parties to the positions they occupied before the contract was made. When rescission and the making of a new contract take place at the same time, the courts frequently are given a choice of applying the preexisting duty rule or allowing rescission and letting the new contract stand.

PAST CONSIDERATION   Promises made in return for actions or events that have already taken place are unenforceable. These promises lack consideration in that the element of bargained-for exchange is missing. In short, you can bargain for something to take place now or in the future but not for something that has already taken place. Therefore, **past consideration** is no consideration.

Suppose, for example, that Elsie, a real estate agent, does her friend Judy a favor by selling Judy's house and not charging any commission. Later, Judy says to Elsie, "In return for your generous act, I will pay you $3,000." This promise is made in return for past consideration and is thus unenforceable; in effect, Judy is stating her intention to give Elsie a gift.

ILLUSORY PROMISES   If the terms of the contract express such uncertainty of performance that the promisor has not definitely promised to do anything, the promise is said to be *illusory*—without consideration and unenforceable. For example, suppose that the president of Tuscan Corporation says to his employees, "All of you have worked hard, and if profits continue to remain high, a 10 percent bonus at the end of the year will be given—if management thinks it is warranted." This is an *illusory promise*, or no promise at all, because performance depends solely on the discretion of the president (the management). There is no bargained-for consideration. The statement declares merely that management may or may not do something in the future.

Option-to-cancel clauses in contracts for specified time periods sometimes present problems in regard to consideration. For example, suppose that Abe contracts to hire Chris for one year at $5,000 per month, reserving the right to cancel the con-

---

20.   See *Foakes v. Beer*, 9 App.Cas. 605 (1884).
21.   Note that under the UCC, any agreement modifying a contract within Article 2 on Sales needs no consideration to be binding. See UCC 2–209(1).

22.   Pronounced reh-*sih*-zhen.

tract at any time. On close examination of these words, you can see that Abe has not actually agreed to hire Chris, as Abe could cancel without liability before Chris started performance. Abe has not given up the opportunity of hiring someone else. This contract is therefore illusory. Now suppose that Abe contracts to hire Chris for a one-year period at $5,000 per month, reserving the right to cancel the contract at any time after Chris has begun performance by giving Chris thirty days' notice. Abe, by saying that he will give Chris thirty days' notice, is relinquishing the opportunity (legal right) to hire someone else instead of Chris for a thirty-day period. If Chris works for one month, at the end of which Abe gives him thirty days' notice, Chris has a valid and enforceable contractual claim for $10,000 in salary.

Settlement of Claims

Businesspersons or others can settle legal claims in several ways. It is important to understand the nature of consideration given in these kinds of settlement agreements, or contracts. A common means of settling a claim is through an *accord and satisfaction,* in which a debtor offers to pay a lesser amount than the creditor purports to be owed. Two other methods that are commonly used to settle claims are the release and the covenant not to sue.

ACCORD AND SATISFACTION The concept of **accord and satisfaction** deals with a debtor's offer of payment and a creditor's acceptance of a lesser amount than the creditor originally purported to be owed. The *accord* is defined as the agreement under which one of the parties undertakes to give or perform, and the other to accept, in satisfaction of a claim, something other than that which was originally agreed on. *Satisfaction* takes place when the accord is executed. Accord and satisfaction deal with an attempt by the obligor to extinguish an obligation. A basic rule is that there can be no satisfaction unless there is first an accord.

For accord and satisfaction to occur, the amount of the debt *must be in dispute.* If a debt is *liquidated,* accord and satisfaction cannot take place. A liquidated debt is one whose amount has been ascertained, fixed, agreed on, settled, or exactly determined. For example, if Baker signs an installment loan contract with her banker in which she agrees to pay a specified rate of interest on a

specified sum of borrowed money at monthly intervals for two years, that is a liquidated debt. The amount owing is precisely known to both of the parties, and reasonable persons will not differ over the amount owed. Suppose that Baker misses her last two payments on the loan and the creditor demands that she pay the overdue debt. Baker makes a partial payment and states that she believes that is all that she should have to pay and that, if the creditor accepts the payment, the debt will be satisfied, or discharged. In the majority of states, acceptance of a lesser sum than the entire amount of a liquidated debt is not satisfaction, and the balance of the debt is still legally owed. The rationale for this rule is that no consideration is given by the debtor to satisfy the obligation of paying the balance to the creditor—because the debtor has a preexisting legal obligation to pay the entire debt.

An *unliquidated debt* is the opposite of a liquidated debt. Here, reasonable persons may differ over the amount owed. It is not settled, fixed, agreed on, ascertained, or determined. In these circumstances, acceptance of payment of the lesser sum can operate as a satisfaction, or discharge, of the debt. For example, suppose that Devereaux goes to the dentist's office. The dentist tells him that he needs three special types of gold inlays. The price is not discussed, and there is no standard fee for this type of work. Devereaux leaves the office. At the end of the month, the dentist sends him a bill for $3,000. Devereaux, believing that this amount is grossly out of proportion with what a reasonable person would believe to be the debt owed, sends a check for $2,000. On the back of the check he writes "payment in full for three gold inlays." The dentist cashes the check. Because we are dealing with an unliquidated debt—the amount has not been agreed on—payment accepted by the dentist normally will eradicate the debt. One argument to support this rule is that the parties give up a legal right to contest the amount in dispute, and thus consideration is given.

RELEASE A **release** is a contract in which one party forfeits the right to pursue a legal claim against the other party. For example, suppose that you are involved in an automobile accident caused by Raoul's negligence. Raoul offers to give you $1,000 if you will release him from further liability resulting from the accident. You believe that this amount will cover your damages, so you agree to the release. Later you discover that it will cost $1,200 to repair your car.

Can you collect the balance from Raoul? The answer is normally no; you are limited to the $1,000 in the release. Why? Because a valid contract existed. You and Raoul both assented to the bargain (hence, agreement existed), and sufficient consideration was present. Your consideration for the contract was the legal detriment you suffered (by releasing Raoul from liability, you forfeited your right to sue to recover damages, should they be more than $1,000). This legal detriment was induced by Raoul's promise to give you the $1,000. Raoul's promise was, in turn, induced by your promise not to pursue your legal right to sue him for damages.

Releases will generally be binding if they are (1) given in good faith, (2) stated in a signed writing (required by many states), and (3) accompanied by consideration.[23] Clearly, persons are better off if they know the extent of their injuries or damages before signing releases.

COVENANT NOT TO SUE   A **covenant not to sue**, unlike a release, does not always bar further recovery. The parties simply substitute a contractual obligation for some other type of legal action based on a valid claim. Suppose (following the earlier example) that you agree with Raoul not to sue for damages in a tort action if he will pay for the damage to your car. If Raoul fails to pay, you can bring an action for breach of contract.

---

23.   Under the UCC, a written, signed waiver or renunciation by an aggrieved party discharges any further liability for a breach, even without consideration. See UCC 1–107.

Promises Enforceable without Consideration — Promissory Estoppel

Sometimes individuals rely on promises, and such reliance may form a basis for contract rights and duties. Under the doctrine of **promissory estoppel** (also called *detrimental reliance*), a person who has reasonably relied on the promise of another can often hope to obtain some measure of recovery. For the doctrine of promissory estoppel to be applied, the following elements are required:

1.   There must be a clear and definite promise.
2.   The promisee must justifiably rely on the promise.
3.   The reliance normally must be of a substantial and definite character.
4.   Justice will be better served by the enforcement of the promise.

Consider some examples. Your uncle tells you, "I'll pay you $150 a week so you won't have to work anymore." You quit your job, but your uncle refuses to pay you. Under the doctrine of promissory estoppel, you may be able to enforce such a promise.[24] Now your uncle makes a promise to give you $10,000 with which to buy a car. If you buy the car and he does not pay you, you may once again be able to enforce the promise under this doctrine. When the doctrine of promissory estoppel is applied, the promisor (the offeror) is **estopped** (barred, or impeded) from revoking the promise.

---

24.   *Ricketts v. Scothorn*, 57 Neb. 51, 77 N.W. 365 (1898).

▌ Terms and Concepts

acceptance 169
accord and satisfaction 175
agreement 161
consideration 172
counteroffer 168
covenant not to sue 176

estopped 176
mailbox rule 172
mirror image rule 169
offer 162
option contract 168
past consideration 174

promissory estoppel 176
release 175
rescission 174
revocation 167

▌Chapter Summary: Agreement and Consideration

AGREEMENT	
Requirements of the Offer *(See pages 162–167.)*	1. *Intent*—There must be a serious, objective intention by the offeror to become bound by the offer. Nonoffer situations include (a) expressions of opinion; (b) statements of intention; (c) preliminary negotiations; (d) generally, advertisements, catalogues, and circulars; (e) solicitations for bids made by an auctioneer; and (f) agreements to agree in the future. 2. *Definiteness*—The terms of the offer must be sufficiently definite to be ascertainable by the parties or by a court. 3. *Communication*—The offer must be communicated to the offeree.

Termination of the Offer *(See pages 167–169.)*	1. *By action of the parties*—
	  a. Revocation—Unless the offer is irrevocable, it can be revoked at any time before acceptance without liability. Revocation is not effective until received by the offeree or the offeree's agent. Some offers, such as the merchant's firm offer and option contracts, are irrevocable.
	  b. Rejection—Accomplished by words or actions that demonstrate a clear intent not to accept the offer; not effective until received by the offeror or the offeror's agent.
	  c. Counteroffer—A rejection of the original offer and the making of a new offer.
	
	2. *By operation of law*—
	  a. Lapse of time—The offer terminates (a) at the end of the time period specified in the offer or (b) if no time period is stated in the offer, at the end of a reasonable time period.
	  b. Destruction of the specific subject matter of the offer—Automatically terminates the offer.
	  c. Death or incompetence—Terminates the offer unless the offer is irrevocable.
	  d. Illegality—Supervening illegality terminates the offer.

Acceptance *(See pages 169–172.)*	1. Can be made only by the offeree or the offeree's agent.
	
	2. Must be unequivocal. Under the common law (mirror image rule), if new terms or conditions are added to the acceptance, it will be considered a counteroffer.
	
	3. Acceptance of a unilateral offer is effective upon full performance of the requested act. Generally, no communication is necessary.
	
	4. Acceptance of a bilateral offer can be communicated by the offeree by any authorized mode of communication and is effective upon dispatch. Unless the mode of communication is expressly specified by the offeror, the following methods are impliedly authorized:
	  a. The same mode used by the offeror (or a faster mode) or, in the sale of goods, any reasonable medium.
	  b. Mail, when the two parties are at a distance.

CONSIDERATION	
Elements of Consideration *(See pages 172–173.)*	Consideration is broken down into two parts: (1) something of *legally sufficient value* must be given in exchange for the promise, and (2) there must be a *bargained-for exchange*. To be legally sufficient, consideration must involve a legal detriment to the promisee, a legal benefit to the promisor, or both. One incurs a legal detriment by doing (or refraining from doing) something that one had no prior legal duty to do (or to refrain from doing).

(Continued)

▌Chapter Summary: Agreement and Consideration—Continued

Adequacy of Consideration *(See page 173.)*	Adequacy of consideration relates to "how much" consideration is given and whether a fair bargain was reached. Courts will inquire into the adequacy of consideration (if the consideration is legally sufficient) only when fraud, undue influence, duress, a gift, or unconscionability may be involved.
Contracts That Lack Consideration *(See pages 173–175.)*	Consideration is lacking in the following situations: 1. *Preexisting duty*—Consideration is not legally sufficient if one is either by law or by contract under a *preexisting duty* to perform the action being offered as consideration for a new contract. 2. *Past consideration*—Actions or events that have already taken place do not constitute legally sufficient consideration. 3. *Illusory promises*—When the nature or extent of performance is too uncertain, the promise is rendered illusory (without consideration and unenforceable).
Settlement of Claims *(See pages 175–176.)*	1. *Accord and satisfaction*—An *accord* is an agreement in which a debtor offers to pay a lesser amount than the creditor purports to be owed. *Satisfaction* takes place when the accord is executed. 2. *Release*—An agreement by which, for consideration, a party is barred from further recovery beyond the terms specified in the release. 3. *Covenant not to sue*—An agreement not to sue on a present, valid claim.
Promises Enforceable without Consideration— Promissory Estoppel *(See page 176.)*	The equitable doctrine of promissory estoppel applies when a promisor reasonably expects a promise to induce definite and substantial action or forbearance by the promisee, and the promisee does act in reliance on the promise. Such a promise is binding if injustice can be avoided only by enforcement of the promise. Also known as the doctrine of detrimental reliance.

▌For Review

1. What elements are necessary for an effective offer? What are some examples of nonoffers?
2. In what circumstances will an offer be irrevocable?
3. What elements are necessary for an effective acceptance?

4. What is consideration? What is required for consideration to be legally sufficient?
5. In what circumstances might a promise be enforced despite a lack of what is normally thought of as consideration?

▌Questions and Case Problems

8–1. Offer. Chernek, operating a sole proprietorship, has a large piece of used farm equipment for sale. He offers to sell the equipment to Bollow for $10,000. Discuss the legal effects of the following events on the offer.

(a) Chernek dies prior to Bollow's acceptance, and at the time she accepts, Bollow is unaware of Chernek's death.

(b) The night before Bollow accepts, fire destroys the equipment.

(c) Bollow pays $100 for a thirty-day option to purchase the equipment. During this period Chernek dies, and later Bollow accepts the offer, knowing of Chernek's death.

(d) Bollow pays $100 for a thirty-day option to purchase the equipment. During this period Bollow dies, and Bollow's estate accepts Chernek's offer within the stipulated time period.

8–2. Offers versus Nonoffers. On June 1, Jason placed an ad in a local newspaper, to be run on the following Sunday, June 5, offering a reward of $100 to anyone who found his wallet. When his wallet had not been returned by June 12, he purchased another wallet and took steps to obtain duplicates of his driver's license, credit cards, and other items that he had lost. On June 15, Sharith, who had seen Jason's ad in the paper, found Jason's wallet, returned it to Jason, and asked for the $100. Is Jason obligated to pay Sharith the $100? Why or why not?

8–3. Offer and Acceptance. Carrie offered to sell a set of legal encyclopedias to Antonio for $300. Antonio said that he would think about her offer and let her know his decision the next day. Norvel, who had overheard the conversation between Carrie and Antonio, said to Carrie, "I accept your offer" and gave her $300. Carrie gave Norvel the books. The next day, Antonio, who had no idea that Carrie had already sold the books to Norvel, told Carrie that he accepted her offer. Has Carrie breached a valid contract with Antonio? Explain.

8–4. Consideration. Ben hired Lewis to drive his racing car in a race. Tuan, a friend of Lewis, promised to pay Lewis $3,000 if he won the race. Lewis won the race, but Tuan refused to pay the $3,000. Tuan contended that no legally binding contract had been formed, because he had received no consideration from Lewis for his promise to pay the $3,000. Lewis sued Tuan for breach of contract, arguing that winning the race was the consideration given in exchange for Tuan's promise to pay the $3,000. What rule of law discussed in this chapter supports Tuan's claim? Explain.

8–5. Acceptance. On Saturday, Arthur mailed Tanya an offer to sell his car to her for $2,000. On Monday, having changed his mind and not having heard from Tanya, Arthur sent her a letter revoking his offer. On Wednesday, before she had received Arthur's letter of revocation, Tanya mailed a letter of acceptance to Arthur. When Tanya demanded that Arthur sell his car to her as promised, Arthur claimed that no contract existed because he had revoked his offer prior to Tanya's acceptance. Is Arthur correct? Explain.

8–6. Promissory Estoppel. Red Owl Stores, Inc., induced the Hoffmans to give up their current business and run a Red Owl franchise. Although no contract was ever signed, the Hoffmans incurred numerous expenses in reliance upon Red Owl's representations. When the deal ultimately fell through because of Red Owl's failure to keep its promise concerning the operation of the franchise agency store, the Hoffmans brought suit to recover their losses under the doctrine of promissory estoppel. What is this doctrine, and what elements must exist before it will be applied by the court? Will the Hoffmans likely succeed in their suit? Discuss fully. [*Hoffman v. Red Owl Stores, Inc.*, 26 Wis.2d 683, 133 N.W.2d 267 (1965)]

8–7. Offers versus Nonoffers. The Olivers were planning to sell some of their ranch land and mentioned this fact to Southworth, a neighbor. Southworth expressed interest in purchasing the property and later notified the Olivers that he had the money available to buy it. The Olivers told Southworth they would let him know shortly about the details concerning the sale. The Olivers later sent a letter to Southworth—and (unknown to Southworth) to several other neighbors—giving information about the sale, including the price, the location of the property, and the amount of acreage involved. When Southworth received the letter, he sent a letter to the Olivers "accepting" their offer. The Olivers stated that the information letter had not been intended as an "offer" but merely as a starting point for negotiations. Southworth brought suit against the Olivers to enforce the "contract." Did a contract exist? Why or why not? Explain fully. [*Southworth v. Oliver*, 284 Or. 361, 587 P.2d 994 (1978)]

8–8. Consideration. Martino was a police officer in Atlantic City. Gray, who lost a significant amount of her jewelry during a burglary of her home, offered a reward for the recovery of the property. Incident to his job, Martino possessed certain knowledge concerning the theft of Gray's jewelry. When Martino informed Gray of his knowledge of the theft, Gray offered Martino $500 to help her recover her jewelry. As a result of Martino's police work, the jewelry was recovered and returned to Gray. Gray, however, did not pay Martino the $500. Martino sued Gray for the reward he claimed she promised him. Was there a valid contract between Gray and Martino? [*Gray v. Martino*, 91 N.J.L. 462, 103 A. 24 (1918)]

8–9. Offer and Acceptance. James sent invitations to a number of potential buyers to submit bids for some timber he wanted to sell. Two bids were received as a result, the highest one submitted by Eames. James changed his mind about selling the timber and did not accept Eames's bid. Eames claimed that a contract for sale existed and sued James for breach. Did a contract exist? Explain. [*Eames v. James*, 452 So.2d 384 (La.App.3d 1984)]

8–10. Acceptance. On September 5, 1987, Ralph Defeo and others offered to purchase a farm that Amfarms Associates had listed for sale in 1986. At one point during the subsequent negotiations, Amfarms made a counteroffer to Defeo and the others, stating that the offer would be valid only until 5 P.M. on October 17. Amfarms's attorney sent the offer to Defeo's attorney via Federal Express. On October 16, Defeo and the others sent their acceptance by certified mail to Amfarms's real estate broker, and Amfarms received it on October 19. On October 16, however, Amfarms had accepted an offer from another party. Defeo and the others sued Amfarms, claiming that their acceptance on October 16 was effective on the day that it was sent.

How should the court decide? Discuss fully. [*Defeo v. Amfarms Associates*, 161 A.D.2d 904, 557 N.Y.S.2d 469 (1990)]

8–11. Consideration. In 1972, Thomas L. Weinsaft signed a written agreement with his son, Nicholas L. Weinsaft. Thomas agreed that during his lifetime he would not transfer any interest in his 765 shares of stock of Crane Manufacturing Co. unless he first gave Nicholas an opportunity to purchase it, and upon Thomas's death, Nicholas would have the "option and right to purchase all of the stock" from the estate. The agreement stated that it was entered into "In consideration of $10.00 and other good and valuable consideration, including the inducement of Second Party [Nicholas] to remain the chief executive officer of said company." Thomas died in 1980. Nicholas gave notice that he intended to buy the stock, but one of the beneficiaries under Thomas's will objected, contending that there was no consideration for Thomas's promises. Nicholas sued to force the estate to transfer the shares. Discuss whether this contract is supported by consideration. [*In re Estate of Weinsaft*, 647 S.W.2d 179 (Mo.App. 1983)]

8–12. Offer and Acceptance. Cora Payne was involved in an automobile accident with Don Chappell, an employee of E & B Carpet Cleaning, Inc. E & B's insurance company offered Payne $18,500 to settle her claim against E & B. Payne did not accept the offer at that time but instead filed suit against E & B and its insurance company (the defendants). Later Payne offered to settle the case for $50,000, but the defendants refused her offer. Ultimately, Payne told the defendants that she would accept the insurance company's original settlement offer of $18,500, but the insurance company stated that the offer was no longer open for acceptance. When Payne sought to compel the defendants to perform the original settlement offer, the defendants contended that Payne's filing of her lawsuit terminated the insurance company's earlier settlement offer. Will the court agree with the defendants? Discuss. [*Payne v. E & B Carpet Cleaning, Inc.*, 896 S.W.2d 650 (Mo.App. 1995)]

Accessing the Internet: Fundamentals of Business Law

To learn more about the requirements of a valid contract, including consideration, you can access the Law Office's site at
http://www.thelawoffice.com/
Select the topic of Business Law from the USA Legal Topics list in the left-hand column. Go to Guide to Business law and then to Contracts.

The 'Lectric Law Library provides extensive information on contract law, including the requirement of consideration for a valid contract. Go to the library's LawCopedia at
http://www.lectlaw.com

To learn more about the requirements of a valid contract, including agreement, you can access the Law Office's site at
http://www.thelawoffice.com/
Select the topic of Business Law from the USA Legal Topics list in the left-hand column. Go to Guide to Business law and then to Contracts.

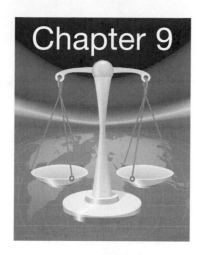

Chapter 9

Capacity and Legality

CHAPTER OBJECTIVES

After reading this chapter, you should be able to:

1. Explain the contractual rights and obligations of minors.
2. Indicate how intoxication affects contractual liability.
3. Outline the effects of mental incompetency on contractual liability.
4. Give examples of some contracts that are contrary to state or federal statutes.
5. Discuss why certain types of contracts and clauses are contrary to public policy.

Courts generally want contracts to be enforceable, and much of the law is made to aid in the enforceability of contracts. Nonetheless, not all people can make legally binding contracts at all times. Contracts entered into by persons lacking the capacity to do so may be unenforceable. Similarly, contracts calling for the performance of an illegal act are illegal and thus void—they are not contracts at all. In this chapter, we examine contractual capacity and some aspects of illegal bargains.

▌ Contractual Capacity

Although the parties to a contract must assume certain risks, the law indicates that neither party should be allowed to benefit from the other party's lack of **contractual capacity**—the legal ability to enter into a contractual relationship. Courts generally presume the existence of contractual capacity, but there are some situations in which capacity is lacking or may be questionable. A person *adjudged*

by a court to be mentally incompetent, for example, cannot form a legally binding contract with another party. In other situations, a party may have the capacity to enter into a valid contract but also have the right to avoid liability under it. For example, minors usually are not legally bound by contracts. In this section, we look at the effect of youth, intoxication, and mental incompetence on contractual capacity.

Minors

Today, in virtually all states, the *age of majority* (when a person is no longer a minor) for contractual purposes is eighteen years for both sexes.[1] In addition, some states provide for the termination of

---

1. The age of majority may still be twenty-one for other purposes, such as the purchase and consumption of alcohol. The word *infant* is usually used synonymously with the word *minor*.

minority upon marriage. Subject to certain exceptions, the contracts entered into by a minor are voidable at the option of that minor.

The general rule is that a minor can enter into any contract an adult can, provided that the contract is not one prohibited by law for minors (for example, the sale of alcoholic beverages). Although minors have the right to avoid their contracts, there are exceptions (to be discussed later).

DISAFFIRMANCE   For a minor to exercise the option to avoid a contract, he or she need only manifest an intention not to be bound by it. The minor "avoids" the contract by disaffirming it. The technical definition of **disaffirmance** is the legal avoidance, or setting aside, of a contractual obligation. Words or conduct may serve to express this intent. The contract can ordinarily be disaffirmed at any time during minority or for a reasonable time after the minor comes of age. In some states, however, when there is a contract for the sale of land by a minor, the minor cannot disaffirm the contract until he or she reaches the age of majority. When a minor disaffirms a contract, all property that he or she has transferred to the adult as consideration can be recovered, even if it is then in the possession of a third party.[2]

Disaffirmance must be timely. If, for example, an individual wishes to disaffirm an executed contract made as a minor but fails to do so until two years after he or she has reached the age of majority, a court will likely hold that the contract has been ratified (see the discussion of ratification below). Additionally, if a minor disaffirms a contract, he or she must disaffirm the *entire* contract. The minor cannot decide to keep part of the goods contracted for and return the remainder.

---

2.   The Uniform Commercial Code, in Section 2–403(1), allows an exception if the third party is a "good faith purchaser for value." See Chapter 14.

Note that an adult who enters into a contract with a minor cannot avoid his or her contractual duties on the ground that the minor can do so. Unless the minor exercises the option to disaffirm the contract (to be discussed shortly), the adult party normally is bound by it.

Minor's Obligations on Disaffirmance   All state laws permit minors to disaffirm contracts (with certain exceptions—to be discussed shortly), including executed contracts. States differ, however, on the extent of a minor's obligations on disaffirmance. Courts in a majority of states hold that the minor need only return the goods (or other consideration) subject to the contract, provided the goods are in the minor's possession or control. For example, suppose that Jim Garrison, a seventeen-year-old, purchases a computer from Radio Shack. While transporting the computer to his home, Garrison, through no fault of his own, is involved in a car accident. As a result of the accident, the plastic casing of the computer is broken. The next day, he returns the computer to Radio Shack and disaffirms the contract. Under the majority view, this return fulfills Garrison's duty even though the computer is now damaged. Garrison is entitled to get a refund of the purchase price (if paid in cash) or to be relieved of any further obligations under an agreement to purchase the computer on credit.

A growing number of states, either by statute or by court decision, place an additional duty on the minor—the duty to restore the adult party to the position he or she held before the contract was made. In the example just given, Garrison would be required not only to return the computer but also to pay Radio Shack for damages to the computer.

In the following case, a minor's father brought an action on behalf of his son to disaffirm the minor's purchase of an automobile and to recover the money paid for the car from a seller who knew that the purchaser was a minor when the contract was made.

CASE 9.1

Quality Motors, Inc. v. Hays

Supreme Court of Arkansas, 1949.
216 Ark. 264,
225 S.W.2d 326.

FACTS   Sixteen-year-old Johnny Hays went to Quality Motors, Inc., to purchase a car. The salesperson refused to sell the car unless the purchase was made by an adult, so Johnny left and later returned with a young man of twenty-three. Hays paid for the car, and a bill of sale was made out to the twenty-three-year-old. The salesperson then drove the two boys into town to a notary public, the young

Case 9.1—Continued

man transferred the title to the car to Johnny, and the salesperson delivered the car to Johnny. Johnny's father attempted to return the car to Quality Motors for a full refund, but Quality Motors refused it. Subsequently, Johnny wrecked the car in an accident. Johnny, through his father, brought suit in an Arkansas state court to disaffirm the contract and recover the purchase price. The trial court ordered the purchase price to be refunded to Hays on his return of the car to Quality Motors. Quality Motors appealed.

ISSUE   Can Johnny disaffirm this contract even though it was nominally (in name only) made by an adult?

DECISION   Yes. The Supreme Court of Arkansas held that Johnny could disaffirm the contract and return the car. He was not held liable for any damages.

REASON   The court reasoned that because the salesperson knew that Johnny was a minor, aided Johnny in obtaining the car by selling it to an adult, and assisted in the transfer of title to Johnny, the sale was essentially made to Johnny. When goods—*other than necessaries* (food, clothing, and so on, as will be discussed shortly)—are sold to a minor, the minor can disaffirm the contract of sale. The court quoted the law as follows: "The law is well settled *   *   * that an infant may disaffirm his contracts, except those made for necessaries, without being required to return the consideration received, except such part as may remain *   *   * in his hands."

FOR CRITICAL ANALYSIS—Cultural Consideration   *What societal values have led to laws governing disaffirmance that weigh so heavily in favor of minors?*

Disaffirmance and Misrepresentation of Age
Suppose that a minor tells a seller she is twenty-one years old when she is really seventeen. Ordinarily, the minor can disaffirm the contract even though she has misrepresented her age. Moreover, the minor is not liable in certain jurisdictions for the tort of deceit for such misrepresentation, the rationale being that such a tort judgment might indirectly force the minor to perform the contract.

Many jurisdictions, however, do find circumstances under which a minor can be bound by a contract when the minor has misrepresented his or her age. First, several states have enacted statutes for precisely this purpose. In these states, misrepresentation of age is enough to prohibit disaffirmance. Other statutes prohibit disaffirmance by a minor who has engaged in business as an adult.

Second, some courts refuse to allow minors to disaffirm executed (fully performed) contracts unless they can return the consideration received. The combination of the minors' misrepresenta-

tions and their unjust enrichment has persuaded these courts to *estop* (prevent) minors from asserting contractual incapacity.

Third, some courts allow a misrepresenting minor to disaffirm the contract, but they hold the minor liable for damages in tort. Here, the defrauded party may sue the minor for misrepresentation or fraud. A split in authority exists on this point, because some courts, as previously noted, have recognized that allowing a suit in tort is equivalent to the indirect enforcement of the minor's contract.

Liability for Necessaries, Insurance, and Loans
A minor who enters into a contract for necessaries may disaffirm the contract but remains liable for the reasonable value of the goods. **Necessaries** are basic needs, such as food, clothing, shelter, and medical services. In some cases, however, courts have not limited necessaries to items required for physical existence but have interpreted the term to

include whatever is believed to be necessary to maintain a person's standard of living or financial and social status. Thus, what will be considered a necessary for one person may be a luxury for another.

Traditionally, insurance has not been viewed as a necessary, so minors can ordinarily disaffirm their insurance contracts and recover all premiums paid. Some jurisdictions, however, prohibit the right to disaffirm insurance contracts—for example, when minors contract for life insurance on their own lives. Financial loans are seldom considered to be necessaries, even if the minor spends the money borrowed on necessaries. If, however, a lender makes a loan to a minor for the express purpose of enabling the minor to purchase necessaries, and the lender personally makes sure the money is so spent, the minor normally is obligated to repay the loan.

RATIFICATION   In contract law, **ratification** is the act of accepting and giving legal force to an obligation that previously was not enforceable. A minor who has reached the age of majority can ratify a contract expressly or impliedly.

Express ratification occurs when the minor expressly states, orally or in writing, that he or she intends to be bound by the contract. Implied ratification exists when the conduct of the minor is inconsistent with disaffirmance (as when the minor enjoys the benefits of the contract) or when the minor fails to disaffirm an executed (fully performed) contract within a reasonable time after reaching the age of majority. If the contract is still executory (not yet performed or only partially performed), however, failure to disaffirm the contract will not necessarily imply ratification.

Generally, the courts base their determination on whether the minor, after reaching the age of majority, has had ample opportunity to consider the nature of the contractual obligations he or she entered into as a minor and the extent to which the adult party to the contract has performed.

PARENTS' LIABILITY   As a general rule, parents are not liable for the contracts made by minor children acting on their own. This is why businesses ordinarily require parents to cosign any contract made with a minor. The parents then become personally obligated under the contract to perform the conditions of the contract, even if their child avoids liability.

Generally, a minor is held personally liable for the torts he or she commits. Therefore, minors cannot disaffirm their liability for their tortious conduct. The parents of the minor can *also* be held liable under certain circumstances. For example, if the minor commits a tort under the direction of a parent or while performing an act requested by a parent, the injured party can hold the parent liable. In addition, parents are liable in many states up to a statutory amount for malicious torts committed by a minor child living in their home.

EMANCIPATION   The release of a minor by his or her parents is known as emancipation. **Emancipation** occurs when a child's parent or legal guardian relinquishes the legal right to exercise control over the child. Normally, a minor who leaves home to support himself or herself is considered emancipated. Several jurisdictions permit minors to petition a court for emancipation themselves. For business purposes, a minor may petition a court to be treated as an adult. If the court grants the minor's request, it removes the minor's lack of contractual capacity and right of disaffirmance for those contracts entered into in conducting the business.

Intoxicated Persons

Another situation in which contractual capacity becomes an issue is when a contract is formed by a person who claims to have been intoxicated at the time the contract was made. The general rule is that if a person who is sufficiently intoxicated to lack mental capacity enters into a contract, the contract is voidable at the option of the intoxicated person. This is true even if the intoxication was purely voluntary. For the contract to be voidable, it must be proved that the intoxicated person's reason and judgment were impaired to the extent that he or she did not comprehend the legal consequences of entering into the contract. If the person was intoxicated but understood these legal consequences, the contract is enforceable.

Simply because the terms of the contract are foolish or are obviously favorable to the other party does not mean the contract is voidable (unless the other party fraudulently induced the person to become intoxicated). Problems often arise in determining whether a party was sufficiently intoxicated to avoid legal duties. Generally, contract avoidance on the ground of intoxication is rarely permitted.

The following case involves an unusual business transaction in which boasts and dares "after a few drinks" resulted in a contract to sell certain property. The issue before the court is whether the seller was sufficiently intoxicated to render the contract voidable at the seller's option.

CASE 9.2

Lucy v. Zehmer

Supreme Court of Appeals of
Virginia, 1954.
196 Va. 493,
84 S.E.2d 516.

FACTS   Lucy and Zehmer had known each other for fifteen or twenty years. For some time, Lucy had been wanting to buy Zehmer's farm. Zehmer had always told Lucy that he was not interested in selling. One night, Lucy stopped in to visit with the Zehmers at a restaurant they operated. Lucy said to Zehmer, "I bet you wouldn't take $50,000 for that place." Zehmer replied, "Yes, I would, too; you wouldn't give fifty." Throughout the evening, the conversation returned to the sale of the farm. At the same time, the parties were drinking whiskey. Eventually, Zehmer wrote up an agreement, on the back of a restaurant check, for the sale of the farm, and he asked his wife to sign it—which she did. When Lucy brought an action in a Virginia state court to enforce the agreement, Zehmer argued that he had been "high as a Georgia pine" at the time and that the offer had been made in jest: "two doggoned drunks bluffing to see who could talk the biggest and say the most." Lucy claimed that he had not been intoxicated and did not think Zehmer had been, either, given the way Zehmer handled the transaction. The trial court ruled in favor of the Zehmers, and Lucy appealed.

ISSUE   Can the agreement be avoided on the basis of intoxication?

DECISION   No. The agreement to sell the farm was binding.

REASON   The opinion of the court was that the evidence given about the nature of the conversation, the appearance and completeness of the agreement, and the signing all tended to show that a serious business transaction, not a casual jest, was intended. The court had to look into the objective meaning of the words and acts of the Zehmers: "An agreement or mutual assent is of course essential to a valid contract, but the law imputes to a person an intention corresponding to the reasonable meaning of his words and acts. If his words and acts, judged by a reasonable standard, manifest an intention to agree, it is immaterial what may be the real but unexpressed state of mind."

FOR CRITICAL ANALYSIS—Cultural Consideration   *How does the court's decision in this case relate to the objective theory of contracts discussed in Chapter 7?*

Mentally Incompetent Persons

If a person has been adjudged mentally incompetent by a court of law and a guardian has been appointed, any contract made by the mentally incompetent person is *void*—no contract exists. Only the guardian can enter into a binding contract on behalf of the mentally incompetent person.

If a mentally incompetent person not previously so adjudged by a court enters into a contract, the contract may be *voidable* if the person does not know he or she is entering into the contract or lacks the mental capacity to comprehend its nature, purpose, and consequences. In such situations, the contract is voidable at the option of the mentally incompetent person but not the other party. The contract may then be disaffirmed or ratified. Ratification must occur after the person has regained mental competence or after a guardian is appointed and ratifies the contract. Like minors and intoxicated persons, mentally incompetent persons are liable for the reasonable value of any necessaries they receive.

A contract entered into by a mentally incompetent person (but not previously so adjudged by a court) may also be deemed valid and enforceable if the contract was formed during a lucid interval. For such a contract to be valid, it must be shown that the person was able to comprehend the nature, purpose, and consequences of the contract *at the time the contract was formed.*

▌ Legality
....

To this point, we have discussed three of the requirements for a valid contract to exist—agreement, consideration, and contractual capacity. Now we examine a fourth—legality. For a contract to be valid and enforceable, it must be formed for a legal purpose. A contract to do something that is prohibited by federal or state statutory law is illegal and, as such, void from the outset and thus unenforceable. Additionally, a contract to commit a tortious act or to commit an action that is contrary to public policy is illegal and unenforceable.

Contracts Contrary to Statute

Statutes sometimes prescribe the terms of contracts. In some instances, the laws are specific, even providing for the inclusion of certain clauses and their wording. Other statutes prohibit certain contracts on the basis of their subject matter, the time at which they are entered into, or the status of the contracting parties. We examine here several ways in which contracts may be contrary to a statute and thus illegal.

USURY   Virtually every state has a statute that sets the maximum rate of interest that can be charged for different types of transactions, including ordinary loans. A lender who makes a loan at an interest rate above the lawful maximum commits **usury**. The maximum rate of interest varies from state to state.

Although usury statutes place a ceiling on allowable rates of interest, exceptions have been made to facilitate business transactions. For example, many states exempt corporate loans from the usury laws. In addition, almost all states have adopted special statutes allowing much higher interest rates on small loans to help those borrowers who are in need of money but simply cannot get loans at interest rates below the normal lawful maximum.

The effects of a usurious loan differ from state to state. A number of states allow the lender to recover only the principal of a loan along with interest up to the legal maximum. In effect, the lender is denied recovery of the excess interest. In other states, the lender can recover the principal amount of the loan but not the interest. In a few states, a usurious loan is a void transaction, and the lender cannot recover either the principal or the interest.

GAMBLING   In general, gambling contracts are illegal and thus void. All states have statutes that regulate gambling—defined as any scheme that involves the distribution of property by chance among persons who have paid valuable consideration for the opportunity (chance) to receive the property.[3] Gambling is the creation of risk for the purpose of assuming it. In some states, such as Nevada and New Jersey, casino gambling is legal. In other states, certain other forms of gambling are legal. California, for example, has not defined draw poker as a crime, although criminal statutes prohibit numerous other types of gambling games. Several states allow horse racing, and about half of the states have recognized the substantial revenues that can be obtained from gambling and have legalized state-operated lotteries, as well as lotteries (such as bingo) arranged for charitable purposes. Many states also allow gambling on Indian reservations.

Sometimes it is difficult to distinguish a gambling contract from the risk sharing inherent in almost all contracts. Suppose that Isaacson takes out a life insurance policy on Donohue, naming himself as beneficiary under the policy. At first glance, this may seem entirely legal; but further examination shows that Isaacson is simply gambling on how long Donohue will live. To prevent that type of practice, insurance contracts can be entered into only by someone with an *insurable interest* (see Chapter 30).

---

3. See *Wishing Well Club v. Akron,* 66 Ohio Law Abs. 406, 112 N.E.2d 41 (1951).

SABBATH (SUNDAY) LAWS Statutes called Sabbath (Sunday) laws prohibit the formation or performance of certain contracts on a Sunday. Under the common law, such contracts are legal in the absence of this statutory prohibition. Under some state and local laws, all contracts entered into on a Sunday are illegal. Laws in other states or municipalities prohibit only the sale of certain types of merchandise, such as alcoholic beverages, on a Sunday.

These laws, which date back to colonial times, are often called **blue laws.** Blue laws get their name from the blue paper on which New Haven, Connecticut, printed its new town ordinance in 1781. The ordinance prohibited all work on Sunday and required all shops to close on the "Lord's Day." A number of states and municipalities enacted laws forbidding the carrying on of "all secular labor and business on the Lord's Day." Exceptions to Sunday laws permit contracts for necessities (such as food) and works of charity. A fully performed (executed) contract that was entered into on a Sunday normally cannot be rescinded (canceled).

Sunday laws are often not enforced, and some of these laws have been held to be unconstitutional on the ground that they are contrary to the freedom of religion. Nonetheless, as a precaution, business owners contemplating doing business in a particular locality should check to see if any Sunday statutes or ordinances will affect their business activities.

LICENSING STATUTES All states require that members of certain professions obtain licenses allowing them to practice. Physicians, lawyers, real estate brokers, architects, electricians, and stockbrokers are but a few of the people who must be licensed. Some licenses are obtained only after extensive schooling and examinations, which indicate to the public that a special skill has been acquired. Others require only that the particular person be of good moral character.

Generally, business licenses provide a means of regulating and taxing certain businesses and protecting the public against actions that could threaten the general welfare. For example, in nearly all states, a stockbroker must be licensed and must file a bond with the state to protect the public from fraudulent transactions in stock. Similarly, a plumber must be licensed and bonded to protect the public against incompetent plumbers and to protect the public health. Only persons or businesses possessing the qualifications and complying with the conditions required by statute are entitled to licenses. Typically, for example, an owner of a saloon or tavern is required to sell food as a condition of obtaining a license to sell liquor for consumption on the premises.

When a person enters into a contract with an unlicensed individual, the contract may still be enforceable depending on the nature of the licensing statute. Some states expressly provide that the lack of a license in certain occupations bars the enforcement of work-related contracts. If the statute does not expressly state this, one must look to the underlying purpose of the licensing requirements for a particular occupation. If the purpose is to protect the public from unauthorized practitioners, a contract involving an unlicensed individual is illegal and unenforceable. If, however, the underlying purpose of the statute is to raise government revenues, a contract with an unlicensed practitioner is enforceable—although the unlicensed person is usually fined. In the following case, the court looked at the purpose of an attorney registration statute to decide whether an unregistered attorney could collect fees for legal services.

CASE 9.3

Benjamin v. Koeppel

Court of Appeals of New York, 1995.
85 N.Y.2d 549,
650 N.E.2d 829,
626 N.Y.S.2d 982.

FACTS Donald Benjamin, an attorney, agreed to a fee-sharing arrangement with Koeppel, Del Casino & Martone, P.C. (professional corporation), a law firm. Under the agreement, Benjamin was to receive one-third of any fees the firm obtained from a client whom Benjamin referred to it. When the firm refused to pay, Benjamin filed a suit against it and Adolph Koeppel, one of the partners, in a New York state court. The firm discovered that Benjamin was not registered with the state according to the state's attorney registration rules and claimed that payment to Benjamin would therefore violate public policy. The court ruled in Benjamin's favor, and the firm appealed. The appellate court affirmed the

(Continued)

Case 9.3—Continued

lower court's ruling, and the law firm appealed to New York's highest state court, the New York Court of Appeals.

ISSUE   May an attorney who has not complied with a state's statutory registration requirements recover fees for legal services provided in that state?

DECISION   Yes. The New York Court of Appeals affirmed the lower court's ruling. The appellate court held, among other things, that the registration requirements were revenue-raising measures.

REASON   The court determined that the state's attorney registration system "more closely resembles a revenue-raising measure than a program for 'the protection of public health or morals or the prevention of fraud.'" The court pointed out that when the registration statute was enacted, its express purpose was to "generate $1,750,000 in estimated [annual] fee revenues." The court also found that amendments to the statute "only serve to underscore [its] essential purpose as a revenue-raising mechanism." For example, "[t]he 1990 amendments tripled the $100 biannual fee and provided for the allocation of the resulting revenues."

FOR CRITICAL ANALYSIS—Political Consideration   *When a licensing statute provides for a fine for noncompliance, is it still appropriate to deny an individual his or her fee, even after the fine has been paid?*

Contracts Contrary to Public Policy

Although contracts involve private parties, some are not enforceable because of the negative impact they would have on society. These contracts are said to be *contrary to public policy*. Examples include a contract to commit an immoral act (such as a surrogate-parenting contract, which several courts and state statutes equate with "baby selling") and a contract that prohibits marriage. As an example of the latter, suppose that Everett offers a young man $500 if he refrains from marrying Everett's daughter. If the young man accepts, no contract is formed (the contract is void) because it is contrary to public policy. Thus, if the man marries Everett's daughter, Everett cannot sue him for breach of contract. Business contracts that may be contrary to public policy include contracts in restraint of trade and unconscionable contracts or clauses.

CONTRACTS IN RESTRAINT OF TRADE   Contracts in restraint of trade (anticompetitive agreements) usually adversely affect the public, which favors competition in the economy. Typically, such contracts also violate one or more federal or state

statutes.[4] An exception is recognized when the restraint is reasonable and it is *ancillary to* (is a subsidiary part of) a contract, such as a contract for the sale of a business or an employment contract. Many such exceptions involve a type of restraint called a *covenant not to compete*, or a restrictive covenant.

Covenants Not to Compete   Covenants not to compete are often contained in contracts concerning the sale of an ongoing business. A covenant not to compete is created when a seller agrees not to open a new store in a certain geographical area surrounding the old store. Such an agreement, when it is ancillary to a sales contract and reasonable in terms of time and geographic area, enables the seller to sell, and the purchaser to buy, the "goodwill" and "reputation" of an ongoing business. If, for example, a well-known merchant sells his or her store and opens a competing business a block

---

4.   Such as the Sherman Antitrust Act, the Clayton Act and the Federal Trade Commission Act.

away, many of the merchant's customers will likely do business at the new store. This renders valueless the good name and reputation sold to the other merchant for a price. If a covenant not to compete was not ancillary to a sales agreement, however, it would be void, because it unreasonably restrains trade and is contrary to public policy.

Agreements not to compete can also be contained in employment contracts. It is common for many people in middle-level and upper-level management positions to agree not to work for competitors or not to start a competing business for a specified period of time after terminating employment. Such agreements are legal so long as the specified period of time is not excessive in duration and the geographical restriction is reasonable. Basically, the restriction on competition must be reasonable—that is, not any greater than necessary to protect a legitimate business interest. The following case illustrates this point.

CASE 9.4

Superior Consulting Corp. v. Walling

United States District Court,
Eastern District of Michigan, 1994.
851 F.Supp. 839.

FACTS   Michael Walling began work for SCC as an executive director in 1990. Two years later, when he was promoted to vice president, he signed a new employment contract that contained a covenant not to compete. The covenant prohibited Walling from accepting a job with "any health-care information systems consulting business for a period of six months following his termination" of employment with SCC. The express purpose of the agreement was to protect SCC's trade secrets. Walling resigned from SCC in 1994. In less than a week, he agreed to work for Ernst & Young to provide health-care information systems consulting services. SCC filed a suit in a federal district court against Walling to enforce the covenant not to compete.

ISSUE   Were the terms of this covenant not to compete reasonable?

DECISION   Yes. The court ordered Walling to comply with the covenant not to compete.

REASON   Six months was reasonable, the court concluded, pointing out that "[l]onger periods have been approved, particularly *   *   * to protect proprietary information learned by the employee." The agreement had no geographical limitations, but the court explained that this was reasonable "if the employer actually has legitimate business interests throughout the world," as SCC did. Finally, the agreement was reasonable as to "line of work," because, as limited by the court, it applied only to "actual consulting and management work for competitors of SCC, and only in the competitors' health-care information systems consulting businesses."

FOR CRITICAL ANALYSIS—Social Consideration   *Why wouldn't every company want all of its employees to sign covenants not to compete?*

Reformation of an Illegal Covenant Not to Compete   On occasion, when a covenant not to compete is unreasonable in its essential terms, the court may *reform* the covenant, converting its terms into reasonable ones. Instead of declaring the covenant illegal and unenforceable, the court applies the rule of reasonableness and changes the contract so that its basic, original intent can be enforced. This presents a problem, however, in that the judge becomes a party to the contract. Consequently, contract **reformation** is usually carried out by a court only when necessary to prevent undue burdens or hardships.

UNCONSCIONABLE CONTRACTS OR CLAUSES
Ordinarily, a court does not look at the fairness or equity of a contract; in other words, it does not inquire into the adequacy of consideration. Persons are assumed to be reasonably intelligent, and the court does not come to their aid just because they have made unwise or foolish bargains. In certain circumstances, however, bargains are so oppressive that the courts relieve innocent parties of part or all of their duties. Such a bargain is called an **unconscionable contract** (or **unconscionable clause**). Both the Uniform Commercial Code (UCC) and the Uniform Consumer Credit Code (UCCC) embody the unconscionability concept—the former with regard to the sale of goods and the latter with regard to consumer loans and the waiver of rights.[5]

Procedural Unconscionability Procedural unconscionability has to do with how a term becomes part of a contract and relates to factors bearing on a party's lack of knowledge or understanding of the contract terms because of inconspicuous print, unintelligible language ("legalese"), lack of opportunity to read the contract, lack of opportunity to ask questions about its meaning, and other factors. Procedural unconscionability sometimes relates to purported lack of voluntariness because of a disparity in bargaining power between the two parties. Contracts entered into because of one party's vastly superior bargaining power may be deemed unconscionable. These situations usually involve an **adhesion contract,** which is a contract drafted by the dominant party and then presented to the other—the adhering party—on a "take it or leave it" basis.[6] The following case involved an adhesion contract.

---

5. See, for example, UCC Sections 2–302 and 2–719 (see Chapters 13 and 15, respectively) and UCCC Sections 5.108 and 1.107.

6. See, for example, *Henningsen v. Bloomfield Motors, Inc.,* 32 N.J. 358, 161 A.2d 69 (1960).

CASE 9.5
Phoenix Baptist Hospital & Medical Center, Inc. v. Aiken
Court of Appeals of Arizona, Division 1, Department B, 1994.
179 Ariz. 289,
877 P.2d 1345.

FACTS   Patricia Aiken suffered a heart attack and was hospitalized at Phoenix Baptist Hospital and Medical Center, Inc. At the time of her admission, the Aikens told the hospital that they did not have the money to pay for medical care. At the same time, her husband, Thomas, signed an agreement to pay her medical expenses. He did not read what he signed, no one explained the agreement to him, and he later claimed to have been so upset that he could not remember having signed anything. When the bills were not paid, the hospital filed a suit in an Arizona state court against the Aikens. The court ruled in favor of the hospital, and the Aikens appealed. They argued that the agreement was an adhesion contract obtained under circumstances that made it unenforceable.

ISSUE   Were the circumstances such that the agreement may have been unenforceable?

DECISION   Yes. The state court of appeals reversed the ruling of the lower court and remanded the case. The lower court was instructed to look at the circumstances surrounding Thomas's signing of the agreement.

REASON   The appellate court held that the agreement was "undeniably a contract of adhesion." Whether it was enforceable depended on "the reasonable expectations of the adhering party and whether the contract is unconscionable." The court concluded that there was "a material issue of fact as to Thomas' reasonable expectation," considering the stressful

Case 9.5—Continued

circumstances under which he signed the agreement. As to the form's unconscionability, the court stated that, given the circumstances—Thomas's haste, the failure of the hospital to explain the agreement, and the small print of the form—Thomas either may not have understood "the implications of the agreement" or may have "felt he had no choice but to immediately sign the preprinted form."

FOR CRITICAL ANALYSIS—Ethical Consideration *Under what circumstances would an adhesion contract to pay for medical services be enforceable when an emergency admission to a hospital is at issue?*

Substantive Unconscionability Substantive unconscionability characterizes those contracts, or portions of contracts, that are oppressive or overly harsh. Courts generally focus on provisions that deprive one party of the benefits of the agreement or leave that party without remedy for nonperformance by the other. For example, suppose that a welfare recipient with a fourth-grade education agrees to purchase a refrigerator for $2,000 and signs a two-year installment contract. The same type of refrigerator usually sells for $400 on the market. Some courts have held this type of contract to be unconscionable, despite the general rule that the courts will not inquire into the adequacy of the consideration, because the contract terms are so oppressive as to "shock the conscience" of the court.[7]

EXCULPATORY CLAUSES Often closely related to the concept of unconscionability are **exculpatory clauses,** defined as clauses that release a party from liability in the event of monetary or physical injury, *no matter who is at fault.* Indeed, some courts refer to such clauses in terms of unconscionability. Suppose, for example, that Madison Manufacturing Company hires a laborer and has him sign a contract containing the following clause:

Said employee hereby agrees with employer, in consideration of such employment, that he will take upon himself all risks incident to his position and will in no case hold the company liable for any injury or damage he may sustain, in his person or otherwise, by accidents or injuries in the factory, or which may result from defective machinery or care-

lessness or misconduct of himself or any other employee in service of the employer.

This contract provision attempts to remove Madison's potential liability for injuries occurring to the employee, and it would usually be held contrary to public policy.[8] Exculpatory clauses found in agreements to lease commercial property are also, in the majority of cases, held to be contrary to public policy. Additionally, such clauses are almost universally held to be illegal and unenforceable when they are included in residential property leases.

Generally, an exculpatory clause will not be enforced if the party seeking its enforcement is involved in a business that is important to the public interest. These businesses include public utilities, common carriers, and banks. Because of the essential nature of these services, the companies offering them have an advantage in bargaining strength and could insist that anyone contracting for their services agree not to hold them liable. This would tend to relax their carefulness and increase the number of injuries. Imagine the results, for example, if all exculpatory clauses in contracts between airlines and their passengers were enforced.

Exculpatory clauses may be enforced, however, when the parties seeking their enforcement are not involved in businesses considered important to the public interest. These businesses have included health clubs, amusement parks, horse-rental concessions, golf-cart concessions, and skydiving organizations. Because these services are not essential,

---

7. See, for example, *Jones v. Star Credit Corp.*, 59 Misc.2d 189, 298 N.Y.S.2d 264 (1969). This case is presented in Chapter 13 as Case 13.4.

8. For a case with similar facts, see *Little Rock & Fort Smith Railway Co. v. Eubanks*, 48 Ark. 460, 3 S.W. 808 (1887). In such a case, the exculpatory clause may also be illegal on the basis of a violation of a state workers' compensation law.

the firms offering them are sometimes considered to have no relative advantage in bargaining strength, and anyone contracting for their services is considered to do so voluntarily. The following case involved an exculpatory clause that purported to absolve an alarm company from liability for its own negligence.

CASE 9.6

New Light Co. v. Wells Fargo Alarm Services

Supreme Court of Nebraska, 1994.
247 Neb. 57,
525 N.W.2d 25.

FACTS The New Light Company, which owned and operated the Great Wall Restaurant in Omaha, Nebraska, contracted with Wells Fargo Alarm Services to install and maintain a fire alarm system in the restaurant. The agreement included an exculpatory clause that relieved Wells Fargo of liability for its "negligent acts or omissions." A fire in the restaurant rendered the alarm system inoperative. New Light sued Wells Fargo in a Nebraska state court, claiming in part that the alarm company's failure to install an alarm system that would detect a fire before the system was rendered inoperative amounted to willful, wanton, and intentional misconduct and thus constituted gross negligence. Based on the exculpatory clause, the court issued a summary judgment in favor of Wells Fargo, and New Light appealed. The state appellate court affirmed, and New Light appealed to the Supreme Court of Nebraska.

ISSUE Is an exculpatory clause that relieves a party of liability for its gross negligence or willful and wanton misconduct against public policy?

DECISION Yes. The state supreme court reversed the decision of the lower court and remanded the case for a determination as to whether Wells Fargo had in fact been grossly negligent or was guilty of any willful and wanton misconduct.

REASON There was, the court found, "a sufficiently compelling reason to prevent Wells Fargo from insulating itself by contractual agreement from damages caused by its own gross negligence or willful and wanton misconduct. Such an agreement would have a tendency to be injurious to the public." The court explained that "[t]he right of contract may be restricted for the public good. The greater the threat to the general safety of the community, the greater the restriction on the party's freedom to contractually limit the party's liability." The court stated that "[t]his limitation on the freedom to contract is imposed by law because of the potential risks to human life and property and is, therefore, independent of the agreement of the parties."

FOR CRITICAL ANALYSIS—Ethical Consideration *Under what circumstances should a court uphold an exculpatory clause that partially eliminates a party's duty of care?*

The Effect of Illegality

In general, an illegal contract is void: the contract is deemed never to have existed, and the courts will not aid either party. In most illegal contracts, both parties are considered to be equally at fault—*in pari delicto*. If the contract is executory (not yet fulfilled), neither party can enforce it. If it is executed, there can be neither contractual nor quasi-contractual recovery.

That one wrongdoer in an illegal contract is unjustly enriched at the expense of the other is of no concern to the law—except under certain circumstances (to be discussed shortly). The major justification for this hands-off attitude is that it is improper to place the machinery of justice at the disposal of a plaintiff who has broken the law by entering into an illegal bargain. Another justification is the hoped-for deterrent effect of this general rule. A plaintiff who suffers a loss because of an illegal bargain should presumably be deterred from entering into similar illegal bargains in the future.

There are exceptions to the general rule that neither party to an illegal bargain can sue for breach and neither can recover for performance rendered. We look at these exceptions here.

JUSTIFIABLE IGNORANCE OF THE FACTS When one of the parties to a contract is relatively innocent (has no knowledge or any reason to know that the contract is illegal), that party can often obtain restitution or recovery of benefits conferred in a partially executed contract. The courts do not enforce the contract but do allow the parties to return to their original positions.

It is also possible for an innocent party who has fully performed under the contract to enforce the contract against the guilty party. For example, Debbie contracts with Tucker to purchase ten crates of goods that cannot legally be bought or sold. Tucker hires a trucking firm to deliver the shipment to Debbie and agrees to pay the firm the normal fee of $500. Although the law specifies that the shipment, use, and sale of the goods were illegal, the carrier, being an innocent party, can legally collect the $500 from Tucker.

MEMBERS OF PROTECTED CLASSES When a statute protects a certain class of people, a member of that class can enforce an illegal contract even though the other party cannot. For example, there are statutes that prohibit certain employees (such as flight attendants) from working more than a specified number of hours per month. These employees thus constitute a class protected by statute. An employee who is required to work more than the maximum can recover for those extra hours of service.

Another example of statutes designed to protect a particular class of people are **blue sky laws,** which are state laws that regulate and supervise investment companies for the protection of the public. (The phrase *blue sky laws* dates to a 1917 decision by the United States Supreme Court in which the Court declared that the purpose of such laws was to prevent "speculative schemes which have no more basis than so many feet of 'blue sky.'")[9] These laws are intended to stop the sale of stock in fly-by-night concerns, such as visionary oil wells and distant and perhaps nonexistent gold mines. Investors are protected as a class and can sue to recover the purchase price of stock issued in violation of such laws.

Most states also have statutes regulating the sale of insurance. If an insurance company violates a statute when selling insurance, the purchaser can nevertheless enforce the policy and recover from the insurer.

WITHDRAWAL FROM AN ILLEGAL AGREEMENT If the illegal part of a bargain has not yet been performed, the party tendering performance can withdraw from the bargain and recover the performance or its value. For example, suppose that Martha and Andy decide to wager (illegally) on the outcome of a boxing match. Each deposits money with a stakeholder, who agrees to pay the winner of the bet. At this point, each party has performed part of the agreement, but the illegal part of the agreement will not occur until the money is paid to the winner. Before such payment occurs, either party is entitled to withdraw from the agreement by giving notice to the stakeholder of his or her withdrawal.

FRAUD, DURESS, OR UNDUE INFLUENCE Whenever a plaintiff has been induced to enter into an illegal bargain as a result of fraud, duress, or undue influence, he or she can either enforce the contract or recover for its value.

---

9. *Hall v. Geiger-Jones Co.*, 242 U.S. 539, 37 S.Ct. 217, 61 L.Ed. 480 (1917).

▌ Terms and Concepts

adhesion contract 190
blue law 187
blue sky law 193
contractual capacity 181
disaffirmance 182

emancipation 184
exculpatory clause 191
necessaries 183
ratification 184
reformation 189

unconscionable contract (or unconscionable clause) 190
usury 186

▌ Chapter Summary: Capacity and Legality

CONTRACTUAL CAPACITY	

Minors
(See pages 181–184.)
	A minor is a person who has not yet reached the age of majority. In most states, the age of majority is eighteen for contract purposes. Contracts with minors are voidable at the option of the minor.
	
	1. *Disaffirmance*—Defined as the legal avoidance of a contractual obligation.
	  a. Can take place (in most states) at any time during minority and within a reasonable time after the minor has reached the age of majority.
	  b. If a minor disaffirms a contract, the entire contract must be disaffirmed.
	  c. When disaffirming executed contracts, the minor has a duty to return received goods if they are still in the minor's control or (in some states) to pay their reasonable value.
	  d. A minor who has committed an act of fraud (such as misrepresentation of age) will be denied the right to disaffirm by some courts.
	  e. A minor may disaffirm a contract for necessaries but remains liable for the reasonable value of the goods.
	
	2. *Ratification*—Defined as the affirmation of a voidable legal obligation; may be express or implied.
	  a. Express ratification—Exists when the minor, through a writing or an oral agreement, explicitly assumes the obligations imposed by the contract.
	  b. Implied ratification—Exists when the conduct of the minor is inconsistent with disaffirmance or when the minor fails to disaffirm an executed contract within a reasonable time after reaching the age of majority.
	
	3. *Parents' liability*—Generally, parents are not liable for the contracts made by minor children acting on their own, nor are parents liable for minors' torts except in certain circumstances.
	
	4. *Emancipation*—Occurs when a child's parent or legal guardian relinquishes the legal right to exercise control over the child. Normally, a minor who leaves home to support himself or herself is considered emancipated. In some jurisdictions, minors themselves are permitted to petition for emancipation for limited purposes.

Intoxicated Persons *(See pages 184–185.)*	1. A contract entered into by an intoxicated person is voidable at the option of the intoxicated person if the person was sufficiently intoxicated to lack mental capacity, even if the intoxication was voluntary. 2. A contract with an intoxicated person is enforceable if, despite being intoxicated, the person understood the legal consequences of entering into the contract.
Mentally Incompetent Persons *(See pages 185–186.)*	1. A contract made by a person adjudged by a court to be mentally incompetent is void. 2. A contract made by a mentally incompetent person not adjudged by a court to be mentally incompetent is voidable at the option of the mentally incompetent person.
LEGALITY	
Contracts Contrary to Statute *(See pages 186–188.)*	1. *Usury*—Occurs when a lender makes a loan at an interest rate above the lawful maximum. The maximum rate of interest varies from state to state. 2. *Gambling*—Gambling contracts that contravene (go against) state statutes are deemed illegal and thus void. 3. *Sabbath (Sunday) laws*—Laws prohibiting the formation or the performance of certain contracts on Sunday. Such laws vary widely from state to state, and many states do not enforce them.

▌Chapter Summary: Capacity and Legality—Continued

Contracts Contrary to Statute —Continued	4. *Licensing statutes*—Contracts entered into by persons who do not have a license, when one is required by statute, will not be enforceable *unless* the underlying purpose of the statute is to raise government revenues (and not to protect the public from unauthorized practitioners).
Contracts Contrary to Public Policy (*See pages 188–192.*)	1. *Contracts in restraint of trade*—Contracts to reduce or restrain free competition are illegal. Most such contracts are now prohibited by statutes. An exception is a *covenant not to compete*. It is usually enforced by the courts if the terms are ancillary to a contract (such as a contract for the sale of a business or an employment contract) and are reasonable as to time and area of restraint. Courts tend to scrutinize covenants not to compete closely. If a covenant is overbroad, a court may either reform the covenant to fall within reasonable constraints and then enforce the reformed contract or declare the covenant void and thus unenforceable.
	2. *Unconscionable contracts and clauses*—When a contract or contract clause is so unfair that it is oppressive to one party, it can be deemed unconscionable; as such, it is illegal and cannot be enforced.
	3. *Exculpatory clauses*—An exculpatory clause is a clause that releases a party from liability in the event of monetary or physical injury, no matter who is at fault. In certain situations, exculpatory clauses may be contrary to public policy and thus unenforceable.
Effect of Illegality (*See pages 192–193.*)	In general, an illegal contract is void, and the courts will not aid either party when both parties are considered to be equally at fault (*in pari delicto*). If the contract is executory, neither party can enforce it. If the contract is executed, there can be neither contractual nor quasi-contractual recovery. Exceptions (situations in which recovery is allowed):
	1. When one party to the contract is relatively innocent.
	2. When one party to the contract is a member of a group of persons protected by statute.
	3. When either party seeks to recover consideration given for an illegal contract before the illegal act is performed.
	4. When one party was induced to enter into an illegal bargain through fraud, duress, or undue influence.

▌For Review

1. Generally, a minor can disaffirm any contract. What are some exceptions to this rule?
2. Under what circumstances does intoxication make a contract voidable?
3. Does mental incompetence necessarily render a contract void?

4. Under what circumstances will a covenant not to compete be enforceable? When will such covenants not be enforced?
5. What is an exculpatory clause? In what circumstances might exculpatory clauses be enforced? When will they not be enforced?

▌Questions and Case Problems

9–1. Contracts by Minors. Kalen is a seventeen-year-old minor who has just graduated from high school. He is attending a university two hundred miles from home and has contracted to rent an apartment near the university for one year at $500 per month. He is working at a convenience store to earn enough money to be self-supporting. After living in the apartment and paying monthly rent for four months, a dispute arises between him and the landlord. Kalen, still a minor, moves out and returns the key to the landlord. The landlord wants to hold Kalen liable for the balance of the payments due under the lease. Discuss fully Kalen's liability in this situation.

9–2. Covenants Not to Compete. Joseph, who owns the only pizza parlor in Middletown, learns that Giovanni is about to open a competing pizza parlor in the same small town, just a few blocks from Joseph's restaurant. Joseph offers Giovanni $10,000 in return for Giovanni's promise not to open a pizza parlor in the Middletown area. Giovanni accepts the $10,000 but goes ahead with his plans, in spite of the agreement. When Giovanni opens his restaurant for business, Joseph sues to enjoin (prevent) Giovanni's continued operation of his restaurant or to recover the $10,000. The court denies recovery. On what basis?

9–3. Intoxication. After Katie has several drinks one night, she sells Emily a valuable fur stole for $10. The next day, Katie offers the $10 to Emily and requests the return of her stole. Emily refuses, claiming that they had a valid contract of sale. Katie explains that she was intoxicated at the time the bargain was made, and thus the contract is voidable at her option. Who is right? Explain.

9–4. Mental Incompetence. Jermal has been the owner of a car dealership for a number of years. One day, Jermal sold one of his most expensive cars to Kessler. At the time of the sale, Jermal thought Kessler acted in a peculiar manner, but he gave the matter no further thought until four months later, when Kessler's court-appointed guardian appeared at Jermal's office, tendered back the car, and demanded Kessler's money back. The guardian informed Jermal that Kessler had been adjudicated mentally incompetent two months earlier by a proper court.

(a) Discuss the rights of the parties in this situation.

(b) If Kessler had been adjudicated mentally incompetent before the contract was formed, what would be the legal effect of the contract?

9–5. Licensing Statutes. State X requires that persons who prepare and serve liquor in the form of drinks at commercial establishments be licensed by the state to do so. The only requirement for obtaining a yearly license is that the person be at least eighteen years old. Mickey, aged thirty-five, is hired as a bartender for the Southtown Restaurant. Gerald, a staunch alumnus of a nearby university, brings twenty of his friends to the restaurant to celebrate a football victory one afternoon. Gerald orders four rounds of drinks, and the bill is nearly $200. Gerald learns that Mickey has failed to

renew his bartender's license, and Gerald refuses to pay, claiming that the contract is unenforceable. Discuss whether Gerald is correct.

9–6. Contracts by Minors. In 1982, Webster Street Partnership, Ltd. (Webster), entered into a lease agreement with Matthew Sheridan and Pat Wilwerding. Webster was aware that both Sheridan and Wilwerding were minors. Both tenants were living away from home, apparently with the understanding that they could return home at any time. Sheridan and Wilwerding paid the first month's rent but then failed to pay the rent for the next month and vacated the apartment. Webster sued them for breach of contract. They claimed that the lease agreement was voidable because they were minors. Who will win, and why? [*Webster Street Partnership, Ltd. v. Sheridan*, 220 Neb. 9, 368 N.W.2d 439 (1985)]

9–7. Contracts by Minors. Smith purchased a car on credit from Bobby Floars Toyota, Inc., a month before his eighteenth birthday. Smith made regular monthly payments for eleven months but then returned the car to the dealer and made no further payments on it. The dealer sold the car and sued Smith to recover the difference between the amount obtained by the sale of the car and the money Smith still owed to the dealer. Smith refused to pay on the ground that he had been a minor at the time of purchase and had disaffirmed the contract after he had reached the age of majority. Will the car dealer succeed in its claim that the ten monthly payments made after Smith turned eighteen constituted a ratification of the purchase contract? Discuss. [*Bobby Floars Toyota, Inc. v. Smith*, 48 N.C.App. 580, 269 S.E.2d 320 (1980)]

9–8. Unconscionability. Carolyn Murphy was a welfare recipient with four minor children. After seeing Brian McNamara's advertisement for "rent to own" televisions, Murphy signed a lease agreement with McNamara for a twenty-five-inch Philco color TV at $16 per week. The lease payments were to run for seventy-eight weeks, after which Murphy would become the owner. At no time did McNamara tell Murphy that the total lease payments amounted to $1,268, including the delivery charge. The retail sale price of the set was $499. Murphy had paid about $436 when she read a newspaper article criticizing the lease plan. When she learned that she was required to pay $1,268, Murphy stopped making payments. McNamara's employees attempted to take possession of the TV and made threats through telephone and written communications. Murphy filed suit, alleging, among other things, that the contract terms were unconscionable. Discuss her allegation and whether a court might find the contract unconscionable. [*Murphy v. McNamara*, 36 Conn.Supp. 183, 416 A.2d 170 (1979)]

9–9. Usury. Tony's Tortilla Factory, Inc., had two checking accounts with First Bank. Due to financial difficulties, Tony's wrote a total of 2,165 checks (totaling $88,000) for which there were insufficient funds in the accounts. First Bank paid the overdrawn checks but imposed an "NSF" (nonsufficient funds) fee of $20 for each check paid. The owners of Tony's sued First Bank and one of its officers, alleging, among other things, that the $20-per-check fee was essentially "interest" charged by the bank for Tony's use of the bank's money (the money the bank advanced to cover the bad checks); because the rate of "interest" charged by the bank ($20 per check) exceeded the rate allowed by law, it was usurious. First Bank claimed that its NSF fees were not interest but fees charged to cover its costs in processing checks drawn on accounts with insufficient funds. How should the court decide this issue? Discuss fully. [*First Bank v. Tony's Tortilla Factory, Inc.*, 877 S.W.2d 285 (Tex. 1994)]

9–10. Gambling Contracts. No law prohibits citizens in a state that does not sponsor a state-operated lottery from purchasing lottery tickets in a state that does have such a lottery. Because Georgia did not have a state-operated lottery, Talley and several other Georgia residents allegedly agreed to purchase a ticket in a lottery sponsored by Kentucky and to share the proceeds if they won. They did win, but apparently Talley had difficulty collecting his share of the proceeds. In Talley's suit to obtain his share of the funds, a Georgia trial court held that the "gambling contract" was unenforceable because it was contrary to Georgia's public policy. On appeal, how should the court rule on this issue? Discuss. [*Talley v. Mathis*, 265 Ga. 179, 453 S.E.2d 704 (1995)]

A QUESTION OF ETHICS AND SOCIAL RESPONSIBILITY

9–11. *Michael Niemiec and Judith Polek (the plaintiffs) joined a buyer's club after they had been invited via telephone to visit the club's premises. A salesperson told them that in exchange for a $1,160 membership fee, members could order items from various catalogues at supposedly low prices, but they had to sign the contract then and there or forgo the "once in a lifetime opportunity" to join the club. They signed the contract. When they sought to cancel the contract three days later, they learned that they could not do so. The contract stated that no dues were refundable, even on a member's death; that a membership could not be transferred for any reason; that orders for merchandise could not be canceled even prior to shipment; and that merchandise could not be returned once accepted. Further, although members were to rely on warranties of the supplier for all merchandise, they were forbidden to make any "contact with the suppliers of merchandise." The plaintiffs then sought relief in court. The court held that the contract was unconscionable. [Niemiec v. Kellmark Corp., 153 Misc.2d 347, 581 N.Y.S.2d 569 (1992)]*

1. Courts will sometimes hold contracts unconscionable because of gross inadequacy of consideration. Is that a possibility here? What, for example, did the club offer as consideration for the contract?

2. What might be some other possible reasons for the court's conclusion that this contract was unconscionable?

Accessing the Internet: Fundamentals of Business Law

A good way to learn more about how the courts decide such issues as whether a party lacked capacity due to intoxication or mental incompetence is to look at relevant case law. To find recent cases on contract law decided by the United States Supreme Court and the federal appellate courts, access Cornell University's School of Law site at

http://www.law.cornell.edu/topics/contracts.html

As mentioned in previous chapters, the 'Lectric Law Library provides extensive information on contract requirements. For more information on contractual capacity, access the library's site at

http://www.lectlaw.com

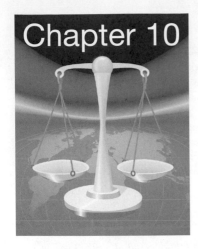

Chapter 10

Assent and Form

CHAPTER OBJECTIVES

After reading this chapter, you should be able to:

1. Distinguish between a mistake of value or quality and a mistake of fact.
2. Describe fraudulent misrepresentation and its elements.
3. Discuss the effects of undue influence and duress on contract enforceability.
4. Identify the types of contracts that must be in writing to be enforceable.
5. State the parol evidence rule, and indicate when parol evidence will be admissible.

A contract has been entered into by two parties, each with full legal capacity and for a legal purpose. The contract is also supported by consideration. Nonetheless, the contract may be unenforceable if the parties have not genuinely assented to the terms. Lack of genuine assent is a *defense* to the enforcement of a contract. If the law were to enforce contracts not genuinely assented to by the contracting parties, injustice would result. The first part of this chapter focuses on what kinds of factors indicate that genuineness of assent to a contract may be lacking.

A contract that is otherwise valid may also be unenforceable if it is not in the proper form. For example, if a contract is required by law to be in writing, and there is no written evidence of the contract, it may not be enforceable. In the second part of this chapter, we examine the kinds of contracts that require a writing under what is called the *Statute of Frauds.* The chapter concludes with a discussion of the *parol evidence rule,* under which courts determine the admissibility at trial of evidence extraneous (external) to written contracts.

▌Genuineness of Assent

Genuineness of assent may be lacking because of mistake, fraudulent misrepresentation, undue influence, or duress. Generally, a party who demonstrates that he or she did not genuinely assent to the terms of a contract can choose either to carry out the contract or to rescind (cancel) it, and thus avoid the entire transaction.

Mistakes

We all make mistakes, and it is not surprising that mistakes are made when contracts are created. In certain circumstances, contract law allows a contract to be avoided on the basis of mistake. Realize, though, that the concept of mistake in contract law has to do with mistaken assumptions relating to contract formation. For example, if you send your monthly bank loan payment to your plumber "by mistake," that is a kind of mistake totally different from the kind of mistake that we are discussing here. In contract law, a mistake may be a defense to the enforcement of a contract if it can be proved that the parties entered into the contract under different assumptions relating to the subject matter of the contract.

Courts have considerable difficulty in specifying the circumstances that justify allowing a mistake to invalidate a contract. Thus, the results in cases with similar facts can be different, and finding clearly defined rules governing the effects of mistakes can be difficult. Generally, though, courts distinguish between *mistakes as to judgment of market value or conditions* and *mistakes as to fact.* Only the latter normally have legal significance.

Suppose, for example, that Jud Wheeler contracts to buy ten acres of land because he believes that he can resell the land at a profit to Bart. Can Jud escape his contractual obligations if it later turns out that he was mistaken? Not likely. Jud's overestimation of the value of the land or of Bart's interest in it is an ordinary risk of business for which a court will not normally provide relief. Now suppose that Jud purchases a painting of a landscape from Roth's Gallery. Both Jud and Roth believe that the painting is by the artist Van Gogh. Jud later discovers that the painting is a very clever fake. Because neither Jud nor Roth was aware of this fact when they made their deal, Jud can rescind the contract and recover the purchase price of the painting.

Mistakes occur in two forms—*unilateral* and *bilateral (mutual).* A unilateral mistake is made by only one of the contracting parties; a mutual mistake is made by both.

UNILATERAL MISTAKES   A unilateral mistake involves some *material fact*—that is, a fact important to the subject matter of the contract. In general, a unilateral mistake does not afford the mistaken party any right to relief from the contract. In other words, the contract normally is enforceable. For example, Ellen intends to sell her motor home for $17,500. When she learns that Chin is interested in buying a used motor home, she faxes him an offer to sell her vehicle to him, but when typing the fax, she mistakenly keys in the price of $15,700. Chin writes back, accepting Ellen's offer. Even though Ellen intended to sell her motor home for $17,500, she has made a unilateral mistake and is bound by contract to sell the vehicle to Chin for $15,700.

There are at least two exceptions.[1] First, if the *other* party to the contract knows or should have known that a mistake of fact was made, the contract may not be enforceable. In the above example, if Chin knew that Ellen intended to sell her motor home for $17,500, then Ellen's unilateral mistake (stating $15,700 in her offer) may render the resulting contract unenforceable. The second exception arises when a unilateral mistake of fact was due to a mathematical mistake in addition, subtraction, division, or multiplication and was made inadvertently and without gross (extreme) negligence. If a contractor's bid was low because he or she made a mistake in addition when totaling the estimated costs, any contract resulting from the bid may be rescinded. Of course, in both situations, the mistake must still involve some *material* fact. In the following case, a unilateral mistake was made when a typist erroneously transformed $500 to $500,000 in a settlement offer.

---

1. *The Restatement (Second) of Contracts,* Section 153, liberalizes the general rule to take into account the modern trend of allowing avoidance in some circumstances even though only one party has been mistaken.

CASE 10.1

Whitaker v. Associated Credit Services, Inc.

United States Court of Appeals, Sixth Circuit, 1991.
946 F.2d 1222.

FACTS   Kenneth and Linda Whitaker had filed an action against Trans Union Corporation and others, alleging violations of the Fair Credit Reporting Act. The lawyer for Trans Union drafted an offer of settlement and presented it to the Whitakers' attorney. The amount of the

(Continued)

Case 10.1—Continued

settlement was supposed to be $500, but the first draft contained a typographical error showing the amount as $500,000. The error went undetected, and the $500,000 figure was typed into the second draft, which was forwarded to Linda Gosnell, Trans Union's attorney, who also did not detect the mistake. Gosnell filed the offer with the clerk of the court and mailed a copy to the Whitakers' lawyer. The Whitakers filed an acceptance of the settlement and forwarded it to Gosnell, who at that time noticed the typing error. The Whitakers refused a substitute offer, and Trans Union filed a motion in a federal district court to set aside the settlement. The district court found for Trans Union, and the Whitakers appealed.

ISSUE   Could the settlement be set aside on the basis of mistake, notwithstanding the fact that the mistake was unilateral?

DECISION   Yes. The U.S. Court of Appeals for the Sixth Circuit affirmed the district court's decision.

REASON   In this case, a clerical error was indisputably the cause of the mistake. The court stated that "any reasonable person would have been shocked by the offer in light of the circumstances of this case[:] *   *   * that before they filed their action, plaintiffs had made no demands for monetary damages; *   *   * that plaintiffs in their complaint had specified only $3,600 in actual damages caused by Trans Union's conduct; and that the purported $500,000 offer was the first offer of any kind that plaintiffs had received from defendants." If the offer was allowed to stand, it would result in unjust enrichment. The court found that there was, in fact, no "meeting of the minds," because the Whitakers were aware of the outrageousness of the $500,000 offer.

FOR CRITICAL ANALYSIS—Social Consideration   *What would be the social ramifications if everybody who received benefits as a result of a mistake retained those benefits?*

MUTUAL MISTAKES   When both parties are mistaken about the same material fact, the contract can be rescinded by either party.[2] Note that, as with unilateral mistakes, the mistake must be about a *material fact* (one that is important and central to the contract). If, instead, a mutual mistake concerns the later market value or quality of the object of the contract, the contract normally can be enforced by either party. This rule is based on the theory that both parties assume certain risks when they enter into a contract. Without this rule, almost any party who did not receive what he or she considered a fair bargain could argue bilateral mistake.

In essence, this would make adequacy of consideration a factor in determining whether a contract existed, and as discussed previously, the courts normally do not inquire into the adequacy of the consideration.

A word or term in a contract may be subject to more than one reasonable interpretation. In that situation, if the parties to the contract attach materially different meanings to the term, their mutual misunderstanding may allow the contract to be rescinded. The following classic case on mutual misunderstanding involved a ship named *Peerless* that was to sail from Bombay with certain cotton goods on board. More than one ship named *Peerless* sailed from Bombay that winter, however.

---

2.   *Restatement (Second) of Contracts,* Section 152.

CASE 10.2

Raffles v. Wichelhaus

Court of Exchequer, England, 1864.
159 Eng.Rep. 375.

FACTS Wichelhaus purchased a shipment of cotton from Raffles to arrive on a ship called the *Peerless* from Bombay, India. Wichelhaus meant a ship called the *Peerless* sailing from Bombay in October; Raffles meant another ship called the *Peerless* sailing from Bombay in December. When the goods arrived on the December *Peerless*, Raffles delivered them to Wichelhaus. By that time, however, Wichelhaus was no longer willing to accept them.

ISSUE Was there a bilateral mistake of fact, which would release Wichelhaus from the contract?

DECISION Yes. The court adjudged that a bilateral mistake of fact had occurred, and hence there was no contract.

REASON When both parties contract under the mistaken, but reasonable, belief that a certain fact is true from an objective viewpoint, neither one is bound by the contract. The British court hearing the case stated, "There is nothing on the face of the contract to show that any particular ship called the 'Peerless' was meant; but the moment it appears that two ships called the 'Peerless' were about to sail from Bombay there is a latent ambiguity. * * * That being so, there was no consensus * * * and therefore no binding contract."

FOR CRITICAL ANALYSIS—Social Consideration *What policy considerations underlie the general rule that contracts involving mutual mistakes of fact may be rescinded, whereas contracts involving unilateral mistakes of fact (with the exceptions discussed earlier) may not be?*

Fraudulent Misrepresentation

Although fraud is a tort, the presence of fraud also affects the genuineness of the innocent party's consent to a contract. When an innocent party consents to a contract with fraudulent terms, the contract usually can be avoided, because he or she has not *voluntarily* consented to the terms.[3] Normally, the innocent party can either rescind (cancel) the contract and be restored to his or her original position or enforce the contract and seek damages for injuries resulting from the fraud.

Typically, there are three elements of fraud:

1. A misrepresentation of a material fact must occur.
2. There must be an intent to deceive.

3. The innocent party must justifiably rely on the misrepresentation.

Additionally, to collect damages, a party must have been injured as a result of the misrepresentation.

MISREPRESENTATION MUST OCCUR The first element of proving fraud is to show that misrepresentation of a material fact has occurred. This misrepresentation can take the form of words or actions. For example, an art gallery owner's statement "This painting is a Picasso" is a misrepresentation of fact if the painting was done by another artist.

A statement of opinion is generally not subject to a claim of fraud. For example, claims such as "This computer will never break down" and "This car will last for years and years" are statements of opinion, not fact, and contracting parties should

---

3. *Restatement (Second) of Contracts*, Sections 163 and 164.

recognize them as such and not rely on them. A fact is objective and verifiable; an opinion is usually subject to debate. Therefore, a seller is allowed to "huff and puff his wares" without being liable for fraud. In certain cases, however, particularly when a naïve purchaser relies on a so-called expert's opinion, the innocent party may be entitled to rescission or reformation (an equitable remedy granted by a court in which the terms of a contract are altered to reflect the true intentions of the parties). The issue in the following case is whether the statements made by instructors at a dancing school to one of the school's dance students qualified as statements of opinion or statements of fact.

CASE 10.3

Vokes v. Arthur Murray, Inc.

Distrist Court of Appeal of Florida, Second District, 1968.
212 So.2d 906.

FACTS Audrey Vokes was a fifty-one-year-old widow. While she was attending a dance party at Davenport's School of Dancing, an Arthur Murray dancing school, an instructor sold her eight half-hour dance lessons for the sum of $14.50. Thereafter, over a period of less than sixteen months, she was sold a total of fourteen dance courses, which amounted to 2,302 hours of dancing lessons for a total cash outlay of $31,090.45. All of these lessons were sold to her by salespersons who continually assured her that she was very talented, that she was progressing in her lessons, that she had great dance potential, and that they were "developing her into a beautiful dancer." Vokes contended that, in fact, she was not progressing in her dancing ability, had no "dance aptitude," and had difficulty even "hearing the musical beat." She filed suit against the school in a Florida state court, seeking rescission of her contract on the ground of fraudulent misrepresentation. When the trial court dismissed her complaint, she appealed.

ISSUE Could Vokes's contract be rescinded because the salespersons misrepresented her dancing ability?

DECISION Yes. The Florida appellate court reinstated Vokes's complaint and remanded the case to the trial court for further proceedings consistent with the appellate court's opinion.

REASON The court held that Vokes could avoid the contract because it was procured by false representations that she had a promising career in dancing. The court acknowledged that ordinarily, to be grounds for rescission, a misrepresentation must be one of fact rather than of opinion. The court concluded that "[a] statement of a party having * * * superior knowledge may be regarded as a statement of fact although it would be considered as opinion if the parties were dealing on equal terms. It could be reasonably supposed here that defendants [the dance studio] had 'superior knowledge' as to whether plaintiff had 'dance potential.'"

FOR CRITICAL ANALYSIS—Social Consideration *If the law imposed liability for fraudulent misrepresentation on all persons who make false statements of opinion (such as "This car is the best on the road"), as well as on those persons who make false statements of fact (such as "This car has only been driven twelve thousand miles"), would society benefit? Explain.*

Misrepresentation by Conduct Misrepresentation can occur by conduct, as well as through express oral or written statements. For example, if a seller, by his or her actions, prevents a buyer from learning of some fact that is material to the contract, such an action constitutes misrepresentation by conduct. Suppose that Cummings contracts to purchase a racehorse from Garner. The horse is blind in one eye, but when Garner shows the horse, he skillfully conceals this fact by keeping the horse's head turned so that Cummings does not see the defect. The concealment constitutes fraud.[4] Another example of misrepresentation by conduct is the false denial of knowledge or information concerning facts that are material to the contract when such knowledge or information is requested.

Misrepresentation of Law Misrepresentation of law does not *ordinarily* entitle a party to be relieved of a contract. For example, Debbie has a parcel of property that she is trying to sell to Barry. Debbie knows that a local ordinance prohibits building anything higher than three stories on the property. Nonetheless, she tells Barry, "You can build a condominium fifty stories high if you want to." Barry buys the land and later discovers that Debbie's statement is false. Normally, Barry cannot avoid the contract, because under the common law, people are assumed to know state and local laws. Exceptions to this rule occur, however, when the misrepresenting party is in a profession known to require greater knowledge of the law than the average citizen possesses.

Misrepresentation by Silence Ordinarily, neither party to a contract has a duty to come forward and disclose facts, and a contract normally will not be set aside because certain pertinent information has not been volunteered. For example, suppose that you are selling a car that has been in an accident and has been repaired. You do not need to volunteer this information to a potential buyer. If, however, the purchaser asks you if the car has had extensive body work and you lie, you have committed a fraudulent misrepresentation.

Generally, if a *serious* defect or a *serious* potential problem is known to the seller but cannot reasonably be suspected to be known by the buyer, the seller may have a duty to speak. For example,

suppose a city fails to disclose to bidders for sewer-construction contracts the fact that subsoil conditions will cause great expense in constructing the sewer. In this situation, the city has committed fraud.[5] Also, when the parties are in a fiduciary relationship (one of trust, such as partners, doctor and patient, or attorney and client), there is a duty to disclose material facts; failure to do so may constitute fraud.

INTENT TO DECEIVE The second element of fraud is knowledge on the part of the misrepresenting party that facts have been falsely represented. This element, normally called *scienter*,[6] or "guilty knowledge," generally signifies that there was an *intent to deceive*. *Scienter* clearly exists if a party knows that a fact is not as stated. *Scienter* also exists if a party makes a statement that he or she believes not to be true or makes a statement recklessly, without regard to whether it is true or false. Finally, this element is met if a party says or implies that a statement is made on some basis, such as personal knowledge or personal investigation, when it is not.

For example, suppose that Rolando, when selling a house to Cariton, tells Cariton that the plumbing pipe is of a certain quality. Rolando knows nothing about the quality of the pipe but does not believe it to be what she is representing it to be (and in fact it is not what she says it is). Rolando's statement induces Cariton to buy the house. Rolando's statement is a misrepresentation, because Rolando does not believe that what she says is true and because she knows that she does not have any basis for making the statement. Cariton can avoid the contract.

RELIANCE ON THE MISREPRESENTATION The third element of fraud is *justifiable reliance* on the misrepresentation of fact. The deceived party must have a justifiable reason for relying on the misrepresentation, and the misrepresentation must be an important factor (but not necessarily the sole factor) in inducing the party to enter into the contract.

---

4. *Restatement (Second) of Contracts*, Section 160.

5. *City of Salinas v. Souza & McCue Construction Co.*, 66 Cal. 2d 217, 424 P.2d 921, 57 Cal.Rptr. 337 (1967). Normally, the seller must disclose only "latent" defects—that is, defects that would not readily be discovered. Thus, termites in a house would not be a latent defect, because a buyer could normally discover their presence.

6. Pronounced sy-*en*-ter.

Reliance is not justified if the innocent party knows the true facts or relies on obviously extravagant statements. Suppose that a used-car dealer tells you, "This old Cadillac will get over sixty miles to the gallon." You normally would not be justified in relying on this statement. Suppose, however, that Merkel, a bank director, induces O'Connell, a co-director, to sign a statement that the bank's assets will satisfy its liabilities by telling O'Connell, "We have plenty of assets to satisfy our creditors." If O'Connell knows the true facts, he is not justified in relying on Merkel's statement. If O'Connell does not know the true facts, however, *and has no way of finding them out*, he may be justified in relying on the statement. The same rule applies to defects in property sold. If the defects are obvious, the buyer cannot justifiably rely on the seller's representations. If the defects are hidden or latent (that is, not apparent on examination), the buyer is justified in relying on the seller's statements.

Can a lawyer justifiably rely on the representations of another lawyer, when the two are on opposite sides in a lawsuit? That was one of the questions in the following case.

CASE 10.4

Fire Insurance Exchange v. Bell

Supreme Court of Indiana, 1994.
643 N.E.2d 310.

FACTS A fire at the Indianapolis home of Joseph Moore severely burned Moore's sixteen-month-old grandson, Jason Bell. Jason's mother, Ruby, hired attorney Robert Collins to negotiate a payment for Jason's injuries with Moore's insurer, the Fire Insurance Exchange. Phillip Scaletta, the attorney for the insurer, told Collins that the limit on Moore's policy was $100,000. After the parties settled, Ruby learned that the limit was actually $300,000. Through Ruby, Jason filed a suit in an Indiana state court against Scaletta and others, alleging, among other things, fraudulent misrepresentation of the policy limits. The defendants filed a motion for summary judgment, which the court denied. The defendants appealed, the state court of appeals affirmed, and the defendants appealed to the Supreme Court of Indiana.

ISSUE Did Jason's attorney have a right to rely on the allegedly fraudulent misrepresentations of the insurer's attorney?

DECISION Yes. The Supreme Court of Indiana affirmed this part of the lower court's decision and remanded the case for further proceedings.

REASON The state supreme court reasoned that it would "burden unnecessarily the courts and litigation process with discovery to verify the truthfulness of material representations made by opposing counsel." Relying on such statements "is an integral component of the fair and efficient administration of justice." The court believed that "[t]he law should promote lawyers' care in making statements that are accurate and trustworthy and should foster the reliance upon such statements by others."

FOR CRITICAL ANALYSIS—Economic Consideration *If attorneys were not held to the standard the court upholds in this case, what would be the effect on negotiations and trial tactics in the course of litigation?*

INJURY TO THE INNOCENT PARTY Most courts do not require a showing of injury when the action is to *rescind* the contract—these courts hold that because rescission returns the parties to the positions they held before the contract was made, a showing of injury to the innocent party is unnecessary.[7]

7. See, for example, *Kaufman v. Jaffe*, 244 App.Div. 344, 279 N.Y.S. 392 (1935).

For a person to recover damages caused by fraud, however, proof of an injury is universally required. The measure of damages is ordinarily equal to the property's value had it been delivered as represented, less the actual price paid for the property. In actions based on fraud, courts often award *punitive*, or *exemplary, damages*—which are granted to a plaintiff over and above the proved, actual compensation for the loss. Punitive damages are based on the public-policy consideration of punishing the defendant or setting an example to deter similar wrongdoing by others.

Undue Influence

Undue influence arises from relationships in which one party can greatly influence another party, thus overcoming that party's free will. Minors and elderly people, for example, are often under the influence of guardians. If a guardian induces a young or elderly *ward* (a person placed by a court under the care of a guardian) to enter into a contract that benefits the guardian, the guardian may have exerted undue influence.

Undue influence can arise from a number of confidential relationships or relationships founded on trust, including attorney-client, doctor-patient, guardian-ward, parent-child, husband-wife, and trustee-beneficiary relationships. The essential feature of undue influence is that the party being taken advantage of does not, in reality, exercise free will in entering into a contract. A contract entered into under excessive or undue influence lacks genuine assent and is therefore voidable.[8]

Duress

Assent to the terms of a contract is not genuine if one of the parties is *forced* into the agreement. Forcing a party to enter into a contract because of the fear created by threats is legally defined as *duress*.[9] In addition, blackmail or extortion to induce consent to a contract constitutes duress. Duress is both a defense to the enforcement of a contract and a ground for rescission, or cancellation, of a contract. Therefore, a party who signs a contract under duress can choose to carry out the contract or to avoid the entire transaction. (The wronged party usually has this choice in cases in which assent is not real or genuine.)

Economic need is generally not sufficient to constitute duress, even when one party exacts a very high price for an item the other party needs. If the party exacting the price also creates the need, however, economic duress may be found. For example, the Internal Revenue Service (IRS) assessed a large tax and penalty against Weller. Weller retained Eyman to resist the assessment. Two days before the deadline for filing a reply with the IRS, Eyman declined to represent Weller unless Weller agreed to pay a very high fee for Eyman's services. The agreement was unenforceable.[10] Although Eyman had threatened only to withdraw his services, something that he was legally entitled to do, he was responsible for delaying his withdrawal until the last days. Because it would have been impossible at that late date to obtain adequate representation elsewhere, Weller was forced into either signing the contract or losing his right to challenge the IRS assessment.

The Statute of Frauds— Requirement of a Writing

Today, almost every state has a statute that stipulates what types of contracts must be in writing. In this text, we refer to such statutes as the **Statute of Frauds.** The primary purpose of the statute is to ensure that there is reliable evidence of the existence and terms of certain classes of contracts deemed historically to be important or complex. Although the statutes vary slightly from state to state, all require the following types of contracts to be in writing or evidenced by a written memorandum:

1. Contracts involving interests in land.
2. Contracts that cannot *by their terms* be performed within one year from the date of formation.
3. Collateral contracts, such as promises to answer for the debt or duty of another.
4. Promises made in consideration of marriage.
5. Contracts for the sale of goods priced at $500 or more.

---

8. *Restatement (Second) of Contracts,* Section 177.
9. *Restatement (Second) of Contracts,* Sections 174 and 175.

10. *Thompson Crane & Trucking Co. v. Eyman,* 123 Cal.App.2d 904, 267 P.2d 1043 (1954).

Certain exceptions are made to the applicability of the Statute of Frauds in some circumstances. These exceptions are discussed later in this section.

The actual name of the Statute of Frauds is misleading, because it does not apply to fraud. Rather, the statute denies enforceability to certain contracts that do not comply with its requirements. The name derives from an English act passed in 1677.

Contracts Involving Interests in Land

Land is real property, which includes not only land but all physical objects that are permanently attached to the soil, such as buildings, plants, trees, and the soil itself. Under the Statute of Frauds, a contract involving an interest in land, to be enforceable, must be evidenced by a writing.[11] If Carol, for example, contracts orally to sell Seaside Shelter to Axel but later decides not to sell, Axel cannot enforce the contract. Similarly, if Axel refuses to close the deal, Carol cannot force Axel to pay for the land by bringing a lawsuit. The Statute of Frauds is a *defense* to the enforcement of this type of oral contract.

A contract for the sale of land ordinarily involves the entire interest in the real property, including buildings, growing crops, vegetation, minerals, timber, and anything else affixed to the land. Therefore, a *fixture* (personal property so affixed or so used as to become a part of the realty—see Chapter 29) is treated as real property.

The Statute of Frauds requires written contracts not just for the sale of land but also for the transfer of other interests in land, such as mortgages and leases. We describe these other interests in Chapter 29.

The One-Year Rule

Contracts that cannot, *by their own terms*, be performed within one year from the day after the contract is formed must be in writing to be enforceable. Because disputes over such contracts are unlikely to occur until some time after the contracts are made, resolution of these disputes is difficult unless the contract terms have been put in writing. The one-year period begins to run *the day after the contract is made*.[12] Exhibit 10–1 illustrates the one-year rule.

The test for determining whether an oral contract is enforceable under the one-year rule of the statute is not whether the agreement is *likely* to be performed within one year from the date of contract formation but whether performance within a year is *possible*. When performance of a contract is

---

11. In some states, the contract will be enforced, however, if each party admits to the existence of the oral contract in court or admits to its existence during discovery before trial (see Chapter 2).

12. Arthur Corbin, *Corbin on Contracts* (St. Paul: West Publishing Co., 1952), Section 444.

♦ **Exhibit 10–1**
   The One-Year Rule

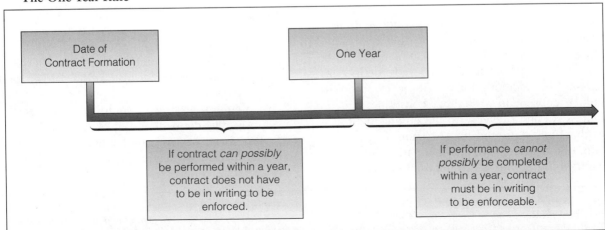

objectively impossible during the one-year period, the oral contract will be unenforceable.

Collateral Promises

A **collateral promise,** or secondary promise, is one that is ancillary (subsidiary) to a principal transaction or primary contractual relationship. In other words, a collateral promise is one made by a third party to assume the debts or obligations of a primary party to a contract if that party does not perform. Any collateral promise of this nature falls under the Statute of Frauds and therefore must be in writing to be enforceable. To understand this concept, it is important to distinguish between primary and secondary promises and obligations.

PRIMARY VERSUS SECONDARY OBLIGATIONS Suppose that Kenneth orally contracts with Joanne's Floral Boutique to send his mother a dozen roses for Mother's Day. Kenneth promises to pay the boutique when he receives the bill for the flowers. Kenneth is a direct party to this contract and has incurred a *primary* obligation under the contract. Because he is a party to the contract and has a primary obligation to Joanne's Floral Boutique, this contract does *not* fall under the Statute of Frauds and does not have to be in writing to be enforceable. If Kenneth fails to pay the florist and the florist sues him for payment, Kenneth cannot raise the Statute of Frauds as a defense. He cannot claim that the contract is unenforceable because it was not in writing.

Now suppose that Kenneth's mother borrows $1,000 from the Medford Trust Company on a promissory note payable six months later. Kenneth promises the bank officer handling the loan that he will pay the $1,000 *if his mother does not pay the loan on time.* Kenneth, in this situation, becomes what is known as a *guarantor* on the loan. That is, he is guaranteeing to the bank (the *creditor*) that he will pay the loan if his mother fails to do so. This kind of collateral promise, in which the guarantor states that he or she will become responsible *only* if the primary party does not perform, must be in writing to be enforceable. We return to the concept of guaranty and the distinction between primary and secondary obligations in Chapter 22, in the context of creditors' rights.

AN EXCEPTION—THE "MAIN PURPOSE" RULE An oral promise to answer for the debt of another is covered by the Statute of Frauds *unless* the guarantor's main purpose in accepting secondary liability is to secure a personal benefit. Under the "main purpose" rule, this type of contract need not be in writing.[13] The assumption is that a court can infer from the circumstances of a case whether the "leading objective" of the promisor was to secure a personal benefit and thus, in effect, to answer for his or her own debt.

Consider an example. Oswald contracts with Machine Manufacturing Company to have some machines custom-made for Oswald's factory. She promises Allrite Materials Supply Company, Machine Manufacturing's supplier, that if Allrite continues to deliver materials to Machine Manufacturing, she will guarantee payment. This promise need not be in writing, even though the effect may be to pay the debt of another, because Oswald's main purpose is to secure a benefit for herself.[14]

Another typical application of the so-called main purpose doctrine is the situation in which one creditor guarantees the debtor's debt to another creditor to forestall litigation. This allows the debtor to remain in business long enough to generate profits sufficient to pay *both* creditors.

Promises Made in Consideration of Marriage

A unilateral promise to pay a sum of money or to give property in consideration of a promise to marry must be in writing. If Mr. Baumann promises to pay Joe Villard $10,000 if Villard promises to marry Baumann's daughter, the promise must be in writing. The same rule applies to **prenuptial agreements**—agreements made before marriage (also called *antenuptial agreements*) that define each partner's ownership rights in the other partner's property. For example, a prospective wife may wish to limit the amount her prospective husband could obtain if the marriage ended in divorce. Prenuptial agreements made in consideration of marriage must be in writing to be enforceable.

Generally, courts tend to give more credence to prenuptial agreements that are accompanied by consideration. For example, assume that Maureen,

---

13. *Restatement (Second) of Contracts,* Section 116.
14. See *Kampman v. Pittsburgh Contracting and Engineering Co.,* 316 Pa. 502, 175 A. 396 (1934).

who has little money, marries Kaiser, who has a net worth of $300 million. Kaiser has several children, and he wants them to receive most of his wealth upon his death. Prior to their marriage, Maureen and Kaiser draft and sign a prenuptial agreement in which Kaiser promises to give Maureen $100,000 per year for the rest of her life should they divorce. As consideration for her consenting to this amount, Kaiser offers Maureen $500,000. If Maureen consents to the agreement and accepts the $500,000, very likely a court would hold this to be a valid prenuptial agreement should the agreement ever be contested.

Contracts for the Sale of Goods

The Uniform Commercial Code (UCC) contains several Statute of Frauds provisions that require written evidence of a contract. Section 2–201 contains the major provision, which generally requires a writing or memorandum for the sale of goods priced at $500 or more. A writing that will satisfy the UCC requirement need only state the quantity term; other terms agreed upon need not be stated "accurately" in the writing, as long as they adequately reflect both parties' intentions. The contract will not be enforceable, however, for any quantity greater than that set forth in the writing. In addition, the writing must be signed by the person against whom enforcement is sought. Beyond these two requirements, the writing need not designate the buyer or the seller, the terms of payment, or the price.

Exceptions to the Statute of Frauds

Exceptions to the applicability of the Statute of Frauds are made in certain situations. We describe those situations here.

PARTIAL PERFORMANCE   In cases involving contracts relating to the transfer of interests in land, if the purchaser has paid part of the price, taken possession, and made permanent improvements to the property, and if the parties cannot be returned to their status quo prior to the contract, a court may grant *specific performance* (performance of the contract according to its precise terms). Whether the courts will enforce an oral contract for an interest in land when partial performance has taken place is usually determined by the degree of injury that

would be suffered if the court chose *not* to enforce the oral contract. In some states, mere reliance on certain types of oral contracts is enough to remove them from the Statute of Frauds.

Under the UCC, an oral contract is enforceable to the extent that a seller accepts payment or a buyer accepts delivery of the goods.[15] For example, if Ajax Corporation ordered by telephone twenty crates of bleach from Cloney, Inc., and repudiated the contract after ten crates had been delivered and accepted, Cloney could enforce the contract to the extent of the ten crates accepted by Ajax.

ADMISSIONS   In some states, if a party against whom enforcement of an oral contract is sought "admits" in pleadings, testimony, or otherwise in court proceedings that a contract for sale was made, the contract will be enforceable.[16] A contract subject to the UCC will be enforceable, but only to the extent of the quantity admitted.[17] Thus, if the president of Ajax Corporation admits under oath that an oral agreement was made with Cloney, Inc., for twenty crates of bleach, the agreement will be enforceable to that extent.

PROMISSORY ESTOPPEL   In some states, an oral contract that would otherwise be unenforceable under the Statute of Frauds may be enforced under the doctrine of promissory estoppel, or detrimental reliance. Recall from Chapter 8 that if a promisor makes a promise on which the promisee justifiably relies to his or her detriment, a court may *estop* (prevent) the promisor from denying that a contract exists. Section 139 of the *Restatement (Second) of Contracts* provides that in these circumstances, an oral promise can be enforceable notwithstanding the Statute of Frauds if the reliance was foreseeable to the person making the promise and if injustice can be avoided only by enforcing the promise.

SPECIAL EXCEPTIONS UNDER THE UCC   Special exceptions to the applicability of the Statute of Frauds apply to sales contracts. Oral contracts for customized goods may be enforced in certain circumstances. Another exception has to do with oral contracts *between merchants* that have been confirmed in writing. We will examine these exceptions in Chapter 13.

---

15.   UCC 2–201(3)(c). See Chapter 13.
16.   *Restatement (Second) of Contracts*, Section 133.
17.   UCC 2–201(3)(b). See Chapter 13.

The Statute of Frauds—Sufficiency of the Writing

A written contract will satisfy the writing requirement of the Statute of Frauds. A *written memorandum* signed by the party against whom enforcement is sought will also satisfy the writing requirement.[18] A writing can consist of any confirmation, invoice, sales slip, check, or fax—or such items in combination. The writing need not consist of a single document to constitute an enforceable contract. One document may incorporate another document by expressly referring to it. Several documents may form a single contract if they are physically attached, by staple, paper clip, or glue. Several documents may form a single contract even if they are only placed in the same envelope.

The signature need not be placed at the end of the document but can be anywhere in the writing; it can even be initials rather than the full name. For example, Sam orally agrees to sell to Terry some land next to a shopping mall. Sam gives to Terry an unsigned memo that contains a legal description of the property, and Terry gives to Sam an unsigned first draft of their contract. Sam writes a signed letter to Terry that refers to the memo and to the first and final drafts of the contract. Terry sends to Sam an unsigned copy of the final draft of the contract with a signed check stapled to it. Together, the documents can constitute a writing sufficient to satisfy the Statute of Frauds and bind both parties to the terms of the contract.

A memorandum evidencing the oral contract need only contain the essential terms of the contract. Under most provisions of the Statute of Frauds, the writing must name the parties, subject matter, consideration, and quantity. With respect to contracts for the sale of land, some states require that the memorandum also state the essential terms of the contract, such as location and price, with sufficient clarity to allow the terms to be determined from the memo itself, without reference to any outside sources.[19] Under the UCC, in regard to the sale of goods, the writing need only name the quantity term and be signed by the party against whom enforcement is sought.

Because only the party against whom enforcement is sought need have signed the writing, a contract may be enforceable by one of its parties but not by the other. Suppose that Rock agrees to buy Devlin's lake house and lot for $150,000. Devlin writes Rock a letter confirming the sale by identifying the parties and the essential terms of the sales contract—price, method of payment, and legal address—and signs the letter. Devlin has made a written memorandum of the oral land contract. Because she signed the letter, she normally can be held to the oral contract by Rock. Rock, however, because he has not signed or entered into a written contract or memorandum, can plead the Statute of Frauds as a defense, and Devlin cannot enforce the contract against him. The following classic case illustrates what may be considered a "signed writing" by the court.

---

18. Under the UCC Statute of Frauds, a writing is only required for contracts for the sale of goods priced at $500 or more. See Chapter 13.

---

19. *Rhodes v. Wilkins*, 83 N.M. 782, 498 P.2d 311 (1972).

CASE 10.5

Drury v. Young

Court of Appeals of Maryland, 1882.
58 Md. 546.

FACTS The plaintiff, Young, formed an oral agreement with the defendant, Drury, to buy several carloads of tomatoes. Afterward, Drury wrote a memorandum concerning the agreement and all its terms for his own records and put it in his safe. The memo, which Drury did not sign, was created on Drury's letterhead (which is a sufficient signing in the eyes of the court) and contained Young's name in the text. Subsequently, Drury wrote a letter to Young stating he was not going to sell Young the tomatoes as agreed. When Young sued Drury in a Maryland state court for breach of contract, Drury used the Statute of Frauds as a defense. The trial court held in Young's favor, claiming that

(Continued)

Case 10.5—Continued

Drury's memo (even if it was never delivered to Young), combined with the subsequent letter, satisfied the writing requirement of the Statute of Frauds. Drury appealed. Ultimately, the Court of Appeals of Maryland (that state's highest court) reviewed the case.

ISSUE   Does the memo written by Drury satisfy the writing requirement under the Statute of Frauds?

DECISION   Yes. The Court of Appeals of Maryland affirmed the trial court's judgment.

REASON   The court stated that the Statute of Frauds is not concerned with whether or not a writing has been delivered, or with the custody of a writing, but just with the *existence* of a writing evidencing the agreement. Drury's memo with the terms of the agreement, kept in his own safe, in conjunction with the subsequent letter to Young denying delivery, provided sufficient evidence to the court that the Statute of Frauds had been satisfied.

FOR CRITICAL ANALYSIS—Technological Consideration   *How does the existence of electronic mail (e-mail) affect the writing requirements under the Statute of Frauds?*

▌The Parol Evidence Rule

The **parol evidence rule** prohibits the introduction at trial of evidence of the parties' prior negotiations, prior agreements, or contemporaneous oral agreements if that evidence contradicts or varies the terms of written contracts. The written contract is ordinarily assumed to be the complete embodiment of the parties' agreement. Because of the rigidity of the parol evidence rule, however, courts make several exceptions:

1. Evidence of a *subsequent modification* of a written contract can be introduced in court. Keep in mind that the oral modifications may not be enforceable if they come under the Statute of Frauds—for example, if they increase the price of the goods for sale to $500 or more or increase the term for performance to more than one year. Also, oral modifications will not be enforceable if the original contract provides that any modification must be in writing.[20]
2. Oral evidence can be introduced in all cases to show that the contract was voidable or void (for example, induced by mistake, fraud, or misrepresentation). In this situation, if deception led one of the parties to agree to the terms of a written contract, oral evidence indicating fraud should not be excluded. Courts frown upon bad faith and are quick to allow such evidence when it establishes fraud.
3. When the terms of a written contract are ambiguous, evidence is admissible to show the meaning of the terms.
4. Evidence is admissible when the written contract is incomplete in that it lacks one or more of the essential terms. The courts allow evidence to "fill in the gaps."
5. Under the UCC, evidence can be introduced to explain or supplement a written contract by showing a prior dealing, course of performance, or usage of trade.[21] We discuss these terms in further detail in Chapter 13, in the context of sales contracts. Here, it is sufficient to say that when buyers and sellers deal with each other over extended periods of time, certain customary practices develop. These practices are often overlooked in the writing of the contract, so courts allow the introduction of evidence to show how the parties have acted in the past.
6. The parol evidence rule does not apply if the existence of the entire written contract is subject to an orally agreed-on condition. Proof of the condition does not alter or modify the written terms but

---

20.   UCC 2–209(2), (3). See Chapter 13.

21.   UCC 1–205, 2–202.

affects the *enforceability* of the written contract. Suppose, for example, that Jelek agrees to purchase Armand's car for $4,000, but only if Jelek's mechanic, Frank, inspects the car and approves of the purchase. Armand agrees to this condition, but because he is leaving town for the weekend and Jelek wants to use the car (if he buys it) before Armand returns, Jelek writes up a contract of sale, and they both sign it. Frank does not approve of the purchase, and when Jelek does not buy the car, Armand sues him, alleging that he breached the contract. In this case, Jelek's oral agreement did not alter or modify the terms of the written agreement but concerned whether or not the contract would exist at all.

7. When an *obvious* or *gross* clerical (or typographic) error exists that clearly would not represent the agreement of the parties, parol evidence is admissible to correct the error. For example, Sharon agrees to lease 1,000 square feet of office space at the current monthly rate of $3 per square foot from Stone Enterprises. The signed written lease provides for a monthly lease payment of $300 rather than the $3,000 agreed to by the parties. Because the error is obvious, Stone Enterprises would be allowed to admit parol evidence to correct the mistake.

The determination of whether evidence will be allowed basically depends on whether the written contract is intended to be a complete and final embodiment of the terms of the agreement. If it is so intended, it is referred to as an **integrated contract**, and extraneous evidence is excluded. If it is only partially integrated, evidence of consistent additional terms is admissible to supplement the written agreement.[22]

---

22. *Restatement (Second) of Contracts*, Section 216.

▮ Terms and Concepts

collateral promise 207	parol evidence rule 210	*scienter* 203
integrated contract 211	prenuptial agreement 207	Statute of Frauds 205

▮ Chapter Summary: Assent and Form

GENUINENESS OF ASSENT	
Mistakes *(See pages 199–201.)*	1. *Unilateral*—Generally, the mistaken party is bound by the contract *unless* (a) the other party knows or should have known of the mistake or (b) the mistake is an inadvertent mathematical error—such as an error in addition or subtraction—committed without gross negligence. 2. *Mutual (bilateral)*—When both parties are mistaken about the same material fact, such as identity, either party can avoid the contract. If the mistake concerns value or quality, either party can enforce the contract.
Fraudulent Misrepresentation *(See pages 201–205.)*	When fraud occurs, usually the innocent party can enforce or avoid the contract. The elements necessary to establish fraud are as follows: 1. A misrepresentation of a material fact must occur. 2. There must be an intent to deceive. 3. The innocent party must justifiably rely on the misrepresentation.
Undue Influence *(See page 205.)*	Undue influence arises from special relationships, such as fiduciary or confidential relationships, in which one party's free will has been overcome by the undue influence exerted by the other party. Usually, the contract is voidable.
Duress *(See page 205.)*	Duress is defined as the tactic of forcing a party to enter a contract under the fear of a threat—for example, the threat of violence or serious economic loss. The party forced to enter the contract can rescind the contract.

(Continued)

▌Chapter Summary: Assent and Form—Continued

FORM	
Contracts Subject to the Statute of Frauds *(See pages 205–208.)*	*Applicability*—The following types of contracts fall under the Statute of Frauds and must be in writing to be enforceable: 1. *Contracts involving interests in land*—The statute applies to any contract for an interest in realty, such as a sale, a lease, or a mortgage. 2. *Contracts whose terms cannot be performed within one year*—The statute applies only to contracts objectively impossible to perform fully within one year from (the day after) the contract's formation. 3. *Collateral promises*—The statute applies only to express contracts made between the guarantor and the creditor whose terms make the guarantor secondarily liable. Exception: "main purpose" rule. 4. *Promises made in consideration of marriage*—The statute applies to promises to pay money or give property in consideration of a promise to marry and to prenuptial agreements made in consideration of marriage. 5. *Contracts for the sale of goods priced at $500 or more*—Under the UCC Statute of Frauds provision in UCC 2–201. *Exceptions*—Partial performance, admissions, and promissory estoppel.
Sufficiency of the Writing *(See pages 209–210.)*	To constitute an enforceable contract under the Statute of Frauds, a writing must be signed by the party against whom enforcement is sought, must name the parties, must identify the subject matter, and must state with reasonable certainty the essential terms of the contract. In a sale of land, the price and a description of the property may need to be stated with sufficient clarity to be determined without reference to outside sources. Under the UCC, a contract for a sale of goods is not enforceable beyond the quantity of goods shown.
Parol Evidence Rule *(See pages 210–211.)*	The parol evidence rule prohibits the introduction at trial of evidence of the parties' prior negotiations, prior agreements, or contemporaneous oral agreements that contradicts or varies the terms of written contracts. The written contract is assumed to be the complete embodiment of the parties' agreement. Exceptions are made in the following circumstances: 1. To show that the contract was subsequently modified. 2. To show that the contract was voidable or void. 3. To clarify the meaning of ambiguous terms. 4. To clarify the terms of the contract when the written contract lacks one or more of its essential terms. 5. Under the UCC, to explain the meaning of contract terms in light of a prior dealing, course of performance, or usage of trade. 6. To show that the entire contract is subject to an orally agreed-on condition. 7. When an obvious clerical or typographic error was made.

▌For Review

1. In what types of situations might genuineness of assent to a contract's terms be lacking?

2. What is the difference between a mistake of value or quality and a mistake of fact?

▌ For Review—Continued

3. What elements must exist for fraudulent misrepresentation to occur?

4. What contracts must be in writing to be enforceable?

5. What is parol evidence? When is it admissible to clarify the terms of a written contract?

▌ Questions and Case Problems

10–1. Genuineness of Assent. Jerome is an elderly man who lives with his nephew, Philip. Jerome is totally dependent on Philip's support. Philip tells Jerome that unless Jerome transfers a tract of land he owns to Philip for a price 15 percent below market value, Philip will no longer support and take care of him. Jerome enters into the contract. Discuss fully whether Jerome can set aside this contract.

10–2. Collateral Promises. Gemma promises a local hardware store that she will pay for a lawn mower that her brother is purchasing on credit if the brother fails to pay the debt. Must this promise be in writing to be enforceable? Why or why not?

10–3. One-Year Rule. On January 1, Dominic, for consideration, orally promised to pay Francis $300 a month for as long as Francis lived, with the payments to be made on the first day of every month. Dominic made the payments regularly for nine months and then made no further payments. Francis claimed that Dominic had breached the oral contract and sued Dominic for damages. Dominic contended that the contract was unenforceable because, under the Statute of Frauds, contracts that cannot be performed within one year must be in writing. Discuss whether Dominic will succeed in this defense.

10–4. Fraudulent Misrepresentation. Larry offered to sell Stanley his car and told Stanley that the car had been driven only 25,000 miles and had never been in an accident. Stanley hired Cohen, a mechanic, to appraise the condition of the car, and Cohen said that the car probably had at least 50,000 miles on it and probably had been in an accident. In spite of this information, Stanley still thought the car would be a good buy for the price, so he purchased it. Later, when the car developed numerous mechanical problems, Stanley sought to rescind the contract on the basis of Larry's fraudulent misrepresentation of the auto's condition. Will Stanley be able to rescind his contract? Discuss.

10–5. Collateral Promises. Jeffrey took his mother on a special holiday to Mountain Air Resort. Jeffrey was a frequent patron of the resort and was well known by its manager. The resort required of each of its patrons a large deposit to ensure payment of the room rental. Jeffrey asked the manager to waive the requirement for his mother and told the manager that if his mother for any reason failed to pay the resort for her stay there, he would cover the bill. Relying on Jeffrey's promise, the manager waived the deposit requirement for Jeffrey's mother. After she returned home from her holiday, Jeffrey's mother refused to pay the resort bill. The resort manager tried to collect the sum from Jeffrey, but Jeffrey also refused to pay, stating that his promise was not enforceable under the Statute of Frauds. Is Jeffrey correct? Explain.

10–6. Genuineness of Assent. Steven Lanci was involved in an automobile accident with an uninsured motorist. Lanci was insured with Metropolitan Insurance Co., although he did not have a copy of the insurance policy. Lanci and Metropolitan entered settlement negotiations, during which Lanci told Metropolitan that he did not have a copy of his policy. Ultimately, Lanci agreed to settle all claims for $15,000, noting in a letter to Metropolitan that $15,000 was the "sum you have represented to be the . . . policy limits applicable to this claim." After signing a release, Lanci learned that the policy limits were actually $250,000, and he refused to accept the settlement proceeds. What defense could Lanci assert to avoid his obligations under the release (contract)? Explain. [*Lanci v. Metropolitan Insurance Co.*, 388 Pa.Super. 1, 564 A.2d 972 (1989)]

10–7. Statute of Frauds. The plaintiffs—the Nicols, Hoerrs, Turners, and Andersons—purchased subdivision lots from Ken Nelson. The lots bordered an undeveloped tract and offered scenic views of an adjacent lake. When Nelson and his partners began taking steps to develop the previously undeveloped tract, the plaintiffs sued to enjoin (prevent) the development of the tract. The plaintiffs argued (and the trial court found) that the plaintiffs had purchased their lots only after receiving oral assurances from Nelson that (1) the tract would remain undeveloped open space, (2) the property was owned by a company that had no plans to build on the land, (3) he held an option to purchase the property if it became available, and (4) he would not develop the land if it came under his ownership. Nelson argued that the Statute of Frauds barred the enforcement of his oral promises. Did it? Explain. [*Nicol v. Nelson*, 776 P.2d 1144 (Colo.App. 1989)]

10–8. Fraudulent Misrepresentation. Nosrat, a citizen of Iran, owned a hardware store with his brother-in-law, Edwin. Edwin induced Nosrat to sign a promissory note written in English, for $11,400, payable to a third party, telling Nosrat that the document was a credit application for the hardware store. Although Nosrat could read and write English, he failed to read the note or to notice that the document was clearly entitled "PROMISSORY NOTE (SECURED) and Security Agreement." Edwin and others spent the money received from the third party in exchange for the note. When the third party sued for payment, Nosrat sought to void the note on the basis of Edwin's fraudulent inducement. Will Nosrat succeed in his attempt? Discuss. [*Waldrep v. Nosrat*, 426 So.2d 822 (Ala. 1983)]

10–9. One-Year Rule. Fernandez orally promised Pando that if Pando helped her win the New York state lottery, she would share the proceeds equally with him. Pando agreed to purchase the tickets in Fernandez's name, select the lottery numbers, and pray for the divine intervention of a saint to help them win. Fernandez won $2.8 million in the lottery, which was to be paid over a ten-year period. When Fernandez failed to share the winnings equally, Pando sued for breach of her contractual obligation. Fernandez countered that their contract was unenforceable under the Statute of Frauds, because the contract could not be performed within one year. Could the contract be performed within one year? Explain. [*Pando by Pando v. Fernandez*, 127 Misc.2d 224, 485 N.Y.S.2d 162 (1984)]

10–10. Genuineness of Assent. Linda Lorenzo purchased Lurlene Noel's home in 1988 without having it inspected. The basement started leaking in 1989. In 1991, Lorenzo had the paneling removed from the basement walls and discovered that the walls were bowed inward and cracked. Lorenzo then had a civil engineer inspect the basement walls, and he found that the cracks had been caulked and painted over before the paneling was installed. He concluded that the "wall failure" had existed "for at least thirty years" and that the basement walls were "structurally unsound." Does Lorenzo have a cause of action against Noel? If so, on what ground? Discuss. [*Lorenzo v. Noel*, 206 Mich.App. 682, 522 N.W.2d 724 (1994)]

10–11. One-Year Rule. Adam Curry worked as a videodisc jockey for MTV Networks (MTVN). In discussions during 1993, Curry and MTVN executives orally agreed that Curry could develop, at his own expense, an Internet site address ("mtv.com") and that MTVN would not interfere with Curry's development of the site. By early 1994, Curry's mtv.com address had been accessed by millions of Internet users, in part because of a computer bulletin board (developed by Curry) that facilitated communication between performers and other music professionals. In the meantime, MTVN decided to offer on-line services through America On-Line. These services were to include a bulletin board similar to that developed by Curry. In mid-January 1994, MTVN requested that Curry cease using the mtv.com address. A dispute ensued, and eventually MTVN sued Curry on several grounds. Curry counterclaimed that MTVN had breached its oral contract with him. MTVN argued that because the contract could not be performed within one year, the Statute of Frauds barred its enforcement. How should the court decide this issue? Explain. [*MTV Networks, A Division of Viacom International, Inc. v. Curry*, 867 F.Supp. 202 (S.D.N.Y. 1994)]

Accessing the Internet: Fundamentals of Business Law

The Library of Congress offers online links to an extensive menu of topics concerning contract law at

http://www.loc.gov/

You can find a research project report on the nature and enforceability of electronic contracts at

http://www.uchastings.edu/plri/fall94/whipple.html

The report discusses critical issues with respect to satisfying the writing requirements of the Statute of Frauds.

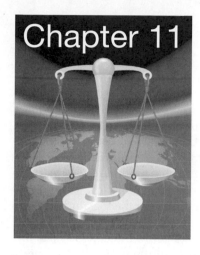

Chapter 11

Third Party Rights and Discharge

CHAPTER OBJECTIVES

After reading this chapter, you should be able to:

1. Identify noncontracting parties who have rights under a contract.
2. Discuss assignments of contract rights, and describe what rights can or cannot be assigned.
3. Explain what a contract condition is and the different kinds of conditions that may exist.
4. Indicate how contract obligations are commonly discharged.
5. Differentiate between complete and substantial performance of a contract, and indicate when a breach of contract occurs.

Because a contract is a private agreement between the parties who have entered into it, it is fitting that these parties alone should have rights and liabilities under the contract. This concept is referred to as **privity of contract,** and it establishes the basic principle that third parties have no rights in contracts to which they are not parties.

You are probably convinced by now that for every rule of contract law there is an exception. As times change, so must the laws, as indicated in the opening quotation. When justice cannot be served by adherence to a rule of law, exceptions to the rule must be made. There are two important exceptions to the rule of privity of contract. One exception allows a party to a contract to transfer the rights arising from the contract to another or to free himself or herself from the duties of a contract by having another person perform them. Legally, the first of these actions is referred to as

an *assignment of rights* and the second, as a *delegation of duties.* A second exception to the rule of privity of contract involves a *third party beneficiary* contract. Here, the rights of a third party against the promisor arise from the original contract, as the parties to the original contract normally make it with the intent to benefit the third party. We discuss the law relating to assignments, delegations, and third party beneficiary contracts in the first half of this chapter.

At some point, parties to a contract must know when their duties are at an end and when their contract is terminated. The second part of this chapter deals with the *discharge* of a contract, which is normally accomplished when both parties have performed the acts promised in the contract. We look at the degree of performance required, as well as at some other ways in which contract discharge can occur.

215

▌Assignments and Delegations

When third parties acquire rights or assume duties arising from contracts to which they were not parties, the rights are transferred to them by *assignment*, and the duties are transferred by *delegation*. Assignment and delegation occur *after* the original contract is made, when one of the parties transfers to another party a right or obligation arising from the contract.

Assignments

In a bilateral (mutual) contract, the two parties have corresponding rights and duties. One party has a right to require the other to perform some task, and the other has a duty to perform it. The transfer of *rights* to a third person is known as an **assignment.** When rights under a contract are assigned unconditionally, the rights of the *assignor* (the party making the assignment) are extinguished.[1] The third party (the *assignee*, or party

---

1. *Restatement (Second) of Contracts*, Section 317.

receiving the assignment) has a right to demand performance from the other original party to the contract (the *obligor*).

Consider Exhibit 11–1, which illustrates assignment relationships. Suppose that Brent owes Alex $1,000, and Alex assigns to Carmen the right to receive the $1,000. Here, a valid assignment of a debt exists. Once Alex has assigned to Carmen his rights under the original contract with Brent, Carmen can enforce the contract against Brent if Brent fails to perform.

The assignee takes only those rights that the assignor originally had. Furthermore, the assignee's rights are subject to the defenses that the obligor has against the assignor. For example, assume that in the above example, Brent owes Alex the $1,000 under a contract in which Brent agreed to buy Alex's personal computer. Brent, in deciding to purchase the computer, relied on Alex's fraudulent misrepresentation that the computer's hard drive had a storage capacity of 1 gigabyte. When Brent discovered that the computer could store only 500 megabytes, he told Alex that he was going to return the computer to him and cancel the contract. Even

♦ **Exhibit 11–1**
  Assignment Relationships
  In the assignment relationship illustrated here, Alex assigns his *rights* under a contract that he made with Brent to a third party, Carmen. Alex thus becomes the *assignor* and Carmen the *assignee* of the contractual rights. Brent, the *obligor* (the party owing performance under the contract), now owes performance to Carmen instead of Alex. Alex's original contract rights are extinguished after assignment.

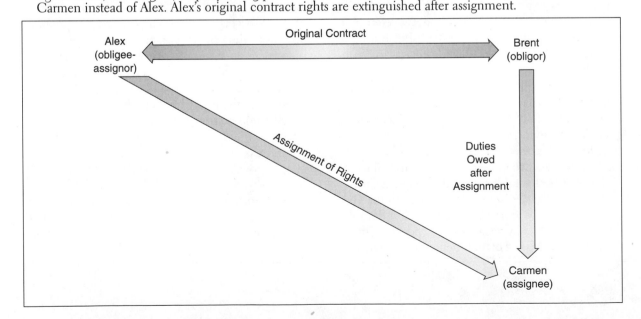

though Alex had assigned his "right" to receive the $1,000 to Carmen, Brent need not pay Carmen the $1,000—Brent can raise the defense of Alex's fraudulent misrepresentation to avoid payment.

Assignments are important because they are involved in much business financing. Banks, for example, frequently assign the rights to receive payments under their loan contracts to other firms, which pay for those rights. For example, if you obtain a loan from your local bank to purchase a car, you might later receive in the mail a notice stating that your bank has transferred (assigned) its rights to receive payments on the loan to another firm and that, when the time comes to repay your loan, you must make the payments to that other firm.

Banks that make *mortgage loans* (loans to allow prospective home buyers to purchase land or a home) often assign their rights to collect the mortgage payments to a third party, such as GMAC Mortgage Corporation. Following the assignment, the home buyers are notified that they must make future payments not to the bank that loaned them the funds but to the third party. Millions of dollars change hands daily in the business world in the form of assignments of rights in contracts. If it were not possible to transfer (assign) contractual rights, many businesses could not continue to operate.

RIGHTS THAT CANNOT BE ASSIGNED   As a general rule, all rights can be assigned. Exceptions are made, however, in the following special circumstances:

1.   If a statute expressly prohibits assignment, the particular right in question cannot be assigned. Suppose that Marn is a new employee of CompuFuture, Inc. CompuFuture is an employer under workers' compensation statutes (see Chapter 32) in this state, and thus Marn is a covered employee. Marn has a relatively high-risk job. In need of a loan, Marn borrows some money from Stark, assigning to Stark all workers' compensation benefits due her should she be injured on the job. The assignment of *future* workers' compensation benefits is prohibited by state statute, and thus such rights cannot be assigned.
2.   When a contract is *personal* in nature, the rights under the contract cannot be assigned unless all that remains is a money payment.[2] Suppose that

Brent signs a contract to be a tutor for Alex's children. Alex then attempts to assign to Carmen his right to Brent's services. Carmen cannot enforce the contract against Brent. Brent may not like Carmen's children or may for some other reason not want to tutor them. Because personal services are unique to the person rendering them, rights to receive personal services cannot be assigned.

3.   A right cannot be assigned if assignment will materially increase or alter the risk or duties of the obligor.[3] Assume that Alex has a hotel, and to insure it he takes out a policy with Northwest Insurance Company. The policy insures against fire, theft, floods, and vandalism. Alex attempts to assign the insurance policy to Carmen, who also owns a hotel. The assignment is ineffective because it may substantially alter the insurance company's duty of performance and the risk that the company undertakes. An insurance company evaluates the particular risk of a certain party and tailors its policy to fit that risk. If the policy is assigned to a third party, the insurance risk is materially altered.

4.   If a contract stipulates that the right cannot be assigned, then *ordinarily* it cannot be assigned. For example, suppose that Brent agrees to build a house for Alex. The contract between Brent and Alex states, "This contract cannot be assigned by Alex without Brent's consent. Any assignment without such consent renders this contract void, and all rights hereunder will thereupon terminate." Alex then assigns his rights to Carmen, without first obtaining Brent's consent. Carmen cannot enforce the contract against Brent.

There are several exceptions to the fourth rule. These exceptions are as follows:

1.   A contract cannot prevent an assignment of the right to receive money. This exception exists to encourage the free flow of money and credit in modern business settings.
2.   The assignment of rights in real estate often cannot be prohibited, because such a prohibition is contrary to public policy. Prohibitions of this kind are called restraints against **alienation** (transfer of land ownership).
3.   The assignment of *negotiable instruments* (see Chapter 17) cannot be prohibited.

---

2.   *Restatement (Second) of Contracts*, Sections 317 and 318.

3.   See UCC 2–210(2).

4.   In a contract for the sale of goods, the right to receive damages for breach of contract or for payment of an account owed may be assigned even though the sales contract prohibits such assignment.[4]

In the following case, the central issue was whether a covenant not to compete contained in an employment contract could be assigned.

---

4.   UCC 2–210(2).

CASE 11.1

Pino v. Spanish Broadcasting System of Florida, Inc.

District Court of Appeal of Florida, Third District, 1990.
564 So.2d 186.

FACTS   In October 1985, Beatriz Pino signed a five-year employment contract as a radio announcer and disc jockey with two radio stations. The contract provided that Pino would not "engage directly or indirectly in the broadcasting business * * * in Dade or Broward Counties, Florida, for a period of twelve (12) months after the termination of her employment by the stations." The contract also provided that it was assignable. In December 1986, the stations sold their assets to Spanish Broadcasting System of Florida, Inc. (SBS), and as part of the sale, Pino's contract was assigned to SBS. In October 1989, Pino contracted with Viva, a broadcasting competitor of SBS, to begin working for Viva when her SBS contract terminated in March 1990. SBS asked a Florida state court to grant a temporary injunction to enforce the agreement not to compete. Pino contended that the assignment of the clause containing the covenant not to compete was invalid. Although a Florida statute provided that covenants not to compete could be enforced, it said nothing about such covenants being assignable. The trial court held for SBS, and Pino appealed.

ISSUE   Was the covenant not to compete assignable?

DECISION   Yes. The appellate court affirmed the trial court's decision.

REASON   The appellate court held that because the contract contained a provision permitting its assignment, the covenant not to compete was assignable. The court explained that its holding "conform[ed] with the policy of preserving the sanctity of contract and providing uniformity and certainty in commercial transactions."

FOR CRITICAL ANALYSIS—Social Consideration   *What interests must a court balance when deciding whether a covenant not to compete is assignable?*

NOTICE OF ASSIGNMENT   Once a valid assignment of rights has been made to a third party, the third party should notify the obligor of the assignment (for example, in Exhibit 11–1, Carmen should notify Brent). Giving notice is not legally necessary to establish the validity of the assignment, because an assignment is effective immediately, whether or not notice is given. Two major problems arise, however, when notice of the assignment is not given to the obligor:

1.   If the assignor assigns the same right to two different persons, the question arises as to which one has priority—that is, which one has the right to the performance by the obligor. Although the rule most often observed in the United States is that the

first assignment in time is the first in right, some states follow the English rule, which basically gives priority to the first assignee who gives notice. For example, suppose that Brent owes Alex $1,000 on a contractual obligation. On May 1, Alex assigns this monetary claim to Carmen. Carmen gives no notice of the assignment to Brent. On June 1, for services Dorman has rendered to Alex, Alex assigns the same monetary claim (to collect $1,000 from Brent) to Dorman. Dorman immediately notifies Brent of the assignment. In the majority of states, Carmen would have priority, because the assignment to Carmen was first in time. In some states, however, Dorman would have priority, because Dorman gave first notice.

2.   Until the obligor has notice of assignment, the obligor can discharge his or her obligation by performance to the assignor, and performance by the obligor to the assignor constitutes a discharge to the assignee. Once the obligor receives proper notice, only performance to the assignee can discharge the obligor's obligations. To illustrate: Suppose that in the above example Alex assigns to Carmen his right to collect $1,000 from Brent. Carmen does not give notice to Brent. Brent subsequently pays Alex the $1,000. Although the assignment was valid, Brent's payment to Alex was a discharge of the debt, and Carmen's failure to give notice to Brent of the assignment caused her to lose the right to collect the money from Brent. If Carmen had given Brent notice of the assignment, however, Brent's payment to Alex would not have discharged the debt.

Delegations

Just as a party can transfer rights to a third party through an assignment, a party can also transfer duties. Duties are not assigned, however; they are *delegated*. Normally, a **delegation of duties** does not relieve the party making the delegation (the *delegator*) of the obligation to perform in the event that the party to whom the duty has been delegated (the *delegatee*) fails to perform. No special form is required to create a valid delegation of duties. As long as the delegator expresses an intention to make the delegation, it is effective; the delegator need not even use the word *delegate*. Exhibit 11–2 graphically illustrates delegation relationships.

DUTIES THAT CANNOT BE DELEGATED   As a general rule, any duty can be delegated. There are,

however, some exceptions to this rule. Delegation is prohibited in the following circumstances:

1.   When performance depends on the *personal* skill or talents of the obligor.
2.   When special trust has been placed in the obligor.
3.   When performance by a third party will vary materially from that expected by the obligee (the one to whom performance is owed) under the contract.
4.   When the contract expressly prohibits delegation.

The following examples will help to clarify the kinds of duties that can and cannot be delegated:

1.   Brent contracts with Alex to tutor Alex in the various aspects of financial underwriting and investment banking. Brent, an experienced businessperson known for his expertise in finance, delegates his duties to a third party, Carmen. This delegation is ineffective, because Brent contracted to render a service that is founded on Brent's *expertise*, and the delegation changes Alex's expectancy under the contract.
2.   Brent contracts with Alex *personally* to mow Alex's lawn during June, July, and August. Then Brent decides that he would rather spend the summer at the beach. Brent delegates his lawn-mowing duties to Carmen, who is in the business of mowing lawns and doing other landscaping work to earn money to pay for college. The delegation is not effective, no matter how competent Carmen is, without Alex's consent. The contract was for *personal* performance.
3.   Brent contracts with Alex to pick up and deliver heavy construction machinery to Alex's property. Brent delegates this duty to Carmen, who is in the business of delivering heavy machinery. This delegation is effective. The performance required is of a *routine* and *nonpersonal* nature, and the delegation does not change Alex's expectancy under the contract.

EFFECT OF A DELEGATION   If a delegation of duties is enforceable, the *obligee* (the one to whom performance is owed) must accept performance from the delegatee (the one to whom the duties are delegated). Consider the third example in the above list, in which Brent delegates his duty (to pick up and deliver heavy construction machinery

◆ **Exhibit 11–2**
Delegation Relationships
In the delegation relationship illustrated here, Brent delegates his *duties* under a contract that he made with Alex to a third party, Carmen. Brent thus becomes the *delegator* and Carmen the *delegatee* of the contractual duties. Carmen now owes performance of the contractual duties to Alex. Note that a delegation of duties does not normally relieve the delegator (Brent) of liability if the delegatee (Carmen) fails to perform the contractual duties.

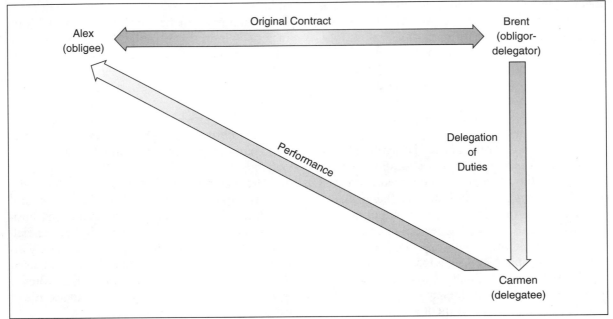

to Alex's property) to Carmen. In that situation, Alex (the obligee) must accept performance from Carmen (the delegatee), because the delegation was effective. The obligee can legally refuse performance from the delegatee only if the duty is one that cannot be delegated.

A valid delegation of duties does not relieve the delegator of obligations under the contract.[5] For example, in the above example, if Carmen (the delegatee) fails to perform, Brent (the delegator) is still liable to Alex (the obligee). The obligee can also hold the delegatee liable if the delegatee made a promise of performance that will directly benefit the obligee. In this situation, there is an "assumption of duty" on the part of the delegatee, and breach of this duty makes the delegatee liable to the obligee. For example, if Carmen (the delegatee) promises Brent (the delegator), in a contract, to pick up and deliver the construction equipment to Alex's property but fails to do so, Alex (the obligee) can sue Brent, Carmen, or both. Although there are many exceptions, the gen-

eral rule today is that the obligee can sue both the delegatee and the delegator.

"Assignment of All Rights"

Sometimes, a contract provides for an "assignment of all rights." The traditional view was that under this type of assignment, the assignee did not assume any duties. This view was based on the theory that the assignee's agreement to accept the benefits of the contract was not sufficient to imply a promise to assume the duties of the contract.

Modern authorities, however, take the view that the probable intent in using such general words is to create both an assignment of rights and an assumption of duties.[6] Therefore, when general words are used (for example, "I assign the contract" or "all my rights under the contract"), the contract is construed as implying both an assignment of rights and an assumption of duties.

---

5.   *Crane Ice Cream Co. v. Terminal Freezing & Heating Co.*, 147 Md. 588, 128 A. 280 (1925).

6.   See UCC 2–210(1), (4); *Restatement (Second) of Contracts*, Section 328.

▮ Third Party Beneficiaries

To have contractual rights, a person normally must be a party to the contract. In other words, privity of contract must exist. As mentioned earlier in this chapter, an exception to the doctrine of privity exists when the original parties to the contract intend at the time of contracting that the contract performance directly benefit a third person. In this situation, the third person becomes a **third party beneficiary** of the contract. As an **intended beneficiary** of the contract, the third party has legal rights and can sue the promisor directly for breach of the contract.

Who, though, is the promisor? In bilateral contracts, both parties to the contract are promisors, because they both make promises that can be enforced. In third party beneficiary contracts, courts will determine the identity of the promisor by asking which party made the promise that benefits the third party—that person is the promisor. Allowing a third party to sue the promisor directly in effect circumvents the "middle person" (the promisee) and thus reduces the burden on the courts. Otherwise, a third party would sue the promisee, who would then sue the promisor.

Types of Intended Beneficiaries

The law distinguishes between *intended* beneficiaries and *incidental* beneficiaries. Only intended beneficiaries acquire legal rights in a contract. One type of intended beneficiary is a *creditor beneficiary*. A creditor beneficiary is one who benefits from a contract in which one party (the promisor) promises another party (the promisee) to pay a debt that the promisee owes to a third party (the creditor beneficiary). As an intended beneficiary, the creditor beneficiary can sue the promisor directly to enforce the contract.

Another type of intended beneficiary is a *donee beneficiary*. When a contract is made for the express purpose of giving a *gift* to a third party, the third party (the donee beneficiary) can sue the promisor directly to enforce the promise.[7] The most common donee beneficiary contract is a life insurance contract. Consider the following example of a typical life insurance contract: Akins (the promisee) pays premiums to Standard Life, a life insurance company, and Standard Life (the promisor) promises to pay a certain amount of money on Akins's death to anyone Akins designates as a beneficiary. The designated beneficiary is a donee beneficiary under the life insurance policy and can enforce the promise made by the insurance company to pay him or her on Akins's death.

As the law concerning third party beneficiaries evolved, numerous cases arose in which the third party beneficiary did not fit readily into either category—creditor beneficiary or donee beneficiary. Thus, the modern view, and the one adopted by the *Restatement (Second) of Contracts*, does not draw such clear lines and distinguishes only between intended beneficiaries (who can sue to enforce contracts made for their benefit) and incidental beneficiaries (who cannot sue, as will be discussed shortly).

Can an intended beneficiary recover on the basis of a contract between an attorney and client for legal services, if a transfer of property from the client to the beneficiary fails due to the attorney's negligence? That is the issue in the following case.

---

7. *Seaver v. Ransom*, 224 N.Y. 233, 120 N.E. 639 (1918).

Case 11.2

Holsapple v. McGrath
Supreme Court of Iowa, 1994.
521 N.W.2d 711.

FACTS Don and Beulah DeVoss hired attorney James McGrath to handle the transfer of title to a farm they wished to give to Bobby and Barbara Holsapple. The transfer failed because McGrath did not have the new deed notarized. The DeVosses died before a corrected deed could be signed. The Holsapples filed a suit in an Iowa state court against McGrath, alleging negligence. McGrath filed a motion to dismiss for failure to state a claim, which the court granted on the ground that the Holsapples were not parties to the lawyer-client

(Continued)

Case 11.2—Continued

relationship between McGrath and the DeVosses and thus McGrath owed them no duty. The Holsapples appealed to the Supreme Court of Iowa.

ISSUE Can the Holsapples recover by establishing that they were intended beneficiaries of the DeVosses' transfer of their property and that the transfer failed only because of McGrath's negligence?

DECISION Yes. The Supreme Court of Iowa reversed the decision of the lower court and remanded the case.

REASON The state supreme court held that plaintiffs such as the Holsapples must plead two elements for their cases to proceed. First, a cause of action for professional negligence arises only when a plaintiff is a "specifically identifiable" beneficiary, as expressed by the grantor (the DeVosses). The court explained that "more than an unrealized expectation of benefits must be shown; a plaintiff must show that the * * * grantor attempted to put the donative wishes into effect and failed to do so only because of the intervening negligence of a lawyer." Second, "a cause of action ordinarily will arise only when as a direct result of the lawyer's professional negligence * * * the [benefit] is * * * lost." Because the Holsapples' petition alleged both elements, "it was error for the district court to dismiss it."

FOR CRITICAL ANALYSIS—Social Consideration *What are the policy reasons for allowing intended beneficiaries to enforce contracts made between other parties for their benefit (or, as in the* Holsapple *case, to sue for negligence in the execution of such a contract)?*

When the Rights of an Intended Beneficiary Vest

An intended third party beneficiary cannot enforce a contract against the original parties until the rights of the third party have *vested*, which means the rights have taken effect and cannot be taken away. Until these rights have vested, the original parties to the contract—the promisor and the promisee—can modify or rescind the contract without the consent of the third party. When do the rights of third parties vest? Generally, the rights vest when either of the following occurs:

1. When the third party demonstrates *manifest assent* to the contract, such as sending a letter or note acknowledging awareness of and consent to a contract formed for his or her benefit.
2. When the third party materially alters his or her position in *detrimental reliance* on the contract.

If the contract expressly reserves to the contracting parties the right to cancel, rescind, or modify the contract, the rights of the third party beneficiary are subject to any changes that result. In such a situation, the vesting of the third party's rights does not terminate the power of the original contracting parties to alter their legal relationships.[8] This is particularly true in most life insurance contracts, in which the right to change the beneficiary is reserved to the policyholder.

Incidental Beneficiaries

The benefit that an **incidental beneficiary** receives from a contract between two parties is unintentional. Therefore, an incidental beneficiary cannot enforce a contract to which he or she is not a party. The following are examples of *incidental* beneficiaries:

---

8. Defenses that can be raised against third party beneficiaries are given in *Restatement (Second) of Contracts*, Section 309.

1.   Jules contracts with Vivian to build a cottage on Vivian's land. Jules's plans specify that Super Insulation Company's insulation materials must be used in constructing the house. Super Insulation Company is an incidental beneficiary and cannot enforce the contract against Jules.

2.   Ed contracts with Ona to build a recreational facility on Ona's land. Once the facility is constructed, it will greatly enhance the property values in the neighborhood. If Ed subsequently refuses to build the facility, Tandy, Ona's neighbor, cannot enforce the contract against Ed.

Intended versus Incidental Beneficiaries

In determining whether a third party beneficiary is an intended or an incidental beneficiary, the courts generally use the *reasonable person* test. That is, a beneficiary will be considered an intended beneficiary if a reasonable person in the position of the beneficiary would believe that the promisee *intended* to confer upon the beneficiary the right to bring suit to enforce the contract. In determining whether a party is an intended or an incidental beneficiary, the courts also look at a number of other factors. The presence of one or more of the following factors strongly indicates that the third party is an *intended* (rather than an incidental) beneficiary to the contract:

1.   Performance is rendered directly to the third party.
2.   The third party has the right to control the details of performance.
3.   The third party is expressly designated as a beneficiary in the contract.

▌Contract Discharge

The most common way to **discharge**, or terminate, one's contractual duties is by the **performance** of those duties. The duty to perform under a contract may be *conditioned* on the occurrence or nonoccurrence of a certain event, or the duty may be *absolute*. In addition to performance, there are numerous other ways in which a contract can be discharged, including discharge by agreement of

the parties and discharge based on impossibility of performance.

Conditions of Performance

In most contracts, promises of performance are not expressly conditioned or qualified. Instead, they are *absolute promises*. They must be performed, or the party promising the act will be in breach of contract. For example, JoAnne contracts to sell Alfonso a painting for $1,000. The parties' promises are unconditional: JoAnne's transfer of the painting to Alfonso and Alfonso's payment of $1,000 to JoAnne. The payment does not have to be made if the painting is not transferred.

In some situations, however, contractual promises are conditioned. A **condition** is a possible future event, the occurrence or nonoccurrence of which will trigger the performance of a legal obligation or terminate an existing obligation under a contract. If the condition is not satisfied, the obligations of the parties are discharged. Suppose that Alfonso, in the above example, offers to purchase JoAnne's painting only if an independent appraisal indicates that it is worth at least $1,000. JoAnne accepts Alfonso's offer. Their obligations (promises) are conditioned upon the outcome of the appraisal. Should this condition not be satisfied (for example, if the appraiser deems the value of the painting to be only $500), their obligations to each other are discharged and cannot be enforced.

We look here at three types of conditions that can be present in any given contract: conditions precedent, conditions subsequent, and concurrent conditions.

CONDITIONS PRECEDENT   A condition that must be fulfilled before a party's promise becomes absolute is called a **condition precedent.** The condition precedes the absolute duty to perform. For example, in the JoAnne-Alfonso example just given, Alfonso's promise is subject to the condition precedent that the appraised value of the painting be at least $1,000. Until the condition is fulfilled, Alfonso's promise is not absolute. Insurance contracts frequently specify that certain conditions, such as passing a physical examination, must be met before the insurance company will be obligated to perform under the contract. The issue in the following case involves a condition precedent.

CASE 11.3

**Cal Wadsworth
Construction v. City
of St. George**

Supreme Court of Utah, 1995.
898 P.2d 1372.

FACTS   The city of St. George asked for bids to expand its municipal airport terminal. Cal Wadsworth Construction submitted the lowest bid. Because even the lowest (Wadsworth's) bid was more than the city had budgeted, the city council accepted the bid only on the condition that Wadsworth reduce it to conform to the city's budget. When Wadsworth did not meet the condition, the city reopened the bidding process. Wadsworth sued the city in a Utah state court for breach of contract. The court ruled in favor of the city on the ground that there was no contract, and Wadsworth appealed. The state appellate court affirmed. Wadsworth appealed to the Supreme Court of Utah.

ISSUE   Did Wadsworth's failure to fulfill the condition regarding reduction of the bid mean that there was no contract between Wadsworth and the city?

DECISION   Yes. The Supreme Court of Utah affirmed the lower court's decision.

REASON   The Supreme Court of Utah pointed out that "the City Council clearly and unambiguously imposed a condition of price reduction on its acceptance of Wadsworth's bid." The court stated that Wadsworth's bid constituted an offer, and the city's modification of the offer (the condition that the price be reduced) constituted a counteroffer, which Wadsworth had not accepted unconditionally. According to the court, "Merely expressing confidence that the requested reduction could be made later [as Wadsworth had done] was insufficient as an acceptance. We therefore hold *   *   * that the court of appeals did not err in concluding that a contract did not come into existence between Wadsworth and the City."

FOR CRITICAL ANALYSIS—Political Consideration   *Why would a government agency impose a price reduction as a condition rather than reject the bidder's offer outright and request the bidder to submit a lower bid?*

CONDITIONS SUBSEQUENT   When a condition operates to terminate a party's absolute promise to perform, it is called a **condition subsequent.** The condition follows, or is subsequent to, the absolute duty to perform. If the condition occurs, the party need not perform any further. For example, assume that a law firm hires Julia Darby, a recent law-school graduate and a newly licensed attorney. Their contract provides that the firm's obligation to continue employing Darby is discharged if Darby fails to maintain her license to practice law. This is a condition subsequent, because a failure to main-

tain the license would discharge a duty that has already arisen.[9]

Generally, conditions precedent are common; conditions subsequent are rare. The *Restatement*

---

9.   The difference between conditions precedent and conditions subsequent is relatively unimportant from a substantive point of view but very important procedurally. Normally, the plaintiff must prove conditions precedent, because usually it is he or she who claims there is a duty to be performed. Similarly, the defendant must usually prove conditions subsequent, because usually it is he or she who claims that a duty no longer exists.

(Second) of Contracts deletes the terms *condition subsequent* and *condition precedent* and refers to both simply as "conditions."[10]

CONCURRENT CONDITIONS   When each party's absolute duty to perform is conditioned on the other party's absolute duty to perform, there are **concurrent conditions.** These conditions exist only when the parties expressly or impliedly are to perform their respective duties *simultaneously.* For example, if a buyer promises to pay for goods when they are delivered by the seller, each party's absolute duty to perform is conditioned upon the other party's absolute duty to perform. The buyer's duty to pay for the goods does not become absolute until the seller either delivers or attempts to deliver the goods. Likewise, the seller's duty to deliver the goods does not become absolute until the buyer pays or attempts to pay for the goods. Therefore, neither can recover from the other for breach without first tendering performance.

Discharge by Performance

The contract comes to an end when both parties fulfill their respective duties by performance of the acts they have promised. Performance can also be accomplished by tender. **Tender** is an unconditional offer to perform by a person who is ready, willing, and able to do so. Therefore, a seller who places goods at the disposal of a buyer has tendered delivery and can demand payment according to the terms of the agreement. A buyer who offers to pay for goods has tendered payment and can demand delivery of the goods. Once performance has been tendered, the party making the tender has done everything possible to carry out the terms of the contract. If the other party then refuses to perform, the party making the tender can consider the duty discharged and sue for **breach of contract**.

COMPLETE VERSUS SUBSTANTIAL PERFORMANCE
Normally, conditions expressly stated in the contract must fully occur in all aspects for *complete performance* (strict performance) of the contract to occur. Any deviation breaches the contract and dis-

charges the other party's obligations to perform. Although in most contracts the parties fully discharge their obligations by complete performance, sometimes a party fails to fulfill all of the duties or completes the duties in a manner contrary to the terms of the contract. The issue then arises as to whether the performance was nonetheless sufficiently substantial to discharge the contractual obligations.

To qualify as *substantial performance*, the performance must not vary greatly from the performance promised in the contract, and it must create substantially the same benefits as those promised in the contract. If performance is substantial, the other party's duty to perform remains absolute (less damages, if any, for the minor deviations).

For example, a couple contracts with a construction company to build a house. The contract specifies that Brand X plasterboard be used for the walls. The builder cannot obtain Brand X plasterboard, and the buyers are on holiday in France and virtually unreachable. The builder decides to install Brand Y instead, which he knows is identical in quality and durability to Brand X plasterboard. All other aspects of construction conform to the contract. Does this deviation constitute a breach of contract? Can the buyers avoid their contractual obligation to pay the builder because Brand Y plasterboard was used instead of Brand X? Very likely, a court would hold that the builder had substantially performed his end of the bargain, and therefore the couple is obligated to pay the builder.[11]

What if the plasterboard substituted for Brand X had been inferior in quality to Brand X, reducing the value of the house by $1,000? Again, a court would likely hold that the contract was substantially performed and that the contractor should be paid the price agreed on in the contract, less that $1,000.

PERFORMANCE TO THE SATISFACTION OF ANOTHER   Contracts often state that completed work must personally satisfy one of the parties or a third person. The question is whether this satisfaction becomes a condition precedent, requiring

---

10.   *Restatement (Second) of Contracts*, Section 224.

11.   For a classic case on substantial performance, see *Jacobs & Young, Inc. v. Kent*, 230 N.Y. 239, 129 N.E. 889 (1921).

actual personal satisfaction or approval for discharge, or whether the test of satisfaction is performance that would satisfy a *reasonable person* (substantial performance).

When the subject matter of the contract is personal, a contract to be performed to the satisfaction of one of the parties is conditioned, and performance must actually satisfy that party. For example, contracts for portraits, works of art, and tailoring are considered personal. Therefore, only the personal satisfaction of the party fulfills the condition—unless a jury finds the party is expressing dissatisfaction only to avoid payment or otherwise is not acting in good faith.

Contracts that involve mechanical fitness, utility, or marketability need only be performed to the satisfaction of a reasonable person unless they *expressly state otherwise.* When such contracts require performance to the satisfaction of a third party (for example, "to the satisfaction of Robert Ames, the supervising engineer"), the courts are divided. A majority of courts require the work to be satisfactory to a reasonable person, but some courts hold that the personal satisfaction of the third party (Robert Ames) must be met. Again, the personal judgment must be made honestly, or the condition will be excused.

MATERIAL BREACH OF CONTRACT   When a breach of contract is *material*[12]—that is, when performance is not deemed substantial—the nonbreaching party is excused from the performance of contractual duties and has a cause of action to sue for damages caused by the breach. If the breach is *minor* (not material), the nonbreaching party's duty to perform can sometimes be suspended until the breach is remedied, but the duty is not entirely excused. Once the minor breach is cured, the nonbreaching party must resume performance of the contractual obligations undertaken.

A breach entitles the nonbreaching party to sue for damages, but only a material breach discharges the nonbreaching party from the contract. The policy underlying these rules is that contracts should go forward when only minor problems occur, but contracts should be terminated if major problems arise.[13] The issue in the following case is whether performance was substantial or so inferior as to constitute a material breach of contract.

---

12.   *Restatement (Second) of Contracts,* Section 241.
13.   See UCC 2–612, which provides that an installment contract for the sale of goods is breached only when one or more nonconforming installments *substantially impairs* the value of the *whole* contract.

CASE 11.4

Warren v. Denison

Court of Appeals of Texas, Amarillo, 1978.
563 S.W.2d 299.

FACTS   Denison was a building contractor hired by the Warrens to construct a house on their property. The parties formed a written contract in which the Warrens agreed to pay Denison $73,400 for the work. Further writings gave Denison the right to foreclose on the house if the Warrens refused to make payments. After the Warrens took possession of the house, they noted several flaws in the construction of the home and refused to pay the $48,400 that they still owed to Denison. Denison initiated foreclosure proceedings, and the Warrens sued Denison in a Texas state court, alleging that Denison had breached their contract by his poor workmanship. The trial court ruled for Denison, and the Warrens appealed.

ISSUE   Had Denison, despite his poor workmanship, discharged his duty under the contract?

DECISION   Yes. The Texas appellate court affirmed the trial court's judgment.

REASON   The court noted that "literal performance of each and every particular of such [construction] contracts is virtually impossible. *   *   * [S]ubstantial performance is regarded as full performance in allowing the builder to recover on the contract. *   *   * [A] job can be substantially performed with some breaches of workmanlike construction pre-

Case 11.4—Continued

venting * * * perfect performance." The Warrens were thus ordered to pay the $48,400 still owed to Denison, minus $2,161.50, which the Warrens felt was necessary to undertake repairs on the house necessitated by Denison's "construction flaws."

FOR CRITICAL ANALYSIS—Economic Consideration *If courts routinely held that only strict (complete) performance could discharge contractual obligations, how would this affect the construction industry? How would it affect homeowners?*

ANTICIPATORY REPUDIATION OF A CONTRACT
Before either party to a contract has a duty to perform, one of the parties may refuse to perform his or her contractual obligations. This is called **anticipatory repudiation**.[14] When anticipatory repudiation occurs, it is treated as a material breach of contract, and the nonbreaching party is permitted to bring an action for damages immediately, even though the scheduled time for performance under the contract may still be in the future.[15] Until the nonbreaching party treats this early repudiation as a breach, however, the breaching party can retract his or her anticipatory repudiation by proper notice and restore the parties to their original obligations.[16]

There are two reasons for treating an anticipatory repudiation as a present, material breach. First, the nonbreaching party should not be required to remain ready and willing to perform when the other party has already repudiated the contract. Second, the nonbreaching party should have the opportunity to seek a similar contract elsewhere and should have the duty to do so to minimize his or her loss.

Quite often, an anticipatory repudiation occurs when a sharp fluctuation in market prices creates a situation in which performance of the contract would be extremely unfavorable to one of the parties. For example, Shasta Manufacturing Company contracts to manufacture and sell 100,000 personal computers to New Age, Inc., a computer retailer with 500 outlet stores. Delivery is to be made eight months from the date of the contract. One month later, three suppliers of computer parts raise their prices to Shasta. Because of these higher prices, Shasta stands to lose $500,000 if it sells the computers to New Age at the contract price. Shasta writes to New Age, informing New Age that it cannot deliver the 100,000 computers at the agreed-on contract price. Even though you might sympathize with Shasta, its letter is an anticipatory repudiation of the contract, allowing New Age the option of treating the repudiation as a material breach and proceeding immediately to pursue remedies, even though the actual contract delivery date is still seven months away.[17]

Discharge by Agreement

Any contract can be discharged by the agreement of the parties. The agreement can be contained in the original contract, or the parties can form a new contract for the express purpose of discharging the original contract.

DISCHARGE BY RESCISSION As discussed in an earlier chapter, *rescission* is the process in which the parties cancel the contract and are returned to the positions they occupied prior to the contract's formation. For *mutual rescission* to take place, the parties must make another agreement that also satisfies the legal requirements for a contract—there must be an *offer*, an *acceptance*, and *consideration*. Ordinarily, if the parties agree to rescind the original contract, their promises *not* to perform those

---

14. *Restatement (Second) of Contracts,* Section 253, and UCC 2–610.
15. The doctrine of anticipatory repudiation first arose in the landmark case of *Hochster v. De La Tour,* 2 Ellis and Blackburn Reports 678 (1853), when the English court recognized the delay and expense inherent in a rule requiring a nonbreaching party to wait until the time of performance before suing on an anticipatory repudiation.
16. See UCC 2–611.

17. Another illustration can be found in *Reliance Cooperage Corp. v. Treat,* 195 F.2d 977 (8th Cir. 1952).

acts promised in the original contract will be legal consideration for the second contract.

Mutual rescission can occur in this manner when the original contract is executory on both sides (that is, neither party has completed performance). The agreement to rescind an executory contract is generally enforceable, even if it is made orally and even if the original agreement was in writing.[18] When one party has fully performed, however, an agreement to rescind the original contract is not usually enforceable. Because the performing party has received no consideration for the promise to call off the original bargain, additional consideration is necessary.[19]

DISCHARGE BY NOVATION   The process of **novation** substitutes a third party for one of the original parties. Essentially, the parties to the original contract and one or more new parties all get together and agree to the substitution. The requirements of a novation are as follows:

1. The existence of a previous, valid obligation.
2. Agreement by all of the parties to a new contract.
3. The extinguishing of the old obligation (discharge of the prior party).
4. A new, valid contract.

An important distinction between an assignment or delegation and a novation is that a novation involves a new contract, and an assignment or delegation involves the old contract.

Suppose that you contract with A. Logan Enterprises to sell it your office-equipment business. Logan later learns that it should not expand at this time but knows of another party, MBI Corporation, that is interested in purchasing your business. All three of you get together and agree to a novation. As long as the new contract is supported by consideration, the novation discharges the original contract between you and Logan and replaces it with the new contract between you and

MBI Corporation. Logan prefers the novation to an assignment because it discharges all the contract liabilities stemming from its contract with you. For example, if an installment sales contract had been involved, requiring twelve monthly payments, and Logan had merely assigned the contract (assigned its rights *and* delegated its duties under the contract) to MBI Corporation, Logan would have remained liable to you for the payments if MBI Corporation defaulted.

DISCHARGE BY ACCORD AND SATISFACTION   As discussed in Chapter 8, in an *accord and satisfaction*, the parties agree to accept performance different from the performance originally promised. An *accord* is defined as an executory contract (one that has not yet been performed) to perform some act in order to satisfy an existing contractual duty that is not yet discharged.[20] A *satisfaction* is the performance of the accord agreement. An *accord* and its *satisfaction* discharge the original contractual obligation.

Once the accord has been made, the original obligation is merely suspended until the accord agreement is fully performed. If it is not performed, the party to whom performance is owed can bring an action on the original obligation. Suppose that Shea obtains a judgment against Marla for $4,000. Later, both parties agree that the judgment can be satisfied by Marla's transfer of her automobile to Shea. This agreement to accept the auto in lieu of $4,000 in cash is the accord. If Marla transfers her automobile to Shea, the accord agreement is fully performed, and the $4,000 debt is discharged. If Marla refuses to transfer her car, the accord is breached. Because the original obligation is merely suspended, Shea can bring an action to enforce the judgment for $4,000 in cash.

When Performance Is Impossible

After a contract has been made, performance may become impossible in an objective sense. This is known as **impossibility of performance** and may discharge a contract.[21]

---

18. Agreements to rescind contracts involving transfers of realty, however, must be evidenced by a writing. Another exception has to do with the sale of goods under the UCC, when the sales contract requires written rescission.
19. Under UCC 2–209(1), however, no consideration is needed to modify a contract for a sale of goods. See Chapter 13. Also see UCC 1–107.

20. *Restatement (Second) of Contracts*, Section 281.
21. *Restatement (Second) of Contracts*, Section 261.

OBJECTIVE IMPOSSIBILITY *Objective impossibility* ("It can't be done") must be distinguished from *subjective impossibility* ("I'm sorry, I simply can't do it"). Examples of subjective impossibility include contracts in which goods cannot be delivered on time because of a freight car shortage[22] and contracts in which money cannot be paid on time because the bank is closed.[23] In effect, the nonperforming party is saying, "It is impossible for *me* to perform," not "It is impossible for *anyone* to perform." Accordingly, such excuses do not discharge a contract, and the nonperforming party is normally held in breach of contract. Four basic types of situations will generally qualify as grounds for the discharge of contractual obligations based on impossibility of performance:[24]

1. *When one of the parties to a personal contract dies or becomes incapacitated prior to performance.* For example, Fred, a famous dancer, contracts with Ethereal Dancing Guild to play a leading role in its new ballet. Before the ballet can be performed, Fred becomes ill and dies. His personal performance was essential to the completion of the contract. Thus, his death discharges the contract and his estate's liability for his nonperformance.

2. *When the specific subject matter of the contract is destroyed.* For example, A-1 Farm Equipment agrees to sell Gudgel the green tractor on its lot and promises to have it ready for Gudgel to pick up on Saturday. On Friday night, however, a truck veers off the nearby highway and smashes into the tractor, destroying it beyond repair. Because the contract was for this specific tractor, A-1's performance is rendered impossible owing to the accident.

3. *When a change in the law renders performance illegal.* An example is a contract to build an apartment building, when the zoning laws are changed to prohibit the construction of residential rental property at this location. This change renders the contract impossible to perform.

4. *When performance becomes commercially impracticable.* The inclusion of this type of "impossibility" as a basis for contract discharge results from a growing trend to allow parties to discharge contracts in which the originally contemplated performance turns out to be much more difficult or expensive than anticipated. In such situations, courts may excuse parties from their performance obligations under the doctrine of *commercial impracticability*. For example, in one case, a court held that a contract could be discharged because a party would have to pay ten times more than the original estimate to excavate a certain amount of gravel.[25] We will discuss this doctrine in more detail in Chapter 15, in the context of sales contracts.

TEMPORARY IMPOSSIBILITY An occurrence or event that makes performance temporarily impossible operates to *suspend* performance until the impossibility ceases. Then, ordinarily, the parties must perform the contract as originally planned. If, however, the lapse of time and the change in circumstances surrounding the contract make it substantially more burdensome for the parties to perform the promised acts, the contract is discharged.

The leading case on the subject, *Autry v. Republic Productions*,[26] involved an actor who was drafted into the army in 1942. Being drafted rendered the actor's contract temporarily impossible to perform, and it was suspended until the end of the war. When the actor got out of the army, the value of the dollar had so changed that performance of the contract would have been substantially burdensome to him. Therefore, the contract was discharged.

---

22. *Minneapolis v. Republic Creosoting Co.*, 161 Minn. 178, 201 N.W. 414 (1924).
23. *Ingham Lumber Co. v. Ingersoll & Co.*, 93 Ark. 447, 125 S.W. 139 (1910).
24. *Restatement (Second) of Contracts*, Sections 262–266, and UCC 2–615.

25. *Mineral Park Land Co. v. Howard*, 172 Cal. 289, 156 P. 458 (1916).
26. 30 Cal.2d 144, 180 P.2d 888 (1947).

▌ Terms and Concepts

alienation 217
anticipatory repudiation 227
assignment 216

breach of contract 225
concurrent condition 225
condition 223

condition precedent 223
condition subsequent 224
delegation of duties 219

▌Terms and Concepts—Continued

discharge 223
impossibility of
   performance 228
incidental beneficiary 222

intended beneficiary 221
novation 228
performance 223
privity of contract 215

tender 225
third party beneficiary 221

▌Chapter Summary: Third Party Rights and Discharge

THIRD PARTY RIGHTS	

Assignment
(See pages 216–219.)
	1. An assignment is the transfer of rights under a contract to a third party. The person assigning the rights is the *assignor,* and the party to whom the rights are assigned is the *assignee.* The assignee has a right to demand performance from the other original party to the contract.
	
	2. Generally, all rights can be assigned, except in the following circumstances:
	  a. When assignment is expressly prohibited by statute (for example, workers' compensation benefits).
	  b. When a contract calls for the performance of personal services.
	  c. When the assignment will materially increase or alter the risks or duties of the *obligor* (the party that is obligated to perform).
	  d. When the contract itself stipulates that the rights cannot be assigned (except a money claim).
	
	3. Notice of the assignment should be given by the assignee to the obligor.
	  a. If the assignor assigns the same right to two different persons, generally the first assignment in time is the first in right, although in some states the first assignee to give notice takes priority.
	  b. Until the obligor is notified of the assignment, the obligor can tender performance to the assignor; and if performance is accepted by the assignor, the obligor's duties under the contract are discharged without benefit to the assignee.

Delegation
(See pages 219–220.)
	1. A delegation is the transfer of duties under a contract to a third party (the delegatee), who then assumes the obligation of performing the contractual duties previously held by the one making the delegation (the delegator).
	
	2. As a general rule, any duty can be delegated, except in the following circumstances:
	  a. When performance depends on the personal skill or talents of the obligor.
	  b. When special trust has been placed in the obligor.
	  c. When performance by a third party will vary materially from that expected by the obligee (the one to whom the duty is owed) under the contract.
	  d. When the contract expressly prohibits delegation.
	
	3. A valid delegation of duties does not relieve the delegator of obligations under the contract. If the delegatee fails to perform, the delegator is still liable to the obligee.
	
	4. An "assignment of all rights" or an "assignment of contract" is often construed to mean that both the rights and duties arising under the contract are transferred to a third party.

Third Party Beneficiary Contract *(See pages 220–223.)*	A third party beneficiary contract is one made for the purpose of benefiting a third party.

▌Chapter Summary: Third Party Rights and Discharge—Continued

Third Party Beneficiary Contract —Continued	1. *Intended beneficiary*—One for whose benefit a contract is created. When the promisor (the one making the contractual promise that benefits a third party) fails to perform as promised, the third party can sue the promisor directly. Examples of third party beneficiaries are creditor beneficiaries and donee beneficiaries.
	2. *Incidental beneficiary*—A third party who indirectly (incidentally) benefits from a contract but for whose benefit the contract was not specifically intended. Incidental beneficiaries have no rights to the benefits received and cannot sue to have the contract enforced.
WAYS TO DISCHARGE A CONTRACT	
Conditions of Performance *(See pages 223–225.)*	Contract obligations may be subject to the following types of conditions:
	1. *Condition precedent*—A condition that must be fulfilled before a party's promise becomes absolute.
	2. *Condition subsequent*—A condition that operates to terminate a party's absolute promise to perform.
	3. *Concurrent conditions*—Each party's absolute duty to perform is conditioned on the other party's absolute duty to perform.
Discharge by Performance *(See pages 225–227.)*	A contract may be discharged by complete (strict) or by substantial performance. In some cases, performance must be to the satisfaction of another. Totally inadequate performance constitutes a material breach of contract. An anticipatory repudiation of a contract allows the other party to sue immediately for breach of contract.
Discharge by Agreement *(See pages 227–228.)*	Parties may agree to discharge their contractual obligations in several ways:
	1. *By rescission*—The parties mutually agree to rescind (cancel) the contract.
	2. *By novation*—A new party is substituted for one of the primary parties to a contract.
	3. *By accord and satisfaction*—The parties agree to render performance different from that originally agreed on.
Discharge by Objective Impossibility of Performance *(See pages 228–229.)*	Parties' obligations under contracts may be discharged by objective impossibility of performance owing to one of the following events:
	1. The death or incapacity of a person whose performance is essential to the completion of the contract.
	2. The destruction of the specific subject matter of the contract prior to transfer.
	3. A change in the law that renders the performance called for by the contract illegal.
	4. Commercial impracticability of performance.

▌For Review

1. What is the difference between an assignment and a delegation?

2. State what rights can be assigned despite a contract clause expressly prohibiting assignment.

3. What factors indicate that a third party beneficiary is an intended beneficiary?

4. How are most contracts discharged?

5. What is a contractual condition, and how might a condition affect contractual obligations?

▌Questions and Case Problems

11–1. Substantial Performance. Complete performance is strict performance according to the terms of a contract. What is substantial performance?

11–2. Third Party Beneficiaries. Wilken owes Rivera $2,000. Howie promises Wilken to pay Rivera the $2,000 in return for Wilken's promise to give Howie's children guitar lessons. Is Rivera an intended beneficiary of the Howie-Wilken contract? Explain.

11–3. Assignments. Aron is a student attending college. He signs a one-year lease agreement that runs from September 1 to August 31. The lease agreement specifies that the lease cannot be assigned without the landlord's consent. In late May, Aron decides not to go to summer school and assigns the balance of the lease (three months) to a close friend, Erica. The landlord objects to the assignment and denies Erica access to the apartment. Aron claims that Erica is financially sound and should be allowed the full rights and privileges of an assignee. Discuss fully whether the landlord or Aron is correct.

11–4. Novation versus Accord and Satisfaction. Doug owes creditor Cartwright $1,000, which is due and payable on June 1. Doug has a car accident, misses several months of work, and consequently does not have the money to pay Cartwright on June 1. Doug's father, Bert, offers to pay Cartwright $1,100 in four equal installments if Cartwright will discharge Doug from any further liability on the debt. Cartwright accepts. In view of these events, answer the following questions.

   (a) Is the transaction a novation, or is it an accord and satisfaction? Explain.

   (b) Does the contract between Bert and Cartwright have to be in writing to be enforceable? (Review the Statute of Frauds.) Explain.

11–5. Impossibility of Performance. Millie contracted to sell Frank 1,000 bushels of corn to be grown on Millie's farm. Owing to drought conditions during the growing season, Millie's yield was much less than anticipated, and she could deliver only 250 bushels to Frank. Frank accepted the lesser amount but sued Millie for breach of contract. Can Millie defend successfully on the basis of objective impossibility of performance? Explain.

11–6. Third Party Beneficiaries. Rensselaer Water Co. was under contract to the city of Rensselaer, New York, to provide water to the city, including water at fire hydrants. A warehouse owned by H. R. Moch Co. was totally destroyed by a fire that could not be extinguished because of inadequate water pressure at the fire hydrants. Moch brought suit against Rensselaer Water Co. for damages, claiming that Moch was a third party beneficiary to the city's contract with the water com-

pany. Will Moch be able to recover damages from the water company on the basis that the water company breached its contract with the city? Explain. [*H. R. Moch Co. v. Rensselaer Water Co.*, 247 N.Y. 160, 159 N.E. 896 (1928)]

11–7. Third Party Beneficiaries. Owens, a federal prisoner, was transferred from federal prison to the Nassau County Jail pursuant to a contract between the U.S. Bureau of Prisons and the county. The contract included a policy statement that required the receiving prison to provide for the safekeeping and protection of transferred federal prisoners. While in the Nassau County Jail, Owens was beaten severely by prison officials and suffered lacerations, bruises, and a lasting impairment that caused blackouts. Can Owens, as a third party beneficiary, sue the county for breach of its agreement with the U.S. Bureau of Prisons? [*Owens v. Haas*, 601 F.2d 1242 (2d Cir. 1979)]

11–8. Performance and Discharge. John Agosta and his brother Salvatore had formed a corporation, but disagreements between the two brothers caused John to petition for voluntary dissolution of the corporation. According to the dissolution agreement, the total assets of the corporation, which included a warehouse and inventory, would be split between the brothers by Salvatore's selling his stock to John for $500,000. This agreement was approved, but shortly before the payment was made, a fire totally destroyed the warehouse and inventory, which were the major assets of the corporation. John refused to pay Salvatore the $500,000, and Salvatore brought suit for breach of contract. Discuss whether the destruction of the major assets of the corporation affects John's required performance under the contract. [*In the Matter of Fontana v. D'Oro Foods, Inc.*, 122 Misc.2d 1091, 472 N.Y.S.2d 528 (1983)]

11–9. Assignments. Abby's Cakes on Dixie, Inc., agreed in a lease contract to lease space in a shopping center from Colonial Palms Plaza, Ltd. The contract provided that Colonial would pay Abby's a construction allowance of up to $11,250 after Abby's had satisfactorily completed certain improvements to the rented premises. The contract also prohibited any "assignment, encumbrance or subletting" of the premises by Abby's without Colonial's prior consent. Before the improvements were completed, Abby's assigned its right to receive the first $8,000 of the construction allowance to Robert Aldana (without first obtaining Colonial's consent). In return, Aldana loaned Abby's $8,000 to finance the construction. Aldana notified Colonial of the assignment by certified mail. After Abby's had completed the improvements, Colonial ignored the assignment and paid Abby's the construction allowance. Will

Aldana succeed in his suit against Colonial for the $8,000 due him pursuant to the assignment? Explain. [*Aldana v. Colonial Palms Plaza, Ltd.*, 591 So.2d 953 (Fla.App. 1992)]

11–10. Conditions Precedent. Larry McLanahan's 1985 Lamborghini was stolen, and by the time McLanahan recovered the car, it had been extensively damaged. The car was insured by Farmers Insurance Co. of Washington under a policy providing comprehensive coverage, including theft. A provision in the policy stated that the coverage for theft damages was subject to certain terms and conditions, including the condition that any person claiming coverage under the policy must allow Farmers "to inspect and appraise the damaged vehicle before its repair or disposal." McLanahan, without notifying Farmers and without giving Farmers an opportunity to inspect the vehicle, sold the car to a wholesale car dealer. Farmers then denied coverage, and McLanahan brought suit to recover for the damages caused to his car by the theft. Did McLanahan have a valid claim against the insurance company? Explain. [*McLanahan v. Farmers Insurance Co. of Washington*, 66 Wash.App. 36, 831 P.2d 160 (1992)]

11–11. Third Party Beneficiaries. When Charles and Judy Orr were divorced in 1970, their divorce agreement included a provision that Charles would pay for the college or professional school education of the couple's two children, then minors. In 1990, when Charles's daughter Jennifer was attending college, Charles refused to pay her college tuition. Can Jennifer, who was not a party to her parents' divorce agreement, bring a court action to compel her father to pay her college expenses? Discuss fully. [*Orr v. Orr*, 228 Ill.App.3d 234, 592 N.E.2d 553, 170 Ill.Dec. 117 (1992)]

11–12. Assignments. Joseph LeMieux, of Maine, won $373,000 in a lottery operated by the Tri-State Lotto Commission. The lottery is sponsored by the three northern New England states and is administered in Vermont. Per its usual payment plan, Tri-State was to pay the $373,000 to LeMieux in annual installments over a twenty-year period. LeMieux assigned his rights to the lottery installment payments for the years 1996 through 2006 to Singer Freidlander Corp. for the sum of $80,000. LeMieux and Singer Freidlander (the plaintiffs) sought a declaratory judgment from a court authorizing the assignment agreement between them despite Tri-State's regulation barring the assignment of lottery proceeds. The trial court granted Tri-State's motion for summary judgment. On appeal, the plaintiffs argued that Tri-State's regulation was invalid. Is it? Discuss. [*LeMieux v. Tri-State Lotto Commission*, 666 A.2d 1170 (Vt. 1995)]

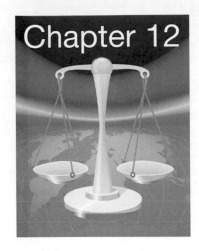

Chapter 12

Breach and Remedies

CHAPTER OBJECTIVES

After reading this chapter, you should be able to:

1. Define the different types of damages that may be obtainable on the breach of a contract.
2. Describe the usual measure of damages for breach of various types of contracts.
3. Distinguish between liquidated damages and penalties.
4. List the equitable remedies that may be granted by courts, and indicate when they will be granted.
5. Explain the common law doctrine of election of remedies.

Normally, the reason a person enters into a contract with another is to secure an advantage. When it is no longer advantageous for a party to fulfill his or her contractual obligations, breach of contract may result. As discussed in Chapter 11, a *breach of contract* occurs when a party fails to perform part or all of the required duties under a contract.[1] Once a party fails to perform or performs inadequately, the other party—the nonbreaching party—can choose one or more of several remedies.

The most common remedies available to a nonbreaching party include damages, rescission and restitution, specific performance, and reformation. As discussed in Chapter 1, courts distinguish between *remedies at law* and *remedies in equity*. Today, the remedy at law is normally money dam-

ages. We discuss this remedy in the first part of this chapter. Equitable remedies include rescission and restitution, specific performance, and reformation, all of which we examine later in the chapter. Usually a court will not award an equitable remedy unless the remedy at law is inadequate. In the final pages of this chapter, we look at some special legal doctrines and concepts relating to remedies.

▌Damages

A breach of contract entitles the nonbreaching party to sue for money damages. As you read in Chapter 4, damages are designed to compensate a party for harm suffered as a result of another's wrongful act. In the context of contract law, damages are designed to compensate the nonbreaching party for the loss of the bargain. Often, courts say

---

1. *Restatement (Second) of Contracts*, Section 235(2).

234

that innocent parties are to be placed in the position they would have occupied had the contract been fully performed.[2]

Types of Damages

There are basically four kinds of damages: compensatory, consequential, punitive, and nominal damages.

COMPENSATORY DAMAGES As discussed in Chapter 4, *compensatory damages* compensate an injured party for injuries or damages actually sustained by that party. The nonbreaching party must prove that the actual damages arose directly from the loss of the bargain caused by the breach of contract. The amount of compensatory damages is the difference between the value of the breaching party's promised performance under the contract and the value of his or her actual performance. This amount is reduced by any loss that the injured party has avoided, however.

Suppose that you contract with Marinot Industries to perform certain personal services exclusively for Marinot during August for a payment of $3,500. Marinot cancels the contract and is in breach. You are able to find another job during August but can only earn $1,000. You normally can sue Marinot for breach and recover $2,500 as compensatory damages. You may also recover from Marinot the amount you spent to find the other job. Expenses or costs that are caused directly by a breach of contract—such as those incurred to obtain performance from another source—are *incidental damages.*

The measurement of compensatory damages varies by type of contract. Certain types of contracts deserve special mention—contracts for the sale of goods, contracts for the sale of land, and construction contracts.

Sale of Goods In a contract for the sale of goods, the usual measure of compensatory damages is an amount equal to the difference between the contract price and the market price.[3] Suppose that MediQuick Laboratories contracts with Cal Computer Industries to purchase ten Model X-15 computer workstations for $8,000 each. If Cal Computer fails to deliver the ten workstations, and the current market price of the workstations is $8,150, MediQuick's measure of damages is $1,500 (10 × $150). In cases in which the buyer breaches and the seller has not yet produced the goods, compensatory damages normally equal the lost profits on the sale, not the difference between the contract price and the market price.

Sale of Land The measure of damages in a contract for the sale of land is ordinarily the same as it is for contracts involving the sale of goods—that is, the difference between the contract price and the market price of the land. The majority of states follow this rule regardless of whether it is the buyer or the seller who breaches the contract.

A minority of states, however, follow a different rule when the seller breaches the contract and the breach is not deliberate. An example of a nondeliberate breach of a contract to sell land occurs when a previously unknown easement (a right of use over the property of another) is discovered and renders title to the land unmarketable. (In real property law, *title* means the right to own property or the evidence of that right.) In such a situation, these states allow the prospective purchaser to recover any down payment plus any expenses incurred (such as fees for title searches or attorneys). This minority rule effectively places a purchaser in the position that he or she occupied prior to the contract of sale.

Construction Contracts With construction contracts, the measure of damages often varies depending on which party breaches and at what stage the breach occurs. See Exhibit 12–1 for illustrations. In the following case, the issue centers on the proper measure of damages in a breached construction contract.

---

2. *Restatement (Second) of Contracts,* Section 347, and UCC 1–106(1).

3. That is, the difference between the contract price and the market price at the time and place at which the goods were to be delivered or tendered. See UCC 2–708 and 2–713 (discussed in Chapter 15).

CASE 12.1

Shadow Lakes, Inc. v. Cudlipp Construction and Development Co.

District Court of Appeal of Florida, Second District, 1995.
658 So.2d 116.

FACTS Cudlipp Construction and Development Company agreed to build up to 375 houses for Shadow Lakes, Inc., near Tampa, Florida. Under the contract, the parties were bound to complete fourteen of the houses, but either party had the right to terminate the agreement with regard to future houses if prices could not be mutually agreed on by the parties. For each house, Shadow Lakes agreed to pay a fixed price, which included the costs of construction and a fee for Cudlipp's services. The contract indicated that the fee covered "off-site and on-site supervision, office overhead and general support," as well as Cudlipp's profit—which, according to Cudlipp's testimony at trial—was to be $10,000 per house. Problems developed between the parties after Cudlipp had begun to construct eight houses. Cudlipp filed a suit in a Florida state court against Shadow Lakes, alleging, among other things, breach of contract. The damages Cudlipp sought included lost profits of $3,670,000 ($10,000 for 367 houses—375 houses less the 8 houses already under construction). The jury awarded Cudlipp $3,670,000 in lost profits, and Shadow Lakes appealed.

ISSUE Was $10,000 an accurate figure for the amount of Cudlipp's lost profits for each house?

DECISION No. The District Court of Appeal of Florida reversed the award and remanded for a new trial on the amount.

REASON The state appellate court concluded in part that the amount of profit to be realized on each home was "speculative." Additionally, stated the court, "Whether or not the parties would have come to a meeting of the minds regarding other houses beyond the original fourteen is pure speculation and conjecture. Not only did the parties have to agree on price, but the acreage needed for the project had to be purchased by Shadow Lakes." The court pointed out that the contract indicated, and Cudlipp later acknowledged, that "certain overhead and other expenses should be subtracted from" the $10,000 per house. Moreover, Cudlipp's owner testified that "the $10,000 figure also included possible upgrades to the houses by the ultimate purchasers."

FOR CRITICAL ANALYSIS—Economic Consideration *What might be an appropriate measure of damages if in fact a contractor was realizing no profit, or was even actually losing money, on a contract?*

CONSEQUENTIAL DAMAGES Foreseeable damages that result from a party's breach of contract are referred to as **consequential damages,** or *special damages.* Consequential damages differ from compensatory damages in that they are caused by special circumstances beyond the contract itself. When a seller does not deliver goods, *knowing* that a buyer is planning to resell those goods immediately, consequential damages are awarded for the loss of profits from the planned resale. For example, Gilmore contracts to have a specific item shipped to her—one that she desperately needs to repair her printing press. In contracting with the shipper, Gilmore tells him that she must receive the item by Monday or she will not be able to print her paper and will lose $750. If the shipper is late, Gilmore normally can recover the consequential damages caused by the delay (that is, the $750 in losses).

♦ **Exhibit 12–1**
Measurement of Damages—Breach of Construction Contracts

PARTY IN BREACH	TIME OF BREACH	MEASUREMENT OF DAMAGES
Owner	Before construction begins	Profits (contract price less cost of materials and labor)
Owner	After construction begins	Profits plus costs incurred up to time of breach
Owner	After construction is completed	Contract price
Contractor	Before construction is completed	Generally, all costs incurred by owner to complete construction

For a nonbreaching party to recover consequential damages, the breaching party must know (or have reason to know) that special circumstances will cause the nonbreaching party to suffer an additional loss.[4] When damages are awarded, compensation is given only for those injuries that the defendant *could reasonably have foreseen* as a probable result of the usual course of events following a breach. If the injury complained of is outside the usual and foreseeable course of events, the plaintiff must show specifically that the defendant had reason to know the facts and foresee the injury.

PUNITIVE DAMAGES Recall from Chapter 4 that *punitive damages* are designed to punish a wrongdoer and set an example to deter similar conduct in the future. Punitive damages, which are also referred to as *exemplary damages,* are generally not recoverable in an action for breach of contract. Such damages have no legitimate place in contract law because they are, in essence, penalties, and a breach of contract is not unlawful in a criminal sense. A contract is simply a civil relationship between the parties. The law may compensate one party for the loss of the bargain—no more and no less.

In a few situations, a person's actions can cause both a breach of contract and a tort. For example, the parties can establish by contract a certain reasonable standard or duty of care. Failure to live up to that standard is a breach of contract, and the act itself may constitute negligence. An intentional tort (such as fraud) may also be tied to a breach of contract. In such a situation, it is possible for the nonbreaching party to recover punitive damages for the tort in addition to compensatory and consequential damages for the breach of contract.

NOMINAL DAMAGES Damages that are awarded to an innocent party when only a technical injury is involved and no actual damage (no financial loss) has been suffered are called **nominal damages.** Nominal damage awards are often small, such as one dollar, but they do establish that the defendant acted wrongfully.

For example, suppose that Parrott contracts to buy potatoes at fifty cents a pound from Lentz. Lentz breaches the contract and does not deliver the potatoes. Meanwhile, the price of potatoes falls. Parrott is able to buy them in the open market at half the price he agreed to pay Lentz. Parrott is clearly better off because of Lentz's breach. Thus, in a suit for breach of contract, Parrott may be awarded only nominal damages for the technical injury he sustained, as no monetary loss was involved. Most lawsuits for nominal damages are brought as a matter of principle under the theory that a breach has occurred and some damages must be imposed regardless of actual loss.

Mitigation of Damages

In most situations, when a breach of contract occurs, the injured party is held to a duty to mitigate, or reduce, the damages that he or she suffers. Under this doctrine of **mitigation of damages,** the required action depends on the nature of the situation. For

---

4.   UCC 2–715(2). See Chapter 15.

example, in the majority of states, wrongfully terminated employees have a duty to mitigate damages suffered by their employers' breach. The damages they will be awarded are their salaries less the incomes they would have received in similar jobs obtained by reasonable means. It is the employer's burden to prove the existence of such jobs and to prove that the employee could have been hired. An employee is, of course, under no duty to take a job that is not of the same type and rank. This is illustrated in the following case.

CASE 12.2

Parker v. Twentieth Century-Fox Film Corp.
Supreme Court of California, 1970.
3 Cal.3d 176,
474 P.2d 689,
89 Cal.Rptr. 737.

FACTS Twentieth Century-Fox Film Corporation planned to produce a musical, *Bloomer Girl,* and contracted with Shirley MacLaine Parker to play the leading female role. According to the contract, Fox was to pay Parker $53,571.42 per week for fourteen weeks, for a total of $750,000. Fox later decided not to produce *Bloomer Girl* and tried to substitute another contract for the existing contract. Under the terms of this second contract, Parker would play the leading role in a Western movie for the same amount of money guaranteed by the first contract. Fox gave Parker one week in which to accept the new contract. Parker filed suit in a California state court against Fox to recover the amount of compensation guaranteed in the first contract because, she maintained, the two roles were not at all equivalent. The *Bloomer Girl* production was a musical, to be filmed in California, and it could not be compared with a "western-type" production that Fox tentatively planned to produce in Australia. When the trial court held for Parker, Fox appealed. Ultimately, the California Supreme Court reviewed the case.

ISSUE May Fox's substitute offer of the Western movie contract be used in mitigating the damages ensuing from the breach of the first contract?

DECISION No. The California Supreme Court affirmed the judgment for Parker.

REASON The court noted that the "measure of recovery by a wrongfully discharged employee is the amount of salary agreed upon for the period of service, less the amount which the employer affirmatively proves the employee has earned or with reasonable effort might have earned from other employment. Before projected earnings from other employment opportunities not sought or accepted by the discharged employee can be applied in mitigation, however, the employer must show that the other employment was comparable, or substantially similar, to that of which the employee has been deprived." The court held that the two roles were substantially dissimilar—that is, one called for Parker's dancing and acting abilities, and the other was simply an acting role in a Western movie. The court asserted that "by no stretch of the imagination" could the latter "be considered the equivalent of or substantially similar to the lead in a song-and-dance production."

FOR CRITICAL ANALYSIS—International Consideration *Many legal systems, including that of France, have no clear requirement that damages must be mitigated. Can justice be better served by requiring that damages be mitigated? If so, how?*

Liquidated Damages versus Penalties

A **liquidated damages** provision in a contract specifies that a certain amount of money is to be paid in the event of a future default or breach of contract. (*Liquidated* means determined, settled, or fixed.) Liquidated damages differ from penalties. A **penalty** specifies a certain amount to be paid in the event of a default or breach of contract and is designed to penalize the breaching party. Liquidated damages provisions normally are enforceable; penalty provisions are not.[5]

To determine whether a particular provision is for liquidated damages or for a penalty, the court must answer two questions: First, at the time the contract was formed, was it difficult to estimate the potential damages that would be incurred if the contract was not performed on time? Second, was the amount set as damages a reasonable estimate of those potential damages and not excessive?[6] If the answers to both questions are yes, the provision will be enforced. If either answer is no, the provision will normally not be enforced. In a construction contract, it is difficult to estimate the amount of damages that might be caused by a delay in completing construction, so liquidated damages clauses are often used.

The following case involved a contract clause that required a client to pay an attorney substantial damages if the client terminated its relationship with the attorney. The issue before the court was whether the clause was a liquidated damages clause or a penalty clause.

---

5. This is also the rule under the Uniform Commercial Code. See UCC 2–718(1).

6. *Restatement (Second) of Contracts*, Section 356(1).

CASE 12.3

AFLAC, Inc. v. Williams

Supreme Court of Georgia, 1994.
264 Ga. 351,
444 S.E.2d 314.

FACTS AFLAC, Inc., hired Peter Williams, an attorney, under a seven-year contract to give the company legal advice as needed. The contract provided that if AFLAC terminated the relationship, it would pay Williams 50 percent of whatever amount was due for the remaining term. After four years, AFLAC terminated the contract with Williams and asked a Georgia state court to determine the enforceability of the termination payment provision. The court declared the provision unenforceable, and Williams appealed. The state appellate court reversed this decision, and AFLAC appealed.

ISSUE Does a contract clause that requires a client to pay his or her attorney unreasonably high damages for discharging the attorney constitute an improper penalty?

DECISION Yes. The Supreme Court of Georgia, holding that the provision was an unenforceable penalty clause, reversed the decision of the intermediate appellate court.

REASON The state supreme court explained that the contract "requires AFLAC to pay an unreasonably high sum as damages, requires payment without considering Williams' duty to mitigate his damages, and obligates AFLAC to pay even if Williams is discharged for cause." Thus, the provision "is not a reasonable estimate of Williams' damages and instead is a penalty imposed to punish AFLAC."

FOR CRITICAL ANALYSIS—Ethical Consideration *Why shouldn't parties to a contract be allowed to agree to the imposition of whatever penalty they wish in the event of a breach?*

Rescission and Restitution

As discussed in Chapter 11, *rescission* is essentially an action to undo, or cancel, a contract—to return nonbreaching parties to the positions that they occupied prior to the transaction. When fraud, mistake, duress, or failure of consideration is present, rescission is available. The failure of one party to perform under a contract entitles the other party to rescind the contract.[7] The rescinding party must give prompt notice to the breaching party. Furthermore, both parties must make **restitution** to each other by returning goods, property, or money previously conveyed.[8] If the goods or property can be restored *in specie*—that is, if they can be returned—they must be. If the goods or property have been consumed, restitution must be made in an equivalent amount of money.

Essentially, restitution refers to the recapture of a benefit conferred on the defendant through which the defendant has been unjustly enriched. For example, Andrea pays $10,000 to Miles in return for Miles's promise to design a house for her. The next day Miles calls Andrea and tells her that he has taken a position with a large architectural firm in another state and cannot design the house. Andrea decides to hire another architect that afternoon. Andrea can get restitution of $10,000, because she conferred an unjust benefit of $10,000 on Miles.

Specific Performance

The equitable remedy of **specific performance** calls for the performance of the act promised in the contract. This remedy is often attractive to a nonbreaching party, because it provides the exact bargain promised in the contract. It also avoids some of the problems inherent in a suit for money damages. First, the nonbreaching party need not worry about collecting the judgment.[9] Second, the nonbreaching party need not look around for another contract. Third, the actual performance may be more valuable than the money damages. Although the equitable remedy of specific performance is often preferable to other remedies, normally it is not granted unless the party's legal remedy (money damages) is inadequate.[10]

For example, contracts for the sale of goods that are readily available on the market rarely qualify for specific performance. Money damages ordinarily are adequate in such situations, because substantially identical goods can be bought or sold in the market. If the goods are unique, however, a court of equity will decree specific performance. For example, paintings, sculptures, and rare books and coins are often unique, and money damages will not enable a buyer to obtain substantially identical substitutes in the market. The same principle applies to contracts relating to sales of land or interests in land, because each parcel of land is unique by legal description.

Courts normally refuse to grant specific performance of contracts for personal services. Sometimes the remedy at law may be adequate if substantially identical services are available from other persons (as with lawn-mowing services). Even for individually tailored personal-service contracts, courts are very hesitant to order specific performance by a party, because public policy strongly discourages involuntary servitude.[11] Moreover, the courts do not want to monitor a personal-service contract. For example, if you contract with a brain surgeon to perform brain surgery on you and the surgeon refuses to perform, the court would not compel (and you certainly would not want) the

---

7. The rescission discussed here refers to *unilateral* rescission, in which only one party wants to undo the contract. In *mutual* rescission, both parties agree to undo the contract. Mutual rescission discharges the contract; unilateral rescission is generally available as a remedy for breach of contract.
8. *Restatement (Second) of Contracts*, Section 370.
9. Courts dispose of cases, after trials, by entering judgments. A judgment may order the losing party to pay money damages to the winning party. Collection of judgments, however, poses problems—such as when the judgment debtor is insolvent (cannot pay his or her bills when they become due) or has only a small net worth, or when the debtor's assets cannot be seized, under exemption laws, by a creditor to satisfy a debt (see Chapter 20).
10. *Restatement (Second) of Contracts*, Section 359.
11. The Thirteenth Amendment to the U.S. Constitution prohibits involuntary servitude, but negative injunctions (that is, prohibiting rather than ordering certain conduct) are possible. Thus, you may not be able to compel a person to perform under a personal-service contract, but you may be able to restrain that person from engaging in similar contracts with others for a period of time.

surgeon to perform under these circumstances. There is no way the court can assure meaningful performance in such a situation.[12]

Reformation

When the parties have imperfectly expressed their agreement in writing, the equitable remedy of *reformation* allows the contract to be rewritten to reflect the parties' true intentions. This remedy applies most often when fraud or mutual mistake (for example, a clerical error) has occurred. If Keshan contracts to buy a certain piece of equipment from Shelley but the written contract refers to a different piece of equipment, a mutual mistake has occurred. Accordingly, a court could reform the contract so that the writing conforms to the parties' original intention as to which piece of equipment is being sold.

Two other examples deserve mention. The first involves two parties who have made a binding oral contract. They further agree to reduce the oral contract to writing, but in doing so, they make an error in stating the terms. Universally, the courts allow into evidence the correct terms of the oral contract, thereby reforming the written contract.

The second example has to do with written covenants not to compete. As discussed in Chapter 9, if a covenant not to compete is for a valid and legitimate purpose (such as the sale of a business), but the area or time restraints of the covenant are unreasonable, some courts reform the restraints by making them reasonable and enforce the entire contract as reformed. Other courts throw the entire restrictive covenant out as illegal.

Recovery Based on Quasi Contract

Recall from Chapter 7 that a quasi contract is not a true contract but a fictional contract that is imposed on the parties to obtain justice and prevent unjust enrichment. Hence, a quasi contract becomes an equitable basis for relief. Generally,

when one party confers a benefit on another, justice requires that the party receiving the benefit pay a reasonable value for it so as not to be unjustly enriched at the other party's expense.

Quasi-contractual recovery is useful when one party has *partially* performed under a contract that is unenforceable. It can be an alternative to suing for damages, and it allows the party to recover the reasonable value of the partial performance. For quasi-contractual recovery to occur, the party seeking recovery must show the following:

1. A benefit was conferred on the other party.
2. The party conferring the benefit did so with the expectation of being paid.
3. The party seeking recovery did not act as a volunteer in conferring the benefit.
4. Retaining the benefit without paying for it would result in an unjust enrichment of the party receiving the benefit.

For example, suppose that Ericson contracts to build two oil derricks for Petro Industries. The derricks are to be built over a period of three years, but the parties do not create a written contract. Enforcement of the contract will therefore be barred by the Statute of Frauds.[13] Ericson completes one derrick, and then Petro Industries informs him that it will not pay for the derrick. Ericson can sue in quasi contract because (1) a benefit (one oil derrick) has been conferred on Petro Industries; (2) Ericson conferred the benefit (built the derrick) expecting to be paid; (3) Ericson did not volunteer to build the derrick but built it under an unenforceable oral contract; and (4) allowing Petro Industries to retain the derrick without paying would enrich the company unjustly. Therefore, Ericson should be able to recover the reasonable value of the oil derrick (under the theory of *quantum meruit*[14]—"as much as he deserves"). The reasonable value is ordinarily equal to the fair market value.

Election of Remedies

In many cases, a nonbreaching party has several remedies available. Because the remedies may be

---

12. Similarly, courts often refuse to order specific performance of construction contracts, because courts are not set up to operate as construction supervisors or engineers.

13. Contracts that by their terms cannot be performed within one year must be in writing to be enforceable. See Chapter 10.
14. Pronounced *kwahn*-tuhm *mehr*-oo-wuht.

inconsistent with one another, the common law of contract requires the party to choose which remedy to pursue. This is called *election of remedies*.

The purpose of the doctrine of election of remedies is to prevent double recovery. Suppose that Jefferson agrees to sell his land to Adams. Then Jefferson changes his mind and repudiates the contract. Adams can sue for compensatory damages or for specific performance. If she receives damages as a result of the breach, she should not also be granted specific performance of the sales contract, because that would mean she would end up with both the land *and* damages, which would be unfair. In effect, she would recover twice for the same breach of contract. The doctrine of election of remedies requires Adams to choose the remedy she wants, and it eliminates any possibility of double recovery.

Unfortunately, the doctrine has been applied in a rigid and technical manner, leading to some harsh results. For example, in a Wisconsin case, a man named Carpenter was fraudulently induced to buy a piece of land for $100. He spent $140 moving onto the land and then discovered the fraud. Instead of suing for damages, Carpenter sued to rescind the contract. The court denied recovery of the $140 because the seller, Mason, had not received the $140 and was therefore not required to reimburse Carpenter for his moving expenses. So Carpenter suffered a net loss of $140 on the transaction. If Carpenter had sued for damages, he could have recovered the $100 purchase price and the $140.[15]

In the following case, the frustrated sellers of a house were apparently attempting to avoid the doctrine of election of remedies in order to, as the old saying goes, "have their cake and eat it, too."

---

15. See *Carpenter v. Mason*, 181 Wis. 114, 193 N.W. 973 (1923). Because of the harsh results of the doctrine of election of remedies, the Uniform Commercial Code expressly rejects it. Remedies under the UCC, discussed in Chapter 15, are essentially *cumulative* in nature (see UCC 2–703 and 2–711).

Case 12.4

Palmer v. Hayes

Court of Appeals of Utah, 1995.
892 P.2d 1059.

FACTS Kenneth and Rebecca Palmer wanted to sell their house. Edward and Stephanie Hayes signed a proposed contract of sale, under which they agreed to give the Palmers' real estate agent, Maple Hills Realty, $2,000 as a deposit on the house. The agreement provided that in the event of default, the Palmers could either keep the deposit or sue to enforce their rights. The Palmers accepted the Hayeses' offer and signed the contract. Before the property changed hands, however, the Hayeses changed their minds and asked for the return of their deposit. The Palmers refused and filed a suit against the Hayeses in a Utah state court, seeking damages. The Hayeses filed a motion for summary judgment on the ground that, by not releasing the deposit, the Palmers had elected their remedy. The court ruled in favor of the Hayeses on this point, and the Palmers appealed.

ISSUE Did the Palmers' failure to release the deposit money before filing their suit for damages constitute an election of remedies?

DECISION Yes. The Court of Appeals of Utah, concluding that the Palmers had elected the remedy of retaining the deposit, affirmed the lower court's ruling.

REASON The state appellate court held that "a seller's failure to offer to return * * * deposits precludes the seller from pursuing other remedies." The court explained that the Palmers "needed only to indicate to Maple Hills Realty, in writing, that they released the deposit money to the Hayeses. Then they could have proceeded with their suit for damages." The court concluded that "by failing to release the deposit money, the Palmers elected to retain it as liquidated damages."

Case 12.4—Continued   **FOR CRITICAL ANALYSIS—Economic Consideration** *What are the reasons for applying the doctrine of election of remedies to preclude sellers who keep deposits from suing for damages?*

▌ Provisions Limiting Remedies

A contract may include provisions stating that no damages can be recovered for certain types of breaches or that damages must be limited to a maximum amount. The contract may also provide that the only remedy for breach is replacement, repair, or refund of the purchase price. Provisions stating that no damages can be recovered are called *exculpatory clauses* (see Chapter 10). Provisions that affect the availability of certain remedies are called *limitation-of-liability clauses.*

Whether these contract provisions and clauses will be enforced depends on the type of breach that is excused by the provision. For example, a provision excluding liability for fraudulent or intentional injury will not be enforced. Likewise, a clause excluding liability for illegal acts or violations of law will not be enforced. A clause excluding liability for negligence may be enforced in some cases. When an exculpatory clause for negligence is contained in a contract made between parties who have roughly equal bargaining positions, the clause usually will be enforced.

The UCC provides that in a contract for the sale of goods, remedies can be limited. We will examine the UCC's provisions on limited remedies in Chapter 15, in the context of the remedies available on the breach of a sales contract.

▌ Terms and Concepts

consequential damages 236	nominal damages 237	restitution 240
liquidated damages 239	penalty 239	specific performance 240
mitigation of damages 237		

▌ Chapter Summary: Breach and Remedies

COMMON REMEDIES AVAILABLE TO THE NONBREACHING PARTY	

Damages
(See pages 234–239.)
	The legal remedy of damages is designed to compensate the nonbreaching party for the loss of the bargain. By awarding money damages, the court tries to place the parties in the positions that they would have occupied had the contract been fully performed. The nonbreaching party frequently has a duty to *mitigate* (lessen or reduce) the damages incurred as a result of the contract's breach. There are five broad categories of damages:
	
	1. *Compensatory damages*—Damages that compensate the nonbreaching party for injuries actually sustained and proved to have arisen directly from the loss of the bargain resulting from the breach of contract.
	   a. In breached contracts for the sale of goods, the usual measure of compensatory damages is an amount equal to the difference between the contract price and the market price.
	   b. In breached contracts for the sale of land, the measure of damages is ordinarily the same as in contracts for the sale of goods.
	   c. In breached construction contracts, the measure of damages depends on which party breaches and at what stage of construction the breach occurs.
	
	2. *Consequential damages*—Damages resulting from special circumstances beyond the contract itself; the damages flow only from the consequences of a breach. For a party to recover consequential damages, the damages must be the foreseeable result
	<div align="right">*(Continued)*</div>

▌Chapter Summary: Breach and Remedies—Continued

Damages—Continued	of a breach of contract, and the breaching party must have known at the time the contract was formed that special circumstances existed and that the nonbreaching party would incur additional loss upon breach of the contract. Also called *special damages*. 3. *Punitive damages*—Damages awarded to punish the breaching party. Usually not awarded in an action for breach of contract unless a tort is involved. 4. *Nominal damages*—Damages small in amount (such as one dollar) that are awarded when a breach has occurred but no actual damages have been suffered. Awarded only to establish that the defendant acted wrongfully. 5. *Liquidated damages*—Damages that may be specified in a contract as the amount to be paid to the nonbreaching party in the event the contract is later breached. Clauses providing for liquidated damages are enforced if the damages were difficult to estimate at the time the contract was formed and if the amount stipulated is reasonable. If construed to be a penalty, the clause will not be enforced.
Rescission and Restitution *(See page 240.)*	1. *Rescission*—A remedy whereby a contract is canceled and the parties are restored to the original positions that they occupied prior to the transaction. Available when fraud, a mistake, duress, or failure of consideration is present. The rescinding party must give prompt notice of the rescission to the breaching party. 2. *Restitution*—When a contract is rescinded, both parties must make restitution to each other by returning the goods, property, or money previously conveyed. Restitution prevents the unjust enrichment of the defendant.
Specific Performance *(See pages 240–241.)*	An equitable remedy calling for the performance of the act promised in the contract. Specific performance is only available in special situations—such as those involving contracts for the sale of unique goods or land—and when monetary damages would be an inadequate remedy. Specific performance is not available as a remedy in breached contracts for personal services.
Reformation *(See page 241.)*	An equitable remedy allowing a contract to be "reformed," or rewritten, to reflect the parties' true intentions. Available when an agreement is imperfectly expressed in writing.
Recovery Based on Quasi Contract *(See page 241.)*	An equitable theory imposed by the courts to obtain justice and prevent unjust enrichment in a situation in which no enforceable contract exists. The party seeking recovery must show the following: 1. A benefit was conferred on the other party. 2. The party conferring the benefit did so with the expectation of being paid. 3. The benefit was not volunteered. 4. Retaining the benefit without paying for it would result in the unjust enrichment of the party receiving the benefit.
CONTRACT DOCTRINES RELATING TO REMEDIES	
Election of Remedies *(See pages 241–243.)*	A common law doctrine under which a nonbreaching party must choose one remedy from those available. This doctrine prevents double recovery.
Provisions Limiting Remedies *(See page 243.)*	A contract may provide that no damages (or only a limited amount of damages) can be recovered in the event the contract is breached. Clauses excluding liability for fraudulent or intentional injury or for illegal acts cannot be enforced. Clauses excluding liability for negligence may be enforced if both parties hold roughly equal bargaining power. Under the UCC, in contracts for the sale of goods, remedies may be limited.

▌ For Review

1. What is the difference between compensatory damages and consequential damages? What are nominal damages, and when might they be awarded by a court?
2. What is the usual measure of damages on a breach of contract for a sale of goods?
3. Under what circumstances will the remedy of rescission and restitution be available?

4. When might specific performance be granted as a remedy?
5. What is the rationale underlying the doctrine of election of remedies? Does the UCC accept or reject the doctrine?

▌ Questions and Case Problems

12–1. Liquidated Damages. Carnack contracts to sell his house and lot to Willard for $100,000. The terms of the contract call for Willard to pay 10 percent of the purchase price as a deposit toward the purchase price, or as a down payment. The terms further stipulate that should the buyer breach the contract, the deposit will be retained by Carnack as liquidated damages. Willard pays the deposit, but because her expected financing of the $90,000 balance falls through, she breaches the contract. Two weeks later Carnack sells the house and lot to Balkova for $105,000. Willard demands her $10,000 back, but Carnack refuses, claiming that Willard's breach and the contract terms entitle him to keep the deposit. Discuss who is correct.

12–2. Election of Remedies. Perez contracts to buy a new Oldsmobile from Central City Motors, paying $2,000 down and agreeing to make twenty-four monthly payments of $350 each. He takes the car home and, after making one payment, learns that his Oldsmobile has a Chevrolet engine in it rather than the famous Olds Super V-8 engine. Central City never informed Perez of this fact. Perez immediately notifies Central City of his dissatisfaction and returns the car to Central City. Central City accepts the car and returns to Perez the $2,000 down payment plus the one $350 payment. Two weeks later Perez, without a car and feeling angry, files a suit against Central City, seeking damages for breach of warranty and fraud. Discuss the effect of Perez's actions.

12–3. Specific Performance. In which of the following situations might a court grant specific performance as a remedy for the breach of contract?

(a) Tarrington contracts to sell her house and lot to Rainier. Then, on finding another buyer willing to pay a higher purchase price, she refuses to deed the property to Rainier.

(b) Marita contracts to sing and dance in Horace's nightclub for one month, beginning June 1. She then refuses to perform.

(c) Juan contracts to purchase a rare coin from Edmund, who is breaking up his coin collec-

tion. At the last minute, Edmund decides to keep his coin collection intact and refuses to deliver the coin to Juan.

(d) There are three shareholders of Astro Computer Corp.: Coase, who owns 48 percent of the stock; De Valle, who owns 48 percent; and Cary, who owns 4 percent. Cary contracts to sell his 4 percent to De Valle but later refuses to transfer the shares to him.

12–4. Measure of Damages. Johnson contracted to lease a house to Fox for $700 a month, beginning October 1. Fox stipulated in the contract that before he moved in, the interior of the house had to be completely repainted. On September 9, Johnson hired Keever to do the required painting for $1,000. He told Keever that the painting had to be finished by October 1 but did not explain why. On September 28, Keever quit for no reason, having completed approximately 80 percent of the work. Johnson then paid Sam $300 to finish the painting, but Sam did not finish until October 4. Fox, when the painting had not been completed as stipulated in his contract with Johnson, leased another home. Johnson found another tenant who would lease the property at $700 a month, beginning October 15. Johnson then sued Keever for breach of contract, claiming damages of $650. This amount included the $300 Johnson paid Sam to finish the painting and $350 for rent for the first half of October, which Johnson had lost as a result of Keever's breach. Johnson had not yet paid Keever anything for Keever's work. Can Johnson collect the $650 from Keever? Explain.

12–5. Measure of Damages. Ben owns and operates a famous candy store. He makes most of the candy sold in the store, and business is particularly heavy during the Christmas season. Ben contracts with Sweet, Inc., to purchase ten thousand pounds of sugar, to be delivered on or before November 15. Ben informs Sweet that this particular order is to be used for the Christmas season business. Because of production problems, the sugar is not tendered to Ben until December 10, at which time Ben refuses the order because it is so late. Ben has been unable to purchase the quantity of sugar needed to meet the Christmas orders and has had to turn down numerous regular customers, some of whom have indicated that they will purchase candy elsewhere in the future. The sugar that Ben has been able to purchase has cost him ten cents per pound above Sweet's price. Ben sues Sweet for breach of contract, claiming as damages the higher price paid for the sugar from others, lost profits from this year's lost Christmas sales, future lost profits from customers who have indicated that they will discontinue doing business with him, and punitive damages for failure to meet the contracted-for delivery date. Sweet claims Ben is limited to compensatory damages only. Discuss who is correct and why.

12–6. Consequential Damages. Kerr Steamship Co. delivered to Radio Corp. of America (RCA) a twenty-nine-word, coded message to be sent to Kerr's agent in Manila. The message included instructions on loading cargo onto one of Kerr's vessels. Kerr's profits on the carriage of the cargo were to be about $6,600. RCA mislaid the coded message, and it was never sent. Kerr sued RCA for the $6,600 in profits that it lost because RCA failed to send the message. Can Kerr recover? Explain. [*Kerr Steamship Co. v. Radio Corp. of America*, 245 N.Y. 284, 157 N.E. 140 (1927)]

12–7. Liquidated Damages versus Penalties. Dewerff was a teacher and basketball coach for Unified School District No. 315. The employment contract included a clause that read, in part: "Penalty for breaking contracts: . . . In all cases where a teacher under contract fails to honor the full term of his or her contract, a lump sum of $400 is to be collected if the contract is broken before August 1." Dewerff resigned on June 28, 1978, and he was told that the school would accept his resignation on his payment of the $400 stipulated in the contract. When Dewerff refused to make the $400 payment, the school district sued for $400 as "liquidated damages" on the basis of the contract clause. Dewerff argued that the contract provision was a "penalty" clause and unenforceable in this situation. Is Dewerff correct? Discuss. [*Unified School District No. 315, Thomas County v. Dewerff*, 6 Kan.App.2d 77, 626 P.2d 1206 (1981)]

12–8. Limitation of Liability. Westinghouse Electric Corp. entered into a contract with New Jersey Electric to manufacture and install a turbine generator for producing electricity. The contract price was over $10 million. The parties engaged in three years of negotiations and bargaining before they agreed on a suitable contract. The ultimate contract provided, among other things, that Westinghouse would not be liable for any injuries to the property belonging to the utility or to its customers or employees. Westinghouse warranted only that it would repair any defects in workmanship and materials appearing within one year of installation. After installation, part of New Jersey Electric's plant was damaged, and several of its employees were injured

because of a defect in the turbine. New Jersey Electric sued Westinghouse, claiming that Westinghouse was liable for the damages because the exculpatory provisions in the contract were unconscionable. What was the result? [*Royal Indemnity Co. v. Westinghouse Electric Corp.*, 385 F.Supp. 520 (S.D.N.Y. 1974)]

12–9. Liquidated Damages versus Penalties. The Ivanovs, who were of Russian origin, agreed to purchase the Sobels' home for $300,000. A $30,000 earnest money deposit was placed in the trust account of Kotler Realty, Inc., the broker facilitating the transaction. Tiasia Buliak, one of Kotler's salespersons, negotiated the sale because she spoke fluent Russian. To facilitate the closing without the Ivanovs' having to be present, Buliak suggested they form a Florida corporation, place the cash necessary to close the sale in a corporate account, and give her authority to draw checks against it. The Ivanovs did as Buliak had suggested. Before the closing date of the sale, Buliak absconded with all of the closing money, which caused the transaction to collapse. Subsequently, because the Ivanovs had defaulted, Kotler Realty delivered the $30,000 earnest money deposit in its trust account to the Sobels. The Ivanovs then sued the Sobels, seeking to recover the $30,000. Was the clause providing that the seller could retain the earnest money if the buyer defaulted an enforceable liquidated damages clause or an unenforceable penalty clause? Discuss. [*Ivanov v. Sobel*, 654 So.2d 991 (Fla.App.3d 1995)]

12–10. Mitigation of Damages. Charles Kloss had worked for Honeywell, Inc., for over fifteen years when Honeywell decided to transfer the employees at its Ballard facility to its Harbour Pointe facility. Honeywell planned to hire a medical person at the Harbour Pointe facility and promised Kloss that if he completed a nursing program and became a registered nurse (RN), the company would hire him for the medical position. When Kloss graduated from his RN program, however, Honeywell did not assign him to a nursing or medical position. Instead, the company gave Kloss a job in its maintenance department. Shortly thereafter, Kloss left the company and eventually sued Honeywell for damages (lost wages) resulting from Honeywell's breach of the employment contract. One of the issues facing the court was whether Kloss, by voluntarily leaving the maintenance job at Honeywell, had failed to mitigate his damages. How should the court rule on this issue? Discuss. [*Kloss v. Honeywell, Inc.*, 77 Wash.App. 294, 820 P.2d 480 (1995)]

CASE BRIEFING ASSIGNMENT

U.S. F2d

12–11. *Examine Case A.3 [Potter v. Oster, 426 N.W.2d 148 (Iowa 1988)] in Appendix A.* The case has been excerpted there in great detail. Review and then brief the case, making sure that you include answers to the following questions in your brief.

1. Why was Oster appealing the trial court's decision?
2. Why did Oster assert that allowing the remedy of rescission and restitution in this case would lead to an inequitable result?
3. According to the court, what three requirements must be met before rescission will be granted?

4. Did the Potters meet these three requirements, and if so, why?
5. What reasons did the court give for its conclusion that remedies at law were inadequate in this case?
6. Why are remedies at law presumed to be inadequate for breach of real estate contracts?

▌Unit Three—Cumulative Hypothetical Problem

 12–12. *Corelli offers to purchase Bach's coin collection for $5,000, and Bach accepts Corelli's offer. Assuming that the contract has met all of the requirements for a valid contract, answer the questions raised in each of the following situations.*

1. The contract is in writing. Bach is a minor, and Corelli is an adult. Bach gives the coin collection to Corelli and receives the $5,000. Bach then has a change of heart and wants to recover his coin collection from Corelli. Can he do so? Explain. What if Bach was a minor at the time of the sale but did not decide that he wanted the coin collection back until a year after he had turned eighteen?

2. The contract is oral, and both parties are adults. Bach creates a memorandum of the transaction, indicating the names of the parties, the date, and the exact terms of the contract; Bach places the memorandum in his file. Corelli refuses to go through with the agreement. Is the contract enforceable against Corelli? Against Bach?

3. The contract is in writing, and both parties are adults. Although Bach represented to Corelli that the coin collection was worth at least $5,000, in fact, Bach had just had it appraised and knew that it was worth only $2,000. Corelli later learns that the collection is worth only $2,000 and wants to sue Bach. What remedies are available to Corelli?

4. The contract is in writing, and both parties are adults. Corelli pays Bach $5,000, but Bach, having had a change of heart, decides to keep the collection and offers to return the $5,000 to Corelli. Corelli wants the coin collection, not the money. In Corelli's suit against Bach, will the court grant the equitable remedy of specific performance? Explain.

5. The contract is in writing, and both parties are adults. Corelli takes possession of the coin collection and promises to pay Bach the $5,000 in three weeks. Bach, in urgent need of money, borrows $5,000 from his friend Viva and assigns to Viva his rights to collect $5,000 from Corelli in return for the loan. Viva notifies Corelli of the assignment. Corelli pays Bach the $5,000 on the date stipulated in their contract. Bach refuses to give the money to Viva, and Viva sues Corelli. Is Corelli obligated to pay Viva $5,000 also? Discuss.

Accessing the Internet: Fundamentals of Business Law

For a discussion of how "smart contracts" in the future might make breach of contract expensive to the breaching party, go to

http://www.best.com/~szabo/smart.contracts.2.html

There you will find a document entitled "Smart Contracts: Building Blocks for Digital Markets." The article discusses a future in which contracts could be electronically attached to property, and such contracts might be enforced without having to resort to court action.

The following sites offer information on contract law, including breach of contract and remedies:

http://www.nolo.com/Chunkcm/CM9.html

http://www.law.cornell.edu/topics/contracts.html

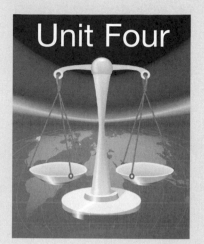

Unit Four

Sales and Lease Contracts

▌Unit Contents

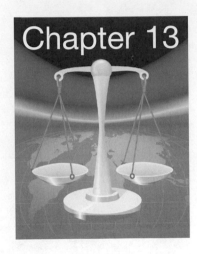

Chapter 13

The Formation of Sales and Lease Contracts

CHAPTER OBJECTIVES

After reading this chapter, you should be able to:

1. Discuss the scope of the UCC's Article 2 (on sales of goods) and Article 2A (on leases of goods).
2. Indicate the ways in which the UCC changes the common law of contracts in respect to contract formation.
3. Describe how the UCC attempts to avoid the "battle of the forms."
4. Identify some rules that apply only to contracts between merchants.
5. Compare and contrast the law governing domestic contracts with the law governing contracts for the international sale of goods.

When we turn to sales and lease contracts, we move away from common law principles and into the area of statutory law. State statutory law governing sales and lease transactions is based on the Uniform Commercial Code (UCC). The UCC facilitates commercial transactions by making the laws governing sales and lease contracts clearer, simpler, and more readily applicable to the numerous difficulties that can arise during such transactions.

We open this chapter with a discussion of the general coverage of the UCC and its significance as a legal landmark. We then look at the scope of the UCC's Article 2 (on sales) and Article 2A (on leases) as a background to the focus of this chapter, which is the formation of contracts for the sale and lease of goods. Because international sales transactions are increasingly commonplace in the business world, the chapter concludes with an examination of the United Nations Convention on Contracts for the International Sale of Goods (CISG), which governs international sales contracts.

The Scope of the UCC

The UCC attempts to provide a consistent and integrated framework of rules to deal with all phases *ordinarily arising* in a commercial sales transaction from start to finish. For example, consider the following events, all of which may be involved in a single sales transaction:

1. *A contract for the sale or lease of goods is formed and performed.* Article 2 and Article 2A of the UCC provide rules governing all the facets of this transaction.
2. *The transaction may involve a payment—by check, electronic fund transfer, or other means.* Arti-

cle 3 (on negotiable instruments), Article 4 (on bank deposits and collections), and Article 4A (on fund transfers) cover this part of the transaction.

3. *If the goods purchased are shipped or stored, they may be covered by a bill of lading or a warehouse receipt.* Article 7 (on documents of title) deals with this subject.

4. *The transaction may involve the acceptance of some form of security for a remaining balance owed.* Article 9, on secured transactions, covers this part of the transaction.

Two articles of the UCC seemingly do not address the "ordinary" commercial sales transaction. Article 6, on bulk transfers, has to do with merchants who sell off the major part of their inventory. Such bulk sales are not part of the ordinary course of business. Article 8, which covers investment securities, deals with transactions involving negotiable securities (stocks and bonds), transactions that do not involve the sale of *goods*. The subject matter of Articles 6 and 8, however, was considered by the UCC's drafters to be related *sufficiently* to commercial transactions to warrant its inclusion in the UCC. Excerpts from the most recent version of the UCC are included in Appendix C in this text.

The UCC has been adopted by all of the states, and it is impossible for a person to be in the business world without coming into contact with some aspect of the UCC.

▌ The Scope of Article 2—Sales

Article 2 of the UCC governs **sales contracts,** or contracts for the sale of goods. To facilitate commercial transactions, Article 2 modifies some of the common law contract requirements that were discussed in the previous chapters. To the extent that it has not been modified by the UCC, however, the common law of contracts also applies to sales contracts. For example, the common law requirements for a valid contract—agreement (offer and acceptance), consideration, capacity, and legality—are applicable to sales contracts as well. Thus, you should reexamine these common law principles when studying sales. In general, the rule is that whenever there is a conflict between a common law contract rule and the UCC, the UCC controls. In other words, when a UCC provision addresses a

certain issue, the UCC governs; when the UCC is silent, the common law governs.

In regard to Article 2, you should keep in mind two things. First, Article 2 deals with the sale of *goods*; it does not deal with real property (real estate), services, or intangible property such as stocks and bonds. Thus, if the subject matter of a dispute is goods, the UCC governs. If it is real estate or services, the common law applies. The relationship between general contract law and the law governing sales of goods is illustrated in Exhibit 13–1. Second, in some cases, the rules may vary quite a bit, depending on whether the buyer or the seller is a *merchant*. We look now at how the UCC defines a *sale, goods,* and *merchant status.*

What Is a Sale?

The UCC defines a **sale** as "the passing of title from the seller to the buyer for a price," where *title* refers to the formal right of ownership of property [UCC 2–106(1)]. The price may be payable in money or in other goods, services, or realty (real estate).

What Are Goods?

To be characterized as a *good*, the item of property must be *tangible*, and it must be *movable*. **Tangible property** has physical existence—it can be touched or seen. Intangible property—such as corporate stocks and bonds, patents and copyrights, and ordinary contract rights—have only conceptual existence and thus do not come under Article 2. A *movable* item can be carried from place to place. Hence, real estate is excluded from Article 2.

Two areas of dispute arise in determining whether the object of the contract is goods and thus whether Article 2 is applicable. One problem has to do with *goods associated with real estate,* such as crops or timber, and the other concerns contracts involving a combination of *goods and services.*

GOODS ASSOCIATED WITH REAL ESTATE Goods associated with real estate often fall within the scope of Article 2. Section 2–107 provides the following rules:

1. A contract for the sale of minerals or the like (including oil and gas) or a structure (such as a building) is a contract for the sale of goods *if*

◆ **Exhibit 13–1**
Law Governing Contracts
This exhibit graphically illustrates the relationship between general contract law and the law governing contracts for the sale of goods. Sales contracts are not governed exclusively by Article 2 of the Uniform Commercial Code but also by general contract law whenever it is relevant and has not been modified by the UCC.

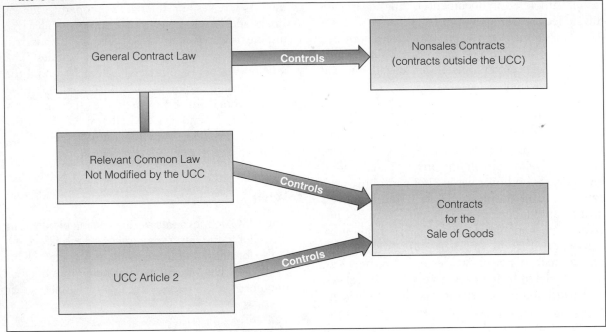

severance, or separation, is to be made by the seller. If the *buyer* is to sever (separate) the minerals or structure from the land, the contract is considered to be a sale of real estate governed by the principles of real property law, not the UCC.
2.   A sale of growing crops or timber to be cut is considered to be a contract for the sale of goods *regardless of who severs them.*
3.   Other "things attached" to realty but capable of severance without material harm to the land are considered goods *regardless of who severs them.*[1] Examples of "things attached" that are severable without harm to realty are a heater, a window air conditioner in a house, and counters and stools in a restaurant. Thus, removal of one of these things would be considered a sale of goods. The test is whether removal will cause substantial harm to the real property to which the item is attached.

GOODS AND SERVICES COMBINED   In cases in which goods and services are combined, courts disagree. For example, is the blood furnished to a patient during an operation a "sale of goods" or the "performance of a medical service"? Some courts say it is a good; others say it is a service. Similarly, contracts to sell and install software have posed the question of whether such contracts are primarily contracts for the sale of goods or contracts for the sale of services.[2] Because the UCC does not provide the answers to such questions, the courts try to determine which factor is predominant—the good or the service.

The UCC does stipulate, however, that serving food or drink to be consumed either on or off restaurant premises is a "sale of goods," at least for the purpose of an implied warranty of merchantability (to be explained in Chapter 16) [UCC 2–314(1)]. Other special transactions are also explicitly characterized as sales of goods by the UCC, including sales of unborn animals and rare coins. Whether the

---

1.   The UCC avoids the term *fixtures* here because of the numerous definitions of the word. A fixture is anything so firmly or permanently attached to land or to a building as to become a part of it. Once personal property becomes a fixture, it is governed by real estate law. See Chapter 29.

---

2.   See, for example, *Richard Haney Ford v. Ford Dealer Computer Services,* 218 Ga.App. 315, 461 S.E.2d 282 (1995).

transaction in question involves the sale of goods or services is important, because the majority of courts treat services as being excluded by the UCC. If the transaction is not covered by the UCC, then UCC provisions, including those relating to implied warranties, would not apply. The court in the following case considered whether electricity is a "product" and thus subject to laws that apply to goods.

CASE 13.1

Bryant v. Tri-County Electric Membership Corp.

United States District Court, Western District of Kentucky, 1994. 844 F.Supp. 347.

FACTS   A fire in April 1988 destroyed the sawmill at the Bryant Lumber Company. The fire started when an electrical switch on one of the machines exploded. The mill owners claimed that the switch failed because of voltage surges that had plagued the mill for years. Seeking to recover for the damage, the owners filed a suit in a federal district court against the Tri-County Electric Membership Corporation (the utility that supplied the electricity causing the surges) and others. The owners argued in part that electricity is a "product" and thus subject to warranty laws and other laws that apply to goods. The defendants filed motions for summary judgment, contending in effect that electricity is not a "product."

ISSUE   Is ordinary electricity a product?

DECISION   Yes. The court refused to grant Tri-County's motion for summary judgment.

REASON   The court pointed out that "the majority rule *   *   * considers ordinary electricity to be a 'product.'" The court explained that this view "sensibly accounts for the fact that electricity is created, harnessed, measured, transported, bought and sold, like products generally." The court recognized, however, that "in some respects electricity is different from traditional products. These real differences will be considered by the Court and by the jury" in determining, during the trial, whether Tri-County is liable.

FOR CRITICAL ANALYSIS—Social Consideration   *If electricity was not considered a "product," under what legal theory might a supplier be held liable for injuries attributable to its actions in connection with providing the electricity?*

Who Is a Merchant?

Article 2 governs the sale of goods in general. It applies to sales transactions between all buyers and sellers. In a limited number of instances, however, the UCC presumes that in certain phases of sales transactions involving merchants, special business standards ought to be imposed because of the merchants' relatively high degree of commercial expertise.[3] Such standards do not apply to the casual or inexperienced seller or buyer ("consumer"). Section 2–104 defines three ways in which merchant status can arise:

1. A merchant is a person who *deals in goods of the kind* involved in the sales contract. Thus, a retailer, a wholesaler, or a manufacturer is a merchant of those goods sold in the business. A merchant for one type of goods is not necessarily a merchant for another type. For example, a sporting-equipment retailer is a merchant when selling tennis equipment but not when selling a used computer.

2. A merchant is a person who, by occupation, holds himself or herself out as having knowledge and skill unique to the practices or goods involved

---

3. The provisions that apply only to merchants deal principally with the Statute of Frauds, firm offers, confirmatory memoranda, warranties, and contract modification. These special rules reflect expedient business practices commonly known to merchants in the commercial setting. They will be discussed later in this chapter.

In the transaction. This broad definition may include banks or universities as merchants.

3. A person who *employs a merchant as a broker, agent, or other intermediary* has the status of merchant in that transaction. Hence, if a "gentleman farmer" who ordinarily does not run the farm hires a broker to purchase or sell livestock, the farmer is considered a merchant in the transaction.

In summary, a person is a **merchant** when he or she, acting in a mercantile capacity, possesses or uses an expertise specifically related to the goods being sold. This basic distinction is not always clear-cut. For example, courts in some states have determined that farmers may be merchants, while courts in other states have determined that it was not within the contemplation of the drafters of the UCC to include farmers as merchants.

❚ The Scope of Article 2A—Leases

In the past few decades, leases of personal property (goods) have become increasingly common. Consumers and business firms lease automobiles, industrial equipment, items for use in the home (such as floor sanders), and many other types of goods. Until Article 2A was added to the UCC, no specific body of law addressed the legal problems that arose when goods were leased, rather than sold. In cases involving leased goods, the courts generally applied a combination of common law rules, real estate law, and principles expressed in Article 2 of the UCC.

Article 2A of the UCC was created to fill the need for uniform guidelines in this area. Article 2A covers any transaction that creates a lease of goods, as well as subleases of goods [UCC 2A–102, 2A–103(k)]. Article 2A is essentially a repetition of Article 2, except that it applies to leases of goods, rather than sales of goods, and thus varies to reflect differences between sale and lease transactions.

Definition of a Lease

Article 2A defines a **lease agreement** as the lessor and lessee's bargain, as found in their language and as implied by other circumstances, including course of dealing and usage of trade or course of performance [UCC 2A–103(k)]. A **lessor** is one who sells the right to the possession and use of goods under a lease [UCC 2A–103(p)]. A **lessee** is one who acquires the right to the possession and use of goods under a lease [UCC 2A–103(o)]. Article 2A applies to all types of leases of goods, including commercial leases and consumer leases. Special rules apply to certain types of leases, however, including consumer leases and finance leases.

Consumer Leases

A *consumer lease* involves three elements: (1) a lessor who regularly engages in the business of leasing or selling, (2) a lessee (except an organization) who leases the goods "primarily for a personal, family, or household purpose," and (3) total lease payments that are less than $25,000 [UCC 2A–103(1)(e)]. In the interest of providing special protection for consumers, certain provisions of Article 2A apply only to consumer leases. For example, one provision states that a consumer may recover attorneys' fees if a court finds that a term in a consumer lease contract is unconscionable [UCC 2A–108(4)(a)].

Finance Leases

A *finance lease* involves a lessor, a lessee, and a supplier. The lessor buys or leases goods from a supplier and leases or subleases them to the lessee [UCC 2A–103(g)]. Typically, in a finance lease, the lessor is simply financing the transaction. For example, suppose that Marlin Corporation wants to lease a crane for use in its construction business. Marlin's bank agrees to purchase the equipment from Jennco, Inc., and lease the equipment to Marlin. In this situation, the bank is the lessor-financer, Marlin is the lessee, and Jennco is the supplier.

Article 2A, unlike ordinary contract law, makes the lessee's obligations under a commercial finance lease irrevocable and independent from the financer's obligations [UCC 2A–407]. That is, the lessee must perform whether or not the financer performs. The lessee also must look almost entirely to the supplier for warranties.

❚ The Formation of Sales and Lease Contracts

In regard to the formation of sales and lease contracts, the UCC modifies the common law in several ways. We look here at how Article 2 and Article 2A of the UCC modify common law contract rules. Remember that parties to sales contracts are free to establish whatever terms they wish. The UCC comes into play when the parties have not, in their contract, provided for a contingency that later gives rise to a dispute. The UCC makes this very clear time and again by its use of such phrases as "unless the parties otherwise agree" or "absent a contrary agreement by the parties."

Offer

In general contract law, the moment a definite offer is met by an unqualified acceptance, a binding contract is formed. In commercial sales transactions, the verbal exchanges, the correspondence, and the actions of the parties may not reveal exactly when a binding contractual obligation arises. The UCC states that an agreement sufficient to constitute a contract can exist even if the moment of its making is undetermined [UCC 2–204(2), 2A–204(2)].

OPEN TERMS   According to contract law, an offer must be definite enough for the parties (and the courts) to ascertain its essential terms when it is accepted. The UCC states that a sales or lease contract will not fail for indefiniteness even if one or more terms are left open as long as (1) the parties intended to make a contract and (2) there is a reasonably certain basis for the court to grant an appropriate remedy [UCC 2–204(3), 2A–204(3)].

For example, Mike agrees to lease from CompuQuik a highly specialized computer workstation. Mike and one of CompuQuick's sales representatives sign a lease agreement that leaves some of the details blank, to be "worked out" the following week, when the leasing manager will be back from her vacation. In the meantime, CompuQuick obtains the necessary equipment from one of its suppliers and spends several days modifying the equipment to suit Mike's needs. When the leasing manager returns, she calls Mike and tells him that his workstation is ready. Mike says he is no longer interested in the workstation, as he has arranged to lease the same type of equipment for a lower price from another firm. CompuQuik sues Mike to recover its costs in obtaining and modifying the equipment, and one of the issues before the court is whether the parties had an enforceable contract. The court will likely hold that they did, based on their intent and conduct, despite the blanks in their written agreement.

Although the UCC has radically lessened the requirement of definiteness of terms, keep in mind that the more terms left open, the less likely a court will find that the parties intended to form a contract.

Open Price Term   If the parties have not agreed on a price, the court will determine a "reasonable price at the time for delivery" [UCC 2–305(1)]. If either the buyer or the seller is to determine the price, the price is to be fixed in good faith [UCC 2–305(2)].

Sometimes the price fails to be fixed through the fault of one of the parties. In that case, the other party can treat the contract as canceled or fix a reasonable price. For example, Johnson and Merrick enter into a contract for the sale of goods and agree that Johnson will fix the price. Johnson refuses to fix the price. Merrick can either treat the contract as canceled or set a reasonable price [UCC 2–305(3)].

Open Payment Term   When parties do not specify payment terms, payment is due at the time and place at which the buyer is to receive the goods [UCC 2–310(a)]. The buyer can tender payment using any commercially normal or acceptable means, such as a check or credit card. If the seller demands payment in cash, however, the buyer must be given a reasonable time to obtain it [UCC 2–511(2)]. This is especially important when the contract states a definite and final time for performance.

Open Delivery Term   When no delivery terms are specified, the buyer normally takes delivery at the seller's place of business [UCC 2–308(a)]. If the seller has no place of business, the seller's residence is used. When goods are located in some other place and both parties know it, delivery is made there. If the time for shipment or delivery is not clearly specified in the sales contract, the court infers a "reasonable" time for performance [UCC 2–309(1)].

Duration of an Ongoing Contract   A single contract might specify successive performances but not indicate how long the parties are required to deal with each other. Although either party may terminate the ongoing contractual relationship, principles of good faith and sound commercial practice call for reasonable notification before termination so as to give the other party reasonable time to seek a substitute arrangement [UCC 2–309(2), (3)].

Options and Cooperation Regarding Performance

When specific shipping arrangements have not been made but the contract contemplates shipment of the goods, the *seller* has the right to make these arrangements in good faith, using commercial reasonableness in the situation [UCC 2–311].

When terms relating to the assortment of goods are omitted from a sales contract, the *buyer* can specify the assortment. For example, Marconi's Dental Supply and Petry Drugs, Inc., contract for the sale of one thousand toothbrushes. The toothbrushes come in a variety of colors, but the contract does not specify color. Petry, the buyer, has the right to take six hundred blue toothbrushes and four hundred green ones if it wishes. Petry, however, must exercise good faith and commercial reasonableness in making the selection [UCC 2–311].

Open Quantity Term

Normally, if the parties do not specify a quantity, a court will have no basis for determining a remedy. The UCC recognizes two exceptions in requirements and output contracts [UCC 2–306(1)]. In a **requirements contract,** the buyer agrees to purchase and the seller agrees to sell all or up to a stated amount of what the buyer *needs* or *requires*. There is implicit consideration in a requirements contract, for the buyer gives up the right to buy from any other seller, and this forfeited right creates a legal detriment. Requirements contracts are common in the business world and are normally enforceable. If, however, the buyer promises to purchase only if the buyer *wishes* to do so, or if the buyer reserves the right to buy the goods from someone other than the seller, the promise is illusory (without consideration) and unenforceable by either party.

In an **output contract,** the seller agrees to sell and the buyer agrees to buy all or up to a stated amount of what the seller *produces*. Again, because the seller essentially forfeits the right to sell goods to another buyer, there is implicit consideration in an output contract.

The UCC imposes a *good faith limitation* on requirements and output contracts. The quantity under such contracts is the amount of requirements or the amount of output that occurs during a *normal* production year. The actual quantity purchased or sold cannot be unreasonably disproportionate to normal or comparable prior requirements or output [UCC 2–306].

MERCHANT'S FIRM OFFER Under regular contract principles, an offer can be revoked at any time before acceptance. The major common law exception is an *option contract* (discussed in Chapter 8), in which the offeree pays consideration for the offeror's irrevocable promise to keep the offer open for a stated period. The UCC creates a second exception, which applies only to firm offers for the sale or lease of goods made by a merchant (regardless of whether or not the offeree is a merchant). A **firm offer** arises when a merchant-offeror gives *assurances* in a *signed writing* that the offer will remain open. The merchant's firm offer is irrevocable without the necessity of consideration[4] for the stated period or, if no definite period is stated, a reasonable period (neither to exceed three months) [UCC 2–205, 2A–205].

It is necessary that the offer be both *written* and *signed* by the offeror.[5] When a firm offer is contained in a form contract prepared by the offeree, the offeror must also sign a separate firm offer assurance also. This requirement ensures that the offeror will be made aware of the offer. If the firm offer is buried amid copious language in one of the pages of the offeree's form contract, the offeror may inadvertently sign the contract without realizing that there is a firm offer, thus defeating the purpose of the rule—which is to give effect to a merchant's deliberate intent to be bound to a firm offer.

Acceptance

The following sections examine the UCC's provisions governing acceptance. As you will see, acceptance of an offer to buy, sell, or lease goods generally may be made in any reasonable manner and by any reasonable means.

---

4. If the offeree pays consideration, then an option contract (not a merchant's firm offer) is formed.

5. "Signed" includes any symbol executed or adopted by a party with a present intention to authenticate a writing [UCC 1–201(39)]. A complete signature is not required. Therefore, initials, a thumbprint, a trade name, or any mark used in lieu of a written signature will suffice, regardless of its location on the document.

METHODS OF ACCEPTANCE The general common law rule is that an offeror can specify, or authorize, a particular means of acceptance, making that means the only one effective for contract formation. Even an unauthorized means of communication is effective, however, as long as the acceptance is received by the specified deadline. For example, suppose that the offer states, "Answer by fax within five days." If the offeree sends a letter, and the offeror receives it within five days, a valid contract is formed. (For a review of the requirements relating to mode and timeliness of acceptance, see Chapter 8.)

Any Reasonable Means When the offeror does not specify a means of acceptance, the UCC provides that acceptance can be made by any means of communication reasonable under the circumstances [UCC 2–206(1), 2A–206(1)]. This broadens the common law rules concerning authorized means of acceptance.

For example, Anodyne Corporation writes Bethlehem Industries a letter offering to lease $1,000 worth of goods. The offer states that Anodyne will keep the offer open for only ten days from the date of the letter. Before the ten days have lapsed, Bethlehem sends Anodyne an acceptance by fax. The fax is misdirected by someone at Anodyne's offices and does not reach the right person at Anodyne until after the ten-day deadline has passed. Is a valid contract formed? The answer is yes, because acceptance by fax is a commercially reasonable medium of acceptance under the circumstances. Acceptance would be effective upon Bethlehem's transmission of the fax, which occurred before the offer lapsed.

Promise to Ship or Prompt Shipment The UCC permits acceptance of an offer to buy goods for current or prompt shipment by either a prompt promise to ship the goods to the buyer or the prompt shipment of conforming goods (that is, goods that accord with the contract's terms) to the buyer [UCC 2–206(1)(b)]. The prompt shipment of nonconforming goods constitutes both an acceptance (a contract) and a breach of that contract. This rule does not apply if the seller seasonably (within a reasonable amount of time) notifies the buyer that the nonconforming shipment is offered only as an accommodation, or as a favor. The notice of accommodation must clearly indicate to the buyer that the shipment does not constitute an

acceptance and that, therefore, no contract has been formed.

For example, suppose that McIntosh orders five thousand *blue* widgets from Halderson. If Halderson ships five thousand *black* widgets instead, the shipment acts as both an acceptance of McIntosh's offer and a *breach* of the resulting contract. McIntosh may sue Halderson for any appropriate damages. If, however, Halderson notifies McIntosh that the black widgets are being shipped *as an accommodation*—because Halderson has only black widgets in stock—the shipment will not constitute an acceptance but a counteroffer. A contract will be formed only if McIntosh (the buyer) accepts the black widgets.

NOTICE OF ACCEPTANCE Under the common law, because a unilateral offer invites acceptance by a performance, the offeree need not notify the offeror of performance unless the offeror would not otherwise know about it. The UCC is more stringent than the common law, stating that when "the beginning of requested performance is a reasonable mode of acceptance[,] an offeror who is not notified of acceptance within a reasonable time may treat the offer as having lapsed before acceptance" [UCC 2–206(2), 2A–206(2)].

ADDITIONAL TERMS Under the common law, if Alderman makes an offer to Beale, and Beale in turn accepts but adds some slight modification, there is no contract. The so-called *mirror image rule*, which requires that the terms of the acceptance exactly match those of the offer (see Chapter 8), makes Beale's action a rejection of—and a counter-offer to—Alderman's offer. This rule often results in the so-called *battle of the forms.*

Say, for example, that a buyer negotiates with a seller over the phone to purchase a certain piece of equipment. The parties agree to all of the specific terms of the sale—price, quantity, delivery date, and so on. The buyer then offers to buy the equipment, using its standard purchase order form, and sends the form to the seller. At the same time, the seller accepts the offer, using its standard sales form. Because the parties presume that they have reached an agreement, discrepancies in the terms and conditions contained in their respective forms may go unnoticed. (See Exhibit 13–2 for an illustration of the kinds of terms and conditions that may be included in a standard purchase order form.) If a dispute arises, however, the discrepancies become significant, and a "battle of the forms" begins, in which each party claims that its form represents the true terms of the agreement.

Under the common law, the courts tended to resolve this difficulty by holding that no contract was formed, because the last form to be sent was not an acceptance but a counteroffer. To avoid the battle of the forms, the UCC dispenses with the mirror image rule. The UCC generally takes the position that if the offeree's response indicates a *definite* acceptance of the offer, a contract is formed, even if the acceptance includes additional or different terms from those contained in the offer [UCC 2–207(1)]. What happens to these additional terms? The answer to this question depends, in part, on whether the parties are nonmerchants or merchants.

One Party or Both Parties Are Nonmerchants If one (or both) of the parties is a *nonmerchant*, the contract is formed according to the terms of the original offer submitted by the original offeror and not according to the additional terms of the acceptance [UCC 2–207(2)]. For example, Tolsen offers in writing to sell his personal computer to Valdez for $1,500. Valdez faxes a reply to Tolsen in which Valdez states, "I accept your offer to purchase your computer for $1,500. I *would like* a box of computer paper and ten diskettes to be included in the purchase price." Valdez has given Tolsen a definite expression of acceptance (creating a contract), even though Valdez's acceptance also suggests an added term for the offer. Because Tolsen is not a merchant, the additional term is merely a proposal (suggestion), and Tolsen is not legally obligated to comply with that term.

Both Parties Are Merchants In contracts *between merchants* (that is, when both parties to the contract are merchants), the additional terms automatically become part of the contract unless (1) the original offer expressly limits acceptance to the terms of the offer, (2) the new or changed terms materially alter the contract, or (3) the offeror objects to the new or changed terms within a reasonable period of time [UCC 2–207(2)].

What constitutes a material alteration is frequently a question of fact that only a court can decide. Generally, if the modification involves no unreasonable element of surprise or hardship for the offeror, the court will hold that the modification did not materially alter the contract. The issue in the following case concerns whether an additional term in the acceptance (subjecting any disputes to arbitration) constituted a material alteration of the contract terms.

CASE 13.2

Wilson Fertilizer & Grain, Inc. v. ADM Milling Co.

Court of Appeals of Indiana, 1995.
654 N.E.2d 848.

FACTS In October 1992, Wilson Fertilizer & Grain, Inc., agreed to sell grain to the ADM Milling Company. ADM sent Wilson a confirmation stating that "[t]his contract is also subject to the Trade Rules of the National Grain and Feed Association [NGFA]." The NGFA rules require the arbitration of disputes and limit the time for filing a complaint to one year. Wilson did not respond to the confirmation. A dispute arose under the contract, and Wilson filed suit against ADM in an Indiana state court. ADM moved to dismiss the action, claiming that the Trade Rules of the NGFA require the parties to arbitrate the dispute. Wilson argued that the arbitration provisions were not included within the terms of its agreement with ADM. The trial court granted ADM's motion and ordered the parties to arbitration. By that time, however, the one-year limit had expired. Wilson appealed, arguing in part that ADM's confirmation materially altered the contract and thus did not become a part of the contract, because the one-year limit imposed a hardship on Wilson.

ISSUE Was the confirmation clause that required the arbitration of disputes a material alteration of the contract terms?

DECISION No. The Court of Appeals of Indiana affirmed the order of the lower court.

Case 13.2—Continued

REASON   The state appellate court pointed out that "the test for whether additional terms materially alter an agreement is whether their 'incorporation into the contract without express awareness by the other party would result in surprise or hardship.'" The court concluded that the arbitration provision and the requirement that claims must be filed within one year did not impose an undue hardship on Wilson. First, the court stated that the UCC "specifically permits parties to a contract for sale to reduce the time for filing claims to one year." Second, "and even more significantly," the court noted "Wilson's apparent ability to have submitted its claim for arbitration within the one-year limit." The court explained that the contract was formed in October 1992, and Wilson filed the complaint in September 1993. "If Wilson was able to file its complaint in court within one year" after ADM allegedly breached the contract, "we fail to see how a contract provision requiring Wilson to submit its claim for arbitration in the same time period imposes a hardship."

FOR CRITICAL ANALYSIS—Social Consideration   *For what reasons might a company prefer to litigate a dispute rather than submit it to arbitration?*

Conditioned on Offeror's Assent   Regardless of merchant status, the UCC provides that the offeree's expression cannot be construed as an acceptance if additional or different terms in the acceptance are expressly conditioned on the offeror's assent to the additional or different terms [UCC 2–207(1)]. For example, Philips offers to sell Hundert 650 pounds of turkey thighs at a specified price and with specified delivery terms. Hundert responds, "I accept your offer for 650 pounds of turkey thighs *on the condition that you agree that the weight will be evidenced by a city scale weight certificate.*" Hundert's response will be construed not as an acceptance but as a counteroffer, which Philips may or may not accept.

Additional Terms May Be Stricken   The UCC provides yet another option for dealing with conflicting terms in the parties' writings. Section 2–207(3) states that conduct by both parties that recognizes the existence of a contract is sufficient to establish a contract for sale even though the writings of the parties do not otherwise establish a contract. In this situation, "the terms of the particular contract will consist of those terms on which the writings of the parties agree, together with any supplementary terms incorporated under any other provisions of this Act." In a dispute over contract terms, this provision allows a court simply to strike from the contract those terms on which the parties do not agree.

Consideration

The common law rule that a contract requires consideration also applies to sales and lease contracts. Unlike the common law, however, the UCC does not require a contract modification to be supported by new consideration. An agreement modifying a contract for the sale or lease of goods "needs no consideration to be binding" [UCC 2–209(1), 2A–208(1)].

MODIFICATIONS MUST BE MADE IN GOOD FAITH
Of course, contract modification must be sought in good faith [UCC 1–203]. For example, Jim agrees to lease certain goods to Louise for a stated price. Subsequently, a sudden shift in the market makes it difficult for Jim to lease the items to Louise at the given price without suffering a loss. Jim tells Louise of the situation, and Louise agrees to pay an additional sum for the goods. Later Louise reconsiders and refuses to pay more than the original price. Under the UCC, Louise's promise to modify the contract needs no consideration to be binding. Hence, Louise is bound by the modified contract.

♦ Exhibit 13–2
An Example of a Purchase Order (Front)

IBM® **Purchase Order**

IBM DATA

SUPPLIER	MACH	U/M	O C	SUC	P P E C	R E X P	COMMODITY	M M	DEPT. ORDER	A L T	JOB NO.	DEPT. CHG.	APPROP.	C C	PR ORIG.	CHG. RN

NUMBER   DATE

REC. NO. | B.J. S.O. OR REF. NO. | ACCOUNT NO. | COMMITMENT

REMIT TO ⟶

NOTIFY BUYER IMMEDIATELY IF REMIT TO
ADDRESS IS DIFFERENT ON INVOICE

CODE	**TAXES**	**SPECIFICATION CODE**
	DO NOT CHARGE TEXAS SALES USE TAX SINCE WE PAY DIRECT OUR DIRECT PAY AUTHORIZATION NUMBER IS: **3-000001-7281-4**	1. Print Attached. 2. Specifications Attached. 3. Sample Attached. 4. Print in Your Possession. 5. Specification in Your Possession. 6. Sample in your Possession.

S H I P   T O

IBM® 11400 BURNET ROAD AUSTIN, TEXAS 78758   BLDG.
OTHER THAN ABOVE

SEE CODE BELOW	SHIP VIA	IBM DATA	F.O.B. SHIP POINT **DESTINATION**	IBM DATA	YOUR TERMS OF PAYMENT

IMPORTANT
1. SHOW OUR COMPLETE ORDER NUMBER, ITEM NUMBER AND IBM PART NUMBER (IF ANY) ON ALL INVOICES, SHIPPING CONTAINERS, PACKING LISTS AND CORRESPONDENCE.
2. SECURELY ATTACH PACKING SLIP TO OUTSIDE OF CARTON.
3. PACKAGES WEIGHING OVER 75 LBS. MUST BE PACKAGED FOR HANDLING WITH A MECHANICAL DEVICE.

TRANSPORTATION ROUTING GUIDELINES
(DO NOT INSURE OR DECLARE VALUE)
0-99 (45kg.) United Parcel Service, if available. If not, 0-40 (18kg.) Parcel Post (Zones 1-8) up to $1000 value. All other Ship as indicated in "ship via" block.

ITEM	PART NUMBER	E/C LEVEL	SHIP TO ARRIVE	QUANTITY	U/M	UNIT PRICE	U/M

*TOTAL QUANTITY OF ITEM ORDERED

"SUBJECT TO THE TERMS AND CONDITIONS ON THE BACK HEREOF WHICH ARE INCORPORATED AND MADE A PART HEREOF"

ADDRESS ALL INVOICES TO:
INTERNATIONAL BUSINESS MACHINES CORP.
Attn: Accounts Payable
P.O. Box 9928
Austin, Texas 78766

AUTHORIZED SIGNATURE   512-838-3300
EXT.

942-0262-4

♦ **Exhibit 13–2—Continued**
An Example of a Purchase Order (Back)

STANDARD TERMS AND CONDITIONS

IBM EXPRESSLY LIMITS ACCEPTANCE TO THE TERMS SET FORTH ON THE FACE AND REVERSE SIDE OF THIS PURCHASE ORDER AND ANY ATTACHMENTS HERETO:

PURCHASE ORDER CONSTITUTES COMPLETE AGREEMENT	This Purchase order, including the terms and conditions on the face and reverse side hereof and any attachments hereto, contains the complete and final agreement between International Business Machines Corporation (IBM) and Seller. Reference to Seller's bids or proposals, if noted on this order, shall not affect terms and conditions hereof, unless specifically provided to the contrary herein, and no other agreement or quotation in any way modifying any of said terms and conditions will be binding upon IBM unless made in writing and signed by IBM's authorized representative.
ADVERTISING	Seller shall not, without first obtaining the written consent of IBM, in any manner advertise, publish or otherwise disclose the fact that Seller has furnished, or contracted to furnish to IBM, the material and/or services ordered hereunder.
APPLICABLE LAW	The agreement arising pursuant to this order shall be governed by the laws of the State of New York. No rights, remedies and warranties available to IBM under this contact or by operation of law are waived or modified unless expressly waived or modified by IBM in writing.
CASH DISCOUNT OR NET PAYMENT PERIOD	Calculations will be from the date an acceptable invoice is received by IBM. Any other arrangements agreed upon must appear on this order and on the invoice.
CONFIDENTIAL INFORMATION	Seller shall not disclose to any person outside of its employ, or use for any purpose other than to fulfill its obligations under this order, any information received from IBM pursuant to this order, which has been disclosed to Seller by IBM in confidence, except such information which is otherwise publicly available or is publicly disclosed by IBM subsequent to Seller's receipt of such information or is rightfully received by Seller from a third party. Upon termination of this order, Seller shall return to IBM upon request all drawings, blueprints, descriptions or other material received from IBM and all materials containing said confidential information. Also, Seller shall not disclose to IBM any information which Seller deems to be confidential, and it is understood that any information received by IBM, including all manuals, drawings and documents will not be of a confidential nature or restrict, in any manner, the use of such information by IBM. Seller agrees that any legend or other notice on any information supplied by Seller, which is inconsistent with the provisions of this article, does not create any obligation on the part of IBM.
GIFTS	Seller shall not make or offer gifts or gratuities of any type to IBM employees or members of their families. Such gifts or offerings may be construed as Seller's attempt to improperly influence our relationship.
IBM PARTS	All parts and components bailed by IBM to Seller for incorporation in work being performed for IBM shall be used solely for such purposes.
OFF-SPECIFICATION	Seller shall obtain from IBM written approval of all off-specification work.
PACKAGES	Packages must bear IBM's order number and show gross, tare and net weights and/or quantity.
PATENTS	Seller will settle or defend, at Seller's expense (and pay any damages, costs or fines resulting from), all proceedings or claims against IBM, its subsidiaries and affiliates and their respective customers, for infringement, or alleged infringement, by the goods furnished under this order, or any part or use thereof of patents (including utility models and registered designs) now or hereafter granted in the United States or in any country where Seller, its subsidiaries or affiliates, heretofore has furnished similar goods. Seller will, at IBM's request, identify the countries in which Seller, its subsidiaries or affiliates, heretofore has furnished similar goods.
PRICE	If price is not stated on this order, Seller shall invoice at lowest prevailing market price.
QUALITY	Material is subject to IBM's inspection and approval within a reasonable time after delivery. If specifications are not met, material may be returned at Seller's expense and risk for all damages incidental to the rejection. Payment shall not constitute an acceptance of the material nor impair IBM's right to inspect or any of its remedies.
SHIPMENT	Shipment must be made within the time stated on this order, failing which IBM reserves the right to purchase elsewhere and charges Seller with any loss incurred, unless delay in making shipment is due to unforeseeable causes beyond the control and without the fault or negligence of Seller.
SUBCONTRACTS	Seller shall not subcontract or delegate its obligations under this order without the written consent of IBM. Purchase of parts and materials normally purchased by Seller or required by this order shall be construed as subcontracts or delegations.
(NON-U.S. LOCATIONS ONLY)	Seller further agrees that during the process of bidding or production of goods and services hereunder, it will not re-export or divert to others any IBM specifications, drawing or other data, or any product of such data.
TAXES	Unless otherwise directed, Seller shall pay all sales and use taxes imposed by law upon or on account of this order. Where appropriate, IBM will reimburse Seller for this expense.
TOOLS	IBM owned tools held by Seller are to be used only for making parts for IBM. Tools of any kind held by Seller for making IBM's parts must be repaired and renewed by Seller at Seller's expense.
TRANSPORTATION	Routing—As indicated in transportation routing guidelines on face of this order. F.O.B.—Unless otherwise specified, ship collect, F.O.B. origin. Prepaid Transportation (when specified)—Charges must be supported by a paid freight bill or equivalent. Cartage) No charge allowed Premium Transportation) unless authorized Insurance) by IBM Consolidation—Unless otherwise instructed, consolidate all daily shipments to one destination on one bill of lading.
COMPLIANCE WITH LAWS AND REGULATIONS	Seller shall at all times comply with all applicable Federal, State and local laws, rules and regulations.
EQUAL EMPLOYMENT OPPORTUNITY	There are incorporated in this order the provisions of Executive Order 11246 (as amended) of the President of the United States on Equal Employment Opportunity and the rules and regulations issued pursuant thereto with which the Seller represents that he will comply, unless exempt.
EMPLOYMENT AND PROCUREMENT PROGRAMS	There are incorporated in this order the following provisions as they apply to performing work under Government procurement contracts: Utilization of Small Business Concerns (if in excess of $10,000) (Federal Procurement Regulation (FPR) 1-1.710-3(a)); Small Business Subcontracting Program (if in excess of $500,000) (FPR 1-1.710-3 (b)); Utilization of Labor Surplus Area Concerns (if in excess of $10,000) (FPR 1-1.805-3(a)); Labor Surplus Area Subcontracting Program (if in excess of $500,000) (FPR 1-1.805-3 (b)); Utilization of Minority Enterprises (if in excess of $10,000) (FPR 1-1.1310-2 (a)); Minority Business Enterprises Subcontracting Program (if in excess of $50,000) (FPR 1-1.1310-2(b)); Affirmative Action for Handicapped Workers (if $2,500 or more) (41 CFR 60-741.4); Affirmative Action for Disabled Veterans and Veterans of the Vietnam Era (if $10,000 or more) (41 CFR 60-250.4); Utilization of Small Business Concerns and Small Business Concerns Owned and Controlled by Socially and Economically Disadvantaged Individuals (if in excess of $10,000) (44 Fed. Reg. 23610 (April 20, 1979)); Small Business and Small Disadvantaged Business Subcontracting Plan (if in excess of $500,000) (44 Fed. Reg. 23610 (April 20, 1979)).
WAGES AND HOURS	Seller warrants that in the performance of this order Seller has complied with all of the provisions of the Fair Labor Standards Act of 1938 of the United States as amended.
WORKERS' COMPENSATION, EMPLOYERS' LIABILITY INSURANCE	If Seller does not have Workers' Compensation or Employer's Liability Insurance, Seller shall indemnify IBM against all damages sustained by IBM resulting from Seller's failure to have such insurance.

In this example, a shift in the market is a *good faith* reason for contract modification. What if there really was no shift in the market, however, and Jim knew that Louise needed the goods immediately but refused to deliver them unless Louise agreed to pay an additional sum of money? This sort of extortion of a modification without a legitimate commercial reason would be ineffective, because it would violate the duty of good faith. Jim would not be permitted to enforce the higher price.

WHEN MODIFICATION WITHOUT CONSIDERATION REQUIRES A WRITING   In some situations, modification of a sales or lease contract without consideration must be in writing to be enforceable. For example, if the contract itself prohibits any changes to the contract unless they are in a signed writing, only those changes agreed to in a signed writing are enforceable. If a consumer (nonmerchant buyer) is dealing with a merchant *and* the merchant supplies the form that contains a prohibition against oral modification, the consumer must sign a separate acknowledgment of such a clause [UCC 2–209(2), 2A–208(2)].

Also, any modification that brings a sales contract under the Statute of Frauds must usually be in writing to be enforceable. Thus, if an oral contract for the sale of goods priced at $400 is modified so that the contract goods are now priced at $600, the modification must be in writing to be enforceable [UCC 2–209(3)]. If, however, the buyer accepts delivery of the goods after the modification, he or she is bound to the $600 price [UCC 2–201(3)(c)]. Unlike Article 2, Article 2A does not say whether a lease as modified needs to satisfy the Statute of Frauds.

Statute of Frauds

The UCC contains Statute of Frauds provisions covering sales and lease contracts. Under these provisions, sales contracts for goods priced at $500 or more and lease contracts requiring payments that are $1,000 or more must be in writing to be enforceable [UCC 2–201(1), 2A–201(1)].

SUFFICIENCY OF THE WRITING   The UCC has greatly relaxed the requirements for the sufficiency of a writing to satisfy the Statute of Frauds. A writing or a memorandum will be sufficient as long as it indicates that the parties intended to form a contract and as long as it is signed by the party (or agent of the party) against whom enforcement is sought. The contract normally will not be enforceable beyond the quantity of goods shown in the writing, however. All other terms can be proved in court by oral testimony. For leases, the writing must reasonably identify and describe the goods leased and the lease term.

WRITTEN CONFIRMATION BETWEEN MERCHANTS   Once again, the UCC provides a special rule for merchants. Merchants can satisfy the requirements of a writing for the Statute of Frauds if, after the parties have agreed orally, one of the merchants sends a signed written confirmation to the other merchant. The communication must indicate the terms of the agreement, and the merchant receiving the confirmation must have reason to know of its contents. Unless the merchant who receives the confirmation gives written notice of objection to its contents within ten days after receipt, the writing is sufficient against the receiving merchant, even though he or she has not signed anything [UCC 2–201(2)].[6]

For example, Alfonso is a merchant buyer in Cleveland. He contracts over the telephone to purchase $4,000 worth of goods from Goldstein, a New York City merchant seller. Two days later, Goldstein sends written confirmation detailing the terms of the oral contract, and Alfonso subsequently receives it. If Alfonso does not give Goldstein written notice of objection to the contents of the written confirmation within ten days of receipt, Alfonso cannot raise the Statute of Frauds as a defense against the enforcement of the oral contract.

EXCEPTIONS   The UCC defines three exceptions to the writing requirements of the Statute of Frauds. An oral contract for the sale of goods priced at $500 or more or the lease of goods involving total payments of $1,000 or more will be enforceable despite the absence of a writing in the following circumstances [UCC 2–201(3), 2A–201(4)]. These exceptions and other ways in which sales law differs from general contract law are summarized in Exhibit 13–3.

---

6. According to the Comments accompanying UCC 2A–201 (Article 2A's Statute of Frauds), the "between merchants" provision was not included because the number of such transactions involving leases, as opposed to sales, was thought to be modest.

♦ **Exhibit 13–3**
Major Differences between Contract Law and Sales Law

	CONTRACT LAW	**SALES LAW**
Contract Terms	Contract must contain all material terms.	Open terms are acceptable if parties intended to form a contract, but contract not enforceable beyond quantity term.
Acceptance	Mirror image rule applies. If additional terms are added in acceptance, counteroffer is created.	Additional terms will not negate acceptance unless acceptance is made expressly conditional on assent to the additional terms.
Contract Modification	Requires consideration.	Does not require consideration.
Irrevocable Offers	Option contracts (with consideration).	Merchants' firm offers (without consideration).
Statute of Frauds Requirements	All material terms must be included in the writing.	Writing required only in sale of goods of $500 or more but not enforceable beyond quantity specified. *Between merchants:* Contract is enforceable if merchant fails to object in writing to confirming memorandum within ten days. *Exceptions:* 1. Contracts for specially manufactured goods. 2. Contracts admitted to by party against whom enforcement is sought. 3. Contracts will be enforced to extent goods delivered or paid for.

Specially Manufactured Goods An oral contract is enforceable if it is for (1) goods that are specially manufactured for a particular buyer or specially manufactured or obtained for a particular lessee, (2) these goods are not suitable for resale or lease to others in the ordinary course of the seller's or lessor's business, and (3) the seller or lessor has substantially started to manufacture the goods or has made commitments for the manufacture or procurement of the goods. In this situation, once the seller or lessor has taken action, the buyer or lessee cannot repudiate the agreement claiming the Statute of Frauds as a defense.

For example, suppose Womach orders custom-made draperies for her new boutique. The price is $1,000, and the contract is oral. When the merchant seller manufactures the draperies and ten-ders delivery to Womach, Womach refuses to accept them even though the quality of the work is satisfactory and the job has been completed on time. Womach claims that she is not liable because the contract was oral. Clearly, if the unique style and color of the draperies makes it improbable that the seller can find another buyer, Womach is liable to the seller. Note that the seller must have made a substantial beginning in manufacturing the specialized item prior to the buyer's repudiation. (Here, the manufacture was completed.) Of course, the court must still be convinced by evidence of the terms of the oral contract.

Admissions An oral contract for the sale or lease of goods is enforceable if the party against whom enforcement of a contract is sought admits in pleadings, testimony, or other court proceedings, that a contract for sale was made. In this situation, the contract will be enforceable even though it was oral, but enforceability will be limited to the quantity of goods admitted.

For example, Lane and Sugg negotiate an agreement over the telephone. During the negotiations, Lane requests a delivery price for five hundred gallons of gasoline and a separate price for seven hundred gallons of gasoline. Sugg replies that the price would be the same, $1.10 per gallon. Lane orally orders five hundred gallons. Sugg honestly believes that Lane ordered seven hundred gallons and tenders that amount. Lane refuses the shipment of seven hundred gallons, and Sugg sues for breach. In his pleadings and testimony, Lane admits that an oral contract was made, but only for five hundred gallons. Because Lane admits the existence of the oral contract, Lane cannot plead the Statute of Frauds as a defense. The contract is enforceable, however, only to the extent of the quantity admitted (five hundred gallons).

Partial Performance   An oral contract for the sale or lease of goods is enforceable if payment has been made and accepted or goods have been received and accepted. This is the "partial performance" exception. The oral contract will be enforced at least to the extent that performance *actually* took place.

Suppose that Allan orally contracts to lease Opus a thousand chairs at $1 each to be used during a one-day rock concert. Before delivery, Opus sends Allan a check for $500, which Allan cashes. Later, when Allan attempts to deliver the chairs, Opus refuses delivery, claiming the Statute of Frauds as a defense, and demands the return of his $500. Under the UCC's partial performance rule, Allan can enforce the oral contract by tender of delivery of five hundred chairs for the $500 accepted. Similarly, if Opus had made no payment but had accepted the delivery of five hundred chairs from Allan, the oral contract would have been enforceable against Opus for $500, the price of the five hundred chairs delivered.

Parol Evidence

If the parties to a contract set forth its terms in a confirmatory memorandum (a writing expressing offer and acceptance of the deal) or in a writing intended as their final expression, the terms of the contract cannot be contradicted by evidence of any prior agreements or contemporaneous oral agreements. The terms of the contract may, however, be explained or supplemented by *consistent additional terms* or by *course of dealing, usage of trade,* or *course of performance* [UCC 2–202, 2A–202].

CONSISTENT ADDITIONAL TERMS   If the court finds an ambiguity in a writing that is supposed to be a complete and exclusive statement of the agreement between the parties, it may accept evidence of consistent additional terms to clarify or remove the ambiguity. The court will not, however, accept evidence of contradictory terms. This is the rule under both the UCC and the common law of contracts.

COURSE OF DEALING AND USAGE OF TRADE   Under the UCC, the meaning of any agreement, evidenced by the language of the parties and by their actions, must be interpreted in light of commercial practices and other surrounding circumstances. In interpreting a commercial agreement, the court will assume that the *course of prior dealing* between the parties and the *usage of trade* were taken into account when the agreement was phrased.

A **course of dealing** is a sequence of previous actions and communications between the parties to a particular transaction that establishes a common basis for their understanding [UCC 1–205(1)]. A course of dealing is restricted to the sequence of actions and communications between the parties that has occurred prior to the agreement in question. The UCC states, "A course of dealing between the parties and any usage of trade in the vocation or trade in which they are engaged or of which they are or should be aware give particular meaning to [the terms of the agreement] and supplement or qualify the terms of [the] agreement" [UCC 1–205(3)].

Usage of trade is defined as any practice or method of dealing having such regularity of observance in a place, vocation, or trade as to justify an expectation that it will be observed with respect to the transaction in question [UCC 1–205(2)]. Further, the express terms of an agreement and an applicable course of dealing or usage of trade will be construed to be consistent with each other whenever reasonable. When such a construction is *unreasonable,* however, the express terms in the agreement will prevail [UCC 1–205(4)]. In the following case, the issue concerned whether evidence of usage and custom in the trade could be used to explain the meaning of the quantity figures specified by the parties when the contract was formed.

CASE 13.3

Heggblade-Marguleas-Tenneco, Inc. v. Sunshine Biscuit, Inc.

Court of Appeal of California,
Fifth District, 1976.
59 Cal.App.3d 948,
131 Cal.Rptr. 183.

FACTS   In 1970, Heggblade-Marguleas-Tenneco, Inc. (HMT), contracted with Sunshine Biscuit, Inc., to supply potatoes to be used in the 1971 production of snack foods. HMT had never marketed processing potatoes before. The quantity mentioned in its contract negotiations was 100,000 sacks of potatoes. The parties agreed that the amount of potatoes to be supplied would vary somewhat with Sunshine Biscuit's needs. Subsequently, a decline in demand for Sunshine Biscuit's products severely reduced its need for potatoes. Sunshine Biscuit was able to take only 60,105 sacks out of the 100,000 previously estimated. HMT filed suit against Sunshine Biscuit in a California state court. Sunshine Biscuit attempted to introduce evidence that it is customary in the potato-processing industry for the number of potatoes specified in sales contracts to be reasonable estimates rather than exact numbers that a buyer intends to purchase. The trial court held for Sunshine Biscuit, and HMT appealed.

ISSUE   Could evidence of custom in the potato-processing trade be admissible?

DECISION   Yes. The California appellate court affirmed the trial court's decision.

REASON   UCC Section 2–202 states that even though evidence of prior agreements or contemporaneous oral agreements that contradict a written contract is inadmissible, evidence of a course of dealing or of trade usage is admissible to explain or supplement a written contract. The fact that specific numbers were used to designate what quantities of potatoes Sunshine Biscuit thought it would need does not dispose of the issue. In its statement that evidence of trade usage was admissible, the court quoted an official comment to the UCC: "[I]n order that the true understanding of the parties as to the agreement may be [reached, such] writings are to be read on the assumption that *   *   * the usages of trade were taken for granted when the document was phrased. Unless carefully negated they have become an element of the meaning of the words used." HMT was held to have sufficient knowledge of the "trade custom."

FOR CRITICAL ANALYSIS—Ethical Consideration   *If HMT had not been aware of the prevailing customs in the potato-processing trade, would evidence of those customs still be admissible? Should it be?*

COURSE OF PERFORMANCE   A **course of performance** is the conduct that occurs under the terms of a particular agreement. Presumably, the parties themselves know best what they meant by their words, and the course of performance actually undertaken under their agreement is the best indication of what they meant [UCC 2–208(1), 2A–207(1)].

For example, suppose that Janson's Lumber Company contracts with Barrymore to sell

Barrymore a specified number of "2 by 4s." The lumber in fact does not measure 2 inches by 4 inches but rather 1⅞ inches by 3¾ inches. Janson's agrees to deliver the lumber in five deliveries, and Barrymore, without objection, accepts the lumber in the first three deliveries. On the fourth delivery, however, Barrymore objects that the two-by-fours do not measure 2 inches by 4 inches.

The course of performance in this transaction—that is, the fact that Barrymore accepted three deliveries without objection under the agreement—is relevant in determining that here the words "2 by 4" actually mean "1⅞ by 3¾." Janson's can also prove that two-by-fours need not be exactly 2 inches by 4 inches by applying usage of trade, course of prior dealing, or both. Janson's can, for example, show that in previous transactions, Barrymore took 1⅞-inch-by-3¾-inch lumber without objection. In addition, Janson's can show that in the trade, two-by-fours are commonly 1⅞ inches by 3¾ inches.

RULES OF CONSTRUCTION   The UCC provides *rules of construction* for interpreting contracts. Express terms, course of performance, course of dealing, and usage of trade are to be construed together when they do not contradict one another. When such a construction is unreasonable, however, the following order of priority controls: (1) express terms, (2) course of performance, (3) course of dealing, and (4) usage of trade [UCC 1–205(4), 2–208(2), 2A–207(2)].

Unconscionability

As discussed in Chapter 9, an unconscionable contract is one that is so unfair and one sided that it would be unreasonable to enforce it. The UCC allows the court to evaluate a contract or any clause in a contract, and if the court deems it to have been unconscionable *at the time it was made*, the court can (1) refuse to enforce the contract, (2) enforce the remainder of the contract without the unconscionable clause, or (3) limit the application of any unconscionable clauses to avoid an unconscionable result [UCC 2–302, 2A–108].

The inclusion of Sections 2–302 and 2A–108 in the UCC reflects an increased sensitivity to certain realities of modern commercial activities. Classical contract theory holds that a contract is a bargain in which the terms have been worked out *freely* between parties that are equals. In many modern commercial transactions, this premise is invalid. Standard-form contracts and leases are often signed by consumer-buyers who understand few of the terms used and who often do not even read them. Virtually all of the terms are advantageous to the party supplying the standard-form contract. The UCC's unconscionability provisions give the courts a powerful weapon for policing such transactions, as the next case illustrates.

CASE 13.4

Jones v. Star Credit Corp.

Supreme Court of New York,
Nassau County, 1969.
59 Misc. 2d 189,
298 N.Y.S.2d 264.

FACTS   The Joneses, the plaintiffs, were welfare recipients who agreed to purchase a freezer for $900 as the result of a salesperson's visit to their home. Tax and financing charges raised the total price to $1,234.80. At trial, the freezer was found to have a maximum retail value of approximately $300. The plaintiffs, who had made payments totaling $619.88, brought a suit in a New York state court to have the purchase contract declared unconscionable under the UCC.

ISSUE   Can this contract be denied enforcement on the ground of unconscionability?

DECISION   Yes. The court held that the contract was not enforceable as it stood, and the contract was reformed so that no further payments were required.

Case 13.4—Continued

REASON   The court relied on UCC 2–302(1), which states that if "the court as a matter of law finds the contract or any clause of the contract to have been unconscionable at the time it was made the court may * * * so limit the application of any unconscionable clause as to avoid any unconscionable result." The court then examined the disparity between the $900 purchase price and the $300 retail value, as well as the fact that the credit charges alone exceeded the retail value. These excessive charges were exacted despite the seller's knowledge of the plaintiffs' limited resources. The court reformed the contract so that the plaintiffs' payments, amounting to more than $600, were regarded as payment in full.

FOR CRITICAL ANALYSIS—Ethical Consideration   *What if the plaintiffs had made payments totaling $300—the retail value of the freezer? Would the court regard that $300 as "payment in full"? Should the court consider the seller's interests in a case such as this one, in which the seller was deemed to have acted unconscionably?*

Contracts for the International Sale of Goods

International sales contracts between firms or individuals located in different countries are governed by the 1980 United Nations Convention on Contracts for the International Sale of Goods (CISG)—if the countries of the parties to the contract have ratified the CISG (and if the parties have not agreed that some other law will govern their contract). As of 1996, thirty-eight countries had ratified or acceded to the CISG, including the United States, Canada, Mexico, some Central and South American countries, and most of the European nations. Four other nations have signed the CISG and indicated their intent to ratify it.

Applicability of the CISG

Essentially, the CISG is to international sales contracts what Article 2 of the UCC is to domestic sales contracts. As discussed in this chapter, in domestic transactions the UCC applies when the parties to a contract for a sale of goods have failed to specify in writing some important term concerning price, delivery, or the like. Similarly, whenever the parties to international transactions have failed to specify in writing the precise terms of a contract, the CISG will be applied. Although the UCC applies to consumer sales, the CISG does not, and neither applies to contracts for services.

Businesspersons must take special care when drafting international sales contracts to avoid problems caused by distance, including language differences and different national laws. Exhibit 13–4 shows an actual international sales contract used by Starbucks Coffee Company, illustrating many of the special terms and clauses that are typically contained in international contracts for the sale of goods. Annotations in the exhibit explain the meaning and significance of specific clauses in the contract.

A Comparison of CISG and UCC Provisions

The provisions of the CISG, although similar for the most part to those of the UCC, differ from them in some respects. We have already mentioned some of these differences. For example, the CISG does not include the requirements imposed by the UCC's Statute of Frauds. Rather, Article 11 of the CISG states that an international sales contract "need not be concluded in or evidenced by writing and is not subject to any other requirements as to form."

In respect to contract formation, some other differences between the CISG and the UCC merit attention. First, under the UCC, if the price term is left open, the court will determine "a reasonable price at the time for delivery" [UCC 2–305(1)]. Under the CISG, however, the price term must be specified, or at least provisions for its specification must be included in the agreement; otherwise, normally no contract will exist.

Second, like UCC 2–207, the CISG provides that a contract can be formed even though the acceptance contains additional terms, unless the

◆ **Exhibit 13–4   An Example of a Contract for the International Sale of Coffee**

① OVERLAND COFFEE IMPORT CONTRACT
OF THE
GREEN COFFEE ASSOCIATION
OF
② NEW YORK CITY, INC.*
Effective May 9, 1991

Contract Seller's No.:   **504617**
Buyer's No.:   **P9264**
Date: **9/11/99**

SOLD BY: **XYZ Co.**
TO: **Starbucks**

③ QUANTITY: **Five Hundred** (**500** (Bags) Tons of   **Mexican**   coffee
weighing about **152.117 lbs.** per bag.

PACKAGING: Coffee must be packed in clean sound bags of uniform size made of sisal, henequen, jute, burlap, or
④ similar woven material, without inner lining or outer covering of any material properly sewn by hand
and/or machine.
Bulk shipments are allowed if agreed by mutual consent of Buyer and Seller.

DESCRIPTION: **High grown Mexican Altura**
⑤

PRICE: At   **Ten/$10.00 dollars**   U. S. Currency, per **lb.**   net, (U.S. Funds)
Upon delivery in Bonded Public Warehouse at **Laredo, TX**
(City and State)

PAYMENT: **Cash against warehouse receipts**
⑥

Bill and tender to DATE when all import requirements and governmental regulations have been satisfied,
and coffee delivered or discharged (as per contract terms). Seller is obliged to give the Buyer two (2)
calendar days free time in Bonded Public Warehouse following but not including date of tender.

ARRIVAL: During **December** via **truck**
(Period)   (Method of Transportation)
⑦   from **Mexico**   for arrival at **Laredo, TX**
(Country of Exportation)   (Country of Importation)
Partial shipments permitted.

ADVICE OF   Advice of arrival with warehouse name and location, together with the quantity, description, marks and
ARRIVAL: place of entry, must be transmitted directly, or through Seller's Agent/Broker, to the Buyer or his Agent/
Broker. Advice will be given as soon as known but not later than the fifth business day following arrival
at the named warehouse. Such advice may be given verbally with written confirmation to be sent the
same day.

WEIGHTS: (1) DELIVERED WEIGHTS: Coffee covered by this contract is to be weighed at location named in
⑧   tender. Actual tare to be allowed.
(2) SHIPPING WEIGHTS: Coffee covered by this contract is sold on shipping weights. Any loss in
weight exceeding **1/2** percent at location named in tender is for account of Seller at contract price.
(3) Coffee is to be weighed within fifteen (15) calendar days after tender. Weighing expenses, if any, for
account of **Seller**   (Seller or Buyer)

MARKINGS: Bags to be branded in English with the name of Country of Origin and otherwise to comply with laws
and regulations of the Country of Importation, in effect at the time of entry, governing marking of import
merchandise. Any expense incurred by failure to comply with these regulations to be borne by
Exporter/Seller.

⑨ RULINGS: The "Rulings on Coffee Contracts" of the Green Coffee Association of New York City, Inc., in effect on
the date this contract is made, is incorporated for all purposes as a part of this agreement, and together
herewith, constitute the entire contract. No variation or addition hereto shall be valid unless signed by
the parties to the contract.
Seller guarantees that the terms printed on the reverse hereof, which by reference are made a part hereof,
are identical with the terms as printed in By-Laws and Rules of the Green Coffee Association of New
⑩ York City, Inc., heretofore adopted.
Exceptions to this guarantee are:

ACCEPTED: COMMISSION TO BE PAID BY:
XYZ Co.   **seller**

⑪   BY _____   Seller
_____   Agent
Starbucks

BY _____   Buyer
_____   Agent   **ABC Brokerage**
Broker(s)
⑫   When this contract is executed by a person acting for another, such person hereby represents that he is
fully authorized to commit his principal.

⑬

* Reprinted with permission of The Green Coffee Association of New York City, Inc.

♦ **Exhibit 13–4 (Continued)**

❶ This is a contract for a sale of coffee to be *imported* internationally. If the parties have their principal places of business located in different countries, the contract may be subject to the United Nations Convention on Contracts for the International Sale of Goods (CISG). If the parties' principal places of business are located in the United States, the contract may be subject to the Uniform Commercial Code (UCC).

❷ Quantity is one of the most important terms to include in a contract. Without it, a court may not be able to enforce the contract.

❸ Weight per unit (bag) can be exactly stated or approximately stated. If it is not so stated, usage of trade in international contracts determines standards of weight.

❹ Packaging requirements can be conditions for acceptance and payment. Bulk shipments are not permitted without the consent of the buyer.

❺ A description of the coffee and the "Markings" constitute express warranties. Warranties in contracts for domestic sales of goods are discussed generally in Chapter 16. International contracts rely more heavily on descriptions and models or samples.

❻ Under the UCC, parties may enter into a valid contract even though the price is not set. Under the CISG, a contract must provide for an exact determination of the price.

❼ The terms of payment may take one of two forms: credit or cash. Credit terms can be complicated. A cash term can be simple, and payment may be by any means acceptable in the ordinary course of business (for example, a personal check or a letter of credit). If the seller insists on actual cash, the buyer must be given a reasonable time to get it. See Chapter 15.

❽ *Tender* means the seller has placed goods that conform to the contract at the buyer's disposition. What constitutes a valid tender is explained in Chapter 15. This contract requires that the coffee meet all import regulations and that it be ready for pickup by the buyer at a "Bonded Public Warehouse." (A *bonded warehouse* is a place in which goods can be stored without paying taxes until the goods are removed.)

❾ The delivery date is significant because, if it is not met, the buyer may hold the seller in breach of the contract. Under this contract, the seller can be given a "period" within which to deliver the goods, instead of a specific day, which could otherwise present problems. The seller is also given some time to rectify goods that do not pass inspection (see the "Guarantee" clause on page two). For a discussion of the remedies of the buyer and seller, see Chapter 15.

❿ As part of a proper tender, the seller (or its agent) must inform the buyer (or its agent) when the goods have arrived at their destination. The responsibilities of agents are set out in Chapter 22.

⓫ In some contracts, delivered and shipped weights can be important. During shipping, some loss can be attributed to the type of goods (spoilage of fresh produce, for example) or to the transportation itself. A seller and buyer can agree on the extent to which either of them will bear such losses.

⓬ Documents are often incorporated in a contract by reference, because including them word-for-word can make a contract difficult to read. If the document is later revised, the whole contract might have to be reworked. Documents that are typically incorporated by reference include detailed payment and delivery terms, special provisions, and sets of rules, codes, and standards.

⓭ In international sales transactions, and for domestic deals involving certain products, brokers are used to form the contracts. When so used, the brokers are entitled to a commission. See Chapter 22.

(Continued)

♦ **Exhibit 13–4** (Continued)

TERMS AND CONDITIONS

⑭ ARBITRATION: All controversies relating to, in connection with, or arising out of this contract, its modification, making or the authority or obligations of the signatories hereto, and whether involving the principals, agents, brokers, or others who actually subscribe hereto, shall be settled by arbitration in accordance with the "Rules of Arbitration" of the Green Coffee Association of New York City, Inc., as they exist at the time of the arbitration (including provisions as to payment of fees and expenses). Arbitration is the sole remedy hereunder, and it shall be held in accordance with the law of New York State, and judgment of any award may be entered in the courts of that State, or in any other court of competent jurisdiction. All notices or judicial service in reference to arbitration or enforcement shall be deemed given if transmitted as required by the aforesaid rules.

⑮ GUARANTEE: (a) If all or any of the coffee is refused admission into the country of importation by reason of any violation of governmental laws or acts, which violation existed at the time the coffee arrived at Bonded-Public Warehouse, seller is required, as to the amount not admitted and as soon as possible, to deliver replacement coffee in conformity to all terms and conditions of this contract, excepting only the Arrival terms, but not later than thirty (30) days after the date of the violation notice. Any payment made and expenses incurred for any coffee denied entry shall be refunded within ten (10) calendar days of denial of entry, and payment shall be made for the replacement delivery in accordance with the terms of this contract. Consequently, if Buyer removes the coffee from the Bonded Public Warehouse, Seller's responsibility as to such portion hereunder ceases.

⑯ (b) Contracts containing the overstamp "No Pass-No Sale" on the face of the contract shall be interpreted to mean: If any or all of the coffee is not admitted into the country of Importation in its original condition by reason of failure to meet requirements of the government's laws or Acts, the contract shall be deemed null and void as to that portion of the coffee which is not admitted in its original condition. Any payment made and expenses incurred for any coffee denied entry shall be refunded within ten (10) calendar days of denial of entry.

CONTINGENCY: This contract is not contingent upon any other contract.

CLAIMS: Coffee shall be considered accepted as to quality unless within *fifteen* (15) calendar days after delivery at Bonded Public Warehouse or within *fifteen* (15) calendar days after all Government clearances have been received, whichever is later, either:
(a) Claims are settled by the parties hereto, or,
(b) Arbitration proceedings have been filed by one of the parties in accordance with the provisions hereof.
⑰ (c) If neither (a) nor (b) has been done in the stated period or if any portion of the coffee has been removed from the Bonded Public Warehouse before representative sealed samples have been drawn by the Green Coffee Association of New York City, Inc., in accordance with its rules, Seller's responsibility for quality claims ceases for that portion so removed.
(d) Any question of quality submitted to arbitration shall be a matter of allowance only, unless otherwise provided in the contract.

⑱ DELIVERY: (a) No more than three (3) chops may be tendered for each lot of 250 bags.
(b) Each chop of coffee tendered is to be uniform in grade and appearance. All expense necessary to make coffee uniform shall be for account of seller.
(c) Notice of arrival and/or sampling order constitutes a tender, and must be given not later than the fifth business day following arrival at Bonded Public Warehouse stated on the contract.

INSURANCE: Seller is responsible for any loss or damage, or both, until Delivery and Discharge of coffee at the Bonded Public Warehouse in the Country of Importation.

All Insurance Risks, costs and responsibility are for Seller's Account until Delivery and Discharge of coffee at the Bonded Public Warehouse in the Country of Importation.

⑲ Buyer's insurance responsibility begins from the day of importation or from the day of tender, whichever is later.

⑳ FREIGHT: Seller to provide and pay for all transportation and related expenses to the Bonded Public Warehouse in the Country of Importation.

Exporter is to pay all Export taxes, duties or other fees or charges, if any, levied because of exportation.

㉑ EXPORT DUTIES/TAXES:

IMPORT DUTIES/TAXES: Any Duty or Tax whatsoever, imposed by the government or any authority of the Country of Importation, shall be borne by the Importer/Buyer.

INSOLVENCY OR FINANCIAL FAILURE OF BUYER OR SELLER: If, at any time before the contract is fully executed, either party hereto shall meet with creditors because of inability generally to make payment of obligations when due, or shall suspend such payments, fail to meet his general trade obligations in the regular course of business, shall file a petition in bankruptcy or, for an arrangement, shall become insolvent, or commit an act of bankruptcy, then the other party may at his option, expressed in writing, declare the aforesaid to constitute a breach and default of this contract, and may, in addition to other remedies, decline to deliver further or make payment or may sell or purchase for the defaulter's account, and may collect damage for any injury or loss, or shall account for the profit, if any, occasioned by such sale or purchase.

㉒ This clause is subject to the provisions of (11 USC 365 (e) 1) if invoked.

㉓ BREACH OR DEFAULT OF CONTRACT: In the event either party hereto fails to perform, or breaches or repudiates this agreement, the other party shall subject to the specific provisions of this contract be entitled to the remedies and relief provided for by the Uniform Commercial Code of the State of New York. The computation and ascertainment of damages, or the determination of any other dispute as to relief, shall be made by the arbitrators in accordance with the Arbitration Clause herein.

Consequential damages shall not, however, be allowed.

♦ **Exhibit 13–4 (Continued)**

⑭ Arbitration is the settling of a dispute by submitting it to a disinterested party (other than a court) that renders a decision. The procedures and costs can be provided for in an arbitration clause or incorporated through other documents. To enforce an award rendered in an arbitration, the winning party can "enter" (submit) the award in a court "of competent jurisdiction." For a general discussion of arbitration and other forms of dispute resolution (other than courts), see Chapter 3.

⑮ When goods are imported internationally, they must meet certain import requirements before being released to the buyer. Because of this, buyers frequently want a guaranty clause that covers the goods not admitted into the country and that either requires the seller to replace the goods within a stated time or allows the contract for those goods not admitted to be void.

⑯ In the "Claims" clause, the parties agree that the buyer has a certain time within which to reject the goods. The right to reject is a right by law and does not need to be stated in a contract. If the buyer does not exercise the right within the time specified in the contract, the goods will be considered accepted. See Chapter 15.

⑰ Many international contracts include definitions of terms so that the parties understand what they mean. Some terms are used in a particular industry in a specific way. Here, the word "chop" refers to a unit of like-grade coffee bean. The buyer has a right to inspect ("sample") the coffee. If the coffee does not conform to the contract, the seller must correct the nonconformity.

⑱ The "Delivery," "Insurance," and "Freight" clauses, with the "Arrival" clause on page one, indicate that this is a destination contract. The seller has the obligation to deliver the goods to the destination, not simply deliver them into the hands of a carrier. Under this contract, the destination is a "Bonded Public Warehouse" in a specific location. The seller bears the risk of loss until the goods are delivered at their destination. Typically, the seller will have bought insurance to cover the risk.

⑲ Delivery terms are commonly placed in all sales contracts. Such terms determine who pays freight and other costs, and, in the absence of an agreement specifying otherwise, who bears the risk of loss. International contracts may use these delivery terms or they may use INCOTERMS, which are published by the International Chamber of Commerce. For example, the INCOTERM "DDP" ("delivered duty paid") requires the seller to arrange shipment, obtain and pay for import or export permits, and get the goods through customs to a named destination.

⑳ Exported and imported goods are subject to duties, taxes, and other charges imposed by the governments of the countries involved. International contracts spell out who is responsible for these charges.

㉑ This clause protects a party if the other party should become financially unable to fulfill the obligations under the contract. Thus, if the seller cannot afford to deliver, or the buyer cannot afford to pay, for the stated reasons, the other party can consider the contract breached. This right is subject to "11 USC 365(e)(1)," which refers to a specific provision of the U.S. Bankruptcy Code dealing with executory contracts. Bankruptcy provisions are covered in Chapter 21.

㉒ In the "Breach or Default of Contract" clause, the parties agreed that the remedies under this contract are the remedies (except for consequential damages) provided by the UCC, as in effect in the state of New York. The amount and "ascertainment" of damages, as well as other disputes about relief, are to be determined by arbitration. Breach of contract and contractual remedies in general are explained in Chapter 15. Arbitration is discussed in Chapter 2.

㉓ Three clauses frequently included in international contracts are omitted here. There is no "Choice of Language" clause designating the official language to be used in interpreting the contract terms. There is no "Choice of Forum" clause designating the place in which disputes will be litigated, except for arbitration (law of New York State). Finally, there is no *"Force Majeure"* clause relieving the sellers or buyers from nonperformance due to events beyond their control.

additional terms materially alter the contract. The definition of a "material alteration" under the CISG, however, involves virtually any differences in terms. In its effect, then, the CISG requires that the terms of the acceptance mirror those of the offer.

Third, under the UCC, an acceptance is effective on dispatch. Under the CISG, however, a contract is created not at the time the acceptance is transmitted but only on its receipt by the offeror. (The offer becomes *irrevocable*, however, when the acceptance is sent.) Additionally, in contrast to the UCC, the CISG provides that acceptance by performance does not require that the offeror be notified of the performance.

In the following chapters, we continue to point out differences between the CISG and the UCC as they relate to the topics covered. These topics include risk of loss, performance, remedies, and warranties.

▌Terms and Concepts

course of dealing 264
course of performance 265
firm offer 256
lease agreement 254
lessee 254

lessor 254
merchant 254
output contract 256
requirements contract 256
sale 251

sales contract 251
seasonably 257
tangible property 251
usage of trade 264

▌Chapter Summary: The Formation of Sales and Lease Contracts

The Scope of the UCC *(See pages 250–251.)*	The UCC attempts to provide a consistent and integrated framework of rules to deal with all phases *ordinarily arising* in a commercial sales or lease transaction, including contract formation, passage of title and risk of loss, performance, remedies, payment for goods, warehoused goods, and secured transactions. If there is a conflict between a common law rule and the UCC, the UCC controls.
The Scope of Article 2—Sales *(See pages 251–254.)*	Article 2 governs contracts for the sale of goods (tangible, movable personal property). The common law of contracts also applies to sales contracts to the extent that the common law has not been modified by the UCC.
The Scope of Article 2A—Leases *(See page 254.)*	Article 2A governs contracts for the lease of goods. Article 2A is essentially a repetition of Article 2, except that it applies to leases, instead of sales, of goods and thus varies to reflect differences between sale and lease transactions.

Offer and Acceptance *(See pages 254–259.)*	1. *Offer—*
	  a. Not all terms have to be included for a contract to be formed (only the subject matter and quantity term must be specified).
	  b. The price does not have to be included for a contract to be formed.
	  c. Particulars of performance can be left open.
	  d. A written and signed firm offer by a *merchant*, covering a period of three months or less, is irrevocable without payment of consideration.
	
	2. *Acceptance—*
	  a. Acceptance may be made by any reasonable means of communication; it is effective when dispatched.
	  b. The acceptance of a unilateral offer can be made by a promise to ship or by prompt shipment of conforming goods.
	  c. Acceptance by performance requires notice within a reasonable time; otherwise, the offer can be treated as lapsed.
	  d. A definite expression of acceptance creates a contract even if the terms of the acceptance vary from those of the offer.

▌Chapter Summary: The Formation of Sales and Lease Contracts—Continued

Consideration *(See pages 259–262.)*	A modification of a contract for the sale of goods does not require consideration.

Requirements under the Statute of Frauds
(See pages 262–264.)
	1. All contracts for the sale of goods priced at $500 or more must be in writing. A writing is sufficient as long as it indicates a contract between the parties and is signed by the party against whom enforcement is sought. A contract is not enforceable beyond the quantity shown in the writing.
	
	2. When written confirmation of an oral contract *between merchants* is not objected to in writing by the receiver within ten days, the contract is enforceable.
	
	3. Exceptions to the requirement of a writing exist in the following situations:
	   a. When the oral contract is for specially manufactured goods not suitable for resale to others, and the seller has substantially started to manufacture the goods.
	   b. When the defendant admits in pleadings, testimony, or other court proceedings that an oral contract for the sale of goods was made. In this case, the contract will be enforceable to the extent of the quantity of goods admitted.
	   c. The oral agreement will be enforceable to the extent that payment has been received and accepted or to the extent that the goods have been received and accepted.

Parol Evidence Rule
(See pages 264–266.)
	1. The terms of a clearly and completely worded written contract cannot be contradicted by evidence of prior agreements or contemporaneous oral agreements.
	
	2. Evidence is admissible to clarify the terms of a writing in the following situations:
	   a. If the contract terms are ambiguous.
	   b. If evidence of course of dealing, usage of trade, or course of performance is necessary to learn or to clarify the intentions of the parties to the contract.

Unconscionability *(See pages 266–267.)*	An unconscionable contract or clause is one that is so unfair and one sided that it would be unreasonable to enforce it. If the court deems a contract to have been unconscionable at the time it was made, the court can (1) refuse to enforce the contract, (2) refuse to enforce the unconscionable clause of the contract, or (3) limit the application of any unconscionable clauses to avoid an unconscionable result.
Contracts for the International Sale of Goods *(See pages 267–272.)*	International sales contracts are governed by the United Nations Convention on Contracts for the International Sale of Goods (CISG)—if the countries of the parties to the contract have ratified the CISG (and if the parties have not agreed that some other law will govern their contract). Essentially, the CISG is to international sales contracts what Article 2 of the UCC is to domestic sales contracts. Whenever the parties to international transactions have failed to specify in writing the precise terms of a contract, the CISG will be applied.

▌For Review

1. Describe the scope and coverage of Article 2 and Article 2A of the UCC.

2. What is a merchant's firm offer?

3. If an offeree includes additional or different terms in an acceptance, will a contract result? If so, what happens to these terms?

4. Article 2 and Article 2A of the UCC both define three exceptions to the writing requirements of the Statute of Frauds. What are these three exceptions?

5. What law governs contracts for the international sale of goods?

▌ Questions and Case Problems

13–1. Terms of the Offer. The UCC changes the effect of the common law of contracts in several ways. For instance, at common law, an offer must be definite enough for the parties to ascertain its essential terms when it is accepted. What happens under the UCC if some of an offer's terms—the price term, for example—are left open? What if the quantity term is left open?

13–2. Statute of Frauds. Fresher Foods, Inc., orally agreed to purchase from Dale Vernon, a farmer, one thousand bushels of corn for $1.25 per bushel. Fresher Foods paid $125 down and agreed to pay the remainder of the purchase price upon delivery, which was scheduled for one week later. When Fresher Foods tendered the balance of $1,125 on the scheduled day of delivery and requested the corn, Vernon refused to deliver it. Fresher Foods sued Vernon for damages, claiming that Vernon had breached their oral contract. Can Fresher Foods recover? If so, to what extent?

13–3. Merchant's Firm Offer. On September 1, Jennings, a used-car dealer, wrote a letter to Wheeler in which he stated, "I have a 1955 Thunderbird convertible in mint condition that I will sell you for $13,500 at any time before October 9. [signed] Peter Jennings." By September 15, having heard nothing from Wheeler, Jennings sold the Thunderbird to another party. On September 29, Wheeler accepted Jennings's offer and tendered the $13,500. When Jennings told Wheeler he had sold the car to another party, Wheeler claimed Jennings had breached their contract. Is Jennings in breach? Explain.

13–4. Accommodation Shipments. M. M. Salinger, Inc., a retailer of television sets, orders one hundred Model Color-X sets from manufacturer Fulsom. The order specifies the price and that the television sets are to be shipped via Interamerican Freightways on or before October 30. Fulsom receives the order on October 5. On October 8, Fulsom writes Salinger a letter indicating that it has received the order and that it will ship the sets as directed, at the specified price. Salinger receives this letter on October 10. On October 28, Fulsom, in preparing the shipment, discovers it has only ninety Color-X sets in stock. Fulsom ships the ninety Color-X sets and ten television sets of a different model, stating clearly on the invoice that the ten sets are being shipped only as an accommodation. Salinger claims that Fulsom is in breach of contract. Fulsom claims that the shipment was not an acceptance, and therefore no contract was formed. Explain who is correct, and why.

13–5. Statute of Frauds. Loeb & Co. entered into an oral agreement with Schreiner, a farmer, in which Schreiner agreed to sell Loeb 150 bales of cotton, each weighing 480 pounds. Shortly thereafter, Loeb sent Schreiner a letter confirming the terms of the oral contract. Schreiner neither acknowledged receipt of the letter nor objected to its terms. When delivery came due, Schreiner ignored the oral agreement and sold his cotton on the open market, because the price of cotton had more than doubled (from 37 cents to 80 cents per pound) since the oral agreement had been made. In the lawsuit by Loeb & Co. against Schreiner, did Loeb recover? Explain. [*Loeb & Co. v. Schreiner*, 294 Ala. 722, 321 So.2d 199 (1975)]

13–6. Additional Terms in Acceptance. The Carpet Mart, a carpet dealer, telephoned an order (offer) for carpet to Collins & Aikman Corp., a carpet manufacturer. Collins & Aikman then sent Carpet Mart an acknowledgment form (acceptance), which specified the quantity and price agreed to in the telephone conversation. The reverse side of the printed acknowledgment form stated that Collins & Aikman's acceptance was subject to the buyer's agreement to submit all disputes to arbitration. Collins & Aikman shipped the carpet to Carpet Mart, which received the acknowledgment form and shipment without objection. Later, a dispute arose, and Carpet Mart brought a civil suit against Collins & Aikman, claiming misrepresentation as to the quality of the carpet. Collins & Aikman filed a motion to compel arbitration. Will the court enforce the arbitration clause? Discuss. [*Dorton v. Collins & Aikman Corp.*, 453 F.2d 1161 (6th Cir. 1972)]

13–7. Statute of Frauds. Peggy Holloway was a real estate broker who guaranteed payment for shipment of over $11,000 worth of mozzarella cheese sold by Cudahy Foods Co. to Pizza Pride in Jamestown, North Carolina. The entire arrangement was made orally. Cudahy mailed to Holloway an invoice for the order, and Holloway did not object in writing to the invoice within ten days of receipt. Later, when Cudahy demanded payment from Holloway, Holloway denied ever having guaranteed payment for the cheese and raised the Statute of Frauds [UCC 2–201] as a defense. Cudahy claimed that the Statute of Frauds could not be used as a defense, as both Cudahy and Holloway were merchants and Holloway failed to object within ten days to Cudahy's invoice. Discuss Cudahy's argument. [*Cudahy Foods Co. v. Holloway*, 286 S.E.2d 606 (N.C.App. 1982)]

13–8. Statute of Frauds. Harry Starr orally contracted to purchase a new automobile from Freeport Dodge, Inc. Starr signed an order form describing the car and made a down payment of $25. The dealer did not sign the form, and the form stated that "this order is not valid unless signed and accepted by the dealer." The dealer deposited the $25, and that was noted on the order form. On the day scheduled for delivery, a sales representative for the dealer told Starr that an error had been made in determining the price and that Starr would be required to pay an additional $175 above the price on the order form. Starr refused to pay the additional amount and sued for breach of contract. Freeport Dodge claimed that the contract fell under the Statute of Frauds and that because Freeport Dodge had not signed the contract, the oral contract was not enforceable. Discuss Freeport Dodge's contention. [*Starr v. Freeport Dodge, Inc.*, 54 Misc.2d 271, 282 N.Y.S.2d 58 (Dist. 1967)]

13–9. Statute of Frauds. R-P Packaging, Inc., is a manufacturer of cellophane wrapping material. The plant manager for Flowers Baking Co. decided to improve its packaging of cookies. The plant manager contacted R-P Packaging for the possible purchase of cellophane wrap imprinted with designed "artwork." R-P took measurements to determine the appropriate size of the wrap and submitted to Flowers a sample size with the artwork to be imprinted. After agreeing that the artwork was satisfactory, Flowers gave a verbal order to R-P for the designed cellophane wrap at a price of $13,000. When the wrap was tendered, although it conformed to the measurements and design, Flowers complained that the wrap was too short and the design off center. Flowers rejected the shipment. R-P sued. Flowers contended that the oral contract was unenforceable under the Statute of Frauds. Discuss this contention. [*Flowers Baking Co. v. R-P Packaging, Inc.*, 229 Va. 370, 329 S.E.2d 462 (1985)]

13–10. Merchant Status. Albert Reifschneider was raised on a farm and had been in the business of selling corn and in the business of selling other crops under futures contracts (contracts for goods to be harvested in the future) for twenty years. In April 1988, Reifschneider orally agreed to sell Colorado-Kansas Grain Co. 12,500 bushels of corn after the harvest in the fall. The company sent Reifschneider a written confirmation of the agreement with instructions to sign it and return it. In June, Reifschneider told the company that he would not sign the confirmation and that no contract existed between the parties. The company demanded that

Reifschneider deliver the corn, but the demand was to no avail. The company sued Reifschneider for breach of contract, and the issue turned on whether Reifschneider was a "merchant" within the meaning of the UCC. How should the court rule? Discuss. [*Colorado-Kansas Grain Co. v. Reifschneider*, 817 P.2d 637 (Colo.App. 1991)]

13–11. Goods and Services Combined. Jane Pittsley contracted with Donald Houser, who was doing business as the Hilton Contract Carpet Co., for the installation of carpet in her home. Following installation, Pittsley complained to Hilton that some seams were visible, gaps appeared, the carpet did not lie flat in all areas, and the carpet failed to reach the wall in certain locations. Although Hilton made various attempts to fix the installation by attempting to stretch the carpet and other methods, Pittsley was not satisfied with the work and eventually sued Hilton to recover the $3,500 she had paid toward the $4,319.50 contract price for the carpet and its installation. Hilton paid the installers $700 for the work done in laying Pittsley's carpet. One of the issues before the court was whether the contract was a contract for the sale of goods or a contract for the sale of services. How should the court decide this issue? Discuss fully. [*Pittsley v. Houser*, 125 Idaho 820, 875 P.2d 232 (1994)]

CASE BRIEFING ASSIGNMENT

13–12. *Examine Case A.4 [Goldkist, Inc. v. Brownlee, 182 Ga.App. 287, 355 S.E.2d 733 (1987)] in Appendix A. The case has been excerpted there in great detail. Review and then brief the case, making sure that you include answers to the following questions in your brief.*

1. What defense did the Brownlees raise against Goldkist's claim that the Brownlees had formed a contract with Goldkist for the sale of goods?
2. Why is the question as to whether the Brownlees were merchants significant?
3. Summarize the court's reasons for reversing the trial court's summary judgment for the Brownlees.

▌Accessing the Internet: Fundamentals of Business Law

For the most updated information on the Uniform Commercial Code, including drafts of revised articles, go to

http://www.law.cornell.edu/ucc/ucc.table.html

Or go to

http://www.kentlaw.edu/ulc/ulc.html

You can obtain information on current commercial law topics from the law firm of Hale and Dorr at

http://www.haledorr.com/

Cornell Law School's Legal Information Institute offers online access to the Uniform Commercial Code as enacted in several of the states at

http://www.law.cornell.edu/statutes.html#state

If you use the commercial service CompuServe, you can view the text of the United Nations Convention on Contracts for the International Sale of Goods (CISG) by doing the following: Type in

Go itforum

From your Library Menu, you should choose

Browse

Then select

IT Practices

Then you should select

International Sales Agreements

The Pace University School of Law's Institute of International Commercial Law maintains a Web site that contains the full text of the CISG, as well as relevant cases and discussions of the law. Go to

http://cisgw3.law.pace.edu/

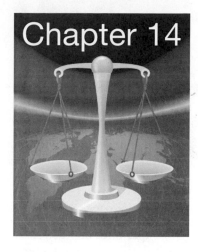

Chapter 14

Title and Risk of Loss

CHAPTER OBJECTIVES

After reading this chapter, you should be able to:

1. Indicate when title to goods passes from seller to buyer.
2. Explain the problems that can arise when persons who acquire goods with imperfect title attempt to resell the goods.
3. Define various contract terms that help to determine when the risk of loss passes from a seller or lessor to a buyer or lessee.
4. Identify who bears the risk of loss when a contract is breached.
5. Indicate when each party to a sales or lease contract has an insurable interest in the goods.

The sale of goods transfers ownership (title) from the seller to the buyer. Often, a sales contract is signed before the actual goods are available. For example, a sales contract for oranges might be signed in May, but the oranges may not be ready for picking and shipment until October. Any number of things can happen between the time the sales contract is signed and the time the goods are actually transferred to the buyer's possession. For example, fire, flood, or frost may destroy the orange groves, or the oranges may be lost or damaged in transit. The same problems may occur under a lease contract. Because of these possibilities, it is important to know the rights and liabilities of the parties between the time the contract is formed and the time the goods are actually received by the buyer or lessee.

Before the creation of the Uniform Commercial Code (UCC), *title*—the right of ownership—was the central concept in sales law, controlling all issues of rights and remedies of the parties to a sales con-

tract. There were numerous problems attending this concept. For example, frequently it was difficult to determine when title actually passed from a seller to a buyer, and therefore it was also difficult to predict which party a court would decide had title at the time of a loss. Because of such problems, the UCC divorced the question of title as completely as possible from the question of the rights and obligations of buyers, sellers, and third parties (such as subsequent purchasers, creditors, or the tax collector).

In some situations, title is still relevant under the UCC, and the UCC has special rules for locating title. These rules will be discussed in the sections that follow. In most situations, however, the UCC has replaced the concept of title with three other concepts: (1) identification, (2) risk of loss, and (3) insurable interest. By breaking down the transfer of ownership into these three components, the drafters of the UCC have essentially followed Aristotle's advice in the chapter-opening quotation and created greater precision in the law governing sales—leaving as few points of law as possible "to the decision of the judges."

In lease contracts, of course, title to the goods is retained by the lessor-owner of the goods. Hence, the UCC's provisions relating to passage of title do not apply to leased goods. Other concepts discussed in this chapter, though, including identification, risk of loss, and insurable interest, relate to lease contracts as well as to sales contracts.

▌Identification

Before any interest in specific goods can pass from the seller or lessor to the buyer or lessee, two conditions must prevail: (1) the goods must be in existence, and (2) they must be identified as the specific goods designated in the contract. Identification is a designation of goods as the subject matter of a sales or lease contract. Title cannot pass from buyer to seller unless the goods are identified to the contract. (As mentioned, title to leased goods remains with the lessor—or, if the owner is a third party, with that party. The lessee does not acquire title to leased goods.) Identification is significant because it gives the buyer or lessee the right to insure (or an insurable interest in) the goods and the right to recover from third parties who damage the goods.

In their contract, the parties can agree on when identification will take place. If they do not so specify, however, the UCC provisions discussed here determine when identification takes place [UCC 2–501(1), 2A–217].

Existing Goods

If the contract calls for the sale or lease of specific and ascertained goods that are already in existence, identification takes place at the time the contract is made. For example, you contract to purchase or lease a fleet of five cars by the serial numbers listed for the cars.

Future Goods

If a sale involves unborn animals to be born within twelve months after contracting, identification takes place when the animals are conceived. If a lease involves any unborn animals, identification occurs when the animals are conceived. If a sale involves crops that are to be harvested within twelve months (or the next harvest season occurring after contracting, whichever is longer), identification takes place when the crops are planted or begin to grow. In a sale or lease of any other future goods, identification occurs when the goods are shipped, marked, or otherwise designated by the seller or lessor as the goods to which the contract refers.

Goods That Are Part of a Larger Mass

Goods that are part of a larger mass are identified when the goods are marked, shipped, or somehow designated by the seller or lessor as the particular goods to pass under the contract. Suppose that a buyer orders 1,000 cases of beans from a 10,000-case lot. Until the seller separates the 1,000 cases of beans from the 10,000-case lot, title and risk of loss remain with the seller.

A common exception to this rule deals with fungible goods. Fungible goods are goods that are alike by physical nature, by agreement, or by trade usage. Typical examples are specific grades or types of wheat, oil, and wine, usually stored in large containers. If these goods are held or intended to be held by owners as tenants in common (owners having shares undivided from the entire mass), a seller-owner can pass title and risk of loss to the buyer without an actual separation. The buyer replaces the seller as an owner in common [UCC 2–105(4)].

For example, Anselm, Braudel, and Carpenter are farmers. They deposit, respectively, 5,000 bushels, 3,000 bushels, and 2,000 bushels of grain of the same grade and quality in a bin. The three become owners in common, with Anselm owning 50 percent of the 10,000 bushels, Braudel 30 percent, and Carpenter 20 percent. Anselm could contract to sell 5,000 bushels of grain to Tareyton and, because the goods are fungible, pass title and risk of loss to Tareyton without physically separating 5,000 bushels. Tareyton now becomes an owner in common with Braudel and Carpenter.

▌Passage of Title

Once goods exist and are identified, the provisions of UCC 2–401 apply to the passage of title. In virtually all subsections of UCC 2–401, the words "unless otherwise explicitly agreed" appear, meaning that any explicit understanding between the buyer and the seller determines when title passes. Unless an agreement is explicitly made, title passes to the buyer at the time and the place the seller performs the *physical* delivery of the goods [UCC 2–401(2)]. This rule is applied in the following case.

CASE 14.1

Synergistic Technologies, Inc. v. IDB Mobile Communications, Inc.

Unitee States District Court, District of Columbia, 1994. 871 F.Supp. 24.

FACTS Synergistic Technologies, Inc. (SynTech), developed three computer software systems for IDB Mobile Communications, Inc., to provide IDB's customers with satellite voice and data communications services. SynTech installed the systems in IDB's computers under a "Statement of Work" negotiated between the two firms. During the installation, IDB discovered that the systems would not allow it to make back-up copies of the software. If IDB's computers crashed, a return to full operation would thus be delayed. When IDB hired another company to make back-up copies, SynTech filed a suit in a federal district court against IDB, seeking damages and other relief for, among other things, alleged infringement of SynTech's copyrights. IDB responded in part by filing a motion for summary judgment. One of the issues was whether IDB was the "owner" of the software.

ISSUE Had title to the software passed to IDB?

DECISION Yes. The federal district court granted IDB's motion for summary judgment on this issue.

REASON The court found that the parties' "Statement of Work is not clear on the issue of transfer of ownership of the software," adding that "[i]f this matter turned solely on the Statement of Work, the Court would be unable to resolve the issue." The court pointed out, however, that the question was "also governed by [Section] 2–401 of the Uniform Commercial Code, which provides that '[u]nless otherwise explicitly agreed title passes to the buyer at the time and place at which the seller completes his performance with reference to the physical delivery of the goods.' " Thus, because the parties had not explicitly agreed otherwise, title to "the software passed to IDB at the time of delivery of the goods."

FOR CRITICAL ANALYSIS—Technological Consideration *Why would Synergistic Technologies be concerned about the fact that its client was making back-up copies of the software?*

Shipment and Destination Contracts

Delivery arrangements can determine when title passes from the seller to the buyer. In a **shipment contract,** the seller is required or authorized to ship goods by carrier, such as a trucking company. Under a shipment contract, the seller is required only to deliver conforming goods into the hands of a carrier, and title passes to the buyer at the time and place of shipment [UCC 2–401(2)(a)]. Generally, *all contracts are assumed to be shipment contracts if nothing to the contrary is stated in the contract.*

In a **destination contract,** the seller is required to deliver the goods to a particular destination, usually directly to the buyer, but sometimes the buyer designates that the goods should be delivered to another party. Title passes to the buyer when the goods are *tendered* at that destination [UCC 2–401(2)(b)]. A tender of delivery is the seller's placing or holding of conforming goods at the buyer's disposition (with any necessary notice), enabling the buyer to take delivery [UCC 2–503(1)].

Delivery without Movement of the Goods

When the contract of sale does not call for the seller's shipment or delivery of the goods (when the buyer is to pick up the goods), the passage of title depends on whether the seller must deliver a **document of title,** such as a bill of lading or a warehouse receipt, to the buyer. A *bill of lading* is a receipt for goods that is signed by a carrier and that serves as a contract for the transportation of the goods. A *warehouse receipt* is a receipt issued by a warehouser for goods stored in a warehouse. (See Exhibits 14–1 and 14–2.)

When a document of title is required, title passes to the buyer *when and where the document is delivered.* Thus, if the goods are stored in a warehouse, title passes to the buyer when the appropriate documents are delivered to the buyer. The goods never move. In fact, the buyer can choose to leave the goods at the same warehouse for a period of time, and the buyer's title to those goods will be unaffected.

When no documents of title are required, and delivery is made without moving the goods, title passes at the time and place the sales contract is made, if the goods have already been identified. If the goods have not been identified, title does not pass until identification occurs. Consider an example. Rogers sells lumber to Bodan. It is agreed that Bodan will pick up the lumber at the yard. If the lumber has been identified (segregated, marked, or in any other way distinguished from all other lumber), title passes to Bodan when the contract is signed. If the lumber is still in storage bins at the mill, title does not pass to Bodan until the particular pieces of lumber to be sold under this contract are identified [UCC 2–401(3)].

Sales or Leases by Nonowners

Problems occur when persons who acquire goods with imperfect titles attempt to sell or lease them. Sections 2–402 and 2–403 of the UCC deal with the rights of two parties who lay claim to the same goods, sold with imperfect titles. Generally, a buyer acquires at least whatever title the seller has to the goods sold.

The UCC also protects a person who leases such goods from the person who bought them. Of course, a lessee does not acquire whatever title the lessor has to the goods. A lessee acquires a right to possess and use the goods—that is, a *leasehold interest.* A lessee acquires whatever leasehold interest the lessor has or has the power to transfer, subject to the lease contract [UCC 2A–303, 2A–304, 2A–305].

VOID TITLE   A buyer may unknowingly purchase goods from a seller who is not the owner of the goods. If the seller is a thief, the seller's title is *void*—legally, no title exists. Thus, the buyer acquires no title, and the real owner can reclaim the goods from the buyer. The same result would occur if the goods were only leased, because the lessor has no leasehold interest to transfer.

For example, if Jim steals goods owned by Maren, Jim has a *void title* to those goods. If Jim sells the goods to Shidra, Maren can reclaim them from Shidra even though Shidra acted in good faith and honestly was not aware that the goods were stolen. Article 2A contains similar provisions for leases.

VOIDABLE TITLE   A seller has a *voidable title* if the goods that he or she is selling were obtained by fraud, paid for with a check that is later dishonored, purchased from a minor, or purchased on credit when the seller was insolvent. (Under the UCC, a person is **insolvent** when that person ceases to pay "his debts in the ordinary course of business or cannot pay his debts as they become due or is insolvent within the meaning of federal bankruptcy law" [UCC 1–201(23)].)

In contrast to a seller with *void title,* a seller with *voidable title* has the power to transfer a good title to a good faith purchaser for value. A **good faith purchaser** is one who buys without knowledge of circumstances that would make a person of ordinary prudence inquire about the validity of the seller's title to the goods. One who purchases *for value* gives legally sufficient consideration (value) for the goods purchased. The real, or original, owner cannot recover goods from a good faith purchaser for value [UCC 2–403(1)].[1] If the buyer of the goods is not a good faith purchaser for value, then the actual owner of the goods can reclaim them from the buyer (or from the seller, if the goods are still in the seller's possession). Exhibit 14–3 illustrates these concepts.

The same rules apply in circumstances involving leases. A lessor with voidable title has the power to transfer a valid leasehold interest to a good faith lessee for value. The real owner cannot recover the goods, except as permitted by the terms of the lease. The real owner can, however, receive all proceeds arising from the lease, as well as a transfer of

---

1.   The real, or original, owner could, of course, sue the purchaser who initially obtained voidable title to the goods.

Exhibit 14–1
A Sample Negotiable Bill of Lading

UNIFORM MOTOR CARRIER ORDER BILL OF LADING	1st Sheet

Original—Domestic

Shipper's No. _____

Agent's No. _____

CENTRAL FREIGHT LINES INC.

RECEIVED, subject to the classifications and tariffs in effect on the date of the issue of this Bill of Lading,

From		Date	19

At	Street	City	County	State

the property described below, in apparent good order, except as noted (contents and condition of contents of packages unknown) marked, consigned and destined as shown below, which said company (the word company being understood throughout this contract as meaning any person or corporation in possession of the property under the contract) agrees to carry to its usual place of delivery at said destination, if within the scope of its lawful operations, otherwise to deliver to another carrier on the route to said destination. It is mutually agreed, as to each carrier of all or any of said property over all or any portion of said route to destination, and as to each party at any time interested in all or any of said property, that every service to be performed hereunder shall be subject to all the conditions not prohibited by law, whether printed or written, herein contained, including the conditions on back hereof, which are hereby agreed to by the shipper and accepted for himself and his assigns.

The surrender of this Original ORDER Bill of Lading properly indorsed shall be required before the delivery of the property. Inspection of property covered by this bill of lading will not be permitted unless provided by law or unless permission is indorsed on this original Bill of lading or given in writing by the shipper.

Consigned to Order of

Destination	Street,	City,	County,	State

Notify

At	Street,	City,	County,	State

I.C.C. No.	Vehicle No.

Routing

No. Pack- ages	Description of Articles, Special Marks, and Exceptions	*Weight (Subject to Correction)	Class or Rate	Check Column	
					Subject to Section 7 of Conditions, if this shipment is to be delivered to the consignee without recourse on the consignor, the consignor shall sign the following statement: The carrier shall not make delivery of this shipment without payment of freight and all other lawful charges.
					(signature of consignor.)
					If charges are to be prepaid write or stamp here, "To be Prepaid."
					Received $ _____ to apply in prepayment of the charges of the property described hereon.
					Agent or Cashier.
					Per _____ (the signature here acknowledges only the amount prepaid.)

SAMPLE

*If the shipment moves between two ports by a carrier by water, the law requires that the bill of lading shall state whether it is "carrier's or shipper's weight."

Note--Where the rate is dependent on value, shippers are required to state specifically in writing the agreed or declared value of the property.

The agreed or declared value of the property is hereby specifically stated by the shipper to be not exceeding

_____ per _____

Charges advanced:

$ _____

Shipper	Agent.
Per	Per

Permanent address of Shipper	Street	City,	State

MOORE BUSINESS FORMS, INC. WACO, TEX. M

Source: Reprinted with permission of Central Freight Lines, Inc. © 1985 Central Freight Lines, Inc.
Note: This form is printed in yellow to warn holders that it is a bill lading. The back of the form permits negotiation by indorsement.

♦ **Exhibit 14–2**
A Sample Nonnegotiable Warehouse Receipt

HART

Warehouse Receipt – Not Negotiable

Agreement No. _____   Vault No. _____

Service Order _____   _____

Receipt and
Lot Number _____   Date of Issue _____ 19____

Received for the account of and deliverable to • _____

whose latest known address is _____ SAMPLE _____

_____ the goods enumerated on the inside or attached schedule to be

stored in Company warehouse, located at _____
which goods are accepted only upon the following conditions set forth below:

READ CAREFULLY ☞ That the value of all goods stored, including the contents of any container, and all goods hereafter stored for Depositor's account to be not over $ _____ per pound† per article unless a higher value is noted in the schedule, for which an additional monthly storage charge of _____ ¢ on each $_____ valuation in excess of $ _____ per pound † per article or fraction thereof will be made.

If there are any items enumerated in this receipt valued in excess of the above limitations per pound per article and not so noted in the schedule, return this receipt within 10 days with proper values so indicated in writing in order that the receipt may be re-issued and proper higher storage rates assessed.

OWNERSHIP. The Customer, Shipper, Depositor, or Agent represents and warrants that he is lawfully possessed of goods to be stored and/or has the authority to store or ship said goods. (If the goods are mortgaged, notify the Company the name and address of the mortgagee.)

PAYMENT OF CHARGES. Storage bills are payable monthly in advance for each month's storage or fraction thereof. Labor charges, cartage and other services rendered are payable upon completion of work. All charges shall be paid at the warehouse location shown hereon, and if delinquent, shall incur interest monthly at the rate of _____ per cent ( ) per year.
The Depositor will pay reasonable attorney's fee incurred by The Company in collecting delinquent accounts.

LIABILITY OF COMPANY. The company shall be liable for any loss or injury to the goods caused by its failure to exercise such care as a reasonably careful man would exercise under like circumstances. The company will not be liable for loss or damage to fragile articles not packed, or articles packed or unpacked by other than employees of this company. Depositor specifically agrees that the warehouse will not be liable for contamination or for insect damage to articles placed in drawer of furniture by the depositor. Periodic spraying of the warehouse premises shall constitute ordinary and proper care, unless the depositor requests in writing and pays for anti-infestation treatment of articles in drawers and compartments of stored furniture.

CHANGE OF ADDRESS. Notice of change of address must be given the Company in writing, and acknowledged in writing by the Company.

TRANSFER OR WITHDRAWAL OF GOODS. The warehouse receipt is not negotiable and shall be produced and all charges must be paid before delivery to the Depositor, or transfer of goods to another person; however, a written direction to the Company to transfer the goods to another person or deliver the goods may be accepted by the Company at its option without requiring tender of the warehouse receipt

ACCESS TO STORAGE PARTIAL WITHDRAWAL. A signed order from the person in whose name the receipt is issued is required to enable others to remove or have access to goods. A charge is made for stacking and unstacking, and for access to stored goods.
BUILDING-FIRE-WATCHMAN. The Company does not represent or warrant that its building cannot be destroyed by fire or that the contents of said buildings including the said property cannot be destroyed by fire. The Company shall not be required to maintain a watchman or sprinkler system and its failure to do so shall not constitute negligence.
CLAIMS OR ERRORS. All claims for non-delivery of any article or articles and for damage, breakage, etc., must be made in writing within ninety (90) days from delivery of goods stored or they are waived. Failure to return the warehouse receipt for correction within ( ) days after receipt thereof by the depositor will be conclusive that it is correct and delivery will be made only in accordance therewith.
FUTURE SERVICE. This Contract shall extend and apply to future services rendered to the Depositor by the Company and to any additional goods deposited with the Company by the Depositor.
WAREHOUSEMAN'S LIEN. The Company reserves the right to sell the goods stored, in accordance with the provisions of the Uniform Commercial Code (Business and Commerce Code if stored in Texas), for all lawful charges in arrears.
TERMINATION OF STORAGE. The Company reserves the right to terminate the storage of the goods at any time by giving to the Depositor thirty (30) days' written notice of its intention so to do, and, unless the Depositor removes such goods within that period, the Company is hereby empowered to have the same removed at the cost and expense of the Depositor, or the Company may sell them at auction in accordance with state law.

DEPOSITOR WILL PAY REASONABLE LEGAL FEES INCURRED BY WAREHOUSE IN COLLECTING DELINQUENT CHARGES.

THIS DOCUMENT CONTAINS THE WHOLE CONTRACT BETWEEN THE PARTIES AND THERE ARE NO OTHER TERMS, WARRANTIES, REPRESENTATIONS, OR AGREEMENTS OF EITHER DEPOSITOR OR COMPANY NOT HEREIN CONTAINED.

Storage per month
or fraction thereof. . . . $_____
Warehouse labor . . . . $_____
Cartage. . . . . $_____
Packing at residence . . . $_____
Wrapping and preparing
for storage. . . . . . $_____
Charges advanced . . . . $_____
_____ $_____
_____ $_____

By _____

• Insert "Mr. and/or Mrs." or, if military personnel, appropriate rank or grade.
†Delete the words "per pound" if the declared value is per article.
  For goods stored for military personnel under PL 245, the contractor's liability for care of goods is as provided in Basic Agreement with U.S. Goverment

THIS PROPERTY HAS NOT BEEN INSURED BY THIS COMPANY FOR FIRE OR ANY OTHER CASUALTY
SCHEDULE OF GOODS ON FOLLOWING PAGE OR ATTACHED

W-1 (9-81) Approved by SW WT4©   Re-order from Hart Graphics, Austin, Texas

♦ **Exhibit 14–3**
Void and Voidable Title
If goods are transferred from their owner to another by theft, the thief acquires no ownership rights. Because the thief's title is *void*, a later buyer can acquire no title, and the owner can recover the goods. If the transfer occurs by fraud, the transferee acquires a *voidable* title. A later good faith purchaser for value can acquire good title, and the original owner cannot recover the goods.

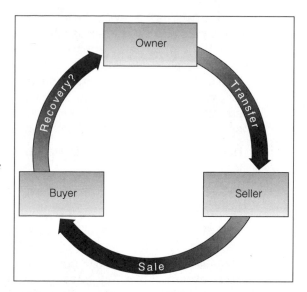

all rights, title, and interest as lessor under the lease, including the lessor's interest in the return of the goods when the lease expires.

THE ENTRUSTMENT RULE   According to Section 2–403(2), entrusting goods to a merchant *who deals in goods of that kind* gives the merchant the power to transfer all rights to a *buyer in the ordinary course of business*. Entrusting includes both delivering the goods to the merchant and leaving the purchased goods with the merchant for later delivery or pickup [UCC 2–403(3)]. A buyer in the ordinary course of business is a person who, in good faith and without knowledge that the sale violates the ownership rights or security interest of a third party, buys in ordinary course from a person (other than a pawnbroker) in the business of selling goods of that kind [UCC 1–201(9)]. (A *security interest* is any interest in personal property that secures payment or the performance of an obligation—see Chapter 19.)

For example, Jan leaves her watch with a jeweler to be repaired. The jeweler sells both new and used watches. The jeweler sells Jan's watch to Kim,

a customer, who does not know that the jeweler has no right to sell it. Kim, as a good faith buyer, gets good title against Jan's claim of ownership.[2] Kim, however, obtains only those rights held by the person entrusting the goods (here, Jan). Suppose that in the example just given, Jan had stolen the watch from Greg and then left it with the jeweler to be repaired. The jeweler then sells it to Kim. Kim gets good title against Jan, who entrusted the watch to the jeweler, but not against Greg (the real owner), who neither entrusted the watch to Jan nor authorized Jan to entrust it.

Article 2A provides a similar rule for leased goods. If a lessor entrusts goods to a lessee-merchant who deals in goods of that kind, the lessee-merchant has the power to transfer all of the rights the lessor had in the goods to a buyer or sublessee in the ordinary course of business [UCC 2A–305(2)].

The following case involved the application of the entrustment doctrine to protect a good faith buyer.

---

2.   Jan, of course, can sue the jeweler for the equivalent money value of the watch.

CASE 14.2

Heinrich v. Titus-Will Sales, Inc.

Court of Appeals of Washington, Division 2, 1994.
73 Wash.App. 147,
868 P.2d 169.

FACTS   James Wilson held himself out as a dealer/broker, licensed to buy and sell motor vehicles. Michael Heinrich hired Wilson to buy a new Ford pickup. Wilson made a deal with Titus-Will Ford Sales, Inc., for the truck. Heinrich gave Wilson checks totaling more than $22,000. Titus-Will gave Wilson a variety of documents, including the owner's manual, an odometer disclosure statement, and a warranty
(Continued)

Case 14.2—Continued

card, as well as the keys to the truck. Wilson gave Titus-Will a check for half of the purchase price. Because the check was dated for three days later, Titus-Will did not release the truck's certificate of origin, which a buyer needs to obtain title. When Wilson's check bounced, Titus-Will refused to give up title to the truck. Heinrich sued Titus-Will and Wilson in a Washington state court to obtain the title and damages. The court applied the entrustment doctrine to award Heinrich what he asked for, and Titus-Will appealed. Titus-Will argued that the entrustment doctrine did not apply.

ISSUE   Did Titus-Will "entrust" the truck to Wilson for purposes of applying the entrustment doctrine?

DECISION   Yes. The Court of Appeals of Washington affirmed the award of the lower court.

REASON   The state appellate court pointed out that "[t]he UCC definition of 'entrusting' is broad." Under UCC 2–403, "any delivery and any acquiescence in retention of possession" can constitute entrustment. The court explained that "[a] person can entrust goods to a merchant by a variety of methods, such as consigning them, creating a bailment, taking a security interest in inventory, leaving them with the merchant after purchase, and delivering them for purposes of repair." The court also noted that "[a] sale can *   *   * constitute an entrustment when some aspect of the transaction remains incomplete."

FOR CRITICAL ANALYSIS—Social Consideration   *What policies support protecting innocent buyers, such as Heinrich, under the entrustment doctrine?*

▌Risk of Loss

Under the UCC, risk of loss does not necessarily pass with title. When risk of loss passes from a seller or lessor to a buyer or lessee is generally determined by the contract between the parties. Sometimes, the contract states expressly when the risk of loss passes. At other times, it does not, and a court must interpret the performance and delivery terms of the contract to determine whether the risk has passed. In the following case, the court had to decide whether, under the terms of the parties' agreement, the risk of loss had passed from the seller to the buyer.

CASE 14.3

In re Thomas[a]

United States Bankruptcy Court,
Southern District of Florida, 1995.
182 Bankr. 347,
26 UCC Rep.Serv.2d 774.

FACTS   Marilyn Thomas contracted with Sunkissed Pools for an "installed pool heater" for her home. One afternoon, Thomas noticed that a heating unit had been placed in her driveway. When Sunkissed returned to install the heater, it had been stolen. Thomas subsequently filed for personal bankruptcy. Sunkissed filed a claim for the price of the heater. Thomas objected. She argued that when she had noticed the heater in her driveway, she had called Sunkissed and told them they needed to move the unit because the neighborhood was not safe. She said that the unit sat in her driveway for four days before it disappeared, after which she again called Sunkissed and was told "not

a.   *In re* means "in the matter of, concerning, or regarding." The use of *in re* is the usual method of entitling a judicial proceeding in which judicial action is to be taken on some matter, such as a debtor's estate in bankruptcy, in which there are no adversary parties. *In re, Matter of,* and *Estate of,* or some combination of these phrases (such as *In re Estate of*) , are all commonly used in the titles of cases involving actions of the kind just mentioned.

Case 14.3—Continued

to worry." Sunkissed's president testified that the firm did not receive any calls from Thomas and that he had gone to her home the day after the unit was left in her driveway and found that it was gone.

ISSUE   Had the risk of loss of the pool heater passed from the seller to the buyer?

DECISION   No. The court dismissed Sunkissed's claim.

REASON   The court stated that the parties' "conflicting views of the events" were "worrisome" but pointed out that "they are not controlling or truly relevant." Instead, the court found it more significant that both parties "testified that [Thomas] had purchased an 'installed' pool heater, and that the pool heater had not been installed as agreed and contracted for." Thus, the court concluded that "there simply was no delivery by the seller." For this reason, "the risk of loss always remained with the seller, and never shifted."

FOR CRITICAL ANALYSIS—Social Consideration   *What if Thomas had purchased a different product, such as a set of poolside chairs, and Sunkissed Pools simply delivered them to her driveway? Would the risk have passed to Thomas in such a situation?*

Delivery with Movement of the Goods— Carrier Cases

When there is no specification in the agreement, the following rules apply to cases involving movement of the goods (carrier cases).

SHIPMENT CONTRACTS   In a shipment contract, if the seller or lessor is required or authorized to ship goods by carrier (but not required to deliver them to a particular destination), risk of loss passes to the buyer or lessee when the goods are duly delivered to the carrier [UCC 2–509(1)(a), 2A–219(2)(a)].

For example, a seller in Texas sells five hundred cases of grapefruit to a buyer in New York, F.O.B. Houston (free on board in Houston—that is, the buyer pays the transportation charges from Houston). The contract authorizes a shipment by carrier; it does not require that the seller tender the grapefruit in New York. Risk passes to the buyer when conforming goods are properly placed in the possession of the carrier. If the goods are damaged in transit, the loss is the buyer's. (Actually, buyers have recourse against carriers, subject to certain limitations, and they usually insure the goods from the time the goods leave the seller.)

DESTINATION CONTRACTS   In a destination contract, the risk of loss passes to the buyer or lessee when the goods are tendered to the buyer or lessee at the specified destination [UCC 2–509(1)(b), 2A–219(2)(b)]. In the preceding example, if the con-

tract had been F.O.B. New York, risk of loss during transit to New York would have been the seller's.

CONTRACT TERMS   Specific terms in the contract help determine when risk of loss passes to the buyer. These terms, which are listed and defined in Exhibit 14–4, relate generally to the determination of which party will bear the costs of delivery.

Delivery without Movement of the Goods

The UCC also addresses situations in which the seller or lessor is required neither to ship nor to deliver the goods. Frequently, the buyer or lessee is to pick up the goods from the seller or lessor, or the goods are held by a bailee. Under the UCC, a **bailee** is a party who, by a bill of lading, warehouse receipt, or other document of title, acknowledges possession of goods and contracts to deliver them. A warehousing company, for example, or a trucking company that normally issues documents of title for the goods it receives is a bailee. (Bailments are discussed in detail in Chapter 28.)

GOODS HELD BY THE SELLER   If the goods are held by the seller, a document of title is usually not used. If the seller is a merchant, risk of loss to goods held by the seller passes to the buyer when the buyer *actually takes physical possession of the goods* [UCC 2–509(3)]. If the seller is not a merchant, the risk of loss to goods held by the seller passes to the buyer upon *tender of delivery* [UCC 2–509(3)].

♦ **Exhibit 14–4**
Contract Terms—Definitions

F.O.B. (free on board)—Indicates that the selling price of goods includes transportation costs (and that the seller carries risk of loss) to the specific F.O.B. place named in the contract. The place can be either the place of initial shipment (for example, the seller's city or place of business) or the place of destination (for example, the buyer's city or place of business) [UCC 2–319(1)].
F.A.S. (free alongside)—Requires that the seller, at his or her own expense and risk, deliver the goods alongside the ship before risk passes to the buyer [UCC 2–319(2)].
C.I.F. or C.&F. (cost, insurance, and freight, or just cost and freight)—Requires, among other things, that the seller "put the goods in possession of a carrier" before risk passes to the buyer [UCC 2–320(2)]. (These are basically pricing terms, and the contracts remain shipment contracts, not destination contracts.)
Delivery ex-ship (delivery from the carrying ship)—Means that risk of loss does not pass to the buyer until the goods leave the ship or are otherwise properly unloaded [UCC 2–322].

In respect to leases, the risk of loss passes to the lessee on the lessee's receipt of the goods if the lessor—or supplier, in a finance lease (see Chapter 13)—is a merchant. Otherwise, the risk passes to the lessee on tender of delivery [UCC 2A–219(c)].

GOODS HELD BY A BAILEE When a bailee is holding goods for a person who has contracted to sell them and the goods are to be delivered without being moved, the goods are usually represented by a negotiable or nonnegotiable document of title (a bill of lading or a warehouse receipt—see Exhibits 14–1 and 14–2). Risk of loss passes to the buyer when (1) the buyer receives a negotiable document of title for the goods, (2) the bailee acknowledges the buyer's right to possess the goods, or (3) the buyer receives a nonnegotiable document of title *and* has had a *reasonable time* to present the document to the bailee and demand the goods. Obviously, if the bailee refuses to honor the document, the risk of loss remains with the seller [UCC 2–503(4)(b), 2–509(2)].

In respect to leases, if goods held by a bailee are to be delivered without being moved, the risk of loss passes to the lessee on acknowledgment by the bailee of the lessee's right to possession of the goods [UCC 2A–219(2)(b)].

Conditional Sales

Buyers and sellers sometimes form sales contracts that are conditioned either on the buyer's approval of the goods or on the buyer's resale of the goods. Under such contracts, the buyer is in possession of the goods. Sometimes, however, problems arise as to whether the buyer or seller should bear the loss if, for example, the goods are damaged or stolen while in the possession of the buyer.

SALE OR RETURN A sale or return (sometimes called a *sale and return*) is a type of contract by which the seller delivers a quantity of goods to the buyer on the understanding that if the buyer wishes to retain any portion of those goods (for use or resale), the buyer will consider the portion retained as having been sold to him or her and will pay accordingly. The balance will be returned to the seller. When the buyer receives possession of the goods under a sale-or-return contract, the title and risk of loss pass to the buyer. Title and risk of loss remain with the buyer until the buyer returns the goods to the seller within the time period specified. If the buyer fails to return the goods within this time period, the sale is finalized. The return of the goods is made at the buyer's risk and expense. Goods held under a sale-or-return contract are subject to the claims of the buyer's creditors while they are in the buyer's possession (even if the buyer has not paid for the goods).

The UCC treats a **consignment** as a sale or return. Under a consignment, the owner of goods (the *consignor*) delivers them to another (the *consignee*) for the consignee to sell. If the consignee sells the goods, the consignee must pay the consignor for them. If the consignee does not sell the goods, they may simply be returned to the consignor. While the goods are in the possession of the consignee, the consignee holds title to them, and creditors of the consignee will prevail over the consignor in any action to repossess the goods [UCC 2–326(3)].

SALE ON APPROVAL When a seller offers to sell goods to a buyer and permits the buyer to take the goods on a trial basis, a **sale on approval** is usually made. The term *sale* here is a misnomer, as only an *offer* to sell has been made, along with a *bailment* created by the buyer's possession. (A bailment is a temporary delivery of personal property into the care of another—see Chapter 28.)

Therefore, title and risk of loss (from causes beyond the buyer's control) remain with the seller until the buyer accepts (approves) the offer. Acceptance can be made expressly, by any act inconsistent with the *trial* purpose or the seller's ownership, or by the buyer's election not to return the goods within the trial period. If the buyer does not wish to accept, the buyer may notify the seller of that fact within the trial period, and the return is made at

the seller's expense and risk [UCC 2–327(1)]. Goods held on approval are not subject to the claims of the buyer's creditors until acceptance.

It is often difficult to determine from a particular transaction which exists—a contract for a sale on approval, a contract for a sale or return, or a contract for sale. The UCC states that (unless otherwise agreed) "if the goods are delivered primarily for use," the transaction is a sale on approval; "if the goods are delivered primarily for resale," the transaction is a sale or return [UCC 2–326(1)]. The court in the following case had to determine whether a particular transaction was a contract for a sale on approval or a contract for sale.

CASE 14.4

Houghton Wood Products, Inc. v. Badger Wood Products, Inc.

Court of Appeals of Wisconsin, 1995.
196 Wis.2d 457,
538 N.W.2d 621.

FACTS Badger Wood Products, Inc., a manufacturer of cabinets and other wood products, owed Associated Bank Green Bay over $3.7 million dollars. As collateral for the debt, Badger had promised all of its raw materials and work in process. When Badger failed to repay the money, it gave its assets to the bank, including three shipments of wood that had been delivered to Badger from Houghton Wood Products, Inc., but that had not been paid for. Houghton filed a suit in a Wisconsin state court against Badger and the bank, seeking the wood or the full purchase price of the wood. Houghton contended that it owned the wood because it was delivered pursuant to a sale on approval. The court agreed and issued a judgment in Houghton's favor. The bank appealed.

ISSUE Was the transaction between Badger and Houghton a sale on approval?

DECISION No. The Court of Appeals of Wisconsin reversed the lower court's ruling and remanded the case with an order to enter a judgment in the bank's favor.

REASON The court explained that "the wood delivered to Badger was to be made into cabinets that Badger would then sell to customers. Once the wood is made into cabinets, it undergoes substantial transformation and cannot be returned." If the sale was on approval, "title in the transformed wood would remain with Houghton until payment is made." The court reasoned that it "violates common sense and the rules of commerce to permit transformed goods to remain titled to the seller." Thus, the court held that "when a good is used in the manufacturing process where it undergoes transformation and is subsequently resold, it is not delivered for 'use,'" as that term is used in the UCC. Because the transaction was not a delivery for use, the court concluded that it was a contract for sale, not a sale on approval.

FOR CRITICAL ANALYSIS—Economic Consideration *For what reasons would a seller ever agree to a sale on approval, given the fact that in a sale on approval the seller retains the risk of loss and is also responsible for the expenses involved in the buyer's returning of the goods?*

Risk of Loss When a Sales or Lease Contract Is Breached

There are many ways to breach a sales or lease contract, and the transfer of risk operates differently depending on which party breaches. Generally, the party in breach bears the risk of loss.

WHEN THE SELLER OR LESSOR BREACHES If the goods are so nonconforming that the buyer has the right to reject them, the risk of loss does not pass to the buyer until the defects are **cured** (that is, until the goods are repaired, replaced, or discounted in price by the seller) or until the buyer accepts the goods in spite of their defects (thus waiving the right to reject). For example, a buyer orders blue widgets from a seller, F.O.B. seller's plant. The seller ships black widgets instead. The black widgets (nonconforming goods) are damaged in transit. The risk of loss falls on the seller. Had the seller shipped blue widgets (conforming goods) instead, the risk would have fallen on the buyer [UCC 2–510(2)].

If a buyer accepts a shipment of goods and later discovers a defect, acceptance can be revoked. Revocation allows the buyer to pass the risk of loss back to the seller, at least to the extent that the buyer's insurance does not cover the loss [UCC 2–510(2)].

In regard to leases, Article 2A states a similar rule. If the lessor or supplier tenders goods that are so nonconforming that the lessee has the right to reject them, the risk of loss remains with the lessor or the supplier until cure or acceptance [UCC 2A–220(1)(a)]. If the lessee, after acceptance, revokes his or her acceptance of nonconforming goods, the revocation passes the risk of loss back to the seller or supplier, to the extent that the lessee's insurance does not cover the loss [UCC 2A–220(1)(b)].

In the following case, the buyer claimed that the seller should bear the risk of loss for nonconforming goods that were stolen before the buyer was able to return them to the seller.

CASE 14.5

Graybar Electric Co. v. Shook

Supreme Court of North Carolina, 1973.
283 N.C. 213,
195 S.E.2d 514.

FACTS Harold Shook agreed with Graybar Electric Company to purchase three reels of burial cable for use in Shook's construction work. When the reels were delivered, each carton was marked "burial cable," but two of the reels were in fact aerial cable. Shook accepted the conforming reel of cable and notified Graybar that he was rejecting the two reels of aerial cable. Because of a truckers' strike, Shook was unable to return the reels to Graybar. He stored the reels in a well-lighted space near a grocery store owner's dwelling, which was close to Shook's work site. About four months later, Shook noticed that one of the reels had been stolen. On the following day, he notified Graybar of the loss and, worried about the safety of the second reel, arranged to have it transported to a garage for storage. Before the second reel was transferred, however, it was also stolen, and Shook notified Graybar of the second theft. Graybar sued Shook in a North Carolina state court for the purchase price, claiming that Shook had agreed to return to Graybar the nonconforming reels and had failed to do so. Shook contended that he had agreed only to contact a trucking company to return the reels, and because he had contacted three trucking firms to no avail (owing to the strike), his obligation had been fulfilled. The trial court ruled for Shook, and Graybar appealed.

ISSUE Who should bear the risk of loss for the reels?

DECISION Graybar. The Supreme Court of North Carolina affirmed the lower court's judgment in Shook's favor.

REASON The court relied on UCC 2–510(1), which states, "Where tender or delivery of goods so fails to conform to the contract as to give a right of rejection the risk of their loss remains on the seller until cure or

Case 14.5—Continued

acceptance." The court held that Shook had formed no contract with Graybar to return the nonconforming goods, although Shook had attempted to facilitate the aerial cable's return at the owner's request. Graybar, however, "with full notice of the place of storage which was at the place of delivery did nothing but sleep on its rights for more than three months." Thus, Graybar had evidenced neither promptness of action nor good faith.

FOR CRITICAL ANALYSIS—Ethical Consideration *Did the fact that Graybar "did nothing but sleep on its rights for more than three months" have anything to do with the outcome of this case? Should it have?*

WHEN THE BUYER OR LESSEE BREACHES The general rule is that when a buyer or lessee breaches a contract, the risk of loss *immediately* shifts to the buyer or lessee. There are three important limitations to this rule:

1. The seller or lessor must already have identified the contract goods.
2. The buyer or lessee bears the risk for only a *commercially reasonable time* after the seller has learned of the breach.
3. The buyer or lessee is liable only to the extent of any deficiency in the seller's insurance coverage [UCC 2–510(3), 2A–220(2)].

▌Insurable Interest

Parties to sales and lease contracts often obtain insurance coverage to protect against damage, loss, or destruction of goods. Any party purchasing insurance, however, must have a sufficient interest in the insured item to obtain a valid policy. Insurance laws—not the UCC—determine sufficiency. The UCC is helpful, however, because it contains certain rules regarding insurable interests in goods.

Insurable Interest of the Buyer or Lessee

A buyer or lessee has an **insurable interest** in *identified* goods. The moment the contract goods are identified by the seller or lessor, the buyer or lessee has a special property interest that allows the buyer or lessee to obtain necessary insurance coverage for those goods even before the risk of loss has passed [UCC 2–501(1), 2A–218(1)].

Consider an example: In March, a farmer sells a cotton crop he hopes to harvest in October. The buyer acquires an insurable interest in the crop

when it is planted, because those goods (the cotton crop) are identified to the sales contract between the seller and the buyer. The rule stated in UCC 2–501(1)(c) is that such buyers obtain an insurable interest in crops by identification, which occurs when the crops are planted or otherwise become growing crops, providing that the contract is for "the sale of crops to be harvested within twelve months or the next normal harvest season after contracting, whichever is longer."

Insurable Interest of the Seller or Lessor

A seller has an insurable interest in goods as long as he or she retains title to the goods. Even after title passes to a buyer, however, a seller who has a security interest in the goods (a right to secure payment—see Chapter 19) still has an insurable interest and can insure the goods [UCC 2–501(2)]. Hence, both a buyer and a seller can have an insurable interest in identical goods at the same time. Of course, the buyer or seller must sustain an actual loss to have the right to recover from an insurance company. In regard to leases, the lessor retains an insurable interest in leased goods until an option to buy has been exercised by the lessee and the risk of loss has passed to the lessee [UCC 2A–218(3)].

▌Bulk Transfers

Bulk transfers are the subject of UCC Article 6. A *bulk transfer* is defined as any transfer of a major part of the transferor's material, supplies, merchandise, or other inventory *not made in the ordinary course of the transferor's business* [UCC 6–102(1)]. Difficulties sometimes occur with bulk transfers. For example, when a business that owes debts to numerous creditors sells a substantial part of its equipment and inventories to a buyer, the business should use the proceeds to pay off the debts. What happens, though, if the merchant instead spends the money on a trip, leaving the creditors without payment? Can the creditors lay any claim to the goods that were transferred in bulk to the buyer? The purpose of Article 6 is to protect creditors in such situations. UCC 6–104 and 6–105 provide that the following requirements must be met when a bulk transfer is undertaken:

1. The seller must furnish to the buyer a sworn list of his or her existing creditors. The list must include those whose claims are disputed and must state names, business addresses, and amounts due.
2. The buyer and the seller must prepare a schedule of the property to be transferred.
3. The buyer must preserve the list of creditors and the schedule of property for six months and permit inspection of the list by any creditor of the seller or must file the list and the schedule of property in a designated public office.
4. The buyer must give notice of the proposed bulk transfer to each of the seller's creditors at least ten days before the buyer takes possession of the goods or makes payments for them, whichever happens first.

If these requirements are met, the buyer acquires title to the goods free of all claims by the seller's creditors. If the requirements are not met, goods in the possession of the buyer continue to be subject to the claims of the unpaid creditors of the seller for six months [UCC 6–111].

In 1988, the National Conference of Commissioners on Uniform State Laws recommended that those states that have adopted Article 6 repeal it, because changes in the business and legal contexts in which bulk sales are conducted have made their regulation unnecessary. For states disinclined to do so, Article 6 has been revised to provide creditors with better protection while reducing the burden imposed on good faith purchasers. To date, over half of the states have repealed Article 6, and an increasing number of states have opted for the revised version.

The revised Article 6 limits its application to bulk sales by sellers whose principal business is the sale of inventory from bulk stock. It does not apply to transactions involving property valued at less than $10,000 or more than $25 million. If a seller has more than two hundred creditors, a buyer, rather than having to send individual notice to each creditor, can give notice by public filing (for example, in the office of a state's secretary of state). The notice period is increased from ten to forty-five days, and the statute of limitations is extended from six months to one year.

▌ Terms and Concepts

bailee 285
consignment 286
cure 288
destination contract 279
document of title 280

fungible goods 278
good faith purchaser 280
identification 278
insolvent 280

insurable interest 289
sale on approval 287
sale or return 286
shipment contract 279

▌ Chapter Summary: Title and Risk of Loss

Shipment Contracts (*See page 279.*)	In the absence of an agreement, title and risk pass upon the seller's or lessor's delivery of conforming goods to the carrier [UCC 2–401(2)(a), 2–509(1)(a), 2A–219(2)(a)].
Destination Contracts (*See page 279.*)	In the absence of an agreement, title and risk pass upon the seller's or lessor's *tender* of delivery of conforming goods to the buyer or lessee at the point of destination [UCC 2–401(2)(b), 2–509(1)(b), 2A–219(2)(b)].

▌Chapter Summary: Title and Risk of Loss—Continued

Delivery without Movement of the Goods *(See page 280.)*	1. In the absence of an agreement, if the goods are not represented by a document of title: a. Title passes upon the formation of the contract [UCC 2–401(3)(b)]. b. Risk passes to the buyer or lessee, if the seller or lessor (or supplier, in a finance lease) is a merchant, upon the buyer's or lessee's receipt of the goods or, if the seller or lessor is a nonmerchant, upon the seller's or lessor's *tender* of delivery of the goods [UCC 2–509(3), 2A–219(c)]. 2. In the absence of an agreement, if the goods are represented by a document of title: a. If the document is negotiable and the goods are held by a bailee, title and risk pass upon the buyer's *receipt* of the document [UCC 2–401(3)(a), 2–509(2)(a)]. b. If the document is nonnegotiable and the goods are held by a bailee, title passes upon the buyer's receipt of the document, but risk does *not* pass until the buyer, after receipt of the document, has had a reasonable time to present the document to demand the goods [UCC 2–401(3)(a), 2–509(2)(c), 2–503(4)(b)]. 3. In the absence of an agreement, if the goods are held by a bailee and no document of title is transferred, risk passes to the buyer when the bailee acknowledges the buyer's right to the possession of the goods [UCC 2–509(2)(b)]. 4. In respect to leases, if goods held by a bailee are to be delivered without being moved, the risk of loss passes to the lessee upon acknowledgment by the bailee of the lessee's right to possession of the goods [UCC 2A–219(2)(b)].
Sales by Nonowners *(See pages 280 and 283–284.)*	Between the owner and a good faith purchaser or sublessee: 1. *Void title*—Owner prevails [UCC 2–403(1)]. 2. *Voidable title*—Buyer prevails [UCC 2–403(1)]. 3. *Entrusting to a merchant*—Buyer or sublessee prevails [UCC 2–403(2), (3); 2A–305(2)].
Sale-or-Return Contracts *(See page 286.)*	When the buyer receives possession of the goods, title and risk of loss pass to the buyer, with the buyer's option to return to the seller the goods, title, and risk [UCC 2–327(2)].
Sale-on-Approval Contracts *(See pages 286–287.)*	Title and risk of loss (from causes beyond the buyer's control) remain with the seller until the buyer approves (accepts) the offer [UCC 2–327(1)].
Risk of Loss When a Sales or Lease Contract Is Breached *(See pages 288–289.)*	1. If the seller or lessor breaches by tendering nonconforming goods that are rejected by the buyer or lessee, the risk of loss does not pass to the buyer or lessee until the defects are cured (unless the buyer or lessee accepts the goods in spite of their defects, thus waiving the right to reject) [UCC 2–510(1), 2A–220(1)]. 2. If the buyer or lessee breaches the contract, the risk of loss to identified goods immediately shifts to the buyer or lessee. Limitations to this rule are as follows [UCC 2–510(3), 2A–220(2)]: a. The seller or lessor must already have identified the contract goods. b. The buyer or lessee bears the risk for only a commercially reasonable time after the seller or lessor has learned of the breach. c. The buyer or lessee is liable only to the extent of any deficiency in the seller's or lessor's insurance coverage.
Insurable Interest *(See page 289.)*	1. Buyers and lessees have an insurable interest in goods the moment the goods are identified to the contract by the seller or the lessor [UCC 2–510(3), 2A–218(1)]. *(Continued)*

▋ Chapter Summary: Title and Risk of Loss—Continued

Insurable Interest—Continued	2. Sellers have an insurable interest in goods as long as they have (1) title to the goods or (2) a security interest in the goods [UCC 2–501(2)]. Lessors have an insurable interest in leased goods until an option to buy has been exercised by the lessee and the risk of loss has passed to the lessee [UCC 2A–218(3)].
Bulk Transfers *(See pages 289–290.)*	1. In a bulk transfer of assets, in those states that have not repealed Article 6 of the UCC or replaced it with the revised Article 6, the buyer acquires title to the goods free of all claims of the seller's creditors if the following requirements are met: a. The transferor (seller) furnishes to the transferee (buyer) a sworn list of existing creditors, listing their names, business addresses, amounts due, and any disputed claims [UCC 6–104(1)(a)]. b. The buyer and seller prepare a schedule of the property to be transferred [UCC 6–104(1)(b)]. c. The buyer preserves the list of creditors and the schedule of property for six months, allowing any creditors of the seller to inspect it, or files the list and schedule of property in a designated public office [UCC 6–104(1)(c)]. d. Notice of the proposed bulk transfer is given by the buyer to each creditor of the seller at least ten days before the buyer takes possession of the goods or pays for them, whichever happens first [UCC 6–105]. 2. The revised Article 6 limits its application to bulk sales by sellers whose principal business is the sale of inventory from bulk stock and to transactions involving property valued between $10,000 and $25 million. If a seller has more than two hundred creditors, the buyer can give notice of the sale to the creditors by public filing.

▋ For Review

1. What is the significance of identifying goods to a contract?

2. If the parties to a contract do not expressly agree on when title to goods passes, what determines when title passes?

3. Risk of loss does not necessarily pass with title. If the parties to a contract did not expressly agree when risk passes and the goods are to be delivered without movement by the seller, when does risk pass?

4. Under what circumstances will the seller's title to goods being sold be void? Under what circumstances will a seller have voidable title? What is the legal effect on a good faith purchaser of the goods of the seller's having a void title versus a voidable title?

5. At what point does the buyer acquire an insurable interest in goods subject to a sales contract? Can the buyer and seller both have an insurable interest in the goods simultaneously?

▋ Questions and Case Problems

14–1. Sales by Nonowners. In the following situations, two parties lay claim to the same goods sold. Discuss which of the parties would prevail in each situation.

   (a) Terry steals Dom's television set and sells the set to Blake, an innocent purchaser, for value. Dom learns that Blake has the set and demands its return.

   (b) Karlin takes her television set for repair to Orken, a merchant who sells new and used television sets. By accident, one of Orken's employees sells the set to Grady, an innocent purchaser-customer, who takes possession. Karlin wants her set back from Grady.

14–2. Risk of Loss. When will risk of loss pass from the seller to the buyer under each of the following contracts, assuming the parties have not expressly agreed on when risk of loss would pass?

    (a) A New York seller contracts with a San Francisco buyer to ship goods to the buyer F.O.B. San Francisco.

    (b) A New York seller contracts with a San Francisco buyer to ship goods to the buyer in San Francisco. There is no indication as to whether the shipment will be F.O.B. New York or F.O.B. San Francisco.

    (c) A seller contracts with a buyer to sell goods located on the seller's premises. The buyer pays for the goods and makes arrangements to pick them up the next week at the seller's place of business.

    (d) A seller contracts with a buyer to sell goods located in a warehouse.

14–3. Sales by Nonowners. Julian Makepeace, who had been declared mentally incompetent by a court, sold his diamond ring to Golding for value. Golding later sold the ring to Carmichael for value. Neither Golding nor Carmichael knew that Makepeace had been adjudged mentally incompetent by a court. Farrel, who had been appointed as Makepeace's guardian, subsequently learned that the diamond ring was in Carmichael's possession and demanded its return from Carmichael. Who has legal ownership of the ring? Why?

14–4. Risk of Loss. Alberto's Food Stores contracts to purchase from Giant Food Distributors, Inc., one hundred cases of Golden Rod corn to be shipped F.O.B. seller's warehouse by Janson Truck Lines. Giant Food Distributors, by mistake, delivers one hundred cases of Gold Giant corn to Janson Truck Lines. While in transit, the Gold Giant corn is stolen. Between Alberto's and Giant Food Distributors, who suffers the loss? Explain.

14–5. Sale on Approval. Chi Moy, a student, contracted to buy a television set from Ted's Electronics. Under the terms of the contract, Moy was to try out the set for thirty days, and if he liked it, he was to pay for the set at the end of the thirty-day period. If he did not want to purchase the set after thirty days, he could return the TV to Ted's Electronics with no obligation. Ten days after Moy took the set home, it was stolen from Moy's apartment, although Moy had not been negligent in his care of the set in any way. Ted's Electronics claimed that Moy had to pay for the stolen set. Moy argued that the risk of loss fell on Ted's Electronics. Which party will prevail?

14–6. Risk of Loss. Isis Foods, Inc., located in St. Louis, wanted to purchase a shipment of food from Pocasset Food Sales, Inc. The sale of food was initiated by a purchase order from Isis stating that the shipment was to be made "F.O.B. St. Louis." Pocasset made the shipment by delivery of the goods to the carrier. Pocasset's invoices contained a provision stating, "Our liability ceases upon delivery of merchandise to carrier." The shipment of food was destroyed before it reached St. Louis. Discuss which party bears the risk of loss, and why. [*In re Isis Foods, Inc.,* 38 Bankr. 48 (Bankr.W.D.Mo. 1983)]

14–7. Sales by Nonowners. A new car owned by a New Jersey car-rental agency was stolen in 1967. The agency collected the full price of the car from its insurance company, Home Indemnity Co., and assigned all its interest in the automobile to the insurer. Subsequently, the thief sold the car to an automobile wholesaler, who in turn sold it to a retail car dealer. Schrier purchased the car from the dealer without knowledge of the theft. Home Indemnity sued Schrier to recover the car. Can Home Indemnity recover? [*Schrier v. Home Indemnity Co.,* 273 A.2d 248 (D.C. 1971)]

14–8. Sales by Nonowners. Fred Lane was the owner of Lane's Outboard and was engaged in the business of selling boats, motors, and trailers. He sold a new boat, motor, and trailer to a person who called himself John Willis. Willis took possession of the goods and paid for them with a check for $6,285. The check was later dishonored. About six months later, Jimmy Honeycutt bought the boat, motor, and trailer from a man identified as "Garrett," who was renting a summer beach house to the Honeycutts that year and whom Honeycutt had known for several years. Honeycutt paid $2,500 for the boating equipment and did not receive an official certificate of title. Lane sought to recover the boat, motor, and trailer from Honeycutt. Honeycutt's sole defense was that he was a good faith purchaser and therefore Lane should not be able to recover from him. Discuss whether Honeycutt will succeed in his defense. [*Lane v. Honeycutt,* 14 N.C.App. 436, 188 S.E.2d 604 (1972)]

14–9. Sale or Return. Hargo Woolen Mills had purchased bales of surplus wool fibers, which Hargo used in its manufacture of woolen cloth, from Shabry Trading Co. for many years. On one occasion, however, Shabry shipped twenty-four bales to Hargo without an order. Rather than pay for reshipment, both parties decided that Hargo would retain possession of the bales and pay for what it used. Hargo kept the bales separate inside its warehouse and eventually used, and was billed for, eight bales. Hargo still kept the remaining sixteen bales separate. Hargo went bankrupt, and the receiver, Meinhard-Commercial Corp., took everything in Hargo's warehouse. Shabry claimed that it was the owner and title holder of the bales and requested their return, but Meinhard-Commercial refused to return them. Should Shabry be able to retake possession of the bales? [*Meinhard-Commercial Corp. v. Hargo Woolen Mills,* 112 N.H.500, 300 A.2d 321 (1972)]

14–10. Risk of Loss. Donald Hayward agreed to buy a thirty-foot Revel Craft Playmate Yacht from Herbert F. Postma, a yacht dealer, on February 7, 1967. The boat was to be delivered to a slip on Lake Macatawa during

April 1967. Hayward signed a security agreement on March 1, 1967, and gave a promissory note for $13,095.60 to Postma's dealership. The note was subsequently assigned to a bank. The security agreement contained clauses requiring the buyer to keep the boat in first-class order or repair and to keep the boat fully insured at all times. After Hayward had made some payments, but before the boat was delivered to Hayward, it was destroyed by fire. Neither Postma nor Hayward had insured the boat, and Hayward requested that Postma pay off the note or reimburse him for payments made. Postma refused, and Hayward sued. Discuss whether Hayward or Postma bears the risk of loss as to the boat destroyed in the fire. [*Hayward v. Postma,* 31 Mich.App. 720, 188 N.W.2d 31 (1971)]

14–11. Entrustment Rule. Bobby Locke, the principal stockholder and chief executive officer (CEO) of Worthco Farm Center, Inc., hired Mr. Hobby as the company's manager. Subsequently, it was discovered that during the approximately thirteen months of Locke's tenure as CEO, Hobby had sold corn stored with Worthco to Arabi Grain & Elevator Co. and pocketed the proceeds. When Locke brought an action against Arabi to recover the corn, Arabi alleged, among other things, that Locke had entrusted the corn to Hobby and that because Arabi was a purchaser in the ordinary course of business, Hobby had transferred ownership rights in the corn to Arabi. Assuming that Arabi was a buyer in the ordinary course of business, how should the court rule? Discuss. [*Locke v. Arabi Grain & Elevator Co.,* 197 Ga.App. 854, 399 S.E.2d 705 (1991)]

14–12. Sales by Nonowners. Doyle Alexander sold his 1986 Mercury to another person (called the "initial buyer," because the identity of this person was not disclosed in the court record). Alexander signed the back of the certificate of title to the car but did not indicate the name of the person to whom he was selling the car. The initial buyer, posing as Doyle Alexander, then sold the car to Express Drive Away. Express Drive Away resold the car to Hodges Wholesale Cars through an auction conducted by Auto Dealer's Exchange of Birmingham. The car was later resold several other times. In the meantime, Alexander, upon learning that the initial buyer's check had bounced, informed the authorities that his car had been "stolen." Ultimately, Hodges Wholesale Cars sued Auto Dealer's Exchange of Birmingham to recover payments that Hodges Wholesale Cars had made to a later purchaser (who had demanded a refund of the purchase price it had paid for the "stolen" car). A central issue before the court was whether the initial buyer had acquired voidable title or void title to the car. How should the court rule on this issue, and why? Discuss fully. [*Hodges Wholesale Cars v. Auto Dealer's Exchange of Birmingham,* 628 So.2d 608 (Ala. 1993)]

Accessing the Internet: Fundamentals of Business Law

To view the UCC provisions discussed in this chapter, including Official Comments, go to
http://www.law.cornell.edu/ucc/ucc.table.html
To review bills of lading, access the following Web site:
http://www.showtrans.com/bl.htm

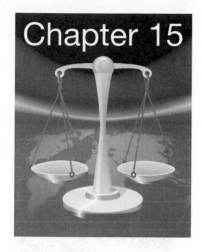

Chapter 15

Performance and Breach of Sales and Lease Contracts

CHAPTER OBJECTIVES

After reading this chapter, you should be able to:

1. Outline the performance obligations of sellers and lessors under the UCC.
2. State the perfect tender rule, and identify and discuss its exceptions.
3. Describe the performance obligations of buyers and lessees under the UCC.
4. Point out the options available in the event that one of the parties to a sales or lease contract repudiates the contract prior to the time for performance.
5. List and discuss the remedies available to the nonbreaching party when a sales or lease contract is breached.

Billions of sales and lease contracts are carried out every year in the United States. Most of these contracts involve virtually no problems. This is because most people try to fulfill their contractual obligations.

The performance that is required of the parties under a sales or lease contract consists of the duties and obligations each party has assumed under the terms of the contract. Keep in mind that "duties and obligations" under the terms of the contract include those specified by the agreement, by custom, and by the Uniform Commercial Code (UCC). In this chapter, we examine the basic performance obligations of the parties under a sales or lease contract.

Sometimes circumstances make it difficult for a person to carry out the promised performance, in which case the contract may be breached. When

breach occurs, the aggrieved party looks for remedies—which we deal with in the second half of the chapter.

■ Performance Obligations

The standards of good faith and commercial reasonableness are read into every contract. These standards provide a framework in which the parties can specify particulars of performance. Thus, when one party delays specifying particulars of performance for an unreasonable period of time or fails to cooperate with the other party, the innocent party is excused from any resulting delay in performance. In addition, the innocent party can proceed to perform in any reasonable manner. If the innocent party has performed as far as is reasonably possible under the circumstances, the other party's failure to specify particulars or to cooperate can be treated as a breach of contract. Good faith is a question of fact for the jury.

In the performance of a sales or lease contract, the basic obligation of the seller or lessor is to *transfer and deliver conforming goods*. The basic obligation of the buyer or lessee is to *accept and pay for conforming goods* in accordance with the contract [UCC 2–301, 2A-516(1)]. Overall performance of a sales or lease contract is controlled by the agreement between the parties. When the contract is unclear and disputes arise, the courts look to the UCC.

Obligations of the Seller or Lessor

The major obligation of the seller or lessor under a sales or lease contract is to *tender* conforming goods to the buyer or lessee.

Tender of Delivery

Tender of delivery requires that the seller or lessor have and hold *conforming* goods at the disposal of the buyer or lessee and give the buyer or lessee whatever notification is reasonably necessary to enable the buyer or lessee to take delivery [UCC 2–503(1), 2A–508(1)].

Tender must occur at a *reasonable hour* and in a *reasonable manner*. In other words, a seller cannot call the buyer at 2:00 A.M. and say, "The goods are ready. I'll give you twenty minutes to get them." Unless the parties have agreed otherwise, the goods must be tendered for delivery at a reasonable time and kept available for a reasonable period of time to enable the buyer to take possession of them [UCC 2–503(1)(a)].

All goods called for by a contract must be tendered in a single delivery unless the parties agree otherwise, or the circumstances are such that either party can rightfully request delivery in lots [UCC 2–307, 2–612, 2A–510]. Hence, an order for 1,000 shirts cannot be delivered 2 shirts at a time. If, however, the seller and the buyer contemplate that the shirts will be delivered in four orders of 250 each, as they are produced (for summer, fall, winter, and spring stock), and the price can be apportioned accordingly, it may be commercially reasonable to deliver the shirts in this way.

Place of Delivery

The UCC provides for the place of delivery pursuant to a contract if the contract does not. Of course, the parties may agree on a particular destination, or their contract's terms or the circumstances may indicate the place.

NONCARRIER CASES If the contract does not designate the place of delivery for the goods, and the buyer is expected to pick them up, the place of delivery is the *seller's place of business* or, if the seller has none, the *seller's residence* [UCC 2–308]. If the contract involves the sale of *identified goods*, and the parties know when they enter into the contract that these goods are located somewhere other than at the seller's place of business (such as at a warehouse), then the *location of the goods* is the place for their delivery [UCC 2–308].

For example, Rogers and Aguirre live in San Francisco. In San Francisco, Rogers contracts to sell Aguirre five used trucks, which both parties know are located in a Chicago warehouse. If nothing more is specified in the contract, the place of delivery for the trucks is Chicago. The seller may tender delivery by either giving the buyer a *negotiable or nonnegotiable document of title* or obtaining the *bailee's (warehouser's) acknowledgment* that the buyer is entitled to possession.[1]

CARRIER CASES In many instances, attendant circumstances or delivery terms in the contract make it apparent that the parties intend that a carrier be used to move the goods. There are two ways a seller can complete performance of the obligation to deliver the goods in carrier cases—through a shipment contract and through a destination contract.

Shipment Contracts Recall from Chapter 14 that a *shipment contract* requires or authorizes the

---

1. If the seller delivers a nonnegotiable document of title or merely writes instructions to the bailee to release the goods to the buyer without the bailee's *acknowledgment* of the buyer's rights, this is also a sufficient tender, unless the buyer objects [UCC 2–503(4)]. Risk of loss, however, does not pass until the buyer has a reasonable amount of time in which to present the document or the instructions.

seller to ship goods by a carrier. The contract does not require that the seller deliver the goods at a particular destination [UCC 2–319, 2–509]. Unless otherwise agreed, the seller must do the following:

1. Put the goods into the hands of the carrier.
2. Make a contract for their transportation that is reasonable according to the nature of the goods and their value. (For example, certain types of goods need refrigeration in transit.)
3. Obtain and promptly deliver or tender to the buyer any documents necessary to enable the buyer to obtain possession of the goods from the carrier.
4. Promptly notify the buyer that shipment has been made [UCC 2–504].

If the seller fails to notify the buyer that shipment has been made or fails to make a proper contract for transportation, and a *material loss* of the goods or a significant *delay* results, the contract has been breached and the buyer can reject the shipment. Of course, the parties can agree that a lesser amount of loss or any delay will be grounds for rejection.

Destination Contracts Under a *destination contract,* the seller agrees to see that conforming goods will be duly tendered to the buyer at a particular destination. The goods must be tendered at a reasonable hour and held at the buyer's disposal for a reasonable length of time. The seller must also give the buyer appropriate notice. In addition, the seller must provide the buyer with any documents of title necessary to enable the buyer to obtain delivery from the carrier. This is often done by tendering the documents through ordinary banking channels [UCC 2–503].

The Perfect Tender Rule

As previously noted, the seller or lessor has an obligation to ship or tender *conforming goods,* and this entitles the buyer or lessee to accept and pay for the goods according to the terms of the contract. Under the common law, the seller was obligated to deliver goods in conformity with the terms of the contract in every detail. This was called the *perfect tender* doctrine. The UCC preserves the perfect tender doctrine by stating that if goods or tender of delivery fail *in any respect* to conform to

the contract, the buyer or lessee has the right to accept the goods, reject the entire shipment, or accept part and reject part [UCC 2–601, 2A–509].

For example, a lessor contracts to lease fifty Vericlear computers to be delivered at the lessee's place of business on or before October 1. On September 28, the lessor discovers that there are only thirty Vericlear computers in inventory, but there will be another forty Vericlear computers within the next two weeks. The lessor tenders delivery of the thirty Vericlear computers on October 1, with the promise that the other computers will be delivered within three weeks. Because the lessor failed to make a perfect tender of fifty Vericlear computers, the lessee has the right to reject the entire shipment and hold the lessor in breach.

Exceptions to Perfect Tender

Because of the rigidity of the perfect tender rule, several exceptions to the rule have been created, some of which are discussed here.

AGREEMENT OF THE PARTIES Exceptions to the perfect tender rule may be established by agreement. If the parties have agreed, for example, that defective goods or parts will not be rejected if the seller or lessor is able to repair or replace them within a reasonable period of time, the perfect tender rule does not apply.

CURE The UCC does not specifically define the term *cure,* but it refers to the right of the seller or lessor to repair, adjust, or replace defective or nonconforming goods [UCC 2–508, 2A–513]. When any tender of delivery is rejected because of nonconforming goods and the time for performance has not yet expired, the seller or lessor can notify the buyer or lessee promptly of the intention to cure and can then do so *within the contract time for performance* [UCC 2–508(1), 2A–513(1)]. Once the time for performance under the contract has expired, the seller or lessor can still exercise the right to cure in respect to the rejected goods if he or she had *reasonable grounds to believe that the nonconforming tender would be acceptable to the buyer or lessee* [UCC 2–508(2), 2A–513(2)].

Sometimes, a seller or lessor will tender nonconforming goods with some type of price allowance. The allowance serves as the "reasonable grounds" for the seller or lessor to believe that the nonconforming tender will be acceptable to the buyer or lessee. Other reasons might also serve as the basis for the assumption that a buyer or lessee will accept a nonconforming tender. For example, if in the past a buyer frequently accepted a particular substitute for a good when the good ordered was not available, the seller has reasonable grounds to believe the buyer will again accept such a substitute. If the buyer rejects the substitute good on a particular occasion, the seller nonetheless had reasonable grounds to believe that the substitute would be acceptable. Therefore, the seller can cure within a reasonable time, even though conforming delivery will occur after the time limit for performance allowed under the contract.

The right to cure substantially restricts the right of the buyer or lessee to reject goods. For example, if a lessee refuses a tender of goods as nonconforming but does not disclose the nature of the defect to the lessor, the lessee cannot later assert the defect as a defense if the defect is one that the lessor could have cured. Generally, buyers and lessees must act in good faith and state specific reasons for refusing to accept goods [UCC 2–605, 2A–514].

SUBSTITUTION OF CARRIERS When an agreed-on manner of delivery (such as which carrier will be used to transport the goods) becomes impracticable or unavailable through no fault of either party, but a commercially reasonable substitute is available, the seller must use this substitute performance, which is sufficient tender to the buyer [UCC 2–614(1)]. For example, a sales contract calls for the delivery of a large piece of machinery to be shipped by Roadway Trucking Corporation on or before June 1. The contract terms clearly state the importance of the delivery date. The employees of Roadway Trucking go on strike. The seller will be entitled to make a reasonable substitute tender, perhaps by rail. Note that the seller here is responsible for any additional shipping costs, unless contrary arrangements have been made in the sales contract.

INSTALLMENT CONTRACTS An **installment contract** is a single contract that requires or authorizes delivery in two or more separate lots to be accepted and paid for separately. In an installment contract, a buyer or lessee can reject an installment *only if the nonconformity substantially impairs the value* of the installment and cannot be cured [UCC 2–612(2), 2–307, 2A–510(1)].

Unless the contract provides otherwise, the entire installment contract is breached only when one or more nonconforming installments *substantially* impair the value of the *whole contract*. If the buyer or lessee subsequently accepts a nonconforming installment and fails to notify the seller or lessor of cancellation, however, the contract is reinstated [UCC 2–612(3), 2A–510(2)].

A major issue to be determined is what constitutes substantial impairment of the "value of the whole contract." For example, consider an installment contract for the sale of twenty carloads of plywood. The first carload does not conform to the contract because 9 percent of the plywood deviates from the thickness specifications. The buyer cancels the contract, and immediately thereafter the second and third carloads of plywood arrive at the buyer's place of business. If a lawsuit ensued, the court would have to grapple with the question of whether the 9 percent of nonconforming plywood substantially impaired the value of the whole.[2]

The point to remember is that the UCC substantially alters the right of the buyer or lessee to reject the entire contract if the contract requires delivery to be made in several installments. The UCC strictly limits rejection to cases of *substantial* nonconformity.

COMMERCIAL IMPRACTICABILITY As mentioned in Chapter 11, occurrences unforeseen by either party when a contract was made may make performance commercially impracticable. When this occurs, the rule of perfect tender no longer holds. According to UCC 2–615(a) and 2A–405(a), delay in delivery or nondelivery in whole or in part is not a breach when performance has been made impracticable "by the occurrence of a contingency the nonoccurrence of which was a basic assumption on which the contract was made." The seller or lessor must, however, notify the buyer or lessee as soon as practicable that there will be a delay or nondelivery.

Foreseeable versus Unforeseeable Contingencies
An increase in cost resulting from inflation does not in and of itself excuse performance, as this kind

---

2. *Continental Forest Products, Inc. v. White Lumber Sales, Inc.*, 256 Or. 466, 474 P.2d 1 (1970). The court held that the deviation did not substantially impair the value of the whole contract. Additionally, the court stated that the nonconformity could be cured by an adjustment in the price.

of risk is ordinarily assumed by a seller or lessor conducting business. The unforeseen contingency must be one that would have been impossible to contemplate in a given business situation. For example, a major oil company that receives its supplies from the Middle East has a contract to supply a buyer with 100,000 gallons of oil. Because of an oil embargo by the Organization of Petroleum Exporting Countries (OPEC), the seller is prevented from securing oil supplies to meet the terms of the contract. Because of the same embargo, the seller cannot secure oil from any other source. This situation comes fully under the commercial-impracticability exception to the perfect tender doctrine.

Can unanticipated increases in a seller's costs, which make performance "impracticable," constitute a valid defense to performance on the basis of commercial impracticability? The court deals with this question in the following case.

CASE 15.1

Maple Farms, Inc. v. City School District of Elmira

Supreme Court of New York, 1974.
76 Misc.2d 1080.
352 N.Y.S.2d 784.

FACTS On June 15, 1973, Maple Farms, Inc., formed an agreement with the city school district of Elmira, New York, to supply the school district with milk for the 1973–1974 school year. The agreement was in the form of a requirements contract, under which Maple Farms would sell to the school district all the milk the district required at a fixed price—which was the June market price of milk. By December 1973, the price of raw milk had increased by 23 percent over the price specified in the contract. This meant that if the terms of the contract were fulfilled, Maple Farms would lose $7,350. Because it had similar contracts with other school districts, Maple Farms stood to lose a great deal if it was held to the price stated in the contracts. When the school district would not agree to release Maple Farms from its contract, Maple Farms brought an action in a New York state court for a declaratory judgment (a determination of the parties' rights under a contract). Maple Farms contended that the substantial increase in the price of raw milk was an event not contemplated by the parties when the contract was formed and that, given the increased price, performance of the contract was commercially impracticable.

ISSUE Can Maple Farms be released from the contract on the ground of commercial impracticability?

DECISION No. The court ruled that performance in this case was not impracticable.

REASON The court reasoned that commercial impracticability arises when an event occurs that is totally unexpected and unforeseeable by the parties. The increased price of raw milk was not totally unexpected, given the facts that in the previous year the price of milk had risen 10 percent and that the price of milk had traditionally varied. Additionally, the general inflation of prices in the United States should have been anticipated. Maple Farms had reason to know these facts and could have placed a clause in its contract with the school district to protect itself from its present situation. The court also noted that the primary purpose of the contract, on the part of the school district, was to protect itself (for budgeting purposes) against price fluctuations.

FOR CRITICAL ANALYSIS—Economic Consideration *What would be the result for society if courts routinely allowed parties to avoid their contractual obligations because of steep price increases?*

Partial Performance　Sometimes the unforeseen event only *partially* affects the capacity of the seller or lessor to perform, and the seller or lessor is thus able to fulfill the contract *partially* but cannot tender total performance. In this event, the seller or lessor is required to allocate in a fair and reasonable manner any remaining production and deliveries among those to whom it is contractually obligated to deliver the goods [UCC 2–615(b), 2A–405(b)]. The buyer or lessee must receive notice of the allocation and has the right to accept or reject the allocation [UCC 2–615(c), 2A–405(c)].

For example, a Florida orange grower, Best Citrus, Inc., contracts to sell this season's production to a number of customers, including Martin's grocery chain. Martin's contracts to purchase two thousand crates of oranges. Best Citrus has sprayed *some* of its orange groves with a chemical called Karmoxin. The Department of Agriculture discovers that persons who eat products sprayed with Karmoxin may develop cancer. The department issues an order prohibiting the sale of these products. Best Citrus picks all of the oranges not sprayed with Karmoxin, but the quantity does not fully meet all the contracted-for deliveries. In this situation, Best Citrus is required to allocate its production, and it notifies Martin's that it cannot deliver the full quantity agreed on in the contract and specifies the amount it will be able to deliver under the circumstances. Martin's can either accept or reject the allocation, but Best Citrus has no further contractual liability.

DESTRUCTION OF IDENTIFIED GOODS　The UCC provides that when an unexpected event, such as a fire, totally destroys *goods identified at the time the contract is formed* through no fault of either party and *before risk passes to the buyer or lessee*, the parties are excused from performance [UCC 2–613, 2A–221]. If the goods are only partially destroyed, however, the buyer or lessee can inspect them and either treat the contract as void or accept the damaged goods with a reduction of the contract price.

Consider an example. Atlas Sporting Equipment agrees to lease to River Bicycles sixty of a particular model of bicycle that has been discontinued. No other bicycles of that model are available. River specifies that it needs the bicycles to rent to tourists. Before Atlas can deliver the bikes, they are destroyed by a fire. In this situation, Atlas is not liable to River for failing to deliver the bikes. The goods were destroyed through no fault of either

party, before the risk of loss passed to the lessee. The loss was total, so the contract is avoided. Clearly, Atlas has no obligation to tender the bicycles, and River has no obligation to pay for them.

Obligations of the Buyer or Lessee

Once the seller or lessor has adequately tendered delivery, the buyer or lessee is obligated to accept the goods and pay for them according to the terms of the contract. In the absence of any specific agreements, the buyer or lessee must make payment at the time and place the buyer or lessee *receives* the goods [UCC 2–310(a), 2A–516(1)].

Payment

When a sale is made on credit, the buyer is obliged to pay according to the specified credit terms (for example, 60, 90, or 120 days), *not* when the goods are received. The credit period usually begins on the *date of shipment* [UCC 2–310(d)]. Under a lease contract, a lessee must pay the lease payment specified in the contract [2A–516(1)].

Payment can be made by any means agreed on between the parties—cash or any other method generally acceptable in the commercial world. If the seller demands cash when the buyer offers a check, credit card, or the like, the seller must permit the buyer reasonable time to obtain legal tender [UCC 2–511].

Right of Inspection

Unless otherwise agreed, or for C.O.D. (collect on delivery) transactions, the buyer or lessee has an absolute right to inspect the goods. This right allows the buyer or lessee to verify, before making payment, that the goods tendered or delivered are what were contracted for or ordered. If the goods are not what the buyer or lessee ordered, the buyer or lessee has no duty to pay. *An opportunity for inspection is therefore a condition precedent to the right of the seller or lessor to enforce payment* [UCC 2–513(1), 2A–515(1)].

Unless otherwise agreed, inspection can take place at any reasonable place and time and in any reasonable manner. Generally, what is reasonable is determined by custom of the trade, past practices of the parties, and the like. Costs of inspecting conforming goods are borne by the buyer unless otherwise agreed [UCC 2–513(2)].

C.O.D. Shipments   If a seller ships goods to a buyer C.O.D. (or under similar terms) and the buyer has not agreed to a C.O.D. shipment in the contract, the buyer can rightfully *reject* the goods. This is because a C.O.D. shipment does not permit inspection before payment, which is a denial of the buyer's right of inspection. When the buyer has agreed to a C.O.D. shipment in the contract, however, or has agreed to pay for the goods upon the presentation of a bill of lading, no right of inspection exists, because it was negated by the agreement [UCC 2–513(3)].

Payment Due—Documents of Title   Under certain contracts, payment is due upon the receipt of the required documents of title even though the goods themselves may not have arrived at their destination. With C.I.F. and C.&F. contracts (see Exhibit 14–4 in Chapter 14), payment is required upon receipt of the documents unless the parties have agreed otherwise. Thus, payment may be required prior to inspection, and payment must be made unless the buyer knows that the goods are nonconforming [UCC 2–310(b), 2–513(3)].

Acceptance

A buyer or lessee can manifest assent to the delivered goods in the following ways, each of which constitutes acceptance:

1.   The buyer or lessee can expressly accept the shipment by words or conduct. For example, there is an acceptance if the buyer or lessee, after having had a reasonable opportunity to inspect the goods, signifies agreement to the seller or lessor that the goods are either conforming or are acceptable despite their nonconformity [UCC 2–606(1)(a), 2A–515(1)(a)].

2.   Acceptance is presumed if the buyer or lessee has had a reasonable opportunity to inspect the goods and has failed to reject them within a reasonable period of time [UCC 2–606(1)(b), 2–602(1), 2A–515(1)(b)].

Additionally, in sales contracts, the buyer will be deemed to have accepted the goods if he or she performs any act inconsistent with the seller's ownership. For example, any use or resale of the goods generally constitutes an acceptance. Limited use for the sole purpose of testing or inspecting the goods is not an acceptance, however [UCC 2–606(1)(c)].

If some of the goods delivered do not conform to the contract and the seller or lessor has failed to cure, the buyer or lessee can make a *partial* acceptance [UCC 2–601(c), 2A–509(1)]. The same is true if the nonconformity was not reasonably discoverable before acceptance. (In the latter situation, the buyer or lessee may be able to revoke the acceptance, as will be discussed later in this chapter.) A buyer or lessee cannot accept less than a single commercial unit, however. A *commercial unit* is defined by the UCC as a unit of goods that, by commercial usage, is viewed as a "single whole" for purposes of sale, division of which would materially impair the character of the unit, its market value, or its use [UCC 2–105(6), 2A–103(1)(c)]. A commercial unit can be a single article (such as a machine), a set of articles (such as a suite of furniture or an assortment of sizes), a quantity (such as a bale, a gross, or a carload), or any other unit treated in the trade as a single whole.

In the following case, the court considered whether a buyer's actions, in regard to goods shipped to it by the seller, were "inconsistent with the seller's ownership" so as to constitute acceptance under UCC 2–606(1)(c).

Case 15.2

Industria de Calcados Martini Ltda.[a] v. Maxwell Shoe Co.

Appeals Court of Massachusetts, 1994.

36 Mass.App.Ct. 268,
630 N.E.2d 299.

FACTS   The Maxwell Shoe Company agreed to buy 12,042 pairs of shoes from Industria de Calcados Martini Ltda. (Martini), a Brazilian shoe manufacturer. Maxwell paid part of the price with a check. When the shoes arrived, they were cracked and peeling. Maxwell stopped payment on the check and told Martini that it

a.   *Ltda.* is an abbreviation for *Limitada*, a business organization form involving limited liability for the owners (see Chapter 24).

(Continued)

302 UNIT FOUR: SALES AND LEASE CONTRACTS

Case 15.2—Continued

was rejecting the shoes. Martini did not respond. Two months later, Maxwell shipped the shoes to Maine to have them refinished, sold the refinished shoes, and kept the money. Martini filed a suit in a Massachusetts state court against Maxwell for, among other things, breach of contract. The court held in part that Maxwell had accepted the shoes when it shipped them to Maine to be refinished, "on the grounds that an alteration or repair of a defect in goods is an act inconsistent with the seller's ownership" under UCC 2–606(1)(c). The court awarded damages to Martini, reduced by the amount that Maxwell had paid for the refinishing. Both parties appealed.

ISSUE   Did Maxwell accept the shoes?

DECISION   Yes. The Appeals Court of Massachusetts affirmed the lower court's decision.

REASON   The court pointed out that "Maxwell received no * * * instructions from Martini" and instead "acted on its own in sending the shoes for refinishing and then selling them and retaining the proceeds for its own benefit." The court concluded, "Accordingly, we do not think the judge's ruling * * * was clearly erroneous."

FOR CRITICAL ANALYSIS—Economic Consideration   *What might have been Maxwell's recovery if, instead of refinishing and reselling the shoes, Maxwell had simply sent them back?*

▌Anticipatory Repudiation

What if, before the time for contract performance, one party clearly communicates to the other the intention not to perform? Such an action is a breach of the contract by *anticipatory repudiation*. When anticipatory repudiation occurs, the nonbreaching party has a choice of two responses. He or she can treat the repudiation as a final breach by pursuing a remedy; or he or she can wait, hoping that the repudiating party will decide to honor the obligations required by the contract despite the avowed intention to renege [UCC 2–610, 2A–402]. In either situation, the nonbreaching party may suspend performance.

Should the latter course be pursued, the UCC permits the breaching party (subject to some limitations) to "retract" his or her repudiation. This can be done by any method that clearly indicates an intent to perform. Once retraction is made, the rights of the repudiating party under the contract are reinstated [UCC 2–611, 2A–403].

▌Remedies of the Seller or Lessor

There are numerous remedies available under the UCC to a seller or lessor when the buyer or lessee is in breach. Generally, the remedies available to the seller or lessor depend on the circumstances existing at the time of the breach, such as which party has possession of the goods, whether the goods are in transit, whether the buyer or lessee has rejected or accepted the goods, and so on.

When the Goods Are in the Possession of the Seller or Lessor

Under the UCC, if the buyer or lessee breaches the contract before the goods have been delivered to the buyer or lessee, the seller or lessor has the right to pursue the remedies discussed here.

THE RIGHT TO CANCEL THE CONTRACT   One of the options available to a seller or lessor when the buyer or lessee breaches the contract is simply to cancel the contract [UCC 2–703(f), 2A–523(1)(a)]. The seller must notify the buyer or lessee of the cancellation, and at that point all remaining obligations of the seller or lessor are discharged. The buyer or lessee is not discharged from all remaining obligations, however; he or she is in breach, and the seller or lessor can pursue remedies available under the UCC for breach.

THE RIGHT TO WITHHOLD DELIVERY In general, sellers and lessors can withhold or discontinue performance of their obligations under sales or lease contracts when the buyers or lessees are in breach. If a buyer or lessee has wrongfully rejected or revoked acceptance of contract goods (rejection and revocation of acceptance will be discussed later), failed to make proper and timely payment, or repudiated a part of the contract, the seller or lessor can withhold delivery of the goods in question [UCC 2–703(a), 2A–523(1)(c)]. If the breach results from the buyer's or the lessee's insolvency (inability to pay debts as they become due), the seller or lessor can refuse to deliver the goods unless the buyer or lessee pays in cash [UCC 2–702(1), 2A–525(1)].

THE RIGHT TO RESELL OR DISPOSE OF THE GOODS When a buyer or lessee breaches or repudiates a sales contract while the seller or lessor is still in possession of the goods, the seller or lessor can resell or dispose of the goods, retaining any profits made as a result of the breach or holding the buyer or lessee liable for any loss [UCC 2–703(d), 2–706(1), 2A–523(1)(e), 2A–527(1)].

When the goods contracted for are unfinished at the time of breach, the seller or lessor can do one of two things: (1) cease manufacturing the goods and resell them for scrap or salvage value or (2) complete the manufacture and resell or dispose of them, holding the buyer or lessee liable for any deficiency. In choosing between these two alternatives, the seller or lessor must exercise reasonable commercial judgment in order to mitigate the loss and obtain maximum value from the unfinished goods [UCC 2–704(2), 2A–524(2)]. Any resale of the goods must be made in good faith and in a commercially reasonable manner.

In sales transactions, the seller can recover any deficiency between the resale price and the contract price, along with **incidental damages,** defined as those costs to the seller resulting from the breach

[UCC 2–706(1), 2–710]. The resale can be private or public, and the goods can be sold as a unit or in parcels. The seller must give the original buyer reasonable notice of the resale, unless the goods are perishable or will rapidly decline in value [UCC 2–706(2), (3)]. A good faith purchaser in a resale takes the goods free of any of the rights of the original buyer, even if the seller fails to comply with these requirements of the UCC [UCC 2–706(5)].

In lease transactions, the lessor may lease the goods to another party and recover from the original lessee, as damages, any unpaid lease payments up to the beginning date of the lease term under the new lease. The lessor can also recover any deficiency between the lease payments due under the original lease contract and under the new lease contract, along with incidental damages [UCC 2A–527(2)].

THE RIGHT TO RECOVER THE PURCHASE PRICE OR LEASE PAYMENTS DUE Under the UCC, an unpaid seller or lessor can bring an action to recover the purchase price or payments due under the lease contract, plus incidental damages, if the seller or lessor is unable to resell or dispose of the goods [UCC 2–709(1), 2A–529(1)].

For example, suppose that Southern Realty contracts with Gem Point, Inc., to purchase one thousand pens with Southern Realty's name inscribed on them. Gem Point tenders delivery of the one thousand pens, but Southern Realty wrongfully refuses to accept them. In this situation, Gem Point has, as a proper remedy, an action for the purchase price. Gem Point tendered delivery of conforming goods, and Southern Realty, because it failed to accept the goods, is in breach. Gem Point obviously cannot sell to anyone else the pens inscribed with the buyer's business name, so this situation falls under UCC 2–709.

If a seller or lessor sues for the contract price of, or lease payments for, goods that he or she has been unable to resell or dispose of, the goods must be held for the buyer or lessee. The seller or lessor can resell or dispose of the goods at any time prior to collection (of the judgment) from the buyer or lessee, but the net proceeds from the sale must be credited to the buyer or lessee. This is an example of the duty to mitigate damages. In the following case, the court had to determine whether a seller was entitled to recover the purchase price of specially manufactured goods after the buyer had breached the sales contract.

CASE 15.3

Royal Jones & Associates, Inc. v. First Thermal Systems, Inc.

District Court of Appeals of Florida, 1990.
566 So.2d 853.

FACTS Royal Jones & Associates, Inc., ordered three steel rendering tanks from First Thermal Systems, Inc., for use in its business of constructing rendering plants (factories that process livestock carcasses into hides, fertilizer, and so on). The contract provided that First Thermal would manufacture the tanks according to Royal Jones's specifications for a price of $64,350. When the manufacture of the tanks was completed, Royal Jones refused to accept or pay for the tanks. First Thermal brought an action in a Florida state court for the contract price of the tanks. The trial court, finding that Royal Jones had breached the contract and that the specially manufactured goods were not suitable for sale in the ordinary course of First Thermal's business, awarded First Thermal the full contract price as damages. Royal Jones appealed.

ISSUE Is First Thermal entitled to the full contract price as damages?

DECISION Yes. The Florida appellate court affirmed the trial court's judgment.

REASON The appellate court held that First Thermal was entitled to the full contract price of the specially manufactured tanks as damages because the evidence showed that efforts to resell the tanks would be useless. The court pointed to evidence that the rendering tanks "were the only ones First Thermal ever made, the tanks were manufactured according to Royal Jones's specifications, [and] First Thermal had no other customers to which it could resell the tanks[.]" Furthermore, First Thermal did not know how to market the tanks for resale, and the "tanks were built without needed internal components and to a special size" and "could not be used as rendering tanks without special engineering to which First Thermal had no access." The court also noted that the scrap value of the tanks to First Thermal was only about $700.

FOR CRITICAL ANALYSIS—Social Consideration *What factors must a court consider when determining whether to allow a seller to recover the purchase price for specially manufactured goods?*

THE RIGHT TO RECOVER DAMAGES

If a buyer or lessee repudiates a contract or wrongfully refuses to accept the goods, a seller or lessor can maintain an action to recover the damages that were sustained. Ordinarily, the amount of damages equals the difference between the contract price or lease payments and the market price or lease payments (at the time and place of tender of the goods), plus incidental damages [UCC 2–708(1), 2A–528(1)]. The time and place of tender are frequently given by such terms as F.O.B., F.A.S., C.I.F., and the like, which determine whether there is a shipment or destination contract.

If the difference between the contract price or payments due under the lease contract and the market price or payments due under a new lease contract is too small to place the seller or lessor in the position that he or she would have been in if the buyer or lessee had fully performed, the proper measure of damages is the lost profits of the seller or lessor, including a reasonable allowance for overhead and other expenses [UCC 2–708(2), 2A–528(2)].

When the Goods Are in Transit

If the seller or lessor has delivered the goods to a carrier or a bailee but the buyer or lessee has not as yet received them, the goods are said to be *in transit*. If, while the goods are in transit, the seller or lessor learns that the buyer or lessee is insolvent, the seller or lessor can stop the carrier or bailee from delivering the goods, regardless of the quantity of goods shipped. If the buyer or lessee is in breach but is not insolvent, the seller or lessor can stop the goods in transit only if the quantity shipped is at least a carload, a truckload, a plane-load, or a larger shipment [UCC 2–705(1), 2A–526(1)].

To stop delivery, the seller or lessor must *timely notify* the carrier or other bailee that the goods are to be returned or held for the seller or lessor. If the carrier has sufficient time to stop delivery, the goods must be held and delivered according to the instructions of the seller or lessor, who is liable to the carrier for any additional costs incurred [UCC 2–705(3), 2A–526(3)].

UCC 2–705(2) and 2A–526(2) provide that the right of the seller or lessor to stop delivery of goods in transit is lost when any of the following events occur:

1. The buyer or lessee obtains possession of the goods.
2. The carrier acknowledges the rights of the buyer or lessee by reshipping or storing the goods for the buyer or lessee.
3. A bailee of the goods other than a carrier acknowledges that he or she is holding the goods for the buyer or lessee.

Additionally, in sales transactions, the seller loses the right to stop delivery of goods in transit when a negotiable document of title covering the goods has been negotiated (properly transferred, giving the buyer ownership rights in the goods) to the buyer [UCC 2–705(2)].

Once the seller or lessor reclaims the goods in transit, he or she can pursue the remedies allowed to sellers and lessors when the goods are in their possession. In other words, the seller or lessor who has reclaimed goods may do the following:

1. Cancel the contract.
2. Resell the goods and recover any deficiency.
3. Sue for any deficiency between the contract price (or lease payments due) and the market price (or market lease payments).
4. Sue to recover the purchase price or lease payments due if the goods cannot be resold.

When the Goods Are in the Possession of the Buyer or Lessee

When the buyer or lessee breaches a sales or lease contract and the goods are in the buyer's or lessee's possession, the UCC gives the seller or lessor the right to choose among various remedies.

THE RIGHT TO RECOVER THE PURCHASE PRICE OR PAYMENTS DUE UNDER THE LEASE CONTRACT

If the buyer or lessee has accepted the goods but refuses to pay for them, the seller or lessor can sue for the purchase price of the goods or for the lease payments due, plus incidental damages [UCC 2–709(1), 2A–529(1)].

THE RIGHT TO RECLAIM THE GOODS

In regard to sales contracts, if a seller discovers that the buyer has received goods on credit and is insolvent, the seller can demand return of the goods, if the demand is made within ten days of the buyer's receipt of the goods. The seller can demand and reclaim the goods at any time if the buyer misrepresented his or her solvency in writing within three months prior to the delivery of the goods [UCC 2–702(2)]. The seller's right to reclaim the goods, however, is subject to the rights of a good faith purchaser or other buyer in the ordinary course of business who purchases the goods from the buyer before the seller reclaims.

Under the UCC, a seller seeking to exercise the right to reclaim goods receives preferential treatment over the buyer's other creditors—the seller need only demand the return of the goods within ten days after the buyer has received them.[3] Because of this preferential treatment, the UCC provides that reclamation *bars* the seller from pursuing any other remedy as to these goods [UCC 2–702(3)].

In regard to lease contracts, if the lessee is in default (fails to make payments that are due, for example), the lessor may reclaim the leased goods that are in the possession of the lessee [UCC 2A–525(2)].

---

3. A seller who has delivered goods to an insolvent buyer also receives preferential treatment if the buyer enters into bankruptcy proceedings (discussed in Chapter 20).

▌Remedies of the Buyer or Lessee

Under the UCC, there are numerous remedies available to the buyer or lessee when the seller or lessor breaches the contract. As with the remedies available to sellers and lessors, the remedies of buyers and lessees depend on the circumstances existing at the time of the breach.

When the Seller or Lessor Refuses to Deliver the Goods

If the seller or lessor refuses to deliver the goods to the buyer or lessee, the remedies available to the buyer or lessee include those discussed here.

THE RIGHT TO CANCEL THE CONTRACT   When a seller or lessor fails to make proper delivery or repudiates the contract, the buyer or lessee can cancel, or rescind, the contract. Upon notice of cancellation, the buyer or lessee is relieved of any further obligations under the contract but retains all rights to other remedies against the seller [UCC 2–711(1), 2A–508(1)(a)].

THE RIGHT TO RECOVER THE GOODS   If a buyer or lessee has made a partial or full payment for goods that remain in the possession of the seller or lessor, the buyer or lessee can recover the goods if the seller or lessor becomes insolvent within ten days after receiving the first payment and if the goods are identified to the contract. To exercise this right, the buyer or lessee must tender to the seller any unpaid balance of the purchase price [UCC 2–502, 2A–522].

THE RIGHT TO OBTAIN SPECIFIC PERFORMANCE A buyer or lessee can obtain specific performance when the goods are unique and when the remedy at law is inadequate [UCC 2–716(1), 2A–521(1)]. Ordinarily, a suit for money damages is sufficient to place a buyer or lessee in the position he or she would have occupied if the seller or lessor had fully performed. When the contract is for the purchase of a particular work of art or a similarly unique item, however, money damages may not be sufficient. Under these circumstances, equity will require that the seller or lessor perform exactly by delivering the particular goods identified to the contract (a remedy of specific performance).

THE RIGHT OF COVER   In certain situations, buyers and lessees can protect themselves by obtaining **cover**—that is, by substituting goods for those that were due under the sales contract. This option is available when the seller or lessor repudiates the contract or fails to deliver the goods. (The right to obtain cover is also available to a buyer or lessee who has rightfully rejected goods or revoked acceptance.)

In obtaining cover, the buyer or lessee must act in good faith and without unreasonable delay [UCC 2–712, 2A–518]. After purchasing or leasing substitute goods, the buyer or lessee can recover from the seller or lessor the difference between the cost of cover and the contract price (or lease payments), plus incidental and consequential damages, less the expenses (such as delivery costs) that were saved as a result of the breach [UCC 2–712, 2–715, 2A–518]. Consequential damages are any losses suffered by the buyer or lessee that the seller or lessor could have foreseen (had reason to know about) at the time of contract and any injury to the buyer's or lessee's person or property proximately resulting from the contract's breach [UCC 2–715(2), 2A–520(2)].

Buyers and lessees are not required to cover, and failure to do so will not bar them from using any other remedies available under the UCC. A buyer or lessee who fails to cover, however, may *not* be able to collect consequential damages that could have been avoided had he or she purchased or leased substitute goods.

If, by obtaining cover and reselling the substitute goods, a buyer is able to recoup all or most of his or her loss from a source other than the breaching party, should the buyer's recovery under UCC 2–712 be reduced? That was the issue confronting the court in the following case.

CASE 15.4

KGM Harvesting Co. v. Fresh Network

California Court of Appeal, Sixth District, 1995. 36 Cal.App. 4th 376, 42 Cal.Rptr.2d 286.

FACTS   McDonald's buys its lettuce from the KGM Harvesting Company, which also sells lettuce to other companies. For example, in 1988, KGM also agreed to deliver fourteen loads of lettuce each week to Fresh Network. Fresh Network then sold the lettuce to the Castellini Company, which in turn sold it to Club Chef. Club Chef then chopped and shredded it for Burger King, Taco Bell, and

Case 15.4—Continued

Pizza Hut. In the spring of 1991, the market price of lettuce rose dramatically. KGM chose to sell only to McDonald's and some of its other customers rather than to deliver to Fresh Network the usual fourteen loads at the contract price. Consequently, to fulfill its obligation to Castellini, Fresh Network bought lettuce on the open market at a higher price. Castellini agreed to pay the difference, which it charged to its customer, Club Chef, which in turn passed the higher price on to its customers. In an attempt to recover the extra amount it had to pay for lettuce, Fresh Network refused to pay KGM for previous shipments. KGM filed a suit in a California state court for the balance due. Fresh Network responded with a demand for damages. The court awarded Fresh Network an amount equal to the difference between the contract price and the price it had paid for the substitute lettuce, minus the amount that it owed KGM. KGM appealed, arguing that the court should have taken into consideration the fact that Fresh Network had passed on most of its loss to Castellini.

ISSUE   In assessing a buyer's recovery under the UCC's cover provision, should all of the events affecting the buyer's ultimate profit or loss be taken into consideration?

DECISION   No. The California Court of Appeal affirmed the lower court's award.

REASON   The court pointed out that "the object of contract damages is to give the aggrieved party as nearly as possible the equivalent of the benefits of performance." The court explained that buying replacement lettuce did not put Fresh Network in "as good a position as if the other party had fully performed," because Fresh Network paid more than the contract price for the replacement lettuce. Only when Fresh Network was reimbursed for the additional cost could it "truly receive the benefit of the bargain." This, the court held, is the measure of damages set forth in UCC 2–712. "What the buyer chooses to do with that bargain is not relevant."

FOR CRITICAL ANALYSIS—Economic Consideration   *Is it fair for Fresh Network to, in essence, recover twice—once from KGM and once from Castellini?*

THE RIGHT TO REPLEVY GOODS   Buyers and lessees also have the right to replevy goods. Replevin[4] is an action to recover specific goods in the hands of a party who is wrongfully withholding them from the other party. Outside the UCC, the term *replevin* refers to a prejudgment process (a proceeding that takes place prior to a court's judgment) that permits the seizure of specific personal property in which a party claims a right or an interest. Under the UCC, the buyer or lessee can replevy goods subject to the contract if the seller or lessor has repudiated or breached the contract. To maintain an action to replevy goods, buyers and lessees must usually show that they are unable to cover for the goods after a reasonable effort [UCC 2–716(3), 2A–521(3)].

THE RIGHT TO RECOVER DAMAGES   If a seller or lessor repudiates the sales contract or fails to deliver the goods, the buyer or lessee can sue for damages. The measure of recovery is the difference between the contract price (or lease payments) and the market price of (or lease payments that could be obtained for) the goods at the time the buyer (or lessee) *learned* of the breach. The market price or market lease payments are determined at the place where the seller or lessor was supposed to deliver the goods. The buyer or lessee can also recover incidental and consequential damages less the expenses that were saved as a result of the breach [UCC 2–713, 2A–519].

---

4.   Pronounced ruh-*pleh*-vun.

Consider an example. Schilling orders ten thousand bushels of wheat from Valdone for $5 a bushel, with delivery due on June 14 and payment due on June 20. Valdone does not deliver on June 14. On June 14, the market price of wheat is $5.50 per bushel. Schilling chooses to do without the wheat. He sues Valdone for damages for nondelivery. Schilling can recover $0.50 × 10,000, or $5,000, plus any expenses the breach may have caused him. The measure of damages is the market price less the contract price on the day Schilling was to have received delivery. (Any expenses Schilling saved by the breach would be deducted from the damages.)

When the Seller or Lessor Delivers Nonconforming Goods

When the seller or lessor delivers nonconforming goods, the buyer or lessee has several remedies available under the UCC.

THE RIGHT TO REJECT THE GOODS   If either the goods or the tender of the goods by the seller or lessor fails to conform to the contract *in any respect*, the buyer or lessee can reject the goods. If some of the goods conform to the contract, the buyer or lessee can keep the conforming goods and reject the rest [UCC 2–601, 2A–509]. If the buyer or lessee rejects the goods, he or she may then obtain cover, cancel the contract, or sue for damages for breach of contract, just as if the seller or lessor had refused to deliver the goods (see the earlier discussion of these remedies).

Timeliness and Reason for Rejection Required The buyer or lessee must reject the goods within a reasonable amount of time, and the seller or lessor must be notified seasonably—that is, in a timely fashion or at the proper time [UCC 2–602(1), 2A–509(2)]. Furthermore, the buyer or lessee must designate defects that would have been apparent to the seller or lessor on reasonable inspection. Failure to do so precludes the buyer or lessee from using such defects to justify rejection or to establish breach when the seller could have cured the defects if they had been stated seasonably [UCC 2–605, 2A–514].

Duties of Merchant Buyers and Lessees When Goods Are Rejected   If a *merchant buyer or lessee*

rightfully rejects goods, and the seller or lessor has no agent or business at the place of rejection, the buyer or lessee is required to follow any reasonable instructions received from the seller or lessor with respect to the goods controlled by the buyer or lessee. The buyer or lessee is entitled to reimbursement for the care and cost entailed in following the instructions [UCC 2–603, 2A–511]. The same requirements hold if the buyer or lessee rightfully revokes his or her acceptance of the goods at some later time [UCC 2–608(3), 2A–517(5)]. (Revocation of acceptance will be discussed shortly.)

If no instructions are forthcoming and the goods are perishable or threaten to decline in value quickly, the buyer or lessee can resell the goods in good faith, taking the appropriate reimbursement from the proceeds [UCC 2–603(1), 2A–511(1)]. If the goods are not perishable, the buyer or lessee may store them for the seller or lessor or reship them to the seller or lessor [UCC 2–604, 2A–512].

Buyers who rightfully reject goods that remain in their possession or control have a *security interest* in the goods (basically, a legal claim to the goods to the extent necessary to recover expenses, costs, and the like—see Chapter 19). The security interest encompasses any payments the buyer has made for the goods, as well as any expenses incurred with regard to inspection, receipt, transportation, care, and custody of the goods [UCC 2–711(3)]. A buyer with a security interest in the goods is a "person in the position of a seller." This gives the buyer the same rights as an unpaid seller. Thus, the buyer can resell, withhold delivery of, or stop delivery of the goods. A buyer who chooses to resell must account to the seller for any amounts received in excess of the security interest [UCC 2–711, 2–706(6)].

REVOCATION OF ACCEPTANCE   Acceptance of the goods precludes the buyer or lessee from exercising the right of rejection, but it does not necessarily preclude the buyer or lessee from pursuing other remedies. In certain circumstances, a buyer or lessee is permitted to *revoke* his or her acceptance of the goods. Acceptance of a lot or a commercial unit can be revoked if the nonconformity *substantially* impairs the value of the lot or unit and if one of the following factors is present:

1. If acceptance was predicated on the reasonable assumption that the nonconformity would

be cured, and it has not been cured within a reasonable period of time [UCC 2–608(1)(a), 2A–517(1)(a)].

2. If the buyer or lessee did not discover the nonconformity before acceptance, either because it was difficult to discover before acceptance or because assurances made by the seller or lessor that the goods were conforming kept the buyer or lessee from inspecting the goods [UCC 2–608(1)(b), 2A–517(1)(b)].

Revocation of acceptance is not effective until notice is given to the seller or lessor, which must occur within a reasonable time after the buyer or lessee either discovers *or should have discovered* the grounds for revocation. Additionally, revocation must occur before the goods have undergone any substantial change (such as spoilage) not caused by their own defects [UCC 2–608(2), 2A–517(4)].

THE RIGHT TO RECOVER DAMAGES FOR ACCEPTED GOODS A buyer or lessee who has accepted nonconforming goods may also keep the goods and recover damages caused by the breach. The buyer or lessee, however, must *notify* the seller or lessor of the breach within a reasonable time after the defect was or should have been discovered. Failure of the buyer or lessee to give notice of the defects (breach) to the seller or lessor bars the buyer or lessee from pursuing any remedy to recover damages. [UCC 2–607(3), 2A–516(3)]. In addition, the parties to a sales or lease contract can insert a provision requiring that the buyer or lessee give notice of any defects in the goods within a prescribed period.

When the goods delivered are not as promised, the measure of damages equals the difference between the value of the goods as accepted and their value if they had been delivered as promised [UCC 2–714(2), 2A–519(4)]. For this and other types of breaches in which the buyer or lessee has accepted the goods, the buyer or lessee is entitled to recover for any loss "resulting in the ordinary course of events . . . as determined in any manner which is reasonable" [UCC 2–714(1), 2A–519(3)]. The UCC also permits the buyer or lessee, with proper notice to the seller or lessor, to deduct all or any part of the damages from the price or lease payments still due and payable to the seller or lessor [UCC 2–717, 2A–516(1)].

▌ Statute of Limitations

An action for breach of contract under the UCC must be commenced *within four years after the cause of action accrues*—that is, within four years after the breach occurs. In addition to filing suit within the four-year period, an aggrieved party who has accepted nonconforming goods usually must notify the breaching party of the breach within a reasonable time, or the buyer or lessee is barred from pursuing any remedy [UCC 2–607(3)(a), 2A–516(3)]. By agreement in the contract, the parties can reduce this period to not less than one year but *cannot* extend it beyond four years [UCC 2–725(1), 2A–506(1)]. A cause of action accrues for breach of warranty when the seller or lessor *tenders* delivery. This is the rule even if the aggrieved party is unaware that the cause of action has accrued [UCC 2–725(2), 2A–506(2)].

▌ Limitation of Remedies

The parties to a sales or lease contract can vary their respective rights and obligations by contractual agreement. For example, a seller and buyer can expressly provide for remedies in addition to those provided in the UCC. They can also provide remedies in lieu of those provided in the UCC, or they can change the measure of damages. The seller can provide that the buyer's only remedy upon breach of warranty will be repair or replacement of the item, or the seller can limit the buyer's remedy to return of the goods and refund of the purchase price. In sales and lease contracts, an agreed-on remedy is in addition to those provided in the UCC unless the parties expressly agree that the remedy is exclusive of all others [UCC 2–719(1), 2A–503(1)].

If the parties state that a remedy is exclusive, then it is the sole remedy. When circumstances cause an exclusive remedy to fail in its essential purpose, however, it is no longer exclusive [UCC 2–719(2), 2A–503(2)]. For example, a sales contract that limits the buyer's remedy to repair or replacement fails in its essential purpose if the item cannot be repaired and no replacements are available.

A contract can limit or exclude consequential damages, provided the limitation is not unconscionable. When the buyer or lessee is a consumer, the limitation of consequential damages for personal injuries resulting from nonconforming goods is *prima facie* (on its face) unconscionable. The limitation of consequential damages is not necessarily unconscionable when the loss is commercial in nature—for example, lost profits and property damage [UCC 2–719(3), 2A–503(3)]. In the following case, the court had to decide whether a contract clause that excluded liability for consequential damages was unconscionable.

CASE 15.5

Transport Corp. of America, Inc. v. International Business Machines Corp.

United States Court of Appeals. Eighth Circuit, 1994. 30 F.3d 953.

FACTS Innovative Computing Corporation (ICC) sold an International Business Machines Corporation (IBM) computer to TCA. As part of the deal, TCA expressly agreed to a disclaimer that stated, in part, "IN NO EVENT SHALL ICC BE LIABLE FOR ANY * * * CONSEQUENTIAL DAMAGES * * * IN CONNECTION WITH * * * THIS AGREEMENT." One year later, the computer failed. The downtime was nearly thirty-four hours. TCA spent more than $4,500 to replace lost data and purportedly lost nearly $470,000 in income while the computer was down. TCA filed a suit in a Minnesota state court against IBM and ICC, alleging, among other things, breach of warranty. The case was moved to a federal district court, and IBM and ICC filed a motion for summary judgment. The court granted the motion, based in part on the disclaimer. TCA appealed, arguing in part that the disclaimer was unconscionable.

ISSUE Was the disclaimer of consequential damages unconscionable?

DECISION No. The U.S. Court of Appeals for the Eighth Circuit affirmed the lower court's decision.

REASON The court explained that "[t]he U.C.C. encourages negotiated agreements in commercial transactions * * *. It is at the time of contract formation that experienced parties define the product, identify the risks, and negotiate a price of the goods that reflects the relative benefits and risks to each. An exclusion of consequential damages set forth in advance in a commercial agreement between experienced business parties represents a bargained-for allocation of risk that is conscionable." The court concluded that "the damages claimed by TCA, for business interruption losses and replacement media, were consequential damages," but that "TCA and ICC were sophisticated business entities of relatively equal bargaining power." Thus "ICC's disclaimer was not unconscionable and TCA is * * * precluded from recovering consequential damages."

FOR CRITICAL ANALYSIS—Social Consideration *Why is a limitation on consequential damages considered unconscionable when one of the parties is a consumer but not when both parties are business entities?*

▌ Terms and Concepts

Chapter Summary: Performance and Breach of Sales and Lease Contracts

PERFORMANCE OBLIGATIONS	
Obligations of the Seller or Lessor *(See pages 296–300.)*	1. The seller or lessor must tender *conforming* goods to the buyer. Tender must take place at a *reasonable hour* and in a *reasonable manner*. Under the perfect tender doctrine, the seller or lessor must tender goods that exactly conform to the terms of the contract [UCC 2–503(1), 2A–508(1)]. 2. If the seller or lessor tenders nonconforming goods and the buyer or lessee rejects them, the seller or lessor may *cure* (repair or replace the goods) within the contract time for performance [UCC 2–508(1), 2A–513(1)]. If the seller or lessor has reasonable grounds to believe the buyer or lessee would accept the goods, on the buyer's or lessee's rejection, the seller or lessor has a reasonable time to substitute conforming goods without liability [UCC 2–508(2), 2A–513(2)]. 3. If the agreed-on means of delivery becomes impracticable or unavailable, the seller must substitute a reasonable alternative means (such as a different carrier) if one is available [UCC 2–614(1)]. 4. If a seller or lessor tenders nonconforming goods in any one installment under an installment contract, the buyer or lessee may reject the installment only if its value is substantially impaired and cannot be cured. The entire installment contract is breached when one or more installments *substantially* impair the value of the *whole* contract [UCC 2–612, 2A–510]. 5. When performance becomes commercially impracticable owing to circumstances unforeseen when the contract was formed, the perfect tender rule no longer holds [UCC 2–615, 2A–405].
Obligations of the Buyer or Lessee *(See pages 300–302.)*	1. Upon tender of delivery by the seller, the buyer or lessee must pay for the goods at the time and place the buyer or lessee *receives* the goods, even if the place of shipment is the place of delivery, unless the sale is made on credit. Payment may be made by any method generally acceptable in the commercial world [UCC 2–310, 2–511]. In lease contracts, the lessee must pay lease payments in accordance with the contract [UCC 2A–516(1)]. 2. Unless otherwise agreed, the buyer or lessee has an absolute right to inspect the goods before acceptance [UCC 2–513(1), 2A–515(1)]. 3. The buyer or lessee can manifest acceptance of delivered goods expressly in words or by conduct, or by failing to reject the goods after a reasonable period of time following inspection or after having had a reasonable opportunity to inspect them [UCC 2–606(1), 2A–515(1)]. A buyer will be deemed to have accepted goods if he or she performs any act inconsistent with the seller's ownership [UCC 2–606(1)(c)]. 4. Following the acceptance of delivered goods, the buyer or lessee may revoke acceptance only if the nonconformity *substantially* impairs the value of the unit or lot and if one of the following factors is present: a. Acceptance was predicated on the reasonable assumption that the nonconformity would be cured and it was not cured within a reasonable time [UCC 2–608(1)(a), 2A–517(1)(a)]. b. The buyer or lessee did not discover the nonconformity before acceptance, either because it was difficult to discover before acceptance or because the seller's or lessor's assurance that the goods were conforming kept the buyer or lessee from inspecting the goods [UCC 2–608(1)(b), 2A–517(1)(b)].

(Continued)

▌Chapter Summary: Performance and Breach—Continued

Anticipatory Repudiation *(See page 302.)*	If, before the time for performance, either party clearly indicates to the other an intention not to perform, under UCC 2–610 and 2A–402 the aggrieved party may do the following: 1. Await performance by the repudiating party for a commercially reasonable time. 2. Resort to any remedy for breach. 3. In either situation, suspend performance.
	**REMEDIES FOR BREACH OF CONTRACT**
Remedies of the Seller or Lessor *(See pages 302–305.)*	1. *When the goods are in the possession of the seller or lessor*—The seller or lessor may do the following: 　a. Cancel the contract [UCC 2–703(f), 2A–523(1)(a)]. 　b. Withhold delivery [UCC 2–703(a), 2A–523(1)(c)]. 　c. Resell or dispose of the goods [UCC 2–703(d), 2–706(1), 2A–523(1)(e), 2A–527(1)]. 　d. Sue to recover the purchase price or lease payments due [UCC 2–709(1), 2A–529(1)]. 　e. Sue to recover damages [UCC 2–708, 2A–528]. 2. *When the goods are in transit*—The seller may stop the carrier or bailee from delivering the goods [UCC 2–705, 2A–526]. 3. *When the goods are in the possession of the buyer or lessee*—The seller or lessor may do the following: 　a. Sue to recover the purchase price or lease payments due [UCC 2–709(1), 2A–529(1)]. 　b. Reclaim the goods. A seller may reclaim goods received by an insolvent buyer if the demand is made within ten days of receipt (excludes all other remedies on reclamation) [UCC 2–702]; a lessor may repossess goods if the lessee is in default [UCC 2A–525(2)].
Remedies of the Buyer or Lessee *(See pages 306–309.)*	1. *When the seller or lessor refuses to deliver the goods*—The buyer or lessee may do the following: 　a. Cancel the contract [UCC 2–711(1), 2A–508(1)(a)]. 　b. Recover the goods if the seller or lessor becomes insolvent within ten days after receiving the first payment and the goods are identified to the contract [UCC 2–502, 2A–522]. 　c. Obtain specific performance (when the goods are unique or when the remedy at law is inadequate) [UCC 2–716(1), 2A–521(1)]. 　d. Obtain cover [UCC 2–712, 2A–518]. 　e. Replevy the goods (if cover is unavailable) [UCC 2–716(3), 2A–521(3)]. 　f. Sue to recover damages [UCC 2–713, 2A–519]. 2. *When the seller or lessor delivers nonconforming goods*—The buyer or lessee may do the following: 　a. Reject the goods [UCC 2–601, 2A–509]. 　b. Revoke acceptance (in certain circumstances) [UCC 2–608, 2A–517]. 　c. Sue to recover damages [UCC 2–607, 2–714, 2A–519].
Statute of Limitations *(See page 309.)*	The UCC has a four-year statute of limitations for actions involving breach of contract. By agreement, the parties to a sales or lease contract can reduce this period to not less than one year, but they cannot extend it beyond four years [UCC 2–725(1), 2A–506(1)].
Limitation of Remedies *(See pages 309–310.)*	Remedies may be limited in sales or lease contracts by agreement of the parties. If the contract states that a remedy is exclusive, then that is the sole remedy—unless the remedy fails in its essential purpose. Sellers and lessors can also limit the rights of buyers and lessees to receive consequential damages—unless the limitation is unconscionable [UCC 2–719, 2A–503].

▌For Review

1. What are the respective obligations of the parties under a contract for the sale or lease of goods?

2. What is the perfect tender rule? What are some important exceptions to this rule that apply to sales and lease contracts?

3. What options are available to the nonbreaching party when the other party to a sales or lease contract repudiates the contract prior to the time for performance?

4. What remedies are available to a seller or lessor when the buyer or lessee breaches the contract? What remedies are available to a buyer or lessee if the seller or lessor breaches the contract?

5. In contracts subject to the UCC, are parties free to limit the remedies available to the nonbreaching party on a breach of contract?

▌Questions and Case Problems

15–1. Revocation of Acceptance. What events or circumstances must occur before a buyer can rightfully revoke his or her acceptance of a sales contract?

15–2. Remedies. Genix, Inc., has contracted to sell Larson five hundred washing machines of a certain model at list price. Genix is to ship the goods on or before December 1. Genix produces one thousand washing machines of this model but has not yet prepared Larson's shipment. On November 1, Larson repudiates the contract. Discuss the remedies available to Genix in this situation.

15–3. Right of Inspection. Cummings ordered two Model-X Super Fidelity speakers from Jamestown Wholesale Electronics, Inc. Jamestown shipped the speakers via United Parcel Service, C.O.D. (collect on delivery), although Cummings had not requested or agreed to a C.O.D. shipment of the goods. When the speakers were delivered, Cummings refused to accept them because he would not be able to inspect them before payment. Jamestown claimed that Cummings had breached their contract, because Jamestown had shipped conforming goods. Had Cummings breached the contract? Explain.

15–4. Anticipatory Repudiation. Moore contracted in writing to sell her 1994 Ford Taurus to Hammer for $8,500. Moore agreed to deliver the car on Wednesday, and Hammer promised to pay the $8,500 on the following Friday. On Tuesday, Hammer informed Moore that he would not be buying the car after all. By Friday, Hammer had changed his mind again and tendered $8,500 to Moore. Moore, although she had not sold the car to another party, refused the tender and refused to deliver. Hammer claimed that Moore had breached their contract. Moore contended that Hammer's repudiation released her from her duty to perform under the contract. Who is correct, and why?

15–5. Remedies. Rodriguez is an antique car collector. He contracts to purchase spare parts for a 1938 engine from Gerrard. These parts are not made anymore and are scarce. To get the contract with Gerrard, Rodriguez has to pay 50 percent of the purchase price in advance. On May 1, Rodriguez sends the payment, which is received on May 2. On May 3, Gerrard, having found another buyer willing to pay substantially more for the parts, informs Rodriguez that he will not deliver as contracted. That same day, Rodriguez learns that Gerrard is insolvent. Gerrard has the parts, and Rodriguez wants them. Discuss fully any available remedies that would allow Rodriguez to obtain these car parts.

15–6. Commercial Impracticability. In November 1975, Sun Maid Raisin Growers of California contracted to purchase 1,900 tons of raisins from Victor Packing Co. The first 100 tons were priced at 39 cents per pound and the remainder at 40 cents per pound. No delivery date was specified in the contract. On August 10, 1976, Victor informed Sun Maid that it would not complete performance, as it was unable to deliver the last 610 tons. Sun Maid was able to purchase 200 tons of raisins at 43 cents per pound from another supplier. In September 1976, heavy rains damaged the new crop of raisins, causing the price of raisins to increase dramatically. Sun Maid sued Victor for damages, including lost profits (consequential damages). Victor claimed that it should not be liable for lost profits because the disastrous rain was not foreseeable. Discuss Victor's claim. [*Sun Maid Raisin Growers of California v. Victor Packing Co.*, 146 Cal.App.3d 787, 194 Cal.Rptr. 612 (1983)]

15–7. Right to Cure. Wilson purchased a new television set from Scampoli in 1965. When the set was delivered, Wilson found that it did not work properly; the color was defective. Scampoli's repairperson could not correct the problem, and Wilson refused to allow the repairperson to dismantle the set and take it back to the shop to determine the cause of the difficulty. Instead, Wilson demanded that Scampoli deliver a new television set or return the purchase price. Scampoli refused to refund Wilson's money and insisted that he receive the opportunity to correct the malfunctioning of Wilson's set before replacing it or issuing a refund. Discuss whether Scampoli has the right to attempt to cure the product, according to UCC 2–508. [*Wilson v. Scampoli*, 228 A.2d 848 (D.C.App. 1967)]

15–8. Measure of Damages. Bigelow-Sanford, Inc., entered into a contract to buy 100,000 yards of jute (a strong, coarse fiber used for sacking and cordage) at $0.64 per yard from Gunny Corp. Gunny delivered 22,228 yards to Bigelow but informed the company that it would deliver no more. Several other suppliers to Bigelow defaulted, and Bigelow was forced to go into the market one month later to purchase a total of 164,503 yards of jute for $1.21 per yard. Bigelow sued Gunny for the difference between the market price and the contract price of the amount of jute that Gunny had not delivered. Discuss whether Bigelow could recover this amount from Gunny. [*Bigelow-Sanford, Inc. v. Gunny Corp.*, 649 F.2d 1060 (5th Cir. 1981)]

15–9. Limited Remedies. In 1983, Canal Electric Co. purchased some new rotating blades from Westinghouse Electric Corp. to use in a generator that Canal had purchased several years earlier from Westinghouse. The contract for the sale of the blades warranted that Westinghouse would repair or replace any defective parts for a one-year period and limited Westinghouse's total liability under the contract to the purchase price of the blades, which was $40,750. Liability for incidental and consequential damages was specifically disclaimed. A few months later, the blades developed cracks, and Canal had to shut down operations for 124 days while the blades were being replaced. As a result, Canal incurred costs (which were significantly higher than the purchase price of the blades) to obtain replacement power during this period. Ultimately, Canal sued Westinghouse for breach of warranty and negligence. Westinghouse claimed that its liability to Canal was limited to the purchase price of the blades, $40,750. Will the court enforce the limitation-of-liability clause? What factors will the court consider in deciding the issue? Discuss fully. [*Canal Electric Co. v. Westinghouse Electric Corp.*, 756 F.Supp. 620 (D.Mass. 1991)]

15–10. Remedies of the Buyer or Lessee. Marine Indemnity Insurance Co. of America purchased a "toploader" (a piece of ship-loading equipment) from Hapag-Lloyd, A.G. (A.G. is an abbreviation of the German *Aktiengesellschaft*—the German equivalent of the English term *company*.) Marine Indemnity was aware of the fact that the wiring in the toploader's engine was defective but nevertheless used the equipment in its defective state without notifying the seller. After Marine Indemnity had used the toploader for about four weeks, the wiring caused an explosion in the engine, which severely damaged the equipment. Marine Indemnity

then sued Hapag-Lloyd for breach of express warranty. The trial court held for Marine Indemnity. Hapag-Lloyd appealed, contending that Marine Indemnity's failure to give timely notice of the breach barred it from pursuing any remedy. Will the appellate court agree with Hapag-Lloyd? Discuss fully. [*Hapag-Lloyd, A.G. v. Marine Indemnity Insurance Co. of America*, 576 So.2d 1330 (Fla.App.3d 1991)]

15–11. Notice of Defect. Rachel Hebron bought an Isuzu Trooper four-wheel-drive sports vehicle from American Isuzu Motors, Inc. Their contract required her to give notice of any defects in the car within two years of their discovery. In June 1991, Hebron was driving the Trooper when another vehicle pulled in front of her. She swerved to avoid hitting it, and the Trooper rolled over, causing her permanent injuries. Hebron waited, for no apparent reason, until July 1993 to file a suit in a federal district court against American, seeking damages for alleged defects in the car. She had already disposed of the Trooper, without notifying American. American filed a motion for summary judgment based on the contract requirement of notice within two years. How should the court rule? Discuss fully. [*Hebron v. American Isuzu Motors, Inc.*, 60 F.3d 1095 (4th Cir. 1995)]

15–12. Limitation of Remedies. Wilk Paving, Inc., bought a street-paving asphalt roller from Southworth-Milton, Inc. In large capital letters, on the front of the contract, was printed, "ADDITIONAL TERMS AND CONDITIONS ON REVERSE SIDE." A clause on the back stated that "under no circumstances shall seller . . . be held liable for any . . . consequential damages." In a hurry to close the deal, Wilk's representative did not notice this clause, and Southworth's representative did not call attention to it. Within sixty days, the roller needed the first of what became continuous repairs for mechanical problems. Wilk asked Southworth for its money back. When Southworth refused, Wilk sued Southworth, seeking the purchase price and consequential damages. Was the clause limiting damages enforceable in these circumstances? Explain. [*Wilk Paving, Inc. v. Southworth-Milton, Inc.*, 649 A.2d 778 (Vt. 1995)]

A QUESTION OF ETHICS AND SOCIAL RESPONSIBILITY

15–13. *In March 1985, Bruce Young purchased from Hessel Tractor & Equipment Co., a John Deere equipment dealer, a machine to shear trees in his logging business. The only warranty in the contract was a one-year warranty against defects in the equipment with an exclusive remedy of repair and replacement for any defect in materials or workmanship. All other warranties were expressly and conspicuously disclaimed. Young began to have serious problems with the equipment after less than a month of use. After over a year of continuing* *unsuccessful attempts at repair and after the one-year warranty had expired, Hessel stopped repairing the machine. Given these facts, consider the following questions.* [Young v. Hessel Tractor & Equipment Co., 782 P.2d 164 (Or.App. 1989)]

1. Do you think that it is fair for a seller to limit available remedies under a sales contract to just one exclusive remedy, such as repair and replacement of parts? Is there anything unethical about this practice?

2. When an exclusive remedy leads to unfair results, as in this case, what, if anything, can be done about it?

3. What UCC provisions might Young cite to persuade the court that he is entitled to revoke his acceptance of the machine and recover the purchase price? How do these provisions reflect the UCC's attempt to balance freedom of contract against the need for fairness and justice in commercial transactions?

Accessing the Internet: Fundamentals of Business Law

To obtain information on performance requirements in relation to contracts for the international sale of goods, you can access the Institute of International Commercial Law at Pace University at:

http://cisgw3.law.pace.edu/

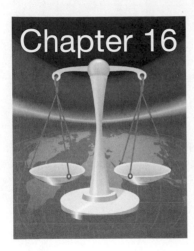

Chapter 16

Warranties and Product Liability

CHAPTER OBJECTIVES

After reading this chapter, you should be able to:

1. Describe the types of warranties that may arise in a sales or lease transaction.
2. Indicate how warranties may be disclaimed and the legal effect of warranty disclaimers.
3. Discuss how negligence and misrepresentation can provide a basis for a product liability action.
4. List the requirements for an action in strict liability.
5. Summarize the defenses that can be raised against product liability claims.

Warranty is an age-old concept. In sales and lease law, a warranty is an assurance by one party of the existence of a fact upon which the other party can rely. Sellers and lessors warrant to those who purchase or lease their goods that the goods are as represented or will be as promised.

The Uniform Commercial Code (UCC) has numerous rules governing the concept of product warranty as it occurs in sales and lease contracts. That will be the subject matter of the first part of this chapter. A natural addition to the discussion is *product liability:* Who is liable to consumers, users, and bystanders for physical harm and property damage caused by a particular good or the use thereof? Product liability encompasses the contract theory of warranty, as well as the tort theories of negligence and strict liability (discussed in Chapter 4).

▌ Warranties

Article 2 (on sales) and Article 2A (on leases) of the UCC designate several types of warranties that

can arise in a sales or lease contract, including warranties of title, express warranties, and implied warranties.

Warranties of Title

Title warranty arises automatically in most sales contracts. The UCC imposes three types of warranties of title.

GOOD TITLE In most cases, sellers warrant that they have good and valid title to the goods sold and that transfer of the title is rightful [UCC 2–312(1)(a)]. For example, Sharon steals goods from Miguel and sells them to Carrie, who does not know that the goods are stolen. If Miguel reclaims the goods from Carrie, which he has a right to do, Carrie can then sue Sharon for breach of warranty. When Sharon sold Carrie the goods, Sharon *automatically* warranted to her that the title conveyed was valid and that its transfer was rightful. Because this was not in fact the case, Sharon

316

breached the warranty of title imposed by UCC 2–312(1)(a) and became liable to the buyer for the appropriate damages.

NO LIENS   A second warranty of title provided by the UCC protects buyers who are *unaware* of any encumbrances (claims, charges, or liabilities—usually called **liens**[1]) against goods at the time the contract was made [UCC 2–312(1)(b)]. This warranty protects buyers who, for example, unknowingly purchase goods that are subject to a creditor's security interest (see Chapter 19). If a creditor legally repossesses the goods from a buyer *who had no actual knowledge of the security interest*, the buyer can recover from the seller for breach of warranty.

Article 2A affords similar protection for lessees. Section 2A–211(1) provides that during the term of the lease, no claim of any third party will interfere with the lessee's enjoyment of the leasehold interest.

NO INFRINGEMENTS   A merchant is also deemed to warrant that the goods delivered are free from any copyright, trademark, or patent claims of a third person[2] [UCC 2–312(3), 2A–211(2)]. If this warranty is breached and the buyer is sued by the party holding copyright, trademark, or patent rights in the goods, the buyer *must notify the seller* of litigation within a reasonable time to enable the seller to decide whether to defend the lawsuit. If the seller states in writing that he or she has decided to defend and agrees to bear all expenses, including that of an adverse judgment, then the buyer must let the seller undertake litigation; otherwise, the buyer loses all rights against the seller if any infringement liability is established [UCC 2–607(3)(b), 2–607(5)(b)].

Article 2A provides for the same notice of litigation in situations that involve leases rather than sales [UCC 2A–516(3)(b), 2A–516(4)(b)]. There is an exception for leases to individual consumers for personal, family, or household purposes. A con-

sumer who fails to notify the lessor within a reasonable time does not lose his or her remedy against the lessor for any liability established in the litigation [UCC 2A–516(3)(b)].

DISCLAIMER OF TITLE WARRANTY   In an ordinary sales transaction, the title warranty can be disclaimed or modified only by *specific language* in the contract [UCC 2–312(2)]. For example, sellers can assert that they are transferring only such rights, title, and interest as they have in the goods. In a lease transaction, the disclaimer must "be specific, be by a writing, and be conspicuous" [UCC 2A–214(4)].

Express Warranties

A seller or lessor can create an **express warranty** by making representations concerning the quality, condition, description, or performance potential of the goods. Under UCC 2–313 and 2A–210, express warranties arise when a seller or lessor indicates any of the following:

1.   That the goods conform to any *affirmation or promise of fact that the seller or lessor makes to the buyer or lessee about the goods.* Such affirmations or promises are usually made during the bargaining process. Statements such as "these drill bits will penetrate stainless steel—and without dulling" are express warranties.

2.   That the goods conform to any *description* of them. For example, a label that reads "Crate contains one 150-horsepower diesel engine" or a contract that calls for the delivery of a "camel's-hair coat" creates an express warranty.

3.   That the goods conform to any *sample or model* of the goods shown to the buyer or lessee.

To create an express warranty, a seller or lessor does not have to use formal words such as *warrant* or *guarantee*. It is only necessary that a reasonable buyer or lessee would regard the representation as part of the basis of the bargain [UCC 2–313(2), 2A–210(2)].

BASIS OF THE BARGAIN   The UCC requires that for an express warranty to be created, the affirmation, promise, description, or sample must become part of the "basis of the bargain" [UCC 2–313(1),

---

1.   Pronounced *leens*. The term *lien* is derived from the Latin word *liqare*, which means "to bind."

2.   Recall from Chapter 13 that a *merchant* is defined in UCC 2–104(1) as a person who deals in goods of the kind involved in the sales contract or who, by occupation, presents himself or herself as having knowledge or skill peculiar to the goods involved in the transaction.

2A–210(1)]. Just what constitutes the basis of the bargain is hard to say. The UCC does not define the concept, and it is a question of fact in each case whether a representation was made at such a time and in such a way that it induced the buyer or lessee to enter into the contract. In the following case, the issue was whether warranties contained in a booklet in the glove compartment of a new truck were part of the basis of the bargain for the purchase of the truck.

CASE 16.1

Harris v. Ford Motor Co.

United States District Court,
Middle District of Alabama, 1994.
845 F.Supp. 1511.

FACTS William Harris purchased a new 1989 Ford F350 pickup truck from Quality Motors, Inc. The truck came with a "New Car Warranty" booklet, which had been placed in the glove compartment of the truck. A few months later, after the right rear fender on the truck began to discolor, Harris discovered that the truck's fender had been scratched in transit from the manufacturer (Ford Motor Company) to the dealership (Quality Motors) and that Quality Motors had repaired the scratched fender and repainted the truck before it sold the truck to Harris. Harris sued Quality Motors and Ford in a federal district court for, among other things, breach of express warranty, claiming in part that the truck was represented as being "new" when in fact it was not—it was damaged. In defending against Harris's claim, the defendants pointed to a clause in the "New Car Warranty" booklet. The clause provided as follows: "A defect or damage may occur in an appearance item while a vehicle is being assembled at the factory or shipped to the dealer. Usually such a defect or damage is found and repaired during the inspection processes at the factory and the dealership." Harris, in response, contended that the warranty booklet was not a part of the "basis of the bargain," because the booklet was delivered long after Harris obligated himself to purchase the vehicle. All of the parties filed motions for summary judgment.

ISSUE Was the warranty expressed in the booklet part of the basis of the bargain?

DECISION Yes. The court granted summary judgment in favor of the defendants.

REASON According to the court, "[t]he evidence demonstrates that, at the time William Harris purchased the vehicle, the 'New Car Warranty' was in the glove compartment of the truck and that the plaintiff was aware of its presence." The court thus held that "the warranty was delivered to the plaintiff at the time of the sale and was part of the 'basis of the bargain.'"

FOR CRITICAL ANALYSIS—Social Consideration *What are some of the factors that a court must consider in deciding whether a seller's oral or written statement about a product, such as the new car in this case, was part of the "basis of the bargain"?*

STATEMENTS OF OPINION Statements of fact create express warranties. If the seller or lessor merely makes a statement that relates to the value or worth of the goods, or makes a statement of opinion or recommendation about the goods, however, the seller or lessor is not creating an express warranty [UCC 2–313(2), 2A–210(2)].

For example, a seller claims that "this is the best used car to come along in years; it has four new tires and a 350-horsepower engine just rebuilt this year." The seller has made several *affirmations of fact* that can create a warranty: the automobile has an engine; it has a 350-horsepower engine; it was rebuilt this year; there are four tires on the automobile; and the tires are new. The seller's *opinion* that the vehicle is "the best used car to come along in years," however, is known as "puffing" and creates no warranty. (Puffing is the expression of opinion by a seller or lessor that is not made as a representation of fact.) A statement relating to the value of the goods, such as "it's worth a fortune" or "anywhere else you'd pay $10,000 for it," does not usually create a warranty. If the seller or lessor is an expert and gives an opinion as an expert to a layperson, however, then a warranty can be created.

It is not always easy to determine what constitutes an express warranty and what constitutes puffing. The reasonableness of the buyer's or lessee's reliance appears to be the controlling criterion in many cases. For example, a salesperson's statements that a ladder "will never break" and will "last a lifetime" are so clearly improbable that no reasonable buyer should rely on them. Additionally, the context within which a statement is made might be relevant in determining the reasonableness of the buyer's or lessee's reliance. For example, a reasonable person is more likely to rely on a written statement made in an advertisement than on a statement made orally by a salesperson.

Implied Warranties

An **implied warranty** is one that *the law derives* by implication or inference from the nature of the transaction or the relative situation or circumstances of the parties. In an action based on breach of implied warranty, it is necessary to show that an implied warranty existed and that the breach of the warranty proximately caused the damage sustained. We look here at some of the implied warranties that arise under the UCC.

IMPLIED WARRANTY OF MERCHANTABILITY
Every sale or lease of goods made *by a merchant who deals in goods of the kind* sold or leased automatically gives rise to an **implied warranty of merchantability** [UCC 2–314, 2A–212]. Thus, a merchant who is in the business of selling ski equipment makes an implied warranty of merchantability every time the merchant sells a pair of skis, but a neighbor selling his or her skis at a garage sale does not.

Merchantable Goods Goods that are *merchantable* are "reasonably fit for the ordinary purposes for which such goods are used." They must be of at least average, fair, or medium-grade quality. The quality must be comparable to quality that will pass without objection in the trade or market for goods of the same description. To be merchantable, the goods must also be adequately packaged and labeled as provided by the agreement, and they must conform to the promises or affirmations of fact made on the container or label, if any.

An implied warranty of merchantability also imposes on the merchant liability for the safe performance of the product. It makes no difference whether the merchant knew of or could have discovered a defect that makes the product unsafe— he or she is liable in either situation. Of course, merchants are not absolute insurers against *all* accidents arising in connection with the goods. For example, a bar of soap is not unmerchantable merely because a user could slip and fall by stepping on it.

Merchantable Food The UCC recognizes the serving of food or drink to be consumed on or off the premises as a sale of goods subject to the implied warranty of merchantability [UCC 2–314(1)]. "Merchantable" food means food that is fit to eat. Courts generally determine whether food is fit to eat on the basis of consumer expectations. For example, the courts assume that consumers should reasonably expect to find on occasion bones in fish fillets, cherry pits in cherry pie, a nutshell in a package of shelled nuts, and so on—because such substances are natural incidents of the food. In contrast, consumers would not reasonably expect to find an inchworm in a can of peas or a piece of glass in a soft drink—because these substances are not natural to the food product.[3] In the following classic case, the court had to determine whether a fish bone was a substance that one should reasonably expect to find in fish chowder.

---

3. See, for example, *Mexicali Rose v. Superior Court*, 1 Cal.4th 617, 4 Cal.Rptr.2d 145, 822 P.2d 1292 (1992).

CASE 16.2

Webster v. Blue Ship Tea Room, Inc.

Supreme Judicial Court of Massachusetts, 1964.
347 Mass. 421, 198 N.E.2d 309.

FACTS Blue Ship Tea Room, Inc., was located in Boston in an old building overlooking the ocean. Webster, who had been born and raised in New England, went to the restaurant and ordered fish chowder. The chowder was milky in color. After three or four spoonfuls, she felt something lodged in her throat. As a result, she underwent two esophagoscopies; in the second esophagoscopy, a fish bone was found and removed. Webster filed suit against the restaurant in a Massachusetts state court for breach of the implied warranty of merchantability. The jury rendered a verdict for Webster, and the restaurant appealed to the state's highest court.

ISSUE Does serving fish chowder that contains a bone constitute the breach of an implied warranty of merchantability on the part of the restaurant?

DECISION No. The Supreme Judicial Court of Massachusetts held that Webster could not recover against Blue Ship Tea Room, because no breach of warranty had occurred.

REASON The court, citing UCC Section 2–314, stated that "a warranty that goods shall be merchantable is implied in a contract for their sale if the seller is a merchant with respect to goods of that kind. Under this section the serving for value of food or drink to be consumed either on the premises or elsewhere is a sale. * * * Goods to be merchantable must at least be * * * fit for the ordinary purposes for which such goods are used." The question here is whether a fish bone made the chowder unfit for eating. In the judge's opinion, "the joys of life in New England include the ready availability of fresh fish chowder. We should be prepared to cope with the hazards of fish bones, the occasional presence of which in chowders is, it seems to us, to be anticipated, and which, in the light of a hallowed tradition, do not impair their fitness or merchantability."

FOR CRITICAL ANALYSIS—Cultural Consideration *If the fish chowder had been served in a restaurant located in, say, Nebraska, instead of a restaurant in New England, would the outcome of this case have been different? Should it have?*

IMPLIED WARRANTY OF FITNESS FOR A PARTICULAR PURPOSE The **implied warranty of fitness for a particular purpose** arises when *any seller or lessor* (merchant or nonmerchant) knows the particular purpose for which a buyer or lessee will use the goods *and* knows that the buyer or lessee is relying on the skill and judgment of the seller or lessor to select suitable goods [UCC 2–315, 2A–213].

A "particular purpose" of the buyer or lessee differs from the "ordinary purpose for which goods are used" (merchantability). Goods can be merchantable but unfit for a particular purpose. For example, suppose that you need a gallon of paint to match the color of your living room walls—a light shade somewhere between coral and peach. You take a sample to your local hardware store and request a gallon of paint of that color. Instead, you are given a gallon of bright blue paint. Here, the salesperson has not breached any warranty of implied merchantability—the bright blue paint is of high quality and suitable for interior walls—but he or she has breached an implied warranty of fitness for a particular purpose.

A seller or lessor does not need to have actual knowledge of the buyer's or lessee's particular purpose. It is sufficient if a seller or lessor "has reason to know" the purpose. The buyer or lessee, however, must have *relied* on the skill or judgment of the seller or lessor in selecting or furnishing suitable goods for an implied warranty to be created.

For example, Bloomberg leases a computer from Future Tech, a lessor of technical business equipment. Bloomberg tells the clerk that she wants a computer with enough memory to operate certain brands of software and to produce and store complicated engineering graphics and plans. Future Tech leases Bloomberg an Architex One computer. The computer works, but its memory is too limited. Bloomberg wants her money back. Here, because Future Tech has breached the implied warranty of fitness for a particular purpose, Bloomberg normally will be able to recover. The clerk knew specifically that Bloomberg wanted a computer with enough memory to run certain software and store certain information. Furthermore, Bloomberg relied on the clerk to furnish a computer that would fulfill this purpose. Because Future Tech did not do so, the warranty was breached.

OTHER IMPLIED WARRANTIES Implied warranties can also arise (or be excluded or modified) as a result of course of dealing, course of performance, or usage of trade [UCC 2–314(3), 2A–212(3)]. In the absence of evidence to the contrary, when both parties to a sales or lease contract have knowledge of a well-recognized trade custom, the courts will infer that both parties intended for that custom to apply to their contract. For example, if an industry-wide custom is to lubricate a new car before it is delivered and a dealer fails to do so, the dealer can be held liable to a buyer for damages resulting from the breach of an implied warranty. This, of course, would also be negligence on the part of the dealer.

Overlapping Warranties

Sometimes two or more warranties are made in a single transaction. An implied warranty of merchantability, an implied warranty of fitness for a particular purpose, or both, can exist in addition to an express warranty. For example, when a sales contract for a new car states that "this car engine is warranted to be free from defects for 36,000 miles or thirty-six months, whichever occurs first," there is an express warranty against all defects and an implied warranty that the car will be fit for normal use.

The rule under the UCC is that express and implied warranties are construed as *cumulative* if they are consistent with one another [UCC 2–317, 2A–215]. If the warranties are *inconsistent*, the courts usually hold as follows:

1. *Express* warranties displace inconsistent *implied* warranties, except implied warranties of fitness for a particular purpose.
2. Samples take precedence over inconsistent general descriptions.
3. Technical specifications displace inconsistent samples or general descriptions.

In the example described earlier, suppose that when Bloomberg leases the computer from Future Tech, the contract contains an express warranty concerning the amount of memory in the computer and the application programs that the computer is capable of running. Bloomberg does not realize that the memory expressly warranted in the contract is insufficient for her needs. When she tries to load the software and some engineering plans, the computer memory is quickly filled. Bloomberg claims that Future Tech has breached the implied warranty of fitness for a particular purpose. Here, although the express warranty would take precedence over any implied warranty of merchantability, it normally would not take precedence over an implied warranty of fitness for a particular purpose. Bloomberg therefore has a good claim for the breach of implied warranty of fitness for a particular purpose, because she made it clear that she was leasing the computer to perform certain tasks.

Third Party Beneficiaries of Warranties

One of the general principles of contract law is that unless you are one of the parties to a contract, you have no rights under the contract. In other words, *privity of contract* must exist between a plaintiff and a defendant before any action based on a contract can be maintained. Two notable exceptions to the rule of privity are assignments and third party beneficiary contracts (discussed in Chapter 11). Another exception is made under warranty laws so that third parties can recover for harms suffered as a result of breached warranties.

There is sharp disagreement among the states as to how far warranty liability should extend, however. In view of this disagreement, the UCC offers three alternatives for liability to third parties [UCC 2–318, 2A–216]. All three alternatives are intended to eliminate the privity requirement with respect to certain enumerated types of injuries (personal versus property) for certain beneficiaries (for example, household members or bystanders). The following case involves a third party who suffered injuries as a result of a faulty lock on the door of a walk-in freezer, which was located in a church. The issue is whether the seller's express and implied warranties extended to the injured third party under the UCC alternative adopted by the state of North Carolina.

CASE 16.3

Crews v. W. A. Brown & Son, Inc.

Court of Appeals of North Carolina, 1992.
106 N.C.App. 324, 416 S.E.2d 924.

FACTS   Thirteen-year-old Vickie Crews was working as a volunteer at her church on the evening of July 2, 1985. At about 8:45 P.M., Vickie went to the church's kitchen and thought she heard a noise in the walk-in freezer. Crews, barefoot and wearing shorts, stepped inside the freezer, and the door closed behind her. She pushed the red emergency release button on the inside of the door, but the door did not open. At approximately 10:00 P.M., someone discovered Crews, and she was taken to a hospital and treated for severe frostbite. During the next two months, she endured five separate operations and the amputation of most of her toes. Crews and her mother (the plaintiffs) brought suit in a North Carolina state court against W. A. Brown & Son, Inc. (the manufacturer of the freezer), Foodcraft Equipment Company (the firm that had assembled and installed the freezer and sold it to the church), and the church. The plaintiffs alleged, among other things, breach of express and implied warranties. The court granted Foodcraft's motion for summary judgment, holding that the plaintiffs' claims were barred by a lack of privity with Foodcraft. The plaintiffs appealed.

ISSUE   Were the plaintiffs' breach of warranty claims barred by a lack of privity with Foodcraft?

DECISION   Yes. The appellate court affirmed the trial court's decision.

REASON   The court stated that under North Carolina law, the ultimate purchaser of a product may sue a seller for breach of express or implied warranties. Additionally, "any natural person who is in the family or household of [the] buyer or who is a guest in his home if it is reasonable to expect that such person may use, consume or be affected by the goods and who is injured in person by breach of the warranty" has standing to sue a seller for breach of warranty. The court stressed that the statute did not extend warranty coverage to persons beyond those specifically enumerated, and Vickie Crews was not among them. "Because a church does not have a 'family' or a 'household' in the ordinary meanings of those terms, Crews cannot be classified as a member of [the church's] 'family' or 'household.'" Furthermore, because "a church is not a 'home,' * * * she was not a guest in the buyer's 'home.'"

FOR CRITICAL ANALYSIS—Social Consideration   *For what reasons might a state, such as North Carolina in this case, restrict recovery for breach of implied warranties to only those persons who are in the family or household of the buyer or who are guests in the buyer's home?*

Warranty Disclaimers

Because each type of warranty is created in a special way, the manner in which warranties can be disclaimed or qualified by a seller or lessor varies depending on the type of warranty.

EXPRESS WARRANTIES As already stated, any affirmation of fact or promise, description of the goods, or use of samples or models by a seller or lessor creates an express warranty. Obviously, then, express warranties can be excluded if the seller or lessor carefully refrains from making any promise or affirmation of fact relating to the goods, describing the goods, or using a sample or model.

The UCC does permit express warranties to be negated or limited by specific and unambiguous language, provided that this is done in a manner that protects the buyer or lessee from surprise. Therefore, a written disclaimer in language that is clear and conspicuous, and called to a buyer's or lessee's attention, could negate all oral express warranties not included in the written sales contract [UCC 2–316(1), 2A–214(1)]. This allows the seller or lessor to avoid false allegations that oral warranties were made, and it ensures that only representations made by properly authorized individuals are included in the bargain.

Note, however, that a buyer or lessee must be made aware of any warranty disclaimers or modifications *at the time the contract is formed*. In other words, any oral or written warranties—or disclaimers—made during the bargaining process cannot be modified at a later time by the seller or lessor.

IMPLIED WARRANTIES Generally speaking, unless circumstances indicate otherwise, the implied warranties of merchantability and fitness are disclaimed by the expressions "as is," "with all faults," and other similar expressions that in common understanding for *both* parties call the buyer's or lessee's attention to the fact that there are no implied warranties [UCC 2–316(3)(a), 2A–214(3)(a)].

The UCC also permits a seller or lessor to specifically disclaim an implied warranty either of fitness or of merchantability [UCC 2–316(2), 2A–214(2)]. To disclaim an implied warranty of fitness for a particular purpose, the disclaimer *must* be in writing and be conspicuous. The word *fitness*

does not have to be mentioned in the writing; it is sufficient if, for example, the disclaimer states, **"THERE ARE NO WARRANTIES THAT EXTEND BEYOND THE DESCRIPTION ON THE FACE HEREOF."**

A merchantability disclaimer must be more specific; it must mention *merchantability*. It need not be written; but if it is, the writing must be conspicuous [UCC 2–316(2), 2A–214(4)]. According to UCC 1–201(10),

> A term or clause is conspicuous when it is so written that a reasonable person against whom it is to operate ought to have noticed it. A printed heading in capitals . . . is conspicuous. Language in the body of a form is conspicuous if it is in larger or other contrasting type or color.

For example, Forbes, a merchant, sells Maves a particular lawn mower selected by Forbes with the characteristics clearly requested by Maves. At the time of the sale, Forbes orally tells Maves that he does not warrant the merchantability of the mower, as it is last year's model. If the mower proves to be defective and does not work, Maves can hold Forbes liable for breach of the warranty of fitness for a particular purpose but not for breach of the warranty of merchantability. Forbes's oral disclaimer mentioning the word *merchantability* is a proper disclaimer. For Forbes to have disclaimed the implied warranty of fitness for a particular purpose, however, a conspicuous writing would have been required. Because he made no written disclaimer, Forbes can still be held liable.

BUYER'S OR LESSEE'S REFUSAL TO INSPECT If a buyer or lessee actually examines the goods (or a sample or model) as fully as desired before entering into a contract, or if the buyer or lessee refuses to examine the goods on the seller's or lessor's demand that he or she do so, *there is no implied warranty with respect to defects that a reasonable examination would reveal or defects that are accidentally found* [UCC 2–316(3)(b), 2A–214(2)(b)].

For example, suppose that Joplin buys an ax at Gershwin's Hardware Store. No express warranties are made. Joplin, even after Gershwin asks, refuses to inspect the ax before buying it. Had she done so, she would have noticed that the handle of the ax was obviously cracked. If she is later injured by the defective ax, she normally will not be able to hold

Gershwin liable for breach of the warranty of merchantability, because she could have spotted the defect during an inspection.

WARRANTY DISCLAIMERS AND UNCONSCIONABILITY

The UCC sections dealing with warranty disclaimers do not refer specifically to unconscionability as a factor. Ultimately, however, the courts will test warranty disclaimers with reference to the UCC's unconscionability standards [UCC 2–302, 2A–108]. Such things as lack of bargaining position, "take-it-or-leave-it" choices, and a buyer's or lessee's failure to understand or know of a warranty disclaimer will become relevant to the issue of unconscionability. In the following landmark decision, which was decided before the UCC was effective in New Jersey, the court gave significant weight to a consumer's lack of bargaining power with respect to a large auto manufacturer in determining whether a warranty disclaimer was unconscionable.

CASE 16.4

Henningsen v. Bloomfield Motors, Inc.

Supreme Court of New Jersey, 1960.
32 N.J. 358, 161 A.2d 69.

FACTS   Henningsen purchased a new Chrysler from Bloomfield Motors, Inc., for his wife. Subsequently, his wife suffered severe injuries as a result of an apparent defect in the steering wheel mechanism. The standard-form purchase order used in the transaction contained an express ninety-day/four-thousand-mile warranty. In addition, the purchase order contained a disclaimer, in fine print, of any and all other express or implied warranties. Thus, Bloomfield Motors and Chrysler Corporation refused to pay for Mrs. Henningsen's injuries, asserting that the sales contract, which warranted that Bloomfield would repair defects at no charge, disclaimed warranty liabilities for injuries suffered. A lawsuit in a New Jersey state court followed, based in part on breach of the implied warranty of merchantability. The trial court held for the Henningsens, and Bloomfield appealed.

ISSUE   Can the Henningsens recover from Bloomfield Motors and Chrysler despite the disclaimer contained in the sales contract?

DECISION   Yes. The Supreme Court of New Jersey affirmed the trial court's judgment.

REASON   The liability of Bloomfield Motors and Chrysler Corporation was based on an implied warranty of merchantability contained in the Uniform Sales Act (the warranty is now included in the UCC). The court stated that the legislature's purpose in implying a warranty of merchantability in the sale of goods was to protect buyers and "not to limit the liability of the seller or manufacturer." In the opinion of the court, "[t]he disclaimer of the implied warranty and exclusion of all obligations except those specifically assumed by the express warranty signify a studied effort to frustrate the protection." Although the Uniform Sales Act allowed parties to modify warranty obligations, "[t]he lawmakers did not authorize the automobile manufacturer to use its grossly disproportionate bargaining power [and the unfair surprise of fine print] to relieve itself from liability and to impose on the ordinary buyer, who in effect has no real freedom of choice, the grave danger of injury to himself and others that attends the sale of such a dangerous instrumentality as a defectively made automobile."

FOR CRITICAL ANALYSIS—Economic Consideration   *Why would a buyer ever accept a deal in which the seller disclaims all warranties?*

Magnuson-Moss Warranty Act

The Magnuson-Moss Warranty Act of 1975[4] was designed to prevent deception in warranties by making them easier to understand. The act is mainly enforced by the Federal Trade Commission (FTC). Additionally, the attorney general or a consumer who has been injured can enforce the act if informal procedures for settling disputes prove to be ineffective. The act modifies UCC warranty rules to some extent when *consumer* transactions are involved. The UCC, however, remains the primary codification of warranty rules for industrial and commercial transactions.

No seller or lessor is *required* to give a written warranty for consumer goods sold under the Magnuson-Moss Act. If a seller or lessor chooses to make an express written warranty, however, and the cost of the consumer goods is more than $10, the warranty must be labeled as "full" or "limited." In addition, if the cost of the goods is more than $15, by FTC regulation, the warrantor must make certain disclosures fully and conspicuously in a single document in "readily understood language." This disclosure states the names and addresses of the warrantor(s), what specifically is warranted, procedures for enforcement of the warranty, any limitations on warranty relief, and that the buyer has legal rights.

FULL WARRANTY Although a *full warranty* may not cover every aspect of the consumer product sold, what it covers ensures some type of consumer satisfaction in case the product is defective. A full warranty requires free repair or replacement of any defective part; if the product cannot be repaired within a reasonable time, the consumer has the choice of either a refund or a replacement without charge. The full warranty frequently does not have a time limit on it. Any limitation on consequential damages must be *conspicuously* stated. Additionally, the warrantor need not perform warranty services if the problem with the product was caused by damage to the product or unreasonable use by the consumer.

LIMITED WARRANTY A *limited warranty* arises when the written warranty fails to meet one of the minimum requirements of a full warranty. The fact that only a limited warranty is being given must be conspicuously designated. If it is only a time limitation that distinguishes a limited warranty from a full warranty, the Magnuson-Moss Warranty Act allows the warrantor to identify the warranty as a full warranty by such language as "full twelve-month warranty."

IMPLIED WARRANTIES Implied warranties are not covered under the Magnuson-Moss Warranty Act; they continue to be created according to UCC provisions. When an express warranty is made, the Magnuson-Moss Warranty Act prevents disclaimers or modifications of the implied warranties of merchantability and fitness for a particular purpose. A warrantor can impose a time limit on the duration of an implied warranty, but it has to correspond to the duration of the express warranty.[5]

▌Lemon Laws

Some purchasers of defective automobiles—called "lemons"—found that the remedies provided by the UCC, after limitations had been imposed by the seller, were inadequate. In response to the frustrations of these buyers, the majority of states have enacted *lemon laws*. Basically, lemon laws provide that if an automobile under warranty possesses a defect that significantly affects the vehicle's value or use, and the defect has not been remedied by the seller within a specified number of opportunities (usually four), the buyer is entitled to a new car, replacement of defective parts, or return of all consideration paid.

In most states, lemon laws require an aggrieved new-car owner to notify the dealer or manufacturer of the problem and to provide the dealer or manufacturer with an opportunity to solve it. If the problem remains, the owner must then submit complaints to the arbitration program specified in the manufacturer's warranty before taking the case to court. Decisions by arbitration panels are binding on the manufacturer (that is, cannot be appealed by the manufacturer to the courts) but are not usually binding on the purchaser.

Most major automobile companies use their own arbitration panels. Some companies, however,

---

4.　15 U.S.C. Sections 2301–2312.

5.　The time limit on an implied warranty occurring by virtue of the warrantor's express warranty must, of course, be reasonable, conscionable, and set forth in clear and conspicuous language on the face of the warranty.

subscribe to independent arbitration services, such as those provided by the Better Business Bureau. Although arbitration boards must meet state and/or federal standards of impartiality, industry-sponsored arbitration boards have been criticized for not being truly impartial in their decisions. In response to this criticism, some states have established mandatory, government-sponsored arbitration programs for lemon-law disputes.

▋ Product Liability

Manufacturers, sellers, and lessors of goods can be held liable to consumers, users, and bystanders for physical harm or property damage that is caused by the goods. This is called **product liability.** Product liability may be based on the warranty theories just discussed, as well as on the theories of negligence, misrepresentation, and strict liability.

Negligence

Chapter 4 defined *negligence* as the failure to exercise the degree of care that a reasonable, prudent person would have exercised under the circumstances. If a manufacturer fails to exercise "due care" to make a product safe, a person who is injured by the product may sue the manufacturer for negligence.

Due care must be exercised in designing the product, in selecting the materials, in using the appropriate production process, in assembling and testing the product, and in placing adequate warnings on the label informing the user of dangers of which an ordinary person might not be aware. The duty of care also extends to the inspection and testing of any purchased products that are used in the final product sold by the manufacturer.

A product liability action based on negligence does not require privity of contract between the injured plaintiff and the negligent defendant-manufacturer. Section 395 of the *Restatement (Second) of Torts* states as follows:

> A manufacturer who fails to exercise reasonable care in the manufacture of a chattel [movable good] which, unless carefully made, he should recognize as involving an unreasonable risk of causing physical harm to those who lawfully use it for a purpose for which the manufacturer should expect it to be used and to those whom he should expect to be

endangered by its probable use, is subject to liability for physical harm caused to them by its lawful use in a manner and for a purpose for which it is supplied.

In other words, a manufacturer is liable for its failure to exercise due care to any person who sustained an injury proximately caused by a negligently made (defective) product, regardless of whether the injured person is in privity of contract with the negligent defendant-manufacturer or lessor.

Misrepresentation

When a fraudulent misrepresentation has been made to a user or consumer, and that misrepresentation ultimately results in an injury, the basis of liability may be the tort of fraud. Examples are the intentional mislabeling of packaged cosmetics and the intentional concealment of a product's defects.

Strict Liability

Under the doctrine of strict liability (discussed in Chapter 4), people may be liable for the results of their acts regardless of their intentions or their exercise of reasonable care. Under this doctrine, liability does not depend on privity of contract. The injured party does not have to be the buyer or a third party beneficiary, as required under contract warranty theory. Indeed, this type of liability in law is not governed by the provisions of the UCC because it is a tort doctrine, not a principle of contract law.

The *Restatement (Second) of Torts* designates how the doctrine of strict liability should be applied. It is a precise and widely accepted statement of the liabilities of sellers of goods (including manufacturers, processors, assemblers, packagers, bottlers, wholesalers, distributors, retailers, and lessors) and deserves close attention. Section 402A of the *Restatement (Second) of Torts* states as follows:

(1) One who sells any product in a defective condition unreasonably dangerous to the user or consumer or to his property is subject to liability for physical harm thereby caused to the ultimate user or consumer or to his property, if
   (a) the seller is engaged in the business of selling such a product, and
   (b) it is expected to and does reach the user or consumer without substantial change in the condition in which it is sold.

(2) The rule stated in Subsection (1) applies although
  (a) the seller has exercised all possible care in the preparation and sale of his product, and
  (b) the user or consumer has not bought the product from or entered into any contractual relation with the seller.

Strict liability is imposed by law as a matter of public policy. This policy rests on the threefold assumption that (1) consumers should be protected against unsafe products; (2) manufacturers and distributors should not escape liability for faulty products simply because they are not in privity of contract with the ultimate user of those products; and (3) manufacturers, sellers, and lessors of products are in a better position to bear the costs associated with injuries caused by their products—costs that they can ultimately pass on to all consumers in the form of higher prices.

California was the first state to impose strict liability in tort on manufacturers. In the landmark decision that follows, the California Supreme Court sets out the reason for applying tort law rather than contract law to cases in which consumers are injured by defective products.

CASE 16.5

Greenman v. Yuba Power Products, Inc.

Supreme Court of California, 1962.
59 Cal.2d 57,
377 P.2d 897,
27 Cal.Rptr. 697.

FACTS The plaintiff, Greenman, wanted a Shopsmith—a combination power tool that could be used as a saw, drill, and wood lathe—after seeing a Shopsmith demonstrated by a retailer and studying a brochure prepared by the manufacturer. The plaintiff's wife bought and gave him one for Christmas. More than a year later, a piece of wood flew out of the lathe attachment of the Shopsmith while the plaintiff was using it, inflicting serious injuries on him. About ten and a half months later, the plaintiff filed suit in a California state court against both the retailer and the manufacturer for breach of warranties and negligence. The trial court jury found for the plaintiff. The case was ultimately appealed to the Supreme Court of California.

ISSUE Can the manufacturer and retailer be held liable for the plaintiff's injuries?

DECISION Yes. The Supreme Court of California upheld the verdict for the plaintiff.

REASON The plaintiff had successfully proved that the design and construction of the Shopsmith were defective, that statements in the manufacturer's brochure constituted express warranties and were untrue, and that the plaintiff's injuries were caused by the breach of these express warranties. The manufacturer argued that the plaintiff had waited too long to give notice of the breach of warranty, but the court, in imposing strict liability upon the manufacturer, held that it was not necessary for the plaintiff to establish an express warranty or a breach of warranty. The court stated that "a manufacturer is strictly liable in tort when an article he places on the market, knowing that it is to be used without inspection for defects, proves to have a defect that causes injury to a human being." The court stated that the "purpose of such liability is to [e]nsure that the costs of injuries resulting from defective products are borne by the manufacturers * * * rather than by the injured persons who are powerless to protect themselves."

FOR CRITICAL ANALYSIS—Ethical Consideration *What UCC rule did the manufacturer refer to when it argued that the plaintiff had "waited too long" to give notice of the breach of warranty? What ethical doctrine underlies this rule?*

REQUIREMENTS OF STRICT PRODUCT LIABILITY—SUMMARIZED The bases for an action in strict liability as set forth in Section 402A of the *Restatement (Second) of Torts* and as the doctrine is commonly applied can be summarized as a series of six requirements, which are listed here. If these requirements are met, the manufacturer's liability to an injured party may be virtually unlimited.[6]

1. The product must be in a defective condition when the defendant sells it.
2. The defendant must normally be engaged in the business of selling (or otherwise distributing) that product.
3. The product must be unreasonably dangerous to the user or consumer because of its defective condition (in most states).
4. The plaintiff must incur physical harm to self or property by use or consumption of the product.
5. The defective condition must be the proximate cause of the injury or damage.
6. The goods must not have been substantially changed from the time the product was sold to the time the injury was sustained.

Thus, in any action against a manufacturer, seller, or lessor, the plaintiff does not have to show why or in what manner the product became defective. To recover damages, however, the plaintiff must show that the product was so defective as to be unreasonably dangerous; that the product caused the plaintiff's injury; and that at the time the injury was sustained, the condition of the product was essentially the same as when it left the hands of the defendant manufacturer, seller, or lessor.

PRODUCT DEFECT AND STRICT LIABILITY CLAIMS A court may consider a product so defective as to be an **unreasonably dangerous product** if either (1) the product was dangerous beyond the expectation of the ordinary consumer or (2) a less dangerous alternative was economically feasible for the manufacturer, but the manufacturer failed to pro-

duce it. Generally, claims that a product is so defective as to be unreasonably dangerous fall into the three categories discussed here.

Flaw in the Manufacturing Process A plaintiff may allege that a product was unreasonably dangerous because of a flaw in the manufacturing process. As discussed earlier, manufacturers are required to use due care in the manufacture, assembly, and testing of the goods they produce. A manufacturer that fails to exercise proper care in manufacturing a product may be liable in strict liability for harms suffered by users of the product.

Design Defect A product, although perfectly manufactured, may nonetheless be unreasonably dangerous because of a defect in design. Generally, a plaintiff claiming a design defect must show that a safer alternative was available and economically feasible for the manufacturer, but the manufacturer failed to produce it. When determining whether a less dangerous alternative was economically feasible for the manufacturer, courts will consider a number of factors, including the product's social utility and desirability, the availability of—and economic feasibility of producing—a safer alternative, the obviousness of the danger posed by the product, the probability of injury and its likely seriousness, and the possibility of eliminating the danger without appreciably impairing the product's function.

People often cut themselves on knives, but because there is no way to avoid injuries without making the product useless and because the danger is obvious to users, a court normally would not find a knife to be unreasonably dangerous and would not hold a supplier of knives liable. In contrast, a court may consider a snowblower without a safety guard over the opening through which the snow is blown to be in a condition that is unreasonably dangerous, even if the snowblower carries warnings to stay clear of the opening. The danger may be within the users' expectations, but the court will also consider the likelihood of injury and its probable seriousness, as well as the cost of putting a guard over the opening and the guard's effect on the blower's operation.

Some products are safe when used as their manufacturers and distributors intend but not safe when used in other ways. Suppliers are generally required to expect reasonably foreseeable misuses and to design products that are either safe when

6. Some states have enacted what are called *statutes of repose*. Basically, these statutes provide that after a specific statutory period of time from the date of manufacture or sale, a plaintiff is precluded from pursuing a cause of action for injuries or damages sustained from a product, even though the product is defective. The states of Illinois, Indiana, Alabama, Tennessee, Florida, Texas, and Nebraska are illustrative.

misused or marketed with some protective device—for example, a childproof cap. The following case required the court to determine whether a misuse of a product was reasonably foreseeable.

CASE 16.6

Lutz v. National Crane Corp.

Supreme Court of Montana, 1994.
884 P.2d 455.

FACTS   Gerald Lutz and another employee of Montana Ready-Mix were using a crane to retrieve drilling pipe from beneath power lines when the crane cable touched one of the lines. The cable did not have an insulated link and thus conducted electricity from the line to the pipe, electrocuting Lutz. Lutz's widow, Lori Lutz, filed a suit in a Montana state court against the National Crane Corporation, which manufactured the crane, and others, alleging, among other things, that the crane—without an insulated link—was defectively designed and unreasonably dangerous. National Crane argued, among other things, that the employees had been using the crane to sideload and that sideloading was an unreasonable misuse. The court awarded Lori Lutz $815,400, less 20 percent, which it attributed, in part, to Gerald Lutz's unreasonable misuse. Both parties appealed. Lori Lutz sought the full $815,400. She admitted that sideloading was a misuse but claimed that it was reasonably foreseeable.

ISSUE   Was sideloading a reasonably foreseeable misuse of the crane?

DECISION   Yes. The Supreme Court of Montana remanded the case to the lower court with the instruction to reinstate the full award.

REASON   The Supreme Court of Montana explained that "cranes are often operated in close proximity to live electrical lines and that *   *   * sideloading is not an uncommon, albeit improper, practice." The court pointed out that National Crane admitted that its cranes could be misused through sideloading and knew that if sideloading occurred near power lines, the crane cables might contact the lines. The court reasoned that the alleged misuse was thus reasonably foreseeable, making the defense of "unreasonable misuse" unavailable to National Crane.

FOR CRITICAL ANALYSIS—Social Consideration   *Who would bear the consequences if the law did not allow for reasonably foreseeable misuses?*

Inadequate Warning   A plaintiff in a strict liability action may claim that a product is unreasonably dangerous because it lacks adequate warnings or instructions. Manufacturers and other suppliers of products have a duty to warn product users of product-associated risks and dangers, unless the risks and dangers are commonly known. (As will be discussed later in this chapter, an assertion that a danger is commonly known can be used as a defense to product liability.) A pharmaceutical company, for example, must warn of possible side effects of its drugs or of the risks associated with using a certain drug in conjunction with other medications.

Generally, a manufacturer must warn those who purchase its product of the harms that can result from the misuse of the product as well. If a particular misuse of a product is foreseeable, a court normally will hold that the manufacturer had a duty to warn of the dangers associated with such misuse.

MARKET-SHARE LIABILITY   Generally, in all cases involving product liability, a plaintiff must prove that the defective product that caused his or her injury was the product of a specific defendant. In the last decade or so, in cases in which plaintiffs could not prove which of many distributors of a harmful product supplied the particular product that caused the plaintiffs' injuries, courts have dropped this requirement.

This has occurred, for example, in several cases involving DES (diethylstilbestrol), a drug administered in the past to prevent miscarriages. DES's harmful character was not realized until, a generation later, daughters of the women who had taken DES developed health problems, including vaginal carcinoma, that were linked to the drug. Partly because of the passage of time, a plaintiff-daughter often could not prove which pharmaceutical company—out of as many as three hundred—had marketed the DES her mother had ingested. In these cases, some courts applied *market-share liability*, holding that all firms that manufactured and distributed DES during the period in question were liable for the plaintiffs' injuries in proportion to the firms' respective shares of the market.[7]

Market-share liability has also been applied in other situations. In one case, for example, a plaintiff who was a hemophiliac received injections of a blood protein known as antihemophiliac factor (AHF) concentrate. The plaintiff later tested positive for the AIDS (acquired immune deficiency syndrome) virus. Because it was not known which manufacturer was responsible for the particular AHF received by the plaintiff, the court held that all of the manufacturers of AHF could be held liable under a market-share theory of liability.[8] In another case, the New York Court of Appeals (that state's highest court) held that even if a firm can prove that it did not manufacture the particular product that caused injuries to the plaintiff, the firm can be held liable based on the firm's share of the national market.[9]

OTHER APPLICATIONS OF STRICT LIABILITY
Although the drafters of the *Restatement (Second) of Torts*, Section 402A, did not take a position on bystanders, all courts extend the strict liability of manufacturers and other sellers to injured bystanders. For example, in one case, an automobile manufacturer was held liable for injuries caused by the explosion of a car's motor. A cloud of steam that resulted from the explosion caused multiple collisions because other drivers could not see well.[10]

The rule of strict liability also applies to suppliers of component parts. Thus, if General Motors buys brake pads from a subcontractor and puts them in Chevrolets without changing their composition, and those pads are defective, both the supplier of the brake pads and General Motors will be held strictly liable for the damages caused by the defects.

Defenses to Product Liability

There are several defenses that manufacturers, sellers, or lessors can raise to avoid liability for harms caused by their products. We look at some of these defenses here.

ASSUMPTION OF RISK   Assumption of risk can sometimes be used as a defense in a product liability action. To establish such a defense, the defendant must show that (1) the plaintiff knew and appreciated the risk created by the product defect and (2) the plaintiff voluntarily assumed the risk, even though it was unreasonable to do so. (See Chapter 4 for a more detailed discussion of assumption of risk.)

PRODUCT MISUSE   Similar to the defense of voluntary assumption of risk is that of misuse of the product. Here, the injured party *does not know that the product is dangerous for a particular use* (contrast this with assumption of risk), but the use is not the one for which the product was designed. The courts have severely limited this defense, however. Even if the injured party does not know about the inherent danger of using the product in a wrong way, if the misuse is foreseeable, the seller must take measures to guard against it.

COMPARATIVE NEGLIGENCE   Developments in the area of comparative negligence (discussed in Chapter 4) have even affected the doctrine of strict liability—the most extreme theory of product lia-

---

7. See, for example, *Martin v. Abbott Laboratories*, 102 Wash.2d 581, 689 P.2d 368 (1984).

8. *Smith v. Cutter Biological, Inc.*, 72 Haw. 416, 823 P.2d 717 (1991).

9. *Hymowitz v. Eli Lilly and Co.*, 73 N.Y.2d 487, 539 N.E.2d 1069, 541 N.Y.S.2d 941 (1989).

10. *Giberson v. Ford Motor Co.*, 504 S.W.2d 8 (Mo. 1974).

bility. Whereas previously the plaintiff's conduct was not a defense to strict liability, today many jurisdictions consider the negligent or intentional actions of both the plaintiff and the defendant in the apportionment of liability and damages. This means that even if a product was misused by the plaintiff, the plaintiff may nonetheless be able to recover at least some damages for injuries caused by the defendant's defective product.

COMMONLY KNOWN DANGERS The dangers associated with certain products (such as sharp knives and guns) are so commonly known that manufacturers need not warn users of those dangers. If a defendant succeeds in convincing the court that a plaintiff's injury resulted from a *commonly known danger*, the defendant will not be liable.

A classic case on this issue involved a plaintiff who was injured when an elastic exercise rope that she had purchased slipped off her foot and struck her in the eye, causing a detachment of the retina. The plaintiff claimed that the manufacturer should

be liable because it had failed to warn users that the exerciser might slip off a foot in such a manner. The court stated that to hold the manufacturer liable in these circumstances "would go beyond the reasonable dictates of justice in fixing the liabilities of manufacturers." After all, stated the court, "[a]lmost every physical object can be inherently dangerous or potentially dangerous in a sense. . . . A manufacturer cannot manufacture a knife that will not cut or a hammer that will not mash a thumb or a stove that will not burn a finger. The law does not require [manufacturers] to warn of such common dangers."[11]

A related defense is the *knowledgeable user* defense. If a particular danger (such as electrical shock) is or should be commonly known by particular users of the product (such as electricians), the manufacturer of electrical equipment need not warn these users of the danger. The following case illustrates this concept.

---

11. *Jamieson v. Woodward & Lothrop*, 247 F.2d 23, 101 D.C.App. 32 (1957).

CASE 16.7

Travelers Insurance Co. v. Federal Pacific Electric Co.

Supreme Court of New York, Appellate Division, First Department, 1995.
211 A.D.2d 40,
625 N.Y.S.2d 121.

FACTS A water pipe burst, flooding a switchboard at the offices of RCA Global Communications, Inc. This tripped the switchboard circuit breakers. RCA employees assigned to reactivate the switchboard included an electrical technician with twelve years of on-the-job training, a licensed electrician, and an electrical engineer with twenty years of experience who had studied power engineering in college. The employees attempted to switch one of the circuit breakers back on without testing for short circuits, which they later admitted they knew how to do and should have done. The circuit breaker failed to engage but ignited an explosive fire. RCA filed a claim with its insurer, the Travelers Insurance Company. Travelers paid the claim and filed a suit in a New York state court against, among others, the Federal Pacific Electric Company, the supplier of the circuit breakers. Travelers alleged that Federal had been negligent in failing to give RCA adequate warnings and instructions regarding the circuit breakers. The court apportioned 15 percent of the responsibility for the fire to Federal. Federal appealed.

ISSUE Did Federal fail to give RCA adequate warnings and instructions regarding the circuit breakers?

DECISION No. The Supreme Court of New York, Appellate Division, reversed the judgment of the lower court and dismissed the complaint against Federal.

REASON The appellate court explained that "[t]here is 'no necessity to warn a customer already aware—through common knowledge or

(Continued)

Case 16.7—Continued

learning—of a specific hazard.' " The court concluded that, "[g]iven the * * * common knowledge of the minimal accepted practices in the field and the level of expertise, training and experience of the RCA electricians which encompassed the specific situation they faced, the * * * court should have found that there was no necessity on the part of Federal to warn RCA."

FOR CRITICAL ANALYSIS—Technological Consideration *What might have been the result in this case if the training, experience, and expertise of the employees dispatched to check the circuit breakers had been with a different, out-of-date technology?*

OTHER DEFENSES A defendant can also defend against product liability by showing that there is no basis for the plaintiff's claim. For example, suppose that a plaintiff alleges that a seller breached an implied warranty. If the seller can prove that he or she effectively disclaimed all implied warranties, the plaintiff cannot recover. Similarly, in a product liability case based on negligence, a defendant who can show that the plaintiff has not met the requirements (such as causation) for an action in negligence will not be liable. In regard to strict liability, a defendant could claim that the plaintiff failed to meet one of the requirements for an action in strict liability. For example, if the defendant establishes that the goods have been subsequently altered, the defendant will not be held liable.

▌ Terms and Concepts

express warranty 317	implied warranty of	unreasonably dangerous
implied warranty 319	merchantability 319	product 328
implied warranty of fitness for	lien 317	
a particular purpose 320	product liability 326	

▌ Chapter Summary: Warranties and Product Liability

WARRANTIES	
Warranties of Title *(See pages 316–317.)*	The UCC provides for the following warranties of title [UCC 2–312, 2A–211]: 1. *Good title*—A seller warrants that he or she has the right to pass good and rightful title to the goods. 2. *No liens*—A seller warrants that the goods sold are free of any encumbrances (claims, charges, or liabilities—usually called *liens*). A lessor warrants that the lessee will not be disturbed in his or her possession of the goods by the claims of a third party. 3. *No infringements*—A merchant seller warrants that the goods are free from infringement claims (claims that a patent, trademark, or copyright has been infringed) by third parties. Lessors make similar warranties.
Express Warranties *(See pages 317–319.)*	1. *Under the UCC*—An express warranty arises under the UCC when a seller or lessor indicates any of the following [UCC 2–313, 2A–210]: a. An affirmation or promise of fact. b. A description of the goods. c. A sample shown as conforming to the contract goods.

▌Chapter Summary: Warranties and Product Liability—Continued

Express Warranties—Continued	2. *Under the Magnuson-Moss Warranty Act*—Express written warranties covering consumer goods priced at more than $10, *if made*, must be labeled as one of the following: a. Full warranty—Free repair or replacement of defective parts; refund or replacement for goods if they cannot be repaired in a reasonable time. b. Limited warranty—When less than a full warranty is being offered.
Implied Warranty of Merchantability *(See pages 319–320.)*	When a seller or lessor is a merchant who deals in goods of the kind sold or leased, the seller or lessor warrants that the goods sold or leased are properly packaged and labeled, are of proper quality, and are reasonably fit for the ordinary purposes for which such goods are used [UCC 2–314, 2A–212].
Implied Warranty of Fitness for a Particular Purpose *(See pages 320–321.)*	Arises when the buyer's or lessee's purpose or use is expressly or impliedly known by the seller or lessor, and the buyer or lessee purchases or leases the goods in reliance on the seller's or lessor's selection [UCC 2–315, 2A–213].
Other Implied Warranties *(See page 321.)*	Other implied warranties can arise as a result of course of dealing, course of performance, or usage of trade [UCC 2–314(3), 2A–212(3)].
PRODUCT LIABILITY	
Liability Based on Negligence *(See page 326.)*	1. Due care must be used by the manufacturer in designing the product, selecting materials, using the appropriate production process, assembling and testing the product, and placing adequate warnings on the label or product. 2. Privity of contract is not required. A manufacturer is liable for failure to exercise due care to any person who sustains an injury proximately caused by a negligently made (defective) product.
Liability Based on Misrepresentation *(See page 326.)*	Fraudulent misrepresentation of a product may result in product liability based on the tort of fraud.
Strict Liability—Requirements *(See pages 326–328.)*	1. The defendant must sell the product in a defective condition. 2. The defendant must normally be engaged in the business of selling that product. 3. The product must be unreasonably dangerous to the user or consumer because of its defective condition (in most states). A court may consider a product so defective as to be unreasonably dangerous if either (a) the product was dangerous beyond the expectation of the ordinary consumer or (b) a less dangerous alternative was economically feasible for the manufacturer, but the manufacturer failed to produce it. 4. The plaintiff must incur physical harm to self or property by use or consumption of the product. (Courts will also extend strict liability to include injured bystanders.) 5. The defective condition must be the proximate cause of the injury or damage. 6. The goods must not have been substantially changed from the time the product was sold to the time the injury was sustained.
Strict Liability—Product Defect *(See pages 328–329.)*	Claims that a product is so defective as to be unreasonably dangerous generally allege that the product is unreasonably dangerous for one of the following reasons: 1. Because of a flaw in the manufacturing process. 2. Because of a design defect. 3. Because the manufacturer failed to warn adequately of harms associated with the product's use.

(Continued)

▌Chapter Summary: Warranties and Product Liability—Continued

Market-Share Liability (See pages 329–330.)	In cases in which plaintiffs cannot prove which of many distributors of a harmful product supplied the particular product that caused the plaintiffs' injuries, some courts have applied market-share liability. All firms that manufactured and distributed the harmful product during the period in question are then held liable for the plaintiffs' injuries in proportion to the firms' respective shares of the market, as directed by the court.
Other Applications of Strict Liability (See page 330.)	1. Manufacturers and other sellers are liable for harms suffered by injured bystanders due to defective products. 2. Suppliers of component parts are strictly liable for defective parts that, when incorporated into a product, cause injuries to users.
Defenses to Product Liability (See pages 330–332.)	1. *Assumption of risk*—The user or consumer knew of the risk of harm and voluntarily assumed it. 2. *Product misuse*—The user or consumer misused the product in a way unforeseeable by the manufacturer. 3. *Comparative negligence*—Liability may be distributed between plaintiff and defendant under the doctrine of comparative negligence. 4. *Commonly known dangers*— If a defendant succeeds in convincing the court that a plaintiff's injury resulted from a commonly known danger, such as the danger associated with using a sharp knife, the defendant will not be liable. 5. *Other defenses*—A defendant can also defend against a strict liability claim by showing that there is no basis for the plaintiff's claim (that the plaintiff has not met the requirements for an action in negligence or strict liability, for example).

▌For Review

1. What factors determine whether a seller's or lessor's statement constitutes an express warranty or merely "puffing"?

2. What implied warranties arise under the UCC?

3. Can a manufacturer be held liable to *any* person who suffers an injury proximately caused by the manufacturer's negligently made product?

4. What are the elements of a cause of action in strict product liability?

5. What defenses to liability can be raised in a product liability lawsuit?

▌Questions and Case Problems

16–1. Product Liability. Under what contract theory can a seller be held liable to a consumer for physical harm or property damage that is caused by the goods sold? Under what tort theories can the seller be held liable?

16–2. Product Liability. Carmen buys a television set manufactured by AKI Electronics. She is going on vacation, so she takes the set to her mother's house for her mother to use. Because the set is defective, it explodes,

causing considerable damage to her mother's house. Carmen's mother sues AKI for the damages to her house. Discuss the theories under which Carmen's mother can recover from AKI.

16–3. Warranty Disclaimers. Tandy purchased a washing machine from Marshall Appliances. The sales contract included a provision explicitly disclaiming all express or implied warranties, including the implied warranty of merchantability. The disclaimer was printed in the same size and color as the rest of the contract. The machine turned out to be a "lemon" and never functioned properly. Tandy sought a refund of the purchase price, claiming that Marshall had breached the implied warranty of merchantability. Can Tandy recover her money, notwithstanding the warranty disclaimer in the contract? Explain.

16–4. Implied Warranties. Sam, a farmer, needs to place a two-thousand-pound piece of equipment in his barn. The equipment must be lifted thirty feet into a hayloft. Sam goes to Durham Hardware and tells Durham that he needs some heavy-duty rope to be used on his farm. Durham recommends a one-inch-thick nylon rope, and Sam purchases two hundred feet of it. Sam ties the rope around the piece of equipment, puts it through a pulley, and with the aid of a tractor lifts the equipment off the ground. Suddenly the rope breaks. In the crash to the ground, the equipment is extensively damaged. Sam files suit against Durham for breach of the implied warranty of fitness for a particular purpose. Discuss how successful Sam will be with his suit.

16–5. Product Liability. George Nesselrode lost his life in an airplane crash. The plane had been manufactured by Beech Aircraft Corp. and sold to Executive Beechcraft, Inc. Shortly before the crash occurred, Executive Beechcraft had conducted a routine inspection of the plane and found that some of the parts needed to be replaced. The new parts were supplied by Beech Aircraft but installed by Executive Beechcraft. These particular airplane parts could be installed backward, and if they were, the plane would crash. Nesselrode's crash resulted from just such an incorrect installation of the airplane parts. Nesselrode's wife, Jane, and three daughters sued Executive Beechcraft, Beech Aircraft, and Gerald Hultgren, the pilot who had flown the plane, for damages. Beech Aircraft claimed that it was not at fault because it had not installed the parts. Will Beech Aircraft be held liable for Nesselrode's death? Discuss. [*Nesselrode v. Executive Beechcraft, Inc.*, 707 S.W.2d 371 (Mo. 1986)]

16–6. Strict Liability. Embs was buying some groceries at Stamper's Cash Market. Unnoticed by her, a carton of 7-Up was sitting on the floor at the edge of the produce counter about one foot from where she was standing. Several of the 7-Up bottles exploded. Embs's leg was injured severely enough that she had to be taken to the hospital by a managing agent of the store. Embs sued the manufacturer of 7-Up, Pepsi-Cola Bottling Co. of Lexington, Kentucky, Inc., claiming that the manufacturer should be held strictly liable for the harm caused by its products. The trial court dismissed her claim. On appeal, what will the court decide? Discuss fully. [*Embs v. Pepsi-Cola Bottling Co. of Lexington, Kentucky, Inc.*, 528 S.W.2d 703 (Ky.App. 1975)]

16–7. Duty to Warn. William Mackowick, who had worked as an electrician for thirty years, was installing high-voltage capacitors in a switchgear room in a hospital when he noticed that a fellow electrician had removed the cover from an existing capacitor manufactured by Westinghouse Electric Corp. A warning label that Westinghouse had placed inside the cover of the metal box containing the capacitor instructed users to ground the electricity before handling. Nothing was said on the label about the propensity of electricity to arc. (Arcing occurs when electricity grounds itself by "jumping" to a nearby object or instrument.) Mackowick, while warning the other electrician of the danger, pointed his screwdriver toward the capacitor box. The electricity flowing through the fuses arced to the screwdriver and sent a high-voltage electric current through Mackowick's body. As a result, he sustained severe burns and was unable to return to work for three months. Should Westinghouse be held liable because it failed to warn users of arcing—a principle of electricity? Discuss. [*Mackowick v. Westinghouse Electric Corp.*, 575 A.2d 100 (Pa. 1990)]

16–8. Strict Liability. David Jordon, a ten-year-old boy, lost control of his sled, hit a tree, and was injured. The sled was a plastic toboggan-like sled that had been purchased from K-Mart. David's parents brought suit against K-Mart, alleging that the sled was defective and unreasonably dangerous because (1) the sled contained design defects (the molded runners on the sled rendered the sled unsteerable, and the sled lacked any independent steering or braking mechanisms), and (2) there were no warnings of the dangers inherent in the use of the sled. K-Mart moved for summary judgment. Should the court grant K-Mart's motion? Discuss fully. [*Jordon v. K-Mart Corp.*, 416 Pa.Super. 186, 611 A.2d 1328 (1992)]

16–9. Defenses to Product Liability. The Campbell Soup Co. manufactured, sold, and shipped packages of chicken-flavored Campbell's Ramen Noodle Soup to a distributor. The distributor sold and shipped the packages to Associated Grocers. Associated Grocers shipped the packages to Warehouse Foods, a retail grocer. Six weeks after Campbell first shipped the soup to the distributor, Warehouse Foods sold it to Kathy Jo Gates. Gates prepared the soup. Halfway through eating her second bowl, she discovered beetle larvae in the noodles. She filed a product liability suit against Campbell and others. Gates argued, in effect, that the mere presence of the bugs in the soup was sufficient to hold Campbell strictly liable. How might Campbell defend itself? [*Campbell Soup Co. v. Gates*, 319 Ark. 54, 889 S.W.2d 750 (1994)]

16–10. Product Liability. John Whitted bought a Chevrolet Nova from General Motors Corp. (GMC). Six years later, Whitted crashed the Nova into two trees. During the impact, the seat belt broke, and Whitted was thrust against the steering wheel, which broke, and the windshield, which shattered. He suffered fractures in his left arm and cuts to his forehead. Whitted sued GMC and the manufacturer, asserting, among other things, that because the seat belt broke, the defendants were strictly liable for his injuries. What does Whitted have to show in order to prove his case? [*Whitted v. General Motors Corp.*, 58 F.3d 1200 (7th Cir. 1995)]

▌Unit Four—Cumulative Hypothetical Problem

 16–11. *Lesa, who owns a small restaurant on the Oregon coast, orders three new tables and twelve new chairs from Larson's Furniture Plaza, a local furniture store. She gives the store a check for $2,000, the purchase price of the tables and chairs, and Larson, the store's owner, agrees to have the furniture delivered to her restaurant the following week.*

1. Larson only has only one table-and-chair set in stock. When he calls the manufacturer and orders two more sets, however, he learns that the manufacturer has increased the price of the furniture. Larson telephones Lesa and informs her of the price increase. Lesa agrees to pay the additional price for the remaining two sets when they are delivered. After the furniture is delivered, however, Lesa refuses to pay the extra amount. She claims that her oral agreement to pay the extra cost is not enforceable because the modification of her contract with Larson was not supported by any new consideration. Is Lesa correct? Why or why not?

2. The manufacturer shipped the furniture to Larson via truck, F.O.B. Portland, from its warehouse located in Portland, Oregon. If the manufacturer and Larson do not specify when risk of loss will pass from the seller to the buyer, when will risk pass? Explain.

3. Suppose that when Lesa receives the furniture, she notices a large crack in the top of one of the tables. She tells Larson about the problem and asks him to replace the cracked table with a new, undamaged one. Larson refuses to do so. What remedies might Lesa pursue in this situation?

4. One day, Jane, an elderly diner, was sitting at one of the new tables in Lesa's restaurant. The table leg suddenly buckled under, causing the table to fall on Jane and injure her hip. In spite of several hip operations, Jane was never able to walk normally again. Under what theories discussed in Chapter 17 might Jane be able to recover damages from the manufacturer of the table?

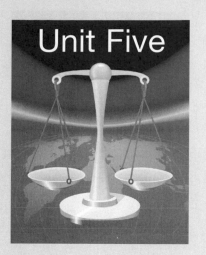

Unit Five

Negotiable Instruments

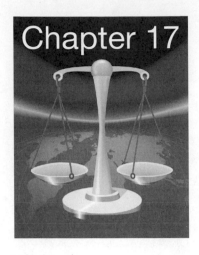

Chapter 17

Negotiability, Transferability, and Liability

CHAPTER OBJECTIVES

After reading this chapter, you should be able to:

1. Summarize the requirements that must be met for an instrument to be negotiable.
2. Explain the process of negotiation.
3. Summarize the requirements for HDC status.
4. Explain the liability of parties who sign negotiable instruments.
5. Identify the defenses that can be raised to avoid liability for payment on negotiable instruments.

The vast number of commercial transactions that take place daily in the modern business world would be inconceivable without negotiable instruments. A **negotiable instrument** can be defined as a signed writing that contains an unconditional promise or order to pay an exact sum of money on demand or at an exact future time to a specific person or order, or to bearer. The checks you write to pay for groceries and other items are negotiable instruments.

A negotiable instrument can function in two ways—as a substitute for money or as an extension of credit. For example, when a buyer writes a check to pay for goods, the check serves as a substitute for money. When a buyer gives a seller a promissory note in which the buyer promises to pay the seller the purchase price within sixty days, the seller has essentially extended credit to the buyer for a sixty-day period. For a negotiable instrument to operate *practically* as either a substitute for money or a credit device, or both, it is essential that the instrument be easily transferable without danger of being uncollectible. This is an

essential function of negotiable instruments. Each rule described in the following pages can be examined in light of this function.

▌ Article 3 of the UCC

Negotiable instruments must meet special requirements relating to form and content. These requirements, which are imposed by Article 3 of the Uniform Commercial Code (UCC), will be discussed at length in this chapter. When an instrument is negotiable, its transfer from one person to another is also governed by Article 3. Indeed, UCC 3–104(b) defines *instrument* as a "negotiable instrument." For that reason, whenever the term *instrument* is used in this book, it refers to a negotiable instrument.

In 1990, a revised version of Article 3 was promulgated for adoption by the states. Many of the changes to Article 3 simply clarified old sections; some significantly altered the former UCC Article

3 provisions. As of this writing, most of the states have adopted the revised article. Therefore, references to Article 3 in this chapter and in the following two chapters are to the *revised* Article 3. When the revised Article 3 has made important changes in the law, however, we discuss the previous law in footnotes.

Article 4 of the UCC, which governs bank deposits and collections (discussed in Chapter 18), was also revised in 1990. In part, these changes were necessary to reflect changes in Article 3 that affect Article 4 provisions. The revised Articles 3 and 4 are included in their entirety in Appendix C.

▌ Types of Instruments

The UCC specifies four types of negotiable instruments: *drafts*, *checks*, *promissory notes*, and *certificates of deposit (CDs)*. These instruments are frequently divided into the two classifications that we will discuss in the following subsections: *orders to pay* (drafts and checks) and *promises to pay* (promissory notes and CDs).

Negotiable instruments may also be classified as either demand instruments or time instruments. A *demand instrument* is payable on demand; that is, it is payable immediately after it is issued and

thereafter for a reasonable period of time. (Instruments payable on demand include those payable at sight, or on **presentment,** and those in which no time for payment is stated [UCC 3-108(a)].) All checks are demand instruments, because by definition, they must be payable on demand. A *time instrument* is payable at a future date.

Drafts and Checks (Orders to Pay)

A **draft** (bill of exchange) is an unconditional written order that involves *three parties*. The party creating the draft (the **drawer**) orders another party (the **drawee**) to pay money, usually to a third party (the **payee**). A *time draft* is payable at a definite future time. A *sight draft* (or demand draft) is payable on sight—that is, when it is presented for payment. A draft can be both a time and a sight draft; such a draft is one payable at a stated time after sight.

Exhibit 17–1 shows a typical time draft. The drawee must be obligated to the drawer either by agreement or through a debtor-creditor relationship for the drawee to be obligated to the drawer to honor the order. For example, on November 16, the Bank of Ourtown orders $1,000 worth of office supplies from Stephen Eastman, with payment due January 16. On December 16, Eastman borrows

◆ **Exhibit 17–1**
A Typical Time Draft

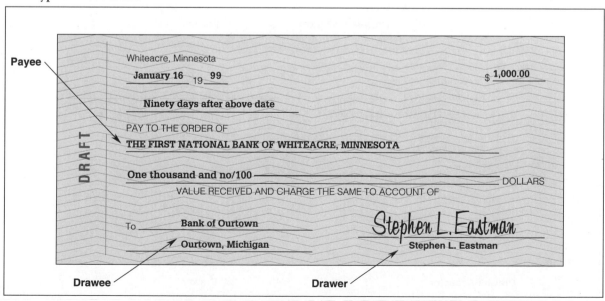

$1,000 from the First National Bank of Whiteacre, with payment also due January 16. The First National Bank of Whiteacre might agree to accept a draft drawn by Eastman on the Bank of Ourtown as payment for the loan.

A trade acceptance is a type of draft that is frequently used in the sale of goods. The seller is both the drawer and the payee on this draft. Essentially, the draft orders the buyer to pay a specified sum of money to the seller, usually at a stated time in the future. For example, Jackson River Fabrics sells fabric priced at $50,000 to Comfort Creations, Inc., each fall on terms requiring payment to be made in ninety days. One year Jackson River needs cash, so it draws a *trade acceptance* (see Exhibit 17–2) that orders Comfort Creations to pay $50,000 to the order of Jackson River Fabrics ninety days hence. Jackson River presents the paper to Comfort Creations. Comfort Creations *accepts* the draft, by signing the face of the draft, and returns it to Jackson River Fabrics. The acceptance by Comfort Creations creates an enforceable obligation to pay the draft when it comes due in ninety days. Jackson River can then sell the trade acceptance in the commercial money market.

The most commonly used type of draft is a check. The writer of the check is the drawer, the bank upon which the check is drawn is the drawee, and the person to whom the check is payable is the payee. As mentioned earlier, checks, because they are payable on demand, are demand instruments.

Checks will be discussed more fully in Chapter 18, but it should be noted here that with certain types of checks, such as *cashier's checks*, the bank is both the drawer and the drawee. The bank customer purchases a cashier's check from the bank—that is, pays the bank the amount of the check—and indicates to whom the check should be made payable. The bank, not the customer, is the drawer of the check (as well as the drawee).

Promissory Notes and Certificates of Deposit (Promises to Pay)

A promissory note is a written promise made by one person (the **maker** of the promise to pay) to another (the payee, or the one to whom the promise is made). A promissory note, which is often referred to simply as a *note*, can be made payable at a definite time or on demand. It can name a specific payee or merely be payable to bearer (bearer instruments are discussed later in this chapter). For example, on April 30, Laurence and Margaret Roberts sign a writing unconditionally promising to pay "to the order of" the First

♦ Exhibit 17–2
A Typical Trade Acceptance

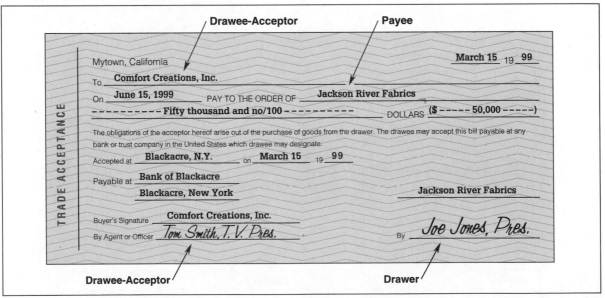

♦ Exhibit 17–3
A Typical Promissory Note

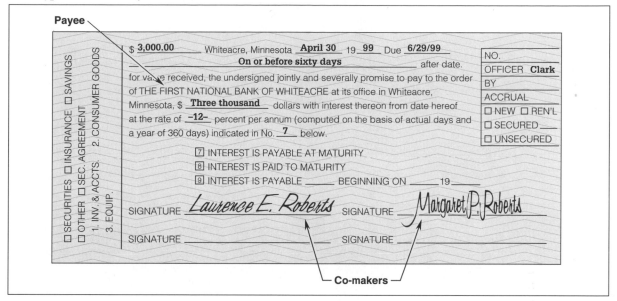

National Bank of Whiteacre $3,000 (with 12 percent interest) on or before June 29. This writing is a promissory note. A typical promissory note is shown in Exhibit 17–3.

Notes are used in a variety of credit transactions and often carry the name of the transaction involved. For example, a note that is secured by personal property, such as an automobile, is called a *collateral note*, because the property pledged as security for the satisfaction of the debt is called *collateral* (see Chapter 19). A note payable in installments, such as for payment for an entertainment center over a twelve-month period, is called an *installment note*.

A **certificate of deposit (CD)** is a type of note. A CD is issued when a party deposits money with a bank, and the bank promises to repay the money, with interest, on a certain date [UCC 3–104(j)]. The bank is the maker of the note, and the depositor is the payee. For example, on February 15, Sara Levin deposits $5,000 with the First National Bank of Whiteacre. The bank promises to repay the $5,000, plus 7½ percent interest, on August 15.

Certificates of deposit in small denominations (for amounts up to $100,000) are often sold by savings and loan associations, savings banks, and commercial banks. Certificates of deposit for amounts over $100,000 are called large (or jumbo) CDs. Exhibit 17–4 shows a typical small CD.

Requirements for Negotiability

For an instrument to be negotiable, it must meet the following requirements:

1. Be in writing.
2. Be signed by the maker or the drawer.
3. Be an unconditional promise or order to pay.
4. State a fixed amount of money.
5. Be payable on demand or at a definite time.
6. Be payable to order or to bearer, unless it is a check.

The UCC grants extreme latitude in regard to what constitutes a signature. UCC 1–201(39) provides that a **signature** may include "any symbol executed or adopted by a party with present intention to authenticate a writing." UCC 3–401(b) expands on this by stating that a "signature may be made (i) manually or by means of a device or machine, and (ii) by the use of any name, including a trade or assumed name, or by a word, mark, or symbol executed or adopted by a person with present intention to authenticate a writing." Thus, initials, an X, or a thumbprint will suffice as a signature. A trade name or an assumed name is also sufficient. Signatures that are placed onto instruments by means of rubber stamps are permitted and frequently used in the business world.

♦ **Exhibit 17–4**
  A Typical Small CD

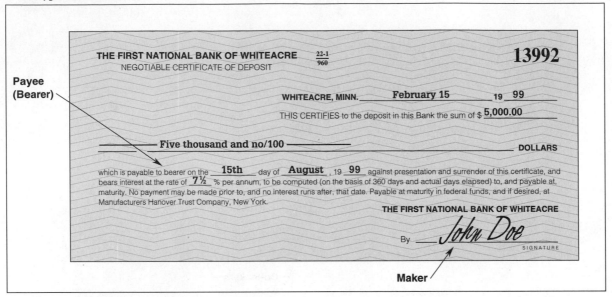

For an instrument to be negotiable, it must contain an express order or promise to pay. A mere acknowledgment of the debt, which might logically *imply* a promise, is not sufficient under the UCC, because the promise must be an *affirmative* (express) undertaking [UCC 3–103(a)(9)]. For example, the traditional I.O.U. is only an acknowledgment of indebtedness. Although the I.O.U. might logically *imply* a promise, it is not a negotiable instrument, because it does not contain an express promise to repay the debt. If such words as "to be paid on demand" or "due on demand" are added to the I.O.U., however, the need for an express promise is satisfied.

A promise or order is conditional (and *not* negotiable) if it states (1) an express condition to payment, (2) that the promise or order is subject to or governed by another writing, or (3) that the rights or obligations with respect to the promise or order are stated in another writing. A reference to another writing, however, does not of itself make the promise or order conditional [UCC 3–106(a)]. For example, the words "As per contract" or "This debt arises from the sale of goods X and Y" do not render an instrument nonnegotiable.

The term *fixed amount* means an amount that is ascertainable from the face of the instrument. A demand note payable with 12 percent interest meets the requirement of a fixed amount because its amount can be determined at the time it is payable [UCC 3–104(a)].[1] The rate of interest also may be determined with reference to information that is not contained in the instrument but that is readily ascertainable by reference to a formula or a source described in the instrument [UCC 3–112(b)].[2] For example, when an instrument is payable at the *legal rate of interest* (a rate of interest fixed by statute), the instrument is negotiable. Mortgage notes tied to a variable rate of interest (a rate that fluctuates as a result of market conditions) can also be negotiable. The requirement that to be negotiable a writing must contain a promise or order to pay a fixed amount applies only to the principal [UCC 3–104].

An **order instrument** is an instrument that is payable (1) "to the order of an identified person" or (2) "to an identified person or order" [UCC 3–109(b)]. An identified person is the person "to whom the instrument is initially payable" as determined by the intent of the maker or drawer [UCC 3–110(a)]. The identified person, in turn, may transfer the instrument to whomever he or she wishes. Thus, the maker or drawer is agreeing to

---

1. Under Section 3–104(1)(b) of the unrevised Article 3, the amount to be paid was called a *sum certain*.

2. This was not possible under the unrevised Article 3, which required that an amount or rate of interest could be determined only from the instrument without reference to any outside source [UCC 3–106].

pay either the person specified on the instrument or whomever that person might designate. In this way, the instrument retains its transferability. Suppose an instrument states, "Payable to the order of Rocky Reed" or "Pay to Rocky Reed or order." Clearly, the maker or drawer has indicated that a payment will be made to Reed or to whomever Reed designates. The instrument is negotiable.

A **bearer instrument** is an instrument that does not designate a specific payee [UCC 3–109(a)]. The term **bearer** refers to a person in the possession of an instrument that is payable to bearer or indorsed in blank (with a signature only, as will be discussed shortly) [UCC 1–201(5), 3–109(a), 3–109(c)]. This means that the maker or drawer agrees to pay anyone who presents the instrument for payment.

∎ Transfer of Instruments

Once issued, a negotiable instrument can be transferred by *assignment* or by *negotiation*.

Transfer by Assignment

Recall from Chapter 11 that an assignment is a transfer of rights under a contract. Under general contract principles, a transfer by assignment to an assignee gives the assignee only those rights that the assignor possessed. Any defenses that can be raised against an assignor can normally be raised against the assignee. This same principle applies when an instrument, such as a promissory note, is transferred by assignment. The transferee is then an *assignee* rather than a *holder*. Sometimes, a transfer fails to qualify as a negotiation because it fails to meet one or more of the requirements of a negotiable instrument, discussed above. When this occurs, the transfer becomes an assignment.

Transfer by Negotiation

Negotiation is the transfer of an instrument in such form that the transferee (the person to whom the instrument is transferred) becomes a holder [UCC 3–201(a)]. A **holder** is any person in the possession of an instrument drawn, issued, or indorsed to him or her, to his or her order, to bearer, or in blank [see UCC 1–201(20)]. (The terms *indorse* and *in*

blank are explained below.) Under UCC principles, a transfer by negotiation creates a holder who, at the very least, receives the rights of the previous possessor [UCC 3–203(b)]. Unlike an assignment, a transfer by negotiation can make it possible for a holder to receive *more* rights in the instrument than the prior possessor had [UCC 3–202(b), 3–305, 3–306]. A holder who receives greater rights is known as a *holder in due course*, a concept we discuss later in this chapter.

There are two methods of negotiating an instrument so that the receiver becomes a holder. The method used depends on whether the instrument is order paper or bearer paper.

NEGOTIATING ORDER INSTRUMENTS An order instrument contains the name of a payee capable of indorsing, as in "Pay to the order of Lloyd Sorenson." If the instrument is an order instrument, it is negotiated by delivery with any necessary indorsements. An **indorsement** is a signature placed on an instrument, such as on the back of a check, for the purpose of transferring one's ownership rights in the instrument. An *indorsement in blank* specifies no particular indorsee and can consist of a mere signature. For example, National Express Corporation issues a payroll check "to the order of Lloyd Sorenson." Sorenson takes the check to the supermarket, signs his name on the back (an indorsement), gives it to the cashier (a delivery), and receives cash. Sorenson has *negotiated* the check to the supermarket [UCC 3–201(b)]. Types of indorsements and their consequences are listed in Exhibit 17–5.

NEGOTIATING BEARER INSTRUMENTS If an instrument is payable to bearer, it is negotiated by delivery—that is, by transfer into another person's possession. Indorsement is not necessary [UCC 3–201(b)]. The use of bearer instruments thus involves more risk through loss or theft than the use of order instruments.

Assume that Richard Kraychek writes a check "payable to cash" and hands it to Jessie Arnold (a delivery). Kraychek has issued the check (a bearer instrument) to Arnold. Arnold places the check in her wallet, which is subsequently stolen. The thief has possession of the check. At this point, negotiation has not occurred, because delivery must be *voluntary* on the part of the transferor. If the thief "delivers" the check to an innocent third person, however, negotiation will be complete. All rights to the check will be passed *absolutely* to that third

♦ Exhibit 17–5
Types of Indorsements and Their Consequences

WORDS CONSTITUTING THE INDORSEMENT	TYPE OF INDORSEMENT	INDORSER'S SIGNATURE LIABILITY[a]
"Rosemary White"	Blank	Unqualified signature liability on proper presentment and notice of dishonor.[b]
"Pay to Sam Wilson, Rosemary White"	Special	Unqualified signature liability on proper presentment and notice of dishonor.
"Without recourse, Rosemary White"	Qualified (blank for further negotiation)	No signature liability. Transfer warranty liability if breach occurs.[c]
"Pay to Sam Wilson, without recourse, Rosemary White"	Qualified (special for further negotiation)	No signature liability. Transfer warranty liability if breach occurs.
"Pay to Sam Wilson on condition he completes painting my house at 23 Elm Street by 9/1/99, Rosemary White"	Restrictive—conditional (special for further negotiation)	Signature liability only if condition is met. If condition is met, signature liability on proper presentment and notice of dishonor.
"Pay to Sam Wilson only, Rosemary White"	Restrictive—prohibitive (special for further negotiation)	Signature liability only on Sam Wilson receiving payment. If Wilson receives payment, signature liability on proper presentment and notice of dishonor.
"For deposit, Rosemary White"	Restrictive—for deposit (blank for further negotiation)	Signature liability only on White having amount deposited in her account. If deposit is made, signature liability on proper presentment and notice of dishonor.
"Pay to Ann South in trust for John North, Rosemary White"	Restrictive—trust (special for further negotiation)	Signature liability only on payment to Ann South for John North's benefit. If restriction is met, signature liability on proper presentment and notice of dishonor

a. *Signature liability* refers to the liability of a party who signs an instrument. The basic questions include whether there is any liability and, if so, whether it is unqualified or restricted.
b.   When an instrument is dishonored—that is, when, for example, a drawer's bank refuses to cash the drawer's check on proper presentment—an indorser of the check may be liable on it if he or she is given proper *notice of dishonor*.
c.   The transferor of an instrument makes certain warranties to the transferee and subsequent holders, and thus, even if the transferor's signature does not render him or her liable on the instrument, he or she may be liable for breach of a transfer warranty. Transfer warranties are discussed later in this chapter.

person, and Arnold will lose all right to recover the proceeds of the check from him or her [UCC 3–306]. Of course, Arnold can recover the money from the thief if the thief can be found.

▌Holder in Due Course (HDC)

An ordinary holder obtains only those rights that the transferor had in the instrument. In this

respect, a holder has the same status as an assignee (see Chapter 11). Like an assignee, a holder normally is subject to the same defenses that could be asserted against the transferor.

In contrast, a **holder in due course (HDC)** is a holder who, by meeting certain acquisition requirements (to be discussed shortly), takes the instrument *free* of most of the defenses and claims that could be asserted against the transferor. Stated another way, an HDC can normally acquire a higher level of immunity than can an ordinary holder in regard to defenses against payment on the instrument or ownership claims to the instrument by other parties.

The basic requirements for attaining HDC status are set forth in UCC 3–302. A holder of a negotiable instrument is an HDC if he or she takes the instrument (1) for value; (2) in good faith; and (3) without notice that it is overdue, that it has been dishonored, that any person has a defense against it or a claim to it, or that the instrument contains unauthorized signatures, alterations, or is so irregular or incomplete as to call into question its authenticity. We now examine each of these requirements.

Taking for Value

An HDC must have given *value* for the instrument [UCC 3–302(a)(2)(i)]. A person who receives an instrument as a gift or who inherits it has not met the requirement of value. In these situations, the person normally becomes an ordinary holder and does not possess the rights of an HDC.

The concept of *value* in the law of negotiable instruments is not the same as the concept of *consideration* in the law of contracts. A promise to give value in the future is clearly sufficient consideration to support a contract [UCC 1–201(44)]. A promise to give value in the future, however, normally does not constitute value sufficient to make one an HDC. A holder takes an instrument for value only to the extent that the promise has been performed [UCC 3–303(a)(1)]. Therefore, if the holder plans to pay for the instrument later or plans to perform the required services at some future date, the holder has not yet given value. In that situation, the holder is not yet an HDC.

Under UCC 3–303(a), a holder can take an instrument for value in one of five ways:

1. By performing the promise for which the instrument was issued or transferred.
2. By acquiring a security interest or other lien in the instrument, excluding a lien obtained by a judicial proceeding. (Security interests and liens are discussed in Chapters 19 and 20.)
3. By taking an instrument in payment of (or as security for) an antecedent debt.
4. By giving a negotiable instrument as payment.
5. By giving an irrevocable commitment as payment.

Taking in Good Faith

The second requirement for HDC status is that the holder take the instrument in *good faith* [UCC 3–302(a)(2)(ii)]. This means that the holder must have acted honestly in the process of acquiring the instrument. Article 3 defines *good faith* as "honesty in fact and the observance of reasonable commercial standards of fair dealing." The good faith requirement applies only to the *holder*. It is immaterial whether the transferor acted in good faith. Thus, even a person who in good faith takes a negotiable instrument from a thief may become an HDC.

Because of the good faith requirement, one must ask whether the purchaser, when acquiring the instrument, honestly believed that the instrument was not defective. If a person purchases a $10,000 note for $300 from a stranger on a street corner, the issue of good faith can be raised on the grounds of both the suspicious circumstances and the grossly inadequate consideration (value). The UCC does not provide clear guidelines to determine good faith, so each situation must be examined separately. In the following case, the court considered whether a casino fulfilled the good faith requirement to qualify as an HDC.

CASE 17.1

Adamar of New Jersey, Inc. v. Chase Lincoln First Bank, N.A.[a]

Supreme Court of New York, Appellate Division, Fourth Department, 1994. 615 N.Y.S.2d 550.

FACTS Joseph Thomas stole two signed cashier's checks from a loan officer's desk at Chase Lincoln First Bank, N.A. Thomas wrote $200,000 as the amount of one check and $300,000 as the amount of the other, and made them payable to the order of his brother-in-law. Posing as his brother-in-law, Thomas presented the checks to the Tropicana Casino. A casino employee who contacted Chase was told that the $200,000 check was "good," that there were adequate

a.   The initials *N.A.* stand for National Association.

(Continued)

Case 17.1—Continued

funds to cover it, and that there was no stop-payment order on the $300,000 check. Thomas gambled away most of the money before Chase stopped payment on the checks. The owner of the Tropicana, Adamar of New Jersey, Inc., filed a suit in a New York state court against the bank to recover the $500,000. When the court denied Adamar's motion for summary judgment, Adamar appealed.

ISSUE   Had Adamar taken the checks in good faith, as required for HDC status?

DECISION   Yes. The Supreme Court of New York, Appellate Division, held that the casino was entitled to payment.

REASON   The court framed the issue as follows: Did the casino have "knowledge of some fact which would prevent a commercially honest individual from taking up the instruments"? The court pointed out that the casino did not violate either state gaming regulations or its own internal procedures in verifying Thomas's identity and the validity of the checks. The court concluded that the Chase employee's statement, in response to the casino's inquiries, that the $200,000 check was "good," with adequate funds to cover it, satisfied a relevant state regulation. The regulation required that "[p]rior to acceptance of any cash equivalent from a patron, the general cashier shall determine the validity of such cash equivalent by performing the necessary verification for each type of cash equivalent." Besides, the court added, "the Casino was expressly informed that there was no stop payment on the $300,000 check."

FOR CRITICAL ANALYSIS—Ethical Consideration   *Why should good faith be a requirement to attain HDC status?*

Taking without Notice

The final requirement for HDC status involves *notice* [UCC 3–302]. A person will not be afforded HDC protection if he or she acquires an instrument and is *on notice* (knows or has reason to know) that it is defective in any one of the following ways [UCC 3–302(a)]:

1.   It is overdue.
2.   It has been dishonored.
3.   There is an uncured (uncorrected) default with respect to another instrument issued as part of the same series.
4.   The instrument contains an unauthorized signature or has been altered.
5.   There is a defense against the instrument or a claim to the instrument.
6.   The instrument is so irregular or incomplete as to call into question the instrument's authenticity.

WHAT CONSTITUTES NOTICE?   Notice of a defective instrument is given whenever the holder (1) has actual knowledge of the defect; (2) has received a notice of the defect (such as a bank's receipt of a letter listing the serial numbers of stolen bearer instruments); or (3) has reason to know that a defect exists, given all the facts and circumstances known at the time in question [UCC 1–201(25)]. The holder must also have received the notice "at a time and in a manner that gives a reasonable opportunity to act on it" [UCC 3–302(f)]. A purchaser's knowledge of certain facts, such as insolvency proceedings against the maker or drawer of the instrument, does not constitute notice that the instrument is defective [UCC 3–302(b)].

OVERDUE INSTRUMENTS   What constitutes notice that an instrument is overdue depends on whether it is a demand instrument (payable on demand) or a time instrument (payable at a definite time).

A purchaser has notice that a *demand instrument* is overdue if he or she either takes the instrument knowing that demand has been made or takes the instrument an unreasonable length of time after its issue. A "reasonable time" for the taking of a check is ninety days, but for other demand instruments, what will be considered a reasonable time depends on the circumstances [UCC 3–304(a)].[3]

A holder of a *time instrument* who takes the instrument at any time after its expressed due date is on notice that it is overdue [UCC 3–304(b)(2)]. Nonpayment by the due date should indicate to any purchaser that the instrument may be defective. Thus, a promissory note due on May 15 must be acquired before midnight on May 15. If it is purchased on May 16, the purchaser will be an ordinary holder, not an HDC.

Sometimes, an instrument reads, "Payable in thirty days." A promissory note dated December 1 that is payable in thirty days is due by midnight on December 31. If the payment date falls on a Sunday or holiday, the instrument is payable on the next business day. If a debt is to be paid in installments or through a series of notes, the maker's default on any installment of prinicpal (not interest) or on any one note of the series will constitute notice to the purchaser that the instrument is overdue [UCC 3–304(b)(1)].

▌ Holder through an HDC

A person who does not qualify as an HDC but who derives his or her title through an HDC can acquire the rights and privileges of an HDC. According to UCC 3–203(b),

> Transfer of an instrument, whether or not the transfer is a negotiation, vests in the transferee any right of the transferor to enforce the instrument, including any right as a holder in due course, but the transferee cannot acquire rights of a holder in due course by a transfer, directly or indirectly, from a holder in due course if the transferee engaged in fraud or illegality affecting the instrument.

Under this rule, which is sometimes called the **shelter principle,** anyone—no matter how far removed from an HDC—who can trace his or her title ultimately back to an HDC has the rights of an HDC.

There are some limitations on the shelter principle, however. Certain persons who formerly held instruments cannot improve their positions by later reacquiring the instruments from HDCs [UCC 3–203(b)]. Thus, if a holder was a party to fraud or illegality affecting the instrument or if, as a prior holder, he or she had notice of a claim or defense against an instrument, that holder is not allowed to improve his or her status by repurchasing from a later HDC.

▌ Signature Liability

The key to liability on a negotiable instrument is a *signature*. The general rule is as follows: Every party, except a qualified indorser,[4] who signs a negotiable instrument is either primarily or secondarily liable for payment of that instrument when it comes due. The following subsections discuss these two types of liability, as well as the conditions that must be met before liability can arise.

Primary Liability

A person who is primarily liable on a negotiable instrument is absolutely required to pay the instrument—unless, of course, he or she has a valid defense to payment [UCC 3–305]. Only *makers* and *acceptors* of instruments are primarily liable.

The maker of a promissory note promises to pay the note. It is the maker's promise to pay that makes the note a negotiable instrument. The words "I promise to pay" embody the maker's obligation to pay the instrument according to the terms as written at the time of the signing. If the instrument is incomplete when the maker signs it, then the maker's obligation is to pay it to an HDC according to the terms written when it is completed [UCC 3–115, 3–407(a), 3–412].

A drawee that promises to pay an instrument when it is presented later for payment is an **acceptor.** A drawee's acceptance of a draft, which it makes by signing the draft, guarantees that the drawee will pay the draft when it is presented in the future for payment [UCC 3–409(a)]. A drawee that

---

3. Under the unrevised Article 3, a reasonable time for the taking of a domestic check is *presumed* to be thirty days [UCC 3–304(3)(c)].

4. A qualified indorser—one who indorses "without recourse"—undertakes no contractual obligation to pay. A qualified indorser merely assumes warranty liability, which is discussed later in this chapter.

refuses to accept a draft that requires the drawee's acceptance (such as a trade acceptance, discussed earlier in this chapter) has dishonored the instrument. Acceptance of a check is called *certification* (discussed in Chapter 18). Certification is not necessary on checks, and a bank is under no obligation to certify checks. Upon certification, however, the drawee bank occupies the position of an acceptor and is primarily liable on the check to any holder [UCC 3–409(d)].

Secondary Liability

Drawers and indorsers are secondarily liable. Secondary liability on a negotiable instrument is similar to the liability of a guarantor in a simple contract (described in Chapter 11) in the sense that it is *contingent liability*. In other words, a drawer or an indorser will be liable only if the party that is primarily liable on the instrument dishonors it or, in regard to drafts and checks, the drawee fails to pay or to accept the instrument, whichever is required [UCC 3–412, 3–415].

Dishonor of an instrument thus triggers the liability of parties who are secondarily liable on the instrument—that is, the drawer and *unqualified* indorsers. For example, Nina Lee writes a check on her account at Universal Bank payable to the order of Stephen Miller. Universal Bank refuses to pay the check when Miller presents it for payment, thus dishonoring the check. In this situation, Lee will be liable to Miller on the basis of her secondary liability. Drawers are secondarily liable on drafts unless they disclaim their liability by drawing the instruments "without recourse" (unless the draft is a check, in which circumstance a drawer cannot disclaim liability) [UCC 3–414(e)].

Parties that are secondarily liable on a negotiable instrument promise to pay on that instrument only if the following events occur:[5]

1. The instrument is properly and timely presented.
2. The instrument is dishonored.
3. Timely notice of dishonor is given to the secondarily liable party.

_____
5. These requirements are necessary for a secondarily liable party to have signature liability on a negotiable instrument, but they are not necessary for a secondarily liable party to have warranty liability (to be discussed later in the chapter).

PROPER AND TIMELY PRESENTMENT   The UCC requires that presentment by a holder must be made to the proper person, must be made in a proper manner, and must be timely [UCC 3–414(f), 3–415(e), 3–501]. The party to whom the instrument must be presented depends on what type of instrument is involved. A note or certificate of deposit (CD) must be presented to the maker for payment. A draft is presented by the holder to the drawee for acceptance, payment, or both, whichever is required. A check is presented to the drawee for payment [UCC 3–501(a), 3–502(b)].

Presentment can be properly made in any of the following ways, depending on the type of instrument involved [UCC 3–501(b)]:

1. By any commercially reasonable means, including oral, written, or electronic communication (but presentment is not effective until the demand for payment or acceptance is received).
2. Through a clearinghouse procedure used by banks, such as for deposited checks (see Chapter 18).
3. At the place specified in the instrument for acceptance or payment.

One of the most crucial criteria for proper presentment is timeliness [UCC 3–414(f), 3–415(e), 3–501(b)(4)]. Failure to present on time is the most common reason for improper presentment and consequent discharge of unqualified indorsers from secondary liability. The time for proper presentment for different types of instruments is shown in Exhibit 17–6.

DISHONOR   An instrument is dishonored when the required acceptance or payment is refused or cannot be obtained within the prescribed time, or when required presentment is excused (as it would be, for example, if the maker had died) and the instrument is not properly accepted or paid [UCC 3–502(e), 3–504].

PROPER NOTICE   Once an instrument has been dishonored, proper notice must be given to secondary parties for them to be held liable. Notice may be given in any reasonable manner. This includes oral notice, written notice (including notice by fax, E-mail, and the like), and notice written or stamped on the instrument itself. Any necessary notice must be given by a bank before its

◆ **Exhibit 17–6**
Time for Proper Presentment

TYPE OF INSTRUMENT	FOR ACCEPTANCE	FOR PAYMENT
Time	On or before due date.	On due date.
Demand	Within a reasonable time (after date or issue or after secondary party becomes liable on the instrument).	
Check	Not applicable.	Within thirty days of its date, to hold drawer secondarily liable
		Within thirty days of indorsement to hold indorser secondarily lliable.[a]
a. Under the unrevised Article 3, these periods were *presumed* to be thirty days to hold drawer secondarily liable, and seven days to hold indorser secondarily liable.		

midnight deadline (midnight of the next banking day after receipt). Notice by any party other than a bank must be given within thirty days following the day on which the person receives notice of dishonor [UCC 3–503].[6]

Unauthorized Signatures

People normally are not liable to pay on negotiable instruments unless their signatures appear on the instruments. As already stated, the general rule is that an unauthorized signature is wholly inoperative and will not bind the person whose name is forged. Assume, for example, that Parra finds Dolby's checkbook lying on the street, writes out a check to himself, and forges Dolby's signature. If a bank fails to ascertain that Dolby's signature is not genuine (which banks normally have a duty to do) and cashes the check for Parra, the bank will generally be liable to Dolby for the amount. (The liability of banks for paying over forged signatures is discussed further in Chapter 18.) There are two exceptions to this rule:

1. Any unauthorized signature will bind the person whose name is forged if the person whose name is signed ratifies (affirms) it [UCC 3–403(a)]. For example, a signature made by an agent who exceeded the scope of his or her authority can be

ratified by the principal, either expressly, by affirming the validity of the signature, or impliedly, by other conduct, such as keeping any benefits received in the transaction or failing to repudiate the signature. The parties involved need not be principal and agent. For example, a mother may ratify her daughter's forgery of the mother's name so that her daughter will not be prosecuted for forgery.

2. A person may be precluded from denying the effectiveness of an unauthorized signature if the person's negligence led to the forgery. For example, Jonathan signs a check, leaving blank the amount and the name of the payee, and then leaves the check in a public place. Jonathan can be estopped (prevented), on the basis of negligence, from denying liability for payment of the check [UCC 3–115, 3–406, 4–401(d)(2)].

An unauthorized signature operates as the signature of the unauthorized signer in favor of an HDC. A person who forges a check, for example, can be held personally liable for payment by an HDC [UCC 3–403(a)].

Special Rules for Unauthorized Indorsements

Generally, when there is a forged or unauthorized indorsement, the burden of loss falls on the first party to take the instrument with the forged or unauthorized indorsement. If the indorsement was made by an imposter or by a fictitious payee, however, the loss falls on the maker or drawer. We look at these two situations here.

---

6.   Under the unrevised Article 3, notice by a person other than a bank has to be given "before midnight of the third business day after dishonor or receipt of notice of dishonor" [UCC 3–508(2)].

IMPOSTERS   An **imposter** is one who, by use of the mails, telephone, or personal appearance, induces a maker or drawer to issue an instrument in the name of an impersonated payee. If the maker or drawer believes the imposter to be the named payee at the time of issue, the indorsement by the imposter is not treated as unauthorized when the instrument is transferred to an innocent party. This is because the maker or drawer *intended* the imposter to receive the instru-ment. In this situation, under the UCC's *imposter rule*, the imposter's indorsement will be effective—that is, not considered a forgery—insofar as the drawer or maker is concerned [UCC 3–404(a)].

In the following case, a financial adviser pretended to be one of his clients so that he could obtain checks in the client's name and then cash the checks. The court had to decide whether the financial adviser was an imposter or a mere forger.

CASE 17.2

Dominion Bank, N.A. v. Household Bank, F.S.B.[a]

United States District Court, Southern District of Ohio, 1993. 827 F.Supp. 463.

FACTS   Lawrence Pompili was in charge of his firm's employee-benefits plans. Robert Grossman was a financial adviser. Pompili gave Grossman over $80,000 to buy an annuity from the Fidelity Bankers' Life Insurance Company. After buying the annuity, Grossman wrote to Fidelity by mail, using Pompili's name and personal stationery, and asked for a check for $35,000. Later, Grossman followed the same procedure to request a check for $29,037.17. Both times, Fidelity issued checks payable to Pompili and mailed them to Grossman. Grossman forged Pompili's signature on the checks, added his own indorsement, and deposited them into his own account in Household Bank. Household obtained payment for the checks from the Dominion Bank, Fidelity's bank. When the scam was uncovered, Dominion filed a suit in a federal district court against Household. Household filed a motion for summary judgment, arguing that Grossman was an imposter and that under the imposter rule Household was not liable for the amount of the checks.

ISSUE   Was Grossman an imposter?

DECISION   Yes. The court held that Grossman was an imposter. Household was thus not liable for the amount of the checks.

REASON   The court explained that a "distinction exists between impersonation and mere forgery." If a person, through simple forgery, causes a drawer "to issue a check to him in the name of another, his actions do not trigger the application of the [imposter] rule." Instead, said the court, "the forger must have actively impersonated the payee by holding himself out to be that person." The court pointed out that Grossman corresponded with Fidelity in the name of Pompili, using Pompili's stationery. In fact, emphasized the court, throughout the letters were references by Grossman to himself as Pompili. "The record is so replete with such references" that the only conclusion to be drawn is that Grossman assumed the identity of *   *   * Pompili in all of his communications with Fidelity and did not merely forge *   *   * Pompili's signature."

FOR CRITICAL ANALYSIS—Social Consideration   *Why should the drawer of a check suffer the loss under the imposter rule?*

---

a.   *F.S.B.* is an abbreviation of Federal Savings Bank.

FICTITIOUS PAYEES Another situation in which an unauthorized indorsement will be effective is when a person causes an instrument to be issued to a payee who will have *no interest* in the instrument [UCC 3–404(b), 3–405]. In this situation, the payee is referred to as a **fictitious payee.** Situations involving fictitious payees most often arise when (1) a dishonest employee deceives the employer into signing an instrument payable to a party with no right to receive payment on the instrument or (2) a dishonest employee or agent has the authority to issue an instrument on behalf of the employer. Under the UCC's *fictitious payee rule*, the payee's indorsement is not treated as a forgery, and the employer can be held liable on the instrument by an innocent holder.

Assume that Flair Industries, Inc., gives its bookkeeper, Axel Ford, general authority to issue checks in the company name drawn on First State Bank so that Ford can pay employees' wages and other corporate bills. Ford decides to cheat Flair Industries out of $10,000 by issuing a check payable to Erica Nied, an old acquaintance. Neither Flair nor Ford intends Nied to receive any of the money, and Nied is not an employee or creditor of the company. Ford indorses the check in Nied's name, naming himself as indorsee. He then cashes the check at a local bank, which collects payment from the drawee bank, First State Bank.

First State Bank charges the Flair Industries account $10,000. Flair Industries discovers the fraud and demands that the account be recredited.

Who bears the loss? UCC 3–404(b)(2) provides the answer. Neither the local bank that first accepted the check nor First State Bank is liable. Because Ford's indorsement in the name of a payee with no interest in the instrument is "effective," there is no "forgery." Hence, the collecting bank is protected in paying on the check, and the drawee bank is protected in charging Flair's account. It is the employer-drawer, Flair Industries, that bears the loss. Of course, Flair Industries has recourse against Axel Ford, if Ford has not absconded with the money.

Regardless of whether a dishonest employee actually signs the check or merely supplies his or her employer with names of fictitious creditors (or with true names of creditors having fictitious debts), the UCC makes no distinction in result. Assume that Nathan Holtz draws up the payroll list from which employees' salary checks are written. He fraudulently adds the name Sally Slight (a fictitious person) to the payroll, thus causing checks to be issued to her. Again, it is the employer-drawer who bears the loss. In the following case, the court had to determine whether a bank should bear the loss for forged indorsements on checks payable to fictitious payees.

CASE 17.3

Golden Years Nursing Home (No. 2), Inc. v. Gabbard

Court of Appeals of Ohio, Butler County, 1994.
640 N.E.2d 1186.

FACTS Nancy Gabbard was the office manager at Golden Years Nursing Home (No. 2), Inc. She was given a signature stamp to issue checks to the nursing home's employees for up to $100 as advances on their pay. The checks were drawn on Golden Years's account at the First National Bank. Over a seven-year period, Gabbard wrote a number of checks to employees exclusively for the purpose of embezzling the money. She forged the employees' indorsements on the checks, signed her name as a second indorser, and deposited the checks in her personal account at Star Bank. The employees whose names were on the checks never actually requested them. When the scheme was uncovered, Golden Years filed a suit in an Ohio state court against Gabbard, Star Bank, and others to recover the money. Star Bank filed a motion for summary judgment, which the court granted. Golden Years appealed.

ISSUE Did the fictitious payee rule bar Golden Years from recovering the amount of the checks from the bank?

DECISION Yes. The Court of Appeals of Ohio affirmed this part of the lower court's decision.

(Continued)

Case 17.3—Continued

REASON The appellate court pointed out that "[t]he padded-payroll or fictitious-payee defense * * * validates a forged payee's indorsement whenever the drawer or his employee has designated as payee someone who is not really intended to have an interest in the instrument." In that situation, "the instrument will be properly payable out of the drawer/employer's bank account." The court explained that because Gabbard provided her employer with the names of employees "who had not really requested loans for the specific purpose of embezzling money without ever intending that the employees have an interest in the checks, * * * the padded-payroll defense * * * precluded Golden Years, the drawer of the checks, from asserting the forged payee indorsements against Star Bank."

FOR CRITICAL ANALYSIS—Social Consideration *Why should an employer, rather than a bank, have to suffer the loss in a fictitious payee case?*

▌ Warranty Liability

In addition to the signature liability discussed in the preceding pages, transferors make certain implied warranties regarding the instruments that they are negotiating. Liability under these warranties is not subject to the conditions of proper presentment, dishonor, or notice of dishonor. These warranties arise even when a transferor does not indorse the instrument (as in the delivery of a bearer instrument) [UCC 3–416, 3–417]. Warranties fall into two categories: those that arise on the *transfer* of a negotiable instrument and those that arise on *presentment*. Both transfer and presentment warranties attempt to shift liability back to a wrongdoer or to the person who dealt face to face with the wrongdoer and thus was in the best position to prevent the wrongdoing.

Transfer Warranties

The UCC describes five transfer warranties [UCC 3–416]. Any person who transfers an instrument *for consideration* makes the following warranties to all subsequent transferees and holders who take the instrument in good faith (with some exceptions, as will be noted shortly):

1. The transferor is entitled to enforce the instrument.
2. All signatures are authentic and authorized.
3. The instrument has not been altered.
4. The instrument is not subject to a defense or claim of any party that can be asserted against the transferor.[7]
5. The transferor has no knowledge of any insolvency proceedings against the maker, the acceptor, or the drawer of the instrument.

The manner of transfer and the negotiation that is used determine how far and to whom a transfer warranty will run. Transfer by indorsement and delivery of order paper extends warranty liability to any subsequent holder who takes the instrument in good faith. The warranties of a person who transfers without indorsement (by the delivery of a bearer instrument), however, will extend the transferor's warranties only to the immediate transferee [UCC 3–416(a)].

Suppose that Abraham forges Peter's name as a maker of a promissory note. The note is made payable to Abraham. Abraham indorses the note in blank, negotiates it to Carla, and then leaves the country. Carla, without indorsement, delivers the note to Frank. Frank, in turn without indorsement, delivers the note to Ricardo. On Ricardo's presentment of the note to Peter, the forgery is discovered. Ricardo can hold Frank (the immediate transferor) liable for breach of the transfer warranty that all signatures are genuine. Ricardo cannot hold Carla liable, because the transfer warranties made by

---

7. Under the unrevised Article 3, a qualified indorser who indorses an instrument "without recourse" limits this warranty to a warranty that he or she has "no knowledge" of such a defense (rather than that there is no defense). This limitation does not apply under the revised Article 3.

Carla, who negotiated the bearer instrument by delivery only, extend only to Frank, the immediate transferee.

Note that if Abraham had added a special indorsement ("Payable to Carla") instead of a blank indorsement, the instrument would have remained an order instrument. In that situation, to negotiate the instrument to Frank, Carla would have had to indorse the instrument, and her transfer warranties would extend to all subsequent holders, including Ricardo. This example shows the importance of the distinction between a transfer by indorsement and delivery (of an order instrument) and a transfer by delivery only, without indorsement (of a bearer instrument).

Presentment Warranties

Any person who presents an instrument for payment or acceptance makes the following **presentment warranties** to any other person who in good faith pays or accepts the instrument [UCC 3–417(a), 3–417(d)]:

1. The person obtaining payment or acceptance is entitled to enforce the instrument or is authorized to obtain payment or acceptance on behalf of a person who is entitled to enforce the instrument. (This is, in effect, a warranty that there are no missing or unauthorized indorsements.)

2. The instrument has not been altered.

3. The person obtaining payment or acceptance has no knowledge that the signature of the issuer of the instrument is unauthorized.

These warranties are referred to as presentment warranties because they protect the person to whom the instrument is presented. The second and third warranties do not apply in certain situations (to certain persons). It is assumed, for example, that a drawer or a maker will recognize his or her own signature and that a maker or an acceptor will recognize whether an instrument has been materially altered.

▌Defenses to Liability

Persons who would otherwise be liable on negotiable instruments may be able to avoid liability by raising certain defenses. There are two general categories of defenses—*universal defenses* and *personal defenses*.

Universal Defenses

Universal defenses (also called *real defenses*) are valid against *all* holders, including HDCs and holders who take through an HDC. Universal defenses include those described here.

FORGERY Forgery of a maker's or drawer's signature cannot bind the person whose name is used unless that person ratifies (approves or validates) the signature or is precluded from denying it (because the forgery was made possible by the maker's or drawer's negligence, for example) [UCC 3–403(a)]. Thus, when a person forges an instrument, the person whose name is used normally has no liability to pay any holder or any HDC the value of the forged instrument.

FRAUD IN THE EXECUTION If a person is deceived into signing a negotiable instrument, believing that he or she is signing something other than a negotiable instrument (such as a receipt), *fraud in the execution*, or fraud in the inception, is committed against the signer. For example, a salesperson asks a consumer to sign a paper, which the salesperson says is a request for an estimate. In fact, the paper is a promissory note, but the consumer, who is unfamiliar with the English language, does not realize this. In this situation, even if the note is negotiated to an HDC, the consumer has a valid defense against payment [UCC 3–305(a)(1)].

The defense of fraud in the execution cannot be raised, however, if a reasonable inquiry would have revealed the nature and terms of the instrument.[8] Thus, the signer's age, experience, and intelligence are relevant, because they frequently determine whether the signer should have known the nature of the transaction before signing.

MATERIAL ALTERATION An alteration is material if it changes the contract terms between any two parties in any way. Examples of material alterations include completing an incomplete instrument, adding words or numbers to an instrument, or making any other change to an instrument in

---

8. *Burchett v. Allied Concord Financial Corp.*, 74 N.M. 575, 396 P.2d 186 (1964).

an unauthorized manner that affects the obligation of a party to the instrument [UCC 3–407(a)].

Thus, cutting off part of the paper of a negotiable instrument; adding clauses; or making any change in the amount, the date, or the rate of interest—even if the change is only one penny, one day, or 1 percent—is material. It is not a material alteration, however, to correct the maker's address, for example, or to change the figures on a check so that they agree with the written amount (words outweigh figures if there is a conflict between the written amount and the amount given in figures). If the alteration is not material, any holder is entitled to enforce the instrument according to its terms.

Material alteration is a *complete defense* against an ordinary holder. An ordinary holder can recover nothing on an instrument if it has been materially altered [UCC 3–407(b)]. Material alteration, however, may be only a *partial defense* against an HDC. When the holder is an HDC, if an original term, such as the monetary amount payable, has been *altered*, the HDC can enforce the instrument against the maker or drawer according to the original terms but not for the altered amount. If the instrument was originally incomplete and was later completed in an unauthorized manner, however, alteration no longer can be claimed as a defense against an HDC, and the HDC can enforce the instrument as completed [UCC 3–407(b)]. This is because the drawer or maker of the instrument, by issuing an incomplete instrument, will normally be held responsible for the alteration, which could have been avoided by the exercise of greater care. If the alteration is readily apparent, then obviously the holder has notice of some defect or defense and therefore cannot be an HDC [UCC 3–302(a)(1)].

DISCHARGE IN BANKRUPTCY

Discharge in bankruptcy is an absolute defense on any instrument regardless of the status of the holder, because the purpose of bankruptcy is to settle finally all of the insolvent party's debts [UCC 3–305(a)(1)].

MINORITY

Minority, or infancy, is a universal defense only to the extent that state law recognizes it as a defense to a simple contract (see Chapter 9). Because state laws on minority vary, so do determinations of whether minority is a universal defense against an HDC [UCC 3–305(a)(1)(i)].

ILLEGALITY

Certain types of illegality constitute universal defenses. Other types constitute personal defenses—that is, defenses that are effective against ordinary holders but not against HDCs. The difference lies in the state statutes or ordinances that make the transactions illegal. If a statute provides that an illegal transaction is *void*, then the defense is universal—that is, absolute against both an ordinary holder and an HDC. If the law merely makes the instrument *voidable*, then the illegality is still a defense against an ordinary holder but not against an HDC. The courts are sometimes prone to treat the word *void* in a statute as meaning *voidable* to protect an HDC [UCC 3–305(a)(1)(ii)].

MENTAL INCAPACITY

If a person is adjudged mentally incompetent by state proceedings, then any instrument issued by that person thereafter is void. The instrument is *void ab initio* (void from the beginning) and unenforceable by any holder or HDC [UCC 3–305(a)(1)(ii)]. Mental incapacity in these circumstances is thus a universal defense. If a person has not been adjudged mentally incompetent by state proceedings, mental incapacity operates as a defense against an ordinary holder but not against an HDC.

EXTREME DURESS

When a person signs and issues a negotiable instrument under such extreme duress as an immediate threat of force or violence (for example, at gunpoint), the instrument is void and unenforceable by any holder or HDC [UCC 3–305(a)(1)(ii)]. (Ordinary duress is a defense against ordinary holders but not against HDCs.)

Personal Defenses

Personal defenses (sometimes called *limited defenses*), such as those described here, can be used to avoid payment to an ordinary holder of a negotiable instrument, but not an HDC or a holder with the rights of an HDC.

BREACH OF CONTRACT OR BREACH OF WARRANTY

When there is a breach of the underlying contract for which the negotiable instrument was issued, the maker of a note can refuse to pay it, or the drawer of a check can order his or her bank to stop payment on the check. Breach of warranty can

CHAPTER 17: NEGOTIABILITY, TRANSFERABILITY, AND LIABILITY

also be claimed as a defense to liability on the instrument.

For example, Rhodes purchases several sets of imported china from Livingston. The china is to be delivered in four weeks. Rhodes gives Livingston a promissory note for $2,000, which is the price of the china. The china arrives, but many of the pieces are broken, and several others are chipped or cracked. Rhodes refuses to pay the note on the basis of breach of contract and breach of warranty. (Under sales law, a seller impliedly promises that the goods are at least merchantable—see Chapter 16.) The payee-seller cannot enforce payment on the note because of the breach of contract and breach of warranty. If the payee-seller has negotiated the note to a third party, however, and the third party is an HDC, the maker-buyer will not be able to use breach of contract or warranty as a defense against liability on the note.

LACK OR FAILURE OF CONSIDERATION

The absence of consideration (value) may be a successful defense in some instances [UCC 3–303(b), 3–305(a)(2)]. For example, Tara gives Clem, as a gift, a note that states "I promise to pay you $100,000," and Clem accepts the note. There is no consideration for Tara's promise, and a court will not enforce the promise.

FRAUD IN THE INDUCEMENT (ORDINARY FRAUD)

A person who issues a negotiable instrument based on false statements by the other party will be able to avoid payment on that instrument, unless the holder is an HDC. Suppose that Jerry agrees to purchase Howard's used tractor for $24,500. Howard, knowing his statements to be false, tells Jerry that the tractor is in good working order and that it has been used for only one harvest. In addition, he tells Jerry that he owns the tractor free and clear of all claims. Jerry pays Howard $4,500 in cash and issues a negotiable promissory note for the balance. As it turns out, Howard still owes the original seller $10,000 on the purchase of the tractor. In addition, the tractor is three years old and has been used in three harvests. Jerry can refuse to pay the note if it is held by an ordinary holder. If Howard has negotiated the note to an HDC, however, Jerry must pay the HDC. Of course, Jerry can then sue Howard to recover the money.

ILLEGALITY

As mentioned, if a statute provides that an illegal transaction is void, a universal defense exists. If, however, the statute provides that an illegal transaction is voidable, the defense is personal. For example, a state may make gambling contracts illegal and void but be silent on payments of gambling debts. Thus, the payment of a gambling debt becomes voidable and is a personal defense.

MENTAL INCAPACITY

As mentioned, if a maker or drawer has been declared by a court to be mentally incompetent, any instrument issued by the maker or drawer is void. Hence, mental incapacity can serve as a universal defense [UCC 3–305(a)(1)(ii)]. If a maker or drawer issues a negotiable instrument while mentally incompetent but before a formal court hearing has declared him or her to be so, however, the instrument is voidable. In this situation, mental incapacity can serve only as a personal defense.

OTHER PERSONAL DEFENSES

Other personal defenses can be used to avoid payment to an ordinary holder of a negotiable instrument, including the following:

1. Discharge by payment or cancellation [UCC 3–601(b), 3–602(a), 3–603, 3–604].
2. Unauthorized completion of an incomplete instrument [UCC 3–115, 3–302, 3–407, 4–401(d)(2)].
3. Nondelivery of the instrument [UCC 1–201(14), 3–105(b), 3–305(a)(2)].
4. Ordinary duress or undue influence rendering the contract voidable [UCC 3–305(a)(1)(ii)].

Discharge from Liability

Discharge from liability on an instrument can occur in several ways. The liability of all parties to an instrument is discharged when the party primarily liable on it pays to a holder the amount due in full [UCC 3–602, 3–603]. Payment by any other party discharges only the liability of that party and subsequent parties.

Intentional cancellation of an instrument discharges the liability of all parties [UCC 3–604]. Intentionally writing "Paid" across the face of an instrument cancels it. Intentionally tearing up an instrument cancels it. If a holder intentionally crosses out a party's signature, that party's liability and the liability of subsequent indorsers who have already indorsed the instrument are discharged. Materially altering an instrument may discharge the liability of any party affected by the alteration, as previously discussed [UCC 3–407(b)]. (An HDC may be able to enforce a materially altered instrument against its maker or drawer according to the instrument's original terms, however.)

Discharge of liability can also occur when a party's right of recourse is impaired [UCC 3–605].

A right of recourse is a right to seek reimbursement. Ordinarily, when a holder collects the amount of an instrument from an indorser, the indorser has a right of recourse against prior indorsers, the maker or drawer, and accommodation parties. If the holder has adversely affected the indorser's right to seek reimbursement from these other parties, however, the indorser is not liable on the instrument. This occurs when, for example, the holder releases or agrees not to sue a party against whom the indorser has a right of recourse.

▌Terms and Concepts

acceptor 347
bearer 343
bearer instrument 343
certificate of deposit (CD) 341
check 340
draft 339
drawee 339
drawer 339
fictitious payee 351

holder 343
holder in due course 344
imposter 350
indorsement 343
maker 340
negotiable instrument 338
negotiation 343
order instrument 342
payee 339
personal defense 354

presentment 339
presentment warranties 353
promissory note 340
shelter principle 347
signature 341
trade acceptance 340
transfer warranties 352
universal defense 353

▌Chapter Summary: Negotiability, Transferability, and Liability

Types of Instruments (*See pages 339–341.*)	The UCC specifies four types of negotiable instruments: drafts, checks, promissory notes, and certificates of deposit (CDs). These instruments fall into two basic classifications: 1. *Demand instruments versus time instruments*—A demand instrument is payable on demand (when the holder presents it to the maker or drawer). A time instrument is payable at a future date. 2. *Orders to pay versus promises to pay*—Checks and drafts are *orders* to pay. Promissory notes and certificates of deposit (CDs) are *promises* to pay.
Requirements for Negotiability (*See pages 341–343.*)	1. Must be in writing. 2. Must be signed by the maker or drawer. 3. Must be an unconditional promise or order to pay. 4. Must state a fixed amount of money. 5. Must be payable on demand or at a definite time. 6. Must be payable to order or bearer.
Transfer of Instruments (*See pages 343–344.*)	1. *Transfer by assignment*— A transfer by assignment to an assignee gives the assignee only those rights that the assignor possessed. Any defenses that can be raised against an assignor can normally be raised against the assignee. 2. *Transfer by negotiation*—An order instrument is negotiated by indorsement and delivery; a bearer instrument is negotiated by delivery only.

▌Chapter Summary: Negotiability, Transferability, and Liability—Continued

Holder versus Holder in Due Course (HDC) (*See page 344.*)	1. *Holder*—A person in the possession of an instrument drawn, issued, or indorsed to him or her, to his or her order, or to bearer or in blank. A holder obtains only those rights that the transferor had in the instrument [UCC 1–201(20)]. 2. *Holder in due course (HDC)*—A holder who, by meeting certain acquisition requirements (summarized next), takes the instrument free of most defenses and claims to which the transferor was subject.

Requirements for HDC Status (*See pages 344–347.*)	To be an HDC, a holder must take the instrument:
	
	 1. *For value*—A holder can take an instrument for value in one of five ways [UCC 3–303]:
	   a. By performing the promise for which the instrument was issued or transferred.
	   b. By acquiring a security interest or other lien in the instrument, excluding a lien obtained by a judicial proceeding.
	   c. By taking an instrument in payment of (or as security for) an antecedent debt.
	   d. By giving a negotiable instrument as payment.
	   e. By giving an irrevocable commitment as payment.
	
	 2. *In good faith*—Good faith is defined as "honesty in fact and the observance of reasonable commercial standards of fair dealing" [UCC 3–103(a)(4)].
	
	 3. *Without notice*—To be an HDC, a holder must not be on notice that the instrument is defective in any of the following ways [UCC 3–302, 3–304]:
	   a. It is overdue.
	   b. It has been dishonored.
	   c. There is an uncured (uncorrected) default with respect to another instrument issued as part of the same series.
	   d. The instrument contains an unauthorized signature or has been altered.
	   e. There is a defense against the instrument or a claim to the instrument.
	   f. The instrument is so irregular or incomplete as to call into question its authenticity.

The Shelter Principle (*See page 347.*)	A holder who cannot qualify as an HDC has the *rights* of an HDC if he or she derives title through an HDC unless the holder engaged in fraud or illegality affecting the instrument [UCC 3–203(b)].

Signature Liability (*See pages 347–352.*)	Every party (except a qualified indorser) who signs a negotiable instrument is either primarily or secondarily liable for payment of the instrument when it comes due.
	
	 1. *Primary liability*—Makers and acceptors are primarily liable (an acceptor is a drawee that promises to pay an instrument when it is presented for payment at a later time) [UCC 3–115, 3–407, 3–409, 3–412].
	
	 2. *Secondary liability*—Drawers and indorsers are secondarily liable [UCC 3–412, 3–414, 3–415, 3–501, 3–502, 3–503]. Parties who are secondarily liable on an instrument promise to pay on that instrument only if the following events occur:
	   a. The instrument is properly and timely presented.
	   b. The instrument is dishonored.
	   c. Timely notice of dishonor is given to the secondarily liable party.
	
	 3. *Unauthorized signatures*—An unauthorized signature is wholly inoperative *unless*:
	   a. The person whose name is signed ratifies (affirms) it or is precluded from denying it [UCC 3–115, 3–401, 3–403, 3–406].
	   b. The instrument has been negotiated to an HDC [UCC 3–403].
	
	 4. *Special rules for unauthorized indorsements*—An unauthorized signature will not bind the person whose name is forged except in the following circumstances:
	 <div align="right">*(Continued)*</div>

▌Chapter Summary: Negotiability, Transferability, and Liability—Continued

Signature Liability—Continued	a. When an imposter induces the maker or drawer of an instrument to issue it to the imposter (imposter rule) [UCC 3–404(a)]. b. When a person signs as or on behalf of a maker or drawer, intending that the payee will have no interest in the instrument, or when an agent or employee of the maker or drawer has supplied him or her with the name of the payee, also intending the payee to have no such interest (fictitious payee rule) [UCC 3–404(b), 3–405].
Warranty Liability *(See pages 352–353.)*	1. *Transfer warranties*—Any person who transfers an instrument for consideration makes the following warranties to all subsequent transferees and holders who take the instrument in good faith (but when a bearer instrument is transferred by delivery only, the transferor's warranties extend only to the immediate transferee) [UCC 3–416]: a. The transferor is entitled to enforce the instrument. b. All signatures are authentic and authorized. c. The instrument has not been altered. d. The instrument is not subject to a defense or claim of any party that can be asserted against the transferor. e. The transferor has no knowledge of any insolvency proceedings against the maker, the acceptor, or the drawer of the instrument. 2. *Presentment warranties*—Any person who presents an instrument for payment or acceptance makes the following warranties to any other person who in good faith pays or accepts the instrument [UCC 3–417(a), 3–417(d)]: a. The person obtaining payment or acceptance is entitled to enforce the instrument or is authorized to obtain payment or acceptance on behalf of a person who is entitled to enforce the instrument. (This is, in effect, a warranty that there are no missing or unauthorized indorsements.) b. The instrument has not been altered. c. The person obtaining payment or acceptance has no knowledge that the signature of the drawer of the instrument is unauthorized.
Defenses to Liability *(See pages 353–355.)*	1. *Universal (real) defenses*—The following defenses are valid against all holders, including HDCs and holders with the rights of HDCs [UCC 3–305, 3–401, 3–403, 3–407]: a. Forgery. b. Fraud in the execution. c. Material alteration. d. Discharge in bankruptcy. e. Minority—if the contract is voidable under state law. f. Illegality, mental incapacity, or extreme duress—if the contract is void under state law. 2. *Personal (limited) defenses*—The following defenses are valid against ordinary holders but not against HDCs or holders with the rights of HDCs [UCC 3–105, 3–115, 3–302, 3–305, 3–306, 3–407, 3–601, 3–602, 3–603, 3–604, 4–401]: a. Breach of contract or breach of warranty. b. Lack or failure of consideration. c. Fraud in the inducement. d. Illegality and mental incapacity—if the contract is voidable. e. Previous payment of the instrument. f. Unauthorized completion of the instrument. g. Nondelivery of the instrument. h. Ordinary duress or undue influence that renders the contract voidable.

▌Chapter Summary: Negotiability, Transferability, and Liability—Continued

Discharge from Liability (See pages 355–356.)	All parties to a negotiable instrument will be discharged when the party primarily liable on it pays to a holder the amount due in full. Discharge can also occur in other circumstances (if the instrument has been canceled, materially altered, and so on) [UCC 3–601 through 3–606].

▌For Review

1. What requirements must an instrument meet to be negotiable?
2. What are the requirements for attaining HDC status?
3. What is the key to liability on a negotiable instrument? What is the difference between signature liability and warranty liability?
4. Certain defenses are valid against all holders, including HDCs. What are these defenses called? Name four defenses that fall within this category.

5. Certain defenses can be used to avoid payment to an ordinary holder of a negotiable instrument but are not effective against an HDC. What are these defenses called? Name four defenses that fall within this category.

▌Questions and Case Problems

17–1. Parties to Negotiable Instruments. A note has two original parties. What are these parties called? A check has three original parties. What are these parties called?

17–2. Unauthorized Indorsements. What are the exceptions to the rule that a bank will be liable for paying a check over an unauthorized indorsement?

17–3. Requirements for Negotiability. The following note is written by Muriel Evans on the back of an envelope: "I, Muriel Evans, promise to pay Karen Marvin or bearer $100 on demand." Is this a negotiable instrument? Discuss fully.

17–4. Requirements for Negotiability. The following instrument was written on a sheet of paper by Jeff Nolan: "I, the undersigned, do hereby acknowledge that I owe Stephanie Craig one thousand dollars, with interest, payable out of the proceeds of the sale of my horse, Swiftfoot, next month. Payment is to be made on or before six months from date." Discuss specifically why this instrument is not negotiable.

17–5. Defenses. Jules sold Alfred a small motorboat for $1,500; Jules maintained to Alfred that the boat was in excellent condition. Alfred gave Jules a check for $1,500, which Jules indorsed and gave to Sherry for value. When Alfred took the boat for a trial run, he discovered that the boat leaked, needed to be painted, and needed a new motor. Alfred stopped payment on his

check, which had not yet been cashed. Jules has disappeared. Can Sherry recover from Alfred as a holder in due course? Discuss.

17–6. Defenses. Fox purchased a used car from Emerson for $1,000. Fox paid for the car with a check, written in pencil, payable to Emerson for $1,000. Emerson, through careful erasures and alterations, changed the amount on the check to read $10,000 and negotiated the check to Sanderson. Sanderson took the check for value, in good faith, and without notice of the alteration and thus met the UCC requirements for holder-in-due-course status. Can Fox successfully raise the universal defense of material alteration to avoid payment on the check? Explain.

17–7. Signature Liability. Marion makes a promissory note payable to the order of Perry. Perry indorses the note by writing "without recourse, Perry" and transfers the note for value to Steven. Steven, in need of cash, negotiates the note to Harriet by indorsing it with the words "Pay to Harriet, Steven." On the due date, Harriet presents the note to Marion for payment, only to learn that Marion has filed for bankruptcy and will have all debts (including the note) discharged in bankruptcy. Discuss fully whether Harriet can hold Marion, Perry, or Steven liable on the note.

17–8. Requirements for Negotiability. Emil Amberboy and others invested in oil and gas partnerships formed by Vanguard Group International, Inc. Each investor made a down payment in cash and signed a promissory note payable to the partnership for the balance of the investment. Each note stated that its interest rate was to be determined by reference to a certain bank's published prime rate. Several months later, Vanguard sold the notes to Société de Banque Privée. Suspecting that the investments were being handled fraudulently, Amberboy and the other investors stopped making payments on the notes and filed a lawsuit against Société de Banque Privée and others. One of the issues before the court was whether the notes were negotiable. The plaintiffs contended that because the interest rate on the notes could be calculated only by reference to a source outside the notes, the notes could not be negotiable instruments. How should the court rule? [*Amberboy v. Société de Banque Privée*, 831 S.W.2d 793 (Tex. 1992)]

17–9. HDC Status. An employee of Epicycle Corp. cashed a payroll check at Money Mart Check Cashing Center, Inc. Money Mart deposited the check, with others, into its bank account. When the check was returned marked "Payment stopped," Money Mart sought to recover from Epicycle for the value of the check. Money Mart claimed that it was a holder in due course on the instrument because it had accepted the check for value, in good faith, and without notice that a stop-payment order had been made. Epicycle argued that Money Mart was not a holder in due course, because it had failed to verify that the check was good before it cashed the check. Did Money Mart's failure to inquire into the validity of the check preclude it from being a holder in due course? Explain. [*Money Mart Check Cashing Center, Inc. v. Epicycle Corp.*, 667 P.2d 1372 (Colo. 1983)]

17–10. Unauthorized Indorsements. Edward Bauerband contacted Minster State Bank by phone and requested a $25,000 loan, purportedly on behalf of himself and his wife, Michelle. The Bauerbands had a long-standing relationship with the bank, and the request was not so unusual as to put the bank on notice. The bank mailed a promissory note to Edward to be signed by both him and his wife. Edward forged his wife's signature on the note, signed it himself, and returned the note and other loan documents to the bank. On its receipt of the documents, the bank issued a cashier's check in the amount of $25,000, payable to Edward and Michelle jointly, and mailed the check to the Bauerbands' home. Edward indorsed the check in his name, forged his wife's indorsement, and deposited the check in his business account at another bank, Baybank Middlesex. Michelle knew nothing about the loan transaction or the check. Ultimately, the forgery was discovered, and Minster State Bank sued Baybank Middlesex to recover the funds. Baybank contended that it was precluded from liability under the UCC's "imposter rule." Was it? Explain. [*Minster State Bank v. Bauerband*, 1992 Mass.App.Div. 61 (1992)]

17–11. Discharge. Richard and Coralea Triplett signed two promissory notes—one for $14,000 and one for $3,500—in favor of FirsTier Bank, N.A. The Tripletts sent the bank a check for $7,200 as payment on the notes. A clerk divided the $7,200 payment to pay the second note in full and to reduce the amount owed on the first note. The clerk then incorrectly stamped the first note "PAID," signed it, and mailed it to the Tripletts. Later, a different clerk stamped the second note "PAID," signed it, and returned it to the Tripletts. When FirsTier sued the Tripletts in a Nebraska state court for the rest of the money due on the first note, the Tripletts asserted that the bank had stamped "PAID" on the note and returned it. The bank contended that it had not intended to release both notes. In deciding whether the first note was discharged, what factors should the court take into consideration? [*FirsTier Bank, N.A. v. Triplett*, 242 Neb. 614, 497 N.W.2d 339 (1993)]

**A QUESTION OF ETHICS
AND SOCIAL RESPONSIBILITY**

17–12. *One day, while Ort, a farmer, was working alone in his field, a stranger approached him. The stranger said he was the state agent for a manufacturer of iron posts and wire fence. Eventually the stranger persuaded Ort to accept a township-wide agency for the same manufacturer. The stranger then asked Ort to sign a document that purportedly was an agency agreement. Because Ort did not have his glasses with him and could read only with great difficulty, he asked the stranger to read what the document said. The stranger then pretended to read the document to Ort, not mentioning that it was a promissory note. Both men signed the note, and Ort assumed that he was signing a document of agency. The stranger later negotiated the note to a good faith purchaser for value. When that person sued Ort, Ort attempted to defend on the basis of fraud in the execution. In view of these facts, consider the following questions.* [*Ort v. Fowler*, 31 Kan. 478, 2 P. 580 (1884)]

1. Although this classic case was decided long before the UCC was drafted, the court applied essentially the same rule that would apply under Article 3. What is this rule, and how would it be applied to Ort's attempted defense on the ground of fraud in the execution?

2. This case provides a clear example of a situation in which one of two innocent parties (Ort and the purchaser of the note) must bear the loss caused by a third party (the stranger, who was the perpetrator of the fraud). Under Article 3, which party should bear the loss, and why?

CASE BRIEFING ASSIGNMENT

17–13. *Examine Case A.5 [Federal Deposit Insurance Corp. v. Trans Pacific Industries, Inc., 14 F.3d 10 (5th Cir. 1994] in Appendix A. The case has been excerpted there in great detail. Review and then brief the case, making sure that you include answers to the following questions in your brief.*

1. What was the procedural background to this case?
2. What issue was being appealed and by which party?
3. Which UCC provision applied to this issue?
4. How did the appellate court rule on the issue, and why?

▌Accessing the Internet: Fundamentals of Business Law

For the most updated information on the Uniform Commercial Code, including the revised Article 3 and 4, along with Official Comments, go to

http://www.law.cornell.edu/ucc/ucc.table.html

Or go to

http://www.law.upenn.edu/library/ulc/ulc.htm

Cornell Law School's Legal Information Institute offers online access to the Uniform Commercial Code, including Articles 3 and 4, as enacted in several of the states at

http://www.laaw.cornell.edu/statutes.html#state

For an article discussing the future of checks as negotiable instruments, go to Create-A-Check at the URL given below and select Appendix A.

http://www.createacheck.com/Chksdie.htm

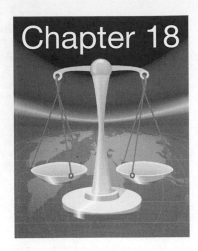

Chapter 18

Checks and the Banking System

CHAPTER OBJECTIVES

After reading this chapter, you should be able to:

1. Identify the different types of checks.
2. Indicate when a bank may dishonor a customer's check without liability to the customer.
3. Outline a bank's responsibilities regarding stale checks, stop-payment orders, and forged or altered checks.
4. Describe how banks collect payment on checks deposited by their customers.
5. Explain the laws governing consumer electronic fund transfers and commercial fund transfers.

Checks are the most common kind of negotiable instruments regulated by the Uniform Commercial Code (UCC). It is estimated that over sixty billion personal and commercial checks are written each year in the United States. Checks are more than a daily convenience; they are an integral part of the American economic system. Most people accept checks—because they serve as substitutes for money.

Issues relating to checks are governed by Article 3 and Article 4 of the UCC. Recall from Chapter 17 that Article 3 establishes the requirements that all negotiable instruments, including checks, must meet. Article 3 also sets forth the rights and liabilities of parties to negotiable instruments. Article 4 of the UCC governs the relationships of banks with one another as they process checks for payment, and it establishes a framework for deposit and checking agreements between a bank and its customers. A check therefore may fall within the scope of Article 3 and yet be subject to the provisions of Article 4 while the check is in the course of collec-

tion. If a conflict between Article 3 and Article 4 arises, Article 4 controls [UCC 4–102(a)].

In this chapter, we first identify the legal characteristics of checks and the legal duties and liabilities that arise when a check is issued. Then we examine the check deposit and collection process—that is, the actual procedure by which the checks deposited into bank accounts move through banking channels, causing the underlying cash dollars to be shifted from one bank account to another. Increasingly, credit cards, debit cards, and other devices and methods to transfer funds electronically are being used to pay for goods and services. In the latter part of this chapter, we look at the law governing electronic fund transfers.

▌ Checks

A **check** is a special type of draft that is drawn on a bank, ordering the bank to pay a fixed amount of

362

money on demand [UCC 3–104(f)]. Article 4 defines a *bank* as "a person engaged in the business of banking, including a savings bank, savings and loan association, credit union or trust company" [UCC 4–105(1)]. If any other institution handles a check for payment or for collection, the check is not covered by Article 4.

Recall from the discussion of negotiable instruments in Chapter 17 that a person who writes a check is called the *drawer*. The drawer is a depositor in the bank on which the check is drawn. The person to whom the check is payable is the *payee*. The bank or financial institution on which the check is drawn is the *drawee*. If Anita Cruzak writes a check from her checking account to pay her college tuition, she is the drawer, her bank is the drawee, and her college is the payee. We now look at some special types of checks.

Cashier's Checks

Checks are usually three-party instruments, but on certain types of checks, the bank can serve as both the drawer and the drawee. For example, when a bank draws a check upon itself, the check is called a **cashier's check** and is a negotiable instrument upon issue (see Exhibit 18–1) [UCC 3–104(g)]. Normally, a cashier's check indicates a specific payee. In effect, with a cashier's check, the bank assumes responsibility for paying the check, thus making the check more readily negotiable.

For example, Kramer needs to pay a moving company $6,000 for moving his household goods to a new home in another state. The moving company requests payment in the form of a cashier's check. Kramer goes to a bank (he need not have an account at the bank) and purchases a cashier's check, payable to the moving company, in the amount of $6,000. Kramer has to pay the bank the $6,000 for the check, plus a small service fee. He then gives the check to the moving company.

Cashier's checks are sometimes used in the business community as nearly the equivalent of cash. Except in very limited circumstances, the issuing bank must honor its cashier's checks when they are presented for payment. If a bank wrongfully dishonors a cashier's check, a holder can recover from the bank all expenses incurred, interest, and consequential damages [UCC 3–411]. This same rule applies if a bank wrongfully dishonors a certified check (to be discussed shortly) or a teller's check. (A *teller's check* is a check drawn by a bank on another bank or, when drawn on a nonbank, payable at or through a bank [UCC 3–104(h)]). In the following case, the court considered whether a bank could legitimately refuse to honor its own cashier's checks.

CASE 18.1

First Railroad Community Federal Credit Union v. Columbia County Bank

United States District Court, Middle District of Florida, Jacksonville Division, 1994. 849 F.Supp. 780.

FACTS   Clark Crapps operated two automobile dealerships with bank accounts in the First Railroad Community Federal Credit Union and the Columbia County Bank. On one occasion, checks drawn on the account with First Railroad were deposited into the Columbia account. Unaware that the First Railroad account did not have enough funds to pay the checks, Columbia credited the account in its bank and issued two cashier's checks, each for $300,000, based on the credit. Both checks were immediately deposited into the First Railroad account. When Columbia learned of the financial misdealings, it refused to honor the cashier's checks. Seeking payment, First Railroad filed a suit in a federal district court against Columbia. Both parties filed motions for summary judgment.

ISSUE   Did Columbia have to pay its cashier's checks?

DECISION   Yes. The court held that First Railroad was entitled to payment and granted summary judgment in its favor.

(Continued)

Case 18.1—Continued

REASON   The court explained that unlike an ordinary check, a cashier's check "stands on its own foundation as an independent, unconditional, and primary obligation of the bank. People accept a cashier's check as a substitute for cash because the bank stands behind the check, rather than an individual." The court reasoned that "the parties' expectation is that the cashier's check will remove doubt as to whether the instrument will be returned to the holder unpaid due to insufficient funds in the account, a stop payment order, or insolvency." Therefore, "the only inquiry a bank may make upon presentment of a cashier's check is whether or not the payee or [i]ndorsee is in fact a legitimate holder, i.e., whether the cashier's check is being presented by a thief or one who simply found a lost check, or whether the check has been materially altered."

FOR CRITICAL ANALYSIS—Economic Consideration   *Why are the grounds on which a bank can refuse to pay a cashier's check so limited?*

Traveler's Checks

A **traveler's check** has the characteristics of a teller's check. It is an instrument that is payable on demand, drawn on or payable at a bank, and designated as a traveler's check. The institution is directly obligated to accept and pay its traveler's check according to the check's terms. The purchaser is required to sign the check at the time it is bought and again at the time it is used [UCC 3–104(i)]. Exhibit 18–2 shows an example of a traveler's check.

Certified Checks

A **certified check** is a check that has been *accepted* by the bank on which it is drawn [UCC 3–409(d)]. When a drawee bank certifies (accepts) a check, it immediately charges the drawer's account with the amount of the check and transfers those funds to its own certified check account. In effect, the bank is agreeing in advance to accept that check when it is presented for payment and to make payment from those funds reserved in the certified check account. Essentially, certification prevents the bank from

♦ **Exhibit 18–1**
  A Cashier's Check

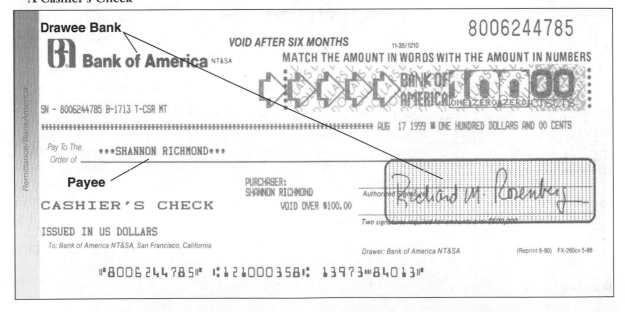

♦ **Exhibit 18–2**
  A Traveler's Check

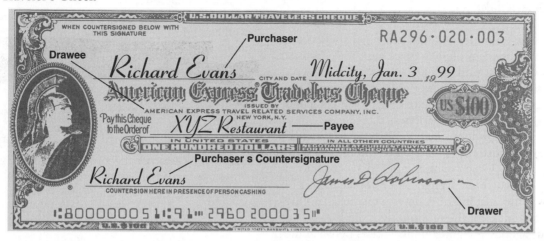

denying liability. It is a promise that sufficient funds are on deposit and *have been set aside* to cover the check. Exhibit 18–3 shows a sample certified check.

A drawee bank is not obligated to certify a check, and failure to do so is not a dishonor of the check [UCC 3–409(d)]. If a bank does certify a check, however, the bank should write on the check the amount that it will pay. If the certification does not state an amount, and the amount is later increased and the instrument negotiated to a holder in due course (HDC), the obligation of the certifying bank is the amount of the instrument when it was taken by the HDC [UCC 3–413(b)].

Certification may be requested by a holder (to ensure that the check will not be dishonored for insufficient funds) or by the drawer. In either circumstance, on certification the drawer and any prior indorsers are completely discharged from liability on the instrument [UCC 3–414(c), 3–415(d)].[1]

---

1. Under Section 3–411 of the unrevised Article 3, the legal liability of a drawer varies according to whether certification is requested by the drawee or a holder. The drawer who obtains certification remains *secondarily liable* on the instrument if the certifying bank does not honor the check when it is presented for payment. If the check is certified at the request of a holder, the drawer and anyone who indorses the check before certification are completely discharged.

♦ **Exhibit 18–3**
  A Certified Check

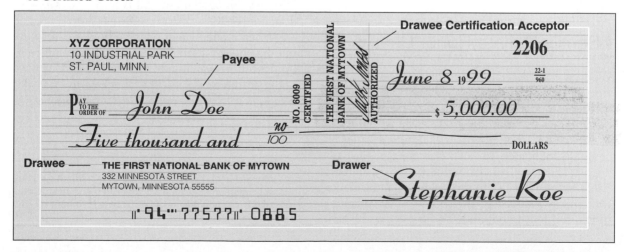

The Bank-Customer Relationship

The bank-customer relationship begins when the customer opens a checking account and deposits money that the bank will use to pay for checks written by the customer. The rights and duties of the bank and the customer are contractual and depend on the nature of the transaction.

A creditor-debtor relationship is created between a customer and a bank when, for example, the customer makes cash deposits into a checking account. When a customer makes a deposit, the customer becomes a creditor, and the bank a debtor, for the amount deposited.

An agency relationship also arises between the customer and the bank when the customer writes a check on his or her account. In effect, the customer is ordering the bank to pay the amount specified on the check to the holder when the holder presents the check to the bank for payment. In this situation, the bank becomes the customer's agent and is obligated to honor the customer's request. Similarly, if the customer deposits a check into his or her account, the bank, as the customer's agent, is obligated to collect payment on the check from the bank on which the check was drawn. To transfer checkbook dollars among different banks, each bank acts as the agent of collection for its customer [UCC 4–201(a)].

Whenever a bank-customer relationship is established, certain contractual rights and duties arise. The respective rights and duties of banks and their customers are discussed in detail in the following pages.

Bank's Duty to Honor Checks

When a commercial bank provides checking services, it agrees to honor the checks written by its customers with the usual stipulation that there be sufficient funds available in the account to pay each check [UCC 4–401(a)]. The customer is generally obligated to keep sufficient money on deposit to cover all checks written. The customer is liable to the payee or to the holder of a check in a civil suit if a check is dishonored for insufficient funds. If intent to defraud can be proved, the customer can also be subject to criminal prosecution for writing a bad check.

When the bank properly dishonors a check for insufficient funds, it has no liability to the customer. When a drawee bank *wrongfully* fails to honor a customer's check, however, it is liable to its customer for damages resulting from its refusal to pay [UCC 4–402].

Clearly, the bank's duty to honor its customers' checks is not absolute. As noted, the bank, is under no duty to honor a check when there are insufficient funds in the customer's account. There are other circumstances as well in which the bank may rightfully refuse payment on a customer's check. We look here at the rights and duties of both the bank and its customers in relation to specific situations.

Overdrafts

When the bank receives an item properly payable from its customer's checking account but there are insufficient funds in the account to cover the amount of the check, the bank has two options. It can either (1) dishonor the item or (2) pay the item and charge the customer's account, thus creating an overdraft, providing that the customer has authorized the payment and the payment does not violate any bank-customer agreement [UCC 4–401(a)].[2] The bank can subtract the difference from the customer's next deposit, because the check carries with it an enforceable implied promise to reimburse the bank. A bank can expressly agree with a customer to accept overdrafts through what is sometimes called an "overdraft protection agreement." If such an agreement is formed, any failure of the bank to honor a check because it would create an overdraft breaches this agreement and is treated as wrongful dishonor [UCC 4–402(a)].

When a check "bounces," a holder can resubmit the check, hoping that at a later date sufficient funds will be available to pay it. The holder must notify any indorsers on the check of the first dishonor, however; otherwise, they will be discharged from their signature liability.

---

2.   If there is a joint account, the bank cannot hold any joint-account customer liable for payment of an overdraft unless the customer has signed the check or has benefited from the proceeds of the check [UCC 4–401(b)].

Postdated Checks

A bank may also charge a postdated check against a customer's account, unless the customer notifies the bank not to pay the check until the stated date in a timely manner—that is, in time to allow the bank to act on the notice before the bank commits itself to pay on the check. If the bank receives timely notice from the customer and nonetheless charges the customer's account before the date on the postdated check, the bank may be liable for any damages incurred by the customer as a result [UCC 4–401(c)].[3]

Stale Checks

Commercial banking practice regards a check that is presented for payment more than six months from its date as a **stale check**. A bank is not obligated to pay an uncertified check presented more than six months from its date [UCC 4–404]. When receiving a stale check for payment, the bank has the option of paying or not paying the check. The bank may consult the customer before paying the check. If a bank pays a stale check in good faith without consulting the customer, however, the bank has the right to charge the customer's account for the amount of the check.

Stop-Payment Orders

A **stop-payment order** is an order by a customer to his or her bank not to pay or certify a certain check. Only a customer or a person authorized to draw on the account can order the bank not to pay the check when it is presented for payment [UCC 4–403(a)]. For a deceased customer, any person claiming a legitimate interest in the account may issue a stop-payment order [UCC 4–405]. A customer has no right to stop payment on a check that

has been certified or accepted by a bank, however. Also, a stop-payment order must be received within a reasonable time and in a reasonable manner to permit the bank to act on it [UCC 4–403(a)]. Although a stop-payment order can be given orally, usually by phone, it is binding on the bank for only fourteen calendar days unless confirmed in writing.[4] A written stop-payment order (see Exhibit 18–4) or an oral order confirmed in writing is effective for six months, at which time it must be renewed in writing [UCC 4–403(b)].

If the bank pays the check over the customer's properly instituted stop-payment order, the bank will be obligated to recredit the customer's account—but only for the amount of the actual loss suffered by the drawer because of the wrongful payment [UCC 4–403(c)]. For example, Arlene Drury orders six bamboo palms from a local nursery at $50 each and gives the nursery a check for $300. Later that day, the nursery tells Drury that it will not deliver the palms as arranged. Drury immediately calls her bank and stops payment on the check. If the bank nonetheless honors the check, the bank will be liable to Drury for the full $300. The result would be different, however, if the nursery had delivered five palms. In that situation, Drury would owe the nursery $250 for the delivered palms, and her actual losses would be only $50. Consequently, the bank would be liable to Drury for only $50.

A stop-payment order has its risks for a customer. The customer-drawer must have a *valid legal ground* for issuing such an order; otherwise, the holder can sue the drawer for payment. Moreover, defenses sufficient to refuse payment against a payee may not be valid grounds to prevent payment against a subsequent holder in due course [UCC 3–305, 3–306]. A person who wrongfully stops payment on a check not only will be liable to the payee for the amount of the check but also may be liable for consequential damages incurred by the payee as a result of the wrongful stop-payment order.

At issue in the following case was whether a bank wrongfully honored a check by making payment on the check after its customer had given the bank a stop-payment order.

---

3. Under the UCC, postdating does not affect the negotiability of a check. Instead of treating postdated checks as checks payable on demand, however, many courts treat them as time drafts. Thus, regardless of whether the customer notified the bank of the postdating, a bank could not charge a customer's account for a postdated check without facing potential liability for the payment of later checks. Under the automated check-collection system in use today, however, a check is usually paid without respect to its date.

---

4. Some states do not recognize oral stop-payment orders; they must be in writing.

CASE 18.2

Thomas v. Marine Midland Tinkers National Bank

Civil Court of the City of New York, 1976.
86 Misc.2d 284,
381 N.Y.S.2d 797.

FACTS   On December 8, 1973, the plaintiff (Thomas) gave Ralph Gallo a check for $2,500 as a down payment on two rugs that Thomas was purchasing from Gallo. The check was postdated December 10 and drawn on the Marine Midland Tinkers National Bank. Having changed his mind about the purchase, Thomas went to the Marine Midland bank on the morning of December 10 and arranged with a bank officer whom he knew to have a stop-payment order placed on the check. Thomas gave the bank officer all the required information but described the check as #22 instead of #221, the correct number. On the afternoon of the following day, the check was presented for payment at the same bank, and the bank cashed it and debited the plaintiff's account in the amount of the $2,500. When Thomas called Gallo, demanding the return of the $2,500, Gallo refused to pay and threatened to enforce the purchase agreement. Thomas then brought an action in a New York court against the bank for wrongful payment. The bank moved for dismissal of the charge on the basis of the incorrect information (the erroneous check number) given by Thomas on the stop-payment order.

ISSUE   Can Thomas recover the $2,500 from the bank?

DECISION   Yes. The bank was held responsible for its act of improperly making payment on the check.

REASON   The court held that "[a] day and a half is more than reasonable notice to enforce a stop order on a check presented at the very same branch, and payment of the item by the bank thereafter constitutes a breach of its obligations to honor the stop order. The normal problem of reasonable computer lag when dealing with a great number of other branches of a large bank has no relevancy to the facts at bar [the facts in this case], where all transactions occurred in a single branch." As to the error regarding the check number, the court stated, "The single digital mistake in describing the check in the stop order is deemed trivial, and insignificant. Enough information was supplied to the bank to reasonably provide it with sufficient information to comply with the stop payment order. The bank is therefore held responsible for its act of improperly making payment upon the check."

FOR CRITICAL ANALYSIS—Economic Consideration   *If Thomas did not have a legally sufficient reason to stop payment on the check, would that circumstance affect the court's decision that the bank had improperly paid the check? Should it?*

Death or Incompetence of a Customer

A customer's death or incompetence does not affect the bank's authority to honor a check until the bank knows of the situation and has had a reasonable period of time to act on the information. Article 4 provides that if, at the time a check is issued or its collection has been undertaken, a bank does not know of an adjudication of incompetence or of the death of its customer, an item can be paid, and the bank will not incur liability.

Even when a bank knows of the death of its customer, for ten days after the *date of death,* it can pay or certify checks drawn on or before the date of death—unless a person claiming an interest in that account, such as an heir, orders the bank to stop payment [UCC 4–405]. Without this provision,

♦ **Exhibit 18–4**
A Stop-Payment Order

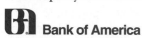

**Checking Account
Stop Payment Order**

To: Bank of America NT&SA
I want to stop payment on the following check(s).

ACCOUNT NUMBER: ☐☐☐☐☐☐ — ☐☐☐☐☐

SPECIFIC STOP

*ENTER DOLLAR AMOUNT: [   ]   *CHECK
                                        NUMBER: [   ]

THE CHECK WAS SIGNED BY: _____

THE CHECK IS PAYABLE TO: _____

THE REASON FOR THIS STOP PAYMENT IS: _____

STOP RANGE   (Use for lost or stolen check(s) only.)

DOLLAR AMOUNT: 000

                    *ENTER [   ]   *END [   ]
STARTING CHECK NUMBER: CHECK NUMBER:

THE REASON FOR THIS STOP PAYMENT IS: _____

I agree that this order (1) is effective only if the above check(s) has (have) not yet been cashed or paid against my account, (2) will end six months from the date it is delivered to you unless I renew it in writing, and (3) is not valid if the check(s) was (were) accepted on the strength of my Bank of America courtesy-check guarantee card by a merchant participating in that program. I also agree (1) to notify you immediately to cancel this order if the reason for the stop apyment no laonger exists or (2) that closing the account on which the check(s) is (are) drawn automatically cancels this order.

IF ANOTHER BRANCH OF THIS BANK OR ANOTHER PERSON OR ENTITY BECOMES A "HOLDER IN DUE COURSE" OF THE ABOVE CHECK, I UNDERSTAND THAT PAYMENT MAY BE ENFORCED AGAINST THE CHECK'S MAKER (SIGNER).

*I CERTIFY THE AMOUNT AND CHECK NUMBER(S) ABOVE ARE CORRECT.
☐ I have written a replacement check (number and date of check).

_____

(Optional—please circle one: Mr., Ms., Mrs., Miss) CUSTOMER'S SIGNATURE **X** _____ DATE _____

BANK USE ONLY

TRANCODE:

☐ 21—ENTER STOP PAYMENT
(SEE OTHER SIDE TO REMOVE)

NON READS: _____

UNPROC. STMT HIST: _____

PRIOR STMT CYCLE: _____

HOLDS ON COOLS: __

REJECTED CHKS: _____

LARGE ITEMS: _____

FEE COLLECTED: _____

DATE ACCEPTED: _____

TIME ACCEPTED: _____

---

banks would constantly be required to verify the continued life and competence of their drawers.

Forged Drawers' Signatures

When a bank pays a check on which the drawer's signature is forged, generally the bank is liable. A bank, however, may be able to recover at least some of the loss—from the customer (if the customer's negligence contributed to the forgery), from the forger of the check (if he or she can be found), or from the holder who presented the check for payment (if the holder knew that the signature was forged).

THE GENERAL RULE A forged signature on a check has no legal effect as the signature of a drawer [UCC 3–403(a)]. For this reason, banks require signature cards from each customer who opens a checking account. Signature cards allow the bank to verify whether the signatures on their customers' checks are genuine. The general rule, illustrated in the following case, is that the bank must recredit the customer's account when it pays a check with a forged signature.

CASE 18.3

SCCI, Inc. v. United States National Bank of Oregon

Court of Appeals of Oregon, 1986.
78 Or.App. 176,
714 P.2d 1113.

FACTS Susan Wolf, who was employed as a secretary and bookkeeper for SCCI, Inc., a construction contractor, forged her employer's name on more than ninety checks drawn on SCCI's account at the United States National Bank of Oregon. The bank cashed the checks and debited SCCI's account, and Susan Wolf wrongfully received a total of approximately $22,600. SCCI brought a criminal action

(Continued)

Case 18.3—Continued

against Wolf when the forgeries were discovered but later dropped the charges because SCCI's president "was acquainted with the parents of Susan Wolf, had no desire that [she] go to jail and was content to let the attorneys work the matter out." Wolf and her father gave SCCI a signed promissory note for $10,000. Meanwhile, SCCI demanded that the bank credit its account for the $22,600 worth of forged checks. The bank refused, claiming that the out-of-court settlement between SCCI and Wolf would undermine its ability to collect from Wolf (which it would attempt to do if it credited SCCI's account). SCCI filed a suit in an Oregon state court against the bank, arguing that it was the bank's duty, under its contractual responsibilities to SCCI, to cash checks only when they were authorized by SCCI. The court granted the bank's request for summary judgment. SCCI appealed.

ISSUE   Can the bank be held liable for cashing the forged checks?

DECISION   Yes. The Oregon appellate court reversed the trial court's judgment and remanded the case.

REASON   The court reasoned that because there was no evidence that "plaintiff's [SCCI's] negligence substantially contributed to the forgery, plaintiff was not obligated for the forged checks that the bank had honored *   *   * and the bank lacked authority to debit plaintiff's account for the checks. Plaintiff was entitled to have the bank credit its account."

FOR CRITICAL ANALYSIS—Ethical Consideration   *One of the general principles underlying the UCC's provisions governing negotiable instruments is that between two innocent parties, the one in the better position to prevent the loss should bear the burden of the loss. How might one argue that in the above case, SCCI, and not the bank, was in the better position to prevent the loss?*

CUSTOMER NEGLIGENCE   When the customer's negligence substantially contributes to the forgery, the bank will not normally be obligated to recredit the customer's account for the amount of the check [UCC 3–406]. Suppose, for example, that Gemco Corporation uses special check-writing equipment to write its payroll and business checks. Gemco discovers that one of its employees used the equipment to write himself a check for $10,000 and that the bank subsequently honored it. Gemco requests the bank to recredit $10,000 to its account for improperly paying the forged check.

If the bank can show that Gemco failed to take reasonable care in controlling access to the check-writing equipment, Gemco cannot require the bank to recredit its account for the amount of the forged check. Gemco's liability may be reduced, however, by the amount of loss caused by negligence on the part of the bank (or other "person") paying the instrument or taking it for value if the negligence substantially contributes to the loss [UCC 3–406(b)].[5]

Timely Examination of Bank Statements Required   Banks typically send their customers monthly statements detailing activity on their checking accounts. Banks are not obligated to include the canceled checks themselves with the statement sent to the customer. If the bank does not send the canceled checks (or photocopies of the canceled checks), however, it must provide the customer with information (check number, amount, and date of payment) on the statement that will allow the customer to reasonably identify the checks that the bank has paid [UCC 4–406(a), 4–406(b)]. If the bank retains the canceled checks, it must keep the checks—or legible copies of the checks—for a period of seven years [UCC

---

5.   The unrevised Article 4 does not include a similar provision.

4–406(b)]. The customer may obtain a check (or a copy of the check) during this period of time.

The customer has a duty to examine bank statements (and canceled checks or photocopies, if they are included with the statements) promptly and with reasonable care, and to report any alterations or forged signatures promptly [UCC 4–406(c)]. This includes forged signatures of indorsers, to be discussed later. If the customer fails to fulfill this duty and the bank suffers a loss as a result, the customer will be liable for the loss [4–406(d)]. Even if the customer can prove that he or she took reasonable care against forgeries, the UCC provides that discovery of such forgeries and notice to the bank must take place within specific time frames in order for the customer to require the bank to recredit his or her account.

Consequences of Failing to Detect Forgeries

When a series of forgeries by the same wrongdoer has taken place, the UCC provides that the customer, to recover for all the forged items, must have discovered and reported the first forged check to the bank within thirty calendar days of the receipt of the bank statement (and canceled checks or copies, if they are included) [UCC 4–406(d)(2)].[6] Failure to notify the bank within this period of time discharges the bank's liability for all forged checks that it pays prior to notification.

When the Bank Is Also Negligent

There is one situation in which a bank customer can escape liability, at least in part, for failing to notify the bank of forged or altered checks within the required thirty-day period. If the customer can prove that the bank was also negligent—that is, that the bank failed to exercise ordinary care—then the bank will also be liable, and an allocation of the loss between the bank and the customer will be made on the basis of comparative negligence [UCC 4–406(e)].[7] In other words, even though a customer may have been negligent, the bank may still have to recredit the customer's account for a portion of the loss if the bank failed to exercise ordinary care.

Does a bank fail to exercise ordinary care if it fails to examine *every* signature on every check? Not according to UCC 3–103(a)(7). That section defines *ordinary care* to mean the "observance of reasonable commercial standards, prevailing in the area in which [a] person is located, with respect to the business in which that person is engaged." It is customary in the banking industry to manually examine signatures only on checks over a certain amount (such as $1,000, $2,500, or some higher amount). Thus, if a bank, in accordance with prevailing banking standards, fails to examine a signature on a particular check, the bank has not breached its duty to exercise ordinary care.

Prior to the 1990 revision of Article 3, bank customers whose own negligence contributed to forgeries sometimes sought to avoid liability by claiming that their banks were also negligent—that is, customers claimed that the banks' failure to examine *every* signature on the checks they paid constituted a breach of the banks' duty to exercise ordinary care. Some courts agreed; others did not. The revised Article 3 put an end to the problem by clarifying the meaning of ordinary care in the context of today's banking system.

Regardless of the degree of care exercised by the customer or the bank, the UCC places an absolute time limit on the liability of a bank for paying a check with a forged customer signature. A customer who fails to report a forged signature within one year from the date that the statement was made available for inspection loses the legal right to have the bank recredit his or her account [UCC 4–406(f)].

Forged Indorsements

A bank that pays a customer's check bearing a forged indorsement must recredit the customer's account or be liable to the customer-drawer for breach of contract. Suppose that Brian issues a $50 check "to the order of Antonio." Jimmy steals the check, forges Antonio's indorsement, and cashes the check. When the check reaches Brian's bank, the bank pays it and debits Brian's account. The bank must recredit the $50 to Brian's account because it failed to carry out Brian's order to pay "to the order of Antonio" [UCC 4–401(a)]. Of course, Brian's bank can in turn recover—under breach of warranty principles (see Chapter 17)—from the bank that paid the check when Jimmy presented it [UCC 4–207(a)(2)].

Eventually, the loss usually falls on the first party to take the instrument bearing the forged

---

6. The unrevised Article 4 limits the period for examining and reporting to *fourteen* days [UCC 4–406(2)(b)].

7. Under the unrevised Article 4, if both parties are negligent, the bank is wholly liable [UCC 4–406(3)].

indorsement, because a forged indorsement does not transfer title. Thus, whoever takes an instrument with a forged indorsement cannot become a holder.

In any event, the customer has a duty to examine the returned checks (or copies of the checks) and statements received from the bank and to report forged indorsements promptly. A customer's failure to report forged indorsements within a three-year period after the forged items have been made available to the customer relieves the bank of liability [UCC 4–111].

Altered Checks

The customer's instruction to the bank is to pay the exact amount on the face of the check to the holder. The bank has a duty to examine each check before making final payment. If it fails to detect an alteration, it is liable to its customer for the loss, because it did not pay as the customer ordered. The loss is the difference between the original amount of the check and the amount actually paid. Suppose that a check written for $11 is raised to $111. The customer's account will be charged $11 (the amount the customer ordered the bank to pay). The bank will normally be responsible for the $100 [UCC 4–401(d)(1)].

The bank is entitled to recover the amount of loss from the transferor, who, by presenting the check for payment, warrants that the check has not been materially altered. If the bank is the drawer

(as it is on a cashier's check and a teller's check), however, it cannot recover on this ground from the presenting party if the party is an HDC acting in good faith [UCC 3–417(a)(2), 4–208(a)(2)]. The reason is that an instrument's drawer is in a better position than an HDC to know whether the instrument has been altered. Similarly, an HDC, acting in good faith in presenting a certified check for payment, does not warrant that the check was not altered before the HDC acquired it [UCC 3–417(a)(2), 4–207(a)(2)].

For example, Selling draws a check for $500 payable to Deffen. Deffen alters the amount to $5,000. The First National Bank of Whiteacre, the drawee bank, certifies the check for $5,000. Deffen negotiates the check to Evans, an HDC. The drawee bank pays Evans $5,000. On discovering the mistake, the bank cannot recover from Evans the $4,500 paid by mistake, even though the bank was not in a superior position to detect the alteration. This is in accord with the purpose of certification, which is to obtain the definite obligation of a bank to honor a definite instrument.

As in a situation involving a forged drawer's signature, when payment is made on an altered check, a customer's negligence can shift the loss (unless the bank was also negligent). A common example occurs when a person carelessly writes a check and leaves large gaps around the numbers and words so that additional numbers and words can be inserted (see Exhibit 18–5). Similarly, a person who signs a check and leaves the dollar amount for someone else to fill in is barred from

♦ **Exhibit 18–5**
A Poorly Filled-Out Check

protesting when the bank unknowingly and in good faith pays whatever amount is shown [UCC 4–401(d)(2)]. Finally, if the bank can trace its loss on successive altered checks to the customer's failure to discover the initial alteration, then the bank can reduce its liability for reimbursing the customer's account [UCC 4–406]. The law governing the customer's duty to examine monthly statements and canceled checks (or copies), and to discover and report unauthorized signatures to the drawee bank, applies to altered instruments as well as forgeries.

■ Bank's Duty to Accept Deposits

A bank has a duty to its customer to accept the customer's deposits of cash and checks. When checks are deposited, the bank must make the funds represented by those checks available within certain time frames. A bank also has a duty to collect payment on any checks payable or indorsed to its customer and deposited by the customer into his or her account. Cash deposits made in U.S. currency are received into the customer's account without being subject to further collection procedures.

Availability Schedule for Deposited Checks

The Expedited Funds Availability Act of 1987[8] and Regulation CC,[9] which was issued by the Federal Reserve Board of Governors (the Federal Reserve System will be discussed shortly) to implement the act, require that any local check deposited must be available for withdrawal by check or as cash within one business day from the date of deposit. A check is classified as a local check if the first bank to receive the check for payment and the bank on which the check is drawn are located in the same check processing region (check processing regions are designated by the Federal Reserve Board of Governors). For nonlocal checks, the funds must be available for withdrawal within not more than five business days.

In addition, the act requires the following:

1. That funds be available on the *next business day* for cash deposits and wire transfers, government checks, the first $100 of a day's check deposits, cashier's checks, certified checks, and checks for which the depositary and payor banks are branches of the same institution.

2. That the first $100 of any deposit be available for cash withdrawal on the opening of the next business day after deposit. If a local check is deposited, the next $400 is to be available for withdrawal by no later than 5:00 P.M. the next business day. If, for example, you deposit a local check for $500 on Monday, you can withdraw $100 in cash at the opening of the business day on Tuesday, and an additional $400 must be available for withdrawal by no later than 5:00 P.M. on Wednesday.

A different availability schedule applies to deposits made at *nonproprietary* automated teller machines (ATMs). These are ATMs that are not owned or operated by the depositary institution. Basically, a five-day hold is permitted on all deposits, including cash deposits, made at nonproprietary ATMs.

Other exceptions also exist. A depository institution has eight days to make funds available in new accounts (those open less than thirty days). It has an extra four days on deposits over $5,000 (except deposits of government and cashier's checks), on accounts with repeated overdrafts, and on checks of questionable collectibility (if the institution tells the depositor it suspects fraud or insolvency).

Truth-in-Savings Act

Under the Truth-in-Savings Act (TISA) of 1991[10] and Regulation DD,[11] the act's implementing regulation, banks must pay interest on the full balance of a customer's account each day. For example, Furman has an interest-bearing checking account with the First National Bank. Furman keeps a $500 balance in the account for most of the month but withdraws all but $50 the day before the bank posts the interest. The bank cannot pay interest on only the $50. The interest must be adjusted to account for all of the days that Furman's balance was higher.

---

8. 12 U.S.C. Sections 4001–4010.
9. 12 C.F.R. Sections 229.1–229.42.

10. 12 U.S.C. Sections 4301–4313.
11. 12 C.F.R. Sections 230.1–230.9.

Before opening a deposit account, new customers must be given certain information in a brochure, pamphlet, or other handout. The information, which must also appear in all advertisements, includes the following:

1. The minimum balance required to open an account and to be paid interest.
2. The interest, stated in terms of the annual percentage yield on the account.
3. Whether interest is calculated daily.
4. Any fees, charges, and penalties, and how they are calculated.

Also, under the TISA and Regulation DD, a customer's monthly statement must declare the interest earned on the account, any fees that were charged, how the fees were calculated, and the number of days that the statement covers.

The Collection Process

Usually, deposited checks involve parties who do business at different banks, but sometimes checks are written between customers of the same bank. Either situation brings into play the bank collection process as it operates within the statutory framework of Article 4 of the UCC.

DESIGNATIONS OF BANKS INVOLVED IN THE COLLECTION PROCESS The first bank to receive a check for payment is the **depositary bank**.[12] For example, when a person deposits an IRS tax-refund check into a personal checking account at the local bank, that bank is the depositary bank. The bank on which a check is drawn (the drawee bank) is called the **payor bank**. Any bank except the payor bank that handles a check during some phase of the collection process is a **collecting bank**. Any bank except the payor bank or the depositary bank to which an item is transferred in the course of this collection process is called an **intermediary bank**.

During the collection process, any bank can take on one or more of the various roles of depositary, payor, collecting, and intermediary bank. To illustrate: A buyer in New York writes a check on her New York bank and sends it to a seller in San Francisco. The seller deposits the check in her San Francisco bank account. The seller's bank is both a *depositary bank* and a *collecting bank*. The buyer's bank in New York is the *payor bank*. As the check travels from San Francisco to New York, any collecting bank handling the item in the collection process (other than the ones acting as a depositary bank and a payor bank) is also called an *intermediary bank*. Exhibit 18–6 illustrates how various banks function in the collection process.

CHECK COLLECTION BETWEEN CUSTOMERS OF THE SAME BANK An item that is payable by the depositary bank (also the payor bank) that receives it is called an "on-us item." If the bank does not dishonor the check by the opening of the second banking day following its receipt, the check is considered paid [UCC 4–215(e)(2)]. For example, Williams and Merkowitz both have checking accounts at State Bank. On Monday morning, Merkowitz deposits into his own checking account a $300 check drawn by Williams. That same day, State Bank issues Merkowitz a "provisional credit" for $300. When the bank opens on Wednesday, Williams's check is considered honored, and Merkowitz's provisional credit becomes a final payment.

CHECK COLLECTION BETWEEN CUSTOMERS OF DIFFERENT BANKS Once a depositary bank receives a check, it must arrange to present it either directly or through intermediary banks to the appropriate payor bank. Each bank in the collection chain must pass the check on before midnight of the next banking day following its receipt [UCC 4–202(b)].[13] A "banking day" is any part of a day that the bank is open to carry on substantially all of its banking functions. Thus, if a bank has only its drive-through facilities open, a check deposited on Saturday would not trigger a bank's midnight deadline until the following Monday. When the check reaches the payor bank, unless the payor bank dishonors the check or returns it by midnight on the next banking day following receipt, the payor bank

12. All definitions in this section are found in UCC 4–105. The terms *depositary* and *depository* have different meanings in the banking context. A depository bank refers to a *physical* place (a bank or other institution) in which deposits or funds are held or stored.

13. A bank may take a "reasonably longer time," such as when the bank's computer system is down due to a power failure, but the bank must show that it is still timely [UCC 4–202(b)].

♦ **Exhibit 18–6**
The Check Collection Process

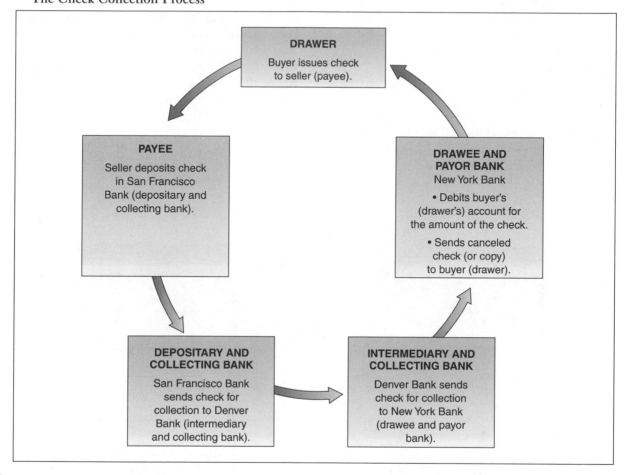

is accountable for the face amount of the check [UCC 4–302].[14]

Because of this deadline and because banks need to maintain an even work flow in the many items they handle daily, the UCC permits what is called *deferred posting*. According to UCC 4–108, "a bank may fix an afternoon hour of 2:00 P.M. or later as a cutoff hour for the handling of money and items and the making of entries on its books." Any checks received after that hour "may be treated as being received at the opening of the next

banking day." Thus, if a bank's "cutoff hour" is 3:00 P.M., a check received by a payor bank at 4:00 P.M. on Monday would be deferred for posting until Tuesday. In this situation, the payor bank's deadline would be midnight Wednesday.

HOW THE FEDERAL RESERVE SYSTEM CLEARS CHECKS The **Federal Reserve System** is a network of twelve central banks, located around the country and headed by the Federal Reserve Board of Governors. Most banks in the United States have Federal Reserve accounts. The Federal Reserve System has greatly simplified the check collection process by acting as a **clearinghouse**—a system or a place where banks exchange checks and drafts drawn on each other and settle daily balances.

For example, suppose that Pamela Moy of Philadelphia writes a check to Jeanne Sutton in San Francisco. When Sutton receives the check in

---

14. Most checks are cleared by a computerized process, and communication and computer facilities may fail because of weather, equipment malfunction, or other conditions. If such conditions arise and a bank fails to meet its midnight deadline, the bank is "excused" from liability if the bank has exercised "such diligence as the circumstances require" [UCC 4–109(d)].

the mail, she deposits it in her bank. Her bank then deposits the check in the Federal Reserve Bank of San Francisco, which transfers it to the Federal Reserve Bank of Philadelphia. That Federal Reserve bank then sends the check to Moy's bank, which deducts the amount of the check from Moy's account. Exhibit 18–7 illustrates this process.

ELECTRONIC CHECK PRESENTMENT   In the past, most checks were processed manually—the employees of each bank in the collection chain would physically handle each check that passed through the bank for collection or payment. Today, however, most checks are being processed electronically. In contrast to manual check processing, which can take days, *electronic check presentment* can be done on the day of the deposit. With electronic check presentment, items may be encoded with information (such as the amount of the check) that is read and processed by other banks' computers. In some situations, a check may be

♦ **Exhibit 18–7**
  How a Check Is Cleared

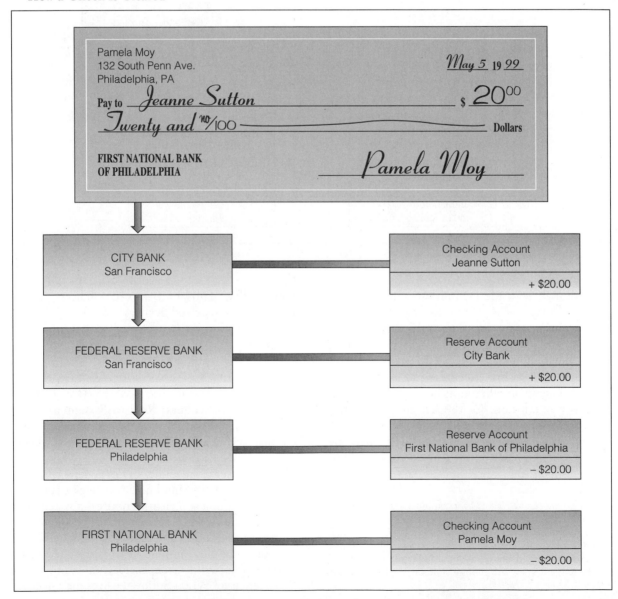

retained at its place of deposit, and only its image or information describing it is presented for payment under a Federal Reserve agreement, clearinghouse rule, or truncation agreement [UCC 4–110]. The term *truncation* refers to presentment by notice rather than by delivery.

Electronic Fund Transfers

The application of computer technology to banking, in the form of *electronic fund transfer systems*, has been helping to relieve banking institutions of the burden of having to move mountains of paperwork to process fund transfers. An **electronic fund transfer (EFT)** is a transfer of money made by the use of an electronic terminal, a telephone, a computer, or magnetic tape.

The benefits of electronic banking are obvious. Automatic payments, direct deposits, and other fund transfers are now made electronically; no physical transfers of cash, checks, or other negotiable instruments are involved. Through the use of EFT systems, transactions that would otherwise take days can now be completed in seconds. For example, Harlan in New York can pay a debt to Lesley in Los Angeles by entering into a computer a bank order to pay it. Chase Manhattan, the drawee bank, can instantly debit Harlan's account and transfer the credit to the Bank of America, Lesley's bank, which can immediately credit her account. Not surprisingly, though, electronic banking also poses difficulties on occasion, including the following:

1. It is difficult to issue stop-payment orders.
2. Fewer records are available to prove or disprove that a transaction took place.
3. The possibilities for tampering (with a resulting decrease in privacy) are increased.
4. The time between the writing of a check and its deduction from an account (float time) is lost.

Types of EFT Systems

Most banks today offer EFT services to their customers. The four most common types of EFT systems used by bank customers are (1) automated teller machines, (2) point-of-sale systems, (3) systems handling direct deposits and withdrawals, and (4) pay-by-telephone systems. We look here at each of these types of EFT systems. Vast amounts of money are also transferred daily through electronic transfers between financial institutions. We look at these *commercial transfers* of funds later in the chapter.

AUTOMATED TELLER MACHINES Automated teller machines (ATMs) are located either on the bank's premises or at convenient locations such as supermarkets, drugstores and other stores, airports, and shopping centers. Automated teller machines receive deposits, dispense funds from checking or savings accounts, make credit-card advances, and receive payments. The devices are connected online to the banks' computers. To access an account through an ATM, the bank customer uses a plastic card (debit card, access card), issued to him or her by the bank, plus a secret *personal identification number (PIN)*. The PIN protects the customer from someone else's use of a lost or stolen access card.

POINT-OF-SALE SYSTEMS Point-of-sale systems allow consumers to transfer funds to merchants to pay for purchases. On-line terminals are located in, for example, grocery stores. When a purchase is made, the customer's *debit card* (issued by the bank to the customer) is inserted into the terminal, which reads the data encoded on it. The computer at the customer's bank verifies that the card and identification code are valid and that there is enough money in the customer's account to cover the purchase. After the purchase is made, the customer's account is debited for the amount of the purchase.

DIRECT DEPOSITS AND WITHDRAWALS A direct deposit may be made to a customer's account through an electronic terminal when the customer has authorized the deposit in advance. The federal government often uses this type of EFT to deposit Social Security payments directly into beneficiaries' accounts. Similarly, an employer may agree to make payroll and pension payments directly into an employee's account at specified intervals.

A customer may also authorize the bank (or other financial institution at which the customer's funds are on deposit) to make automatic payments at regular, recurrent intervals to a third party. For example, insurance premiums, utility bills, and automobile installment loan payments may often be made automatically.

PAY-BY-TELEPHONE SYSTEMS When it is undesirable to arrange in advance for an automatic payment—as, for example, when the amount of a regular payment varies—some financial institutions permit customers to pay bills through a pay-by-telephone system. This allows the customer to access the institution's computer system by telephone and direct a transfer of funds. Customers frequently pay utility bills directly using pay-by-telephone systems. Customers may also be permitted to transfer funds between accounts—for example, to withdraw funds from a savings account and make a deposit in a checking account—in this way.

Consumer Fund Transfers

Consumer fund transfers are governed by the Electronic Fund Transfer Act (EFTA)[15] of 1978. This act provides a basic framework for the rights, liabilities, and responsibilities of users of EFT systems. Additionally, the act gave the Federal Reserve Board authority to issue rules and regulations to help implement the act's provisions. The Federal Reserve Board's implemental regulation is called Regulation E.

The EFTA governs financial institutions that offer electronic fund transfers involving consumer accounts. The types of accounts covered include checking accounts, savings accounts, and any other asset accounts established for personal, family, or household purposes. Note that telephone transfers are covered by the EFTA only if they are made in accordance with a prearranged plan under which periodic or recurring transfers are contemplated.[16]

MAJOR RULES UNDER THE EFTA Congress passed the EFTA "to provide a basic framework establishing the rights, liabilities, and responsibilities of participants in electronic fund transfers." The EFTA is designed to protect consumers. It is not concerned with commercial electronic fund transfers—transfers between businesses or between businesses and financial institutions. (Commercial fund transfers are governed by Article 4A of the UCC.)

The EFTA is essentially a disclosure law benefiting consumers. The act requires financial institutions to inform consumers of their rights and responsibilities, including those listed here, with respect to EFT systems.

1. If a customer's debit card is lost or stolen and used without his or her permission, the customer may be required to pay no more than $50. The customer, however, must notify the bank of the loss or theft within two days of learning about it. Otherwise, the liability increases to $500. The customer may be liable for more than $500 if he or she does not report the unauthorized use within sixty days after it appears on the customer's statement. (Even the $50 limit does not apply if the customer gives his or her card to someone who uses it improperly or if fraud is committed.)

2. The customer must discover any error on the monthly statement within sixty days, and he or she must notify the bank. The bank then has ten days to investigate and must report its conclusions to the customer in writing. If the bank takes longer than ten days, it must return the disputed amount of money to the customer's account until it finds the error. If there is no error, the customer has to return the money to the bank.

3. The bank must furnish receipts for transactions made through computer terminals, but it is not obligated to do so for telephone transfers.

4. The bank must make a monthly statement for every month in which there is an electronic transfer of funds. Otherwise, the bank must make statements every quarter. The statement must show the amount and date of the transfer, the names of the retailers or other third parties involved, the location or identification of the terminal, and the fees. Additionally, the statement must give an address and a phone number for inquiries and error notices.

5. Any authorized prepayment for utility bills and insurance premiums can be stopped three days before the scheduled transfer.

UNAUTHORIZED ELECTRONIC FUND TRANSFERS Unauthorized electronic fund transfers are one of the hazards of electronic banking. A paper check leaves visible evidence of a transaction, and a customer can easily detect a forgery or an alteration on a check with ordinary vigilance. Evidence of an electronic transfer, however, is in many cases only an entry in a computer printout of the various deb-

---

15. 15 U.S.C. Sections 1693 *et seq.* The EFTA is Title IX of the Consumer Credit Protection Act.
16. *Kashanchi v. Texas Commerce Medical Bank, N.A.,* 703 F.2d 936 (5th Cir. 1983).

its and credits made to a particular account during a specified time period.

Because of the vulnerability of EFT systems to fraudulent activities, the EFTA of 1978 clearly defined what constitutes an unauthorized transfer. Under the act, a transfer is unauthorized if (1) it is initiated by a person other than the consumer who has no actual authority to initiate the transfer; (2) the consumer receives no benefit from it; and (3) the consumer did not furnish the person "with the card, code, or other means of access" to his or her account.

In the following case, the court had to determine whether an account holder had authorized an imposter to withdraw funds from the customer's account. The first two parts of the definition of an unauthorized transfer just cited were obviously not relevant—the customer had not initiated or authorized the transfer, nor had he benefited from it. He had, however, unwittingly furnished the imposter with his EFT card and bank code. The case contains a lesson for all ATM users.

CASE 18.4

Ognibene v. Citibank, N.A.

Civil Court of New York City, 1981.
112 Misc.2d 219,
446 N.Y.S.2d 845.

FACTS Frederick Ognibene stopped at an ATM outside a Citibank branch to make a $20 withdrawal from his account. Two ATMs were close together. In between them was a customer service telephone that a man appeared to be using. After Ognibene made his withdrawal, the man asked if he could try Ognibene's card in the other ATM to see if it would activate the machine. Ognibene, who thought the man was a bank employee, gave the man his card. The man inserted it in the other machine and punched in Ognibene's personal identification number (which the man had seen when Ognibene made his withdrawal). The man said into the phone that the machine was functioning and then hung up, returned Ognibene's card, thanked him, and left. Later, Ognibene realized that $400 had been withdrawn from his account at that time. He brought an action against Citibank in a New York court to recover the money.

ISSUE Was the stranger's withdrawal from Ognibene's account "authorized" by Ognibene, in view of the fact that Ognibene had voluntarily allowed the stranger to use his card?

DECISION No. The court ordered the bank to credit the $400 to Ognibene's account.

REASON The court emphasized that Ognibene did not intend to authorize the stranger's withdrawal of funds from his account. The court also concluded that Ognibene was not negligent—he believed he was assisting a bank employee. Instead, the court pointed out that the bank had received reports of fraudulent withdrawals conducted by imposters posing as bank employees and gaining access to accounts in the same manner as in Ognibene's case. Because "the bank had knowledge of the scam and its operational details," it was in a better position than Ognibene to prevent the fraud. Thus, the court concluded that the bank "was negligent in failing to provide plaintiff-customer with information sufficient to alert him to the danger," so that, for example, he could have kept his personal identification number private.

FOR CRITICAL ANALYSIS—Ethical Consideration *Was the bank really in a better position than the customer to protect against fraud in this case? What kind of message does this case send to bank customers?*

ERROR RESOLUTION AND DAMAGES Banks must strictly follow the error-resolution procedures prescribed by the EFTA. If a bank fails to investigate an error and report its conclusion promptly to the customer, in the specific manner designated by the EFTA, it will be in violation of the act and subject to civil liability. Its liability extends to any actual damages sustained by a customer and to all the costs of a successful action brought against the bank by a customer, including attorneys' fees. In addition, the bank may be liable for punitive damages ranging from $100 to $1,000 in an individual action. Failure to investigate an error in good faith makes the bank liable for treble damages. Even when a customer has sustained no actual damage, the bank may be liable for legal costs and punitive damages if it fails to follow the proper procedures outlined by the EFTA in regard to error resolution.

Commercial Transfers

The transfer of funds "by wire" between commercial parties is another way in which funds are transferred electronically. In fact, the dollar volume of payments by wire transfer is more than $1 trillion a day—an amount that far exceeds the dollar volume of payments made by other means. The two major wire payment systems are the Federal Reserve wire transfer network (Fedwire) and the New York Clearing House Interbank Payments Systems (CHIPS).

Unauthorized wire transfers are obviously possible and, indeed, have become a problem. If an imposter, for example, succeeds in having funds wired from another's account, the other party will bear the loss (unless he or she can recover from the imposter). In the past, any disputes arising as a result of unauthorized or incorrectly made transfers were settled by the courts under the common law principles of tort law or contract law. To clarify the rights and liabilities of parties involved in fund transfers not subject to the EFTA or other federal or state statutes, Article 4A of the UCC was promulgated in 1989. Most states have adopted this article.

The type of fund transfer covered by Article 4A is illustrated in the following example. Jellux, Inc., owes $5 million to Perot Corporation. Instead of sending Perot a check or some other instrument that would enable Perot to obtain payment, Jellux tells its bank, East Bank, to credit $5 million to Perot's account in West Bank. East Bank instructs West Bank to credit $5 million to Perot's account. In more complex transactions, additional banks would be involved.

In these and similar circumstances, ordinarily a financial institution's instruction is transmitted electronically. Any means may be used, however, including first-class mail. To reflect this fact, Article 4A uses the term *funds transfer* rather than *wire transfer* to describe the overall payment transaction. The full text of Article 4A is included in Appendix C, following Article 4 of the Uniform Commercial Code.

▌ Terms and Concepts

cashier's check 363
certified check 364
check 362
clearinghouse 375
collecting bank 374

depositary bank 374
electronic fund transfer (EFT) 377
Federal Reserve System 375
intermediary bank 374

overdraft 366
payor bank 374
stale check 367
stop-payment order 367
traveler's check 364

▌ Chapter Summary: Checks and the Banking System

Checks (See pages 362–365.)	1. *Cashier's check*—A check drawn by a bank on itself (the bank is both the drawer and the drawee) and purchased by a customer. In effect, the bank lends its credit to the purchaser of the check, thus making the funds available for immediate use in banking circles.

▮ Chapter Summary: Checks and the Banking System—Continued

Checks—Continued	2. *Teller's check*—A check drawn by a bank on another bank or, when drawn on a nonbank, payable at or through a bank.
	3. *Traveler's check*—An instrument payable on demand, drawn on or through a bank, and designated as a traveler's check. The purchaser must provide his or her signature for a traveler's check to become a negotiable instrument.
	4. *Certified check*—A check for which the drawee bank certifies that it will set aside funds in the drawer's account to ensure payment of the check upon presentation. On certification, the drawer and all prior indorsers are completely discharged from liability on the check.
The Bank-Customer Relationship *(See page 366.)*	1. *Contractual relationship*—The bank's relationship with its customer is contractual; both the bank and the customer assume certain contractual duties when a customer opens a bank account.
	2. *Creditor-debtor relationship*—The relationship is also a creditor-debtor relationship (the bank is the debtor, because it holds the customer's funds on deposit).
	3. *Agency relationship*—Because a bank must act in accordance with the customer's orders in regard to the customer's deposited money, an agency relationship also arises—the bank is the agent for the customer, who is the principal.
Bank's Duty to Honor Checks *(See pages 366–373.)*	Generally, a bank has a duty to honor its customers' checks, provided that the customers have sufficient funds on deposit to cover the checks [UCC 4–401(a)]. The bank is liable to its customers for actual damages caused by the bank's wrongful dishonor. The following list summarizes the rights and liabilities of the bank and the customer in various situations.
	1. *Overdrafts*—The bank has the right to charge a customer's account for any item properly payable, even if the charge results in an overdraft [UCC 4–401(a)].
	2. *Postdated checks*—A bank may charge a postdated check against a customer's account, unless the customer notifies the bank of the postdating in time to allow the bank to act on the notice before the bank commits itself to pay on the check [UCC 4–401(c)].
	3. *Stale checks*—The bank is not obligated to pay an uncertified check presented more than six months after its date, but it may do so in good faith without liability [UCC 4–404].
	4. *Stop-payment orders*—The customer must make a stop-payment order in time for the bank to have a reasonable opportunity to act. Oral orders are binding for only fourteen days unless they are confirmed in writing. Written orders are effective for only six months unless renewed in writing. The bank is liable for wrongful payment over a timely stop-payment order, but only to the extent of the loss suffered by the drawer-customer [UCC 4–403].
	5. *Death or incompetence of a customer*—So long as the bank does not know of the death or incompetence of a customer, the bank can pay an item without liability to the customer's estate. Even with knowledge of a customer's death, a bank can honor or certify checks (in the absence of a stop-payment order) for ten days after the date of the customer's death [UCC 4–405].
	6. *Forged drawers' signatures, forged indorsements, and altered checks*—The customer has a duty to examine account statements with reasonable care upon receipt and to notify the bank promptly of any forged or unauthorized signatures or indorsements, or alterations. On a series of unauthorized signatures or alterations by the same wrongdoer, examination and report must occur within thirty calendar days of receipt of the statement. Failure to comply releases the bank from any liability unless the

(Continued)

▌Chapter Summary: Checks and the Banking System—Continued

Banks Duty to Honor Checks— Continued	bank failed to exercise ordinary care. Regardless of care or lack of care, the customer is estopped from holding the bank liable after one year for unauthorized customer signatures or alterations and after three years for unauthorized indorsements [UCC 3–403, 4–111, 4–401(a), 4–406].
Bank's Duty to Accept Deposits *(See pages 373–374.)*	A bank has a duty to accept deposits made by its customers into their accounts. Funds represented by checks deposited must be made available to the customer according to a schedule mandated by the Expedited Funds Availability Act of 1987 and Regulation CC. A bank also has a duty to collect payment on any checks deposited by its customers. When checks deposited by a customer are drawn on other banks, as they often are, the check collection process comes into play (discussed next). Under the Truth-in-Savings Act of 1991 and its implementing regulation, banks must pay interest on the full balance of a customer's account each day on any interest-bearing account.
The Collection Process *(See pages 374–377.)*	1. *Definitions of banks*—UCC 4–105 provides the following definitions of banks involved in the collection process: a. Depository bank—The first bank to accept a check for payment. b. Payor bank—The bank on which a check is drawn. c. Collecting bank—Any bank except the payor bank that handles a check during the collecting process. d. Intermediary bank—Any bank except the payor bank or the depositary bank to which an item is transferred in the course of the collection process. 2. *Check collection between customers of the same bank*—A check payable by the depository bank that receives it is an "on-us item"; if the bank does not dishonor the check by the opening of the second banking day following its receipt, the check is considered paid [UCC 4–215(e)(2)]. 3. *Check collection between customers of different banks*—Each bank in the collection process must pass the check on to the next appropriate bank before midnight of the next banking day following its receipt [UCC 4–108, 4–202(b), 4–302]. 4. *How the Federal Reserve System clears checks*—The Federal Reserve System facilitates the check clearing process by serving as a clearinghouse for checks. 5. *Electronic check presentment*—When checks are presented electronically, items may be encoded with information (such as the amount of the check) that is read and processed by other banks' computers. In some situations, a check may be retained at its place of deposit, and only its image or information describing it is presented for payment under a Federal Reserve agreement, clearinghouse rule, or other agreement [UCC 4–110].
Electronic Fund Transfers *(See pages 377–380.)*	1. *Types of EFT systems*— a. Automated teller machines (ATMs). b. Point-of-sale systems. c. Direct deposits and withdrawals. d. Pay-by-telephone systems. 2. *Consumer fund transfers*—Consumer fund transfers are governed by the Electronic Fund Transfer Act (EFTA) of 1978. The EFTA is basically a disclosure law that sets forth the rights and duties of the bank and the customer in respect to electronic fund transfer systems. Banks must comply strictly with EFTA requirements. 3. *Commercial transfers*—Disputes arising as a result of unauthorized or incorrectly made fund transfers between financial institutions are not covered under the EFTA. Article 4A of the UCC, which has been adopted by the majority of the states, governs fund transfers not subject to the EFTA or other federal or state statutes.

▌For Review

1. Checks are usually three-party instruments. On what type of check, however, does a bank serve as both the drawer and the drawee? What type of check does a bank agree in advance to accept when the check is presented for payment?
2. When may a bank properly dishonor a customer's check without liability to the customer?
3. In what circumstances might a bank not be liable for payment of a check containing a forged signature of the drawer?

4. Under the Electronic Fund Transfer Act, under what conditions will a bank be liable for an unauthorized fund transfer? When will the consumer be liable?
5. Are commercial electronic fund transfers between businesses governed by the Electronic Fund Transfer Act? If not, what law governs commercial fund transfers?

▌Questions and Case Problems

18–1. Error Resolution. Sheridan has a checking account at Gulf Bank. She frequently uses her access card to obtain money from the automatic teller machines. She always withdraws $50 when she makes a withdrawal, but she never withdraws more than $50 in any one day. When she received the April statement on her account, she noticed that on April 13 two withdrawals for $50 each had been made from the account. Believing this to be a mistake, she went to her bank on May 10 to inform the bank of the error. A bank officer told her that the bank would investigate and inform her of the result. On May 26, the bank officer called her and said that bank personnel were having trouble locating the error but would continue to try to find it. On June 20, the bank sent her a full written report advising her that no error had been made. Sheridan, unhappy with the bank's explanation, filed suit against the bank, alleging that it had violated the Electronic Fund Transfer Act. What was the outcome of the suit? Would it matter if the bank could show that on the day in question it had deducted $50 from Sheridan's account to cover a check that Sheridan had written to a local department store and that had cleared the bank on that day?

18–2. Forged Signatures. Gary goes grocery shopping and carelessly leaves his checkbook in his shopping cart. Dolores steals his checkbook, which has two blank checks remaining. On May 5, Dolores forges Gary's name on a check for $10 and cashes the check at Gary's bank, Citizens Bank of Middletown. Gary has not reported the theft of his blank checks to his bank. On June 1, Gary receives his monthly bank statement and canceled checks from Citizens Bank, including the forged check, but he does not examine the canceled checks. On June 20, Dolores forges Gary's last check. This check is for $1,000 and is cashed at Eastern City Bank, a bank with which Dolores has previously done

business. Eastern City Bank puts the check through the collection process, and Citizens Bank honors it. On July 1, Gary receives his bank statement and canceled checks. On July 4, Gary discovers both forgeries and immediately notifies Citizens Bank. Dolores cannot be found. Gary claims that Citizens Bank must recredit his account for both checks, as his signature was forged. Discuss fully Gary's claim.

18–3. Death of Bank Customer/Stale Checks. Brian, on January 5, drafts a check for $3,000 drawn on the Southern Marine Bank and payable to his assistant, Shanta. Brian puts last year's date on the check by mistake. On January 7, before Shanta has had a chance to go to the bank, Brian is killed in an automobile accident. Southern Marine is aware of Brian's death. On January 10, Shanta presents the check to the bank, and the bank honors the check by payment to Shanta. Brian's widow, Joyce, claims that the bank wrongfully paid Shanta, because it knew of Brian's death and also paid a check that was by date over one year old. Joyce, as executor of Brian's estate and sole heir by his will, demands that Southern Marine recredit Brian's estate for the check paid to Shanta. Discuss fully Southern Marine's liability in light of Joyce's demand.

18–4. Overdrafts. In September 1976, Edward and Christine McSweeney opened a joint checking account with the United States Trust Co. of New York. Between April 1978 and July 1978, 195 checks totaling $99,063 were written. In July 1978, activity in the account ceased. Christine wrote 95 of the 195 checks, totaling $16,811, and Edward wrote the rest of the checks. After deposits were credited for that period, the checks created a cumulative overdraft of $75,983. Can a bank knowingly honor a check when payment creates an overdraft, or must the bank dishonor the check? If the bank pays a check and thereby creates an overdraft, can the bank collect the amount of the overdraft from its customer? [*United States Trust Co. of New York v. McSweeney,* 91 A.D.2d 7, 457 N.Y.S.2d 276 (1982)]

18–5. Unauthorized Transfers. Parviz Haghighi Abyaneh and Iran Haghighi were co-owners of a savings account at First State Bank. On May 23, 1984, a person identifying himself as Abyaneh entered the Raleigh, North Carolina, office of Citizens Savings and Loan Association of Rocky Mount and opened a savings account. He then called First State Bank and asked a bank employee to transfer funds from Abyaneh's First State account into the newly created account. As a result, $53,825.66 was transferred to the new account, and subsequently the funds were withdrawn. When the true owners of the First State Bank account learned of the transfer, they filed suit against Merchants Bank, North, successor by merger to First State Bank, for violating the Electronic Fund Transfer Act. Discuss whether Abyaneh will be able to recover the $53,825.66. [*Abyaneh v. Merchants Bank, North,* 670 F.Supp. 1298 (M.D.Pa. 1987)]

18–6. Commercial Transfers. Dr. As'ad M. Masri and his wife borrowed $150,000 from First Virginia Bank–Colonial (FVBC). Masri then signed a wire-transfer request directing FVBC to transfer the funds to the Amro Bank in Amsterdam. The request also stated that the funds were to be deposited to the Lenex Corporation's account in that bank. FVBC transferred the funds to the Bank of Nova Scotia, an intermediary bank, and sent disbursal instructions directly to Amro. The following day, the funds were credited to the Lenex account at the Amro Bank. They were withdrawn, however, by someone other than the person intended by Masri to do so. When the Masris later defaulted on the loan, FVBC sought full repayment. The Masris

claimed that FVBC breached the wire-transfer agreement. Has FVBC breached the transfer agreement? Where does FVBC's responsibility end? Discuss fully. [*First Virginia Bank–Colonial v. Masri, M.D.,* 245 Va. 461, 428 S.E.2d 903 (1993)]

18–7. Stale Checks. RPM Pizza, Inc., issued a $96,000 check to Systems Marketing but immediately placed a written stop-payment order on the check. Three weeks after the order expired, Systems cashed the check. Bank One Cambridge, RPM's bank, paid the check with funds from RPM's account. Because the check was more than six months old, it was stale and thus, according to standard banking procedures as well as Bank One's own procedures, the signature on the check should have been specially verified. RPM filed a suit in a federal district court against Bank One to recover the amount of the check. What should the court consider in deciding whether the bank's payment of the check violated the UCC? [*RPM Pizza, Inc. v. Bank One Cambridge,* 69 F.Supp. 517 (E.D.Mich. 1994)]

18–8. Article 3 versus Article 4. Gary Morgan Chevrolet and Oldsmobile, Inc., issued four checks payable to General Motors Acceptance Corp. (GMAC) on Morgan's account with the Bank of Richmondville. There were insufficient funds in Morgan's account, and the bank gave GMAC oral notice of dishonor. The bank returned the checks two days later. GMAC filed a suit against the bank in a New York state court, claiming that the bank failed to dishonor the checks before its midnight deadline, because notice of dishonor must be in writing under Article 4. The bank countered that notice of dishonor may be made orally under Article 3. Which article controls when there is such a conflict? [*General Motors Acceptance Corp. v. Bank of Richmondville,* 203 A.D.2d 851, 611 N.Y.S.2d 338 (1994)]

▌Unit Five—Cumulative Hypothetical Problem

18–9. *Marva Cummings works as a bookkeeper for Albatross Printing Corp., a small printing firm. Marva has worked for the firm for years. She is authorized to sign company checks, on which Albatross's name and address are printed, and generally handles the firm's accounts. One of her tasks is to reconcile the monthly bank statement from the firm's bank.*

1. Albatross owes White Paper Co. $350 for paper supplies that Albatross ordered and received. Marva, who is distracted by personal problems, writes a check to White Paper but inadvertently fails to add the date. She also enters $300 in the box on the check indicating the amount in fig-

ures, but writes out "Three hundred and fifty and no/100" before the word "Dollars"—which is preprinted on the check. Is this check negotiable? If so, for what amount? If White Paper Co. crosses out the numerical amount $300 and writes "$350" above it, will this constitute a material alteration of the check?

2. Marva writes a check for $250 to Tony Malmo for some repairs Tony performed on the printing press. Tony indorses the check in blank and delivers it to Amber, who qualifies as a holder in due course. Amber loses the check. Felix finds it, indorses the check in blank, and deposits it into his bank account. In the meantime, Marva's employer discovers that Tony had not performed

the repairs as promised on the printing press and asks Marva to stop payment on the check, which she does. Describe the rights and liabilities of each of the parties in this situation.

3. Marva writes and signs a corporate check for $3,500 payable to Latham Manufacturing Co. to pay for new printing equipment ordered and received by Albatross. When the check reaches Albatross's bank for collection, the bank refuses payment because Albatross has insufficient funds in its account to cover the check. Latham learns that Albatross is having financial difficulties and decides to sue Marva, claiming that she is personally liable on the check because she signed her name without indicating in her signature that she was acting as an agent for Albatross. Will the court hold Marva liable? Why or why not?

4. Business at Albatross is booming, and its profits have been increasing each month for over a year. Marva's employer refuses to give her a raise, which she feels she deserves. She decides to pay herself some extra money by engaging in some deception. Each month, she writes a check payable to Ann Barkley for $500, indorses Ann's name on the check, and then deposits the check in her bank account, indorsing the check "For deposit only." Marva assumes that Albatross will never learn of her deception, because normally she is the only one who sees the bank statements and copies of the canceled checks. Unfortunately for Marva, after she has written six monthly checks in this way, for a total of $3,000, her employer discovers the scheme. The employer insists that the bank recredit its account for the $3,000 it paid to Marva over the forged indorsements. Must the bank recredit Albatross's account? Why or why not?

▌Accessing the Internet: Fundamentals of Business Law

To discover the major legal issues in banking and finance today, you can use the Legal Research Center of the commercial service CompuServe. When on CompuServe type in

Go legal

Select

Legal Research Center

The law firm of Reinhart et al. offers current information on banking law at

http://www.rbvdnr.com/

You can obtain a tremendous amount of information on banking regulation from the Federal Deposit Insurance Corporation (FDIC) at

http://www.fdic.gov/

Additional information about banking can be obtained from the Federal Reserve System at

http://woodrow.mpls.frb.fed.us/info/policy/

The American Bankers Association is the largest banking trade association in the United States. To learn more about the banking industry, go to

http://www.aba.com/

For a discussion of electronic banking, select the link to the ATA Payments System Task Force Executive Summary.

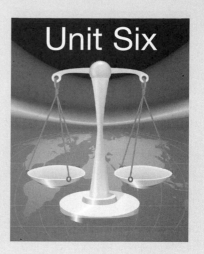

Debtor-Creditor Relationships

▌Unit Contents

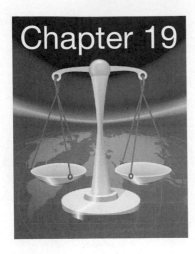

Chapter 19

Secured Transactions

CHAPTER OBJECTIVES

After reading this chapter, you should be able to:

1. List and define the various terms used in secured transactions.
2. State what is necessary to create an enforceable security interest.
3. Explain how and why security interests are perfected.
4. Indicate how priority disputes among creditors are decided.
5. Discuss the remedies available to a secured creditor when the debtor defaults.

Whenever the payment of a debt is guaranteed, or *secured*, by personal property owned by the debtor or in which the debtor has a legal interest, the transaction becomes known as a **secured transaction**. The concept of the secured transaction is as basic to modern business practice as the concept of credit. Logically, sellers and lenders do not want to risk nonpayment, so they usually will not sell goods or lend money unless the promise of payment is somehow guaranteed. Indeed, business as we know it could not exist without laws permitting and governing secured transactions. As will become evident, the law of secured transactions tends to favor the rights of creditors; but to a lesser extent, it offers debtors some protection, too.

The Terminology of Secured Transactions

The UCC's terminology is now uniformly adopted in all documents used in situations involving secured transactions. A brief summary of the UCC's definitions of terms relating to secured transactions follows.

1. A **security interest** is any interest "in personal property or fixtures which secures payment or performance of an obligation" [UCC 1–201(37)].
2. A **secured party** is a lender, a seller, or any person in whose favor there is a security interest, including a person to whom accounts or *chattel paper* (any writing evidencing a debt secured by personal property) has been sold [UCC 9–105(1)(m)]. The terms *secured party* and *secured creditor* are used interchangeably.
3. A **debtor** is the party who owes payment or performance of the secured obligation, whether or not that party actually owns or has rights in the collateral [UCC 9–105(1)(d)].
4. A **security agreement** is the agreement that creates or provides for a security interest between the debtor and a secured party [UCC 9–105(1)(*l*)].
5. **Collateral** is the property subject to a security interest, including accounts and chattel paper that have been sold [UCC 9–105(1)(c)].

These basic definitions form the concept under which a debtor-creditor relationship becomes a secured transaction relationship (see Exhibit 19–1).

388

◆ **Exhibit 19–1**
Secured Transactions—Concept and Terminology
In a security agreement, a debtor and creditor agree that the creditor will have a security interest in collateral in which the debtor has rights. In essence, the collateral secures the loan and ensures the creditor of payment should the debtor default.

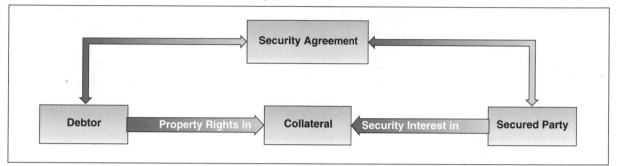

Creating and Perfecting a Security Interest

A creditor has two main concerns if the debtor **defaults** (fails to pay the debt as promised): (1) satisfaction of the debt through the possession and (usually) sale of the collateral and (2) priority over any other creditors or buyers who may have rights in the same collateral. We look here at how these two concerns are met through the creation and perfection of a security interest.

Creating a Security Interest

To become a secured party, the creditor must obtain a security interest in the collateral of the debtor. Three requirements must be met for a creditor to have an enforceable security interest:

1. Either (a) the collateral must be in the possession of the secured party in accordance with an agreement, or (b) there must be a written security

agreement describing the collateral and signed by the debtor.
2. The secured party must give value.
3. The debtor must have rights in the collateral.

Once these requirements have been met, the creditor's rights are said to *attach* to the collateral. **Attachment** gives the creditor an enforceable security interest in the collateral [UCC 9–203].

WRITTEN SECURITY AGREEMENT When the collateral is not in the possession of the secured party, a security agreement must be in writing to be enforceable. To be effective, (1) the security agreement must be signed by the debtor, (2) it must contain a description of the collateral, and (3) the description must reasonably identify the collateral [UCC 9–203(1), 9–110]. See Exhibit 19–2 for a sample security agreement.

At issue in the following case was whether a security agreement had reasonably identified the collateral and had, in fact, been signed by the debtor.

CASE 19.1

In re Ziluck

United States District Court,
Southern District of Florida, 1992.
139 Bankr. 44.

FACTS David Ziluck applied for a Radio Shack credit card. The front of the application contained blanks for various personal and employment information and a space for the applicant to sign. Above the signature line was the following statement: "I have read the Radio Shack Credit Account and Security Agreement, including the notice provisions in the last paragraph, and it contains no blanks or blank spaces. I agree to the terms of the Agreement and acknowledge

(Continued)

Case 19.1—Continued

a copy of the agreement." The back of the application contained a "Radio Shack Credit Account and Security Agreement," which stated in part, "We retain a security interest under the Uniform Commercial Code in all merchandise charged to your Account. If you do not make payments on your Account as agreed, the security interest allows us to repossess only the merchandise that has not been paid in full." When Ziluck later filed for bankruptcy protection, the bankruptcy court had to decide whether the application form constituted a valid security agreement. The court concluded that it did not, for two reasons. First, Ziluck's signature was not effective, because it was not on the back side of the form, which stated the terms of the security agreement. Second, the security agreement's description of the collateral ("all merchandise charged to your Account") was not sufficiently descriptive. The bankruptcy court's decision was appealed.

ISSUE   The issue in this case is twofold: (1) Had Ziluck effectively signed the security agreement? (2) Was the security agreement's description of the collateral sufficient?

DECISION   Yes, to both questions.

REASON   As to whether Ziluck had signed the security agreement, the court found that the language on the front of the credit-card application, above the signature line, made it clear that Ziluck was signing a security agreement. As to whether the collateral had been adequately described, the court stated that under UCC 9–110, "any description of personal property * * * is sufficient whether or not it is specific if it reasonably identifies what is described." In the court's view, the words "all merchandise charged to your Account" reasonably identified "the property subject to the security interest—namely any property purchased with the subject credit card."

FOR CRITICAL ANALYSIS—Ethical Consideration   *Should the court have considered whether Ziluck had actually read the full agreement?*

SECURED PARTY MUST GIVE VALUE   The secured party must give value. Value, according to UCC 1–201(44), is any consideration that supports a simple contract, security given for a pre-existing (antecedent) obligation, or any binding commitment to extend credit. Normally, the value given by a secured party is in the form of a direct loan, or it involves a commitment to sell goods on credit.

DEBTOR MUST HAVE RIGHTS IN THE COLLATERAL   The debtor must have rights in the collateral; that is, the debtor must have some ownership interest or right to obtain possession of that collateral. The debtor's rights can represent either a current or a future legal interest in the collateral. For example,

a retail seller-debtor can give a secured party a security interest not only in existing inventory owned by the retailer but also in *future* inventory to be acquired by the retailer.

In the following case, a creditor held a security interest in a pharmacist's accounts receivable (payments yet to be made to the pharmacist by his customers). Among these receivables were Medicaid payments—payments to be made to the pharmacist by the state government for services rendered to customers who received government assistance through the Medicaid program. Federal and state laws prohibit the assignment of Medicaid payments. Did this mean that the pharmacist had insufficient rights in these accounts to use them as collateral for a loan?

♦ **Exhibit 19–2**
A Sample Security Agreement

Date

| Name | No. and Street | City | County | State |

(hereinafter called "Debtor") hereby grants to _____

Name

| No. and Street | City | County | State |

(hereinafter called "Secured Party") a security interest in the following property (hereinafter called the "Collateral"): _____

_____

_____

to secure payment and performance of obligations identified or set out as follows (hereinafter called the "Obligations"): _____

_____

_____

Default in payment or performance of any of the Obligations or default under any agreement evidencing any of the Obligations is a default under this agreement. Upon such default Secured Party may declare all Obligations immediately due and payable and shall have the remedies of a secured party under the _____ Uniform Commercial Code.

Signed in (duplicate) triplicate.

Debtor
By _____

Secured Party
By _____

CASE 19.2

Estate of Angiulli

Surrogate's Court, Oneida County, 1990.
148 Misc.2d 796,
561 N.Y.S.2d 626.

FACTS When Frank Angiulli died in 1988, the pharmacy he owned in Utica, New York, was insolvent. At the time of his death, Angiulli owed H. K. Hineline Company, a supplier of pharmaceutical supplies, $34,469.63. The debt was secured by the pharmacy's accounts receivable, in which Hineline had earlier acquired a security interest. The administrator of Angiulli's estate collected funds from several accounts due to the pharmacy, including Medicaid payments, and used the monies to pay funeral and administrative costs. Hineline objected to this use of the funds, contending that Hineline's security interest in the accounts receivable entitled it to receive the payments. When the issue came before a New York state court, the administrator moved to dismiss

(Continued)

Case 19.2—Continued

Hineline's objections. The administrator argued that because Medicaid payments are not assignable under either federal or state law, Angiulli never acquired sufficient rights in those accounts to use them as collateral. Therefore, Hineline's security interest in the Medicaid accounts was not valid, because the security interest had never attached to the collateral.

ISSUE   Did Hineline have a valid security interest in the Medicaid accounts receivable?

DECISION   Yes. The court denied the administrator's motion to dismiss Hineline's objection.

REASON   The court acknowledged that under both federal and state law, Medicaid payments were not assignable. In other words, the New York State Department of Social Services, the agency that issued Medicaid payments, could not issue them to anyone other than the provider of the services that were being paid for by the Medicaid payments. The administrator had argued that in view of this law, it necessarily followed that the Medicaid receivables could not have served as collateral for a security interest. The court disagreed. The court found that the reason behind the law prohibiting assignments of Medicaid payments was "to enable the social services district to pay the supplier regardless of any assignment and to relieve the district from the potential liability and increased administrative burdens involved in such assignments." The law did not prohibit the recipient of the payments from assigning them to another party once the funds had been disbursed by the relevant government agency, however. The court therefore concluded that "Hineline's security interest in the Medicaid Receivable attached once the Department approved decedent's claim and authorized payment." Hineline's security interest was therefore effective, and Hineline was entitled to the payments. The payments "could not properly be used to pay funeral and administrative expenses."

FOR CRITICAL ANALYSIS—Economic Consideration   *What was the significance of the fact that Angiulli's pharmacy was insolvent?*

Perfecting a Security Interest

Perfection represents the legal process by which secured parties protect themselves against the claims of third parties who may wish to have their debts satisfied out of the same collateral. Usually, perfection is accomplished by the filing of a financing statement with the appropriate government official. In some circumstances, however, a security interest becomes perfected without the filing of a financing statement. The classification of collateral is important in determining the proper method of perfection. Exhibit 19–3 summarizes the various classifications of collateral and the methods of perfecting a security interest in them.

PERFECTION BY FILING   A secured party can perfect a security interest by filing a financing

statement (or the security agreement) with the appropriate state or local official. The UCC requires a **financing statement** to contain (1) the signature of the debtor, (2) the addresses of both the debtor and the secured party, and (3) a description of the collateral by type or item [UCC 9–402(1)]. Filing is the most common means of perfection to use. A sample financing statement is shown in Exhibit 19–4.

An improper filing reduces a secured party's claim in bankruptcy to that of an unsecured creditor. If the debtor's name on the financing statement is inaccurate, for example, or the collateral is not sufficiently described on the statement, the filing may not be effective.

The Debtor's Name   The UCC requires that a financing statement be filed under the name of the debtor [UCC 9–402(1)]. If the debtor is an individual, the financing statement must be filed under the name of the individual, but if the debtor is a partnership or a corporation, the financing statement must be filed under the partnership or corporate name [UCC 9–402(7)]. If a financing statement identifies the debtor by an incorrect name, the statement may be ineffective to perfect a security interest.

♦ **Exhibit 19–3**
Types of Collateral and Methods of Perfection

TYPE OF COLLATERAL	DEFINITION	PERFECTION METHOD	UCC SECTIONS
Tangible	All things that are *movable* at the time the security interest attaches or that are *fixtures* [UCC 9-105(1)(h)]. This includes timber to be cut, growing crops, and unborn animals.		
1. Consumer Goods	Goods used or bought primarily for personal, family, or household purposes—for example, household furniture [UCC 9–109(1)].	For purchase-money security interest, attachment is sufficient; for boats, motor vehicles, and trailers, there is a requirement of filing or compliance with a certificate of title statute; for other consumer goods, general rules of filing or possession apply.	9–302(1)(d), (3), (4); 9–305
2. Equipment	Goods bought for or used primarily in business—for example, a delivery truck [UCC 9–109(2)].	Filing or possession by secured party.	9–302(1); 9–305
3. Farm Products	Crops, livestock, and supplies used or produced in a farming operation in the possession of a farmer-debtor. This includes products of crops or livestock—for example, milk, eggs, maple syrup, and ginned cotton [UCC 9–109(3)].	Filing or possession by secured party.	9–302(1); 9–305
4. Inventory	Goods held for sale or lease and materials used or consumed in the course of business—for example, raw materials or floor stock of a retailer [UCC 9–109(4)].	Filing or possession by secured party.	9–302(1); 9–305
5. Fixtures	Goods that become so affixed to realty that an interest in them arises under real estate law—for example, a central air-conditioning unit [UCC 9–313(1)(a)].	Filing only.	9–313(1)

(Continued)

♦ Exhibit 19–3
Types of Collateral and Methods of Perfection—Continued

TYPE OF COLLATERAL	DEFINITION	PERFECTION METHOD	UCC SECTIONS
Intangible	Nonphysical property that exists only in connection with something else.		
1. Chattel Paper	Any writing that evidences both a *monetary obligation and a security interest*—for example, a thirty-six-month-payment retail security agreement signed by a buyer to purchase a car [UCC 9–105(1)(b)].	Filing or possession by secured party.	9–304(1); 9–305
2. Documents of Title	Papers that entitle the person in possession to hold, receive, or dispose of the paper or goods the documents cover—for example, bills of lading, warehouse receipts, and dock warrants [UCC 9–105(1)(f), 1–201(15), 7–201].	Filing or possession by secured party.	9–304(1), (3); 9–305
3. Instruments	Any writing that evidences a right to payment of money that is not a security agreement or lease, and any negotiable instrument or certificated security that in the ordinary course of business is transferred by delivery with any necessary indorsement or assignment—for example, stock certificates, promissory notes, and certificates of deposit [UCC 9–105)(1)(i), 3–104, 8–102(1)(a)].	Except for temporary perfected status,	9–304(1), (4), (5); 9–305
4. Accounts	Any right to payment for goods sold or leased or for services *rendered* that is not evidenced by an instrument or chattel paper—for example, accounts receivable and contract right payments [UCC 9–106].	Filing required (with exceptions).	9–302(1)(e), (g)
5. General Intangibles	Any personal property other than that defined above—for example, a patent, a copyright, goodwill, or a trademark [UCC 9–106].	Filing only.	9–302(1)

♦ **Exhibit 19–4**
A Sample Financing Statement

This FINANCING STATEMENT is presented for filing pursuant to the California Uniform Commercial Code.

1. DEBTOR (LAST NAME FIRST—IF AN INDIVIDUAL)	**1A.** SOCIAL SECURITY OR FEDERAL TAX NO.

1B. MAILING ADDRESS	**1C.** CITY, STATE	**1D.** ZIP CODE

2. ADDITIONAL DEBTOR (IF ANY) (LAST NAME FIRST—IF AN INDIVIDUAL)	**2A.** SOCIAL SECURITY OR FEDERAL TAX NO.

2B. MAILING ADDRESS	**2C.** CITY, STATE	**2D.** ZIP CODE

3. DEBTOR'S TRADE NAMES OR STYLES (IF ANY)	**3A.** FEDERAL TAX NUMBER

4. SECURED PARTY NAME MAILING ADDRESS CITY STATE ZIP CODE	**4A.** SOCIAL SECURITY NO., FEDERAL TAX NO. OR BANK TRANSIT AND A.B.A. NO.

5. ASSIGNEE OF SECURED PARTY (IF ANY) NAME MAILING ADDRESS CITY STATE ZIP CODE	**5A.** SOCIAL SECURITY NO., FEDERAL TAX NO. OR BANK TRANSIT AND A.B.A. NO.

6. This FINANCING STATEMENT covers the following types or items of property **(include description of real property on which located and owner of record when required by instruction 4)**.

As security for and in consideration of all present and any future advances or other obligations debtor hereby grants United California Bank a security interest in all of the following types or items of property ("Collateral" herein) in which the debtor now has or hereafter acquires any right, title, or interest, or rights present and future, wheresoever located and whether in the possession of the debtor, a warehouseman, bailee, trustee or any other person, and all increases, therein and replacements, products, and proceeds thereof. Proceeds include but are not limited to inventory, returned merchandise, accounts, chattel paper, general intangibles, insurance proceeds, documents, money, goods, equipment, instruments, and any other tangible or intangible property arising under the sale, lease or other disposition of collateral:

7. CHECK IF APPLICABLE [X]	**7A.** [ ] PRODUCTS OF COLLATERAL ARE ALSO COVERED	**7B.** DEBTOR(S) SIGNATURE NOT REQUIRED IN ACCORDANCE WITH INSTRUCTION 5(c) ITEM: [ ] (1) [ ] (2) [ ] (3) [ ] (4)

8. CHECK IF APPLICABLE [X]	[ ] DEBTOR IS A "TRANSMITTING UTILITY" IN ACCORDANCE WITH UCC § 9105 (1) (n)

9. ▶ SIGNATURE(S) of DEBTOR(S) DATE:	C O D E	**10.** THIS SPACE FOR USE OF FILING OFFICER (DATE, TIME, FILE NUMBER AND FILING OFFICER)
TYPE OR PRINT NAME(S) OF DEBTOR(S)	1	
▶	2	
SIGNATURE(S) OF SECURED PARTY(IES)	3	
	4	
TYPE OR PRINT NAME(S) OF SECURED PARTY(IES)		
11. Return copy to:	5	
NAME	6	
ADDRESS	7	
CITY	8	
STATE	9	
ZIP CODE	0	
(1) FILING OFFICER COPY FORM UCC-1—FILING FEE $3.00 Approved by the Secretary of State		

MS-336 10-78

Description of the Collateral The UCC requires that both the security agreement and the financing statement contain a description of the collateral in which the secured party has a security interest. The security agreement must include a description of the collateral because no security interest in goods can exist unless the parties agree on which goods are subject to the security interest. The financing statement must include a description of the collateral because the purpose of filing the statement is to give public notice of the fact that certain goods in the debtor's possession are subject to a security interest. Other parties who might later wish to lend money to the debtor or buy the collateral can thus learn of the security interest by checking with the state or local office in which a financing statement for that type of collateral would be filed (where financing statements are filed will be discussed shortly).

Sometimes, the descriptions in the two documents vary, with the description in the security agreement being more precise and the description in the financing statement more general. For example, a security agreement for a commercial loan to a manufacturer may list all of the manufacturer's equipment subject to the loan by serial number, whereas the financing statement may simply state "all equipment owned or hereafter acquired." To avoid problems arising from such variations in descriptions, a secured party may repeat exactly the security agreement's description in the financing statement or file the security agreement itself as a financing statement—assuming the security agreement meets the previously discussed criteria. Alternatively, where permitted, the secured party might file a combination security agreement–financing statement form. If the financing statement is too general or vague, a court may find it insufficient to perfect a security interest.

Where to File Depending on how collateral is classified, filing is done either centrally with the secretary of state, locally with the county clerk or other official, or both, according to state law. According to UCC 9–401, a state may choose one of three alternatives.[1] In general, financing statements for consumer goods should be filed with the county clerk. Other kinds of collateral require filing with the secretary of state [UCC 9–401].

PERFECTION WITHOUT FILING   In two types of situations, security interests can be perfected without the secured party's having to file a financing statement. First, when the collateral is transferred into the possession of the secured party, the secured party's security interest in the collateral is perfected. Second, a purchase-money security interest in consumer goods and an assignment of a beneficial interest in a trust or a decedent's estate are perfected automatically.

Perfection by Possession Under the common law, one of the most common means of obtaining financing was to **pledge** certain collateral as security for the debt and transfer the collateral into the creditor's possession. When the debt was paid, the collateral would be returned to the debtor. Usually, the transfer of collateral was accompanied by a written security agreement, but the agreement did not have to be in writing. In other words, an oral security agreement was effective as long as the secured party possessed the collateral. Article 9 of the UCC retained the common law pledge and the principle that the security agreement need not be in writing to be enforceable if the collateral is transferred to the secured party [UCC 9–203(1)(a)].

For most collateral, possession by the secured party is impractical because it denies the debtor the right to use or derive income from the property to pay off the debt. For example, if a farmer took out a loan to finance the purchase of a piece of heavy farm equipment, using the equipment as collateral, the purpose of the purchase would be defeated if the farmer transferred the collateral into the creditor's possession. Certain items, however, such as stocks, bonds, and jewelry, are commonly transferred into the creditor's possession when they are used as collateral for loans. With respect to negotiable instruments and certain securities (such as stocks and bonds), with a few exceptions, the *only* way to properly perfect a security interest is through possession by the secured party.

If a secured party is in possession of the collateral, he or she must use reasonable care in preserving it. Otherwise, the secured party is liable to the debtor [UCC 9–207(1), 9–207(3)].

Purchase-Money Security Interest Often, sellers of consumer goods (defined as goods bought or

---

1. See UCC 9–401 in Appendix C for these three alternatives. Approximately half the states have adopted the second alternative. Filing fees range from as low as $3 to as high as $25.

used by the debtor primarily for personal, family, or household purposes) agree to extend credit for part or all of the purchase price of those goods. Additionally, lenders, such as financial institutions, that are not necessarily in the business of selling such goods often agree to lend much of the purchase price for them. There is a special name for the security interest that the seller or the lender obtains when such a transaction occurs. It is called a **purchase-money security interest (PMSI)**, because the lender or seller has essentially provided a buyer with the "purchase money" to buy goods [UCC 9–107].

Suppose that Jamie wants to purchase a new entertainment center from ABC Electronics. The purchase price is $1,500. Not being able to pay cash, Jamie signs a purchase agreement to pay $300 down and $100 per month until the balance plus interest is fully paid. ABC Electronics is to retain a security interest in the purchased goods until full payment has been made. Because the security interest was created as part of the purchase agreement, it is a PMSI.

A PMSI in consumer goods is perfected automatically at the time of a credit sale—that is, at the time that the PMSI is created. The seller in this situation need do nothing more to protect his or her interest. There are exceptions to this rule, however, that cover security interests in fixtures and in motor vehicles [UCC 9–302(1)(d)]. In a few states, a PMSI in farm equipment under a certain statutory value may also be perfected automatically by attachment.

PERFECTION OF SECURITY INTERESTS IN MOTOR VEHICLES

Most states require a certificate of title for any motor vehicle, boat, or motor home. The normal methods described above for the perfection of a security interest typically do not apply to such vehicles. Rather, the perfection of a security interest only occurs when a notation of such an interest appears on the certificate of title that covers the vehicle.

As an example, suppose that your commercial bank lends you 80 percent of the money necessary to purchase a new BMW. You live in a state that requires certificates of title for all automobiles. If your bank fails to have its security interest noted on the certificate of title, its interest is not perfected. That means that a good faith purchaser of your BMW would take it free of the bank's interest. In most states, purchasers of motor vehicles can buy

vehicles with the confidence that no security interest exists that is not disclosed on the certificate of title.[2]

COLLATERAL MOVED TO ANOTHER JURISDICTION

Obviously, collateral may be moved by the debtor from one jurisdiction (state) to another. In general, a properly perfected security interest in collateral moved into a new jurisdiction continues to be perfected in the new jurisdiction for priority purposes (priority disputes will be examined later in the chapter) for a period of up to four months from the date the collateral was moved into the new jurisdiction or for the period of time remaining under the perfection in the original jurisdiction, whichever expires first [UCC 9–103(1)(d), 9–103(3)(e)]. Collateral moved from county to county within a state (if local filing is required), rather than from one state to another, however, may not have a four-month limitation [UCC 9–403(3)].

To illustrate: Suppose that on January 1, Wheeler secures a loan from a Nebraska bank by putting up all his wheat-threshing equipment as security. The Nebraska bank files the security interest centrally with the secretary of state. In June, Wheeler has an opportunity to harvest wheat crops in South Dakota and moves his equipment into that state on June 15. The law just mentioned means that the Nebraska bank's perfection remains effective in South Dakota for a period of four months from June 15. If the Nebraska bank wishes to retain its perfection priority, the bank must perfect properly in South Dakota during this four-month period. Should the bank fail to do so, its perfection would be lost after four months, and subsequent perfected security interests in the same collateral in South Dakota would prevail.

Among mobile goods, automobiles pose one of the biggest problems. If the original jurisdiction does not require a certificate of title as part of its perfection process for an automobile, perfection automatically ends four months after the automobile is moved into another jurisdiction. When a security interest exists on an automobile in a state in which title registration is required and when the security interest is noted on the certificate of title,

2. In the few states that do not require title registration of motor vehicles, one must examine the appropriate statutes to determine the priority of conflicting security interests.

the perfection of the security interest continues after the automobile is moved to another state requiring a certificate of title until the automobile is registered in the new state [UCC 9–103(2)]. This rule protects the secured party against anyone purchasing the car in the new state prior to the new registration. Moreover, because each certificate-of-title state requires that the old certificate of title be surrendered to obtain a new one, and because the secured party typically holds the certificate, the secured party usually is able to ensure that the security interest is noted on the new certificate of title.

EFFECTIVE TIME OF PERFECTION A financing statement is effective for five years from the date of filing [UCC 9–403(2)]. If a **continuation statement** is filed *within six months* prior to the expiration date, the effectiveness of the original statement is continued for another five years, starting with the expiration date of the first five-year period [UCC 9–403(3)]. The effectiveness of the statement can be continued in the same manner indefinitely.

In the following case, a perfected secured party filed a continuation statement two days early—that is, six months and two days before the expiration date of the original filing. At issue was whether the filing had occurred "within six months," as required under UCC 9–403(3).

CASE 19.3

Banque Worms v. Davis Construction Co.

Court of Appeals of Kentucky, 1992.
831 S.W.2d 921.

FACTS A New York bank, Banque Worms, provided the Big Oak Coal Company and the Dollar Branch Coal Corporation with a loan. As collateral for the loan, the mining companies granted Banque Worms a security interest in a "Euclid R-25 rock truck," as well as in other mining equipment. Banque Worms properly perfected its security interest in the equipment by filing a financing statement, effective for five years, on October 12, 1982. Banque Worms later filed a continuation statement on April 10, 1987, to maintain its priority status as a perfected secured party. Later that year, on November 23, the mining companies sold the rock truck to the Davis Construction Company to satisfy a $36,192 debt. Davis filed suit in a Kentucky state court to clear title to the rock truck once it became aware of Banque Worms's security interest. The trial court, holding in favor of Davis, found that Banque Worms had failed to comply with UCC 9–403. Banque Worms appealed.

ISSUE Is the continuation statement effective?

DECISION No. The Court of Appeals of Kentucky held that Banque Worms became an unperfected secured creditor on the lapse of the five-year perfection period.

REASON The court stated that "[b]ecause the continuation statement was not filed within six months prior to the lapse of the financing statement's effective period, [Banque Worms's] security interest in the rock truck became unperfected on October 12, 1987, which was five years after the date on which the financing statement was filed." In response to Banque Worms's argument for liberal construction of the UCC's time-limiting provision, the court stated that "the statute cannot be employed to overlook and defeat the clear and unambiguous statutory requirement as to timely filing which is imposed by [UCC 9–403(3)]."

FOR CRITICAL ANALYSIS—Ethical Consideration *Is it ever appropriate for a court to "overlook" a "clear and unambiguous statutory requirement"? Did the court in the above case have any alternative option?*

▌ The Scope of a Security Interest

In addition to covering collateral already in the debtor's possession, a security agreement can cover various other types of property, including the proceeds of the sale of collateral, after-acquired property, and future advances.

Proceeds

Proceeds include whatever is received when collateral is sold or otherwise disposed of, such as by exchange. A secured party's security interest in the collateral includes a security interest in the proceeds of the sale of that collateral. For example, suppose that a bank has a perfected security interest in the inventory of a retail seller of heavy farm machinery. The retailer sells a tractor out of this inventory to a farmer, a buyer in the ordinary course of business. The farmer agrees, in a retail security agreement, to pay monthly payments for a period of twenty-four months. If the retailer should go into default on the loan from the bank, the bank is entitled to the remaining payments the farmer owes to the retailer as proceeds.

A security interest in proceeds perfects automatically upon perfection of the secured party's security interest in the collateral and remains perfected for ten days after receipt of the proceeds by the debtor. One way to extend the ten-day automatic period is to provide for such extended coverage in the original security agreement. This is typically done when the collateral is the type that is likely to be sold, such as a retailer's inventory. The UCC provides that in the following circumstances the security interest in proceeds remains perfected for longer than ten days after the receipt of the proceeds by the debtor:

1.   When a filed financing statement covers the original collateral and the proceeds are collateral in which a security interest may be perfected by a filing in the office or offices with which the financing statement has been filed. Furthermore, a secured party's interest automatically perfects in property that the debtor acquires with cash proceeds, if the original filing would have been effective as to that property and the financing statement indicates that type of property [UCC 9–306(3)(a)]. Thus, in the farm equipment example above, if the retailer used the farmer's monthly payments to

acquire additional inventory, the bank would be entitled to that inventory, providing that the bank's original filing was effective as to that property and the financing statement indicated that type of property.

2.   Whenever there is a filed financing statement that covers the original collateral and the proceeds are identifiable cash proceeds [UCC 9–306(3)(b)].

3.   Whenever the security interest in the proceeds is perfected before the expiration of the ten-day period [UCC 9–306(3)(c)].

After-Acquired Property

After-acquired property of the debtor is property acquired after the execution of the security agreement. The security agreement may provide for coverage of after-acquired property [UCC 9–204(1)]. This is particularly useful for inventory financing arrangements, because a secured party whose security interest is in existing inventory knows that the debtor will sell that inventory, thereby reducing the collateral subject to the security interest. Generally, the debtor will purchase new inventory to replace the inventory sold. The secured party wants this newly acquired inventory to be subject to the original security interest. Thus, the after-acquired property clause continues the secured party's claim to any inventory acquired thereafter. This is not to say that the original security interest will be superior to the rights of all other creditors with regard to this after-acquired inventory, as will be discussed later.

Consider a typical example. Amato buys factory equipment from Bronson on credit, giving as security an interest in all of her equipment—both what she is buying and what she already owns. The security interest with Bronson contains an after-acquired property clause. Six months later, Amato pays cash to another seller of factory equipment for more equipment. Six months after that, Amato goes out of business before she has paid off her debt to Bronson. Bronson has a security interest in all of Amato's equipment, even the equipment bought from the other seller.

Future Advances

Often, a debtor will arrange with a bank to have a continuing *line of credit* under which the debtor can borrow funds intermittently. Advances against lines of credit can be subject to a properly perfected security interest in certain collateral. The security agreement may provide that any future advances made against that line of credit are also subject to the security interest in the same collateral. For example, Stroh is the owner of a small manufacturing plant with equipment valued at $1 million. He has an immediate need for $50,000 of working capital, so he obtains a loan from Midwestern Bank and signs a security agreement, putting up all of his equipment as security. The security agreement provides that Stroh can borrow up to $500,000 in the future, using the same equipment as collateral for any future advances. In this situation, Stroh does not have to execute a new security agreement and perfect a security interest in the collateral each time an advance is made [UCC 9–204(3)].

The Floating-Lien Concept

A security agreement that provides for a security interest in proceeds, in after-acquired property, or in property purchased under a line of credit (or in all three) is often characterized as a **floating lien.** When a creditor places a lien on a debtor's property, the creditor's rights are bound (attached) to the property, and the creditor acquires the right to sell or hold the property of a debtor as security or payment for a debt (see Chapter 20 for a further discussion of liens). Floating liens commonly arise in the financing of inventories. A creditor is not interested in specific pieces of inventory, because they are constantly changing, so the lien "floats" from one item to another, as the inventory changes.

For example, suppose that Cascade Sports, Inc., a cross-country ski dealer, has a line of credit with Portland First Bank to finance an inventory of cross-country skis. Cascade and Portland First enter into a security agreement that provides for coverage of proceeds, after-acquired inventory, present inventory, and future advances. This security interest in inventory is perfected by filing centrally (with the secretary of state). One day, Cascade sells a new pair of the latest cross-country skate skis, for which it receives a used pair in trade. That same day, it purchases two new pairs of skate skis from a local manufacturer with an additional amount of money obtained from Portland First.

Portland First gets a perfected security interest in the used pair of skis under the proceeds clause, has a perfected security interest in the two new pairs of skis purchased from the local manufacturer under the after-acquired property clause, and has the new amount of money advanced to Cascade secured by the future-advances clause. All of this is accomplished under the original perfected security agreement. The various items in the inventory have changed, but Portland First still has a perfected security interest in Cascade's inventory, and hence it has a floating lien on the inventory.

The concept of the floating lien can also apply to a shifting stock of goods. Under Section 9–205, the lien can start with raw materials; follow them as they become finished goods and inventories; and continue as the goods are sold and are turned into accounts receivable, chattel paper, or cash.

▌ Priorities among Security Interests

Whether a secured party's security interest is perfected or unperfected may have serious consequences for the secured party if the debtor defaults on the debt or files for bankruptcy. For example, what if the debtor has borrowed money from two different creditors, using the same property as collateral for both loans? If the debtor defaults on both loans, which of the two creditors has first rights to the collateral? In this situation, the creditor with a perfected security interest will prevail. Generally, the following UCC rules apply when more than one creditor claims rights in the same collateral:

1. *Conflicting perfected security interests.* When two or more secured parties have perfected security interests in the same collateral, generally the first to perfect (file or take possession of the collateral) has priority [UCC 9–312(5)(a)].
2. *Conflicting unperfected security interests.* When two conflicting security interests are unperfected, the first to attach has priority [UCC 9–312(5)(b)].
3. *Conflicting perfected security interests in commingled or processed goods.* When goods to which two or more perfected security interests attach are so manufactured or commingled that they lose their identities into a product or mass, the perfected parties' security interests attach to the

new product or mass "according to the ratio that the cost of goods to which each interest originally attached bears to the cost of the total product or mass" [UCC 9–315(2)].

Under certain circumstances, on the debtor's default, the perfection of a security interest will not protect a secured party against certain other third parties having claims to the collateral. For example, the UCC provides that under certain conditions a PMSI, properly perfected, will prevail over another security interest in after-acquired collateral, even though the other was perfected first [UCC 9–312].

Because buyers should not be required to find out if there is an outstanding security interest in, for example, a merchant's inventory, the UCC also provides that a person who buys "in the ordinary course of business" will take the goods free from any security interest created by the seller in the purchased collateral.[3] This is so even if the security interest is perfected and *even if the buyer knows of its existence* [UCC 9–307(1)]. The UCC defines a *buyer in the ordinary course of business* as any person who in good faith, and without knowledge that the sale is in violation of the ownership rights or security interest of a third party in the goods, buys in ordinary course from a person in the business of selling goods of that kind [UCC 1–201(9)]. The priority of claims to a debtor's collateral is detailed in Exhibit 19–5.

---

3. Under the Food Security Act of 1985, buyers in the ordinary course of business include buyers of farm products from a farmer. Under this act, these buyers are protected from prior perfected security interests unless the secured parties perfected centrally by a special form called an effective financing statement (EFS) or the buyers received proper notice.

♦ **Exhibit 19–5**
Priority of Claims to a Debtor's Collateral

PARTIES	PRIORITY
Unperfected Secured Party	Prevails over unsecured creditors and creditors who have obtained judgments against the debtor but who have not begun the legal process to collect on those judgments [UCC 9–301].
Purchaser of Debtor's Collateral	1. Goods purchased in the ordinary course of the seller's business—Purchaser prevails over a secured party's security interest, even if perfected and even if the purchaser knows of the security interest [UCC 9–307(1)].
	2. Consumer goods purchased out of the ordinary course of business—Purchaser prevails over a secured party's interest, even if perfected, providing purchaser purchased as follows: a. For value. b. Without actual knowledge of the security interest. c. For use as a consumer good. d. Prior to secured party's perfection by *filing* [UCC 9–307(2)].
Perfected Secured Parties to Same Collateral	Between two perfected secured parties in the same collateral, the general rule is that first in time of perfection is first in right to the collateral [UCC 9–312(5)]. Exceptions follow: 1. Crops—New value to produce crops given within three months of planting has priority over prior six-month perfected interest [UCC 9–312(2)]. 2. Purchase-money security interest—Even if second in time of perfection, it has priority, providing the following: a. Inventory—PMSI is perfected and proper written notice is given to the other security-interest holder *on* or *before* the time that debtor takes possession [UCC 9–312(3)]. b. Other collateral—PMSI has priority, providing it is perfected within ten days after debtor receives possession [UCC 9–312(4)].

Rights and Duties of Debtors and Creditors

The security agreement itself determines most of the rights and duties of the debtor and the secured party. The UCC, however, imposes some rights and duties that are applicable in the absence of a security agreement to the contrary.

Information Requests

Under UCC 9–407(1), a secured party has the option, when making the filing, of asking the filing officer to make a note of the file number, the date, and the hour of the original filing on a copy of the financing statement. The filing officer must send this copy to the person making the request. Under UCC 9–407(2), a filing officer must also give information to a person who is contemplating obtaining a security interest from a prospective debtor. The filing officer must give a certificate that provides information on possible perfected financing statements with respect to the named debtor. The filing officer will charge a fee for the certification and for any information copies provided.

Assignment, Amendment, and Release

Whenever desired, a secured party of record can release part or all of the collateral described in a filed financing statement. This ends his or her security interest in the collateral [UCC 9–406]. A secured party can assign part or all of the security interest to another, called the assignee. That assignee becomes the secured party of record if, for example, he or she either makes a notation of the assignment somewhere on the financing statement or files a written statement of assignment [UCC 9–405(2)].

It is also possible to amend a financing statement that has already been filed. The amendment must be signed by both parties. The debtor signs the security agreement, the original financing statement, and the amendments [UCC 9–402]. All other secured transaction documents, such as releases, assignments, continuations of perfection, perfections of collateral moved into another jurisdiction, and termination statements, need only be signed by the secured party.

The Status of the Debt

At any time that the secured debt is outstanding, the debtor may wish to know the status of the debt. If so, the debtor need only sign a statement that indicates the aggregate amount of the unpaid debt at a specific date (and perhaps a list of the collateral covered by the security agreement). The secured party (creditor) must then approve or correct this statement in writing. The creditor must comply with the request within two weeks of receipt; otherwise, the creditor is liable for any loss caused to the debtor by the failure to comply [UCC 9–208(2)]. One such request is allowed without charge every six months. For each additional request, the secured party (creditor) can require a fee not exceeding $10 per request [UCC 9–208(3)].

Termination Statement

When a secured debt is paid, the secured party may send a termination statement to the debtor or file such a statement with the filing officer to whom the original financing statement was given. If the financing statement covers consumer goods, the termination statement must be filed by the secured party within one month after the debt is paid, or—if the debtor requests the termination statement in writing—it must be filed within ten days of receipt of such request after the debt is paid, whichever is earlier [UCC 9–404(1)].

In all other circumstances, the termination statement must be filed or furnished to the debtor within ten days after a written request is made by the debtor. If the affected secured party fails to file such a termination statement, as required by UCC 9–404(1), or fails to send the termination statement within ten days after proper demand, the secured party will be liable to the debtor for $100. Additionally, the secured party will be liable for any loss caused to the debtor.

Default

Article 9 defines the rights, duties, and remedies of the secured party and of the debtor upon the debtor's default. Should the secured party fail to comply with his or her duties, the debtor is afforded particular rights and remedies.

The topic of default is one of great concern to secured lenders and to the lawyers who draft security agreements. What constitutes default is not always clear. In fact, Article 9 does not define the term. Consequently, parties are encouraged in practice and by the UCC to include in their security agreements certain standards to be applied should default occur. In so doing, parties can stipulate the conditions that will constitute a default [UCC 9–501(1)]. Typically, because of the disparity in bargaining position between a debtor and a creditor, these critical terms are shaped by the creditor in an attempt to provide the maximum protection possible. The ultimate terms, however, are not allowed to go beyond the limitations imposed by the good faith requirement of UCC 1–203 and the unconscionability doctrine.

Although any breach of the terms of the security agreement can constitute default, default occurs most commonly when the debtor fails to meet the scheduled payments that the parties have agreed on or when the debtor becomes bankrupt. Another breach that could constitute default is a debtor's breach of the warranty of title (see Chapter 16) to property offered as collateral.

Basic Remedies

A secured party's remedies can be divided into two basic categories:

1. A secured party can relinquish a security interest and proceed to judgment on the underlying debt, followed by execution and levy. (**Execution** is an action to carry into effect the directions in a court decree or judgment. **Levy** is the obtaining of money by legal process through the seizure and sale of property, usually done after a writ of execution has been issued.) Execution and levy are rarely undertaken unless the value of the secured collateral has been reduced greatly below the amount of the debt and the debtor has other assets available that may be legally seized to satisfy the debt [UCC 9–501(1)].[4]
2. A secured party can take possession of the collateral covered by the security agreement [UCC 9–503]. Upon taking possession, the secured party can either retain the collateral for satisfaction of

the debt [UCC 9–505(2)] or resell the goods and apply the proceeds toward the debt [UCC 9–504].

The rights and remedies under UCC 9–501(1) are *cumulative.* Therefore, if a creditor is unsuccessful in enforcing rights by one method, he or she can pursue another method.[5]

When a security agreement covers both real and personal property, the secured party can proceed against the personal property in accordance with the remedies of Article 9. Alternatively, the secured party can proceed against the entire collateral under procedures set down by local real estate law, in which case the UCC does not apply [UCC 9–501(4)]. Determining whether particular collateral is personal or real property can prove difficult, especially in dealing with fixtures—things affixed to real property. Under certain circumstances, the UCC allows the removal of fixtures upon default; such removal, however, is subject to the provisions of Article 9 [UCC 9–313].

Repossession of Collateral

UCC 9–503 states that "[u]nless otherwise agreed, a secured party has on default the right to take possession of the collateral. In taking possession, a secured party may proceed without judicial process if this can be done without a breach of the peace." The underlying rationale for this "self-help" provision of Article 9 is that it simplifies the process of repossession for creditors and reduces the burden on the courts. Because the UCC does not define *breach of the peace,* however, it is not always easy to predict what will or will not constitute a breach of the peace.

Generally, the secured party or the secured party's agent cannot enter a debtor's house, garage, or place of business without permission. Consider a situation in which an automobile is collateral. If the repossessing party walks onto the debtor's premises, proceeds up the driveway, enters the vehicle without entering the garage, and drives off, it probably will not amount to a breach of the peace. In some states, however, an action for wrongful trespass could start a cause of action for breach of the peace or other tortious action.

4. Some assets are exempt from creditors' claims—see Chapter 20.

5. See James J. White and Robert S. Summers, *Uniform Commercial Code,* 4th ed. (St. Paul: West Publishing Co., 1995), pp. 908–909.

Disposition of Collateral

Once default has occurred and the secured party has obtained possession of the collateral, the secured party may sell, lease, or otherwise dispose of the collateral in any commercially reasonable manner [UCC 9–504(1)]. Any sale is always subject to procedures established by state law.

RETENTION OF COLLATERAL BY THE SECURED PARTY The UCC acknowledges that parties are sometimes better off if they do not sell the collateral. Therefore, a secured party can retain collateral, but this general right is subject to several conditions. The secured party must send written notice of the proposal to the debtor if the debtor has not signed a statement renouncing or modifying his or her rights after default. If the collateral is consumer goods, the secured party does not need to give any other notice. In all other situations, the secured party must also send notice to any other secured party from whom the secured party has received written notice of a claim of interest in the collateral in question.

If within twenty-one days after the notice is sent, the secured party receives an objection in writing from a person entitled to receive notification, then the secured party must sell or otherwise dispose of the collateral in accordance with the provisions of UCC 9–504 (disposition procedures under UCC 9–504 will be discussed shortly). If no such written objection is forthcoming, the secured party can retain the collateral in full satisfaction of the debtor's obligation [UCC 9–505(2)].

CONSUMER GOODS When the collateral is consumer goods with a PMSI and the debtor has paid 60 percent or more of the purchase price, then the secured party must sell or otherwise dispose of the repossessed collateral in accordance with the provisions of UCC 9–504 within ninety days. Failure to comply opens the secured party to an action for conversion or other liability under UCC 9–507(1) unless the consumer-debtor signed a written statement *after default* renouncing or modifying the right to demand the sale of the goods [UCC 9–505(1)].

DISPOSITION PROCEDURES A secured party who does not choose to retain the collateral must resort to the disposition procedures prescribed under UCC 9–504. The UCC allows a great deal of flexibility with regard to disposition. The only real limitations are that (1) the sale must be accomplished in a commercially reasonable manner and (2) the debtor must be notified of the sale.

What Qualifies as a Commercially Reasonable Sale? A secured party is not compelled to resort to public sale to dispose of the collateral. The party is given latitude under the UCC to seek out the best terms possible in a private sale. Generally, no specific time requirements must be met; however, the time must ultimately meet the standard of commercial reasonableness. Additionally, UCC 9–507(2) states as follows:

> The fact that a better price could have been obtained by a sale at a different time or in a different method from that selected by the secured party is not of itself sufficient to establish that the sale was not made in a commercially reasonable manner. If the secured party either sells the collateral in the usual manner in any recognized market therefor or if he sells at the price current in such a market at the time of sale or if he has otherwise sold in conformity with reasonable commercial practices among dealers in the type of property sold, he has sold in a commercially reasonable manner.

In the following case, the court had to decide whether a sale was conducted in a commercially reasonable manner.

CASE 19.4

First Westside Bank v. For-Med, Inc.

Supreme Court of Nebraska, 1995.
247 Neb. 641,
529 N.W.2d 66.

FACTS David Anderson and For-Med, Inc., signed a security agreement with the First Westside Bank for $79,924.89, plus interest. The collateral for the loan was Anderson's Blue Bird motor home. Anderson and For-Med defaulted, and the bank took possession of the Blue Bird. The bank solicited bids for the motor home by

Case 19.4—Continued

word of mouth from other financial institutions, Blue Bird dealers, and some of its customers. Ultimately, the bank sold the motor home to a bank customer for $60,000. The buyer repaired the motor home at a cost of $22,000 and sold it two and a half years later for $58,000. Meanwhile, the bank sued For-Med and Anderson in a Nebraska state court for the difference between the amount due on the loan and the proceeds from the Blue Bird's sale. The court entered a judgment in favor of the bank. For-Med and Anderson appealed, acknowledging that although the price in the bank's sale had not been "wholly unreasonable," the sale had not been commercially reasonable, because it had not been advertised sufficiently.

ISSUE   Was the sale of the collateral commercially reasonable, despite the bank's failure to advertise?

DECISION   Yes. The Supreme Court of Nebraska affirmed the lower court's decision.

REASON   The state supreme court agreed that a secured party must "use all fair and reasonable means to obtain the best price under the circumstances," but the court added that "the creditor need not use extraordinary means." Depending on the circumstances, the court stated, "a sale may be commercially reasonable notwithstanding the lack of advertising." Factors to be considered in determining whether a sale was commercially reasonable include "the adequacy or insufficiency of the price at which [the collateral] was sold. Here, the collateral was resold 2½ years after the purchaser acquired it, for an amount far less than he had invested in its purchase and repair. In light of that circumstance and the admission of For-Med and Anderson that the price * * * was not 'wholly unreasonable,' it cannot be said that the [lower] court's finding that the sale was commercially reasonable is clearly wrong."

FOR CRITICAL ANALYSIS—Economic Consideration   *Why should a court consider what the buyer of collateral does with it, or sells it for, after the secured party has disposed of it?*

Notice to the Debtor   The secured party must send to the debtor notice of any sale if the debtor has not signed a statement renouncing or modifying the right to notification of the sale after default. For consumer goods, no other notification need be sent. In all other cases, notification must be sent to any other secured party from whom the secured party has received written notice of a claim of interest in the collateral [UCC 9–504(3)]. Such notice is not necessary, however, when the collateral is perishable or threatens to decline speedily in value, or when it is of a type customarily sold on a recognized market. Generally, notice of the place, time, and manner of the sale is required if the sale is to be classified as a sale conducted in a commercially reasonable manner.

PROCEEDS FROM DISPOSITION   Proceeds from the disposition of collateral after default on the underlying debt must be applied in the following order:

1.   Reasonable expenses stemming from the retaking, holding, or preparing for sale are paid first. When authorized by law and if provided for in the agreement, these can include reasonable attorneys' fees and other legal expenses.
2.   Satisfaction of the balance of the debt owed to the secured party is then made.
3.   Creditors with subordinate security interests whose written demands have been received prior to the completion of distribution of the proceeds are then entitled to receive the remaining proceeds from the sale [UCC 9–504(1)].
4.   Any surplus generally goes to the debtor.

DEFICIENCY JUDGMENT   Often, after proper disposition of the collateral, the secured party has not collected all that the debtor still owes. Unless otherwise agreed, the debtor is liable for any deficiency, and the creditor can obtain a **deficiency judgment** from a court to collect the deficiency. Note, however, that if the underlying transaction was a sale of accounts or of chattel paper, the debtor is entitled to any surplus or is liable for any deficiency only if the security agreement so provides [UCC 9–504(2)].

REDEMPTION RIGHTS   At any time before the secured party disposes of the collateral or enters into a contract for its disposition, or before the debtor's obligation has been discharged through the secured party's retention of the collateral, the debtor or any other secured party can exercise the right of *redemption* of the collateral. The debtor or other secured party can do this by tendering performance of all obligations secured by the collateral and by paying the expenses reasonably incurred by the secured party in retaking and maintaining the collateral [UCC 9–506].

▌Terms and Concepts

after-acquired property 399
attachment 389
collateral 388
continuation statement 398
debtor 388
default 389
deficiency judgment 406

execution 403
financing statement 392
floating lien 400
levy 403
perfection 392
pledge 396
proceeds 399

purchase-money security
  interest (PMSI) 397
secured party 388
secured transaction 388
security agreement 388
security interest 388

▌Chapter Summary: Secured Transactions

Creating a Security Interest *(See pages 389–392.)*	1. Unless the creditor has possession of the collateral, there must be an agreement in writing, signed by the debtor, describing and reasonably identifying the collateral. 2. The secured party must give value to the debtor. 3. The debtor must have rights in the collateral—some ownership interest or right to obtain possession of the specified collateral.

Perfecting a Security Interest *(See pages 392–398.)*	1. *Perfection by filing*—The most common method of perfection is by filing a financing statement containing the names and addresses of the secured party and the debtor and describing the collateral by type or item. The financing statement must be signed by the debtor.
	  a. State laws determine where the financing statement is to be filed—with the secretary of state, county clerk (or other local official), or both.
	  b. Classification of collateral determines whether filing is necessary and the place of filing (see Exhibit 19–3).
	2. *Perfection without filing*—
	  a. By transfer of collateral—The debtor can transfer possession of the collateral itself to the secured party. This type of transfer is called a *pledge*.
	  b. By attachment of a *purchase-money security interest* in consumer goods—If the secured party has a purchase-money security interest in consumer goods (goods bought or used by the debtor for personal, family, or household purposes), the secured party's security interest is perfected automatically. Exceptions: security interests in fixtures or motor vehicles.

▌Chapter Summary: Secured Transactions—Continued

The Scope of a Security Interest *(See pages 399–400.)*	A security agreement can cover the following types of property: 1. *Collateral in the present possession of the debtor.* 2. *Proceeds from a sale, exchange, or disposition of secured collateral.* 3. *After-acquired property*—A security agreement may provide that property acquired after the execution of the security agreement will also be secured by the agreement. This provision often accompanies security agreements covering a debtor's inventory. 4. *Future advances*—A security agreement may provide that any future advances made against a line of credit will be subject to the security interest in the same collateral.
Priorities among Security Interests *(See pages 400–401.)*	See Exhibit 19–5.

Rights and Duties of Debtors and Creditors *(See page 402.)*	1. *Information requests*—Upon request by any person, the filing officer must send a statement listing the file number, the date, and the hour of original filing of financing statements covering collateral of a particular debtor; a fee is charged.
	
	2. *Assignment, amendment, and release*—A secured party may (a) release part or all of the collateral described in a filed financing statement, thus ending the creditor's security interest; (b) assign part or all of the security interest to another party; and (c) amend a filed financing statement.
	
	3. *The status of the debt*—If a debtor wishes to know the status of a secured debt, he or she may sign a descriptive statement of the amount of the unpaid debt (and may include a list of the covered collateral) as of a specific date. The creditor must then approve or correct this statement in writing within two weeks of receipt or be liable for any loss caused to the debtor by failure to do so. Only one request without charge is permitted per six-month period.
	
	4. *Termination statement*—When a debt is paid, the secured party generally must send to the debtor or file with the filing officer to whom the original financing statement was given a *termination statement*. Failure to comply results in the secured party's liability to the debtor for $100 plus any loss caused to the debtor.
	  a. If the financing statement covers consumer goods, the termination statement must be filed by the secured party within one month after the debt is paid, or if the debtor requests the termination statement in writing, it must be filed within ten days of the request after the debt is paid—whichever is earlier.
	  b. In all other cases, the termination statement must be filed or furnished to the debtor within ten days after a written request is made by the debtor.

Default *(See pages 402–406.)*	On the debtor's default, the secured party may do either of the following:
	
	1. Relinquish the security interest and proceed to judgment on the underlying debt, followed by execution and levy on the nonexempt assets of the debtor. This remedy is rarely pursued.
	
	2. Take possession (peacefully or by court order) of the collateral covered by the security agreement and then pursue one of two alternatives:
	  a. Retain the collateral (unless the secured party has a purchase-money security interest in consumer goods and the debtor has paid 60 percent or more of the selling price or loan), in which case the secured party—
	    (1) Must give written notice to the debtor if the debtor has not signed a statement renouncing or modifying his or her rights after default. With consumer goods, no other notice is necessary.
	<div align="right">*(Continued)*</div>

▐ Chapter Summary: Secured Transactions—Continued

Default—Continued	
	(2) Must send notice to any other secured party with an interest in the same collateral. If an objection is received from the debtor or any other secured party within twenty-one days, in writing, the creditor must dispose of the collateral according to the requirements of UCC 9–504. Otherwise, the secured party may retain the collateral in full satisfaction of the debt.
	b. Sell the collateral, in which case the secured party—
	(1) Must sell the goods in a commercially reasonable manner at a public or private sale.
	(2) Must notify the debtor and (except in sales of consumer goods) other secured parties who have notified the secured party of claims to the collateral of the sale (unless the collateral is perishable or will decline rapidly in value).
	(3) Must generally apply the proceeds in the following order:
	(a) Expenses incurred by the sale (which may include reasonable attorneys' fees and other legal expenses).
	(b) Balance of the debt owed to the secured party.
	(c) Subordinate security interests of creditors whose written demands have been received prior to the completion of the distribution of the proceeds.
	(d) Surplus to the debtor.

▐ For Review

1. What is a security interest? Who is a secured party? What is a security agreement? What is a financing statement?

2. What three requirements must be met to create an enforceable security interest?

3. What is the most common method of perfecting a security interest under Article 9?

4. If two secured parties have perfected security interests in the collateral of the debtor, which party has priority to the collateral on the debtor's default?

5. What rights does a secured creditor have on the debtor's default?

▐ Questions and Case Problems

19–1. Priority Disputes. Redford is a seller of electric generators. He purchases a large quantity of generators from a manufacturer, Mallon Corp., by making a down payment and signing an agreement to make the balance of payments over a period of time. The agreement gives Mallon Corp. a security interest in the generators and the proceeds. Mallon Corp. files a financing statement on its security interest centrally. Redford receives the generators and immediately sells one of them to Garfield on an installment contract, with payment to be made in twelve equal installments. At the time of sale, Garfield knows of Mallon's security interest. Two months later Redford goes into default on his payments to Mallon. Discuss Mallon's rights against purchaser Garfield in this situation.

19–2. Oral Security Agreements. Marsh has a prize horse named Arabian Knight. Marsh is in need of working capital. She borrows $5,000 from Mendez, with Mendez's taking possession of Arabian Knight as security for the loan. No written agreement is signed. Discuss whether, in the absence of a written agreement, Mendez has a security interest in Arabian Knight. If Mendez does have a security interest, is it a perfected security interest?

19–3. Default. Delgado is a retail seller of television sets. He sells a color television set to Cummings for $600. Cummings cannot pay cash, so she signs a security agreement, paying $100 down and agreeing to pay the balance in twelve equal installments of $50 each. The security agreement gives Delgado a security interest in the television set sold. Cummings makes six payments on time; then she goes into default because of unexpected financial problems. Delgado repossesses the set and wants to keep it in full satisfaction of the debt. Discuss Delgado's rights and duties in this matter.

19–4. The Scope of a Security Interest. Edward owned a retail sporting goods shop. A new ski resort was being created in his area, and to take advantage of the potential business, Edward decided to expand his operations. He borrowed a large sum of money from his bank, which took a security interest in his present inventory and any after-acquired inventory as collateral for the loan. The bank properly perfected the security interest by filing a financing statement. A year later, just a few months after the ski resort had opened, an avalanche destroyed the ski slope and lodge. Edward's business consequently took a turn for the worse, and he defaulted on his debt to the bank. The bank sought possession of his entire inventory, even though the inventory was now twice as large as it had been when the loan was made. Edward claimed that the bank only had rights to half his inventory. Is Edward correct? Explain.

19–5. Sale of Collateral. In 1969, Jones and Percell executed a promissory note and a security agreement covering a converted military aircraft built in the 1950s. Upon their default, the Bank of Nevada repossessed the aircraft. After providing the required notice to Jones and Percell, the bank placed advertisements to sell the aircraft in several trade journals, as well as in major newspapers in several large cities. In addition, the bank sent 2,000 brochures to 240 sales organizations. It hired a sales representative to market the aircraft. The plane was later sold for $71,000 to an aircraft broker, who in turn resold it for $123,000 after spending $33,000 on modifications. Because the price obtained on the sale of the plane was about $75,000 less than the amount Jones and Percell owed the bank, the bank initiated a lawsuit to obtain the amount of the deficiency. Jones and Percell claim that the sale was not conducted in a commercially reasonable manner. Will they succeed in their claim? Why or why not? [*Jones v. Bank of Nevada*, 91 Nev. 368, 535 P.2d 1279 (1975)]

19–6. Priority Disputes. In 1977, the Marcuses sold their drugstore business to Mistura, Inc. Mistura made a down payment on the purchase price, and the Marcuses took a security interest in the fixtures and personal property of the business for the unpaid portion of the debt. Arizona law requires that financing statements relating to security interests in personal property be filed with the secretary of state. Because the Marcuses had filed their statement with the Maricopa County recorder, only their security interest in the fixtures was properly perfected. Mistura later obtained a loan from McKesson, using the same property secured by its transaction with the Marcuses as collateral. McKesson properly perfected a security interest in this

collateral by filing with the secretary of state. McKesson had actual knowledge at the time of the loan that the Marcuses had not properly perfected their security interest in the personal property of Mistura's business. A few days after McKesson's filing, the Marcuses filed a financing statement with the secretary of state. Which party had a superior security interest in the collateral, McKesson or the Marcuses? Explain. [*In re Mistura, Inc.*, 705 F.2d 1496 (9th Cir. 1983)]

19–7. Oral Security Agreements. John and Melody Fish bought various pieces of expensive jewelry, including a diamond ring, a diamond necklace, and a wedding band, from Odom's Jewelers. The Fishes agreed to make monthly installment payments to Odom's until the purchase price was paid in full. In 1988, the Fishes fell behind in their monthly payments on the account. The Fishes and Odom's orally agreed that the Fishes would return the jewelry to Odom's and that Odom's would hold the items for the Fishes until the account was paid. In 1991, the Fishes filed for bankruptcy protection. The jewelry was still in the possession of Odom's. One of the issues before the bankruptcy court was whether Odom's had a security interest in the jewelry. Did it? Explain. [*In re Fish*, 128 Bankr. 468 (N.D.Okla. 1991)]

19–8. Purchase-Money Security Interest. Barbara Wiegert and her daughter, Darcie Wiegert, went shopping at Sears, and Darcie bought a mattress and box spring for $396.11. Barbara later purchased from Sears a television set for $239.96. Both purchases of consumer goods were charged to the credit card of Barbara (and her husband, Harold). On both credit slips was printed the following statement: "I grant Sears a security interest or lien in this merchandise, unless prohibited by law, until paid in full." When the Wiegerts filed their bankruptcy petition, the balance due to Sears was $587.26, plus interest. The Wiegerts claimed that Sears was an unsecured creditor. Sears claimed that it had a purchase-money security interest in the goods and that the security interest was perfected. Was Sears correct in making these claims? Discuss fully. [*In the Matter of Wiegert*, 145 Bankr. 621 (D.Neb. 1991)]

19–9. Perfection. Richard E. Walker, Kelly E. Walker, and Kenneth W. Walker were partners in the Walker Brothers Dairy, a general partnership located in Florida. The Walkers purchased a "Model 2955 utility tractor, a round bale saw, and a feed mixer box" from the John Deere Co. John Deere took a security interest in the equipment. The security agreement stated that the debtor was a partnership known as "Walker Brothers Dairy." John Deere filed a financing statement, however, that listed the debtors as "Richard Walker, Kelly Walker, and Kenneth Wendell Walker." Each of the three partners signed the statement. Their signatures were followed by a typewritten statement indicating that the partners were doing business as "Walker Brothers

Dairy." When Walker Brothers Dairy voluntarily filed for bankruptcy, John Deere sought to repossess the equipment. The issue before the court was whether the financing statement, which listed as debtors the partners rather than the partnership, was sufficient to perfect John Deere's security interest in the partnership equipment. What should the court decide? Discuss. [*In re Walker*, 142 Bankr. 482 (M.D.Fla. 1992)]

19–10. Sale of Collateral. To pay for the purchases of several aircraft, Robert Wall borrowed money from the Cessna Finance Corp., using the aircraft as collateral. Wall defaulted on the loans. Cessna took possession of the collateral (the aircraft) and sold it. Cessna filed a suit in a federal district court against Wall for the difference between the amount due on the loans and the amount received from the sale of the aircraft. Wall claimed that he could have obtained a higher price for the aircraft if he had sold it himself. What effect does the issue concerning whether a better price could have been obtained have on whether the sale was commercially reasonable? Discuss. [*Cessna Finance Corp. v. Wall*, 876 F.Supp. 273 (M.D.Ga. 1994)]

▮ Accessing the Internet: Fundamentals of Business Law

For the most updated information on the Uniform Commercial Code, including Article 9, along with Official Comments, go to

http://www.law.cornell.edu/ucc/ucc.table.html

Or go to

http://www.kentlaw.edu/ulc/ulc.html

Cornell Law School's Legal Information Institute offers online access to the Uniform Commercial Code, including Article 9 as enacted in several states, at

http://www.law.cornell.edu/statutes.html#state

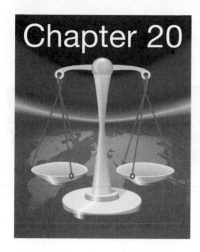

Chapter 20

Creditors' Rights and Bankruptcy

CHAPTER OBJECTIVES

After reading this chapter, you should be able to:

1. Summarize the various remedies available to creditors, and indicate how and when creditors use these remedies to collect debts.
2. Differentiate between suretyship and guaranty arrangements.
3. Outline the typical steps in a bankruptcy proceeding.
4. Describe what property constitutes a debtor's estate in a bankruptcy proceeding and what property is exempt.
5. Compare and contrast the types of relief available under Chapter 7, Chapter 11, Chapter 12, and Chapter 13 of the Bankruptcy Code.

Historically, debtors and their families have been subjected to punishment, including involuntary servitude and imprisonment, for their inability to pay debts. The modern legal system, however, has moved away from a punishment philosophy in dealing with debtors. In fact, many observers say that it has moved too far in the other direction, to the detriment of creditors.

Normally, creditors have no problem collecting the debts owed to them. When disputes arise over the amount owed, however, or when the debtor simply cannot or will not pay, what happens? What remedies are available to creditors when debtors default? We have already discussed, in Chapter 19, the remedies available to secured creditors under Article 9 of the Uniform Commercial Code (UCC). In the first part of this chapter, we focus on other laws that assist the debtor and creditor in resolving their disputes without the debtor's having to resort to bankruptcy. The second part of this chapter discusses bankruptcy as a last resort in resolving debtor-creditor problems.

■ Laws Assisting Creditors

Both the common law and statutory laws other than Article 9 of the UCC create various rights and remedies for creditors. We discuss here some of these rights and remedies.

Liens

As discussed earlier in this text, a *lien* is an encumbrance on property to satisfy a debt or protect a claim for the payment of a debt. Creditors' liens include the mechanic's lien, the artisan's lien, the innkeeper's lien, and judicial liens.

MECHANIC'S LIEN When a person contracts for labor, services, or materials to be furnished for the purpose of making improvements on real property (land and things attached to the land, such as buildings and trees—see Chapter 29) but does not immediately pay for the improvements, the creditor can file a **mechanic's lien** on the property. This

411

creates a special type of debtor-creditor relationship in which the real estate itself becomes security for the debt.

For example, a painter agrees to paint a house for a homeowner for an agreed-on price to cover labor and materials. If the homeowner refuses to pay for the work or pays only a portion of the charges, a mechanic's lien against the property can be created. The painter is the lienholder, and the real property is encumbered with a mechanic's lien for the amount owed. If the homeowner does not pay the lien, the property can be sold to satisfy the debt. Notice of the *foreclosure* (the process by which the creditor deprives the debtor of his or her property) and sale must be given to the debtor in advance, however. Note that state law governs mechanic's liens. The time period within which a mechanic's lien must be filed is usually 60 to 120 days from the last date labor or materials were provided.

ARTISAN'S LIEN An artisan's lien is a security device created at common law through which a creditor can recover payment from a debtor for labor and materials furnished in the repair or improvement of personal property. For example, Cindy leaves her diamond ring at the jeweler's to be repaired and to have her initials engraved on the band. In the absence of an agreement, the jeweler can keep the ring until Cindy pays for the services that the jeweler provides. Should Cindy fail to pay, the jeweler has a lien on Cindy's ring for the amount of the bill and normally can sell the ring in satisfaction of the lien.

In contrast to a mechanic's lien, an artisan's lien is *possessory*. The lienholder ordinarily must have retained possession of the property and have expressly or impliedly agreed to provide the services on a cash, not a credit, basis. Usually, the lienholder retains possession of the property. When this occurs, the lien remains in existence as long as the lienholder maintains possession, and the lien is terminated once possession is voluntarily surrendered—unless the surrender is only temporary. If it is a temporary surrender, there must be an agreement that the property will be returned to the lienholder. Even with such an agreement, if a third party obtains rights in that property while it is out of the possession of the lienholder, the lien is lost.

Modern statutes permit the holder of an artisan's lien to foreclose and sell the property subject to the lien to satisfy payment of the debt. As with the mechanic's lien, the holder of an artisan's lien is required to give notice to the owner of the property prior to foreclosure and sale. The sale proceeds are used to pay the debt and the costs of the legal proceedings, and the surplus, if any, is paid to the former owner.

In the following case, a creditor with a purchase-money security interest (PMSI) in an automobile tried to repossess the property but failed to do so because an artisan's lien had also been placed on the car.

CASE 20.1

National Bank of Joliet v. Bergeron Cadillac, Inc.

Appellate Court of Illinois, 1977.
66 Ill.2d 140,
361 N.E.2d 116,
5 Ill.Dec. 588.

FACTS   In February 1973, Gladys Schmidt borrowed $4,120 from the National Bank of Joliet to finance the purchase of a Cadillac. The bank held a security interest in the automobile and had perfected this interest by filing in the office of the secretary of state. In August 1973, Schmidt took the car to Bergeron Cadillac, Inc., for repairs, which cost approximately $2,000. When Schmidt failed to pay for the repairs, Bergeron Cadillac retained possession of the car and placed an artisan's lien on it. In September, Schmidt defaulted on her payments to the bank, and the bank later filed an action in an Illinois state court to gain possession of the Cadillac from Bergeron. The trial court held for Bergeron Cadillac, and the bank appealed.

ISSUE   Which party has a right to possession of the vehicle—Bergeron Cadillac or the National Bank?

DECISION   Bergeron Cadillac. The Illinois appellate court affirmed the trial court's judgment.

Case 20.1—Continued

REASON The court looked to both the common law and the UCC in its determination: "The plain language of Section 9–310 gives the lien of persons furnishing services or materials upon goods in their possession prior-ity over a perfected security interest unless the lien is created by statute and the statute expressly provides otherwise." In response to the bank's contention that the common law possessory lien had been superseded in Illinois by two statutes providing for artisan's liens, the court ruled that in both cases "the statutes expressly provide that the liens created shall be in addition to, and shall not exclude, any lien existing by virtue of the common law."

FOR CRITICAL ANALYSIS—Ethical Consideration *Is the fact that artisan's liens "arise from work intended to enhance or preserve the value of collateral" a sufficient reason to give artisan's liens priority over perfected security interests?*

INNKEEPER'S LIEN An innkeeper's lien is another security device created at common law. An innkeeper's lien is placed on the baggage of guests for the agreed-on hotel charges that remain unpaid. If no express agreement has been made on the amount of those charges, then the lien will be for the reasonable value of the accommodations furnished. The innkeeper's lien is terminated either by the guest's payment of the hotel charges or by the innkeeper's surrender of the baggage to the guest, unless the surrender is temporary. Additionally, the lien is terminated by the innkeeper's foreclosure and sale of the property.

JUDICIAL LIENS When a debt is past due, a creditor can bring a legal action against the debtor to collect the debt. If a creditor is successful in the action, the court awards the creditor a judgment against the debtor (usually for the amount of the debt plus any interest and legal costs incurred in obtaining the judgment). Frequently, however, the creditor is unable to collect the awarded amount.

To ensure that a judgment in the creditor's favor will be collectible, creditors are permitted to request that certain nonexempt property of the debtor be seized to satisfy the debt. (As will be discussed later in this chapter, under state or federal statutes, certain property is exempt from attachment by creditors.) If the court orders the debtor's property to be seized prior to a judgment in the creditor's favor, the court's order is referred to as a *writ of attachment.* If the court orders the debtor's property to be seized following a judgment in the creditor's favor, the court's order is referred to as a *writ of execution.*

Attachment Recall from Chapter 19 that *attachment,* in the context of secured transactions, refers to the process through which a security interest in a debtor's collateral becomes enforceable. In the context of judicial liens, attachment is a court-ordered seizure and taking into custody of property prior to the securing of a judgment for a past-due debt. Attachment rights are created by state statutes. Attachment is a *prejudgment* remedy, because it occurs either at the time of or immediately after the commencement of a lawsuit and before the entry of a final judgment. By statute, the restrictions and requirements for a creditor to attach before judgment are specific and limited. The due process clause of the Fourteenth Amendment to the Constitution limits the courts' power to authorize seizure of a debtor's property without notice to the debtor or a hearing on the facts.

To use attachment as a remedy, the creditor must have an enforceable right to payment of the debt under law, and the creditor must follow certain procedures. Otherwise, the creditor can be liable for damages for wrongful attachment. He or she must file with the court an *affidavit* (a written or printed statement, made under oath or sworn to) stating that the debtor is in default and stating the statutory grounds under which attachment is sought. The creditor must also post a bond to cover at least court costs, the value of the loss of use of the good suffered by the debtor, and the value of the property attached. When the court is satisfied that all the requirements have been met, it issues a **writ of attachment,** which directs the sheriff or other officer to seize nonexempt property. If the creditor prevails at trial, the seized property can be sold to satisfy the judgment.

Writ of Execution If the debtor will not or cannot pay the judgment, the creditor is entitled to go back to the court and obtain a court order, directing the sheriff to seize (levy) and sell any of the debtor's nonexempt real or personal property that is within the court's geographical jurisdiction (usually the county in which the courthouse is located). This order is called a **writ of execution.** The proceeds of the sale are used to pay off the judgment, accrued interest, and the costs of the sale. Any excess is paid to the debtor. The debtor can pay the judgment and redeem the nonexempt property any time before the sale takes place. Because of exemption laws and bankruptcy laws, however, many judgments are virtually uncollectible.

Garnishment

Garnishment occurs when a creditor is permitted to collect a debt by seizing property of the debtor that is being held by a third party. Typically, a garnishment judgment is served on a debtor's employer so that part of the debtor's usual paycheck will be paid to the creditor. As a result of a garnishment proceeding, the court orders the debtor's employer to turn over a portion of the debtor's wages to pay the debt.

The legal proceeding for a garnishment action is governed by state law, and garnishment operates differently from state to state. According to the laws in some states, the creditor needs to obtain only one order of garnishment, which will then continuously apply to the debtor's weekly wages until the entire debt is paid. In other states, the creditor must go back to court for a separate order of garnishment for each pay period.

Both federal laws and state laws limit the amount of money that can be garnished from a debtor's weekly take-home pay.[1] Federal law provides a minimal framework to protect debtors from losing all their income in order to pay judgment debts.[2] State laws also provide dollar exemptions, and these amounts are often larger than those provided by federal law. Under federal law, garnishment of an employee's wages for any one indebtedness cannot be a ground for dismissal of an employee.

One of the questions courts have faced in recent years has to do with whether a debtor's pension fund can be attached by creditors, through garnishment or other proceedings, to satisfy a debt. Under federal law, certain types of pension funds may not be attached. The law is less clear, however, on whether pension funds, *after* they have been received by a retiree, can be subject to attachment by creditors. This issue is before the court in the following case.

---

1. Some states (for example, Texas) do not permit garnishment of wages by private parties except under a child-support order.
2. For example, the federal Consumer Credit Protection Act of 1968, 15 U.S.C. Sections 1601–1693r, provides that a debtor can retain either 75 percent of the disposable earnings per week or the sum equivalent to thirty hours of work paid at federal minimum wage rates, whichever is greater.

CASE 20.2

United States v. Smith

United States Court of Appeals,
Fourth Circuit, 1995.
47 F.3d 681.

FACTS   For nine years, Charles Smith asked his friends and acquaintances to invest their money in his business schemes. Smith used most of the money—estimated to be more than $350,000—for personal expenses. Smith was indicted for criminal fraud and pleaded guilty to that crime in a federal district court. The court imposed a prison sentence and ordered Smith to repay his victims as much as possible by turning over, each month, the entire amount of his pension benefits. Smith appealed the order, claiming that it violated the "anti-alienation" provision of ERISA.

ISSUE   Was the order to Smith to turn over his pension benefits in violation of federal law?

Case 20.2—Continued

DECISION   Yes. The U.S. Court of Appeals for the Fourth Circuit vacated (removed) the lower court's order and remanded the case. The appellate court ordered the lower court to redetermine the amount that Smith should pay to his victims, based on "a balance of the victims' interest in compensation and Smith's other financial resources."

REASON   The appellate court "recognized a 'strong public policy against the alienability [transferability] of *   *   * ERISA [pension] benefits.'" The court pointed out that the "Supreme Court, as well, has found that it is not 'appropriate to approve any *   *   * exception.'" The appellate court acknowledged that "[u]nderstandably, there may be a natural distaste for the result we reach here" but reasoned that "[t]he statute *   *   * is clear. Congress has made a policy decision to protect the ERISA income of retirees, even if that decision prevents others from securing relief for the wrongs done them."

FOR CRITICAL ANALYSIS—Political Consideration   *Why does the law protect certain pension benefits from court-ordered transfers?*

Creditors' Composition Agreements

Creditors may contract with the debtor for discharge of the debtor's liquidated debts (debts that are definite, or fixed, in amount) on payment of a sum less than that owed. These agreements are called **creditors' composition agreements** or *composition agreements* and are usually held to be enforceable.

Mortgage Foreclosure

Mortgage holders have the right to foreclose on mortgaged property in the event of a debtor's default. The usual method of foreclosure is by judicial sale of the property, although the statutory methods of foreclosure vary from state to state. If the proceeds of the foreclosure sale are sufficient to cover both the costs of the foreclosure and the mortgaged debt, the debtor receives any surplus. If the sale proceeds are insufficient to cover the foreclosure costs and the mortgaged debt, however, the mortgagee (the creditor-lender) can seek to recover the difference from the mortgagor (the debtor) by obtaining a *deficiency judgment* representing the difference between the mortgaged debt and the amount actually received from the proceeds of the foreclosure sale. The mortgagee obtains a deficiency judgment in a separate legal action that he or she pursues subsequent to the foreclosure action. The deficiency judgment entitles the mortgagee to recover the amount of the deficiency from other property owned by the debtor.

Suretyship and Guaranty

When a third person promises to pay a debt owed by another in the event the debtor does not pay, either a *suretyship* or a *guaranty* relationship is created. Suretyship and guaranty have a long history under the common law and provide creditors with the right to seek payment from the third party if the primary debtor defaults on his or her obligations. Exhibit 20–1 illustrates the relationship between a suretyship or guaranty party and the creditor.

SURETY   A contract of strict **suretyship** is a promise made by a third person to be responsible for the debtor's obligation. It is an express contract between the **surety** (the third party) and the creditor. The surety in the strictest sense is *primarily* liable for the debt of the principal. The creditor need not exhaust all legal remedies against the principal debtor before holding the surety responsible for payment. The creditor can demand payment from the surety from the moment the debt is due.

For example, Robert Delmar wants to borrow money from the bank to buy a used car. Because Robert is still in college, the bank will not lend him the money unless his father, Joseph Delmar, who has dealt with the bank before, will cosign the note (add his signature to the note, thereby becoming a surety and thus jointly liable for payment of the

♦ **Exhibit 20–1**
Suretyship and Guaranty Parties
In a suretyship or guaranty arrangement, a third party promises to be responsible for a debtor's obligations. A third party who agrees to be responsible for the debt even if the primary debtor does not default is known as a surety; a third party who agrees to be *secondarily* responsible for the debt only if the primary debtor defaults is known as a guarantor. As noted in Chapter 10, normally a promise of guaranty (a collateral, or secondary, promise) must be in writing to be enforceable.

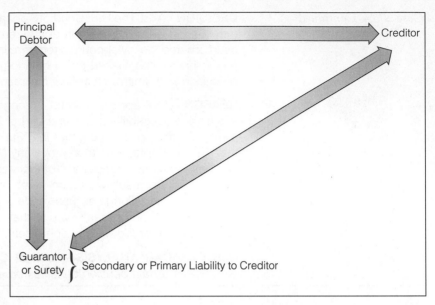

debt). When Joseph Delmar cosigns the note, he becomes primarily liable to the bank. On the note's due date, the bank has the option of seeking payment from either Robert or Joseph Delmar, or both jointly.

GUARANTY A guaranty contract is similar to a suretyship contract in that it includes a promise to answer for the debt or default of another. With a guaranty arrangement, the **guarantor**—the third person making the guaranty—is *secondarily* liable. The guarantor can be required to pay the obligation *only after the principal debtor defaults*, and default usually takes place only after the creditor has made an attempt to collect from the debtor.

For example, a small corporation, BX Enterprises, needs to borrow money to meet its payroll. The bank is skeptical about the creditworthiness of BX and requires Dawson, its president, who is a wealthy businessperson and the owner of 70 percent of BX Enterprises, to sign an agreement making himself personally liable for payment if BX does not pay off the loan. As a guarantor of the loan, Dawson cannot be held liable until BX Enterprises is in default.

The Statute of Frauds requires that a guaranty contract between the guarantor and the creditor must be in writing to be enforceable unless the *main purpose* exception applies. As discussed in Chapter 10, this exception provides that if the

main purpose of the guaranty agreement is to benefit the guarantor, then the contract need not be in writing to be enforceable.

DEFENSES OF THE SURETY AND THE GUARANTOR
The defenses of the surety and the guarantor are basically the same. Therefore, the following discussion applies to both, although it refers only to the surety.

Certain actions will release the surety from the obligation. For example, any binding material modification in the terms of the original contract made between the principal debtor and the creditor—including the awarding of a binding extension of time for making payment—without first obtaining the consent of the surety will discharge a gratuitous surety completely and a compensated surety to the extent that the surety suffers a loss. (An example of a gratuitous surety is a father who agrees to assume responsibility for his daughter's obligation; an example of a compensated surety is a venture capitalist who will profit from a loan made to the principal debtor.)

Naturally, if the principal obligation is paid by the debtor or by another person on behalf of the debtor, the surety is discharged from the obligation. Similarly, if valid tender of payment is made, and the creditor rejects it with knowledge of the surety's existence, then the surety is released from any obligation on the debt.

Generally, the surety can use any defenses available to a principal debtor to avoid liability on the obligation to the creditor. Defenses available to the principal debtor that the surety *cannot* use include the principal debtor's incapacity or bankruptcy and the statute of limitations. The ability of the surety to assert any defenses the debtor may have against the creditor is the most important concept in suretyship, because most of the defenses available to the surety are also those of the debtor.

Obviously, a surety may also have his or her own defenses—for example, incapacity or bankruptcy. If the creditor fraudulently induced the surety to guarantee the debt of the debtor, the surety can assert fraud as a defense. In most states, the creditor has a legal duty to inform the surety, prior to the formation of the suretyship contract, of material facts known by the creditor that would substantially increase the surety's risk. Failure to do so is fraud and makes the suretyship obligation voidable. In addition, if a creditor surrenders the collateral to the debtor or impairs the collateral while knowing of the surety and without the surety's consent, the surety is released to the extent of any loss suffered from the creditor's actions. The primary reason for this requirement is to protect the surety who agreed to become obligated only because the debtor's collateral was in the possession of the creditor.

RIGHTS OF THE SURETY AND THE GUARANTOR

The rights of the surety and the guarantor are basically the same. Therefore, again, the following discussion applies to both.

When the surety pays the debt owed to the creditor, the surety is entitled to certain rights. First, the surety has the legal **right of subrogation**. Simply stated, this means that any right the creditor had against the debtor now becomes the right of the surety. Included are creditor rights in bankruptcy, rights to collateral possessed by the creditor, and rights to judgments secured by the creditor. In short, the surety now stands in the shoes of the creditor and may pursue any remedies that were available to the creditor against the debtor.

Second, the surety has the **right of reimbursement** from the debtor. Basically, the surety is entitled to receive from the debtor all outlays made on behalf of the suretyship arrangement. Such outlays can include expenses incurred as well as the actual amount of the debt paid to the creditor.

Third, in the case of **co-sureties** (two or more sureties on the same obligation owed by the debtor), a surety who pays more than his or her proportionate share on a debtor's default is entitled to recover from the co-sureties the amount paid above the surety's obligation. This is the **right of contribution.** Generally, a co-surety's liability either is determined by agreement or, in the absence of agreement between the co-sureties, can be specified in the suretyship contract itself.

For example, assume that two co-sureties are obligated under a suretyship contract to guarantee the debt of a debtor. Together, the sureties' maximum liability is $25,000. As specified in the suretyship contract, surety A's maximum liability is $15,000, and surety B's is $10,000. The debtor owes $10,000 and is in default. Surety A pays the creditor the entire $10,000. In the absence of any agreement between the two co-sureties, surety A can recover $4,000 from surety B ($10,000/$25,000 × $10,000 = $4,000).

▌Laws Assisting Debtors

The law protects debtors as well as creditors. Certain property of the debtor, for example, is exempt from creditors' actions. Probably the most familiar of these exemptions is the **homestead exemption**. Each state permits the debtor to retain the family home, either in its entirety or up to a specified dollar amount, free from the claims of unsecured creditors or trustees in bankruptcy. The purpose of the homestead exemption is to ensure that the debtor will retain some form of shelter.

Suppose that Van Cleave owes Acosta $40,000. The debt is the subject of a lawsuit, and the court awards Acosta a judgment of $40,000 against Van Cleave. The homestead of Van Cleave is valued at $50,000, and the state exemption on homesteads is $25,000. There are no outstanding mortgages or other liens on his homestead. To satisfy the judgment debt, Van Cleave's family home is sold at public auction for $45,000. The proceeds of the sale are distributed as follows:

1. Van Cleave is given $25,000 as his homestead exemption.
2. Acosta is paid $20,000 toward the judgment debt, leaving a $20,000 deficiency judgment that

can be satisfied from any other nonexempt property (personal or real) that Van Cleave may have, if allowed by state law.

State exemption statutes usually include both real and personal property. Personal property that is most often exempt from satisfaction of judgment debts includes the following:

1. Household furniture up to a specified dollar amount.
2. Clothing and certain personal possessions, such as family pictures or a Bible.
3. A vehicle (or vehicles) for transportation (at least up to a specified dollar amount).
4. Certain classified animals, usually livestock but including pets.
5. Equipment that the debtor uses in a business or trade, such as tools or professional instruments, up to a specified dollar amount.

Consumer protection statutes also protect debtors' rights. Of course, bankruptcy laws, which are discussed in the next section, are designed specifically to assist debtors in need of relief from their debts.

▌ Bankruptcy and Reorganization

At one time, debtors who could not pay their debts as they came due faced harsh consequences, including imprisonment and involuntary servitude. Today, in contrast, debtors have numerous rights. Some of these rights have already been mentioned. We now look at another significant right of debtors: the right to petition for bankruptcy relief under federal law.

Bankruptcy law in the United States has two goals—to protect a debtor by giving him or her a fresh start, free from creditors' claims; and to ensure equitable treatment to creditors who are competing for a debtor's assets. Bankruptcy law is federal law, but state laws on secured transactions, liens, judgments, and exemptions also play a role in federal bankruptcy proceedings. Current bankruptcy law is based on the Bankruptcy Reform Act of 1978, as amended. In this chapter, we refer to this act, as amended, as the Bankruptcy Code (or, more simply, the Code).

Bankruptcy Courts

Bankruptcy proceedings are held in federal bankruptcy courts. A bankruptcy court's primary function is to hold *core proceedings*[3] dealing with the procedures required to administer the estate of the debtor in bankruptcy. Bankruptcy courts are under the authority of U.S. district courts (see Exhibit 2–2 on the federal court system in Chapter 2), and rulings from bankruptcy courts can be appealed to the district courts. Fundamentally, a bankruptcy court fulfills the role of an administrative court for the district court concerning matters in bankruptcy. A bankruptcy court can conduct a jury trial if the appropriate district court has authorized it and if the parties to the bankruptcy consent to a jury trial.

Types of Bankruptcy Relief

The Bankruptcy Code is contained in Title 11 of the U.S. Code (U.S.C.). Chapters 1, 3, and 5 of the Code include general definitional provisions and provisions governing case administration and procedures, creditors, the debtor, and the estate. These three chapters of the Code apply generally to all types of bankruptcies. The next five chapters set forth the different types of relief that debtors may seek. Chapter 7 provides for **liquidation** proceedings (the selling of all nonexempt assets and the distribution of the proceeds to the debtor's creditors). Chapter 9 governs the adjustment of the debts of municipalities. Chapter 11 governs reorganizations. Chapter 12 (for family farmers) and Chapter 13 (for individuals) provide for adjustment of the debts of parties with regular income.[4]

In the following pages, we deal first with liquidation proceedings under Chapter 7 of the Code. We then examine the procedures required for

---

3. Core proceedings are procedural functions, such as allowance of claims, decisions on preferences, automatic-stay proceedings, confirmation of bankruptcy plans, discharge of debts, and so on. These terms and procedures are defined and discussed in the following sections of this chapter.
4. There are no Chapters 2, 4, 6, 8, or 10 in Title 11. Such "gaps" are not uncommon in the U.S.C. This is because chapter numbers (or other subdivisional unit numbers) are sometimes reserved for future use when a statute is enacted. (A gap may also appear if a law has been repealed.)

Chapter 11 reorganizations and for Chapter 12 and Chapter 13 plans.

Chapter 7—Liquidation

Liquidation is the most familiar type of bankruptcy proceeding and is often referred to as an *ordinary*, or *straight*, *bankruptcy*. Put simply, debtors in straight bankruptcies state their debts and turn their assets over to trustees. The trustees sell the assets and distribute the proceeds to creditors. With certain exceptions, the remaining debts are then **discharged** (extinguished), and the debtors are relieved of the obligation to pay the debts.

Any "person"—defined as including individuals, partnerships, and corporations—may be a debtor under Chapter 7. Railroads, insurance companies, banks, savings and loan associations, investment companies licensed by the Small Business Administration, and credit unions *cannot* be Chapter 7 debtors, however. Other chapters of the Code or other federal or state statutes apply to them. A husband and wife may file jointly for bankruptcy under a single petition.

Filing the Petition

A straight bankruptcy may be commenced by the filing of either a voluntary or an involuntary petition in bankruptcy—the document that is filed with a bankruptcy court to initiate bankruptcy proceedings.

VOLUNTARY BANKRUPTCY   A voluntary petition is brought by the debtor, who files official forms designated for that purpose in the bankruptcy court. A **consumer-debtor** (defined as an individual whose debts are primarily consumer debts) who has selected Chapter 7 must state in the petition, at the time of filing, that he or she understands the relief available under other chapters and has chosen to proceed under Chapter 7. If the consumer-debtor is represented by an attorney, the attorney must file an affidavit stating that he or she has informed the debtor of the relief available under each chapter. Any debtor who is liable on a claim held by a creditor can file a voluntary petition. The debtor does not even have to be insolvent to do so.[5] The voluntary petition contains the following schedules:

1. A list of both secured and unsecured creditors, their addresses, and the amount of debt owed to each.
2. A statement of the financial affairs of the debtor.
3. A list of all property owned by the debtor, including property claimed by the debtor to be exempt.
4. A listing of current income and expenses.

The official forms must be completed accurately, sworn to under oath, and signed by the debtor. To conceal assets or knowingly supply false information on these schedules is a crime under the bankruptcy laws. If the voluntary petition for bankruptcy is found to be proper, the filing of the petition will itself constitute an order for relief. An **order for relief** relieves the debtor of the immediate obligation to pay the debts listed in the petition. Once a consumer-debtor's voluntary petition has been filed, the clerk of the court (or person directed) must give the trustee and creditors mailed notice of the order for relief not more than twenty days after the entry of the order.

As mentioned previously, debtors do not have to be insolvent to file for voluntary bankruptcy. Debtors do not have unfettered access to Chapter 7 bankruptcy proceedings, however. Section 707(b) of the Bankruptcy Code allows a bankruptcy court to dismiss a petition for relief under Chapter 7 if the granting of relief would constitute "substantial abuse" of Chapter 7.

For example, the court might determine, after evaluating the debtor's schedule listing current income and expenses, that the debtor would be able to pay creditors a reasonable amount from future income. In this situation, the court might conclude that it would be a substantial abuse of Chapter 7 to allow the debtor to have his or her debts completely discharged. The court might

---

5. The inability to pay debts as they become due is known as *equitable* insolvency. A *balance-sheet* insolvency, which exists when a debtor's liabilities exceed assets, is not the test. Thus, it is possible for debtors to petition voluntarily for bankruptcy even though their assets far exceed their liabilities. This situation may occur when a debtor's cash flow problems become severe.

dismiss the consumer-debtor's Chapter 7 petition after a hearing and encourage the debtor to file a repayment plan under Chapter 13 of the Code, when that would result in a substantial improve-ment in a creditor's receipt of payment. In the fol-lowing case, the court had to decide whether grant-ing a Chapter 7 discharge to the debtor would constitute substantial abuse.

CASE 20.3

Matter of Blair

United States Bankruptcy Court,
Northern District of Alabama,
Eastern Division, 1995.
180 Bankr. 656.

FACTS   James Blair, Jr., owed primarily consumer debts of less than $7,000, and his income exceeded his living expenses by more than $200 a month. When he filed a petition for relief under Chapter 7, the court con-cluded that if he were to file a repayment plan under Chapter 13, his debts would be paid off in forty months. The bankruptcy administrator filed a motion to dismiss Blair's petition.

ISSUE   Should Blair's petition be dismissed on the ground of substantial abuse?

DECISION   Yes. The court dismissed the petition.

REASON   The court held that substantial abuse must be determined on a case-by-case basis, according to the following factors: "(1) Whether the bankruptcy petition was filed because of sudden illness, calamity, disability, or unemployment; (2) Whether the debtor incurred cash advances and made consumer purchases far in excess of his ability to pay; (3) Whether the debtor's proposed family budget is excessive or unreason-able; (4) Whether the debtor's schedules and statement of current income and expenses reasonably and accurately reflect the true financial condition; and (5) Whether the petition was filed in good faith." The court concluded that to grant Blair relief under Chapter 7 would constitute substantial abuse, because he could pay off most, if not all, of his debt under a Chapter 13 repayment plan.

FOR CRITICAL ANALYSIS—Economic Consideration
The court also stated that granting Blair relief under Chapter 7 would be "perverting the purpose of the Bankruptcy Code." What did the court mean by this statement?

INVOLUNTARY BANKRUPTCY   An involuntary bank-ruptcy occurs when the debtor's creditors force the debtor into bankruptcy proceedings. An involuntary case cannot be commenced against a farmer[6] or a charitable institution (or those entities not eligible for Chapter 7 relief—mentioned earlier), however. For an involuntary action to be filed against other debtors, the following requirements must be met: If the debtor has twelve or more creditors, three or more of those creditors having unsecured claims totaling at least $10,775 must join in the petition. If a debtor has fewer than twelve creditors, one or more creditors having a claim of $10,775 may file.

If the debtor challenges the involuntary peti-tion, a hearing will be held, and the bankruptcy court will enter an order for relief if it finds either of the following:

1.   That the debtor is generally not paying debts as they become due.

---

6.   *Farmers* are defined as persons who receive more than 80 percent of their gross income from farming operations, such as tilling the soil; dairy farming; ranching; or the production or raising of crops, ßpoultry, or livestock. Corporations and part-nerships, as well as individuals, can be farmers.

2. That a general receiver, custodian, or assignee took possession of, or was appointed to take charge of, substantially all of the debtor's property within 120 days before the filing of the petition.

If the court grants an order for relief, the debtor will be required to supply the same information in the bankruptcy schedules as in a voluntary bankruptcy.

An involuntary petition should not be used as an everyday debt-collection device, and the Code provides penalties for the filing of frivolous (unjustified) petitions against debtors. Judgment may be granted against the petitioning creditors for the costs and attorneys' fees incurred by the debtor in defending against an involuntary petition that is dismissed by the court. If the petition is filed in bad faith, damages can be awarded for injury to the debtor's reputation. Punitive damages may also be awarded.

Automatic Stay

The filing of a petition, either voluntary or involuntary, operates as an **automatic stay** on (suspension of) virtually all litigation and other action by creditors against the debtor or the debtor's property. In other words, once a petition is filed, creditors cannot commence or continue most legal actions against the debtor to recover claims or to repossess property in the hands of the debtor. A secured creditor, however, may petition the bankruptcy court for relief from the automatic stay in certain circumstances. Additionally, the automatic stay does not apply to paternity, alimony, or family maintenance and support debts.

A creditor's failure to abide by an automatic stay imposed by the filing of a petition can be costly. If a creditor *knowingly* violates the automatic-stay provision (a willful violation), any party injured is entitled to recover actual damages, costs, and attorneys' fees and may also be entitled to recover punitive damages.

Creditors' Meeting and Claims

Within a reasonable time after the order of relief is granted (not less than ten days or more than thirty days), the bankruptcy court must call a meeting of the creditors listed in the schedules filed by the debtor. The bankruptcy judge does not attend this meeting. The debtor must attend this meeting (unless excused by the court) and submit to an examination under oath. Failure to appear or making false statements under oath may result in the debtor's being denied a discharge of bankruptcy. At the meeting, the trustee ensures that the debtor is advised of the potential consequences of bankruptcy and of his or her ability to file under a different chapter.

In a bankruptcy case in which the debtor has no assets (called a "no-asset" case), creditors are notified of the debtor's petition for bankruptcy but are instructed not to file a claim. In such a situation, the creditors will receive no payment, and most, if not all, of the debtor's debts will be discharged. If there are sufficient assets to be distributed to creditors, however, each creditor must normally file a *proof of claim* with the bankruptcy court clerk within ninety days of the creditors' meeting to be entitled to receive a portion of the debtor's estate. The proof of claim lists the creditor's name and address, as well as the amount that the creditor asserts is owed to the creditor by the debtor. If a creditor fails to file a proof of claim, the bankruptcy court or trustee may file the proof of claim on the creditor's behalf but is not obligated to do so. If a claim is for a disputed amount, the bankruptcy court will set the value of the claim.

Creditors' claims are automatically allowed unless contested by the trustee, the debtor, or another creditor. The Code, however, does not allow claims for breach of employment contracts or real estate leases for terms longer than one year. These claims are limited to one year's wages or rent, despite the remaining length of either contract in breach.

Property of the Estate

Upon the commencement of a liquidation proceeding under Chapter 7, an estate in property is created. The estate consists of all the debtor's legal and equitable interests in property presently held, wherever located, together with certain jointly owned property, property transferred in transactions voidable by the trustee, proceeds and profits from the property of the estate, and certain after-acquired property. Interests in certain property—such as gifts, inheritances, property settlements (resulting from divorce), or life insurance death proceeds—to which the debtor becomes entitled *within 180 days after filing* may also become part of the estate. Thus, the filing of a bankruptcy petition generally fixes a dividing line: property acquired prior to the filing becomes property of the estate, and property acquired after the filing, except as just noted, remains the debtor's.

Exempted Property

Any individual debtor is entitled to exempt certain property from the property of the estate. The Bankruptcy Code establishes a federal exemption scheme under which the following property is exempt:[7]

1. Up to $16,150 in equity in the debtor's residence and burial plot (the homestead exemption).

2. Interest in a motor vehicle up to $2,575.

3. Interest in household goods and furnishings, wearing apparel, appliances, books, animals, crops, and musical instruments up to $425 in a particular item but limited to $8,625 in total.

4. Interest in jewelry up to $1,075.

5. Any other property worth up to $800, plus any unused part of the $16,150 homestead exemption up to an amount of $8,075.

6. Interest in any tools of the debtor's trade, up to $1,625.

7. Certain life insurance contracts owned by the debtor.

8. Certain interests in accrued dividends or interests under life insurance contracts owned by the debtor.

9. Professionally prescribed health aids.

10. The right to receive Social Security and certain welfare benefits, alimony and support payments, and certain pension benefits.

11. The right to receive certain personal injury and other awards, up to $16,150.

Individual states have the power to pass legislation precluding debtors in their states from using the federal exemptions. At least thirty-five states have done this. In those states, debtors may use only state (not federal) exemptions. In the rest of the states, an individual debtor (or husband and wife who file jointly) may choose between the exemptions provided under state law and the federal exemptions. State laws may provide significantly greater protection for debtors than federal law. For example, Florida and Texas traditionally have provided for generous exemptions for homeowners. State laws may also define the property coming within an exemption differently than the federal law.

The Trustee's Role

Promptly after the order for relief has been entered, an interim, or provisional, trustee is appointed by the **U.S. trustee** (a government official who performs certain administrative tasks that a bankruptcy judge would otherwise have to perform). The interim trustee administers the debtor's estate until the first meeting of creditors, at which time either a permanent trustee is elected or the interim trustee becomes the permanent trustee. Trustees are entitled to compensation for services rendered, plus reimbursement for expenses.

The basic duty of the trustee is to collect the debtor's available estate and reduce it to money for distribution, preserving the interests of *both* the debtor and unsecured creditors. In other words, the trustee is accountable for administering the debtor's estate. To enable the trustee to accomplish this duty, the Code gives him or her certain powers, stated in both general and specific terms.

TRUSTEE'S POWERS The trustee has the power to require persons holding the debtor's property at the time the petition is filed to deliver the property to the trustee. To enable the trustee to implement this power, the Code provides that the trustee occupies a position equivalent in rights to that of certain other parties. For example, in some situations, the trustee has the same rights as creditors and can obtain a judicial lien or levy execution on the debtor's property. This means that a trustee has priority over an unperfected secured party to the debtor's property. The trustee also has rights equivalent to those of the debtor.

In addition, the trustee has the power to avoid (cancel) certain types of transactions, including those transactions that the debtor could rightfully avoid, *preferences*, certain statutory *liens*, and *fraudulent transfers* by the debtor. Avoidance powers must be exercised within two years of the order for relief (the period runs even if a trustee has not been appointed). These powers of the trustee are discussed in more detail in the following subsections.

---

7. The dollar amounts stated in the Bankruptcy Code are adjusted automatically every three years based on changes in the Consumer Price Index.

VOIDABLE RIGHTS A trustee steps into the shoes of the debtor. Thus, any reason that a debtor can use to obtain the return of his or her property can be used by the trustee as well. These grounds (for recovery) include fraud, duress, incapacity, and mutual mistake.

For example, Rob sells his boat to Inga. Inga gives Rob a check, knowing that there are insufficient funds in her bank account to cover the check. Inga has committed fraud. Rob has the right to avoid that transfer and recover the boat from Inga. Once an order for relief has been entered for Rob, the trustee can exercise the same right to recover the boat from Inga. If the trustee does not take action to enforce one of his or her rights, the debtor in a Chapter 7 bankruptcy will nevertheless be able to enforce that right.[8]

PREFERENCES A debtor is not permitted to transfer property or to make a payment that favors—or gives a **preference** to—one creditor over others. The trustee is allowed to recover payments made both voluntarily and involuntarily to one creditor in preference over another.

To have made a preferential payment that can be recovered, an *insolvent* debtor generally must have transferred property, for a *preexisting* debt, within *ninety days* of the filing of the petition in bankruptcy. The transfer must give the creditor more than the creditor would have received as a result of the bankruptcy proceedings. The trustee does not have to prove insolvency, as the Code provides that the debtor is presumed to be insolvent during this ninety-day period.

Sometimes the creditor receiving the preference is an insider—an individual, a partner, a partnership, or an officer or a director of a corporation (or a relative of one of these) who has a close relationship with the debtor. If this is the case, the avoidance power of the trustee is extended to transfers made within *one year* before filing; however, the *presumption* of insolvency is confined to the ninety-day period. Therefore, the trustee must prove that the debtor was insolvent at the time of an earlier transfer.

Not all transfers are preferences. To be a preference, the transfer must be made for something other than current consideration. Therefore, it is generally assumed by most courts that payment for services rendered within ten to fifteen days prior to the payment of the current consideration is not a preference. If a creditor receives payment in the ordinary course of business, such as payment of last month's telephone bill, the payment cannot be recovered by the trustee in bankruptcy. To be recoverable, a preference must be a transfer for an antecedent (preexisting) debt, such as a year-old printing bill. In addition, the Code permits a consumer-debtor to transfer any property to a creditor up to a total value of $600, without the transfer's constituting a preference. Also, payment of paternity, alimony, maintenance, and support debts is not a preference.

If a preferred creditor has sold the property to an innocent third party, the trustee cannot recover the property from the innocent party. The creditor, however, generally can be held accountable for the value of the property.

LIENS ON DEBTOR'S PROPERTY The trustee is permitted to avoid the fixing of certain statutory liens, such as a mechanic's lien, on property of the debtor. Liens that first become effective at the time of the bankruptcy or insolvency of the debtor are voidable by the trustee. Liens that are not perfected or enforceable against a good faith purchaser on the date of the petition are also voidable.

FRAUDULENT TRANSFERS The trustee may avoid fraudulent transfers or obligations if they were made within one year of the filing of the petition or if they were made with actual intent to hinder, delay, or defraud a creditor. Transfers made for less than a reasonably equivalent consideration are also vulnerable if the debtor thereby became insolvent, was left engaged in business with an unreasonably small amount of capital, or intended to incur debts that would be beyond his or her ability to pay. When a fraudulent transfer is made outside the Code's one-year limit, creditors may seek alternative relief under state laws. State laws often allow creditors to recover for transfers made up to three years prior to the filing of a petition.

The court in the following case had to determine whether the debtors' contributions to their church, in the year preceding their filing of a Chapter 7 petition, could be recovered as "fraudulent transfers."

8. In a Chapter 11 reorganization (to be discussed later), for which generally no trustee is appointed, the debtor has the same avoiding powers as a trustee in a Chapter 7 liquidation. In repayment plans under Chapters 12 and 13 (also to be discussed later), a trustee must be appointed.

CASE 20.4

In re Newman
United States Bankruptcy Court,
District of Kansas, 1995.
183 Bankr. 239.

FACTS   Paul and Myrtle Newman filed a Chapter 7 petition. They listed their monthly income as $1,556 and monthly expenses as $2,458. Their debts totaled more than $25,000, consisting mostly of credit-card and medical bills. Despite the Newmans' circumstances, within the year preceding their petition, they had donated more than $2,400 to the Midway Southern Baptist Church. The donations were pursuant to their "sincere and firmly held belief in tithing."[a] In return for most of the donations, the Newmans received "spiritual benefits" but nothing tangible. Michael Morris, the Newmans' bankruptcy trustee, filed a suit in a federal bankruptcy court against the church to recover the money that the Newmans had donated in the preceding year.

ISSUE   Did the Newmans' donations to their church constitute a fraudulent transfer?

DECISION   Yes. The court granted the trustee's request.

REASON   The court acknowledged that the Newmans and the church had no fraudulent intent but pointed out that fraudulent intent was not required. The Code allows for recovery of those transfers of a debtor's property that occur within one year of the bankruptcy filing, while the debtor is insolvent, and that are not given in exchange for "reasonably equivalent value." The court concluded that "[t]he transfers in question involved interests of the debtors in property, occurred within one year of the debtors' bankruptcy filing, and * * * the debtors were insolvent" when they made their donations. As to whether the Newmans received "reasonably equivalent value," the court noted that in bankruptcy statutes and cases, the term "has long meant tangible benefit or economic value." The court concluded that "[s]uch economic benefit is clearly lacking in this case."

FOR CRITICAL ANALYSIS—Economic Consideration   *What is the policy behind allowing for the recovery of certain transfers made prior to bankruptcy? Who benefits from this recovery?*

a.   *Tithing* means contributing part of one's income (the term *tithe* means "one-tenth") to a church to support the clergy and church administration costs.

Property Distribution

Creditors are either secured or unsecured. As discussed in Chapter 19, a *secured* creditor has a security interest in collateral that secures the debt. An *unsecured* creditor does not have any security interest.

SECURED CREDITORS   The Code provides that a consumer-debtor, within thirty days of the filing of a Chapter 7 petition or before the date of the first meeting of the creditors (whichever is first), must file with the clerk a statement of intention with respect to the secured collateral. The statement must indicate whether the debtor will retain the collateral or surrender it to the secured party. Additionally, if applicable, the debtor must specify whether the collateral will be claimed as exempt property and whether the debtor intends to redeem the property or reaffirm the debt secured by the collateral. The trustee is obligated to enforce the debtor's statement within forty-five days after the statement is filed.

If the collateral is surrendered to the perfected secured party, the secured creditor can enforce the security interest either by accepting the property in full satisfaction of the debt or by foreclosing on the collateral and using the proceeds to pay off the debt. Thus, the secured party has priority over unsecured parties to the proceeds from the disposition of the secured collateral. Indeed, the Code provides that if the value of the secured collateral exceeds the secured party's claim, the secured party also has priority to the proceeds in an amount that will cover reasonable fees (including attorneys' fees, if provided for in the security agreement) and costs incurred because of the debtor's default. Any excess over this amount is used by the trustee to satisfy the claims of unsecured creditors. Should the secured collateral be insufficient to cover the secured debt owed, the secured creditor becomes an unsecured creditor for the difference.

UNSECURED CREDITORS Bankruptcy law establishes an order or priority for classes of debts owed to *unsecured* creditors, and they are paid in the order of their priority. Each class of debt must be fully paid before the next class is entitled to any of the proceeds—if there are sufficient funds to pay the entire class. If not, the proceeds are distributed *proportionately* to each creditor in the class, and all classes lower in priority on the list receive nothing. The order of priority among classes of unsecured creditors is as follows:

1. Administrative expenses—including court costs, trustee fees, and bankruptcy attorneys' fees.
2. In an involuntary bankruptcy, expenses incurred by the debtor in the ordinary course of business from the date of the filing of the petition up to the appointment of the trustee or the issuance by the court of an order for relief.
3. Unpaid wages, salaries, and commissions earned within ninety days of the filing of the petition, limited to $4,300 per claimant. Any claim in excess of $4,300 is treated as a claim of a general creditor (listed as number 9 below).
4. Unsecured claims for contributions to be made to employee benefit plans, limited to services performed during 180 days prior to the filing of the bankruptcy petition and $4,300 per employee.
5. Claims by farmers and fishers, up to $4,300, against debtor operators of grain storage or fish storage or processing facilities.
6. Consumer deposits of up to $1,950 given to the debtor before the petition was filed in connection with the purchase, lease, or rental of property or the purchase of services that were not received or provided. Any claim in excess of $1,950 is treated as a claim of a general creditor (listed as number 9 below).
7. Paternity, alimony, maintenance, and support debts.

8. Certain taxes and penalties due to government units, such as income and property taxes.
9. Claims of general creditors.

If any amount remains after the priority classes of creditors have been satisfied, it is turned over to the debtor.

Discharge

From the debtor's point of view, the purpose of a liquidation proceeding is to obtain a fresh start through the discharge of debts.[9] Certain debts, however, are not dischargeable in a liquidation proceeding. Also, certain debtors may not qualify—because of their conduct—to have all debts discharged in bankruptcy.

EXCEPTIONS TO DISCHARGE Claims that are not dischargeable under Chapter 7 include the following:

1. Claims for back taxes accruing within three years prior to bankruptcy.
2. Claims for amounts borrowed by the debtor to pay federal taxes.
3. Claims against property or money obtained by the debtor under false pretenses or by false representations.
4. Claims by creditors who were not notified of the bankruptcy; these claims did not appear on the schedules the debtor was required to file.
5. Claims based on fraud or misuse of funds by the debtor while he or she was acting in a fiduciary capacity or claims involving the debtor's embezzlement or larceny.
6. Alimony, child support, and (with certain exceptions) property settlements.
7. Claims based on willful or malicious conduct by the debtor toward another or the property of another.
8. Certain government fines and penalties.
9. Certain student loans, unless payment of the loans imposes an undue hardship on the debtor and the debtor's dependents.
10. Consumer debts of more than $1,000 for luxury goods or services owed to a single creditor

---

9. Discharges are granted under Chapter 7 only to *individuals*, not to corporations or partnerships. The latter may use Chapter 11, or they may terminate their existence under state law.

incurred within sixty days of the order for relief. This denial of discharge is a rebuttable presumption (that is, the denial may be challenged by the debtor), however, and any debts reasonably incurred to support the debtor or dependents are not classified as luxuries.

11. Cash advances totaling more than $1,000 that are extensions of open-end consumer credit obtained by the debtor within sixty days of the order for relief. A denial of discharge of these debts is also a rebuttable presumption.

12. Judgments or consent decrees against a debtor as a result of the debtor's operation of a motor vehicle while intoxicated.

In the following case, the debtor sought to have her student loans discharged in bankruptcy. The question before the court was whether payment of the loan would constitute an "undue hardship" for the debtor.

CASE 20.5

In re Baker
United States Bankruptcy Court,
Eastern District of Tennessee, 1981.
10 Bankr. 870.

FACTS   Mary Lou Baker attended three different institutions of higher learning. At these three schools, she received educational loans totaling $6,635. After graduation, she was employed, but her monthly take-home pay was less than $650. Monthly expenses for herself and her three children were approximately $925. Her husband had left town and provided no child or other financial support. She received no public aid and had no other income. In January 1981, just prior to this action, Baker's church paid her gas bill so that she and her children could have heat in their home. One child had reading difficulty, and another required expensive shoes. Baker had not been well and had been unable to pay her medical bills. She filed for bankruptcy. In her petition, she sought a discharge of her educational loans based on the hardship provision.

ISSUE   Would paying the debt pose an undue hardship for Baker?

DECISION   Yes. The student loans were discharged.

REASON   The purpose of the prohibition against discharge was "to remedy an abuse by students who, immediately upon graduation, would file bankruptcy to secure a discharge of educational loans." In this case, Baker did not file bankruptcy to secure a discharge only from her educational loans. The bankruptcy court found that Baker could reduce her expenses somewhat but that her reasonable expenses each month far exceeded her income. Given Baker's circumstances, the court found that forcing payment of Baker's debts would create an undue hardship and that the Bankruptcy Code was drafted to provide a fresh start for those such as Baker "who have truly fallen on hard times."

FOR CRITICAL ANALYSIS— Economic Consideration   *Why does the Bankruptcy Code generally prohibit the discharge of student loans, such as those obtained through government-guaranteed educational loan programs?*

OBJECTIONS TO DISCHARGE   In addition to the exceptions to discharge previously listed, the following circumstances (relating to the debtor's *conduct* and not the debt) will cause a discharge to be denied:

1. The debtor's concealment or destruction of property with the intent to hinder, delay, or defraud a creditor.

2. The debtor's fraudulent concealment or destruction of financial records.

3. The granting of a discharge to the debtor within six years of the filing of the petition.[10]

When a discharge is denied under these circumstances, the assets of the debtor are still distributed to the creditors, but the debtor remains liable for the unpaid portions of all claims.

EFFECT OF DISCHARGE   The primary effect of a discharge is to void, or set aside, any judgment on a discharged debt and prohibit any action to collect a discharged debt. A discharge does not affect the liability of a co-debtor.

REVOCATION OF DISCHARGE   The Code provides that a debtor's discharge may be revoked. Upon petition by the trustee or a creditor, the bankruptcy court may, within one year, revoke the discharge decree if it is discovered that the debtor was fraudulent or dishonest during the bankruptcy proceedings. The revocation renders the discharge void, allowing creditors not satisfied by the distribution of the debtor's estate to proceed with their claims against the debtor.

REAFFIRMATION OF DEBT   A debtor may voluntarily agree to pay off a debt—for example, a debt owed to a family member, close friend, or some other party—notwithstanding the fact that the debt could be discharged in bankruptcy. An agreement to pay a debt dischargeable in bankruptcy is referred to as a *reaffirmation agreement*. To be enforceable, reaffirmation agreements must be made before a debtor is granted a discharge, and they must be filed with the court. If the debtor is represented by an attorney, court approval is not required if the attorney files a declaration or affidavit stating that (1) the debtor has been fully informed of the consequences of the agreement (and a default under the agreement), (2) the agreement is made voluntarily, and (3) the agreement does not impose undue hardship on the debtor or the debtor's family. If the debtor is not represented by an attorney, court approval is required, and the agreement will be approved only if the court finds that the agreement will result in no undue hardship to the debtor and is in the best interest of the debtor.

The agreement must contain a clear and conspicuous statement advising the debtor that reaffirmation is not required. The debtor can rescind, or cancel, the agreement at any time prior to discharge or within sixty days of filing the agreement, whichever is later. This rescission period must be stated *clearly* and *conspicuously* in the reaffirmation agreement.

▮ Chapter 11—Reorganization

The type of bankruptcy proceeding used most commonly by a corporate debtor is the Chapter 11 *reorganization*. In a reorganization, the creditors and the debtor formulate a plan under which the debtor pays a portion of his or her debts and is discharged of the remainder. The debtor is allowed to continue in business. Although this type of bankruptcy is commonly a corporate reorganization, any debtor (except a stockbroker or a commodities broker) who is eligible for Chapter 7 relief is eligible for relief under Chapter 11.[11] Railroads are also eligible.

The same principles that govern the filing of a liquidation petition apply to reorganization proceedings. The case may be brought either voluntarily or involuntarily. The same principles govern the entry of the order for relief. The automatic-stay provision is also applicable in reorganizations.

In some instances, creditors may prefer private, negotiated debt-adjustment agreements, also known as **workouts,** to bankruptcy proceedings. Often these out-of-court workouts are much more flexible and thus more conducive to a speedy settlement. Speed is critical, because delay is one of the most costly elements in any bankruptcy proceeding. Another advantage of workouts is that they avoid the various administrative costs of bankruptcy proceedings.

A bankruptcy court, after notice and a hearing, may dismiss or suspend all proceedings in a case at any time if dismissal or suspension would better serve the interests of the creditors. The Code also allows a court, after notice and a hearing, to dismiss a case under reorganization "for cause." *Cause* includes the absence of a reasonable likelihood of rehabilitation, the inability to effect a plan, and an

---

10. A discharge under Chapter 13 of the Code within six years of the filing of the petition does not bar a subsequent Chapter 7 discharge when a good faith Chapter 13 plan paid at least 70 percent of all allowed unsecured claims and was the debtor's "best effort."

---

11. *Toibb v. Radloff*, 501 U.S. 157, 111 S.Ct. 2197, 115 L.Ed.2d 145 (1991).

unreasonable delay by the debtor that is prejudicial to (may harm the interests of) creditors.[12] In the following widely publicized case, creditors of Johns-Manville Corporation sought to dismiss a voluntary Chapter 11 petition filed by Manville.

_____

12.   See 11 U.S.C. Section 1112(b).

CASE 20.6

In re Johns-Manville Corp.

United States Bankruptcy Court, Southern District of New York, 1984. 36 Bankr. 727.

FACTS   On August 26, 1982, Johns-Manville Corporation a highly successful industrial enterprise, filed for protection under Chapter 11 of the Bankruptcy Code. This filing came as a surprise to some of Manville's creditors, as well as to some of the other corporations that were also being sued, along with Manville, for injuries caused by asbestos exposure. Manville asserted that the approximately sixteen thousand lawsuits pending as of the filing date and the potential lawsuits of people who had been exposed but who would not manifest the asbestos-related diseases until sometime in the future necessitated its filing. Manville's creditors, on motion to the bankruptcy court, contended that Manville did not file in good faith, that Manville was not insolvent, and that therefore the voluntary Chapter 11 petition should be dismissed.

ISSUE   Was Manville eligible to file a voluntary petition for Chapter 11 reorganization under the Bankruptcy Code?

DECISION   Yes. The court held that bankruptcy proceedings were appropriate in this situation and denied the motions to dismiss Manville's petition.

REASON   With respect to voluntary petitions, the court noted that "it is no longer necessary for a petitioner for reorganization to allege or show insolvency or inability to pay debts as they mature." Manville clearly met all of the threshold eligibility requirements for filing a voluntary petition. Furthermore, in determining whether to dismiss a Chapter 11 case, a court is not necessarily required to consider the debtor's good faith in filing, because "good faith" is not specifically necessary for filing under the Code. Rather, good faith emerges as a requirement for confirmation of the plan; that is, good faith is required to come out of Chapter 11, but not to get into it. A "principal goal" of the Code is to provide open and easy access to the bankruptcy process. Here, liquidation would be inefficient and wasteful; it would destroy the utility of Manville's assets, as well as jobs. More important, liquidation would preclude compensation of future asbestos claimants. Ultimately, the court concluded that Manville needed the protection of the Bankruptcy Code and should not be required to wait until its economic picture deteriorated beyond salvation to file for reorganization.

FOR CRITICAL ANALYSIS—Ethical Consideration   *In view of the fact that Manville was a solvent corporation, did it deserve the "fresh start" it achieved through Chapter 11 proceedings?*

Debtor in Possession

Upon entry of the order for relief, the debtor generally continues to operate his or her business as a **debtor in possession (DIP)**. The court, however, may appoint a trustee (often referred to as a *receiver*) to operate the debtor's business if gross mismanagement of the business is shown or if appointing a trustee is in the best interests of the estate.

The DIP's role is similar to that of a trustee in a liquidation. The DIP is entitled to avoid preferential payments made to creditors and fraudulent transfers of assets that occurred prior to the filing of the Chapter 11 petition. The DIP has the power to decide whether to cancel or assume obligations under executory contracts (contracts that have not yet been performed) that were made prior to the petition.

Creditors' Committees

As soon as practicable after the entry of the order for relief, a creditors' committee of unsecured creditors is appointed. The committee may consult with the trustee or the DIP concerning the administration of the case or the formulation of the reorganization plan. Additional creditors' committees may be appointed to represent special interest creditors. Orders affecting the estate generally will not be entered without either the consent of the committee or a hearing in which the judge hears the position of the committee.

Businesses with debts of less than $2 million that do not own or manage real estate can avoid creditors' committees. In these cases, orders can be entered without a committee's consent.

The Reorganization Plan

A reorganization plan to rehabilitate the debtor is a plan to conserve and administer the debtor's assets in the hope of an eventual return to successful operation and solvency. The plan must be fair and equitable and must do the following:

1. Designate classes of claims and interests.
2. Specify the treatment to be afforded the classes. (The plan must provide the same treatment for each claim in a particular class.)
3. Provide an adequate means for execution.

FILING THE PLAN Only the debtor may file a plan within the first 120 days after the date of the order for relief. If the debtor does not meet the 120-day deadline, however, or if the debtor fails to obtain the required creditor consent (see below) within 180 days, any party may propose a plan. The plan need not provide for full repayment to unsecured creditors. Instead, unsecured creditors receive a percentage of each dollar owed to them

by the debtor. If a small-business debtor chooses to avoid creditors' committees, the time for the debtor's filing is shortened to 100 days, and any other party's plan must be filed within 160 days.

ACCEPTANCE AND CONFIRMATION OF THE PLAN Once the plan has been developed, it is submitted to each class of creditors for acceptance. Each class must accept the plan unless the class is not adversely affected by the plan. A class has accepted the plan when a majority of the creditors, representing two-thirds of the amount of the total claim, vote to approve it. Even when all classes of claims accept the plan, the court may refuse to confirm it if it is not "in the best interests of the creditors." A spouse or child of the debtor can block the plan if it does not provide for payment of his or her claims in cash.

Even if only one class of claims has accepted the plan, the court may still confirm the plan under the Code's so-called **cram-down provision.** In other words, the court may confirm the plan over the objections of a class of creditors. Before the court can exercise this right of cram-down confirmation, it must be demonstrated that the plan "does not discriminate unfairly" against any creditors and that the plan is "fair and equitable."

The plan is binding on confirmation. The debtor is given a reorganization discharge from all claims not protected under the plan. This discharge does not apply to any claims that would be denied discharge under liquidation.

▐ Chapter 13—Repayment Plan

Chapter 13 of the Bankruptcy Code provides for the "Adjustment of Debts of an Individual with Regular Income." Individuals (not partnerships or corporations) with regular income who owe fixed unsecured debts of less than $269,250 or fixed secured debts of less than $807,750 may take advantage of bankruptcy repayment plans. This includes salaried employees; individual proprietors; and individuals who live on welfare, Social Security, fixed pensions, or investment income. Many small-business debtors have a choice of filing under either Chapter 11 or Chapter 13. There are several advantages to repayment plans. One advantage is that they are less expensive and less complicated than reorganization proceedings or liquidation proceedings.

A Chapter 13 case can be initiated only by the filing of a voluntary petition by the debtor. Certain liquidation and reorganization cases may be converted to Chapter 13 cases with the consent of the debtor. A Chapter 13 case may be converted to a Chapter 7 case at the request of either the debtor or, under certain circumstances, a creditor. A Chapter 13 case also may be converted to a Chapter 11 case after a hearing. Upon the filing of a petition under Chapter 13, a trustee must be appointed. The automatic stay previously discussed also takes effect. Although the stay applies to all or part of a consumer debt, it does not apply to any business debt incurred by the debtor.

The Repayment Plan

Shortly after the petition is filed, the debtor must file a repayment plan. This plan may provide either for payment of all obligations in full or for payment of a lesser amount. A plan of rehabilitation by repayment provides for the turnover to the trustee of such future earnings or income of the debtor as is necessary for execution of the plan. The time for payment under the plan may not exceed three years unless the court approves an extension. The term, with extension, may not exceed five years.

The Code requires the debtor to make "timely" payments, and the trustee is required to ensure that the debtor commences these payments. The debtor must begin making payments under the proposed plan within thirty days after the plan has been filed with the court. If the plan has not been confirmed, the trustee is instructed to retain the payments until the plan is confirmed and then distribute them accordingly. If the plan is denied, the trustee will return the payments to the debtor less any costs. Failure of the debtor to make timely payments or to begin payments within the thirty-day period will allow the court to convert the case to a liquidation bankruptcy or to dismiss the petition.

CONFIRMATION OF THE PLAN   After the plan is filed, the court holds a confirmation hearing, at which interested parties may object to the plan. The court will confirm a plan with respect to each claim of a secured creditor under any of the following circumstances:

1. If the secured creditors have accepted the plan.
2. If the plan provides that creditors retain their claims against the debtor's property and if the value of the property to be distributed to the creditors under the plan is not less than the secured portion of their claims.
3. If the debtor surrenders the property securing the claim to the creditors.

OBJECTION TO THE PLAN   Unsecured creditors do not have a vote to confirm a repayment plan, but they can object to it. The court can approve a plan over the objection of the trustee or any unsecured creditor only in either of the following situations:

1. When the value of the property to be distributed under the plan is at least equal to the amount of the claims.
2. When all the debtor's projected disposable income to be received during the three-year plan period will be applied to making payments. Disposable income is all income received *less* amounts needed to support the debtor and dependents and/or amounts needed to meet ordinary expenses to continue the operation of a business.

MODIFICATION OF THE PLAN   Prior to the completion of payments, the plan may be modified at the request of the debtor, the trustee, or an unsecured creditor. If any interested party has an objection to the modification, the court must hold a hearing to determine approval or disapproval of the modified plan.

Discharge

After the completion of all payments, the court grants a discharge of all debts provided for by the repayment plan. Except for allowed claims not provided for by the plan, certain long-term debts provided for by the plan, and claims for alimony and child support, all other debts are dischargeable. A discharge of debts under a Chapter 13 repayment plan is sometimes referred to as a "superdischarge." One of the reasons for this is that the law allows a Chapter 13 discharge to include fraudulently incurred debt and claims resulting from malicious or willful injury. Therefore, a discharge under Chapter 13 may be much more beneficial to some debtors than a liquidation discharge under Chapter 7 might be.

Even if the debtor does not complete the plan, a hardship discharge may be granted if failure to complete the plan was due to circumstances beyond the debtor's control and if the value of the property distributed under the plan was greater than creditors would have received in a liquidation proceeding. A discharge can be revoked within one year if it was obtained by fraud.

Chapter 12— Family-Farmer Plan

The Bankruptcy Code defines a *family farmer* as one whose gross income is at least 50 percent farm dependent and whose debts are at least 80 percent farm related. The total debt must not exceed $1.5 million. A partnership or closely held corporation that is at least 50 percent owned by the farm family can also take advantage of Chapter 12.

The procedure for filing a family-farmer bankruptcy plan is very similar to the procedure for filing a repayment plan under Chapter 13. The farmer-debtor must file a plan not later than ninety days after the order for relief. The filing of the petition acts as an automatic stay against creditors' actions against the estate.

The content of a family-farmer plan is basically the same as that of a Chapter 13 repayment plan. The plan can be modified by the farmer-debtor but, except for cause, must be confirmed or denied within forty-five days of the filing of the plan.

Court confirmation of the plan is the same as for a repayment plan. In summary, the plan must provide for payment of secured debts at the value of the collateral. If the secured debt exceeds the value of the collateral, the remaining debt is unsecured. For unsecured debtors, the plan must be confirmed if either the value of the property to be distributed under the plan equals the amount of the claim or the plan provides that all of the farmer-debtor's disposable income to be received in a three-year period (or longer, by court approval) will be applied to making payments. Completion of payments under the plan discharges all debts provided for by the plan.

A farmer who has already filed a reorganization or repayment plan may convert the plan to a family-farmer plan. The farmer-debtor may also convert a family-farmer plan to a liquidation plan.

Terms and Concepts

artisan's lien 412
attachment 413
automatic stay 421
consumer-debtor 419
co-surety 417
cram-down provision 429
creditors' composition agreement 415
debtor in possession (DIP) 428
discharge 419

estate in property 421
garnishment 414
guarantor 416
homestead exemption 417
innkeeper's lien 413
liquidation 418
mechanic's lien 411
mortgagee 415
mortgagor 415
order for relief 419
petition in bankruptcy 419

preference 423
right of contribution 417
right of reimbursement 417
right of subrogation 417
surety 415
suretyship 415
U. S. Trustee 422
workout 427
writ of attachment 414
writ of execution 414

Chapter Summary: Creditors' Rights and Bankruptcy

LAWS ASSISTING CREDITORS	
Liens *(See pages 411–414.)*	1. *Mechanic's lien*—A nonpossessory, filed lien on an owner's real estate for labor, services, or materials furnished to or made on the realty.
	(Continued)

▌ Chapter Summary: Creditors' Rights and Bankruptcy—Continued

Liens—Continued	2. *Artisan's lien*—A possessory lien on an owner's personal property for labor performed or value added.
	
	 3. *Innkeeper's lien*—A possessory lien on a hotel guest's baggage for hotel charges that remain unpaid.
	
	 4. *Judicial Liens*—
	    a. *Attachment*—A court-ordered seizure of property prior to a court's final determination of the creditor's rights to the property. Attachment is available only on the creditor's posting of a bond and in strict compliance with the applicable state statutes.
	    b. *Writ of execution*—A court order directing the sheriff to seize (levy) and sell a debtor's nonexempt real or personal property to satisfy a court's judgment in the creditor's favor.

Garnishment *(See pages 414–415.)*	A collection remedy that allows the creditor to attach a debtor's money (such as wages owed) and property that are held by a third person.
Creditors' Composition Agreement *(See page 415.)*	A contract between a debtor and his or her creditors by which the debtor's debts are discharged by payment of a sum less than the sum that is actually owed.
Mortgage Foreclosure *(See page 415.)*	On the debtor's default, the entire mortgage debt is due and payable, allowing the creditor to foreclose on the realty by selling it to satisfy the debt.
Suretyship or Guaranty *(See pages 415–417.)*	Under contract, a third person agrees to be primarily or secondarily liable for the debt owed by the principal debtor. A creditor can turn to this third person for satisfaction of the debt.

LAWS ASSISTING DEBTORS

Exemptions
 (See pages 417–418.)
	Numerous laws, including consumer protection statutes, assist debtors. Additionally, state laws exempt certain types of real and personal property from levy of execution or attachment.
	
	 1. *Real property*—Each state permits a debtor to retain the family home, either in its entirety or up to a specified dollar amount, free from the claims of unsecured creditors or trustees in bankruptcy (homestead exemption).
	
	 2. *Personal property*—Personal property that is most often exempt from satisfaction of judgment debts includes the following:
	    a. Household furniture up to a specified dollar amount.
	    b. Clothing and certain personal possessions.
	    c. Transportation vehicles up to a specified dollar amount.
	    d. Certain classified animals, such as livestock and pets.
	    e. Equipment used in a business or trade up to a specified dollar amount.

BANKRUPTCY—A COMPARISON OF CHAPTERS 7, 11, 12, AND 13
(See pages 418–431.)

ISSUE	CHAPTER 7	CHAPTER 11	CHAPTERS 12 AND 13
Purpose	Liquidation.	Reorganization.	Adjustment.
Who Can Petition	Debtor (voluntary) or creditors (involuntary).	Debtor (voluntary) or creditors (involuntary).	Debtor (voluntary) only.

▌Chapter Summary: Creditors' Rights and Bankruptcy—Continued

	CHAPTER 7	CHAPTER 11	CHAPTERS 12 AND 13
Who Can Be a Debtor	Any "person" (including partnerships and corporations) except railroads, insurance companies, banks, savings and loan institutions, investment companies licensed by the Small Business Administration, and credit unions. Farmers and charitable institutions cannot be involuntarily petitioned.	Any debtor eligible for Chapter 7 relief; railroads are also eligible.	*Chapter 12*—Any family farmer (one whose gross income is at least 50 percent farm dependent and whose debts are at least 80 percent farm related) or any partnership or closely held corporation at least 50 percent owned by a farm family, when total debt does not exceed $1.5 million. *Chapter 13*—Any individual (not partnerships or corporations) with regular income who owes fixed unsecured debts of less than $269,250 or fixed secured debts of less than $807,750.
Procedure Leading to Discharge	Nonexempt property is sold with proceeds to be distributed (in order) to priority groups. Dischargeable debts are terminated.	Plan is submitted; if it is approved and followed, debts are discharged.	Plan is submitted and must be approved if the debtor turns over disposable income for a three-year period; if the plan is followed, debts are discharged.
Advantages	Upon liquidation and distribution, most debts are discharged, and the debtor has an opportunity for a fresh start.	Debtor continues in business. Creditors can either accept the plan, or it can be "crammed down" on them. The plan allows for the reorganization and liquidation of debts over the plan period.	Debtor continues in business or possession of assets. If the plan is approved, most debts are discharged after a three-year period.

▌For Review

1. What is a prejudgment attachment? What is a writ of execution? How does a creditor use these remedies?

2. What is garnishment? When might a creditor undertake a garnishment proceeding?

3. In a bankruptcy proceeding, what constitutes the debtor's estate in property? What property is exempt from the estate under federal bankruptcy law?

4. What is the difference between an exception to discharge and an objection to discharge?

5. In a Chapter 11 reorganization, what is the role of the debtor in possession?

▌Questions and Case Problems

20–1. Creditors' Remedies. In what circumstances would a creditor resort to each of the following remedies when trying to collect on a debt?

(a) Mechanic's lien.

(b) Artisan's lien.

(c) Innkeeper's lien.

(d) Writ of attachment.

(e) Writ of execution.

(f) Garnishment.

20–2. Rights of the Surety. Meredith, a farmer, borrowed $5,000 from Farmer's Bank and gave the bank $4,000 in bearer bonds to hold as collateral for the loan. Meredith's neighbor, Peterson, who had known Meredith for years, signed as a surety on the note. Because of a drought, Meredith's harvest that year was only a fraction of what it normally was, and he was forced to default on his payments to Farmer's Bank. The bank did not immediately sell the bonds but instead requested $5,000 from Peterson. Peterson paid the $5,000 and then demanded that the bank give him the $4,000 in securities. Can Peterson enforce this demand? Explain.

20–3. Rights of the Guarantor. Sabrina is a student at Sunnyside University. In need of funds to pay for tuition and books, she attempts to secure a short-term loan from University Bank. The bank agrees to make a loan if Sabrina will have someone financially responsible guarantee the loan payments. Abigail, a well-known businessperson and a friend of Sabrina's family, calls the bank and agrees to pay the loan if Sabrina cannot. Because of Abigail's reputation, the bank makes the loan. Sabrina makes several payments on the loan, but because of illness she is not able to work for one month. She requests that University Bank extend the loan for three months. The bank agrees and raises the interest rate for the extended period. Abigail has not been notified of the extension (and therefore has not consented to it). One month later, Sabrina drops out of school. All attempts to collect from Sabrina have failed. University Bank wants to hold Abigail liable. Will the bank succeed? Explain.

20–4. Distribution of Property. Runyan voluntarily petitions for bankruptcy. He has three major claims against his estate. One is by Calvin, a friend who holds Runyan's negotiable promissory note for $2,500; one is by Kohak, an employee who is owed three months' back wages of $4,500; and one is by the First Bank of Sunny Acres on an unsecured loan of $5,000. In addition, Martinez, an accountant retained by the trustee, is owed $500, and property taxes of $1,000 are owed to Micanopa County. Runyan's nonexempt property has been liquidated, with the proceeds totaling $5,000. Discuss fully what amount each party will receive, and why.

20–5. Creditors' Remedies. Orkin owns a relatively old home valued at $45,000. He notices that the bathtubs and fixtures in both bathrooms are leaking and need to be replaced. He contracts with Pike to replace the bathtubs and fixtures. Pike replaces them and submits her bill of $4,000 to Orkin. Because of financial difficulties, Orkin does not pay the bill. Orkin's only asset is his home, which under state law is exempt up to $40,000 as a homestead. Discuss fully Pike's remedies in this situation.

20–6. Writ of Attachment. Topjian Plumbing and Heating, Inc., the plaintiff, sought prejudgment writs of attachment to satisfy an anticipated judgment in a contract action against Bruce Topjian, Inc., the defendant. The plaintiff did not petition the court for permission to effect the attachments but merely completed the forms, served them on the defendant and on the Fencers (the owners of a parcel of land that had previously belonged to the defendant), and recorded them at the registry of deeds. On what grounds might the court invalidate the attachments? [*Topjian Plumbing and Heating, Inc. v. Bruce Topjian, Inc.*, 129 N.H. 481, 529 A.2d 391 (1987)]

20–7. Rights of the Guarantor. Hallmark Cards, Inc., sued Edward Peevy, who had guaranteed an obligation owed to Hallmark by Garry Peevy. At the time of Edward Peevy's guaranty, Hallmark had in its possession property pledged as security by Garry Peevy. Before the suit was filed, Hallmark sold the pledged property without giving notice to Edward Peevy. Because the property sold did not cover the loan balance, Hallmark sued for the balance, seeking a deficiency judgment. Edward Peevy contended that because Hallmark had sold the property pledged by Garry Peevy as security for the obligation without notifying him (Edward Peevy), Hallmark was not entitled to a deficiency judgment against him. Hallmark contended that Edward Peevy was not entitled to notice of the sale of the collateral and was not required to give consent. Which party will prevail in court? Discuss. [*Hallmark Cards, Inc. v. Peevy*, 293 Ark. 594, 739 S.W.2d 691 (1987)]

20–8. Preferences. Fred Currey purchased cattle from Itano Farms, Inc. As payment for the cattle, Currey gave Itano Farms worthless checks in the amount of $50,250. Currey was later convicted of passing bad checks, and the state criminal court ordered him to pay Itano Farms restitution in the amount of $50,250. About four months after this court order, Currey and his wife filed for Chapter 7 bankruptcy protection. During the ninety days prior to the filing of the petition, Currey had made three restitution payments to Itano, totaling $14,821. The Curreys sought to recover these payments as preferences. What should the court decide? Explain. [*In re Currey*, 144 Bankr. 490 (D.Ida. 1992)]

20–9. Dismissal of Chapter 7 Case. Ellis and Bonnie Jarrell filed a Chapter 7 petition. The petition was not filed due to a calamity, sudden illness, disability, or unemployment—both Jarrells were employed. Their petition was full of inaccuracies that understated their income and overstated their obligations. For example, they declared as an expense a monthly contribution to an investment plan. The truth was that they had monthly income of $3,197.45 and expenses of $2,159.44. They were attempting to discharge a total of $15,391.64 in unsecured debts. Most of these were credit-card debts, at least half of which had been taken as cash advances. Should the court dismiss the petition? If so, why? Discuss. [*In re Jarrell*, 189 Bankr. 374 (M.D.N.C. 1995)]

U.S. v. F2d **CASE BRIEFING ASSIGNMENT**

20–10. *Examine Case A.6 [Hawley v. Clement Industries, Inc., 51 F.3d 246 (11th Cir. 1995)] in Appendix A. The case has been excerpted there in great detail. Review and then brief the case, making sure that you include answers to the following questions in your brief.*

1. How did the case originate, and who are the parties?
2. What was the central issue to be decided?
3. What law governs the issue?
4. How did the lower court decide the case?
5. What was the appellate court's decision on the matter?

▋Unit Six—Cumulative Hypothetical Problem

 20–11. *Dmitri Peter ("Pete") Darin is president of Southside Equipment Corp., a small electronics store. Darin owns 80 percent of the corporation's shares, and Oliver Castle owns the remaining 20 percent. Business is booming, and Darin and Castle decide to expand their business. To do so, they borrow $50,000 from First Bank and Trust. As collateral for the loan, Southside agrees to give the bank a security interest in all of the firm's current and after-acquired inventory. The bank properly perfects its interest in Southside's collateral by filing a financing statement with the appropriate government office.*

1. Southside later obtains a loan from Central Bank, using the same inventory as collateral. Central Bank properly perfects its security interest by filing a financing statement. In a priority contest, which bank will have superior rights to the inventory? If First Bank, on its financial statement, had identified the debtor only as "Pete Darin," which creditor would have superior rights to the collateral?
2. Southside is experiencing financial setbacks and defaults on its payments to First Bank. Assuming that First Bank's security interest was properly perfected and that no other creditor has rights in the collateral, what basic remedies are available to First Bank?
3. Suppose that Darin has done business with First Bank for years, and First Bank knows that Darin is a good credit risk. The bank also knows that Darin has substantial personal assets. Instead of taking a security interest in Southside's inventory to secure the $50,000 loan, First Bank asks Darin to promise that if Southside defaults, Darin will personally pay the loan. Is Darin a surety or a guarantor in this situation? Is Darin's liability on the loan primary or secondary? Must Darin's promise be in writing to be enforceable? Explain.
4. Darin is experiencing personal financial problems. The amount of income he receives from the corporation is barely sufficient to cover his living expenses, the payments due on his mortgage, various credit-card debts, and some loans that he took out to pay for his son's college tuition. He would like to file for Chapter 7 liquidation to just be rid of the debts entirely, but he knows that he could probably pay them off over a four-year period if he really scrimped and used every cent available to pay his creditors. Darin decides to file for bankruptcy relief under Chapter 7. Are all of Darin's debts dischargeable under Chapter 7, including the debts incurred for his son's education? Given the fact that Darin could foreseeably pay off his debts over a four-year period, will the court allow Darin to obtain relief under Chapter 7? Why or why not?

▋Accessing the Internet: Fundamentals of Business Law

The Legal Information Institute at Cornell University offers a collection of law materials concerning debtor-creditor relationships, including federal statutes and recent Supreme Court decisions on this topic, at

http://www.law.cornell.edu/topics/debtor_creditor.html

The U.S. Bankruptcy Code is online at

http://www.law.cornell.edu:80/uscode/11

Cornell Law School's Legal Information Institute provides a general introduction to bankruptcy law and links to related Internet resources at

http://www.law.cornell.edu/topics/bankruptcy.html

You can find links to an extensive number of bankruptcy resources on the Internet by accessing the Bankruptcy Lawfinder at

http://www.agin.com/lawfind/

The American Bankruptcy Institute (ABI) is also a good resource for bankruptcy information. The ABI site includes a collection of selected bankruptcy court decisions, daily and weekly summaries of important bankruptcy news, legislative updates, and so on. You can access the site at

http://www.abiworld.org

For a discussion of alternatives to bankruptcy, go to

http://apocalypse.berkshire.net/~mkb/

The site includes information on the following alternatives: Debt Workout, Do Nothing, and Pay Creditors.

Dockets, records, and some of the decisions of the bankruptcy courts can be accessed online through the federal courts' electronic bulletin board system, PACER (see the Accessing the Internet section at the end of Chapter 2 for information on PACER).

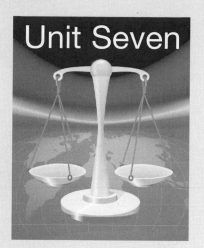

Unit Seven

Employment Relations

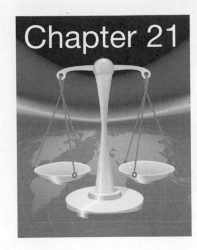

Chapter 21

Agency Relationships

CHAPTER OBJECTIVES

After reading this chapter, you should be able to:

1. Distinguish between employees and independent contractors.
2. Outline the ways in which an agency relationship can arise.
3. Specify the duties that agents and principals owe to each other.
4. Describe the liability of the principal and the agent with respect to third parties.
5. List the ways in which an agency relationship can be terminated.

One of the most common, important, and pervasive legal relationships is that of **agency**. In an agency relationship between two parties, one of the parties, called the *agent*, agrees to represent or act for the other, called the *principal*. The principal has the right to control the agent's conduct in matters entrusted to the agent, and the agent must exercise his or her powers for the benefit of the principal only. By using agents, a principal can conduct multiple business operations simultaneously in various locations. Thus, for example, contracts that bind the principal can be made at different places with different persons at the same time.

A familiar example of an agent is a corporate officer who serves in a representative capacity for the owners of the corporation. In this capacity, the officer has the authority to bind the principal (the corporation) to a contract. Indeed, agency law is essential to the existence and operation of a corporate entity, because only through its agents can a corporation function and enter into contracts. Because agency relationships permeate the business world, an understanding of the law of agency is crucial to understanding business law.

▮ Agency Relationships

Section 1(1) of the *Restatement (Second) of Agency*[1] defines *agency* as "the fiduciary relation which results from the manifestation of consent by one person to another that the other shall act in his behalf and subject to his control, and consent by the other so to act." The term **fiduciary** is at the heart of agency law. The term can be used both as a noun and as an adjective. When used as a noun, it refers to a person having a duty created by his or her undertaking to act primarily for another's benefit in matters connected with the undertaking. When used as an adjective, as in "fiduciary relationship," it means that the relationship involves trust and confidence.

In a principal-agent relationship, the parties have agreed that the agent will act *on behalf and instead of* the principal in negotiating and transacting business with third persons. Agency relation-

---

1. The *Restatement (Second) of Agency* is an authoritative summary of the law of agency and is often referred to by jurists in their decisions and opinions.

438

ships commonly exist between employers and employees. A salesperson in a department store, for example, is an agent of the store's owner (the principal) and acts on the owner's behalf. Any sale of goods made by the salesperson to a customer is binding on the principal. Similarly, most representations of fact made by the salesperson with respect to the goods sold are binding on the principal. Agency relationships may sometimes also exist between employers and independent contractors who are hired to perform special tasks or services.

Employer-Employee Relationships

Normally, all employees who deal with third parties are deemed to be agents. All employment laws (state and federal) apply only to the employer-employee relationship. Statutes governing Social Security, withholding taxes, workers' compensation, unemployment compensation, workplace safety laws, employment discrimination, and the like (see Chapter 22) are applicable only if there is an employer-employee status. *These laws do not apply to the independent contractor.*

Because employees who deal with third parties are normally deemed agents of their employers, agency law and employment law overlap considerably. Agency relationships, though, as will become apparent, can exist outside an employee-employer relationship and thus have a broader reach than employment laws do. Additionally, bear in mind that agency law is based on the common law. In the employment realm, many common law doctrines have been displaced by statutory law and government regulations governing employment relationships.

Employer–Independent Contractor Relationships

Independent contractors are not employees, because by definition, those who hire them have no control over the details of their physical performance. Section 2 of the *Restatement (Second) of Agency* defines an **independent contractor** as follows:

> [An independent contractor is] a person who contracts with another to do something for him but who is not controlled by the other nor subject to the

other's right to control with respect to his physical conduct in the performance of the undertaking. He may or may not be an agent.

Building contractors and subcontractors are independent contractors, and a property owner does not control the acts of either of these professionals. Truck drivers who own their equipment and hire out on a per-job basis are independent contractors, but truck drivers who drive company trucks on a regular basis are usually employees.

The relationship between a person or firm and an independent contractor may or may not involve an agency relationship. To illustrate: An owner of real estate who hires a real estate broker to negotiate a sale of his or her property not only has contracted with an independent contractor (the real estate broker) but also has established an agency relationship for the specific purpose of assisting in the sale of the property. Another example is an insurance agent, who is both an independent contractor and an agent of the insurance company for which he or she sells policies. (Note that an insurance *broker*, in contrast to an insurance agent, normally is not an agent of the insurance company but of the person obtaining insurance.)

Criteria for Determining Employee Status

A question the courts frequently face in determining liability under agency law is whether a person hired by another to do a job is an employee or an independent contractor. Because employers are normally held liable as principals for the actions made by their employee-agents within the scope of employment (as will be discussed later in this chapter), the court's decision as to employee versus independent-contractor status can be significant for the parties. In making this determination, courts often consider the following questions:

1.   How much control can the employer exercise over the details of the work? (If an employer can exercise considerable control over the details of the work, this would indicate employee status.)
2.   Is the worker engaged in an occupation or business distinct from that of the employer? (If so, this would point to independent-contractor status, not employee status.)

3. Is the work usually done under the employer's direction or by a specialist without supervision? (If the work is usually done under the employer's direction, this would indicate employee status.)
4. Does the employer supply the tools at the place of work? (If so, this would indicate employee status.)
5. For how long is the person employed? (If the person is employed for a long period of time, this would indicate employee status.)
6. What is the method of payment—by time period or at the completion of the job? (Payment by time period, such as once every two weeks or once a month, would indicate employee status.)
7. What degree of skill is required of the worker? (If a great degree of skill is required, this may indicate that the person was an independent contractor who was hired for a specialized job and not an employee.)

Often, the criteria for determining employee status are established by a statute or administrative agency regulation. The Internal Revenue Service (IRS), for example, establishes its own criteria for determining whether a worker is an independent contractor or an employee. In the past, these criteria consisted of a list of twenty factors. In 1996, however, these twenty factors were abolished in favor of rules that essentially encourage IRS examiners to look more closely at just one of the factors—the degree of control the business exercises over the worker.

The IRS tends to scrutinize closely a firm's classification of a worker as an independent contractor rather than an employee, because independent contractors can avoid certain tax liabilities by taking advantage of business organizational forms available to small businesses (see Chapter 23). Regardless of the firm's classification of a worker's status as an independent contractor, if the IRS decides that the worker should be classified as an employee, then the employer will be responsible for paying any applicable Social Security, withholding, and unemployment taxes.

Sometimes, it is advantageous to have independent-contractor status—for tax purposes, for example. At other times, employee status may confer desirable benefits on the worker. In the following case, for example, an insurance broker who lost her job wanted to take advantage of the protection against discrimination offered to employees under a state statute. Because that statute governed only employer-employee relationships, the plaintiff tried to convince the court that she was an employee rather than an independent contractor.

CASE 21.1

Scott v. Massachusetts Mutual Life Insurance Co.

Court of Appeals of New York, 1995.
86 N.Y.2d 429,
657 N.E.2d 769,
633 N.Y.S.2d 754.

FACTS James Blatt hired Marilyn Scott to sell insurance for the Massachusetts Mutual Life Insurance Company. Their contract stated, "Nothing in this contract shall be construed as creating the relationship of employer and employee," and that the contract was terminable at will by either party. Scott hired and trained other agents according to Massachusetts Mutual's guidelines, but she financed her own office and staff, was paid according to performance, had no taxes withheld from her checks, and could sell products of Massachusetts Mutual's competitors. When Blatt terminated their contract, Scott filed a suit in a New York state court against him and Massachusetts Mutual. Scott claimed that she had been discriminated against on the basis of her gender, age, and marital status in violation of a state law prohibiting employment discrimination. The defendants filed a motion for summary judgment on the ground that the law applied only to employees and Scott was an independent contractor. The court granted the motion, which an appellate court upheld. Scott appealed to New York's highest state court.

ISSUE Was Scott an independent contractor?

Case 21.1—Continued

DECISION   Yes. The Court of Appeals of New York dismissed Scott's claim.

REASON   The court emphasized that Scott "was responsible for financing her own operating expenses and support staff, was paid by performance rather than a salary, did not have Federal, State or local taxes withheld from her pay, could sell competitors' products and had agreed by contract to operate as an independent contractor." The court acknowledged that one of Scott's duties was "to recruit and train agents according to defendant Massachusetts Mutual's guidelines" but pointed out that "that was true only for agents whose hiring was financed by defendant * * * . [A]t most, * * * defendants exercised minimal control over plaintiff's own daily work product." The court concluded that Scott "operated her office with a high degree of independence not found in a traditional employer/employee relationship."

FOR CRITICAL ANALYSIS—Social Consideration   *Which factor seems to have most influenced the court to rule that Scott was an independent contractor?*

▌Agency Formation

Agency relationships are *consensual*; that is, they come about by voluntary consent and agreement between the parties. Generally, the agreement need not be in writing,[2] and consideration is not required.

A principal must have contractual capacity. A person who cannot legally enter into contracts directly should not be allowed to do so indirectly through an agent. Because an agent derives the authority to enter into contracts from the principal and because a contract made by an agent is legally viewed as a contract of the principal, it is immaterial whether the agent personally has the legal capacity to make that contract. Thus, a minor can be an agent but in some states cannot be a principal appointing an agent.[3] (When a minor is permitted to be a principal, however, any resulting contracts will be voidable by the minor principal but not by the adult third party.) In sum, any person can be an agent, regardless of whether he or she has the capacity to contract. Even a person who is legally incompetent can be appointed an agent.

An agency relationship can be created for any legal purpose. An agency relationship created for an illegal purpose or contrary to public policy is unenforceable. If Sharp (as principal) contracts with Blesh (as agent) to sell illegal narcotics, the agency relationship is unenforceable, because selling illegal narcotics is a felony and is contrary to public policy. It is also illegal for medical doctors and other licensed professionals to employ unlicensed agents to perform professional actions.

Generally, there are four ways in which an agency relationship can arise: by agreement of the parties, by ratification, by estoppel, and by operation of law. We look here at each of these possibilities.

Agency by Agreement

Because an agency relationship is, by definition, consensual, normally it must be based on an express or implied agreement that the agent will act for the principal and the principal agrees to have the agent so act. An agency agreement can take the form of an express written contract. For example, Renato enters into a written agreement with Troy, a real estate agent, to sell Renato's house. An agency relationship exists between

---

2.   There are two main exceptions to the statement that agency agreements need not be in writing: (1) Whenever agency authority empowers the agent to enter into a contract that the Statute of Frauds requires to be in writing, then the agent's authority from the principal must likewise be in writing (this is called the *equal dignity rule,* to be discussed later in this chapter). (2) A power of attorney, which confers authority to an agent, must be in writing.

3.   Some courts have granted exceptions to allow a minor to appoint an agent for the limited purpose of contracting for the minor's necessities of life. See *Casey v. Kastel,* 237 N.Y. 305, 142 N.E. 671 (1924).

Renato and Troy for the sale of the house and is detailed in a document that both parties sign.

Many express agency agreements are oral. If Renato asks Cary, a gardener, to contract with others for the care of his lawn on a regular basis, and Cary agrees, an agency relationship exists between Renato and Cary for the lawn care.

An agency agreement can also be implied by conduct. For example, a hotel expressly allows only Boris Koontz to park cars, but Boris has no employment contract there. The hotel's manager tells Boris when to work, as well as where and how to park the cars. The hotel's conduct amounts to a manifestation of its willingness to have Boris park its customers' cars, and Boris can infer from the hotel's conduct that he has authority to act as a parking valet. It can be inferred that Boris is an agent for the hotel, his purpose being to provide valet parking services for hotel guests.

Agency by Ratification

On occasion, a person who is in fact not an agent (or who is an agent acting outside the scope of his or her authority) may make a contract on behalf of another (a principal). If the principal approves or affirms that contract by word or by action, an agency relationship is created by **ratification.** Ratification is a question of intent, and intent can be expressed by either words or conduct. The basic requirements for ratification are discussed later in this chapter.

Agency by Estoppel

When a principal causes a third person to believe that another person is his or her agent, and the third person deals with the supposed agent, the principal is "estopped to deny" the agency relationship. In such a situation, the principal's actions create the *appearance* of an agency that does not in fact exist.

Suppose that Andrew accompanies Charles, a seed sales representative, to call on a customer, Steve, the proprietor of the General Seed Store. Andrew has done independent sales work but has never signed an employment agreement with Charles at this time. Charles boasts to Steve that he wishes he had three more assistants "just like Andrew." Steve has reason to believe from Charles's statements that Andrew is an agent for Charles. Steve then places seed orders with Andrew. If Charles does not correct the impression that Andrew is an agent, Charles will be bound to fill the orders just as if Andrew were really Charles's agent. Charles's representation to Steve created the impression that Andrew was Charles's agent and had authority to solicit orders.

The acts or declarations of a purported *agent* in and of themselves do not create an agency by estoppel. Rather, it is the deeds or statements of the *principal* that create an agency by estoppel. Suppose that Olivia walks into Dru's Dress Boutique and claims to be a sales agent for an exclusive Paris dress designer, Pierre Dumont. Dru has never had business relations with Pierre Dumont. Based on Olivia's claim, however, Dru gives Olivia an order and prepays 15 percent of the sales price. Olivia is not an agent, and the dresses are never delivered. Dru cannot hold Pierre Dumont liable. Olivia's acts and declarations alone do not create an agency by estoppel.

In addition, to assert the creation of an agency by estoppel, the third person must prove that he or she *reasonably* believed that an agency relationship existed and that the agent had authority. Facts and circumstances must show that an ordinary, prudent person familiar with business practice and custom would have been justified in concluding that the agent had authority.

The court in the following case considered whether an agency existed by estoppel between the owner of a jewelry cart in a mall and the seller of "The Only Completely Safe, Sterile Ear Piercing Method."

Case 21.2
Williams v. Inverness Corp.
Supreme Judicial Court of Maine, 1995.
664 A.2d 1244.

FACTS The Inverness Corporation markets the Inverness Ear Piercing System, which includes a training course, an "eye-catching assortment of selling aids" such as counter displays, and release forms that tout the system as "The Only Completely Safe, Sterile Ear Piercing Method." Margaret Barrera, the owner of a jewelry cart in a mall, bought the system, took the course, and set up the displays. Seventeen-year-old Angela Williams paid Barrera to pierce

Case 21.2—Continued

Williams's ear. The ear became infected, which led to complications. Williams's mother filed a suit on Angela's behalf in a Maine state court against Inverness and Barrera, claiming in part that Inverness was liable on a theory of agency by estoppel. When the court issued a judgment in Williams's favor, Inverness appealed to Maine's highest court.

ISSUE   Was there an agency by estoppel between Inverness and Barrera?

DECISION   Yes. The Supreme Judicial Court of Maine affirmed the lower court's judgment.

REASON   The Supreme Judicial Court of Maine pointed to evidence that Inverness held Barrera out as its agent. "Most important," said the court, "a jury reasonably could infer that Inverness knew, or should have known, that Barrera distributed Inverness's release forms *   *   * , that Barrera was using the Inverness Ear Piercing System, that she displayed Inverness's 'eye-catching assortment of selling aids,' and that she used Inverness's training program." The court also referred to "evidence that Angela believed that Barrera was Inverness's agent, that Angela relied on Inverness's manifestations of agency, and that Angela's reliance on Barrera's care and skill was justifiable." For example, "[t]he release form and display promote the Inverness Ear Piercing System as 'The Only Completely Safe, Sterile Ear Piercing Method.' "

FOR CRITICAL ANALYSIS—Social Consideration   *What are the policy reasons for holding a firm liable on a theory of agency by estoppel?*

Agency by Operation of Law

There are other situations also in which the courts will find an agency relationship in the absence of a formal agreement. This may occur in family relationships. For example, suppose one spouse purchases certain basic necessaries and charges them to the other spouse's charge account. The courts will often rule that the latter is liable for payment of the necessaries, either because of a social policy of promoting the general welfare of the spouse or because of a legal duty to supply necessaries to family members.

Agency by operation of law may also occur in emergency situations, when the agent's failure to act outside the scope of his or her authority would cause the principal substantial loss. If the agent is unable to contact the principal, the courts will often grant this emergency power. For example, a railroad engineer may contract on behalf of his or her employer for medical care for an injured motorist hit by the train.

▌ Duties of Agents and Principals

Once the principal-agent relationship has been created, both parties have duties that govern their conduct. As discussed previously, the principal-agent relationship is *fiduciary*—one of trust. In a fiduciary relationship, each party owes the other the duty to act with the utmost good faith.

We now examine the various duties of agents and principals. In general, for every duty of the principal, the agent has a corresponding right, and vice versa. When one party to the agency relationship violates his or her duty to the other party, the remedies available to the party not in breach arise out of contract and tort law. These remedies include monetary damages, termination of the agency relationship, injunction, and required accountings.

Agent's Duties to the Principal

Generally, the agent owes the principal five duties—performance, notification, loyalty, obedience, and accounting.

PERFORMANCE   An implied condition in every agency contract is the agent's agreement to use reasonable diligence and skill in performing the work. When an agent fails to perform his or her duties entirely, liability for breach of contract normally will result. The degree of skill or care required of an agent is usually that expected of a reasonable person under similar circumstances. Generally, this is interpreted to mean ordinary care. An agent may, however, have represented himself or herself as possessing special skills (such as those that an accountant or attorney possesses). In these situations, the agent is expected to exercise the skill or skills claimed. Failure to do so constitutes a breach of the agent's duty.

Not all agency relationships are based on contract. In some situations, an agent acts gratuitously—that is, not for money. A gratuitous agent cannot be liable for breach of contract, as there is no contract; he or she is subject only to tort liability. Once a gratuitous agent has begun to act in an agency capacity, he or she has the duty to continue to perform in that capacity in an acceptable manner and is subject to the same standards of care and duty to perform as other agents. For example, Peterson's friend, Stendhof, is a real estate broker. Stendhof gratuitously offers to sell Peterson's farm. If Stendhof never attempts to sell the farm, Peterson has no legal cause of action to force Stendhof to do so. If Stendhof does find a buyer, however, but fails to provide a sales contract within a reasonable period of time, thus causing the buyer to seek other property, then Peterson has a cause of action in tort for negligence.

NOTIFICATION There is a maxim in agency law that notice to the agent is notice to the principal. An agent is thus required to notify the principal of all matters that come to his or her attention concerning the subject matter of the agency. This is the duty of notification. The law assumes that the principal knows of any information acquired by the agent that is relevant to the agency—regardless of whether the agent actually passes on this information to the principal.

LOYALTY Loyalty is one of the most fundamental duties in a fiduciary relationship. Basically stated, the agent has the duty to act solely for the benefit of his or her principal and not in the interest of the agent or a third party. For example, an agent cannot represent two principals in the same transaction unless both know of the dual capacity and consent to it. The duty of loyalty also means that any information or knowledge acquired through the agency relationship is considered confidential. It would be a breach of loyalty to disclose such

information either during the agency relationship or after its termination. Typical examples of confidential information are trade secrets and customer lists compiled by the principal.

In short, the agent's loyalty must be undivided. The agent's actions must be strictly for the benefit of the principal and must not result in any secret profit for the agent. For example, suppose that Ryder contracts with Alton, a real estate agent, to sell Ryder's property. Alton knows that he can find a buyer who will pay substantially more for the property than Ryder is asking. If Alton secretly purchased Ryder's property, however, and then sold it at a profit to another buyer, Alton would breach his duty of loyalty as Ryder's agent. Alton has a duty to act in Ryder's best interests and can only become the purchaser in this situation with Ryder's knowledge and approval.

OBEDIENCE When an agent is acting on behalf of the principal, a duty is imposed on that agent to follow all lawful and clearly stated instructions of the principal. Any deviation from such instructions is a violation of this duty. During emergency situations, however, when the principal cannot be consulted, the agent may deviate from such instructions without violating this duty. Whenever instructions are not clearly stated, the agent can fulfill the duty of obedience by acting in good faith and in a manner reasonable under the circumstances.

ACCOUNTING Unless an agent and a principal agree otherwise, the agent has the duty to keep and make available to the principal an account of all property and money received and paid out on behalf of the principal. This includes gifts from third persons in connection with the agency. For example, a gift from a customer to a salesperson for prompt deliveries made by the salesperson's firm belongs to the firm. The agent has a duty to maintain separate accounts for the principal's funds and for the agent's personal funds, and no intermingling of these accounts is allowed. Whenever a licensed professional (such as an attorney) violates this duty to account, he or she may be subject to disciplinary proceedings carried out by the appropriate regulatory institution (such as the state bar association) in addition to being liable to the principal (the professional's client) for failure to account.

Principal's Duties to the Agent

The principal also has certain duties to the agent. These duties relate to compensation, reimbursement and indemnification, cooperation, and safe working conditions.

COMPENSATION In general, when a principal requests certain services from an agent, the agent reasonably expects payment. The principal therefore has a duty to pay the agent for services rendered. For example, when an accountant or an attorney is asked to act as an agent, an agreement to compensate the agent for such service is implied. The principal also has a duty to pay that compensation in a timely manner. Except in a gratuitous agency relationship, in which an agent does not act for money, the principal must pay the agreed-on value for an agent's services. If no amount has been expressly agreed on, then the principal owes the agent the customary compensation for such services.

REIMBURSEMENT AND INDEMNIFICATION Whenever an agent disburses sums of money to fulfill the request of the principal or to pay for necessary expenses in the course of a reasonable performance of his or her agency duties, the principal has the duty to reimburse the agent for these payments. Agents cannot recover for expenses incurred by their own misconduct or negligence, however.

Subject to the terms of the agency agreement, the principal has the duty to compensate, or *indemnify*, an agent for liabilities incurred because of authorized and lawful acts and transactions. For example, if the agent, on the principal's behalf, forms a contract with a third party, and the principal fails to perform the contract, the third party may sue the agent for damages. In this situation, the principal is obligated to compensate the agent for any costs incurred by the agent as a result of the principal's failure to perform the contract. Additionally, the principal must indemnify (pay) the agent for the value of benefits that the agent confers upon the principal. The amount of indemnification is usually specified in the agency contract. If it is not, the courts will look to the nature of the business and the type of loss to determine the amount.

COOPERATION A principal has a duty to cooperate with the agent and to assist the agent in per-

forming his or her duties. The principal must do nothing to prevent such performance. For example, when a principal grants an agent an exclusive territory, creating an *exclusive agency*, the principal cannot compete with the agent or appoint or allow another agent to so compete in violation of the exclusive agency. If the principal did so, he or she would be exposed to liability for the agent's lost sales or profits.

SAFE WORKING CONDITIONS The common law requires the principal to provide safe working premises, equipment, and conditions for all agents and employees. The principal has a duty to inspect working conditions and to warn agents and employees about any unsafe areas. When the agency is one of employment, the employer's liability and the safety standards with which the employer must comply normally are covered by federal and state statutes and regulations (see Chapter 22).

▌Agent's Authority

An agent's authority to act can be either *actual* (express or implied) or *apparent*. If an agent contracts outside the scope of his or her authority, the principal may still become liable by ratifying the contract.

Actual Authority

As indicated, an agent's actual authority can be express or implied. *Express authority* is authority declared in clear, direct, and definite terms. Express authority can be given orally or in writing. The **equal dignity rule** in most states requires that if the contract being executed is or must be in writing, then the agent's authority must also be in writing.[4] Failure to comply with the equal dignity rule can make a contract voidable *at the option of the principal*. The law regards the contract at that point as a mere offer. If the principal decides to accept the offer, acceptance must be in writing. Assume that

---

4.   An exception to the equal dignity rule exists in modern business practice. An executive officer of a corporation, when acting for the corporation in an ordinary business situation, is not required to obtain written authority from the corporation.

Klee (the principal) orally asks Parkinson (the agent) to sell a ranch that Klee owns. Parkinson finds a buyer and signs a sales contract (a contract for an interest in realty must be in writing) on behalf of Klee to sell the ranch. The buyer cannot enforce the contract unless Klee subsequently ratifies Parkinson's agency status *in writing*. Once Parkinson's agency status is ratified, either party can enforce rights under the contract.

The equal dignity rule does not apply when an agent acts in the presence of a principal or when the agent's act of signing is merely perfunctory. Thus, if Dickens (the principal) negotiates a contract but is called out of town the day it is to be signed and orally authorizes Santini to sign the contract, the oral authorization is sufficient.

Giving an agent a **power of attorney** confers express authority.[5] The power of attorney normally is a written document and is usually notarized. (A document is notarized when a **notary public**—a public official authorized to attest to the authenticity of signatures—signs and dates the document and imprints it with his or her seal of authority.) A power of attorney can be special (permitting the agent to do specified acts only), or it can be general (permitting the agent to transact all business for the principal). An agent holding a power of attorney for a client is authorized to act *only* on the principal's behalf when exercising that power. An ordinary power of attorney terminates on the incapacity of the person giving the power.[6] Exhibit 21–1 shows a sample power of attorney.

Implied authority can be (1) conferred by custom, (2) inferred from the position the agent occupies, or (3) inferred as being reasonably necessary to carry out express authority. For example, Mueller is employed by Al's Supermarket to manage one of its stores. Al has not expressly stated that Mueller has authority to contract with third persons. In this situation, however, authority to manage a business implies authority to do what is reasonably required (as is customary or can be inferred from a manager's position) to operate the

business. Reasonably required actions include creating contracts to hire employees, to buy merchandise and equipment, and to arrange for advertising the products sold in the store.

Apparent Authority

Actual authority arises from what the principal manifests *to the agent*. Apparent authority exists when the principal, by either words or actions, causes a *third party* reasonably to believe that an agent has authority to act, even though the agent has no express or implied authority. If the third party changes his or her position in reliance on the principal's representations, the principal may be *estopped* from denying that the agent had authority. Note that here, in contrast to agency formation by estoppel, the issue has to do with the apparent authority of an *agent*, not the apparent authority of a person who is in fact not an agent.

To illustrate: Suppose that a traveling salesperson, Anderson (the agent), is authorized to take customers' orders. Anderson, however, does not deliver the ordered goods and is not authorized to collect payments for the goods. A customer, Byron, pays Anderson for a solicited order. Anderson then takes the payment to the principal's accounting department, and an accountant accepts the payment and sends Byron a receipt. This procedure is thereafter followed for other orders solicited and paid for by Byron. Later, Anderson solicits an order, and Byron pays her as before. This time, however, Anderson absconds with the money. Can Byron claim that the payment to the agent was authorized and was thus, in effect, a payment to the principal?

The answer is normally yes, because the principal's *repeated* acts of accepting Byron's payment led Byron reasonably to expect that Anderson had authority to receive payments for goods solicited. Although Anderson did not have express or implied authority, the principal's conduct gave Anderson *apparent* authority to collect. In this situation, the principal would be estopped from denying that Anderson had authority to collect payments.

Ratification

As already mentioned, ratification is the affirmation of a previously unauthorized contract. Ratification can be either express or implied. If the principal does not ratify, there is no contract binding on the

---

5.   An agent who holds the power of attorney is called an *attorney-in-fact* for the principal. The holder does not have to be an attorney-at-law (and often is not).

6.   A *durable* power of attorney, however, provides an agent with very broad powers to act and make decisions for the principal and specifies that it is not affected by the principal's incapacity. An elderly person, for example, might grant a durable power of attorney to provide for the handling of property and investments should he or she become incompetent.

♦ **Exhibit 21–1   A Sample Power of Attorney**

POWER OF ATTORNEY
GENERAL

Know All Men by These Presents: That I, _____
_____
the undersigned (jointly and severally, if more than one) hereby make, constitute and appoint _____
_____
as a true and lawful Attorney for me and in my name, place and stead and for my use and benefit:

(a)   To ask, demand, sue for, recover, collect and receive each and every sum of money, debt, account, legacy, bequest, interest, dividend, annuity and demand (which now is or hereafter shall become due, owing or payable) belonging to or claimed by me, and to use and take any lawful means for the recovery thereof by legal process or otherwise, and to execute and deliver a satisfaction or release therefore, together with the right and power to compromise or compound any claim or demand;

(b)   To exercise any or all of the following powers as to real property, any interest therein and/or any building thereon: To contract for, purchase, receive and take possession thereof and or evidence of title thereto; to lease the same for any term or purpose, including leases for business, residence, and oil and/or mineral development; to sell, exchange, grant or convey the same with or without warranty; and to mortgage, transfer in trust, or otherwise encumber or hypothecate the same to secure payment of a negotiable or non-negotiable note or performance of any obligation or agreement;

(c)   To exercise any or all of the following powers as to all kinds of personal property and goods, wares and merchandise, choses in action and other property in possession or in action: To contract for, buy, sell, exchange, transfer and in any legal manner deal in and with the same; and to mortgage, transfer in trust, or otherwise encumber or hypothecate the same to secure payment of a negotiable or non-negotiable note or performance of any obligation or agreement;

(d)   To borrow money and to execute and deliver negotiable or non-negotiable notes therefore with or without security; and to loan money and receive negotiable or non-negotiable notes therefore with such security as he shall deem proper;

(e)   To create, amend, supplement and terminate any trust and to instruct and advise the trustee of any trust wherein I am or may be trustor or beneficiary; to represent and vote stock, exercise stock rights, accept and deal with any dividend, distribution or bonus, join in any corporate financing, reorganization, merger, liquidation, consolidation or other action and the extension, compromise, conversion, adjustment, enforcement or foreclosure, singly or in conjunction with others, of any corporate stock, bond, note, debenture or other security; to compound, compromise, adjust, settle and satisfy any obligation, secured or unsecured, owing by or to me and to give or accept any property and/or money whether or not equal to or less in value than the amount owing in payment, settlement or satisfaction thereof;

(f)   To transact business of any kind or class and as my act and deed to sign, execute, acknowledge and deliver any deed, lease, assignment of lease, covenant, indenture, indemnity, agreement, mortgage, deed of trust, assignment of mortgage or of the beneficial interest under deed of trust, extension or renewal of any obligation, subordination or waiver of priority, hypothecation, bottomry, charter-party, bill of lading, bill of sale, bill, bond, note, whether negotiable or non-negotiable, receipt, evidence of debt, full or partial release or satisfaction of mortgage, judgment and other debt, request for partial or full reconveyance of deed of trust and such other instruments in writing of any kind or class as may be necessary or proper in the premises.

Giving and Granting unto my said Attorney full power and authority to do so and perform all and every act and thing whatsoever requisite, necessary or appropriate to be done in and about the premises as fully to all intents and purposes as I might or could do if personally present, hereby ratifying all that my said Attorney shall lawfully do or cause to be done by virtue of these presents. The powers and authority hereby conferred upon my said Attorney shall be applicable to all real and personal property or interests therein now owned or hereafter acquired by me and wherever situated.

My said Attorney is empowered hereby to determine in his sole discretion the time when, purpose for and manner in which any power herein conferred upon him shall be exercised, and the conditions, provisions and covenants of any instrument or document which may be executed by him pursuant hereto; and in the acquisition or disposition of real or personal property, my said Attorney shall have exclusive power to fix the terms thereof for cash, credit and/or property, and if on credit with or without security.

The undersigned, if a married woman, hereby further authorizes and empowers my said Attorney, as my duly authorized agent, to join in my behalf, in the execution of any instrument by which any community real property or any interest therein, now owned or hereafter acquired by my spouse and myself, or either of us, is sold, leased, encumbered, or conveyed.

When the context so requires, the masculine gender includes the feminine and/or neuter, and the singular number includes the plural.

WITNESS my hand this _____ day of _____, 19 ____

_____   _____

_____   _____

State of California ⎫
  County of _____ ⎬ SS.
On _____, before me, the undersigned, a Notary Public in and for said
State, personally appeared _____
_____
known to me to be the person _____ whose name _____ subscribed
to the within instrument and acknowledged that _____ executed the same.
Witness my hand and official seal.
                                    (Seal) _____
                                              Notary Public in and for said State.

principal, and the third party's agreement with the agent is viewed merely as an unaccepted offer. The third party can revoke the offer at any time prior to the principal's ratification without liability. Death or incapacity of the third party before ratification will void an unauthorized contract.

The requirements for ratification can be summarized as follows:

1.   The purported agent must have acted on behalf of a principal who subsequently ratified the action.
2.   The principal must know of all material facts involved in the transaction.
3.   The agent's act must be affirmed in its entirety by the principal.
4.   The principal must have the legal capacity to authorize the transaction at the time the agent engages in the act and at the time the principal ratifies.
5.   The principal's affirmance must occur prior to the withdrawal of the third party from the transaction.
6.   The principal must observe the same formalities when he or she approves the act purportedly done by the agent on his or her behalf as would have been required to authorize it initially.

▌ Liability in Agency Relationships

Frequently, the issue arises as to which party, the principal or the agent, should be held liable for the contracts formed by the agent or for the torts or crimes committed by the agent. We look here at these aspects of agency law.

Liability for Contracts

An important consideration in determining liability for a contract formed by an agent is whether the third party knew the identity of the principal at the time the contract was made. The *Restatement (Second) of Agency*, Section 4, classifies principals as disclosed, partially disclosed, or undisclosed.

DISCLOSED OR PARTIALLY DISCLOSED PRINCIPAL

A principal whose identity is known to the third party at the time the agent makes the contract is a **disclosed principal.** For example, Joan, a purchasing agent for Maxwell Graphics, signs a contract for the purchase of office supplies. Joan signs her name on the contract as purchasing agent for Maxwell Graphics. In this situation, Maxwell Graphics is a disclosed principal.

The identity of a **partially disclosed principal** is not known by the third party, but the third party knows that the agent is or may be acting for a principal at the time the contract is made. For example, a seller of real estate may wish to keep his or her identity a secret, yet the agent with whom the seller has contracted can make it perfectly clear to the purchaser of the real estate that the agent is acting in an agency capacity for a principal.

A disclosed or partially disclosed principal is liable to a third party for a contract made by an agent who is acting within the scope of his or her authority. Ordinarily, if the principal is disclosed, the agent has no contractual liability if the principal or the third party does not perform the contract. If the principal is only partially disclosed, in most states the agent is also liable for nonperformance. If the agent *exceeds* the scope of his or her authority and the principal fails to ratify the contract, however, the third party cannot hold the principal liable for nonperformance. In such situations, the agent is generally liable unless the third party knew of the agent's lack of authority.

In the following case, the issue was whether an agent, through a written agreement, had incurred liability for a contract with a third party when the identity of the principal was fully disclosed to the third party.

CASE 21.3

Fairchild Publications Division of Capital Cities Media, Inc. v. Rosston, Kremer & Slawter, Inc.

Supreme Court, New York County, 1992.
584 N.Y.S.2d 389.

FACTS Fabrican, Inc., a home furnishings manufacturer, hired an advertising agency, Rosston, Kremer & Slawter, Inc. (RKS), to advertise Fabrican's products in national magazines. In early 1989, RKS arranged for Fabrican's ads to be placed in two magazines published by Fairchild Publications Division of Capital Cities Media, Inc. Daniel Kremer of RKS signed two contracts covering the advertising arrangement, both of which clearly designated Fabrican as the "advertiser." Both contracts, which consisted of preprinted forms containing

Case 21.3—Continued

filled-in blanks and typed and handwritten additions, provided that Fairchild agreed to publish the ads subject to the terms of advertising contracts adopted by the AAAA, "which terms are hereby incorporated herein and made part of this contract." The attached AAAA form stated that the advertising agency and the publisher agreed that the publisher would hold the advertising agency solely liable for payment. Fairchild published Fabrican's ads and sent invoices to RKS totaling $85,157. Neither Fabrican (which had since filed for bankruptcy) nor RKS paid the invoices, and Fairchild Publications sued RKS in a New York state court to recover the price of the ads. RKS argued that it could not be liable, because (1) RKS was unaware of the AAAA term holding the advertising agency solely liable for payment and (2) RKS was acting as an agent for a disclosed principal.

ISSUE Can RKS be held liable for payment of the price of the ads?

DECISION Yes.

REASON The court stated that "in order to prevail, Fairchild must prove either that RKS agreed to be liable for Fabrican's debts or that custom and usage rendered RKS liable." The court concluded that based on the evidence, Fairchild "met its burden of proof on both grounds." Even though Kremer was unaware that the AAAA terms regarding agency liability were incorporated by reference into the contracts, Kremer's lack of awareness "does not affect their validity. Under these terms, RKS is liable for payment." Furthermore, the court found that when the contracts were formed, RKS had been placing ads in Fairchild publications for more than forty years and, as a regular customer of Fairchild's, knew or should have known of Fairchild's policy of holding advertising agencies solely liable for payment of the ads. "RKS acknowledged familiarity with the concept of sole agency liability, and did not dispute its liability, despite receiving regular bills, invoices, and dunning letters, until a number of months after executing the Contracts. All these factors combine to estop RKS from denying liability."

FOR CRITICAL ANALYSIS—Ethical Consideration *If RKS had never contracted with Fairchild before for the placement of ads for a third party, would the court have viewed the matter differently?*

UNDISCLOSED PRINCIPAL The identity of an **undisclosed principal** is totally unknown to the third party. Furthermore, the third party has no knowledge that the agent is acting in an agency capacity at the time the contract is made. For example, Albright agrees to sell two truckloads of apples to Zimmer. Zimmer believes that he is buying the apples from Albright; but actually Albright is the agent for Henderson, who legally owns the apples. In this situation, Henderson is an undisclosed principal.

When neither the fact of agency nor the identity of the principal is disclosed, a third party is deemed to be dealing with the agent personally, and the agent is liable as a party to the contract. If an agent has acted within the scope of his or her authority, the undisclosed principal is also liable as a party to the contract, just as if the principal had been fully disclosed at the time the contract was made. The undisclosed principal is liable unless (1) the undisclosed principal was expressly excluded as a party in the contract, (2) the contract is a negotiable instrument signed by the agent with no indication of signing in a representative capacity, or (3) the performance of the agent is personal to the contract, allowing the third party to refuse the principal's performance.

Liability for Torts and Crimes

Obviously, an agent is liable for his or her own torts and crimes. Whether the principal can also be held liable depends on several factors, which we examine here. In some situations, a principal may be held liable not only for the torts of an agent but also for the torts committed by an independent contractor.

LIABILITY FOR AGENT'S TORTS   As mentioned, an agent is liable for his or her own torts. A principal may also be liable for an agent's torts under the doctrine of *respondeat superior,*[7] a Latin term meaning "let the master respond." This doctrine is similar to the theory of strict liability discussed in Chapter 4. The doctrine imposes vicarious (indirect) liability on the employer without regard to the personal fault of the employer for torts committed by an employee in the course or scope of employment.

Scope of Employment   The key to determining whether a principal may be liable for the torts of the agent under the doctrine of *respondeat superior* is whether the torts are committed within the scope of the agency or employment. The *Restatement (Second) of Agency*, Section 229, indicates the factors that courts will consider in determining whether or not a particular act occurred within the course and scope of employment. These factors are as follows:

1.   Whether the act was authorized by the employer.
2.   The time, place, and purpose of the act.
3.   Whether the act was one commonly performed by employees on behalf of their employers.

4.   The extent to which the employer's interest was advanced by the act.
5.   The extent to which the private interests of the employee were involved.
6.   Whether the employer furnished the means or instrumentality (for example, a truck or a machine) by which the injury was inflicted.
7.   Whether the employer had reason to know that the employee would do the act in question and whether the employee had ever done it before.
8.   Whether the act involved the commission of a serious crime.

A useful insight into the "scope of employment" concept may be gained from Baron Parke's classic distinction between a "detour" and a "frolic" in the case of *Joel v. Morison* (1834):[8]

> If the servants, being on their master's business took a *detour* . . . the master will be responsible. . . . The master is only liable where the servant is acting in the course of his employment. If he was going out of his way, against his master's implied commands, when driving on his master's business, he will make his master liable; but if he was going on a *frolic of his own*, without being at all on his master's business, the master will not be liable.

Courts often refer to the "detour-frolic" distinction when deciding whether a given action was within the scope of employment. At issue in the following case is whether a truck driver's actions fell within the scope of employment or constituted a "frolic of his own."

---

7.   Pronounced ree-*spahn*-dee-uht soo-*peer*-ee-your.

8.   6 Car. & P. 501, 172 Eng. Reprint 1338 (1834).

CASE 21.4

McNair v. Lend Lease Trucks, Inc.

United States Court of Appeals, Fourth Circuit, 1995.
62 F.3d 651.

FACTS   Lend Lease Trucks, Inc., employed Thomas Jones as an interstate truck driver. While on an assignment, Jones parked on the shoulder of U.S. Highway 301 near Kenly, North Carolina, and crossed the highway to the Dry Dock Lounge. In the lounge, Jones drank enough liquor for his blood-alcohol level to rise to eighteen points above the level at which he could legally drive his truck. After a few hours, Jones left the lounge. As he started across the highway to his truck, he darted into the path of a motorcycle driven by Edward McNair. In the collision, Jones and McNair were killed. McNair's wife, Catherine, filed a suit in a North Carolina state court against Lend Lease Trucks, Inc., and others, claiming in part that Jones was acting within the scope of employment at the time of the accident. The case was removed

Case 21.4—Continued

to a federal district court. Lend Lease filed a motion to dismiss, the court granted the motion, and Catherine appealed.

ISSUE Was Jones acting within the scope of employment at the time of the accident?

DECISION No. The U.S. Court of Appeals for the Fourth Circuit affirmed the order of the lower court.

REASON The court held that "an employee can go 'on a frolic of his own' * * * by engaging in conduct which * * * is in no way 'about,' or 'in furtherance of,' 'his master's business.'" The court explained that Jones departed from the scope of his employment when he took a break of three to fours hours, "during which he consume[d] sufficient alcohol to make it illegal for him to drive his truck." The court concluded that this departure "could only have ceased * * * when his blood-alcohol content dropped at least to the legal limit for performing his duty. That obviously had not occurred by the time of the collision."

FOR CRITICAL ANALYSIS—Social Consideration *What effect might it have had on the outcome of this case if, during his break, Jones had not "consume[d] sufficient alcohol to make it illegal for him to drive his truck"?*

Misrepresentation A principal is exposed to tort liability whenever a third person sustains a loss due to the agent's misrepresentation. The principal's liability depends on whether or not the agent was actually or apparently authorized to make representations and whether such representations were made within the scope of the agency. The principal is always directly responsible for an agent's misrepresentation made within the scope of the agent's authority, whether the misrepresentation was made fraudulently or simply by the agent's mistake or oversight.

LIABILITY FOR INDEPENDENT CONTRACTOR'S TORTS Generally, the principal is not liable for physical harm caused to a third person by the negligent act of an independent contractor in the performance of the contract. This is because the employer does not have the *right to control* the details of an independent contractor's performance. An exception to this doctrine is made when exceptionally hazardous activities are involved, such as blasting operations, the transportation of highly volatile chemicals, or the use of poisonous gases. In these situations, a principal cannot be shielded from liability merely by using an independent contractor. Strict liability is imposed on the principal as a matter of law and, in some states, by statute. In the following case, one of the issues before the court was whether the "self-help" repossession of collateral is an inherently dangerous activity, in which case the secured creditor could be held liable for damages caused by the independent contractor's tortious actions.

CASE 21.5

Sanchez v. MBank of El Paso

Court of Appeals of Texas—El Paso, 1990.
792 S.W.2d 530.

FACTS MBank of El Paso contracted with El Paso Recovery Service (El Paso) to have El Paso repossess Yvonne Sanchez's 1978 Pontiac Trans Am, which had been purchased through MBank financing. Two men hired by El Paso went to Sanchez's home with a tow truck and proceeded to hook the tow truck to the car, which was in the driveway. Sanchez, who was in the yard cutting the grass at the time, asked them their purpose and demanded that they cease their

(Continued)

Case 21.5—Continued

attempt to take the automobile and leave the premises. When they ignored her, she entered and locked herself in the car in an effort to stall them until the police or her husband could arrive. It was only after they got the automobile in the street that they identified their purpose and told her to get out of the car, which she refused to do. They then took the vehicle, with Sanchez locked in it, on a high-speed ride from her home to the repossession lot and parked the car in a fenced and locked yard with a loose guard dog. She was rescued some time later by her husband and the police. Sanchez filed suit in a Texas state court against MBank for damages, alleging that El Paso and its employees were MBank's agents and that they had willfully breached the peace in violation of UCC 9–503. The trial court granted the bank's motion for summary judgment, holding that the bank could not be liable, because El Paso was an independent contractor and not an employee or agent of MBank. Sanchez appealed.

ISSUE   Can MBank be held liable for the tortious actions of El Paso, notwithstanding the fact that El Paso was an independent contractor?

DECISION   Yes. The Texas appellate court reversed the trial court's decision and remanded the case for trial.

REASON   The appellate court pointed out that two situations represent exceptions to the general rule that an employer is not liable for the tortious acts of an independent contractor: "(1) where the employer is by the statute * * * under a duty to provide specific safeguards for the safety of others" and "(2) where the employer employs an independent contractor to do work involving a special or inherent danger to others." The court concluded that MBank had a nondelegable duty under UCC 9–503 to avoid breaching the peace when repossessing collateral and thus could be liable to Sanchez for a breach of the peace by El Paso. The court also concluded that self-help repossession—"[a]lways bordering on the edge of illegality if not carried out carefully"—is an inherently dangerous activity.

FOR CRITICAL ANALYSIS—Economic Consideration   *In determining liability for a breach of the peace under UCC 9–503, should the court take into consideration the behavior of the person from whom the collateral was possessed (in this case, Sanchez)?*

LIABILITY FOR AGENT'S CRIMES   An agent is liable for his or her own crimes. A principal or employer is not liable for an agent's crime even if the crime was committed within the scope of authority or employment—unless the principal participated by conspiracy or other action. In some jurisdictions, under specific statutes, a principal may be liable for an agent's violation, in the course and scope of employment, of regulations, such as those governing sanitation, prices, weights, and the sale of liquor.

Agency Termination

Agency law is similar to contract law in that both an agency and a contract can be terminated by an act of the parties or by operation of law. Once the relationship between the principal and the agent has ended, the agent no longer has the right to bind the principal. For an agent's apparent authority to be terminated, third persons may also need to be notified when the agency has been terminated.

Termination by Act of the Parties

An agency may be terminated by act of the parties in several ways, including those discussed here.

LAPSE OF TIME   An agency agreement may specify the time period during which the agency relationship will exist. If so, the agency ends when that time period expires. Thus, if Allen signs an agreement of agency with Proust "beginning January 1, 1998, and ending December 31, 1999," the agency is automatically terminated on December 31, 1999. Of course, the parties can agree to continue the relationship, in which case the same terms will apply. If no definite time is stated, then the agency continues for a reasonable time and can be terminated at will by either party. What constitutes a "reasonable time" depends, of course, on the circumstances and the nature of the agency relationship.

PURPOSE ACHIEVED   An agent can be employed to accomplish a particular objective, such as the purchase of stock for a cattle rancher. In that situation, the agency automatically ends after the cattle have been purchased. If more than one agent is employed to accomplish the same purpose, such as the sale of real estate, the first agent to complete the sale automatically terminates the agency relationship for all the others.

OCCURRENCE OF A SPECIFIC EVENT   An agency can be created to terminate upon the happening of a certain event. If Posner appoints Rubik to handle his business affairs while he is away, the agency automatically terminates when Posner returns.

Sometimes, one aspect of the agent's authority terminates on the occurrence of a particular event, but the agency relationship itself does not terminate. Suppose that William, a banker, permits Calvin, the bank's credit manager, to grant a credit line of $2,000 to certain depositors who maintain $2,000 in a savings account. If any customer's savings account falls below $2,000, Calvin can no longer continue making the credit line available to that customer. Calvin's right to extend credit to the other customers maintaining the minimum balance will continue, however.

MUTUAL AGREEMENT   Recall from the chapters on contract law that parties can cancel (rescind) a contract by mutually agreeing to terminate the contractual relationship. The same holds true under agency law regardless of whether the agency contract is in writing or whether it is for a specific duration.

TERMINATION BY ONE PARTY   As a general rule, either party can terminate the agency relationship. The agent's act is called a *renunciation of authority*. The principal's act is referred to as a *revocation of authority*. Although both parties have the *power* to terminate the agency, however, they may not possess the *right*. Wrongful termination can subject the canceling party to a suit for damages. For example, Rawlins has a one-year employment contract with Munro to act as an agent in return for $35,000. Munro can discharge Rawlins before the contract period expires (Munro has the *power* to breach the contract); however, Munro will be liable to Rawlins for money damages, because Munro has no *right* to breach the contract.

A special rule applies in an agency *coupled with an interest*. This type of agency is not an agency in the usual sense, because it is created for the agent's benefit instead of for the principal's benefit. For example, suppose that Julie borrows $5,000 from Rob, giving Rob some of her jewelry and signing a letter giving Rob the power to sell the jewelry as her agent if she fails to repay the loan. Julie, after she has received the $5,000 from Rob, then attempts to revoke Rob's authority to sell the jewelry as her agent. Julie would not succeed in this attempt, because a principal cannot revoke an agency created for the agent's benefit.

NOTICE OF TERMINATION   If the parties themselves have terminated the agency, it is the principal's duty to inform any third parties who know of the existence of the agency that it has been terminated (although notice of the termination may be given by others).

An agent's authority continues until the agent receives some notice of termination. Notice to third parties follows the general rule that an agent's *apparent* authority continues until the third person receives notice (from any source of information) that such authority has been terminated. The principal is expected to notify directly any third person who the principal knows has dealt with the agent. For third persons who have heard about the agency but have not yet dealt with the agent, *constructive notice* is sufficient.[9]

No particular form is required for notice of agency termination to be effective. The principal can actually notify the agent, or the agent can learn of the termination through some other means. For example, Manning bids on a shipment of steel, and Stone is hired as an agent to arrange transportation of the shipment. When Stone learns that Manning has lost the bid, Stone's authority to make the transportation arrangement terminates.

If the agent's authority is written, it must be revoked in writing, and the writing must be shown to all people who saw the original writing that established the agency relationship. Sometimes, a written authorization (such as a power of attorney) contains an expiration date. The passage of the expiration date is sufficient notice of termination for third parties.

Termination by Operation of Law

Termination of an agency by operation of law occurs in the circumstances discussed here. Note that when an agency terminates by operation of law, there is no duty to notify third persons—unless the agent's authority is coupled with an interest.

DEATH OR INSANITY   The general rule is that the death or mental incompetence of either the principal or the agent automatically and immediately terminates the ordinary agency relationship. Knowledge of the death is not required. Suppose that Geer sends Pyron to the Far East to purchase a rare painting. Before Pyron makes the purchase, Geer dies. Pyron's agent status is terminated at the moment of Geer's death, even though Pyron does not know that Geer has died. Some states, however, have changed this common law rule by statute, and death does not terminate an agency coupled with an interest.

An agent's transactions that occur after the death of the principal are not binding on the prin-

cipal's estate.[10] Assume that Carson is hired by Perry to collect a debt from Thomas (a third party). Perry dies, but Carson, not knowing of Perry's death, still collects the money from Thomas. Thomas's payment to Carson is no longer legally sufficient to discharge Thomas's debt to Perry, because Carson's authority to collect the money ended on Perry's death. If Carson absconds with the money, Thomas is still liable for the debt to Perry's estate.

IMPOSSIBILITY   When the specific subject matter of an agency is destroyed or lost, the agency terminates. If Bullard employs Gonzalez to sell Bullard's house, but prior to the sale the premises are destroyed by fire, then Gonzalez's agency and authority to sell Bullard's house terminate. When it is impossible for the agent to perform the agency lawfully, the agency terminates.

CHANGED CIRCUMSTANCES   When an event occurs that has such an unusual effect on the subject matter of the agency that the agent can reasonably infer that the principal will not want the agency to continue, the agency terminates. For example, Roberts hires Mullen to sell a tract of land for $20,000. Subsequently, Mullen learns that there is oil under the land and that the land is worth $1 million. The agency and Mullen's authority to sell the land for $20,000 are terminated.

BANKRUPTCY AND WAR   Bankruptcy of the principal or the agent usually terminates the agency relationship. When the principal's country and the agent's country are at war with each other, the agency is terminated or at least suspended.

---

9.   Constructive notice is information or knowledge of a fact imputed by law to a person if he or she could have discovered the fact by proper diligence. Constructive notice is often accomplished by newspaper publication.

---

10.   There is an exception to this rule in banking under which the bank, as the agent of the customer, can continue to exercise specific types of authority even after the customer has died or become mentally incompetent unless it has knowledge of the death or incompetence [UCC 4–405]. Even with knowledge of the customer's death, the bank has authority for ten days following the customer's death to honor checks in the absence of a stop-payment order.

▌ Terms and Concepts

● ●

agency 438
disclosed principal 448
equal dignity rule 445
fiduciary 438

independent contractor 439
notary public 446
partially disclosed principal
   448

power of attorney 446
ratification 442
respondeat superior 450
undisclosed principal 449

▌ Chapter Summary: Agency Relationships

● ●

Agency Relationships *(See pages 438–441.)*	In a *principal-agent* relationship, an agent acts on behalf of and instead of the principal, using a certain degree of his or her own discretion. An employee who deals with third parties is normally an agent. An independent contractor is not an employee, and the employer has no control over the details of physical performance. The independent contractor is not usually an agent.
Agency Formation *(See pages 441–443.)*	1. *By agreement*—Through express consent (oral or written) or implied by conduct. 2. *By ratification*—The principal, either by act or agreement, ratifies the conduct of an agent who acted outside the scope of authority or the conduct of a person who is in fact not an agent. 3. *By estoppel*—When the principal causes a third person to believe that another person is his or her agent, and the third person deals with the supposed agent, the principal is "estopped to deny" the agency relationship. 4. *By operation of law*—Based on a social duty (such as the need to support family members) or created in emergency situations when the agent is unable to contact the principal.

Duties of Agents and Principals
(See pages 443–445.)
	1. *Duties of the agent*—
	  a. Performance—The agent must use reasonable diligence and skill in performing his or her duties.
	  b. Notification—The agent is required to notify the principal of all matters that come to his or her attention concerning the subject matter of the agency.
	  c. Loyalty—The agent has a duty to act solely for the benefit of his or her principal and not in the interest of the agent or a third party.
	  d. Obedience—The agent must follow all lawful and clearly stated instructions of the principal.
	  e. Accounting—The agent has a duty to make available to the principal records of all property and money received and paid out on behalf of the principal.
	
	2. *Duties of the principal*—
	  a. Compensation—Except in a gratuitous agency relationship, the principal must pay the agreed-on value (or reasonable value) for an agent's services.
	  b. Reimbursement and indemnification—The principal must reimburse the agent for all sums of money disbursed at the request of the principal and for all sums of money the agent disburses for necessary expenses in the course of reasonable performance of his or her agency duties.
	  c. Cooperation—A principal must cooperate with and assist an agent in performing his or her duties.
	  d. Safe working conditions—A principal must provide safe working conditions for the agent-employee.

Agent's Authority *(See pages 445–448.)*	1. *Actual authority*— a. Express authority—Can be oral or in writing. Authorization must be in writing if the agent is to execute a contract that must be in writing. *(Continued)*

▌Chapter Summary: Agency Relationships—Continued

Agent's Authority—Continued	b. Implied authority—Authority customarily associated with the position of the agent or authority that is deemed necessary for the agent to carry out expressly authorized tasks. 2. *Apparent authority*—Exists when the principal, by word or action, causes a third party reasonably to believe that an agent has authority to act, even though the agent has no express or implied authority. 3. *Ratification*—The affirmation by the principal of an agent's unauthorized action or promise. For the ratification to be effective, the principal must be aware of all material facts.
Liability in Agency Relationships *(See pages 448–452.)*	1. *Liability for contracts*—If the principal's identity is disclosed or partially disclosed at the time the agent forms a contract with a third party, the principal is liable to the third party under the contract (if the agent acted within the scope of his or her authority). If the principal's identity is undisclosed at the time of contract formation, the agent is liable to the third party. If the agent acted within the scope of authority, the principal is bound by the contract. 2. *Liability for torts and crimes*— a. Liability for agent's torts—Under the doctrine of *respondeat superior,* the principal is liable for any harm caused to another through the agent's torts if the agent was acting within the scope of his or her employment at the time the harmful act occurred. The principal is also liable for an agent's misrepresentation, whether made knowingly or by mistake. b. Liability for independent contractor's tort—A principal is not liable for harm caused by an independent contractor's negligence, unless hazardous activities are involved (in which situation the principal is strictly liable for any resulting harm). c. Liability for agent's crimes—An agent is responsible for his or her own crimes, even if the crimes were comitted while the agent was acting within the scope of authority or employment. A principal will be liable for an agent's crime only if the principal participated by conspiracy or other action or (in some jurisdictions) if the agent violated certain government regulations in the course of employment.
Agency Termination *(See pages 452–454.)*	1. *By act of the parties*— a. Lapse of time (when a definite time for the duration of the agency was agreed on when the agency was established). b. Purpose achieved. c. Occurrence of a specific event. d. Mutual rescission (requires mutual consent of principal and agent). e. Termination by act of either the principal (revocation) or the agent (renunciation). (A principal cannot revoke an agency coupled with an interest.) f. When an agency is terminated by act of the parties, all third persons who have previously dealt with the agency must be directly notified; constructive notice will suffice for all other third parties. 2. *By operation of law*— a. Death or mental incompetence of either the principal or the agent (except in an agency coupled with an interest). b. Impossibility (when the purpose of the agency cannot be achieved because of an event beyond the parties' control). c. Changed circumstances (in which it would be inequitable to require that the agency be continued). d. Bankruptcy of the principal or the agent, or war between the principal's and agent's countries. e. When an agency is terminated by operation of law, no notice to third parties is required (unless the agent's authority is coupled with an interest).

▌For Review

1. What formalities are required to create an agency relationship?
2. What duties does the agent owe to the principal? What duties does the principal owe to the agent?
3. How does an agent's apparent authority differ from an agent's actual authority? If an agent acts outside the scope of his or her authority, how might a principal still be held liable for the act?

4. If an agent, acting within the scope of authority, forms a contract with a third party on behalf of an undisclosed principal, will the principal be held liable on the contract?
5. Under what doctrine can a principal-employer be held liable for the torts committed by an agent-employee?

▌Questions and Case Problems

21–1. Agency Formation. Pete Gaffrey is a well-known, wealthy financier living in the city of Takima. Alan Winter, Gaffrey's friend, tells Til Borge that he (Winter) is Gaffrey's agent for the purchase of rare coins. Winter even shows Borge a local newspaper clipping mentioning Gaffrey's interest in coin collecting. Borge, knowing of Winter's friendship with Gaffrey, contracts with Winter to sell to Gaffrey a rare coin valued at $25,000. Winter takes the coin and disappears with it. On the date of contract payment, Borge seeks to collect from Gaffrey, claiming that Winter's agency made Gaffrey liable. Gaffrey does not deny that Winter was a friend, but he claims that Winter was never his agent. Discuss fully whether an agency was in existence at the time the contract for the rare coin was made.

21–2. Ratification by Principal. Springer was a political candidate running for congressional office. He was operating on a tight budget and instructed his campaign staff not to purchase any campaign materials without his explicit authorization. In spite of these instructions, one of his campaign workers ordered Dubychek Printing Co. to print some promotional materials for Springer's campaign. When the printed materials were received, Springer did not return them but instead used them during his campaign. When Dubychek failed to obtain payment from Springer for the materials, he sued for recovery of the price. Springer contended that he was not liable on the sales contract, because he had not authorized his agent to purchase the printing services. Dubychek argued that Springer's use of the materials constituted ratification of his agent's unauthorized purchase. Is Dubychek correct? Explain.

21–3. Agent's Duties to Principal. Iliana is a traveling sales agent. Iliana not only solicits orders but also delivers the goods and collects payments from her customers. Iliana places all payments in her private checking account and at the end of each month draws sufficient cash from her bank to cover the payments made. Giberson Corp., Iliana's employer, is totally unaware of this

procedure. Because of a slowdown in the economy, Giberson tells all its sales personnel to offer 20 percent discounts on orders. Iliana solicits orders, but she offers only 15 percent discounts, pocketing the extra 5 percent paid by customers. Iliana has not lost any orders by this practice, and she is rated as one of Giberson's top salespersons. Giberson now learns of Iliana's actions. Discuss fully Giberson's rights in this matter.

21–4. Liability for Agent's Contracts. Michael Mosely works as a purchasing agent for Suharto Coal Supply, a partnership. Mosely has authority to purchase the coal needed by Suharto to satisfy the needs of its customers. While Mosely is leaving a coal mine from which he has just purchased a large quantity of coal, his car breaks down. He walks into a small roadside grocery store for help. While there, he runs into Wiley, who owns 360 acres back in the mountains with all mineral rights. Wiley, in need of money, offers to sell Mosely the property at $1,500 per acre. Upon inspection, Mosely concludes that the subsurface may contain valuable coal deposits. Mosely contracts to purchase the property for Suharto, signing the contract, "Suharto Coal Supply, Michael Mosely, agent." The closing date is set for August 1. Mosely takes the contract to the partnership. The managing partner is furious, as Suharto is not in the property business. Later, just before August 1, both Wiley and the partnership learn that the value of the land is at least $15,000 per acre. Discuss the rights of Suharto and Wiley concerning the land contract.

21–5. Agent's Duties to Principal. Sam Kademenos was about to sell a $1 million life insurance policy to a prospective customer when he resigned from his position with Equitable Life Assurance Society. Before resigning from the company, he had expended substantial amounts of company money and had utilized Equitable's medical examiners to procure the $1 million sale. After resigning, Kademenos joined a competing insurance firm, Jefferson Life Insurance Co., and made the sale through it. Has he breached any duty to

Equitable? Explain. [*Kademenos v. Equitable Life Assurance Society*, 513 F.2d 1073 (3d Cir. 1975)]

21–6. Respondeat Superior. Richard Lanno worked for Thermal Equipment Corp. as a project engineer. Lanno was allowed to keep a company van and tools at his home because he routinely drove to work sites directly from his home and because he was often needed for unanticipated business trips during his off hours. The arrangement had been made for the convenience of Thermal Equipment, even though Lanno's managers permitted him to make personal use of the van. Lanno was involved in a collision with Lazar while driving the van home from work one day. At the time of the accident, Lanno had taken a detour in order to stop at a store—he had intended to purchase a few items and then go home. Lazar sued Thermal Equipment, claiming that Lanno had acted within the scope of his employment. Discuss whether Lazar was able to recover from Thermal Equipment. Can employees act on behalf of their employers and themselves at the same time? Discuss. [*Lazar v. Thermal Equipment Corp.*, 148 Cal.App.3d 458, 195 Cal.Rptr. 890 (1983)]

21–7. Authority of Agent. The Federal Land Bank (FLB) filed an action to foreclose a mortgage on Tom and Judith Sullivan's real estate. Before the trial, FLB's attorney wrote to the Sullivans' attorney to invite settlement offers. A copy of the letter was sent to Wayne Williamson, an FLB vice president. Nine days later, on September 3, the Sullivans' attorney wrote to FLB's attorney expressing interest in settling the case. A copy of this letter was sent to Williamson. On September 11, FLB's attorney replied with an offer that "[m]y client has authorized me to extend . . . to you." The Sullivans accepted the offer. Three weeks later, FLB's attorney wrote the following to the Sullivans' attorney: "Any compromises regarding Federal Land Bank loans must be cleared through [FLB's] Omaha [office]. The proposed compromise was not approved and therefore we have been requested to proceed through the foreclosure process." The case went to trial, and FLB obtained a judgment of foreclosure. The trial court found that FLB was not bound by the offer made by its attorney. The Sullivans appealed, arguing that the attorney had or appeared to have had authority to settle the case. What should the appellate court decide? [*Federal Land Bank v. Sullivan*, 430 N.W.2d 700 (S.Dak. 1988)]

21–8. Ratification by Principal. Fred Hash worked for Van Stavern Construction Co. as a field supervisor in charge of constructing a new plant facility. Hash entered into a contract with Sutton's Steel & Supply, Inc., to supply steel to the construction site in several installments. Hash gave the name of B. D. Van Stavern, the president and owner of the construction firm, instead of the firm's name as the party for whom he was acting. The contract and the subsequent invoices all

had B. D. Van Stavern's name on them. Sutton delivered several loads. All of the invoices were signed by Van Stavern employees, and corporate checks were made out to Sutton. When Sutton Steel later sued Van Stavern personally for unpaid debts totaling $40,437, it claimed that Van Stavern had ratified the acts of his employee, Hash, by allowing payment on previous invoices. Although Van Stavern had had no knowledge of the unauthorized arrangement, had he legally ratified the agreement by his silence? Explain. [*Sutton's Steel & Supply, Inc. v. Van Stavern*, 496 So.2d 1360 (La.App. 3d Cir. 1986)]

21–9. Respondeat Superior. Justin Jones suffered from genital herpes and sought treatment from Dr. Steven Baisch of Region West Pediatric Services. A nurse's assistant, Jeni Hallgren, who was a Region West employee, told her friends and some of Jones's friends about Jones's condition. This was a violation of the Region West employee handbook, which required employees to maintain the confidentiality of patients' records. Jones filed a suit in a federal district court against Region West, among others, alleging that Region West should be held liable for its employee's actions on the basis of *respondeat superior*. On what basis might the court hold that Region West is not liable for Hallgren's acts? Discuss fully. [*Jones v. Baisch, M.D.*, 40 F.3d 252 (8th Cir. 1994)]

21–10. Employee versus Independent Contractor. Stephen Hemmerling was a driver for the Happy Cab Co. Hemmerling paid certain fixed expenses and abided by a variety of rules relating to the use of the cab, the hours that could be worked, the solicitation of fares, and so on. Rates were set by the state. Happy Cab did not withhold taxes from Hemmerling's pay. While driving a cab, Hemmerling was injured in an accident and filed a claim against Happy Cab in a Nebraska state court for workers' compensation benefits. Such benefits are not available to independent contractors. On what basis might the court hold that Hemmerling is an employee? Explain. [*Hemmerling v. Happy Cab Co.*, 247 Neb. 919, 530 N.W.2d 916 (1995)]

A QUESTION OF ETHICS AND SOCIAL RESPONSIBILITY

21–11. *Kimberly Sierra, suffering from a severe asthma attack, went to Southview Hospital & Family Health Center. She was treated in the emergency room by Dr. Thomas Mucci. At the time, as a result of statements by Southview administrators, brochures, and ads, Sierra believed that the physicians at Southview were "hospital doctors." In fact, however, Mucci's contract with Southview stated, "The relationship between [Southview and Mucci] shall be that of independent contractor." Within a few hours, Sierra was pronounced dead. Sierra's mother, Edna Clark, filed a suit in an Ohio state court against Southview and others, alleging, in part, negligent medical care. Southview argued that it was not responsible*

1936, the Walsh-Healey Act[2] was passed. This act requires that a minimum wage, as well as overtime pay of time and a half, be paid to employees of manufacturers or suppliers entering into contracts with agencies of the federal government.

In 1938, Congress passed the Fair Labor Standards Act[3] (FLSA). The FLSA prohibits oppressive child labor. Children under fourteen years of age are allowed to do certain types of work, such as deliver newspapers, work for their parents, and work in the entertainment and (with some exceptions) agricultural areas. Children who are fourteen or fifteen years of age are allowed to work, but not in hazardous occupations. There are also numerous restrictions on how many hours per day and per week they can work. Persons between the ages of sixteen and eighteen do not face such restrictions on working times and hours, but they cannot be employed in hazardous jobs or in jobs detrimental to their health and well-being.

Under the FLSA, any employee who agrees to work more than forty hours per week must be paid no less than one and a half times his or her regular pay for all hours over forty. Certain employees are exempt from the overtime provisions of the act: executives, administrative employees, professional employees, and outside salespersons.

The FLSA provides that a **minimum wage** of a specified amount must be paid to employees in covered industries. Congress periodically revises such minimum wages. For example, in 1996, Congress raised the minimum wage from $4.25 an hour to $5.15 an hour. Under the FLSA, the term *wages* includes the reasonable cost of the employer in furnishing employees with board, lodging, and other facilities if they are customarily furnished by that employer.

▍Labor Unions

In the 1930s, in addition to wage-hour laws, the government also enacted the first of several labor laws. Initially, the laws were concerned with protecting the rights and interests of workers. Subsequent legislation placed some restraints on unions and granted rights to employers. We look here at four major federal statutes regulating union-employer relations.

Norris-LaGuardia Act

Congress protected peaceful strikes, picketing, and boycotts in 1932 in the Norris-LaGuardia Act.[4] The statute restricted federal courts in their power to issue injunctions against unions engaged in peaceful strikes. In effect, this act declared a national policy permitting employees to organize.

National Labor Relations Act

One of the foremost statutes regulating labor is the National Labor Relations Act (NLRA) of 1935.[5] This act established the rights of employees to engage in collective bargaining and to strike. The act also specifically defined a number of employer practices as unfair to labor:

1. Interference with the efforts of employees to form, join, or assist labor organizations or to engage in concerted activities for their mutual aid or protection.
2. An employer's domination of a labor organization or contribution of financial or other support to it.
3. Discrimination based on union affiliation in the hiring or awarding of tenure to employees.
4. Discrimination against employees for filing charges under the act or giving testimony under the act.
5. Refusal to bargain collectively with the duly designated representative of the employees.

The act also created the National Labor Relations Board (NLRB) to oversee union elections and to prevent employers from engaging in unfair and illegal union activities and unfair labor practices. The purpose of the NLRA was to secure for employees the rights to organize; to bargain collectively through representatives of their own choosing; and to engage in concerted activities for organizing, collective bargaining, and other purposes.

The NLRB has the authority to investigate employees' charges of unfair labor practices and to

---

2. 41 U.S.C. Sections 35–45.
3. 29 U.S.C. Sections 201–260.

4. 29 U.S.C. Sections 101–110, 113–115.
5. 29 U.S.C. Section 151–169.

serve complaints against employers in response to these charges. The NLRB may also issue cease-and-desist orders—orders compelling employers to cease engaging in the unfair practices—when violations are found. Cease-and-desist orders can be enforced by a circuit court of appeals if necessary. Arguments over alleged unfair labor practices are first decided by the NLRB and may then be appealed to a federal court.

Labor-Management Relations Act

The Labor-Management Relations Act (LMRA) of 1947[6] was passed to proscribe certain unfair union practices, such as the *closed shop*. A **closed shop** is a firm that requires union membership by its workers as a condition of employment. Although the act made the closed shop illegal, it preserved the legality of the union shop. A **union shop** does not require membership as a prerequisite for employment but can, and usually does, require that workers join the union after a specified amount of time on the job.

The LMRA also prohibited unions from refusing to bargain with employers, engaging in certain types of picketing, and featherbedding (causing employers to hire more employees than necessary). The act also allowed individual states to pass their own **right-to-work laws**—laws making it illegal for union membership to be required for *continued* employment in any establishment. Thus, union shops are technically illegal in states with right-to-work laws.

Labor-Management Reporting and Disclosure Act

The Labor-Management Reporting and Disclosure Act (LMRDA) of 1959[7] established an employee bill of rights and reporting requirements for union activities. The act strictly regulates internal union business procedures. Union elections, for example, are regulated by the LMRDA, which requires that regularly scheduled elections of officers occur and that secret ballots be used. Ex-convicts and Communists are prohibited from holding union office. Moreover, union officials are accountable for union property and funds. Mem-bers have the right to attend and to participate in union meetings, to nominate officers, and to vote in most union proceedings.

The act also outlawed **hot-cargo agreements**—agreements in which employers voluntarily agree with unions not to handle, use, or deal in nonunion-produced goods of other employers. The act made all such **secondary boycotts** illegal.

∎ Worker Health and Safety

Numerous state and federal statutes protect employees and their families from the risk of accidental injury, death, or disease resulting from their employment. This section discusses the primary federal statute governing health and safety in the workplace, along with state workers' compensation acts.

The Occupational Safety and Health Act

At the federal level, the primary legislation for employee health and safety protection is the Occupational Safety and Health Act of 1970.[8] Congress passed this act in an attempt to ensure safe and healthful working conditions for practically every employee in the country. The act provides for specific standards that employers must meet, plus a general duty to keep workplaces safe.

ENFORCEMENT AGENCIES   Three federal agencies develop and enforce the standards set by the Occupational Safety and Health Act. The Occupational Safety and Health Administration (OSHA) is part of the Department of Labor and has the authority to promulgate standards, make inspections, and enforce the act. OSHA has safety standards governing many workplace details, such as the structural stability of ladders and the requirements for railings. OSHA also establishes standards that protect employees against exposure to substances that may be harmful to their health.

The National Institute for Occupational Safety and Health is part of the Department of Health and Human Services. Its main duty is to conduct research on safety and health problems and to recommend standards for OSHA to adopt. Finally, the

---

6. 29 U.S.C. Sections 141 *et seq.*
7. 29 U.S.C. Sections 401 *et seq.*

---

8. 29 U.S.C. Sections 553, 651–678.

Occupational Safety and Health Review Commission is an independent agency set up to handle appeals from actions taken by OSHA administrators.

PROCEDURES AND VIOLATIONS OSHA compliance officers may enter and inspect facilities of any establishment covered by the Occupational Safety and Health Act.[9] Employees may also file complaints of violations. Under the act, an employer cannot discharge an employee who files a complaint or who, in good faith, refuses to work in a high-risk area if bodily harm or death might result.

Employers with eleven or more employees are required to keep occupational injury and illness records for each employee. Each record must be made available for inspection when requested by an OSHA inspector. Whenever a work-related injury or disease occurs, employers must make reports directly to OSHA. Whenever an employee is killed in a work-related accident or when five or more employees are hospitalized in one accident, the employer must notify the Department of Labor within forty-eight hours. If the company fails to do so, it will be fined. Following the accident, a complete inspection of the premises is mandatory.

Criminal penalties for willful violation of the Occupational Safety and Health Act are limited. Employers may be prosecuted under state laws, however. In other words, the act does not preempt state and local criminal laws.[10] In the following case, an employer argued that it should not be penalized by OSHA for violating a regulation of which the employer was ignorant.

---

9. In the past, warrantless inspections were conducted. In 1978, however, the United States Supreme Court held that warrantless inspections violated the warrant clause of the Fourth Amendment to the Constitution. See *Marshall v. Barlow's, Inc.*, 436 U.S. 307, 98 S.Ct. 1816, 56 L.Ed.2d 305 (1978).

10. *Pedraza v. Shell Oil Co.*, 942 F.2d 48 (1st Cir. 1991); *cert.* denied, *Shell Oil Co. v. Pedraza*, 502 U.S. 1082, 112 S.Ct. 993, 117 L.Ed.2d 154 (1992).

CASE 22.1

Valdak Corp. v. Occupational Safety and Health Review Commission

United States Court of Appeals, Eighth Circuit, 1996.
73 F.3d 1466.

FACTS The Valdak Corporation operates a car wash that uses an industrial dryer to spin-dry towels. The dryer was equipped with a device that was supposed to keep it locked while it spun, but the device often did not work. An employee reached into the dryer while it was spinning, and his arm was cut off above the elbow. OSHA cited Valdak for, among other things, a willful violation of a machine-guarding regulation and assessed a $28,000 penalty. Valdak appealed to the Occupational Safety and Health Review Commission, which upheld the penalty. Valdak appealed to the U.S. Court of Appeals for the Eighth Circuit, arguing in part that it did not know about the specific regulation.

ISSUE Can an employer who is not aware of a specific Occupational Safety and Health Act regulation be cited for a "willful" violation of it?

DECISION Yes. The U.S. Court of Appeals for the Eighth Circuit upheld the agency's finding.

REASON The federal appellate court reasoned that "[w]illfulness can be proved by 'plain indifference' to the [Occupational Safety and Health Act's] requirements. Plain indifference to the machine guarding requirement is amply demonstrated by the facts that the dryer was equipped with an interlocking device, the interlocking device did not work, and Valdak continued to use the dryer with the broken interlock device."

FOR CRITICAL ANALYSIS—Ethical Consideration *For what policy reasons might an employer set up a formal safety program or issue a written safety manual?*

Workers' Compensation

State **workers' compensation laws** establish an administrative procedure for compensating workers injured on the job. Instead of suing, an injured worker files a claim with the administrative agency or board that administers the local workers' compensation claims.

Most workers' compensation statutes are similar. In general, the right to recover benefits is predicated wholly on the existence of an employment relationship and the fact that the injury was *accidental* and *occurred on the job* or *in the course of employment*, regardless of fault. Intentionally inflicted self-injury, for example, would not be considered accidental and hence would not be covered. If an injury occurred while an employee was commuting to or from work, it would not usually be considered to have occurred on the job or in the course of employment and hence would not be covered.

An employee must notify his or her employer promptly (usually within thirty days) of an injury. Generally, an employee also must file a workers' compensation claim with the appropriate state agency or board within a certain period (sixty days to two years) from the time the injury is first noticed, rather than from the time of the accident.

An employee's acceptance of workers' compensation benefits bars the employee from suing for injuries caused by the employer's negligence. By barring lawsuits for negligence, workers' compensation laws also bar employers from raising common law defenses to negligence, such as contributory negligence or assumption of risk. A worker may sue an employer who *intentionally* injures the worker, however.

▌ Income Security

Federal and state governments participate in insurance programs designed to protect employees and their families by covering the financial impact of retirement, disability, death, hospitalization, and unemployment. The key federal law on this subject is the Social Security Act of 1935.[11]

Social Security and Medicare

The Social Security Act provides for old age (retirement), survivors, and disability insurance. The act is

---

11.   42 U.S.C. Sections 301–1397e.

therefore often referred to as OASDI. Both employers and employees must "contribute" under the Federal Insurance Contributions Act (FICA)[12] to help pay for the employees' loss of income on retirement. The basis for the employee's and the employer's contribution is the employee's annual wage base— the maximum amount of the employee's wages that are subject to the tax. The employer withholds the employee's FICA contribution from the employee's wages and then matches this contribution.

Medicare, a health-insurance program, is administered by the Social Security Administration for people sixty-five years of age and older and for some under the age of sixty-five who are disabled. It has two parts, one pertaining to hospital costs and the other to nonhospital medical costs, such as visits to doctors' offices. People who have Medicare hospital insurance can also obtain additional federal medical insurance if they pay small monthly premiums, which increase as the cost of medical care increases. As with Social Security contributions, both the employer and the employee contribute to Medicare.

Private Pension Plans

There has been significant legislation to regulate employee retirement plans set up by employers to supplement Social Security benefits. The major federal act covering these retirement plans is the Employee Retirement Income Security Act (ERISA) of 1974.[13] This act empowers the Labor Management Services Administration of the Department of Labor to enforce its provisions governing employers who have private pension funds for their employees. ERISA does not require an employer to establish a pension plan. When a plan exists, however, ERISA establishes standards for its management.

Unemployment Insurance

The United States has a system of unemployment insurance in which employers pay into a fund, the proceeds of which are paid out to qualified unemployed workers. The Federal Unemployment Tax Act of 1935[14] created a state system that provides

---

12.   26 U.S.C. Sections 3101–3125.
13.   29 U.S.C. Sections 1001 *et seq.*
14.   26 U.S.C. Sections 3301–3310.

unemployment compensation to eligible individuals. Employers that fall under the provisions of the act are taxed at regular intervals. Taxes are typically paid by the employers to the states, which then deposit them with the federal government. The federal government maintains an unemployment insurance fund, in which each state has an account.

COBRA

Federal legislation also addresses the issue of health insurance for workers whose jobs have been terminated—and who are thus no longer eligible for group health-insurance plans. The Consolidated Omnibus Budget Reconciliation Act (COBRA) of 1985[15] prohibits the elimination of a worker's medical, optical, or dental insurance coverage on the voluntary or involuntary termination of the worker's employment. Employers, with some exceptions, must comply with COBRA if they employ twenty or more workers and provide a benefit plan to those workers. This is not a free ride for the worker, however. To receive continued benefits, he or she may be required to pay all of the premium, as well as a 2 percent administrative charge.

Family and Medical Leave

In 1993, Congress passed the Family and Medical Leave Act (FMLA)[16] to assist employees who need time off work for family or medical reasons. A majority of the states also have legislation allowing for a leave from employment for family or medical reasons, and many employers maintain private family-leave plans for their workers.

The FMLA requires employers who have fifty or more employees to provide employees with up to twelve weeks of family or medical leave during any twelve-month period. During the employee's leave, the employer must continue the worker's health-care coverage and guarantee employment in the same position or a comparable position when the employee returns to work. An important exception

---

15. 29 U.S.C. Sections 1161–1169.
16. 29 U.S.C. Sections 2601, 2611–2619, 2651–2654.

to the FMLA, however, allows the employer to avoid reinstatement of a *key employee*—defined as an employee whose pay falls within the top 10 percent of the firm's work force. Additionally, the act does not apply to employees who have worked less than one year or less than twenty-five hours a week during the previous twelve months.

Wrongful Discharge

Whenever an employer discharges an employee in violation of an employment contract or laws protecting employees, the employee may bring an action for **wrongful discharge.** An employee who is protected by a statute, such as one prohibiting employment discrimination (discussed later in this chapter), may bring a cause of action under that statute. If an employer's actions do not violate any statute, then the question is whether the employer has violated an employment contract or a common law doctrine.

As mentioned, under the employment-at-will doctrine, an employer may hire and fire employees at will (regardless of the employees' performance) without liability, unless the decision violates the terms of an employment contract or statutory law. Because of the harsh effects of the employment-at-will doctrine for employees, courts have carved out various exceptions to the doctrine. These exceptions are based on contract theory, tort theory, and public policy.

Exceptions Based on Contract Theory

Some courts have held that an *implied* employment contract exists between the employer and the employee. If the employee is fired outside the terms of the implied contract, he or she may succeed in an action for breach of contract even though no written employment contract exists.

For example, an employer's manual or personnel bulletin may state that, as a matter of policy, workers will be dismissed only for good cause. If the employee is aware of this policy and continues to work for the employer, a court may find that there is an implied contract based on the terms stated in the manual or bulletin. Promises that an employer makes to employees regarding discharge policy may also be considered part of an implied contract. If the employer fires a worker in a manner contrary to the manner promised, a court may hold that the employer has violated the implied contract and is liable for damages. Most state courts will consider this claim and judge it by traditional contract standards.

A few states have gone further and held that all employment contracts contain an implied covenant of good faith. This means that both sides promise to abide by the contract in good faith. If an employer fires an employee for an arbitrary or unjustified reason, the employee can claim that the covenant of good faith was breached and the contract violated.

In the following case, one of the issues was whether there existed between an employer and its employees an implied-in-fact contract not to demote the employees without good cause.

CASE 22.2

Scott v. Pacific Gas and Electric Co.

Supreme Court of California, 1995.
11 Cal.4th 454,
904 P.2d 834
46 Cal.Rptr.2d 427.

FACTS   The Pacific Gas and Electric Company (PG&E) had a system called "Positive Discipline" that, according to its personnel manual, was to apply to all employees. The basic principle was to discipline employees only for good cause. Byron Scott and Al Johnson were engineers working for PG&E as senior managers when they were demoted, allegedly for a conflict of interest from their out-side consulting practice. They filed a suit in a California state court against PG&E, claiming that there was no good cause for the demotions. The court issued a judgment in their favor, and PG&E appealed. The state appellate court reversed, and the engineers appealed to the Supreme Court of California.

ISSUE   Was there an implied-in-fact contract between PG&E and its employees not to demote the employees without good cause? If so, did PG&E breach it?

DECISION   Yes, to both questions. The Supreme Court of California reversed the decision of the intermediate appellate court and remanded the case.

REASON   The state supreme court explained that "PG&E employees had a reasonable expectation that the company would follow its own human resources policy, which had as its basic premise the disciplining of its employees only for good cause." The court pointed out that the trial court had found that "Scott and Johnson committed no significant conflict of interest violations." PG&E failed to give them the chance to correct any relatively minor offenses through the positive discipline process. Therefore, the trial court "reasonably concluded that PG&E had breached its implied contractual agreement by wrongfully demoting Scott and Johnson."

FOR CRITICAL ANALYSIS—Political Consideration   *What incentives do employers have to use basic principles of due process in disciplining employees?*

Exceptions Based on Tort Theory

In a few cases, the discharge of an employee may give rise to an action for wrongful discharge under tort theories. Abusive discharge procedures may result in intentional infliction of emotional distress or defamation. In one case, a restaurant had suffered some thefts of supplies, and the manager announced that he would start firing waitresses alphabetically until the thief was identified. The first waitress fired said that she suffered great emotional distress as a result. The state's highest court upheld her claim as stating a valid cause of action.[17]

Exceptions Based on Public Policy

The most widespread common law exception to the employment-at-will doctrine is an exception made on the basis of public policy. Courts may apply this exception when an employer fires a worker for reasons that violate a fundamental public policy of the jurisdiction. For example, a court may prevent an employer from firing a worker who serves on a jury and therefore cannot work during his or her normally scheduled working hours.

Sometimes, an employer will direct an employee to do something that violates the law. If the employee refuses to perform the illegal act, the employer might decide to fire the worker. Similarly, employees who "blow the whistle" on the wrongdoing of their employers often find themselves disciplined or even out of a job. Whistleblowing occurs when an employee tells a government official, upper-management authorities, or the press that his or her employer is engaged in some unsafe or illegal activity. Whistleblowers on occasion have been protected from wrongful discharge for reasons of public policy. For example, a bank was held to have wrongfully discharged an employee who pressured the employer to comply with state and federal consumer credit laws.[18] In the following case, the plaintiff alleged that his discharge for refusing to participate in illegal eavesdropping was wrongful because it violated public policy.

---

17. *Agis v. Howard Johnson Co.*, 371 Mass. 140, 355 N.E.2d 315 (1976).

18. *Harless v. First National Bank in Fairmont*, 162 W.Va. 116, 246 S.E.2d 270 (1978).

CASE 22.3
Nagy v. Whittlesey Automotive Group
California Court of Appeal, Fourth District, Division 3, 1995. 40 Cal.App.4th 1238, 47 Cal.Rptr.2d 395.

FACTS   Gabor Nagy was a car salesperson for Whittlesey Automotive Group. Whittlesey asked Nagy to allow some of his phone conversations with "customers" to be recorded. The "customers" were actually employees of a company Whittlesey hired to conduct a sales training program. Nagy refused to consent. He was eventually fired for his "negative attitude." Nagy filed a suit in a California state court against Whittlesey. He cited a state statute that makes eavesdropping a crime and alleged in part that he was wrongfully terminated in violation of public policy. The court dismissed the suit, and Nagy appealed.

ISSUE   Is it a violation of public policy to terminate an employee for refusing to be a "victim" of the employer's crime of eavesdropping?

DECISION   Yes. The California Court of Appeal reversed the judgment of the lower court and remanded the case.

REASON   The state appellate court pointed out that "[a]n employer may be held liable in tort for terminating an otherwise 'at will' employee if the termination violates public policy." The court explained that "otherwise the threat of discharge could be used to coerce employees into committing crimes, concealing wrongdoing, or taking other action harmful to the public." The court reasoned that "[w]here, as here, employment is conditioned

(Continued)

Case 22.3—Continued   on the employee's agreement to be a crime victim, public policy is equally violated."

FOR CRITICAL ANALYSIS—Ethical Consideration *Consent is a defense to some crimes. Could it also be a defense to charges of violations of public policy in the employment context?*

▌Whistleblower Statutes

To encourage workers to report employer wrongdoing, such as fraud, a number of states have enacted so-called whistleblower statutes.[19] These statutes protect whistleblowers from subsequent retaliation on the part of employers. On the federal level, the Whistleblower Protection Act of 1989[20] protects federal employees who blow the whistle on their employers from their employers' retaliatory actions. Whistleblower statutes may also provide an incentive to disclose information by providing the whistleblower with a monetary reward. For example, the federal False Claims Reform Act of 1986[21] requires that a whistleblower who has disclosed information relating to a fraud perpetrated against the U.S. government receive between 15 and 25 percent of the proceeds if the government brings suit against the wrongdoer.

▌Employment Discrimination

During the early 1960s we, as a nation, focused our attention on the civil rights of all Americans, including our rights under the Fourteenth Amendment to the equal protection of the laws. Out of this movement grew a body of law protecting workers against discrimination on the basis of race, color, religion, national origin, gender, age, or disability. A class of persons defined by one or more of these criteria is known as a *protected class*.

Several federal statutes prohibit discrimination in the employment context against members of protected classes. The most important statute is Title VII of the Civil Rights Act of 1964.[22] Title VII prohibits discrimination on the basis of race, color, religion, national origin, and gender. Discrimination on the basis of age and disability are prohibited by the Age Discrimination in Employment Act of 1967[23] and the Americans with Disabilities Act of 1990,[24] respectively.

The focus here is on the kinds of discrimination prohibited by these federal statutes. Note, however, that discrimination against employees on the basis of any of the above-mentioned criteria may also violate state human rights statutes or other state laws prohibiting discrimination.

Title VII of the Civil Rights Act of 1964

Title VII of the Civil Rights Act of 1964 and its amendments prohibit **employment discrimination** against employees, applicants, and union members on the basis of race, color, national origin, religion, and gender at any stage of employment. Title VII applies to employers with fifteen or more employees, labor unions with fifteen or more members, labor unions that operate hiring halls (to which members go regularly to be rationed jobs as they become available), employment agencies, and state and local governing units or agencies. A special section of the act prohibits discrimination in most federal government employment.

Compliance with Title VII is monitored by the Equal Employment Opportunity Commission (EEOC). A victim of alleged discrimination, before bringing a suit against the employer, must first file a claim with the EEOC. The EEOC may investigate the dispute and attempt to obtain the parties' voluntary consent to an out-of-court settlement. If voluntary agreement cannot be reached, the EEOC may then file a suit against the employer on the employee's behalf. If the EEOC

---

19. At least thirty-seven states now have whistleblower statutes.
20. 5 U.S.C. Section 1201.
21. 31 U.S.C. Sections 3729–3733. This act amended the False Claims Act of 1863.
22. 42 U.S.C. Sections 2000e–2000e-17.
23. 29 U.S.C. Sections 621–634.
24. 42 U.S.C. Sections 12102–12118.

decides not to investigate the claim, the victim may bring his or her own lawsuit against the employer.

TYPES OF DISCRIMINATION Title VII prohibits both intentional and unintentional discrimination. Intentional discrimination by an employer against an employee is known as **disparate-treatment discrimination**. Because intent may sometimes be difficult to prove, courts have established certain procedures for resolving disparate-treatment cases. Suppose that a woman applies for employment with a construction firm and is rejected. If she sues on the basis of disparate-treatment discrimination in hiring, she must show that (1) she is a member of a protected class, (2) she applied and was qualified for the job in question, (3) she was rejected by the employer, and (4) the employer continued to seek applicants for the position or filled the position with a person not in a protected class.

If the woman can meet these relatively easy requirements, she makes out a *prima facie* case of illegal discrimination. Making out a *prima facie* case of discrimination means that the plaintiff has met her initial burden of proof and will win in the absence of a legally acceptable employer defense (defenses to claims of employment discrimination will be discussed later in this chapter). The burden then shifts to the employer-defendant, who must articulate a legal reason for not hiring the plaintiff.

For example, the employer might say that the plaintiff was not hired because she lacked sufficient experience or training. To prevail, the plaintiff must then show that the employer's reason is a *pretext* (not the true reason) and that discriminatory intent actually motivated the employer's decision.

Employers often find it necessary to use interviews and testing procedures to choose from among a large number of applicants for job openings. Minimum educational requirements are also common. Employer practices, such as those involving educational requirements, may have an unintended discriminatory impact on a protected class. **Disparate-impact discrimination** occurs when, as a result of educational or other job requirements or hiring procedures, an employer's work force does not reflect the percentage of non-whites, women, or members of other protected classes that characterizes qualified individuals in the local labor market. If a person challenging an employment practice having a discriminatory effect can show a connection between the practice and the disparity, he or she makes out a *prima facie* case, and no evidence of discriminatory intent needs to be shown. In such cases, there are two basic questions—whether a standard or policy has a discriminatory impact and, if it does, whether the standard or policy nevertheless has a substantial, demonstrable relationship to the job. These were the questions in the following case.

CASE 22.4

Fickling v. New York State Department of Civil Service

United States District Court,
Southern District of New York, 1995.
909 F.Supp. 185.

FACTS Job applicants for the position of Social Welfare Eligibility Examiner for Westchester County, New York, must pass a New York State Department of Civil Service examination. In 1989 and 1990, the exam tested mainly reading comprehension and arithmetic, skills that were of relatively little importance to the job. When it was revealed that fewer than two African Americans and about one Hispanic passed the exam for every three whites who passed, Juliette Fickling and seven other minority members who failed the test (the plaintiffs) filed a suit in a federal district court against the state and the county. The plaintiffs alleged violations of, among other things, Title VII.

ISSUE Did the exam have a racially disparate impact? Did the exam lack a substantial, demonstrable relationship to the job?

DECISION Yes, to both questions. The court ruled in favor of the plaintiffs.

REASON The court pointed out that "[a] selection rate for any race, sex, or ethnic group which is less than four-fifths * * * (or 80%) of the rate

(Continued)

Case 22.4—Continued

for the group with the highest rate" is evidence of disparate impact. "Here," noted the court, "the disparate racial impact * * * was far below the 80% standard." The court also found that, despite the exam's emphasis on reading and arithmetic, neither ability was important to success on the job, while written and oral expression were generally not tested, "despite the fact that these abilities were found to be very important to successful job performance."

FOR CRITICAL ANALYSIS—Social Consideration   *What are reasons, other than equal opportunity under Title VII, for insisting that a job test have a "substantial, demonstrable relationship" to the job?*

DISCRIMINATION BASED ON RELIGION   Title VII of the Civil Rights Act of 1964 also prohibits government employers, private employers, and unions from discriminating against persons because of their religion. An employer must "reasonably accommodate" the religious practices of its employees, unless to do so would cause undue hardship to the employer's business. For example, if an employee's religion prohibits him or her from working on a certain day of the week or at a certain type of job, the employer must make a reasonable attempt to accommodate these religious requirements. Employers must reasonably accommodate an employee's religious belief even if the belief is not based on the tenets or dogma of a particular church, sect, or denomination. The only requirement is that the belief be sincerely held by the employee.[25]

DISCRIMINATION BASED ON GENDER   Under Title VII, as well as other federal acts, employers are forbidden to discriminate against employees on the basis of gender. Employers are prohibited from classifying jobs as male or female and from advertising in help-wanted columns that are designated male or female unless the employer can prove that the gender of the applicant is essential to the job. Furthermore, employers cannot have separate male and female seniority lists. Generally, to succeed in a suit for gender discrimination, a plaintiff must demonstrate that gender was a determining factor in the employer's decision to hire, fire, or promote him or her. Typically, this involves looking at all of the surrounding circumstances.

The Pregnancy Discrimination Act of 1978,[26] which amended Title VII, expanded the definition

of gender discrimination to include discrimination based on pregnancy. Women affected by pregnancy, childbirth, or related medical conditions must be treated—for all employment-related purposes, including the receipt of benefits under employee-benefit programs—the same as other persons not so affected but similar in ability to work. An employer is required to treat an employee temporarily unable to perform her job owing to a pregnancy-related condition in the same manner as the employer would treat other temporarily disabled employees. The employer must change work assignments, grant paid disability leaves, or grant leaves without pay if that is how it would treat other temporarily disabled employees. Policies concerning an employee's return to work, accrual of seniority, pay increases, and so on must also result in equal treatment.[27]

SEXUAL HARASSMENT   Title VII also protects employees against **sexual harassment** in the workplace. Sexual harassment can take two forms: *quid-pro-quo* harassment and hostile-environment harassment. *Quid pro quo* is a Latin phrase that is often translated to mean "something in exchange for something else." *Quid-pro-quo* harassment occurs when job opportunities, promotions, salary increases, and so on are given in return for sexual favors.

---

25. *Frazee v. Illinois Department of Employment Security,* 489 U.S. 829, 109 S.Ct. 1514, 103 L.Ed.2d 914 (1989).
26. 42 U.S.C. Section 2000e(k).

27. A cause of action under the Pregnancy Discrimination Act is not limited to women—a man may also have standing to sue for discrimination under the act. In *Nicol v. Imagematrix, Inc.,* 773 F.Supp. 802 (E.D.Va. 1991), the court held that the husband of a pregnant woman had standing to sue his former employer. The husband alleged that he had been fired because his wife (who worked for the same employer and was also fired) was pregnant.

Hostile-environment harassment occurs when an employee is subjected to sexual conduct or comments that he or she perceives as offensive. The EEOC's guidelines on harassment state that the following types of verbal or physical conduct constitute hostile-environment harassment:

1. Conduct that has the purpose or effect of creating an intimidating, hostile, or offensive working environment.
2. Conduct that has the purpose or effect of unreasonably interfering with an individual's work performance.
3. Conduct that otherwise adversely affects an individual's employment opportunities.

Employers are generally liable for Title VII violations by the firm's managerial or supervisory personnel. Usually, in *quid-pro-quo* harassment cases, the courts hold employers strictly liable for the harassment. In other words, the employer will be held liable regardless of whether the employer knew about the harassment. In hostile-environment cases, however, the majority of courts tend to hold employers liable only if the employer knew or should have known of the harassment and failed to take prompt remedial action.

Often, employees alleging harassment complain that the actions of co-workers, not supervisors, are responsible for creating a hostile working environment. In such cases, the employee still has a cause of action against the employer. Normally, though, the employer will be held liable only if it knew, or should have known, about the harassment and failed to take immediate remedial action.

The following case raises the issue of whether an employer can be held responsible for harassment even though the harassing employee had voluntarily ceased the harassment.

CASE 22.5

Fuller v. City of Oakland, California

United States Court of Appeals, Ninth Circuit, 1995.
47 F.3d 1522.

FACTS Patricia Fuller and Antonio Romero were police officers with the city of Oakland, California, when they had a brief romantic relationship. When Fuller broke it off, Romero—who was promoted to a supervisory position—began to harass her on and off duty. Fuller complained to their superiors. Romero stopped harassing her, and the superiors took no action, except to officially call Fuller's complaint "[u]nfounded." Fuller resigned and filed a suit against the city in a federal district court under Title VII. The city argued that when the harassment stopped, its own responsibility ceased. The court agreed. Fuller appealed to the U.S. Court of Appeals for the Ninth Circuit.

ISSUE Does an employer have a responsibility to take action in a case of harassment even if the harassment has stopped?

DECISION Yes. The U.S. Court of Appeals for the Ninth Circuit reversed the judgment of the lower court and remanded the case.

REASON The appellate court concluded that "Title VII does not permit employers to stand idly by once they learn that sexual harassment has occurred. To do so amounts to a ratification of the prior harassment." The court explained that "[o]nce an employer knows or should know of harassment, a remedial obligation kicks in. That obligation will not be discharged until action—prompt, effective action—has been taken." The court reasoned that the effectiveness of the action is "measured by the twin purposes of ending the current harassment and deterring future harassment—by the same offender or others."

FOR CRITICAL ANALYSIS—Social Consideration *What steps should an employer take, once harassment has ceased, to deter future misconduct?*

REMEDIES UNDER TITLE VII   Employer liability under Title VII may be extensive. If the plaintiff successfully proves that unlawful discrimination occurred, he or she may be awarded reinstatement, back pay, retroactive promotions, and damages. Compensatory damages are available only in cases of intentional discrimination. Punitive damages may be recovered against a private employer only if the employer acted with malice or reckless indifference to an individual's rights. The sum of the amount of compensatory and punitive damages is limited to specific amounts against specific employers—ranging from $50,000 against employers with one hundred or fewer employees to $300,000 against employers with more than five hundred employees.

Discrimination Based on Age

Age discrimination is potentially the most widespread form of discrimination, because anyone—regardless of race, color, national origin, or gender—could be a victim at some point in life. The Age Discrimination in Employment Act (ADEA) of 1967, as amended, prohibits employment discrimination on the basis of age against individuals forty years of age or older. An amendment to the act prohibits mandatory retirement for nonmanagerial workers. For the act to apply, an employer must have twenty or more employees, and the employer's business activities must affect interstate commerce.

If a plaintiff can establish that he or she (1) was a member of the protected age group, (2) was qualified for the position from which he or she was discharged, and (3) was discharged under circumstances that give rise to an inference of discrimination, the plaintiff has established a *prima facie* case of unlawful age discrimination. The burden then shifts to the employer, who must articulate a legitimate reason for the discrimination. If the plaintiff can prove that the employer's reason is only a pretext and that the plaintiff's age was a determining factor in the employer's decision, the employer will be held liable under the ADEA.

Numerous cases of alleged age discrimination have been brought against employers who, to cut costs, replaced older, higher-salaried employees with younger, lower-salaried workers. Whether a firing is discriminatory or simply part of a rational business decision to prune the company's ranks is not always clear. Companies generally defend a decision to discharge a worker by asserting that the worker could no longer perform his or her duties or that the worker's skills were no longer needed. The employee must prove that the discharge was motivated, at least in part, by age bias. Proof that qualified older employees are generally discharged before younger employees or that co-workers continually made unflattering age-related comments about the discharged worker may be enough.

Discrimination Based on Disability

The Americans with Disabilities Act (ADA) of 1990 is designed to eliminate discriminatory employment practices that prevent otherwise qualified workers with disabilities from fully participating in the national labor force. Basically, the ADA requires that employers "reasonably accommodate" the needs of persons with disabilities unless to do so would cause the employer to suffer an "undue hardship."

To prevail on a claim under the ADA, a plaintiff must show that he or she (1) has a disability, (2) is otherwise qualified for the employment in question, and (3) was excluded from the employment solely because of the disability. As in Title VII cases, a claim alleging violation of the ADA may be commenced only after the plaintiff has pursued the claim through the EEOC. Plaintiffs may sue for many of the same remedies available under Title VII. They may seek reinstatement, back pay, a limited amount of compensatory and punitive damages (for intentional discrimination), and certain other forms of relief. Repeat violators may be ordered to pay fines of up to $100,000.

WHAT IS A DISABILITY?   The ADA is broadly drafted to define persons with disabilities as persons with a physical or mental impairment that "substantially limits" their everyday activities. More specifically, the ADA defines *disability* as "(1) a physical or mental impairment that substantially limits one or more of the major life activities of such individuals; (2) a record of such impairment; or (3) being regarded as having such an impairment."

Health conditions that have been considered disabilities under federal law include blindness, alcoholism, heart disease, cancer, muscular dystrophy, cerebral palsy, paraplegia, diabetes, acquired immune deficiency syndrome (AIDS), and morbid obesity (defined as existing when an individual's weight is two times that of the normal person)[28] The ADA excludes from coverage certain conditions, including homosexuality and kleptomania.

REASONABLE ACCOMMODATION   The ADA does not require that *unqualified* applicants with disabilities be hired or retained. Therefore, employers are not obligated to accommodate the needs of job applicants or employees with disabilities who are not otherwise qualified for the work. If a job applicant or an employee with a disability, with reasonable accommodation, can perform essential job functions, however, then the employer must make the accommodation. Required modifications may include installing ramps for a wheelchair, establishing more flexible working hours, creating or modifying job assignments, and creating or improving training materials and procedures.

Employers who do not accommodate the needs of persons with disabilities must demonstrate that the accommodations will cause "undue hardship." Generally, the law offers no uniform standards for identifying what is an undue hardship other than the imposition of a "significant difficulty or expense" on the employer. Usually, the courts decide whether an accommodation constitutes an undue hardship on a case-by-case basis. In one case, the court decided that paying for a parking space near the office for an employee with a disability was not an undue hardship.[29] In another case, the court held that accommodating the request of an employee with diabetes for indefinite leave until his disease was under control would create an undue hardship for the employer, because the employer would not know when the employee was returning to work. The court stated that reasonable accommodation under the ADA means accommodation so that the employee can perform the job now or "in the immediate future" rather than at some unspecified distant time.[30]

Defenses to Employment Discrimination

The first line of defense for an employer charged with employment discrimination is, of course, to assert that the plaintiff has failed to meet his or her initial burden of proof—proving that discrimination in fact occurred. As noted, plaintiffs bringing cases under the ADA often find it difficult to meet this initial burden, because they must prove that their alleged disabilities are disabilities covered by the ADA. Furthermore, plaintiffs in ADA cases must prove that they were otherwise qualified for the job and that the reason they were not hired or were fired was solely because of their disabilities.

Once a plaintiff succeeds in proving that discrimination occurred, then the burden shifts to the employer to justify the discriminatory practice. Often, employers attempt to justify the discrimination by claiming that it was a result of a business necessity, a bona fide occupational qualification, or a seniority system. An effective anti-harassment policy and prompt remedial action when harassment occurs also may shield employers from liability under Title VII for sexual harassment in some cases.

BUSINESS NECESSITY   An employer may defend against a claim of discrimination by asserting that a practice that has a discriminatory effect is a business necessity. If requiring a high school diploma, for example, is shown to have a discriminatory effect, an employer might argue that a high school education is required for workers to perform the job at a required level of competence. If the employer can demonstrate to the court's satisfaction that there exists a definite connection between a high school education and job performance, then the employer will succeed in this **business necessity** defense.

BONA FIDE OCCUPATIONAL QUALIFICATION   Another defense applies when discrimination against a protected class is essential to a job—that is, when a particular trait is a **bona fide occupational qualification (BFOQ)**. For example, a men's fashion magazine might legitimately hire only male models. Similarly, the Federal Aviation Administration can legitimately impose age limits for airline pilots. Race, however, can never be a BFOQ. Generally, courts have restricted the BFOQ defense to instances in which the employee's gender is essential to the job. In 1991, the United States Supreme Court held that even a fetal-protection policy that was adopted to protect the unborn children of female employees from the harmful effects of exposure to lead was an unacceptable BFOQ.[31]

---

28.   *Cook v. Rhode Island Department of Mental Health*, 10 F.3d 17 (1st Cir. 1993).
29.   See *Lyons v. Legal Aid Society*, 68 F.3d 1512 (2d Cir. 1995).
30.   *Myers v. Hase*, 50 F.3d 278 (4th Cir. 1995).

31.   *United Automobile Workers v. Johnson Controls, Inc.*, 499 U.S. 187, 111 S.Ct. 1196, 113 L.Ed.2d 158. (This case is presented in Chapter 3 as Case 3.1.)

SENIORITY SYSTEMS An employer with a history of discrimination may have no members of protected classes in upper-level positions. Even if the employer now seeks to be unbiased, it may face a lawsuit seeking an order that minorities be promoted ahead of schedule to compensate for past discrimination. If no present intent to discriminate is shown, and promotions or other job benefits are distributed according to a fair **seniority system** (in which workers with more years of service are promoted first, or laid off last), however, the employer has a good defense against the suit.

Affirmative Action

Federal statutes and regulations providing for equal opportunity in the workplace were designed to reduce or eliminate discriminatory practices with respect to hiring, retaining, and promoting employees. **Affirmative action** programs go a step further and attempt to "make up" for past patterns of discrimination by giving members of protected classes preferential treatment in hiring or promotion.

Affirmative action programs have caused much controversy, particularly when they result in what is frequently called "reverse discrimination"—discrimination against "majority" workers, such as white males (or discrimination against other minority groups that may not be given preferential

treatment under a particular affirmative action program). At issue is whether affirmative action programs, because of their inherently discriminatory nature, violate the equal protection clause of the Fourteenth Amendment to the Constitution.

State Statutes

Most states also have statutes that prohibit employment discrimination. Generally, the kinds of discrimination prohibited under federal legislation are also prohibited by state laws. In addition, state statutes often provide protection for certain individuals, such as homosexuals, who are not protected under Title VII. Furthermore, state laws prohibiting discrimination may provide additional damages, such as damages for emotional distress, that are not provided for under Title VII.

One of the problems faced by employees of very small business firms is that they may have no cause of action for discrimination under federal statutes (because the statutes apply only to firms with a specified number of employees). Some state statutes have similar requirements. In California, for example, the state employment antidiscrimination statute—the Fair Employment and Housing Act—applies only to employers with five or more employees. Many small businesses, like the medical office in the following case, employ less than five people.

CASE 22.6	

Badih v. Myers

California Court of Appeal,
First District, Division 1, 1995.
36 Cal.App.4th 1289,
43 Cal.Rptr.2d 229.

FACTS Fatmeh Badih was a medical assistant for Dr. Leonard Myers. When Badih married her boyfriend and became pregnant, Myers fired her. Badih filed a suit in a California state court against Myers, alleging in part discrimination on the basis of pregnancy in violation of public policy. The court awarded Badih damages. Myers appealed, asserting that he was not subject to any state law prohibiting discrimination in employment on the basis of pregnancy. Badih argued that pregnancy discrimination in employment is a form of sex discrimination prohibited by the California Constitution, which states that "[a] person may not be disqualified from *   *   * employment because of sex."

ISSUE Is pregnancy discrimination a form of sex discrimination under the California Constitution?

DECISION Yes. The state appellate court affirmed the lower court's decision.

REASON The court agreed with Badih that the state constitution "expresses a fundamental public policy against sex discrimination in employment." The court reasoned that, although there were no cases

Case 22.6—Continued

interpreting this provision of the state constitution, federal and state laws "strongly support the notion that pregnancy discrimination in employment should be treated as a form of sex discrimination." In the context of the state constitution, "there is no reason why a different definition of sex discrimination should be applied."

FOR CRITICAL ANALYSIS—Political Consideration *Why are state antidiscrimination laws necessary?*

▌Terms and Concepts

affirmative action 474
bona fide occupational
   qualification (BFOQ) 473
business necessity 473
closed shop 462
disparate-impact
   discrimination 469
disparate-treatment
   discrimination 469

employment at will 460
employment discrimination
   468
hot-cargo agreement 462
minimum wage 461
prima facie case 469
right-to-work law 462
secondary boycott 462
seniority system 474

sexual harassment 470
union shop 462
whistleblowing 467
workers' compensation laws
   464
wrongful discharge 465

▌Chapter Summary: Employment Law

Wage-Hour Laws (See pages 460–461.)	1. *Davis-Bacon Act (1931)*—Requires the payment of "prevailing wages" to employees of contractors and subcontractors working on government construction projects. 2. *Walsh-Healey Act (1936)*—Requires that a minimum wage and overtime pay be paid to employees of firms that contract with federal agencies. 3. *Fair Labor Standards Act (1938)*—Extended wage-hour requirements to cover all employers whose activities affected interstate commerce. The act has specific requirements in regard to child labor, maximum hours, and minimum wages.
Labor Unions (See pages 461–462.)	Federal labor laws include: 1. Norris-LaGuardia Act (1932)—Protects peaceful strikes, picketing, and boycotts. 2. National Labor Relations Act (1935)—Established the rights of employees to engage in collective bargaining and to strike; also defined specific employer practices as unfair to labor. The National Labor Relations Board (NLRB) was created to administer and enforce the act. 3. Labor-Management Relations Act (1947)—Proscribes certain unfair union practices, such as the closed shop. 4. Labor-Management Reporting and Disclosure Act (1959)—Established an employee bill of rights and reporting requirements for internal control of union activities.
Worker Health and Safety (See pages 462–464.)	1. The Occupational Safety and Health Act of 1970 requires employers to meet specific safety and health standards that are established and enforced by the Occupational Safety and Health Administration (OSHA). 2. State workers' compensation laws establish an administrative procedure for compensating workers who are injured in accidents that occur on the job, regardless of fault.

(Continued)

▌Chapter Summary: Employment Law—Continued

Income Security *(See pages 464–465.)*	1. *Social Security and Medicare*—The Social Security Act of 1935 provides for old-age (retirement), survivors, and disability insurance. Both employers and employees must make contributions under the Federal Insurance Contributions Act (FICA) to help pay for the employees' loss of income on retirement. The Social Security Administration administers Medicare, a health-insurance program for older or disabled persons.
	2. *Private pension plans*—The federal Employee Retirement Income Security Act (ERISA) of 1974 establishes standards for the management of employer-provided pension plans.
	3. *Unemployment insurance*—The Federal Unemployment Tax Act of 1935 created a system that provides unemployment compensation to eligible individuals. Covered employers are taxed to help cover the costs of unemployment compensation.
COBRA *(See page 465.)*	The Consolidated Omnibus Budget Reconciliation Act (COBRA) of 1985 requires employers to give employees, on termination of employment, the option of continuing their medical, optical, or dental insurance coverage for a certain period.
Family and Medical Leave *(See page 465.)*	The Family and Medical Leave Act (FMLA) of 1993 requires employers with fifty or more employees to provide their employees (except for key employees) with up to twelve weeks of unpaid family or medical leave during any twelve-month period.
Wrongful Discharge *(See pages 465–468.)*	Wrongful discharge occurs whenever an employer discharges an employee in violation of the law or of an employment contract. To protect employees from some of the harsh results of the common law employment-at-will doctrine (under which employers may hire or fire employees "at will" unless a contract indicates to the contrary), courts have made exceptions to the doctrine on the basis of contract theory, tort theory, and public policy.
Whistleblower Statutes *(See page 468.)*	Most states have passed whistleblower statutes specifically to protect employees who "blow the whistle" on their employers from subsequent retaliation by those employers. The federal Whistleblower Protection Act of 1989 protects federal employees who report their employers' wrongdoing. The federal False Claims Reform Act of 1986 provides monetary rewards for whistleblowers who disclose information relating to fraud perpetrated against the U.S. government.
Title VII of the Civil Rights Act of 1964 *(See pages 468–472.)*	Title VII prohibits employment discrimination based on race, color, national origin, religion, or gender.
	1. *Procedures*—Employees must file a claim with the Equal Employment Opportunity Commission (EEOC). The EEOC may sue the employer on the employee's behalf; if not, the employee may sue the employer directly.
	2. *Intentional versus unintentional discrimination*—Title VII prohibits both intentional (disparate-treatment) and unintentional (disparate-impact) discrimination. Disparate-impact discrimination occurs when an employer's practice, such as hiring only persons with a certain level of education, has the effect of discriminating against a class of persons protected by Title VII.
	3. *Remedies for discrimination under Title VII*—If a plaintiff proves that unlawful discrimination occurred, he or she may be awarded reinstatement, back pay, and retroactive promotions. Damages (both compensatory and punitive) may be awarded for intentional discrimination.
Discrimination Based on Age *(See page 472.)*	The Age Discrimination in Employment Act (ADEA) of 1967 prohibits employment discrimination on the basis of age against individuals forty years of age or older. Procedures for bringing a case under the ADEA are similar to those for bringing a case under Title VII.

▎Chapter Summary: Employment Law—Continued

Discrimination Based on Disability *(See pages 472–473.)*	The Americans with Disabilities Act (ADA) of 1990 prohibits employment discrimination against persons with disabilities who are otherwise qualified to perform the essential functions of the jobs for which they apply. 1. *Procedures and remedies*—To prevail on a claim under the ADA, the plaintiff must show that he or she has a disability, is otherwise qualified for the employment in question, and was excluded from the employment solely because of the disability. Procedures under the ADA are similar to those required in Title VII cases; remedies are also similar to those under Title VII. 2. *Definition of disability*—The ADA defines the term *disability* as a physical or mental impairment that substantially limits one or more major life activities; a record of such impairment; or being regarded as having such an impairment. 3. *Reasonable accommodation*—Employers are required to reasonably accommodate the needs of persons with disabilities. Reasonable accommodations may include altering job-application procedures, modifying the physical work environment, and permitting more flexible work schedules. Employers are not required to accommodate the needs of all workers with disabilities. For example, employers need not accommodate workers who pose a definite threat to health and safety in the workplace or those who are not otherwise qualified for their jobs.
Defenses to Employment Discrimination *(See pages 473–474.)*	If a plaintiff proves that employment discrimination occurred, employers may avoid liability by successfully asserting certain defenses. Employers may assert that the discrimination was required for reasons of business necessity, to meet a bona fide occupational qualification, or to maintain a legitimate seniority system. Evidence of prior employee misconduct acquired after the employee has been fired is not a defense to discrimination.
Affirmative Action *(See page 474.)*	Affirmative action programs attempt to "make up" for past patterns of discrimination by giving members of protected classes preferential treatment in hiring or promotion. Increasingly, such programs are being strictly scrutinized by the courts.
State Statutes *(See pages 174–475.)*	Generally, the kinds of discrimination prohibited by federal statutes are also prohibited by state laws. State laws may provide for more extensive protection and remedies than federal laws.

▎For Review

1. What is the employment-at-will doctrine? When and why are exceptions to this doctrine made?

2. What federal statute governs working hours and wages? What federal statutes govern labor unions and collective bargaining?

3. What federal act was enacted to protect the health and safety of employees? What are workers' compensation laws?

4. Generally, what kind of conduct is prohibited by Title VII of the Civil Rights Act of 1964, as amended?

5. What remedies are available under Title VII of the 1964 Civil Rights Act, as amended?

▎Questions and Case Problems

22–1. Workers' Compensation. Galvin Strang worked for a tractor company in one of its factories. Near his work station there was a conveyor belt that ran through a large industrial oven. Sometimes, the workers would use the oven to heat their meals. Thirty-inch-high flasks containing molds were fixed at regular intervals on the conveyor and were transported into the oven. Strang had to walk between the flasks to get to his work station. One day, the conveyor was not moving, and Strang used the oven to cook a frozen pot pie. As he was removing the pot pie from the oven, the conveyor came on. One of the flasks struck Strang and seriously injured him. Strang sought recovery under the state workers' compensation law. Should he recover? Why or why not?

22–2. Title VII Violations. Discuss fully whether any of the following actions would constitute a violation of Title VII of the 1964 Civil Rights Act, as amended:

(a) Tennington, Inc., is a consulting firm and has ten employees. These employees travel on consulting jobs in seven states. Tennington has an employment record of hiring only white males.

(b) Novo Films, Inc., is making a film about Africa and needs to employ approximately one hundred extras for this picture. Novo advertises in all major newspapers in southern California for the hiring of these extras. The ad states that only African Americans need apply.

22–3. Discrimination Based on Age. Tavo Jones had worked since 1974 for Westshore Resort, where he maintained golf carts. During the first decade, he received positive job evaluations and numerous merit pay raises. He was promoted to the position of supervisor of golf-cart maintenance at three courses. Then a new employee, Ben Olery, was placed in charge of the golf courses. He demoted Jones, who was over the age of forty, to running only one of the three cart facilities, and he froze Jones's salary indefinitely. Olery also demoted five other men over the age of forty. Another cart facility was placed under the supervision of Blake Blair. Later, the cart facilities for the three courses were again consolidated, but Blair—not Jones—was put in charge. At the time, Jones was still in his forties, and Blair was in his twenties. Jones overheard Blair say that "we are going to have to do away with these . . . old and senile" men. Jones quit and sued Westshore for employment discrimination. Should he prevail? Explain.

22–4. Health and Safety Regulations. At an REA Express, Inc., shipping terminal, a conveyor belt was inoperative because an electrical circuit had shorted out. The manager called a licensed electrical contractor. When the contractor arrived, REA's maintenance supervisor was in the circuit breaker room. The floor was wet, and the maintenance supervisor was using sawdust to try to soak up the water. While REA's maintenance supervisor was standing on the wet floor and attempting to fix the short circuit, he was electrocuted. Simultaneously, the licensed electrical contractor, who was standing on a wooden platform, was burned and knocked unconscious. The Occupational Safety and Health Administration (OSHA) sought to fine REA Express $1,000 for failure to furnish a place of employ-

ment free from recognized hazards. Will the court uphold OSHA's decision? Discuss fully. [*REA Express, Inc. v. Brennan*, 495 F.2d 822 (2d Cir. 1974)]

22–5. Whistleblowing. Richard Winters was an at-will employee for the Houston *Chronicle* from April 1977 to June 1986. Beginning in 1980, he became aware of alleged illegal activities carried out by other employees. He claimed that the *Chronicle* was falsely reporting an inflated number of paid subscribers, that several employees were engaged in inventory theft, and that his supervisor had offered him an opportunity to participate in a kickback scheme with the manufacturers of plastic bags. Winters reported all these activities to upper-level management in January 1986 but made no report to law enforcement agencies. He was fired six months later. He sued the *Chronicle* for wrongful termination. How should the court decide? Discuss fully. [*Winters v. Houston Chronicle Publishing*, 795 S.W.2d 723 (Tex. 1990)]

22–6. Employment at Will. Robert Adams worked as a delivery truck driver for George W. Cochran & Co. Adams persistently refused to drive a truck that lacked a required inspection sticker and was subsequently fired as a result of his refusal. Adams was an at-will employee, and Cochran contended that because there was no written employment contract stating otherwise, Cochran was entitled to discharge Adams at will—that is, for cause or no cause. Adams sought to recover $7,094 in lost wages and $200,000 in damages for the "humiliation, mental anguish and emotional distress" that he had suffered as a result of being fired from his job. Under what legal doctrines discussed in this chapter—or exceptions to those doctrines—might Adams be able to recover damages from Cochran? Discuss fully. [*Adams v. George W. Cochran & Co.*, 597 A.2d 28 (D.C.App. 1991)]

22–7. Workers' Compensation. Linda Burnett Kidwell, employed as a state traffic officer by the California Highway Patrol (CHP), suffered an injury at home, off duty, while practicing the standing long jump. The jump is part of a required test during the CHP's annual physical performance program fitness test. Kidwell filed a claim for workers' compensation benefits. The CHP and the California workers' compensation appeals board denied her claim. Kidwell appealed to a state appellate court. What is the requirement for granting a workers' compensation claim? Should Kidwell's claim be granted? [*Kidwell v. Workers' Compensation Appeals Board*, 33 Cal.App.4th 1130, 39 Cal.Rptr.2d 540 (1995)]

22–8. Discrimination Based on Gender. Beginning in June 1966, Corning Glass Works started to open up jobs on the night shift to women. The previously separate male and female seniority lists were consolidated, and the women became eligible to exercise their seniority on the same basis as men and to bid for higher-paid night inspection jobs as vacancies occurred. On January 20, 1969, however, a new collective bargaining agreement went into effect; it established a new job evaluation system for setting wage rates. This agreement abolished (for the future) separate base wages for night-shift and day-shift inspectors and imposed a uniform base wage for inspectors that exceeded the wage rate previously in effect for the night shift. The agreement, though, did allow for a higher "red circle" rate for employees hired prior to January 20, 1969, when they were working as inspectors on the night shift. This "red circle" wage served essentially to perpetuate the differential in base wages between day and night inspectors. Had Corning violated Title VII of the Civil Rights Act of 1964? Discuss. [*Corning Glass Works v. Brennan*, 417 U.S. 188, 94 S.Ct. 2223, 41 L.Ed.2d 1 (1974)]

22–9. Defenses to Employment Discrimination. Dorothea O'Driscoll had worked as a quality control inspector for Hercules, Inc., for six years when her employment was terminated in 1986. O'Driscoll, who was over forty years of age, sued Hercules for age discrimination in violation of the Age Discrimination in Employment Act of 1967. While preparing for trial, Hercules discovered evidence of misconduct on the part of O'Driscoll that it had been unaware of when it terminated her employment. Among other things, Hercules learned that O'Driscoll had misrepresented her age on both her employment application and her application for a government security clearance (necessary to handle confidential information). She also did not disclose a previous employer, falsely represented that she had never applied for work with Hercules before, and falsely stated that she had completed two quarters of study at a technical college. Additionally, on her application for group insurance coverage, she misrepresented the age of her son, who would otherwise have been ineligible for coverage as her dependent. Hercules defended against O'Driscoll's claim of age discrimination by stating that had it known of this misconduct, it would have terminated her employment anyway. What should the court decide? Discuss fully. [*O'Driscoll v. Hercules, Inc.*, 12 F.3d 176 (10th Cir. 1994)]

22–10. Discrimination Based on Disability. When the University of Maryland Medical System Corp. learned that one of its surgeons was HIV positive, the university offered him transfers to positions that did not involve surgery. The surgeon refused, and the university terminated him. The surgeon filed a suit in a federal district court against the university, alleging in part a violation of the Americans with Disabilities Act. The surgeon claimed that he was "otherwise qualified" for his former position. What does he have to prove to win his case? Should he be reinstated? [*Doe v. University of Maryland Medical System Corp.*, 50 F.3d 1261 (4th Cir. 1995)]

▎Unit Seven—Cumulative Hypothetical Problem

22–11. *Falwell Motors, Inc., is a large corporation that manufactures automobile batteries.*

1. One of Falwell's salespersons, Loren, puts in long hours every week. He spends most of his time away from the office generating sales. Less than 10 percent of his work time is devoted to other duties. Usually, he receives a substantial bonus at the end of each year from his employer, and Loren now relies on this supplement to his annual salary and commission. One year, the employer does not give any of its employees year-end bonuses. Loren calculates the amount of hours he had worked during the year beyond the required forty hours a week. Then he tells Falwell's president that if he is not paid for these overtime hours, he will sue the company for the overtime pay he has "earned." Falwell's president tells Loren that Falwell is not obligated to pay Loren overtime because Loren is a salesperson. What federal statute governs this dispute? Under this statute, is Falwell required to pay Loren for the "overtime hours"? Why or why not?

2. One day Barry, one of the salespersons, anxious to make a sale, intentionally quotes a price to a customer that is $500 lower than Falwell has authorized for that particular product. The customer purchases the product at the quoted price. When Falwell learns of the deal, it claims that it is not legally bound to the sales contract because it did not authorize Barry to sell the product at that price. Is Falwell bound by the contract? Discuss fully.

3. One day Gina, a Falwell employee, suffered a serious burn when she accidentally spilled some acid on her hand. The accident occurred because another employee, who was suspected of using illegal drugs, carelessly bumped into her. The hand required a series of skin-grafting operations before it healed sufficiently to allow Gina to return to work. Gina wants to obtain compensation for her lost wages and medical expenses. Can she do so? If so, how?

4. Aretha, a Falwell employee, is disgusted by the sexually offensive behavior of several male employees. She has complained to her supervisor on several occasions about the offensive behavior, but the supervisor merely laughs at her concerns.

Aretha decides to bring a legal action against the company for sexual harassment. Does Aretha's complaint concern *quid pro quo* harassment or hostile-environment harassment? What federal statute protects employees from sexual harassment? What remedies are available under that statute? What procedures must Aretha follow in pursuing her legal action?

▌Accessing the Internet: Fundamentals of Business Law

The 'Lectric Law Library's Lawcopedia contains a summary of agency laws at
http://www.lectlaw.com/d-a.htm
Scroll down through the A's and select the link to Agent for useful information on this area of the law.

If you are interested in learning more about "intelligent agents," you can read the article entitled "Can Programs Bind Humans to Contracts?" at
http://www.ljx.com/internet/0113shrink.html
The Institute of Labor Relations at Cornell University and Human Resource Executive magazine have compiled an extensive index of resources on labor law. You can find these resources at
http://www.workindex.com
A similar index of Web links on labor relations is Employee Relations Web Picks at
http://www.nyper.com
The site of the American Federation of Labor-Congress of Industrial Organizations (AFL-CIO) provides links to a broad variety of labor-related resources. Go to
http://www.aflcio.org/
The National Labor Relations Board is now online at the following URL:
http://www.nlrb.gov

Unit Eight

Business Organizations

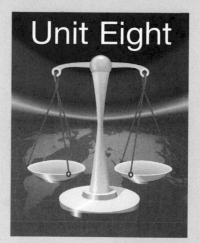

▌Unit Contents

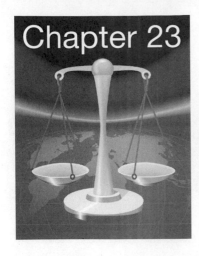

Chapter 23

Sole Proprietorships, Partnerships, and Limited Liability Companies

CHAPTER OBJECTIVES

After reading this chapter, you should be able to:

1. Identify and describe two of the three major traditional forms of business organization.
2. Summarize the advantages and disadvantages of doing business as a partnership.
3. Specify how the limited liability company addresses needs that are not met by traditional forms of business.
4. Explain how a partnership can be terminated.
5. Indicate the similarities and differences between limited partnerships and general partnerships.

An entrepreneur's primary motive for undertaking a business enterprise is to make profits. An **entrepreneur** is by definition one who initiates and *assumes the financial risks* of a new enterprise and undertakes to provide or control its management.

In this chapter, we first briefly discuss the variety of options available to entrepreneurs. We then examine the basic features of two of the major traditional business forms—sole proprietorships and partnerships. We then look at a relatively new, but significant, business form: the limited liability company, or LLC. The LLC is rapidly becoming an attractive alternative to the traditional corporate form. The limited liability partnership, or LLP, which is a variation of the LLC, is also discussed in this chapter.

▌ The Entrepreneur's Options

One of the questions faced by any entrepreneur who wishes to start up a business is what form of business organization she or he should choose for the business endeavor. The three basic organizational options are a sole proprietorship, a partnership (general or limited), or a corporation. Other organizational forms exist, but for the most part they are hybrid organizations—that is, they have characteristics similar to those of partnerships or corporations or they combine features of both.

A *joint venture*, for example, is treated much like a partnership, but it differs in that its creation is in contemplation of a limited activity or a single transaction. The form of a *syndicate* or an *investment group* can vary considerably. They may exist as corporations or as general or limited partnerships. In some cases, the members merely own property jointly and have no legally recognized business arrangement. The *joint stock company* is a true hybrid of a partnership and a corporation. It is similar to a corporation in that it is a shareholder organization; because of the personal liability of its members and other characteristics, however, it is usually treated like a partnership.

The *business trust*, a popular form of business organization in nineteenth-century America, is somewhat similar to the corporation. Although legal ownership and management of the property of the business stay with one or more of the trustees, the beneficiaries—who receive profits from the enterprise—are not personally responsible for the debts or obligations of the business trust, and in some states business trusts must pay corporate taxes. The *cooperative* is a nonprofit organization formed to provide an economic service to its members. Unincorporated cooperatives are often treated like partnerships; incorporated cooperatives, as with all corporations, are subject to state corporate law.

One can also venture into business by purchasing a franchise. About 25 percent of all retail sales and an increasing part of the gross national product of the United States are generated by private franchises. A **franchise** is any arrangement in which the owner of a trademark, a trade name, or a copyright has licensed others to use the trademark, trade name, or copyright in selling goods or services. As a **franchisee** (a purchaser of a franchise), you are generally legally independent of, but economically dependent on, the integrated business system of the **franchisor** (the seller of the franchise). In other words, you can operate as an independent businessperson but still obtain the advantages of a regional or national organization. Well-known franchises include Hilton Hotels, McDonald's, and Burger King. Franchising is not so much a *form* of business organization as a way of doing business. Sole proprietorships, partnerships, and corporations can all buy and sell franchises.

▌ Sole Proprietorships

The simplest form of business is a **sole proprietorship.** In this form, the owner is the business; thus, anyone who does business without cre-

ating a separate business organization has a sole proprietorship. Sole proprietorships constitute over two-thirds of all American businesses. They are also usually small enterprises—about 1 percent of the sole proprietorships existing in the United States have revenues that exceed $1 million per year. Sole proprietors can own and manage any type of business from an informal, home-office undertaking to a large restaurant or construction firm.

A major advantage of the sole proprietorship is that the proprietor receives all of the profits (because he or she assumes all of the risk). In addition, it is often easier and less costly to start a sole proprietorship than to start any other kind of business, as few legal forms are involved. This type of business organization also entails more flexibility than does a partnership or a corporation. The sole proprietor is free to make any decision he or she wishes to concerning the business—whom to hire, when to take a vacation, what kind of business to pursue, and so on. A sole proprietor pays only personal income taxes on profits, which are reported as personal income on the proprietor's personal income tax form. Sole proprietors are also allowed to establish tax-exempt retirement accounts in the form of Keogh plans.[1]

The major disadvantage of the sole proprietorship is that, as sole owner, the proprietor alone bears the burden of any losses or liabilities incurred by the business enterprise. In other words, the sole proprietor has unlimited liability, or legal responsibility, for all obligations incurred in doing business. This unlimited liability is a major factor to be considered in choosing a business form. Another disadvantage is that the proprietor's opportunity to raise capital is limited to personal funds and the funds of those who are willing to make loans. The sole proprietorship also has the disadvantage of lacking continuity upon the death of the proprietor. When the owner dies, so does the business—it is automatically dissolved. If the business is transferred to family members or other heirs, a new proprietorship is created.

---

1. A *Keogh plan* is a retirement program designed for self-employed persons through which a certain percentage of their income can be contributed to the plan, and interest earnings will not be taxed until funds are withdrawn from the plan.

▌ Partnerships

A **partnership** arises from an agreement, express or implied, between two or more persons to carry on a business for profit. When two or more persons agree to do business as partners, they enter into a special relationship with one another. To an extent, their relationship is similar to an agency relationship, because each partner is deemed to be the agent of the other partners and of the partnership. The agency concepts outlined in Chapter 21 thus apply—specifically, the imputation of knowledge of, and responsibility for, acts done within the scope of the partnership relationship. In their relations with one another, partners, like agents, are bound by fiduciary ties.

In one important way, however, partnership law is distinct from agency law. A partnership is based on a voluntary contract between two or more competent persons who agree to place money, labor, and skill in a business with the understanding that profits and losses will be shared. In a non-partnership agency relationship, the agent usually does not have an ownership interest in the business, nor is he or she obliged to bear a portion of the ordinary business losses.

The Uniform Partnership Act (UPA) governs the operation of partnerships *in the absence of express agreement* and has done much to reduce controversies in the law relating to partnerships. Except for Louisiana, all of the states, as well as the District of Columbia, have adopted the UPA. The entire text of the UPA is presented in Appendix D of this book. A revised version of the UPA, known as the Revised Uniform Partnership Act (RUPA), was formally adopted by the National Conference of Commissioners on Uniform State Laws in 1992 and has already been adopted in some states. The RUPA significantly changes some of the rules governing partnerships. We indicate the most important changes in footnotes throughout this chapter.

▌ Definition of Partnership

Conflicts commonly arise over whether a business enterprise is legally a partnership, especially in the absence of a formal, written partnership agreement. The UPA defines a *partnership* as "an asso-

ciation of two or more persons to carry on as co-owners a business for profit" [UPA 6(1)]. The *intent* to associate is a key element of a partnership, and one cannot join a partnership unless all other partners consent [UPA 18(g)].

Partnership Status

In resolving disputes over whether partnership status exists, courts will usually look for the following three essential elements of partnership implicit in the UPA's definition of the term:

1. A sharing of profits and losses.
2. A joint ownership of the business.
3. An equal right in the management of the business.

If the evidence in a particular case is insufficient to establish all three factors, the UPA provides a set of guidelines to be used. For example, the sharing of profits and losses from a business is considered *prima facie* ("on the face of it") evidence that a partnership has been created. No such inference is made, however, if the profits were received as payment of any of the following [UPA 7(4)]:

1. A debt by installments or interest on a loan.
2. Wages of an employee.
3. Rent to a landlord.
4. An annuity to a widow or representative of a deceased partner.
5. A sale of goodwill of a business or property.

Joint ownership of property, obviously, does not in and of itself create a partnership. Therefore, if Ablat and Burke own real property as joint tenants or as tenants in common (forms of joint ownership, to be discussed in Chapter 28), this does not mean that they are partners in a partnership. In fact, the sharing of gross returns and even profits from such ownership is usually not enough to create a partnership [UPA 7(2), (3)]. Thus, if Ablat and Burke jointly own a piece of rural property and lease the land to a farmer, the sharing of the profits from the farming operation conducted by the farmer in lieu of set rental payments would ordinarily not make Ablat, Burke, and the farmer partners. Note, though, that although the sharing of profits in itself does not prove the existence of a partnership, sharing *both profits and losses* usually does.

In the following case, three brothers and their sister bought a ranch from their parents. They owned the property as tenants in common. The issue was whether their ownership was a partnership.

CASE 23.1

Leavell v. Linn

Supreme Court of Wyoming, 1994.
884 P.2d 1364.

FACTS Connie, Bennie, Peter, and Eugene Linn agreed, in writing, to buy a ranch from their parents. The intent was to keep the property in the family, not to run the ranch as a business for profit. The siblings decided specifically not to form a partnership, but they routinely referred to themselves as "partners," and each year they filed a partnership tax return. Many years later, Connie and her husband, Harold Leavell, wanted to obtain sole ownership of a large part of the ranch. When the brothers refused to accommodate their sister, the Leavells filed a suit against the brothers and their spouses in a Wyoming state court. Among other things, the Leavells sought to have the siblings' ownership of the ranch declared to be a partnership (so that the property could then be divided according to partnership law, which the Leavells believed would be to their advantage). The court concluded that there was no partnership. The Leavells appealed to the Supreme Court of Wyoming.

ISSUE Did a partnership exist among the siblings?

DECISION No. The Supreme Court of Wyoming affirmed the lower court's decision.

REASON The state supreme court pointed out that one of the basic indications of partnership status was lacking: the agreement to carry on a business as co-owners for a profit. The court held that "the most obvious inference which might be drawn from the evidence" in this case is that "the agreement entered into by this family was not one intended to be a business for profit." The court also emphasized that the siblings did not intend to form a partnership when they bought the ranch. "While it cannot be denied that the agreement in question has many of the characteristics which might also be found in a partnership agreement," reasoned the court, "on its face it is not a partnership agreement." The court pointed out that the agreement did not use the words "partner" or "partnership" and that "the parties specifically decided not to form a partnership." The court concluded that "unless the intent is clearly proved, this court will not construe a family arrangement as a partnership. *   *   * It is in just such circumstances of disagreement and disarray as those in which this family finds itself that it is especially important to read and strictly construe formal agreements."

FOR CRITICAL ANALYSIS—Economic Consideration *Which, if any, of the requirements for the creation of a partnership did the agreement among the Linn siblings satisfy?*

Entity versus Aggregate

A partnership is sometimes called a *firm* or a *company*, terms that connote an entity separate and apart from its aggregate members. Sometimes the law of partnership recognizes a partnership as an *independent entity*, but for most other purposes, the law treats it as an *aggregate of the individual partners*.

At common law, a partnership was never treated as a separate legal entity. Thus, at common law a suit could never be brought by or against the firm in its own name; each individual partner had to sue or be sued. Today, most states provide specifically that the partnership can be treated as an entity for certain purposes. For example, a partnership usually can sue or be sued, collect judgments, and have all accounting procedures in the name of the partnership entity. In addition, the UPA recognizes that partnership property may be held in the name of the partnership rather than in the names of the individual partners. Finally, federal procedural laws frequently permit the partnership to be treated as an entity in such matters as suits in federal courts, bankruptcy proceedings, and informational federal tax returns.

When the partnership is not regarded as a separate legal entity, it is treated as an aggregate of the individual partners. For example, for federal income tax purposes, a partnership is not a taxpaying entity. The income and losses it incurs are passed through the partnership framework and attributed to the partners on their individual tax returns.

▌Partnership Formation

A partnership is ordinarily formed by an explicit agreement among the parties, although the law recognizes another form of partnership—*partnership by estoppel*—which arises when persons who are not partners represent themselves as partners when dealing with third parties. This section will describe the requirements for the creation of a partnership, including references to the liability of alleged partners.

The Partnership Agreement

As a general rule, agreements to form a partnership can be oral, written, or implied by conduct. Some partnership agreements, however, must be in writing to be legally enforceable within the Statute of Frauds (discussed in Chapter 10). For example, a partnership agreement that, by its terms, is to continue for more than one year must be evidenced by a sufficient writing.

A partnership agreement, called **articles of partnership**, usually specifies the name and location of the business, the duration of the partnership, the purpose of the business, each partner's share of the profits, how the partnership will be managed, how assets will be distributed on dissolution, and other provisions. As mentioned, the UPA applies only in the absence of the parties' agreement on a particular issue. The partnership agreement is thus binding on the parties, even if certain provisions, such as the distribution of profits, seem to be unfair. A sample partnership agreement is shown in Exhibit 23–1.[2]

Partnership Duration

The partnership agreement can specify the duration of the partnership in terms of a date or the completion of a particular project. A partnership that is specifically limited in duration is called a *partnership for a term*. A dissolution without the consent of all the partners prior to the expiration of the partnership term constitutes a breach of the agreement, and the responsible partner can be liable for any losses resulting from it. If no fixed duration is specified, the partnership is a *partnership at will*. This type of partnership can be dissolved at any time by any partner without violating the agreement and without incurring liability for losses to other partners resulting from the termination.

The Corporation as Partner

General partners are personally liable for the debts incurred by the partnership. If one of the general partners is a corporation, however, what does personal liability mean? Basically, the capacity of corporations to contract is a question of corporation law. Many states have restrictions on corporations becoming partners, although such restrictions have become less common over the years. The Revised

---

2. The RUPA provides for the voluntary filing of a partnership statement, containing such information as the agency authority of the partners, with the secretary of state. The statement must be executed by at least two partners, a copy must be sent to all of the partners, and a certified copy must be filed in the office for recording transfers of real property (in most states, in the county in which the property is located).

◆ **Exhibit 23–1**
A Sample Partnership Agreement

PARTNERSHIP AGREEMENT

This agreement, made and entered into as of the _____ , by and among _____
_____ (hereinafter collectively sometimes referred to as "Partners").

WITNESSETH:

Whereas, the Parties hereto desire to form a General Partnership (hereinafter referred to as the "Partnership"), for the term and upon the conditions hereinafter set forth;

Now, therefore, in consideration of the mutual covenants hereinafter contained, it is agreed by and among the Parties hereto as follows:

Article I
BASIC STRUCTURE

Form. The Parties hereby form a General Partnership pursuant to the Laws of _____
_____.

Name. The business of the Partnership shall be conducted under the name of _____
_____.

Place of Business. The principal office and place of business of the Partnership shall be located at _____ , or such other place as the Partners may from time to time designate.

Term. The Partnership shall commence on _____ , and shall continue for _____ years, unless earlier terminated in the following manner: (a) By the completion of the purpose intended, or (b) Pursuant to this Agreement, or (c) By applicable _____ law, or (d) By death, insanity, bankruptcy, retirement, withdrawal, resignation, expulsion, or disability of all of the then Partners.

Purpose—General. The purpose for which the Partnership is organized is _____
_____ .

Article II
FINANCIAL ARRANGEMENTS

Each Partner has contributed to the initial capital of the Partnership property in the amount and form indicated on Schedule A attached hereto and made a part hereof. Capital contributions to the Partnership shall not earn interest. An individual capital account shall be maintained for each Partner. If at any time during the existence of the Partnership it shall become necessary to increase the capital with which the said Partnership is doing business, then (upon the vote of the Managing Partner(s)): each party to this Agreement shall contribute to the capital of this Partnership within _____ days notice of such need in an amount according to his then Percentage Share of Capital as called for by the Managing Partner(s).

The Percentage Share of Profits and Capital of each Partner shall be (unless otherwise modified by the terms of this Agreement) as follows:

Names	Initial Percentage Share of Profits and Capital

No interest shall be paid on any contribution to the capital of the Partnership. No Partner shall have the right to demand the return of his capital contributions except as herein provided. Except as herein provided, the individual Partners shall have no right to any priority over each other as to the return of capital contributions except as herein provided.

Distributions to the Partners of net operating profits of the Partnership, as hereinafter defined, shall be made at _____ . Such contributions shall be made to the Partners simultaneously.

For the purpose of this Agreement, net operating profit for any accounting period shall mean the gross receipts of the Partnership for such period, less the sum of all cash expenses of operation of the Partnership, and such sums as may be necessary to establish a reserve for operating expenses. In determining net operating profit, deductions for depreciation, amortization, or other similar charges not requiring actual current expenditures of cash shall *not* be taken into account in accordance with generally accepted accounting principles.

(Continued)

♦ **Exhibit 23–1**
A Sample Partnership Agreement—Continued

No partner shall be entitled to receive any compensation from the Partnership, nor shall any Partner receive any drawing account from the Partnership.

Article III
MANAGEMENT

The Managing Partner(s) shall be ———————————————————.
The Managing Partner(s) shall have the right to vote as to the management and conduct of the business of the Partnership as follows:

Names   **Vote**

Article IV
DISSOLUTION

In the event that the Partnership shall hereafter be dissolved for any reason whatsoever, a full and general account of its assets, liabilities and transactions shall at once be taken. Such assets may be sold and turned into cash as soon as possible and all debts and other amounts due the Partnership collected. The proceeds thereof shall thereupon be applied as follows:
    (a) To discharge the debts and liabilities of the Partnership and the expenses of liquidation.
    (b) To pay each Partner or his legal representative any unpaid salary, drawing account, interest or profits to which he shall then be entitled and in addition, to repay to any Partner his capital contributions in excess of his original capital contribution.
    (c) To divide the surplus, if any, among the Partners or their representatives as follows: (1) First (to the extent of each Partner's then capital account) in proportion to their then capital accounts. (2) Then according to each Partner's then Percentage Share of [*Capital/Income*].
No Partner shall have the right to demand and receive property in kind for his distribution.

Article V
MISCELLANEOUS

The Partnership's fiscal year shall commence on January 1st of each year and shall end on December 31st of each year. Full and accurate books of account shall be kept at such place as the Managing Partner(s) may from time to time designate, showing the condition of the business and finances of the Partnership; and each Partner shall have access to such books of account and shall be entitled to examine them at any time during ordinary business hours. At the end of each year, the Managing Partner(s) shall cause the Partnership's accountant to prepare a balance sheet setting forth the financial position of the Partnership as of the end of that year and a statement of operations (income and expenses) for that year. A copy of the balance sheet and statement of operations shall be delivered to each Partner as soon as it is available.

Each Partner shall be deemed to have waived all objections to any transaction or other facts about the operation of the Partnership disclosed in such balance sheet and/or statement of operations unless he shall have notified the Managing Partner(s) in writing of his objections within thirty (30) days of the date on which statement is mailed.

The Partnership shall maintain a bank account or bank accounts in the Partnership's name in a national or state bank in the State of ———————————. Checks and drafts shall be drawn on the Partnership's bank account for Partnership purposes only and shall be signed by the Managing Partner(s) or their designated agent.

Any controversy or claim arising out of or relating to this Agreement shall only be settled by arbitration in accordance with the rules of the American Arbitration Association, one Arbitrator, and shall be enforceable in any court having competent jurisdiction.

Witnesses   **Partners**

———————————————————   ———————————————————

———————————————————   ———————————————————

Date: ——————————

Model Business Corporation Act (discussed in Chapter 24), however, generally allows corporations to make contracts and incur liabilities, and the UPA specifically permits a corporation to be a partner. By definition, "a partnership is an association of two or more persons," and the UPA defines *person* as including corporations [UPA 2].

Partnership by Estoppel

Parties who are not partners sometimes represent themselves as such and cause third persons to rely on their representations. The law of partnership does not confer any partnership rights on these persons, but it may impose liability on them. This is also true when a partner represents, expressly or impliedly, that a nonpartner is a member of the firm. Whenever a third person has reasonably and detrimentally relied on the representation that a nonpartner was part of the partnership, *partnership by estoppel* is deemed to exist. When this occurs, the nonpartner is regarded as an agent whose acts are binding on the partnership. In the following case, an attorney's corporate client claimed to have relied on a representation that the attorney was a partner in a law firm.

CASE 23.2

Atlas Tack Corp. v. Dimasi

Appeals Court of Massachusetts, Suffolk, 1994.
37 Mass.App.Ct. 66, 637 N.E.2d 230.

FACTS Attorneys Salvatore DiMasi, Ralph Donabed, and Stephen Karll shared office space, which they designated the "Law Offices of DiMasi, Donabed, & Karll, A Professional Association." They also shared stationery that bore the same heading and that listed their names, along with the names of other attorneys, in the margin. Atlas Tack Corporation hired Donabed to handle a certain legal matter. All correspondence and invoices from Donabed to Atlas were on the "Law Offices" stationery, and Atlas's payment for the services was in the form of checks payable to "DiMasi, Donabed & Karll." Believing that Donabed had done something wrong in his handling of its matter, Atlas filed a suit in a Massachusetts state court against Donabed, DiMasi, and Karll. Donabed settled out of court, but Atlas maintained the suit against DiMasi and Karll, alleging that they were Donabed's partners and were thus liable for Donabed's acts. The court granted the defendants' motion for summary judgment, and Atlas appealed.

ISSUE Can the members of a professional association be considered partners by estoppel?

DECISION Yes. The Appeals Court of Massachusetts reversed the lower court's judgment and remanded the case for trial.

REASON The appeals court pointed out that DiMasi and Karll consented to Donabed's use of stationery with the heading "DiMasi, Donabed & Karll," as well as the legend "a professional association" and a list in the margin of attorneys "including themselves [and] Donabed." The court pointed out that the bills to Atlas came on stationery with this letterhead, with no indication that payment should be made to Donabed specifically "or that the bill was submitted by Donabed instead of the law office of DiMasi, Donabed & Karll." The court also reasoned that "the use of the term 'professional association' may well suggest a partnership to the public * * *. At the very least, the use of the term in the circumstances of this case presents a question * * * as to whether a partnership by estoppel exists."

FOR CRITICAL ANALYSIS—Social Consideration *What could the members of a professional association do to avoid liability for the wrongful acts of other members?*

▌Rights among Partners

The rights and duties of partners are governed largely by the specific terms of their partnership agreement. In the absence of provisions to the contrary in the partnership agreement, the law imposes the rights and duties discussed here. The character and nature of the partnership business generally influence the application of these rights and duties.

Interest in the Partnership

A partner's interest in the partnership is a personal asset consisting of a proportionate share of the profits earned [UPA 26] and a return of capital after the partnership is terminated. Each partner is entitled to the proportion of business profits and losses designated in the partnership agreement.

PROFITS AND LOSSES   If the agreement does not apportion profits or losses, the UPA provides that *profits shall be shared equally* and *losses shall be shared in the same ratio as profits* [UPA 18(a)]. To illustrate: The partnership agreement for Ponce and Brent provides for capital contributions of $6,000 from Ponce and $4,000 from Brent, but it is silent as to how Ponce and Brent will share profits or losses. In this situation, Ponce and Brent will share both profits and losses equally. If the partnership agreement provided for profits to be shared in the same ratio as capital contributions, however, 60 percent of the profits would go to Ponce, and 40 percent of the profits would go to Brent. If their partnership agreement was silent as to losses, losses would be shared in the same ratio as profits (60 percent to 40 percent).

ASSIGNMENT OF PARTNERSHIP INTEREST   A partner may assign (transfer) his or her interest in the partnership to another party. When a partner's interest is assigned, the assignee (the person to whom the interest was transferred) has the right to receive the partner's share of the profits and, on the partnership's termination, the partner's capital contribution. The assignee, however, does not become a partner in the partnership and thus has no say in the management or administration of the partnership affairs and no right to inspect the partnership books. Rather, the partner who assigned his or her interest remains a partner with the full rights of a

partner with respect to those rights that cannot be assigned.

CREDITOR'S LIEN ON PARTNERSHIP INTEREST   A partner's interest is also subject to a judgment creditor's lien (described in Chapter 20). A judgment creditor can attach a partner's interest by petitioning the court that entered the judgment to grant the creditor a **charging order.** This order entitles the creditor to the profits of the partner and to any assets available to the partner on the firm's dissolution [UPA 28].

Management Rights

Under the UPA, all partners have equal rights in managing the partnership [UPA 18(e)]. Each partner has one vote in management matters *regardless of the proportional size of his or her interest in the firm.* Often, in a large partnership, partners will agree to delegate daily management responsibilities to a management committee made up of one or more of the partners.

The majority rule controls decisions in ordinary matters connected with partnership business, unless otherwise specified in the agreement. Decisions to undertake any of the actions listed below, however, if they are to be binding on the partnership, require the *unanimous* consent of the partners. This is because these decisions significantly affect the nature of the partnership.

1.   To alter the essential nature of the firm's business as expressed in the partnership agreement or to alter the capital structure of the partnership.
2.   To admit new partners or to enter a wholly new business [UPA 18(g), (h)].
3.   To assign partnership property into a trust for the benefit of creditors.
4.   To dispose of the partnership's goodwill.
5.   To confess judgment against the partnership or to submit partnership claims to arbitration. (A **confession of judgment** is the act of a debtor in permitting a judgment to be entered against him or her by a creditor, for an agreed sum, without the institution of legal proceedings.)
6.   To undertake any act that would make further conduct of partnership business impossible [UPA 9(3)].
7.   To amend the articles of the partnership agreement.

Compensation

A partner has a duty to expend time, skill, and energy on behalf of the partnership business, and such services are generally not compensable in the form of a salary. Rather, as mentioned, a partner's income from the partnership takes the form of a distribution of profits according to the partner's share in the business. Partners can, however, agree otherwise. For example, the managing partner of a law firm often receives a salary in addition to his or her share of profits for performing special administrative duties in office and personnel management. When a partnership must be terminated because a partner dies, a surviving partner is entitled to reasonable compensation for services relating to the final settlement of partnership affairs (and reimbursement for expenses incurred in the process) above and apart from his or her share in the partnership profits [UPA 18(f)].

Each partner impliedly promises to subordinate his or her interests to those of the partnership. Assume that Hall, Banks, and Porter enter into a partnership. Porter undertakes independent consulting, in the same area in which the partnership specializes, for an outside firm without the consent of Hall and Banks. Porter's compensation from the outside firm is considered partnership income [UPA 21]. A partner cannot engage in any independent business that involves the partnership's time unless expressly agreed on by the partnership.

Inspection of Books

Partnership books and records must be kept accessible to all partners. Each partner has the right to receive (and each partner has the corresponding duty to produce) full and complete information concerning the conduct of all aspects of partnership business [UPA 20]. Each firm keeps books in which to record and preserve such information. Partners contribute the information, and a bookkeeper or an accountant typically has the duty to preserve it. The books must be kept at the firm's principal business office and cannot be removed without the consent of all of the partners [UPA 19]. Every partner, whether active or inactive, is entitled to inspect all books and records on demand and can make copies of the materials. The personal representative of a deceased partner's estate has the same right of access to partnership books and records that the decedent would have had.

Accounting of Assets

An accounting of partnership assets or profits is required to determine the value of each partner's share in the partnership. An accounting can be performed voluntarily, or it can be compelled by a court. Under UPA 22, a partner has the right to a formal accounting in the following situations:

1. When the partnership agreement provides for a formal accounting.
2. When a partner is wrongfully excluded from the business, from access to the books, or both.
3. When any partner is withholding profits or benefits belonging to the partnership in breach of the fiduciary duty.
4. When circumstances "render it just and reasonable."

Formal accounting also occurs by right in connection with *dissolution* proceedings (discussed later in this chapter). Generally, the principal remedy of a partner against co-partners is a suit for dissolution, an accounting, or both. With minor exceptions, a partner cannot maintain an action against other firm members for damages until partnership affairs are settled and an accounting is done. This rule is necessary because legal disputes between partners invariably involve conflicting claims to shares in the partnership. Logically, the value of each partner's share must first be determined by an accounting.

Property Rights

One of the property rights of partners—the right to a share of the profits made by the partnership—has already been discussed. A partner also has ownership rights in any real or personal property owned by the partnership. Property owned by the partnership, or *partnership property*, is defined by the UPA as "all property originally brought into the partnership's stock or subsequently acquired, by purchase or otherwise, on account of the partnership" [UPA 8(1)].

For example, in the formation of a partnership, a partner may bring into the partnership any property that he or she owns as a part of his or her capital contribution. This property becomes partnership property even though title to it may still be in the name of the contributing partner. The intention that certain assets are to be partnership assets is the heart of the phrase "on account of the partnership." Thus, the more closely an asset is associated with the business operations of the partnership, the more likely it is to be a partnership asset.[3]

UPA 25(1) states that partners are *tenants in partnership*. This means that every partner is a co-owner with all other partners of specific partnership property, such as office equipment, paper supplies, and vehicles. Each partner has equal rights to possess partnership property for business purposes or in satisfaction of firm debts, but not for any other purpose without the consent of all the other partners. Tenancy in partnership has several important effects. If a partner dies, the surviving partners, not the heirs of the deceased partner, have the right of survivorship to the specific property. Although surviving partners are entitled to possession, they have a duty to account to the decedent's estate for the *value* of the deceased partner's interest in the property [UPA 25(2)(d), (e)].

A partner has no right to sell, assign, or in any way deal with a particular item of partnership property as an exclusive owner [UPA 25(2)(a), (b)]. Therefore, creditors cannot use partnership property to satisfy the personal debts of a partner. Partnership property is available only to satisfy partnership debts, to enhance the firm's credit, or to achieve other business purposes of the partnership.

▌Duties and Liabilities of Partners

The duties and liabilities of partners are basically derived from agency law. Each partner is an agent of every other partner and acts as both a principal and an agent in any business transaction within the scope of the partnership agreement. Each partner is also a general agent of the partnership in carrying out the usual business of the firm.[4] Thus, every act of a partner concerning partnership business and every contract signed in the partnership name bind the firm [UPA 9(1)]. The UPA affirms general principles of agency law that pertain to the authority of a partner to bind a partnership in contract or tort.

We examine here the fiduciary duties of partners, the authority of partners, the joint and several liability that characterizes partnerships, and the limitations imposed on the liability of incoming partners for preexisting partnership debts.

Fiduciary Duties

Partners stand in a fiduciary relationship to one another just as principals and agents do (see Chapter 21). A fiduciary relationship is one of extraordinary trust and loyalty. Each partner has a fiduciary duty to act in good faith and for the benefit of the partnership. Each partner must also subordinate his or her personal interests to those of the partnership if a conflict of interests arises.[5]

This fiduciary duty underlies the entire body of law pertaining to partnership and agency. From it, certain other duties are commonly implied. Thus, a partner must account to the partnership for personal profits or benefits derived from any partnership transaction that is undertaken without the consent of all of the partners.[6] The following case illustrates this underlying principle of partnership law.

---

3. Under the RUPA, property that is not acquired in the name of the partnership is nonetheless partnership property if the instrument transferring title either refers to (1) a person who is taking title as a partner or (2) indicates the existence of the partnership [RUPA 204(a)(2)]. Also, the property is presumed to be partnership property if it is acquired with partnership funds [RUPA 204(c)]. If none of the above occurs, the property is presumed to be the property of individual partners, even if it is used in the partnership business [RUPA 204(d)].

4. The RUPA adds "or business of the kind carried on by the partnership" [RUPA 301(1)]. Basically, this addition gives added protection to third persons who deal with an unfamiliar partnership.
5. The RUPA states that partners may pursue their own interests without automatically violating their fiduciary duties [RUPA 404(e)].
6. In this sense, to account to the partnership means not only to divulge the information but also to determine the value of any benefits or profits derived and to hold that money or property in trust on behalf of the partnership.

CASE 23.3

Murphy v. Canion

Court of Appeals of Texas—
Houston (14th District), 1990.
797 S.W.2d 944.

FACTS David Murphy and James Canion formed a partnership to conduct real estate business. A provision in their partnership agreement provided that all personal earnings from personal services would be included as partnership income and that any real estate or other partnership business conducted by either partner during the term of the partnership agreement should be for the joint account of the partnership. Through his business associates and contacts, Canion learned of several profitable real estate opportunities. Canion never informed Murphy of these opportunities but instead secretly took advantage of them for his own gain. When Murphy found out about Canion's activities, he told Canion that he was canceling the partnership under a clause in the partnership agreement that allowed termination by a partner with ninety days' notice. In the lawsuit that followed, Murphy alleged that Canion had breached the partnership agreement and his fiduciary duty to the partnership. The trial court agreed with Murphy and awarded him, as damages, half of the profits made by Canion from certain real estate sales made by Canion without Murphy's knowledge. On appeal, Canion contended, among other things, that because he received income from those sales only after the partnership had been terminated, Murphy had no claim to that income.

ISSUE Is Murphy entitled to his share of the income received by Canion after the partnership's termination?

DECISION Yes. The appellate court affirmed the trial court's ruling that Murphy had a right to his share of the income, even though it was received by Canion after the partnership had ended.

REASON The appellate court concluded, as had the trial court, that the income Canion received after the partnership's dissolution resulted from efforts undertaken during the life of the partnership. By these efforts, Canion had taken advantage of partnership opportunities secretly, for his self-gain, in breach of his fiduciary duty to Murphy. Therefore, Murphy had a right to his share of the profits from Canion's usurpation of partnership opportunities.

FOR CRITICAL ANALYSIS—Historical Consideration *How does the imposition of fiduciary duties on partners affect the value of the partnership as a business form?*

Authority of Partners

Agency concepts relating to actual authority (express and implied), apparent authority, and ratification are also applicable to partnerships. In an ordinary partnership, firm members can exercise all implied powers reasonably necessary and customary to carry on that particular business. Some customarily implied powers include the authority to make warranties on goods in the sales business,

the power to convey real property in the firm's name when such conveyances are part of the ordinary course of partnership business, the power to enter into contracts consistent with the firm's regular course of business, and the power to make admissions and representations concerning partnership affairs [UPA 11].

When a partner acts within the scope of authority, the partnership is bound to third parties by these acts. For example, a partner's authority to sell partnership products carries with it the implied authority to transfer title and to make the usual warranties. Hence, in a partnership that operates a retail tire store, any partner negotiating a contract with a customer for the sale of a set of tires can warrant that "each tire will be warranted for normal wear for 40,000 miles."

This same partner, however, does not have the authority to sell office equipment, fixtures, or the partnership office building without the consent of all of the other partners. In addition, because partnerships are formed to create profits, a partner does not generally have the authority to make charitable contributions without the consent of the other partners. Such actions are not binding on the partnership unless they are ratified by all of the other partners.

As in the law of agency, the law of partnership imputes one partner's knowledge to all other partners, because members of a partnership stand in a fiduciary relationship to one another. This relationship implies that each partner will fully disclose to every other partner all information pertaining to the business of the partnership.

Joint Liability

In most states, partners are subject to joint liability on partnership debts and contracts [UPA 15(b)]. **Joint liability** means that if a third party sues a partner on, for example, a partnership debt, the partner has the right to insist that the other partners be sued with him or her. If the third party does not sue all of the partners, the partners sued cannot be required to pay a judgment, and the assets of the partnership cannot be used to satisfy the judgment. (Similarly, a release of one partner releases all partners.) In other words, to bring a successful claim against the partnership on a debt or contract, a plaintiff must name all the partners as defendants.

To simplify this rule, some states, such as California, have enacted statutes providing that a partnership may be sued in its own name and that a judgment will bind the partnership's and the individual partners' property even though not all the partners are named in the complaint. If the third party is successful, he or she may collect on the judgment against the assets of one or more of the partners. Otherwise stated, each partner is liable and may be required to pay the entire amount of the judgment. When one partner pays the entire amount, the partnership is required to indemnify

that partner [UPA 18(b)]. If the partnership cannot do so, the obligation falls on the other partners.

Joint and Several Liability

In some states, partners are both jointly liable and *severally*, or individually, liable for partnership debts and contracts. In all states, partners are jointly and severally liable for torts and breaches of trust [UPA 15(a)].[7] **Joint and several liability** means that a third party may sue any one or more of the partners without suing all of them or the partnership itself. In other words, a third party may sue one or more of the partners separately (severally) or all of the partners together (jointly), at his or her option. This is true even if the partner did not participate in, ratify, or know about whatever it was that gave rise to the cause of action.[8]

A judgment against one partner on his or her several liability does not extinguish the others' liability. (Similarly, a release of one partner discharges the partners' joint but not several liability.) Thus, those not sued in the first action may be sued subsequently. The first action, however, may have been conclusive on the question of liability. If, for example, in an action against one partner, the court held that the partnership was in no way liable, the third party cannot bring an action against another partner and succeed on the issue of the partnership's liability.

If the third party is successful, he or she may collect on the judgment only against the assets of those partners named as defendants. The partner who committed the tort is required to indemnify the partnership for any damages it pays.

Liability of Incoming Partner

A newly admitted partner to an existing partnership normally has limited liability for whatever debts and obligations the partnership incurred prior to the new partner's admission. The new partner's liability can be satisfied only from partnership assets [UPA 17]. This means that the new partner usually has no personal liability for these debts and obliga-

---

7. Under the RUPA, partners' liability is joint and several for all debts [RUPA 306].
8. The RUPA prevents creditors from bringing an action to collect debts from the partners of a nonbankrupt partnership without first attempting unsuccessfully to collect from the partnership (or convincing a court that the attempt would be unsuccessful) [RUPA 307(d)].

tions, but any capital contribution made by him or her to the partnership is subject to these debts.

In cases involving old debts and new partners, there are two dates of great significance: the date on which the debt arose and the date on which the partner joined the firm. The court in the following case had to determine the date on which a partnership debt arose.

CASE 23.4

Citizens Bank of Massachusetts v. Parham-Woodman Medical Associates

United States District Court, Eastern District of Virginia, Richmond Division, 1995. 874 F.Supp. 705.

FACTS   The Citizens Bank of Massachusetts agreed to lend Parham-Woodman Medical Associates, a partnership, $2 million to construct a new office building. Their agreement, which was signed on April 30, 1985, provided for the money to be disbursed in installments. Most of the funds had been disbursed before Richard Hunley, Nada Tas, and Joseph Tas joined the firm. When the partnership failed to repay the loan, the bank sold the building and obtained a deficiency judgment for more than $1.2 million. The bank filed a suit in a federal district court against the firm and the partners to recover this amount.

ISSUE   Were the partners who joined the firm after the date of the loan, but before disbursement of all of the funds, liable for the debt beyond the amount of their interest in partnership assets?

DECISION   No. The court held that Hunley and the Tases were liable only to the extent of the partnership property.

REASON   The court noted that UPA 17 makes an incoming partner liable for "all the obligations of the partnership arising before his admission" but provides that "this liability shall be satisfied only out of partnership property." The court concluded that "a partnership obligation arises * * * when the creditor extends the credit to the partnership." In this case, "that occurred on April 30, 1985 and not on the occasion when the bank disbursed each advance." In other words, "long before Dr. Hunley and the Tases joined Parham-Woodman," the loan documents "were binding obligations on both Citizens Bank and the partnership. That is not changed," said the court, "merely because the passage of part of the consideration was delayed pursuant to a schedule which also was set before Dr. Hunley and the Tases became partners."

FOR CRITICAL ANALYSIS—Economic Consideration   *Does the rule of UPA 17 favor debtors or creditors? Why?*

▍Partnership Termination

Any change in the relations of the partners that demonstrates unwillingness or inability to carry on partnership business dissolves the partnership, resulting in termination [UPA 29]. If one of the partners wishes to continue the business, he or she is free to reorganize into a new partnership with the remaining members.

The termination of a partnership has two stages, both of which must take place before termination is complete. The first stage, **dissolution,** occurs when any partner (or partners) indicates an intention to disassociate from the partnership. The second stage, **winding up,**[9] is the actual process of collecting and distributing the partnership assets.

---

9.   Although "winding down" would seem to describe more accurately the process of settling accounts and liquidating the assets of a partnership, "winding up" has been traditionally used in English and U.S. statutory and case law to denote this final stage of a partnership's existence.

Dissolution

Dissolution of a partnership can be brought about by the acts of the partners, by the operation of law, and by judicial decree. Each of these events will be discussed here.

DISSOLUTION BY ACTS OF PARTNERS   Dissolution of a partnership may come about through the acts of the partners in several ways. First, the partnership can be dissolved by the partners' agreement. For example, when a partnership agreement expresses a fixed term or a particular business objective to be accomplished, the passing of the date or the accomplishment of the objective dissolves the partnership.

Second, because a partnership is a voluntary association, a partner has the power to disassociate himself or herself from the partnership at any time and thus dissolve the partnership. Any change in the partnership, whether by the withdrawal of a partner or by the admission of a new partner, results in dissolution.[10] In practice, this is modified by the provision that the remaining or new partners may continue in the firm's business. Nonetheless, a new partnership arises. Creditors of the prior partnership become creditors of the new partnership [UPA 41].

Finally, the UPA provides that neither a voluntary assignment of a partner's interest nor an involuntary sale of a partner's interest for the benefit of creditors [UPA 28] by itself dissolves the partnership. Either occurrence, however, can ultimately lead to judicial dissolution of the partnership (judicial dissolution will be discussed shortly).

DISSOLUTION BY OPERATION OF LAW   If one of the partners dies, the partnership is dissolved by operation of law, even if the partnership agreement provides for carrying on the business with the executor of the decedent's estate.[11] The bankruptcy of a partner will also dissolve a partnership, and naturally, the bankruptcy of the firm itself will result in dissolution.

Additionally, any event that makes it unlawful for the partnership to continue its business or for any partner to carry on in the partnership will result in dissolution. Note, however, that even if the illegality of the partnership business is a cause for dissolution, the partners can decide to change the nature of their business and continue in the partnership. When the illegality applies to an individual partner, then dissolution is mandatory. For example, suppose the state legislature passes a law making it illegal for judges to engage in the practice of law. If an attorney in a law firm is appointed a judge, the attorney must leave the law firm, and the partnership must be dissolved.

DISSOLUTION BY JUDICIAL DECREE   For dissolution of a partnership by judicial decree to occur, an application or petition must be made in an appropriate court. The court then either denies the petition or grants a decree of dissolution. UPA 32 cites situations in which a court can dissolve a partnership. One situation occurs when a partner is adjudicated mentally incompetent or is shown to be of unsound mind. Another situation arises when a partner appears incapable of performing his or her duties under the partnership agreement. If the incapacity is likely to be permanent and to affect substantially the partner's ability to discharge his or her duties to the firm, a court will dissolve the partnership by decree.

Dissolution may also be ordered by a court when it becomes obviously impractical for the firm to continue—for example, if the business can only be operated at a loss. Additionally, a partner's impropriety involving partnership business (for example, fraud perpetrated on the other partners) or improper behavior reflecting unfavorably on the firm may provide grounds for a judicial decree of dissolution. Finally, if dissension between partners becomes so persistent and harmful as to undermine the confidence and cooperation necessary to carry on the firm's business, dissolution may also be granted.

NOTICE OF DISSOLUTION   The intent to dissolve or to withdraw from a firm must be communicated clearly to each partner. A partner can express this notice of intent by either actions or words. All partners will share liability for the acts of any partner who continues conducting business for the firm without knowing that the partnership has been dissolved.

---

10.   The RUPA distinguishes the withdrawal of a partner that causes a breakup of a partnership from a withdrawal that causes only the end of a partner's participation in the business (and results in a buyout of that partner's interest) [RUPA 601, 701, 801]. Dissolution results only if the partnership must be liquidated [RUPA 801].

11.   Under the RUPA, the death of a partner represents that partner's "dissociation" from the partnership, but it is not an automatic ground for the partnership's dissolution [RUPA 601(7)].

Dissolution of a partnership by the act of a partner requires notice to all affected third persons as well. Any third person who has extended credit to the firm must receive *actual notice* (notice given to the party directly and personally). For all others, *constructive notice* (a newspaper announcement or similar public notice) is sufficient. Dissolution resulting from the operation of law generally requires no notice to third parties.[12]

Winding Up

Once dissolution occurs and the partners have been notified, the partners cannot create new obligations on behalf of the partnership. Their only authority is to complete transactions begun but not finished at the time of dissolution and to wind up the business of the partnership. *Winding up* includes collecting and preserving partnership assets, discharging liabilities (paying debts), and accounting to each partner for the value of his or her interest in the partnership.

Both creditors of the partnership and creditors of the individual partners can make claims on the partnership's assets. In general, creditors of the partnership have priority over creditors of individual partners in the distribution of partnership assets; the converse priority is usually followed in the distribution of individual partner assets, except under bankruptcy law. The priorities in the distribution of a partnership's assets are as follows:[13]

1. Payment of third party debts.
2. Refund of advances (loans) made to or for the firm by a partner.
3. Return of capital contribution to a partner.
4. Distribution of the balance, if any, to partners in accordance with their respective shares in the profits.

If the partnership's liabilities are greater than its assets, the partners bear the losses—in the absence of a contrary agreement—in the same proportion in which they shared the profits (rather than, for example, in proportion to their contributions to the

partnership's capital). Partners continue in their fiduciary relationship until the winding-up process is completed.

▎Limited Partnerships

In many ways, *limited partnerships* are like general partnerships, but they also differ from general partnerships in several ways. Because of this, they are sometimes referred to as *special partnerships*. **Limited partnerships** consist of at least one *general partner* and one or more *limited partners*. The **general partner** (or partners) assumes management responsibility for the partnership and so has full responsibility for the partnership and for all debts of the partnership. The **limited partner** (or partners) contributes cash (or other property) and owns an interest in the firm but does not undertake any management responsibilities and is not personally liable for partnership debts beyond the amount of his or her investment. A limited partner can forfeit limited liability by taking part in the management of the business. A comparison of the basic characteristics of partnerships appears in Exhibit 23–2.[14]

Until 1976, the law governing limited partnerships in all states except Louisiana was the Uniform Limited Partnership Act (ULPA) of 1916. In 1976, the ULPA was revised, and most states and the District of Columbia have adopted its revision, which is known as the Revised Uniform Limited Partnership Act (RULPA). Because the RULPA is the dominant law governing limited partnerships in the United States, we will refer to the RULPA in our discussion of limited partnerships.

Formation

Compared with the informal, private, and voluntary agreement that usually suffices for a general partnership, the formation of a limited partnership is a public and formal proceeding that must follow statutory requirements. A limited partnership must have at least one general partner and one limited

---

12. *Childers v. United States*, 442 F.2d 1299 (5th Cir. 1971).
13. Under the RUPA, partner creditors are included among creditors who take first priority [RUPA 808(a)]. Capital contributions and profits or losses are then calculated together to determine the amounts that the partners receive or the amounts that they must pay.

14. Under the RUPA, a general partnership can be converted into a limited partnership and vice versa [RUPA 901, 902]. The RUPA also provides for the merger of a general partnership with one or more general or limited partnerships under rules that are similar to those governing corporate mergers [RUPA 905].

♦ Exhibit 23–2
A Comparison of General Partnerships and Limited Partnerships

CHARACTERISTIC	GENERAL PARTNERSHIP (UPA)	LIMITED PARTNERSHIP (RULPA)
Creation	By agreement of two or more persons to carry on a business as co-owners for profit.	By agreement of two or more persons to carry on a business as co-owners for profit. Must include one or more general partners and one or more limited partners. Filing of a certificate with the secretary of state is required.
Sharing of Profits and Losses	By agreement; or, in the absence of agreement, profits are shared equally by the partners, and losses are shared in the same ratio as profits.	Profits are shared as required in the certificate agreement, and losses are shared likewise, up to the amount of the limited partners' capital contributions. In the absence of a provision in the certificate agreement, profits and losses are shared on the basis of percentages of capital contributions.
Liability	Unlimited personal liability of all partners.	Unlimited personal liability of all general partners; limited partners liable only to the extent of their capital contributions.
Capital Contribution	No minimum or mandatory amount; set by agreement.	Set by agreement.
Management	By agreement, or in the absence of agreement, all partners have an equal voice.	General partners by agreement, or else each has an equal voice. Limited partners have no voice or else are subject to liability as general partners (but *only* if a third party has reason to believe that the limited partner is a general partner). A limited partner may act as an agent or employee of the partnership and vote on amending the certificate or on the sale or dissolution of the partnership.
Duration	By agreement, or can be dissolved by action of the partners (withdrawal), operation of law (death or bankruptcy), or court decree.	By agreement in the certificate or by withdrawal, death, or mental incompetence of a general partner in the absence of the right of the other general partners to continue the partnership. Death of a limited partner, unless he or she is the only remaining limited partner, does not terminate the partnership.
Distribution of Assets on Liquidation—Order of Priorities	1. Outside creditors. 2. Partner creditors. 3. Partners, according to capital contributions. 4. Partners, according to profits.	1. Outside creditors and partner creditors. 2. Partners and former partners entitled to distributions before withdrawal under the agreement or the RULPA. 3. Partners, according to capital contributions. 4. Partners, according to profits.

partner, as mentioned previously. Additionally, the partners must sign a **certificate of limited partnership,** which requires information similar to that found in a corporate charter (see Chapter 24). The certificate must be filed with the designated state official—under the RULPA, the secretary of state. The certificate is usually open to public inspection.

Rights and Liabilities of Partners

General partners, unlike limited partners, are personally liable to the partnership's creditors; thus, at least one general partner is necessary in a limited partnership so that someone has personal liability. This policy can be circumvented in states that allow a corporation to be the general partner in a partnership. Because the corporation has limited liability by virtue of corporate laws, if a corporation is the general partner, no one in the limited partnership has personal liability.

RIGHTS OF LIMITED PARTNERS Subject to the limitations that will be discussed here, limited partners have essentially the same rights as general partners, including the right of access to partnership books and the right to other information regarding partnership business. Upon dissolution, limited partners are entitled to a return of their contributions in accordance with the partnership certificate [RULPA 201(a)(10)]. They can also assign their interests subject to the certificate [RULPA 702, 704].

The RULPA provides a limited partner with the right to sue an outside party on behalf of the firm if the general partners with authority to do so have refused to file suit [RULPA 1001]. In addition, investor protection legislation, such as securities laws (discussed in Chapter 27), may give some protection to limited partners.

LIABILITIES OF LIMITED PARTNERS In contrast to the virtually unlimited liability of a general partner for partnership indebtedness, the liability of a limited partner is limited to the capital that he or she contributes or agrees to contribute to the partnership [RULPA 502].

A limited partnership is formed by good faith compliance with the requirements for signing and filing the certificate, even if it is incomplete or defective. When a limited partner discovers a defect in the formation of the limited partnership,

he or she can avoid future liability by causing an appropriate amendment or certificate to be filed or by renouncing an interest in the profits of the partnership [RULPA 304]. If the limited partner takes neither of these actions on the discovery of the defect, however, the partner can be held personally liable by the firm's creditors. Liability for false statements in a partnership certificate runs in favor of persons relying on the false statements and against members who know of the falsity but still sign the certificate [RULPA 207].

LIMITED PARTNERS AND MANAGEMENT Limited partners enjoy limited liability so long as they do not participate in management [RULPA 303]. A limited partner who participates in management will be just as liable as a general partner to any creditor who transacts business with the limited partnership and believes, based on a limited partner's conduct, that the limited partner is a general partner [RULPA 303]. How much actual review and advisement a limited partner can engage in before being exposed to liability is an unsettled question.[15] A limited partner who knowingly permits his or her name to be used in the name of the limited partnership is liable to creditors who extend credit to the limited partnership without knowledge that the limited partner is not a general partner [RULPA 102, 303(d)].

Dissolution

A limited partnership is dissolved in much the same way as an ordinary partnership. The retirement, death, or mental incompetence of a general partner can dissolve the partnership, but not if the business can be continued by one or more of the other general partners in accordance with their certificate or by the consent of all of the members [RULPA 801]. The death or assignment of interest of a limited partner does not dissolve the limited partnership [RULPA 702, 704, 705]. A limited partnership can be dissolved by court decree [RULPA 802].

Bankruptcy or the withdrawal of a general partner dissolves a limited partnership. Bankruptcy of a limited partner, however, does not dissolve the partnership unless it causes the bankruptcy of the firm.

---

15. It is an unsettled question partly because there are differences among the laws in different states. Factors to be considered under the RULPA are listed in RULPA 303(b), (c).

The retirement of a general partner causes a dissolution unless the members consent to a continuation by the remaining general partners or unless this contingency is provided for in the certificate.

Upon dissolution, creditors' rights, including those of partners who are creditors, take first priority. Then partners and former partners receive unpaid distributions of partnership assets and, except as otherwise agreed, amounts representing returns on their contributions and amounts proportionate to their shares of the distributions [RULPA 804].

▉ Limited Liability Companies

The **limited liability company (LLC)** is a relatively new form of business enterprise that offers the limited liability of a corporation and the tax advantages of a partnership. Although LLCs have existed for over a century in other areas, including several European and South American nations, it was only in 1977 that they first appeared in the United States. In that year, Wyoming passed legislation authorizing the creation of an LLC. Interest in LLCs mushroomed after a 1988 ruling by the Internal Revenue Service (IRS) that Wyoming LLCs would be taxed as partnerships instead of as corporations. Because of this tax advantage, by 1997 all states had enacted LLC statutes.

Like the limited partnership, an LLC must be formed and operated in compliance with state law. To form an LLC, *articles of organization* must be filed with a central state agency, such as the secretary of state's office. The business's name must include the words "Limited Liability Company" or the initials "L.L.C."

A major advantage of the LLC is that it does not pay taxes as an entity; rather, profits are "passed through" the LLC and paid personally by the owners of the company, who are called *members*. Another advantage is that the liability of members is limited to the amount of their investments. In an LLC, members are allowed to participate fully in management activities, and under at least one state's statute, the firm's managers need not even be members of the LLC. Yet another advantage is that corporations and partnerships, as well as foreign investors, can be LLC members. Additionally, in contrast to S corporations, there is no limit on the number of shareholder-members of the LLC.

Finally, part of the LLC's attractiveness to businesspersons is the flexibility it offers. The members can themselves decide how to operate the various aspects of the business through a simple operating agreement.

The disadvantages of the LLC are relatively few. One disadvantage of the LLC is that state statutes are not uniform. For example, until state LLC statutes are revised to correspond to new IRS rules, as they probably will be in the near future, businesses must comply with existing requirements. Additionally, state laws may continue to vary with respect to *state* taxation.

▉ Limited Liability Partnerships

The **limited liability partnership (LLP)** is similar to the LLC. The difference between an LLP and an LLC is that the LLP is designed more for professionals who normally do business as partners in a partnership. The first state to enact an LLP statute was Texas, in 1991. Other states quickly followed suit, and by 1997, virtually all of the states had enacted LLP statutes. Like LLCs, LLPs must be formed and operated in compliance with state statutes. The appropriate form must be filed with a central state agency, usually the secretary of state's office, and the business's name must include either "Limited Liability Partnership" or "L.L.P."

The major advantage of the LLP is that it allows a partnership to continue as a pass-through entity for tax purposes but limits the personal liability of the partners for partnership tort liability. Consider a group of lawyers operating as a partnership. A client sues one of the attorneys for malpractice and wins a large judgment, and the firm's malpractice insurance is insufficient to cover the obligation. Under traditional partnership law, the partners are jointly and severally (individually) liable. This means, in the example here, that when the attorney's personal assets are exhausted, the personal assets of the other, innocent partners can be used to satisfy the judgment.

Although LLP statutes vary from state to state, generally each state statute limits in some way the liability of partners. For example, Delaware law protects each innocent partner from the "debts and obligations of the partnership arising from negligence, wrongful acts, or misconduct." In North Carolina, Texas, and Washington, D.C., the statutes protect innocent partners from obligations rising from "errors, omissions, negligence, incompetence, or malfeasance."

In most states, it is relatively easy to convert a traditional partnership into an LLP because the firm's basic organizational structure remains the same. Additionally, all of the statutory and common law rules governing partnerships still apply (apart from those modified by the LLP statute). Normally, LLP statutes are simply amendments to a state's already existing partnership law.

Besides professional services firms, such as accounting firms and law firms, family businesses are expected, more than others, to use the LLP. A **family limited liability partnership (FLLP)** is a limited liability partnership in which the majority of the partners are persons related to each other, essentially as spouses, parents, grandparents, siblings, cousins, nephews, or nieces. A person acting in a fiduciary capacity for persons so related can also be a partner. All of the partners must be natural persons or persons acting in a fiduciary capacity for the benefit of natural persons.

Probably the most significant use of the FLLP form of business organization is in agriculture. Family-owned farms sometimes find this form to their benefit. The FLLP has the same advantages as other LLPs with some additional advantages, such as, in Iowa, an exemption from real estate transfer taxes when partnership real estate is transferred among partners.[16]

Limited Liability Limited Partnerships

A **limited liability limited partnership (LLLP)** is a type of limited partnership. The difference between a limited partnership and an LLLP is that the liability of a general partner in an LLLP is the same as the liability of a partner in a limited liability partnership. That is, the liability of all partners is limited to the amount of their investments in the firm.

A few states provide expressly for LLLPs.[17] In states that do not provide for LLLPs but do allow for limited partnerships and limited liability partnerships, a limited partnership should probably still be able to register with the state as an LLLP.

---

16. Iowa Statutes Section 428A.
17. See, for example, Colorado Rev. Stat. Ann. Section 7-62-109. Other states that provide expressly for limited liability limited partnerships include Delaware, Florida, Missouri, Pennsylvania, Texas, and Virginia.

Terms and Concepts

articles of partnership 486
certificate of limited
   partnership 499
charging order 490
confession of judgment 490
dissolution 495
entrepreneur 482
family limited liability
   partnership (FLLP) 501

franchise 483
franchisee 483
franchisor 483
general partner 497
joint and several liability 494
joint liability 494
limited liability
   company (LLC) 500

limited liability limited
   partnership (LLLP) 501
limited liability partnership
   (LLP) 500
limited partner 497
limited partnership 497
partnership 484
sole proprietorship 483
winding up 495

Chapter Summary: Sole Proprietorships, Partnerships, and Limited Liability Companies

Sole Proprietorship *(See page 483.)*	The simplest form of business; used by anyone who does business without creating an organization. The owner is the business. The owner pays personal income taxes on all profits and is personally liable for all business debts.
General Partnership *(See pages 484–497.)*	1. Created by agreement of the parties. *(Continued)*

▌Chapter Summary: Sole Proprietorships, Partnerships, and Limited Liability Companies—Continued

General Partnership— Continued	2. Not treated as an entity except for limited purposes.
	3. Partners have unlimited liability for partnership debts.
	4. Each partner has an equal voice in management unless otherwise provided for in the partnership agreement.
	5. The capital contribution of each partner is determined by agreement.
	6. Each partner pays a proportionate share of income taxes on the net profits of the partnership, whether or not they are distributed; the partnership files only an information return with the Internal Revenue Service.
	7. Terminated by agreement or can be dissolved by action of the partners (withdrawal), operation of law (death or bankruptcy), or court decree.
Limited Partnership *(See pages 497–500.)*	1. Must be formed in compliance with statutory requirements.
	2. Consists of one or more general partners and one or more limited partners.
	3. Only general partners can participate in management. Limited partners have no voice in management; if they do participate in management activities, they risk having general-partner liability.
	4. General partners have unlimited liability for partnership losses; limited partners are liable only to the extent of their contributions.
Limited Liability Company (LLC) *(See page 500.)*	The limited liability company (LLC) is a hybrid form of business organization that offers the limited liability feature of corporations but the tax benefits of partnerships. Unlike limited partners, LLC members participate in management. Unlike shareholders in S corporations, members of LLCs may be corporations or partnerships, are not restricted in number, and may be residents of other countries.
Limited Liability Partnership (LLP) *(See page 501.)*	1. Must be formed in compliance with statutory requirements.
	2. Most state statutes make it relatively easy to establish an LLP, particularly if a firm is already doing business as a partnership.
	3. Statutes vary from state to state, but generally, each state statute limits in some way the personal liability of innocent partners for the wrongful acts of other partners.

▌For Review

1. Which form of business organization is the simplest? Which form arises from an agreement between two or more persons to carry on a business for profit?

2. What are the three essential elements of a partnership?

3. What is meant by joint and several liability? Why is this often considered to be a disadvantage of the partnership form of business?

4. Can a partner continue the business of a terminated partnership if he or she wishes to do so? How?

5. What are the key differences between the rights and liabilities of general partners and limited partners?

▌ Questions and Case Problems

23–1. Forms of Business Organization. In each of the following situations, determine whether Georgio's Fashions is a sole proprietorship, a partnership, a limited partnership, or a corporation.

- (a) Georgio's defaults on a payment to supplier Dee Creations. Dee sues Georgio's and each of the owners of Georgio's personally for payment of the debt.
- (b) At tax time, Georgio's files a tax return with the IRS and pays taxes on the firm's net profits.
- (c) Georgio's is owned by three persons, two of whom are not allowed to participate in the firm's management.

23–2. Distribution of Partnership Assets. Shawna and David formed a partnership. At the time of the partnership's formation, Shawna's capital contribution was $10,000, and David's was $15,000. Later, Shawna made a $10,000 loan to the partnership when it needed working capital. The partnership agreement provided that profits were to be shared, 40 percent for Shawna and 60 percent for David. The partnership was dissolved by David's death. At the end of the dissolution and the winding up of the partnership, the partnership's assets were $50,000, and the partnership's debts were $8,000. Discuss fully how the assets should be distributed.

23–3. Partnership Property. Schwartz and Zenov were partners in an accounting firm. Because business was booming and profits were better than ever, they decided to invest some of the firm's profits in Munificent Corp. stock. The investment turned out to be a good one, as the stock continued to increase in value. On Schwartz's death several years later, Zenov assumed full ownership of the business, including the Munificent Corp. stock, a partnership asset. Schwartz's daughter Rosalie, however, claimed a 50 percent ownership interest in the Munificent Corp. stock as Schwartz's sole heir. Can Rosalie enforce her claim? Explain.

23–4. Liability of Limited Partners. Asher and Breem form a limited partnership with Asher as the general partner and Breem as the limited partner. Breem puts up $15,000, and Asher contributes some office equipment that he owns. A certificate of limited partnership is properly filed, and business is begun. One month later, Asher becomes ill. Instead of hiring someone to manage the business, Breem takes over complete management himself. While Breem is in control, he makes a contract with Thaler involving a large sum of money. Asher returns to work. Because of other commitments, Asher and Breem breach the Thaler contract. Thaler contends that Asher and Breem will be personally liable for damages caused by the breach if the damages cannot be satisfied out of the assets of the limited partnership. Discuss this contention.

23–5. Partner's Property Rights. Maruta, Samms, and Ortega were partners in a business firm. The firm's business equipment included several expensive computers. One day, Maruta borrowed one of the computers for use in his home, but he never bothered to return it. When the other partners asked him about it, Maruta claimed that because the computer represented less than one-third of the computers owned by the partnership, and because he owned one-third of the business, he had a right to keep the equipment. Was he right? Explain.

23–6. Partnership by Estoppel. Alvin and Carol Volkman negotiated with David McNamee, a construction contractor, to have a house built. McNamee informed the Volkmans that he was going into business with Phillip Carroll. Carroll was present on several occasions when the Volkmans went to McNamee's offices, and by all indications he was a partner in the decisions concerning the construction of the Volkmans' house. On one occasion, for example, Carroll said to the Volkmans, "I hope we'll be working together." Correspondence to the Volkmans from McNamee was written on stationery carrying the letterhead "DP Associates," and the Volkmans assumed the "DP" represented David and Phillip. When the construction contract was not performed as agreed, the Volkmans brought suit against DP Associates, McNamee, and Carroll. Carroll petitioned the trial court to dismiss the suit against him, as he was not a partner in DP Associates. Will the court find Carroll to be a partner by estoppel? Explain. [*Volkman v. DP Associates*, 48 N.C.App. 155, 268 S.E.2d 265 (1980)]

23–7. Rights among Partners. Jebeles and Costellos were partners in "Dino's Hot Dogs," doing business on the Montgomery Highway in Alabama. From the outset, Costellos worked at the business full-time, while Jebeles involved himself only to a small extent in the actual running of the business. Jebeles was married to Costellos's sister, and when marital difficulties developed between Jebeles and his wife, Costellos barred Jebeles from the premises. Jebeles sued for an accounting of the partnership's profits and for dissolution of the partnership, claiming a partnership at will and that the relationship between the partners made it impossible to conduct partnership business. Will the court grant the petition? Explain. [*Jebeles v. Costellos*, 391 So.2d 1024 (Ala. 1980)]

23–8. Partnership Dissolution. Carola and Grogan were partners in a law firm. The partnership began business in 1974 and was created by an oral agreement. On September 6, 1976, Carola withdrew from the partnership some of its files, furniture, and books, along with various other items of office equipment. The next day, Carola informed Grogan he had withdrawn from the partnership. Discuss whether Carola's actions on September 6, 1976, constituted effective notice of dissolution to Grogan. [*Carola v. Grogan,* 102 A.D.2d 934, 477 N.Y.S.2d 525 (1984)]

23–9. Liability of General Partners. Pat McGowan, Val Somers, and Brent Roberson were general partners in Vermont Place, a limited partnership formed to construct duplexes on a tract of land in Fort Smith, Arkansas. In 1984, the partnership mortgaged the property so that it could build there. McGowan owned a separate company, Advance Development Corp., which was hired by the partnership to develop the project. On September 3, 1984, Somers and Roberson discovered that McGowan had not been paying the suppliers to the project, including National Lumber Co., and had not been making the mortgage payments. The suppliers and the bank sued the partnership and the general partners individually. Discuss whether Somers and Roberson could be held individually liable for the debts incurred by McGowan. [*National Lumber Co. v. Advance Development Corp.,* 293 Ark. 1, 732 S.W.2d 840 (1987)]

23–10. Distribution of Assets. Robert Lowther, Fred Riggleman, and Granville Zopp were equal partners in the Four Square Partnership. The partnership was created to acquire and develop real estate for commercial retail use. In the course of the partnership, Riggleman loaned $30,000 to the partnership, and Zopp loaned the partnership $50,000. Donald H. Lowther, Robert's brother and not a partner in the firm, loaned Four Square $80,000 and took a promissory note signed by the three partners. Four Square encountered financial difficulties shortly after the commercial venture began and eventually defaulted on payments due on a construction loan it had received from a bank. The bank foreclosed on the property securing the debt. The proceeds of the subsequent foreclosure sale satisfied the bank's interest and left a surplus of $87,783 to be returned to the partnership. In the meantime, the partnership had been dissolved and was in the process of winding up its affairs. Donald H. Lowther maintained that, as a nonpartner creditor, his claim against the firm's assets took priority over those of Riggleman and Zopp. Is Lowther correct? Explain. [*Lowther v. Riggleman,* 189 W.Va. 68, 428 S.E.2d 49 (1993)]

23–11. Rights among Partners. B&R Communications was a general partner in Amarillo CellTelco. Under the partnership agreement, each partner had the right to inspect partnership records "at reasonable times during business hours," so long as the inspection did not "unreasonably interfere with the operation of the partnership." B&R believed that the managers of the firm were using partnership money to engage in lawsuits that were too costly. B&R and other general partners filed a suit in a Texas state court against the managers. B&R wanted to inspect the firm's records to discover information about the lawsuits, but the court denied B&R's request. B&R asked a state appellate court to order the trial judge to grant the request. On what ground did the appellate court issue the order? [*B&R Communications v. Lopez,* 890 S.W.2d 224 (Tex.App.—Amarillo 1994)]

23–12. Liability of Incoming Partner. Conklin Farm sold land to LongView Estates, a general partnership, to build condominiums. LongView gave a promissory note to Conklin for $9 million as payment. A few years later, Doris Leibowitz joined LongView as a general partner. Leibowitz left the firm before the note came due, but while she was a partner, interest accrued on the balance. The condominium project failed, and LongView went out of business. Conklin filed a suit in a New Jersey state court against Leibowitz to recover some of the interest on the note. Conklin acknowledged that Leibowitz was not liable for debt incurred before she joined the firm but argued that the interest that accrued while she was a partner was "new" debt for which she was personally liable. To what extent, if any, is Leibowitz liable to Conklin? [*Conklin Farm v. Leibowitz,* 140 N.J. 417, 658 A.2d 1257 (1995)]

▌Accessing the Internet: Fundamentals of Business Law

The Web site of the law firm of Reinhart et al. provides extensive information about business organizations. The URL for this site is

http://www.rbvdnr.com/

For information on limited liability companies, go to

http://www.mgovg.com/

You can find the full text of the Internal Revenue Service rule concerning the taxation of limited liability companies and limited liability partnerships by accessing the Treasure Chest of Important Documents at the following site:

http://www.LWeekly.com

For daily news on the world of business, you can access Money Online at

http://www.money.com/

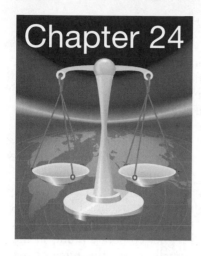

Chapter 24

Corporate Formation and Financing

CHAPTER OBJECTIVES

After reading this chapter, you should be able to:

1. Describe the basic characteristics of the corporate entity.
2. Identify the express and implied powers of a corporation.
3. Summarize the ways in which corporations are classified.
4. Outline the steps involved in forming a corporation, and point out the effects of improper incorporation.
5. Indicate how corporations are financed, and discuss the difference between stocks and bonds.

A corporation can be owned by a single person, or it can have hundreds, thousands, or even millions of shareholders. The shareholder form of business organization was developed in Europe at the end of the seventeenth century. Called *joint stock companies*, these organizations frequently collapsed because their organizers absconded with the funds or proved to be incompetent. Because of this history of fraud and collapse, organizations resembling corporations were regarded with suspicion in the United States during its early years. Although several business corporations were formed after the Revolutionary War, it was not until the nineteenth century that the corporation came into common use for private business. Today, the corporation is one of the most important forms of business organization in the United States.

A corporation is an artificial being, existing in law only and neither tangible nor visible. The corporation is a creature of statute. Its existence depends generally on state law, although some corporations, especially public organizations, can be created under federal law.

Each state has its own body of corporate law, and these laws are not entirely uniform. The Model Business Corporation Act (MBCA) is a codification of modern corporation law that has been influential in the drafting and revision of state corporation statutes. Today, the majority of state statutes are guided by the revised version of the MBCA, known as the Revised Model Business Corporation Act (RMBCA). You should keep in mind, however, that there is considerable variation among the statutes of the states that have used the MBCA or the RMBCA as a basis for their statutes, and several states do not follow either act. Because of this, individual state corporation laws should be relied on rather than the MBCA or RMBCA.

∎ The Nature of the Corporation

A *corporation* can consist of one or more *natural* persons (as opposed to the artificial "person" of the corporation) identified under a common name. The corporation substitutes itself for its shareholders in conducting corporate business and in incurring liability, yet its authority to act and the liability for its actions are separate and apart from the individuals who own it. (In certain limited situations, the "corporate veil" can be pierced; that is, liability for the corporation's obligations can be extended to shareholders, a topic to be discussed later in this chapter.)

Corporate Personnel

Responsibility for the overall management of the corporation is entrusted to a *board of directors,* which is elected by the shareholders. The board of directors hires *corporate officers* and other employees to run the daily business operations of the corporation.

When an individual purchases a share of stock in a corporation, that person becomes a *shareholder* and an owner of the corporation. Unlike the members in a partnership, the body of shareholders can change constantly without affecting the continued existence of the corporation. A shareholder can sue the corporation, and the corporation can sue a shareholder. Additionally, under certain circumstances, a shareholder can sue on behalf of a corporation. The rights and duties of all corporate personnel will be examined in Chapter 25.

Corporate Taxation

Corporate profits are taxed by state and federal governments. Corporations can do one of two things with corporate profits—retain them or pass them on to shareholders in the form of **dividends.** The corporation receives no tax deduction for dividends distributed to shareholders. Dividends are again taxable (except when they represent distributions of capital) as ordinary income to the shareholder receiving them. This double-taxation feature of the corporation is one of its major disadvantages, as mentioned in Chapter 23.

Profits not distributed are retained by the corporation. These **retained earnings,** if invested properly, will yield higher corporate profits in the future and thus normally cause the price of the company's stock to rise. Individual shareholders can then reap the benefits of these retained earnings in the capital gains they receive when they sell their shares.

The consequences of a failure to pay corporate taxes can be severe. As will be discussed in Chapter 26, the state may dissolve a corporation for this reason. Alternatively, corporate status may be suspended until the taxes are paid. In the following case, the state had suspended a corporation's **corporate charter** (the document issued by a state agency or authority—usually the secretary of state—that grants a corporation legal existence and the right to function) because of the corporation's failure to pay certain taxes. The issue before the court is whether a shareholder who was unaware of the suspension could be held personally liable on a corporate contract.

CASE 24.1

Charles A. Torrence Co. v. Clary
Court of Appeals of
North Carolina, 1995.
464 S.E.2d 502.

FACTS In 1989, the architectural firm of Clary, Martin, McMullen & Associates, Inc. (CMMA, Inc.), failed to pay its North Carolina franchise taxes,[a] and the state suspended its corporate charter. Between April 1991 and March 1992, the Charles A. Torrence Company provided graphics services for the firm. In September 1992, Moodye Clary—a shareholder, the president, and the director of marketing of CMMA, Inc.—learned that his firm's corporate charter had been suspended. When CMMA, Inc., failed to pay Torrence's bill, Torrence filed a suit in a North Carolina state court against CMMA, Inc., as well as against Moodye Clary personally, for the money. The court dismissed the claim against Moodye Clary, and Torrence appealed.

a.   A *franchise tax* is an annual tax imposed for the privilege of doing business in a state.

Case 24.1—Continued

ISSUE Is a corporate officer who does not know that the firm's corporate charter has been suspended personally liable for debts incurred by the firm during the suspension?

DECISION No. The Court of Appeals of North Carolina affirmed the lower court's decision.

REASON The state appellate court explained that "the suspension was only designed to put 'additional bite' into the collection of franchise taxes, but not to deprive the shareholders of the normal protection of limited liability." The court acknowledged that "directors and officers are personally liable for corporate obligations incurred by them on behalf of the corporation, or by others with their acquiescence, if at that time they were aware that the corporate charter was suspended." Moodye Clary, however, "had no knowledge, at the time the debt was incurred on behalf of the Corporation, that the corporate charter was suspended."

FOR CRITICAL ANALYSIS—Social Consideration *Why wouldn't a court permit a shareholder who* knows *that the charter of his or her firm has been suspended to retain limited liability for corporate debts?*

Constitutional Rights of Corporations

A corporation is recognized under state and federal law as a "person," and it enjoys many of the same rights and privileges that U.S. citizens enjoy. The Bill of Rights guarantees a person, as a citizen, certain protections, and corporations are considered persons in most instances. Accordingly, a corporation has the same right as a natural person to equal protection of the laws under the Fourteenth Amendment. It has the right of access to the courts as an entity that can sue or be sued. It also has the right of due process before denial of life, liberty, or property, as well as freedom from unreasonable searches and seizures and from double jeopardy.

Under the First Amendment, corporations are entitled to freedom of speech, but commercial speech (such as advertising) and political speech (such as contributions to political causes or candidates) receive significantly less protection than noncommercial speech.

Only the corporation's individual officers and employees possess the Fifth Amendment right against self-incrimination.[1] Additionally, the privileges and immunities clause of the Constitution (Article IV, Section 2) does not protect corporations.[2] This clause requires each state to treat citizens of other states equally with respect to access to courts, travel rights, and so forth.

Torts and Criminal Acts

A corporation is liable for the torts committed by its agents or officers within the course and scope of their employment. This principle applies to a corporation exactly as it applies to the ordinary agency relationships discussed in Chapter 21. It follows the doctrine of *respondeat superior*.

Under modern criminal law, a corporation can sometimes be held liable for the criminal acts of its agents and employees, provided the punishment is one that can be applied to the corporation. Corporate criminal prosecutions were at one time relatively rare, but in the past decade they have increased significantly in number. Obviously, corporations cannot be imprisoned, but they can be fined. (Of course, corporate directors and officers can be imprisoned, and in recent years, many have faced criminal penalties for their own actions or for the actions of employees under their supervision.

---

1. *In re Grand Jury No. 86–3 (Will Roberts Corp.),* 816 F.2d 569 (11th Cir. 1987).

2. *W. C. M. Window Co. v. Bernardi,* 730 F.2d 486 (7th Cir. 1984).

The liability of corporate directors and officers is examined in Chapter 25.)

Recall from Chapter 6 that the U.S. Sentencing Commission, which was established by the Sentencing Reform Act of 1984, created standardized sentencing guidelines for federal crimes. These guidelines went into effect in 1987. The commission subsequently created specific sentencing guidelines for crimes committed by corporate employees (white-collar crimes). The net effect of the guidelines has been a fivefold to tenfold increase in criminal penalties for crimes committed by corporate personnel.

∎ Partnerships and Corporations

Exhibit 24–1 lists the essential advantages and disadvantages of partnerships and corporations. We select for discussion here four important concerns for anyone starting a business—the ease of creation, the liability of the owners, tax features, and the need for capital.

Ease of Creation

A general partnership can be organized easily and inexpensively. A corporation must be organized according to specific statutory procedures, must have sufficient capitalization, and must pay other costs of formal incorporation. In fact, throughout its life, a corporation is subject to more governmental supervision and reporting requirements than a partnership normally is.

Liability of Owners

Generally, general partners have personal liability, whereas the liability of limited partners and shareholders of corporations is limited to their investments. The issue of liability is an important one for the firm's owners, who may not want to place their personal assets at risk in the event the business cannot meet its obligations. The form of the organization does not always in and of itself determine the liability of the owners, however. For example, a court may "pierce the corporate veil" in certain circumstances (as will be discussed in Chapter 25) and hold corporate shareholders personally liable for corporate obligations.

Furthermore, creditors may not be willing to extend credit to a newly formed or small corporation precisely because of the limited liability of corporate owners. Typically, if a corporation has relatively few shareholders, a bank or other lender will require the shareholders to cosign or guarantee personally any loans made to the corporation. That is, the shareholders agree to become personally liable for the loan if the corporation cannot meet its debts or goes bankrupt. In essence, the shareholders become guarantors for the corporation's debt. Hence, the corporate form of business does not prevent the shareholders from having personal liability in such a situation, because they have assumed the liability voluntarily.

Tax Considerations

Various tax considerations must be taken into account when one decides how best to organize a business. Tax aspects of partnerships and corporations are summarized in Exhibit 24–2.

The Need for Capital

One of the most common reasons for changing from a sole proprietorship to a partnership or a corporation is the need for additional capital to finance expansion. A sole proprietor can seek partners who will bring capital with them. The partnership might be able to secure more funds from potential lenders than could the sole proprietor.

When a firm wants to expand greatly, however, simply increasing the number of partners can result in too many partners and make it difficult for the firm to operate effectively. Therefore, incorporation might be the best choice for an expanding business organization because a corporation can obtain more capital by issuing shares of stock. The original owners will find that, although their proportionate ownership of the company is reduced, they are able to expand much more rapidly by selling shares in the company.

∎ Corporate Powers

When a corporation is created, the express and implied powers necessary to achieve its purpose also come into existence. The express powers of a corporation are found in its articles of

♦ Exhibit 24–1
Partnerships and Corporations Compared

CHARACTERISTIC	PARTNERSHIP	CORPORATION
Method of Creation	Created by agreement of the parties.	Charter issued by the state—created by statutory authorization.
Legal Position	Not a separate legal entity in some states.	Always a legal entity separate and distinct from its owners—a legal fiction for the purposes of owning property and being a party to litigation.
Liability	Unlimited liability	Limited liability of shareholders—shareholders are not liable for the debts of the corporation.
Duration	Terminated by agreement of the partners, by the death of one or more of the partners, by withdrawal of a partner, by bankruptcy, and so on.	Can have perpetual existence.
Transferability of Interest	Although a partnership interest can be assigned, the assignee normally does not have the full rights of a partner.	Shares of stock can be transferred.
Management	Each general partner has a direct and equal voice in management unless expressly agreed otherwise in the partnership agreement.	Shareholders elect directors, who set policy and appoint officers.
Taxation	Each partner pays income taxes based on a pro rata share of net profits, whether or not they are distributed.	Double taxation—the corporation pays income tax on net profits, with no deduction for dividends, and shareholders pay income tax on disbursed dividends they receive.
Organizational Fees, Annual License Fees, and Annual Reports	None.	All required.
Transaction of Business in Other States	Generally no limitation.[a]	Normally must qualify to do business and obtain a certificate of authority.

a. A few states have enacted statutes requiring that foreign (out-of-state) partnerships qualify to do business there—for example, 3 N.H.Rev.Stat.Ann. Chapter 305-A in New Hampshire.

incorporation (a document containing information about the corporation, including its organization and functions), in the law of the state of incorporation, and in the state and federal constitutions. Corporate **bylaws** (rules of management adopted by the corporation at its first organizational meeting) and the resolutions of the corporation's board of directors also grant or restrict certain powers. The following order of priority is used when conflicts arise among documents involving corporations:

♦ Exhibit 24–2
Tax Aspects of Partnerships and Corporations[a]

TAX ASPECT	PARTNERSHIP	CORPORATION
Federal Income Tax	Partners are taxed on proportionate shares of partnership income, even if not distributed; the partnership files information returns only.	The income of the corporation is taxed; stockholders are also taxed on distributed dividends. The corporation files corporate income tax forms.
Accumulation	Partners are taxed on accumulated as well as distributed earnings.	Corporate stockholders are not taxed on accumulated earnings. There is, however, a penalty tax, in some instances, that the corporation must pay for "unreasonable" accumulations of income.
Capital Gains	Partners are taxed on their proportionate shares of capital gains, which are taxed at the ordinary income rate.	The corporation is taxed on capital gains and losses.
Exempt Income	Partners are not taxed on exempt income received from the firm.	Any exempt income distributed by a corporation is fully taxable income to the stockholders.
Pension Plan	Partners can adopt a Keogh plan, an Individual Retirement Account (IRA), or a 401-K plan.	Employees and officers who are also stockholders can be beneficiaries of a pension trust. The corporation can deduct its payments to the trust.
Social Security	Partners must pay a self-employment tax (in 1998, 12.4 percent on income up to $68,400, plus 2.9 percent Medicare tax on all income).	All compensation to officers and employee-stockholders is subject to Social Security taxation up to the maximum.
Death Benefits (excluding those provided by Insurance)	There is no exemption for payments to partners' beneficiaries.	Benefits up to $5,000 can be received tax-free by employees' beneficiaries.
State Taxes	The partnership is not subject to taxes. State income taxes are paid by each partner.	The corporation is subject to state income taxes (although these taxes can be deducted on federal returns).

a.   *As of 1996.*

1.   The U.S. Constitution.
2.   State constitutions.
3.   State statutes.
4.   The articles of incorporation.
5.   Bylaws.
6.   Resolutions of the board of directors.

Certain implied powers attach when a corporation is created. Barring express constitutional, statutory, or other prohibitions, the corporation has the implied power to perform all acts reasonably appropriate and necessary to accomplish its corporate purposes. For this reason, a corporation has the implied power to borrow money within certain limits, to lend money or to extend credit to those with whom it has a legal or contractual relationship, and to make charitable contributions.[3] To borrow money, the corporation acts through its board of directors to authorize the loan. Most often, the president or chief executive officer of the corporation will execute the necessary papers on behalf of the corporation. In so doing, corporate officers have the implied power to bind the corporation in matters directly connected with the *ordinary* business affairs of the enterprise.

The term **ultra vires** means "beyond the powers." In corporate law, acts of a corporation that are beyond its express and implied powers are *ultra vires* acts. Under Section 3.04 of the RMBCA, the following remedies are available for *ultra vires* acts:

1. The shareholders may sue on behalf of the corporation to obtain an injunction (to prohibit the corporation from engaging in the *ultra vires* transactions) or to obtain damages for the harm caused by the transactions.
2. The corporation itself can sue the officers and directors who were responsible for the *ultra vires* transactions to recover damages.
3. The attorney general of the state may institute a proceeding to obtain an injunction against the *ultra vires* transactions or to institute dissolution proceedings against the corporation for *ultra vires* acts.

In the following case, the court had to decide whether the board of directors of a cooperative housing corporation had exceeded its authority when it set minimum prices for the cooperative's housing units.

---

3.   A corporation is prohibited from making political contributions in federal elections by the Federal Elections Campaign Act of 1974 (18 U.S.C. Section 321). Early law held that a corporation had no implied authority to make charitable contributions, because charitable activities were contrary to the primary purpose of the corporation to make a profit. Modern law, by statutes and court decisions, holds that a corporation has such implied authority.

CASE 24.2

Oakley v. Longview Owners, Inc.

Supreme Court of New York, Westchester County, 1995.
165 Misc.2d 192,
628 N.Y.S.2d 468.

FACTS Dorothy Oakley owned shares in Longview Owners, Inc., a cooperative housing corporation in New York. When she tried to sell her shares—that is, her apartment—the Longview board of directors refused to approve the sale, in part because the price was less than a minimum price for the apartments set by the board two months earlier. The board set the minimum in a resolution without notifying the shareholder-owners or giving them the opportunity to vote on it. Neither the Longview bylaws nor the certificate of incorporation gave the board the authority to set prices. Oakley filed a suit in a New York state court against the board, alleging that it had exceeded its authority in refusing to approve the sale. The board filed a motion to dismiss.

ISSUE Did the Longview board have the authority to set minimum prices for apartments in the cooperative?

DECISION No. The court denied the board's motion to dismiss the suit and scheduled the case for trial.

REASON The court explained that "[a] cooperative board of directors may only act upon the authority which they are given. That authority may be found by looking to the by-laws of the corporation *   *   * and the certificate of incorporation." In this case, the board was not granted "by language expressed, or implied," authority to impose price restraints. The court also pointed out that the shareholder-owners had not been given

(Continued)

Case 24.2—Continued

prior notice of the restraints or an opportunity to vote on "this significant restriction affecting the stock of the corporation."

FOR CRITICAL ANALYSIS—Economic Consideration *Is it possible that the setting of a minimum sale price by the cooperative's board could somehow benefit the owners of the cooperative?*

▌Classification of Corporations

The classification of a corporation depends on its purpose, ownership characteristics, and location.

Domestic, Foreign, and Alien Corporations

A corporation is referred to as a **domestic corporation** by its home state (the state in which it incorporates). A corporation formed in one state but doing business in another is referred to in that other state as a **foreign corporation.** A corporation formed in another country—say, Mexico—but doing business in the United States is referred to in the United States as an **alien corporation.**

A corporation does not have an automatic right to do business in a state other than its state of incorporation. It normally must obtain a *certificate of authority* in any state in which it plans to do business. Once the certificate has been issued, the powers conferred upon a corporation by its home state generally can be exercised in the other state.

Public and Private Corporations

A public corporation is one formed by the government to meet some political or governmental purpose. Cities and towns that incorporate are common examples. In addition, many federal government organizations, such as the U.S. Postal Service, the Tennessee Valley Authority, and AMTRAK, are public corporations. Note that a public corporation is not the same as a *publicly held* corporation. A publicly held corporation is any corporation whose shares are publicly traded in securities markets, such as the New York Stock Exchange or the over-the-counter market.

In contrast to public corporations, private corporations are created either wholly or in part for private benefit. Most corporations are private. Although they may serve a public purpose, as a

public utility does, they are owned by private persons rather than by the government.[4]

Nonprofit Corporations

Corporations formed without a profit-making purpose are called *nonprofit* or *not-for-profit* corporations. Private hospitals, educational institutions, charities, and religious organizations, for example, are frequently organized as nonprofit corporations. The nonprofit corporation is a convenient form of organization that allows various groups to own property and to form contracts without the individual members' being personally exposed to liability.

Close Corporations

Most corporate enterprises in the United States fall into the category of close corporations. A **close corporation** is one whose shares are held by members of a family or by relatively few persons. Close corporations are also referred to as *closely held, family,* or *privately held* corporations. Usually, the members of the small group constituting a close corporation are personally known to each other. Because the number of shareholders is so small, there is no trading market for the shares.

Some states have enacted special statutory provisions that apply to close corporations. These provisions expressly permit close corporations to depart significantly from certain formalities required by traditional corporation law.[5] Additionally, Section 7.32 of the RMBCA, a provision added to the RMBCA in 1991 and adopted in several states, gives close corporations a substantial

---

4. For a landmark case on the distinction between private and public corporations, and the rights of private corporations, see *The Trustees of Dartmouth College v. Woodward,* 17 U.S. (4 Wheaton) 518, 4 L.Ed. 629 (1819).

5. For example, in some states (such as Maryland), the close corporation need not have a board of directors.

amount of flexibility in determining the rules by which they will operate. Under Section 7.32, if all of the shareholders of a corporation agree in writing, the corporation can operate without directors, bylaws, annual or special shareholders' or directors' meetings, stock certificates, or formal records of shareholders' or directors' decisions.[6]

MANAGEMENT OF CLOSE CORPORATIONS The close corporation has a single shareholder or a closely knit group of shareholders, who usually hold the positions of directors and officers. Management of a close corporation resembles that of a sole proprietorship or a partnership. As a corporation, however, the firm must meet specific legal requirements, as mentioned previously.

To prevent a majority shareholder from dominating a close corporation, the corporation may require that action can be taken by the board only on approval of more than a simple majority of the directors. Typically, this would not be required for ordinary business decisions but only for extraordinary actions, such as changing the amount of dividends or dismissing an employee-shareholder.

TRANSFER OF SHARES IN CLOSE CORPORATIONS Because, by definition, a close corporation has a small number of shareholders, the transfer of one shareholder's shares to someone else can cause serious management problems. The other shareholders may find themselves required to share control with someone they do not know or like.

Consider an example. Three brothers, Terry, Damon, and Henry Johnson, are the only shareholders of Johnson's Car Wash, Inc. Terry and Damon do not want Henry to sell his shares to an unknown third person. To avoid this situation, the articles of incorporation could restrict the transferability of shares to outside persons by stipulating that shareholders must offer their shares to the corporation or other shareholders before selling them to an outside purchaser. In fact, a few states have statutes under which close corporation shares cannot be transferred unless certain persons—including shareholders, family members, and the corporation—are first given the opportunity to purchase the shares for the same price.

Another way that control of a close corporation can be stabilized is through the use of a shareholder agreement. A shareholder agreement can provide that when one of the original shareholders dies, his or her shares of stock in the corporation will be divided in such a way that the proportionate holdings of the survivors, and thus their proportionate control, will be maintained. Courts are generally reluctant to interfere with private agreements, including shareholder agreements. Whether a shareholder agreement should be enforced is at issue in the following case.

---

6. Shareholders cannot agree, however, to eliminate certain rights of shareholders, such as the right to inspect corporate books and records or the right to bring derivative actions (lawsuits on behalf of the corporation—see Chapter 25).

CASE 24.3

Rosiny v. Schmidt

New York Supreme Court,
Appellate Division, 1992.
185 A.D.2d 727,
587 N.Y.S.2d 929.

FACTS In 1981, the four shareholders of Ched Realty, each of whom held 25 percent of the shares, formed a shareholder agreement. The agreement provided that in the event of a shareholder's death, the surviving shareholders could buy the decedent's shares at "book value" or $200 per share, whichever was greater. Two of the shareholders, Allen and Frank Rosiny, were young, well-educated attorneys. The other two shareholders, Charles McGuire and Jeanette Priddy, were elderly, and neither of them had completed high school. Both, however, had signed several shareholder agreements prior to 1981, and a 1971 agreement included basically the same "book value" buy-out agreement. The other agreements provided for a book value formula to determine the value of a decedent's shares. At the time of the 1981 agreement, the book value was negative, but the market value was $4,225 per share and gaining. When Priddy and McGuire died in 1988, their stock had a market value of $41,500 per share. The Rosinys sued in a New York state

(Continued)

Case 24.3—Continued

court to enforce the buy-out provision of the shareholder agreement. The heirs of McGuire and Priddy argued that there was no mutual assent when the 1981 agreement was formed. They also claimed that the agreement was unconscionable, because the younger shareholders, knowing that neither McGuire nor Priddy was aware of what was being signed, took advantage of this fact. The court agreed with the heirs, and the Rosinys appealed.

ISSUE Is the shareholder agreement enforceable?

DECISION Yes. The appellate court ruled in favor of the Rosinys.

REASON The court pointed out that this was the fourth Ched shareholders' agreement, three of which provided for a book value formula to determine the value of a decedent's shares. There was no evidence that "because of the disparity in age and educational background, the decedents were deceived by the young attorneys." Additionally, "[d]espite representation by counsel, neither Priddy nor McGuire opted to sell the property or dissolve the corporation during the seven years following their execution of the 1981 agreement," which included those options. The court also noted that a 1971 shareholder agreement, which was signed by Priddy and McGuire before the Rosinys became shareholders, contained the identical buy-out provision in rejection of a fair market value approach contained in an earlier agreement. "The return to the use of 'book value,' an unambiguous term, from fair market value, as well as the use of this term in previous agreements, evinces a meeting of the minds as to this term of the agreement."

FOR CRITICAL ANALYSIS—Social Consideration *Even assuming (as the court did) that Priddy's and McGuire's consent to the agreement was genuine, were there any other grounds on which the court might have decided that the agreement was unenforceable?*

S Corporations

The Subchapter S Revision Act of 1982 was passed "to permit the incorporation and operation of certain small businesses without the incidence of income taxation at both the corporate and shareholder level."[7] Additionally, Congress divided corporations into two groups: **S corporations,** which have elected Subchapter S treatment, and *C corporations,* which are all other corporations. Certain close corporations can choose to qualify under Subchapter S of the Internal Revenue Code to avoid the imposition of income taxes at the corporate level while retaining many of the advantages of a corporation, particularly limited liability.

QUALIFICATION REQUIREMENTS FOR S CORPORATIONS Among the numerous requirements for S corporation status, the following are the most important:

1. The corporation must be a domestic corporation.
2. The corporation must not be a member of an affiliated group of corporations.
3. The shareholders of the corporation must be individuals, estates, or certain trusts. Partnerships and nonqualifying trusts cannot be shareholders.
4. The corporation must have seventy-five or fewer shareholders.
5. The corporation must have only one class of stock, although not all shareholders need have the same voting rights.

7. Senate Report No. 640, 97th Congress, 1st Session (1981).

6.   No shareholder of the corporation may be a nonresident alien.

BENEFITS OF S CORPORATIONS   At times, it is beneficial for a regular corporation to elect S corporation status. Benefits include the following:

1.   When the corporation has losses, the S election allows the shareholders to use the losses to offset other income.

2.   When the shareholder's tax bracket is lower than the corporation's tax bracket, the S election causes the corporation's pass-through net income to be taxed in the shareholder's bracket. This is particularly attractive when the corporation wants to accumulate earnings for some future business purpose.

3.   As mentioned, a single tax on corporate income is imposed at individual income tax rates at the shareholder level. (The income is taxable to shareholders whether or not it is actually distributed.)

Professional Corporations

Professional persons such as physicians, lawyers, dentists, and accountants can incorporate. Professional corporations are typically identified by the letters S.C. (service corporation), P.C. (professional corporation), or P.A. (professional association). In general, the laws governing professional corporations are similar to those governing ordinary business corporations, but three basic areas of liability deserve special attention.

First, a court might, for liability purposes, regard the professional corporation as a partnership in which each partner can be held liable for whatever malpractice liability is incurred by the others within the scope of the partnership. Second, a shareholder in a professional corporation is protected from the liability imposed because of any torts (unrelated to malpractice) committed by other members. Third, many professional corporation statutes retain personal liability of professional persons for their acts and the professional acts performed under their supervision.

State statutes providing for limited liability companies and limited liability partnerships (discussed in Chapter 23) offer alternative forms of business organizations for professionals. Many of these statutes allow professionals to operate as a professional limited liability company (PLLC) or a professional limited liability partnership (PLLP). These options allow professionals to obtain the limited liability of the professional corporation while enjoying the tax advantages characteristic of the partnership.

In the following case, a law partnership incorporated as a professional corporation in 1977 primarily for the purpose of obtaining certain tax benefits. In fact, however, the firm continued to operate as a partnership. A central question before the court in this case was whether the firm should be governed by partnership law or corporation law.

CASE 24.4

Boyd, Payne, Gates & Farthing, P.C. v. Payne, Gates, Farthing & Radd, P.C.

Supreme Court of Virginia, 1992.
422 S.E.2d 784.

FACTS   Robert Boyd, Charles Payne, Ronald Gates, and Philip Farthing practiced law together as a partnership. In 1977, for tax advantages, the partners formed a professional corporation—Boyd, Payne, Gates & Farthing, P.C. (Boyd P.C.). Corporate stock was issued to each partner in proportion to the amount of profit his work generated for the firm. No partnership assets were transferred to the corporation. The members of the firm continued to refer to one another as "partners" and to Boyd as the "managing partner." "Partner" meetings were held to discuss business matters. In 1983, Anthony Radd joined the practice, but four years later, Radd, Payne, Gates, and Farthing formed their own professional corporation—Payne, Gates, Farthing & Radd, P.C. In a dispute over Boyd P.C.'s assets, a Virginia state court found that Boyd P.C. was a partnership and applied partnership law to distribute the assets. Boyd P.C. appealed.

(Continued)

Case 24.4—Continued

ISSUE Was the trial court justified in applying partnership law to Boyd P.C.?

DECISION Yes. The Supreme Court of Virginia affirmed the trial court's judgment.

REASON The Supreme Court of Virginia found, as the trial court had, that Boyd P.C. was merely a corporate "shell" formed to gain tax advantages. The evidence sufficiently indicated that the firm continued to operate as a partnership. The court also found it significant that after the corporation had been formed, the partners "executed an agreement dealing with the possibility of a tax audit" in which it was provided that if the firm was audited, each partner's tax liability would be based on the percentage of profits that the partner received in that particular year. This agreement effectively indicated that "tax liability was apportioned on the basis of partnership percentages, not stock ownership." The court cited a previous case in which partnership law was applied to a corporation because members of the corporation "utterly disregarded [the] corporate entity, and dealt with its rights, property and business as if they belonged to a partnership." The court concluded that "[b]ecause Boyd P.C. was a close corporation and its shareholders validly conducted the internal affairs of their law practice as a partnership, we hold that the trial court properly settled their rights and liabilities according to partnership law."

FOR CRITICAL ANALYSIS—Economic Consideration *What benefits can be gained by switching from a partnership form of business to a corporation?*

▌Corporate Formation

Up to this point, we have discussed some of the general characteristics of corporations. We now examine the process in which corporations come into existence. Generally, this process involves two steps: (1) preliminary organizational and promotional undertakings—particularly obtaining capital for the future corporation—and (2) the legal process of incorporation.

Promotional Activities

Before a corporation becomes a reality, **promoters**—those who, for themselves or others, take the preliminary steps in organizing a corporation—frequently make contracts with investors and others on behalf of the future corporation. One of the tasks of the promoter is to issue a prospectus. A **prospectus** is a document required by federal or state securities laws (discussed in Chapter 27) that describes the financial operations of the corporation, thus allowing investors to make informed decisions. The promoter also secures the corporate charter.

PROMOTER'S LIABILITY A promoter may purchase or lease property with a view to selling it to the corporation when the corporation is formed. A promoter may also enter into contracts with attorneys, accountants, architects, or other professionals whose services will be needed in planning for the proposed corporation. Finally, a promoter induces people to purchase stock in the corporation.

As a general rule, a promoter is held personally liable on preincorporation contracts. Courts simply hold that promoters are not agents when a corporation has yet to come into existence. If, however, the promoter secures the contracting party's agreement to hold only the corporation (and not the promoter) liable on the contract, the promoter will not be liable in the event of any breach of contract. Basically, the personal liability of the promoter continues even after incorporation unless the third party *releases* the promoter. In most states, this rule is applied whether or not the promoter made the agreement in the name of, or with reference to, the proposed corporation.

Once the corporation is formed (the charter issued), the promoter remains personally liable until the corporation assumes the preincorporation contract by *novation* (discussed in Chapter 11). Novation releases the promoter and makes the corporation liable for performing the contractual obligations. In some situations, the corporation *adopts* the promoter's contract by undertaking to perform it. Most courts hold that adoption in and of itself does not discharge the promoter from contractual liability. A corporation cannot normally *ratify* a preincorporation contract, as no principal was in existence at the time the contract was made.

SUBSCRIBERS AND SUBSCRIPTIONS Prior to the actual formation of the corporation, the promoter can contact potential individual investors, and they can agree to purchase capital stock in the future corporation. This agreement is usually called a *subscription agreement*, and the potential investor is called a *subscriber*. Depending on state law, subscribers become shareholders as soon as the corporation is formed or as soon as the corporation accepts the agreement.

Most courts view preincorporation subscriptions as continuing offers to purchase corporate stock. On or after its formation, the corporation can choose to accept the offer to purchase stock. Many courts also treat a subscription as irrevocable except with the consent of all of the subscribers. A subscription is irrevocable for a period of six months unless the subscription agreement provides otherwise or unless all the subscribers agree to the revocation of the subscription [RMBCA 6.20]. In some courts and jurisdictions, the preincorporation subscriber can revoke the offer to purchase before acceptance without liability, however.

Incorporation Procedures

Exact procedures for incorporation differ among states, but the basic requirements are similar.

STATE CHARTERING The first step in the incorporation procedure is to select a state in which to incorporate. Because state incorporation laws differ, individuals often incorporate in a state that offers the most advantageous tax or incorporation provisions. Delaware has historically had the least restrictive laws. Consequently, many corporations, including a number of the largest, have incorporated there. Delaware's statutes permit firms to incorporate in Delaware and carry out business and locate operating headquarters elsewhere. (Most other states now permit this.) Closely held corporations, however, particularly those of a professional nature, generally incorporate in the state in which their principal shareholders live and work.

ARTICLES OF INCORPORATION The primary document needed to begin the incorporation process is called the *articles of incorporation* (see Exhibit 24–3). The articles include basic information about the corporation and serve as a primary source of authority for its future organization and business functions. The person or persons who execute the articles are called *incorporators*. Generally, the articles of incorporation should include the elements discussed in the following subsections.

Corporate Name The choice of a corporate name is subject to state approval to ensure against duplication or deception. State statutes usually require that the secretary of state run a check on the proposed name in the state of incorporation. Some states require that the incorporators, at their own expense, run a check on the proposed name for the newly formed corporation. Once cleared, a name can be reserved for a short time, for a fee, pending the completion of the articles of incorporation. All corporate statutes require the corporation name to include the word *Corporation, Incorporated, Company,* or *Limited,* or abbreviations of these terms.

A corporate name is prohibited from being the same as (or deceptively similar to) the name of an existing corporation doing business within the state. For example, if an existing corporation is named General Dynamics, Inc., the state will not allow another corporation to be called General Dynamic, Inc.—because that name is deceptively similar to the first, and it impliedly transfers a part of the goodwill established by the first corporate user to the second corporation.

Duration A corporation can have perpetual existence under most state corporate statutes. A few

♦ Exhibit 24–3
Articles of Incorporation

ARTICLE ONE

The name of the corporation is _____ .

ARTICLE TWO

The period of its duration is perpetual (may be a number of years or until a certain date).

ARTICLE THREE

The purpose (or purposes) for which the corporation is organized is (are) _____
_____ .

ARTICLE FOUR

The aggregate number of shares that the corporation shall have authority to issue is _____ of the par value of
_____ dollar(s) each (or without par value).

ARTICLE FIVE

The corporation will not commence business until it has received for the issuance of its shares consideration of the
value of $1,000 (can be any sum not less that $1,000).

ARTICLE SIX

The address of the corporation's registered office is _____ ,
New Pacum, and the name of its registered agent at such address is _____
_____ .

(Use the street or building or rural address of the registered office, not a post office box number.)

ARTICLE SEVEN

The number of initial directors is _____ , and the names and addresses of the directors are
_____
_____

ARTICLE EIGHT

The name and address of the incorporator is _____
_____ .

(signed) _____
                                        Incorporator

Sworn to on _____ by the above-named incorporator.
               (date)

                                    _____
                                    Notary Public _____ County, New Pacum

(Notary Seal)

states, however, prescribe a maximum duration, after which the corporation must formally renew its existence.

Nature and Purpose   The articles must specify the intended business activities of the corporation, and naturally, these activities must be lawful. A general statement of corporate purpose is usually sufficient to give rise to all of the powers necessary or convenient to the purpose of the organization. The articles of incorporation can state, for exam-

ple, that the corporation is organized "to engage in the production and sale of agricultural products." There is a trend toward allowing corporate articles to state that the corporation is organized for "any legal business," with no mention of specifics, to avoid unnecessary future amendments to the corporate articles.

Capital Structure   The articles generally set forth the capital structure of the corporation. A few state statutes require a very small capital investment for ordinary business corporations but a greater capital investment for those engaged in insurance or banking. The articles often must outline the number of shares of stock authorized for issuance; their valuation; the various types or classes of stock authorized for issuance; and other relevant information concerning equity, capital, and credit.

Internal Organization The articles should describe the internal management structure of the corporation, although this can be included in bylaws adopted after the corporation is formed. The articles of incorporation commence the corporation; the bylaws are formed after commencement by the board of directors. Bylaws cannot conflict with the incorporation statute or the corporation's charter [RMBCA 2.06].

Under the RMBCA, shareholders may amend or repeal bylaws. The board of directors may also amend or repeal bylaws unless the articles of incorporation or provisions of the incorporation statute reserve this power to shareholders exclusively [RMBCA 10.20]. Typical bylaw provisions describe such things as voting requirements for shareholders, the election of the board of directors, the methods of replacing directors, and the manner and time of scheduling shareholder and board meetings (these corporate activities will be discussed in Chapter 25).

Registered Office and Agent The corporation must indicate the location and address of its registered office within the state. Usually, the registered office is also the principal office of the corporation. The corporation must give the name and address of a specific person who has been designated as an *agent* and who can receive legal documents (such as orders to appear in court) on behalf of the corporation.

Incorporators Each incorporator must be listed by name and must indicate an address. An incorporator is a person—often, the corporate promoter—who applies to the state on behalf of the corporation to obtain its corporate charter. The incorporator need not be a subscriber and need not have any interest at all in the corporation. Many states do not impose residency or age requirements for incorporators. States vary on the required number of incorporators; it can be as few as one or as many as three. Incorporators are required to sign the articles of incorporation when they are submit-

ted to the state; often this is their only duty. In some states, they participate at the first organizational meeting of the corporation.

CERTIFICATE OF INCORPORATION　Once the articles of incorporation have been prepared, signed, and authenticated by the incorporators, they are sent to the appropriate state official, usually the secretary of state, along with the appropriate filing fee. In many states, the secretary of state then issues a **certificate of incorporation** representing the state's authorization for the corporation to conduct business. (This may be referred to as the *corporate charter*.) The certificate and a copy of the articles are returned to the incorporators.

FIRST ORGANIZATIONAL MEETING　The first organnizational meeting is provided for in the articles of incorporation but is held after the charter has actually been granted. At this meeting, the incorporators elect the first board of directors and complete the routine business of incorporation (pass bylaws and issue stock, for example). Sometimes, the meeting is held after the election of the board, and the business transacted depends on the requirements of the state's incorporation statute, the nature of the business, the provisions made in the articles, and the desires of the promoters. Adoption of bylaws—the internal rules of management for the corporation—is probably the most important function of the meeting. The shareholders, directors, and officers must abide by the bylaws in conducting corporate business.

▌Corporate Status

The procedures for incorporation are very specific. If they are not followed precisely, others may be able to challenge the existence of the corporation.

Errors in the incorporation procedures can become important when, for example, a third person who is attempting to enforce a contract or bring suit for a tort injury learns of them. On the basis of improper incorporation, the plaintiff could seek to make the would-be shareholders personally liable. Additionally, when the corporation seeks to enforce a contract against a defaulting party, if the defaulting party learns of a defect in the incorporation procedure, he or she may be able to avoid liability on that ground.

To prevent injustice, courts will sometimes attribute corporate status to an improperly formed corporation by holding it to be a *de jure* corporation or a *de facto* corporation. Occasionally, a corporation may be held to exist by estoppel. Additionally, in certain circumstances involving abuse of the corporate form, a court may disregard the corporate entity and hold the shareholders personally liable.

De Jure and *De Facto* Corporations

In the event of substantial compliance with all conditions precedent to incorporation, the corporation is said to have *de jure* (rightful and lawful) existence. In most states and under the RMBCA, the certificate of incorporation is viewed as evidence that all mandatory statutory provisions have been met. This means that the corporation is properly formed, and neither the state nor a third party can attack its existence. If, for example, an incorporator's address was incorrectly listed, this would technically mean that the corporation was improperly formed; but the law does not regard such inconsequential procedural defects as detracting from substantial compliance, and courts will uphold the *de jure* status of the corporate entity.

Sometimes, there is a defect in complying with statutory mandates—for example, the corporation charter may have expired. Under these circumstances, the corporation may have *de facto* (actual) status, meaning that the corporation in fact exists, even if not rightfully or lawfully. A corporation with *de facto* status cannot be challenged by third persons (except for the state). The following elements are required for *de facto* status:

1. There must be a state statute under which the corporation can be validly incorporated.
2. The parties must have made a good faith attempt to comply with the statute.
3. The enterprise must already have undertaken to do business as a corporation.

Corporation by Estoppel

If an association that is neither an actual corporation nor a *de facto* or *de jure* corporation holds itself out as being a corporation, it normally will be estopped from denying corporate status in a lawsuit by a third party. This usually occurs when a third party contracts with an association that claims to be a corporation but does not hold a certificate of incorporation. When the third party brings suit naming the so-called corporation as the defendant, the association may not escape from liability on the ground that no corporation exists. When justice requires, the courts treat an alleged corporation as if it were an actual corporation for the purpose of determining the rights and liabilities involved in a particular situation. Corporation by estoppel is thus determined by the situation. It does not extend recognition of corporate status beyond the resolution of the problem at hand.

Disregarding the Corporate Entity

Occasionally, the owners use a corporate entity to perpetuate a fraud, circumvent the law, or in some other way accomplish an illegitimate objective. In these situations, the court will ignore the corporate structure by "piercing the corporate veil" and exposing the shareholders to personal liability. The following are some of the factors that frequently cause the courts to pierce the corporate veil:

1. A party is tricked or misled into dealing with the corporation rather than the individual.
2. The corporation is set up never to make a profit or always to be insolvent, or it is too "thinly" capitalized—that is, it has insufficient capital at the time of formation to meet its prospective debts or potential liabilities.
3. Statutory corporate formalities, such as holding required corporation meetings, are not followed.
4. Personal and corporate interests are commingled (mixed together) to the extent that the corporation has no separate identity.

To elaborate on the fourth factor in the preceding list, consider a close corporation that is formed according to law by a single person or by a few family members. In such a situation, the separate status of the corporate entity and the sole stockholder (or family-member stockholders) must be carefully preserved. Certain practices invite trouble for the one-person or family-owned corporation: the commingling of corporate and personal funds, the failure to hold and record minutes of board of directors' meetings, or the shareholders' continuous personal use of corporate property (for example, vehicles).

Corporation laws usually do not specifically prohibit a stockholder from lawfully lending money to his or her corporation. When an officer or director lends the corporation money and takes back security in the form of corporate assets, however, the courts will scrutinize the transaction closely. Any such transaction must be made in good faith and for fair value.

Generally, when the corporate privilege is abused for personal benefit or when the corporate business is treated in such a careless manner that the corporation and the shareholder in control are no longer separate entities, the court usually will require an owner to assume personal liability to creditors for the corporation's debts. In short, when the facts show that great injustice would result from the use of a corporation to avoid individual responsibility, a court of equity will look behind the corporate structure to the individual stockholder. The following case is illustrative.

CASE 24.5

J-Mart Jewelry Outlets, Inc. v. Standard Design

Court of Appeals of Georgia, 1995.
218 Ga.App. 459,
462 S.E.2d 406.

FACTS Jim Halter, the sole shareholder of J-Mart Jewelry Outlets, Inc., knew that as a result of financial difficulties, J-Mart would soon go out of business. Eight days before the firm stopped doing business, it paid the balance due on Halter's personal credit card. At the same time, Halter paid J-Mart $1 for a Cadillac that the firm had bought new for his personal use and on which it had made three payments. Four of J-Mart's creditors, including Standard Design, filed a suit in a Georgia state court against Halter and others to recover for J-Mart's unpaid debts. The jury "pierced the corporate veil" to hold Halter personally responsible. Halter appealed.

ISSUE Is it proper to pierce the corporate veil when, shortly before a corporation goes out of business, the corporation pays the balance on its sole shareholder's personal credit card and makes unauthorized payments on a car for the shareholder's personal benefit?

DECISION Yes. The Court of Appeals of Georgia affirmed the judgment of the lower court.

REASON The state appellate court explained that "[t]he concept of piercing the corporate veil is applied in Georgia to remedy injustices which arise where a party has overextended his privilege in the use of a corporate entity in order to defeat justice, perpetrate fraud or to evade contractual or tort responsibility." The court noted that shortly before J-Mart went out of business, it paid off the balance on Halter's personal credit card and made unauthorized payments on a car for his personal benefit.

FOR CRITICAL ANALYSIS—Ethical Consideration *Why shouldn't the sole owner of a corporation be held liable for* all *corporate acts?*

▌ Corporate Financing

Part of the process of corporate formation involves corporate financing. Corporations are financed by the issuance and sale of corporate securities. **Securities** (stocks and bonds) evidence the obligation to pay money or the right to participate in earnings and the distribution of corporate property. **Stocks,** or *equity securities,* represent the purchase of ownership in the business firm. **Bonds** (debentures), or *debt securities,* represent the borrowing of money by firms (and governments). Of course, not all debt is in the form of debt securities. For example, some debt is in the form of accounts payable and notes payable. Accounts and notes payable are typically short-term debts. Bonds are simply a way for the corporation to split up its long-term debt so that it can market it more easily.

Bonds

Bonds are issued by business firms and by governments at all levels as evidence of the funds they are borrowing from investors. Bonds normally have a designated *maturity date*—the date when the principal, or face, amount of the bond is returned to the investor. They are sometimes referred to as *fixed-income securities* because their owners (that is, the creditors) receive fixed-dollar interest payments during the period of time prior to maturity, usually semiannually.

Because debt financing represents a legal obligation on the part of the corporation, various features and terms of a particular bond issue are specified in a lending agreement called a **bond indenture**. A corporate trustee, often a commercial bank trust department, represents the collective well-being of all bondholders in ensuring that the corporation meets the terms of the bond issue. The bond indenture specifies the maturity date of the bond and the pattern of interest payments until maturity. The different types of corporate bonds are described in Exhibit 24–4.

Stocks

Issuing stocks is another way that corporations can obtain financing. The ways in which stocks differ from bonds are summarized in Exhibit 24–5. Basically, as mentioned, stocks represent ownership in a business firm, whereas bonds represent borrowing by the firm.

The most important characteristics of stocks are as follows:

1. Stockholders need not be paid back.
2. Stockholders receive dividends only when so voted by the directors.
3. Stockholders are the last investors to be paid off on dissolution.
4. Stockholders vote for management and on major issues.

Exhibit 24–6 summarizes the types of stocks issued by corporations. We look now at the two major types of stock—*common stock* and *preferred stock.*

COMMON STOCK   The true ownership of a corporation is represented by **common stock.** Common stock provides a proportionate interest in the corporation with regard to (1) control, (2) earnings, and (3) net assets. A shareholder's interest is generally in proportion to the number of shares he or she owns out of the total number of shares issued.

Voting rights in a corporation apply to the election of the firm's board of directors and to any proposed changes in the ownership structure of the firm. For example, a holder of common stock generally has the right to vote in a decision on a proposed merger, as mergers can change the proportion of ownership. State corporation law specifies the types of actions for which shareholder approval must be obtained.

◆ Exhibit 24–4
Types of Corporate Bonds

Debenture Bonds	Bonds for which no specific assets of the corporation are pledged as backing. Rather, they are backed by the general credit rating of the corporation, plus any assets that can be seized if the corporation allows the debentures to go into default.
Mortgage Bonds	Bonds that pledge specific property. If the corporation defaults on the bonds, the bondholders can take the property.
Convertible Bonds	Bonds that can be exchanged for a specified number of shares of common stock under certain conditions.
Callable Bonds	Bonds that may be called in and the principal repaid at specified times or under conditions specified in the bond when it is issued.

♦ **Exhibit 24–5**
How Do Stocks and Bonds Differ?

STOCKS	BONDS
1. Stocks represent ownership.	1. Bonds represent debt.
2. Stocks (common) do not have a fixed dividend rate.	2. Interest on bonds must always be paid, whether or not any profit is earned.
3. Stockholders can elect a board of directors, which controls the corporation.	3. Bondholders usually have no voice in, or control over, management of the corporation.
4. Stocks do not have a maturity date; the corporation does not usually repay the stockholder.	4. Bonds have a maturity date, when the corporation is to repay the bondholder the face value of the bond.
5. All corporations issue or offer to sell stocks. This is the usual definition of a corporation.	5. Corporations do not necessarily issue bonds.
6. Stockholders have a claim against the property and income of a corporation after all creditors' claims have been met.	6. Bondholders have a claim against the property and income of a corporation that must be met before the claims of stockholders.

♦ **Exhibit 24–6**
Types of Stocks

Common Stock	Voting shares that represent ownership interest in a corporation. Common stock has the lowest priority with respect to payment of dividends and distribution of assets on the corporation's dissolution.
Preferred Stock	Shares of stock that have priority over common-stock shares as to payment of dividends and distribution of assets on dissolution. Dividend payments are usually a fixed percentage of the face value of the share.
Cumulative Preferred Stock	Required dividends not paid in a given year must be paid in a subsequent year before any common-stock dividends are paid.
Participating Preferred Stock	Stock entitling the owner to receive the preferred-stock dividend and additional dividends after the corporation has paid dividends on common stock.
Convertible Preferred Stock	Stock entitling the owners to convert their shares into a specified number of common shares either in the issuing corporation or, sometimes, in another corporation.
Redeemable, or Callable, Preferred Stock	Preferred shares issued with the express condition that the issuing corporation has the right to repurchase the shares as specified.

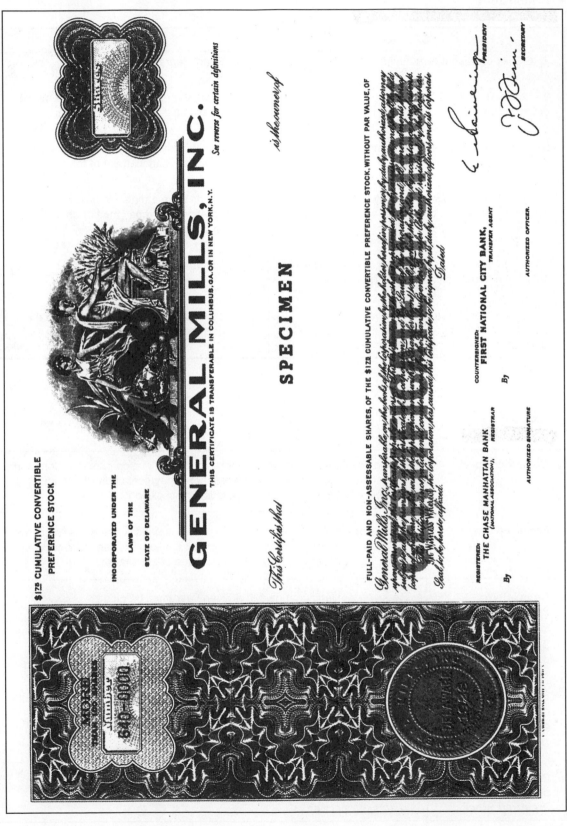

◆ Exhibit 24-7
Cumulative Convertible Preferred-Stock Certificate

Firms are not obligated to return a principal amount per share to each holder of common stock, because no firm can ensure that the market price per share of its common stock will not decline over time. The issuing firm also does not have to guarantee a dividend; indeed, some corporations never pay dividends.

Holders of common stock are a group of investors who assume a *residual* position in the overall financial structure of a business. In terms of receiving payment for their investments, they are last in line. The earnings to which they are entitled are those left after preferred stockholders, bondholders, suppliers, employees, and other groups have been paid. Once those groups are paid, however, the owners of common stock may be entitled to *all* the remaining earnings as dividends. (The board of directors is not normally under any duty to declare the remaining earnings as dividends, however.)

PREFERRED STOCK **Preferred stock** is stock with *preferences*. Usually, this means that holders of preferred stock have priority over holders of common stock as to dividends and as to payment on dissolution of the corporation. Holders of preferred stock may or may not have the right to vote.

Preferred stock is not included among the liabilities of a business, because it is equity. Like other equity securities, preferred shares have no fixed maturity date on which the firm must pay them off. Although occasionally firms buy back preferred stock, they are not legally obligated to do so. A sample cumulative convertible preferred-stock certificate is shown in Exhibit 24–7.

Holders of preferred stock are investors who have assumed a rather cautious position in their relationship to the corporation. They have a stronger position than common shareholders with respect to dividends and claims on assets, but as a result, they will not share in the full prosperity of the firm if it grows successfully over time. This is because the value of preferred shares will not rise as rapidly as that of common shares during a period of financial success. Preferred stockholders do receive fixed dividends periodically, however, and they may benefit to some extent from changes in the market price of the shares.

The return and the risk for preferred stock lie somewhere between those for bonds and those for common stock. Preferred stock is more similar to bonds than to common stock, even though preferred stock appears in the ownership section of the firm's balance sheet. As a result, preferred stock is often categorized with corporate bonds as a fixed-income security, even though the legal status is not the same.

❚ Terms and Concepts

❚ Chapter Summary: Corporate Formation and Financing

The Nature of the Corporation *(See pages 505–508.)*	The corporation is a legal entity distinct from its owners. Formal statutory requirements, which vary somewhat from state to state, must be followed in forming a corporation. The corporation can have perpetual existence or be chartered for a specific period of time.
	1. *Corporate personnel*—The shareholders own the corporation. They elect a board of directors to govern the corporation. The board of directors hires corporate officers and other employees to run the daily business of the firm.

(Continued)

▌Chapter Summary: Corporate Formation and Financing—Continued

The Nature of the Corporation— Continued	2. *Corporate taxation*—The corporation pays income tax on net profits; shareholders pay income tax on the disbursed dividends that they receive from the corporation (double-taxation feature). 3. *Torts and criminal acts*—The corporation is liable for the torts committed by its agents or officers within the course and scope of their employment (under the doctrine of *respondeat superior*). In some circumstances, a corporation can be held liable (and be fined) for the criminal acts of its agents and employees. In certain situations, corporate officers may be held personally liable for corporate crimes.
Corporate Powers *(See pages 508–512.)*	1. *Express powers*—The express powers of a corporation are granted by the following laws and documents (listed according to their priority): federal constitution, state constitutions, state statutes, articles of incorporation, bylaws, and resolutions of the board of directors. 2. *Implied powers*—Barring express constitutional, statutory, or other prohibitions, the corporation has the implied power to do all acts reasonably appropriate and necessary to accomplish its corporate purposes. 3. *Ultra vires doctrine*—Any act of a corporation that is beyond its express or implied powers to undertake is an *ultra vires* act. 　a. *Ultra vires* contracts may or may not be enforced by the courts, depending on the circumstances. 　b. The corporation (or shareholders on behalf of the corporation) may sue to enjoin or recover damages for *ultra vires* acts of corporate officers or directors. In addition, the state attorney general may bring an action either to institute an injunction against the transaction or to institute dissolution proceedings against the corporation for *ultra vires* acts.
Classification of Corporations *(See pages 512–516.)*	1. *Domestic, foreign, and alien corporations*—A corporation is referred to as a *domestic corporation* within its home state (the state in which it incorporates). A corporation is referred to as a *foreign corporation* by any state that is not its home state. A corporation is referred to as an *alien corporation* if it originates in another country but does business in the United States. 2. *Public and private corporations*—A public corporation is one formed by government (e.g., cities, towns, and public projects). A private corporation is one formed wholly or in part for private benefit. Most corporations are private corporations. 3. *Nonprofit corporations*—Corporations formed without a profit-making purpose (e.g., charitable, educational, and religious organizations and hospitals). 4. *Close corporations*—Corporations owned by a family or a relatively small number of individuals; transfer of shares is usually restricted, and the corporation cannot make a public offering of its securities. 5. *S corporations*—Small domestic corporations (must have thirty-five or fewer shareholders as members) that, under Subchapter S of the Internal Revenue Code, are given special tax treatment. These corporations allow shareholders to enjoy the limited legal liability of the corporate form but avoid its double-taxation feature (taxes are paid by shareholders as personal income, and the S corporation is not taxed separately). 6. *Professional corporations*—Corporations formed by professionals (e.g., doctors, lawyers) to obtain the benefits of incorporation (such as tax benefits and limited liability). In most situations, the professional corporation is treated like other corporations, but sometimes the courts will disregard the corporate form and treat the shareholders like partners.

▮ Chapter Summary: Corporate Formation and Financing—Continued

Corporate Formation
(See pages 516–519.)
	1. *Promotional activities*—A corporate promoter is one who takes the preliminary steps in organizing a corporation (issues a prospectus, secures the charter, interests investors in the purchase of corporate stock, forms subscription agreements, and so on).
	
	2. *Incorporation procedures*—
	   a. A state in which to incorporate is selected.
	   b. The articles of incorporation are prepared and filed. The articles generally should include the corporate name, duration, nature and purpose, capital structure, internal organization, registered office and agent, and incorporators.
	   c. The certificate of incorporation (or charter), which authorizes the corporation to conduct business, is received from the appropriate state office (usually the secretary of state) after the articles of incorporation have been filed.
	   d. The first organizational meeting is held after the charter is granted. The board of directors is elected and other business completed (bylaws passed, stock issued, and so on).

Corporate Status *(See pages 519–521.)*	1. *De jure or de facto corporation*—If a corporation has been improperly incorporated, courts will sometimes impute corporate status to the firm by holding that the firm is a *de jure* corporation (cannot be challenged by the state or third persons) or a *de facto* corporation (can be challenged by the state but not by third persons). 2. *Corporation by estoppel*—If a firm is neither a *de jure* nor a *de facto* corporation but represents itself to be a corporation and is sued as such by a third party, it may be held to be a corporation by estoppel. 3. *Disregarding the corporate entity*—To avoid injustice, courts may "pierce the corporate veil" and hold a shareholder or shareholders personally liable for a judgment against the corporation. This usually occurs only when the corporation was established to circumvent the law, when the corporate form is used for an illegitimate or fraudulent purpose, or when the controlling shareholder commingles his or her own interests with those of the corporation to such an extent that the corporation no longer has a separate identity.
Corporate Financing—Bonds *(See page 522.)*	Corporate bonds are securities representing *corporate debt*—money borrowed by a corporation. Types of corporate bonds include the following: 1. *Debenture bonds*—Bonds backed by the general credit rating of the corporation; no corporate assets are pledged as security. 2. *Mortgage bonds*—Bonds pledging as security specific corporate property. 3. *Convertible bonds*—Bonds that can be exchanged for a specified number of shares of common stock at the option of the bondholder. 4. *Callable bonds*—Bonds that may be called in and the principal repaid at specified times or under specified conditions.

Corporate Financing—Stocks
(See pages 522–525.)
	Stocks are equity securities issued by a corporation that represent the purchase of ownership in the business firm.
	
	1. *Important characteristics of stocks*—
	   a. Stockholders need not be paid back.
	   b. Stockholders receive dividends only when so voted by the directors.
	   c. Stockholders are the last investors to be paid on dissolution.
	   d. Stockholders vote for management and on major issues.
	
	2. *Types of stock (see Exhibit 26–4 for details)*—
	   a. Common stock—Represents the true ownership of the firm. Holders of common stock share in the control, earning capacity, and net assets of the

(Continued)

▌ Chapter Summary: Corporate Formation and Financing—Continued

Corporate Financing—Stocks —Continued	corporation. Common stockholders carry more risk than preferred stockholders but, if the corporation is successful, are compensated for this risk by greater returns on their investments. b. Preferred stock—Stock whose holders have a preferred status. Preferred stockholders have a stronger position than common stockholders with respect to dividends and claims on assets, but as a result, they will not share in the full prosperity of the firm if it grows successfully over time. The return and risk for preferred stock lie somewhere between those for bonds and common stock.

▌ For Review

1. What are the express and implied powers of corporations? On what sources are these powers based?

2. What are the steps for bringing a corporation into existence? Who is liable for preincorporation contracts?

3. What is the difference between a *de jure* corporation and a *de facto* corporation?

4. In what circumstances might a court disregard the corporate entity ("pierce the corporate veil") and hold the shareholders personally liable?

5. How are corporations financed? What is the difference between stocks and bonds?

▌ Questions and Case Problems

24–1. Corporate Status. Three brothers inherited a small paper-supply business from their father, who had operated the business as a sole proprietorship. The brothers decided to incorporate under the name of Gomez Corp. and retained an attorney to draw up the necessary documents. The attorney drew up the papers and had the brothers sign them but neglected to send the application for a corporate charter to the secretary of state's office. The brothers assumed that all necessary legal work had been taken care of, and they proceeded to do business as Gomez Corp. One day, a Gomez Corp. employee, while making a delivery to one of Gomez's customers, negligently ran a red light and caused a car accident. Baxter, the driver of the other vehicle, was injured as a result and sued Gomez Corp. for damages. Baxter then learned that no state charter had ever been issued to Gomez Corp., so he sued each of the brothers personally for damages. Can the brothers avoid personal liability for the tort of their employee? Explain.

24–2. Liability for Preincorporation Contracts. Christy, Briggs, and Dobbs are recent college graduates who want to form a corporation to manufacture and sell personal computers. Perez tells them that he will set in motion the formation of their corporation. Perez first

makes a contract with Oliver for the purchase of a parcel of land for $25,000. Oliver does not know of the prospective corporate formation at the time the contract is signed. Perez then makes a contract with Kovac to build a small plant on the property being purchased. Kovac's contract is conditional on the corporation's formation. Perez secures all necessary subscription agreements and capitalization, and he files the articles of incorporation. A charter is issued.

(a) Discuss whether the newly formed corporation or Perez (or both) is liable on the contracts with Oliver and Kovac.

(b) Discuss whether the corporation, on coming into legal existence, is automatically liable to Kovac.

24–3. Corporate Powers. Kora Nayenga and two business associates formed a corporation called Nayenga Corp. for the purpose of selling computer services. Kora, who owned 50 percent of the corporate shares, served as the corporation's president. Kora wished to obtain a personal loan from his bank for $250,000, but the bank required the note to be cosigned by a third party. Kora cosigned the note in the name of the corporation. Later, Kora defaulted on the note, and the bank sued the corporation for payment. The corporation asserted, as a defense, that Kora had exceeded his authority when he cosigned the note. Had he? Explain.

24–4. Liability of Shareholders. Charles Wolfe was the sole shareholder and president of Wolfe & Co., a firm that leased tractor-trailers. The corporation had no separate bank account. Banking transactions were conducted through Wolfe's personal accounts, and employees were paid from them. Wolfe never consulted with any other corporate directors. During the tax years 1974–1976, the corporation incurred $114,472.91 in federal tax liabilities. The government held Wolfe personally liable for the taxes. Wolfe paid the tax bill and then brought an action against the government for disregarding his corporate entity. Discuss whether the government can "pierce the corporate veil" in Wolfe's case and hold Wolfe personally liable for corporate taxes. [*Wolfe v. United States*, 798 F.2d 1241 (9th Cir. 1961)]

24–5. Liability for Preincorporation Contracts. Skandinavia, Inc., manufactured and sold polypropylene underwear. Following two years of poor sales, Skandinavia entered into negotiations to sell the business to Odilon Cormier, an individual who was an experienced textile manufacturer. Skandinavia and Cormier agreed that Cormier would take Skandinavia's underwear inventory and use it in a new corporation, which would be called Polypro, Inc. In return, Skandinavia would receive a commission on future sales from Polypro. Polypro was subsequently established and began selling the underwear. Skandinavia, however, having never received any commissions from the sales, sued Polypro and Cormier to recover its promised commissions. Is Cormier personally liable for the contract he signed in the course of setting up a new corporation? Discuss. [*Skandinavia, Inc. v. Cormier*, 128 N.H. 215, 214 A.2d 1250 (1986)]

24–6. Professional Corporations. Cohen, Stracher & Bloom, P.C., a law firm organized as a professional corporation under New York law, entered into an agreement with We're Associates Co. for the lease of office space located in Lake Success, New York. The lease was signed for We're Associates by one of the partners of that company and for the professional corporation by Paul J. Bloom, as vice president. Bloom, Cohen, and Stracher were the sole officers, directors, and shareholders of the professional corporation. The corporation became delinquent in paying its rent, and We're Associates brought an action to recover rents and other charges of approximately $9,000 alleged to be due under the lease. The complaint was filed against the professional corporation and each individual shareholder of the corporation. The individual shareholders moved to dismiss the action against them individually. Will the court grant their motion? Discuss. [*We're Associates Co. v. Cohen, Stracher & Bloom, P.C.*, 103 A.D.2d 130, 478 N.Y.S.2d 670 (1984)]

24–7. *Ultra Vires* Acts. The Midtown Club, Inc., was a nonprofit corporation whose certificate of incorporation stated that the sole purpose of the club was "to provide facilities for the serving of luncheon or other meals to members." Samuel Cross, a member of the club, brought a female guest to lunch at the club, but he and his friend were both refused seating. On several occasions, Cross made applications on behalf of females for their admission to the club, but the club ignored or rejected them. Cross brought an action against the club, alleging that its actions were *ultra vires*. Did he succeed? Explain. [*Cross v. Midtown Club, Inc.*, 33 Conn.Supp. 150, 365 A.2d 127 (1976)]

24–8. Liability of Shareholders. In the early 1950s, Mary Emmons opened an account at M&M Wholesale Florist, Inc., to purchase flowers and florist supplies for her flower shop, called Bay Minette Flower Shop, which she operated as a sole proprietorship. In 1973, the flower shop was incorporated as Bay Minette Flower Shop, Inc. Emmons continued to order supplies from M&M, as did her son when he began to manage the day-to-day operations of the shop during the 1980s. M&M, which had no knowledge that Bay Minette was now a corporation, sued Emmons and her son personally to recover a balance due on the Bay Minette account (for purchases made after Bay Minette had incorporated). Is the fact that M&M was never informed of the incorporation of Bay Minette Flower Shop a sufficient ground for piercing the corporate veil and holding Emmons and her son personally liable for the debt? Explain. [*M & M Wholesale Florist, Inc. v. Emmons*, 600 So.2d 998 (Ala. 1992)]

24–9. Liability of Shareholders. Moseley Group Management Co. (MGM) provided management services to apartment complexes. MGM's only assets were equipment worth $500 and a bank account with an average balance of $1,500. Richard Moseley ran the company and owned half of the stock. MGM contracted with Property Tax Research Co. (PTR) to obtain a lower property tax assessment on one of its complexes. PTR performed, but MGM refused to pay and transferred its assets and employees to Terrace Management, Inc., a corporation controlled by Moseley. PTR filed a suit in a Missouri state court against Moseley and others to recover the unpaid fees. Should the court pierce the corporate veil and hold Moseley personally liable for the debt? If so, on what basis? [*Sansone v. Moseley*, 912 S.W.2d 666 (Mo.App., W.D. 1995)]

24–10. Corporate Powers. Soda Dispensing Systems, Inc., was owned by two shareholders, each of whom owned half of the stock. One shareholder was the president of the corporation, and the other was vice president. Their shareholder agreement stated that neither shareholder could "encumber any corporate property . . . without the written consent of the other." When Soda Dispensing went out of business, the two shareholders agreed to sell the assets, split the proceeds, and pay $9,900 to their accountants, Cooper, Selvin &

Strassberg. Later, the president committed Soda Dispensing to pay Cooper, Selvin more than $24,000, claiming that he had the authority, as president, to make that commitment. When the accountants tried to collect, the vice president objected, asserting that the president had exceeded his authority. Will the court order Soda Dispensing to pay? Explain. [*Cooper, Selvin & Strassberg v. Soda Dispensing Systems, Inc.*, 212 A.D.2d 498, 622 N.Y.S.2d 312 (1995)]

▌Accessing the Internet: Fundamentals of Business Law

The Center for Corporate Law at the University of Cincinnati College of Law is a good source of information on corporate law. Go to
http://www.law.uc.edu/CCL/

At last count, the corporation statutes of about one-fourth of the states were online. Cornell University's Legal Information Institute has links to these statutes at
http://fatty.law.cornell.edu/topics/state_statutes.html

You can find an online newsletter dealing with corporate officers' and employees' personal liability for business taxes at
http://www.integritax.com

Hoover's Online has an extensive collection of data on U.S. corporations. To access this site, go to
http://www.hoovers.com

Switchboard, a nationwide residential and business directory, can be accessed at
http://www.switchboard.com/

For daily news on the world of business, including corporate activities, you can access Money Online at
http://www.money.com

You can find nearly all of the stories from the printed editions of the *Wall Street Journal* at
http://wsj.com

Fortune magazine also is now on line. Go to
http://fortune.com

To access the current edition of *Business Week*, go to
http://www.businessweek.com/

CNN, the financial network, provides features and news briefs of interest to businesspersons at
http://www.cnnfn.com/

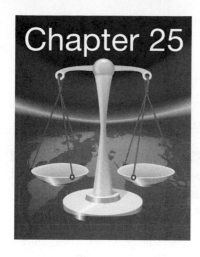

Chapter 25

Corporate Directors, Officers, and Shareholders

CHAPTER OBJECTIVES

After reading this chapter, you should be able to:

1. Describe the role of corporate directors and officers.
2. Summarize the duties owed to the corporation by directors and officers.
3. Explain the effect of the business judgment rule on directors' liability for their decisions.
4. Identify the rights of shareholders, including the right to bring a derivative suit.
5. Discuss the liability of shareholders and the duties owed by majority shareholders.

A corporation is not a "natural" person but a legal fiction. No one individual shareholder or director bears sole responsibility for the corporation and its actions. Rather, a corporation joins the efforts and resources of a large number of individuals for the purpose of producing returns greater than the returns those persons could have obtained individually.

Sometimes, actions that benefit the corporation as a whole do not coincide with the separate interests of the individuals making up the corporation. In such situations, it is important to know the rights and duties of all participants in the corporate enterprise. This chapter focuses on the rights and duties of directors, managers, and shareholders and the ways in which conflicts among them are resolved.

∎ Role of Directors

A corporation typically is governed by a board of directors. A director occupies a position of respon-

sibility unlike that of other corporate personnel. Directors are sometimes inappropriately characterized as *agents* because they act on behalf of the corporation. No *individual* director, however, can act as an agent to bind the corporation; and as a group, directors collectively control the corporation in a way that no agent is able to control a principal. Directors are often incorrectly characterized as *trustees* because they occupy positions of trust and control over the corporation. Unlike trustees, however, they do not own or hold title to property for the use and benefit of others.

Election of Directors

Subject to statutory limitations, the number of directors is set forth in the corporation's articles or bylaws. Historically, the minimum number of directors has been three, but today many states permit fewer. Indeed, the Revised Model Business Corporation Act (RMBCA), in Section 8.01, permits corporations with fewer than fifty shareholders to eliminate the board of directors.

The first board of directors is normally appointed by the incorporators on the creation of the corporation, or directors are named by the corporation itself in the articles. The first board serves until the first annual shareholders' meeting. Subsequent directors are elected by a majority vote of the shareholders.

The term of office for a director is usually one year—from annual meeting to annual meeting. Longer and staggered terms are permissible under most state statutes. A common practice is to elect one-third of the board members each year for a three-year term. In this way, there is greater management continuity.

A director can be removed *for cause* (that is, for failing to perform a required duty), either as specified in the articles or bylaws or by shareholder action. Even the board of directors itself may be given power to remove a director for cause, subject to shareholder review. In most states, unless the shareholders have reserved the right at the time of election, a director cannot be removed without cause.

Vacancies can occur on the board of directors because of death or resignation, or when a new position is created through amendment of the articles or bylaws. In these situations, either the shareholders or the board itself can fill the position, depending on state law or on the provisions of the bylaws.

Directors' Qualifications and Compensation

Few legal requirements exist concerning directors' qualifications. Only a handful of states impose minimum age and residency requirements. A director is sometimes a shareholder, but this is not a necessary qualification—unless, of course, statutory provisions or corporate articles or bylaws require ownership.

Compensation for directors is ordinarily specified in the corporate articles or bylaws. Because directors have a fiduciary relationship to the shareholders and to the corporation, an express agreement or provision for compensation often is necessary for them to receive money from the funds that they control and for which they have responsibilities.

Board of Directors' Meetings

The board of directors conducts business by holding formal meetings with recorded minutes. The date on which regular meetings are held is usually established in the articles or bylaws or by board resolution, and no further notice is customarily required. Special meetings can be called, with notice sent to all directors.

Quorum requirements can vary among jurisdictions. A **quorum** is the minimum number of members of a body of officials or other group that must be present in order for business to be validly transacted. Many states leave the decision as to quorum requirements to the corporate articles or bylaws. In the absence of specific state statutes, most states provide that a quorum is a majority of the number of directors authorized in the articles or bylaws. Voting is done in person (unlike voting at shareholders' meetings, which can be done by proxy, as discussed later in this chapter).[1] The rule is one vote per director. Ordinary matters generally require a simple majority vote; certain extraordinary issues may require a greater-than-majority vote.

Rights of Directors

A director of a corporation has a number of rights, including the rights of participation, inspection, compensation, and indemnification.

PARTICIPATION AND INSPECTION A corporate director must have certain rights to function properly in that position. The main right is one of participation—meaning that the director must be notified of board of directors' meetings so as to participate in them. As pointed out earlier in this chapter, regular board meetings are usually established by the bylaws or by board resolution, and no notice of these meetings is required. If special meetings are called, however, notice is required unless waived by the director.

A director must have access to all of the corporate books and records to make decisions and to exercise the necessary supervision over corporate officers and employees. This right of inspection is virtually absolute and cannot be restricted.

COMPENSATION AND INDEMNIFICATION Historically, directors have had no inherent right to com-

---

1. Except in Louisiana, which allows a director to vote by proxy under certain circumstances. Some states, such as Michigan and Texas, and Section 8.20 of the RMBCA permit telephone conferences for board of directors' meetings.

pensation for their services as directors. Nominal sums are often paid as honorariums to directors, however. In many corporations, directors are also chief corporate officers (president or chief executive officer, for example) and receive compensation in their managerial positions. Most directors, however, gain through indirect benefits, such as business contacts, prestige, and other rewards, such as stock options. There is a trend toward providing more than nominal compensation for directors, especially in large corporations in which directorships can be enormous burdens in terms of time, work, effort, and risk. Many states permit the corporate articles or bylaws to authorize compensation for directors, and in some cases the board can set its own compensation unless the articles or bylaws provide otherwise.

Corporate directors may become involved in lawsuits by virtue of their positions and their actions as directors. Most states (and RMBCA 8.51) permit a corporation to indemnify (guarantee reimbursement to) a director for legal costs, fees, and judgments involved in defending corporation-related suits. Many states specifically permit a corporation to purchase liability insurance for the directors and officers to cover indemnification. When the statutes are silent on this matter, the power to purchase such insurance is usually considered to be part of the corporation's implied power.

Management Responsibilities

Directors have responsibility for all policymaking decisions necessary to the management of corporate affairs. Just as shareholders cannot act individually to bind the corporation, the directors must act as a body in carrying out routine corporate business. One director has one vote, and generally the majority rules. The general areas of responsibility of the board of directors include the following:

1. Declaration and payment of corporate dividends to shareholders.

2. Authorization for major corporate policy decisions—for example, the initiation of proceedings for the sale or lease of corporate assets outside the regular course of business, the determination of new product lines, and the overseeing of major contract negotiations and major management-labor negotiations.

3. Appointment, supervision, and removal of corporate officers and other managerial employees and the determination of their compensation.

4. Financial decisions, such as the issuance of authorized shares and bonds.

The board of directors can delegate some of its functions to an executive committee or to corporate officers. In doing so, the board is not relieved of its overall responsibility for directing the affairs of the corporation, but corporate officers and managerial personnel are empowered to make decisions relating to ordinary, daily corporate affairs within well-defined guidelines.

Role of Corporate Officers and Executives

The officers and other executive employees are hired by the board of directors or, in rare instances, by the shareholders. In addition to carrying out the duties articulated in the bylaws, corporate and managerial officers act as agents of the corporation, and the ordinary rules of agency (discussed in Chapter 21) normally apply to their employment. The qualifications required of officers and executive employees are determined at the discretion of the corporation and are included in the articles or bylaws. In most states, a person can hold more than one office and can be both an officer and a director of the corporation.

The rights of corporate officers and other high-level managers are defined by employment contracts, because these persons are employees of the company. Corporate officers normally can be removed by the board of directors at any time with or without cause and regardless of the terms of the employment contracts—although in so doing, the corporation may be liable for breach of contract. The duties of corporate officers are the same as those of directors, because both groups are involved in decision making and are in similar positions of control. Hence, officers are viewed as having the same fiduciary duties of care and loyalty in their conduct of corporate affairs as directors have, a subject to which we now turn.

Duties of Directors and Officers

Directors and officers are deemed *fiduciaries* of the corporation, because their relationship with the corporation and its shareholders is one of trust and confidence. The fiduciary duties of the directors and officers include the duty of care and the duty of loyalty.

Duty of Care

Directors and officers must exercise due care in performing their duties. The standard of *due care* has been variously described in judicial decisions and codified in many corporation codes. Generally, a director or officer is expected to act in good faith, to exercise the care that an ordinarily prudent person would exercise in similar circumstances, and to act in what he or she considers to be the best interests of the corporation.[2] Directors and officers who have not exercised the required duty of care can be held liable for the harms suffered by the corporation as a result of their negligence.

DUTY TO MAKE INFORMED AND REASONABLE DECISIONS Directors and officers are expected to be informed on corporate matters. To be informed, the director or officer must do what is necessary to become informed: attend presentations, ask for information from those who have it, read reports, review other written materials such as contracts—in other words, carefully study a situation and its alternatives. Depending on the nature of the business, directors and officers are often expected to act in accordance with their own knowledge and training. Most states (and Section 8.30 of the RMBCA), however, allow a director to make decisions in reliance on information furnished by competent officers or employees, professionals such as attorneys and accountants, or even an executive committee of the board without being accused of acting in bad faith or failing to exercise due care if such information turns out to be faulty.

Directors are also expected to make reasonable decisions. For example, a director should not accept a **tender offer** (an offer to purchase shares in the company that is made by another company directly to the shareholders, sometimes referred to as a "takeover" bid) with only a moment's consideration based solely on the market price of the corporation's shares.

DUTY TO EXERCISE REASONABLE SUPERVISION Directors are also expected to exercise a reasonable amount of supervision when they delegate work to

corporate officers and employees. For example, suppose that a corporate bank director fails to attend any board of directors' meetings for five years, never inspects any of the corporate books or records, and generally fails to supervise the efforts of the bank president and the loan committee. Meanwhile, a corporate officer, the bank president, makes various improper loans and permits large overdrafts. In this situation, the corporate director may be held liable to the corporation for losses resulting from the unsupervised actions of the bank president and the loan committee.

DISSENTING DIRECTORS Directors are expected to attend board of directors' meetings, and their votes should be entered into the minutes of corporate meetings. Unless a dissent is entered, the director is presumed to have assented. Directors who dissent are rarely held individually liable for mismanagement of the corporation. For this reason, a director who is absent from a given meeting sometimes registers with the secretary of the board a dissent to actions taken at the meeting.

Duty of Loyalty

Loyalty can be defined as faithfulness to one's obligations and duties. In the corporate context, the duty of loyalty requires directors and officers to subordinate their personal interests to the welfare of the corporation.

For example, directors may not use corporate funds or confidential corporate information for personal advantage. Similarly, they must refrain from self-dealing. For instance, a director should not oppose a tender offer that is in the corporation's best interest simply because its acceptance may cost the director his or her position. Cases dealing with fiduciary duty typically involve one or more of the following:

1. Competing with the corporation.
2. Usurping (taking advantage of) a corporate opportunity.
3. Having an interest that conflicts with the interest of the corporation.
4. Engaging in insider trading (using information that is not public to make a profit trading securities, as discussed in Chapter 27).
5. Authorizing a corporate transaction that is detrimental to minority shareholders.
6. Selling control over the corporation.

2.   RMBCA 8.30.

The usurping of a corporate opportunity occurs when an officer or director, for his or her personal gain, takes advantage of a business opportunity that is financially within the corporation's reach, is in line with the firm's business, is to the firm's practi-cal advantage, and is one in which the corporation has an interest. Whether buying certain stock constitutes the usurping of a corporate opportunity is at issue in the following case.

CASE 25.1

Yiannatsis v. Stephanis
Supreme Court of Delaware, 1995.
653 A.2d 275.

FACTS Demos and Stella Yiannatsis and Demos's cousins John and Costas Stephanis were the directors of the Sunview Corporation. Demos, John, and Costas were also Sunview's shareholders. In 1975, the three shareholders agreed that if any shareholder—or after the shareholder's death, the executor of his or her estate—wished to sell Sunview stock, the stock must be offered to the corporation first. If the shareholders could not agree on a price, they would hire appraisers to determine the value. The purpose of this agreement was to prevent the stock from being sold to a fourth party. In 1984, Costas died. At the next Sunview board meeting, Costas's executor offered to sell Costas's stock for $150,000 cash plus $55,000 payable over time. The directors (Demos, Stella, and John) voted to refuse the offer. The next day, Stella offered to buy the stock, on slightly different terms. The executor agreed. John filed a suit in a Delaware state court against Stella and Demos, alleging that they had usurped a corporate opportunity. The court ruled in John's favor, and the defendants appealed.

ISSUE Did buying the stock without complying with the shareholder agreement constitute the usurping of a corporate opportunity?

DECISION Yes. The Supreme Court of Delaware affirmed the judgment of the lower court.

REASON The state supreme court found that "Sunview's opportunity to purchase the Costas Stock was never properly presented to Sunview, and that Demos and Stella acted without regard for the 1975 Agreement or the fiduciary duties they owed to Sunview and John." The court pointed out that "the Costas Stock price was determined at the meeting where Stella agreed to purchase the Costas Stock. Given this fact," noted the court, "it would be impossible for Sunview to explore adequately the possibility of purchasing the relevant stock before Stella decided to buy it." The court concluded that "Demos' and Stella's actions are classic examples of the acts of faithless fiduciaries, and they should not benefit from their wrongful actions."

FOR CRITICAL ANALYSIS—Ethical Consideration *How could Stella and Demos have met their fiduciary obligations to the corporation?*

Conflicts of Interest

The duty of loyalty also requires officers and directors to disclose fully to the board of directors any possible conflict of interest that might occur in conducting corporate transactions. The various state statutes contain different standards, but a con-tract will generally *not* be voidable if it was fair and reasonable to the corporation at the time it was made, if there was a full disclosure of the interest of the officers or directors involved in the transaction, and if the contract was approved by a majority of the disinterested directors or shareholders.

For example, Southwood Corporation needs office space. Lambert Alden, one of its five directors, owns the building adjoining the corporation's main office building. He negotiates a lease with Southwood for the space, making a full disclosure to Southwood and the other four board directors. The lease arrangement is fair and reasonable, and it is unanimously approved by the corporation's board of directors. In this situation, Alden has not breached his duty of loyalty to the corporation, and the contract is thus valid. The rule is one of reason. If it were otherwise, directors would be prevented from ever giving financial assistance to the corporations they serve.

▌ Liability of Directors and Officers

Directors and officers are exposed to liability on many fronts. Shareholders may perceive that the corporate directors are not acting in the best interests of the corporation and may sue the directors, in what is called a *shareholder's derivative suit*, on behalf of the corporation. (This type of action is discussed later in this chapter, in the context of shareholders' rights.) In addition, corporate directors and officers may be held liable for the torts and crimes committed by themselves or by corporate employees under their supervision.

In this section, we first examine the so-called *business judgment rule*, under which a corporate director or officer may be able to avoid liability to the corporation or to its shareholders for poor business judgments. We then look at the liability of corporate directors and officers for torts and crimes.

The Business Judgment Rule

Directors and officers are expected to exercise due care and to use their best judgment in guiding corporate management, but they are not insurers of business success. Honest mistakes of judgment and poor business decisions on their part do not make them liable to the corporation for resulting damages. This is the **business judgment rule**. The rule generally immunizes directors and officers from liability for the consequences of a decision that is within managerial authority, as long as the decision complies with management's fiduciary duties and as long as acting on the decision is within the powers of the corporation. Consequently, if there is a

reasonable basis for a business decision, it is unlikely that the court will interfere with that decision, even if the corporation suffers as a result.

To benefit from the rule, directors and officers must act in good faith, in what they consider to be the best interests of the corporation, and with the care that an ordinarily prudent person in a similar position would exercise in similar circumstances. This requires an informed decision, with a rational basis, and with no conflict between the decision maker's personal interest and the interest of the corporation.

Liability for Torts and Crimes

As mentioned in previous chapters, the corporation as an entity is liable for the torts and crimes that corporate agents and employees commit when they are acting within the scope of their employment. Liability for the actions of its corporate agents and employees is imputed to the corporation (the principal) under agency law. Directors, officers, and corporate employees also are personally liable for the torts and crimes that they commit within the scope of their employment. In other words, even though the corporation as an entity may assume liability for, say, a corporate agent's tort, that does not mean that the agent can avoid personal liability for the tort. Additionally, directors and officers can be held criminally liable under federal or state statute (employment laws, for example—see Chapter 22).

Corporate directors and officers may also be held personally liable for the torts and crimes committed by corporate personnel under their direct supervision. Normally, the court must show that the wrongful actions were committed at the officer's direction or with his or her permission. Increasingly, however, liability is imposed on corporate officers because of their failure to supervise adequately their employees or because of their ability to exercise such pervasive control over corporate affairs that they should be treated as employers. We look now at these two bases of liability.

"RESPONSIBLE CORPORATE OFFICER" DOCTRINE Under what has become known as the "responsible corporate officer" doctrine, a court may impose criminal liability on a corporate officer regardless of whether he or she participated in, directed, or even knew about a given criminal violation. In

United States v. Park,[3] for example, the chief executive officer of a national supermarket chain was held personally liable for sanitation violations in corporate warehouses in which food was exposed to contamination by rodents. The court imposed personal liability on the corporate officer not because he intended the crime[4] or even knew about it. Rather, liability was imposed because the officer was in a "responsible relationship" to the corporation and had the power to prevent the violation. Since the *Park* decision, courts have applied this "responsible corporate officer" doctrine numerous times to hold corporate officers liable for their employees' statutory violations.

PERVASIVENESS OF CONTROL   In *United States v. Cusack,*[5] the court enunciated yet another basis for imposing personal liability on a corporate officer. In that case, the court held that a corporate officer's control over corporate operations was so pervasive that, in effect, the officer was not only a corporate agent-employee but also an employer. Therefore, as an employer, the officer could be subject to liability for the statutory violations of corporate employees.

∎ Role of Shareholders

The acquisition of a share of stock makes a person an owner and shareholder in a corporation. Shareholders thus own the corporation. Although they have no legal title to corporate property, such as buildings and equipment, they do have an *equitable* (ownership) interest in the firm.

As a general rule, shareholders have no responsibility for the daily management of the corporation, although they are ultimately responsible for choosing the board of directors, which does have such control. Ordinarily, corporate officers and other employees owe no direct duty to individual shareholders. Their duty is to the corporation as a whole. A director, however, is in a fiduciary relationship to the corporation and therefore serves the interests of the shareholders. Generally, there is no legal relationship between shareholders and creditors of the corporation. Shareholders can, in fact, be creditors of the corporation and thus have the same rights of recovery against the corporation as any other creditor.

In this section, we look at the powers and voting rights of shareholders, which are generally established in the articles of incorporation and under the state's general incorporation law.

Shareholders' Powers

Shareholders must approve fundamental corporate changes before the changes can be effected. Hence, shareholders are empowered to amend the articles of incorporation (charter) and bylaws, approve a merger or the dissolution of the corporation, and approve the sale of all or substantially all of the corporation's assets. Some of these powers are subject to prior board approval. Directors are elected to (and removed from) the board of directors by a vote of the shareholders. The first board of directors is either named in the articles of incorporation or chosen by the incorporators to serve until the first shareholders' meeting. From that time on, the selection and retention of directors are exclusively shareholder functions.

Directors usually serve their full terms; if they are unsatisfactory, they are simply not reelected. Shareholders have the inherent power, however, to remove a director from office *for cause* (breach of duty or misconduct) by a majority vote.[6] Some state statutes (and some corporate charters) even permit removal of directors *without cause* by the vote of a majority of the holders of outstanding shares entitled to vote.

Shareholders' Meetings

Shareholders' meetings must occur at least annually, and additional, special meetings can be called as needed to take care of urgent matters.

NOTICE OF MEETINGS   Each shareholder must receive written notice of the date, time, and place

---

3.   421 U.S. 658, 95 S.Ct. 1903, 44 L.Ed.2d 489 (1975).
4.   Recall from Chapter 6 that two elements must be present for a crime to exist: a criminal act and criminal intent. In *Park*, the court dispensed with the latter requirement.
5.   806 F.Supp. 47 (D.N.J. 1992).

---

6.   A director can often demand court review of removal for cause.

of a shareholders' meeting.[7] The notice must be received within a reasonable length of time prior to the date of the meeting. Notice of a special meeting must include a statement of the purpose of the meeting, and business transacted at the meeting is limited to that purpose.

PROXIES AND PROXY MATERIALS Because it is usually not practical for owners of only a few shares of stock of publicly traded corporations to attend shareholders' meetings, such stockholders normally give third parties written authorization to vote their shares at the meeting. This authorization is called a **proxy** (from the Latin *procurare*, "to manage, take care of"). Proxies are often solicited by management, but any person can solicit proxies to concentrate voting power. Proxies have been used by a group of shareholders as a device for taking over a corporation (corporate takeovers are discussed in Chapter 26). Proxies are normally revocable (that is, they can be withdrawn), unless they are specifically designated as irrevocable. Under RMBCA 7.22(c), proxies last for eleven months, unless the proxy agreement provides for a longer period.

When shareholders want to change a company policy, they can put their idea up for a shareholder vote. They can do this by submitting a shareholder proposal to the board of directors and asking the board to include the proposal in the proxy materials that are sent to all shareholders before meetings. The Securities and Exchange Commission (SEC), which regulates the purchase and sale of securities (see Chapter 27), has special provisions relating to proxies and shareholder proposals. SEC Rule 14a-8 requires that when a company sends proxy materials to its shareholders, the company must also include whatever proposals will be considered at the meeting and provide shareholders with the opportunity to vote on the proposals by marking and returning their proxy cards. SEC Rule 14a-8 provides that all shareholders who own stock worth at least $1,000 are eligible to submit proposals for inclusion in corporate proxy material. Only those proposals that relate to significant policy considerations must be included, however.

Shareholder Voting

Shareholders exercise ownership control through the power of their votes. Each shareholder is entitled to one vote per share, although the voting techniques that will be discussed shortly all enhance the power of the shareholder's vote. The articles of incorporation can exclude or limit voting rights, particularly for certain classes of shares. For example, owners of preferred shares are usually denied the right to vote.

QUORUM REQUIREMENTS For shareholders to act during a meeting, a quorum must be present. Generally, a quorum exists when shareholders holding more than 50 percent of the outstanding shares are present. Corporate business matters are presented in the form of *resolutions*, which shareholders vote to approve or disapprove. Some state statutes have set forth specific voting requirements, and corporations' articles or bylaws must abide by these statutory requirements. Some states provide that the unanimous written consent of shareholders is a permissible alternative to holding a shareholders' meeting. Once a quorum is present, a majority vote of the shares represented at the meeting is usually required to pass resolutions.

For example, assume that Novo Pictures, Inc., has 10,000 outstanding shares of voting stock. Its articles of incorporation set the quorum at 50 percent of outstanding shares and provide that a majority vote of the shares present is necessary to pass resolutions concerning ordinary matters. Therefore, for this firm, a quorum of shareholders representing 5,000 outstanding shares must be present at a shareholders' meeting to conduct business. If exactly 5,000 shares are represented at the meeting, a vote of at least 2,501 of those shares is needed to pass a resolution. If 6,000 shares are represented, a vote of 3,001 will be required, and so on.

At times, a larger-than-majority vote will be required either by a statute or by the corporate charter. Extraordinary corporate matters, such as a merger, consolidation, or dissolution of the corporation (see Chapter 27), require a higher percentage of the representatives of all corporate shares entitled to vote, not just a majority of those present at that particular meeting.

---

7. The shareholder can waive the requirement of written notice by signing a waiver form. In some states, a shareholder who does not receive written notice, but who learns of the meeting and attends without protesting the lack of notice, is said to have waived notice by such conduct. State statutes and corporate bylaws typically set forth the time within which notice must be sent, what methods can be used, and what the notice must contain.

VOTING LISTS Voting lists are prepared by the corporation prior to each shareholders' meeting. Persons whose names appear on the corporation's shareholder records as owners are the ones ordinarily entitled to vote.[8] The voting list contains the name and address of each shareholder as shown on the corporate records on a given cutoff date, or record date. (Under RMBCA 7.07, the record date may be as much as seventy days before the meeting.) The voting list also includes the number of voting shares held by each owner. The list is usually kept at the corporate headquarters and is available for shareholder inspection.

CUMULATIVE VOTING Most states permit or even require shareholders to elect directors by *cumulative voting,* a method of voting designed to allow minority shareholders representation on the board of directors.[9] When cumulative voting is allowed or required, the number of members of the board to be elected is multiplied by the total number of voting shares. The result equals the number of votes a shareholder has, and this total can be cast for one or more nominees for director. All nominees stand for election at the same time. When cumulative voting is not required either by statute or under the articles, the entire board can be elected by a simple majority of shares at a shareholders' meeting.

Cumulative voting can best be understood by an example. Suppose that a corporation has 10,000 shares issued and outstanding. One group of shareholders (the minority shareholders) holds only 3,000 shares, and the other group of shareholders (the majority shareholders) holds the other 7,000 shares. Three members of the board are to be elected. The majority shareholders' nominees are Acevedo, Barkley, and Craycik. The minority shareholders' nominee is Drake. Can Drake be elected by the minority shareholders?

If cumulative voting is allowed, the answer is yes. The minority shareholders have 9,000 votes among them (the number of directors to be elected times the number of shares held by the minority shareholders equals 3 times 3,000, which equals 9,000 votes). All of these votes can be cast to elect Drake. The majority shareholders have 21,000 votes (3 times 7,000 equals 21,000 votes), but these votes have to be distributed among their three nominees. The principle of cumulative voting is that no matter how the majority shareholders cast their 21,000 votes, they will not be able to elect all three directors if the minority shareholders cast all of their 9,000 votes for Drake, as illustrated in Exhibit 25–1.

OTHER VOTING TECHNIQUES A group of shareholders can agree in writing prior to a shareholders' meeting, in a *shareholder voting agreement,* to vote their shares together in a specified manner. Such agreements usually are held to be valid and enforceable. A shareholder can also appoint a voting agent and vote by proxy. As mentioned, a proxy is a written authorization to cast the shareholder's vote, and a person can solicit proxies from a number of shareholders in an attempt to concentrate voting power.

Another technique is for shareholders to enter into a voting trust, which is an agreement (a trust contract) under which legal title (record ownership on the corporate books) is transferred to a trustee who is responsible for voting the shares.

---

8. When the legal owner is deceased, bankrupt, incompetent, or in some other way under a legal disability, his or her vote can be cast by a person designated by law to control and manage the owner's property.
9. See, for example, California Corporate Code Section 708. Under RMBCA 7.28, however, no cumulative voting rights exist unless the articles of incorporation so provide.

◆ **Exhibit 25–1   Results of Cumulative Voting**
This exhibit illustrates how cumulative voting gives minority shareholders a greater chance of electing a director of their choice. By casting all of their 9,000 votes for one candidate (Drake), the minority shareholders will succeed in electing Drake to the board of directors.

BALLOT	MAJORITY SHAREHOLDERS' VOTES			MINORITY SHAREHOLDERS' VOTES	DIRECTORS ELECTED
	Acevedo	Barkley	Craycik	Drake	
1	10,000	10,000	1,000	9,000	Acevedo/Barkley/Drake
2	9,001	9,000	2,999	9,000	Acevedo/Barkley/Drake
3	6,000	7,000	8,000	9,000	Barkley/Craycik/Drake

The agreement can specify how the trustee is to vote, or it can allow the trustee to use his or her discretion. The trustee takes physical possession of the stock certificate and in return gives the shareholder a *voting trust certificate*. The shareholder retains all of the rights of ownership (for example, the right to receive dividend payments) except for the power to vote the shares.

▌ Rights of Shareholders

Shareholders possess numerous rights. A significant right—the right to vote their shares—has already been discussed. We now look at some additional rights of shareholders.

Stock Certificates

A **stock certificate** is a certificate issued by a corporation that evidences ownership of a specified number of shares in the corporation. In jurisdictions that require the issuance of stock certificates, shareholders have the right to demand that the corporation issue certificates. In most states (and under RMBCA 6.26), boards of directors may provide that shares of stock be uncertificated (that is, that physical stock certificates need not be issued). In that circumstance, the corporation may be required to send the holders of uncertificated shares letters or some other form of notice containing the same information as that included on stock certificates.

Stock is intangible personal property, and the ownership right exists independently of the certificate itself. A stock certificate may be lost or destroyed, but ownership is not destroyed with it. A new certificate can be issued to replace one that has been lost or destroyed.[10] Notice of shareholders' meetings, dividends, and operational and financial reports are all distributed according to the recorded ownership listed in the corporation's books, not on the basis of possession of the certificate.

Preemptive Rights

A **preemptive right** is a common law concept under which a preference is given to shareholders over all other purchasers to subscribe to or purchase shares of a *new issue* of stock in proportion to the percentage of total shares they already hold. This allows each shareholder to maintain his or her portion of control, voting power, or financial interest in the corporation. Most statutes either (1) grant preemptive rights but allow them to be negated in the corporation's articles or (2) deny preemptive rights except to the extent that they are granted in the articles. The result is that the articles of incorporation determine the existence and scope of preemptive rights. Generally, preemptive rights apply only to additional, newly issued stock sold for cash, and the preemptive rights must be exercised within a specified time period (usually thirty days).

For example, Detering Corporation authorizes and issues 1,000 shares of stock. Lebow purchases 100 shares, making her the owner of 10 percent of the company's stock. Subsequently, Detering, by vote of the shareholders, authorizes the issuance of another 1,000 shares (by amending the articles of incorporation). This increases its capital stock to a total of 2,000 shares. If preemptive rights have been provided, Lebow can purchase one additional share of the new stock being issued for each share she currently owns—or 100 additional shares. Thus, she can own 200 of the 2,000 shares outstanding, and she will maintain her relative position as a shareholder. If preemptive rights are not allowed, her proportionate control and voting power may be diluted from that of a 10 percent shareholder to that of a 5 percent shareholder because of the issuance of the additional 1,000 shares.

Preemptive rights can be very important for shareholders in close corporations. This is because of the relatively small number of shares and the substantial interest that each shareholder controls in a close corporation. Without preemptive rights, it would be possible for a shareholder to lose his or her proportionate control over the firm.

Stock Warrants

Usually, when preemptive rights exist and a corporation is issuing additional shares, each shareholder is given **stock warrants**, which are transferable options to acquire a given number of shares from

---

10.   For a lost or destroyed certificate to be reissued, a shareholder normally must furnish an indemnity bond to protect the corporation against potential loss should the original certificate reappear at some future time in the hands of a bona fide purchaser [UCC 8–302, 8–405(2)].

the corporation at a stated price. Warrants are often publicly traded on securities exchanges. When the option to purchase is in effect for a short period of time, the stock warrants are usually referred to as *rights*.

Dividends

As mentioned in Chapter 24, a *dividend* is a distribution of corporate profits or income *ordered by the directors* and paid to the shareholders in proportion to their respective shares in the corporation. Dividends can be paid in cash, property, stock of the corporation that is paying the dividends, or stock of other corporations.[11]

State laws vary, but each state determines the general circumstances and legal requirements under which dividends are paid. State laws also control the sources of revenue to be used; only certain funds are legally available for paying dividends. Depending on state law, dividends may be paid from the following sources:

1. *Retained earnings.* All state statutes allow dividends to be paid from the undistributed net profits earned by the corporation, including capital gains from the sale of fixed assets. The undistributed net profits are called *retained earnings.*
2. *Net profits.* A few state statutes allow dividends to be issued from current net profits without regard to deficits in prior years.
3. *Surplus.* A number of statutes allow dividends to be paid out of any surplus.

---

11. Technically, dividends paid in stock are not dividends. They maintain each shareholder's proportional interest in the corporation. On one occasion, a distillery declared and paid a "dividend" in bonded whiskey.

ILLEGAL DIVIDENDS A dividend paid while the corporation is insolvent is automatically an illegal dividend, and shareholders may be liable for returning the payment to the corporation or its creditors. Furthermore, as just discussed, dividends are generally required by statute to be distributed only from certain authorized corporate accounts. Sometimes dividends are improperly paid from an unauthorized account, or their payment causes the corporation to become insolvent. Generally, in such cases, shareholders must return illegal dividends only if they knew that the dividends were illegal when they received them. Whenever dividends are illegal or improper, the board of directors can be held personally liable for the amount of the payment. When directors can show that a shareholder knew that a dividend was illegal when it was received, however, the directors are entitled to reimbursement from the shareholder.

DIRECTORS' FAILURE TO DECLARE A DIVIDEND When directors fail to declare a dividend, shareholders can ask a court to compel the directors to meet and to declare a dividend. For the shareholders to succeed, they must show that the directors have acted so unreasonably in withholding the dividend that the directors' conduct is an abuse of their discretion.

Often, large money reserves are accumulated for a bona fide purpose, such as expansion, research, or other legitimate corporate goals. The mere fact that sufficient corporate earnings or surplus is available to pay a dividend is not enough to compel directors to distribute funds that, in the board's opinion, should not be paid. The courts are circumspect about interfering with corporate operations and will not compel directors to declare dividends unless abuse of discretion is clearly shown. In the following classic case, the shareholders brought a court action to compel Ford Motor Company to declare a dividend.

CASE 25.2

Dodge v. Ford Motor Co.

Supreme Court of Michigan, 1919.
204 Mich. 459,
170 N.W. 668.

FACTS Henry Ford was the president and major shareholder of Ford Motor Company. In the company's early years, business expanded rapidly, and in addition to regular quarterly dividends, special dividends were often paid. By 1916, surplus above capital was still $111,960,907. That year, however, Henry Ford declared that the company would no longer pay special dividends but would put

(Continued)

Case 25.2—Continued

back into the business all the earnings of the company above the regular dividend of 5 percent. According to the court, Ford stated as follows: "My ambition is to employ still more men, to spread the benefits of this industrial system to the greatest possible number, to help them build up their lives and their homes. To do this, we are putting the greatest share of our profits back into the business." The minority shareholders (who owned 10 percent of the stock) filed a lawsuit in a Michigan state court against Ford and others to force the declaration of a dividend. The court ordered the Ford directors to declare a dividend, and the plaintiffs appealed.

ISSUE   Was Ford's refusal to pay a dividend an abuse of managerial discretion?

DECISION   Yes. Because of the special circumstances of this case, the court compelled Ford to pay a dividend.

REASON   The undisputed facts were that Ford had a surplus of $112 million—approximately $54 million in cash on hand. It had made profits of $59 million in the past year and expected to make $60 million in the coming year. The board of directors gave no reason to justify withholding a dividend. Thus, in doing so, it violated the stated purpose of the corporation's existence. According to the court, "Courts of equity will not interfere in the management of the directors unless it is clearly made to appear that they are guilty of fraud or misappropriation of the corporate funds, or refuse to declare a dividend when the corporation has a surplus of net profits which it can, without detriment to its business, divide among its stockholders, and when a refusal to do so would amount to such an abuse of discretion as would constitute a fraud, or breach of that good faith which they are bound to exercise towards the stockholders."

FOR CRITICAL ANALYSIS—Social Consideration   *Generally, how can a court determine when directors should pay dividends?*

Inspection Rights

Shareholders in a corporation enjoy both common law and statutory inspection rights.[12] The shareholder's right of inspection is limited, however, to the inspection and copying of corporate books and records for a *proper purpose,* provided the request is made in advance. The shareholder can inspect in person, or an attorney, agent, accountant, or other type of assistant can do so. The RMBCA requires the corporation to maintain an alphabetical voting list of shareholders with addresses and number of shares owned; this list must be kept open at the annual meeting for inspection by any shareholder of record [RMBCA 7.20].

The power of inspection is fraught with potential abuses, and the corporation is allowed to pro-

tect itself from them. For example, a shareholder can properly be denied access to corporate records to prevent harassment or to protect trade secrets or other confidential corporate information. Some states require that a shareholder must have held his or her shares for a minimum period of time immediately preceding the demand to inspect or must hold a minimum number of outstanding shares. The RMBCA provides, however, that every shareholder is entitled to examine specified corporate records [RMBCA 16.02].

In the following case, a shareholder sought to inspect and copy corporate records in order to locate other shareholders who might want to join in an action against the corporation for alleged wrongdoing. The question before the court was whether the shareholder's reason for inspecting the corporate records, given these circumstances, qualified as a "proper purpose."

---

12.   See, for example, *Schwartzman v. Schwartzman Packing Co.*, 99 N.M. 436, 659 P.2d 888 (1983).

CASE 25.3

Compaq Computer Corp. v. Horton

Supreme Court of Delaware, 1993. 631 A.2d 1.

FACTS In July 1991, Charles Horton and seventy-eight other shareholders of Compaq Computer Corporation sued Compaq and some of its advisors and managers in a Delaware state court, alleging fraud and other misconduct. The plaintiffs contended that Compaq misled the public as to the true value of its stock at a time when members of management were selling their shares. In September 1992, Horton sought to inspect Compaq's stock ledger and related records. Horton's demand letter stated that the purpose of the request was to inform other Compaq shareholders of the lawsuit and to learn whether any of them wanted to join in the action against the defendants. Compaq refused Horton's demand, stating that the purpose described in the letter was not a "proper purpose" under Delaware law. The court entered a judgment in the plaintiffs' favor, and Compaq appealed.

ISSUE Was Horton's purpose for inspecting Compaq's records a "proper purpose" under Delaware law?

DECISION Yes. The Supreme Court of Delaware affirmed the lower court's decision.

REASON Compaq argued that because Horton's objective to solicit additional parties to the litigation could impose substantial expenses on the company, it was *per se* ("in itself") improper. The court reasoned, however, that Horton, as a current stockholder, had nothing to gain "by harming the legitimate interests of the company," that the litigation posed "no legitimate threat to Compaq's interests," and that "the litigation [was] already pending with seventy-nine plaintiffs." The court stated that the "real risk to Compaq is that any additional plaintiffs [may] potentially increase the damage award against the company. Yet, * * * for breaches of their duties to shareholders Compaq has no legitimate interest in avoiding the payment of compensatory damages which it, its management or advisors may owe to those who own the enterprise. Thus, common sense and public policy dictate that a proper purpose may be stated in these circumstances, notwithstanding the lack of a direct benefit flowing to the corporation." The court also pointed out that if damages were assessed, Compaq could seek indemnification from its "codefendant managers and advisors" or pursue its own claims against them, thus diminishing any possible harm suffered by Compaq.

FOR CRITICAL ANALYSIS—Ethical Consideration *What did the court mean when it stated that Horton had nothing to gain "by harming the legitimate interests of the company"?*

Transfer of Shares

Stock certificates generally are negotiable and freely transferable by indorsement and delivery. Transfer of stock in closely held corporations, however, usually is restricted by the bylaws, by a restriction stamped on the stock certificate, or by a shareholder agreement (see Chapter 24). The existence of any restrictions on transferability must always be noted on the face of the stock certificate, and these restrictions must be reasonable.

Sometimes, corporations or their shareholders restrict transferability by reserving the option to purchase any shares offered for resale by a shareholder. This **right of first refusal** remains with the corporation or the shareholders for only a specified time or a reasonable time. Variations on the purchase option are possible. For example, a shareholder might be required to offer the shares to other shareholders first or to the corporation first.

When shares are transferred, a new entry is made in the corporate stock book to indicate the new owner. Until the corporation is notified and the entry is complete, the current record owner has the right to be notified of (and attend) shareholders' meetings, the right to vote the shares, the right to receive dividends, and all other shareholder rights.

Corporate Dissolution

When a corporation is dissolved and its outstanding debts and the claims of its creditors have been satisfied, the remaining assets are distributed to the shareholders in proportion to the percentage of shares owned by each shareholder. Certain classes of preferred stock can be given priority. If no preferences to distribution of assets on liquidation are given to any class of stock, then the shareholders are entitled to the remaining assets.

In some circumstances, shareholders may petition a court to have the corporation dissolved. Suppose, for example, that a minority shareholder knows that the board of directors is mishandling corporate assets. The minority shareholder is not powerless to intervene. He or she can petition a court to appoint a **receiver**—who will wind up corporate affairs and liquidate the business assets of the corporation.

The RMBCA permits any shareholder to initiate such an action in any of the following circumstances [RMBCA 14.30]:

1. The directors are deadlocked in the management of corporate affairs. Shareholders are unable to break that deadlock, and irreparable injury to the corporation is being suffered or threatened.
2. The acts of the directors or those in control of the corporation are illegal, oppressive, or fraudulent.
3. Corporate assets are being misapplied or wasted.
4. The shareholders are deadlocked in voting power and have failed, for a specified period (usually two annual meetings), to elect successors to directors whose terms have expired or would have expired with the election of successors.

When the shareholders themselves are deadlocked, a court may order the dissolution of a corporation. This was the circumstance in the following case.

CASE 25.4

Black v. Graham
Supreme Court of Georgia, 1996.
464 S.E.2d 814.

FACTS   Black and Graham each owned 50 percent of the stock of a building supplies corporation; they also served as the corporation's directors. When the two shareholder-directors deadlocked over differences of opinion on how to run their business, Graham filed a petition in a Georgia state court to dissolve the corporation. The parties agreed to the appointment of a custodian to run their firm while the court considered Graham's petition. Ultimately, the court ordered each shareholder to offer to buy the other out. This attempt to resolve the matter failed. The court then converted the custodian into a receiver, directed him to wind up the affairs of the business, and told him to liquidate the corporation. Both parties appealed to the Supreme Court of Georgia.

ISSUE   Were the shareholders and directors so deadlocked that dissolution was warranted?

DECISION   Yes. The Supreme Court of Georgia affirmed the orders of the lower court.

Case 25.4—Continued

REASON   The state supreme court explained that a deadlock occurs "[w]here stock of [a] corporation is owned in equal shares by two contending parties, which condition threatens to result in destruction of business, and it appears that [the] parties cannot agree upon management of [the] business, and under existing circumstances neither one is authorized to impose its views upon the other." This case, the court said, "portrays a classic situation of deadlock. Black and Graham as sole and equal shareholders functioned as *de facto* directors who were wholly unable to agree on the management of the business. Neither had the authority to prevail in his view and the hostile and static situation threatened irreparable injury to the corporation."

FOR CRITICAL ANALYSIS—Political Consideration   *What steps might a corporation with an even number of shareholders and directors take to avoid a deadlock?*

Shareholder's Derivative Suit

When those in control of a corporation—the corporate directors—fail to sue in the corporate name to redress a wrong suffered by the corporation, shareholders are permitted to do so "derivatively" in what is known as a **shareholder's derivative suit.** Some wrong must have been done to the corporation, and before a derivative suit can be brought, the shareholders must first state their complaint to the board of directors. Only if the directors fail to solve the problem or take appropriate action can the derivative suit go forward.

The right of shareholders to bring a derivative action is especially important when the wrong suffered by the corporation results from the actions of corporate directors or officers. This is because the directors and officers would probably want to prevent any action against themselves.

The shareholder's derivative suit is singular in that those suing are not pursuing rights or benefits for themselves personally but are acting as guardians of the corporate entity. Therefore, any damages recovered by the suit normally go into the corporation's treasury, not to the shareholders personally.

▌ Liability of Shareholders

One of the hallmarks of the corporate organization is that shareholders are not personally liable for the debts of the corporation. If the corporation fails, shareholders can lose their investments, but that is generally the limit of their liability. As discussed in Chapter 24, in certain instances of fraud, undercapitalization, or careless observance of corporate formalities, a court will pierce the corporate veil (disregard the corporate entity) and hold the shareholders individually liable. These situations are the exception, however, not the rule. Although they are rare, certain other instances arise where a shareholder can be personally liable. One relates to illegal dividends, which were discussed previously. Two others relate to *stock subscriptions* and *watered stock,* which we discuss here.

Sometimes stock-subscription agreements— written contracts by which one agrees to buy capital stock of a corporation—exist prior to incorporation. Normally, these agreements are treated as continuing offers and are irrevocable (for up to six months under RMBCA 6.20). Once the corporation has been formed, it can sell shares to shareholder investors. In either situation, once the subscription agreement or stock offer is accepted, a binding contract is formed. Any refusal to pay constitutes a breach resulting in the personal liability of the shareholder.

Shares of stock can be paid for by property or by services rendered instead of cash. They cannot be purchased with promissory notes, however. The general rule is that for **par-value shares** (shares that have a specific face value, or formal cash-in value, written on them, such as one penny or one dollar), the corporation must receive a value at least equal to the par-value amount. For **no-par shares** (shares that have no face value—no specific amount printed on their face), the corporation must receive the value of the shares as determined by the board or the shareholders when the stock was issued. When the corporation issues shares for less than these stated values, the shares are referred to as **watered stock**.[13] Usually, the shareholder who receives watered stock must pay the difference to the corporation (the shareholder is personally liable). In some states, the shareholder who receives watered stock may be liable to creditors of the corporation for unpaid corporate debts.

To illustrate the concept of watered stock, suppose that during the formation of a corporation, Gomez, one of the incorporators, transfers his property, Sunset Beach, to the corporation for ten thousand shares of stock. The stock has a par value of $100 per share, and thus the total price of the ten thousand shares is $1 million. After the property is transferred and the shares are issued, Sunset Beach is carried on the corporate books at a value of $1 million. Upon appraisal, it is discovered that the market value of the property at the time of transfer was only $500,000. The shares issued to Gomez are therefore watered stock, and he is liable to the corporation for the difference.

Duties of Majority Shareholders

In some cases, a majority shareholder is regarded as having a fiduciary duty to the corporation and to the minority shareholders. This occurs when a single shareholder (or a few shareholders acting in concert) owns a sufficient number of shares to exercise *de facto* control over the corporation. In these situations, majority shareholders owe a fiduciary duty to the minority shareholders when they sell their shares, because such a sale would be, in fact, a transfer of control of the corporation. Whether the controlling majority of shareholders owed a fiduciary duty to a minority shareholder was at issue in the following case.

---

13. The phrase *watered stock* was originally used to describe cattle that—kept thirsty during a long drive—were allowed to drink large quantities of water just prior to their sale. The increased weight of the "watered stock" allowed the seller to reap a higher profit.

CASE 25.5

Pedro v. Pedro

Court of Appeals of Minnesota, 1992.
489 N.W.2d 798.

FACTS Alfred, Carl, and Eugene Pedro each owned a one-third interest in The Pedro Companies (TPC), a close corporation that manufactured and sold luggage and leather products. All of the brothers had worked for the corporation for most of their adult lives. The relationship between Alfred and the other two brothers began to deteriorate in 1987 after Alfred discovered a discrepancy between the internal accounting records and the TPC checking account. At Alfred's insistence, two different accountants examined the records, but neither could identify the source of a $140,000 discrepancy, and one accountant said that he was denied access to numerous documents during the investigation. Alfred stated that his brothers told him that if he did not forget about the discrepancy, they would fire him—which they did in December 1987. Alfred filed suit in a Minnesota state court against his brothers, alleging that they had breached their fiduciary duties and that he had been wrongfully discharged. The trial court held for Alfred and awarded him over $1.8 million in damages, plus interest, for the value of his shares, lost wages, and attorneys' fees. The brothers appealed.

ISSUE Had the brothers breached their fiduciary duties to Alfred by terminating his employment with TPC?

Case 25.5—Continued

DECISION   Yes. The Minnesota Court of Appeals affirmed the trial court's judgment.

REASON   The appellate court emphasized that the relationship among shareholders in closely held corporations is "analogous to that of partners" and that they owe one another a fiduciary duty. "Owing a fiduciary duty," stated the court, "includes dealing 'openly, honestly and fairly with other shareholders.'" The court found that the brothers had not acted openly, honestly, and fairly with Alfred. Furthermore, the court found that Alfred justifiably assumed that he had an implied contract with the corporation for lifetime employment, a contract that the brothers breached when they fired him. Given the fact that Alfred's father had worked for the company until his death and that Eugene, who had worked for TPC for over fifty years, testified that he intended to always work for the company, Alfred's expectation of a lifetime job was reasonable. The court concluded that "[b]ased upon this evidence[,] it was reasonable for the trial court to determine that the parties did in fact have a contract that was not terminable at will."

FOR CRITICAL ANALYSIS—Economic Consideration   *Is there anything Alfred could have done to ensure that he would be employed "for life" by the corporation?*

▌ Terms and Concepts

business judgment rule 536	quorum 532	stock certificate 540
no-par share 546	receiver 544	stock warrant 540
par-value share 545	right of first refusal 543	tender offer 534
preemptive right 540	shareholder's derivative	voting trust 539
proxy 538	suit 545	watered stock 546

▌ Chapter Summary: Corporate Directors, Officers, and Shareholders

Role of Directors (*See pages 531–533.*)	1. *Election of directors*—The first board of directors is usually appointed by the incorporators; thereafter, directors are elected by the shareholders. Directors usually serve a one-year term, although longer and staggered terms are permitted under most state statutes.
	2. *Directors' qualifications and compensation*—Few qualifications are required; a director can be a shareholder but is not required to be. Compensation is usually specified in the corporate articles or bylaws.
	3. *Board of directors' meetings*—The board of directors conducts business by holding formal meetings with recorded minutes. The date of regular meetings is usually established in the corporate articles or bylaws; special meetings can be called, with

(Continued)

Chapter Summary: Corporate Directors, Officers, and Shareholders—Continued

Role of Director—Continued	notice sent to all directors. Quorum requirements vary from state to state; usually, a quorum is the majority of the corporate directors. Voting must usually be done in person, and in ordinary matters only a majority vote is required. 4. *Rights of directors*—Directors' rights include the rights of participation, inspection, compensation, and indemnification. 5. *Directors' management responsibilities*—Directors are responsible for declaring and paying corporate dividends to shareholders; authorizing major corporate decisions; appointing, supervising, and removing corporate officers and other managerial employees; determining employees' compensation; making financial decisions necessary to the management of corporate affairs; and issuing authorized shares and bonds. Directors may delegate some of their responsibilities to executive committees and corporate officers and executives.
Role of Corporate Officers and Executives *(See page 533.)*	Corporate officers and other executive employees are normally hired by the board of directors. In most states, a person can hold more than one office and can be both an officer and a director of a corporation. The rights of corporate officers and executives are defined by employment contracts. The duties of corporate officers are the same as those of directors.
Duties of Directors and Officers *(See pages 533–536.)*	1. *Duty of care*—Directors are obligated to act in good faith, to use prudent business judgment in the conduct of corporate affairs, and to act in the corporation's best interests. If a director fails to exercise this duty of care, he or she can be answerable to the corporation and to the shareholders for breaching the duty. 2. *Duty of loyalty*—Directors have a fiduciary duty to subordinate their own interests to those of the corporation in matters relating to the corporation. 3. *Conflicts of interest*—To fulfill their duty of loyalty, directors and officers must make a full disclosure of any potential conflicts of interest between their personal interests and those of the corporation.
Liability of Directors and Officers *(See pages 536–537.)*	1. *Business judgment rule*—This rule immunizes a director from liability for a corporate decision as long as the decision was within the powers of the corporation and the authority of the director to make and was an informed, reasonable, and loyal decision. 2. *Liability for torts and crimes*—Corporate directors and officers are personally liable for their own torts and crimes; additionally, they may be held personally liable for the torts and crimes committed by corporate personnel under their direct supervision.
Role of Shareholders *(See pages 537–540.)*	1. *Shareholders' powers*—Shareholders' powers include the approval of all fundamental changes affecting the corporation and the election of the board of directors. 2. *Shareholders' meetings*—Shareholders' meetings must occur at least annually; special meetings can be called when necessary. Notice of the date, time, and place of the meeting (and its purpose, if it is specially called) must be sent to shareholders. Shareholders may vote by proxy (authorizing someone else to vote their shares) and may submit proposals to be included in the company's proxy materials sent to shareholders before meetings. 3. *Shareholder voting*—Shareholder voting requirements and procedures are as follows:

▌Chapter Summary: Corporate Directors, Officers, and Shareholders— Continued

Role of Shareholders— Continued	a. A minimum number of shareholders (a quorum—generally, more than 50 percent of shares held) must be present at a meeting for business to be conducted; resolutions are passed (usually) by simple majority vote. b. The corporation must prepare voting lists of shareholders on record prior to each shareholders' meeting. c. Cumulative voting may or may not be required or permitted. Cumulative voting gives minority shareholders a better chance to be represented on the board of directors. d. A shareholder voting agreement (an agreement of shareholders to vote their shares together) is usually held to be valid and enforceable. e. A shareholder may appoint a proxy (substitute) to vote his or her shares. f. A shareholder may enter into a voting trust agreement by which title (record ownership) of his or her shares is given to a trustee, and the trustee votes the shares in accordance with the trust agreement.
Rights of Shareholders *(See pages 540–545.)*	Shareholders have numerous rights, which may include the following: 1. The right to a stock certificate, preemptive rights, and the right to stock warrants (depending on the corporate charter). 2. The right to obtain a dividend (at the discretion of the directors). 3. Voting rights. 4. The right to inspect the corporate records. 5. The right to transfer shares (this right may be restricted in close corporations). 6. The right to a share of corporate assets when the corporation is dissolved. 7. The right to sue on behalf of the corporation (bring a shareholder's derivative suit) when the directors fail to do so.
Liability of Shareholders *(See pages 545–546.)*	Shareholders may be liable for the retention of illegal dividends, for breach of a stock-subscription agreement, and for the value of watered stock.
Duties of Majority Shareholders *(See pages 546–547.)*	In certain situations, majority shareholders may be regarded as having a fiduciary duty to minority shareholders and will be liable if that duty is breached.

▌For Review

1. What are the duties of the directors and officers of a corporation?

2. Directors are expected to use their best judgment in managing the corporation. What must directors do to avoid liability for honest mistakes of judgment and poor business decisions?

3. What is a voting proxy? What is cumulative voting?

4. If a group of shareholders perceives that the corporation has suffered a wrong and the directors refuse to take action, can the shareholders compel the directors to act? If so, how?

5. From what sources may dividends be paid legally? In what circumstances is a dividend illegal? What happens if a dividend is illegally paid?

▌ Questions and Case Problems

25–1. Rights of Shareholders. Dmitri has acquired one share of common stock of a multimillion-dollar corporation with over 500,000 shareholders. Dmitri's ownership is so small that he is questioning what his rights are as a shareholder. For example, he wants to know whether this one share entitles him to attend and vote at shareholders' meetings, inspect the corporate books, and receive periodic dividends. Discuss Dmitri's rights in these matters.

25–2. Voting Techniques. Algonquin Corp. has issued and has outstanding 100,000 shares of common stock. Four stockholders own 60,000 of these shares, and for the past six years they have nominated a slate of people for membership on the board, all of whom have been elected. Sergio and twenty other shareholders, owning 20,000 shares, are dissatisfied with corporate management and want a representative on the board who shares their views. Explain under what circumstances Sergio and the minority shareholders can elect their representative to the board.

25–3. Duties of Directors. Starboard, Inc., has a board of directors consisting of three members (Ellsworth, Green, and Morino) and approximately five hundred shareholders. At a regular meeting of the board, the board selects Tyson as president of the corporation by a two-to-one vote, with Ellsworth dissenting. The minutes of the meeting do not register Ellsworth's dissenting vote. Later, during an audit, it is discovered that Tyson is a former convict and has openly embezzled $500,000 from Starboard. This loss is not covered by insurance. The corporation wants to hold directors Ellsworth, Green, and Morino liable. Ellsworth claims no liability. Discuss the personal liability of the directors to the corporation.

25–4. Liability of Shareholders. Mallard has made a preincorporation subscription agreement to purchase 500 shares of a newly formed corporation. The shares have a par value of $100 per share. The corporation is formed, and it accepts Mallard's subscription. Mallard transfers a piece of land he owns to the corporation as payment for 250 of the shares, and the corporation issues 250 shares for it. Mallard pays for the other 250 shares with cash. One year later, with the corporation in serious financial difficulty, the board declares and pays a $5-per-share dividend. It is now learned that the land transferred by Mallard had a market value of $18,000. Discuss any liability that shareholder Mallard has to the corporation or to the creditors of the corporation.

25–5. Duties of Directors. Overland Corp. is negotiating with Wharton Construction Co. for the renovation of Overland's corporate headquarters. Wharton, the owner of Wharton Construction, is also one of the five members of the board of directors of Overland. The contract terms are standard for this type of contract. Wharton has previously informed two of the other Overland directors of his interest in the construction company. Overland's board approves the contract on a three-to-two vote, with Wharton voting with the majority. Discuss whether this contract is binding on the corporation.

25–6. Duties of Directors. Midwest Management Corp. was looking for investment opportunities. Morris Stephens, one of Midwest's directors and the chairman of the investment committee, proposed that Midwest provide financing for Stephens's son and his business colleagues, who were in need of financing to open a broker-dealer business. Midwest agreed to propose to the shareholders for their approval an investment of $250,000 in the new business on the condition that Stephens would manage the business and would purchase 100,000 shares of stock in the new firm. At each of two shareholders' meetings, the directors informed the shareholders that Stephens had agreed to the condition. Stephens was present at both meetings and did not deny that he had agreed to purchase the 100,000 shares of stock and manage the new corporation. On the shareholders' approval, the $250,000 investment was made, and later another $150,000 was invested when the new business suffered losses. About a year after it had opened, the business closed, and Midwest ended up losing over $325,000. Midwest then learned that Stephens had not kept his agreement to purchase stock in and manage the corporation. Midwest sued Stephens for breaching his fiduciary duties and asked for compensatory and punitive damages. Did Midwest succeed? Explain. [*Midwest Management Corp. v. Stephens*, 353 N.W.2d 76 (Iowa 1984)]

25–7. Duties of Directors and Officers. Klinicki and Lundgren formed Berlinair, a closely held Oregon corporation, to provide air transportation out of West Germany. Klinicki, who owned 33 percent of the company stock, was the vice president and a director. Lundgren, who also owned 33 percent of the stock, was the president and a director. Lelco, Inc., a corporation owned by Lundgren and his family, owned 33 percent of Berlinair, and Berlinair's attorney owned the last 1 percent of stock. One of the goals of Berlinair was to obtain a contract with BFR, a West German consortium of travel agents, to provide BFR with air charter service. Later, Lundgren learned that the BFR contract might become available. Lundgren then incorporated Air Berlin Charter Co., of which he was the sole owner, and bid for the BFR contract. Lundgren won the BFR contract for Air Berlin while using Berlinair working time, staff, money, and facilities without the knowledge of Klinicki.

Has Lundgren breached any fiduciary duty to Berlinair or to Klinicki? If so, what duty, and how was it breached? Explain. [*Klinicki v. Lundgren*, 67 Or.App. 160, 678 P.2d 1250 (1984)]

25-8. Rights of Shareholders. Jacob Schachter and Herbert Kulik, the founders of Ketek Electric Corp., each owned 50 percent of the corporation's shares and served as the corporation's only officers. Arnold Glenn, as trustee, and Kulik brought a shareholder's derivative suit in a New York state court against Schachter, alleging that Schachter had diverted Ketek assets and opportunities to Hoteltron Systems, Inc., a corporation wholly owned by Schachter. The trial court held for Glenn and Kulik, and it awarded damages to Kulik, not to Ketek. On appeal, the appellate court ruled that the damages should be awarded to the injured corporation, Ketek, rather than to the innocent shareholder, Kulik. Kulik appealed to the state supreme court, arguing that awarding damages to the corporation was inequitable because Schachter, as a shareholder of Ketek, would ultimately share in the proceeds of the award. How should the state supreme court rule, and why? [*Glenn v. Hoteltron Systems, Inc.*, 74 N.Y.2d 386, 547 N.E.2d 71, 547 N.Y.S.2 816 (1989)]

25-9. Duties of Directors and Officers. While working for Veco Corp., an Illinois financial services company, officers Robert Babcock and Margaret Michails, after discussions with other employees, prepared a business plan for their own financial services company, CorMac, Inc. The plan listed other Veco employees who would join CorMac and detailed the "taking over" of an important Veco client. Veco's founder and sole shareholder, David Vear, discovered what Babcock had done and fired him. Michails and other Veco employees quit to work for CorMac. As a result, Veco was left with no personnel who were experienced in handling one of its major accounts. Veco sued Babcock and Michails, alleging that they had breached their fidu-

ciary duties to Veco. Had they breached any fiduciary duty? If so, what duty had they breached? How should the court rule on this issue? [*Veco Corp. v. Babcock*, 243 Ill.App.3d 153, 611 N.E.2d 1054, 183 Ill.Dec. 406 (1993)]

25-10. Rights of Shareholders. Melissa and Gary Callicoat each owned 50 percent of Callicoat, Inc. They were also Callicoat's only directors. They could not agree on the day-to-day management of the firm. They also could not agree on whether a debt owed to Arthur Baz was a personal or corporate debt. Melissa suggested that they dissolve the corporation. Gary refused and shut her out from the operations of the firm. Melissa filed a petition in an Ohio state court against Gary and Callicoat, asking the court to dissolve the corporation. On what basis might the court order the dissolution? [*Callicoat v. Callicoat*, 73 Ohio Misc.2d 38, 657 N.E.2d 874 (1994)]

25-11. Business Judgment Rule. William Bear was the president of the William R. Bear Agency, Inc. (Bear Agency). Timothy Schirmer was a shareholder. In 1990, the YMCA was an important client of Bear Agency, and Bear spent company funds for family memberships in the YMCA. The same year, Bear put his wife on the payroll because, at the time, she was the only one in the office with computer experience. He decided not to declare a bonus for the employees in 1990, in part to invest the money in computers for the firm. The next April, Bear bought a BMW with company funds to use as a company car. Disapproving these actions, Schirmer filed a suit against Bear, Bear Agency, and others in an Illinois state court, asking the court to dissolve the corporation, among other things. Discuss how the decision not to dissolve Bear Agency might be supported by the business judgment rule. [*Schirmer v. Bear*, 271 Ill.App.3d 778, 648 N.E.2d 1131, 208 Ill.Dec. 209 (1994)]

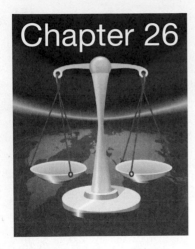

Chapter 26

Corporate Merger, Consolidation, and Termination

CHAPTER OBJECTIVES

After reading this chapter, you should be able to:

1. Summarize the procedures involved in a merger or a consolidation.
2. Indicate what appraisal rights are and how they function.
3. Analyze the effects of a corporation's purchase of all or substantially all of another corporation's assets.
4. Discuss the effects of a corporation's purchase of a substantial number of voting shares of another corporation's stock.
5. Explain the phases of corporate termination.

Corporations increase the size of their operations for a number of reasons. They may wish to enlarge their physical plants, for example, or to increase their property or investment holdings. They may wish to acquire the assets, know-how, or goodwill of another corporation. Sometimes, the acquisition of another company is motivated by a desire to eliminate a competitor, to accomplish diversification, or to ensure adequate resources and markets for the acquiring corporation's product. Whatever the reason, during the 1980s, the acquisition of corporations by other corporations became a common phenomenon, and corporate takeovers continue in the 1990s.

A corporation typically extends its operations by combining with another corporation through a merger, a consolidation, a purchase of assets, or a purchase of a controlling interest in the other corporation. This chapter will examine these four types of corporate expansion. Dissolution and liquidation are the combined processes by which a corporation terminates its existence. The last part of this chapter will discuss the typical reasons

552

for—and methods used in—terminating a corporation's existence.

▌ Merger and Consolidation

The terms *merger* and *consolidation* often are used interchangeably, but they refer to two legally distinct proceedings. The rights and liabilities of the corporation, its shareholders, and its creditors are the same for both, however.

Merger

A **merger** involves the legal combination of two or more corporations in such a way that only one of the corporations continues to exist. For example, Corporation A and Corporation B decide to merge. It is agreed that A will absorb B, so upon merger, B ceases to exist as a separate entity, and A continues as the *surviving corporation*. Exhibit 26–1 graphically illustrates this process.

♦ **Exhibit 26–1 Merger**
In this illustration, Corporation A and
Corporation B decide to merge. They agree that
A will absorb B, so after the merger, B no longer
exists as a separate entity, and A continues as the
surviving corporation.

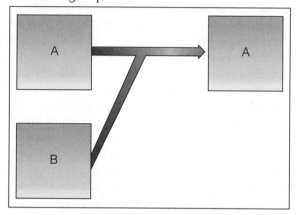

After the merger, A is recognized as a single
corporation, possessing all the rights, privileges,
and powers of itself and B. It automatically
acquires all of B's property and assets without the
necessity of formal transfer. Additionally, A
becomes liable for all of B's debts and obligations.
Finally, A's articles of incorporation are deemed
amended to include any changes that are stated in
the *articles of merger* (a document setting forth the
terms and conditions of the merger that is filed
with the secretary of state).

In a merger, the surviving corporation inherits
the disappearing corporation's preexisting legal
rights and obligations. For example, if the disappearing corporation had a right of action against a
third party, the surviving corporation can bring
suit after the merger to recover the disappearing
corporation's damages. The corporation statutes of
many states provide that a successor (surviving)
corporation inherits a **chose**[1] **in action** (a right to
sue for a debt or sum of money) from a merging
corporation as a matter of law. The common law
similarly recognizes that, following a merger, a
chose in action to enforce a property right will vest
with the successor (surviving) corporation, and no
right of action will remain with the disappearing
corporation.

_____
1. The word *chose* is French for "thing."

Consolidation

In a **consolidation,** two or more corporations combine in such a way that each corporation ceases to
exist and a new one emerges. For example, Corporation A and Corporation B consolidate to form an
entirely new organization, Corporation C. In the
process, A and B both terminate, and C comes into
existence as an entirely new entity. Exhibit 26–2
graphically illustrates this process.

As a result of the consolidation, C is recognized
as a new corporation and a single entity; A and B
cease to exist. C inherits all of the rights, privileges,
and powers that A and B previously held. Title to
any property and assets owned by A and B passes to
C without formal transfer. C assumes liability for all
of the debts and obligations owed by A and B. The
terms and conditions of the consolidation are set
forth in the *articles of consolidation,* which are filed
with the secretary of state. These articles *take the
place of* A's and B's original corporate articles and
are thereafter regarded as C's corporate articles.

Procedure for Merger or Consolidation

All states have statutes authorizing mergers and
consolidations for domestic (in-state) corporations,
and most states allow the combination of domestic
and foreign (out-of-state) corporations. Although
the procedures vary somewhat among jurisdictions,

♦ **Exhibit 26–2 Consolidation**
In this illustration, Corporation A and
Corporation B consolidate to form an entirely
new organization, Corporation C. In the process,
A and B terminate, and C comes into existence
as an entirely new entity.

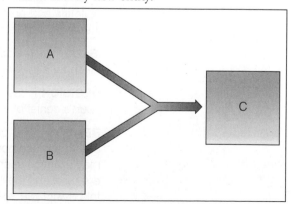

the basic requirements for a merger or a consolidation are as follows:

1. The board of directors of each corporation involved must approve a merger or consolidation plan.
2. The shareholders of each corporation must approve the plan, by vote, at a shareholders' meeting. Most state statutes require the approval of two-thirds of the outstanding shares of voting stock, although some states require only a simple majority, and others require a four-fifths vote. Frequently, statutes require that each class of stock approve the merger; thus, the holders of nonvoting stock must also approve. A corporation's bylaws can provide for a stricter requirement.
3. Once approved by all of the directors and shareholders, the plan (articles of merger or consolidation) is filed, usually with the secretary of state.
4. When state formalities are satisfied, the state issues a certificate of merger to the surviving corporation or a certificate of consolidation to the newly consolidated corporation.

RMBCA 11.04 provides for a simplified procedure for the merger of a substantially owned subsidiary corporation into its parent corporation. Under these provisions, a **short-form merger** can be accomplished *without the approval of the shareholders* of either corporation. The short-form merger can be used only when the parent corporation owns at least 90 percent of the outstanding shares of each class of stock of the subsidiary corporation. The simplified procedure requires that a plan for the merger be approved by the board of directors of the parent corporation before it is filed with the state. A copy of the merger plan must be sent to each shareholder of record of the subsidiary corporation. In the following case, a minority group of shareholders objected to a short-form merger undertaken to "cash out" public shareholders (including the plaintiffs in this case).

CASE 26.1

Roland International Corp. v. Najjar
Supreme Court of Delaware, 1979.
407 A.2d 1032.

FACTS Roland International Corporation was 97.6 percent owned by Hyatt Corporation and others. This controlling group of shareholders created Landro Corporation for the purpose of merging it with Roland. All of the statutory requirements for a short-form merger were met, and the minority (public) shareholders were offered $5.25 per share for each share of Roland stock that they owned. If this price was not acceptable, the minority group could have their shares evaluated under the Delaware appraisal statute. Najjar brought a class-action suit in a Delaware state court on behalf of the minority shareholders, seeking damages. Najjar claimed that the merger was simply an effort to eliminate the public shareholders and that it had been grossly unfair to those shareholders. The defendants (the majority group) moved for dismissal, contending that a proper purpose is conclusively presumed when the conditions of the short-form merger statutes are met; thus the plaintiffs had no cause of action. The trial court denied the motion, and the defendants appealed.

ISSUE May a court examine a short-form merger to see if it was undertaken for a proper purpose?

DECISION Yes. The Supreme Court of Delaware affirmed the trial court's denial of the defendants' motion to dismiss.

REASON The court held that the short-form merger statute does not create a presumption that the merger serves a valid purpose. The court may examine such mergers to determine whether the majority shareholders have met their fiduciary duty to the minority. When a merger is undertaken with the sole purpose of eliminating the minority shareholders, it constitutes a breach of that duty. The plaintiff thus had a cause of action, and the defendants' motion to dismiss was properly denied.

Shareholder Approval

Shareholders invest in a corporate enterprise with the expectation that the board of directors will manage the enterprise and will approve ordinary business matters. Actions taken on extraordinary matters must be authorized by the board of directors and the shareholders. Often, modern statutes require that the shareholders approve certain types of extraordinary matters—such as the sale, lease, or exchange of all or substantially all corporate assets outside of the corporation's regular course of business. Other examples of matters requiring shareholder approval include amendments to the articles of incorporation, transactions concerning merger or consolidation, and dissolution.

Hence, when any extraordinary matter arises, the corporation must proceed as authorized by law to obtain the approval of the shareholders and the board of directors. Sometimes, a transaction can be characterized in such a way as not to require shareholder approval, but in that event, a court will use its equity powers to require such approval. To determine the nature of the transaction, the courts will look not only to the details of the transaction but also to its consequences.

Appraisal Rights

What if a shareholder disapproves of a merger or a consolidation but is outvoted by the other shareholders? The law recognizes that a dissenting shareholder should not be forced to become an unwilling shareholder in a corporation that is new or different from the one in which the shareholder originally invested. The shareholder has the right to dissent and may be entitled to be paid the *fair value* for the number of shares held on the date of the merger or consolidation. This right is referred to as the shareholder's **appraisal right.**

Appraisal rights are available only when a state statute specifically provides for them. Appraisal rights normally extend to regular mergers, consolidations, short-form mergers, and sales of substantially all of the corporate assets not in the ordinary course of business.

Shareholders may lose their appraisal rights if they do not follow precisely the elaborate statutory procedures. Whenever they lose the right to an appraisal, dissenting shareholders must go along with the transaction despite their objections. One of the usual basic requirements is a written notice of dissent filed by dissenting shareholders prior to the vote of the shareholders on the proposed transaction. This notice of dissent is also basically a notice to all shareholders of the costs that dissenting shareholders may impose should the merger or consolidation be approved. In addition, after approval, the dissenting shareholders must make a written demand for payment and for the fair value of their shares.

Valuation of shares is often a point of contention between the dissenting shareholder and the corporation. RMBCA 13.01 provides that the "fair value of shares" normally is the value on the day prior to the date on which the vote was taken. The corporation must make a *written* offer to purchase a dissenting shareholder's stock, accompanying the offer with a current balance sheet and income statement for the corporation. If the shareholder and the corporation do not agree on the fair value, a court will determine it.

Once a dissenting shareholder elects appraisal rights under a statute, in some jurisdictions, the shareholder loses his or her shareholder status. Without that status, a shareholder cannot vote, receive dividends, or sue to enjoin whatever action prompted his or her dissent. In some of those jurisdictions, statutes provide, or courts have held, that shareholder status may be reinstated during the appraisal process (for example, if the shareholder decides to withdraw from the process and the corporation approves). In other jurisdictions, shareholder status may not be reinstated until the appraisal is concluded. Even if an individual loses his or her shareholder status, courts may allow the individual to sue on the ground of fraud or other illegal conduct associated with the merger.

A shareholder cannot sue on the ground of fraud or other illegal conduct, however, if the shareholder's complaint is really about the price that he or she received for the stock. For complaints about price, appraisal rights are the exclusive remedy, as illustrated in the following case.

CASE 26.2

Grace Brothers, Ltd. v. Farley Industries, Inc.

Supreme Court of Georgia, 1994.
264 Ga. 817,
450 S.E.2d 814.

FACTS   William Farley, through Farley Industries, Inc., and other companies, made a tender offer (an offer to purchase shares in the company made by another company directly to the target company's shareholders) of $58 per share for the stock of WPP. This was far more than the price of WPP stock on the New York Stock Exchange. WPP's board of directors approved the offer and sold 95 percent of the stock to Farley. WPP also agreed to merge with West Point Tender Corporation (WPTC), a Farley entity, after which the last 5 percent of WPP shareholders would be paid $58 per share. Before the WPP-WPTC merger could take place, Farley encountered financial troubles and announced that he could pay no more than $46 per share to Grace Brothers, Ltd., and other minority shareholders. Grace and the others filed a suit in a Georgia state court against Farley, alleging, among other things, that Farley breached a fiduciary duty by not paying $58 per share, as promised in the merger agreement. The court dismissed the claim, and the plaintiffs appealed.

ISSUE   Are appraisal rights the exclusive remedy for dissenting shareholders' complaints about stock prices?

DECISION   Yes. The Supreme Court of Georgia affirmed the dismissal.

REASON   The state supreme court concluded that the shareholders' claim "boils down to nothing more than a complaint about stock price." For such complaints, "our statutory appraisal remedy is exclusive. It permits a dissenting shareholder to be paid the fair value of his shares and preempts any other remedy." As for the alleged wrongdoing, "any facts which shed light on the value of the dissenting shareholders' interests are to be considered in arriving at 'fair value.'"

FOR CRITICAL ANALYSIS—Economic Consideration   *Besides Farley's "alleged wrongdoing," what other facts might "shed light on the value of the dissenting shareholders' interests" in determining the fair value of shares?*

▌ Purchase of Assets

When a corporation acquires all or substantially all of the assets of another corporation by direct purchase, the purchasing, or *acquiring*, corporation simply extends its ownership and control over more physical assets. Because no change in the legal entity occurs, the acquiring corporation is not required to obtain shareholder approval for the purchase.[2]

Although the acquiring corporation may not be required to obtain shareholder approval for such an acquisition, the U.S. Department of Justice and the Federal Trade Commission have issued guidelines that significantly constrain and often prohibit mergers that could result from a purchase of assets, including takeover bids. These guidelines are discussed in Chapter 30, in the context of federal antitrust laws.

Note that the corporation that is selling all its assets is substantially changing its business position

---

2.   If the acquiring corporation plans to pay for the assets with its own corporate stock and not enough authorized unissued shares are available, the shareholders must vote to approve issuance of additional shares by amendment of the corporate articles. Additionally, acquiring corporations whose stock is

---

traded in a national stock exchange can be required to obtain their own shareholders' approval if they plan to issue a significant number of shares, such as a number equal to 20 percent or more of the outstanding shares.

and perhaps its ability to carry out its corporate purposes. For that reason, the corporation whose assets are acquired must obtain the approval of both the board of directors and the shareholders. In most states and under RMBCA 13.02, a dissenting shareholder of the selling corporation can demand appraisal rights.

Generally, a corporation that purchases the assets of another corporation is not responsible for the liabilities of the selling corporation. Exceptions to this rule are made in the following circumstances:

1. When the purchasing corporation impliedly or expressly assumes the seller's liabilities.

2. When the sale amounts to what in fact is a merger or consolidation.

3. When the purchaser continues the seller's business and retains the same personnel (same shareholders, directors, and officers).

4. When the sale is fraudulently executed to escape liability.

In any of these situations, the acquiring corporation will be held to have assumed both the assets and the liabilities of the selling corporation.

There are several factors for determining whether a purchase of assets is in fact a merger. The court considers these factors in the following case.

CASE 26.3

Sedbrook v. Zimmerman Design Group, Ltd.

Court of Appeals of Wisconsin, 1994.
190 Wis.2d 14,
526 N.W.2d 758.

FACTS When EG&G, Inc., took over the E. Van Noorden Company, the manufacturer of Vanco-brand skylights, Van Noorden shareholders traded their stock for EG&G stock. Van Noorden ceased to exist. EG&G assumed Van Noorden's customer and supplier relationships and acquired all of Van Noorden's assets. EG&G continued to make Vanco skylights, using the same factory and employees, as well as at least two key Van Noorden officers. EG&G also assumed all of the obligations of Van Noorden necessary for uninterrupted operations. Clarence Sedbrook fell through a Vanco skylight on a hospital roof and suffered permanent injuries. Sedbrook and his family filed a suit in a Wisconsin state court against Zimmerman Design Group, Ltd. (the firm that designed the roof), EG&G, and others. EG&G asked to be dismissed from the suit on the ground that Van Noorden had manufactured the skylight before EG&G had purchased Van Noorden's assets. The court granted the request. Sedbrook appealed.

ISSUE Did EG&G, when it acquired Van Noorden's assets, assume Van Noorden's liability for manufacturing a defective product?

DECISION Yes. The Court of Appeals of Wisconsin reversed the lower court's decision and remanded the case for trial.

REASON The state appellate court held, among other things, that EG&G's acquisition of Van Noorden qualified as a merger. The court listed four factors for determining whether a purchase of assets is in fact a merger: "(1) the assets of the seller corporation are acquired with shares of the stock in the buyer corporation * * * ; (2) the seller ceases operations and dissolves soon after the sale; (3) the buyer continues the enterprise of the seller corporation so that there is a continuity of management, employees, business location, assets and general business operations; and (4) the buyer assumes those liabilities of the seller necessary for the uninterrupted continuation of normal business operations." The court found all of those factors present in this case. "[A]s a result, there is no

(Continued)

Case 26.3—Continued

legal bar to Sedbrook's asserting a * * * claim against EG&G for its predecessor's potential liability."

FOR CRITICAL ANALYSIS—Social Consideration *In determining whether a merger occurred, which of the four factors listed by the court do you think was the most important, and why?*

▌Purchase of Stock

An alternative to the purchase of another corporation's assets is the purchase of a substantial number of the voting shares of its stock. This enables the acquiring corporation to control the acquired corporation. The acquiring corporation deals directly with the target company's shareholders in seeking to purchase the shares they hold. It does this by making a *tender offer* to all of the shareholders of the corporation to be acquired, or the **target corporation.** The tender offer is publicly advertised and addressed to all shareholders of the target company. The price of the stock in the tender offer is generally higher than the market price of the target stock prior to the announcement of the tender offer. The higher price induces shareholders to tender their shares to the acquiring firm.

The tender offer can be conditioned on the receipt of a specified number of outstanding shares by a specified date. The offering corporation can make an *exchange tender offer* in which it offers target stockholders its own securities in exchange for their target stock. In a *cash tender offer,* the offering corporation offers the target stockholders cash in exchange for their target stock.

Federal securities laws strictly control the terms, duration, and circumstances under which most tender offers are made. In addition, a majority of states have passed takeover statutes that impose additional regulations on tender offers.

A firm may respond to a tender offer in numerous ways. Sometimes, a target firm's board of directors will see a tender offer as favorable and will recommend to the shareholders that they accept it. To resist a takeover, a target company may make a *self-tender,* which is an offer to acquire stock from its own shareholders and thereby retain corporate control. Alternatively, a target corporation might resort to one of several other tactics to resist a takeover (see Exhibit 26–3).

▌Termination

The termination of a corporation's existence has two phases. **Dissolution** is the legal death of the artificial "person" of the corporation. **Liquidation** is the process by which corporate assets are converted into cash and distributed among creditors and shareholders according to specific rules of preference (see Chapter 24).

Dissolution

Dissolution of a corporation can be brought about in any of the following ways:

1. An act of a legislature in the state of incorporation.
2. Expiration of the time provided in the certificate of incorporation.
3. Voluntary approval of the shareholders and the board of directors.
4. Unanimous action by all shareholders.
5. A court decree brought about by the attorney general of the state of incorporation for any of the following reasons: (a) the failure to comply with administrative requirements (for example, failure to pay annual franchise taxes, to submit an annual report, or to have a designated registered agent), (b) the procurement of a corporation charter through fraud or misrepresentation on the state, (c) the abuse of corporate powers (*ultra vires* acts), (d) the violation of the state criminal code after the demand to discontinue has been made by the secretary of state, (e) the failure to commence business operations, or (f) the abandonment of operations before starting up [RMBCA 14.20].

As discussed in Chapter 25, sometimes a shareholder or a group of shareholders petitions a court for corporate dissolution. For example, the board of directors may be deadlocked. Courts

◆ Exhibit 26–3
The Terminology of Takeover Defenses

TERM	DEFINITION
Crown Jewel	When threatened with a takeover, management makes the company less attractive to the raider by selling to a third party the company's most valuable asset (hence the term *crown jewel*).
Golden Parachute	When a takeover is successful, top management is usually changed. With this in mind, a company may establish special termination or retirement benefits that must be paid to top management if they are "retired." In other words, a departing high-level manager's parachute will be "golden" when he or she is forced to "bail out" of the company.
Greenmail	To regain control, a target company may pay a higher-than-market price to repurchase the stock that the acquiring corporation bought. When a takeover is attempted through a gradual accumulation of target stock rather than a tender offer, the intent may be to get the target company to buy back the accumulated shares at a premium price—a concept similar to blackmail.
Lobster Trap	Lobster traps are designed to catch large lobsters but to allow small lobsters to escape. In the "lobster trap" defense, holders of convertible securities (corporate bonds or stock that is convertible into common shares) are prohibited from converting the securities into common shares if the holders already own, or would own after conversion, 10 percent or more of the voting shares of stock.
Pac-Man	Named after the Atari video game, this is an aggressive defense by which the target corporation attempts its own takeover of the acquiring corporation.
Poison Pill	The target corporation issues to its stockholders shares that can be turned in for cash if a takeover is successful. This makes the takeover undesirably or even prohibitively expensive for the acquiring corporation.
Scorched Earth	The target corporation sells off assets or divisions or takes out loans that it agrees to repay in the event of a takeover, thus making itself less financially attractive to the acquiring corporation.
Shark Repellent	To make a takeover more difficult, a target company may change its articles of incorporation or bylaws. For example, the bylaws may be amended to require that a large number of shareholders approve the firm's combination. This tactic casts the acquiring corporation in the role of a shark that must be repelled.
White Knight	The target corporation solicits a merger with a third party, which then makes a better (often simply a higher) tender offer to the target's shareholders. The third party that "rescues" the target is the "white knight."

hesitate to order involuntary dissolution in such circumstances unless there is specific statutory authorization to do so. If the deadlock cannot be resolved by the shareholders and if it will irreparably injure the corporation, however, the court will proceed with an involuntary dissolution. Courts can also dissolve a corporation in other circumstances, such as when the controlling shareholders or directors are committing fraudulent or oppressive acts or when management is misapplying or wasting corporate assets [RMBCA 14.30].

Liquidation

When dissolution takes place by voluntary action, the members of the board of directors act as trustees of the corporate assets. As trustees, they are responsible for winding up the affairs of the corporation for the benefit of corporate creditors and shareholders. This makes the board members personally liable for any breach of their fiduciary trustee duties.

Liquidation can be accomplished without court supervision unless the members of the board do not wish to act as trustees of the corporate assets, or unless shareholders or creditors can show cause to the court why the board should not be permitted to assume the trustee function. In either case, the court will appoint a receiver to wind up the corporate affairs and liquidate corporate assets. A receiver is always appointed by the court if the dissolution is involuntary.

▌Terms and Concepts

appraisal right 555
chose in action 553
consolidation 553

dissolution 558
liquidation 558
merger 552

short-form merger 554
target corporation 558

▌Chapter Summary: Corporate Merger, Consolidation, and Termination

Merger and Consolidation *(See pages 552–556.)*	1. *Merger*—The legal combination of two or more corporations, the result of which is that the surviving corporation acquires all the assets and obligations of the other corporation, which then ceases to exist.
	2. *Consolidation*—The legal combination of two or more corporations, the result of which is that each corporation ceases to exist and a new one emerges. The new corporation assumes all the assets and obligations of the former corporations.
	3. *Procedure*—Determined by state statutes. Basic requirements are the following: a. The board of directors of each corporation involved must approve the merger or consolidation plan. b. The shareholders of each corporation must approve the merger or consolidation plan at a shareholders' meeting. c. Articles of merger or consolidation (the plan) must be filed, usually with the secretary of state. d. The state issues a certificate of merger (or consolidation) to the surviving (or newly consolidated) corporation.
	4. *Short-form merger (parent-subsidiary merger)*—Possible when the parent corporation owns at least 90 percent of the outstanding shares of each class of stock of the subsidiary corporation. a. Shareholder approval is not required. b. The merger must be approved only by the board of directors of the parent corporation. c. A copy of the merger plan must be sent to each shareholder of record. d. The merger plan must be filed with the state.
	5. *Appraisal rights*—Rights of shareholders (given by state statute) to receive the *fair value* for their shares when a merger or consolidation takes place. If the shareholder and the corporation do not agree on the fair value, a court will determine it.

▌Chapter Summary: Corporate Merger, Consolidation, and Termination—Continued

Purchase of Assets *(See pages 556–558.)*	A purchase of assets occurs when one corporation acquires all or substantially all of the assets of another corporation. 1. *Acquiring corporation*—The acquiring (purchasing) corporation is not required to obtain shareholder approval; the corporation is merely increasing its assets, and no fundamental business change occurs. 2. *Acquired corporation*—The acquired (purchased) corporation is required to obtain the approval of both its directors and its shareholders for the sale of its assets, because this creates a substantial change in the corporation's business position.
Purchase of Stock *(See page 558.)*	A purchase of stock occurs when one corporation acquires a substantial number of the voting shares of the stock of another (target) corporation. 1. *Tender offer*—A public offer to all shareholders of the target corporation to purchase its stock at a price generally higher than the market price of the target stock prior to the announcement of the tender offer. Federal and state securities laws strictly control the terms, duration, and circumstances under which most tender offers are made. 2. *Target responses*—Ways in which target corporations respond to takeover bids. These include self-tender (the target firm's offer to acquire its own shareholders' stock), the Pac-Man defense (the target firm's takeover of the acquiring corporation), and numerous other strategies (see Exhibit 26–3).
Termination *(See pages 558–560.)*	The termination of a corporation involves the following two phases: 1. *Dissolution*—The legal death of the artificial "person" of the corporation. Dissolution can be brought about in any of the following ways: a. An act of a legislature in the state of incorporation. b. Expiration of the time provided in the corporate charter. c. Voluntary approval of the shareholders and the board of directors. d. Unanimous action by all shareholders. e. Court decree. 2. *Liquidation*—The process by which corporate assets are converted into cash and distributed to creditors and shareholders according to specified rules of preference. May be supervised by members of the board of directors (when dissolution is voluntary) or by a receiver appointed by the court to wind up corporate affairs.

▌For Review

1. What is the difference between a merger and a consolidation?

2. What are the four steps of the merger or consolidation procedure?

3. Under what circumstances is a corporation that purchases the assets of another corporation responsible for the liabilities of the selling corporation?

4. A target corporation can use a number of defenses to resist a takeover. Name five such defenses.

5. What are the two ways in which a corporation can be voluntarily dissolved? Under what circumstances might a corporation be involuntarily dissolved by state action?

▌Questions and Case Problems

26–1. Consolidations. Determine which of the following situations describes a consolidation:
  (a) Arkon Corp. purchases all of the assets of Botrek Co.
  (b) Arkon Corp. and Botrek Co. combine their firms, with Arkon Corp. as the surviving corporation.
  (c) Arkon Corp. and Botrek Co. agree to combine their assets, dissolve their old corporations, and form a new corporation under a new name.
  (d) Arkon Corp. agrees to sell all its accounts receivable to Botrek Co.

26–2. Corporate Combinations. Jolson is chairman of the board of directors of Artel, Inc., and Douglas is chairman of the board of directors of Fox Express, Inc. Artel is a manufacturing corporation, and Fox Express is a transportation corporation. Jolson and Douglas meet to consider the possibility of combining their corporations and activities into a single corporate entity. They consider two alternative courses of action: Artel could acquire all of the stock and assets of Fox Express, or the corporations could combine to form a new corporation, called A&F Enterprises, Inc. Both chairmen are concerned about the necessity of a formal transfer of property, liability for existing debts, and the problem of amending the articles of incorporation. Discuss what the two proposed combinations are called and the legal effect each has on the transfer of property, the liabilities of the combined corporations, and the need to amend the articles of incorporation.

26–3. Mergers. Tally Ho Co. was merged into Perfecto Corp., with Perfecto being the surviving corporation in the merger. Hanjo, a creditor of Tally Ho, brought suit against Perfecto Corp. for payment of the debt. The directors of Perfecto refused to pay, stating that Tally Ho no longer existed and that Perfecto had never agreed to assume any of Tally Ho's liabilities. Discuss fully whether Hanjo will be able to recover from Perfecto.

26–4. Purchase of Assets. Fuju Enterprises, Inc., purchased all the assets of Grosmont Corp. The directors of both corporations approved the sale, and 80 percent of Grosmont's shareholders approved. The shareholders of Fuju Enterprises, however, were never consulted. Some of these shareholders claimed that the purchase was invalid. Are they correct?

26–5. Corporate Dissolution. Two brothers, Albert and Raymond Martin, each owned 50 percent of the stock in Martin's News Service, Inc. Albert and Raymond had difficulty working together and communicated only through their accountant. For ten years, there were no corporate meetings, elections to the board of directors, or other corporate formalities. During that time, Raymond operated the business much as a sole proprietorship, failing to consult Albert on any matter and making all of the decisions himself. The corporation, however, was a viable concern that had grown successfully through the years. Albert sued to have the corporation dissolved. Should he succeed? Discuss. [*Martin v. Martin's News Service, Inc.*, 9 Conn.App. 304, 518 A.2d 951 (1986)]

26–6. Corporate Dissolution. I. Burack, Inc., was a family-operated close corporation that sold plumbing supplies in New York. The founder, Israel Burack, transferred his shares in the corporation to other family members, and when Israel died in 1974, the position of president passed to his son, Robert Burack. Robert held a one-third interest in the company, and the remainder was divided among Israel's other children and grandchildren. All of the shareholders participated in the corporation as employees or officers and thus relied on salaries and bonuses, rather than dividends, for distribution of the corporation's earnings. In 1976, several of the family-member employees requested a salary increase from Robert, who claimed that company earnings were not sufficient to warrant any employee salary increases. Shortly thereafter, a shareholders' meeting was held (the first in the company's fifty-year history), and Robert was removed from his position as president and denied the right to participate in any way in the corporation. Robert sued to have the company dissolved because he had been "frozen out" of the business by the allegedly oppressive tactics of the other shareholders. Discuss whether Robert should succeed in his suit or whether the court would choose another alternative. [*Burack v. I. Burack, Inc.*, 137 A.D.2d 523, 524 N.Y.S.2d 457 (1988)]

26–7. Mergers and Consolidations. Edward Antar and William Markowitz were the sole stockholders and directors of E.B.M., Inc., a corporation formed for the purpose of buying and managing real estate. Antar and Markowitz were also the controlling shareholders and directors of Acousti-Phase, Inc., a corporation that manufactured and sold stereo speakers. In 1982, Acousti-Phase was effectively shut down when a fire destroyed the manufacturing and storage facility that it was renting from E.B.M. Shortly after the fire, E.B.M. contracted with a New York firm to assemble the speakers, affix the Acousti-Phase name, and sell the final product, primarily to former customers of Acousti-Phase. At the time of the fire, Acousti-Phase owed $26,470 to Cab-Tek, Inc., a corporation that supplied it with cabinet housings for its stereo speakers. In 1985, Cab-Tek sued E.B.M. to recover the debt owed by Acousti-Phase. Discuss fully whether E.B.M. can be held liable for Acousti-Phase's debt. [*Cab-Tek, Inc. v. E.B.M., Inc.*, 153 Vt. 432, 571 A.2d 671 (1990)]

26–8. Purchase of Assets. In 1987, William Myers sustained injuries to his hand while operating a concrete cement pump that had been designed and manufactured by Thomsen Equipment Co. and purchased from Thomsen in 1981. Myers alleged that the pump was unreasonably dangerous because it had an "unguarded nip point in a flapper valve." Putzmeister, Inc., had purchased Thomsen's assets in 1982. Assuming that Myers has a valid product liability claim, what factors will the court consider in determining whether Putzmeister, as a successor corporation, can be held liable for injuries caused by Thomsen's product? [*Myers v. Putzmeister, Inc.*, 232 Ill.App.3d 419, 596 N.E.2d 754, 173 Ill.Dec. 130 (1992)]

26–9. Purchase of Assets. Lori Nilsson, while working as a machine operator, was injured by a pipe and tube cutoff machine that had been manufactured and sold by Continental Machine Co. (CM) prior to 1978. In 1986, Fredor Corp. purchased all of the production assets of CM, including the pipe and tube machine product line, and formed Continental Machine Manufacturing Co. (CMM). CMM continued to manufacture the same product lines as CM had. The shareholders of CM did not become shareholders, officers, or employees of Fredor or CMM. Most of the employees of CM became employees of CMM, however. There was no evidence that the transaction was undertaken for a fraudulent purpose, nor did Fredor or CMM agree to assume CM's liabilities. After the sale of assets, CM continued to exist, but it had no productive assets. CM continued to own the building in which the assets had been located, however, and leased the building to CMM. Nilsson brought a product liability suit against CMM. Should CMM be held liable for injuries caused by a machine manufactured by CM? How will

the court decide this issue? Discuss fully. [*Nilsson v. Continental Machine Manufacturing Co.*, 251 Ill.App.3d 415, 621 N.E.2d 1032, 190 Ill.Dec. 579 (1993)]

26–10. Purchase of Assets. MRS Manufacturing, Inc., manufactured tractors, which it sold to Glades Equipment, Inc. Glades Equipment sold one of the tractors to the U.S. Sugar Corp. Later, Glade and Grove Supply, Inc., bought the Glades Equipment dealership under a contract that stated the sale covered only such property "as [Glades Equipment] has on hand at the time of the . . . sale." kDaniel Brown, an employee of the U.S. Sugar Corp., was operating an MRS tractor when it rolled over and killed him. His wife, Patricia, filed a product liability suit against, among others, Glade and Grove. What factors will the court consider in determining whether Glade and Grove is liable? [*Brown v. Glade and Grove Supply, Inc.*, 647 So.2d 1033 (Fla.App. 1994)]

26–11. Appraisal Rights. Travelers Corp. announced that it would merge with Primerica Corp. At a special shareholders meeting, a vote of the Travelers shareholders revealed that 95 percent approved of the merger. Robert Brandt and other shareholders who did not approve of the merger sued Travelers and others, complaining that the defendants had not obtained "the highest possible price for shareholders." Travelers asked the court to dismiss the suit, contending that Brandt and the others had, as a remedy for their complaint, their statutory appraisal rights. On what basis might the court dismiss the suit? Discuss. [*Brandt v. Travelers Corp.*, 44 Conn.Supp. 12, 665 A.2d 616 (1995)]

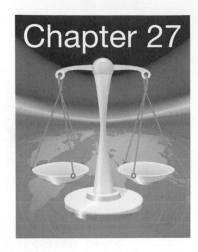

Chapter 27

Investor Protection

CHAPTER OBJECTIVES

After reading this chapter, you should be able to:

1. Define what is meant by the term *securities.*
2. Describe the purpose and provisions of the Securities Act of 1933.
3. Explain the purpose and provisions of the Securities Exchange Act of 1934.
4. Identify federal laws that specifically regulate investment companies.
5. Point out some of the features of state securities laws.

After the great stock market crash of 1929, various studies showed a need for regulating securities markets. Basically, legislation for such regulation was enacted to provide investors with more information to help them make buying and selling decisions about **securities**—generally defined as any documents evidencing corporate ownership (stock) or debts (bonds)—and to prohibit deceptive, unfair, and manipulative practices. Today, the sale and transfer of securities are heavily regulated by federal and state statutes and by government agencies. This chapter will discuss the nature of federal securities regulations and their effects on the business world.

▌ Securities Act of 1933

The Securities Act of 1933[1] was designed to prohibit various forms of fraud and to stabilize the securities industry by requiring that all essential information concerning the issuance of securities be made available to the investing public. Essentially, the purpose of this act is to require disclosure.

What Is a Security?

Section 2(1) of the Securities Act states that securities include the following:

> [A]ny note, stock, treasury stock, bond, debenture, evidence of indebtedness, certificate of interest or participation in any profit-sharing agreement, collateral-trust certificate, preorganization certificate or subscription, transferable share, investment contract, voting-trust certificate, certificate of deposit for a security, fractional undivided interest in oil, gas, or other mineral rights, or, in general, any interest or instrument commonly known as a "security," or any certificate of interest or participation in, temporary or interim certificate for, receipt for, guarantee of, or warrant or right to subscribe to or purchase, any of the foregoing.[2]

---

1. 15 U.S.C. Sections 77–77aa.

2. 15 U.S.C. Section 77b(1). Amendments in 1982 added stock options.

Generally, the courts have interpreted Section 2(1) of the Securities Act to mean that a security exists in any transaction in which a person (1) invests (2) in a common enterprise (3) reasonably expecting profits (4) derived *primarily* or *substantially* from others' managerial or entrepreneurial efforts.[3]

For our purposes, it is probably most convenient to think of securities in their most common forms—stocks and bonds issued by corporations. Bear in mind, however, that securities can take many forms and have been held to include whiskey, cosmetics, worms, beavers, boats, vacuum cleaners, muskrats, and cemetery lots, as well as investment contracts in condominiums, franchises, limited partnerships, oil or gas or other mineral rights, and farm animals accompanied by care agreements.

Registration Statement

Section 5 of the Securities Act of 1933 broadly provides that if a security does not qualify for an exemption, that security must be *registered* before it is offered to the public either through the mails or through any facility of interstate commerce, including securities exchanges. Issuing corporations must file a *registration statement* with the Securities and Exchange Commission (SEC). Investors must be provided with a *prospectus* that describes the security being sold, the issuing corporation, and the investment or risk attaching to the security. In principle, the registration statement and the prospectus supply sufficient information to enable unsophisticated investors to evaluate the financial risk involved.

CONTENTS OF THE REGISTRATION STATEMENT The registration statement must include the following:

1. A description of the significant provisions of the security offered for sale, including the relationship between that security and the other capital securities of the registrant. Also, the corporation must disclose how it intends to use the proceeds of the sale.
2. A description of the registrant's properties and business.

3. A description of the management of the registrant and its security holdings; remuneration; and other benefits, including pensions and stock options. Any interests of directors or officers in any material transactions with the corporation must be disclosed.
4. A financial statement certified by an independent public accounting firm.
5. A description of pending lawsuits.

In 1996, the SEC undertook steps to simplify corporate securities-offering procedures that will make it easier for small businesses to raise capital. Generally, the SEC intends to eliminate many of its regulations and required forms, and streamline the disclosure process, so that requirements will be easier to understand. The SEC may also create broader exemptions from registration requirements for small businesses (exemptions under the 1933 act will be discussed shortly).

OTHER REQUIREMENTS Before filing the registration statement and the prospectus with the SEC, the corporation is allowed to obtain an underwriter—a company that agrees to purchase the new issue of securities for resale to the public. There is a twenty-day waiting period (which can be accelerated by the SEC) after registration before the sale can take place. During this period, oral offers between interested investors and the issuing corporation concerning the purchase and sale of the proposed securities may take place; very limited written advertising is allowed. At this time, the so-called **red herring** prospectus may be distributed. It gets its name from the red legend printed across it stating that the registration has been filed but has not become effective.

After the waiting period, the registered securities can be legally bought and sold. Written advertising is allowed in the form of a **tombstone ad,** so named because historically the format resembles a tombstone. Such ads simply tell the investor where and how to obtain a prospectus. Normally, any other type of advertising is prohibited.

VIOLATIONS As mentioned, the SEC has the power to investigate and bring civil enforcement actions against companies that violate federal securities laws, including the Securities Act of 1933. Criminal violations are prosecuted by the Department of Justice. When the SEC was formed, Congress intended that the SEC also would rely on private lawsuits as a supplement to its efforts to

---

3. *SEC v. W. J. Howey Co.,* 328 U.S. 293, 66 S.Ct. 1100, 90 L.Ed. 1244 (1946).

enforce securities laws. Thus, private parties, such as shareholders, can bring suits against those who violate federal securities laws.

Registration violations of the 1933 act are not treated lightly. In the following classic case, purchasers of the corporation's debentures (deben- tures were discussed in Chapter 26) sued BarChris Construction Corporation under Section 11 of the Securities Act of 1933. Section 11 imposes liability when a registration statement contains material false statements or material omissions.

CASE 27.1

Escott v. BarChris Construction Corp.

United States District Court,
Southern District of New York, 1968.
283 F.Supp. 643.

FACTS BarChris Construction Corporation was an expanding company that built bowling alleys and was in constant need of cash to finance its operations. In 1961, BarChris issued securities, in the form of debenture bonds, after filing the appropriate registration statement with the Securities and Exchange Commission. By early 1962, the company's financial difficulties had become insurmountable, and BarChris defaulted on the interest due on the debentures one month after petitioning for bankruptcy. Purchasers of the BarChris bonds sued BarChris in a federal district court, alleging that BarChris had violated Section 11 of the Securities Act of 1933. The plaintiffs challenged the accuracy of the registration statement filed with the Securities and Exchange Commission and charged that the text of the prospectus was false and that material information had been omitted. There were three categories of defendants: BarChris and all of the signers of the registration statement, the underwriters, and BarChris's auditors.

ISSUE Had BarChris violated the 1933 Securities Act requirements concerning the registration statement and prospectus accompanying its bond issue?

DECISION Yes. The court held that BarChris and all of the signers of the registration statement, the underwriters, and the corporation's auditors were all liable.

REASON The court found that the registration statement contained false statements of fact and omitted other facts that should have been included to prevent the statement from being misleading. The misstatements included overstatement of sales and gross profits; understatement of contingent liabilities; overstatement of orders on hand; and failure to disclose true facts with respect to officers' loans, customers' delinquencies, application of proceeds, and the prospective operation of several bowling alleys. The facts that were falsely stated or omitted were "material" within the meaning of the Securities Act of 1933. The court found that "[t]he average prudent investor is not concerned with minor inaccuracies or with errors as to matters which are of no interest to him. The facts which tend to deter him from purchasing a security are facts which have an important bearing upon the nature or condition of the issuing corporation or its business. Judged by this test, there is no doubt that many of the misstatements and omissions in this prospectus were material."

FOR CRITICAL ANALYSIS—Social Consideration *Under what common law theory might a buyer sue a seller for the seller's failure to disclose material facts about the goods being sold?*

Exempt Securities

A number of specific securities are exempt from the registration requirements of the Securities Act of 1933. These securities—which can also generally be resold without being registered—include the following:[4]

1. All bank securities sold prior to July 27, 1933.
2. Commercial paper, if the maturity date does not exceed nine months.
3. Securities of charitable organizations.
4. Securities resulting from a corporate reorganization issued for exchange with the issuer's existing security holders and certificates issued by trustees, receivers, or debtors in possession under the bankruptcy laws (bankruptcy is discussed in Chapter 20).
5. Securities issued exclusively for exchange with the issuer's existing security holders, provided no commission is paid (for example, stock dividends and stock splits).
6. Securities issued to finance the acquisition of railroad equipment.
7. Any insurance, endowment, or annuity contract issued by a state-regulated insurance company.
8. Government-issued securities.
9. Securities issued by banks, savings and loan associations, farmers' cooperatives, and similar institutions subject to supervision by governmental authorities.
10. In consideration of the "small amount involved,"[5] an issuer's offer of up to $5 million in securities in any twelve-month period (including up to $1.5 million in nonissuer resales).

For the last exemption, under Regulation A,[6] the issuer must file with the SEC a notice of the issue and an offering circular, which must also be provided to investors before the sale. This is a much simpler and less expensive process than the procedures associated with full registration. Companies are allowed to "test the waters" for potential interest before preparing the offering circular. To *test the waters* means to determine potential interest without actually selling any securities or requiring any commitment on the part of those who are interested. Small-business issuers (companies with less than $25 million in annual revenues and less than $25 million in outstanding voting stock) can also use an integrated registration and reporting system that uses simpler forms than the full registration system.

Exhibit 27–1 summarizes the securities and transactions (discussed next) that are exempt from the registration requirements under the Securities Act of 1933 and SEC regulations.

Exempt Transactions

An issuer of securities that are not exempt under one of the categories listed above can avoid the high cost and complicated procedures associated with registration by taking advantage of certain transaction exemptions. An offering may qualify for more than one exemption. These exemptions are very broad, and thus most sales occur without registration. The exemptions are available only in the transaction in which the securities are issued, however (except for securities issued under Rule 504, which will be discussed shortly). A resale may be made only after registration (unless the resale qualifies as an exempt transaction).

REGULATION D The SEC's Regulation D contains four separate exemptions from registration requirements for limited offers (offers that involve either a small amount of money or are made in a limited manner). Regulation D provides that any of these offerings made during any twelve-month period are exempt from the registration requirements.

Rule 504 Noninvestment company offerings up to $1 million in any twelve-month period are exempt.[7] In contrast to investment companies (discussed later in this chapter), noninvestment companies are firms that are not engaged primarily in the business of investing or trading in securities.

Rule 504a Offerings up to $500,000 in any one year by so-called blank check companies—companies with no specific business plans except to locate

---

4. 15 U.S.C. Section 77c.
5. 15 U.S.C. Section 77c(b).
6. 17 C.F.R. Sections 230.251–230.263.

---

7. 17 C.F.R. Section 230.504. Rule 504 is the exemption currently used by most small businesses, but that could change under SEC Rule 1001. This rule permits, under certain circumstances, "testing the waters" for offerings of up to $5 million *per transaction*.

◆ **Exhibit 27–1**
Exemptions under the 1933 Securities Act

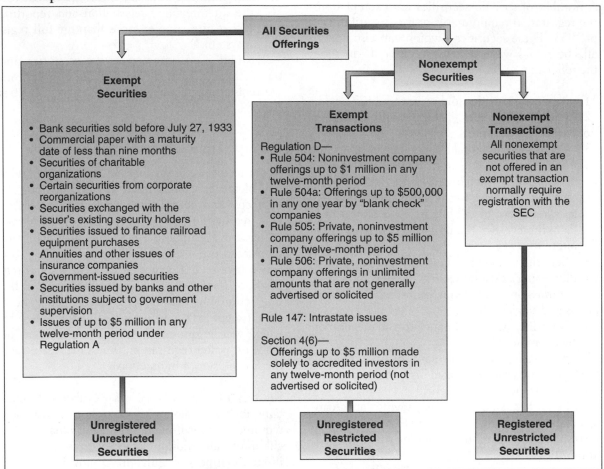

and acquire presently unknown businesses or opportunities—are exempt if no general solicitation or advertising is used; the SEC is notified of the sales; and precaution is taken against nonexempt, unregistered resales.[8] The limits on advertising and unregistered resales do not apply if the offering is made solely in states that provide for registration and disclosure and the securities are sold in compliance with those provisions.[9]

Rule 505 Private, noninvestment company offerings up to $5 million in any twelve-month period are exempt, regardless of the number of **accredited investors** (banks, insurance companies, investment companies, the issuer's executive officers and directors, and persons whose income or net worth exceeds certain limits), so long as there are no more than thirty-five unaccredited investors; no general solicitation or advertising is used; the SEC is notified of the sales; and precaution is taken against nonexempt, unregistered resales. If the sale involves *any* unaccredited investors, *all* investors must be given material information about the offering company, its business, and the securities before the sale. The issuer is not required to believe that each unaccredited investor "has such knowledge and experience in financial and business matters

---

8. Precautions to be taken against nonexempt, unregistered resales include asking the investor whether he or she is buying the securities for others; before the sale, disclosing to each purchaser in writing that the securities are unregistered and thus cannot be resold, except in an exempt transaction, without first being registered; and indicating on the certificates that the securities are unregistered and restricted.
9. 17 C.F.R. Section 230.504a.

that he is capable of evaluating the merits and the risks of the prospective investment."[10]

Rule 506 Private offerings in unlimited amounts that are not generally solicited or advertised are exempt if the SEC is notified of the sales; precaution is taken against nonexempt, unregistered resales; and the issuer believes that each unaccredited investor has sufficient knowledge or experience in financial matters to be capable of evaluating the investment's merits and risks. There may be no more than thirty-five unaccredited investors, although there may be an unlimited number of accredited investors. If there are *any* unaccredited investors, the issuer must provide to *all* purchasers material information about itself, its business, and the securities before the sale.[11]

This exemption is perhaps most important to those firms that want to raise funds through the sale of securities without registering them. It is often referred to as the *private placement* exemption, because it exempts "transactions not involving any public offering."[12] This provision applies to private offerings to a limited number of persons who are sufficiently sophisticated and in a sufficiently strong bargaining position to be able to assume the risk of the investment (and who thus have no need for federal registration protection), as well as to private offerings to similarly situated institutional investors.

RULE 147—INTRASTATE ISSUES Also exempt are intrastate transactions involving purely local offerings.[13] This exemption applies to most offerings that are restricted to residents of the state in which the issuing company is organized and doing business. For nine months after the last sale, virtually no resales may be made to nonresidents, and precautions must be taken against this possibility. These offerings remain subject to applicable laws in the state of issue.

SECTION 4(6) Under Section 4(6) of the Securities Act of 1933, an offer made *solely* to accredited investors is exempt if its amount is not more than $5 million. Any number of accredited investors may participate, but no unaccredited investors may do so. No general solicitation or advertising may be used; the SEC must be notified of all sales; and precaution must be taken against nonexempt, unregistered resales (because these are restricted securities and may be resold only by registration or in an exempt transaction).[14]

RESALES Most securities can be resold without registration (although some resales may be subject to certain restrictions, which were discussed previously in connection with specific exemptions). The Securities Act of 1933 provides exemptions for resales by most persons other than issuers or underwriters. Resales of restricted securities acquired under Rule 504a, Rule 505, Rule 506, or Section 4(6), however, trigger the registration requirements unless the party selling them complies with Rule 144 or Rule 144A. These rules are sometimes referred to as "safe harbors."

Rule 144 Rule 144 exempts restricted securities from registration on resale if there is adequate current public information about the issuer, the person selling the securities has owned them for at least two years, they are sold in certain limited amounts in unsolicited brokers' transactions, and the SEC is given notice of the resale.[15] "Adequate current public information" consists of the reports that certain companies are required to file under the Securities Exchange Act of 1934.

Rule 144A Securities that at the time of issue are not of the same class as securities listed on a national securities exchange or quoted in a U.S. automated interdealer quotation system may be resold under Rule 144A.[16] They may be sold only to a qualified institutional buyer (an institution, such as an insurance company, an investment company, or a bank, that owns and invests at least $100 million in securities). The seller must take reasonable steps to ensure that the buyer knows that the seller is relying on the exemption under Rule 144A. A sample restricted stock certificate is shown in Exhibit 27–2.

---

10. 17 C.F.R. Section 230.505.
11. 17 C.F.R. Section 230.506.
12. 15 U.S.C. Section 77d(2).
13. 15 U.S.C. Section 77c(a)(11); 17 C.F.R. Section 230.147.

14. 15 U.S.C. Section 77d(6).
15. 17 C.F.R. Section 230.144.
16. 17 C.F.R. Section 230.144A.

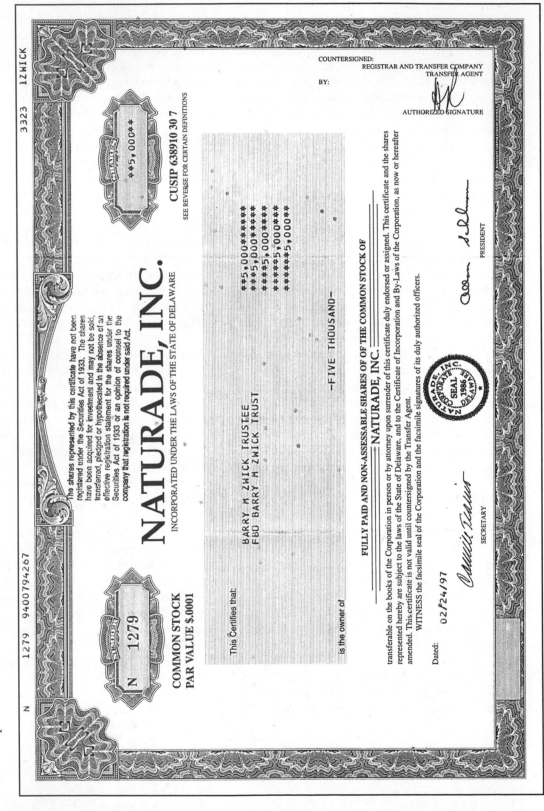

◆ Exhibit 27–2
A Sample Restricted Stock Certificate

∎ Securities Exchange Act of 1934

The Securities Exchange Act of 1934 provides for the regulation and registration of securities exchanges; brokers; dealers; and national securities associations, such as the National Association of Securities Dealers (NASD). The SEC regulates the markets in which securities are traded by maintaining a continuous disclosure system for all corporations with securities on the securities exchanges and for those companies that have assets in excess of $10 million and five hundred or more shareholders. These corporations are referred to as Section 12 companies, because they are required to register their securities under Section 12 of the 1934 act.

The act regulates proxy solicitation for voting (discussed in Chapter 25) and allows the SEC to engage in market surveillance to regulate undesirable market practices such as fraud, market manipulation, misrepresentation, and stabilization. (*Stabilization* is a market-manipulating technique by which securities underwriters bid for securities to stabilize the prices of securities during their issuance.)

Section 10(b), SEC Rule 10b-5, and Insider Trading

Section 10(b) is one of the most important sections of the Securities Exchange Act of 1934. This section proscribes the use of "any manipulative or deceptive device or contrivance in contravention of such rules and regulations as the [SEC] may prescribe." Among the rules that the SEC has promulgated pursuant to the 1934 act is **SEC Rule 10b-5**, which prohibits the commission of fraud in connection with the purchase or sale of any security.

One of the most important purposes of Section 10(b) and SEC Rule 10b-5 relates to so-called **insider trading.** Because of their positions, corporate directors and officers often obtain advance inside information that can affect the future market value of the corporate stock. Obviously, their positions can give them a trading advantage over the general public and shareholders. The 1934 Securities Exchange Act defines inside information and extends liability to officers and directors for taking advantage of such information in their personal transactions when they know that it is unavailable to the persons with whom they are dealing.

Section 10(b) of the 1934 act and SEC Rule 10b-5 cover not only corporate officers, directors, and majority shareholders but also any persons having access to or receiving information of a nonpublic nature on which trading is based.[17] Those found liable under SEC Rule 10b-5 have a right to seek reimbursement from persons or entities that may have shared responsibility for the violations, including accountants, attorneys, and corporations.[18]

DISCLOSURE UNDER SEC RULE 10b-5 Any material omission or misrepresentation of material facts in connection with the purchase or sale of a security may violate not only Section 11 of the Securities Act of 1933 but also the antifraud provisions of Section 10(b) and SEC Rule 10b-5 of the 1934 act. The key to liability (which can be civil or criminal) under Section 10(b) and SEC Rule 10b-5 is whether the insider's information is *material.* The following are some examples of material facts calling for a disclosure under the rule:

1. A new ore discovery.
2. Fraudulent trading in the company stock by a broker-dealer.
3. A dividend change (whether up or down).
4. A contract for the sale of corporate assets.
5. A new discovery (process or product).
6. A significant change in the firm's financial condition.

Courts have struggled with the problem of when information becomes public knowledge. Clearly, when inside information becomes public knowledge, all insiders should be allowed to trade without disclosure. The courts have suggested that insiders should refrain from trading for a "reasonable waiting period" when the news is not readily translatable into investment action. Presumably, this gives the news time to filter down to, and to be evaluated by, the investing public.

---

17. Note that a private cause of action under Section 10(b) and SEC Rule 10b-5 cannot be brought against accountants, attorneys, and others who "aid and abet" violations of the act. Only the SEC can bring actions against so-called aiders and abettors. See *Central Bank of Denver, N.A. v. First Interstate Bank of Denver, N.A.,* 511 U.S. 164, 114 S.Ct. 1439, 128 L.Ed.2d 119 (1994).
18. *Musick, Peeler & Garrett v. Employers Insurance of Wausau,* 508 U.S. 286, 113 S.Ct. 2085, 124 L.Ed.2d 194 (1993).

The following is one of the landmark cases interpreting SEC Rule 10b-5. The SEC sued Texas Gulf Sulphur Company for issuing a misleading press release. The release underestimated the magnitude and the value of a mineral discovery. The SEC also sued several of Texas Gulf Sulphur's directors, officers, and employees under SEC Rule 10b-5 for purchasing large amounts of the corporate stock prior to the announcement of the corporation's rich ore discovery.

CASE 27.2
SEC v. Texas Gulf Sulphur Co.
United States Court of Appeals, Second Circuit, 1968. 401 F.2d 833.

FACTS The Texas Gulf Sulphur Company drilled a hole on November 12, 1963, that appeared to yield a core with an exceedingly high mineral content. TGS kept secret the results of the core sample. Officers and employees of the company made substantial purchases of TGS's stock or accepted stock options after learning of the ore discovery, even though further drilling was necessary to establish whether there was enough ore to be mined commercially. On April 11, 1964, an unauthorized report of the mineral find appeared in the newspapers. On the following day, April 12, TGS issued a press release that played down the discovery and stated that it was too early to tell whether the ore finding would be a significant one. Later on, TGS announced a strike of at least twenty-five million tons of ore, substantially driving up the price of TGS stock. The SEC brought suit in a federal district court against the officers and employees of TGS for violating the insider-trading prohibition of SEC Rule 10b-5. The officers and employees argued that the prohibition did not apply. They reasoned that the information on which they had traded was not material, as the mine had not been commercially proved. The court held that most of the defendants had not violated SEC Rule 10b-5, and the SEC appealed.

ISSUE Had the officers and employees of TGS violated SEC Rule 10b-5 by purchasing the stock, even though they did not know the full extent and profit potential of the mine at the time they purchased the stock?

DECISION Yes. The federal appellate court reversed the lower court's decision and remanded the case to the trial court, holding that the employees and officers violated SEC Rule 10b-5's prohibition against insider trading.

REASON For SEC Rule 10b-5 purposes, the test of materiality is whether the information would affect the judgment of reasonable investors. Reasonable investors include speculative as well as conservative investors. "[A] major factor in determining whether the * * * discovery [of the ore] was a material fact is the importance attached to the drilling results by those who knew about it. * * * [T]he timing by those who knew of it of their stock purchases and their purchases of short-term calls [rights to buy shares at a specified price within a specified time period]—purchases in some cases by individuals who had never before purchased calls or even TGS stock—virtually compels the inference that the insiders were influenced by the drilling results. * * * We hold, therefore, that all transactions in TGS stock or calls by individuals apprised of the drilling results * * * were made in violation of Rule 10b–5."

FOR CRITICAL ANALYSIS—Economic Consideration *Who is hurt by insider trading?*

APPLICABILITY OF SEC RULE 10b-5 SEC Rule 10b-5 applies in virtually all cases concerning the trading of securities, whether on organized exchanges, in over-the-counter markets, or in private transactions. The rule covers notes, bonds, certificates of interest and participation in any profit-sharing agreement, agreements to form a corporation, and joint-venture agreements; in short, it covers just about any form of security. It is immaterial whether a firm has securities registered under the 1933 act for the 1934 act to apply.

Although SEC Rule 10b-5 is applicable only when the requisites of federal jurisdiction—such as the use of the mails, of stock exchange facilities, or of any instrumentality of interstate commerce—are present, virtually no commercial transaction can be completed without such contact. In addition, the states have corporate securities laws, many of which include provisions similar to SEC Rule 10b-5.

OUTSIDERS AND SEC RULE 10b-5 The traditional insider-trading case involves true insiders—corporate officers, directors, and majority shareholders who have access to (and trade on) inside information. Increasingly, liability under Section 10(b) of the 1934 act and SEC Rule 10b-5 has been extended to include certain "outsiders"—those who trade on inside information acquired *indirectly*. Two theories have been developed under which outsiders may be held liable for insider trading: the *tipper/tippee theory* and the *misappropriation theory*.

Tipper/Tippee Theory Anyone who acquires inside information as a result of a corporate insider's breach of his or her fiduciary duty can be liable under SEC Rule 10b-5. This liability extends to **tippees** (those who receive "tips" from insiders) and even remote tippees (tippees of tippees).

The key to liability under this theory is that the inside information be obtained as a result of someone's breach of a fiduciary duty to the corporation whose shares are involved in the trading. Unless there is a breach of a duty not to disclose inside

information, the disclosure was in exchange for personal benefit, and the tippee knows of this breach (or should know of it) and benefits from it, there is no liability under this theory.[19]

Misappropriation Theory Liability for insider trading may also be established under the misappropriation theory. This theory holds that if an individual wrongfully obtains (misappropriates) inside information and trades on it for his or her personal gain, then the individual should be held liable because, in essence, the individual stole information rightfully belonging to another.

The misappropriation theory significantly extends the reach of SEC Rule 10b-5 to outsiders who would not ordinarily be deemed fiduciaries of the corporations in whose stock they trade. Courts will normally hold, however, that some fiduciary duty to some lawful possessor of material nonpublic information must have been violated and some harm to the defrauded party must have occurred for liability to exist. For example, suppose that an employee of a printing shop that handles takeover bids learns of a takeover and trades on the information. Clearly, the employee has no fiduciary duty to the shareholders of either corporation involved in the takeover. The employee does, however, have a duty of loyalty to his or her employer—who lawfully possesses material nonpublic information.[20]

The following case raises the question of whether, for the tippee to be held liable under SEC Rule 10b-5, the tipper, must have known that his or her breach of a fiduciary obligation would lead to the tippee's trading on the misappropriated information.

---

19. See, for example, *Chiarella v. United States*, 445 U.S.222, 100 S.Ct. 1108, 63 L.Ed.2d 348 (1980); and *Dirks v. SEC*, 463 U.S. 646, 103 S.Ct. 3255, 77 L.Ed.2d 911 (1983).
20. Note that in contrast to several other federal circuit courts of appeals, the U.S. Court of Appeals for the Fourth Circuit has refused to impose liability under the misappropriation theory for SEC Rule 10b-5 violations. See *United States v. Bryan*, 58 F.3d 933 (4th Cir. 1994).

CASE 27.3

United States v. Libera

United States Court of Appeals,
Seventh Circuit, 1993.
989 F.2d 596.

FACTS R. R. Donnelley & Sons Company operates a printing plant that prints *Business Week* (owned by McGraw-Hill, Inc.). McGraw-Hill and Donnelley had a policy of keeping the contents of each issue confidential until 5:00 P.M. on Thursday, because the contents could affect the price of particular stocks and, before release, were

(Continued)

Case 27.3—Continued

regarded as inside information by the Securities and Exchange Commission. William Dillon observed that trading in stocks mentioned favorably in the magazine often began increasing on the Wednesday before publication and continued through the next Monday. Dillon, recognizing the value of receiving advance copies of *Business Week*, sought out Donnelley employees who would give him copies on Thursday mornings. Dillon, Benjamin Libera, and Francis Sablone used the information to trade regularly on Thursday mornings in the securities reported in *Business Week*. When their scheme was discovered, Dillon pleaded guilty to certain criminal charges and testified against Libera and Sablone, who were convicted of violations of Section 10(b) under the misappropriation theory. Libera and Sablone appealed, arguing that they could not be liable for insider trading unless the tipper (in this case, the Donnelly employees who gave them advance copies) knew that the breach of a fiduciary obligation would lead to the tippee's trading on the misappropriated information.

ISSUE   Must the tipper know that a tippee will trade on misappropriated information for the tippee to be held liable under Section 10(b)?

DECISION   No. The U.S. Court of Appeals for the Seventh Circuit affirmed the convictions of Libera and Sablone.

REASON   The federal appellate court stated that "[t]he misappropriation theory requires the establishment of two elements: (i) a breach by the tipper of a duty owed to the owner of the nonpublic information; and (ii) the tippee's knowledge that the tipper had breached the duty." The court held that "these two elements, without more, are sufficient for tippee liability. The tipper's knowledge that he or she was breaching a duty to the owner of confidential information suffices to establish the tipper's expectation that the breach will lead to some kind of a misuse of the information," because "it may be presumed that the tippee's interest in the information is, in contemporary jargon, not for nothing. To allow a tippee to escape liability solely because the government cannot prove *   *   * that the tipper knew exactly what misuse would result from the tipper's wrongdoing would not fulfill the purpose of the misappropriation theory, which is to protect property rights in information."

FOR CRITICAL ANALYSIS—Social Consideration   *From whom was the information misappropriated?*

Insider Reporting and Trading—Section 16(b)

Officers, directors, and certain large stockholders[21] of Section 12 corporations (corporations that are required to register their securities under Section 12 of the 1934 act) must file reports with the SEC concerning their ownership and trading of the corporations' securities.[22] To discourage such insiders from using nonpublic information about their companies for their personal benefit in the stock market, Section 16(b) of the 1934 act provides for the recapture by the corporation of all profits realized by an insider on any purchase and sale or sale and purchase of the corporation's stock within any six-month period.[23] It is irrelevant

---

21.   Those stockholders owning 10 percent of the class of equity securities registered under Section 12 of the 1934 act.
22.   15 U.S.C. Section 78*l*.

23.   When a decline is predicted in the market for a particular stock, one can realize profits by "selling short"—selling at a high price and repurchasing later at a lower price to cover the "short sale." The short seller typically has to borrow the stock in the meantime (and pay interest on the borrowed stock).

whether the insider actually uses inside information; all such *short-swing* profits must be returned to the corporation.

Section 16(b) applies not only to stock but to warrants, options, and securities convertible into stock. In addition, the courts have fashioned complex rules for determining profits. Corporate insiders are wise to seek competent counsel prior to trading in the corporation's stock. Exhibit 27–3 compares the effects of SEC Rule 10b-5 and Section 16(b).

People resort to various tactics to avoid liability under Section 16(b). These tactics include creative forms for the exchange of money for stock, as illustrated by the following case.

CASE 27.4

Tristar Corp. v. Freitas
United States District Court,
Eastern District of New York, 1994.
867 F.Supp. 149.

FACTS Ross Freitas and Carolyn Kenner were officers and directors of the Tristar Corporation. They were also Tristar shareholders, as they had bought Tristar stock between February 2 and June 15, 1989. Meanwhile, on May 31, they agreed to transfer their Tristar shares to Starion International Ltd. Under a contract titled "Periodic Loan Agreement," Freitas and Kenner gave their shares to Starion's attorney. Starion paid Freitas and Kenner in periodic installments. With each payment, the attorney gave a block of the stock to Starion. When Tristar learned of the deal, the firm filed a suit in a federal district court against Freitas and Kenner, under Section 16(b), to obtain their profits. Tristar filed a motion for summary judgment.

ISSUE For the purposes of Section 16(b), was the so-called Periodic Loan Agreement actually a contract to sell shares?

DECISION Yes. The federal district court ruled in favor of Tristar on this point. The court set for trial the issue of how much money Freitas and Kenner should pay to Tristar.

REASON The court pointed out that under Section 16(b), a sale occurs when "the insider has incurred an 'irrevocable liability' to dispose of the stock so that his 'rights and obligations' have become fixed." The court was "persuaded that the Loan Agreement has the ordinary indicia [signs or indications] of an installment sales contract." The court found that Freitas and Kenner did "contract to sell or otherwise dispose of" their stock on May 31.

FOR CRITICAL ANALYSIS—Economic Consideration *Had the shares of stock simply been used as collateral, would this case have been decided differently?*

Insider-Trading Sanctions

The Insider Trading Sanctions Act of 1984 permits the SEC to bring suit in a federal district court against anyone violating or aiding in a violation of the 1934 act or SEC rules by purchasing or selling a security while in the possession of material nonpublic information.[24] The violation must occur on or through the facilities of a national securities exchange or through a broker or dealer. Transactions connected with a public offering by an issuer of securities are excepted.

The Insider Trading and Securities Fraud Enforcement Act of 1988 extended the class of persons who may be subject to civil liability for insider-trading violations and gave the SEC authority to award **bounty payments** (rewards given by government officials for acts beneficial to the state) to persons providing information leading to the prosecution of insider-trading violations. The act

---

24.   15 U.S.C. Section 78u–1(a)(1).

♦ Exhibit 27–3
Comparison of Coverage, Application, and
Liabilities under SEC Rule 10b-5 and Section 16(b)

	SEC RULE 10b-5	SECTION 16(b)
What is the subject matter of the transaction?	Any security (does not have to be registered).	Any security (does not have to be registered).
What transactions are covered?	Purchase or sale.	Short-swing purchase and sale or short-swing sale and purchase.
Who is subject to liability?	Virtually anyone with inside information under a duty to disclose—including officers, directors, controlling stock-holders, and tippees.	Officers, directors, and certain 10 percent stockholders.
Is omission or misrepresentation necessary for liability?	Yes.	No.
Are there any exempt transactions?	No.	Yes, there are a variety of exemptions.
Is direct dealing with the party necessary?	No.	No.
Who may bring an action?	A person transacting with an insider, the SEC, or a purchaser or seller damaged by a wrongful act.	A corporation or a shareholder by derivative action.

also gave the SEC rulemaking authority to require specific policies and procedures in order to prevent insider trading, in addition to increasing the criminal penalties for violations. Maximum jail terms were increased from five to ten years, and fines were increased to $1 million for individuals and $2.5 million for partnerships and corporations.[25] Neither act has any effect on other actions the SEC or private investors may take.

In imposing sanctions for insider trading, the court may assess as a penalty as much as triple the profits gained or the loss avoided by the guilty party. For purposes of the act, profit or loss is defined as "the difference between the purchase or sale price of the security and the value of that security as measured by the trading price of the security at a reasonable period of time after public dissemination of the nonpublic information."[26] The following case provides an example, in a securities fraud case, of the computation of "avoided losses"—that is, the amount of the loss a violator avoids by selling his or her stock before a disclosure of negative information about a company.

---

25. 15 U.S.C. Section 78ff(a).

26. 15 U.S.C. Section 78u–1(d)(5)(f).

SEC v. Patel
United States Court of Appeals,
Second Circuit, 1995.
61 F.3d 137.

FACTS In November 1987, Par Pharmaceutical, Inc., submitted to the Food and Drug Administration (FDA) an application for a new generic drug. The application falsely stated that the drug had been tested as required. Ratilal Patel, an officer and director of Par Pharmaceutical, knew that the application contained false information

Case 27.5—Continued

and subsequently (in early 1988) sold 75,000 shares of his stock in Par Pharmaceutical at a price of approximately $21 per share. In 1988 and 1989, Par Pharmaceutical became the target of investigations and indictments for various improprieties, including bribery. By Friday, July 21, 1989, the price of Par stock was $10 per share. On Monday, July 24, Par Pharmaceutical publicly disclosed the facts about the falsified drug application. On Tuesday, the price of Par Pharmaceutical stock dropped to $7.125 per share. The SEC filed a suit in a federal district court against Patel, alleging that he had violated securities laws. The court ordered Patel to, among other things, pay the amount of the loss he avoided by selling his stock before the announcement of the false FDA application. The court computed the amount based on the difference between the price of Par Pharmaceutical stock on July 21 and the price on July 25. Patel appealed, contending in part that the earlier investigations and indictments had affected the price of the stock.

ISSUE Did the computation of Patel's "avoided losses" reasonably approximate the amount that was causally connected to his securities fraud violations?

DECISION Yes. The U.S. Court of Appeals for the Second Circuit affirmed this part of the lower court's decision.

REASON The federal appellate court acknowledged that "calculations of this nature are not capable of exactitude" but added that any "risk of uncertainty [in calculating losses] should fall on the wrongdoer whose illegal conduct created that uncertainty." At any rate, the court stated that "[t]here certainly was a rational basis" to conclude that the investigations and indictments "had been fully taken into account by the market and that the July 24, 1989 disclosure alone accounted for the 28.75% decline identified as of July 25."

FOR CRITICAL ANALYSIS—Social Consideration *What penalty, among those that a court can impose, might a corporate officer and director consider worse than paying out "avoided losses"?*

Proxy Statements

Section 14(a) of the Securities Exchange Act of 1934 regulates the solicitation of proxies from shareholders of Section 12 companies. The SEC regulates the content of proxy statements, which (as discussed in Chapter 25) are statements sent to shareholders by corporate officials who are requesting authority to vote on behalf of the shareholders in a particular election on specified issues. Whoever solicits a proxy must fully and accurately disclose in the proxy statement all of the facts that are pertinent to the matter on which the shareholders are to vote. SEC Rule 14a-9 is similar to the antifraud provisions of SEC Rule 10b-5. Remedies for violation are extensive; they range from injunctions that prevent a vote from being taken to monetary damages.

The Expanding Powers of the SEC

In recent years, Congress has expanded significantly the SEC's powers. For example, to further curb securities fraud, the Securities Enforcement Remedies and Penny Stock Reform Act of 1990 amended existing securities laws to expand greatly the types of securities violation cases that SEC administrative law judges can hear and the SEC's enforcement options. The act also provides that courts may bar persons who have engaged in securities fraud from serving as officers and directors of publicly held corporations.

The 1990 Securities Acts Amendments authorized the SEC to seek sanctions against those who violate foreign securities laws. These amendments increase the ability of the SEC to cooperate in international securities law enforcement. Under the Market Reform Act of 1990, the SEC can suspend trading in securities in the event that the prices rise and fall excessively in a short period of time.

Regulation of Investment Companies

Investment companies, and mutual funds in particular, grew rapidly after World War II. **Investment companies** act on behalf of many smaller shareholders by buying a large portfolio of securities and professionally managing that portfolio. A **mutual fund** is a specific type of investment company that continually buys or sells to investors shares of ownership in a portfolio. Such companies are regulated by the Investment Company Act of 1940,[27] which provides for SEC regulation of their activities. The act was expanded by the 1970 amendments to the Investment Company Act. Further minor changes were made in the Securities Act Amendments of 1975 and in later years.

The 1940 act requires that every investment company register with the SEC and imposes restrictions on the activities of these companies and persons connected with them. For the purposes of the act, an investment company is defined as any entity that (1) is engaged primarily "in the business of investing, reinvesting, or trading in securities" or (2) is engaged in such business and has more than 40 percent of its assets in investment securities. Excluded from coverage by the act are banks, insurance companies, savings and loan associations, finance companies, oil and gas drilling firms, charitable foundations, tax-exempt pension funds, and other special types of institutions, such as closely held corporations.

All investment companies must register with the SEC by filing a notification of registration. Each year, registered investment companies must file reports with the SEC. To safeguard company assets, all securities must be held in the custody of a bank or stock exchange member, and that bank or stock exchange member must follow strict procedures established by the SEC.

No dividends may be paid from any source other than accumulated, undistributed net income. Furthermore, there are some restrictions on investment activities. For example, investment companies are not allowed to purchase securities on the margin (pay only part of the total price, borrowing the rest), sell short (sell shares not yet owned), or participate in joint trading accounts.

State Securities Laws

Today, all states have their own corporate securities laws, or "blue sky laws," that regulate the offer and sale of securities within individual state borders.[28] (As mentioned in Chapter 9, the phrase *blue sky laws* dates to a 1917 decision by the United States Supreme Court in which the Court declared that the purpose of such laws was to prevent "speculative schemes which have no more basis than so many feet of 'blue sky.' ")[29] Article 8 of the Uniform Commercial Code, which has been adopted by all of the states, also imposes various requirements relating to the purchase and sale of securities. State securities laws apply only to intrastate transactions. Since the adoption of the 1933 and 1934 federal securities acts, the state and federal governments have regulated securities concurrently. Issuers must comply with both federal and state securities laws, and exemptions from federal law are not exemptions from state laws.

There are differences in philosophy among state statutes, but certain features are common to all state blue sky laws. Typically, state laws have disclosure requirements and antifraud provisions, many of which are patterned after Section 10(b) of the Securities Exchange Act of 1934 and SEC Rule 10b-5. State laws also provide for the registration or qualification of securities offered or issued for sale within the state and impose disclosure requirements. Unless an applicable exemption from registration is found, issuers must register or qualify their stock with the appropriate state official, often called a *corporations commissioner*. Additionally, most state securities laws regulate

---

27. 15 U.S.C. Sections 80a-1 to 80a-64.

28. These laws are catalogued and annotated in the Commerce Clearing House's *Blue Sky Law Reporter*, a loose-leaf service.
29. *Hall v. Geiger-Jones Co.*, 242 U.S. 539, 37 S.Ct. 217, 61 L.Ed. 480 (1917).

securities brokers and dealers. The Uniform Securities Act, which has been adopted in part by several states, was drafted to be acceptable to states with differing regulatory philosophies.

▌Terms and Concepts

▌Chapter Summary: Investor Protection

The Securities Act of 1933 *(See pages 564–570.)*	Prohibits fraud and stabilizes the securities industry by requiring disclosure of all essential information relating to the issuance of stocks to the investing public. 1. *Registration requirements*—Securities, unless exempt, must be registered with the SEC before being offered to the public through the mails or any facility of interstate commerce (including securities exchanges). The *registration statement* must include detailed financial information about the issuing corporation; the intended use of the proceeds of the securities being issued; and certain disclosures, such as interests of directors or officers and pending lawsuits. 2. *Prospectus*—A *prospectus* must be provided to investors, describing the security being sold, the issuing corporation, and the risk attaching to the security. 3. *Exemptions*—The SEC has exempted certain offerings from the requirements of the Securities Act of 1933. Exemptions may be determined on the basis of the size of the issue, whether the offering is private or public, and whether advertising is involved. Exemptions are summarized in Exhibit 27–1.

The Securities Exchange Act of 1934 *(See pages 570–578.)*	Provides for the regulation and registration of securities exchanges, brokers, dealers, and national securities associations (such as the NASD). Maintains a continuous disclosure system for all corporations with securities on the securities exchanges and for those companies that have assets in excess of $10 million and five hundred or more shareholders (Section 12 companies).
	
	1. *SEC Rule 10b-5 [under Section 10(b) of the 1934 act]*—
	  a. Applies to insider trading by corporate officers, directors, majority shareholders, and any persons receiving information not available to the public who base their trading on this information.
	  b. Liability for violation can be civil or criminal.
	  c. May be violated by failing to disclose "material facts" that must be disclosed under this rule.
	  d. Applies in virtually all cases concerning the trading of securities—a firm does not have to have its securities registered under the 1933 act for the 1934 act to apply.
	  e. Applies only when the requisites of federal jurisdiction (such as use of the mails, stock exchange facilities, or any facility of interstate commerce) are present.
	
	2. *Insider trading [under Section 16(b) of the 1934 act]*—To prevent corporate officers and directors from taking advantage of inside information (information not available to the investing public), the 1934 act requires officers, directors, and shareholders owning 10 percent or more of the issued stock of a corporation to turn over to the corporation all short-term profits (called short-swing profits) realized
	
	(Continued)

▌Chapter Summary: Investor Protection—Continued

The Securities Exchange Act of 1934—Continued	from the purchase and sale or sale and purchase of corporate stock within any six-month period. 3. *Proxies [under Section 14(a) of the 1934 act]*—The SEC regulates the content of proxy statements sent to shareholders by corporate managers of Section 12 companies who are requesting authority to vote on behalf of the shareholders in a particular election on specified issues. Section 14(a) is essentially a disclosure law, with provisions similar to the antifraud provisions of SEC Rule 10b-5.
Regulation of Investment Companies *(See page 578.)*	The Investment Company Act of 1940 provides for SEC regulation of investment company activities. It was altered and expanded by the amendments of 1970 and 1975.
State Securities Laws *(See pages 578–579.)*	All states have corporate securities laws (*blue sky laws*) that regulate the offer and sale of securities within state borders; designed to prevent "speculative schemes which have no more basis than so many feet of 'blue sky.'" States regulate securities concurrently with the federal government.

▌For Review

1. What is the essential purpose of the Securities Act of 1933? What is the essential purpose of the Securities Exchange Act of 1934?
2. What is a registration statement? What must it include? What is a prospectus?
3. Basically, what constitutes a *security* under the Securities Act of 1933?

4. What is SEC Rule 10b-5? What is the key to liability under this rule? To what kinds of transactions does SEC Rule 10b-5 apply?
5. Name two theories under which "outsiders" can be held liable for violating SEC Rule 10b-5.

▌Questions and Case Problems

27–1. Registration Requirements. Langley Brothers, Inc., a corporation incorporated and doing business in Kansas, decides to sell no-par common stock worth $1 million to the public. The stock will be sold only within the state of Kansas. Joseph Langley, the chairman of the board, says the offering need not be registered with the SEC. His brother, Harry, disagrees. Who is right? Explain.

27–2. Registration Requirements. Huron Corp. had 300,000 common shares outstanding. The owners of these outstanding shares lived in several different states. Huron decided to split the 300,000 shares two for one. Will Huron Corp. have to file a registration statement and prospectus on the 300,000 new shares to be issued as a result of the split? Explain.

27–3. Definition of a Security. The W. J. Howey Co. (Howey) owned large tracts of citrus acreage in Lake County, Florida. For several years, it planted about five hundred acres annually, keeping half of the groves itself and offering the other half to the public to help finance

additional development. Howey-in-the-Hills Service, Inc., was a service company engaged in cultivating and developing these groves, including the harvesting and marketing of the crops. Each prospective customer was offered both a land sales contract and a service contract, after being told that it was not feasible to invest in a grove unless service arrangements were made. Of the acreage sold by Howey, 85 percent was sold with a service contract with Howey-in-the-Hills Service. Howey did not register with the SEC or meet the other administrative requirements that issuers of securities must fulfill. The SEC sued to enjoin Howey from continuing to offer the land sales and service contracts. Howey responded that no SEC violation existed, because no securities had been issued. Evaluate the definition of a security given in this chapter, and then determine which party should prevail in court, Howey or the SEC. [*SEC v. W. J. Howey Co.*, 328 U.S. 293, 66 S.Ct. 1100, 90 L.Ed. 1244 (1946)]

27–4. Definition of a Security. U.S. News & World Report, Inc., set up a profit-sharing plan in 1962 that allotted to certain employees specially issued stock known as bonus or anniversary stock. The stock was given to the employees for past services and could not be traded or sold to anyone other than the corporate issuer, U.S. News. This special stock was issued only to employees and for no other purpose than as bonuses. Because there was no market for the stock, U.S. News hired an independent appraiser to estimate the fair value of the stock so that the employees could redeem the shares. Charles Foltz and several other employees held stock through this plan and sought to redeem the shares with U.S. News, but Foltz disputed the value set by the appraisers. Foltz sued U.S. News for violation of securities regulations. What defense would allow U.S. News to resist successfully Foltz's claim? [*Foltz v. U.S. News & World Report, Inc.*, 627 F.Supp. 1143 (D.D.C. 1986)]

27–5. Short-Swing Profits. Emerson Electric Co. purchased 13.2 percent of Dodge Manufacturing Co.'s stock in an unsuccessful takeover attempt in June 1967. Less than six months later, when Dodge merged with Reliance Electric Co., Emerson decided to sell its shares. To avoid being subject to the short-swing profit restrictions of Section 16(b) of the Securities Exchange Act of 1934, Emerson decided on a two-step selling plan. First, it sold off sufficient shares to reduce its holdings to 9.96 percent [owners with less than 10 percent are exempt from Section 16(b)], and then it sold the remaining stock –all within a six-month period. Emerson in this way succeeded in avoiding Section 16(b) requirements. Reliance demanded that Emerson return the profits made on both sales. Emerson sought a declaratory judgment from the court that it was not liable, arguing that because at the time of the second sale it had not owned 10 percent of Dodge stock, Section 16(b) did not apply. Does Section 16(b) of the Securities Exchange Act of 1934 apply to Emerson's transactions, and is Emerson liable to Reliance for its profits? Discuss fully. [*Reliance Electric Co. v. Emerson Electric Co.*, 404 U.S. 418, 92 S.Ct. 596, 30 L.E.2d 575 (1972)]

27–6. SEC Rule 10b-5. Energy Resource Group, Inc. (ERG), entered into a written agreement with Ivan West by which West was to find an investor willing to purchase ERG stock. West later formed a partnership, called Investment Management Group (IMG), with Don Peters and another person. According to the terms of the partnership agreement, West's consulting work for ERG was excluded from the work of the IMG partnership. West learned through his consulting position with ERG that ERG was to be acquired by another corporation for $6.00 per share. At the time West learned of the acquisition, ERG stock was trading at $3.50 per share. Apparently, Peters learned of the acquisition from papers on West's desk in the IMG office and then shared the information with Ken Mick, his stockbroker.

Mick then encouraged several clients to buy ERG stock prior to the public announcement of the acquisition. Mick, in return for leaking this inside information to clients, received a special premium from the enriched investors. Mick then paid a portion of the premium to Peters. The SEC brought an action against Peters for violating SEC Rule 10b-5. Under what theory might Peters be held liable for insider trading in violation of SEC Rule 10b-5? Discuss fully. [*SEC v. Peters*, 735 F.Supp. 1505 (D.Kans. 1990)]

27–7. Securities Fraud. William Gotchey owned 50 percent of the shares of First American Financial Consultants, Inc. (FAFC), an investment company registered with the SEC. In the fall of 1987, Paul Hatfield, a client of FAFC, spoke with Gotchey about investing. As a result of their conversations, Hatfield invested $5,000 with FAFC. In December, Hatfield told Gotchey that he wished to invest $20,000, $15,000 of which he wished to place in a secure investment. Gotchey told Hatfield that he would place this $15,000 in mortgage-backed securities to be invested through a mortgage company. For a time, Hatfield received interest payments from FAFC, purportedly from the mortgage-backed investment. He also received statements confirming that the investment had been made. In fact, Gotchey had deposited the entire $20,000 in an FAFC bank account. When Hatfield did not receive the interest payment due at the beginning of July 1988, he confronted Gotchey. Gotchey responded by asking Hatfield to sign an agreement whereby FAFC would repay the $15,000 in monthly installments over ten years. Hatfield refused. Gotchey did not account for the $15,000, and Hatfield received no interest payments after June 1988. Has Gotchey violated Section 10(b) of the Securities Exchange Act? Why or why not? [*SEC v. Gotchey*, 981 F.2d 1251 (4th Cir. 1992)]

27–8. SEC Rule 10b-5. Danny Cherif worked for a Chicago bank from 1979 until 1987, when his position was eliminated because of an internal reorganization. Cherif, through a forged memo to the bank's security department, caused his magnetic identification (ID) card—which he had received as an employee to allow him to enter the bank building—to remain activated after his employment was terminated. Cherif used his ID card to enter the building at night to obtain confidential financial information regarding extraordinary business transactions, such as tender offers. During 1988 and 1989, Cherif made substantial profits by using this information in securities trading. Eventually, Cherif's activities were investigated by the SEC, and he was charged with violating Section 10(b) and SEC Rule 10b-5 by misappropriating and trading on inside information in violation of his fiduciary duties to his former employer. Cherif argued that the SEC had wrongfully applied the misappropriation theory to his activities, because as a former employee, he no longer had a fiduciary duty to the bank.

Will the court agree with Cherif? Discuss fully. [*SEC v. Cherif*, 933 F.2d 403 (7th Cir. 1991)]

27–9. SEC Rule 10b-5. In early 1985, FMC Corp. made plans to buy some of its own stock as part of a restructuring of its balance statement. Unknown to FMC management, the brokerage firm FMC employed—Goldman, Sachs & Co.—disclosed information on the stock purchase that found its way to Ivan Boesky. FMC was one of the seven major corporations in whose stock Boesky allegedly traded using inside information. Boesky made purchases of FMC's stock between February 18 and February 21, 1986, and between March 12 and April 4, 1986. Boesky's purchases amounted to a substantial portion of the total volume of FMC stock traded during these periods. The price of FMC stock increased from $71.25 on February 20, 1986, to $97.00 on April 25, 1986. As a result, FMC paid substantially more for the repurchase of its own stock than anticipated. When FMC discovered Boesky's knowledge of its recapitalization plan, FMC sued Boesky for the excess price it had paid—approximately $220 million. Discuss whether FMC should recover under Section 10(b) of the Securities Exchange Act and SEC Rule 10b-5. [*In re Ivan F. Boesky Securities Litigation*, 36 F.3d 255 (2d Cir. 1994)]

27–10. SEC Rule 10b-5. Louis Ferraro was the chairman and president of Anacomp, Inc. In June 1988, Ferraro told his good friend Michael Maio that Anacomp was negotiating a tender offer for stock in Xidex Corp. Maio passed on the information to Patricia Ladavac, a friend of both Ferraro and Maio. Maio and Ladavac immediately purchased shares in Xidex stock. On the day that the tender offer was announced—an announcement that caused the price of Xidex shares to increase—Maio and Ladavac sold their Xidex stock and made substantial profits (Maio made $211,000 from the transactions, and Ladavac gained $78,750). The SEC brought an action against the three individuals, alleging that they had violated, among other laws, SEC Rule 10b-5. Maio and Ladavac claimed that they had done nothing illegal. They argued that they had no fiduciary duty either to Anacomp or to Xidex, and therefore they had no duty to disclose or abstain from trading in the stock of those corporations. Had Maio and Ladavac violated SEC Rule 10b-5? Discuss fully. [*SEC v. Maio*, 51 F.3d 623 (7th Cir. 1995)]

27–11. Definition of a Security. Life Partners, Inc. (LPI), facilitates the sale of life insurance policies that are owned by persons suffering from AIDS (acquired immune deficiency syndrome) to investors at a discount. The investors pay LPI, and LPI pays the policyholder. Typically, the policyholder, in turn, assigns the policy to LPI, which also obtains the right to make LPI's president the beneficiary of the policy. On the policyholder's death, LPI receives the proceeds of the policy and pays the investor. In this way, the terminally ill sellers secure much-needed income in the final years of life, when employment is unlikely and medical bills are often staggering. The SEC sought to enjoin (prevent) LPI from engaging in further transactions on the ground that the investment contracts were securities, which LPI had failed to register with the SEC in violation of securities laws. Do the investment contracts meet the definition of a security discussed in this chapter? Discuss fully. [*SEC v. Life Partners, Inc.*, 87 F.3d 536 (D.C.Cir. 1996)]

▌Unit Eight—Cumulative Hypothetical Problem

27–12. *Samuel Polson established a publishing business, and over the years it became quite profitable. On his death, three of his children—Joan, Harley, and Kevin Polson—took over the business.*

1. When Samuel Polson ran the business, one of Polson's employees routinely used the firm's van to make deliveries. One day, while delivering some pamphlets to a customer, the employee negligently drove through a red light and crashed into another car. A passenger in the other car was seriously injured and sued both the employee and Samuel Polson for damages. Is the employee liable? Can Polson be held liable for his employee's negligence? Explain.

2. While he lived, Samuel Polson was the sole owner of the business and paid no business income taxes. What was the form of Samuel's business organization? After Samuel died, his children wanted to continue the business. What options, in terms of business organizational forms, do they have? What are the advantages and disadvantages of each option?

3. Joan, Harley, and Kevin decide to incorporate the business under the name Polson Publishing, Inc. They also want to expand the business by setting up branch offices in two other cities. What steps will they need to take to incorporate the business and obtain the capital needed for expansion?

4. Polson Publishing, now a thriving corporate enterprise, decides to merge with another publishing firm, with Polson as the surviving corporation. What procedures must Polson follow in carrying

out the merger? After the merger, would Polson be liable for the debts and obligations of the other company? What if a minority of the shareholders disagree with the merger? What rights and remedies are available to these shareholders?

5. One of Polson Publishing's employees learned that Polson was contemplating a takeover of a rival publishing house. The employee told her husband about the possibility. The husband called their broker, who purchased shares in the target corporation for the employee and her husband, as well as for himself. Has the employee violated any securities law? Has her husband? Has the broker? Explain.

▌Accessing the Internet: Fundamentals of Business Law

The Web site for the Securities and Exchange Commission (SEC) is called EDGAR, for Electronic Data Gathering Analysis and Retrieval system. Corporate financial information in the EDGAR database—including initial public offerings, proxy statements, annual corporate reports, registration statements, and other documents filed with the SEC—is available to the public. The site also contains information about the SEC's operations, the statutes it implements, its proposed and final rules, and its enforcement actions. To access EDGAR, go to

http://www.sec.gov/edgarhp.htm

The Center for Corporate Law at the University of Cincinnati College of Law examines all of the acts discussed in this chapter. Go to

http://www.law.uc.edu/CCL/

To find the Securities Act of 1933, go to

http://www.law.uc.edu/CCL/33Act/index.html

To examine the Securities Exchange Act of 1934, go to

http://www.law.uc.edu/CCL/34Act/index.html

For information on investor protection and securities fraud, including answers to frequently asked questions on the topic of securities fraud, go to

http://www.securitieslaw.com

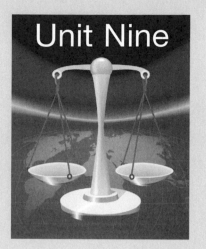

Unit Nine

Property and Its Protection

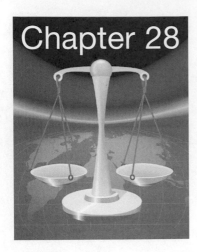

Chapter 28

Personal Property and Bailments

CHAPTER OBJECTIVES

After reading this chapter, you should be able to:

1. Distinguish between personal property and real property.
2. Discuss different types of property ownership and the ways in which property can be acquired.
3. Identify who has rights to mislaid, lost, or abandoned property.
4. List the elements of a bailment.
5. Outline the rights and duties of a bailee and a bailor.

Property consists of the legally protected rights and interests a person has in anything with an ascertainable value that is subject to ownership. Property would have little value (and the word would have little meaning) if the law did not define the right to use it, to sell or dispose of it, and to prevent trespass on it. In the United States, the ownership of property receives unique protection under the law. The Bill of Rights states that "no person shall . . . be deprived of life, liberty, or property, without due process of law; nor shall private property be taken for public use, without just compensation." The Fourteenth Amendment provides that "no State shall . . . deprive any person of life, liberty, or property, without due process of law."

Property is divided into real property and personal property. **Real property** (sometimes called *realty* or *real estate*) means the land and everything permanently attached to it. Everything else is **personal property,** or *personalty*. Attorneys sometimes refer to personal property as **chattel,** a term used under the common law to denote all forms of personal property. Personal property can be tangible or intangible. *Tangible* personal property, such as a TV set or a car, has physical substance.

Intangible personal property represents some set of rights and interests but has no real physical existence. Stocks and bonds, patents, and copyrights are examples of intangible personal property.

In the first part of this chapter, we look at the ways in which title to property is held; the methods of acquiring ownership of personal property; and issues relating to mislaid, lost, and abandoned personal property. In the second part of the chapter, we examine bailment relationships. A **bailment** is created when personal property is temporarily delivered into the care of another without a transfer of title. This is the distinguishing characteristic of a bailment compared with a sale or a gift—there is no passage of title and no intent to transfer title.

▊ Property Ownership

Property ownership[1] can be viewed as a bundle of rights, including the right to possess property and to dispose of it—by sale, gift, lease, or other means.

---

1. The principles discussed in this section apply equally to real property ownership, which is discussed in Chapter 29.

586

Fee Simple

A person who holds the entire bundle of rights to property is said to be the owner in **fee simple.** The owner in fee simple is entitled to use, possess, or dispose of the property as he or she chooses during his or her lifetime, and on this owner's death, the interests in the property descend to his or her heirs. We will return to this form of property ownership in Chapter 29, in the context of ownership rights in real property.

Concurrent Ownership

Persons who share ownership rights simultaneously in a particular piece of property are said to be *concurrent* owners. There are two principal types of concurrent ownership: tenancy in common and joint tenancy. Other types of concurrent ownership include tenancy by the entirety and community property.

TENANCY IN COMMON   The term **tenancy in common** refers to a form of co-ownership in which each of two or more persons owns an undivided interest in the property. The interest is *undivided* because each tenant has rights in the *whole* property. For example, Rosa and Chad own a rare-stamp collection as tenants in common. This does not mean that Rosa owns some particular stamps and Chad others. Rather, it means that Rosa and Chad each have rights in the entire collection. (If Rosa owned some stamps and Chad owned others, then the interest would be *divided.*)

On the death of a tenant in common, that tenant's interest in the property passes to his or her heirs. For example, should Rosa die before Chad, a one-half interest in the stamp collection would become the property of Rosa's heirs. If Rosa sold her interest to Fred before she died, Fred and Chad would be co-owners as tenants in common. If Fred died, his interest in the personal property would pass to his heirs, and they in turn would own the property with Chad as tenants in common.

JOINT TENANCY   In a **joint tenancy,** each of two or more persons owns an undivided interest in the property, and a deceased joint tenant's interest passes to the surviving joint tenant or tenants. The rights of a surviving joint tenant to inherit a deceased joint tenant's ownership interest, which

are referred to as *survivorship rights,* distinguish the joint tenancy from the tenancy in common. A joint tenancy can be terminated before a joint tenant's death by gift or by sale, in which situation the person who received the property as a gift or who purchased the property would become a tenant in common, not a joint tenant.

To illustrate: In the preceding example, if Rosa and Chad held their stamp collection in a joint tenancy and if Rosa died before Chad, the entire collection would become the property of Chad; Rosa's heirs would receive absolutely no interest in the collection. If Rosa, while living, sold her interest to Fred, however, the sale would terminate the joint tenancy, and Fred and Chad would become owners as tenants in common.

TENANCY BY THE ENTIRETY   Concurrent ownership of property can also take the form of a **tenancy by the entirety**—a form of co-ownership between a husband and wife that is similar to a joint tenancy, except that a spouse cannot transfer his or her interest during his or her lifetime without the consent of the other spouse.

COMMUNITY PROPERTY   When property is held as **community property,** each spouse technically owns an undivided one-half interest in property acquired during the marriage. The community property form of ownership occurs in only nine states and Puerto Rico.

Acquiring Ownership of Personal Property

The most common way of acquiring personal property is by purchasing it. We have already discussed the purchase and sale of personal property (goods) in Chapters 13 through 16. Often, property is acquired by will or inheritance, a topic we cover in Chapter 30. Here we look at additional ways in which ownership of personal property can be acquired, including acquisition by possession, production, gift, accession, and confusion.

Possession

One example of acquiring ownership by possession is the capture of wild animals. Wild animals belong to no one in their natural state, and the first person to take possession of a wild animal normally owns it. The killing of a wild animal amounts to assuming ownership of it. Merely being in hot pursuit does not give title, however. There are two exceptions to this basic rule. First, any wild animals captured by a trespasser are the property of the landowner, not the trespasser. Second, if wild animals are captured or killed in violation of wild-game statutes, the capturer does not obtain title to the animals; rather, the state does.

Those who find lost or abandoned property also can acquire ownership rights through mere possession of the property, as will be discussed later in the chapter. (Ownership rights in real property can also be acquired through possession, such as adverse possession—see Chapter 29.)

Production

Production—the fruits of labor—is another means of acquiring ownership of personal property. For example, writers, inventors, and manufacturers all produce personal property and thereby acquire title to it. (In some situations—for example, when a researcher is hired to invent a new product or technique—the producer may not own what is produced, however.)

Gifts

A **gift** is another fairly common means of acquiring and transferring ownership of real and personal property. A gift is essentially a voluntary transfer of property ownership for which no consideration is given. As discussed in Chapter 8, the presence of consideration is what distinguishes a contract from a gift. Certain conditions must exist, however, before a gift will be deemed effective in the eyes of the law. The donor (the one making the gift) must intend to make the gift, the gift must be delivered to the donee (the recipient of the gift), and the donee must accept the gift. We examine each of these requirements here, as well as the requirements of a gift made in contemplation of imminent death.

DONATIVE INTENT   When a gift is challenged in court, the court will determine whether donative intent exists by looking at the surrounding circum-

stances. For example, the court may look at the relationship between the parties and the size of the gift in relation to the donor's other assets. A gift to a mortal enemy is viewed with suspicion. Similarly, when a gift represents a large portion of a person's assets, the courts scrutinize the transaction closely to determine the mental capacity of the donor and whether there is any element of fraud or duress present.

DELIVERY   The gift must be delivered to the donee. An effective delivery requires giving up complete control and **dominion** (ownership rights) over the subject matter of the gift. Delivery is obvious in most cases. Suppose, though, that you want to make a gift of various old rare coins that you have stored in a safe-deposit box. You certainly cannot deliver the box itself to the donee, and you do not want to take the coins out of the bank. In such a situation, when the physical object cannot be delivered, a symbolic, or *constructive*, delivery will be sufficient. **Constructive delivery** is a general term for all those acts that the law holds to be equivalent to acts of real delivery. In the preceding example, the delivery of the key to the safe-deposit box constitutes a constructive delivery of the contents of the box. The delivery of intangible property—such as stocks, bonds, insurance policies, contracts, and so on—is always accomplished by symbolic, or constructive, delivery. This is because the documents represent rights and are not, by themselves, the true property.

Delivery may be accomplished by means of a third party. If the third party is the agent of the donor, the delivery is effective when the agent delivers the gift to the donee. If the third party is the agent of the donee, then the gift is effectively delivered when the donor delivers the property to the donee's agent.[2] Naturally, no delivery is necessary if the gift is already in the hands of the donee.

In the following case, the court focused on the requirement that a donor must give up complete control and dominion over property given to the donee before a gift can be effectively delivered.

2. *Bickford v. Mattocks,* 95 Me. 547, 50 A. 894 (1901).

CASE 28.1

In Re Estate of Piper
Missouri Court of Appeals, 1984.
676 S.W.2d 897.

FACTS   Gladys Piper died intestate (without a will) in 1982. At her death, she owned miscellaneous personal property worth $5,000 and had in her purse $200 in cash and two diamond rings, known as the Andy Piper rings. The contents of her purse were taken by her niece Wanda Brown, allegedly to preserve them for the estate. Clara Kaufmann, a friend of Piper's, filed a claim against the estate for $4,800. From October 1974 until Piper's death, Kaufmann had taken Piper to the doctor, beauty shop, and grocery store; had written her checks to pay her bills; and had helped her care for her home. Kaufmann maintained that Piper had promised to pay her for these services and had given her the diamond rings as a gift. A Missouri state trial court denied her request for payment; the court found that her services had been voluntary. Kaufmann then filed a petition for delivery of personal property, the rings, which was granted by the trial court. Brown, other heirs, and the administrator of Piper's estate appealed.

ISSUE   Had Gladys Piper made an effective gift of the rings to Clara Kaufmann?

DECISION   No. The state appellate court reversed the judgment of the trial court on the ground that Piper had never delivered the rings to Kaufmann.

REASON   Kaufmann claimed that the rings belonged to her by reason of a "consummated gift long prior to the death of Gladys Piper." Two witnesses testified for Kaufmann at the trial that Piper had told them the rings belonged to Kaufmann but that she was going to wear them until she died. The appellate court found "no evidence of any actual delivery." The court held that the essentials of a gift are (1) a present intention to make a gift on the part of the donor, (2) a delivery of the property by the donor to the donee, and (3) an acceptance by the donee. The evidence in the case showed only an intent to make a gift. Because there was no delivery—either actual or constructive—a valid gift was not made. For Piper to have made a gift, her intention would have to have been executed by the complete and unconditional delivery of the property or the delivery of a proper written instrument evidencing the gift. As this did not occur, the court found that there had been no gift.

FOR CRITICAL ANALYSIS—Social Consideration   *What could Piper have done to ensure that Kaufmann received the rings on Piper's death?*

ACCEPTANCE   The final requirement of a valid gift is acceptance by the donee. This rarely presents any problem, as most donees readily accept their gifts. The courts generally assume acceptance unless shown otherwise.

GIFTS *INTER VIVOS* AND GIFTS *CAUSA MORTIS*   Gifts *inter vivos* are gifts made during one's lifetime, whereas **gifts *causa mortis*** (so-called *deathbed gifts*) are made in contemplation of immi-

nent death. A gift *causa mortis* does not become absolute until the donor dies from the contemplated illness, and it is automatically revoked if the donor recovers from the illness. Moreover, the donee must survive to take the gift. To be effective, a gift *causa mortis* must also meet the three requirements discussed earlier—donative intent, delivery, and acceptance by the donee. The question of whether a gift *causa mortis* had been effectively delivered is at issue in the following case.

CASE 28.2

Kesterson v. Cronan

Court of Appeals of Oregon, 1991.
105 Or.App. 551,
806 P.2d 134.

FACTS James Wilson, after learning that he had terminal cancer, arranged for a friend, Harold Buell, to have joint access to his safe-deposit box. Wilson gave Buell a key to the box, which contained, among other things, a copy of a promissory note for $65,000 from Michael Cronan. Wilson told Buell that the debt represented by the note was to be forgiven when he died and that on his (Wilson's) death, Buell was to deliver the copy of the note to Cronan. After Cronan had learned of Wilson's illness, Wilson told Cronan on at least two occasions that Cronan's debt was to be forgiven on Wilson's death. In the meantime, Cronan continued to make payments on the note. On the day after Wilson died, Buell delivered the copy of the note to Cronan, as directed. Wilson's personal representative (a person appointed to look after the deceased's affairs), Carol Kesterson, brought an action in an Oregon state court to recover from Cronan the balance owing on the $65,000 note, the original of which was found among Wilson's personal effects after his death. Cronan claimed that the debt had been forgiven, as a gift to Cronan. The trial court held that the gift had not been adequately delivered prior to Wilson's death, and therefore Cronan was liable on the debt. Cronan appealed.

ISSUE Had Wilson effectively delivered the gift?

DECISION No. The appellate court affirmed the trial court's decision. Wilson's gift to Cronan—the forgiveness of Cronan's debt—was never adequately delivered to Cronan during Wilson's lifetime.

REASON The court stated that "[f]or a gift of personal property * * * to be valid, there must be a donative intent, coupled with the delivery of the subject of the gift to the donee with the intent that the donee have a present interest in it and an acceptance by the donee. * * * The one claiming a gift has the burden to prove the elements by clear and convincing evidence." Cronan argued that Wilson had delivered the copy of the note to Buell and that Buell was acting as Cronan's agent, but the court noted that the evidence did not support the finding that an agency relationship between Buell and Cronan existed. The court found "no evidence that [Cronan] knew that Buell had the key to the safe deposit box or that he had possession of the envelope" that contained the copy of the note, or even that Cronan had given instructions to Buell. Because Buell acted on Wilson's instructions and essentially served as Wilson's agent, the court found that there was no delivery of the note to Cronan before Wilson died.

FOR CRITICAL ANALYSIS—Ethical Consideration *Why does the law impose such strict legal requirements for a gift to be effective?*

Accession

Accession, which means "adding on" to something, occurs when someone adds value to an item of personal property by either labor or materials. Generally, there is no dispute about who owns the property after accession has occurred, especially when the accession is accomplished with the owner's consent. When accession occurs without the permission of the owner, the courts will tend to favor the owner over the improver—the one who improves the property—provided that the accession was wrongful and undertaken in bad faith. In addition, many courts will deny the improver any compensation for the value added; for example, a car thief who puts new tires on the stolen car will obviously not be compensated for the value of the new tires.

If the accession is performed in good faith, however, even without the owner's consent, ownership of the improved item most often depends on whether the accession has increased the value of the property or changed its identity. The greater the increase in value, the more likely it is that ownership will pass to the improver. If ownership so passes, the improver obviously must compensate the original owner for the value of the property prior to the accession. If the increase in value is not sufficient for ownership to pass to the improver, most courts will require the owner to compensate the improver for the value added.

Confusion

Confusion is defined as the commingling (mixing together) of goods so that one person's personal property cannot be distinguished from another's. Confusion frequently occurs when the goods are *fungible*, meaning that each particle is identical with every other particle, as with grain and oil. For example, if two farmers put their Number 2–grade winter wheat into the same storage bin, confusion would occur.

If confusion of goods is caused by a person who wrongfully and willfully mixes the goods for the purpose of rendering them indistinguishable, the innocent party acquires title to the whole. If confusion occurs as a result of agreement, an honest mistake, or the act of some third party, the owners share ownership as tenants in common and will share any loss in proportion to their shares of ownership of the property.

▌Mislaid, Lost, and ▌Abandoned Property

As already mentioned, one of the methods of acquiring ownership of property is to possess it. Simply finding something and holding onto it, however, does not necessarily give the finder any legal rights in the property. Different rules apply, depending on whether the property was mislaid, lost, or abandoned.

Mislaid Property

Property that has been placed somewhere by the owner voluntarily and then inadvertently forgotten is **mislaid property**. Suppose that you go to the theater and leave your gloves on the concession stand. The gloves are mislaid property, and the theater owner is entrusted with the duty of reasonable care for them. When mislaid property is found, the finder does not obtain title to the goods. Instead, the owner of the place where the property was mislaid becomes the caretaker of the property, because it is highly likely that the true owner will return.[3]

Lost Property

Property that is involuntarily left and forgotten is **lost property**. A finder of the property can claim title to the property against the whole world, *except the true owner*.[4] If the true owner demands that the lost property be returned, the finder must return it. If a third party attempts to take possession of lost property from a finder, however, the third party cannot assert a better title than the finder. When a finder knows who the true owner of the property is and fails to return it to that person, the finder is guilty of the tort of *conversion* (the wrongful taking of another's property—see Chapter 5). Finally, many states require the finder to make a reasonably diligent search to locate the true owner of lost property.

For example, suppose that Kormian works in a large library at night. In the courtyard on her way home, she finds a piece of gold jewelry set with stones that look like precious stones to her. She takes it to a jeweler to have it appraised. While pretending to weigh the jewelry, an employee of the jeweler removes several of the stones. If Kormian brings an action to recover the stones from the jeweler, she normally will win, because she found lost property and holds valid title against everyone *except the true owner*. Because the property was lost, rather than mislaid, the finder is not the caretaker of the jewelry. Instead, the finder acquires title good against the whole world (except the true owner).

---

3. The finder of mislaid property is an involuntary bailee (to be discussed later in this chapter).
4. See *Armory v. Delamirie*, 93 Eng.Rep. 664 (K.B. [King's Bench] 1722).

Many states have laws that encourage and facilitate the return of property to its true owner and then reward a finder for honesty if the property remains unclaimed. These laws, called **estray statutes,** provide an incentive for finders to report their discoveries by making it possible for them, after the passage of a specified period of time, to acquire legal title to the property they have found. The statute usually requires the county clerk to advertise the property in an attempt to enhance the opportunity of the owner to recover what has been lost. Some preliminary questions must always be resolved before the estray statute can be employed. The item must be lost property, not merely mislaid property. When the situation indicates that the property was probably lost and not mislaid or abandoned, loss is presumed as a matter of public policy, and the estray statute applies.

The law that finders of lost property may obtain good title to the property has a long history. Under the doctrine of *relativity of title*, if two contestants are before the court, neither of whom can claim absolute title to the property, the one who can claim prior possession will likely have established sufficient rights to the property to win the case.

Abandoned Property

Property that has been discarded by the true owner, who has no intention of reclaiming title to it, is **abandoned property.** Someone who finds abandoned property acquires title to it, and such title is good against the whole world, *including the original owner*. The owner of lost property who eventually gives up any further attempt to find the lost property is frequently held to have abandoned the property. In situations in which the finder is trespassing on the property of another and finds abandoned property, title vests not in the finder but in the owner of the land.

▌ Bailments

A bailment is formed by the delivery of personal property, without transfer of title, by one person, called a **bailor,** to another, called a **bailee,** usually under an agreement for a particular purpose (for example, for storage, repair, or transportation). Upon completion of the purpose, the bailee is

obligated to return the bailed property to the bailor or to a third person or to dispose of it as directed.

Bailments usually are created by agreement but not necessarily by contract, because in many bailments not all of the elements of a contract (such as mutual assent and consideration) are present. For example, if you loan your bicycle to a friend, a bailment is created, but not by contract, because there is no consideration. Many commercial bailments, such as the delivery of your suit to the cleaners for dry cleaning, are based on contract, however.

Virtually every individual or business is affected by the law of bailments at one time or another (and sometimes even on a daily basis). When individuals deal with bailments, whether they realize it or not, they are subject to the obligations and duties that arise from the bailment relationship. The number, scope, and importance of bailments created daily in the business community and in everyday life make it desirable for every person to understand the elements necessary for the creation of a bailment and to know what rights, duties, and liabilities flow from bailments.

Elements of a Bailment

Not all transactions involving the delivery of property from one person to another create a bailment. For such a transfer to become a bailment, three conditions must be met. We look here at each of these conditions.

PERSONAL PROPERTY Bailment involves only personal property; there can be no bailment of persons. Although a bailment of your luggage is created when it is transported by an airline, as a passenger you are not the subject of a bailment. Additionally, you cannot bail realty; thus, leasing your house to a tenant does not create a bailment.

DELIVERY OF POSSESSION In a voluntary bailment, possession of the property must be transferred to the bailee in such a way that (1) the bailee is given exclusive possession and control over the property and (2) the bailee *knowingly* accepts the personal property. If either of these conditions for effective delivery of possession is lacking, there is no bailment relationship. For example, suppose that you take a friend out to dinner at an expensive restaurant. When you enter the restaurant, your friend checks her coat. In the pocket of the coat is a $20,000 diamond necklace. The bailee, by accepting the coat, does not *knowingly* also accept the necklace; thus, a bailment of the coat exists—because the restaurant has exclusive possession and control over the coat and knowingly accepted it—but a bailment of the necklace does not exist.

Two types of delivery—*physical* and *constructive*—will result in the bailee's exclusive possession of and control over the property. As discussed earlier, in the context of gifts, constructive delivery is a substitute, or symbolic, delivery. What is delivered to the bailee is not the actual property bailed (such as a car) but something so related to the property (such as the car keys) that the requirement of delivery is satisfied.

In certain unique situations, a bailment is found despite the apparent lack of the requisite elements of control and knowledge. In particular, the rental of a safe-deposit box is usually held to create a bailor-bailee relationship between the bank and its customer, despite the bank's lack of knowledge of the contents and its inability to have exclusive control of the property.[5] Another example of such a situation occurs when the bailee acquires the property accidentally or by mistake—as in finding someone else's lost or mislaid property. A bailment is created even though the bailor did not voluntarily deliver the property to the bailee. Such bailments are called *constructive* or *involuntary* bailments.

To what extent is a parking lot attendant responsible for undisclosed articles left in the trunk of a car placed in his or her care? This is the question in the following case.

---

5. By statute or by express contract, the rental of a safe-deposit box may be regarded as a lease of space or a license instead of a bailment.

CASE 28.3

Jack Boles Services, Inc. v. Stavely

Court of Appeals of Texas, Austin, 1995.
906 S.W.2d 185.

FACTS   Gerald Stavely entrusted a valuable painting to the care of Patricia Bolger. Bolger put the painting in the trunk of her husband's Cadillac. Her husband left the car at his country club in the care of a parking attendant who worked for Jack Boles Services, Inc. The car and painting were stolen. Bolger's car was eventually returned to him, but the painting was missing. Stavely filed a suit in a Texas state court against Jack Boles Services, Inc., arguing that the bailee was responsible for the theft. The court agreed. Boles appealed.

ISSUE   Is a bailee responsible for the unknown contents of bailed property if the presence of those contents is not reasonably foreseeable?

DECISION   No. The Court of Appeals of Texas (Austin) reversed the lower court's judgment.

REASON   The state appellate court concluded that "[i]t cannot be said * * * that a country club parking attendant should reasonably foresee the presence of valuable artwork in each member's car trunk." Thus, Boles could not be said to have had actual or implied notice of the painting. Without notice, it could "not expressly or implicitly accept Stavely's painting as a bailed piece of property. Without acceptance, no bailor-bailee relationship existed in regard to the painting, and accordingly, Jack Boles had no duty of care in regard to the painting."

FOR CRITICAL ANALYSIS—Social Consideration   *Why did Stavely file suit against Boles instead of against the parking attendant?*

BAILMENT AGREEMENT   A bailment agreement can be express or implied. Although a written agreement is not required for bailments of less than one year (that is, the Statute of Frauds does not apply—see Chapter 10), it is a good idea to have one, especially when valuable property is involved.

The bailment agreement expressly or impliedly provides for the return of the bailed property to the bailor or to a third person, or it provides for disposal by the bailee. The agreement presupposes that the bailee will return the identical goods originally given by the bailor. In certain types of bailments, however, such as bailments of fungible goods, the property returned need only be equivalent property.

For example, if Holman stores his grain (fungible goods) in Joe's Warehouse, a bailment is created. At the end of the storage period, however, the warehouse is not obligated to return to Holman exactly the same grain that he stored. As long as the warehouse returns goods of the same *type*, *grade*, and *quantity*, the warehouse—the bailee—has performed its obligation.

Ordinary Bailments

Bailments are either *ordinary* or *special (extraordinary)*. There are three types of ordinary bailments. The distinguishing feature among them is *which party receives a benefit from the bailment*. Ultimately, the courts may use this factor to determine the standard of care required of the bailee in possession of the personal property, and this factor will dictate the rights and liabilities of the parties. The three types of ordinary bailments are as follows:

1. *Bailment for the sole benefit of the bailor.* This is a gratuitous bailment (a bailment without consideration) for the convenience and benefit of the bailor. For example, if Allen asks his friend, Sumi, to store Allen's car in Sumi's garage, and Sumi agrees to do so, the bailment of the car would be for the sole benefit of the bailor (Allen).
2. *Bailment for the sole benefit of the bailee.* This type of bailment typically occurs when one person loans an item to another person (the bailee) solely for the bailee's convenience and benefit. For example, Allen asks his friend Sumi to borrow Sumi's boat so that Allen can go sailing over the weekend. The bailment of the boat is for Allen's (the bailee's) sole benefit.

3. *Bailment for the mutual benefit of the bailee and the bailor.* This is the most common kind of bailment and involves some form of compensation for storing items or holding property while it is being serviced. It is a contractual bailment and is often referred to as a bailment for hire. For example, leaving your car at a service station for an oil change is a mutual-benefit bailment.

RIGHTS OF THE BAILEE   Certain rights are implicit in the bailment agreement. A hallmark of the bailment agreement is that the bailee acquires the *right to control and possess the property temporarily*. The bailee's right of possession permits the bailee to recover damages from any third person for damage or loss of the property. If the property is stolen, the bailee has a legal right to regain possession of it or to obtain damages from any third person who has wrongfully interfered with the bailee's possessory rights. The bailee's right to regain possession of the property or to obtain damages is important because, as you will read shortly, a bailee is liable to the bailor for any loss or damage to bailed property resulting from the bailee's negligence.

Depending on the type of bailment and the terms of the bailment agreement, a bailee also may have a *right to use the bailed property*. For example, if you borrow a friend's car to drive to the airport, you, as the bailee, would obviously be expected to use the car. In a bailment involving the long-term storage of a car, however, the bailee is not expected to use the car, because the ordinary purpose of a storage bailment does not include use of the property.

Except in a gratuitous bailment, a bailee has a *right to be compensated* as provided for in the bailment agreement, a right to be reimbursed for costs and services rendered in the keeping of the bailed property, or both. Even in a gratuitous bailment, a bailee has a right to be reimbursed or compensated for costs incurred in the keeping of the bailed property. For example, Margo loses her pet dog, which Judith finds. Judith takes Margo's dog to her home and feeds it. Even though she takes good care of the dog, it becomes ill, and she calls a veterinarian. Judith pays the bill for the veterinarian's services and the medicine. Judith normally will be entitled to be reimbursed by Margo for all reasonable costs incurred in the keeping of Margo's dog. To enforce the right of compensation, the bailee has a right to place a *possessory lien* (which entitles a creditor to retain possession of the debtor's goods until a debt is paid) on the specific bailed property until he or she has been fully compensated. This type of lien, sometimes referred to as an *artisan's lien* or a *bailee's lien,* was discussed in Chapter 20.

Ordinary bailees have the *right to limit their liability* as long as the limitations are called to the attention of the bailor and are not against public policy. It is essential that the bailor in some way know of the limitation. Even if the bailor has notice, certain types of disclaimers of liability have been con-

sidered to be against public policy and therefore illegal. For example, certain exculpatory clauses limiting a person's liability for his or her own wrongful acts are often scrutinized by the courts and, in the case of bailments, are routinely held to be illegal. This is particularly true in bailments for the mutual benefit of the bailor and the bailee. Whether a bailee could disclaim liability for the loss of bailed property is at issue in the following case.

CASE 28.4

Brockwell v. Lake Gaston Sales and Service

Court of Appeals of North Carolina, 1992.
105 N.C.App. 226,
412 S.E.2d 104.

FACTS R. W. Brockwell took his boat and its motor to Lake Gaston Sales and Service (Gaston) to be repaired. At the time Brockwell delivered the boat to Gaston, the boat contained many items of personal property, including fishing gear, navigation equipment, and electronic equipment. Before the boat could be repaired, Brockwell had to sign a repair order that contained the following disclaimer: "It is understood and agreed that [Gaston] assumes no responsibility whatsoever for loss or damage by theft, fire, vandalism, water or weather related damages, nor for any items of personal property left with the unit placed with [Gaston] for repair, storage or sale." About ten days later, after the boat had been repaired, Brockwell learned that equipment and other personal property worth over $2,000 were missing from the boat. Gaston contended that the disclaimer in the repair order absolved it from any liability for the missing property. Brockwell sued Gaston in a North Carolina state court for negligence. The trial court held for Brockwell and awarded him damages. Gaston appealed.

ISSUE Did the disclaimer in the repair order absolve Gaston from liability for the missing property?

DECISION No. The appellate court affirmed the trial court's decision. Gaston could not, by contract, disclaim liability for its own negligence.

REASON The court stated that as a general rule, in mutual-benefit bailment contracts, bailees can relieve themselves from the liability imposed on them under the common law so long as contract provisions are not contrary to public policy. The court noted that many courts have held that "where the bailee makes it his business to act as bailee for hire, on a uniform and not an individual basis, it is against the public interest to permit him to exculpate himself from his own negligence. And the decided trend of modern decisions is against the validity of such exculpatory clauses or provisions * * * ." Gaston, the bailee, was in the business of acting as a bailee for hire on a uniform basis and took Brockwell's boat and its contents and attachments "into its sole possession in order to perform repairs on the boat in the regular course of its business, and we hold it was against public policy for [Gaston] to attempt to exculpate itself from the duty of ordinary care it owed to [Brockwell]. We therefore hold the liability disclaimer in the present case is void and unenforceable as a matter of law."

FOR CRITICAL ANALYSIS—Ethical Consideration *Would it matter, in terms of the outcome of this case, whether Brockwell had or had not read the disclaimer?*

DUTIES OF THE BAILEE The bailee has two basic responsibilities: (1) to take proper care of the property and (2) to surrender to the bailor or dispose of the property in accordance with the bailor's instructions at the end of the bailment. The bailee must exercise reasonable care in preserving the bailed property. What constitutes reasonable care in a bailment situation normally depends on the nature and specific circumstances of the bailment. Traditionally, courts have determined the appropriate standard of care on the basis of the type of bailments involved. In a bailment for the sole benefit for the bailor, for example, the bailee need exercise only a slight degree of care. In a bailment for the sole benefit of the bailee, however, the bailee must exercise great care. In a mutual-benefit bailment, courts normally impose a reasonable standard of care—that is, the bailee must exercise the degree of care that a reasonable and prudent person would exercise in the same circumstances. Exhibit 28–1 illustrates these concepts.

A bailee's failure to exercise appropriate care in handling the bailor's property results in tort liability. The duty to relinquish the property at the end of the bailment is grounded in both contract and tort law principles. Failure to return the property constitutes a breach of contract or the tort of conversion, and with one exception, the bailee is liable for damages. The exception is when the obligation is excused because the goods or chattels have been destroyed, lost, or stolen through no fault of the bailee (or claimed by a third party with a superior claim).

Under the law of bailments, a bailor's proof that damage or loss to the property has occurred will, in and of itself, raise a *presumption* that the bailee is guilty of negligence or conversion. In other words, whenever a bailee fails to return bailed property, the bailee's negligence will be *presumed* by the court.

DUTIES OF THE BAILOR It goes without saying that the rights of a bailor are essentially the same as the duties of a bailee. The major duty of the bailor is to provide the bailee with goods or chattels that are free from known defects that could cause injury to the bailee. In the case of a mutual-benefit bailment, the bailor must also notify the bailee of any hidden defects that the bailor could have discovered with reasonable diligence and proper inspection.

The bailor's duty to reveal defects is based on a negligence theory of tort law. A bailor who fails to give the appropriate notice is liable to the bailee and to any other person who might reasonably be expected to come into contact with the defective article. For example, if an equipment rental firm leases equipment with a *discoverable* defect, and the lessee (bailee) is not notified of such a defect and is harmed because of it, the rental firm is liable for negligence under tort law.

An exception to this rule exists if the bailment was created for the sole benefit of the bailee. Thus, if you loaned your car to a friend as a favor to your friend and not for any direct return benefit to yourself, you would be required to notify your friend of any *known* defect of the automobile that could cause injury but not of a defect of which you were unaware (even if it was a *discoverable* defect). If your friend was injured in an accident as a result of a defect unknown to you, you would normally not be liable.

A bailor can also incur *warranty liability* based on contract law (see Chapter 16) for injuries resulting from the bailment of defective articles. Property leased by a bailor must be *fit for the intended purpose of the bailment.* Warranties of fitness arise by law in sales contracts and leases and by judicial interpretation in the case of bailments for hire. Article 2A of the Uniform Commercial Code extends implied warranties of merchantability and fitness for a particular purpose to bailments when-

♦ **Exhibit 28–1**
Degree of Care Required of a Bailee

Bailment for the Sole Benefit of the Bailor	Mutual-Benefit Bailment	Bailment for the Sole Benefit of the Bailee
DEGREE OF CARE →		
SLIGHT	REASONABLE	GREAT

ever the bailments include rights to use the bailed goods.[6]

The resolution of the following case depended on the degree of care owed by a bailor—the

6. UCC 2A–212, 2A–213.

CASE 28.5

Prince v. Atlanta Coca-Cola Bottling Co.

Court of Appeals of Georgia, 1993.
210 Ga.App. 108,
435 S.E.2d 482.

Atlanta Coca-Cola Bottling Company—to an injured third party. In determining the required degree of care, the court evaluates whether the bailment was a bailment for hire or a gratuitous bailment (a bailment without consideration).

FACTS Phar-Mor arranged with the Atlanta Coca-Cola Bottling Company (ACCBC) to use one of its "special events wagons" during a promotion in the store's parking lot. An ACCBC employee delivered the wagon and parked it in accordance with a Phar-Mor employee's instructions. ACCBC did not charge Phar-Mor for the use of the wagon, but only for the beverages and food items (provided by ACCBC) that Phar-Mor employees sold during the event. Water leaked from the wagon, causing a puddle to form. Lisa Prince stepped in the puddle, slipped, fell, and sustained injuries. ACCBC was not aware of the accident for several months. Prince sued ACCBC for negligence in a Georgia state court, claiming, among other things, that ACCBC had failed in its duty, as a bailor, to maintain the premises around the wagon. The trial court granted summary judgment in ACCBC's favor, and Prince appealed.

ISSUE Did ACCBC have a legal duty to maintain the premises around the wagon?

DECISION No. The appellate court affirmed the lower court's decision.

REASON The court reasoned that a gratuitous bailment existed between Phar-Mor and ACCBC, because there was no evidence of Prince's claim that "appellee contracted with Phar-Mor to provide refreshments in the Coca-Cola special events wagon under a bailment for hire." As a gratuitous bailor, ACCBC had no legal duty to maintain the area around the wagon, no legal duty to prevent drain water from accumulating, and no legal duty to warn "of any slippery, dangerous, or unsafe conditions existing in the vicinity," particularly as to water that drained and accumulated after the wagon was delivered and placed under Phar-Mor's sole control.

FOR CRITICAL ANALYSIS—Social Consideration *What might result if bailors were held to the same standard of care in gratuitous bailments as in bailments for hire?*

Special Types of Bailments

Up to this point, our discussion of bailments has been concerned with ordinary bailments—bailments in which bailees are expected to exercise ordinary care in the handling of bailed property. Some bailment transactions warrant special consideration. These include bailments in which the bailee's duty

of care is *extraordinary*—that is, his or her liability for loss or damage to the property is absolute—as is generally true in cases involving common carriers and innkeepers. Warehouse companies have the same duty of care as ordinary bailees; but, like carriers, they are subject to extensive regulation under federal and state laws, including Article 7 of the Uniform Commercial Code (UCC).

COMMON CARRIERS Transportation providers that are publicly licensed to provide transportation services to the general public are known as **common carriers.** Common carriers are distinguished from private carriers, which operate transportation facilities for a select clientele. Whereas a private carrier is not bound to provide service to every person or company making a request, a common carrier must arrange carriage for all who apply, within certain limitations.[7]

The delivery of goods to a common carrier creates a bailment relationship between the shipper (bailor) and the common carrier (bailee). Unlike ordinary bailees, the common carrier is held to a standard of care based on *strict liability*, rather than reasonable care, in protecting the bailed personal property. This means that the common carrier is absolutely liable, regardless of negligence, for all loss or damage to goods except damage caused by one of the following common law exceptions: (1) an act of God, (2) an act of a public enemy, (3) an order of a public authority, (4) an act of the shipper, or (5) the inherent nature of the goods.

Common carriers cannot contract away their liability for damaged goods. Subject to government regulations, however, they are permitted to limit their dollar liability to an amount stated on the shipment contract or rate filing.[8]

WAREHOUSE COMPANIES Warehousing is the business of providing storage of property for compensation.[9] A warehouse company is a professional bailee whose responsibility differs from an ordinary bailee's in two important aspects. First, a warehouse company is empowered to issue documents of title—in particular, warehouse receipts.[10] Second, warehouse companies are subject to an extraordinary network of state and federal statutes, including Article 7 of the UCC.

A warehouse company accepts goods for storage and issues a warehouse receipt describing the property and the terms of the bailment contract. The warehouse receipt can be negotiable or nonnegotiable, depending on how it is written. It is negotiable if its terms provide that the warehouse company will deliver the goods "to the bearer" of the receipt or "to the order of" a person named on the receipt.[11]

The warehouse receipt serves multiple functions. It is a receipt for the goods stored; it is a contract of bailment; it also represents the goods (that is, it indicates title) and hence has value and utility in financing commercial transactions. For example, Ossip, a processor and canner of corn, delivers 6,500 cases of corn to Shaneyfelt, the owner of a warehouse. Shaneyfelt issues a negotiable warehouse receipt payable "to bearer" and gives it to Ossip. Ossip sells and delivers the warehouse receipt to a large supermarket chain, Better Foods, Inc. Better Foods is now the owner of the corn and has the right to obtain the cases from Shaneyfelt. It will present the warehouse receipt to Shaneyfelt, who in return will release the cases of corn to the grocery chain.

Like ordinary bailees, a warehouse company is liable for loss or damage to property resulting from *negligence* (and therefore does not have the same liability as a common carrier). As a professional bailee, however, it is expected to exercise a high degree of care to protect and preserve the goods. A warehouse company can limit the dollar amount of its liability, but the bailor must be given the option of paying an increased storage rate for an increase in the liability limit.

---

7. A common carrier is not required to take any and all property anywhere in all instances. Public regulatory agencies govern common carriers, and carriers can be restricted to geographical areas. They can also be limited to carrying certain kinds of goods or to providing only special types of transportation equipment.

8. Federal laws require common carriers to offer shippers the opportunity to obtain higher dollar limits for loss by paying a higher fee for the transport.

9. UCC 7–102(h) defines the person engaged in the storing of goods for hire as a "warehouseman."

---

10. A document of title is defined in UCC 1–201(15) as any "document which in the regular course of business or financing is treated as adequately evidencing that the person in possession of it is entitled to receive, hold, and dispose of the document and the goods it covers. To be a document of title, a document must purport to be issued by or addressed to a bailee and purport to cover goods in the bailee's possession."

11. UCC 7–104.

INNKEEPERS At common law, innkeepers, hotel owners, and similar operators were held to the same strict liability as common carriers with respect to property brought into the rooms by guests. Today, only those who provide lodging to the public for compensation as a *regular* business are covered under this rule of strict liability. Moreover, the rule applies only to those who are guests, as opposed to lodgers. A lodger is a permanent resident of the hotel or inn, whereas a guest is a traveler.

In many states, innkeepers can avoid strict liability for loss of guests' valuables and money by providing a safe in which to keep them. Each guest must be clearly notified of the availability of such a safe. Statutes often limit the liability of innkeepers with regard to articles that are not kept in the safe or that are of such a nature that they are not normally kept in a safe. These statutes may limit the amount of monetary damages or even provide for no liability in the absence of innkeeper negligence.

Suppose that Joyce stays for a night at the Harbor Hotel. When she returns from eating breakfast in the hotel restaurant, she discovers that the people in the room next door have forced the lock on the door between the two rooms and stolen her suitcase. Joyce claims that the hotel is liable for her loss. The hotel maintains that because it was not negligent, it is not liable. At common law, the hotel would have been liable, because innkeepers were actually insurers of the property of their guests. Today, however, state statutes limit strict liability by limiting the amount of monetary damages for which the innkeeper is liable or providing that the innkeeper has no liability in the absence of negligence. Most statutes require these limitations to be posted or the guest to be notified. Such postings, or notices, are frequently found on the doors of the rooms in the motel or hotel.

Normally, the innkeeper (a motel keeper, for example) assumes no responsibility for the safety of a guest's automobile, because the guest usually retains possession and control over it. If, however, the innkeeper provides parking facilities and the guest's car is entrusted to the innkeeper or to an employee, the innkeeper will be liable under the rules that pertain to parking-lot bailments (which are ordinary bailments).

▮ Terms and Concepts

▮ Chapter Summary: Personal Property and Bailments

PERSONAL PROPERTY	
Definition of Personal Property *(See page 586.)*	Personal property (personalty) is considered to include all property not classified as real property (realty). Personal property can be tangible (such as a TV set or a car) or intangible (such as stocks or bonds). Personal property may be referred to legally as *chattel*—a term used under the common law to denote all forms of personal property.
Property Ownership *(See pages 586–587.)*	1. *Fee simple*—Exists when individuals have the right to use, possess, or dispose of the property as they choose during their lifetimes and to pass on the property to their heirs at death. *(Continued)*

▌Chapter Summary: Personal Property and Bailments—Continued

PERSONAL PROPERTY—Continued	

Property Ownership —Continued	2. *Concurrent ownership—*
	  a. Tenancy in common—Co-ownership in which two or more persons own an undivided interest in the property; on one tenant's death, the property interest passes to his or her heirs.
	  b. Joint tenancy—Exists when two or more persons own an undivided interest in property; on the death of a joint tenant, the property interest transfers to the remaining tenant(s), not to the heirs of the deceased.
	  c. Tenancy by the entirety—A form of co-ownership between a husband and wife that is similar to a joint tenancy, except that a spouse cannot transfer separately his or her interest during his or her lifetime without the consent of the other spouse.
	  d. Community property—A form of co-ownership in which each spouse technically owns an undivided one-half interest in property acquired during the marriage. This type of ownership occurs in only a few states.

Acquiring Ownership of Personal Property *(See pages 587–591.)*	The most common means of acquiring ownership in personal property is by purchasing it (see Chapters 13 through 16). Another way in which personal property is often acquired is by will or inheritance (see Chapter 30). The following are additional methods of acquiring personal property:
	
	1. *Possession*—Ownership may be acquired by possession if no other person has ownership title (for example, capturing wild animals or finding abandoned property).
	
	2. *Production*—Any product or item produced by an individual (with some exceptions) becomes the property of that individual.
	
	3. *Gift*—An effective gift exists when the following conditions exist:
	  a. There is evidence of *intent* to make a gift of the property in question.
	  b. The gift is *delivered* (physically or constructively) to the donee or the donee's agent.
	  c. The gift is *accepted* by the donee or the donee's agent.
	
	4. *Accession*—When someone adds value to a piece of personal property by labor or materials, the added value generally becomes the property of the owner of the original property (includes accessions made in bad faith or wrongfully). Good faith accessions that substantially increase the property's value or change the identity of the property may cause title to pass to the improver.
	
	5. *Confusion*—In the case of fungible goods, if a person wrongfully and willfully commingles goods with those of another in order to render them indistinguishable, the innocent party acquires title to the whole. Otherwise, the owners become tenants in common of the commingled goods.

Mislaid, Lost, and Abandoned Property *(See pages 591–592.)*	1. *Mislaid property*—Property that is placed somewhere voluntarily by the owner and then inadvertently forgotten. A finder of mislaid property will not acquire title to the goods, and the owner of the place where the property was mislaid becomes a caretaker of the mislaid property. 2. *Lost property*—Property that is involuntarily left and forgotten. A finder of lost property can claim title to the property against the whole world *except the true owner.* 3. *Abandoned property*—Property that has been discarded by the true owner, who has no intention of claiming title to the property in the future. A finder of abandoned property can claim title to it against the whole world, *including the original owner.*

▌Chapter Summary: Personal Property and Bailments—Continued

BAILMENTS	
Elements of a Bailment *(See pages 592–594.)*	1. *Personal property*—Bailments involve only personal property. 2. *Delivery of possession*—For an effective bailment to exist, the bailee (the one receiving the property) must be given exclusive possession and control over the property, and in a voluntary bailment, the bailee must knowingly accept the personal property. 3. *The bailment agreement*—Expressly or impliedly provides for the return of the bailed property to the bailor or a third party, or for the disposal of the bailed property by the bailee.

Ordinary Bailments *(See pages 594–597.)*	1. *Types of bailments*—
	  a. Bailment for the sole benefit of the bailor—A gratuitous bailment undertaken for the sole benefit of the bailor (for example, as a favor to the bailor).
	  b. Bailment for the sole benefit of the bailee—A gratuitous bailment of an article to a person (the bailee) solely for the bailee's benefit.
	  c. Mutual-benefit (contractual) bailment—The most common kind of bailment; involves compensation between the bailee and bailor for the service provided.
	
	2. *Rights of a bailee (duties of a bailor)*—
	  a. The right of possession—Allows actions against third persons who damage or convert the bailed property and allows actions against the bailor for wrongful breach of the bailment.
	  b. The right to be compensated and reimbursed for expenses—In the event of nonpayment, the bailee has the right to place a possessory (bailee's) lien on the bailed property.
	  c. The right to limit liability—An ordinary bailee can limit his or her liability for loss or damage, provided proper notice is given and the limitation is not against public policy. In special bailments, limitations on types of liability are usually not allowed, but limitations on the monetary amount of liability are permitted.
	
	3. *Duties of a bailee (rights of a bailor)*—
	  a. A bailee must exercise appropriate care over property entrusted to him or her. What constitutes appropriate care normally depends on the nature and circumstances of the bailment.
	  b. Bailed goods in a bailee's possession must be either returned to the bailor or disposed of according to the bailor's directions. A bailee's failure to return the bailed property constitutes a breach of contract or the tort of conversion.

Special Types of Bailments *(See pages 597–599.)*	1. *Common carriers*—Carriers that are publicly licensed to provide transportation services to the general public. The common carrier is held to a standard of care based on *strict liability* unless the bailed property is lost or destroyed due to (a) an act of God, (b) an act of a public enemy, (c) an order of a public authority, (d) an act of a shipper, or (e) the inherent nature of the goods. 2. *Warehouse companies*—Professional bailees that differ from ordinary bailees because they (a) can issue documents of title (warehouse receipts) and (b) are subject to state and federal statutes, including Article 7 of the UCC (as are common carriers). They must exercise a high degree of care over the bailed property and are liable for loss or damage of property due to negligence. 3. *Innkeepers (hotel operators)*—Those who provide lodging to the public for compensation as a *regular* business. The common law standard of strict liability to which innkeepers were once held is limited today by state statutes, which vary from state to state.

▮ For Review

1. What is real property? What is personal property?
2. What does it mean to own property in fee simple? What is the difference between a joint tenancy and a tenancy in common?
3. What are the three elements necessary for an effective gift? How else can property be acquired?

4. What are the three elements of a bailment?
5. What are the basic rights and duties of the bailee? What are the rights and duties of the bailor?

▮ Questions and Case Problems

28–1. Duties of the Bailee. Discuss the standard of care traditionally required of the bailee for the bailed property in each of the following situations, and determine whether the bailee breached that duty.

(a) Ricardo borrows Steve's lawn mower because his own lawn mower needs repair. Ricardo mows his front yard. To mow the back yard, he needs to move some hoses and lawn furniture. He leaves the mower in front of his house while doing so. When he returns to the front yard, he discovers that the mower has been stolen.

(b) Alicia owns a valuable speedboat. She is going on vacation and asks her neighbor, Maureen, to store the boat in one stall of Maureen's double garage. Maureen consents, and the boat is moved into the garage. Maureen needs some grocery items for dinner and drives to the store. She leaves the garage door open while she is gone, as is her custom, and the speedboat is stolen during that time.

28–2. Gifts. Reineken, very old and ill, wanted to make a gift to his nephew, Gerald. He had a friend obtain $2,500 in cash for him from his bank account, placed this cash in an envelope, and wrote on the envelope, "This is for my nephew, Gerald." Reineken then placed the envelope in his dresser drawer. When Reineken died a month later, his family found the envelope, and Gerald got word of the intended gift. Gerald then demanded that Reineken's daughter, the executor of Reineken's estate (the person appointed by Reineken to handle his affairs after his death), turn over the gift to him. The daughter refused to do so. Discuss fully whether Gerald can successfully claim ownership rights to the $2,500.

28–3. Gifts. In 1968, Armando was about to be shipped to Vietnam for active duty with the U.S. Marines. Shortly before he left, he gave an expensive stereo set and other personal belongings to his girlfriend, Sara, saying, "I'll probably not return from this war, so I'm giving these to you." Armando returned eighteen months later and requested that Sara return

the property. Sara said that because Armando had given her these items to keep, she was not required to return them. Was a gift made in this instance, and can Armando recover his property? Discuss fully.

28–4. Requirements of a Bailment. Calvin is an executive on a business trip to the West Coast. He has driven his car on this trip and checks into the Hotel Ritz. The hotel has a guarded underground parking lot. Calvin gives his car keys to the parking-lot attendant but fails to notify the attendant that his wife's $10,000 diamond necklace is in a box in the trunk. The next day, upon checking out, he discovers that his car has been stolen. Calvin wants to hold the hotel liable for both the car and the necklace. Discuss the probable success of his claim.

28–5. Gifts. Welton, an experienced businessperson, transferred to Gallagher some bearer bonds. He stated that the bonds were hers with "no strings attached" and that she should place the bonds in her safe-deposit box for safekeeping. Later, Welton wanted Gallagher to return the bonds to him, claiming that he was still the owner. Gallagher refused, claiming that Welton's transfer was a gift. Was it? Discuss fully. [*Welton v. Gallagher*, 2 Haw.App. 242, 630 P.2d 1077 (1981)]

28–6. Abandoned Property. Danny Smith and his brother discovered a sixteen-foot boat lying beside a roadway in Alabama. Smith informed the police, who immediately impounded the boat and stored it in a city warehouse. Although Smith acquiesced to the police action, he told the police that if the true owner did not claim the boat, he wanted it. When the true owner did not come forward, the police refused to relinquish the boat to Smith and instead told Smith that they planned to auction it to the highest bidder on behalf of the city. Smith sued for custody of the boat. Because Smith never physically held the boat but rather allowed the police to take possession, should Smith succeed in his claim to title as finder? Could Smith defeat a claim if the true owner sought to retake the boat? Discuss fully. [*Smith v. Purvis*, 474 So.2d 1131 (Ala.Civ.App. 1985)]

28–7. Duties of the Bailee. Wanda Perry, who had an account with Farmers Bank of Greenwood, wanted to rent a safe-deposit box from the bank. The boxes were available only to bank customers, and no fee was charged. When renting the box, Wanda was asked to sign a signature card that stated as follows: "The undersigned customer holds the Farmers Bank harmless for loss of currency or coin left in the box." A little over four years later, the bank was burglarized, and most of the safe-deposit boxes were broken into. Wanda's box was among those burglarized, and she lost all the currency and coins it contained. At trial, evidence showed that the bank had been negligent in failing to restore a burglar alarm system that had been inoperative for more than a week when the bank was burglarized. Wanda sued the bank to recover the value of the currency and coins, alleging negligence on the part of the bank. Discuss fully whether the bank should be held liable for the loss. [*Farmers Bank of Greenwood v. Perry*, 301 Ark. 547, 787 S.W.2d 645 (1990)]

28–8. Gifts. William Yee and S. Hing Woo had been lovers for nearly twenty years. They held themselves out as husband and wife, and Woo wore a wedding band. Two days before his death, Yee told Woo that he felt "terribly bad" and believed he would die. He gave Woo three checks, for $42,700, $80,000, and $1,900, and told her that if he died, he wanted her "to be taken care of." After Yee's death, Woo cashed the $42,700 check and the $1,900 check. She never cashed the $80,000 check. The administrator of Yee's estate petitioned a Virginia state court to declare that Woo was not entitled to the money represented by the checks. What will the court decide, and why? [*Woo v. Smart*, 247 Va. 365, 442 S.E.2d 690 (1994)]

28–9. Bailments. Jole Liddle, a high school student in Salem School District No. 600, played varsity basketball. A letter from Monmouth College of West Long Branch, New Jersey, addressed to Liddle in care of the coach, was delivered to Liddle's school a few days after it was mailed on July 18, 1990. The letter notified Liddle that he was being recruited for a basketball scholarship. The school, which had a policy of delivering promptly any mail sent to students in care of the school, did not deliver the letter to Liddle until seven months later. Because Monmouth College had not heard from Liddle, the college discontinued its efforts to recruit him. Liddle sued the school district, alleging that the coach was negligent in his duties as a bailee of the letter. The school district filed a motion to dismiss the case, arguing that the letter was not bailable property. Was the letter bailable property? Discuss fully. [*Liddle v. Salem School District No. 600*, 249 Ill.App.3d 768, 619 N.E.2d 530, 188 Ill.Dec. 905 (1993)]

28–10. Gifts. Mabel Meredith gave Jeanette Taylor and Ann Dumler each a $25,000 check. Although Meredith owned property worth more than $2 million, she did not have enough in her checking account to cover the checks. Meredith died six years later, and Taylor and Dumler filed claims in a Maryland state court against her estate, represented by William Dulany, to recover the amounts of the checks. Does the receipt of a check represent a completed gift? Should Taylor and Dumler be awarded $25,000 each? [*Dulany v. Taylor*, 105 Md.App. 619, 660 A.2d 1046 (1995)]

U.S. **CASE BRIEFING ASSIGNMENT**
2 F2d **28–11.** *Examine Case A.7 [Strang v. Hollowell, 387 S.E.2d 664 (N.C.App. 1990)]* in Appendix A. The case has been excerpted there in great detail. Review and then brief the case, making sure that you include answers to the following questions in your brief.

1. Are there any facts in dispute in this case?
2. What was the only issue presented on appeal?
3. How was the bailment contract breached?
4. Why did the defendant, Hollowell, contend that he should not be held personally liable for the damages to the plaintiff's automobile?

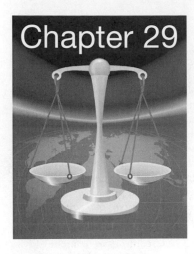

Chapter 29

Real Property

CHAPTER OBJECTIVES

After reading this chapter, you should be able to:

1. Distinguish among different types of possessory ownership interests in real property.
2. Identify three types of nonpossessory interests in real property.
3. Discuss how ownership interests in real property can be transferred.
4. Indicate what a leasehold estate is and how a landlord-tenant relationship comes into existence.
5. Outline the respective rights of landlords and tenants concerning the possession, use, and maintenance of leased property.

From earliest times, property has provided a means for survival. Primitive peoples lived off the fruits of the land, eating the vegetation and wildlife. Later, as the wildlife was domesticated and the vegetation cultivated, property provided pasturage and farmland. In the twelfth and thirteenth centuries, the power of feudal lords was determined by the amount of land that they held; the more land they held, the more powerful they were. After the age of feudalism passed, property continued to be an indicator of family wealth and social position. In the Western world, the protection of an individual's right to his or her property has become one of the most important rights of citizenship.

In this chapter, we first examine closely the nature of real property. We then look at the various ways in which real property can be owned and at how ownership rights in real property are transferred from one person to another. We conclude

the chapter with a discussion of leased property and landlord-tenant relationships.

■ The Nature of Real Property

Real property consists of land and the buildings, plants, and trees that it contains. Real property also includes subsurface and air rights, as well as personal property that has become permanently attached to real property. Whereas personal property is movable, real property—also called *real estate* or *realty*—is immovable.

Land

Land includes the soil on the surface of the earth and the natural or artificial structures that are attached to it. It further includes all the waters contained on or under the surface and much, but not necessarily all, of the airspace above it. The exterior boundaries of land extend down to the center of the earth and up to the farthest reaches of the atmosphere (subject to certain qualifications).

Air and Subsurface Rights

The owner of real property has relatively exclusive rights to the airspace above the land, as well as to the soil and minerals underneath it.

AIR RIGHTS Early cases involving air rights dealt with matters such as the right to run a telephone wire across a person's property when the wire did not touch any of the property[1] and whether a bullet shot over a person's land constituted trespass.[2] Today, disputes concerning air rights may involve the right of commercial and private planes to fly over property and the right of individuals and governments to seed clouds and produce artificial rain. Flights over private land do not normally violate the property owners' rights unless the flights are low and frequent enough to cause a direct interference with the enjoyment and use of the land.[3] Leaning walls or buildings and projecting eave spouts or roofs may also violate the air rights of an adjoining property owner.

SUBSURFACE RIGHTS In many states, the owner of the surface of a piece of land is not the owner of the subsurface, and hence the land ownership may be separated. Subsurface rights can be extremely valuable, as these rights include the ownership of minerals and, in most states, oil and natural gas. Water rights are also extremely valuable, especially in the West. When the ownership is separated into surface and subsurface rights, each owner can pass title to what he or she owns without the consent of the other owner. Each owner has the right to use the land owned, and in some cases a conflict arises between a surface owner's use and the subsurface

owner's need to extract minerals, oil, and natural gas. When this occurs, one party's interest may become subservient to the other party's interest, either by statute or case decision.

Significant limitations on either air rights or subsurface rights normally have to be indicated on the deed transferring title at the time of purchase. (Deeds and the types of warranties they contain are discussed later in this chapter.)

Plant Life and Vegetation

Plant life, both natural and cultivated, is also considered to be real property. In many instances, the natural vegetation, such as trees, adds greatly to the value of the realty. When a parcel of land is sold and the land has growing crops on it, the sale includes the crops, unless otherwise specified in the sales contract. When crops are sold by themselves, however, they are considered to be personal property or goods. Consequently, the sale of crops is a sale of goods, and therefore it is governed by the Uniform Commercial Code rather than by real property law.[4]

Fixtures

Certain personal property can become so closely associated with the real property to which it is attached that the law views it as real property. Such property is known as a **fixture**—a thing *affixed* to realty, meaning it is attached to it by roots; embedded in it; or permanently attached by means of cement, plaster, bolts, nails, or screws. The fixture can be physically attached to real property, be attached to another fixture, or even be without any actual physical attachment to the land (such as a statue). As long as the owner *intends* the property to be a fixture, normally it will be a fixture.

Fixtures are included in the sale of land if the sales contract does not provide otherwise. The sale of a house includes the land and the house and the garage on the land, as well as the cabinets, plumbing, and windows. Because these are permanently affixed to the property, they are considered to be a part of it. Unless otherwise agreed, however, the curtains and throw rugs are not included. Items such as drapes and window-unit air conditioners

---

1. *Butler v. Frontier Telephone Co.*, 186 N.Y. 486, 79 N.E. 716 (1906).
2. *Herrin v. Sutherland*, 74 Mont. 587, 241 P. 328 (1925). Shooting over a person's land constitutes trespass.
3. *United States v. Causby*, 328 U.S. 256, 66 S.Ct. 1062, 90 L.Ed. 1206 (1946).

---

4. See UCC 2–107(2).

are difficult to classify. Thus, a contract for the sale of a house or commercial realty should indicate which items of this sort are included in the sale.

The following case illustrates the court's interpretation of whether a grain storage silo became a fixture to the realty or remained personal property.

CASE 29.1

Metropolitan Life Insurance Co. v. Reeves

Supreme Court of Nebraska, 1986.
223 Neb. 299,
389 N.W.2d 295.

FACTS   Lawrence Reeves was a landowning farmer whose land was being foreclosed upon by his mortgage holder, Metropolitan Life Insurance Company. Prior to the foreclosure, Reeves had contracted with Production Sale Company to erect a grain storage facility on the farm. Its total cost was $171,185.30, of which Reeves had paid only $16,137.77. When Metropolitan brought the foreclosure proceedings, the question arose as to whether the grain storage facility was a fixture to the realty or personal property. If it was considered to be a fixture, Metropolitan would receive the proceeds from the sale; if it was considered to be personal property, the proceeds would go to Production Sale Company. A Nebraska state trial court held that the facility was a fixture. Production Sale Company appealed to the Supreme Court of Nebraska.

ISSUE   Was the facility a fixture to the real property, or was it personal property?

DECISION   The Supreme Court of Nebraska, reversing the district court's ruling, deemed the storage facility to be personal property.

REASON   The court cited three factors that determine whether an article, or combination of articles, is a fixture: (1) whether the article was actually annexed to the realty, (2) whether the article had been appropriated to the use or purpose of that part of the realty with which it was connected, and (3) whether it was the intention of the parties making the contract to affix the article permanently to the land. The last factor was the most important in determining this case, and the court gave much weight to the circumstances of the purchase agreement between Reeves and Production Sale. The court concluded that under the provisions of the purchase agreement, the parties had not intended the grain storage facility to become a part of the real property until full payment had been made. Because full payment had not been made, the facility had not become a fixture.

FOR CRITICAL ANALYSIS—Social Consideration   *In determining whether an article of property is a fixture, why would the intent factor be more important than whether the article was actually annexed to the realty?*

▮ Ownership of Real Property

Ownership of property is an abstract concept that cannot exist independently of the legal system. No one can actually possess or *hold* a piece of land, the air above it, the earth below it, and all the water contained on it. The legal system therefore recognizes certain rights and duties that constitute ownership interests in real property.

Recall from Chapter 28 that property ownership is often viewed as a bundle of rights. One who possesses the entire bundle of rights is said to hold the property in *fee simple,* which is the most complete form of ownership. When only some of the rights in the bundle are transferred to another person, the effect is to limit the ownership rights of both the one transferring the rights and the one receiving them.

Ownership in Fee Simple

The most common type of property ownership today is the fee simple. Generally, the term *fee simple* is used to designate a **fee simple absolute,** in which the owner has the greatest possible aggregation of rights, privileges, and power. The fee simple is limited absolutely to a person and his or her heirs and is assigned forever without limitation or condition. The rights that accompany a fee simple include the right to use the land for whatever purpose the owner sees fit, subject to laws that prevent the owner from unreasonably interfering with another person's land and subject to applicable zoning laws. Furthermore, the owner has the rights of *exclusive* possession and use of the property. A fee simple is potentially infinite in duration and can be disposed of by deed or by will (by selling or giving away). When there is no will, the fee simple passes to the owner's legal heirs.

Ownership in fee simple may become limited whenever the property is transferred to another *conditionally.* When this occurs, the fee simple is known as a **fee simple defeasible** (the word *defeasible* means capable of being terminated or annulled). For example, a **conveyance,** or transfer of real property, "to A and his heirs as long as the land is used for charitable purposes" creates a fee simple defeasible, because ownership of the property is conditioned on the land's being used for charitable purposes. The original owner retains a *partial* ownership interest, because if the specified condition does not occur (if the land ceases to be used for charitable purposes), then the land reverts, or returns, to the original owner. If the original owner is not living at the time, the land passes to his or her heirs.

Life Estates

A **life estate** is an estate that lasts for the life of some specified individual. A conveyance "to A for his life" creates a life estate.[5] In a life estate, the life tenant has fewer rights of ownership than the holder of a fee simple defeasible, because the rights necessarily cease to exist on the life tenant's death. The life tenant has the right to use the land, provided that he or she commits no waste (injury to the land). In other words, the life tenant cannot injure the land in a manner that would adversely affect its value. The life tenant can use the land to harvest crops or, if mines and oil wells are already on the land, can extract minerals and oil from it, but the life tenant cannot exploit the land by creating new wells or mines. The life tenant has the right to mortgage the life estate and create liens, easements, and leases; but none can extend beyond the life of the tenant. In addition, with few exceptions, the owner of a life estate has an exclusive right to possession during his or her life.

Along with these rights, the life tenant also has some duties—to keep the property in repair and to pay property taxes. In short, the owner of the life estate has the same rights as a fee simple owner except that he or she must maintain the value of the property during his or her tenancy, less the decrease in value resulting from the normal use of the property allowed by the life tenancy.

Future Interests

When an owner in fee simple absolute conveys the estate conditionally to another (such as with a fee simple defeasible) or for a limited period of time (such as with a life estate), the original owner still retains an interest in the land. The owner retains the right to repossess ownership of the land if the conditions of the fee simple defeasible are not met or when the life of the life-estate holder ends. The residuary (or leftover) interest in the property that the owner retains is called a **future interest,** because if it arises, it will only arise in the future.

If the owner retains ownership of the future interest, then the future interest is described as a **reversionary interest,** because the property will *revert* to the original owner if the condition specified in a fee simple defeasible fails or when a life tenant dies. If, however, the owner of the future

_____

5. A less common type of life estate is created by the conveyance "to A for the life of B." This is known as an estate *pur autre vie,* or an estate for the duration of the life of another.

interest transfers ownership rights in that future interest to another, the future interest is described as a **remainder.** For example, a conveyance "to A for life, then to B" creates a life estate for A and a remainder (future interest) for B. An **executory interest** is a type of future interest very similar to a remainder, the difference being that an executory interest does not take effect immediately on the expiration of another interest, such as a life estate. For example, a conveyance "to A and his (or her) heirs, as long as the premises are used for charitable purposes, and if not so used for charitable purposes, then to B" creates an executory interest in the property for B.

Nonpossessory Interests

In contrast to the types of property interests just described, some interests in land do not include any rights to possess the property. These interests are thus known as *nonpossessory interests.* Two forms of nonpossessory interests are easements and profits. A license to come onto property is also a nonpossessory interest.

An **easement** is the right of a person to make limited use of another person's real property without taking anything from the property. An easement, for example, can be the right to travel over another's property. In contrast, a **profit**[6] is the right to go onto land in possession of another and take away some part of the land itself or some product of the land. For example, Akmed, the owner of Sandy View, gives Carmen the right to go there and remove all the sand and gravel that she needs for her cement business. Carmen has a profit. Easements and profits can be classified as either *appurtenant* or *in gross.* Because easements and profits are similar and the same rules apply to both, they are discussed together.

EASEMENT OR PROFIT APPURTENANT An easement or profit appurtenant arises when the owner of one piece of land has a right to go onto (or to remove things from) an *adjacent* piece of land owned by another. Suppose that Acosta, the owner of Juniper Hills, has a right to drive his car across Green's land, Greenacres, which is adjacent to Juniper Hills. This right-of-way over Green's prop-

erty is an easement appurtenant to Juniper Hills and can be used only by the owner of Juniper Hills. Acosta can convey the easement when he conveys Juniper Hills. Now suppose that the highway is on the other side of Bancroft's property, which is on the other side of Green's property. To reach the highway, Acosta has an easement across both Green's and Bancroft's properties. Juniper Hills and Bancroft's property are not adjacent, but Green's and Bancroft's properties are, so Acosta has an easement appurtenant.

EASEMENT OR PROFIT IN GROSS An easement or profit in gross exists when one's right to use or take things from another's land does not depend on one's owning an adjacent tract of land. Suppose that Avery owns a parcel of land with a marble quarry. Avery conveys to XYZ Corporation, which owns no land, the right to come onto his land and remove up to five hundred pounds of marble per day. XYZ Corporation owns a profit in gross. When a utility company is granted an easement to run its power lines across another's property, it obtains an easement in gross.

EFFECT OF A SALE OF PROPERTY When a parcel of land that is *benefited* by an easement or profit appurtenant is sold, the property carries the easement or profit along with it. Thus, if Acosta sells Juniper Hills to Thomas and includes the appurtenant right-of-way across Green's property in the deed to Thomas, Thomas will own both the property and the easement that benefits it.

When a parcel of land that has the *burden* of an easement or profit appurtenant is sold, the new owner must recognize its existence only if he or she knew or should have known of it or if it was recorded in the appropriate office of the county. Thus, if Acosta records his easement across Green's property in the appropriate county office before Green conveys the land, the new owner of Green's property will have to allow Acosta, or any subsequent owner of Juniper Hills, to continue to use the path across Green's property.

CREATION OF AN EASEMENT OR PROFIT Easements and profits can be created by deed, by will, or by implication, necessity, or prescription. Creation by *deed* or *will* simply involves the delivery of a deed or a disposition in a will by the owner of an easement stating that the grantee (the person receiving the profit or easement) is granted the owner's rights in the easement or profit.

---

6. The term *profit*, as used here, does not refer to the "profits" made by a business firm. Rather, it means a gain or an advantage.

An easement or profit may be created by *implication* when the circumstances surrounding the division of a parcel of property imply its creation. If Barrow divides a parcel of land that has only one well for drinking water and conveys the half without a well to Jarad, a profit by implication arises, because Jarad needs drinking water.

An easement may also be created by *necessity*. An easement by necessity does not require division of property for its existence. A person who rents an apartment, for example, has an easement by necessity in the private road leading up to it.

Easements and profits by *prescription* are created in much the same way as title to property is obtained by *adverse possession* (discussed later in this chapter). An easement arises by prescription when one person exercises an easement, such as a right-of-way, on another person's land without the landowner's consent, and the use is apparent and continues for a period of time equal to the applicable statute of limitations.

TERMINATION OF AN EASEMENT OR PROFIT   An easement or profit can be terminated or extinguished in several ways. The simplest way is to deed it back to the owner of the land that is burdened by it. Another way is to abandon it and create evidence of intent to relinquish the right to use it. Mere nonuse will not extinguish an easement or profit *unless the nonuse is accompanied by an intent to abandon.* Finally, when the owner of an easement or profit becomes the owner of the property burdened by it, then it is merged into the property.

LICENSE   A **license** is the revocable right of a person to come onto another person's land. It is a personal privilege that arises from the consent of the owner of the land and that can be revoked by the owner. A ticket to attend a movie at a theater is an example of a license. Assume that a Broadway theater owner issues to Carla a ticket to see a play. If Carla is refused entry into the theater because she is improperly dressed, she has no right to force her way into the theater. The ticket is only a revocable license, not a conveyance of an interest in property.

▮ Transfer of Ownership

Ownership of real property can pass from one person to another in a number of ways. Commonly,

ownership interests in land are transferred by sale, in which case the terms of the transfer are specified in a real estate sales contract. When real property is sold or transferred as a gift, title to the property is conveyed by means of a **deed**—the instrument of conveyance of real property. We look here at transfers of real property by deed, as well as some other ways in which ownership rights in real property can be transferred.

Deeds

A valid deed must contain the following elements:

1.   The names of the buyer (grantee) and seller (grantor).
2.   Words evidencing an intent to convey the property (for example, "I hereby bargain, sell, grant, or give").
3.   A legally sufficient description of the land.
4.   The grantor's (and usually the spouse's) signature.

Additionally, to be valid, a deed must be delivered to the person to whom the property is being conveyed or to his or her agent.

WARRANTY DEEDS   Different types of deeds provide different degrees of protection against defects of title. A **warranty deed** warrants the greatest number of things and thus provides the greatest protection for the buyer, or grantee. In most states, special language is required to make a deed a general warranty deed; normally, the deed must include a written promise to protect the buyer against all claims of ownership of the property. A sample warranty deed is shown in Exhibit 29–1. Warranty deeds commonly include a number of *covenants*, or promises, that the grantor makes to the grantee.

A *covenant of seisin*[7] and a *covenant of the right to convey* warrant that the seller has title to the estate that the deed describes and the power to convey the estate, respectively. The covenant of seisin specifically assures the buyer that the grantor has the property in the purported quantity and quality.

A *covenant against encumbrances* is a covenant that the property being sold or conveyed is not

---

7.   Pronounced *see-zuhn.*

◆ **Exhibit 29–1**
A Sample Warranty Deed

Date:　May 31, 1999

Grantor:　GAYLORD A. JENTZ AND WIFE, JOANN H. JENTZ

Grantor's Mailing Address (including county):
　　　4106 North Loop Drive
　　　Austin, Travis County, Texas

Grantee:　DAVID F. FRIEND AND WIFE, JOAN E. FRIEND AS JOINT TENANTS
　　　　　WITH RIGHT OF SURVIVORSHIP
Grantee's Mailing Address (including county):
　　　5929 Fuller Drive
　　　Austin, Travis County, Texas

Consideration:
For and in consideration of the sum of Ten and No/100 Dollars ($10.00) and other
valuable consideration to the undersigned paid by the grantees herein named, the receipt of which is hereby
acknowledged, and for which no lien is retained, either express or implied.

Property (including any improvements):
Lot 23, Block "A", Northwest Hills, Green Acres Addition, Phase 4, Travis County,
Texas, according to the map or plat of record in volume 22, pages 331-336 of the
Plat Records of Travis County, Texas.

Reservations from and Exceptions to Conveyance and Warranty:

This conveyance with its warranty is expressly made subject to the following:

Easements and restrictions of record in Volume 7863, Page 53, Volume 8430,
Page 35, Volume 8133, Page 152 of the Real Property Record of Travis County,
Texas; Volume 22, Pages 335-339, of the Plat Records of Travis County, Texas;
and to any other restrictions and easements affecting said property which are
of record in Travis County, Texas.

　　Grantor, for the consideration and subject to the reservations from and exceptions to conveyance and warranty, grants,
sells, and conveys to Grantee the property, together with all and singular the rights and appurtenances thereto in any wise
belonging, to have and hold it to Grantee, Grantee's heirs, executors, administrators, successors, or assigns forever.　Grantor
binds Grantor and Grantor's heirs, executors, administrators, and successors to warrant and forever defend all and singular
the property to Grantee and Grantee's heirs, executors, administrators, successors, and assigns against every person
whomsoever lawfully claiming or to claim the same or any part thereof, except as to the reservations from and exceptions to
conveyance and warranty.

　　When the context requires, singular nouns and pronouns include the plural.

　　　　　　　　　　　　　　　　　　BY: *Gaylord A. Jentz*
　　　　　　　　　　　　　　　　　　　　Gaylord A. Jentz

　　　　　　　　　　　　　　　　　　BY: *John H. Jentz*
　　　　　　　　　　　　　　　　　　　　JoAnn H. Jentz

　　　　　　　　　　(Acknowledgment)

STATE OF TEXAS
COUNTY OF TRAVIS

　　This instrument was acknowledged before me on the　　31st day of　May　　. 1999
by Gaylord A. and JoAnn H. Jentz

　　　　　　　　　　　　　　Rosemary Potter
　　　　　　　　　　　Notary Public.State of Texas
　　　　　　　　　　　Notary's name (printed): **Rosemary Potter**

　　　　　　Notary Seal
　　　　　　　　　　　Notary's commission expires:　**1/31/2002**

subject to any outstanding rights or interests that will diminish the value of the land, except as explicitly stated. Examples of common encumbrances include mortgages, liens, profits, easements, and private deed restrictions on the use of the land.

A *covenant of quiet enjoyment* guarantees that the buyer will not be disturbed in his or her possession of the land by the seller or any third persons. For example, assume that Julio sells a two-acre lot and office building by warranty deed. Subsequently, a third person shows better title than Julio had and proceeds to evict the buyer. Here, the covenant of quiet enjoyment has been breached, and the buyer can recover the purchase price of the land plus any other damages incurred as a result of the eviction.

QUITCLAIM DEEDS A **quitclaim deed** offers the least amount of protection against defects in the title. Basically, a quitclaim deed conveys to the grantee whatever interest the grantor had; so if the grantor had no interest, then the grantee receives no interest. Quitclaim deeds are often used when the seller, or grantor, is uncertain as to the extent of his or her rights in the property.

RECORDING STATUTES Every jurisdiction has **recording statutes**, which allow deeds to be recorded. Recording a deed gives notice to the public that a certain person is now the owner of a particular parcel of real estate. Thus, prospective buyers can check the public records to see whether there have been earlier transactions creating interests or rights in specific parcels of real property. Placing everyone on notice as to the identity of the true owner is intended to prevent the previous owners from fraudulently conveying the land to other purchasers. Deeds are recorded in the county in which the property is located. Many state statutes require that the grantor sign the deed in the presence of two witnesses before it can be recorded.

Will or Inheritance

Property that is transferred on an owner's death is passed either by will or by state inheritance laws. If the owner of land dies with a will, the land passes in accordance with the terms of the will. If the owner dies without a will, state inheritance statutes prescribe how and to whom the property will pass. Transfers of property by will or inheritance are examined in detail in Chapter 30.

Adverse Possession

Adverse possession is a means of obtaining title to land without delivery of a deed. Essentially, when one person possesses the property of another for a certain statutory period of time (three to thirty years, with ten years being most common), that person, called the *adverse possessor,* acquires title to the land and cannot be removed from it by the original owner. The adverse possessor is vested with a perfect title just as if there had been a conveyance by deed.

For property to be held adversely, four elements must be satisfied:

1. Possession must be actual and exclusive; that is, the possessor must take sole physical occupancy of the property.
2. The possession must be open, visible, and notorious, not secret or clandestine. The possessor must occupy the land for all the world to see.
3. Possession must be continuous and peaceable for the required period of time. This requirement means that the possessor must not be interrupted in the occupancy by the true owner or by the courts.
4. Possession must be hostile and adverse. In other words, the possessor must claim the property as against the whole world. He or she cannot be living on the property with the permission of the owner.

There are a number of public-policy reasons for the adverse possession doctrine. These reasons include society's interest in resolving boundary disputes and determining ownership rights when title to property is in question and in assuring that real property remains in the stream of commerce. More fundamentally, policies behind the doctrine include not rewarding owners who sit on their rights too long and rewarding possessors for putting land to productive use. In the following case, the question before the court was whether a couple had obtained title to a certain portion of land by adverse possession.

CASE 29.2

Klos v. Molenda

Superior Court of Pennsylvania,
1986.
355 Pa.Super. 399,
513 A.2d 490.

FACTS   In September 1950, Michael and Albina Klos purchased part of some property in Pennsylvania owned by John and Anne Molenda. The Kloses' lot was 50 feet wide and 135 feet deep. Rather than surveying the property, the seller and buyer paced off the lot and placed stakes in the ground as boundary markers. The Kloses built a house on the lot in 1952 and put in a sidewalk along the full front. They also put in a driveway thirty inches from the stake line. They planted grass in that thirty inches and maintained it until 1984. In 1983, John Molenda died, and his widow hired a surveyor to inventory the landholdings. The survey located the rightful property line between the Molendas' and the Kloses' land as being thirty inches closer to the Kloses' house than the line established earlier. This placed the property line right along the Kloses' driveway, instead of thirty inches to the side of the driveway. Upon learning this, Anne Molenda erected a fence right along the Kloses' driveway to mark the property line. The Kloses brought an action in a Pennsylvania state court challenging Anne Molenda's conduct, claiming that they held title to the land by adverse possession. The trial court held that the Kloses had title to the land. Anne Molenda appealed.

ISSUE   Who held title to the thirty-inch strip of land?

DECISION   The Kloses held rightful title to the land. The appellate court affirmed the trial court's decision.

REASON   The rule of adverse possession holds that if a person has actual, continuous, exclusive, visible, notorious, distinct, and hostile possession of land for a long period of time (in Pennsylvania, twenty-one years), that person gains title to the land. This means that the adverse possessor must use the land in a regular, normal, and obvious manner so that the original title owner would know, on inspection, of the possessor's use. If the original title owner does not evict the possessor or otherwise exercise his or her ownership rights, then the possessor will obtain title once the statutory time period has lapsed. Here, the Kloses were certainly open, hostile, and notorious in their possession of the land in question, and they possessed the land for over thirty years. They therefore obtained title to the land by adverse possession.

FOR CRITICAL ANALYSIS—Ethical Consideration   *If the Kloses had known from the outset that the Molendas actually owned the thirty-inch strip of land, would this have affected the outcome in this case?*

Eminent Domain

Even ownership in real property in fee simple absolute is limited by a superior ownership. Just as in medieval England the king was the ultimate landowner, so in the United States the government has an ultimate ownership right in all land. This right is known as **eminent domain**, and it is some-times referred to as the condemnation power of the government to take land for public use. It gives the government a right to acquire possession of real property in the manner directed by the Constitution and the laws of the state whenever the public interest requires it. Property may be taken only for public use.

When the government takes land owned by a private party for public use, it is referred to as a **taking,** and the government must compensate the private party. Under the so-called *takings clause* of the Fifth Amendment, the government may not take private property for public use without "just compensation."

The power of eminent domain is generally invoked through condemnation proceedings. For example, when a new public highway is to be built, the government must decide where to build it and how much land to condemn. After the government determines that a particular parcel of land is necessary for public use, it brings a judicial proceeding to obtain title to the land. Then, in another proceeding, the court determines the *fair value* of the land, which is usually approximately equal to its market value.

▌Leasehold Estates

Often, real property is used by those who do not own it. A **lease** is a contract by which the owner of real property (the landlord, or lessor) grants to a person (the tenant, or lessee) an exclusive right to use and possess the property, usually for a specified period of time, in return for rent or some other form of payment. Property in the possession of a tenant is referred to as a **leasehold estate.**

The respective rights and duties of the landlord and tenant that arise under a lease agreement will be discussed shortly. Here we look at the types of leasehold estates, or tenancies, that can be created when real property is leased.

Tenancy for Years

A **tenancy for years** is created by an express contract by which property is leased for a specified period of time, such as a month, a year, or a period of years. For example, signing a one-year lease to occupy an apartment creates a tenancy for years. At the end of the period specified in the lease, the lease ends (without notice), and possession of the apartment returns to the lessor. If the tenant dies during the period of the lease, the lease interest passes to the tenant's heirs as personal property. Often, leases include renewal or extension provisions.

Periodic Tenancy

A **periodic tenancy** is created by a lease that does not specify how long it is to last but does specify that rent is to be paid at certain intervals. This type of tenancy is automatically renewed for another rental period unless properly terminated. For example, a periodic tenancy is created by a lease that states, "Rent is due on the tenth day of every month." This provision creates a tenancy from month to month. This type of tenancy can also extend from week to week or from year to year.

Under the common law, to terminate a periodic tenancy, the landlord or tenant must give one period's notice to the other party. If the tenancy extends from month to month, for example, one month's notice must be given. State statutes may require a different period for notice of termination in a periodic tenancy, however.

Tenancy at Will

Suppose that a landlord rents an apartment to a tenant "for as long as both agree." In such a situation, the tenant receives a leasehold estate known as a **tenancy at will.** Under the common law, either party can terminate the tenancy without notice (that is, "at will"). This type of estate usually arises when a tenant who has been under a tenancy for years retains possession after the termination date of that tenancy with the landlord's consent. Before the tenancy has been converted into a periodic tenancy (by the periodic payment of rent), it is a tenancy at will, terminable by either party without notice. Once the tenancy is treated as a periodic tenancy, termination notice must conform to the one already discussed for that type of tenancy. The death of either party or the voluntary commission of waste by the tenant will terminate a tenancy at will.

Tenancy at Sufferance

The mere possession of land without right is called a **tenancy at sufferance.** It is not a true tenancy. A tenancy at sufferance is not an estate, because it is created when a tenant *wrongfully* retains possession of property. Whenever a tenancy for years, periodic tenancy, or tenancy at will ends and the tenant continues to retain possession of the premises without the owner's permission, a tenancy at sufferance is created.

■ Landlord-Tenant Relationships

In the past several decades, landlord-tenant relationships have become much more complex than they were before, as has the law governing them. Generally, the law has come to apply contract doctrines, such as those providing for implied warranties and unconscionability, to the landlord-tenant relationship. Increasingly, landlord-tenant relationships have become subject to specific state and local statutes and ordinances as well. In 1972, in an effort to create more uniformity in the law governing landlord-tenant relationships, the National Conference of Commissioners on Uniform State Laws issued the Uniform Residential Landlord and Tenant Act (URLTA). We look now at how a landlord-tenant relationship is created and at the respective rights and duties of landlords and tenants.

Creating the Landlord-Tenant Relationship

A landlord-tenant relationship is established by a lease contract. As mentioned, a lease contract arises when a property owner (landlord) agrees to give another party (the tenant) the exclusive right to possess the property—usually for a price and for a specified term.

FORM OF THE LEASE   A lease contract may be oral or written. Under the common law, an oral lease is valid. As with most oral contracts, however, a party who seeks to enforce an oral lease may have difficulty proving its existence. In most states, statutes mandate that leases be in writing for some tenancies (such as those exceeding one year). To

ensure the validity of a lease agreement, it should therefore be in writing and do the following:

1.   Express an intent to establish the relationship.
2.   Provide for the transfer of the property's possession to the tenant at the beginning of the term.
3.   Provide for the landlord's reversionary interest, which entitles the property owner to retake possession at the end of the term.
4.   Describe the property—for example, give its street address.
5.   Indicate the length of the term, the amount of the rent, and how and when it is to be paid.

LEGAL REQUIREMENTS   State or local law often dictates permissible lease terms. For example, a statute or ordinance might prohibit the leasing of a structure that is in a certain physical condition or is not in compliance with local building codes. Similarly, a statute may prohibit the leasing of property for a particular purpose. For instance, a state law might prohibit gambling houses. Thus, if a landlord and tenant intend that the leased premises be used only to house an illegal betting operation, their lease is unenforceable.

A property owner cannot legally discriminate against prospective tenants on the basis of race, color, national origin, religion, gender, or disability. Similarly, a tenant cannot legally promise to do something counter to laws prohibiting discrimination. A tenant, for example, cannot legally promise to do business only with members of a particular race. The public policy underlying these prohibitions is to treat all people equally.

Often, rental properties are leased by agents of the landowner. Recall from Chapter 21 that under the theory of *respondeat superior*, a principal (a landlord, with respect to leases) is liable for the wrongful actions of his or her agent if the actions occurred within the scope of employment. At issue in the following case is whether a landlord can be held liable for his agent's discrimination on the basis of sex against a woman who sought to rent a particular apartment.

CASE 29.3
Walker v. Crigler
United States Court of Appeals,
Fourth Circuit, 1992.
976 F.2d 900.

FACTS   Darlene Walker, a single parent with one son, was looking for an apartment in Falls Church, Virginia. A real estate agent, John Moore, was assisting her in her search and took Walker to view an apartment owned by Frank Whitesell III and managed by Constance Crigler. Walker liked the apartment because it was near a school

Case 29.3—Continued

for her son and near transportation, and Moore called Crigler and told her that he had an applicant for the apartment. Crigler told Moore, and later Walker, that she would never rent to a woman in any circumstances. Walker asked Crigler if she was speaking for the owner, and Crigler said that she was. Walker sued Crigler and Whitesell in a federal district court for violating federal laws prohibiting discrimination in housing. The trial court found Crigler liable for damages in the amount of $5,000 but held that Whitesell was not liable for Crigler's actions, because he had previously instructed her, in writing, not to discriminate illegally against any potential renters. Walker appealed. (Shortly after the appeal was filed, Crigler filed for Chapter 7 bankruptcy, and a few months later the $5,000 judgment against her was discharged.)

ISSUE   Can Whitesell be held liable for Crigler's discrimination against Walker?

DECISION   Yes. The U.S. Court of Appeals for the Fourth Circuit reversed the trial court's decision on this issue. Whitesell was ordered to pay $5,000 in damages to Walker.

REASON   The trial jury had found that Crigler, because she disobeyed Whitesell's instructions, had acted outside the scope of her employment. The appellate court stated that this was an erroneous reading of the law. For one thing, the appellate court doubted whether the "mere act of instructing Crigler not to discriminate would be sufficient to justify a ruling that she was acting outside the scope of employment." In any event, whether Crigler was acting within the scope of her employment was irrelevant in this case, because the duty not to discriminate was nondelegable. The court noted that just as property owners cannot avoid responsibilities for paying taxes and meeting health and safety requirements by delegating those responsibilities to others, neither can owners avoid the duty not to discriminate through delegation of the duty. In sum, said the court, "Whitesell could not insulate himself from liability for sex discrimination in regard to living premises owned by him and managed for his benefit merely by relinquishing the responsibility for preventing such discrimination to another party."

FOR CRITICAL ANALYSIS—Ethical Consideration   *For what policy reasons do courts impose liability on landlords for their agents' actions?*

Rights and Duties

The rights and duties of landlords and tenants generally pertain to four broad areas of concern—the possession, use, and maintenance of leased property and, of course, rent.

POSSESSION   Possession involves both the obligation of the landlord to deliver possession to the tenant at the beginning of the lease term and the right of the tenant to obtain possession and retain it until the lease expires.

The covenant of quiet enjoyment mentioned previously also applies to leased premises. Under this covenant, the landlord promises that during the lease term, neither the landlord nor anyone having a superior title to the property will disturb the tenant's use and enjoyment of the property. This covenant forms the essence of the landlord-tenant relationship, and if it is breached, the tenant can terminate the lease and sue for damages.

If the landlord deprives the tenant of the tenant's possession of the leased property or interferes with the tenant's use or enjoyment of it, an **eviction** occurs. An eviction occurs, for example, when the landlord changes the lock and refuses to give the tenant a new key. A **constructive eviction** occurs when the landlord wrongfully performs or fails to perform any of the undertakings the lease requires, thereby making the tenant's further use and enjoyment of the property exceedingly difficult or impossible. Examples of constructive eviction include a landlord's failure to provide heat in the winter, light, or other essential utilities.

USE AND MAINTENANCE OF THE PREMISES   If the parties do not limit by agreement the uses to which the property may be put, the tenant may make any use of it, as long as the use is legal and reasonably relates to the purpose for which the property is adapted or ordinarily used and does not injure the landlord's interest.

The tenant is responsible for any damages to the premises that he or she causes, intentionally or negligently, and the tenant may be held liable for the cost of returning the property to the physical condition it was in at the lease's inception. Unless the parties have agreed otherwise, the tenant is not responsible for ordinary wear and tear and the property's consequent depreciation in value.

Usually, the landlord must comply with state statutes and city ordinances that delineate specific standards for the construction and maintenance of buildings. Typically, these codes contain structural requirements common to the construction, wiring, and plumbing of residential and commercial buildings. In some jurisdictions, landlords of resi-

dential property are required by statute to maintain the premises in good repair.

IMPLIED WARRANTY OF HABITABILITY   The **implied warranty of habitability** requires a landlord who leases residential property to deliver the premises to the tenant in a habitable condition—that is, in a condition that is safe and suitable for people to live in—at the beginning of a lease term and to maintain them in that condition for the lease's duration. Some state legislatures have enacted this warranty into law. In other jurisdictions, courts have based the warranty on the existence of a landlord's statutory duty to keep leased premises in good repair, or they have simply applied it as a matter of public policy.

Generally, this warranty applies to major, or *substantial*, physical defects that the landlord knows or should know about and has had a reasonable time to repair—for example, a large hole in the roof. An unattractive or annoying feature, such as a crack in the wall, may be unpleasant, but unless the crack is a structural defect or affects the residence's heating capabilities, it is probably not sufficiently substantial to make the place uninhabitable. At issue in the following case is whether specific conditions in an apartment basement constituted a violation of the implied warranty of habitability.

CASE 29.4

Weingarden v. Eagle Ridge Condominiums

Toledo Municipal Court,
Lucas County, Ohio, 1995.
71 Ohio Misc.2d 7,
653 N.E.2d 759.

FACTS   Don Weingarden notified his landlord, Eagle Ridge Condominiums, that his apartment basement leaked when it rained or when snow melted. The water soaked the carpeting and caused the growth of mildew; this rendered the basement—which was one-third of the apartment—useless and spread odor throughout the apartment. For these and other reasons, Weingarden vacated the premises before the end of the term. When his security deposit was not returned, Weingarden filed a suit in an Ohio state court against Eagle Ridge.

ISSUE   Did the conditions in the basement violate the implied warranty of habitability?

DECISION   Yes. The court ruled in Weingarden's favor.

REASON   The court pointed out that "the apartment was rented to the plaintiff with a carpeted basement, leading the tenant to believe that the basement was indeed a habitable part of the unit." The court concluded that the continuing leak, "resulting in thoroughly soaked carpeting and resultant mildew and its odors," made the basement uninhabitable.

Case 29.4—Continued   "[T]his breach of the warranty of habitability resulted in a constructive eviction of the tenant."

FOR CRITICAL ANALYSIS—Ethical Consideration   *What policy reasons justify imposing an implied warranty of habitability on landlords?*

RENT   *Rent* is the tenant's payment to the landlord for the tenant's occupancy or use of the landlord's real property. Generally, the tenant must pay the rent even if he or she refuses to occupy the property or moves out, as long as the refusal or the move is unjustifiable and the lease is in force.

Under the common law, destruction by fire or flood of a building leased by a tenant did not relieve the tenant of the obligation to pay rent and did not permit the termination of the lease. Today, however, state statutes have altered the common law rule. If the building burns down, apartment dwellers in most states are not continuously liable to the landlord for the payment of rent.

In some situations, such as when a landlord breaches the implied warranty of habitability, a tenant is allowed to withhold rent as a remedy. When rent withholding is authorized under a statute (sometimes referred to as a "rent-strike" statute), the tenant must usually put the amount withheld into an *escrow account*. This account is held in the name of the depositor (in this case, the tenant) and an *escrow agent* (in this case, usually the court or a government agency), and the funds are returnable to the depositor if the third person (in this case, the landlord) fails to fulfill the escrow condition. Generally, the tenant may withhold an amount equal to the amount by which the defect rendering the premises unlivable reduces the property's rental value. How much that is may be determined in different ways, and the tenant who withholds more than is legally permissible is liable to the landlord for the excessive amount withheld.

Transferring Rights to Leased Property

Either the landlord or the tenant may wish to transfer his or her rights to the leased property during the term of the lease.

TRANSFERRING THE LANDLORD'S INTEREST   Just as any other real property owner can sell, give away, or otherwise transfer his or her property, so can a landlord—who is, of course, the leased property's owner. If complete title to the leased property is transferred, the tenant becomes the tenant of the new owner. The new owner may collect subsequent rent but must abide by the terms of the existing lease agreement.

TRANSFERRING THE TENANT'S INTEREST   The tenant's transfer of his or her entire interest in the leased property to a third person is an *assignment of the lease*. A lease assignment is an agreement to transfer all rights, title, and interest in the lease to the assignee. It is a complete transfer. Many leases require that the assignment have the landlord's written consent, and an assignment that lacks consent can be avoided (nullified) by the landlord. A landlord who knowingly accepts rent from the assignee, however, will be held to have waived the requirement. An assignment does not terminate a tenant's liabilities under a lease agreement, however, because the tenant may assign rights but not duties. Thus, even though the assignee of the lease is required to pay rent, the original tenant is not released from the contractual obligation to pay the rent if the assignee fails to do so.

The tenant's transfer of all or part of the premises for a period shorter than the lease term is a **sublease**. The same restrictions that apply to an assignment of the tenant's interest in leased property apply to a sublease. To illustrate, a student named Derek leases an apartment for a two-year period. Although Derek had planned on attending summer school, he is offered a job in Europe for the summer months and accepts. Because he does not wish to pay three months' rent for an unoccupied apartment, Derek subleases the apartment to Darwin (the sublessee). (Derek may have to obtain his landlord's consent for this sublease if the lease requires it.) Darwin is bound by the same terms of the lease as Derek, but as in a lease assignment, Derek remains liable for the obligations under the lease if Darwin fails to fulfill them.

▌ Terms and Concepts

adverse possession 611
constructive eviction 615
conveyance 607
deed 609
easement 608
eminent domain 612
eviction 615
executory interest 608
fee simple absolute 607
fee simple defeasible 607
fixture 605

future interest 607
implied warranty of
  habitability 616
lease 613
leasehold estate 613
license 609
life estate 607
periodic tenancy 613
profit 608
quitclaim deed 611
recording statute 611

remainder 608
reversionary interest 607
sublease 617
taking 613
tenancy at sufferance 613
tenancy at will 613
tenancy for years 613
warranty deed 609

▌ Chapter Summary: Real Property

The Nature of Real Property (*See pages 604–606.*)	Real property (also called real estate or realty) is immovable. It includes land, subsurface and air rights, plant life and vegetation, and fixtures.
Ownership of Real Property (*See pages 606–609.*)	1. *Fee simple absolute*—The most complete form of ownership. 2. *Fee simple defeasible*—Ownership in fee simple that can end if a specified event or condition occurs. 3. *Life estate*—An estate that lasts for the life of a specified individual; ownership rights in a life estate are subject to the rights of the future-interest holder. 4. *Future interest*—A residuary interest not granted by the grantor in conveying an estate to another for life, for a specified period of time, or on the condition that a specific event does or does not occur. The grantor may retain the residuary interest (which is then called a reversionary interest) or transfer ownership rights in the future interest to another (the interest is then referred to as a remainder). 5. *Nonpossessory interest*—An interest that involves the right to use real property but not to possess it. Easements, profits, and licenses are nonpossessory interests.
Transfer of Ownership (*See pages 609–613.*)	1. *By deed*—When real property is sold or transferred as a gift, title to the property is conveyed by means of a deed. A deed must meet specific legal requirements. A *warranty deed* warrants the most extensive protection against defects of title. A *quitclaim deed* conveys to the grantee whatever interest the grantor had; it warrants less than any other deed. A deed may be recorded in the manner prescribed by *recording statutes* in the appropriate jurisdiction to give third parties notice of the owner's interest. 2. *By will or inheritance*—If the owner dies after having made a valid will, the land passes as specified in the will. If the owner dies without having made a will, the heirs inherit according to state inheritance statutes. 3. *By adverse possession*—When a person possesses the property of another for a statutory period of time (three to thirty years, with ten years being the most common), that person acquires title to the property, provided the possession is actual and exclusive, open and visible, continuous and peaceable, and hostile and adverse (without the permission of the owner). 4. *By eminent domain*—The government can take land for public use, with just compensation, when the public interest requires the taking.

▮ Chapter Summary: Real Property—Continued

Leasehold Estates *(See pages 613–614.)*	A leasehold estate is an interest in real property that is held only for a limited period of time, as specified in the lease agreement. Types of tenancies relating to leased property include the following: 1. *Tenancy for years*—Tenancy for a period of time stated by express contract. 2. *Periodic tenancy*—Tenancy for a period determined by the frequency of rent payments; automatically renewed unless proper notice is given. 3. *Tenancy at will*—Tenancy for as long as both parties agree; no notice of termination is required. 4. *Tenancy at sufferance*—Possession of land without legal right.

Landlord-Tenant Relationships
(See pages 614–617.)
	1. *Lease agreement*—The landlord-tenant relationship is created by a lease agreement. State or local laws may dictate whether the lease must be in writing and what lease terms are permissible.
	
	2. *Rights and duties*—The rights and duties that arise under a lease agreement generally pertain to the following areas:
	  a. Possession—The tenant has an exclusive right to possess the leased premises, which must be available to the tenant at the agreed-on time. Under the covenant of quiet enjoyment, the landlord promises that during the lease term neither the landlord nor anyone having superior title to the property will disturb the tenant's use and enjoyment of the property.
	  b. Use and maintenance of the premises—Unless the parties agree otherwise, the tenant may make any legal use of the property. The tenant is responsible for any damage that he or she causes. The landlord must comply with laws that set specific standards for the maintenance of real property. The implied warranty of habitability requires that a landlord furnish and maintain residential premises in a habitable condition (that is, in a condition safe and suitable for human life).
	  c. Rent—The tenant must pay the rent as long as the lease is in force, unless the tenant justifiably refuses to occupy the property or withholds the rent because of the landlord's failure to maintain the premises properly.
	
	3. *Transferring rights to leased property*—
	  a. If the landlord transfers complete title to the leased property, the tenant becomes the tenant of the new owner. The new owner may then collect the rent but must abide by the existing lease.
	  b. Generally, tenants may assign their rights (but not their duties) under a lease contract to a third person. Tenants may also sublease leased property to a third person, but the original tenant is not relieved of any obligations to the landlord under the lease. In either case, the landlord's consent may be required.

▮ For Review

1. What can a person who holds property in fee simple absolute do with the property? Can a person who holds property as a life estate do the same?

2. What are the requirements for acquiring property by adverse possession?

3. What limitations may be imposed on the rights of property owners?

4. What is a leasehold estate? What types of leasehold estates, or tenancies, can be created when real property is leased?

5. What are the respective duties of the landlord and tenant concerning the use and maintenance of leased property? Is the tenant responsible for all damages that he or she causes, intentionally or negligently?

▌ Questions and Case Problems

29–1. Tenant's Rights and Responsibilities. You are a student in college and plan to attend classes for nine months. You sign a twelve-month lease for an apartment. Discuss fully each of the following situations.

(a) You have a summer job in another town and wish to assign the balance of your lease (three months) to a fellow student who will be attending summer school. Can you do so?

(b) You are graduating in May. The lease will have three months remaining. Can you terminate the lease without liability by giving a thirty-day notice to the landlord?

29–2. Property Ownership. Antonio is the owner of a lakeside house and lot. He deeds the house and lot "to my wife, Angela, for life, then to my son, Charles." Given these facts, answer the following questions:

(a) Does Antonio have any ownership interest in the lakeside house after making these transfers? Explain.

(b) What is Angela's interest called? Is there any limitation on her rights to use the property as she wishes?

(c) What is Charles's interest called? Why?

29–3. Property Ownership. Lorenz was a wanderer twenty-two years ago. At that time, he decided to settle down on an unoccupied, three-acre parcel of land that he did not own. People in the area indicated to him that they had no idea who owned the property. Lorenz built a house on the land, got married, and raised three children while living there. He fenced in the land, placed a gate with a sign above it that read "Lorenz's Homestead," and had trespassers removed. Lorenz is now confronted by Joe Reese, who has a deed in his name as owner of the property. Reese, claiming ownership of the land, orders Lorenz and his family off the property. Discuss who has the better "title" to the property.

29–4. Deeds. Wiley and Gemma are neighbors. Wiley's lot is extremely large, and his present and future use of it will not involve the entire area. Gemma wants to build a single-car garage and driveway along the present lot boundary. Because of ordinances requiring buildings to be set back fifteen feet from an adjoining property line, and because of the placement of her existing structures, Gemma cannot build the garage. Gemma contracts to purchase ten feet of Wiley's property along their boundary line for $3,000. Wiley is willing to sell but will give Gemma only a quitclaim deed, whereas Gemma wants a warranty deed. Discuss the differences between these deeds as they would affect the rights of the parties if the title to this ten feet of land later proved to be defective.

29–5. Leased Property. The landlord of an apartment building leased a building he owned nearby for use as a cocktail lounge. The residential tenants complained to the landlord about the late evening and early morning music and disturbances coming from the lounge. Although the lease for the lounge provided that entertainment had to be conducted so that it could not be heard outside the building and would not disturb the apartment tenants, the landlord was unsuccessful in remedying the problem. The tenants vacated their apartments. Was the landlord successful in his suit to collect rent from the tenants who vacated the premises? Discuss. [*Blackett v. Olanoff*, 371 Mass. 714, 358 N.E.2d 817 (1977)]

29–6. Easements. In 1882, Moses Webster owned a parcel of land that extended down to the Atlantic Ocean. He conveyed the strip of the property fronting the ocean to another party. The deed included the following statement: "Reserve being had for said Moses Webster the right of way by land or water." The strip of property is now owned by Margaret Williams, and the portion retained by Webster now belongs to Thomas O'Neill. Williams is denying O'Neill access to the ocean. O'Neill has brought an action to establish his title to an easement over Williams's property. What should the court decide? Discuss fully. [*O'Neill v. Williams*, 527 A.2d 322 (Me. 1987)]

29–7. Adverse Possession. As the result of a survey in 1976, the Nolans discovered that their neighbor's garage extended more than a foot onto their property. Nolan requested that his neighbor, Naab, tear down the garage. The Naabs refused to do this, stating that the garage had been built in 1952 and had been on the property when the Naabs purchased it in 1973. In West Virginia, where these properties were located, there is a ten-year statute of limitations covering adverse possession of property. Were the Naabs able to claim title to the land on which the garage was situated by adverse possession? Explain. [*Naab v. Nolan*, 327 S.E.2d 151 (W.Va.1985)]

29–8. Maintenance of Leased Premises. Inwood North Professional Group—Phase I leased medical office space to Joseph Davidow, a physician. The terms of the five-year lease specified that Inwood would provide electricity, hot water, air conditioning, janitorial and maintenance services, light fixtures, and security services. During his tenancy, Davidow encountered a number of problems. The roof leaked, and the air conditioning did not function properly. The premises were not cleaned and maintained by Inwood as promised in the lease agreement, and as a consequence, rodents and pests infested the premises, and trash littered the parking area. There was frequently no hot water, and at one point Davidow was without electricity for several days because Inwood had not paid the bill. About a year prior to the lease's expiration, Davidow moved to another office building and refused to pay the remaining rent due under the lease. Inwood sued for the unpaid rent. Must Davidow pay the remaining rent due under the lease? Discuss. [*Davidow v. Inwood North Professional Group—Phase I*, 747 S.W.2d 373 (Tex. 1988)]

29–9. The Lease Contract. Christine Callis formed a lease agreement with Colonial Properties, Inc., to lease property in a shopping center in Montgomery, Alabama. Callis later alleged that before signing the lease agreement, she had told a representative of Colonial that she wanted to locate in a shopping center that would attract a wealthy clientele, and the representative had assured her that no discount stores would be allowed to lease space in the shopping center. The written lease agreement, which Callis signed, contained a clause stating that "[n]o representation, inducement, understanding or anything of any nature whatsoever made, stated or represented on Landlord's behalf, either orally or in writing (except this Lease), has induced Tenant to enter into this lease." The lease also stipulated that Callis would not conduct any type of business commonly called a discount store, surplus store, or other similar business. Later, Colonial did, in fact, lease space to discount stores, and Callis sued Colonial for breach of the lease contract. Will Callis succeed in her claim? Discuss fully. [*Callis v. Colonial Properties, Inc.*, 597 So.2d 660 (Ala. 1991)]

29–10. Easements. Merton Peterson owned a golf course, a supper club, and the parking lot between them. Both golfers and club patrons always parked in the lot. Peterson sold the club and the lot to the American Legion, which sold them to VBC, Inc. (owned by Richard Beck and others). When VBC demanded rent from Peterson for use of the lot, Peterson filed a suit in a South Dakota state court to determine title. On what basis might the court hold that Peterson has an easement for the use of the lot? Does Peterson have an easement? [*Peterson v. Beck*, 537 N.W.2d 375 (S.Dak. 1995)]

▌Accessing the Internet: Fundamentals of Business Law

Cornell Law University's Legal Information Institute has links to state statutes governing property for several of the states. To access these statutes, go to

http://fatty.law.cornell.edu/topics/state_statutes.html

Homes and Communities is a Web site offered by the U.S. Department of Housing and Urban Development. Information of interest to both consumers and businesses is available at this site, which can be accessed at

http://www.hud.gov/

Information on the buying and financing of homes, as well as the full text of the Real Estate Settlement Procedures Act, is online at

http://www.hud.gov/fha/fhahome.html

For answers to frequently asked questions on Veterans Administration home loans, go to

http://www.va.gov/vas/loan/index.htm

The Internet Law Library of the House of Representatives offers extensive links to sources of law relating to real estate. Go to

http://law.house.gov/home.htm

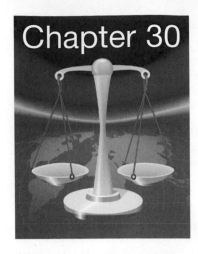

Chapter 30

Insurance, Wills, and Trusts

CHAPTER OBJECTIVES

After reading this chapter, you should be able to:

1. Indicate when an insurable interest arises in regard to life and property insurance.
2. Distinguish between an insurance broker and an insurance agent.
3. Summarize some of the clauses that are typically included in insurance contracts.
4. Describe the requirements of a valid will.
5. Explain how property is transferred when a person dies without a valid will.

Most individuals insure both real and personal property (as well as their lives). By insuring our property, we protect ourselves against damage and loss. After discussing insurance, which is a foremost concern of all property owners, we examine how property is transferred on the death of its owner. Certainly, the laws of succession of property are a necessary corollary to the concept of private ownership of property. Our laws require that on death, title to the property of a decedent (one who has recently died) must be delivered in full somewhere. In this chapter we see that this can be done by will, through trusts, or through state laws prescribing distribution of property among heirs or next of kin.

▌ Insurance

Insurance is a contract by which the insurance company (the insurer) promises to pay a sum of money or give something of value to another (either the insured or the beneficiary) in the event that the insured is injured, dies, or sustains damage to his or her property as a result of particular, stated contingencies. Basically, insurance is an arrangement for *transferring and allocating risk*. In many cases, **risk** can be described as a prediction concerning potential loss based on known and unknown factors. Insurance, however, involves much more than a game of chance.

Many precautions may be taken to protect against the hazards of life. For example, an individual may wear a seat belt to protect against automobile injuries or install smoke detectors to guard against injury from the risk of fire. Of course, no one can predict whether an accident or a fire will ever occur, but individuals and businesses must establish plans to protect their personal and financial interests should some event threaten to undermine their security. This concept is known as **risk management.** The most common method of risk management is the transfer of certain risks from the individual to the insurance company.

Risk is transferred to an insurance company by a contractual agreement. The insurance contract and its provisions will be examined shortly. First, however, we look at the different types of insurance that can be obtained, insurance terminology, and the concept of insurable interest.

Classifications of Insurance

Insurance is classified according to the nature of the risk involved. For example, fire insurance, casualty insurance, life insurance, and title insurance apply to different types of risk. Furthermore, policies of these types differ in the persons and interests that they protect. This is reasonable, because the types of losses that are expected and the types that are foreseeable or unforeseeable vary with the nature of the activity. Exhibit 30–1 presents a list of insurance classifications.

Insurance Terminology

An insurance contract is called a **policy;** the consideration paid to the insurer is called a **premium;** and the insurance company is sometimes called an **underwriter.**

The parties to an insurance policy are the *insurer* (the insurance company) and the *insured* (the person covered by the insurer's provisions or the holder of the policy). Insurance contracts are usually obtained through an *agent*, who ordinarily works for the insurance company, or through a *broker*, who is ordinarily an *independent contractor*. When a broker deals with an applicant for insurance, the broker is, in effect, the applicant's agent. In contrast, an insurance agent is an agent of the insurance company, not of the applicant. As a general rule, the insurance company is bound by the acts of its agents when they act within the agency relationship (discussed in Chapter 21). A broker, however, normally has no relationship with the insurance company and is an agent of the insurance applicant. In most situations, state law determines the status of all parties writing or obtaining insurance.

Insurable Interest

A person can insure anything in which he or she has an **insurable interest**. Without this insurable interest, there is no enforceable contract, and a transaction to insure would have to be treated as a wager. In regard to real and personal property, an insurable interest exists when the insured derives a pecuniary benefit (a benefit consisting of or relating to money) from the preservation and continued existence of the property. Put another way, one has an insurable interest in property when one would sustain a pecuniary loss from its destruction. In regard to life insurance, a person must have a reasonable expectation of benefit from the continued life of another in order to have an insurable interest in that person's life. The benefit may be pecuniary (as with so-called *key-person insurance*, which insures the lives of important employees, usually in small companies), or it may be founded on the relationship between the parties (by blood or affinity).

For property insurance, the insurable interest must exist at the time the loss occurs but need not exist when the policy is purchased. In contrast, for life insurance, the insurable interest must exist at the time the policy is obtained. The existence of an insurable interest is a primary concern in determining liability under an insurance policy.

The Insurance Contract

An insurance contract is governed by the general principles of contract law, although the insurance industry is heavily regulated by each state. Several aspects of the insurance contract will be treated here, including the application for insurance, when the contract takes effect, important contract provisions, cancellation of the policy, and defenses that can be raised by insurance companies against payment on a policy.

APPLICATION The filled-in application form for insurance is usually attached to the policy and

◆ Exhibit 30–1
Insurance Classifications

TYPE OF INSURANCE	COVERAGE
Accident	Covers expenses, losses, and suffering incurred by the insured because of accidents causing physical injury and any consequent disability; sometimes includes a specified payment to heirs of the insured if death results from an accident.
All-risk	Covers all losses that the insured may incur except those resulting from fraud on the part of the insured.
Automobile	May cover damage to automobiles resulting from specified hazards or occurrences (such as fire, vandalism, theft, or collision); normally provides protection against liability for personal injuries and property damage resulting from the operation of the vehicle.
Casualty	Protects against losses that may be incurred by the insured as a result of being held liable for personal injuries or property damage sustained by others.
Credit	Pays to a creditor the balance of a debt on the disability, death, insolvency, or bankruptcy of the debtor; often offered by lending institutions.
Decreasing-term life	Provides life insurance; requires uniform payments over the life (term) of the policy, but with a decreasing face value (amount of coverage).
Employer's liability	Insures employers against liability for injuries or losses sustained by employees during the course of their employment; covers claims not covered under workers' compensation insurance.
Fidelity or guaranty	Provides indemnity against losses in trade or losses caused by the dishonesty of employees, the insolvency of debtors, or breaches of contract.
Fire	Covers losses caused to the insured as a result of fire.
Floater	Covers movable property, as long as the property is within the territorial boundaries specified in the contract.
Group	Provides individual life, medical, or disability insurance coverage but is obtainable through a group of persons, usually employees; the policy premium is paid either entirely by the employer or partially by the employer and partially by the employee.
Health	Covers expenses incurred by the insured resulting from physical injury or illness and other expenses relating to health and life maintenance.
Homeowners'	Protects homeowners against some or all risks of loss to their residences and the residences' contents or liability arising from the use of the property.
Key-person	Protects a business in the event of the death or disability of a key employee.
Liability	Protects against liability imposed on the insured resulting from injuries to the person or property of another.
Life	Covers the death of the policyholder. Upon the death of the insured, an amount specified in the policy is paid by the insurer to the insured's beneficiary.

◆ **Exhibit 30–1**
Insurance Classifications—Continued

TYPE OF INSURANCE	COVERAGE
Major medical	Protects the insured against major hospital, medical, or surgical expenses.
Malpractice	Protects professionals (doctors, lawyers, and others) against malpractice claims brought against them by their patients or clients; a form of liability insurance.
Marine	Covers movable property, including ships, freight, and cargo, against certain perils or navigation risks during a specific voyage or time period.
Mortgage	Covers a mortgage loan; the insurer pays the balance of the mortgage to the creditor on the death or disability of the debtor.
No-fault auto	Covers personal injury and (sometimes) property damage resulting from automobile accidents. The insured submits his or her claims to his or her own insurance company, regardless of who was at fault. A person may sue the party at fault or that party's insurer only in cases involving serious medical injury and consequent high medical costs. Governed by state "no-fault" statutes.
Term life	Provides life insurance for a specified period of time (term) with no cash surrender value; usually renewable.
Title	Protects against any defects in title to real property and any losses incurred as a result of existing claims against or liens on the realty at the time of purchase.

made a part of the insurance contract. Thus, an insurance applicant is bound by any false statements that appear in the application (subject to certain exceptions). Because the insurance company evaluates the risk factors based on the information included in the insurance application, misstatements or misrepresentations can void a policy, especially if the insurance company can show that it would not have extended insurance if it had known the true facts.

EFFECTIVE DATE   The effective date of an insurance contract is important. In some instances, the insurance applicant is not protected until a formal written policy is issued. In other situations, the applicant is protected between the time the application is received and the time the insurance company either accepts or rejects it. Four facts should be kept in mind:

1.   A broker is merely the agent of an applicant. Therefore, until the broker obtains a policy, the applicant normally is not insured.
2.   A person who seeks insurance from an insurance company's agent will usually be protected from the moment the application is made, provided—in the case of life insurance—that some form of premium has been paid. Between the time the application is received and either rejected or accepted, the applicant is covered (possibly subject to medical examination). Usually, the agent will write a memorandum, or **binder,** indicating that a policy is pending and stating its essential terms.
3.   If the parties agree that the policy will be issued and delivered at a later time, the contract is not effective until the policy is issued and delivered or sent to the applicant, depending on the agreement. Thus, any loss sustained between the time of application and the delivery of the policy is not covered.
4.   Parties may agree that a life insurance policy will be binding at the time the insured pays the first premium, or the policy may be expressly contingent on the applicant's passing a physical examination. In the latter situation, if the applicant pays the premium and passes the examination, then the policy coverage is in effect. If the applicant pays the premium but dies before having the physical examination, then to collect, the applicant's estate must show that the applicant would have passed the examination had he or she not died.

In the following case, the court had to decide whether a policy that required an applicant to be "still insurable" on the effective date of the policy should prevent the beneficiary from recovering.

CASE 30.1

Life Insurance Co. of North America v. Cichowlas

District Court of Appeal of Florida, Fourth District, 1995.
659 So.2d 1333.

FACTS Waldemar Cichowlas applied to the Life Insurance Company of North America (LINA) for insurance naming his wife Ewa as beneficiary. The application asked if he had been hospitalized during the past five years and if he had ever been treated for lung disease. A yes answer would have affected his insurability. Waldemar truthfully answered no. The policy required that an applicant be "still insurable" on the effective date of the policy. Three weeks before the policy took effect, Waldemar was hospitalized with a lung disease. He did not tell LINA. When he died of other causes, LINA refused to pay Ewa. She filed a suit in a Florida state court against the insurer. The court ordered LINA to pay. The insurer appealed.

ISSUE Did the requirement that Waldemar be "still insurable" on the effective date of the policy prevent Ewa from recovering?

DECISION Yes. The District Court of Appeal of Florida reversed the judgment of the lower court and remanded the case.

REASON The state intermediate appellate court explained that "[c]lauses requiring that an applicant remain insurable between the filing of the application and the delivery of the policy have traditionally been approved by Florida courts." The court noted that "Mr. Cichowlas was not insurable on the effective date of the policy." Thus, "the 'still insurable' clause precluded recovery for" Ewa.

FOR CRITICAL ANALYSIS—Ethical Consideration *What effect might it have had on the outcome of this case if the court had held that LINA had a continuing duty to ask about the health of its applicants?*

PROVISIONS AND CLAUSES Some of the important provisions and clauses contained in insurance contracts are listed and defined in Exhibit 30–2. The courts are increasingly cognizant of the fact that most people do not have the special training necessary to understand the intricate terminology used in insurance policies. Thus, the words used in an insurance contract have their ordinary meanings. They are interpreted by the courts in light of the nature of the coverage involved.

When there is an ambiguity in the policy, the provision generally is interpreted against the insurance company. When the written policy has not been delivered and it is unclear whether an insurance contract actually exists, the uncertainty normally will be resolved against the insurance company. The court will presume that the policy is in effect unless the company can show otherwise. Similarly, an insurer must take care to make sure that the insured is adequately notified of any change in coverage under an existing policy.

CANCELLATION The insured can cancel a policy at any time, and the insurer can cancel under certain circumstances. When an insurance company can cancel its insurance contract, the policy or a state statute usually requires that the insurer give advance written notice of the cancellation to the insured.

The insurer may cancel an insurance policy for various reasons, depending on the type of insurance. For example, automobile insurance can be canceled for nonpayment of premiums or suspension of the insured's driver's license. Property insur-

♦ **Exhibit 30–2**
Insurance Contract Provisions and Clauses

Incontestability clause	An incontestability clause provides that after a policy has been in force for a specified length of time—usually two or three years—the insurer cannot contest statements made in the application.
Coinsurance clause	A coinsurance clause provides that if the owner insures his or her property up to a specified percentage—usually 80 percent—of its value, he or she will recover any loss up to the face amount of the policy. If the insurance is for less than the fixed percentage, the owner is responsible for a proportionate share of the loss.
Appraisal clause	Insurance policies frequently provide that if the parties cannot agree on the amount of a loss covered under the policy or the value of the property lost, an appraisal, or estimate, by an impartial and qualified third party can be demanded.
Arbitration clause	Many insurance policies include clauses that call for arbitration of disputes that may arise between the insurer and the insured concerning the settlement of claims.
Antilapse clause	An antilapse clause provides that the policy will not automatically lapse if no payment is made on the date due. Ordinarily, under such a provision, the insured has a *grace period* of thirty or thirty-one days within which to pay an overdue premium before the policy is canceled.
Cancellation	Cancellation of an insurance policy can occur for various reasons, depending on the type of insurance. When an insurance company can cancel its insurance contract, the policy or a state statute usually requires that the insurer give advance written notice of the cancellation. An insurer cannot cancel—or refuse to renew—a policy because of the national origin or race of an applicant or because the insured has appeared as a witness in a case against the company.

ance can be canceled for nonpayment of premiums or for other reasons, including the insured's fraud or misrepresentation, conviction for a crime that increases the hazard insured against, or gross negligence that increases the hazard insured against. Life and health policies can be canceled because of false statements made by the insured in the application. An insurer cannot cancel—or refuse to renew—a policy for discriminatory rea-

sons or other reasons that violate public policy, or because the insured has appeared as a witness in a case against the company.

State laws normally impose specific requirements relating to insurance policy cancellations. In the following case, the plaintiff claimed that the insurer had not complied with the state's statutory requirements governing policy cancellation.

CASE 30.2

Clyburn v. Allstate Insurance Co.

United States District Court,
District of South Carolina, 1993.
826 F.Supp. 955.

FACTS William Clyburn's house burned to the ground. Because two years had passed since he had paid a premium on his policy with the Allstate Insurance Company, Allstate refused to cover the loss. Clyburn sued Allstate in a federal district court, claiming that the policy had not been canceled. To cancel a policy, a state statute required an insurer to send written notice to both the insured and the insurer's agent of record. Allstate argued that it had properly notified

(Continued)

Case 30.2—Continued

Clyburn in writing of the cancellation and had also notified Clyburn's agent of record, Thomas Young, by sending Young a computer diskette containing the cancellation notice. The jury found in Clyburn's favor, concluding that Allstate had sent written notice to Clyburn but not to Young, the agent of record. Allstate moved for either a new trial or a judgment notwithstanding the verdict (*n.o.v.*).

ISSUE   Can notice included on a computer diskette constitute "written notice"?

DECISION   Yes. Because the factual issue of whether Allstate had actually sent a diskette to its agent still needed to be resolved, however, the court granted Allstate's motion for a new trial.

REASON   The district court held that notice on a diskette could constitute written notice. The court pointed out that "other media forms," including videotapes and tape recordings, "are recognized as 'writings.'" Referring to "today's 'paperless' society of computer generated information," the court reasoned that "[t]he storage of information on tape recordings and videotapes is not that much different from that on floppy diskettes for computers, but rather is more a difference in the devices used to read the information."

FOR CRITICAL ANALYSIS—Technological Consideration   *Can you think of other examples of how technological changes have challenged traditional legal terminology?*

DEFENSES AGAINST PAYMENT   In attempting to avoid payment on a policy claim, an insurance company can raise any of the defenses that would be valid in any ordinary action on a contract, as well as some defenses that do not apply in ordinary contract actions. If the insurance company can show that the policy was procured by fraud, misrepresentation, or violation of warranties, it may have a valid defense for not paying on a claim. Improper actions, such as those that are against public policy or that are otherwise illegal, can also give the insurance company a defense against the payment of a claim or allow it to rescind the contract.

An insurance company can be prevented from asserting some defenses that are normally available, however. For example, if a company tells an insured that information requested on a form is optional, and the insured provides it anyway, the company cannot use the information to avoid its contractual obligation under the insurance contract. Similarly, incorrect statements as to the age of the insured normally do not allow the insurer to avoid payment on the death of the insured.

▌Wills

Private ownership of property leads logically to both the protection of that property by insurance coverage while the owner is alive and the transfer of that property on the death of the owner to those designated in the owner's will. A **will** is the final declaration of how a person desires to have his or her property disposed of after death.

At common law, people had no way to control the distribution of their property after death. The power of transfer or distribution is derived solely from statutes originating in feudal England that strictly controlled the transfer of property at death. The heir (the one who inherited) was required to pay the feudal lord a sum of money[1] for the privilege of succeeding to his or her ancestor's lands. When a tenant died without heirs, title to the land reverted to the feudal lord of the manor.

---

1.   The sum, called a *relief,* was usually equivalent to one year's rent.

Sweeping land reforms in England during the 1920s replaced inheritance payments and reversion of title to the feudal lord with the right of the Crown to receive inheritance taxes and to take the property of an **intestate** (one who dies without a valid will) who died without heirs. Modern legislation has changed the terminology but not the result. Today, in the United States, title to the land of persons who die intestate and without heirs reverts to the state.

A will, because it is a person's "last will and testament," is referred to as a *testamentary disposition* of property. It is a formal instrument that must follow exactly the requirements of state law to be effective. The reasoning behind such a strict requirement is obvious. A will becomes effective only after death. No attempts to modify it after the death of the maker are allowed, because the court cannot ask the maker to confirm the attempted modifications. (Sometimes, however, the wording of the will must be "interpreted" by the courts.) A will can serve other purposes besides the distribution of property. It can appoint a guardian for minor children or incapacitated adults. It can also appoint a *personal representative* to settle the affairs of the deceased. Exhibit 30–3 presents a copy of one of the many wills purportedly written by Howard Hughes, the reclusive American film producer and manufacturer.

Terminology of Wills

A person who makes out a will is known as a **testator** (from the Latin *testari*, "to make a will"). The court responsible for administering any legal problems surrounding a will is called a *probate court*, as mentioned in Chapter 2. When a person dies, a personal representative administers the estate and settles finally all of the decedent's (deceased person's) affairs. An **executor** is a personal representative named in the will; an **administrator** is a personal representative appointed by the court for a decedent who dies without a will, who fails to name an executor in the will, who names an executor lacking the capacity to serve, or who writes a will that the court refuses to admit to probate.

A gift of real estate by will is generally called a **devise,** and a gift of personal property by will is called a **bequest,** or **legacy.** The recipient of a gift by will is a **devisee** or **legatee,** depending on whether the gift was a devise or a legacy.

Types of Gifts

Gifts by will can be specific, general, or residuary. A *specific* devise or bequest (legacy) describes particular property (such as "Eastwood Estate" or "my gold pocket watch") that can be distinguished from all the rest of the testator's property. A *general* devise or bequest (legacy) uses less restrictive terminology. For example, "I devise all my lands" is a general devise. A general bequest often specifies a sum of money instead of a particular item of property, such as a watch or an automobile. For example, "I give to my nephew, Carleton, $30,000" is a general bequest.

If the assets of an estate are insufficient to pay in full all general bequests provided for in the will, an *abatement*, by which the legatees receive reduced benefits, takes place. If a legatee dies prior to the death of the testator or before the legacy is payable, a *lapsed legacy* results. At common law, the legacy failed. Today, the legacy may not lapse if the legatee is in a certain blood relationship to the testator (such as a child, grandchild, brother, or sister) and has left a child or other surviving descendant.

Sometimes a will provides that any assets remaining after specific gifts have been made and debts are paid—called the *residuum*—are to be distributed through a *residuary* clause. A residuary clause is used when the exact amount to be distributed cannot be determined until all of the other gifts and payouts have been made. A residuary clause can pose problems, however, when the will does not specifically name the beneficiaries to receive the residuum. In such a situation, if the court cannot determine the testator's intent, the residuum passes according to state laws of intestacy.

Probate Procedures

To *probate* a will means to establish its validity and to carry the administration of the estate through a court process. Probate laws vary from state to state. In 1969, however, the American Bar Association and the National Conference of Commissioners on Uniform State Laws approved the Uniform Probate Code (UPC). The UPC codifies general principles and procedures for the resolution of conflicts in settling estates and relaxes some of the requirements for a valid will contained in earlier state laws. About a third of the states have adopted some form of the UPC. Because succession and

♦ Exhibit 30–3
  A Sample Will

Jan. 11/72

    This is my Last Will and Testament

(1)   I hereby revoke all Wills and testamentary dispositions of every nature
or kind whatsoever made by me before this date.

(2)   I nominate, constitute, and appoint my counsel Chester C. Davis, sole
executor and trustee of this my Last Will and Testament . . .

(3)   I give, devise, and bequeath all my monies, holdings, property of every
nature and kind, all of my possessions and any profits of the before
mentioned to the Howard Hughes Medical Institute for the use of medical
research and the betterment of medical and health standards around the
world.

(4)   I hereby direct my trustee Chester Davis and my assistants Nadine Henley
and Frank Gay to continue in their positions and duties, and to also
assume a controlling interest in management in the Medical Institute, to
decide, direct, and implement policies and funds for the proper uses of
the Medical Institute in the areas of medical research and the
betterment of world health and medical standards.

(5)   I hereby request that my trustee make known to any business associates,
aides, or confidants who wish to, or have undertaken a written
documentation of any or all parts of my life, the terms of the Rosemont
Enterprises agreement and possible infringements thereof—because of
the conditions of that document.

(6)   I hereby direct my trustee to instruct Rosemont Enterprises to complete
all written, visual, and audio documentation in the presentation of the
factual representation of my life for public release two years to the
day, after my death.

(7)   I authorize my trustee to make funds available limited to one quarter of
the total estate to a private agency of my trustee's choice, in the event
of my death by unnatural or man-made causes; to apprehend such person or
group of persons and to bring them within full prosecution of the law;
the funds being made available for legal expenses and costs incurred on
behalf of the trustee's appointed agency.

(8)   I wish to make known to my trustee that I did not at any time enter into
any contracts, agreements, or promises either oral or written, that
transferred gave or bequeathed the bulk or any part of my estate to any
person, persons, organizations, or whatever other than the Howard
Hughes Medical Institute. I sign this as my Last Will and Testament.

                                       /S/ Howard R. Hughes
                                       Jan. 11,1972

inheritance laws vary widely among states, one should always check the particular laws of the state involved.[2] Typically, probate procedures vary, depending on the size of the decedent's estate.

INFORMAL PROBATE   For smaller estates, most state statutes provide for the distribution of assets without formal probate proceedings. Faster and less expensive methods are then used. For example, property can be transferred by affidavit (a written statement taken before a person who has authority to affirm it), and problems or questions can be handled during an administrative hearing. In addition, some state statutes provide that title to cars, savings and checking accounts, and certain other property can be passed merely by filling out forms.

A majority of states also provide for *family settlement agreements*, which are private agreements among the beneficiaries. Once a will is admitted to probate, the family members can agree to settle among themselves the distribution of the decedent's assets. Although a family settlement agreement speeds the settlement process, a court order is still needed to protect the estate from future creditors and to clear title to the assets involved. The use of these and other types of summary procedures in estate administration can save time and money.

FORMAL PROBATE   For larger estates, normally formal probate proceedings are undertaken, and the probate court supervises every aspect of the settlement of the decedent's estate. Additionally, in some situations—such as when a guardian for minor children or for an incompetent person must be appointed, and a trust has been created to protect the minor or the incompetent person—more formal probate procedures cannot be avoided. Formal probate proceedings may take several months to complete, and as a result, a sizable portion of the decedent's assets (up to perhaps 10 percent) may have to go toward payment of court costs and fees charged by attorneys and personal representatives.

PROPERTY TRANSFERS OUTSIDE THE PROBATE PROCESS   In the ordinary situation, a person can employ various will substitutes to avoid the cost of probate—for example, *inter vivos* trusts (discussed later in this chapter), life insurance policies with named beneficiaries, or joint-tenancy arrangements. Not all methods are suitable for every estate, but there are alternatives to complete probate administration.

Requirements for a Valid Will

A will must comply with statutory formalities designed to ensure that the testator understood his or her actions at the time the will was made. These formalities are intended to help prevent fraud. Unless they are followed, the will is declared void, and the decedent's property is distributed according to the laws of intestacy of that state. The requirements are not uniform among the jurisdictions. Most states, however, uphold certain basic requirements for executing a will. We now look at these requirements.

TESTAMENTARY CAPACITY   For a will to be valid, the testator must have testamentary capacity—that is, the testator must be of legal age and sound mind *at the time the will is made*. The legal age for executing a will varies, but in most states and under the UPC the minimum age is eighteen years [UPC 2–501]. Thus, the will of a twenty-one-year-old decedent written when the person was sixteen is invalid if, under state law, the legal age for executing a will is eighteen.

The concept of "being of sound mind" refers to the testator's ability to formulate and to comprehend a personal plan for the disposition of property. Generally, a testator must (1) intend the document to be his or her last will and testament, (2) comprehend the kind and character of the property being distributed, and (3) comprehend and remember the "natural objects of his or her bounty" (usually, family members and persons for whom the testator has affection).

In the following case, the question before the court was whether the testator had the required testamentary capacity. As the court notes, testamentary capacity will be presumed unless sufficient evidence exists to call such capacity into question.

---

2.   For example, California law differs substantially from the UPC.

CASE 30.3

Bolan v. Bolan
Supreme Court of Alabama, 1993.
611 So.2d 1051.

FACTS On Charley Bolan's death, he was survived by six children. His will left one dollar to each of three of his children and to each child of his deceased son ("the contestants") and the remainder of his estate to the other three children ("the proponents"). The contestants claimed that the will was invalid, alleging, among other things, that Charley lacked testamentary capacity at the time he made the will. The evidence before the court was conflicting. Witnesses present at the time the will was executed testified that Charley was in sound mental condition on that occasion, and other family members testified to the same effect. Other testimony, including statements made by the contestants, indicated that Charley was "in poor health before the date of execution; that he repeatedly held conversations with his dead wife; that he refused to bathe, change his clothes, or otherwise take care of himself; and that he had rigged up a dangerous spring-gun to protect himself from intruders when no real threat existed." The case was transferred from a probate court to an Alabama state trial court, and the trial jury held for the contestants. The proponents appealed.

ISSUE Was there sufficient evidence to support a finding that Charley Bolan lacked testamentary capacity?

DECISION Yes. The Supreme Court of Alabama affirmed the trial court's judgment.

REASON The court stated that every testator is presumed to have the capacity to make a will, and the burden is on the contestant of a will to prove that testamentary capacity is lacking. "The contestant need not show that the testator suffered from permanent insanity," said the court. All that the contestant must do is show that the testator lacked testamentary capacity at the time the will was made. After reviewing the record, the court concluded that "[a]lthough the evidence was conflicting, the contestants presented sufficient evidence of a lack of testamentary capacity to support the submission of the contest to the jury on this ground."

FOR CRITICAL ANALYSIS—Social Consideration *What policy considerations underlie the courts' presumption that testamentary capacity exists?*

WRITING REQUIREMENTS Generally, a will must be in writing. The writing itself can be informal as long as it substantially complies with the statutory requirements. In some states, a will can be handwritten in crayon or ink. It can be written on a sheet or scrap of paper, on a paper bag, or on a piece of cloth. A will that is completely in the handwriting of the testator is called a **holographic will** (sometimes referred to as an *olographic will*).

In some cases, oral wills are found valid. A **nuncupative will** is an oral will made before witnesses. It is not permitted in most states. Where

authorized by statute, such wills are generally valid only if made during the last illness of the testator and are therefore sometimes referred to as *deathbed wills*. Normally, only personal property can be transferred by a nuncupative will. Statutes frequently permit soldiers and sailors to make nuncupative wills when on active duty.

SIGNATURE REQUIREMENTS It is a fundamental requirement that the testator's signature appear, generally at the end of the will. Each jurisdiction dictates by statute and court decision what constitutes a signature. Initials, an X or other mark, and words like "Mom" have all been upheld as valid when it was shown that the testators *intended* them to be signatures.

WITNESS REQUIREMENTS A will must be attested (sworn to) by two, and sometimes three, witnesses. The number of witnesses, their qualifications, and the manner in which the witnessing must be done are generally set out in a statute. A witness can be required to be disinterested—that is, not a beneficiary under the will. The UPC, however, provides that a will is valid even if it is attested by an interested witness [UPC 2–505]. There are no age requirements for witnesses, but witnesses must be mentally competent.

The purpose of witnesses is to verify that the testator actually executed (signed) the will and had the requisite intent and capacity at the time. A witness does not have to read the contents of the will. Usually, the testator and all witnesses must sign in the sight or the presence of one another, but the UPC deems it sufficient if the testator acknowledges his or her signature to the witnesses [UPC 2–502]. The UPC does not require all parties to sign in the presence of one another.

PUBLICATION REQUIREMENTS A will is *published* by an oral declaration by the maker to the witnesses that the document they are about to sign is his or her "last will and testament." Publication is becoming an unnecessary formality in most states, and it is not required under the UPC.

Undue Influence

A valid will is one that represents the maker's intention to transfer and distribute his or her property. When it can be shown that the decedent's plan of distribution was the result of improper pressure brought by another person, the will is declared invalid. Undue influence may be inferred by the court if the testator ignored blood relatives and named as beneficiary a nonrelative who was in constant close contact and in a position to influence the making of the will. For example, if a nurse or friend caring for the deceased at the time of death was named as beneficiary to the exclusion of all family members, the validity of the will might well be challenged on the basis of undue influence.

Revocation of Wills

An executed will is revocable by the maker at any time during the maker's lifetime. The maker may revoke a will by a physical act, such as tearing up the will, or by a subsequent writing. Wills can also be revoked by operation of law. Revocation can be partial or complete, and it must follow certain strict formalities.

REVOCATION BY A PHYSICAL ACT OF THE MAKER A testator may revoke a will by intentionally burning, tearing, canceling, obliterating, or otherwise destroying it, or by having someone else do so in the presence of the maker and at the maker's direction.[3] In some states, partial revocation by physical act of the maker is recognized. Thus, those portions of a will lined out or torn away are dropped, and the remaining parts of the will are valid. In no circumstances, however, can a provision be crossed out and an additional or substitute provision written in. Such altered portions require reexecution (re-signing) and reattestation (rewitnessing). To revoke a will by physical act, it is necessary to follow the mandates of a state statute exactly. When a state statute prescribes the exact methods for revoking a will by physical act, those are the only methods that will revoke the will.

REVOCATION BY A SUBSEQUENT WRITING A will may also be wholly or partially revoked by a **codicil**, a written instrument separate from the will that amends or revokes provisions in the will. A codicil eliminates the necessity of redrafting an entire will merely to add to it or amend it. It can also be used to revoke an entire will. The codicil must be executed with the same formalities required for a will, and it must refer expressly to the will. In effect, it updates a will, because the will is "incorporated by reference" into the codicil.

A new will (second will) can be executed that may or may not revoke the first or a prior will, depending on the language used. To revoke a prior will, the second will must use language specifically revoking other wills, such as, "This will hereby revokes all prior wills." If the second will is otherwise

---

3. The destruction cannot be inadvertent. The maker's intent to revoke must be shown. Consequently, when a will has been burned or torn accidentally, it is normally recommended that the maker have a new document created so that it will not falsely appear that the maker intended to revoke the will.

valid and properly executed, it will revoke all prior wills. If the express *declaration of revocation* is missing, then both wills are read together. If any of the dispositions made in the second will are inconsistent with the prior will, the second will controls.

REVOCATION BY OPERATION OF LAW   Revocation by *operation of law* occurs when marriage, divorce or annulment, or the birth of a child takes place after a will has been executed. In most states, when a testator marries after executing a will that does not include the new spouse, on the testator's death the spouse can still receive the amount he or she would have taken had the testator died intestate (how an intestate's property is distributed under state laws will be discussed shortly). In effect, this revokes the will to the point of providing the spouse with an intestate share. The rest of the estate is passed under the will [UPC 2–301, 2–508]. If, however, the new spouse is otherwise provided for in the will (or by transfer of property outside the will), the new spouse will not be given an intestate amount.

At common law and under the UPC, divorce does not necessarily revoke the entire will. A divorce or an annulment occurring after a will has been executed will revoke those dispositions of property made under the will to the former spouse [UPC 2–508].

If a child is born after a will has been executed and if it appears that the deceased parent would have made a provision for the child, then the child is entitled to receive whatever portion of the estate he or she is allowed under state laws providing for the distribution of an intestate's property. Most state laws allow a child to receive some portion of a parent's estate if no provision is made in the parent's will, unless it appears from the terms of the will that the testator intended to disinherit the child. Under the UPC, the rule is the same.

Intestacy Laws

Each state regulates by statute how property will be distributed when a person dies intestate (without a valid will). These statutes are called statutes of descent and distribution, or more simply, **intestacy laws.** Intestacy laws attempt to carry out the likely intent and wishes of the decedent. These laws assume that deceased persons would have intended that their natural heirs (spouses, children,

grandchildren, or other family members) inherit their property. Therefore, intestacy statutes set out rules and priorities under which these heirs inherit the property. If no heirs exist, the state will assume ownership of the property. The rules of descent vary widely from state to state.

SURVIVING SPOUSE AND CHILDREN   Usually, state statutes provide that first the debts of the decedent must be satisfied out of his or her estate, and then the remaining assets will pass to the surviving spouse and to the children. A surviving spouse usually receives only a share of the estate—one-half if there is also a surviving child and one-third if there are two or more children. Only if no children or grandchildren survive the decedent will a surviving spouse succeed to the entire estate.

Assume that Allen dies intestate and is survived by his wife, Della, and his children, Duane and Tara. Allen's property passes according to intestacy laws. After Allen's outstanding debts are paid, Della will receive the homestead (either in fee simple or as a life estate) and ordinarily a one-third (to one-half) interest in all other property. The remaining real and personal property will pass to Duane and Tara in equal portions. Under most state intestacy laws and under the UPC, in-laws do not share in an estate. If a child dies before his or her parents, the child's spouse will not receive an inheritance upon the parents' death. For example, if Duane died before his father (Allen), Duane's spouse would not inherit Duane's share of Allen's estate.

When there is no surviving spouse or child, the order of inheritance is grandchildren, then brothers and sisters, and in some states, parents of the decedent. These relatives are usually called *lineal descendants*. If there are no lineal descendants, then *collateral heirs*—nieces, nephews, aunts, and uncles of the decedent—make up the next group to share. If there are no survivors in any of these groups, most statutes provide for the property to be distributed among the next of kin of the collateral heirs.

STEPCHILDREN, ADOPTED CHILDREN, AND ILLE-GITIMATE CHILDREN   Under intestacy laws, stepchildren are not considered kin. Legally adopted children, however, are recognized as lawful heirs of their adoptive parents. Statutes vary from state to state in regard to the inheritance laws governing illegitimate children. Generally, an illegitimate child is treated as the child of the mother and can inherit from her and her relatives. The child is usually not regarded as the legal child of the father with the right of inheritance unless paternity is established through some legal proceeding prior to the father's death.

DISTRIBUTION TO GRANDCHILDREN When an intestate is survived by descendants of deceased children, a question arises as to what share these descendants (that is, grandchildren of the intestate) will receive. *Per stirpes* is a method of dividing an intestate share by which, within a class or group of distributees (for example, grandchildren), the children of any one descendant take the share that their deceased parent *would have been* entitled to inherit. For example, assume that Michael, a widower, has two children, Scott and Jonathan. Scott has two children (Becky and Holly), and Jonathan has one child (Paul). Scott and Jonathan die before their father, and then Michael dies. If Michael's estate is distributed *per stirpes*, Becky and Holly will each receive one-fourth of the estate (dividing Scott's one-half share). Paul will receive one-half of the estate (taking Jonathan's one-half share). Exhibit 30–4 illustrates the *per stirpes* method of distribution.

An estate may also be distributed on a *per capita* basis, which means that each person in a class or group takes an equal share of the estate. If Michael's estate is distributed *per capita*, Becky, Holly, and Paul will each receive a one-third share. Exhibit 30–5 illustrates the *per capita* method of distribution.

▌Trusts

A **trust** is any arrangement through which property is transferred from one person to a trustee to be administered for the transferor's or another party's benefit. It can also be defined as a right or property, real or personal, held by one party for the benefit of another. A trust can be created for any purpose that is not illegal or against public policy. Its essential elements are as follows:

1. A designated beneficiary.
2. A designated trustee.
3. A fund sufficiently identified to enable title to pass to the trustee.
4. Actual delivery by the settlor or grantor to the trustee with the intention of passing title.

◆ **Exhibit 30–4**
   Per Stirpes **Distribution**
   Under this method of distribution, an heir takes the share that his or her deceased parent would have been entitled to inherit, had the parent lived. This may mean that a class of distributees—the grandchildren in this example—will not inherit in equal portions. Note that Becky and Holly only receive one-fourth of Michael's estate while Paul inherits one-half.

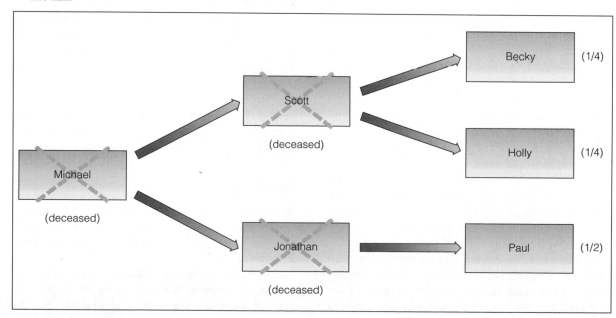

♦ **Exhibit 30–5**
Per Capita **Distribution**
Under this method of distribution, all heirs in a certain class—in this case, the grandchildren—inherit equally. Note that Becky and Holly in this situation each inherit one-third, as does Paul.

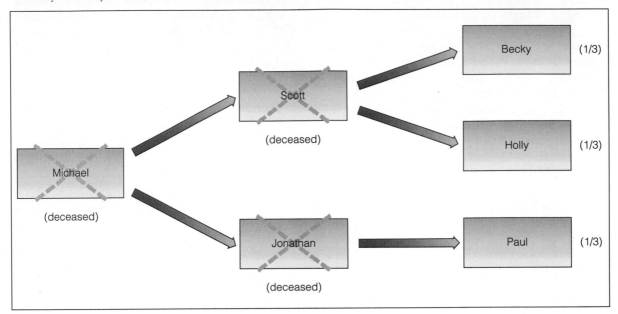

Express Trusts

An *express trust* is one created or declared in explicit terms, usually in writing. Express trusts fall into two categories: *inter vivos* (living) trusts and testamentary trusts (trusts provided for in a last will and testament).

An ***inter vivos*** **trust** is a trust executed by a grantor during his or her lifetime. The grantor (settlor) executes a *trust deed*, and legal title to the trust property passes to the named trustee. The trustee has a duty to administer the property as directed by the grantor for the benefit and in the interest of the beneficiaries. The trustee must preserve the trust property, make it productive, and if required by the terms of the trust agreement, pay income to the beneficiaries, all in accordance with the terms of the trust. Once the *inter vivos* trust is created, the grantor has, in effect, given over the property for the benefit of the beneficiaries. Often, tax-related benefits exist in setting up this type of trust.

A **testamentary trust** is a trust created by a will to come into existence on the settlor's death. Although a testamentary trust has a trustee who maintains legal title to the trust property, actions of the trustee are subject to judicial approval. This trustee can be named in the will or be appointed by the court. Thus, a testamentary trust does not fail because a trustee has not been named in the will. The legal responsibilities of the trustee are the same as in an *inter vivos* trust. If the will setting up a testamentary trust is invalid, then the trust will also be invalid. The property that was supposed to be in the trust will then pass according to intestacy laws, not according to the terms of the trust.

Implied Trusts

Sometimes, a trust will be imposed (implied) by law, even in the absence of an express trust. Implied trusts include resulting trusts and constructive trusts.

A **resulting trust** arises from the conduct of the parties. Suppose that Garrison wants to put one acre of land she owns on the market for sale. Because she is going out of the country for two

---

If James conveys his farm to the First Bank of Minnesota to be held for the benefit of his daughters, he has created a trust. James is the settlor, the First Bank of Minnesota is the trustee, and James's daughters are the beneficiaries. This arrangement is illustrated in Exhibit 30–6. Numerous types of trusts can be established. In this section, we look at some of the major types of trusts and their characteristics.

♦ **Exhibit 30–6**
Trust Arrangement
In a trust, there is a separation of interests in the trust property. The trustee takes *legal* title, which is the complete ownership and possession but which does not include the right to receive any benefits from the property. The beneficiary takes *equitable* title, which is the right to receive benefits from the property.

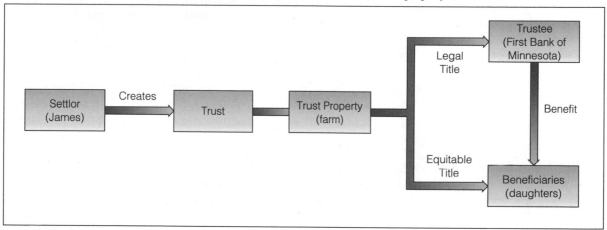

years and would not be able to deed the property to a buyer during that period, Garrison conveys the property to her good friend Oswald. Oswald will attempt to sell the property while Garrison is gone. Because the intent of the transaction to convey the property to Oswald is neither a sale nor a gift, the property will be held in trust (a resulting trust) by Oswald for the benefit of Garrison. Therefore, on Garrison's return, Oswald will be required either to deed back the property to Garrison or, if the property has been sold, to turn over the proceeds (held in trust) to Garrison. Here, the trust arises (*results* from) the *apparent intention* of the parties.

A **constructive trust** is an equitable trust imposed in the interests of fairness and justice. If someone wrongfully holds legal title to property—for example, if the property was obtained through fraud or in breach of a legal duty—a court may require that owner to hold the property in trust for

the person or persons who rightfully should own the property. For instance, suppose that Kraft is a partner in a partnership that purchases and develops real estate. Kraft learns in a partners' meeting that the partnership is considering the purchase of a vacant lot that will soon come on the market. Kraft secretly purchases the property in his own name, thus violating his fiduciary duty of loyalty to the partnership. If the partnership discovers what Kraft has done and brings a legal action against Kraft, a court may impose a constructive trust, thus requiring Kraft to hold the property in trust for the partnership.

Constructive trusts may be imposed for a variety of reasons. In the following case, the issue concerns whether a constructive trust should be imposed to counter the effects of an insurance company's failure to change the beneficiary on a life insurance policy after the insured had requested the change.

CASE 30.4
Zeigler v. Cardona
United States District Court,
Middle District of Alabama, 1993.
830 F.Supp. 1395.

FACTS In March 1990, Antonio Suarez, Sr., bought a $50,000 life insurance policy from Liberty National Life Insurance Company. The beneficiary was Suarez's mother, Guarina Cardona. At the time, Suarez was living with his aunt, Ruby Zeigler. Suarez and Zeigler later met with the insurance agent to change the beneficiary to Zeigler. At the meeting, Suarez made it clear that he wanted the proceeds of the policy to be used for the benefit of his children, Antonio and Ebony, and after Zeigler agreed to implement his wishes, Suarez signed the

(Continued)

Case 30.4—Continued

change-of-beneficiary form. Apparently due to a clerical error, Liberty National never acted on the change-of-beneficiary request. Zeigler paid the premiums. Suarez died in January 1991. Because of Liberty National's error, Cardona was the beneficiary of record. A suit was brought in a federal district court to establish who had rights in the insurance proceeds. The children sought to have the proceeds placed in a constructive trust on their behalf.

ISSUE   Who is entitled to the insurance proceeds?

DECISION   The court held that Zeigler was the proper beneficiary under the policy and was entitled to $10,000. A constructive trust on the remainder of the proceeds was imposed for the benefit of Antonio and Ebony. Cardona received nothing.

REASON   The court explained that "the law of equity regards as having been done that which ought to be done and the courts will give effect to the intention of the insured by holding that a change of beneficiary has been accomplished where he or she has done all that he or she could do in order to comply with the provisions of the policy." The court concluded that in this case, Suarez had done all that he could do, which made Zeigler the beneficiary. In imposing the constructive trust, the court noted that the evidence is undisputed that Suarez intended that the proceeds be used for the children and pointed out that "[a] constructive trust may be imposed on life insurance proceeds even though the designated beneficiary is not guilty of fraud or wrongdoing."

FOR CRITICAL ANALYSIS—Social Consideration   *If Suarez had no proof that he had ever signed a change-of-beneficiary form, would the outcome in this case be different?*

Special Types of Trusts

Certain trusts are created for special purposes. Three of these trusts that warrant discussion are charitable, spendthrift, and Totten trusts. A trust designed for the benefit of a segment of the public or of the public in general is a **charitable trust.** Usually, to be deemed a charitable trust, a trust must be created for charitable, educational, religious, or scientific purposes.

A trust created to provide for the maintenance of a beneficiary by preventing his or her improvidence with the bestowed funds is a **spendthrift trust.** Essentially, the beneficiary is permitted to draw only a certain portion of the total amount to which he or she is entitled at any one time. The majority of states allow spendthrift trust provisions that prohibit creditors from attaching such trusts.

A **Totten trust**[4] is created when one person deposits money in his or her own name as a trustee for another. This trust is tentative in that it is revocable at will until the depositor dies or completes the gift in his or her lifetime by some unequivocal act or declaration (for example, delivery of the funds to the intended beneficiary). If the depositor should die before the beneficiary dies and if the depositor has not revoked the trust expressly or impliedly, the beneficiary obtains property rights to the balance on hand.

_____
4.   This type of trust derives its unusual name from *In the Matter of Totten,* 179 N.Y. 112, 71 N.E. 748 (1904).

▌Terms and Concepts

▌Chapter Summary: Insurance, Wills, and Trusts

INSURANCE	
Classifications *(See pages 623, 624–625.)*	See Exhibit 30–1.
Terminology *(See page 623.)*	1. *Policy*—The insurance contract. 2. *Premium*—The consideration paid to the insurer for a policy. 3. *Underwriter*—The insurance company. 4. *Parties*—Include the insurer (the insurance company), the insured (the person covered by insurance), an agent (a representative of the insurance company) or a broker (ordinarily an independent contractor), and a beneficiary (the person to receive proceeds under the policy).
Insurable Interest *(See page 623.)*	An insurable interest exists whenever an individual or entity benefits from the preservation of the health or life of the insured or the property to be insured. For life insurance, an insurable interest must exist at the time the policy is issued. For property insurance, an insurable interest must exist at the time of the loss.
The Insurance Contract *(See pages 623–628.)*	1. *Laws governing*—The general principles of contract law are applied; the insurance industry is also heavily regulated by the states. 2. *Application*—An insurance applicant is bound by any false statements that appear in the application (subject to certain exceptions), which is part of the insurance contract. Misstatements or misrepresentations may be grounds for voiding the policy. 3. *Effective date*—Coverage on an insurance policy can begin when the binder (a written memorandum indicating that a formal policy is pending and stating its essential terms) is written; when the policy is issued; or depending on the terms of the contract, when certain conditions are met. 4. *Provisions and clauses*—See Exhibit 36–2. Words will be given their ordinary meanings, and any ambiguity in the policy will be interpreted against the insurance company. When the written policy has not been delivered and it is unclear whether an insurance contract actually exists, the uncertainty will be determined against the insurance company. The court will presume that the policy is in effect unless the company can show otherwise. *(Continued)*

▌Chapter Summary: Insurance, Wills, and Trusts—Continued

The Insurance Contract—Continued	5. *Defenses against payment to the insured*—Defenses include misrepresentation, fraud, or violation of warranties by the applicant.
WILLS	
Terminology *(See page 629.)*	1. *Intestate*—One who dies without a valid will. 2. *Testator*—A person who makes out a will. 3. *Personal representative*—A person appointed in a will or by a court to settle the affairs of a decedent. A personal representative named in the will is an *executor*; a personal representative appointed by the court for an intestate decedent is an *administrator*. 4. *Devise*—A gift of real estate by will; may be general or specific. The recipient of a devise is a *devisee*. 5. *Bequest, or legacy*—A gift of personal property by will; may be general or specific. The recipient of a bequest (legacy) is a *legatee*.
Probate Procedures *(See pages 629–631.)*	To probate a will means to establish its validity and to carry the administration of the estate through a court process. Probate laws vary from state to state. Probate procedures may be informal or formal, depending on the size of the estate and other factors, such as whether a guardian for minor children must be appointed.
Requirements for a Valid Will *(See pages 631–633.)*	1. The testator must have testamentary capacity (be of legal age and sound mind at the time the will is made). 2. A will must be in writing (except for nuncupative wills). A holographic will is completely in the handwriting of the testator. 3. A will must be signed by the testator; what constitutes a signature varies from jurisdiction to jurisdiction. 4. A nonholographic will (an attested will) must be witnessed in the manner prescribed by state statute. 5. A will may have to be *published*—that is, the testator may be required to announce to witnesses that this is his or her "last will and testament." Not required under the UPC.

Revocation of Wills *(See pages 633–634.)*	1. By *physical act of the maker*—Tearing up, canceling, obliterating, or deliberately destroying part or all of a will.
	
	2. By *subsequent writing*—
	  a. Codicil—A formal, separate document to amend or revoke an existing will.
	  b. Second will or new will—A new, properly executed will expressly revoking the existing will.
	
	3. *By operation of law*—
	  a. Marriage—Generally revokes part of a will written before the marriage.
	  b. Divorce or annulment—Revokes dispositions of property made under a will to a former spouse.
	  c. Subsequently born child—It is *implied* that the child is entitled to receive the portion of the estate granted under intestacy distribution laws.

Intestacy Laws *(See pages 634–635.)*	1. Vary widely from state to state. Usually, the law provides that the surviving spouse and children inherit the property of the decedent (after the decedent's debts are paid). The spouse usually will inherit the entire estate if there are no children, one-half of the estate if there is one child, and one-third of the estate if there are two or more children.

▌Chapter Summary: Insurance, Wills, and Trusts—Continued

Intestacy Laws—Continued	2. If there is no surviving spouse or child, then, in order, lineal descendants (grandchildren, brothers and sisters, and—in some states—parents of the decedent) inherit. If there are no lineal descendants, then collateral heirs (nieces, nephews, aunts, and uncles of the decedent) inherit.
	TRUSTS
Definition *(See page 635.)*	A trust is any arrangement through which property is transferred from one person to be administered by a trustee for another party's benefit. The essential elements of a trust are (1) a designated beneficiary, (2) a designated trustee, (3) a fund sufficiently identified to enable title to pass to the trustee, and (4) actual delivery to the trustee with the intention of passing title.
Express Trusts *(See page 636.)*	Express trusts are created by expressed terms, usually in writing, and fall into two categories: 1. *Inter vivos trust*—A trust executed by a grantor during his or her lifetime. 2. *Testamentary trust*—A trust created by will and coming into existence on the death of the grantor.
Implied Trusts *(See pages 636–638.)*	Implied trusts, which are imposed by law in the interests of fairness and justice, include the following: 1. *Resulting trust*—Arises from the conduct of the parties when an *apparent intention* to create a trust is present. 2. *Constructive trust*—Arises by operation of law whenever a transaction takes place in which the person who takes title to property is in equity not entitled to enjoy the beneficial interest therein.
Special Types of Trusts *(See page 638.)*	1. *Charitable trust*—A trust designed for the benefit of a public group or the public in general. 2. *Spendthrift trust*—A trust created to provide for the maintenance of a beneficiary by allowing only a certain portion of the total amount to be received by the beneficiary at any one time. 3. *Totten trust*—A trust created when one person deposits money in his or her own name as a trustee for another.

▌For Review

1. What is an insurable interest? To obtain life insurance, when must an insurable interest exist—at the time that the policy is obtained, at the time that the loss occurs, or both? To obtain property insurance, when must an insurable interest exist—at the time that the policy is obtained, at the time that the loss occurs, or both?

2. Is an insurance broker the agent of the insurance applicant or the agent of the insurer? If the broker accepts an applicant's initial premium but fails to obtain coverage, and the applicant is damaged as a result, who may be liable for the damage?

3. Who can make a will? What are the basic requirements for executing a will? How may a will be revoked?

4. What is the difference between a *per stirpes* and a *per capita* distribution of an estate to the grandchildren of the deceased?

5. What are the four essential elements of a trust? What is an express trust? How do implied trusts arise?

▐ Questions and Case Problems

30–1. Timing of Insurance Coverage. On October 10, Joleen Vora applied for a $50,000 life insurance policy with Magnum Life Insurance Co.; she named her husband, Jay, as the beneficiary. Joleen paid the insurance company the first year's policy premium upon making the application. Two days later, before she had a chance to take the physical examination required by the insurance company and before the policy was issued, Joleen was killed in an automobile accident. Jay submitted a claim to the insurance company for the $50,000. Can Jay collect? Explain.

30–2. Validity of Wills. Merlin Winters had three sons. Merlin and his youngest son, Abraham, had a falling out in 1994 and had not spoken to each other since. Merlin made a formal will in 1996, leaving all his property to the two older children and deliberately excluding Abraham. Merlin's health began to deteriorate, and by 1997 he was under the full-time care of a nurse, Julia. In 1998, he made a new will expressly revoking the 1996 will and leaving all his property to Julia. On Merlin's death, the two older children contested the 1998 will, claiming that Julia had exercised undue influence over their father. Abraham claimed that both wills were invalid, because the first one had been revoked by the second will, and the second will was invalid on the ground of undue influence. Is Abraham's contention correct? Explain.

30–3. Wills. Gary Mendel drew up a will in which he left his favorite car, a 1966 red Ferrari, to his daughter, Roberta. A year prior to his death, Mendel sold the 1966 Ferrari and purchased a 1969 Ferrari. Discuss whether Roberta will inherit the 1969 Ferrari under the terms of her father's will.

30–4. Estate Distribution. Benjamin is a widower who has two married children, Edward and Patricia. Patricia has two children, Perry and Paul. Edward has no children. Benjamin dies, and his typewritten will leaves all his property equally to his children, Edward and Patricia, and provides that should a child predecease him, the grandchildren are to take *per stirpes*. The will was witnessed by Patricia and by Benjamin's lawyer and was signed by Benjamin in their presence. Patricia has predeceased Benjamin. Edward claims the will is invalid.

    (a) Discuss whether the will is valid.

    (b) Discuss the distribution of Benjamin's estate if the will is invalid.

    (c) Discuss the distribution of Benjamin's estate if the will is valid.

30–5. Validity of Wills. An elderly, childless widow had nine nieces and nephews. Her will divided her entire estate equally among two nieces and the husband of one of the nieces, who was also the attorney who drafted the will and the executor named in the will. The testator was definitely of sound mind when the will was executed. If you were one of the seven nieces or nephews omitted from the will, could you think of any way to have the will invalidated? [*Estate of Eckert*, 93 Misc.2d 677, 403 N.Y.S.2d 633 (Surrogate's Ct. 1978)]

30–6. Revocation of Wills. Myrtle Courziel executed a valid will that provided for the establishment of a scholarship fund designed to encourage the study of corrosion as it affects metallurgical engineering. The recipients were to be students in the upper halves of their classes at the University of Alabama. Subsequently, Courziel died. John Calhoun, the eventual administrator of her estate, obtained access to her safe-deposit box to search for her will. He found the will intact, except that the last page of the will, which had contained Courziel's signature and the signatures of the witnesses, had been removed from the document and was not in the safe-deposit box or anywhere else to be found. Because Courziel had had sole control over the will, should it be presumed that her removal of the last page (or her having allowed it to be removed) effectively revoked the will? Discuss. [*Board of Trustees of University of Alabama v. Calhoun*, 514 So.2d 895 (Ala. 1987)]

30–7. Insurer's Defenses. Kirk Johnson applied for life insurance with New York Life Insurance Co. on October 7, 1986. In answer to a question about smoking habits, Johnson stated that he had not smoked in the past twelve months and that he had never smoked cigarettes. In fact, Johnson had smoked for thirteen years, and during the month prior to the insurance application, he was smoking approximately ten cigarettes per day. Johnson died on July 17, 1988, for reasons unrelated to smoking. Johnson's father, Lawrence Johnson, who was the beneficiary of the policy, filed a claim for the insurance proceeds. While investigating the claim, New York Life discovered Kirk Johnson's misrepresentation and denied the claim. The company canceled the policy and sent Lawrence Johnson a check for the premiums that had been paid. Lawrence Johnson refused to accept the check, and New York Life brought an action for a declaratory judgment (a court determination of a plaintiff's rights). What should the court decide? Discuss fully. [*New York Life Insurance Co. v. Johnson*, 923 F.2d 279 (3d Cir. 1991)]

30–8. Testamentary Trusts. Edwin Fickes died in 1943. His will provided for the creation of a trust, half of which was to be divided, on the death of Fickes's last surviving child, "in equal portions between [the testator's] grandchildren then living." At the time of the death of Fickes's last surviving child, there were four biological grandchildren and four adopted grandchildren living. Two of the adopted grandchildren, both boys, had been adopted prior to Fickes's death. The other two, both girls, had been adopted after Fickes died. The trustee, Connecticut National Bank and Trust Co., sought a court determination of whether the adopted grandchildren were entitled to share in the trust distribution. The trial court found that the testator, Fickes, had intended to include his adopted grandsons as "grandchildren" within the meaning of his will but could not have intended to include his adopted granddaughters as "grandchildren," so they were not entitled to a share of the trust. What will happen on appeal? Discuss fully. [*Connecticut National Bank and Trust Co. v. Chadwick*, 217 Conn. 260, 585 A.2d 1189 (1991)]

30–9. Spendthrift Trusts. Billy Putman rented and occupied a house trailer owned by Douglas Sanders. Because Putman damaged the trailer while it was in his possession, Sanders sought and acquired a judgment against Putman for $2,429.36 in damages, plus court costs and interest. Sanders garnished Putman's bank account and learned of a certificate of deposit (CD) worth $20,000, which was held by a trustee (Georgia Putman) on behalf of Billy Putman as the beneficiary. The CD was purchased with the proceeds from Billy Putman's deceased father's life insurance policy. Sanders claimed that the insurance proceeds, or the CD, could be garnished. Billy Putman argued that the CD funds were part of a spendthrift trust and therefore could not be reached by creditors, including Sanders. The only evidence in support of a spendthrift trust was the insurance company's check made payable to Billy Putman's trustee. How should the court decide? Explain. [*Sanders v. Putman*, 315 Ark. 251, 866 S.W.2d 827 (1993)]

30–10. Validity of Wills. In the last fourteen years of Evelyn Maheras's life, William Cook, a Baptist pastor, became her spiritual adviser and close personal friend. Cook—and no one else—actively participated in helping Maheras draft her will. He gave Maheras a church-sponsored booklet on will drafting, recommended an attorney (a church member) to do the drafting, and reviewed the terms of the will with Maheras. When Maheras died, she left most of her estate to Cook's church. Cook personally received nothing under the will. Maheras's nephew and only heir, Richard Suagee, filed a suit against Cook in an Oklahoma state court to contest the will, arguing that Cook unduly influenced Maheras. Can a party who receives nothing under a will be regarded as having exercised undue influence over the testator? What should the court in Maheras's case do? [*Estate of Maheras*, 897 P.2d 268 (Okla. 1995)]

▌Unit Nine—Cumulative Hypothetical Problem

30–11. *Joel and Marsha Cummings operate a consulting business out of their home. Most of their work consists of creating and maintaining "home pages" on the Internet for various clients. Business is thriving, and to obtain tax benefits, they recently organized their business as an S corporation. They are contemplating leasing office space and hiring some assistants.*

1. Joel and Marsha own their home and both of their cars as joint tenants. They have never gotten around to making a will. Assume that Joel dies and is survived by his wife (Marsha) and their two children. Who will inherit the home and the two automobiles?

2. One day, Marsha's computer malfunctions, and she takes it to a computer shop for repairs. The next day, the computer technician calls Marsha and tells her that her computer is missing. Marsha claims that the shop is liable for the value of the computer. The shop contends that it was not negligent in any way and therefore cannot be held liable. Will Marsha succeed in a suit against the shop? Explain.

3. Marsha and Joel, having decided to move their business out of their home, lease office space in a building owned by Dan Silver. The written lease contract, a brief form contract, provides that the term of the lease is one year; that the monthly rent is $900, to be paid on the first of each month; and that Marsha and Joel will pay all utility bills. After they have moved to the new office space, Marsha and Joel learn that the electrical wiring is deficient, that the roof leaks, and that the furnace does not function properly. Silver refuses to make any repairs. What legal options do Marsha and Joel have in this situation? Can they break the lease without liability? Discuss fully.

4. Marsha and Joel are concerned about the potential liability they will incur if a customer is injured while on their business premises. They also want to protect against the loss of income that they would suffer if one of them were disabled or died. What types of insurance policies would best meet each of these needs? Why?

5. Joel dies intestate, and his property is distributed under intestacy laws. Marsha decides she had better write a will so that she will have more control over how her property will be transferred on her death. She particularly wants to make sure that one of her children, Sam, inherits nothing, because he has been so unaffectionate and unhelpful to his parents over the years. In her will, Marsha designated her daughter, Julie, as her sole heir, and said nothing about Sam. If Sam contests

the will, will he succeed in obtaining any of his mother's property?

6. Assume that Marsha, before she died, had a change of heart. She wrote a new will in which she left everything she owned to both of her children in equal shares. In the new will, she said nothing about revoking her prior will. Who will inherit what in these circumstances?

▌Accessing the Internet: Fundamentals of Business Law

If you are interested in reading the wills of some historical figures and celebrities, including John Lennon, Elvis Presley, Jacqueline Kennedy Onassis, and Richard Nixon, go to

http://www.ca-probate.com/wills.htm

The American College of Trust and Estate Counsel (ACTEC) has a site on the Web that offers links to other resources as well as pamphlets on wills and organ donation. You can access the ACTEC site at

http://www.actec.org

The Senior Law Web site offers information on a variety of topics, including elder law, estate planning, and trusts. The URL for this site is

http://www.seniorlaw.com

To learn about some estate-planning software available from a Web site, access

http://www.atlaw.com

Cornell Law University's Legal Information Institute offers links to several states' probate statutes at

http://fatty.law.cornell.edu/topics/state_statutes.html

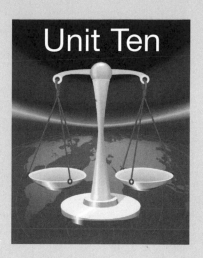

Unit Ten

Special Topics

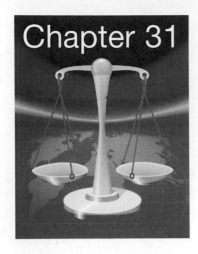

Chapter 31

Professional Liability

CHAPTER OBJECTIVES

After reading this chapter, you should be able to:

1. Summarize areas in which professionals may be liable at common law.
2. Outline liability that may be imposed on accountants under the securities laws.
3. Identify accountants' potential criminal liability.
4. State professionals' duties concerning working papers.
5. Explain the duty of professionals regarding communications with their clients.

Accountants have found themselves increasingly subject to liability in the past decade or so. This more extensive liability has resulted in large part from a greater public awareness of the fact that professionals are required to deliver competent services and are obligated to adhere to standards of performance commonly accepted within their professions.

Considering the many potential sources of legal liability that may be imposed on them, accountants should be well aware of their legal obligations.[1] In the first part of this chapter, we look at the potential common law liability of accountants and then examine the potential liabil-

ity of accountants under securities laws and the Internal Revenue Code. The chapter concludes with a brief examination of the relationship of professionals, particularly accountants and attorneys, with their clients.

Potential Common Law Liability to Clients

Under the common law, accountants may be liable to clients for breach of contract, negligence, or fraud.

Liability for Breach of Contract

Accountants face liability for any breach of contract under the common law. A professional owes a duty to his or her client to honor the terms of the contract and to perform the contract within the stated time period. If the professional fails to perform as

---

1. The recent verdict against the accounting firm of Coopers & Lybrand underscores the potential consequences of not fulfilling those obligations. A jury found the firm guilty of common law fraud and securities law violations for failing to expose a client's $1 billion investment scam. The firm may be ordered to pay investors more than $150 million in damages. Matt Murray, "Coopers & Lybrand Is Found Liable by Jury to Investors," *The Wall Street Journal*, 15 Feb. 1996, p. B3.

agreed in the contract, then he or she has breached the contract, and the client has the right to recover damages from the professional. A professional may be held liable for expenses incurred by his or her client in securing another professional to provide the contracted-for services, for penalties imposed on the client for failure to meet time deadlines, and for any other reasonable and foreseeable monetary losses that arise from the professional's breach.

Liability for Negligence

Accountants may also be held liable under the common law for negligence in the performance of their services. As with any negligence claim, the elements that must be proved to establish negligence on the part of a professional are as follows:

1. A duty of care existed.
2. That duty of care was breached.
3. The plaintiff suffered an injury.
4. The injury was proximately caused by the defendant's breach of the duty of care.

All accountants are subject to standards of conduct established by codes of professional ethics, by state statutes, and by judicial decisions. They are also governed by the contracts they enter into with their clients. In their performance of contracts, accountants must exercise the established standard of care, knowledge, and judgment generally accepted by other accountants. We look below at this duty of care.

ACCOUNTANT'S DUTY OF CARE Accountants play a major role in a business's financial system. Accountants have the necessary expertise and experience in establishing and maintaining accurate financial records to design, control, and audit recordkeeping systems; to prepare reliable statements that reflect an individual's or a business's financial status; and to give tax advice and prepare tax returns.

In the performance of their services, accountants must comply with **generally accepted accounting principles (GAAP)** and **generally accepted auditing standards (GAAS)**. The Financial Accounting Standards Board (FASB, usually pronounced "faz-bee") determines what account-

ing conventions, rules, and procedures constitute GAAP at a given point in time. GAAS are standards concerning an auditor's professional qualities and the judgment that he or she exercises in performing an examination and report. GAAS are established by the American Institute of Certified Public Accountants. As long as an accountant conforms to GAAP and acts in good faith, he or she will not be held liable to the client for incorrect judgment.

As a general rule, an accountant is not required to discover every impropriety, **defalcation** (embezzlement), or fraud in his or her client's books. If, however, the impropriety, defalcation, or fraud has gone undiscovered because of an accountant's negligence or failure to perform an express or implied duty, the accountant will be liable for any resulting losses suffered by his or her client. Therefore, an accountant who uncovers suspicious financial transactions and fails to investigate the matter fully or to inform his or her client of the discovery can be held liable to the client for the resulting loss.

A violation of GAAP and GAAS will be considered *prima facie* evidence of negligence on the part of the accountant. Compliance with GAAP and GAAS, however, does not *necessarily* relieve an accountant of potential legal liability. An accountant may be held to a higher standard of conduct established by state statute and by judicial decisions.

DEFENSES TO NEGLIGENCE If an accountant is deemed guilty of negligence, the client may collect damages for losses that arose from the accountant's negligence. An accountant, however, is not without possible defenses to a cause of action for damages based on negligence. Possible defenses include the following allegations:

1. The accountant was not negligent.
2. If the accountant was negligent, this negligence was not the proximate cause of the client's losses.
3. The client was negligent (depending on whether state law allows contributory negligence as a defense).

UNAUDITED FINANCIAL STATEMENTS Sometimes accountants are hired to prepare unaudited financial statements. (A financial statement is considered unaudited if no auditing procedures have been used in its preparation or if insufficient procedures have been used to justify an opinion.)

Accountants may be subject to liability for failing, in accordance with standard accounting procedures, to delineate a balance sheet as "unaudited." An accountant will also be held liable for failure to disclose to a client facts or circumstances that give reason to believe that misstatements have been made or that a fraud has been committed.

Liability for Fraud

Actual fraud and constructive fraud present two different circumstances under which an accountant may be found liable. Recall from Chapter 10 that fraud, or misrepresentation, consists of the following elements:

1. A misrepresentation of a material fact has occurred.
2. There exists an intent to deceive.
3. The innocent party has justifiably relied on the misrepresentation.
4. For damages, the innocent party must have been injured.

A professional may be held liable for *actual fraud* when he or she intentionally misstates a material fact to mislead his or her client, and the client justifiably relies on the misstated fact to his or her injury. A material fact is one that a reasonable person would consider important in deciding whether to act. In contrast, a professional may be held liable for *constructive fraud* whether or not he or she acted with fraudulent intent. For example, constructive fraud may be found when an accountant is grossly negligent in the performance of his or her duties. The intentional failure to perform a duty in reckless disregard of the consequences of such a failure would constitute gross negligence on the part of a professional. Both actual and constructive fraud are potential sources of legal liability under which a client may bring an action against an accountant or other professional.

When a client is dissatisfied with the performance of an accounting firm, he or she will often sue on several theories. In the following case, the court had to sift through claims for negligence, breach of contract, and constructive fraud. The court concluded that only the last theory presented a ground for proceeding with the case.

CASE 31.1

Barger v. McCoy Hillard & Parks

Court of Appeals of North Carolina, 1995.
120 N.C.App. 326,
462 S.E.2d 252.

FACTS Jerry Barger, Wayne Kennerly, and Harry Young were the shareholders and directors of The Furniture House of North Carolina, Inc. (TFH). They asked David McCoy of the accounting firm of McCoy Hillard & Parks to determine the financial health of TFH. A misapplication of computer data resulted in an overstatement of sales and an understatement of liabilities. Based on these statements, McCoy assured Barger and the others that TFH could repay certain loans. Consequently, Barger and the others personally guaranteed the loans. Ultimately, TFH filed for bankruptcy, and the guarantors were forced to repay the loans with their own money. They filed a suit against the accountants in a North Carolina state court, alleging, in part, fraud. The court granted the accountants' motion for summary judgment. Barger and the others appealed.

ISSUE Could the accountants be held liable for fraud?

DECISION Yes. The Court of Appeals of North Carolina reversed the lower court's grant of summary judgment on this issue and remanded the case for trial.

REASON The appellate court concluded that the plaintiffs alleged sufficient facts to infer that the accountant may have committed fraud. The

Case 31.1—Continued

appellate court pointed out that "the record as to plaintiffs' * * * [constructive] fraud claims arising from the personal guarantees does reflect a genuine issue of material fact * * * . It is possible to infer that defendant McCoy was aware plaintiffs would rely on his opinion in personally guaranteeing loans for TFH, and that the parties may have had a relationship of trust which defendants breached to the detriment of plaintiffs."

FOR CRITICAL ANALYSIS—Technological Consideration *How might the losses in this case have been avoided?*

Auditors' Liability to Third Parties

Traditionally, an accountant did not owe any duty to a third person with whom he or she had no direct contractual relationship—that is, to any person not in *privity of contract* with the professional. An accountant's duty was only to his or her client. Violations of statutory laws, fraud, and other intentional or reckless acts of wrongdoing were the only exceptions to this general rule.

Today, numerous third parties—including investors, shareholders, creditors, corporate managers and directors, regulatory agencies, and others—rely on professional opinions, such as those of auditors, when making decisions. In view of this extensive reliance, many courts have all but abandoned the privity requirement in regard to accountants' liability to third parties.

In this section, we focus on the potential liability of auditors to third parties. Understanding an auditor's common law liability to third parties is critical, because often, when a business fails, its independent auditor (accountant) may be one of the few potentially solvent defendants. The majority of courts now hold that auditors can be held liable to third parties for negligence, but the standard for the imposition of this liability varies. There are generally three different views of accountants' liability to third parties, each of which we discuss below.

The *Ultramares* Rule

The traditional rule regarding an accountant's liability to third parties was enunciated by Chief Judge Benjamin Cardozo in *Ultramares Corp. v. Touche*,[2] a case decided in 1931. In *Ultramares*,

Fred Stern & Company (Stern) hired the public accounting firm of Touche, Niven & Company (Touche) to review Stern's financial records and prepare a balance sheet[3] for the year ending December 31, 1923. Touche prepared the balance sheet and supplied Stern with thirty-two certified copies. According to the certified balance sheet, Stern had a net worth (assets less liabilities) of $1,070,715.26. In reality, however, Stern was insolvent—the company's records had been falsified by Stern's insiders to reflect a positive net worth. In reliance on the certified balance sheets, a lender, Ultramares Corporation, loaned substantial amounts to Stern. After Stern was declared bankrupt, Ultramares brought an action against Touche for negligence in an attempt to recover damages.

The New York Court of Appeals (that state's highest court) refused to impose liability on the accountants and concluded that they owed a duty of care only to those persons for whose "primary benefit" the statements were intended. In this case, Stern was the only person for whose primary benefit the statements were intended. The court held that in the absence of privity or a relationship "so close as to approach that of privity," a party could not recover from an accountant.

The court's requirement of privity or near privity has since been referred to as the *Ultramares* rule, or the New York rule. The rule was restated and somewhat modified in a 1985 New York case, *Credit Alliance Corp. v. Arthur Andersen & Co.*[4] In that case, the court held that if a third party has a sufficiently close relationship or nexus (link or

---

2.   255 N.Y. 170, 174 N.E. 441 (1931).

3.   A balance sheet is often relied on by banks, creditors, stockholders, purchasers, or sellers as a basis for making decisions relating to a company's business.

4.   65 N.Y.2d 536, 483 N.E.2d 110 (1985): A "relationship sufficiently intimate to be equated with privity" is sufficient for a third party to sue another's accountant for negligence.

connection) with an accountant, then the *Ultramares* privity requirement may be satisfied without establishing an accountant-client relationship. The rule enunciated in *Credit Alliance* is often referred to as the "near privity" rule. Only a minority of states have adopted this rule of accountants' liability to third parties.

The *Restatement* Rule

In the past several years, the *Ultramares* rule has been severely criticized. Auditors perform much of their work for use by persons who are not parties to the contract; thus, it is asserted that they owe a duty to these third parties. Consequently, there has been an erosion of the *Ultramares* rule, and accountants have been exposed to potential liability to third parties.

The majority of courts have adopted the position taken by the *Restatement (Second) of Torts*, which states that accountants are subject to liability for negligence not only to their clients but also to *foreseen*, or *known*, users—or classes of users—of their reports or financial statements. Under Section 552(2) of the *Restatement (Second) of Torts*, an accountant's liability extends to those persons for whose benefit and guidance the accountant "intends to supply the information or knows that the recipient intends to supply it" and to those persons whom the accountant "intends the information to influence or knows that the recipient so intends." In other words, if an accountant prepares a financial statement for a client and knows that the client will submit that statement to a bank to secure a loan, the accountant may be held liable to the bank for negligent misstatements or omissions—because the accountant knew that the bank would rely on the accountant's work product when deciding whether to make the loan.

In the following case, the court considers the question of the extent of an accountant's liability to a third party. Note the court's reliance on the *Restatement's* position in determining the issue.

CASE 31.2

Boykin v. Arthur Andersen & Co.

Supreme Court of Alabama, 1994.
639 So.2d 504.

FACTS   Secor Bank hired independent certified public accountants Arthur Andersen & Company to certify the bank's annual reports. The reports did not mention losses resulting from millions of dollars of bad commercial loans. Samuel Boykin and Apon, Inc., were Secor shareholders. When they learned of the losses, they filed a suit in an Alabama state court against Andersen and others, alleging in part professional negligence. The court dismissed the suit, ruling in part that the claim did not satisfy the *Credit Alliance* "near privity" rule. Boykin and Apon appealed to the Supreme Court of Alabama, which adopted the Restatement rule.

ISSUE   Could the accountants be held liable for professional negligence?

DECISION   Yes. The Supreme Court of Alabama adopted the *Restatement* rule, reversed the judgment of the lower court, and remanded the case for trial.

REASON   The state supreme court explained that under the *Restatement* rule, "a restricted group of third parties [may] recover for pecuniary losses attributed to inaccurate financial statements. * * * The restricted group includes third parties whom the accountants intend to influence and those whom the accountants know their clients intend to influence." Thus Boykin and Apon had stated a claim for professional negligence against Andersen. The state supreme court reasoned, "Basic prin-

Case 31.2—Continued   ciples of justice require that an accounting firm be held liable for its intentional or negligent dissemination of inaccurate financial reports to specifically foreseen and limited groups of third parties for whose benefit and guidance the accounting firm supplied the information."

FOR CRITICAL ANALYSIS—Ethical Consideration   *Disregarding the legal issues, what general ethical standards might Andersen have violated?*

Liability to Reasonably Foreseeable Users

A small minority of courts hold accountants liable to any users whose reliance on an accountant's statements or reports was *reasonably foreseeable*. This standard has been criticized as extending liability too far. In *Raritan River Steel Co. v. Cherry, Bekaert & Holland,* for example, the North Carolina Supreme Court stated that "in fairness accountants should not be liable in circumstances where they are unaware of the use to which their opinions will be put. Instead, their liability should be commensurate with those persons or classes of persons whom they know will rely on their work. With such knowledge the auditor can, through purchase of liability insurance, setting fees, and adopting other protective measures appropriate to the risk, prepare accordingly."[5]

The North Carolina court's statement echoes the view of the majority of the courts that the *Restatement's* approach is the more reasonable, because it allows accountants to control their exposure to liability. Liability is "fixed by the accountants' particular knowledge at the moment the audit is published," not by the foreseeability of the harm that might occur to a third party after the report is released.[6]

▌Potential Statutory Liability of Accountants

Both civil and criminal liability may be imposed on accountants under the Securities Act of 1933

and the Securities Exchange Act of 1934, and the Private Securities Litigation Reform Act of 1995.[7]

Liability under the Securities Act of 1933

The Securities Act of 1933 requires registration statements to be filed with the Securities and Exchange Commission (SEC) prior to an offering of securities (see Chapter 27).[8] Accountants frequently prepare and certify the issuer's financial statements that are included in the registration statement.

LIABILITY UNDER SECTION 11   Section 11 of the Securities Act of 1933 imposes civil liability on accountants for misstatements and omissions of material facts in registration statements. Therefore, an accountant may be found liable if he or she prepared any financial statements included in the registration statement that "contained an untrue statement of a material fact or omitted to state a material fact required to be stated therein or necessary to make the statements therein not misleading."[9]

Liability to Purchasers of Securities   Under Section 11, an accountant's liability for a misstatement or omission of a material fact in a registration statement extends to anyone who acquires a security covered by the registration statement. A purchaser of a security need only demonstrate that he or she has suffered a loss on the security. Proof of reliance on the materially false statement or misleading

---

5.   322 N.C. 200, 367 S.E.2d 609 (1988).
6.   *Bethlehem Steel Corp. v. Ernst & Whinney,* 822 S.W.2d 592 (Tenn. 1991).

7.   Other potential sources of civil and criminal liability that may be imposed on accountants include provisions of the Racketeer Influenced and Corrupt Organizations Act (RICO). RICO is discussed in Chapter 5.
8.   Many securities and transactions are expressly exempted from the 1933 act.
9.   15 U.S.C. Section 77k(a).

omission is not ordinarily required. Nor is there a requirement of privity between the accountant and the security purchaser.

The Due Diligence Standard Section 11 imposes a duty on accountants to use **due diligence** in the preparation of financial statements included in the filed registration statements. After the purchaser has proved the loss on the security, the accountant bears the burden of showing that he or she exercised due diligence in the preparation of the financial statements. To avoid liability, the accountant must show that he or she had, "after reasonable investigation, reasonable grounds to believe and did believe, at the time such part of the registration statement became effective, that the statements therein were true and that there was no omission of a material fact required to be stated therein or necessary to make the statements therein not misleading."[10] The failure to follow GAAP and GAAS is proof of a lack of due diligence.

In particular, the due diligence standard places a burden on accountants to verify information furnished by a corporation's officers and directors. The burden of proving due diligence requires an accountant to demonstrate that he or she is free from negligence or fraud. The accountants in *Escott v. Bar Chris Construction Corp.*,[11] for example, were held liable for a failure to detect danger signals in materials that, under GAAS, required further investigation under the circumstances. Merely asking questions is not always sufficient to satisfy the requirement of due diligence.

Defenses to Liability Besides proving that he or she has acted with due diligence, an accountant may raise the following defenses to Section 11 liability:

1. There were no misstatements or omissions.
2. The misstatements or omissions were not of material facts.
3. The misstatements or omissions had no causal connection to the plaintiff's loss.
4. The plaintiff purchaser invested in the securities knowing of the misstatements or omissions.

LIABILITY UNDER SECTION 12(2) Section 12(2) of the Securities Act of 1933 imposes civil liability for fraud on anyone offering or selling a security.[12] Liability is based on the communication to an investor, whether orally or in the written prospectus,[13] of an untrue statement or omission of a material fact.

Before 1994, some courts applied Section 12(2) to accountants who *aided and abetted* the seller or the offeror of the securities in violating Section 12(2). In those jurisdictions, an accountant might have been liable if he or she knew or should have known that an untrue statement or omission of material fact existed in the offer or sale. In light of the United States Supreme Court's decision in *Central Bank of Denver, N.A. v. First Interstate Bank of Denver, N.A.*[14] (discussed later in this chapter)—which regards liability for aiding and abetting under Section 10(b)—accountants are less likely to be held liable in the future, in suits by private individuals, for aiding and abetting their clients' Section 12(2) violations.

PENALTIES AND SANCTIONS FOR VIOLATIONS Those who purchase securities and suffer harm as a result of a false or omitted statement, or some other violation, may bring a suit in a federal court to recover their losses and other damages. The U.S. Department of Justice brings criminal actions against those who commit willful violations. The penalties include fines up to $10,000, imprisonment up to five years, or both. The SEC is authorized to seek, against a willful violator, an injunction against further violations. The SEC can also ask a court to grant other relief, such as an order to a violator to refund profits derived from an illegal transaction.

Liability under the Securities Exchange Act of 1934

Under Sections 18 and 10(b) of the Securities Exchange Act of 1934 and Rule 10b-5 of the Securities and Exchange Commission, an accountant may be found liable for fraud. A plaintiff has a substantially heavier burden of proof under the 1934 act than under the 1933 act. Unlike the 1933 act, which provides that an accountant must prove due diligence to escape liability, the 1934 act relieves

10. 15 U.S.C. Section 77k(b)(3).
11. 283 F.Supp. 643 (S.D.N.Y. 1968). This case is presented in Chapter 27 as Case 27.1.
12. 15 U.S.C. Section 77l.
13. As discussed in Chapter 27, a *prospectus* contains financial disclosures about the corporation for the benefit of potential investors.
14. 511 U.S. 164, 114 S.Ct. 1439, 128 L.Ed.2d 119 (1994).

from liability the accountant who acted in "good faith."

LIABILITY UNDER SECTION 18   Section 18 of the 1934 act imposes civil liability on an accountant who makes or causes to be made in any application, report, or document a statement that at the time and in light of the circumstances was false or misleading with respect to any material fact.[15]

Section 18 liability is narrow in that it applies only to applications, reports, documents, and registration statements filed with the SEC. This remedy is further limited in that it applies only to sellers and purchasers. Under Section 18, a seller or purchaser must prove one of the following:

1.   That the false or misleading statement affected the price of the security.
2.   That the purchaser or seller relied on the false or misleading statement in making the purchase or sale and was not aware of the inaccuracy of the statement.

Even if a purchaser or seller proves these two elements, an accountant can be exonerated of liability on proof of "good faith" in the preparation of the financial statement. To demonstrate good faith, an accountant must show that he or she had no knowledge that the financial statement was false and misleading. Acting in good faith requires the total absence of an intention on the part of the accountant to seek an unfair advantage over or to defraud another party. Proving a lack of intent to deceive, manipulate, or defraud is frequently referred to as proving a lack of *scienter* (knowledge on the part of a misrepresenting party that material facts have been misrepresented or omitted with an intent to deceive). Absence of good faith can be demonstrated not only by proof of *scienter* but also by the accountant's reckless conduct and gross negligence. (Note that "mere" negligence in the preparation of a financial statement does not constitute liability under the 1934 act. This differs from provisions of the 1933 act, under which an accountant is liable for all negligent acts.) In addition to the good faith defense, accountants have available as a defense the buyer's or seller's knowledge that the financial statement was false and misleading.

A court, under Section 18 of the 1934 act, also has the discretion to assess reasonable costs, including attorneys' fees, against accountants.[16] Sellers and purchasers may maintain a cause of action "within one year after the discovery of the facts constituting the cause of action and within three years after such cause of action accrued."[17]

LIABILITY UNDER SECTION 10(b) AND RULE 10b-5
The Securities Exchange Act of 1934 further subjects accountants to potential legal liability in its antifraud provisions. Section 10(b) of the 1934 act and SEC Rule 10b-5 contain the antifraud provisions. As stated in *Herman & MacLean v. Huddleston,* "a private right of action under Section 10(b) of the 1934 act and Rule 10b-5 has been consistently recognized for more than 35 years."[18]

Section 10(b) makes it unlawful for any person, including accountants, to use, in connection with the purchase or sale of any security, any manipulative or deceptive device or contrivance in contravention of SEC rules and regulations.[19] Rule 10b-5 further makes it unlawful for any person, by use of any means or instrumentality of interstate commerce, to do the following:

1.   To employ any device, scheme, or artifice to defraud.
2.   To misrepresent a material fact necessary to make the statements, in light of the circumstances, not misleading.
3.   To engage in any act, practice, or course of business that operates or would operate as a fraud or deceit on any person, in connection with the purchase or sale of any security.[20]

Accountants may be held liable only to sellers or purchasers under Section 10(b) and Rule 10b-5.[21] The scope of these antifraud provisions is extremely wide. Privity is not necessary for a recovery. Under these provisions, an accountant may be found liable not only for fraudulent misstatements of material facts in written material filed with the SEC but also for any fraudulent oral statements or omissions made in connection with the purchase or sale of any security.

---

16.   15 U.S.C. Section 78r(a).
17.   15 U.S.C. Section 78r(c).
18.   459 U.S. 375, 103 S.Ct. 683, 74 L.Ed.2d 548 (1983).
19.   15 U.S.C. Section 78j(b).
20.   17 C.F.R. Section 240.10b-5.
21.   See *Blue Chip Stamps v. Manor Drug Stores,* 421 U.S. 723, 95 S.Ct. 1917, 44 L.Ed.2d 539 (1975).

---

15.   15 U.S.C. Section 78r(a).

The Requirement of Scienter For a plaintiff to recover from an accountant under the antifraud provisions of the 1934 act, he or she must, in addition to establishing status as a purchaser or seller, prove *scienter*,[22] a fraudulent action or deception, reliance, materiality, and causation. A plaintiff who fails to establish these elements cannot recover damages from an accountant under Section 10(b) or Rule 10b-5.

Liability of Aiders and Abettors A significant issue in recent years concerns whether accountants (and others) may be held liable in private actions for "aiding and abetting" violations of various provisions of the securities laws, including Section 10(b) and Rule 10b-5. In a 1994 case, *Central Bank of Denver, N.A. v. First Interstate Bank of Denver, N.A.*,[23] the United States Supreme Court held that private parties could not bring actions against accountants for aiding and abetting violations of Section 10(b) of the 1934 act. The Court stated that "none of the express causes of action in the 1934 Act further imposes liability on one who aids or abets a violation." It was not clear from the Court's opinion, however, whether the logic of *Central Bank* should extend to injunctive actions brought by the SEC against aiders and abettors of Section 10(b) violations. We examine this issue further in the next subsection.

The Private Securities Litigation Reform Act of 1995

The Private Securities Litigation Reform Act of 1995 made some changes to the potential liability of accountants and other professionals in securities fraud cases. For example, the act imposed a new obligation on accountants. An auditor must use adequate procedures in an audit to detect any illegal acts of the company being audited. If something illegal is detected, the auditor must disclose it to the company's board of directors, the audit committee, or the Securities and Exchange Commission, depending on the circumstances.[24]

In terms of liability, the 1995 act provides that in most cases, a party is liable only for that proportion of damages for which he or she is responsible.[25] For example, if an accountant actively participated in defrauding investors, he or she could be liable for the entire loss. If the accountant was not actually aware of the fraud, however, his or her liability could be proportionately less.

The act also stated that aiding and abetting a violation of the Securities Exchange Act of 1934 is a violation in itself. The following case addresses this provision of the 1995 act. The case arose after the SEC issued an injunctive order against an attorney for aiding and abetting violations of Section 10(b) of the 1934 act. (The case involved an attorney, but the point of law applies to accountants and others as well.) The order was issued just two weeks after the Supreme Court had rendered its opinion in the *Central Bank* case. The attorney appealed the order, claiming that the Supreme Court's decision in *Central Bank* precluded the SEC from bringing a civil injunctive action for aiding and abetting securities fraud. A central issue in the case had to do with whether the 1995 Private Securities Litigation Reform Act reversed any impact that *Central Bank* might have had on the SEC's power to enjoin aiding and abetting of Section 10(b).

---

22. See *Ernst & Ernst v. Hochfelder*, 425 U.S. 185, 96 S.Ct. 1375, 47 L.Ed.2d 668 (1976).
23. 511 U.S. 164, 114 S.Ct. 1439, 128 L.Ed.2d 119 (1994).

24. 15 U.S.C. Section 78j-1.
25. 15 U.S.C. Section 78u-4(g).

CASE 31.3

SEC v. Fehn

United States Court of Appeals,
Ninth Circuit, 1996.
97 F.3d 1276.

FACTS CTI Technical, Inc., issued stock in a public offering that violated federal securities laws. The Securities and Exchange Commission (SEC) began an investigation. Thomas Fehn, an attorney who represented CTI during the investigation, prepared certain required reports for CTI and sent them to the SEC. The reports contained material misrepresentations related to the securities violations. The SEC filed a suit in a federal district court against Fehn, charging him with aiding and abetting securities fraud. The court issued an injunction

Case 31.3—Continued

barring Fehn from aiding and abetting any future securities fraud. Fehn appealed to the U.S. Court of Appeals for the Ninth Circuit. Fehn argued, among other things, that the United States Supreme Court's decision in *Central Bank* prevented the SEC from filing suits for aiding and abetting securities violations.

ISSUE Did the Supreme Court's decision in *Central Bank* prevent the SEC from filing suits for aiding and abetting securities violations?

DECISION No. The U.S. Court of Appeals for the Ninth Circuit affirmed the lower court's injunction barring Fehn from participating in any future securities fraud.

REASON The appellate court concluded that the Private Securities Litigation Reform Act of 1995 (PSLRA) precluded the extension of the Supreme Court's decision in *Central Bank* to SEC actions. The court explained that the PSLRA "provides that aiding and abetting a violation of [federal securities laws] is itself a violation, and as such is subject to injunctive actions and civil actions for money penalties by the SEC." The court pointed to legislative history that confirmed the PSLRA "was intended to override *Central Bank*."

FOR CRITICAL ANALYSIS—Economic Consideration *If the Supreme Court had ruled that the SEC could not file suits for aiding and abetting securities violations, what effect might that have had on transactions in securities?*

▮ Potential Criminal Liability

An accountant may be found criminally liable for violations of the Securities Act of 1933, the Securities Exchange Act of 1934, the Internal Revenue Code, and both state and federal criminal codes. Under both the 1933 act and the 1934 act, accountants may be subject to criminal penalties for *willful* violations—imprisonment of up to five years and/or a fine of up to $10,000 under the 1933 act and up to $100,000 under the 1934 act.

The Internal Revenue Code, Section 7206(2),[26] makes aiding or assisting in the preparation of a false tax return a felony punishable by a fine of $100,000 ($500,000 in the case of a corporation) and imprisonment for up to three years. Those who prepare tax returns for others also may face liability under the Internal Revenue Code.

Note that one does not have to be an accountant to be subject to liability for tax-preparer penalties. The Internal Revenue Code defines a tax preparer as any person who prepares for compensation, or who employs one or more persons to prepare for compensation, all or a substantial portion of a tax return or a claim for a tax refund.[27]

Section 6694[28] of the Internal Revenue Code imposes on the tax preparer a penalty of $250 per return for negligent understatement of his or her client's tax liability and a penalty of $1,000 for willful understatement of tax liability or reckless or intentional disregard of rules or regulations. A tax preparer may also be subject to penalties under Section 6695[29] for failing to furnish the taxpayer with a copy of the return, failing to sign the return, or failing to furnish the appropriate tax identification numbers.

---

26. 26 U.S.C. Section 7206(2).

27. 26 U.S.C. Section 7701(a)(36).
28. 26 U.S.C. Section 6694.
29. 26 U.S.C. Section 6695.

Section 6701[30] of the Internal Revenue Code imposes a penalty of $1,000 per document for aiding and abetting an individual's understatement of tax liability (the penalty is increased to $10,000 in corporate cases). The tax preparer's liability is limited to one penalty per taxpayer per tax year. If this penalty is imposed, no penalty can be imposed under Section 6694 with respect to the same document.

In most states, criminal penalties may be imposed for such actions as knowingly certifying false or fraudulent reports; falsifying, altering, or destroying books of account; and obtaining property or credit through the use of false financial statements.

▮ Working Papers

Performing an audit for a client involves an accumulation of **working papers**—the various documents used and developed during the audit. These include notes, computations, memoranda, copies, and other papers that make up the work product of an accountant's services to a client. Under the common law, which in this instance has been codified in a number of states, working papers remain the accountant's property. It is important for accountants to retain these records in the event that they need to defend against lawsuits for negligence or other actions in which their competence is challenged. But because an accountant's working papers reflect his or her client's financial situation, the client has a right of access to them. (An accountant must return to his or her client any of the client's records or journals on the client's request, and failure to do so may result in liability.)

The client must give permission before working papers can be transferred to another accountant. Without the client's permission or a valid court order, the contents of working papers are not to be disclosed. Disclosure would constitute a breach of the accountant's fiduciary duty to the client. On the ground of unauthorized disclosure, the client could initiate a malpractice suit. The accountant's best defense would be that the client gave permission for the papers' release.

▮ Confidentiality and Privilege

Professionals are restrained by the ethical tenets of their professions to keep all communications with their clients confidential. In a few states, the confidentiality of accountant-client communications is also protected by law, which confers a *privilege* on such communications. This privilege is granted because of the need for full disclosure to the accountant of the facts of a client's case. To encourage frankness, confidential communications are normally held in strictest confidence and protected by law. The accountant and his or her employees may not discuss the client's case with anyone—even under court order—without the client's permission. The client holds the privilege, and only the client may waive it—by disclosing privileged information to someone outside the privilege, for example.

The majority of states, however, abide by the common law, which provides that if a court so orders, an accountant must disclose information about his or her clients to the court. Physicians and other professionals may similarly be compelled to disclose in court information given to them in confidence by patients or clients.

Communications between accountants and their clients are not privileged under federal law. In cases involving federal law, state-provided rights to confidentiality of accountant-client communications are not recognized. Thus, in those cases, in response to a court order, an accountant must provide the information sought.

▮ Limiting Professionals' Liability

As mentioned earlier in this chapter, accountants (and other professionals) can limit their liability to some extent by disclaiming it. Depending on the circumstances, a disclaimer that does not meet certain requirements will not be effective, however; and in some situations, a disclaimer may not be effective at all.

Professionals may be able to limit their liability for the misconduct of other professionals with whom they work by organizing their business as a professional corporation (P.C.) or a limited liability partnership (LLP). In some states, a professional who is a member of a P.C. is not personally liable for a co-member's misconduct unless he or she

---

30. 26 U.S.C. Section 6701.

participated in it or supervised the member who acted wrongly. The innocent professional is liable only to the extent of his or her interest in the assets

of the firm. This is also true for professionals who are partners in an LLP. LLPs are covered in Chapter 23.

▮ Terms and Concepts

defalcation 647
due diligence 652

generally accepted accounting
  principles (GAAP) 647

generally accepted auditing
  standards (GAAS) 647
working papers 656

▮ Chapter Summary: Professional Liability

COMMON LAW LIABILITY	
Liability to Client *(See pages 646–649.)*	1. *Breach of contract*—An accountant who fails to perform according to his or her contractual obligations can be held liable for breach of contract and resulting damages. 2. *Negligence*—An accountant, in performance of his or her duties, must use the care, knowledge, and judgment generally used by other accountants in the same or similar circumstances. Failure to do so is negligence. An accountant's violation of generally accepted accounting principles and generally accepted auditing standards is *prima facie* evidence of negligence. 3. *Fraud*—Actual intent to misrepresent a material fact to a client, when the client relies on the misrepresentation, is fraud. Gross negligence in performance of duties is constructive fraud.
Liability to Third Parties *(See pages 649–651.)*	An accountant may be liable for negligence to any third person the accountant knows or should have known will benefit from the accountant's work. The standard for imposing this liability varies, but generally courts follow one of the following three rules: 1. *Ultramares rule*—Liability will be imposed only if the accountant is in privity, or near privity, with the third party. 2. *Restatement rule*—Liability will be imposed only if the third party's reliance is foreseen, or known, or if the third party is among a class of foreseeable, or known, users. The majority of courts apply this rule. 3. *"Reasonably foreseeable user" rule*—Liability will be imposed if the third party's use was reasonably foreseeable.
STATUTORY LIABILITY	
Securities Act of 1933, Section 11 *(See pages 651–652.)*	An accountant who makes a false statement or omits a material fact in audited financial statements required for registration of securities under the law may be liable to anyone who acquires securities covered by the registration statement. The accountant's defense is basically the use of due diligence and the reasonable belief that the work was complete and correct. The burden of proof is on the accountant. Willful violations of this act may be subject to criminal penalties.
Securities Act of 1933, Section 12(2) *(See page 652.)*	In some jurisdictions, an accountant may be liable for aiding and abetting the seller or offeror of securities when a prospectus or communication presented to an investor

(Continued)

▍Chapter Summary: Professional Liability—Continued

Securities Act of 1933, Section 12(2)—Continued	contained an untrue statement or omission of a material fact. To be liable, the accountant must have known, or at least should have known, that an untrue statement or omission of a material fact existed in the offer to sell the security.
Securities Exchange Act of 1934, Sections 18 and 10(b) *(See pages 652–655.)*	Accountants are held liable for false and misleading applications, reports, and documents required under the act. The burden is on the plaintiff, and the accountant has numerous defenses, including good faith and lack of knowledge that what was submitted was false. Willful violations of this act may be subject to criminal penalties.
Internal Revenue Code *(See pages 655–656.)*	1. Aiding or assisting in the preparation of a false tax return is a felony. Aiding and abetting an individual's understatement of tax liability is a separate crime. 2. Tax preparers who negligently or willfully understate a client's tax liability or who recklessly or intentionally disregard Internal Revenue Service rules or regulations are subject to criminal penalties. 3. Tax preparers who fail to provide a taxpayer with a copy of the return, fail to sign the return, or fail to furnish the appropriate tax identification numbers may also be subject to criminal penalties.

▍For Review

1. What are the common law theories under which accountants may be liable to clients?
2. What are the rules concerning an auditor's liability to third parties?
3. How might an accountant violate federal securities laws?

4. What crimes might an accountant commit under the Internal Revenue Code?
5. What restrains accountants to keep communications with their clients confidential?

▍Questions and Case Problems

31–1. Accountant's Liability to Third Parties. Larkin, Inc., retains Howard Perkins to manage its books and prepare its financial statements. Perkins, a certified public accountant, lives in Indiana and practices there. After twenty years, Perkins has become a bit bored with the format of generally accepted accounting principles (GAAP) and has become creative in his accounting methods. Now, though, Perkins has a problem, as he is being sued by Molly Tucker, one of Larkin's creditors. Tucker alleges that Perkins either knew or should have known that Larkin's financial statements would be distributed to various individuals. Furthermore, she asserts that these financial statements were negligently prepared and seriously inaccurate. What are the consequences of Perkins's failure to adopt GAAP? Under the traditional *Ultramares* rule, can Tucker recover damages from Perkins?

31–2. Accountant's Liability to Third Parties. The accounting firm of Goldman, Walters, Johnson & Co.

prepared financial statements for Lucy's Fashions, Inc. After reviewing the various financial statements, Happydays State Bank agreed to loan Lucy's Fashions $35,000 for expansion. When Lucy's Fashions declared bankruptcy under Chapter 11 six months later, Happydays State Bank promptly filed an action against Goldman, Walters, Johnson & Co., alleging negligent preparation of financial statements. Assuming that the court has abandoned the *Ultramares* approach, what is the result? What are the policy reasons for holding accountants liable to third parties with whom they are not in privity?

31–3. Accountant's Liability under Rule 10b-5. In early 1989, Bennett, Inc., offered a substantial number of new common shares to the public. Harvey Helms had a long-standing interest in Bennett because his grandfather had once been president of the company. On receiving a prospectus prepared and distributed by Bennett, Helms was dismayed by the pessimism it embodied. After much debate, Helms decided to delay purchasing stock in the company. A few months later, Helms asserted that the prospectus prepared by the accountants was overly pessimistic. Moreover, Helms alleged that the prospectus contained materially misleading statements. How successful could Helms be in bringing a cause of action under Rule 10b-5 against the accountants of Bennett, Inc.?

31–4. Accountant's Liability to Third Parties. The plaintiffs, Harry and Barry Rosenblum, brought an action against Touche Ross & Co., a prominent accounting firm. The plaintiffs alleged that they had relied on the correctness of audits in acquiring Giant common stock in conjunction with the sale of their business to Giant. The financial statements of Giant were found to be fraudulent, and the stock that the Rosenblums had acquired proved to be worthless. The plaintiffs alleged that Touche's negligence in conducting the audits was the proximate cause of their loss. Does an auditor owe a duty to third persons known and intended by the auditor to be recipients of the audit? Furthermore, does an independent auditor owe a duty to anyone when the opinion he or she furnishes does not include a statement limiting the dissemination of the information contained in the financial statements? [*H. Rosenblum, Inc. v. Adler*, 93 N.J. 324, 461 A.2d 138 (1983)]

31–5. Auditors' Liability to Third Parties. Max Mitchell, a certified public accountant and president of Max Mitchell & Co., went to First Florida Bank, N.A., to negotiate a $500,000 unsecured line of credit for C. M. Systems, Inc. The audited financial statements that Mitchell gave the bank did not indicate that C. M. Systems owed any money. In fact, the company owed at least $750,000 to several banks. First Florida approved the loan, but C. M. Systems never repaid it. The bank filed a suit in a Florida state court against Mitchell and his firm, alleging negligence. Because there was no privity between Mitchell and the bank, the court granted Mitchell summary judgment. The bank appealed. On what basis might the appellate court reverse? [*First Florida Bank, N.A. v. Max Mitchell & Co.*, 558 So.2d 9 (Fla. 1990)]

31–6. Accountant's Liability under Rule 10b-5. The plaintiffs were the purchasers of all the stock in companies owned by the defendant sellers. Alleging fraud under the federal securities law and under the New York common law of fraud, the plaintiffs sued the defendant sellers and their accounting firm. What should be the result with respect to the accounting firm, assuming that the treatment of shipping costs, expenses, and other charges was not in accordance with generally accepted accounting principles and hence created an inaccurate financial picture in the financial statement? [*Berkowitz v. Baron*, 428 F.Supp. 1190 (S.D.N.Y. 1977)]

31–7. Accountant's Liability to Third Parties. Credit Alliance Corp. is a major financial service company

engaged primarily in financing the purchase of capital equipment through installment sales and leasing agreements. As a condition of extending additional major financing to L. B. Smith, Credit Alliance required an audited financial statement. Smith provided Credit Alliance with an audited financial statement prepared by the accounting firm of Arthur Andersen & Co. Later, on Smith's petitioning for bankruptcy, it was discovered that Smith, at the time of the audit, had been in a precarious financial position. Credit Alliance filed suit against Arthur Andersen, claiming that Andersen had failed to conduct investigations in accordance with proper auditing standards and that Andersen's recklessness had resulted in misleading statements that caused Credit Alliance to incur damages. In addition, it was claimed that Andersen knew, or should have known, that Credit Alliance would rely on these statements in issuing credit to Smith. Discuss whether Credit Alliance, as a third party, could hold Arthur Andersen liable in a negligence action. [*Credit Alliance Corp. v. Arthur Andersen & Co.*, 65 N.Y.2d 536, 483 N.E.2d 110, 493 N.Y.S.2d 435 (1985)]

31–8. Accountant's Liability to Third Parties. Toro Co. was a major supplier of equipment and credit to Summit Power Equipment Distributors. Toro required audited reports from Summit to evaluate the distributor's financial condition. Summit supplied Toro with reports prepared by Krouse, Kern & Co., an accounting firm. The reports allegedly contained mistakes and omissions regarding Summit's financial condition. According to Toro, it extended and renewed large amounts of credit to Summit in reliance on the audited reports. Summit was unable to repay these amounts, and Toro brought a negligence action against the accounting firm and the individual accountants. Evidence produced at the trial showed that Krouse knew that the reports it furnished to Summit were to be used by Summit to induce Toro to extend credit, but no evidence was produced to show either a contractual relationship between Krouse and Toro or a link between these companies evidencing Krouse's understanding of Toro's actual reliance on the reports. If the relevant state law followed the *Ultramares* rule, what would be the result? [*Toro Co. v. Krouse, Kern & Co.*, 827 F.2d 155 (7th Cir. 1987)]

31–9. Accountant's Liability under Rule 10b-5. The accounting firm of Arthur Young & Co. was employed by DMI Furniture, Inc., to conduct a review of an audit prepared by Brown, Kraft & Co., certified public accountants, for Gillespie Furniture Co. DMI planned to purchase Gillespie and wished to determine its net worth. Arthur Young, by letter, advised DMI that Brown, Kraft had performed a high-quality audit and that Gillespie's inventory on the audit dates was fairly stated on the general ledger. Allegedly as a result of these representations, DMI went forward with its purchase of Gillespie. Subsequently, DMI charged Brown, Kraft & Co., Arthur Young, and Gillespie's former owners with violations of Section 10(b) of the Securities Exchange Act and SEC Rule 10b-5. DMI complained that Arthur Young's review had proved to be materially inaccurate and misleading, primarily because the inventory reflected in the balance sheet was grossly overstated. Arthur Young was charged "with acting recklessly in failing to detect, and thus failing to disclose, material omissions and reckless conduct on the part of Brown, Kraft, and in making affirmative misstatements in its letter" to DMI. DMI sought $8 million in compensatory damages and $8 million in punitive damages from the accounting firms. Did DMI have a valid cause of action under either Section 10(b) or Rule 10b-5? [*DMI Furniture, Inc. v. Brown, Kraft & Co.,* 644 F.Supp. 1517 (C.D.Cal. 1986)]

A QUESTION OF ETHICS AND SOCIAL RESPONSIBILITY

31–10. *Crawford, a certified public accountant, prepared a financial statement for Erps Construction Co., which was seeking a loan from the First National Bank of Bluefield. Crawford knew at the time he prepared the statement that the bank would rely on the statement in making its decision on whether to extend credit to Erps. The bank later sued Crawford, alleging that he had been professionally negligent in preparing the financial statement, upon which the bank had relied in determining whether to give the construction company a loan. Crawford defended against the suit by asserting that he could not be liable to the bank because of lack of privity. The trial court ruled that in the absence of contractual privity between the parties, the bank could not recover from the accountant. On appeal, the appellate court adopted the rule enunciated by the* Restatement (Second) of Torts *in regard to a professional's liability to third parties. [First National Bank of Bluefield v. Crawford, 386 S.E.2d 310 (W.Va. 1989)]*

1. What is the standard of an accountant's liability to third parties under the *Restatement (Second) of Torts*? What ethical reasoning underlies this standard?

2. Do you think that the standard of liability under the Restatement adequately balances the rights of accountants and the rights of third parties? Can you think of a fairer standard?

3. A few courts have adopted the principle that accountants should be liable for negligence to all persons who use and rely on their work products, provided that this use and reliance was foreseeable by the accountants at the time they prepared the documents relied on. Does such a standard of liability impose too great a burden on accountants and accounting firms? Why or why not?

▌Unit Ten—Cumulative Hypothetical Problem

31–11. *JB Mediquip, Inc., is in the business of manufacturing hospital equipment. The business was formed several years ago by Jerrold Botran, who remains the company's president and major shareholder.*

1. Aaron Falkner, a certified public accountant, provides accounting services to JB Mediquip. The services include preparing JB's financial reports and issuing opinion letters based on those reports. One year, JB falls into serious financial trouble, but neither Falkner's reports nor his opinion letters indicate this situation. Relying on Falkner's portrayal of the company's financial health, JB borrows substantial sums of money to invest in the construction of a new manufacturing plant. The bank, in lending JB the money, relies on an opinion letter from Falkner. Falkner is aware of the bank's reliance on the letter. Assuming that Falkner did not engage in intentional fraud but was negligent, what is his potential liability in this situation? Discuss fully.

GUIDE TO PERSONAL LAW

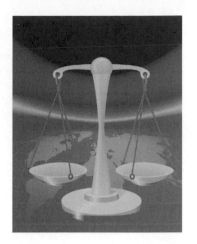

Contents

Note to Student*

Business law and the legal environment do not just consist of theoretical concepts and vague statutes. Rather, you will find that you can use what you have learned from your course in many practical ways throughout your life. In this *Personal Law Handbook* you will discover suggestions for preventing costly legal problems, as well as ideas about how to handle those legal problems that you have not been able to avoid. To a large extent, personal law is preventive—the more you know about the legal consequences of your actions and the actions of those with whom you have dealings, the better you will be able to prevent legal problems.

In no way should you take this *Handbook* to be a substitute for licensed, professional legal assistance. Whenever you think that you have a legal problem, you should consult an attorney.

---

* This handbook was written by Frank B. Cross of the University of Texas at Austin.

Topic 1   **Renting a Home**

Like millions of Americans, you may decide not to own your own home. Instead, you may choose to rent a house, an apartment, a mobile home, or some other form of housing. As a tenant, your relationship with your landlord is *generally governed by the law of the state in which you live.*

▌Leases

The **lease** is the agreement between you and your landlord that sets out rights and duties regarding the rental property. A written lease is a legal document enforceable in court—a signature on a lease is generally proof that the person who signed it read it and agreed to it. Thus, if you sign a lease, you are bound to do what it says. For this reason, you should read an entire lease carefully before you sign it.

Most leases are written to favor the landlord's interests. If you are unsure of the meaning or effect of any of the terms, before signing the lease you should seek the advice of a lawyer, a tenants' rights organization, a legal aid office, or others experienced with leases.

Oral Leases

In almost all states, an oral lease for a period of less than a year is valid and enforceable. The basic problem with an oral lease is the same as the basic problem with other oral contracts: it is difficult to prove the terms of the oral agreement. Generally, it is assumed an oral lease that requires rent to be paid monthly creates a **month-to-month tenancy.** This means that, with a month's written notice, a landlord can raise the rent or end the tenancy. Of course, you can also end the tenancy with a month's written notice. The notice must be given a month (or, if a local statute states thirty days, then thirty days) before the rent is due.

Lease Terms

Leases include such terms as the following items:

1. The names of the parties to the agreement.
2. The address of the rental property.
3. The amount and the due date of the rent.
4. Other fees and charges.
5. The period of time for which the property is rented.

6.   The rights and duties of the parties, which relate to use of the premises, alterations, maintenance, repairs, and other areas of responsibility.
7.   The amount of a security deposit.
8.   The conditions under which the rent can be raised.
9.   Provisions for subleasing the property and terminating the lease.

ALTERATIONS   Can you make changes to rental property after you move in? In most circumstances, the answer depends on the terms of the lease. Most leases include a provision that prohibits alterations without the landlord's written approval. If you do not get the landlord's approval before making alterations, you will violate the lease and may be liable for any presumed destruction of the property. If there is no lease provision concerning alterations, you can make changes to the property that do not reduce the value of the property to the landlord.

If no lease provision applies and you have made a change—for example, if you have added bookshelves or installed new cabinets—who owns the new addition? If you cannot come to an agreement with your landlord, and you ask a court to decide the question, the court will look at the laws of your state to determine who owns what. In some states, the addition may be the property of the landlord; in other states, it may be yours, and you can sell it to the landlord or remove it. If it is your property and you choose to remove it, you should do so carefully to avoid any damage to the rental property. If the property is damaged, you are responsible.

SUBLEASES   Normally, a lease contains a provision that prohibits a tenant from **subleasing** the rental property without the landlord's written approval. If the lease does not require the landlord's approval, in most cases you can sublease for whatever period of time you could remain on the property under the lease. A sublease cannot be for a longer period than you could stay on the property. For instance, if you signed a one-year lease that contains no provision regarding subleasing and there are six months left before the lease expires, you could sublease the property for six months or less. *As the original tenant, however, you are still liable for the rent and any damage to the property.*

Whether or not your lease prohibits subleasing, can you move out before the lease expires? Gener-

ally, the answer is yes. You will be liable for the rent for the rest of the lease, however. There may be a limit on how much you pay: in some states, a landlord must make a reasonable effort to find a new tenant for the same amount of rent and the same period of time. If the property can be rented only for a smaller amount of money or a shorter time, you will be liable for the difference.

To minimize your losses, as soon as you know you will be moving out, send the landlord written notice (via certified or registered mail) of your plan to allow as much time as possible to find a new tenant. Keep a copy of the notice. You might also help find a new tenant by advertising that the property will be available.

RENEWAL   Typically, a lease requires that you move out when it expires. A lease can provide, however, that it renews automatically unless you tell the landlord in advance that you plan to move out. If you do not give the landlord this notice, you will be renewing the lease on the same terms for the same period of time. A different lease might provide that if you stay on the property after the lease expires and the landlord accepts a payment of rent, the lease renews according to the original terms.

If the lease does not mention renewal, in some states the landlord does not need to give you notice that the lease is ending. In these states, the reasoning is that you know when the lease expires because you signed it, and thus you must leave the property when the lease ends without additional notice. In other states, if you remain on the property after the lease ends and the landlord accepts a payment of rent, a new month-to-month tenancy is created or, in some states, the lease renews according to its original terms.

OTHER RIGHTS   You may have other rights and responsibilities as a tenant. Leases often cover such subjects as pets, parking, cleaning, noise, and so on. If you violate any of these rules, the landlord can give you notice to move or take you to court to have you evicted. The other tenants are probably subject to the same rules. If you have any complaints regarding other tenants' behavior under the lease, contact your landlord. If you are unhappy with the landlord's response, or if the complaint concerns a neighbor who is not a tenant, contact your attorney, a legal aid office, or a local tenants' rights organization.

Illegal Terms

A landlord cannot legally discriminate against you on the basis of your race, color, religion, national origin, or gender. Also, a landlord cannot discriminate against you if you have a handicap or, in most cases, if you have children. Similarly, as a tenant, you cannot legally promise to do something counter to the laws prohibiting discrimination. The public policy underlying these prohibitions is to treat all people equally.

One of the reasons to read a lease carefully is to look for, and avoid, illegal terms. Generally, any clause that purports to waive your legal rights is unenforceable. For this reason, clauses that attempt to do any or all of the following may be unenforceable in your state:

1. Waiving your right to a jury trial in eviction proceedings.
2. Permitting your landlord to evict you in a court proceeding without your presence.
3. Providing for a nonrefundable security deposit.
4. Limiting your landlord's liability for hazardous conditions that injure you or your guests.
5. Requiring that you pay an unreasonably high fee or penalty for a late rent payment.
6. Requiring that you assume your landlord's responsibility for maintenance and repair of a private residence.
7. Requiring that you pay your landlord's attorneys' fees if the landlord sues to enforce the lease.

A lease is enforceable in most cases even if it contains an illegal clause. A court will strike the illegal clause from the lease and enforce the other terms. For example, some states prohibit a clause under which you agree to pay the landlord's attorneys' fees if the landlord sues to enforce the lease. If you fail to pay the rent and the landlord sues, the court could enforce the lease but order the landlord to pay his or her own attorneys' fees.

▮ Eviction

Eviction is a legal process by which your landlord can get you off the rental property. In most states, the procedure involves a written notice to you and a hearing in court.

Reasons for Eviction

Your landlord can have you evicted for violating the lease, the law, or other rules that apply to the rental property. Reasons that your landlord might want to evict you include:

1. Failing to pay the rent.
2. Remaining on the property after the lease expires.
3. Damaging the property.
4. Disturbing your neighbors' quiet enjoyment.

The most common reason for eviction is nonpayment of rent. Paying rent late, paying less than is due, and paying it to the wrong person or at the wrong place are related reasons that a landlord might want to evict you. Failing to pay a valid rent increase may justify eviction. If you believe that an increase is not valid, you may defend against an eviction on that ground. Another course of action is to pay the increase under protest and challenge it in court.

Can your landlord refuse to accept rent that is offered on time and evict you for nonpayment of rent? If your landlord refuses to accept your payment, send the landlord a certified, return-receipt-requested letter offering again to pay the rent. Keep a copy of the letter. If your landlord tries to evict you, you can show the copy of the letter and receipt to the court to prove that you offered the rent and it was refused.

Your landlord can evict you for staying on the property after your lease expires. You might avoid an eviction after the last month of the term by offering the landlord the next month's rent. If the landlord accepts the payment, a new month-to-month tenancy begins or, in some states, the lease is renewed.

Eviction Notice

Ordinarily, your landlord has to give you written notice before beginning an eviction, to give you a chance to correct the violation. For example, if you have not paid the rent, you must be given an opportunity to pay it. The notice period is usually short— three days, in most states. Of course, if the lease has expired, in most states the landlord is not required to give notice. Many states have strict requirements about how the notice must be given. Sometimes it must be given to you personally or sent to you by registered or certified mail.

Eviction Proceedings

In most states, eviction requires going to court. An eviction proceeding is generally a brief proceeding in which the court acts quickly to determine who has the right to the rental property. In some states and in some cases, you have the right to a jury trial (ask the clerk of the court). You are not entitled to a court-appointed lawyer in an eviction proceeding, and you are not required to have one, but it is a good idea to be represented because the landlord will probably have an attorney. If you choose to represent yourself, you can do anything an attorney could do, but you will be expected to do it competently. If you do not show up to defend yourself, you normally automatically lose.

In the proceeding, your landlord must prove the truth of what he or she claims and show that what is proved is a cause for eviction. You have a right to prove that the landlord is wrong. For example, if the landlord is attempting to evict you for not paying all of the rent or not paying a rent increase, you might defend yourself on any of the following grounds:

1.   You paid the rent.
2.   No rent was owed.
3.   You rightfully deducted the cost of a repair to the property from the amount of the rent.
4.   The landlord's motive for the eviction or the rent increase violated the lease or was otherwise illegal.
5.   The eviction notice did not give you necessary information within the required time.

The court decides whom to believe and if what is proved is a sufficient cause for eviction or a sufficient defense against it. The court can issue an order to the landlord to leave you alone, or the court can issue a judgment in favor of the landlord for the amount of the rent. The court can also issue an order to an officer (usually a sheriff) to put you out on the street. The officer may give you notice a few days before acting, depending on local law. In many states, the court can order a **stay of eviction**, which temporarily postpones execution of the judgment, usually on the basis of a hardship such as cold winter weather or the lack of another place to live. The entire process, from the day you receive the notice of eviction to the day the sheriff appears at your door, may take as little as three weeks or as much as three months. Either party may appeal the judgment.

▮ Substandard Housing

Landlords must maintain rental property to meet certain minimum health and safety standards. These standards are generally established in state or local laws known as housing codes. In most states, the **implied warranty of habitability** also guarantees that landlords will provide decent, safe, sanitary, and livable housing, as defined by local housing codes.

Local Housing Codes

Housing codes normally include regulations that cover such details as the following:

1.   Room temperature.
2.   Water temperature, water pressure, and plumbing.
3.   Electrical wiring and fire safety, including smoke alarms.
4.   Rodent and insect infestation.
5.   The number of garbage cans.
6.   Building structure and related features, such as the kind of locks required on apartment doors.

To learn the exact requirements of your local housing code, contact your attorney, a legal aid office, a local tenants' rights organization, or the city or county building inspection department. Your local library may also have a reference copy of the housing code and other state and local laws.

The Implied Warranty of Habitability

The implied warranty of habitability applies whether or not it is mentioned in your lease, and a clause in the lease that attempts to reject the warranty is unenforceable. Generally, this warranty covers only the most serious problems—a lack of heat in the winter, for example, rather than a few ants on the kitchen floor. If your landlord fails to fix a serious problem, you can go to court and charge the landlord with violation of the warranty. Your best evidence to prove the substandard condition of your home is your copy of the building inspection department's report (discussed below).

Steps to Take to Fix the Situation

What can you do if your landlord fails to provide decent, safe, sanitary, and livable housing? You can contact the city or county to enforce your local housing code. There are steps you can take on your own, or with other tenants, to remedy the situation. Possible steps that you can take include moving out; repairing the condition that makes the housing unsafe, unsanitary, or unlivable and deducting the cost of the repair from the rent; reducing the amount of the rent that you pay; getting a court order to have the property repaired; and suing your landlord. Your landlord may challenge what you do, and this challenge may involve court action, but if you choose your remedy carefully and follow the appropriate steps, you should have a good defense.

CONTACT YOUR LOCAL BUILDING INSPECTION DEPARTMENT   If you believe that your landlord is in violation of your local housing code, contact your local building inspection department. Explain what you think is wrong and ask for an inspection. When the inspector arrives, point out the conditions that need repair and ask the inspector to check the rest of the building for other violations. When the inspector files a report, get a copy from the building inspection department. If there are mistakes or something is missing, ask for a new inspection.

Your landlord will be given a copy of the report and an order to repair violations within a certain period of time (usually thirty days). The building inspection department and the courts are responsible for seeing that your landlord makes the repairs, but if there will be a hearing, you may want to go to explain what you think is wrong. A landlord who does not make the repairs is subject to a fine. If the violations are very serious, the property may be condemned and the building demolished.

MOVE OUT   If the property is essentially uninhabitable, you can move out. Generally, it does not matter what caused the property to become uninhabitable—a fire, a storm, a flood, or your landlord's failure to maintain the property—so long as the cause was not something that you did. Frequently, you can move out without giving the landlord notice and without being liable for future rent. You should be aware, however, that the option to move out was created by the courts as the **doctrine of constructive eviction.** Its availability varies from state to state and from case to case. If you move out and your landlord sues you, the court may decide that the property was habit-

able, and you can be held liable for unpaid and future rent.

MAKE REPAIRS AND DEDUCT THE COST FROM THE RENT   In some states, if the rental property includes a defective condition that will affect your health or safety (that is, if the condition violates the warranty of habitability), you can pay for the repairs and deduct the cost from the rent. To use this remedy, take the following steps:

1.   Determine that the problem is the landlord's responsibility. This will depend on your local law or lease terms to the contrary. In some states, the condition must concern a basic service, such as heat or water.
2.   Notify the landlord about the problem in writing (certified or registered mail), explaining that you intend to use this remedy if repairs are not made within a reasonable time. Normally, thirty days is sufficient. An emergency might warrant less time.
3.   Make repairs (or hire someone to make repairs) if the landlord does not take steps to fix the problem. Some states require that you get written estimates first. Save all receipts and other paperwork.
4.   Deduct the cost of the repairs from your next rent payment. Give the receipts to the landlord but keep copies. In some states, the deductible amount is restricted to a month's rent or some other fixed amount. To avoid this restriction in making a major repair, you and other tenants might act together and deduct a portion of the cost from each tenant's rent. Before doing so, however, ask your attorney, or someone else familiar with your local law, about this possibility.

If your landlord tries to evict you for nonpayment of rent, you can explain your side of the story in court. Generally, if you have followed the law and used common sense, you should have few problems. If the court decides that you were wrong, you will have to pay the entire rent, regardless of how much you spent on repairs.

WITHHOLD RENT   In some states, if the rental property includes a defective condition that violates the warranty of habitability, you can withhold some of the rent. To use this remedy, take the following steps:

1.   Determine that the condition violates the warranty of habitability.

2.   Notify the landlord of the problem in writing (certified or registered mail).

3.   Allow the landlord a reasonable time to make repairs.

4.   Withhold all or part of your next rental payment. In some states, you may be able to withhold amounts for past months when the property was uninhabitable and you paid the rent. In a few states, you must deposit any withheld amounts in a special **escrow account.** The money in the account will be returned to you if the landlord does not make the repairs.

The basic difficulty with using this remedy is determining how much rent to withhold. Often, the decision is made by a court because usually, when rent is withheld, a landlord tries to evict the tenant for nonpayment of rent or asks a court to order the tenant to pay back rent. The court reviews the condition of the property and decides whether the amount withheld was correct. Generally, the court considers how much the defective condition affects the habitability of the property. There is no penalty for withholding too much rent if you act in good faith. If the court determines that you withheld too much, you pay the difference to the landlord.

SUE THE LANDLORD   You can sue your landlord anytime you believe that the implied warranty of habitability has been breached. In your suit, you can ask the court for any of the following remedies:

1.   A declaration of your rights and remedies in the relationship with your landlord.

2.   An order to the landlord to pay you money for any injury to you or any damage to your property.

3.   An order to the landlord to fix the condition of the property or to stop doing whatever it is that makes the property uninhabitable.

Before asking a court for relief, you should be aware that a court will usually declare parties' rights and remedies, but courts are reluctant to order landlords to do something or to stop doing something when constant supervision is required to ensure that the orders are followed. Also, although a lawsuit is always a possible course of action, it is not always economical.

If a serious dispute develops between you and your landlord, and the dispute cannot be resolved, you may take the matter to court. In some circumstances, this may be required. In most cases and in most states, the appropriate court is a small claims court. When taking a matter to small claims court, you should keep the following points in mind:

1. In many states, no attorney is necessary. In some states, an attorney cannot appear on behalf of a client in small claims court. Assistance can be obtained from the clerk of the court or some other designated official.

2. The proper party must be notified about the suit. You may know only the resident manager of the property, not the actual owner, or you may know the owner only as the name of a corporation. An owner's name may be available through the local tax assessor's office or the county clerk.

3. All relevant documents should be kept available for the court. These may include a copy of the lease, rent receipts, an inventory of the condition of the premises taken before you moved in, canceled checks, receipts and estimates for repairs, and notes taken during any negotiations between you and your landlord.

4. You might be able to recover attorneys' fees, if an attorney was consulted and paid. In some cases, you may recover double or triple the amount of a security deposit wrongfully retained by your landlord. For more information about small claims courts, see the discussion of consumer law later in this *Handbook.*

Retaliatory Eviction

Retaliatory eviction occurs if your landlord evicts you for complaining to a government agency about the condition of the property. If you can prove that your landlord's primary purpose in evicting or attempting to evict you is retaliation for reporting violations—of a housing or sanitation code, for example—you may be entitled to stop the eviction proceedings or collect damages. This can be difficult to prove, unless your landlord admits his or her purpose in a note, in a statement to another person, or in testimony to a court.

In many states, a landlord is presumed to be acting in retaliation if the eviction proceedings are begun within a certain period of time (six to twelve months, in some states) after a tenant has contacted a government agency. In this case, the landlord must prove that he or she did not have a retaliatory purpose. If your landlord shows that you did not pay the rent or that you violated the lease, you could be evicted. If you win, however, you can stay on the premises.

When your lease comes up for renewal, the landlord may raise the rent to help cover the cost of the repairs. Your landlord cannot raise the rent simply to punish you for reporting the violations, however. In most of the states that protect tenants from retaliatory eviction, courts would consider this retaliatory and subject to the same limitations as a retaliatory eviction.

▌Rent

The primary obligation of the tenant is to pay the agreed-upon rent at the time specified. You retain this obligation even after you have subleased the apartment. If the sublessee fails to pay, your lease obliges you to make payment. Rent is typically due on a certain date of the month. If payments are late, the landlord may charge interest for being late. Most leases provide that if rent is late by more than a certain amount, you will be charged a penalty fee. The amount and nature of this fee must be specified in the lease. The amount must also be reasonable. One Vermont case held that a dollar-a-day charge for late rent payments was excessive.

Raising the Rent

As a general rule, your landlord cannot raise your rent during the term of your lease. An exception would exist if the lease itself provides some procedure for rent increases during its term. Such a provision is typically called an **escalation clause,** which permits periodic increases that usually are based upon rising costs for fuel or building upkeep.

After a lease expires, you may continue, with the landlord's consent, renting on a month-to-month basis. This means that the terms of the old lease continue in operation but can be terminated at any time either by you or the landlord (usually with one month's or thirty days' notice). Alternatively, you may execute a new lease with your landlord, who may require a higher rental payment. This is a matter to be negotiated.

Rent Control

While landlords may generally charge whatever the market will bear, many large cities have rent control laws that restrain rent increases. These ordinances place limits on how much rent can be raised by landlords, even after a lease expires. Rent can be increased only by a set percentage, which may be tied to the cost of living. Because the existence and substance of these ordinances vary from place to place and can change over time, those renting property should become familiar with their local laws.

▌Security Deposits

Before renting an apartment, you probably will be required to make a **security deposit** in an amount such as one month's rent. The landlord holds this money during your lease to protect against damage that you may do to the property. Theoretically, you recover this deposit when you move out of the apartment. All security deposits must be potentially refundable. If you caused more damage than covered by your security deposit, the landlord may sue you for the remainder.

Use of the Security Deposit

You may lose your security deposit if the landlord requires the money to repair damages that you have done to the premises. The security deposit is not applied to **ordinary wear and tear.** This term applies to ordinary deterioration of an apartment over time, such as fading paint, carpet wear, etc. The landlord may take your security deposit for larger damages, such as permanent stains or cigarette burns in carpeting, broken appliances or window frames, or holes punched in walls. Even a small hole to hang a picture might permit withholding (though repair costs would be quite small). Some landlords might attempt to use your security deposit to recover fees for late payment of rent, but this is illegal in most states.

Protecting Your Security Deposit

When you attempt to recover your security deposit, a dispute may arise over the nature of damages and the condition of the apartment when you moved in. The following steps will help you protect your deposit:

1.   Get a receipt for the amount of the deposit.

2.   Before moving in, make a list of existing defects or problems and provide a copy of the list to your landlord.
3.   Before moving out, clean the apartment and repair damages insofar as possible.
4.   Before moving out, inspect the apartment yourself along with the landlord or other witness.
5.   After moving out, leave a forwarding address and your keys to the apartment with the landlord.

You might also ask your landlord for interest on your deposit during your lease. This is required only in a few states.

Withholding Your Deposit

The landlord may decide to withhold some of your security deposit for repairs. Most jurisdictions require the landlord to provide you with an itemized list of repairs and their costs. In many states, to avoid a penalty, the landlord must provide this list or refund the deposit within thirty days of the date that you moved out and gave the landlord a forwarding address. If the landlord does not do this, he or she may forfeit the right to withhold any of your security deposit.

You may dispute your landlord's assessment. You may file suit against your landlord for withholding your deposit, probably in small claims court. You can question either the need for the repairs or whether the cost of the repairs was reasonable.

▌ Liability for Injuries

What if a guest of yours is injured while in your apartment? The guest might sue the landlord, or you, or both. Either one of you could be liable.

Common Areas

Liability for injuries in apartments depends on who has legal control over the area in question. **Common areas** are under the control of the landlord, who will be liable for injuries in this area. If your guest trips over a defective stair step on the way to your apartment, the landlord is liable and you probably are not. The landlord may also be responsible for slippery surfaces, inadequate lighting, or rotting wood.

Structural Defects

Even if the injury occurs inside your apartment, the landlord may be liable. A defective water heater or outside railing, for example, is within the landlord's control. Similarly, if the landlord undertakes certain repairs in your apartment and performs the repairs negligently, the landlord is responsible for resultant damages.

Tenant Liability

You are potentially liable for certain injuries occurring within your apartment. You have some control over this area and are responsible for maintaining its safe condition. You are responsible for any injuries resulting from your furnishings or from your misuse of apartment fixtures, such as lights or plumbing. You may purchase renters' insurance to cover this liability, as well as to insure against the damage, loss, or destruction of your belongings.

▌ Lockouts

If a dispute with your landlord has reached an extreme level, your landlord may lock you out of your apartment and seize your possessions. In the vast majority of states, such lockouts are unlawful. The laws provide that a tenant has a right to notice and a hearing, but some landlords continue to conduct illegal lockouts. If you suffer an illegal lockout, you should call the police and complain of a criminal trespass and conversion of your personal property. If the police are unhelpful, you can get an attorney to obtain an order recovering possession. You may recover all your costs from the landlord and may continue to pursue a tort action.

In lieu of a lockout, the landlord may conduct a **utility shutoff,** in an effort to force you off the premises. This action is also illegal, and states provide both civil and criminal penalties against the offending landlord. As with a lockout, you may need to go to court to enforce your rights and get your utilities turned back on.

Topic 2   Family Law

Families ideally work out their relationships internally and settle their own problems without resorting to legal process. In reality, however, courts often become involved in family disputes. Moreover, the law establishes a basic framework through which parties may voluntarily resolve their disputes without going before a judge.

▌Getting Married

The decision to get married has changed in recent decades. Couples are more frequently living together, or cohabiting, without first marrying. This is generally legal, though some states have normally unenforced laws prohibiting extramarital cohabitation. Most couples still get married and there are some practical advantages to marriage. Married couples may have an easier time obtaining insurance, credit, etc. Married partners, upon divorce, are more likely to receive child custody. Married couples also have more adoption opportunities. Many companies offer health insurance to spouses but not to unmarried partners.

Engagement

There are few legal requirements governing engagement. Traditionally, one left at the altar could sue a fiancé for breach of promise to marry. Today, most states have done away with this cause of action. If an engagement is broken, the law probably would force the party to return certain gifts, such as engagement rings, shower gifts, etc.

Marriage Requirements

States place some limitations upon who may marry. The betrothed must be man and woman, currently unmarried, not closely related by blood, and over a certain age (often eighteen). State laws differ, and some actually prohibit marriages among those closely related even if the relation is only by marriage. Those who are underage may marry with parental consent or if judicially emancipated from their parents. Below a certain age, such as fourteen or sixteen, marriage may be absolutely prohibited by state law except with court approval.

Marriage Ceremony

Certain procedures are generally required for a legally recognized marriage. The parties must first obtain a marriage license from the state government. Some states also require a blood test, in which the government checks for diseases, such as venereal diseases. Some states require a waiting period before getting the license or between the time of acquiring the license and officially getting married. In thirteen states and the District of Columbia, a license is the only requirement for a marriage.

In the other thirty-seven states, some form of marriage ceremony is also required. The parties must present the license to someone authorized to perform marriages (a state official or member of the clergy). The ceremony must involve a public statement of agreement to marriage. The remainder of the ceremony is generally within the couple's discretion. After the ceremony, the marriage license must be recorded.

Common Law Marriage

About fifteen states recognize a **common law marriage,** a procedure by which parties become married without a license or ceremony. There are four general requirements for a common law marriage:

1. The parties must be eligible to marry.
2. The parties must have a present and continuing intention and agreement to be husband and wife.
3. The parties must live together as husband and wife.
4. The parties must hold themselves out to the public as husband and wife.

There are a number of misapprehensions about common law marriage. Cohabitation alone cannot produce a common law marriage; the parties must additionally hold themselves out to others as husband and wife. There is no minimum time period required for a common law marriage. The parties may become married as soon as they both live as husband and wife and hold themselves out to the public as married.

There is no common law divorce. Once a couple is regarded as married—and particularly once a court has recognized them as married by common law—they must obtain a court decree to dissolve the marriage.

Duties of Marriage

The law considers marriage to be a form of contract, and historically the marriage contract came complete with a full set of duties for the husband and wife. Formerly, the husband had the duty to be the provider, and could not purchase luxuries for himself until the family was provided with necessities. The wife had certain duties in the home. Times have changed, and courts today enforce few duties arising from the marriage contract. Spouses are generally allowed to arrange their own affairs however they see fit.

The law still holds that a spouse has a duty of financial support, providing such basics as food, shelter, and medical care, insofar as he or she is able. In many states, this duty lasts throughout the marriage, even if the spouses are living apart. Failure to provide support for a child may be a criminal violation. (In non-community property states, except for these basics, one spouse is not responsible for the debts of the other spouse unless he or she is ordered to pay them as part of a divorce decree.)

Additional duties may be created by a separate agreement between the spouses. Some decisions have held that a spouse may not deny sexual relations without good cause, though courts are becoming more hesitant to enforce such a requirement.

Traditional common law provided for **interspousal immunity.** This means that one spouse could not sue the other for torts, such as assault and battery. Most states now have modified this law and permit one spouse to sue the other for at least intentional torts. Interspousal immunity still means that one partner may not be required to testify against a spouse in court, though a spouse may voluntarily so testify. An increasing number of states recognizes the crime of marital rape.

It is, of course, illegal to batter a spouse. Unlawful abuse has been extended to include extreme cases of harassment and threats of physical beating or confinement. A victim of spousal battering should call the police and may seek other legal protection against the abuser, including an emergency restraining order, which requires the abusing spouse to stay away from the victim. Many shelters are available to assist an abused spouse.

▌Financial Aspects of Marriage

Prenuptial Agreements

Brides and grooms are increasingly bringing substantial assets into a marriage, which has led to greater use of the **prenuptial,** or premarital, **agreement.** A prenuptial agreement is a contract between the parties entered into before the wedding occurs. Such an agreement generally provides for disposition of property in the event of the divorce or death of one spouse. One typical use of a prenuptial agreement would be to guarantee that children from a previous marriage receive a certain share of their parent's estate. Prenuptial agreements must be in writing to be enforceable.

There are certain advantages to prenuptial agreements. Such contracts enable the parties to settle possible disagreements in advance and provide some long-term financial certainty to the parties. Note, though, that prenuptial agreements are criticized for evincing a lack of mutual trust and for being unromantic. Such agreements may even prove unfair to a spouse in the event of divorce.

As with any contract, prenuptial agreements are presumptively valid but are not always so. While traditional courts refused to recognize prenuptial agreements, most states now uphold such contracts, even if they eliminate financial support in the event of divorce. Courts do look closely at the agreement for evidence of unfairness. There are several circumstances when courts have refused to enforce prenuptial agreements, such as:

● When the agreement would so impoverish the spouse as to make him or her eligible for welfare.
● When there was unfair bargaining at the time of the agreement, such as a failure to disclose all money and property assets.
● When one party was not represented by counsel.

● When the agreement was entered into immediately before the marriage (such agreements should be made weeks or months in advance).

In general, a party must show that the prenuptial agreement was made voluntarily and without threats or unfair pressure.

Property Ownership

Separate property is property that a spouse owned before the marriage, plus inheritances and gifts acquired during the marriage. This property belongs to the spouse personally and not to the marital unit. Upon dissolution of the marriage, separate property is not divided but retained by the owner.

The separate property right may be lost during marriage, however. If the couple combines separate property with that acquired during the marriage, the two properties may be merged into jointly held property. Suppose that a wife owns a lot on which the couple builds a house after their marriage. The wife has lost her separate property rights in the land. Merely renovating a separately held property (e.g., sprucing up a vacation home) may transform the separate property into joint property. Placing separate property into a jointly held bank account may also transform the money into joint property. The separate property issue is important even if the couple is happy and trusting. For example, a wife's creditors may not attach her husband's separate property but may reach at least a portion of jointly held property.

The converse of separate property occurs when one spouse brings debts into the marriage. In most states, you are not liable for your spouse's premarital debts. In community property states (described below), under certain circumstances, a spouse may become liable for premarital debts.

Ten jurisdictions (Arizona, California, Idaho, Louisiana, Nebraska, New Mexico, Texas, Washington, Wisconsin, and Puerto Rico) have the system known as **community property.** In these jurisdictions, each spouse shares equally in all income earned and most property acquired during the marriage. This is true even if one party supplied all the income and assets. The community property system is significant both for creditors and for the parties upon divorce. In community property states, one spouse may encumber the other with debts. In other states, one party generally may not incur debts for the other.

Separation and Divorce

Divorce is generally preceded by a separation period. Such separation may be due to abandonment or may be through mutual consent. States may require a separation period prior to granting a divorce.

A divorce is a formal court proceeding used to legally dissolve a marriage. Divorce laws vary considerably among the states, with some having much easier procedures. All states provide for some form of **no-fault divorce.** This eliminates the requirement that divorce be justified by some demonstrable reason, such as abuse or abandonment. The most common basis for a no-fault divorce is irreconcilable differences. No-fault divorce laws make it practically impossible for one spouse to prevent a divorce desired by the other. Even in these states, courts may look to fault in deciding financial settlements between the parties.

Lawyers are not strictly required for a divorce proceeding. Most states permit "do-it-yourself divorces," sometimes called *pro se* **divorces.** In this process, the individuals handle everything themselves before the court. Couples can obtain the necessary forms at the local courthouse (or in form books). If a significant amount of money is at stake, however, the divorcing spouses should obtain professional legal and accounting advice.

Most divorces are not actually tried in court. Only about ten percent of divorces go to trial. The parties typically settle their outstanding claims, though often only after lengthy negotiations. Divorcing spouses increasingly use **mediation** to settle disagreements. A mediator is typically trained and meets with the parties in the absence of lawyers. The mediator does not make decisions but tries to prod the parties into a mutually acceptable agreement.

In a divorce settlement, some written agreement is reached on contested issues, such as property settlement, child custody, continued support, etc. This agreement must be presented to the court for its approval. The court may disapprove the agreement as unconscionable (extremely unfair), though this is very rare. If only one side of the divorce had legal representation, courts will scrutinize settlement agreements more closely.

An **annulment** is more than a divorce and means that the marriage was never effective in the first place. Annulment may be available if the marriage is based upon fraud, if the marriage was unconsummated, if there was **bigamy,** and for a limited set of other reasons. Obtaining an annulment is especially significant for those belonging to certain religions (such as Catholicism) in order for a person to remarry.

Property Division and Alimony

Although most divorcing parties settle their financial disputes, this settlement is colored by the requirements of the law. Whether the state has community property laws or not, the court may divide marital property without respect to formal papers of ownership. Judges have almost unlimited discretion in deciding which person receives what property, as long as the division is reasonably equitable.

Courts divide marital property and, in most circumstances, separate property remains with the owner. When deciding how to divide the common property, however, judges consider the existence of the separate property and its effect on the wealth and needs of the divorcing spouses. Retirement benefits are generally considered to be marital property, divided between the spouses. In community property states, the property is presumptively split equally. Judges may change this division to suit the circumstances, however. Courts use a variety of standards in considering how to divide property, including the following:

- The duration of the marriage.
- The health of the parties.
- The individuals' occupations and vocational skills.
- The individuals' relative wealth and income.
- The standard of living during the marriage.
- The relative contributions to the marriage, both financially and in homemaker contributions.
- Needs and concerns of any children.
- Tax and inheritance considerations.

Marital debts must also be divided according to similar criteria.

A typical property controversy in divorce cases concerns rights to the marital residence. If there are minor children, the house is usually given to the parent with custody of the children. It may be difficult to balance the grant of the house with other property (many families have few substantial assets other than their homes). Once the children are grown, the court may order the house to be sold and the proceeds divided.

Alimony is money paid for support of the former spouse. Historically, the husband was the wage earner and was expected to pay alimony to his former wife, to permit her to maintain her standard of living. There are well-known cases involving wealthy entertainers, such as former NBC late-night T.V. host Johnny Carson, who have been directed to pay their ex-wives (or, in a few cases, ex-husbands) hundreds of thousands of dollars in annual alimony. Alimony ends when the recipient remarries.

The law of alimony is changing. One common form of alimony today is called **rehabilitative support.** Rather than providing indefinite support payments, rehabilitative support is designed to provide the ex-spouse with the education, training, or job experience necessary to support himself or herself. This form of alimony assists spouses who devoted their lives to homemaking or who left lucrative opportunities because of the marriage. Such rehabilitative support may only last for a limited period, particularly if the spouse finds a good job. Such temporary rehabilitative support has been criticized, because many divorcees are of an age that hampers their prospects of developing a new career. Many courts still award permanent support, if the recipient's earning prospects are far less than those of the wealthier spouse or if the recipient is of relatively advanced age. About half the states also consider fault in the divorce as a factor in awarding spousal support such as alimony. Alimony may be modified as the parties' situations change.

A common controversy involves one spouse supporting another through graduate school (such as law or medical school), followed by a divorce. The supporting spouse may claim a share of the income subsequently earned by the supported spouse as a lawyer or a doctor. Courts have been hesitant to grant the supporting spouse some property right in the advanced or professional degree obtained by the other spouse but have awarded payments to compensate for the supporting spouse's contributions to the education. One New York decision did hold that an academic degree earned by the husband was marital property.

Palimony

Palimony is a common but nonlegal name for claims made by a member of an unmarried couple after they have split up. After cohabiting for years, a partner may claim some interest in the other's property. There is no statutory provision for such a claim, and courts have been reluctant to recognize an automatic right to palimony. Unmarried couples may enter a contract that specifies legal rights should they break up. Such contracts may be valid, but courts have tended to scrutinize them closely for legality. These contracts should be in writing, although this is not strictly required at law. The California Supreme Court has held that a contract between a cohabiting couple may even be implied from conduct or unspoken understandings. Other states, such as Illinois, are unwilling to recognize palimony actions. Palimony may be especially important for homosexual couples, who are barred from marrying legally.

Child Custody

The most contentious issue in many divorces is child custody—the right to live with and to care for the children on an everyday basis. Traditionally, the mother almost always received custody. Forty-four states have now adopted the Uniform Marriage and Divorce Act, which governs custody determinations. Mothers still usually receive custody, but courts now explicitly consider a list of factors, including:

● The wishes of the child.
● The nature of the relationship and emotional ties with each parent.
● The ability and interest of the parents in providing for the child's needs and education.
● Any required adjustments to a new house or community.
● The stability of the family relationship.

Family stability is probably the most important factor. Some recent decisions have put increased emphasis on whether one parent was a smoker, because secondary smoke may damage the child's lungs. Courts may appoint a **guardian *ad litem***, usually an attorney, who directly represents the child's interests in court. Custody decisions are not permanent and may be changed by a court.

The noncustodial parent generally receives visitation rights. The parent may get to spend weekends or other time periods with the child. Visitation is denied in extreme cases, such as child abuse or when there is a reasonable fear of child snatching by the noncustodial parent.

The court may provide a system of **joint custody,** which many states now prefer. Joint legal custody means that both parents together make major decisions about the child. Some procedure, such as mediation, is available in the event of disagreement. In some states, including California, mediation is mandatory in child custody disputes. This may also involve joint physical custody, in which both parents maintain a home for the child and have roughly comparable time with the child.

Regardless of the custody arrangements, a court must make some provision for financial **child support.** Child support obligations arise even if the parents were never married. States have official guidelines to determine child support duties. These guidelines are often percentage formulas based on parental income. Judges must follow the guidelines, unless special facts justify a departure. Children with particularly large needs (for example, the disabled) may require a greater support award.

It is a common misconception that if one ex-spouse fails to meet his or her obligations under a divorce decree or other court order (such as withholding visitation rights), the other party can withhold payment of child support. Child support is a separate court order—it cannot be withheld because an ex-spouse does something that the other ex-spouse does not like. (What a parent can do is ask the court to modify a decree in some way.) A large number of noncustodial parents are failing to make their child support payments, and states are providing for automatic withholding of support payments from the wages of the parent. Child support orders may also be revised and adjusted according to need and ability to pay. The Uniform Reciprocal Enforcement of Support Act assists states in recovering support payments from parents living in other states. The failure to make child support payments is a crime.

▌Children

The decision whether to have children is a central part of the family relationship. The law of childbearing has become increasingly complex with the advent of new arrangements, such as surrogate parenthood and artificial insemination. The law here is still unsettled. Within a marriage, the decision to have children obviously should be mutually reached. The woman ultimately has the right to use contraceptive devices or to go ahead and bear a child, and she does not need to obtain the husband's permission.

Paternity

If a couple is married, the law presumes that any newborn child is the husband's, and he must support the child unless he can prove that he is not the biological father. Some states do not even allow the husband an opportunity to prove his lack of paternity. An unmarried mother may file a suit to establish the **paternity** of her child. If the unwed mother is on public welfare aid, the government may file a paternity suit to be reimbursed.

The paternity of a child may be proved scientifically. Science has advanced beyond historically used blood tests and now uses DNA testing or comparable procedures that check for genetic factors. Such tests reportedly are 98 to 99 percent accurate in determining parenthood. The biological father of the child has a legal obligation to provide support, regardless of marital status. These obligations are just as great as for married fathers and are determined by the child support guidelines of the state. The obligations usually last until the child is no longer a minor. The mother's subsequent marriage to another man does not necessarily extinguish the child support obligations of the biological father.

While all biological fathers have an obligation to provide child support regardless of marital status, children born out of wedlock still suffer disadvantages. Legally, an illegitimate child has no presumptive right to inherit as an heir of the father. An increasing number of children are born to unmarried parents (about one-third of all first births). In response, the law is evolving to provide added rights and protections to children born out of wedlock. Courts have held that the government cannot discriminate against illegitimate children and that such children have a right to recover damages for the deaths of their parents. In most states, the eventual marriage of the parents "legitimizes" a previous child of theirs.

Adoption

Adoption is a procedure in which persons become the official legal parents of a child that is not their biological child. Adoption may be contrasted with

foster care, which is a temporary arrangement in which a family is paid by the state to care for a child over a limited time period, often pending adoption. There are three minimum requirements for an adoption to be legal:

1.   The legal rights of the biological parents must have been terminated by death or judicial decree.
2.   The adopting parents must follow all procedures required by the state of adoption.
3.   The adoption must be formally approved by a judge.

There may be additional requirements in specific circumstances. For example, adopting a teenage child generally requires the child's official consent.

Adoption is often done through a public or private agency that has received authority to agree to the adoption of children in its custody. The biological parents may convey the authority to the agency to find legal parents for their child. The agency investigates potential adopters and chooses a set of parents. In other circumstances, potential parents may pursue independent adoption, when a doctor or lawyer or other individual puts adopting parents together with a pregnant woman who must give up her child. These parties make their own private arrangements, which usually involve the adopting parents paying for the legal and medical expenses associated with childbirth and adoption. The intermediary also generally receives a fee. This approach has the potential for abuse and is prohibited by some states. There is a growing number of black market adoptions from developing nations (such as China and Romania).

Even entirely independent adoptions must be approved in court. The primary standard for approving an adoption is the best interests of the child. The court (and applicable private agency) considers the financial resources of the adopting parents, their family stability and home environment, their ages, religious and racial compatibility, and other factors relevant to the child's future health and welfare. Most states permit single persons to adopt, though married couples are generally preferred.

After the adoption, many states place the new parents on probation for a time. This period is usually from six months to one year. The agency or court appoints an individual to ensure that the adoptive parents are caring appropriately for the child's well-being. If not, the child may be removed and returned to an agency for placement in another home.

Once an adoption is formally completed, the adoptive parents have all the responsibilities of biological parents. Should they divorce, each adoptive parent still has all the child support obligations associated with biological parents. Depending on the state, the child may retain some legal connection with the biological parents, such as inheritance rights upon their deaths. The adopted child also has rights of inheritance from the adoptive parents.

Children's Rights

The law has special concern for children. Legally, a child is an unmarried minor (under the age of eighteen), who is not emancipated. **Emancipation** occurs when children leave home to support themselves. Parents have duties toward their children to provide food, shelter, clothing, medical care, and other necessities. Parents must also ensure that their children attend school (normally until the age of sixteen). Parents are prohibited from abusing or neglecting their children. Parental duties to children generally end at age eighteen, but these duties may continue longer if the child is seriously disabled.

Along with these duties, parents have certain rights of control over children. Parents can direct the upbringing of their children and control where they live, what school they attend, and even what religion they practice. Parents also generally control the medical care to be given, though parents' refusal to provide for such care in life-threatening situations (usually for religious reasons) can be a crime. Parents have broad legal authority to control the behavior of their children, though this lessens as the children age and become more mature. Parents may punish children but not excessively.

Historically, children could not sue their parents for negligence, due to a governmental interest in family harmony. Today, most states permit such lawsuits, which are generally covered by insurance. The traditional common law rule was that parents were not liable for the tortious actions of their children. About half the states now provide partial parental liability for their children's intentional torts, up to a limit of about $10,000 (depending upon the state).

Child Abuse and Neglect

All states have laws that prohibit the abuse and neglect of children by their parents or others.

Child abuse primarily covers severe physical beatings and sexual molestation of minors by anyone. Child abuse may even extend to emotional abuse, when a person publicly humiliates a child in an extreme way. Child neglect occurs when parents or legal guardians fail to provide for basic needs, such as food, shelter, clothing, and medical treatment. Laws now require doctors and social workers to report suspected cases of child abuse.

In serious cases of child abuse or neglect, the government may remove the child from his or her parents. Ideally, this is temporary and the objective is to reunite the family after the parents' problems have been corrected through counseling or otherwise. If the parents are unrepentant, the state may ask the court to terminate all parental rights and make the children available for adoption.

▌Wills and Estates

In a marriage, each spouse should have a will. State intestacy laws provide that surviving spouses automatically inherit a share of a decedent's property. These laws apply if a person dies **intestate** (without a will). The adjudication of inheritance rights is known as **probate**, and legal probate battles may be protracted and costly. If there is no will, a court will appoint someone to manage the estate. Couples also should revise the terms of their wills to take advantage of changes in the tax laws and the changing needs of their heirs. A will is even more important for unmarried couples. An unmarried partner has no automatic right to assets on death and will inherit only if provided for in a will.

In the absence of a will, the deceased's property is distributed according to a state's intestate succession law. The surviving spouse has a legal right to a certain share of the estate (usually one-third or one-half, depending upon the state). In the absence of a will, children also have a right to a share of the property.

When there is a will, the law restricts its terms in order to protect the surviving family. A married person cannot will an entire estate to charity, for example. The surviving spouse has a right to what is known as the **elective share.** The elective share is a certain guaranteed minimum of the deceased's estate. It is called elective, because the spouse may choose to take what is provided in the will or may elect the minimum share specified by state law. A spouse may lose this elective share option if he or she signed the deceased's will. A child may be disinherited, even when he or she is a minor, and thereby be denied a share of the deceased parent's estate. Such disinheritance must be clearly intended, however. Mere failure to mention a child in the will does not constitute disinheritance. In limited circumstances, the contents of a will may be challenged by potential heirs.

Some families partially avoid probate and wills by using a **living trust.** The living trust is a device in which a person known as the **trustee** holds legal title to property and manages it in the interest of named beneficiaries of the trust. A wife might establish such a trust with herself and her husband as beneficiaries for life. After her death, her husband may receive the property directly or continue the trust, with himself as beneficiary. The latter option requires appointment of a new trustee. The trust option may allow greater flexibility than a will and also avoid certain taxes.

▌Homosexual Families

Some of the most controversial family law topics involve gay or lesbian families. Many homosexual couples live in stable, long-term relationships. They may wish to formally recognize their relationships through a wedding ceremony. No state legally recognizes such same-sex marriages, although Hawaii may soon pass legislation allowing such marriages. Gays and lesbians may hold what have become known as "commitment ceremonies," which are similar to marriage ceremonies. Such commitment ceremonies do not invoke the legal protections surrounding marriage, however. There is no legal provision for community property or alimony in such cases. Homosexual couples may provide for similar protections through a contract.

Some homosexual couples wish to adopt children, though this can be difficult. Two states, Florida and New Hampshire, have explicitly prohibited homosexual adoptions, but some local Florida courts have struck down that state's law as being unconstitutional. Even in the absence of such a law, an Ohio judge held in 1988 that gays and lesbians were ineligible to adopt. Despite the roadblocks, over two hundred homosexual couples have successfully adopted children. Gays and lesbians are also at a disadvantage in child custody battles that follow a divorce.

Topic 3   **Consumer Law**

The typical American undertakes hundreds of consumer transactions every year. Most such purchases prove ordinary and uncontroversial, but an occasional purchase goes awry. The product may be worthless or even dangerous. In these instances, the consumer may need the protection of the law. The traditional common law embraced the doctrine of *caveat emptor*, meaning "let the buyer beware." Consumers had little recourse when purchases went sour. Today, there is an increasing number of consumer protection laws.

▌The Consumer Contract

Whenever you purchase groceries or any other product, you enter a contract. Although grocery shopping does not involve a formal written contract, such purchases are contracts and are governed by the principles of contract law. Consumer purchases must meet all of the requirements of a contract in order to be binding on you and the seller. Most purchases easily satisfy the main requirements of contract law and present no loopholes for escaping a deal. An exception exists when a purchaser is a minor. The general rule is that a minor (someone under eighteen years of age) may disavow and escape a contract even after it has been completed.

Fraud

You can escape a contract if you were fraudulently induced into making the contract. Fraud requires proof of the following elements:

1. A misrepresentation of material fact.
2. An intent to deceive.
3. Justifiable reliance.

A seller who lies about the attributes of a product to make a sale may commit fraud. You must distinguish fraudulent lying from **puffing,** which refers to the seller's qualitative statements about the product. A seller who promises that its product is "of great quality" or "fantastic" is merely puffing about the product. To show fraud you would have to demonstrate a more specific statement of fact, such as a false statement about the number of miles on a used car. If you can prove fraud, you may either rescind (escape) the contract or collect the damages that you suffered as a consequence of the fraud.

Unconscionability

The law ordinarily does not look into the fairness of contracts. It is the responsibility of the parties to obtain the best deal for themselves. Courts usually will not strike down contracts simply for unfairness. A limited exception exists for **unconscionability,** which means such extreme unfairness as to "shock the conscience" of a court. Courts can refuse to enforce unconscionable contracts.

Unconscionability may be found when there is a great disparity of bargaining power. Such disparity may arise with **contracts of adhesion.** These exist when a seller presents you with a "take-it-or-leave-it" form contract and refuses to negotiate over the terms on the form. You have little bargaining power in this circumstance. Note that not all contracts of adhesion are unconscionable—you could simply walk away from the deal. If circumstances force you to make a contract and you cannot bargain over the terms, and if those terms seem manifestly unfair to you, the contract may be deemed unconscionable.

▍Warranties

Most products that you purchase will come with some form of warranty or promise regarding the quality of the product. If the product does not meet the warranted standard, you have a right to a remedy. Generally this remedy is readily provided by the manufacturer or retailer, but in some cases you

may need to go to court. Warranties may come in several forms.

Express Warranties

An **express warranty** is any explicit factual assurance about a product. The express warranty may be a written promise of quality and performance or may be an oral assurance from a salesperson. An express warranty may even be visual. If the retailer shows you a model of the product, it is creating an express warranty that the item purchased will conform to that model. Of course, a written warranty is easier to enforce in court. You should also be aware that puffing does not create a warranty but is merely sales talk.

Many warranties contain a specific remedy should something go wrong with the product. A **full warranty** means that the product will be repaired or replaced free of charge within a reasonable time, or else you will receive a refund. Even a full warranty does not provide absolute protection, because the warranty will also set forth terms and conditions. For example, a microwave oven may be under full warranty for 180 days. After that time you are unprotected. A limited warranty provides even less protection. A limited warranty might provide for repair but not a refund. Moreover, to take advantage of such a warranty you may have to deliver or mail the product to a designated site.

Beware of disclaimers. Even after a salesperson makes detailed promises about a product, you may be expected to sign a written contract that disclaims all express warranties. Although this may seem unfair, it is a legal practice and can nullify anything that the salesperson said, as well as eliminate any other warranty protection. Disclaimers are discussed below. Be sure to read any warranty and understand your rights before you make a purchase.

Implied Warranties

Many consumer contracts come with implied warranties that automatically come with the product. These warranties protect you even if the salesperson made no promises about the product. The law implies these warranties in sales of goods. Implied warranties of merchantability are created only by sellers who are merchants. Thus, a garage sale in your neighborhood would not include such a warranty.

The **implied warranty of merchantability** means that your purchase will be of at least average quality for that type of product and will perform its intended function. This means that if you buy a camera, it will successfully take pictures. The **implied warranty of fitness** applies when the salesperson helps you select a product for a particular purpose. If you inform the retailer of your purpose and rely on him or her to choose a suitable product, the company warrants that the product is suited for that purpose. If you ask for an underwater camera, the product a salesperson picks out must function under water. The **implied warranty of title** simply means that the seller warrants that he or she is the owner (or authorized agent) of the item for sale.

Disclaimers

Companies may choose to disclaim warranties or to limit their potential liability. The disclaimer may bluntly declare that there are no warranties on the product or may state that your only remedy is repair or replacement of the product. Merchants may even disclaim the implied warranties discussed above, but they must use specific and conspicuous language to do so. The implied warranties of merchantability and fitness may be disclaimed by declaring that the product is sold "as is." This language is understood to state that the product is being sold with possible flaws and that the buyer assumes the risk of the flaws.

Most disclaimers are legally effective and prevent you from claiming breach of warranty, but many disclaimers must be conspicuous (for example, in capital letters on the front page of the contract) or in clear and understandable language to be effective. In any event, you are expected to read the contract and be aware of any disclaimers.

▮ Product Liability

If you are physically injured by a product, you may bring a product liability action. Under modern law, you may sue even if you did not personally purchase the product that injured you. This is the doctrine of **strict product liability.**

Under strict product liability, you need not prove that the manufacturer was negligent or careless, but you must show that the product contained a defect causing an unreasonable danger. Suppose

that you received from your toaster a nasty shock that required medical attention. You might recover these damages in strict product liability. You could not get a new toaster, however. You cannot recover if you or anyone else altered the product after it was purchased.

You may recover product liability damages in negligence, though negligence tends to be difficult to prove. A breach of warranty action may also be available for unsafe products. Warranties often are limited to the actual purchasers of the product or family members, however. Warranty actions are limited by the scope of the warranty and any disclaimers.

▮ Deceptive Sales Practices

Most of the protections discussed above are limited by the sales contract. In recent years, many legislatures have passed statutes that provide further protection to consumers against a variety of deceptive sales practices used by merchants.

Bait and Switch

Bait and switch is a sales tactic that has been outlawed. The typical bait-and-switch scheme begins with a store advertising a popular product at an extremely low price. This is the "bait." Consumers see the advertisement and go to the store to purchase the advertised product. The store informs the consumers that it is sold out of the advertised product or otherwise discourages the sale of this product. Salespersons attempt to convince the consumer to purchase an alternative product that has a higher profit margin (the "switch"). The bait-and-switch scheme lures customers into the store, where they can be persuaded to "buy up" by the salesperson.

The federal government has prohibited bait-and-switch tactics. If you believe that a store is using this method, you should complain to the Federal Trade Commission, which enforces the law. Most states and many local government consumer protection agencies also act against unlawful bait-and-switch tactics.

Note the differences between illegal bait-and-switch scams and legal *loss-leader tactics.* Grocery stores may offer a very low price on milk or some other staple to get you into the store. Their theory is that once you buy the milk, you are also likely to purchase other groceries that have higher markups. You should be aware of this tactic, but as long as the milk is available for your purchase, the tactic is a sound business practice and perfectly legal.

Mail Order Sales

Mail order sales are growing rapidly, as tens of millions of Americans rely on the convenience of ordering at home. Mail order purchases obviously represent some risk to consumers, however, because you don't obtain immediate possession of the product. Some laws have been passed to protect against mail order fraud.

A Federal Trade Commission rule states that the seller must inform you when the purchase will be shipped and must conform to promises about shipping. If no shipping date is given, the merchandise must be sent within thirty days. If the product is not shipped within thirty days, you have a right to cancel the order.

Sometimes, unsolicited products are sent to you by mail. You may treat these as gifts, and you have no obli-gation to pay for the unrequested merchandise. Sending you a bill for free samples may be mail fraud, which is a federal crime. This rule does not apply if you belong to a club, such as a book-of-the-month club or a record club. When you joined this club, it is likely that you contractually agreed to purchase the month's selection unless you took affirmative action and sent in a card rejecting the selection. If you failed to send in the card, you are legally obligated to pay for the selection shipped.

"Free" Offers

From time to time, you may receive what appear to be remarkable offers for free merchandise. One common form of such offers is a promise that if you visit a condominium complex you will receive one of a selection of valuable-sounding gifts. These offers are seldom as they appear. In one reported case, a person was promised an "all-terrain vehicle," but this proved to be a lawn chair on wheels. You might have a fraud action in response to such an offer, but it is wisest simply to have a healthy skepticism and protect yourself in the first place. Be particularly suspicious if you must pay any money to take advantage of some later offer.

Door-to-Door Sales

Door-to-door sales occur when a salesperson goes from house to house in a neighborhood offering a product. The law offers special protections for consumers in these transactions.

The law establishes a three-day **cooling-off period** for sales made in your home or anywhere that is not a fixed place of business for the seller. Under this rule, you may cancel the contract for any or no reason within three days of entering into the deal. The three-day period does not begin to run until you have been informed of your cooling-off-period rights. There can be no charge for your canceling the deal. If you have already made payment, the salesperson must refund your money in full within ten business days. If you have received the merchandise, you must make it available to be picked up during this time.

In addition to the cooling-off period, federal and state laws dictate that the door-to-door salesperson provide you with certain information on a receipt or otherwise. This information includes:

● A description of the goods or services sold.
● The seller's identity and place of business.
● The amount of money you paid or the value of the goods delivered to you.
● Your cooling-off-period rights.

▮ Consumer Credit

A large proportion of purchases in today's market is made with credit. While use of credit is convenient, the process creates its own legal issues. Several laws have been passed to settle credit issues.

Credit Cards

Most consumers use credit cards for purchases. These cards may be issued by a specific store or may be all-purpose cards, such as Visa or American Express. While such cards make shopping convenient, be sure that you understand how the cards operate.

Many credit cards, such as Visa and Mastercard and most department store credit cards, use a **revolving credit** system. Each month's purchases are added and a bill is sent to you. Many cards grant you a "free ride period," meaning you need not pay interest during the weeks before you receive the bill. You may pay all or a minimum portion of the bill. The remaining unpaid balance represents a loan to you. Be careful about maintaining an unpaid balance on your charge cards. Interest rates charged on credit cards continue to be high, compared with market rates for bank loans. You may end up paying a considerable premium for use of your credit card. Some companies reserve the right to change their interest rates over time.

Some companies, such as American Express, issue cards that do not permit a revolving credit balance and require you to pay off your debts in full every month. If you fail to pay in full on these cards, you will be charged a contractual penalty that may well exceed the high interest rates of charge cards. Many cards also charge an annual fee for possession of the card. You should compare interest rates and other features before choosing a charge card for regular use.

One concern with credit-card ownership is theft. If your card is stolen, the thief could make many purchases and bill them to you. Indeed, a thief does not need your actual card—learning your card number enables such a person to make mail order purchases on your card. Credit-card theft is increasingly common. The law provides some strong protections for the consumer who suffers from credit-card theft.

Under the Truth-in-Lending Act, you have no liability on your credit card unless the granting company has followed required procedures. The credit grantor must prove that you used the card at least once yourself, that the company notified you of your potential liability, and that the company notified you of how to inform the company in the event the card was stolen or lost. Even if the company follows all these requirements, your potential liability is still quite limited.

The law normally restricts your total liability for improper use of your charge cards to $50 per card. Moreover, you have no liability for any charges that occur after you have reported the card as stolen. Consequently, you should report lost or stolen charge cards as soon as you discover them to be missing.

Another potential credit-card problem involves **billing errors.** Billing errors could include being charged for products you did not purchase, mistakes in computations, or failure to give credit for your payments or returned purchases. If you believe that you have discovered a billing error, the

Fair Credit Billing Act provides procedures for you to use.

First, notify the credit-card company in writing within sixty days after the bill was mailed to you. Notification must be in writing—telephone calls do not protect your rights under the statute. Be sure to include your account number, the date of the error, and a specification of the nature of the error. The credit-card company must acknowledge your letter or correct the error within thirty days. If the error is not corrected, the company must explain to you within ninety days why it believes the bill to be correct. You may continue to correspond with the company. If you protest the company's explanation within ten days, your credit record will reflect the presence of the dispute. The following table summarizes the time limits of the law.

• Notify company of error—*in writing, sixty days from error*
• Company acknowledgment to you—*thirty days from notification*
• Company correction or final response—*ninety days from notification*
• Your notice of protest—*ten days from final response*

If the company fails to follow the required legal procedures, it cannot collect the first $50 of the disputed amount or finance charges but can bill you for any remainder. If you fail to pay the remainder, the company may institute collection proceedings against you. At this point, your choice may be to pay or to go to court.

If you use a credit card to buy goods that are defective or damaged or services that are poor quality, you may withhold payment for the disputed item. You cannot withhold payment, however, unless you notify the merchant of your complaint at the same time and make a real attempt to resolve the problem with the merchant. If you bought the goods or services with a credit card other than the store's credit card, the right to withhold payment is limited to purchases over $50 that occurred in your state, or outside your state within one hundred miles of your home address.

Credit Reports

After using credit cards or paying off other loans, you will establish a **credit record.** It is important to make payments on time, as this will create a good credit record and make it much easier to obtain a loan in the future. If you have a bad credit record, you may face difficulty getting a loan, even if you are gainfully employed.

Your credit record is summarized on **credit reports** that are maintained by credit bureaus and other companies. Despite your best efforts to pay responsibly, there is a risk that an error in your credit report could make you appear to have an unreliable credit record. To help correct this problem, Congress passed the Fair Credit Reporting Act in 1970.

The Fair Credit Reporting Act requires that those who deny you credit based on credit-bureau information must inform you of the name and address of the credit bureau. If you inquire of the bureau, it must disclose the substance of the information in your file, though you do not have a right to actual copies of the file. If the information in your credit record is inaccurate or incomplete, you can demand that the credit bureau investigate and correct these errors. If the disagreement continues, you can have your position included in your file. If the credit bureau refuses to cooperate at all, you may complain to the Federal Trade Commission, which enforces the act.

Bill Collection Practices

If you have an overdue debt, a company may assign it to a debt collector. This is a person or company that effectively receives a percentage of the debt in exchange for efforts to collect overdue debts. In the past, collection agencies have been quite abusive in their efforts to collect past-due accounts.

In response to past abuses, Congress passed the Fair Debt Collection Practices Act in 1978. This act requires the debt collector to notify you of the following facts within five days of the initial contact:

1. The amount that you owe.
2. To whom you owe the money.
3. That the collector accepts the debt as authentic unless you challenge it within thirty days.
4. What to do if you dispute the debt.

Perhaps you accept that you owe the debt but are simply unable to pay at this time. You may be able to negotiate a payment schedule with the debt collector. The act prohibits a specific series of debt-collection practices, such as:

● Informing employers or others of the debt.
● Using obscene or harassing language.
● Using threats to harm you or your reputation.
● Making harassing telephone calls at inconvenient times.
● Misrepresenting the amount of the debt or the collector's identity.
● Threatening you with imprisonment or garnishment other than that provided at law.

If the debt-collection agency violates these provisions you may sue the collector and recover up to $1,000. You should also inform the Federal Trade Commission, any state or local consumer protection departments, and if appropriate, the telephone company.

You may choose to send a letter to the debt collector telling the agency not to contact you any further. The collector must also stop contacting you if you write within thirty days that you dispute the existence or amount of the debt. The collector may respond by sending you proof of the debt. In any event, the collector still may commence a legal collection action against you for the unpaid debt.

If you are sued for an unpaid debt, you should contact a lawyer or go to a legal aid office if you cannot afford an attorney. You may have defenses to the alleged debt, such as your belief that you purchased a defective product. If the court enters a judgment against you for the debt, it may allow the creditor to seize your nonexempt property in the amount owed and sell it to satisfy the debt. In most states, the court might **garnish** your bank accounts or wages. This permits the creditor automatically to receive a portion of your take-home pay from your employer (up to a maximum of 25 percent).

▌ Small Claims Court

Some defective products may cause great harm, such as bodily injury, and these damages should be pursued with a lawyer in a general state court. Many consumer transactions, such as the purchase of a nonfunctioning product, result in only small damages, which make it impractical to hire a lawyer and pursue an ordinary claim. For these smaller harms, every state provides some form of **small claims court** (sometimes called *pro se* courts or magistrate courts).

There are many advantages to the use of small claims court. The cost of bringing an action is much less than in regular court, and you probably will receive a decision much sooner. A typical small claims case is resolved in a couple of months, while ordinary litigation may take years. In small claims court, you will not need to retain a lawyer to represent you; many states prohibit the use of attorneys in small claims court. You will not need complicated forms or special language. You do make some sacrifices, however, such as the absence of a jury trial and pretrial discovery.

Jurisdictional Limits

Not every case can be filed in small claims court. The court's jurisdiction is limited to truly small claims and varies by state. The typical dollar limit for small claims court is about $2,500, which means you may not bring an action seeking more than that amount in damages. Some states have higher limits—for example, Tennessee, which permits small claims court to hear cases for up to $10,000, and Illinois, which places the limit at $15,000. Other states have lower limits, such as Arizona and Ohio, which limit jurisdiction to claims of under $1,000.

You may voluntarily choose to reduce your claim to slip under the jurisdiction of the small claims court. If you believe that you are owed $3,000, you might file a claim for only $2,500 in small claims court. While you lose the opportunity to recover the $500 difference, you gain the reduced costs of proceeding in small claims court. You cannot split a single claim into two separate cases and then try to bring them both in small claims court. In about half the states, small claims cases are limited to damages and the court cannot issue injunctions or other equitable remedies.

Filing a Claim

As in a general court, a small claims court action begins with the filing of a claim at a specific office. Before filing this claim, you should notify the prospective defendant through a **demand letter** that states the amount that you believe you are owed. The claim need follow few formalities but must contain certain essential information, such as:

- Your name and address.
- The correct name and address of the person that you are suing.
- The reason that you are owed money, such as when and where your damages arose or a debt was incurred.
- The amount of damages that you are claiming.

Some states give you a form on which you supply this information. Keep copies of all letters, forms, and other papers for your files.

Statutes of limitations apply to small claims actions. This means that you must bring your case within a reasonably prompt time after you suffered damages or learned of your claim. The statutes of limitations vary by state. In most states, the limitations period for actions under a written contract is four years; under an oral contract it is two years; and for a tort action it is two or three years, depending upon the tort.

There is a fee associated with filing a claim in small claims court. The amount of this fee is typically small (about $25 to $50), and the fee may vary based on the amount of your claim. You must pay this fee at the time that you file the claim. If you win, the fee may be refunded or added to the judgment.

After the claim is filed, the court will notify the person you are suing. That party will receive a summons to appear before the court. You must provide the court with the correct address, however, which is not always easy to obtain for out-of-state corporations. You may obtain this information from your state's secretary of state office, which maintains a roster of companies doing business in the state. In some states, the defendant must respond to your claim (if only by filing a general denial), but in most jurisdictions, the defendant need file no papers in response to your claim.

Pretrial Procedures

In the traditional legal action, trial is preceded by extensive discovery, in which the parties exchange documents, question witnesses, etc.

The small claims court dispenses with most of this expensive and time-consuming process. As a litigant, you can **subpoena** documents if necessary. While this procedure is seldom used in small claims court, it could be that the defendant or other party has documents that you need for your case. You can require the party to turn over these documents, but don't abuse this authority. If extensive discovery is necessary, you should go to a more traditional court.

You should also identify and arrange for the appearance of relevant witnesses. Go over their testimony with witnesses in advance of trial so that you are prepared for what they will say. You can have a subpoena issued to uncooperative witnesses. If a question of value is at issue, you may need an expert witness. If you are disputing the efficacy of an automobile repair, you should have your own mechanic render an opinion.

You will probably receive a hearing on your claim within thirty days. In most jurisdictions, this is an informal pretrial hearing without witnesses. The court may try to arrange a settlement between you and the defendant. If the defendant fails to appear, you can win a **default judgment,** which is a victory without a trial. If you fail to appear, your case may be dismissed. In the absence of a settlement, your case will promptly advance to trial.

Some states do not provide for these pretrial procedures. If the defendant does respond, the matter is scheduled for trial.

Trial Procedures

Because you will be presenting the case in small claims court, you should do some preparation. Arrange all your documentary evidence of support (receipts, canceled checks, contracts, etc.) and other physical evidence, such as the damaged product. Outline your case and go over your presentation. You should also consider sitting in on a few cases before your own trial, in order to familiarize yourself with the court's methods. Sitting in can also alert you to potential pitfalls.

When the trial time comes, you will stand up and present your case, along with your documents, witnesses, and other evidence. You and your witnesses can speak freely, without the constraints of the formal rules of evidence. Indeed, your witness need not appear in person but might provide a written statement. You may prepare maps or charts or write on a court blackboard. The defendant will have an opportunity to present its case to the court as well. The judge will ask questions of both sides.

When presenting your case, stand up. Be clear, organ-ized, and concise. Limit yourself to the facts and treat the defendant with courtesy. Provide only that evidence which is relevant to your particular claim. Present your facts in a conversational manner; do not attempt to read or memorize every word of a prepared statement. Don't act like Perry Mason but simply present your facts in a straightforward fashion.

Judgment and Appeal

After deliberating, the small claims judge will render a decision. If you prevail, you will receive a **final judgment,** which is a document that states that you are authorized to recover a certain amount from the party that you sued. This amount will be whatever the court found you were owed, plus court fees and **prejudgment interest.** The court may provide that the judgment is to be paid out in installments over a period of time.

Even if you win and receive the final judgment, you still must collect the claim. The court does not serve as a collection agency. The court will inform you of how to go about collecting your judgment. If the defendant refuses to pay, you must go back to court to obtain a **writ of execution**—a legal document that you can present to the sheriff, who will seize the defendant's nonexempt property for you. When payment is complete, you file a **satisfaction of judgment** form with the court.

In most states, if you lose your case in small claims court, you may appeal. Some states, including Michigan and California, do not permit plaintiffs to appeal a small claims judgment. If appeal is allowed, you must file a notice of appeal within a brief time following the judgment, such as thirty days. There will be an additional fee to file an appeal, and attorneys may be used on appeal.

Topic 4   Owning and Operating Motor Vehicles

Motor vehicles are a significant part of the average American's life. In many areas of the country, a car or motorcycle is a necessity for commuting, shopping, etc. A car is also one of the most significant expenses that you may have. The laws of owning and operating motor vehicles vary by state jurisdiction, but the state requirements have many common features.

∎ Buying a New Car

When shopping for a new motor vehicle, you will inevitably be drawn to dealer advertising in newspapers or on television. Some states regulate automobile ads, requiring that they state the duration of a sale or the number of vehicles that the dealer has available. Automobile ads may nevertheless mislead you. Published prices may omit necessary or factory-installed option packages, dealer preparation costs, taxes, and other fees.

Once you have settled on a new motor vehicle, its purchase is a fairly standard contractual arrangement in which you obtain title to the vehicle in exchange for cash or loan financing. The contract must be in writing and should clearly set forth all important terms (such as total cost, value for trade-in, terms of financing, etc.). The contract also should set forth the vehicle identification number ("VIN") and any other fundamental understandings between the buyer and seller. For example, the contract should state that the car is in fact new and has not been used as a demonstrator or rental car. Also, be sure to get promised warranties in writing in the contract.

Financing

Most individuals cannot pay cash for a new car and must therefore arrange for financing. You may obtain such financing through a bank, savings and loan, or credit union, but many dealers now offer their own financing, often at a discount rate, in order to attract customers. Compare rates and be aware that dealers may increase the purchase price of the car to compensate for discount financing.

Federal law regulates contracts for financing products such as automobiles. The lender must inform you of the following facts:

1. The annual percentage rate charged.
2. How the lender sets the finance charge.
3. The balance on which the finance charge is computed.
4. The finance charge amount.
5. The amount to be financed.
6. The total dollar amount to be paid.
7. The number, amounts, and due dates of payments.

Lenders who violate the law owe you any damages you have suffered, plus a fine and court costs.

Title

Once financing has been arranged, you obtain the vehicle plus a certificate of title to the vehicle. This title serves as proof of ownership and should be safely kept by the buyer. The title alone does not give you the right to drive the vehicle, however. States require that the car be registered with the state and be issued license plates. The driver also must have a driver's license.

If you fail to make required loan payments, the seller may take back the title and repossess the car. After a car is repossessed, you have a chance to redeem it by paying all overdue payments (and possibly the entire balance due), plus repossession costs.

Warranties

Most new cars come with some form of **express warranty.** This is a promise of quality or service that should be stated in the contract. A typical express warranty would provide that the seller will replace any defective parts without charge, for a certain time period or until the car has been driven a certain number of miles.

Automobile purchasers also automatically receive certain **implied warranties.** These warranties are presumed to be included in all contracts and need not be stated explicitly. The **implied warranty of title** declares that the seller is the true owner of the car and has legal right to transfer that ownership to you. The **implied warranty of**

merchantability states that the vehicle at least meets ordinary standards of mechanical efficiency. This assures you that the car won't break down as soon as you drive it off the seller's lot.

While these implied warranties generally accompany any sale of a new car, the seller may avoid such warranties by using a **disclaimer.** A provision in the contract of sale, if properly worded, could clearly declare that the seller is making no warranties. The sale of a used car "as is" disclaims implied warranties. If you sign such a contract, you lose the legal protections associated with implied warranties of merchantability.

If a warranty or other contract provision is violated, you may cancel the sale of the car within a reasonable time after you have obtained it. A reasonable time is usually no more than a week or two. Alternatively, you may provide the dealer an opportunity to "cure" the defect. Once you cancel the sale of the car, it is no longer yours and you must stop using it.

If the warranty violation is discovered too late for cancellation, you can seek damages. As a general rule, you must continue to make your car payments while seeking legal recourse. If the violation is significant or costly to correct, you may need a lawyer to help you enforce your contractual rights.

Lemon Laws

Forty-five states have passed **lemon laws** to protect those who purchase defective vehicles. These laws provide you protection over and above any warranties. The precise terms of lemon laws vary from state to state. In general, a "lemon" is a vehicle that has a defect substantially affecting its use, value, or safety, even after reasonable efforts of repair. This may mean as many as four repair attempts on the same problem before repair is deemed futile. Alternatively, some states consider a car a lemon if it is out of commission for more than thirty days during the first year of ownership.

In order to take advantage of a lemon law, you must notify the dealer of the defect and keep a copy of all repair records and receipts. In most states, you will be required to take the dispute to **arbitration** before suing. If you win, you may obtain a satisfactory replacement vehicle or a refund of the purchase price plus associated taxes and fees (minus some allowance for the value of your use of the car). The states also provide other consumer protection laws that offer larger damages than those under lemon laws (such as triple the cost of the car), though these laws may require you to prove that the dealer knowingly or willfully sold you a defective vehicle.

▌Buying or Selling a Used Car

Used vehicles represent a significant percentage of sales, and nonmerchants may be on both sides of a used-car sale. The law provides some basic requirements for such a contract. First, if the price is $500 or more, the contract must be in writing to be enforceable in court. Second, the transaction must include a written **bill of sale.** The bill of sale should state the amount paid, the method of payment, and identifying details about the car, including its VIN. The bill of sale or transfer of title should be signed and dated and generally must be submitted to a specific government agency for registration. Note that applicable sales tax must be paid on used-car sales.

Used-car sales are subject to many of the same buyer-protection laws as are new-car sales. Lemon laws are increasingly being extended to apply to used-car sales. Warranties also apply to many used car sales. If you are selling a car with a material latent defect (one that is not readily discoverable by the buyer), you have a duty to disclose that defect. Otherwise you may be liable for fraud. The implied warranty of merchantability, however, only applies to merchants and does not exist if the sale is by an individual who is not in the business of selling used cars. Although an individual seller makes no implied warranty of quality, the seller may make an express warranty of quality.

Additional regulatory requirements apply to dealers in used cars and provide further buyer protection. A dealer is anyone who sells six or more used cars in a twelve-month period. The Federal Trade Commission requires that dealers post a **Buyer's Guide** on the side window of each used car they sell. This includes a warning that oral promises are difficult to enforce as a practical matter and a recommendation that you get all promises in unambiguous writing. The Guide also lists the terms of any warranties provided and supplies details about any service contracts and significant recurrent problems with the car's mechanical or safety systems.

▌ Renting or Leasing a Car

A short-term automobile rental is another form of contractual arrangement subject to the agreement of the parties. Most automobile rental companies require that you have a driver's license and a major credit card, and some require that you be at least twenty-five years old before they will rent you a vehicle. These companies often waive the age requirement if the rental is business related or if you are a member of an established auto club.

The rental agreement contract will contain a variety of detailed terms and provide you some options. The most significant of these options is the **collision damage waiver.** If you pay for this collision protection, you are not liable for accidental damages to the rental car. The coverage does not extend to personal injuries or damage to others' property, however. Accepting the company's collision damage insurance may be unnecessary. Your existing automobile insurance policy may already provide for this coverage, as may your employer's policy (if this is a business rental) or your credit card itself.

Automobile leasing is a growing business and typically substitutes for the purchase of a car. Under a typical lease, you make monthly payments to the dealer for two to four years. These payments are in place of and typically much less than the monthly payments you would make on a new-car loan. Unlike such loan payments, however, lease payments do not provide you with an **equity (ownership) interest** in the vehicle. Leasing a car may in some states avoid the need to pay sales tax and avoid a down payment (although one- or two-months' advance lease payments are typically required).

When the lease expires, you return the vehicle to the dealer. You no longer have any obligation or interest in this car. If you want to keep the car, you may buy it from the dealer at the end of the lease. Some leases specify an end-of-lease purchase price. For other leases, you simply must negotiate a price with the dealer.

The terms of a lease are like any other contract. Many leases provide that you must make additional payments if you drive more than 15,000 miles per year or cause some irreparable damage to the vehicle. Other terms may include insurance, maintenance agreements, loaner-car arrangements, etc. These may be negotiated, but some dealers may be unwilling to modify their standard form leases.

In some respects, a lease of a motor vehicle may be as much of a commitment as a purchase. The contract binds you to keep the car for the duration of the lease, unless you can sublease the vehicle. Some lease contracts contain an early termination clause through which you may escape the lease early if you don't like the car. These clauses typically require you to pay a penalty, however. If your leased car is stolen or destroyed, it is considered to be an early termination, and your insurance probably will not cover the early termination penalty. **Gap insurance** is available to cover this possibility.

▌ Insuring a Car

Categories of Insurance

Many states require you to have automobile **liability insurance** and others require you to demonstrate "financial responsibility" (such as obtaining insurance or posting a bond). The laws specify a minimum basic level of coverage that is required. These requirements vary by state. Insurance laws are designed to ensure that you can pay damages if injury occurs to another person as a result of your careless driving. Failure to maintain such insurance is a driving violation that subjects you to a fine and potential loss of your license.

When you acquire liability insurance, your insurance company must pay for the damages that you caused. If you are sued for negligent driving, your insurance company generally will take charge of the suit and supply its own lawyer. You remain personally liable, however, for damages over and above the policy limits (which may be as low as $50,000). The compulsory liability insurance laws also help protect your ability to recover damages if you are injured by others.

When you obtain insurance, your periodic payment rate will be based upon a number of factors. These include type of car, your age, gender, driving record, and primary use of car, plus local accident rates. Although it may seem unfair, all young males pay an extra premium, because so many young males get into accidents. You may pay a higher rate if your type of car is particularly expensive to repair or especially likely to be stolen. As with any business deal, you can shop around to find the best rates.

When acquiring insurance, you may obtain **uninsured motorist coverage.** Indeed, seventeen states require you to have such a policy. This uninsured motorist coverage enables you to collect for your damages if you are injured by a negligent driver who lacks his or her own insurance. Even in states in which liability insurance is required, a significant number of drivers lack coverage. Under uninsured motorist coverage, your own insurance company pays for your damages and then attempts to recover this payment in an action against the uninsured driver. You are thus covered even if the negligent driver lacks the ability to pay.

To collect under uninsured motorist coverage, you generally must show that the other driver was at fault and lacked liability insurance. Many uninsured motorist policies provide protection even when the other party has insurance, but the party's policy limits are insufficient to cover all your damages. You can recover your damages only once, however, and cannot duplicate payments from both your own and the other party's insurers.

In addition to liability and uninsured motorist coverage, you have other insurance options. Many individuals purchase **collision insurance,** through which the insurer pays for any damages to your car from a collision, regardless of who was at fault. **Comprehensive insurance** protects against non-collision damage to your vehicle (including theft, vandalization, and hail damage). These policies generally do *not* cover personal items left in your vehicle. These policies also generally contain a **deductible,** which means that you must pay a certain amount of your loss, such as the first $200 of damages. You may also obtain insurance to cover medical payments for you and your passengers after an accident.

About half of the states have a system of **no-fault insurance.** This system largely eliminates lawsuits for negligence and requires every driver to carry insurance to pay for his or her own damages, regardless of who was at fault in the accident. Under this system, parties need not go to court to recover and need not worry that the other driver lacks insurance. Damage compensation in no-fault systems tends to be lower than in traditional jurisdictions.

Insurance Coverage

If you obtain automobile insurance and inform your insurance company that others may drive your car, they too are protected by the policy. An automobile insurance policy typically extends coverage to the following parties:

- You and your spouse.
- Other residents of your household that you have declared to the insurance company.
- Other undeclared persons who drive the car with your permission (though this may be limited to infrequent borrowings).
- Nondrivers who may be liable due to your negligence, such as your employer.

If you fail to inform the insurance company that another party will be a regular driver of your car, that person may not be covered by the insurance.

If you purchase a new car, your old automobile insurance policy continues in effect for at least thirty days, while a new policy may be written and acquired. You should notify your insurance company of your purchase and obtain a new policy promptly in order to ensure continued protection. Your policy will also cover you when you drive an automobile owned by another person. If you go on vacation and have an accident while driving your sister's car, you will probably be covered by both your policy and her policy. In many cases, your policy will not provide coverage for driving in foreign countries (except Canada).

▌ Repairing a Car

When your car is damaged and requires repair, you will need to choose a mechanic. In some areas, auto mechanics are notorious for questionable or fraudulent practices. To defend yourself against such practices, investigate the reputation and past practices of mechanics and negotiate a repair contract that legally protects your interests.

The repair contract is often called a **repair order.** This order is customarily a form standard in the industry that describes the work to be done on your vehicle. Signing the order creates a contract authorizing the mechanic to make the described repairs. The repair order contains necessary identifying information about you and your car but does not generally state a price for the repairs.

It is a good practice to receive a cost estimate for repairs before authorizing the work, though some repair shops will charge for such estimates. At common law, this estimate is not binding, and if the cost proves greater than the estimate, you are still bound to pay the difference. Some states have legislation that provides that actual costs cannot exceed the estimate by more than a certain percentage.

After repair work, complaints may arise over the quality of the work, the cost, or warranties made by the mechanic. Most states have laws requiring that you be provided with a detailed invoice of parts and labor as well as the right to receive parts that have been replaced. If you believe that you have been cheated, you may be able to sue in contract or under a deceptive trade practices statute. If you inform your state attorney general, he or she may take action on your behalf.

If you refuse to pay for the repairs, the mechanic may keep your car through an **artisan's lien** (or mechanic's lien), which gives the repair shop the right to sell your car to satisfy your debt. This lien is available only if the shop has complied with legal requirements for repair authorization. If you make payments, or the mechanic has agreed to do the repairs on credit, the mechanic must return your car.

▌ Driving Violations

A long list of criminal laws governs driving. These laws vary greatly in seriousness and in penalties. For the most significant violations, penalties may include prison time.

Stop and Search

The police have a broad right to stop you while you are driving. When you see the police flashing lights in your rearview mirror, you should pull over to the side of the road as promptly and safely as possible. The police have a right to see your driver's license and to have you step out of the car.

After a stop, the officer may want to search your car. The officer need not have a warrant. Your car can only be searched, however, if either (a) you consent or (b) the officer has probable cause to believe that your vehicle contains incriminating evidence. If an illegal item (such as drugs or guns) is in plain view in your car, the officer may seize it without the need for a search warrant. The law defining the scope of police searches is ever changing as new cases are brought. At a minimum, the police may search the area within the driver's

reach, including the glove compartment. Under some circumstances, the police can impound your car. If so, they may do a thorough search without a warrant or even probable cause.

Speeding

A common driving violation is excessive speed. If you are caught speeding, you may be subject to a substantial fine. The officer may choose not to cite you for speeding if you have a particularly good reason (such as a health emergency). Most speeding violations are demonstrated by radar readings of your speed. You may have heard of cases in which radar results were thrown out of court for improper maintenance or other reasons. In the vast majority of cases, however, courts accept the results of radar guns as virtually conclusive evidence that you were speeding. In many jurisdictions, you may take a defensive driving course in lieu of a fine for speeding. Completion of the course may also keep the ticket off your driving record and avoid an increase in insurance rates.

Some people use radar detectors to avoid getting caught speeding. Connecticut and Virginia have outlawed the use of such radar detectors. In a recent New Jersey case, a person was arrested for flashing his headlights to warn oncoming traffic of the presence of a radar trap. The court, however, held that his actions were perfectly legal.

Driving While Intoxicated

Perhaps the most serious driving violation is driving while intoxicated with alcohol or other drugs. Some states call this crime "driving under the influence." Intoxication is typically defined by blood-alcohol level, and different states have different standards for defining intoxication. Drunk driving is responsible for about 20,000 deaths annually.

The blood-alcohol level defining intoxication varies somewhat by state, with most using a .10 standard (meaning one-tenth of one percent blood-alcohol concentration). California and some other states have lowered this threshold to .08. Your blood-alcohol level is a function of your weight and alcohol consumption, plus some other factors. Having two regular-sized drinks (one ounce of alcohol each) within one hour may put you in the danger zone of violation.

The police may pull you over if your driving appears erratic, such as weaving from lane to lane.

Indeed, the police may establish roadblocks in areas frequented by drinkers and stop cars randomly to check for drunk driving. Once you are stopped they will observe your coordination, your speech, whether you smell of alcohol, and the appearance of your eyes. They may administer a simple test of your ability to walk a straight line or your ability to focus your eyes on a point. If they continue to suspect that you were driving while intoxicated, they will ask you to take a breathalyzer examination.

You are not required to take the breathalyzer test, due to the constitutional protection against self-incrimination. If you refuse, however, states are authorized to suspend your driver's license, usually for several months. Many attorneys advise that you should refuse the breathalyzer if you suspect that you are indeed intoxicated beyond the legal limit. If you fail a breathalyzer test, your attorney may subsequently challenge the results, but the test is often powerful evidence. In many states, you have a right to a second, confirmatory test if you fail the first breath-alyzer exam. If you refuse the breathalyzer, the case against you will be built upon the testimony of the police officer and others who observed your condition at the time.

Penalties

The penalty for most driving violations is a fine, ranging from tens to hundreds of dollars. If you have accumulated a number of driving violations, the state may also suspend your license temporarily or revoke your license indefinitely. Revocation is generally limited to serious violations, such as driving while intoxicated, fleeing the police, or using a vehicle to commit a felony crime. You are entitled to notice and a hearing before revocation takes effect.

If you drive without a license (because it has been suspended or revoked), you may be arrested and held in jail until you can post bond. The amount of this bond will depend on your driving record and the nature of any other violation you may have committed to provoke the arrest. In this event, you should find an attorney as promptly as possible.

Serious violations, such as driving while intoxicated, may result in imprisonment. Fourteen states require mandatory imprisonment after the first offense of drunk driving. (The requirement may be only a few days.) Numerous other states require

imprisonment after repeat violations and potential penalties include months or years in prison. A drunk-driving conviction also results in a substantial increase in insurance premiums or even insurance cancellation.

▌Driving Accidents

Liability

Under the law, you have a duty to drive with reasonable care. If your negligent driving injures someone, you and/or your insurance company may be liable for the resultant damages. Negligence is a general term covering any sort of carelessness including driving violations. It is also negligence if you fail to keep your vehicle in good repair. If the accident was unavoidable, you are not liable.

You may be liable even if you were not the driver. The doctrine of **negligent entrustment** applies if you permit an underage, intoxicated, or other incapable person to use your car. In about half the states, parents or guardians are automatically liable if they have signed the driver's license application for their children who subsequently cause an accident. An employer is also typically liable for accidents caused by an employee acting within the scope of employment.

In many accidents, both involved parties were negligent in some manner. In this circumstance, the law provides for **comparative negligence**. Under this doctrine, each party must pay damages in proportion to his or her negligence. In most states, you cannot recover any damages if you were more than 50 percent to blame. Even in these states, the damages you owe will be reduced by the proportion of negligence assigned to the other driver. You also may be liable to passengers in your own car who are injured in an accident that was your fault.

Reporting Requirements

The law requires that you report some driving accidents. A written report is required if the accident causes personal injury or if property damage exceeds a minimum threshold (usually about $250). This report generally must be filed with a specific government agency within five or ten days of the accident, depending on the state. To help ensure the report's accuracy, take careful note of weather and road conditions, speed estimates, time, and other relevant factors.

Failure to file the report is a misdemeanor and may be punishable by suspension of your driver's license. When you submit the report, you are automatically verifying that all the reported facts are true and that you are not omitting any material facts about the accident. Knowingly providing false information may be a felony.

What to Do after Your Accident

If you are in a significant accident, you should first park your car out of traffic, if possible. Driving away from the scene of the accident is illegal. Post warning flares by the side of the road or have a person warn oncoming vehicles. Exchange information with the other driver involved in the accident. This information should include the names and addresses of all passengers, vehicle license number, vehicle registration, and proof of insurance. Today's laws require a person to provide such identification. If police officers arrive on the scene, ask for their names and badge numbers. If you have a camera in your car, take pictures of the scene.

Do not make statements about fault to the other driver, bystanders, or the police. If you have injured someone, you may feel bad. There is nothing to be gained, however, by confessing fault immediately after the accident. At this time, you may be unaware of the true cause of the accident, and an admission of fault may be used against you even if you later realize that you were not at fault. After you are familiar with all the relevant facts and you have consulted with your insurance company and an attorney, you may choose to admit fault.

If someone is hurt or killed in the accident, you should alert the police and emergency medical services immediately. Be cautious about attempting to provide medical assistance unless you are qualified—you could aggravate an injury. After emergency concerns have been addressed, you should file required reports, contact your insurance company, and possibly contact an attorney.

Even if you do not seem to be injured, you should see a doctor for possible hidden or delayed conditions. If the insurance claims adjustor for the other party contacts you, refer the adjustor to your attorney. If you don't have an attorney, be careful what you say. Make no settlement until you have sufficiently explored your medical condition and legal opportunities. If you suspect that the accident was caused by a defect in your own vehicle, do not have the car repaired until after consulting with an attorney. In any event, keep careful records of any repairs done following the accident and retain replaced parts.

Rendering Assistance to Others

If you come across an accident while driving, you may consider stopping and rendering assistance. As a general rule, you have no duty to provide assistance if you were uninvolved in the accident. If you were involved in the accident, all states require you to stop and render assistance, even if you do not believe that you were at fault. Rendering assistance may simply involve telephoning the police and emergency medical services.

If you witness an accident, you may render assistance even when it is not legally required. If you stop and provide assistance to an accident victim, theoretically you could subsequently be sued by the victim for negligence in the manner of providing such assistance. The vast majority of states have adopted **Good Samaritan laws,** which shield you from any liability for simple negligence in assisting an accident victim. You could still be sued, though, for extreme or gross negligence in providing assistance.

Topic 5   **Criminal Law**

It is wise to obey the law and avoid the criminal justice system. Should you be charged with a crime, it is crucial for you to understand the charges and your constitutional rights. Except for the most minor crimes, you must consult an attorney.

The Nature of Crimes

A criminal act is one that is prohibited by the legislature in a statute. An act does not become criminal simply because it is unethical or reprehensible—it must be specifically outlawed to be a crime.

There is considerable overlap between criminal law and civil law. If a person steals your car, that action is the crime of auto theft and also the civil tort of conversion. The responsible party may be prosecuted for the crime and also sued for the tort in separate judicial actions. The criminal action will be brought by the state government and tried by a **prosecutor** employed by the government. If convicted, the defendant will be required to pay a fine and/or do time in jail. The civil action must be brought by you and litigated by your lawyer. If you win, the defendant must pay you damages. The defendant cannot be sentenced to jail in a civil case. Although the two cases deal with the same action, they are pursued independently and employ different procedures, such as different burdens of proof.

Either the state or the federal legislature may make a certain action criminal. Most crimes are state crimes, prosecuted by the state and heard in state court. Other crimes, such as mail fraud or failure to pay federal income tax, are uniquely federal and enforced by federal authorities. A few crimes, such as possession of illegal drugs and bank robbery, are both federal and state crimes.

Types of Crimes

A wide range of activities have been outlawed as criminal acts. The best known are the most serious and violent crimes, such as murder, rape, and kidnapping. These crimes are punishable by death or by an imprisonment sentence for a period such as twenty years to life. The **felony murder rule** makes a person guilty of murder, even if he or she does not personally murder anyone. Suppose an armed robbery of a convenience store involves three persons—two go into the store and one stays in the "getaway car." No violence is planned, but one of the robbers shoots and kills the clerk. All three persons are guilty of murder, even the one who did not go into the store.

The criminal justice system considers lesser but still severe crimes to include those such as armed robbery and manslaughter (for example,

murder through negligence). Careless driving that results in a fatal accident may give rise to a negligent manslaughter prosecution. The sentence for these crimes may be three to five years or longer in prison.

Some crimes against property are also punished severely. For example, arson and extortion may be punished by years of imprisonment. Robbery, the taking of money or property by force from a person, is a more serious crime than burglary, the taking of property from a home in that person's absence. A burglary conviction may have greater penalties if it was conducted with a weapon, at night, or when the home was occupied. Receiving or buying property that you know or should know has been stolen is itself a crime sometimes referred to as obtaining stolen goods.

Crimes against public health, safety, and welfare form another category of criminal action. This category includes the possession, manufacture, or sale of certain prohibited drugs, such as cocaine or heroin. Selling alcohol to a minor is another example of this type of crime. Many of the laws against such crimes are aimed at businesses that may violate environmental laws or food safety laws.

Among the most controversial crimes are those "against public decency and morals." Such crimes include bigamy, prostitution, and illegal gambling. A controversial Supreme Court decision held that it was constitutional to prohibit homosexual sodomy, even in private. A number of states still have statutes that outlaw both homosexual and heterosexual sodomy, but these laws are seldom enforced. By contrast, molestation or other lewd and lascivious behavior toward a child is illegal and strictly enforced.

Misdemeanors versus Felonies

Crimes are deemed to be either **misdemeanors** or **felonies.** A felony is a particularly serious crime. Examples of felonies are homicide, rape, and armed robbery. Misdemeanors are somewhat less serious crimes. Shoplifting, public drunkenness, and mildly resisting arrest are examples of misdemeanors.

The general distinction between felonies and misdemeanors is based upon the potential sentence for the crime. Offenses punishable by a prison sentence of more than one year are considered felonies. Misdemeanors are punishable by sentences of a year or less, and incarceration is in a county or municipal jail rather than a state prison. Those convicted of felonies may also lose other significant rights, including the right to vote or to serve on a jury.

The same basic action may be a misdemeanor or a felony, depending on the circumstances. For example, petty theft involves stealing less than a certain dollar amount and is a misdemeanor. Stealing goods worth more than the statutorily specified dollar amount is grand theft and constitutes a felony. For other crimes, the first offense may be considered a misdemeanor, but subsequent offenses become felonies.

▌ Arrest and Prosecution

Stop and Arrest

The criminal process often commences with a procedure known as **stop and frisk**. This occurs when the police have reason to suspect that you are engaged in a criminal activity and that you may be armed. Such suspicion may arise if you were loitering outside a home or business in a manner to suggest that you might be "casing" the place for a break-in. After the police have stopped you, they may ask you questions. They may also conduct a frisk, which is a patting down of the outside of your clothing. If they feel something that might be a weapon, the police are permitted to reach into your pocket and remove it. If they feel something soft that could not be a dangerous weapon, the police generally cannot search for it. In June 1993, the Supreme Court expanded police authority to allow removal and seizure of a package of drugs felt during a frisk.

Except for the stop-and-frisk rule, the police may not search you, unless you are under arrest or the police have a **search warrant.** The police may ask you to consent to a search, but there is no reason for you to agree. Refusal to cooperate with a stop and frisk, however, may represent independent grounds to arrest you.

The stop and frisk may be followed by an **arrest**. An arrest occurs when a suspect is taken into custody. The police may obtain an arrest warrant in advance, then seek out and arrest the suspect. If a person is caught in the act of committing a crime and the police lack time to obtain a warrant, the police may perform a **warrantless arrest.** A warrantless arrest must be based upon **probable cause.** Probable cause is a concept meaning that the police have a reasonable belief that a specific person has committed a crime. Probable cause is based on more than just a hunch or a stereotype, but involves far less than the evidence required to convict at trial. A tip from an informer is one way of establishing probable cause. Those subjected to warrantless arrest have an opportunity for a prompt hearing on the presence of probable cause.

Warrantless arrests are generally limited to public situations. For the police to seek you out and arrest you in a private place, an arrest warrant is generally required. The police may put you under surveillance at your house and then arrest you without a warrant after you leave home.

If you are arrested, you should be very careful of what you say or do. Don't resist the arrest or fingerprinting, and give the police your name and address. Don't say anything about the arrest to the police until after you have consulted with an attorney. If you are held in jail, you will have an opportunity to call a friend or relative. Inform them of the situation and arrange for legal representation. Be scrupulously honest with your lawyer—confessions to your lawyer cannot be used against you, due to the attorney-client privilege. Have your lawyer present at any police questioning or lineups at which you might be identified by the purported crime victim.

The police may seek to question you immediately after the arrest, before you have an opportunity to consult with an attorney. The U.S. Constitution guarantees you a right against self-incrimination, so that you cannot be forced to testify against yourself, and you need not respond to such questioning. Historically, the police have sometimes used physical or psychological pressure to coerce confessions even from the innocent. To avoid this scenario, the Supreme Court has required that persons in custody be given a set of **Miranda warnings** (named for the case that created the requirement). Police initially carried a "Miranda card" to remind them of the language, but these warnings are now quite well known to police and many ordinary citizens.

MIRANDA WARNINGS

● You have the right to remain silent. Anything you say can be used against you.

● You have the right to a lawyer and to have one present during questioning.

● If you cannot afford a lawyer, one will be appointed for you before questioning commences.

If the police fail to provide Miranda warnings, a suspect may still be prosecuted and convicted. The Miranda warnings are required only for use at trial of statements made by the accused.

Search and Seizure

The Fourth Amendment to the United States Constitution protects the privacy of Americans and restricts the government's ability to conduct searches. The government may search your home if it obtains a *search warrant*. Such a warrant generally must be obtained from a judge. The police go before the court and present evidence of its probable cause to believe that evidence of a crime is present. This warrant must particularly describe the place or person to be searched and the evidence to be seized. With such a warrant, the police may thoroughly search you, your home, your car, your business, or other places.

Under certain defined circumstances, the police may conduct a warrantless search. The stop and frisk is a limited form of such a warrantless search. Some examples of lawful warrantless searches are:

1.   When the police are in hot pursuit of a felon trying to escape the scene of a crime.
2.   When the police have probable cause to believe that a vehicle contains illegal items, the police may search the vehicle without a warrant.
3.   When an item is in plain view of an officer, it may be seized without a warrant.
4.   When the police make a proper arrest, they may search the area immediately surrounding the arrested person.
5.   When a person consents to the search and seizure.
6.   Searches in some special locations, such as at the national border or at an airport.

What if a search is illegal, due to the absence of a warrant or grounds for a warrantless search, and the police then find evidence of a crime? Under the **exclusionary rule,** evidence from the illegal search cannot be introduced at the criminal trial.

❚ Pretrial Procedures

After the arrest, the accused typically is **booked,** fingerprinted, and photographed at the local police station. Booking is the official police processing of the arrest. The defendant may be strip-searched.

Hearing Right

Soon after the booking, the accused has a right to a first appearance before a court. At this point, the judge explains the charges to be brought and the defendant's rights. The court will appoint a lawyer for the defendant if necessary. In a felony case, this appearance is often called a **presentment** or **preliminary arraignment.** This hearing may serve as an **arraignment,** when the defendant is formally advised of the charges and given an opportunity to respond by pleading guilty or not guilty. When the government's case is weak, the judge may dismiss the case in this first appearance.

Release before Trial

The key aspect of this first-appearance hearing is whether the defendant will be released from custody automatically, or if **bail** will be set. Bail involves the payment of a bond by the defendant in order to secure release from custody. The core function of bail is to ensure that the accused does not go into hiding to avoid trial. In many cases, the defendant may obtain a **release on his or her own recognizance** (without posting a bond). This occurs when the defendant promises to return for trial and convinces the court that he or she is a good risk.

In some cases, even bail may be denied and the defendant held in custody without prospect for release. Bail may be denied for particularly horrendous crimes, if the defendant is considered a threat to the community. Bail may also be denied if the defendant was already on parole or probation and if the defendant presents a particular danger of flight from the jurisdiction before trial.

The next major step in a criminal prosecution is either to present the case to a grand jury for indictment or to hold a preliminary hearing. Both events require a closer investigation of the charges against the defendant. A grand jury is a group of up to twenty-three ordinary citizens who hear testimony and evidence presented only by the prosecution. The grand jury then decides whether to indict the accused and send the defendant to trial, or to "no bill" the defendant, releasing the accused from the charges.

At a preliminary hearing, the prosecutor, in the presence of a judge, must present sufficient evidence and witnesses to establish the probable guilt of the defendant. The accused is represented by counsel, who may present witnesses and evidence and may cross-examine prosecution witnesses. The judge decides whether to bind the defendant over for trial. Grand jury indictments are required in federal prosecution of felonies.

If the prosecution proceeds and the defendant maintains innocence, the parties then undergo discovery of evidence. Lawyers may file pretrial motions to the court. For example, the defense may contend that the prosecution's evidence is inadmissible and ask the judge to dismiss the action. If the prosecution prevails, the next step is the criminal trial.

▎ Trial and Defenses

Defendants have a right to a speedy trial which must quickly follow the indictment or arraignment. Typically, a state might guarantee that the trial begin within sixty days. It is common, however, for defendants to waive their right to be tried so promptly, in order to obtain more time to prepare their defenses.

The Trial

The Constitution has been interpreted to give the defendant the right to a jury trial for significant crimes (punishable by imprisonment of six months or more). The defendant has a right to a jury of peers, but this does not mean individuals in the same financial or social position as the defendant. A jury of peers simply means that the jury is selected from residents of the accused's community and that no groups have been artificially excluded from serving on the jury. If the crime has received extensive pretrial publicity, the defendant may ask for a **change of venue,** so that the trial can be held in another location where jurors may not be so prejudiced by media coverage of the crime.

Eventually, the criminal case will come to trial. The prosecution will present its evidence. Such evidence may be in the form of eyewitness testimony; namely, individuals who claim to have seen the defendant commit the crime. The prosecution may present documentary evidence of guilt. The prosecution may also present circumstantial evidence, facts that create a strong inference that the defendant must have committed the crime. The

defendant has the **presumption of innocence.** This means that the prosecution has the burden of proof to establish guilt beyond a reasonable doubt.

Defenses

Several constitutional protections extend to the trial of the accused. The Fifth Amendment contains a general right to **due process,** which requires procedural fairness, such as an impartial judge. The Sixth Amendment gives the accused a right to confront and cross-examine the witnesses against them. As noted, the defendant has a right to an attorney and the right not to testify. The defendant may seek to exclude some prosecution evidence as inadmissible. The exclusionary rule means that most illegally obtained evidence cannot be introduced against you in trial. This includes evidence from illegal searches and seizures or confessions obtained through coercion or without first giving the accused his or her Miranda warnings.

Criminal defendants may have available other procedural or constitutional defenses. One such defense is known as **entrapment.** Defendants often claim entrapment but seldom succeed. The defense is quite narrow, and the defendant has the burden of proof to demonstrate entrapment. It is not enough to show that government agents suggested the commission of a crime. A police officer offering to sell drugs to a college student is generally not a case of entrapment. Entrapment means that the government somehow induced a person to commit a crime that he or she otherwise would never have considered committing. If the government merely affords a person the opportunity to commit a crime, and the person seizes that opportunity, entrapment is not established.

Entrapment might exist when the government continues at great length in its efforts to catch an individual. Suppose that an undercover agent arrived at your door and offered to sell you a stolen stereo. You declined. The agent then appeared at your door and made the same offer day after day. After you declined to purchase the stereo many times, you finally relented. This degree of government perseverance might constitute entrapment.

The accused may of course maintain that no crime was committed or that he or she is not the guilty party. This defense may involve undermining the testimony of the prosecution witnesses, such as challenging the accuracy of eyewitness testimony. The defendant may also present evidence of his or her innocence. This may consist, for example, of an **alibi,** showing that the defendant was somewhere else at the time of the crime's commission. The defendant may testify but is not required to do so.

Another defense to crime is **self-defense** or the defense of others. It is not unlawful to attack someone in self-defense. To demonstrate self-defense, a defendant must show that he or she had a reasonable fear of an imminent danger of bodily harm from an attacker. This same defense is available if you come to the defense of others endangered by an attack. The force used in self-defense must be reasonable. If the attacker runs away from you, you generally may not pursue him to strike him further. Deadly force (such as a gun or knife) may be used in self-defense only when you are threatened with deadly force. You can also use some force in the defense of your property, but you usually cannot use deadly force in defense of property. Some states have exceptions to this rule. In Texas, you can use deadly force if a person is seeking to enter your property at night.

Another defense is available if the defendant is not responsible for his or her actions. Extreme cases of intoxication may mean that the defendant lacked the state of mind to commit certain crimes. Slight drunkenness is not a defense, though, and some states hold that voluntary intoxication cannot be a defense, no matter how drunk the defendant is. Another such defense is **insanity.** The insanity defense is actually rather narrow, and even a significant psychological problem may not qualify. Standards differ somewhat by state but a common test is that the defendant be so insane as to lack the ability to appreciate the nature of the criminal act or that the conduct was wrongful. Insanity is judged as pertaining to the time of the crime. If the defendant remains insane, a trial cannot proceed, because due process requires that the defendant be able to understand the charges brought. Such a defendant is typically held in an institution until sanity is regained.

Yet another defense is the passage of too much time between the act and the prosecution. The **statute of limitations** is a law that requires that legal proceedings (such as a complaint) commence within a certain period of time. A typical state statute of limitations would be one year for misdemeanors and three years for certain felonies. The statute stops running if the defendant is out of the state during this period or changes his or her identity. For very serious crimes, such as murder, there is no statute of limitations.

∎ Sentencing

After a person is convicted of a crime, the court metes out some form of sentence. Sentencing has a variety of purposes. Some of the objectives of sentencing are rehabilitation of the offender, incapacitation of the offender so that the crime is not repeated, and deterrence of future crimes by the offender and others.

Types of Sentences

The law provides for a broad range of sentencing options, depending upon the nature of the crime. The most severe is capital punishment, in which the defendant is executed. Other serious crimes provide for imprisonment for a specified term, often a number of years. Felony sentences are commonly served in state prison, while misdemeanor sentences are typically served in a local jail. In many other cases, the defendant must pay a fine to the state.

A variety of lesser sentences are also available for less serious crimes or first offenders. **Probation** refers to a sentence by which an offender does not go to jail or prison but is released under the supervision of a probation officer. States prohibit probation for certain serious offenses. The offender also agrees to follow certain conditions, such as not carrying a gun, not using illegal drugs, getting a job, and checking in regularly with the probation officer. Probation is for a set period of time, such as one year. If the offender violates the terms of probation during this period, probation may be revoked and he or she may be sent to prison. Revocation of probation requires a hearing to establish the presence of a violation.

In some cases, the convicted criminal may receive a **suspended sentence.** The offender first receives a particular prison sentence (for example, two years in prison), which is then suspended by the judge. The offender is then released without conditions or supervision by a probation officer. In a suspended sentence, the conviction and sentence is a matter of public record and may hamper the job prospects of the convicted. Another procedure is called **deferred sentencing.** After a conviction, the judge will elect to defer sentencing for a period such as a year. If the offender commits no more violations during that year, the judge imposes no sentence at all.

States are increasingly turning to innovative forms of punishment. Many states have **restitution statutes.** Such laws require defendants to pay the victims to compensate them for the losses suffered from the crimes. While conceptually appealing, restitution statutes have limits for the reason that many convicted criminals lack the resources to make restitution. Judges have also turned to public humiliation as a sanction. A convicted criminal may be forced to wear a sign or take out an advertisement in the newspaper confessing his or her guilt. Convicted drunk drivers have been compelled to apply bumper stickers declaring themselves guilty of that crime.

The Eighth Amendment to the Constitution prohibits **cruel and unusual punishment.** This typically concerns punishments such as torture, but courts are extending the amendment to unreasonable prison conditions if the government exhibits "deliberate indifference" to the conditions. A 1993 Supreme Court decision held that being confined to a cell with a smoker could be cruel and unusual punishment if the prisoner could show that the secondhand tobacco smoke presented a serious risk to his or her health.

▌ Juvenile Justice

The United States provides a justice system for juveniles separate from that for adults. This system tends to be more lenient and often refers to "delinquent acts" rather than crimes. Sentences are also lighter. As juveniles are increasingly committing heinous crimes, the relative lenience of juvenile courts has fallen into some disfavor.

The Juvenile

Each state sets its own age limit for determination of whether an accused person should be tried as an adult or as a juvenile. In most states the age of maturity is eight-een, but a number of states have reduced this age to sixteen or seventeen. Underage individuals are presumptively treated as youths and tried in juvenile court. Most states provide that some juveniles may be tried in an adult court and subjected to the full range of penalties. The juvenile

may be transferred to adult court, depending on certain factors. The relevant factors include the seriousness of the crime, the criminal record of the defendant, the age of the defendant, and the likelihood that juvenile status will better enable the rehabilitation of the defendant.

Pretrial

The apprehension of a juvenile is not called an arrest but a *taking into custody.* Juveniles may be taken into custody for the very same criminal acts that would result in the arrest of an adult. Juveniles may also be taken into custody for **status offenses.** Status offenses are not criminal acts proscribed by the legislature but are problems such as repeated truancy at school or habitual disobedience and may apply to those minors who have run away from home. A single episode of misbehavior does not render a youth a status offender. Consistent misbehavior is required. Juveniles charged with status offenses have basically the same legal protections as those charged with crimes.

As juvenile criminal behavior has grown, status offenses have taken a back seat. Such offenses are still significant, however, as they often reflect an emotionally troubled life that may be amenable to rehabilitation. Various programs, such as youth shelters and counseling, have been established to assist runaways and other troubled youths.

After a juvenile is taken into custody for either a crime or a status offense, the police may choose to file a formal charge, refer the case to social workers, or release the youth to the care of parents. If the police detain the juvenile, a process known as **intake** follows. At this stage the authorities question the juvenile, to assess the seriousness of the problem. Many complaints are eliminated at this stage, and the youth may be referred to a social service agency or have the charges dismissed.

Juvenile Court Procedures

Juveniles in custody must first receive an initial hearing on the validity of their detention. The youth has a right to an attorney and may have one appointed by the court if necessary. Instead of a trial, a juvenile is given an **adjudication hearing.** This functions much like an adult trial, and the juvenile has a constitutional right to due process, including the right to present evidence, cross-examine witnesses, and be represented by an attorney. In contrast to the trial of an adult, a juvenile adjudication hearing is not public.

A juvenile may be found delinquent, rather than guilty. In this event juveniles undergo a **dispositional hearing** in which the judge decides what disposition (sentence) the youth should receive. Juvenile dispositions tend to place more emphasis on rehabilitation and less on deterrence or incarceration as compared to adult sentencing. Probation is a common disposition, and the conditions of probation may be particularly strict, such as a curfew. The juvenile may be sentenced to a juvenile institution for an indeterminate amount of time, up to the maximum statutorily allowed for the violation committed. The youth may instead be sent to a halfway house or foster home for rehabilitation.

Disposition is more limited for status offenders, who have committed no adult crime. Parents may actually take their child to a local prosecutor and ask that a status offender complaint be filed against the juvenile. Such a petition might request that the youth be removed from the home and placed in some sort of government institution or foster home. Many states allow such a ruling for a child who continually refuses to obey the directions of parents or fails to attend school. Such a juvenile might be declared a **person in need of supervision.**

Juveniles have many, but not all, of the constitutional protections afforded adults. The Supreme Court has held that juveniles cannot be found in violation of a criminal act without proof beyond a reasonable doubt, though this does not extend to status offenses. Juveniles also have the right to an attorney and to confront their accusers. Juveniles do not have the right to trial by jury, however. An adult can never be tried for status offenses. Most states permit juveniles to appeal their dispositions, but the Supreme Court has never held that this is constitutionally required.

Topic 6   **Jury Duty**

The jury system is central to the American system of justice. Serving on a jury is both a privilege and a responsibility of citizenship. While such service may be a temporary inconvenience, the willingness of citizens to serve is essential to preserve constitutional rights and is reflective of democracy. Community participation in justice is important to public confidence in the system.

▌Jury *Venire* and Selection

The process of jury selection can be lengthy and confusing to the ordinary person. While parts of the process may appear arbitrary, they are designed to help select an impartial jury of the defendant's peers.

Jury *Venire*

Jury selection must begin with a pool of possible jurors. This pool of potential jurors is often called a jury *venire*. Choosing the individuals in this pool for any given case requires a list of all possible jurors in the community. There is no such convenient list. In the past, some communities used lists of property taxpayers or telephone book listings. Such lists created a bias toward the wealthier citizens, who are more likely to own property and have more telephone lines. Consequently, exclusive reliance on such lists may violate the constitutional requirement of a **jury of peers.**

A defendant's right to a jury of peers does not mean that the jurors must come from the same walk of life as the defendant. A hot-rodder charged with drunk driving has no right to a jury composed of automobile fanciers. Rather, the term "jury of peers" simply means that no group in the community has been systematically excluded from the jury. The jury pool must represent a "fair cross section" of the community. Suppose that the jury pool was drawn from all those who voted in the last two presidential elections. The hot-rodder might reasonably complain that this unfairly excluded a large number of younger persons in their twenties.

There is no perfect list for a jury *venire*. Many communities still use phone books but supplement them with lists of registered voters, census rolls, and motor vehicle registration lists. Whatever the list used, the jury pool is selected randomly from the list. The *venire* may consist of hundreds of names, depending on the number of trials to be covered and the potential difficulty of finding impartial individuals. A highly publicized trial may require a larger initial *venire* of potential jurors, because many individuals may already have formed a strong opinion of the case.

If you are in the *venire* of jurors for a given case or cases, you will first receive a card in the mail summoning you to the courthouse. Many people ignore this card—over 50 percent of those summoned to jury duty fail to appear on the designated day and time. It is your civic duty to appear, however, and it is normally a crime if you fail to appear in response to the summons. Failure to appear may result in your arrest, though it is more common for the government to issue a contempt-of-court letter that may result in a fine. Many people on the *venire* will not actually be selected for a jury. One New Jersey study found that 63 percent of those summoned for jury duty never served.

Jury Selection

After responding to your summons to jury duty, you probably will sit in a large courtroom and listen to a judge lecture you on the importance of jury service and your duties. At this point, some jurors will be removed from the pool because of exemptions from jury service. An exemption is a statutory provision declaring that certain groups need not serve on juries, often because their jobs are considered so important that the individuals cannot be taken away from their employment.

Historically, states provided a large number of exemptions from jury service. Even in this century, women were exempted for a variety of reasons, including their duties to home and family. The exemption for women was deemed unconstitutional, but many professional groups are still excluded. A representative list of exemptions might include the clergy, doctors, lawyers, teachers, pharmacists, firefighters, and even embalmers. These professional exemptions do not mean that the individuals *cannot* serve on a jury. The exemptions mean that the professionals are not required to serve.

There is currently a trend toward abolishing all these exemptions. The exclusion of professionals obviously makes the jury less than representative of the community. In some states, even judges serve on juries when summoned. These states still provide some exemption for individuals who would be removed from work necessary for the public health or safety of the community or who can establish some other good cause for being exempted.

States also provide for other exemptions in addition to the named professions. Felons, minors, noncitizens, and those who cannot understand English are typically exempted. Most states also exempt severely disabled individuals. Single parents with minor children or others with special cause may also be excluded. Fear of losing one's job is not a basis for exemption from jury duty.

Suppose that you are summoned for jury duty and have no professional exemption. It also happens that the next month is particularly critical to your business and requires your close attention. You probably can receive a deferral of jury service until a later, more convenient date. Such deferrals are routinely granted.

Voir Dire

Once the exemption process is completed, the court commences *voir dire*. This is a process of questioning jurors to elicit any prejudices that could preclude the individual's impartiality. In some states, the attorneys conduct *voir dire* and question the potential jurors directly. In other states, the attorneys for the parties submit questions to the judge, who does the direct questioning of the *venire*.

Voir dire questions might inquire about whether the individual had a strong prejudice against members of a given race or religion. Other questions relate to the facts of the case, such as whether the juror would be willing to consider imposing capital punishment. A common question is whether the potential jurors have read about the case in the papers and formed an opinion about the guilt or innocence of a criminal defendant. Merely reading about a case does not disqualify a juror as biased, but the formation of a strong opinion about guilt will undermine impartiality. The court or lawyers also will ask about education, relevant experiences, family background, and other factors.

If you wish to avoid jury service, you might be tempted to state that you are biased about the case.

In addition to being dishonest, this approach might not work. In a Massachusetts case, a doctor openly sought to avoid jury service for financial reasons. He stated that he would be biased in the case. The judge believed that he was lying and ordered the doctor to sit in the courtroom as a spectator for the duration of the trial.

Challenges

After a juror is questioned, the attorneys may accept him or her or they may attempt to challenge the individual. Such a challenge may prevent the person from serving on the jury. Each side of the case may raise an unlimited number of **challenges for cause.** A challenge for cause involves the attorney asking the judge to excuse the juror because of disqualifying bias or lack of competence for jury service. The judge makes the ultimate decision whether the individual should serve or not.

Each side of the case also gets a limited number of **peremptory challenges.** In capital cases, the defendant may have as many as twenty peremptories, while for misdemeanors peremptories may be limited to four. In a peremptory challenge, an attorney may excuse a prospective juror from service without giving any reason at all. Lawyers typically use peremptory challenges when they have a hunch that a juror will favor the other side but cannot establish this bias sufficiently to convince the judge to accept a challenge for cause.

The theory of jury selection is to find an impartial jury. In reality, each side is seeking to identify and seat jurors who favor its case, even if only subconsciously. Some lawyers hire psychologists for jury selection to help choose favorable jurors. The tobacco industry, for example, has discovered that current smokers tend to be unsympathetic to smokers suing cigarette companies for health harms. It is hoped that the efforts of both sides will balance each other out so that the resulting jury will be reasonably impartial.

Lawyers' use of peremptory challenges is limited by the Constitution. Such challenges cannot be used to exclude a given race or gender from the jury. For example, in a case when an African American is on trial for a crime, there might be only a few African Americans in the jury *venire*. A prosecutor who uses all his or her peremptory challenges against these African Americans, ensuring an all-white jury, violates the Constitution and denies the defendant a jury of peers.

Alternate Jurors and Jury Size

The *voir dire* and challenge process continues until a full jury can be seated. In complicated cases, *voir dire* can last for weeks. Most juries consist of twelve persons, though a court usually selects a couple of alternate jurors as well. The alternates sit in the courtroom and observe the case just like the real jurors. Should a juror fall sick during the trial or become disqualified for other reasons, an alternate juror may sit in. This avoids the waste of restarting the trial from the beginning with a new jury.

The twelve-person jury is historically traditional but not constitutionally required. Many states today, however, have approved juries of less than twelve persons. A reduced number makes it easier and quicker to empanel a jury.

▌Trial

Once you are selected for a jury, you sit through the trial in a designated spot in the courtroom. You will likely discover that trials are not as exciting as portrayed on television or in movies. Nevertheless, your close attention is required in order that the parties get a fair verdict.

Trial Procedures

The trial usually will begin with opening arguments from the attorneys for each side in the case. These arguments are not evidence but are persuasive appeals that help you understand the theories of the parties. Each side then will present its evidence in the form of physical exhibits, documents, and witnesses. The witnesses probably will be cross-examined. You must follow this presentation closely and decide which witnesses are believable. It is likely that you will be prohibited from taking notes, so you must struggle to remember key facts. After the evidence, the attorneys will present closing arguments, which are not evidence but which summarize the case and seek to persuade you.

Jury Instructions

At the end of the trial, the judge will give you instructions to help decide the case. These instructions inform you of the law that should be applied to the facts, based upon the testimony. A judge's instructions might tell you that you have to find certain facts before you may decide the case for a given side.

It is the jury's general responsibility to apply the law, even if you disagree with the law. Some juries have been known to ignore the law, a process known as jury nullification. Such a jury might decide that marijuana should be legal and therefore refuse to convict a person for possession of that drug. Jury nullification is often criticized, but jury deliberations are secret and there is no known way to prevent a jury from nullifying the law and acquitting a defendant. If the jury obviously ignores the law in a civil case, the decision is more likely to be overturned on appeal.

Deliberations

Different juries may adopt very different approaches to deliberations. Whatever procedure is chosen, you should speak openly about your views and listen closely to the opinions of fellow jurors. You must decide the case on the evidence presented at trial, not on prejudices or outside sources of information known to you. If you forget something that occurred during the trial, you may ask the judge for information. If you wish to examine an exhibit, it generally will be provided. In contrast, courts commonly deny jury requests for transcripts of trial testimony.

It is expected that there will be disagreement among the jurors. After discussion and give-and-take, the jury is expected to reach a verdict. In criminal cases, the verdict must be unanimous. In civil cases, states provide for verdicts by a **supermajority** of the jury, such as a three-fourths or two-thirds vote. In a criminal case, if you cannot reach a verdict it is called a hung jury, and the judge must declare a **mistrial.** This means that the trial must be conducted again before a new jury. For obvious reasons, courts try to avoid such deadlocks and will urge you to compromise and reach a verdict.

It is very difficult to challenge a jury verdict after the fact. It is important that verdicts have finality and not be subject to constant reopening. Suppose that a juror evinces extreme racial bias toward the defendant during deliberations. Courts are still unsettled about whether evidence of such bias will even be considered. Some judges have refused even to listen to such evidence of bias. This makes it all the more important that unbiased jurors work to ensure a fair result. Courts are more

likely to overturn a verdict if a juror lied in *voir dire* about a significant fact such as that he or she has been convicted of a felony. A $45 million verdict against Lockheed Corporation was overturned because of such a lie.

▌ Jurors' Rights

Jury service is a duty that may inconvenience you. In the best case you will lose some time at work. In the worst case, you may be penalized or even fired by your employer for losing this time. The law increasingly provides some protections for jurors.

Employment

In the past under common law, an employer could fire a worker for any reason whatsoever. Today, courts recognize a **wrongful discharge** action that makes it illegal to fire employees for certain public-policy reasons. Courts have consistently found that it is wrongful to fire a person for serving on a jury. The juror will, of course, have to prove that jury service was indeed the cause of the termination. In a 1992 Oklahoma case, the juror successfully proved this point and received $175,000 in actual damages for being fired and another $175,000 in punitive damages.

In addition to private wrongful discharge actions, a number of states make it illegal to fire a worker because of jury duty. In Arizona, for example, companies are prohibited from dismissing workers, demoting workers, or taking away seniority rights for time on jury service. Breaking this law is punishable by both a fine and imprisonment of the responsible individual.

Pay

Jurors are paid a *per diem* (an allowance for daily expenses) for their service. The rate of pay for jury service is set by state law and is far below the minimum wage. A common *per diem* is $5 per day of jury duty. There is momentum to increase the *per diem*, but the most generous states pay only about $30 per day.

Firms are not necessarily required to pay wages for employees' time spent on jury service. Most cases last only two or three days, however, and companies often pay for this time. When a Los

Angeles law firm refused to pay a worker for extended jury duty in 1992, the federal district court reprimanded the firm for evading its civic responsibility. The judge declared that he would "make them" pay her.

Secrecy

Traditionally, the law provides for the **sequestration** of jurors in order to maintain their objectivity. If a trial was receiving great publicity, the jurors would be confined to hotel rooms and denied access to newspapers and television, to prevent them from reading public accounts of their trial. This helped ensure that the jury decided the case only on the facts presented in court.

Today, a more extreme form of sequestration may occur for a different reason. In organized crime prosecutions, jurors have been bribed or threatened by criminals in order to gain an acquittal. In response, the identities of jurors in such trials are kept secret, and the jury may even sit behind a screen. A similar approach may be used in extremely controversial cases, such as certain police-brutality prosecutions. If such a case may produce rioting, jurors may have concern for their safety or fear public blame for bringing in an unpopular verdict. These jurors also may have their identities shielded by the court.

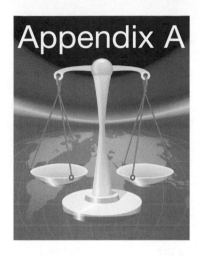

Appendix A

How to Brief a Case and Selected Cases

How to Brief a Case

To fully understand the law with respect to business, you need to be able to read and understand court decisions. To make this task easier, you can use a method of case analysis that is called *briefing*. There is a fairly standard procedure that you can follow when you "brief" any court case. You must first read the case opinion carefully. When you feel you understand the case, you can prepare a brief of it.

Although the format of the brief may vary, typically it will present the essentials of the case under headings such as those listed below.

1. **Citation.** Give the full citation for the case, including the name of the case, the date it was decided, and the court that decided it.
2. **Facts.** Briefly indicate (a) the reasons for the lawsuit; (b) the identity and arguments of the plaintiff(s) and defendant(s), respectively; and (c) the lower court's decision—if appropriate.
3. **Issue.** Concisely phrase, in the form of a question, the essential issue before the court. (If more than one issue is involved, you may have two—or even more—questions here.)
4. **Decision.** Indicate here—with a "yes" or "no," if possible—the court's answer to the question (or questions) in the *Issue* section above.

5. **Reason.** Summarize as briefly as possible the reasons given by the court for its decision (or decisions) and the case or statutory law relied on by the court in arriving at its decision.

Sample Annotated Case

As a guide to briefing cases, we present here excerpts from the actual words of the court in the "sample court case" provided (in a "briefed" version) in Chapter 1. We have added annotations in the margin to explain the meaning of certain terms or phrases, or certain portions of the opinion.

Court opinions can run from a few pages to hundreds of pages in length. For reasons of space, only the essential parts of the opinions are presented in the annotated case as well as in the selected cases for briefing that follow. A series of three asterisks indicates that a portion of the text—other than citations and footnotes—has been omitted. Four asterisks indicate the omission of an entire paragraph (or more). Additionally, when an opinion cites another case or legal source, the citation to the referenced case or source has been omitted to save space and to improve the flow of the text.

SUGGS v. SERVICEMASTER EDUCATION FOOD MANAGEMENT

United States Court of Appeals, Sixth Circuit, 1996.
72 F.3d 1228.

BATCHELDER, Circuit Judge.

* * * *

The first part of the court opinion normally summarizes the facts of the case. The facts include the identities of the plaintiff (the party initiating the lawsuit) and the defendant (the party against whom the suit is brought), the reason for the action, the contentions of the parties, and the judgment of the lower court.

Title VII of the Civil Rights Act of 1964 is a federal law that prohibits employment discrimination on the basis of race, color, national origin, religion, or gender.

This action originated when Sharon L. Suggs * * * filed * * * an employment discrimination charge against ServiceMaster Education Food Management ("ServiceMaster"), claiming that her termination was based on sex or race * * *, in violation of Title VII of the Civil Rights Act of 1964. Following a two-day * * * trial, the district court awarded judgment to Suggs and ordered ServiceMaster to reinstate her. The court awarded Suggs $100,460.03 in back pay from the time of her termination * * * to the end of trial. In addition, the court * * * required ServiceMaster to pay Suggs "additional backpay based on an annual salary of $44,409.63 for the period from the conclusion of trial * * * through the effective date of an offer of reinstatement by ServiceMaster to Ms. Suggs." ServiceMaster timely appealed * * * the district court's judgment in favor of Suggs * * *.

* * * *

Suggs has a B.S. degree in food and nutritional sciences from Tuskegee Institute. ServiceMaster, a corporate/institutional food catering service, hired Suggs as an assistant-director in 1984. In 1988, she was promoted to director and was given responsibility for the ServiceMaster account at Tennessee State University ("TSU"). * * * In September 1989, the health department closed the main campus cafeteria at TSU for several hours to correct significant problems with the facility conditions. Terry Van Booven, the ServiceMaster area manager to whom Suggs reported, conceded that the facilities were a "significant part" of the reason for the shut-down and that Suggs was not authorized to order repairs.

One week after the shut-down, Van Booven approved a four percent pay raise for Suggs. Van Booven then ranked the directors under his supervision according to the profitability of their facilities and quality of service provided to their clients. Suggs was ranked fifth among the twelve directors * * *. Van Booven approved another four percent pay increase for Suggs in October 1990. He rated Suggs' performance in the area of client relations as "satisfactory" on her November 1990 evaluation. * * * Suggs was terminated on January 17, 1991, and was given ten days' severance pay. According to her employment contract, Suggs would have been eligible for severance pay only if she had performed her job adequately. * * * ServiceMaster stated that "major issues concerning [her] separation * * * were: (1) client dissatisfaction; (2) continuing unresolved operational problems; [and] (3) failure to meet financial and budget commitments."

Gordon, the man who replaced Suggs as director of the TSU account * * * , testified that Van Booven told him * * * it was time to show that a man could run the operation better. * * * When ServiceMaster lost the TSU account to another company in June 1991, ServiceMaster offered the male production supervisor of the TSU account three different director positions, in New York, Kentucky, and North Carolina. * * *

Bryant, a male director who had been ranked below Suggs, was promoted to area manager in 1992. Herman, who had been ranked last among the twelve directors, was promoted and transferred when he lost the account for which he was responsible. * * *

* * * *

To prevail on her * * * claim of discriminatory discharge, the plaintiff must prove the following elements: she belongs to a protected class; she was qualified for her position; she was discharged by the defendant; * * * after she was discharged, she was replaced with a similarly qualified person or her employer sought a similarly qualified replacement, who was not a member of her protected class; and her treatment differed from that accorded to otherwise similarly-situated individuals outside her protected group. After a * * * trial, the district court * * * analyzed the evidence * * * , finding that the female plaintiff in this case was indisputably a member of a protected class, that she had been terminated by the defendant and replaced by a man, and that she had demonstrated that she was qualified for the position from which she had been discharged. * * * [T]he district court concluded * * * that ServiceMaster's proffered reasons for removing Suggs from her position and terminating her employment were a pretext to mask unlawful discrimination.

> Under Title VII of the Civil Rights Act of 1964, *protected class* is the legal term used to denote any persons classified because of race, color, national origin, religion, or gender.

> The lower court's decision.

* * * *

The evidence does not support a claim that ServiceMaster's client TSU was dissatisfied with Suggs * * * . Although ServiceMaster's contract with TSU provided that the client could request removal of ServiceMaster employees from the TSU account, no TSU official ever made such a request, and Suggs' manager had, only weeks before her termination, given her a satisfactory rating on client satisfaction. Competent evidence in the record concerning "operational problems" points to the TSU facility itself, rather than to Suggs' management * * * . As to Suggs' purported failure to meet financial and budget commitments, * * * the problems * * * had been ongoing for many years prior to Suggs' promotion to director of the account. She had recently been evaluated favorably for profitability. Suggs received merit raises throughout her period of employment with ServiceMaster. Suggs' manager had consistently rated her performance favorably and had recently approved another increase in her salary. When she was terminated, Suggs was given ten days of severance pay to which she would not have been entitled if she had been discharged for failing to perform her duties adequately.

> The appellate court's conclusion on the first part of the issue.

The court's conclusion on the second part of the issue.

The evidence supports Suggs' claim that ServiceMaster's stated reasons for terminating her employment were pretextual and that Suggs was actually terminated because she was a female. Suggs was qualified for the position she held. She was replaced by a man and was not offered another position with the company when she was removed from the TSU account and later terminated, although ServiceMaster had identified positions available at other locations. In contrast to ServiceMaster's treatment of Suggs, other directors in Suggs' area, who had been ranked below Suggs for profitability and client satisfaction, were offered transfers and relocations when their accounts were lost. Those directors were men. * * *

The judgment of the lower court is affirmed.

* * * *

The district court's judgment that Suggs was terminated in violation of Title VII is AFFIRMED * * * .

▌ Selected Cases for Briefing

The cases presented in the following pages have all been referenced in *Case Briefing Assignments* within the text.

Case A.1   *Reference: Problem 1–9.*

AUSTIN v. BERRYMAN

United States Court of Appeals, Fourth Circuit, 1989.
878 F.2d 786.

MURNAGHAN, Circuit Judge:

We have before us for *en banc* reconsideration [consideration by the whole court] an appeal taken from an action successfully brought by Barbara Austin in the United States District Court for the Western District of Virginia against the Virginia Employment Commission, challenging a denial of unemployment compensation benefits. * * * In brief, Austin charged, *inter alia* [among other things], that the denial of her claim for unemployment benefits, based on a Virginia statute specifically precluding such benefits for any individual who voluntarily quits work to join his or her spouse in a new location, was an unconstitutional infringement upon the incidents of marriage protected by the fourteenth amendment and an unconstitutional burden on her first amendment right to the free exercise of her religion. Her religion happened to command that she fol-

low her spouse wherever he might go and the sincerity of her religious belief was not questioned. The district court found in Austin's favor and awarded injunctive relief and retroactive benefits.

On appeal, Judge Sprouse, writing for a panel majority, found that the denial of benefits did not implicate Austin's fourteenth amendment rights, but that it did unconstitutionally burden Austin's right to the free exercise of her religion. The panel also found, however, that any award of retroactive benefits was barred by the eleventh amendment. One panel member concurred with the panel majority as to the fourteenth and eleventh amendment issues, but dissented as to the existence of a free exercise violation. The panel opinion now, of course, has been vacated by a grant of rehearing *en banc*.

After careful consideration of the additional arguments proffered by both sides, the Court, *en banc*, is convinced that the panel majority correctly concluded that denying Austin unemployment benefits did not infringe upon fundamental marital rights protected by the fourteenth amendment. To this extent, we adopt the majority panel opinion. We also find, however, that the denial of benefits did not unconstitutionally burden Austin's first amendment right to the free exercise of her religion. We are persuaded that the views expressed on the first amendment, free exercise of religion claim in the opinion dissenting in part from the panel majority are correct, and we hereby adopt that opinion as that of the *en banc* court. As we find that Austin is not entitled to any relief, we need not address whether the eleventh amendment bars an award of retroactive benefits.

The decisive consideration, as we see it, is that the proximate cause of Austin's unemployment is geographic distance, not her religious beliefs. There is no conflict between the circumstances of work and Austin's religious precepts. Austin's religious beliefs do not "require" her "to refrain from the work in question." Austin is unable to work simply because she is now too far removed from her employer to make it practical. In striking contrast, if one, for genuine religious beliefs, moves to a new residence in order to continue to live with a spouse, and that residence is not geographically so removed as to preclude regular attendance at the worksite, no unemployment, and hence no unemployment benefits, will arise. That amounts to proof that extent of geographical [distance], not religious belief, led to Austin's disqualification for unemployment benefits.

Austin voluntarily decided to quit her job and join her spouse in a new geographic location 150 miles away. Virginia has stated that every individual who follows such a course, no matter what the reason, religious or non-religious, is disqualified for unemployment benefits. To craft judicially a statutory exception only for those individuals who profess Austin's religious convictions, particularly in the absence of a direct conflict between a given employment practice and a religious belief, would, in our view, result in a subsidy to members of a particular religious belief, impermissible under the Establishment Clause.

Accordingly, the judgment of the district court is REVERSED.

Case A.2   Reference: Problem 4–12.

BURLINGHAM v. MINTZ

Supreme Court of Montana, 1995.
891 P.2d 527.

HUNT, Justice.

* * * *

On March 21, 1990, Candance Burlingham visited Dr. Mintz for a check-up and teeth cleaning. Dr. Mintz determined that she needed further treatment. Dr. Mintz also determined that Candance suffered from temporomandibular joint (TMJ) pain. On April 20, 1990, Candance returned to Dr. Mintz for treatment of her upper left rear molar. After applying a local anesthetic, Dr. Mintz noted that Candance had difficulty keeping her mouth open. To help keep her mouth open, Dr. Mintz placed a bite block between Candance's jaws. A bite block is a rubber coated tapered device with a serrated surface to keep it in place. The bite block was left in for approximately 45 minutes to one hour while Dr. Mintz completed the work. Later that day Candance began to suffer severe TMJ pain which did not abate. Dr. Mintz filled several more of Candance's teeth over the next few months, although he was hindered by her TMJ pain. In October 1990, Dr. Mintz referred Candance to a * * * specialist [in Kalispell, Montana,] who attempted, without success, to relieve Candance's pain. Eventually, Candance underwent restorative arthroscopic surgery in Spokane, Washington, to alleviate her TMJ pain.

On September 18, 1992, appellants filed suit alleging that Dr. Mintz's negligence caused Candance's TMJ injury. Appellants' first standard of care expert, Dr. James McGivney, was deposed on June 11, 1993. On August 12, 1993, appellants filed a motion asking the District Court to qualify Dr. McGivney as an **expert** [a person whose professional training or experience qualifies him or her to testify on a particular subject]. * * *

On February 8, 1994, the District Court denied appellants' motion[,] finding that Dr. McGivney, a suburban St. Louis dentist, was not familiar with the standards of practice or medical facilities available in Eureka, Montana, in a similar locality in Montana, or a similar locality anywhere in the country. The District Court granted appellants until the end of February to find another expert.

* * * *

On June 7, 1994, respondent filed a motion for summary judgment, arguing that appellants were not able to present expert testimony to meet their burden of proof to establish * * * a violation by respondent of his standard of care. The District Court granted respondent's motion. Appellants appeal from the order granting summary judgment.

* * * *

The District Court concluded that appellants' proposed experts had no idea of the standards of practice in Eureka, Montana, in a similar locality in Montana, or in a similar place anywhere else in the country. A review of the testimony of respondent's and appellants' standard of care experts reveals little, if any, contradictory testimony as to the applicable standard of care for a dentist treating a patient suffering from TMJ pain in Eureka, Montana, or any other community in the country. Respondent's first standard of care expert testified that, with the exception of limited specialties, the same standard of care that applies to dentists in San Francisco and Kalispell, applies to dentists in Eureka. He agreed that the standard of care required in the diagnosis of and the treatment decisions regarding TMJ pain would be the same in San Francisco, Kalispell, and Eureka. Respondent's second standard of care expert testified that in non-emergency situations the standard of care for dentists in Eureka is the same as the non-emergency standard of care anywhere else in the United States.

* * * *

We conclude that appellants' standard of care experts were familiar with the applicable non-emergency standard of care for dentists in Eureka if, by either direct or indirect knowledge, they were familiar with the applicable non-emergency standard of care for dentists in their communities, regardless of size or location. As a result, we hold that the District Court erred by excluding appellants' standard of care experts.

* * * *

* * * We reverse the summary judgment and remand this case to the District Court for further proceedings.

Case A.3   Reference: Problem 12–11.
POTTER v. OSTER
Supreme Court of Iowa, 1988.
426 N.W.2d 148.

NEUMAN, Justice.

This is a suit in equity brought by the plaintiffs to rescind an installment land contract based on the seller's inability to convey title. The question on appeal is whether, in an era of declining land values, returning the parties to the status quo works an inequitable result. We think not. Accordingly, we affirm the district court judgment for rescission and restitution.

The facts are largely undisputed. Because the case was tried in equity, our review is *de novo* [as if the case had not been heard and no decision rendered before]. We give weight to the findings of the trial court, particularly where the credibility of witnesses is concerned, but we are not bound thereby.

The parties, though sharing a common interest in agribusiness, present a study in contrasts. We think the disparity in their background and experience is notable insofar as it bears on the equities of the transaction in issue. Plaintiff Charles Potter is a farm laborer and his wife, Sue, is a homemaker and substitute teacher. They have lived all their lives within a few miles of the real estate in question. Defendant Merrill Oster is an agricultural journalist and recognized specialist in land investment strategies. He owns Oster Communications, a multimillion dollar publishing concern devoted to furnishing farmers the latest in commodity market analysis and advice on an array of farm issues.

In May 1978, Oster contracted with Florence Stark to purchase her 160-acre farm in Howard County, Iowa, for $260,000 on a ten-year contract at seven percent interest. Oster then sold the homestead and nine acres to Charles and Sue Potter for $70,000. Potters paid $18,850 down and executed a ten-year installment contract for the balance at 8.5% interest. Oster then executed a contract with Robert Bishop for the sale of the remaining 151 acres as part of a package deal that included the sale of seventeen farms for a sum exceeding $5.9 million.

These back-to-back contracts collapsed like dominoes in March 1985 when Bishop failed to pay Oster and Oster failed to pay Stark the installments due on their respective contracts. Stark commenced **forfeiture proceedings** [proceedings to retake the property, in this case because Oster failed to perform a legal obligation—payment under the contract—and thus forfeited his right to the land]. Potters had paid every installment when due under their contract with Oster and had included Stark as a **joint payee** [one of two or more payees—persons to whom checks or notes are payable] with Oster on their March 1, 1985, payment * * * [The Potters'] interest in the real estate was forfeited along with Oster's and Bishop's and they were forced to move from their home in August 1985.

Potters then sued Oster to rescind their contract with him, claiming restitution damages for all consideration paid * * *

Trial testimony * * * revealed that the market value of the property had decreased markedly since its purchase. Expert appraisers valued the homestead and nine acres between $27,500 and $35,000. Oster himself placed a $28,000 value on the property; Potter $39,000. Evidence was also received placing the reasonable rental value of the property at $150 per month, or a total of $10,800 for the six-year Potter occupancy.

The district court concluded the Potters were entitled to rescission of the contract and return of the consideration paid including principal and interest, cost of improvements, closing expenses, and taxes for a total of $65,169.37. From this the court deducted $10,800 for six years' rental, bringing the final judgment to $54,369.37.

On appeal, Oster challenges the judgment. * * * [H]e claims Potters had an adequate remedy at law for damages which should have been measured by the actual economic loss sustained * * *.

* * * *

Rescission is a restitutionary remedy which attempts to restore the parties to their positions at the time the contract was executed. The remedy calls for a return of the land to the seller, with the buyer given judgment for payments made under the contract plus the value of improvements, less reasonable rental value for the period during which the buyer was in possession. The remedy has long been available in Iowa to buyers under land contracts when the seller has no title to convey.

Rescission is considered an extraordinary remedy, however, and is ordinarily not available to a litigant as a matter of right but only when, in the discretion of the court, it is necessary to obtain equity. Our cases have established three requirements that must be met before rescission will be granted. First, the injured party must not be in default. Second, the breach must be substantial and go to the heart of the contract. Third, remedies at law must be inadequate.

The first two tests are easily met in the present case. Potters are entirely without fault in this transaction. They tendered their 1985 installment payment to Oster before the forfeiture, and no additional payments were due until 1986. On the question of materiality, Oster's loss of **equitable title** [ownership rights protected in equity] to the homestead by forfeiture caused not only substantial, but total breach of his obligation to insure **peaceful possession** [an implied promise made by a landowner, when selling or renting land, that the buyer or tenant will not be evicted or disturbed by the landowner or a person having a lien or superior title] and convey marketable title under the Oster-Potter contract.

Only the third test—the inadequacy of damages at law—is contested by Oster on appeal. * * *

Restoring the status quo is the goal of the restitutionary remedy of rescission. Here, the district court accomplished the goal by awarding Potters a sum representing all they had paid under the contract rendered worthless by Oster's default. Oster contends that in an era of declining land values, such a remedy goes beyond achieving the status quo and results in a windfall to the Potters. Unwilling to disgorge the benefits he has received under the unfulfilled contract, Oster would have the court shift the **"entrepreneural risk"** [the risk assumed by one who initiates, and provides or controls the management of, a business enterprise] of market loss to the Potters by limiting their recovery to the difference between the property's market value at breach ($35,000) and the contract balance ($27,900). In other words, Oster claims the court should have awarded * * * damages. * * *

* * * *

* * * [L]egal remedies are considered inadequate when the damages cannot be measured with sufficient certainty. Contrary to Oster's assertion that Potters' compensation should be limited to the difference between the property's fair market value and contract balance at time of breach, * * * damages are correctly calculated as the difference between contract price and market value at the time for performance. Since the time of performance in this case would have been March 1990, the market value of the homestead and acreage cannot be predicted with any certainty, thus rendering such a formulation inadequate.

Most importantly, the fair market value of the homestead at the time of forfeiture is an incorrect measure of the benefit Potters lost. It fails to account for the special value Potters placed on the property's location and residential features that uniquely suited their family. For precisely this reason, remedies at law are presumed inadequate for breach of a real estate contract. Oster has failed to overcome that presumption here. His characterization of the transaction as a mere market loss for Potters, compensable by a sum which would enable them to make a nominal down payment on an equivalent homestead, has no legal or factual support in this record. * * *

* * * *

In summary, we find no error in the trial court's conclusion that Potters were entitled to rescission of the contract and return of all benefits allowed thereunder, less the value of reasonable rental for the period of occupancy * * *.

AFFIRMED.

Case A.4   Reference: Problem 13–12.

GOLDKIST, INC. v. BROWNLEE

Court of Appeals of Georgia, 1987.
182 Ga.App. 287,
355 S.E.2d 733.

BEASLEY, Judge.

The question is whether the two defendant farmers, who as a partnership both grew and sold their crops, were established by the undisputed facts as not being "merchants" as a matter of law, according to the definition in OCGA [Section] 11-2-104(1) [Official Code of Georgia Annotated; Section 11-2-104(1) corresponds to UCC 2-104(1)]. We are not called upon here to consider the other side of the coin, whether farmers or these farmers in particular are "merchants" as a matter of law.

In November 1983, Goldkist sued under OCGA [Section] 11-2-712 for losses arising out of the necessity to cover [a remedy of the buyer in a breached sales contract; if the seller fails to deliver the goods contracted for, the buyer can purchase them elsewhere and recover any additional price paid, plus damages, from the breaching seller (see Chapter 16)] a contract for soybeans. It produced a written confirmation dated July 22 for 5,000 bushels of soybeans to be delivered to it by defendants between August 22 and September 22 at $6.88 per bushel. A defense was that there was no writing signed by either of the Brownlees, as required by OCGA [Section] 11-2-201(1).

* * * [T]he court agreed with the Brownlees that the circumstances did not fit any of the exceptions provided for in Section 201 and granted summary judgment. On appeal, Goldkist asserts that defendants came within subsection (2), relating to dealings "between merchants."

Appellees admit that their crops are "goods" as defined in OCGA [Section] 11-2-105. The record establishes the following facts. The partnership had been operating the row crop farming business for 14 years, producing peanuts, soybeans, corn, milo, and wheat on 1,350 acres, and selling the crops.

It is also established without dispute that Barney Brownlee, whose deposition was taken, was familiar with the marketing procedure of "booking" crops, which sometimes occurred over the phone between the farmer and the buyer, rather than in person, and a written contract would be signed later. He periodically called plaintiff's agent to check the price, which fluctuated. If the price met his approval, he sold soybeans. At this time the partnership still had some of its 1982 crop in storage, and the price was rising slowly. Mr. Brownlee received a written confirmation in the mail concerning a sale of soybeans and did not contact plaintiff to contest it but simply did nothing. In addition to the agricultural business, Brownlee operated a gasoline service station.

In dispute are the facts with respect to whether or not an oral contract was made between Barney Brownlee for the partnership and agent Harrell for the buyer in a July 22 telephone conversation. The plaintiff's evidence was that it occurred and that it was discussed soon thereafter with Brownlee at the service station on two different occasions, when he acknowledged it, albeit reluctantly, because the market price of soybeans had risen. Mr. Brownlee denies booking the soybeans and denies the nature of the conversations at his service station with Harrell and the buyer's manager.

In this posture, of course, the question of whether an oral contract was made would not yield to summary adjudication, as apparently recognized by the trial court, which based its decision on the preliminary question of whether the Brownlee partnership was a "merchant."

Whether or not the farmers in this case are "merchants" as a matter of law, which is not before us, the evidence does not demand a conclusion that they are outside of that category which is excepted from the requirement of a signed writing to bind a buyer and seller of goods. * * *

* * * *

Defendants' narrow construction of "merchant" would, given the booking procedure used for the sale of farm products, thus guarantee to the farmers the best of both possible worlds (fulfill booking if price goes down after booking and reject it if price improves) and to the buyers the worst of both possible worlds. On the other hand, construing "merchants" in OCGA [Section] 11-2-104(1) as not excluding as a matter of law farmers such as the ones in this case, protects them equally as well as the buyer. If the market price declines after the

booking, they are assured of the higher booking price; the buyer cannot renege, as OCGA [Section] 11-2-201(2) would apply.

* * * *

We believe this is the proper construction to give the two statutes, OCGA [Sections] 11-2-104(1) and 11-2-201(2), as taken together they are thus further branches stemming from the centuries-old simple legal idea *pacta servanda sunt*—agreements are to be kept. So construed, they evince the legislative intent to enforce the accepted practices of the marketplace among those who frequent it.

Judgment reversed.

Case A.5   Reference: Problem 17–13.

FEDERAL DEPOSIT INSURANCE CORP. v. TRANS PACIFIC INDUSTRIES, INC.
United States Court of Appeals, Fifth Circuit, 1994.
14 F.3d 10.

POLITZ, Chief Judge:

The FDIC [Federal Deposit Insurance Corporation,] as receiver for Harris County Bank—Houston, N.A.[,] filed suit to enforce two promissory notes payable to the Bank, one for $67,500 and the other for $100,000. The suit sought recovery from Trans Pacific Industries, Inc. [TPI,] and [W. K.] Robbins, TPI's board chairman. On cross-motions for summary judgment the district court held both defendants liable. Robbins appealed.

* * * *

The top left corner of each note contains a block for designation of "Borrower(s) Name(s) & Address(es)." The only borrower identified in that block is TPI. Underneath, the text begins with the sentence "The undersigned Borrower(s) (if more than one, jointly and severally and hereinafter, whether one or more, called Borrower) promises to pay to the order of the above-named Lender * * * ." The signature block in the bottom right corner has three lines with the designation "Borrower" at the end of each. On each note "TRANS PACIFIC INDUSTRIES" is typewritten on the first line and the name "W. K. Robbins, Jr." is typed and signed below. On the reverse side there is a guaranty which is unsigned.

Robbins contends that he signed only in his capacity as agent for TPI. The government contends that he is bound in his individual capacity as well.

The import of a signature by an authorized representative is governed by section 3-403 of the Uniform Commercial Code. That section provides in pertinent part: ["](2) An authorized representative who signs his own name to an instrument. . . .(b) except as otherwise established between the immediate parties, is personally obligated if the instrument names the person represented but does not show that the representative signed in a representative capacity * * * .["] The FDIC contends that Robbins is personally liable under subsection (2)(b) because the note did not show that Robbins signed in a representative capacity. We are not persuaded.

In order to avoid personal responsibility, the general rule is that an individual signing in a representative capacity must name his principal and must place "by:" before his signature or must follow it with a display of agency status, preferably his title in the represented institution. Thus, "TPI, W. K. Robbins, Jr.," without more, would bind Robbins. Section 3-403(2)(b), however, requires that we consider the face of the entire instrument. When we do so in the context of business expectations, we find it abundantly clear that Robbins signed in a representative capacity only.

The face of the note unambiguously shows that TPI was the sole borrower; it is the only entity listed in the upper left-hand identification block. The FDIC attempts to nullify the import of the identification block by arguing that the first sentence of the text—"The undersigned Borrower(s) * * * promises to pay"—renders each signatory a borrower. It is a basic tenet of contract interpretation, however, that one part of a writing cannot be read to nullify another. Interpreted in harmony with the identification block, the first sentence of the text must mean: TPI, which signs below, promises to pay . . . . The instrument therefore indicates on its face that TPI is the sole borrower and maker of the note.

A corporation can act only through agents. Assuming **per arguendo** [for the sake of argument] that the type-written name of the organization conceivably might pass muster as a signature under U.C.C. section 3-401(2), there are few if any lenders who would accept it as binding. That is both understandable and prudent. The usual business practice is to bind the corporation with the signature of an officer authorized by the corporation to sign on its behalf. On the notes before us,

TPI was bound by the signature of Robbins. That Robbins signed on TPI's behalf would be apparent to any holder of the note. It must have been apparent to the FDIC that Robbins signed for TPI for it sued TPI on the note. The district court agreed for it rendered summary judgment against TPI. "Having secured a judgment on that basis against the corporate defendant, we are at a loss to see how [the FDIC] may now contend that [Robbins'] signature was on his individual behalf and not in a representative capacity. * * *

* * * *

The judgment of the district court is REVERSED, judgment is RENDERED in favor of W. K. Robbins, Jr., and the case is REMANDED for further proceedings consistent herewith.

Case A.6   Reference: Problem 20–10.

HAWLEY v. CEMENT INDUSTRIES, INC.
United States Court of Appeals, Eleventh Circuit, 1995.
51 F.3d 246.

PER CURIAM:

* * * *

In September 1990, Appellant Phillip E. Hawley ("Appellant") filed a Chapter 7 bankruptcy petition, claiming less than $20,000 in assets. In a signed statement dated June 15, 1989, Appellant listed his total assets at $13,822,477, total liabilities at $1,876,814, and total net worth at $11,945,663. Later in 1990, one of Appellant's creditors, Cement Industries, Inc. ("Appellee"), filed an adversary proceeding pursuant to 11 U.S.C. s 727(a)(5), urging the court to deny Appellant's discharge based on his failure to satisfactorily explain the loss of his assets between the filings of his financial statement and his bankruptcy petition.

Section 727(a)(5) of the Bankruptcy Code provides as follows: * * * ["](a) the court shall grant the debtor a discharge, unless— * * * the debtor has failed to explain satisfactorily, before determination of denial of discharge under this paragraph, any loss of assets or deficiency of assets to meet the debtor's liabilities.["]

* * * *

The bankruptcy court denied Appellant's discharge, observing that the Appellant, a "sophisticated and expe-

rienced businessman," had been unable to present documentation to explain the discrepancy between the value of his assets as listed in 1989 and the value he had listed in his bankruptcy petition in 1990. The court found a "complete lack of documentation to support the Debtor's loss of assets" and determined that "when examining the totality of the circumstances, this Court finds a pattern which leads this Court to conclude that the Debtor has not satisfactorily explained the loss or diminution of his assets."

The Appellant appealed to the district court. The district court affirmed and adopted the opinion of the bankruptcy court "as fully as if copied verbatim." The district court dismissed the appeal and Appellant then appealed to this Court * * * .

* * * *

* * * Appellant argues that Appellee failed to carry its burden in showing that Appellant's explanations for the loss of his assets were unsatisfactory. In its [Section] 727(a)(5) action, Appellee had the initial burden of proving its objection to Appellant's discharge. Appellee sustained this burden by showing the vast discrepancies between Appellant's 1989 financial statement and his 1990 Chapter 7 schedules. Once the party objecting to the discharge establishes the basis for its objection, the burden then shifts to the debtor "to explain satisfactorily the loss." "To be satisfactory, 'an explanation' must convince the judge." "Vague and indefinite explanations of losses that are based on estimates uncorroborated by

documentation are unsatisfactory." Obviously, Appellant's explanations did not "convince the judge." The bankruptcy judge clearly found Appellant's testimony and complete lack of documentation unconvincing. Upon review of the record, we find that the bankruptcy judge did not clearly err in finding that Appellant's explanation of his loss of more than $13 million in assets over the course of fifteen months was too vague and indefinite to be "satisfactory." Therefore, the judgment of the district court is AFFIRMED.

Case A.9   Reference: Problem 28–11.

STRANG v. HOLLOWELL

Court of Appeals of North Carolina, 1990.
387 S.E.2d 664.

WELLS, Judge.

On 2 January 1987 plaintiff met with defendants Hollowell and Jones in Cary, North Carolina to negotiate a consignment agreement for the sale of plaintiff's 1974 Pantera automobile which had an estimated value of $23,000 to $25,000. A written consignment contract was executed between plaintiff and Hollowell Auto Sales. Defendant Jones, then employed by Hollowell Auto Sales, signed the contract on behalf of Hollowell Auto Sales. Plaintiff gave defendants the keys to his automobile and they transported it by flatbed trailer to the Hollowell Auto Sales lot in Morehead City. Defendants Jones and Hollowell were unable to sell the Pantera and it was returned to plaintiff in August 1987. At that time plaintiff discovered that the automobile had been damaged to an extent which reduced its value to between $10,000 and $12,000.

On 23 December 1987 plaintiff sued defendants Jones and Hollowell for negligence in their bailment of his automobile. Plaintiff was unaware that Hollowell Auto Sales was a trade name for Solar Center, Inc., whose principal place of business is in Carteret County. Plaintiff was under the impression that Hollowell Auto Sales was a sole proprietorship operated by defendant Hollowell. On motion of defendant Hollowell in open court, defendant Solar Center, Inc. was added as an additional party prior to trial.

Defendant Jones did not file an answer to plaintiff's complaint and default judgment was subsequently entered against him. At a non-jury trial, judgment in the amount of $11,000 was entered against defendants Jones and Hollowell, jointly and severally. Defendant Gene Hollowell appeals.

* * * *

The only issue presented in this appeal is whether defendant Hollowell can be held individually liable for plaintiff's damages. Defendant contends that he was acting as an agent of Hollowell Auto Sales and therefore cannot be held personally liable. Defendant further asserts that, regardless of the fact that plaintiff was unaware that Hollowell Auto Sales was a trade name for Solar Center, Inc., defendant is nevertheless shielded from individual liability because Solar Center, Inc. fulfilled its legal obligation to disclose its relationship with Hollowell Auto Sales by filing an assumed name certificate in [the appropriate county office]. For the following reasons, we disagree.

When plaintiff gave possession of his automobile to defendant under the consignment contract a bailment for the mutual benefit of bailor and bailee was created. This bailment continued until the automobile was returned to plaintiff in August 1987. Defendant was therefore a bailee of plaintiff's automobile while it was in his custody in Morehead City. A bailee is obligated to exercise due care to protect the subject of the bailment from negligent loss, damage, or destruction. His liability depends on the presence or absence of ordinary negligence. While this obligation arises from the relationship created by the contract of bailment, breach of this contractual duty results in a tort. It is well settled that one is personally liable for all torts committed by him, including negligence, notwithstanding that he may have acted as agent for another or as an officer for a corporation. Furthermore, the potential for corporate liability, in addition to individual liability, does not shield the individual tortfeasor from liability. Rather, it provides the injured party a choice as to which party to hold liable for the tort.

Here there is no dispute that plaintiff's automobile was returned to him in a damaged condition. Defendant does not except to the trial court's findings and conclusions that a bailment was created between plaintiff and defendant and that "defendants were negligent in their care and control of the vehicle while it was in their possession." We therefore hold that the trial court correctly ruled that by failing to exercise due care and allowing the automobile to be damaged while in his custody, defendant committed a tort for which he can be held individually liable.

Because the resolution of this case is in tort for negligence, rather than in contract for breach, we need not reach the issue of whether defendant had sufficiently disclosed his agency with Hollowell Auto Sales or with Solar Center, Inc. However, we note that our Supreme Court has said that use of a trade name is not sufficient as a matter of law to disclose the identity of the principal and the fact of agency.

Likewise, the existence of means by which the fact of agency might be discovered is also insufficient to disclose agency.

* * * *

Affirmed.

Appendix B

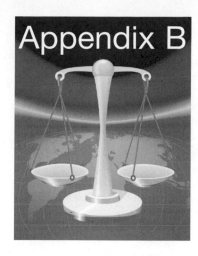

The Constitution of the United States

PREAMBLE

We the People of the United States, in Order to form a more perfect Union, establish Justice, insure domestic Tranquility, provide for the common defence, promote the general Welfare, and secure the Blessings of Liberty to ourselves and our Posterity, do ordain and establish this Constitution for the United States of America.

ARTICLE I

Section 1. All legislative Powers herein granted shall be vested in a Congress of the United States, which shall consist of a Senate and House of Representatives.

Section 2. The House of Representatives shall be composed of Members chosen every second Year by the People of the several States, and the Electors in each State shall have the Qualifications requisite for Electors of the most numerous Branch of the State Legislature.

No Person shall be a Representative who shall not have attained to the Age of twenty five Years, and been seven Years a Citizen of the United States, and who shall not, when elected, be an Inhabitant of that State in which he shall be chosen.

Representatives and direct Taxes shall be apportioned among the several States which may be included within this Union, according to their respective Numbers, which shall be determined by adding to the whole Number of free Persons, including those bound to Service for a Term of Years, and excluding Indians not taxed, three fifths of all other Persons. The actual Enumeration shall be made within three Years after the first Meeting of the Congress of the United States, and within every subsequent Term of ten Years, in such Manner as they shall by Law direct. The Number of Representatives shall not exceed one for every thirty Thousand, but each State shall have at Least one Representative; and until such enumeration shall be made, the State of New Hampshire shall be entitled to chuse three, Massachusetts eight, Rhode Island and Providence Plantations one, Connecticut five, New York six, New Jersey four, Pennsylvania eight, Delaware one, Maryland six, Virginia ten, North Carolina five, South Carolina five, and Georgia three.

When vacancies happen in the Representation from any State, the Executive Authority thereof shall issue Writs of Election to fill such Vacancies.

The House of Representatives shall chuse their Speaker and other Officers; and shall have the sole Power of Impeachment.

Section 3. The Senate of the United States shall be composed of two Senators from each State, chosen by the Legislature thereof, for six Years; and each Senator shall have one Vote.

Immediately after they shall be assembled in Consequence of the first Election, they shall be divided as equally as may be into three Classes. The Seats of the Senators of the first Class shall be vacated at the Expiration of the second Year, of the second Class at the Expiration of the fourth Year, and of the third Class at the Expiration of the sixth Year, so that one third may be chosen every second Year; and if Vacancies happen by Resignation, or otherwise, during the Recess of the Legislature of any State, the Executive thereof may make temporary Appointments until the next Meeting of the Legislature, which shall then fill such Vacancies.

No Person shall be a Senator who shall not have attained to the Age of thirty Years, and been nine Years a Citizen of the United States, and who shall not, when elected, be an Inhabitant of that State for which he shall be chosen.

The Vice President of the United States shall be President of the Senate, but shall have no Vote, unless they be equally divided.

The Senate shall chuse their other Officers, and also a President pro tempore, in the Absence of the Vice President, or when he shall exercise the Office of President of the United States.

The Senate shall have the sole Power to try all Impeachments. When sitting for that Purpose, they shall be on Oath or Affirmation. When the President of the United States is tried, the Chief Justice shall preside: And no Person shall be convicted without the Concurrence of two thirds of the Members present.

Judgment in Cases of Impeachment shall not extend further than to removal from Office, and disqualification to hold and enjoy any Office of honor, Trust, or Profit under the United States: but the Party convicted shall nevertheless be liable and subject to Indictment, Trial, Judgment, and Punishment, according to Law.

Section 4. The Times, Places and Manner of holding Elections for Senators and Representatives, shall be prescribed in each State by the Legislature thereof; but the Congress may at any time by Law make or alter such Regulations, except as to the Places of chusing Senators.

The Congress shall assemble at least once in every Year, and such Meeting shall be on the first Monday in December, unless they shall by Law appoint a different Day.

Section 5. Each House shall be the Judge of the Elections, Returns, and Qualifications of its own Members, and a Majority of each shall constitute a Quorum to do Business; but a smaller Number may adjourn from day to day, and may be authorized to compel the Attendance of absent Members, in such Manner, and under such Penalties as each House may provide.

Each House may determine the Rules of its Proceedings, punish its Members for disorderly Behavior, and, with the Concurrence of two thirds, expel a Member.

Each House shall keep a Journal of its Proceedings, and from time to time publish the same, excepting such Parts as may in their Judgment require Secrecy; and the Yeas and Nays of the Members of either House on any question shall, at the Desire of one fifth of those Present, be entered on the Journal.

Neither House, during the Session of Congress, shall, without the Consent of the other, adjourn for more than three days, nor to any other Place than that in which the two Houses shall be sitting.

Section 6. The Senators and Representatives shall receive a Compensation for their Services, to be ascertained by Law, and paid out of the Treasury of the United States. They shall in all Cases, except Treason, Felony and Breach of the Peace, be privileged from Arrest during their Attendance at the Session of their respective Houses, and in going to and returning from the same; and for any Speech or Debate in either House, they shall not be questioned in any other Place.

No Senator or Representative shall, during the Time for which he was elected, be appointed to any civil Office under the Authority of the United States, which shall have been created, or the Emoluments whereof shall have been increased during such time; and no Person holding any Office under the United States, shall be a Member of either House during his Continuance in Office.

Section 7. All Bills for raising Revenue shall originate in the House of Representatives; but the Senate may propose or concur with Amendments as on other Bills.

Every Bill which shall have passed the House of Representatives and the Senate, shall, before it become a Law, be presented to the President of the United States; If he approve he shall sign it, but if not he shall return it, with his Objections to the House in which it shall have originated, who shall enter the Objections at large on their Journal, and proceed to reconsider it. If after such Reconsideration two thirds of that House shall agree to pass the Bill, it shall be sent together with the Objections, to the other House, by which it shall likewise be reconsidered, and if approved by two thirds of that House, it shall become a Law. But in all such Cases the Votes of both Houses shall be determined by Yeas and Nays, and the Names of the Persons voting for and against the Bill shall be entered on the Journal of each House respectively. If any Bill shall not be returned by the President within ten Days (Sundays excepted) after it shall have been presented to him, the Same shall be a Law, in like Manner as if he had signed it, unless the Congress by their Adjournment prevent its Return in which Case it shall not be a Law.

Every Order, Resolution, or Vote, to which the Concurrence of the Senate and House of Representatives may be necessary (except on a question of Adjournment) shall be presented to the President of the United States; and before the Same shall take Effect, shall be approved by him, or being disapproved by him, shall be repassed by two thirds of the Senate and House of Representatives, according to the Rules and Limitations prescribed in the Case of a Bill.

Section 8. The Congress shall have Power To lay and collect Taxes, Duties, Imposts and Excises, to pay the Debts and provide for the common Defence and general Welfare of the United States; but all Duties, Imposts and Excises shall be uniform throughout the United States;

To borrow Money on the credit of the United States;

To regulate Commerce with foreign Nations, and among the several States, and with the Indian Tribes;

To establish an uniform Rule of Naturalization, and uniform Laws on the subject of Bankruptcies throughout the United States;

To coin Money, regulate the Value thereof, and of foreign Coin, and fix the Standard of Weights and Measures;

To provide for the Punishment of counterfeiting the Securities and current Coin of the United States;

To establish Post Offices and post Roads;

To promote the Progress of Science and useful Arts, by securing for limited Times to Authors and Inventors the exclusive Right to their respective Writings and Discoveries;

To constitute Tribunals inferior to the supreme Court;

To define and punish Piracies and Felonies committed on the high Seas, and Offenses against the Law of Nations;

To declare War, grant Letters of Marque and Reprisal, and make Rules concerning Captures on Land and Water;

To raise and support Armies, but no Appropriation of Money to that Use shall be for a longer Term than two Years;

To provide and maintain a Navy;

To make Rules for the Government and Regulation of the land and naval Forces;

To provide for calling forth the Militia to execute the Laws of the Union, suppress Insurrections and repel Invasions;

To provide for organizing, arming, and disciplining, the Militia, and for governing such Part of them as may be employed in the Service of the United States, reserving to the States respectively, the Appointment of the Officers, and the Authority of training the Militia according to the discipline prescribed by Congress;

To exercise exclusive Legislation in all Cases whatsoever, over such District (not exceeding ten Miles square) as may, by Cession of particular States, and the Acceptance of Congress, become the Seat of the Government of the United States, and to exercise like Authority over all Places purchased by the Consent of the Legislature of the State in which the Same shall be, for the Erection of Forts, Magazines, Arsenals, dock-Yards, and other needful Buildings;—And

To make all Laws which shall be necessary and proper for carrying into Execution the foregoing Powers, and all other Powers vested by this Constitution in the Government of the United States, or in any Department or Officer thereof.

Section 9. The Migration or Importation of such Persons as any of the States now existing shall think proper to admit, shall not be prohibited by the Congress prior to the Year one thousand eight hundred and eight, but a Tax or duty may be imposed on such Importation, not exceeding ten dollars for each Person.

The privilege of the Writ of Habeas Corpus shall not be suspended, unless when in Cases of Rebellion or Invasion the public Safety may require it.

No Bill of Attainder or ex post facto Law shall be passed.

No Capitation, or other direct, Tax shall be laid, unless in Proportion to the Census or Enumeration herein before directed to be taken.

No Tax or Duty shall be laid on Articles exported from any State.

No Preference shall be given by any Regulation of Commerce or Revenue to the Ports of one State over those of another: nor shall Vessels bound to, or from, one State be obliged to enter, clear, or pay Duties in another.

No Money shall be drawn from the Treasury, but in Consequence of Appropriations made by Law; and a regular Statement and Account of the Receipts and Expenditures of all public Money shall be published from time to time.

No Title of Nobility shall be granted by the United States: And no Person holding any Office of Profit or Trust under them, shall, without the Consent of the Congress, accept of any present, Emolument, Office, or Title, of any kind whatever, from any King, Prince, or foreign State.

Section 10. No State shall enter into any Treaty, Alliance, or Confederation; grant Letters of Marque and Reprisal; coin Money; emit Bills of Credit; make any Thing but gold and silver Coin a Tender in Payment of Debts; pass any Bill of Attainder, ex post facto Law, or Law impairing the Obligation of Contracts, or grant any Title of Nobility.

No State shall, without the Consent of the Congress, lay any Imposts or Duties on Imports or Exports, except what may be absolutely necessary for executing its inspection Laws: and the net Produce of all Duties and Imposts, laid by any State on Imports or Exports, shall be for the Use of the Treasury of the United States; and all such Laws shall be subject to the Revision and Controul of the Congress.

No State shall, without the Consent of Congress, lay any Duty of Tonnage, keep Troops, or Ships of War in time of Peace, enter into any Agreement or Compact with another State, or with a foreign Power, or engage in War, unless actually invaded, or in such imminent Danger as will not admit of delay.

ARTICLE II

Section 1. The executive Power shall be vested in a President of the United States of America. He shall hold his Office during the Term of four Years, and, together with the Vice President, chosen for the same Term, be elected, as follows:

Each State shall appoint, in such Manner as the Legislature thereof may direct, a Number of Electors, equal to the whole Number of Senators and Representatives to which the State may be entitled in the Congress; but no Senator or Representative, or Person holding an Office of Trust or Profit under the United States, shall be appointed an Elector.

The Electors shall meet in their respective States, and vote by Ballot for two Persons, of whom one at least shall not be an Inhabitant of the same State with themselves. And they shall make a List of all the Persons voted for, and of the Number of Votes for each; which List they shall sign and certify, and transmit sealed to the Seat of the Government of the United States, directed to the President of the Senate. The President of the Senate shall, in the Presence of the Senate and House of Representatives, open all the Certificates, and the Votes shall then be counted. The Person having the greatest Number of Votes shall be the President, if such Number be a Majority of the whole Number of Electors appointed; and if there be more than one who have such Majority, and have an equal Number of Votes, then the House of Representatives shall immediately chuse by Ballot one of them for President; and if no Person have a Majority, then from the five highest on the List the said House shall in like Manner chuse the President. But in chusing the President, the Votes shall be taken by States, the Representation from each State having one Vote; A quorum for this Purpose shall consist of a Member or Members from two thirds of the States, and a Majority of all the States shall be necessary to a Choice. In every Case, after the Choice of the President, the Person having the greater Number of Votes of the Electors shall be the Vice President. But if there should remain two or more who have equal Votes, the Senate shall chuse from them by Ballot the Vice President.

The Congress may determine the Time of chusing the Electors, and the Day on which they shall give their Votes; which Day shall be the same throughout the United States.

No person except a natural born Citizen, or a Citizen of the United States, at the time of the Adoption of this Constitution, shall be eligible to the Office of President; neither shall any Person be eligible to that Office who shall not have attained to the Age of thirty five Years, and been fourteen Years a Resident within the United States.

In Case of the Removal of the President from Office, or of his Death, Resignation or Inability to discharge the Powers and Duties of the said Office, the same shall devolve on the Vice President, and the Congress may by Law provide for the Case of Removal, Death, Resignation or Inability, both of the President and Vice President, declaring what Officer shall then act as President, and such Officer shall act accordingly, until the Disability be removed, or a President shall be elected.

The President shall, at stated Times, receive for his Services, a Compensation, which shall neither be increased nor diminished during the Period for which he shall have been elected, and he shall not receive within that Period any other Emolument from the United States, or any of them.

Before he enter on the Execution of his Office, he shall take the following Oath or Affirmation: "I do solemnly swear (or affirm) that I will faithfully execute the Office of President of the United States, and will to the best of my Ability, preserve, protect and defend the Constitution of the United States."

Section 2. The President shall be Commander in Chief of the Army and Navy of the United States, and of the Militia of the several States, when called into the actual Service of the United States; he may require the Opinion, in writing, of the principal Officer in each of the executive Departments, upon any Subject relating to the Duties of their respective Offices, and he shall have Power to grant Reprieves and Pardons for Offenses against the United States, except in Cases of Impeachment.

He shall have Power, by and with the Advice and Consent of the Senate to make Treaties, provided two thirds of the Senators present concur; and he shall nominate, and by and with the Advice and Consent of the Senate, shall appoint Ambassadors, other public Ministers and Consuls, Judges of the supreme Court, and all other Officers of the United States, whose Appointments are not herein otherwise provided for, and which shall be established by Law; but the Congress may by Law vest the Appointment of such inferior Officers, as they think proper, in the President alone, in the Courts of Law, or in the Heads of Departments.

The President shall have Power to fill up all Vacancies that may happen during the Recess of the Senate, by granting Commissions which shall expire at the End of their next Session.

Section 3. He shall from time to time give to the Congress Information of the State of the Union, and recommend to their Consideration such Measures as he shall judge necessary and expedient; he may, on extraordinary Occasions, convene both Houses, or either of them, and in Case of Disagreement between them, with Respect to the Time of Adjournment, he may adjourn them to such Time as he shall think proper; he shall receive Ambassadors and other public Ministers; he shall take Care that the Laws be faithfully executed, and shall Commission all the Officers of the United States.

Section 4. The President, Vice President and all civil Officers of the United States, shall be removed from Office on Impeachment for, and Conviction of, Treason, Bribery, or other high Crimes and Misdemeanors.

ARTICLE III

Section 1. The judicial Power of the United States, shall be vested in one supreme Court, and in such inferior Courts as the Congress may from time to time ordain and establish. The Judges, both of the supreme and inferior Courts, shall hold their Offices during good Behaviour, and shall, at stated Times, receive for their Services a Compensation, which shall not be diminished during their Continuance in Office.

Section 2. The judicial Power shall extend to all Cases, in Law and Equity, arising under this Constitution, the Laws of the United States, and Treaties made, or which shall be made, under their Authority;—to all Cases affecting Ambassadors, other public Ministers and Consuls;—to all Cases of admiralty and maritime Jurisdiction;—to Controversies to which the United States shall be a Party;—to Controversies between two or more States;—between a State and Citizens of another State;—between Citizens of different States;—between Citizens of the same State claiming Lands under Grants of different States, and between a State, or the Citizens thereof, and foreign States, Citizens or Subjects.

In all Cases affecting Ambassadors, other public Ministers and Consuls, and those in which a State shall be a Party, the supreme Court shall have original Jurisdiction. In all the other Cases before mentioned, the supreme Court shall have appellate Jurisdiction, both as to Law and Fact, with such Exceptions, and under such Regulations as the Congress shall make.

The Trial of all Crimes, except in Cases of Impeachment, shall be by Jury; and such Trial shall be held in the State where the said Crimes shall have been committed; but when not committed within any State, the Trial shall be at such Place or Places as the Congress may by Law have directed.

Section 3. Treason against the United States, shall consist only in levying War against them, or, in adhering to their Enemies, giving them Aid and Comfort. No Person shall be convicted of Treason unless on the Testimony of two Witnesses to the same overt Act, or on Confession in open Court.

The Congress shall have Power to declare the Punishment of Treason, but no Attainder of Treason shall work Corruption of Blood, or Forfeiture except during the Life of the Person attainted.

ARTICLE IV

Section 1. Full Faith and Credit shall be given in each State to the public Acts, Records, and judicial Proceedings of every other State. And the Congress may by general Laws prescribe the Manner in which such Acts, Records and Proceedings shall be proved, and the Effect thereof.

Section 2. The Citizens of each State shall be entitled to all Privileges and Immunities of Citizens in the several States.

A Person charged in any State with Treason, Felony, or other Crime, who shall flee from Justice, and be found in another State, shall on Demand of the executive Authority of the State from which he fled, be delivered up, to be removed to the State having Jurisdiction of the Crime.

No Person held to Service or Labour in one State, under the Laws thereof, escaping into another, shall, in Consequence of any Law or Regulation therein, be discharged from such Service or Labour, but shall be delivered up on Claim of the Party to whom such Service or Labour may be due.

Section 3. New States may be admitted by the Congress into this Union; but no new State shall be formed or erected within the Jurisdiction of any other State; nor any State be formed by the Junction of two or more States, or Parts of States, without the Consent of the Legislatures of the States concerned as well as of the Congress.

The Congress shall have Power to dispose of and make all needful Rules and Regulations respecting the Territory or other Property belonging to the United States; and nothing in this Constitution shall be so construed as to Prejudice any Claims of the United States, or of any particular State.

Section 4. The United States shall guarantee to every State in this Union a Republican Form of Government, and shall protect each of them against Invasion; and on Application of the Legislature, or of the Executive (when the Legislature cannot be convened) against domestic Violence.

ARTICLE V

The Congress, whenever two thirds of both Houses shall deem it necessary, shall propose Amendments to this Constitution, or, on the Application of the Legislatures of two thirds of the several States, shall call a Convention for proposing Amendments, which, in either Case, shall be valid to all Intents and Purposes, as part of this Constitution, when ratified by the Legislatures of three fourths of the several States, or by Conventions in three fourths thereof, as the one or the other Mode of Ratification may be proposed by the Congress; Provided that no Amendment which may be made prior to the Year One thousand eight hundred and eight shall in any Manner affect the first and fourth Clauses in the Ninth Section of the first Article; and that no State, without its Consent, shall be deprived of its equal Suffrage in the Senate.

ARTICLE VI

All Debts contracted and Engagements entered into, before the Adoption of this Constitution shall be as valid against the United States under this Constitution, as under the Confederation.

This Constitution, and the Laws of the United States which shall be made in Pursuance thereof; and all Treaties made, or which shall be made, under the Authority of the United States, shall be the supreme Law of the Land; and the Judges in every State shall be bound thereby, any Thing in the Constitution or Laws of any State to the Contrary notwithstanding.

The Senators and Representatives before mentioned, and the Members of the several State Legislatures, and all executive and judicial Officers, both of the United States and of the several States, shall be bound by Oath or Affirmation, to support this Constitution; but no religious Test shall ever be required as a Qualification to any Office or public Trust under the United States.

ARTICLE VII

The Ratification of the Conventions of nine States shall be sufficient for the Establishment of this Constitution between the States so ratifying the Same.

AMENDMENT I [1791]

Congress shall make no law respecting an establishment of religion, or prohibiting the free exercise thereof; or abridging the freedom of speech, or of the press; or the right of the people peaceably to assembly, and to petition the Government for a redress of grievances.

AMENDMENT II [1791]

A well regulated Militia, being necessary to the security of a free State, the right of the people to keep and bear Arms, shall not be infringed.

AMENDMENT III [1791]

No Soldier shall, in time of peace be quartered in any house, without the consent of the Owner, nor in time of war, but in a manner to be prescribed by law.

AMENDMENT IV [1791]

The right of the people to be secure in their persons, houses, papers, and effects, against unreasonable searches and seizures, shall not be violated, and no Warrants shall issue, but upon probable cause, supported by Oath or affirmation, and particularly describing the place to be searched, and the persons or things to be seized.

AMENDMENT V [1791]

No person shall be held to answer for a capital, or otherwise infamous crime, unless on a presentment or indictment of a Grand Jury, except in cases arising in the land or naval forces, or in the Militia, when in actual service in time of War or public danger; nor shall any person be subject for the same offence to be twice put in jeopardy of life or limb; nor shall be compelled in any criminal case to be a witness against himself, nor be deprived of life, liberty, or property, without due process of law; nor shall private property be taken for public use, without just compensation.

AMENDMENT VI [1791]

In all criminal prosecutions, the accused shall enjoy the right to a speedy and public trial, by an impartial jury of the State and district wherein the crime shall have been committed, which district shall have been previously ascertained by law, and to be informed of the nature and cause of the accusation; to be confronted with the witnesses against him; to have compulsory process for obtaining witnesses in his favor, and to have the Assistance of Counsel for his defence.

AMENDMENT VII [1791]

In Suits at common law, where the value in controversy shall exceed twenty dollars, the right of trial by jury shall be preserved, and no fact tried by jury, shall be otherwise reexamined in any Court of the United States, than according to the rules of the common law.

AMENDMENT VIII [1791]

Excessive bail shall not be required, nor excessive fines imposed, nor cruel and unusual punishments inflicted.

AMENDMENT IX [1791]

The enumeration in the Constitution, of certain rights, shall not be construed to deny or disparage others retained by the people.

AMENDMENT X [1791]

The powers not delegated to the United States by the Constitution, nor prohibited by it to the States, are reserved to the States respectively, or to the people.

AMENDMENT XI [1798]

The Judicial power of the United States shall not be construed to extend to any suit in law or equity, commenced or prosecuted against one of the United States by Citizens of another State, or by Citizens or Subjects of any Foreign State.

AMENDMENT XII [1804]

The Electors shall meet in their respective states, and vote by ballot for President and Vice-President, one of whom, at least, shall not be an inhabitant of the same state with themselves; they shall name in their ballots the person voted for as President, and in distinct ballots the person voted for as Vice-President, and they shall make distinct lists of all persons voted for as President, and of all persons voted for as Vice-President, and of the number of votes for each, which lists they shall sign and certify, and transmit sealed to the seat of the government of the United States, directed to the President of the Senate;—The President of the Senate shall, in the presence of the Senate and House of Representatives, open all the certificates and the votes shall then be counted;—The person having the greatest number of votes for President, shall be the President, if such number be a majority of the whole number of Electors appointed; and if no person have such majority, then from the persons having the highest numbers not exceeding three on the list of those voted for as President, the House of Representatives shall choose immediately, by ballot, the President. But in choosing the President, the votes shall be taken by states, the representation from each state having one vote; a quorum for this purpose shall consist of a member or members from two-thirds of the states, and a majority of all states shall be necessary to a choice. And if the House of Representatives shall not choose a President whenever the right of choice shall devolve upon them, before the fourth day of March next following, then the Vice-President shall act as President, as in the case of the death or other constitutional disability of the President.—The person having the greatest number of votes as Vice-President, shall be the Vice-President, if such number be a majority of the whole number of Electors appointed, and if no person have a majority, then from the two highest numbers on the list, the Senate shall choose the Vice-President; a quorum for the purpose shall consist of two-thirds of the whole number of Senators, and a majority of the whole number shall be necessary to a choice. But no person constitutionally ineligible to the office of President shall be eligible to that of Vice-President of the United States.

AMENDMENT XIII [1865]

Section 1. Neither slavery nor involuntary servitude, except as a punishment for crime whereof the party shall have been duly convicted, shall exist within the United States, or any place subject to their jurisdiction.

Section 2. Congress shall have power to enforce this article by appropriate legislation.

AMENDMENT XIV [1868]

Section 1. All persons born or naturalized in the United States, and subject to the jurisdiction thereof, are citizens of the United States and of the State wherein they reside. No State shall make or enforce any law which shall abridge the privileges or immunities of citizens of the United States; nor shall any State deprive any person of life, liberty, or property, without due process of law; nor deny to any person within its jurisdiction the equal protection of the laws.

Section 2. Representatives shall be apportioned among the several States according to their respective numbers, counting the whole number of persons in each State, excluding Indians not taxed. But when the right to vote at any election for the choice of electors for President and Vice President of the United States, Representatives in Congress, the Executive and Judicial officers of a State, or the members of the Legislature thereof, is denied to any of the male inhabitants of such State, being twenty-one years of age, and citizens of the United States, or in any way abridged, except for participation in rebellion, or other crime, the basis of representation therein shall be reduced in the proportion which the number of such male citizens shall bear to the whole number of male citizens twenty-one years of age in such State.

Section 3. No person shall be a Senator or Representative in Congress, or elector of President and Vice President, or hold any office, civil or military, under the United States, or under any State, who having previously taken an oath, as a member of Congress, or as an officer of the United States, or as a member of any State legislature, or as an executive or judicial officer of any State, to support the Constitution of the United States, shall have engaged in insurrection or rebellion against the same, or given aid or comfort to the enemies thereof. But Congress may by a vote of two-thirds of each House, remove such disability.

Section 4. The validity of the public debt of the United States, authorized by law, including debts incurred for payment of pensions and bounties for services in suppressing insurrection or rebellion, shall not be questioned. But neither the United States nor any State shall assume or pay any debt or obligation incurred in aid of insurrection or rebellion against the United States, or any claim for the loss or emancipation of any slave; but all such debts, obligations and claims shall be held illegal and void.

Section 5. The Congress shall have power to enforce, by appropriate legislation, the provisions of this article.

AMENDMENT XV [1870]

Section 1. The right of citizens of the United States to vote shall not be denied or abridged by the United States or by any State on account of race, color, or previous condition of servitude.

Section 2. The Congress shall have power to enforce this article by appropriate legislation.

AMENDMENT XVI [1913]

The Congress shall have power to lay and collect taxes on incomes, from whatever source derived, without apportionment among the several States, and without regard to any census or enumeration.

AMENDMENT XVII [1913]

Section 1. The Senate of the United States shall be composed of two Senators from each State, elected by the people thereof, for six years; and each Senator shall have one vote. The electors in each State shall have the qualifications requisite for electors of the most numerous branch of the State legislatures.

Section 2. When vacancies happen in the representation of any State in the Senate, the executive authority of such State shall issue writs of election to fill such vacancies: *Provided*, That the legislature of any State may empower the executive thereof to make temporary appointments until the people fill the vacancies by election as the legislature may direct.

Section 3. This amendment shall not be so construed as to affect the election or term of any Senator chosen before it becomes valid as part of the Constitution.

AMENDMENT XVIII [1919]

Section 1. After one year from the ratification of this article the manufacture, sale, or transportation of intoxicating liquors within, the importation thereof into, or the exportation thereof from the United States and all territory subject to the jurisdiction thereof for beverage purposes is hereby prohibited.

Section 2. The Congress and the several States shall have concurrent power to enforce this article by appropriate legislation.

Section 3. This article shall be inoperative unless it shall have been ratified as an amendment to the Constitution by the legislatures of the several States, as provided in the Constitution, within seven years from the date of the submission hereof to the States by the Congress.

AMENDMENT XIX [1920]

Section 1. The right of citizens of the United States to vote shall not be denied or abridged by the United States or by any State on account of sex.

Section 2. Congress shall have power to enforce this article by appropriate legislation.

AMENDMENT XX [1933]

Section 1. The terms of the President and Vice President shall end at noon on the 20th day of January, and the terms of Senators and Representatives at noon on the 3d day of January, of the years in which such terms would have ended if this article had not been ratified; and the terms of their successors shall then begin.

Section 2. The Congress shall assemble at least once in every year, and such meeting shall begin at noon on the 3d day of January, unless they shall by law appoint a different day.

Section 3. If, at the time fixed for the beginning of the term of the President, the President elect shall have died, the Vice President elect shall become President. If the President shall not have been chosen before the time fixed for the beginning of his term, or if the President elect shall have failed to qualify, then the Vice President elect shall act as President until a President shall have qualified; and the Congress may by law provide for the case wherein neither a President elect nor a Vice President elect shall have qualified, declaring who shall then act as President, or the manner in which one who is to act shall be selected, and such person shall act accordingly until a President or Vice President shall have qualified.

Section 4. The Congress may by law provide for the case of the death of any of the persons from whom the House of Representatives may choose a President whenever the right of choice shall have devolved upon them, and for the case of the death of any of the persons from whom the Senate may choose a Vice President whenever the right of choice shall have devolved upon them.

Section 5. Sections 1 and 2 shall take effect on the 15th day of October following the ratification of this article.

Section 6. This article shall be inoperative unless it shall have been ratified as an amendment to the Constitution by the legislatures of three-fourths of the several States within seven years from the date of its submission.

AMENDMENT XXI [1933]

Section 1. The eighteenth article of amendment to the Constitution of the United States is hereby repealed.

Section 2. The transportation or importation into any State, Territory, or possession of the United States for delivery or use therein of intoxicating liquors, in violation of the laws thereof, is hereby prohibited.

Section 3. This article shall be inoperative unless it shall have been ratified as an amendment to the Constitution by conventions in the several States, as provided in the Constitution, within seven years from the date of the submission hereof to the States by the Congress.

AMENDMENT XXII [1951]

Section 1. No person shall be elected to the office of the President more than twice, and no person who has held the office of President, or acted as President, for more than two years of a term to which some other person was elected President shall be elected to the office of President more than once. But this Article shall not apply to any person holding the office of President when this Article was proposed by the Congress, and shall not prevent any person who may be holding the office of President, or acting as President, during the term within which this Article becomes operative from holding the office of President or acting as President during the remainder of such term.

Section 2. This article shall be inoperative unless it shall have been ratified as an amendment to the Constitution by the legislatures of three-fourths of the several States within seven years from the date of its submission to the States by the Congress.

AMENDMENT XXIII [1961]

Section 1. The District constituting the seat of Government of the United States shall appoint in such manner as the Congress may direct:

A number of electors of President and Vice President equal to the whole number of Senators and Representatives in Congress to which the District would be entitled if it were a State, but in no event more than the least populous state; they shall be in addition to those appointed by the states, but they shall be considered, for the purposes of the election of President and Vice President, to be electors appointed by a state; and they shall meet in the District and perform such duties as provided by the twelfth article of amendment.

Section 2. The Congress shall have power to enforce this article by appropriate legislation.

AMENDMENT XXIV [1964]

Section 1. The right of citizens of the United States to vote in any primary or other election for President or Vice President, for electors for President or Vice President, or for Senator or Representative in Congress, shall not be denied or abridged by the United States, or any State by reason of failure to pay any poll tax or other tax.

Section 2. The Congress shall have power to enforce this article by appropriate legislation.

AMENDMENT **XXV** [1967]

Section 1. In case of the removal of the President from office or of his death or resignation, the Vice President shall become President.

Section 2. Whenever there is a vacancy in the office of the Vice President, the President shall nominate a Vice President who shall take office upon confirmation by a majority vote of both Houses of Congress.

Section 3. Whenever the President transmits to the President pro tempore of the Senate and the Speaker of the House of Representatives his written declaration that he is unable to discharge the powers and duties of his office, and until he transmits to them a written declaration to the contrary, such powers and duties shall be discharged by the Vice President as Acting President.

Section 4. Whenever the Vice President and a majority of either the principal officers of the executive departments or of such other body as Congress may by law provide, transmit to the President pro tempore of the Senate and the Speaker of the House of Representatives their written declaration that the President is unable to discharge the powers and duties of his office, the Vice President shall immediately assume the powers and duties of the office as Acting President.

Thereafter, when the President transmits to the President pro tempore of the Senate and the Speaker of the House of Representatives his written declaration that no inability exists, he shall resume the powers and duties of his office unless the Vice President and a majority of either the principal officers of the executive department or of such other body as Congress may by law provide, transmit within four days to the President pro tempore of the Senate and the Speaker of the House of Representatives their written declaration that the President is unable to discharge the powers and duties of his office. Thereupon Congress shall decide the issue, assembling within forty-eight hours for that purpose if not in session. If the Congress, within twenty-one days after receipt of the latter written declaration, or, if Congress is not in session, within twenty-one days after Congress is required to assemble, determines by two-thirds vote of both Houses that the President is unable to discharge the powers and duties of his office, the Vice President shall continue to discharge the same as Acting President; otherwise, the President shall resume the powers and duties of his office.

AMENDMENT **XXVI** [1971]

Section 1. The right of citizens of the United States, who are eighteen years of age or older, to vote shall not be denied or abridged by the United States or by any State on account of age.

Section 2. The Congress shall have power to enforce this article by appropriate legislation.

AMENDMENT **XXVII** [1992]

No law, varying the compensation for the services of the Senators and Representatives, shall take effect, until an election of Representatives shall have intervened.

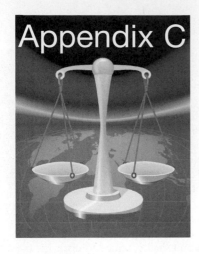

Appendix C

The Uniform Commercial Code

Adopted in fifty-two jurisdictions; all fifty States, although Louisiana has adopted only Articles 1, 3, 4, 7, 8, and 9; the District of Columbia; and the Virgin Islands.)

The Code consists of the following articles:

Art.

Article 1
GENERAL PROVISIONS

Part 1 Short Title, Construction, Application and Subject Matter of the Act

§ 1—101. **Short Title.**

This Act shall be known and may be cited as Uniform Commercial Code.

§ 1—102. **Purposes; Rules of Construction; Variation by Agreement.**

(1) This Act shall be liberally construed and applied to promote its underlying purposes and policies.

(2) Underlying purposes and policies of this Act are

(a) to simplify, clarify and modernize the law governing commercial transactions;

(b) to permit the continued expansion of commercial practices through custom, usage and agreement of the parties;

(c) to make uniform the law among the various jurisdictions.

(3) The effect of provisions of this Act may be varied by agreement, except as otherwise provided in this Act and except that the obligations of good faith, diligence, reasonableness and care prescribed by this Act may not be disclaimed by agreement but the parties may by agreement determine the standards by which the performance of such obligations is to be measured if such standards are not manifestly unreasonable.

(4) The presence in certain provisions of this Act of the words "unless otherwise agreed" or words of similar import does not imply that the effect of other provisions may not be varied by agreement under subsection (3).

(5) In this Act unless the context otherwise requires

(a) words in the singular number include the plural, and in the plural include the singular;

(b) words of the masculine gender include the feminine and the neuter, and when the sense so indicates words of the neuter gender may refer to any gender.

§ 1—103. Supplementary General Principles of Law Applicable.

Unless displaced by the particular provisions of this Act, the principles of law and equity, including the law merchant and the law relative to capacity to contract, principal and agent, estoppel, fraud, misrepresentation, duress, coercion, mistake, bankruptcy, or other validating or invalidating cause shall supplement its provisions.

§ 1—104. Construction Against Implicit Repeal.

This Act being a general act intended as a unified coverage of its subject matter, no part of it shall be deemed to be impliedly repealed by subsequent legislation if such construction can reasonably be avoided.

§ 1—105. Territorial Application of the Act; Parties' Power to Choose Applicable Law.

(1) Except as provided hereafter in this section, when a transaction bears a reasonable relation to this state and also to another state or nation the parties may agree that the law either of this state or of such other state or nation shall govern their rights and duties. Failing such agreement this Act applies to transactions bearing an appropriate relation to this state.

(2) Where one of the following provisions of this Act specifies the applicable law, that provision governs and a contrary agreement is effective only to the extent permitted by the law (including the conflict of laws rules) so specified:

Rights of creditors against sold goods. Section 2—402.

Applicability of the Article on Leases. Sections 2A—105 and 2A—106.

Applicability of the Article on Bank Deposits and Collections. Section 4—102.

Governing law in the Article on Funds Transfers. Section 4A—507.

Letters of Credit, Section 5—116.

Bulk sales subject to the Article on Bulk Sales. Section 6—103.

Applicability of the Article on Investment Securities. Section 8—106.

Perfection provisions of the Article on Secured Transactions. Section 9—103.

§ 1—106. Remedies to Be Liberally Administered.

(1) The remedies provided by this Act shall be liberally administered to the end that the aggrieved party may be put in as good a position as if the other party had fully performed but neither consequential or special nor penal damages may be had except as specifically provided in this Act or by other rule of law.

(2) Any right or obligation declared by this Act is enforceable by action unless the provision declaring it specifies a different and limited effect.

§ 1—107. Waiver or Renunciation of Claim or Right After Breach.

Any claim or right arising out of an alleged breach can be discharged in whole or in part without consideration by a written waiver or renunciation signed and delivered by the aggrieved party.

§ 1—108. Severability.

If any provision or clause of this Act or application thereof to any person or circumstances is held invalid, such invalidity shall not affect other provisions or applications of the Act which can be given effect without the invalid provision or application, and to this end the provisions of this Act are declared to be severable.

§ 1—109. Section Captions.

Section captions are parts of this Act.

Part 2 General Definitions and Principles of Interpretation

§ 1—201. General Definitions.

Subject to additional definitions contained in the subsequent Articles of this Act which are applicable to specific Articles or Parts thereof, and unless the context otherwise requires, in this Act:

(1) "Action" in the sense of a judicial proceeding includes recoupment, counterclaim, set-off, suit in equity and any other proceedings in which rights are determined.

(2) "Aggrieved party" means a party entitled to resort to a remedy.

(3) "Agreement" means the bargain of the parties in fact as found in their language or by implication from other circumstances including course of dealing or usage of trade or course of performance as provided in this Act (Sections 1—205 and 2—208). Whether an agreement has legal consequences is determined by the provisions of this Act, if applicable; otherwise by the law of contracts (Section 1—103). (Compare "Contract".)

(4) "Bank" means any person engaged in the business of banking.

(5) "Bearer" means the person in possession of an instrument, document of title, or certificated security payable to bearer or indorsed in blank.

(6) "Bill of lading" means a document evidencing the receipt of goods for shipment issued by a person engaged in the business of transporting or forwarding goods, and includes an airbill. "Airbill" means a document serving for air transportation as a bill of lading does for marine or rail transportation, and includes an air consignment note or air waybill.

(7) "Branch" includes a separately incorporated foreign branch of a bank.

(8) "Burden of establishing" a fact means the burden of persuading the triers of fact that the existence of the fact is more probable than its non-existence.

(9) "Buyer in ordinary course of business" means a person who in good faith and without knowledge that the sale to him is in violation of the ownership rights or security interest of a third party in the goods buys in ordinary course from a person in the business of selling goods of that kind but does not include a pawnbroker. All persons who sell minerals or the like (including oil and gas) at wellhead or minehead shall be deemed to be persons in the business of selling goods of that kind. "Buying" may be for cash or by exchange of other property or on secured or unsecured credit and includes receiving goods or documents of title under a pre-existing contract for sale but does not include a transfer in bulk or as security for or in total or partial satisfaction of a money debt.

(10) "Conspicuous": A term or clause is conspicuous when it is so written that a reasonable person against whom it is to operate ought to have noticed it. A printed heading in capitals (as: NON-NEGOTIABLE BILL OF LADING) is conspicuous. Language in the body of a form is "conspicuous" if it is in larger or other contrasting type or color. But in a telegram any stated term is "conspicuous". Whether a term or clause is "conspicuous" or not is for decision by the court.

(11) "Contract" means the total legal obligation which results from the parties' agreement as affected by this Act and any other applicable rules of law. (Compare "Agreement".)

(12) "Creditor" includes a general creditor, a secured creditor, a lien creditor and any representative of creditors, including an assignee for the benefit of creditors, a trustee in bankruptcy, a receiver in equity and an executor or administrator of an insolvent debtor's or assignor's estate.

(13) "Defendant" includes a person in the position of defendant in a cross-action or counterclaim.

(14) "Delivery" with respect to instruments, documents of title, chattel paper, or certificated securities means voluntary transfer of possession.

(15) "Document of title" includes bill of lading, dock warrant, dock receipt, warehouse receipt or order for the delivery of goods, and also any other document which in the regular course of business or financing is treated as adequately evidencing that the person in possession of it is entitled to receive, hold and dispose of the document and the goods it covers. To be a document of title a document must purport to be issued by or addressed to a bailee and purport to cover goods in the bailee's possession which are either identified or are fungible portions of an identified mass.

(16) "Fault" means wrongful act, omission or breach.

(17) "Fungible" with respect to goods or securities means goods or securities of which any unit is, by nature or usage of trade, the equivalent of any other like unit. Goods which are not fungible shall be deemed fungible for the purposes of this Act to the extent that under a particular agreement or document unlike units are treated as equivalents.

(18) "Genuine" means free of forgery or counterfeiting.

(19) "Good faith" means honesty in fact in the conduct or transaction concerned.

(20) "Holder" with respect to a negotiable instrument, means the person in possession if the instrument is payable to bearer or, in the cases of an instrument payable to an identified person, if the identified person is in possession. "Holder" with respect to a document of title means the person in possession if the goods are deliverable to bearer or to the order of the person in possession.

(21) To "honor" is to pay or to accept and pay, or where a credit so engages to purchase or discount a draft complying with the terms of the credit.

(22) "Insolvency proceedings" includes any assignment for the benefit of creditors or other proceedings intended to liquidate or rehabilitate the estate of the person involved.

(23) A person is "insolvent" who either has ceased to pay his debts in the ordinary course of business or cannot pay his debts as they become due or is insolvent within the meaning of the federal bankruptcy law.

(24) "Money" means a medium of exchange authorized or adopted by a domestic or foreign government and includes a monetary unit of account established by an intergovernmental organization or by agreement between two or more nations.

(25) A person has "notice" of a fact when

    (a) he has actual knowledge of it; or

    (b) he has received a notice or notification of it; or

    (c) from all the facts and circumstances known to him at the time in question he has reason to know that it exists.

A person "knows" or has "knowledge" of a fact when he has actual knowledge of it. "Discover" or "learn" or a word or phrase of similar import refers to knowledge rather than to reason to know. The time and circumstances under which a notice or notification may cease to be effective are not determined by this Act.

(26) A person "notifies" or "gives" a notice or notification to another by taking such steps as may be reasonably required to inform the other in ordinary course whether or not such other actually comes to know of it. A person "receives" a notice or notification when

(a) it comes to his attention; or

(b) it is duly delivered at the place of business through which the contract was made or at any other place held out by him as the place for receipt of such communications.

(27) Notice, knowledge or a notice or notification received by an organization is effective for a particular transaction from the time when it is brought to the attention of the individual conducting that transaction, and in any event from the time when it would have been brought to his attention if the organization had exercised due diligence. An organization exercises due diligence if it maintains reasonable routines for communicating significant information to the person conducting the transaction and there is reasonable compliance with the routines. Due diligence does not require an individual acting for the organization to communicate information unless such communication is part of his regular duties or unless he has reason to know of the transaction and that the transaction would be materially affected by the information.

(28) "Organization" includes a corporation, government or governmental subdivision or agency, business trust, estate, trust, partnership or association, two or more persons having a joint or common interest, or any other legal or commercial entity.

(29) "Party", as distinct from "third party", means a person who has engaged in a transaction or made an agreement within this Act.

(30) "Person" includes an individual or an organization (See Section 1—102).

(31) "Presumption" or "presumed" means that the trier of fact must find the existence of the fact presumed unless and until evidence is introduced which would support a finding of its non-existence.

(32) "Purchase" includes taking by sale, discount, negotiation, mortgage, pledge, lien, issue or re-issue, gift or any other voluntary transaction creating an interest in property.

(33) "Purchaser" means a person who takes by purchase.

(34) "Remedy" means any remedial right to which an aggrieved party is entitled with or without resort to a tribunal.

(35) "Representative" includes an agent, an officer of a corporation or association, and a trustee, executor or administrator of an estate, or any other person empowered to act for another.

(36) "Rights" includes remedies.

(37) "Security interest" means an interest in personal property or fixtures which secures payment or performance of an obligation. The retention or reservation of title by a seller of goods notwithstanding shipment or delivery to the buyer (Section 2—401) is limited in effect to a reservation of a "security interest". The term also includes any interest of a buyer of accounts or chattel paper which is subject to

Article 9. The special property interest of a buyer of goods on identification of those goods to a contract for sale under Section 2—401 is not a "security interest", but a buyer may also acquire a "security interest" by complying with Article 9. Unless a consignment is intended as security, reservation of title thereunder is not a "security interest," but a consignment is in any event subject to the provisions on consignment sales (Section 2—326).

Whether a transaction creates a lease or security interest is determined by the facts of each case; however, a transaction creates a security interest if the consideration the lessee is to pay the lessor for the right to possession and use of the goods is an obligation for the term of the lease not subject to termination by the lessee, and

(a) the original term of the lease is equal to or greater than the remaining economic life of the goods,

(b) the lessee is bound to renew the lease for the remaining economic life of the goods or is bound to become the owner of the goods,

(c) the lessee has an option to renew the lease for the remaining economic life of the goods for no additional consideration or nominal additional consideration upon compliance with the lease agreement, or

(d) the lessee has an option to become the owner of the goods for no additional consideration or nominal additional consideration upon compliance with the lease agreement.

A transaction does not create a security interest merely because it provides that

(a) the present value of the consideration the lessee is obli-gated to pay the lessor for the right to possession and use of the goods is substantially equal to or is greater than the fair market value of the goods at the time the lease is entered into,

(b) the lessee assumes risk of loss of the goods, or agrees to pay taxes, insurance, filing, recording, or registration fees, or serv-ice or maintenance costs with respect to the goods,

(c) the lessee has an option to renew the lease or to become the owner of the goods,

(d) the lessee has an option to renew the lease for a fixed rent that is equal to or greater than the reasonably predictable fair market rent for the use of the goods for the term of the renewal at the time the option is to be performed, or

(e) the lessee has an option to become the owner of the goods for a fixed price that is equal to or greater than the reasonably predictable fair market value of the goods at the time the option is to be performed.

For purposes of this subsection (37):

(x) Additional consideration is not nominal if (i) when the option to renew the lease is granted to the lessee the rent is stated to be the fair market rent for the use of the goods for the term of the renewal determined at the time the option is to be performed, or (ii) when the option to become the owner of the goods is granted to the lessee the price is stated to be the fair market value of the goods determined at the time the option is to be performed. Additional consideration is nominal if it is less than the lessee's reasonably predictable cost of performing under the lease agreement if the option is not exercised;

(y) "Reasonably predictable" and "remaining economic life of the goods" are to be determined with reference to the facts and circumstances at the time the transaction is entered into; and

(z) "Present value" means the amount as of a date certain of one or more sums payable in the future, discounted to the date certain. The discount is determined by the interest rate specified by the parties if the rate is not manifestly unreasonable at the time the transaction is entered into; otherwise, the discount is determined by a commercially reasonable rate that takes into account the facts and circumstances of each case at the time the transaction was entered into.

(38) "Send" in connection with any writing or notice means to deposit in the mail or deliver for transmission by any other usual means of communication with postage or cost of transmission provided for and properly addressed and in the case of an instrument to an address specified thereon or otherwise agreed, or if there be none to any address reasonable under the circumstances. The receipt of any writing or notice within the time at which it would have arrived if properly sent has the effect of a proper sending.

(39) "Signed" includes any symbol executed or adopted by a party with present intention to authenticate a writing.

(40) "Surety" includes guarantor.

(41) "Telegram" includes a message transmitted by radio, teletype, cable, any mechanical method of transmission, or the like.

(42) "Term" means that portion of an agreement which relates to a particular matter.

(43) "Unauthorized" signature means one made without actual, implied or apparent authority and includes a forgery.

(44) "Value". Except as otherwise provided with respect to negotiable instruments and bank collections (Sections 3—303, 4—210 and 4—211) a person gives "value" for rights if he acquires them

(a) in return for a binding commitment to extend credit or for the extension of immediately available credit whether or not drawn upon and whether or not a chargeback is provided for in the event of difficulties in collection; or

(b) as security for or in total or partial satisfaction of a pre-existing claim; or

(c) by accepting delivery pursuant to a preexisting contract for purchase; or

(d) generally, in return for any consideration sufficient to support a simple contract.

(45) "Warehouse receipt" means a receipt issued by a person engaged in the business of storing goods for hire.

(46) "Written" or "writing" includes printing, typewriting or any other intentional reduction to tangible form.

§1—202. **Prima Facie Evidence by Third Party Documents.**

A document in due form purporting to be a bill of lading, policy or certificate of insurance, official weigher's or inspector's certificate, consular invoice, or any other document authorized or required by the contract to be issued by a third party shall be prima facie evidence of its own authenticity and genuineness and of the facts stated in the document by the third party.

§ 1—203. **Obligation of Good Faith.**

Every contract or duty within this Act imposes an obligation of good faith in its performance or enforcement.

§ 1—204. **Time; Reasonable Time; "Seasonably".**

(1) Whenever this Act requires any action to be taken within a reasonable time, any time which is not manifestly unreasonable may be fixed by agreement.

(2) What is a reasonable time for taking any action depends on the nature, purpose and circumstances of such action.

(3) An action is taken "seasonably" when it is taken at or within the time agreed or if no time is agreed at or within a reasonable time.

§ 1—205. **Course of Dealing and Usage of Trade.**

(1) A course of dealing is a sequence of previous conduct between the parties to a particular transaction which is fairly to be regarded as establishing a common basis of understanding for interpreting their expressions and other conduct.

(2) A usage of trade is any practice or method of dealing having such regularity of observance in a place, vocation or trade as to justify an expectation that it will be observed with respect to the transaction in question. The existence and scope of such a usage are to be proved as facts. If it is established that such a usage is embodied in a written trade code or similar writing the interpretation of the writing is for the court.

(3) A course of dealing between parties and any usage of trade in the vocation or trade in which they are engaged or of which they are or should be aware give particular meaning to and supplement or qualify terms of an agreement.

(4) The express terms of an agreement and an applicable course of dealing or usage of trade shall be construed wherever reasonable as consistent with each other; but when such construction is unreasonable express terms control both course of dealing and usage of trade and course of dealing controls usage trade.

(5) An applicable usage of trade in the place where any part of performance is to occur shall be used in interpreting the agreement as to that part of the performance.

(6) Evidence of a relevant usage of trade offered by one party is not admissible unless and until he has given the other party such notice as the court finds sufficient to prevent unfair surprise to the latter.

§ 1—206. Statute of Frauds for Kinds of Personal Property Not Otherwise Covered.

(1) Except in the cases described in subsection (2) of this section a contract for the sale of personal property is not enforceable by way of action or defense beyond five thousand dollars in amount or value of remedy unless there is some writing which indicates that a contract for sale has been made between the parties at a defined or stated price, reasonably identifies the subject matter, and is signed by the party against whom enforcement is sought or by his authorized agent.

(2) Subsection (1) of this section does not apply to contracts for the sale of goods (Section 2—201) nor of securities (Section 8—113) nor to security agreements (Section 9—203).

§ 1—207. Performance or Acceptance Under Reservation of Rights.

(1) A party who with explicit reservation of rights performs or promises performance or assents to performance in a manner demanded or offered by the other party does not thereby prejudice the rights reserved. Such words as "without prejudice", "under protest" or the like are sufficient.

(2) Subsection (1) does not apply to an accord and satisfaction.

§ 1—208. Option to Accelerate at Will.

A term providing that one party or his successor in interest may accelerate payment or performance or require collateral or additional collateral "at will" or "when he deems himself insecure" or in words of similar import shall be construed to mean that he shall have power to do so only if he in good faith believes that the prospect of payment or performance is impaired. The burden of establishing lack of good faith is on the party against whom the power has been exercised.

§ 1—209. Subordinated Obligations.

An obligation may be issued as subordinated to payment of another obligation of the person obligated, or a creditor may subordinate his right to payment of an obligation by agreement with either the person obligated or another creditor of the person obli-gated. Such a subordination does not create a security interest as against either the common debtor or a subordinated creditor. This section shall be construed as declaring the law as it existed prior to the enactment of this section and not as modifying it. Added 1966.

Note: *This new section is proposed as an optional provision to make it clear that a subordination agreement does not create a security interest unless so intended.*

Article 2
SALES

Part 1 Short Title, General Construction and Subject Matter

§ 2—101. Short Title.

This Article shall be known and may be cited as Uniform Commercial Code—Sales.

§ 2—102. Scope; Certain Security and Other Transactions Excluded From This Article.

Unless the context otherwise requires, this Article applies to transactions in goods; it does not apply to any transaction which although in the form of an unconditional contract to sell or present sale is intended to operate only as a security transaction nor does this Article impair or repeal any statute regulating sales to consumers, farmers or other specified classes of buyers.

§ 2—103. Definitions and Index of Definitions.

(1) In this Article unless the context otherwise requires

    (a) "Buyer" means a person who buys or contracts to buy goods.

    (b) "Good faith" in the case of a merchant means honesty in fact and the observance of reasonable commercial standards of fair dealing in the trade.

    (c) "Receipt" of goods means taking physical possession of them.

    (d) "Seller" means a person who sells or contracts to sell goods.

(2) Other definitions applying to this Article or to specified Parts thereof, and the sections in which they appear are:

"Acceptance". Section 2—606.
"Banker's credit". Section 2—325.
"Between merchants". Section 2—104.
"Cancellation". Section 2—106(4).
"Commercial unit". Section 2—105.
"Confirmed credit". Section 2—325.
"Conforming to contract". Section 2—106.
"Contract for sale". Section 2—106.
"Cover". Section 2—712.
"Entrusting". Section 2—403.
"Financing agency". Section 2—104.
"Future goods". Section 2—105.
"Goods". Section 2—105.
"Identification". Section 2—501.
"Installment contract". Section 2—612.
"Letter of Credit". Section 2—325.
"Lot". Section 2—105.

"Merchant". Section 2—104.

"Overseas". Section 2—323.

"Person in position of seller". Section 2—707.

"Present sale". Section 2—106.

"Sale". Section 2—106.

"Sale on approval". Section 2—326.

"Sale or return". Section 2—326.

"Termination". Section 2—106.

(3) The following definitions in other Articles apply to this Article:

"Check". Section 3—104.

"Consignee". Section 7—102.

"Consignor". Section 7—102.

"Consumer goods". Section 9—109.

"Dishonor". Section 3—507.

"Draft". Section 3—104.

(4) In addition Article 1 contains general definitions and principles of construction and interpretation applicable throughout this Article.

§ 2—104. Definitions: "Merchant"; "Between Merchants"; "Financing Agency".

(1) "Merchant" means a person who deals in goods of the kind or otherwise by his occupation holds himself out as having knowledge or skill peculiar to the practices or goods involved in the transaction or to whom such knowledge or skill may be attributed by his employment of an agent or broker or other intermediary who by his occupation holds himself out as having such knowledge or skill.

(2) "Financing agency" means a bank, finance company or other person who in the ordinary course of business makes advances against goods or documents of title or who by arrangement with either the seller or the buyer intervenes in ordinary course to make or collect payment due or claimed under the contract for sale, as by purchasing or paying the seller's draft or making advances against it or by merely taking it for collection whether or not documents of title accompany the draft. "Financing agency" includes also a bank or other person who similarly intervenes between persons who are in the position of seller and buyer in respect to the goods (Section 2—707).

(3) "Between merchants" means in any transaction with respect to which both parties are chargeable with the knowledge or skill of merchants.

§ 2—105. Definitions: Transferability; "Goods"; "Future" Goods; "Lot"; "Commercial Unit".

(1) "Goods" means all things (including specially manufactured goods) which are movable at the time of identification to the contract for sale other than the money in which the price is to be paid, investment securities (Article 8) and things in action. "Goods" also includes the unborn young of animals and growing crops and other identified things attached to realty as described in the section on goods to be severed from realty (Section 2—107).

(2) Goods must be both existing and identified before any interest in them can pass. Goods which are not both existing and identified are "future" goods. A purported present sale of future goods or of any interest therein operates as a contract to sell.

(3) There may be a sale of a part interest in existing identified goods.

(4) An undivided share in an identified bulk of fungible goods is sufficiently identified to be sold although the quantity of the bulk is not determined. Any agreed proportion of such a bulk or any quantity thereof agreed upon by number, weight or other measure may to the extent of the seller's interest in the bulk be sold to the buyer who then becomes an owner in common.

(5) "Lot" means a parcel or a single article which is the subject matter of a separate sale or delivery, whether or not it is sufficient to perform the contract.

(6) "Commercial unit" means such a unit of goods as by commercial usage is a single whole for purposes of sale and division of which materially impairs its character or value on the market or in use. A commercial unit may be a single article (as a machine) or a set of articles (as a suite of furniture or an assortment of sizes) or a quantity (as a bale, gross, or carload) or any other unit treated in use or in the relevant market as a single whole.

§ 2—106. Definitions: "Contract"; "Agreement"; "Contract for Sale"; "Sale"; "Present Sale"; "Conforming" to Contract; "Termination"; "Cancellation".

(1) In this Article unless the context otherwise requires "contract" and "agreement" are limited to those relating to the present or future sale of goods. "Contract for sale" includes both a present sale of goods and a contract to sell goods at a future time. A "sale" consists in the passing of title from the seller to the buyer for a price (Section 2—401). A "present sale" means a sale which is accomplished by the making of the contract.

(2) Goods or conduct including any part of a performance are "conforming" or conform to the contract when they are in accordance with the obligations under the contract.

(3) "Termination" occurs when either party pursuant to a power created by agreement or law puts an end to the contract otherwise than for its breach. On "termination" all obligations which are still executory on both sides are discharged but any right based on prior breach or performance survives.

(4) "Cancellation" occurs when either party puts an end to the contract for breach by the other and its effect is the same as that of "termination" except that the cancelling party also retains any remedy for breach of the whole contract or any unperformed balance.

§ 2—107. Goods to Be Severed From Realty: Recording. *Goods associated w/ real estate*

(1) A contract for the sale of minerals or the like (including oil and gas) or a structure or its materials to be removed

from realty is a contract for the sale of goods within this Article if they are to be severed by the seller but until severance a purported present sale thereof which is not effective as a transfer of an interest in land is effective only as a contract to sell.

(2) A contract for the sale apart from the land of growing crops or other things attached to realty and capable of severance without material harm thereto but not described in subsection (1) or of timber to be cut is a contract for the sale of goods within this Article whether the subject matter is to be severed by the buyer or by the seller even though it forms part of the realty at the time of contracting, and the parties can by identification effect a present sale before severance.

(3) The provisions of this section are subject to any third party rights provided by the law relating to realty records, and the contract for sale may be executed and recorded as a document transferring an interest in land and shall then constitute notice to third parties of the buyer's rights under the contract for sale.

Part 2 Form, Formation and Readjustment of Contract

§ 2—201. Formal Requirements; Statute of Frauds.

(1) Except as otherwise provided in this section a contract for the sale of goods for the price of $500 or more is not enforceable by way of action or defense unless there is some writing sufficient to indicate that a contract for sale has been made between the parties and signed by the party against whom enforcement is sought or by his authorized agent or broker. A writing is not insufficient because it omits or incorrectly states a term agreed upon but the contract is not enforceable under this paragraph beyond the quantity of goods shown in such writing.

(2) Between merchants if within a reasonable time a writing in confirmation of the contract and sufficient against the sender is received and the party receiving it has reason to know its contents, its satisfies the requirements of subsection (1) against such party unless written notice of objection to its contents is given within ten days after it is received.

(3) A contract which does not satisfy the requirements of subsection (1) but which is valid in other respects is enforceable

(a) if the goods are to be specially manufactured for the buyer and are not suitable for sale to others in the ordinary course of the seller's business and the seller, before notice of repudiation is received and under circumstances which reasonably indicate that the goods are for the buyer, has made either a substantial beginning of their manufacture or commitments for their procurement; or

(b) if the party against whom enforcement is sought admits in his pleading, testimony or otherwise in court that a contract for sale was made, but the contract is not enforceable under this provision beyond the quantity of goods admitted; or

(c) with respect to goods for which payment has been made and accepted or which have been received and accepted (Sec. 2—606).

§ 2—202. Final Written Expression: Parol or Extrinsic Evidence.

Terms with respect to which the confirmatory memoranda of the parties agree or which are otherwise set forth in a writing intended by the parties as a final expression of their agreement with respect to such terms as are included therein may not be contradicted by evidence of any prior agreement or of a contemporaneous oral agreement but may be explained or supplemented

(a) by course of dealing or usage of trade (Section 1—205) or by course of performance (Section 2—208); and

(b) by evidence of consistent additional terms unless the court finds the writing to have been intended also as a complete and exclusive statement of the terms of the agreement.

§ 2—203. Seals Inoperative.

The affixing of a seal to a writing evidencing a contract for sale or an offer to buy or sell goods does not constitute the writing a sealed instrument and the law with respect to sealed instruments does not apply to such a contract or offer.

§ 2—204. Formation in General.

(1) A contract for sale of goods may be made in any manner sufficient to show agreement, including conduct by both parties which recognizes the existence of such a contract.

(2) An agreement sufficient to constitute a contract for sale may be found even though the moment of its making is undetermined.

(3) Even though one or more terms are left open a contract for sale does not fail for indefiniteness if the parties have intended to make a contract and there is a reasonably certain basis for giving an appropriate remedy.

§ 2—205. Firm Offers.

An offer by a merchant to buy or sell goods in a signed writing which by its terms gives assurance that it will be held open is not revocable, for lack of consideration, during the time stated or if no time is stated for a reasonable time, but in no event may such period of irrevocability exceed three months; but any such term of assurance on a form supplied by the offeree must be separately signed by the offeror.

§ 2—206. Offer and Acceptance in Formation of Contract.

(1) Unless other unambiguously indicated by the language or circumstances

(a) an offer to make a contract shall be construed as inviting acceptance in any manner and by any medium reasonable in the circumstances;

(b) an order or other offer to buy goods for prompt or current shipment shall be construed as inviting acceptance either by a prompt promise to ship or by the prompt or current shipment of conforming or non-conforming goods, but such a shipment of non-conforming goods does not constitute an acceptance if the seller seasonably notifies the buyer that the shipment is offered only as an accommodation to the buyer.

(2) Where the beginning of a requested performance is a reasonable mode of acceptance an offeror who is not notified of acceptance within a reasonable time may treat the offer as having lapsed before acceptance.

§ 2–207. Additional Terms in Acceptance or Confirmation.

(1) A definite and seasonable expression of acceptance or a written confirmation which is sent within a reasonable time operates as an acceptance even though it states terms additional to or different from those offered or agreed upon, unless acceptance is expressly made conditional on assent to the additional or different terms.

(2) The additional terms are to be construed as proposals for addition to the contract. Between merchants such terms become part of the contract unless:

(a) the offer expressly limits acceptance to the terms of the offer;

(b) they materially alter it; or

(c) notification of objection to them has already been given or is given within a reasonable time after notice of them is received.

(3) Conduct by both parties which recognizes the existence of a contract is sufficient to establish a contract for sale although the writings of the parties do not otherwise establish a contract. In such case the terms of the particular contract consist of those terms on which the writings of the parties agree, together with any supplementary terms incorporated under any other provisions of this Act.

§ 2–208. Course of Performance or Practical Construction.

(1) Where the contract for sale involves repeated occasions for performance by either party with knowledge of the nature of the performance and opportunity for objection to it by the other, any course of performance accepted or acquiesced in without objection shall be relevant to determine the meaning of the agreement.

(2) The express terms of the agreement and any such course of performance, as well as any course of dealing and usage of trade, shall be construed whenever reasonable as consistent with each other; but when such construction is unreasonable, express terms shall control course of per-

formance and course of performance shall control both course of dealing and usage of trade (Section 1–205).

(3) Subject to the provisions of the next section on modification and waiver, such course of performance shall be relevant to show a waiver or modification of any term inconsistent with such course of performance.

§ 2–209. Modification, Rescission and Waiver.

(1) An agreement modifying a contract within this Article needs no consideration to be binding.

(2) A signed agreement which excludes modification or rescission except by a signed writing cannot be otherwise modified or rescinded, but except as between merchants such a requirement on a form supplied by the merchant must be separately signed by the other party.

(3) The requirements of the statute of frauds section of this Article (Section 2–201) must be satisfied if the contract as modified is within its provisions.

(4) Although an attempt at modification or rescission does not satisfy the requirements of subsection (2) or (3) it can operate as a waiver.

(5) A party who has made a waiver affecting an executory portion of the contract may retract the waiver by reasonable notification received by the other party that strict performance will be required of any term waived, unless the retraction would be unjust in view of a material change of position in reliance on the waiver.

§ 2–210. Delegation of Performance; Assignment of Rights.

(1) A party may perform his duty through a delegate unless otherwise agreed or unless the other party has a substantial interest in having his original promisor perform or control the acts required by the contract. No delegation of performance relieves the party delegating of any duty to perform or any liability for breach.

(2) Unless otherwise agreed all rights of either seller or buyer can be assigned except where the assignment would materially change the duty of the other party, or increase materially the burden or risk imposed on him by his contract, or impair materially his chance of obtaining return performance. A right to damages for breach of the whole contract or a right arising out of the assignor's due performance of his entire obligation can be assigned despite agreement otherwise.

(3) Unless the circumstances indicate the contrary a prohibition of assignment of "the contract" is to be construed as barring only the delegation to the assignee of the assignor's performance.

(4) An assignment of "the contract" or of "all my rights under the contract" or an assignment in similar general terms is an assignment of rights and unless the language or the circumstances (as in an assignment for security) indicate the contrary, it is a delegation of performance of the

duties of the assignor and its acceptance by the assignee constitutes a promise by him to perform those duties. This promise is enforceable by either the assignor or the other party to the original contract.

(5) The other party may treat any assignment which delegates performance as creating reasonable grounds for insecurity and may without prejudice to his rights against the assignor demand assurances from the assignee (Section 2—609).

Part 3 General Obligation and Construction of Contract

§ 2—301. General Obligations of Parties.

The obligation of the seller is to transfer and deliver and that of the buyer is to accept and pay in accordance with the contract.

§ 2—302. Unconscionable Contract or Clause.

(1) If the court as a matter of law finds the contract or any clause of the contract to have been unconscionable at the time it was made the court may refuse to enforce the contract, or it may enforce the remainder of the contract without the unconscionable clause, or it may so limit the application of any unconscionable clause as to avoid any unconscionable result.

(2) When it is claimed or appears to the court that the contract or any clause thereof may be unconscionable the parties shall be afforded a reasonable opportunity to present evidence as to its commercial setting, purpose and effect to aid the court in making the determination.

§ 2—303. Allocations or Division of Risks.

Where this Article allocates a risk or a burden as between the parties "unless otherwise agreed", the agreement may not only shift the allocation but may also divide the risk or burden.

§ 2—304. Price Payable in Money, Goods, Realty, or Otherwise.

(1) The price can be made payable in money or otherwise. If it is payable in whole or in part in goods each party is a seller of the goods which he is to transfer.

(2) Even though all or part of the price is payable in an interest in realty the transfer of the goods and the seller's obligations with reference to them are subject to this Article, but not the transfer of the interest in realty or the transferor's obligations in connection therewith.

§ 2—305. Open Price Term.

(1) The parties if they so intend can conclude a contract for sale even though the price is not settled. In such a case the price is a reasonable price at the time for delivery if

    (a) nothing is said as to price; or

    (b) the price is left to be agreed by the parties and they fail to agree; or

    (c) the price is to be fixed in terms of some agreed market or other standard as set or recorded by a third person or agency and it is not so set or recorded.

(2) A price to be fixed by the seller or by the buyer means a price for him to fix in good faith.

(3) When a price left to be fixed otherwise than by agreement of the parties fails to be fixed through fault of one party the other may at his option treat the contract as cancelled or himself fix a reasonable price.

(4) Where, however, the parties intend not to be bound unless the price be fixed or agreed and it is not fixed or agreed there is no contract. In such a case the buyer must return any goods already received or if unable so to do must pay their reasonable value at the time of delivery and the seller must return any portion of the price paid on account.

§ 2—306. Output, Requirements and Exclusive Dealings.

(1) A term which measures the quantity by the output of the seller or the requirements of the buyer means such actual output or requirements as may occur in good faith, except that no quantity unreasonably disproportionate to any stated estimate or in the absence of a stated estimate to any normal or otherwise comparable prior output or requirements may be tendered or demanded.

(2) A lawful agreement by either the seller or the buyer for exclusive dealing in the kind of goods concerned imposes unless otherwise agreed an obligation by the seller to use best efforts to supply the goods and by the buyer to use best efforts to promote their sale.

§ 2—307. Delivery in Single Lot or Several Lots.

Unless otherwise agreed all goods called for by a contract for sale must be tendered in a single delivery and payment is due only on such tender but where the circumstances give either party the right to make or demand delivery in lots the price if it can be apportioned may be demanded for each lot.

§ 2—308. Absence of Specified Place for Delivery.

Unless otherwise agreed

    (a) the place for delivery of goods is the seller's place of business or if he has none his residence; but

    (b) in a contract for sale of identified goods which to the knowledge of the parties at the time of contracting are in some other place, that place is the place for their delivery; and

    (c) documents of title may be delivered through customary banking channels.

§ 2—309. Absence of Specific Time Provisions; Notice of Termination.

(1) The time for shipment or delivery or any other action under a contract if not provided in this Article or agreed upon shall be a reasonable time.

(2) Where the contract provides for successive performances but is indefinite in duration it is valid for a reasonable time but unless otherwise agreed may be terminated at any time by either party.

(3) Termination of a contract by one party except on the happening of an agreed event requires that reasonable notification be received by the other party and an agreement dispensing with notification is invalid if its operation would be unconscionable.

§ 2—310. Open Time for Payment or Running of Credit; Authority to Ship Under Reservation.

Unless otherwise agreed

(a) payment is due at the time and place at which the buyer is to receive the goods even though the place of shipment is the place of delivery; and

(b) if the seller is authorized to send the goods he may ship them under reservation, and may tender the documents of title, but the buyer may inspect the goods after their arrival before payment is due unless such inspection is inconsistent with the terms of the contract (Section 2—513); and

(c) if delivery is authorized and made by way of documents of title otherwise than by subsection (b) then payment is due at the time and place at which the buyer is to receive the documents regardless of where the goods are to be received; and

(d) where the seller is required or authorized to ship the goods on credit the credit period runs from the time of shipment but post-dating the invoice or delaying its dispatch will correspondingly delay the starting of the credit period.

§ 2—311. Options and Cooperation Respecting Performance.

(1) An agreement for sale which is otherwise sufficiently definite (subsection (3) of Section 2—204) to be a contract is not made invalid by the fact that it leaves particulars of performance to be specified by one of the parties. Any such specification must be made in good faith and within limits set by commercial reasonableness.

(2) Unless otherwise agreed specifications relating to assortment of the goods are at the buyer's option and except as otherwise provided in subsections (1)(c) and (3) of Section 2—319 specifications or arrangements relating to shipment are at the seller's option.

(3) Where such specification would materially affect the other party's performance but is not seasonably made or where one party's cooperation is necessary to the agreed performance of the other but is not seasonably forthcoming, the other party in addition to all other remedies

(a) is excused for any resulting delay in his own performance; and

(b) may also either proceed to perform in any reasonable manner or after the time for a material part of his

own performance treat the failure to specify or to cooperate as a breach by failure to deliver or accept the goods.

§ 2—312. Warranty of Title and Against Infringement; Buyer's Obligation Against Infringement.

(1) Subject to subsection (2) there is in a contract for sale a warranty by the seller that

(a) the title conveyed shall be good, and its transfer rightful; and

(b) the goods shall be delivered free from any security interest or other lien or encumbrance of which the buyer at the time of contracting has no knowledge.

(2) A warranty under subsection (1) will be excluded or modified only by specific language or by circumstances which give the buyer reason to know that the person selling does not claim title in himself or that he is purporting to sell only such right or title as he or a third person may have.

(3) Unless otherwise agreed a seller who is a merchant regularly dealing in goods of the kind warrants that the goods shall be delivered free of the rightful claim of any third person by way of infringement or the like but a buyer who furnishes specifications to the seller must hold the seller harmless against any such claim which arises out of compliance with the specifications.

§ 2—313. Express Warranties by Affirmation, Promise, Description, Sample.

(1) Express warranties by the seller are created as follows:

(a) Any affirmation of fact or promise made by the seller to the buyer which relates to the goods and becomes part of the basis of the bargain creates an express warranty that the goods shall conform to the affirmation or promise.

(b) Any description of the goods which is made part of the basis of the bargain creates an express warranty that the goods shall conform to the description.

(c) Any sample or model which is made part of the basis of the bargain creates an express warranty that the whole of the goods shall conform to the sample or model.

(2) It is not necessary to the creation of an express warranty that the seller use formal words such as "warrant" or "guarantee" or that he have a specific intention to make a warranty, but an affirmation merely of the value of the goods or a statement purporting to be merely the seller's opinion or commendation of the goods does not create a warranty.

§ 2—314. Implied Warranty: Merchantability; Usage of Trade.

(1) Unless excluded or modified (Section 2—316), a warranty that the goods shall be merchantable is implied in a contract for their sale if the seller is a merchant with respect to goods of that kind. Under this section the serving

for value of food or drink to be consumed either on the premises or elsewhere is a sale.

(2) Goods to be merchantable must be at least such as

(a) pass without objection in the trade under the contract description; and

(b) in the case of fungible goods, are of fair average quality within the description; and

(c) are fit for the ordinary purposes for which such goods are used; and

(d) run, within the variations permitted by the agreement, of even kind, quality and quantity within each unit and among all units involved; and

(e) are adequately contained, packaged, and labeled as the agreement may require; and

(f) conform to the promises or affirmations of fact made on the container or label if any.

(3) Unless excluded or modified (Section 2—316) other implied warranties may arise from course of dealing or usage of trade.

§ 2—315. Implied Warranty: Fitness for Particular Purpose.

Where the seller at the time of contracting has reason to know any particular purpose for which the goods are required and that the buyer is relying on the seller's skill or judgment to select or furnish suitable goods, there is unless excluded or modified under the next section an implied warranty that the goods shall be fit for such purpose.

§ 2—316. Exclusion or Modification of Warranties.

(1) Words or conduct relevant to the creation of an express warranty and words or conduct tending to negate or limit warranty shall be construed wherever reasonable as consistent with each other; but subject to the provisions of this Article on parol or extrinsic evidence (Section 2—202) negation or limitation is inoperative to the extent that such construction is unreasonable.

(2) Subject to subsection (3), to exclude or modify the implied warranty of merchantability or any part of it the language must mention merchantability and in case of a writing must be conspicuous, and to exclude or modify any implied warranty of fitness the exclusion must be by a writing and conspicuous. Language to exclude all implied warranties of fitness is sufficient if it states, for example, that "There are no warranties which extend beyond the description on the face hereof."

(3) Notwithstanding subsection (2)

(a) unless the circumstances indicate otherwise, all implied warranties are excluded by expressions like "as is", "with all faults" or other language which in common understanding calls the buyer's attention to the exclusion of warranties and makes plain that there is no implied warranty; and

(b) when the buyer before entering into the contract has examined the goods or the sample or model as fully as he desired or has refused to examine the goods there is no implied warranty with regard to defects which an examination ought in the circumstances to have revealed to him; and

(c) an implied warranty can also be excluded or modified by course of dealing or course of performance or usage of trade.

(4) Remedies for breach of warranty can be limited in accordance with the provisions of this Article on liquidation or limitation of damages and on contractual modification of remedy (Sections 2—718 and 2—719).

§ 2—317. Cumulation and Conflict of Warranties Express or Implied.

Warranties whether express or implied shall be construed as consistent with each other and as cumulative, but if such construction is unreasonable the intention of the parties shall determine which warranty is dominant. In ascertaining that intention the following rules apply:

(a) Exact or technical specifications displace an inconsistent sample or model or general language of description.

(b) A sample from an existing bulk displaces inconsistent general language of description.

(c) Express warranties displace inconsistent implied warranties other than an implied warranty of fitness for a particular purpose.

§ 2—318. Third Party Beneficiaries of Warranties Express or Implied.

Note: If this Act is introduced in the Congress of the United States this section should be omitted. (States to select one alternative.)

Alternative A

A seller's warranty whether express or implied extends to any natural person who is in the family or household of his buyer or who is a guest in his home if it is reasonable to expect that such person may use, consume or be affected by the goods and who is injured in person by breach of the warranty. A seller may not exclude or limit the operation of this section.

Alternative B

A seller's warranty whether express or implied extends to any natural person who may reasonably be expected to use, consume or be affected by the goods and who is injured in person by breach of the warranty. A seller may not exclude or limit the operation of this section.

Alternative C

A seller's warranty whether express or implied extends to any person who may reasonably be expected to use, consume or be affected by the goods and who is injured by breach of the warranty. A seller may not exclude or limit the operation of this section with respect to injury to the person of an individual to whom the warranty extends. As amended 1966.

§ 2—319. F.O.B. and F.A.S. Terms.

(1) Unless otherwise agreed the term F.O.B. (which means "free on board") at a named place, even though used only in connection with the stated price, is a delivery term under which

(a) when the term is F.O.B. the place of shipment, the seller must at that place ship the goods in the manner provided in this Article (Section 2—504) and bear the expense and risk of putting them into the possession of the carrier; or

(b) when the term is F.O.B. the place of destination, the seller must at his own expense and risk transport the goods to that place and there tender delivery of them in the manner provided in this Article (Section 2—503);

(c) when under either (a) or (b) the term is also F.O.B. vessel, car or other vehicle, the seller must in addition at his own expense and risk load the goods on board. If the term is F.O.B. vessel the buyer must name the vessel and in an appropriate case the seller must comply with the provisions of this Article on the form of bill of lading (Section 2—323).

(2) Unless otherwise agreed the term F.A.S. vessel (which means "free alongside") at a named port, even though used only in connection with the stated price, is a delivery term under which the seller must

(a) at his own expense and risk deliver the goods alongside the vessel in the manner usual in that port or on a dock designated and provided by the buyer; and

(b) obtain and tender a receipt for the goods in exchange for which the carrier is under a duty to issue a bill of lading.

(3) Unless otherwise agreed in any case falling within subsection (1)(a) or (c) or subsection (2) the buyer must seasonably give any needed instructions for making delivery, including when the term is F.A.S. or F.O.B. the loading berth of the vessel and in an appropriate case its name and sailing date. The seller may treat the failure of needed instructions as a failure of cooperation under this Article (Section 2—311). He may also at his option move the goods in any reasonable manner preparatory to delivery or shipment.

(4) Under the term F.O.B. vessel or F.A.S. unless otherwise agreed the buyer must make payment against tender of the required documents and the seller may not tender nor the buyer demand delivery of the goods in substitution for the documents.

§ 2—320. C.I.F. and C. & F. Terms.

(1) The term C.I.F. means that the price includes in a lump sum the cost of the goods and the insurance and freight to the named destination. The term C. & F. or C.F.

means that the price so includes cost and freight to the named destination.

(2) Unless otherwise agreed and even though used only in connection with the stated price and destination, the term C.I.F. destination or its equivalent requires the seller at his own expense and risk to

(a) put the goods into the possession of a carrier at the port for shipment and obtain a negotiable bill or bills of lading covering the entire transportation to the named destination; and

(b) load the goods and obtain a receipt from the carrier (which may be contained in the bill of lading) showing that the freight has been paid or provided for; and

(c) obtain a policy or certificate of insurance, including any war risk insurance, of a kind and on terms then current at the port of shipment in the usual amount, in the currency of the contract, shown to cover the same goods covered by the bill of lading and providing for payment of loss to the order of the buyer or for the account of whom it may concern; but the seller may add to the price the amount of the premium for any such war risk insurance; and

(d) prepare an invoice of the goods and procure any other documents required to effect shipment or to comply with the contract; and

(e) forward and tender with commercial promptness all the documents in due form and with any indorsement necessary to perfect the buyer's rights.

(3) Unless otherwise agreed the term C. & F. or its equivalent has the same effect and imposes upon the seller the same obligations and risks as a C.I.F. term except the obligation as to insurance.

(4) Under the term C.I.F. or C. & F. unless otherwise agreed the buyer must make payment against tender of the required documents and the seller may not tender nor the buyer demand delivery of the goods in substitution for the documents.

§ 2—321. C.I.F. or C. & F.: "Net Landed Weights"; "Payment on Arrival"; Warranty of Condition on Arrival.

Under a contract containing a term C.I.F. or C. & F.

(1) Where the price is based on or is to be adjusted according to "net landed weights", "delivered weights", "out turn" quantity or quality or the like, unless otherwise agreed the seller must reasonably estimate the price. The payment due on tender of the documents called for by the contract is the amount so estimated, but after final adjustment of the price a settlement must be made with commercial promptness.

(2) An agreement described in subsection (1) or any warranty of quality or condition of the goods on arrival places upon the seller the risk of ordinary deterioration, shrinkage

and the like in transportation but has no effect on the place or time of identification to the contract for sale or delivery or on the passing of the risk of loss.

(3) Unless otherwise agreed where the contract provides for payment on or after arrival of the goods the seller must before payment allow such preliminary inspection as is feasible; but if the goods are lost delivery of the documents and payment are due when the goods should have arrived.

§ 2—322. Delivery "Ex-Ship".

(1) Unless otherwise agreed a term for delivery of goods "ex-ship" (which means from the carrying vessel) or in equivalent language is not restricted to a particular ship and requires delivery from a ship which has reached a place at the named port of destination where goods of the kind are usually discharged.

(2) Under such a term unless otherwise agreed

(a) the seller must discharge all liens arising out of the carriage and furnish the buyer with a direction which puts the carrier under a duty to deliver the goods; and

(b) the risk of loss does not pass to the buyer until the goods leave the ship's tackle or are otherwise properly unloaded.

§ 2—323. Form of Bill of Lading Required in Overseas Shipment; "Overseas".

(1) Where the contract contemplates overseas shipment and contains a term C.I.F. or C. & F. or F.O.B. vessel, the seller unless otherwise agreed must obtain a negotiable bill of lading stating that the goods have been loaded on board or, in the case of a term C.I.F. or C. & F., received for shipment.

(2) Where in a case within subsection (1) a bill of lading has been issued in a set of parts, unless otherwise agreed if the documents are not to be sent from abroad the buyer may demand tender of the full set; otherwise only one part of the bill of lading need be tendered. Even if the agreement expressly requires a full set

(a) due tender of a single part is acceptable within the provisions of this Article on cure of improper delivery (subsection (1) of Section 2—508); and

(b) even though the full set is demanded, if the documents are sent from abroad the person tendering an incomplete set may nevertheless require payment upon furnishing an indemnity which the buyer in good faith deems adequate.

(3) A shipment by water or by air or a contract contemplating such shipment is "overseas" insofar as by usage of trade or agreement it is subject to the commercial, financing or shipping practices characteristic of international deep water commerce.

§ 2—324. "No Arrival, No Sale" Term.

Under a term "no arrival, no sale" or terms of like meaning, unless otherwise agreed,

(a) the seller must properly ship conforming goods and if they arrive by any means he must tender them on arrival but he assumes no obligation that the goods will arrive unless he has caused the non-arrival; and

(b) where without fault of the seller the goods are in part lost or have so deteriorated as no longer to conform to the contract or arrive after the contract time, the buyer may proceed as if there had been casualty to identified goods (Section 2—613).

§ 2—325. "Letter of Credit" Term; "Confirmed Credit".

(1) Failure of the buyer seasonably to furnish an agreed letter of credit is a breach of the contract for sale.

(2) The delivery to seller of a proper letter of credit suspends the buyer's obligation to pay. If the letter of credit is dishonored, the seller may on seasonable notification to the buyer require payment directly from him.

(3) Unless otherwise agreed the term "letter of credit" or "banker's credit" in a contract for sale means an irrevocable credit issued by a financing agency of good repute and, where the shipment is overseas, of good international repute. The term "confirmed credit" means that the credit must also carry the direct obligation of such an agency which does business in the seller's financial market.

§ 2—326. Sale on Approval and Sale or Return; Consignment Sales and Rights of Creditors.

(1) Unless otherwise agreed, if delivered goods may be returned by the buyer even though they conform to the contract, the transaction is

(a) a "sale on approval" if the goods are delivered primarily for use, and

(b) a "sale or return" if the goods are delivered primarily for resale.

(2) Except as provided in subsection (3), goods held on approval are not subject to the claims of the buyer's creditors until acceptance; goods held on sale or return are subject to such claims while in the buyer's possession.

(3) Where goods are delivered to a person for sale and such person maintains a place of business at which he deals in goods of the kind involved, under a name other than the name of the person making delivery, then with respect to claims of creditors of the person conducting the business the goods are deemed to be on sale or return. The provisions of this subsection are applicable even though an agreement purports to reserve title to the person making delivery until payment or resale or uses such words as "on consignment" or "on memorandum". However, this subsection is not applicable if the person making delivery

(a) complies with an applicable law providing for a consignor's interest or the like to be evidenced by a sign, or

(b) establishes that the person conducting the business is generally known by his creditors to be substantially engaged in selling the goods of others, or

(c) complies with the filing provisions of the Article on Secured Transactions (Article 9).

(4) Any "or return" term of a contract for sale is to be treated as a separate contract for sale within the statute of frauds section of this Article (Section 2—201) and as contradicting the sale aspect of the contract within the provisions of this Article on parol or extrinsic evidence (Section 2—202).

§ 2—327. Special Incidents of Sale on Approval and Sale or Return.

(1) Under a sale on approval unless otherwise agreed

(a) although the goods are identified to the contract the risk of loss and the title do not pass to the buyer until acceptance; and

(b) use of the goods consistent with the purpose of trial is not acceptance but failure seasonably to notify the seller of election to return the goods is acceptance, and if the goods conform to the contract acceptance of any part is acceptance of the whole; and

(c) after due notification of election to return, the return is at the seller's risk and expense but a merchant buyer must follow any reasonable instructions.

(2) Under a sale or return unless otherwise agreed

(a) the option to return extends to the whole or any commercial unit of the goods while in substantially their original condition, but must be exercised seasonably; and

(b) the return is at the buyer's risk and expense.

§ 2—328. Sale by Auction.

(1) In a sale by auction if goods are put up in lots each lot is the subject of a separate sale.

(2) A sale by auction is complete when the auctioneer so announces by the fall of the hammer or in other customary manner. Where a bid is made while the hammer is falling in acceptance of a prior bid the auctioneer may in his discretion reopen the bidding or declare the goods sold under the bid on which the hammer was falling.

(3) Such a sale is with reserve unless the goods are in explicit terms put up without reserve. In an auction with reserve the auctioneer may withdraw the goods at any time until he announces completion of the sale. In an auction without reserve, after the auctioneer calls for bids on an article or lot, that article or lot cannot be withdrawn unless no bid is made within a reasonable time. In either case a bidder may retract his bid until the auctioneer's announcement of completion of the sale, but a bidder's retraction does not revive any previous bid.

(4) If the auctioneer knowingly receives a bid on the seller's behalf or the seller makes or procures such as bid, and notice has not been given that liberty for such bidding is reserved, the buyer may at his option avoid the sale or take the goods at the price of the last good faith bid prior to the completion of the sale. This subsection shall not apply to any bid at a forced sale.

Part 4 Title, Creditors and Good Faith Purchasers

§ 2—401. Passing of Title; Reservation for Security; Limited Application of This Section.

Each provision of this Article with regard to the rights, obligations and remedies of the seller, the buyer, purchasers or other third parties applies irrespective of title to the goods except where the provision refers to such title. Insofar as situations are not covered by the other provisions of this Article and matters concerning title became material the following rules apply:

(1) Title to goods cannot pass under a contract for sale prior to their identification to the contract (Section 2—501), and unless otherwise explicitly agreed the buyer acquires by their identification a special property as limited by this Act. Any retention or reservation by the seller of the title (property) in goods shipped or delivered to the buyer is limited in effect to a reservation of a security interest. Subject to these provisions and to the provisions of the Article on Secured Transactions (Article 9), title to goods passes from the seller to the buyer in any manner and on any conditions explicitly agreed on by the parties.

(2) Unless otherwise explicitly agreed title passes to the buyer at the time and place at which the seller completes his performance with reference to the physical delivery of the goods, despite any reservation of a security interest and even though a document of title is to be delivered at a different time or place; and in particular and despite any reservation of a security interest by the bill of lading

(a) if the contract requires or authorizes the seller to send the goods to the buyer but does not require him to deliver them at destination, title passes to the buyer at the time and place of shipment; but

(b) if the contract requires delivery at destination, title passes on tender there.

(3) Unless otherwise explicitly agreed where delivery is to be made without moving the goods,

(a) if the seller is to deliver a document of title, title passes at the time when and the place where he delivers such documents; or

(b) if the goods are at the time of contracting already identified and no documents are to be delivered, title passes at the time and place of contracting.

(4) A rejection or other refusal by the buyer to receive or retain the goods, whether or not justified, or a justified revocation of acceptance revests title to the goods in the seller. Such revesting occurs by operation of law and is not a "sale".

§ 2—402. Rights of Seller's Creditors Against Sold Goods.

(1) Except as provided in subsections (2) and (3), rights of unsecured creditors of the seller with respect to goods which have been identified to a contract for sale are subject to the buyer's rights to recover the goods under this Article (Sections 2—502 and 2—716).

(2) A creditor of the seller may treat a sale or an identification of goods to a contract for sale as void if as against him a retention of possession by the seller is fraudulent under any rule of law of the state where the goods are situated, except that retention of possession in good faith and current course of trade by a merchant-seller for a commercially reasonable time after a sale or identification is not fraudulent.

(3) Nothing in this Article shall be deemed to impair the rights of creditors of the seller

(a) under the provisions of the Article on Secured Transactions (Article 9); or

(b) where identification to the contract or delivery is made not in current course of trade but in satisfaction of or as security for a pre-existing claim for money, security or the like and is made under circumstances which under any rule of law of the state where the goods are situated would apart from this Article constitute the transaction a fraudulent transfer or voidable preference.

§ 2—403. Power to Transfer; Good Faith Purchase of Goods; "Entrusting".

(1) A purchaser of goods acquires all title which his transferor had or had power to transfer except that a purchaser of a limited interest acquires rights only to the extent of the interest purchased. A person with voidable title has power to transfer a good title to a good faith purchaser for value. When goods have been delivered under a transaction of purchase the purchaser has such power even though

(a) the transferor was deceived as to the identity of the purchaser, or

(b) the delivery was in exchange for a check which is later dishonored, or

(c) it was agreed that the transaction was to be a "cash sale", or

(d) the delivery was procured through fraud punishable as larcenous under the criminal law.

(2) Any entrusting of possession of goods to a merchant who deals in goods of that kind gives him power to transfer all rights of the entruster to a buyer in ordinary course of business.

(3) "Entrusting" includes any delivery and any acquiescence in retention of possession regardless of any condition expressed between the parties to the delivery or acquiescence and regardless of whether the procurement of the entrusting or the possessor's disposition of the goods have been such as to be larcenous under the criminal law.

(4) The rights of other purchasers of goods and of lien creditors are governed by the Articles on Secured Transactions (Article 9), Bulk Transfers (Article 6) and Documents of Title (Article 7).

Part 5 Performance

§ 2—501. Insurable Interest in Goods; Manner of Identification of Goods.

(1) The buyer obtains a special property and an insurable interest in goods by identification of existing goods as goods to which the contract refers even though the goods so identified are non-conforming and he has an option to return or reject them. Such identification can be made at any time and in any manner explicitly agreed to by the parties. In the absence of explicit agreement identification occurs

(a) when the contract is made if it is for the sale of goods already existing and identified;

(b) if the contract is for the sale of future goods other than those described in paragraph (c), when goods are shipped, marked or otherwise designated by the seller as goods to which the contract refers;

(c) when the crops are planted or otherwise become growing crops or the young are conceived if the contract is for the sale of unborn young to be born within twelve months after contracting or for the sale of crops to be harvested within twelve months or the next normal harvest season after contracting whichever is longer.

(2) The seller retains an insurable interest in goods so long as title to or any security interest in the goods remains in him and where the identification is by the seller alone he may until default or insolvency or notification to the buyer that the identification is final substitute other goods for those identified.

(3) Nothing in this section impairs any insurable interest recognized under any other statute or rule of law.

§ 2—502. Buyer's Right to Goods on Seller's Insolvency.

(1) Subject to subsection (2) and even though the goods have not been shipped a buyer who has paid a part or all of the price of goods in which he has a special property under the provisions of the immediately preceding section may on making and keeping good a tender of any unpaid portion of their price recover them from the seller if the seller becomes insolvent within ten days after receipt of the first installment on their price.

(2) If the identification creating his special property has been made by the buyer he acquires the right to recover the goods only if they conform to the contract for sale.

§ 2—503. Manner of Seller's Tender of Delivery.

(1) Tender of delivery requires that the seller put and hold conforming goods at the buyer's disposition and give the buyer any notification reasonably necessary to enable him to take delivery. The manner, time and place for tender are determined by the agreement and this Article, and in particular

(a) tender must be at a reasonable hour, and if it is of goods they must be kept available for the period reasonably necessary to enable the buyer to take possession; but

(b) unless otherwise agreed the buyer must furnish facilities reasonably suited to the receipt of the goods.

(2) Where the case is within the next section respecting shipment tender requires that the seller comply with its provisions.

(3) Where the seller is required to deliver at a particular destination tender requires that he comply with subsection (1) and also in any appropriate case tender documents as described in subsections (4) and (5) of this section.

(4) Where goods are in the possession of a bailee and are to be delivered without being moved

(a) tender requires that the seller either tender a negotiable document of title covering such goods or procure acknowledgment by the bailee of the buyer's right to possession of the goods; but

(b) tender to the buyer of a non-negotiable document of title or of a written direction to the bailee to deliver is sufficient tender unless the buyer seasonably objects, and receipt by the bailee of notification of the buyer's rights fixes those rights as against the bailee and all third persons; but risk of loss of the goods and of any failure by the bailee to honor the non-negotiable document of title or to obey the direction remains on the seller until the buyer has had a reasonable time to pre-sent the document or direction, and a refusal by the bailee to honor the document or to obey the direction defeats the tender.

(5) Where the contract requires the seller to deliver documents

(a) he must tender all such documents in correct form, except as provided in this Article with respect to bills of lading in a set (subsection (2) of Section 2—323); and

(b) tender through customary banking channels is sufficient and dishonor of a draft accompanying the documents constitutes non-acceptance or rejection.

§ 2—504. Shipment by Seller.

Where the seller is required or authorized to send the goods to the buyer and the contract does not require him to deliver them at a particular destination, then unless otherwise agreed he must

(a) put the goods in the possession of such a carrier and make such a contract for their transportation as may be reasonable having regard to the nature of the goods and other circumstances of the case; and

(b) obtain and promptly deliver or tender in due form any document necessary to enable the buyer to obtain possession of the goods or otherwise required by the agreement or by usage of trade; and

(c) promptly notify the buyer of the shipment.

Failure to notify the buyer under paragraph (c) or to make a proper contract under paragraph (a) is a ground for rejection only if material delay or loss ensues.

§ 2—505. Seller's Shipment under Reservation.

(1) Where the seller has identified goods to the contract by or before shipment:

(a) his procurement of a negotiable bill of lading to his own order or otherwise reserves in him a security interest in the goods. His procurement of the bill to the order of a financing agency or of the buyer indicates in addition only the seller's expectation of transferring that interest to the person named.

(b) a non-negotiable bill of lading to himself or his nominee reserves possession of the goods as security but except in a case of conditional delivery (subsection (2) of Section 2—507) a non-negotiable bill of lading naming the buyer as consignee reserves no security interest even though the seller retains possession of the bill of lading.

(2) When shipment by the seller with reservation of a security interest is in violation of the contract for sale it constitutes an improper contract for transportation within the preceding section but impairs neither the rights given to the buyer by shipment and identification of the goods to the contract nor the seller's powers as a holder of a negotiable document.

§ 2—506. Rights of Financing Agency.

(1) A financing agency by paying or purchasing for value a draft which relates to a shipment of goods acquires to the extent of the payment or purchase and in addition to its own rights under the draft and any document of title securing it any rights of the shipper in the goods including the right to stop delivery and the shipper's right to have the draft honored by the buyer.

(2) The right to reimbursement of a financing agency which has in good faith honored or purchased the draft under commitment to or authority from the buyer is not impaired by subsequent discovery of defects with reference to any relevant document which was apparently regular on its face.

§ 2—507. Effect of Seller's Tender; Delivery on Condition.

(1) Tender of delivery is a condition to the buyer's duty to accept the goods and, unless otherwise agreed, to his duty to pay for them. Tender entitles the seller to acceptance of the goods and to payment according to the contract.

(2) Where payment is due and demanded on the delivery to the buyer of goods or documents of title, his right as against the seller to retain or dispose of them is conditional upon his making the payment due.

§ 2—508. Cure by Seller of Improper Tender or Delivery; Replacement.

(1) Where any tender or delivery by the seller is rejected because non-conforming and the time for performance

has not yet expired, the seller may seasonably notify the buyer of his intention to cure and may then within the contract time make a conforming delivery.

(2) Where the buyer rejects a non-conforming tender which the seller had reasonable grounds to believe would be acceptable with or without money allowance the seller may if he seasonably notifies the buyer have a further reasonable time to substitute a conforming tender.

§ 2—509. Risk of Loss in the Absence of Breach.

(1) Where the contract requires or authorizes the seller to ship the goods by carrier

(a) if it does not require him to deliver them at a particular destination, the risk of loss passes to the buyer when the goods are duly delivered to the carrier even though the shipment is under reservation (Section 2—505); but

(b) if it does require him to deliver them at a particular destination and the goods are there duly tendered while in the possession of the carrier, the risk of loss passes to the buyer when the goods are there duly so tendered as to enable the buyer to take delivery.

(2) Where the goods are held by a bailee to be delivered without being moved, the risk of loss passes to the buyer

(a) on his receipt of a negotiable document of title covering the goods; or

(b) on acknowledgment by the bailee of the buyer's right to possession of the goods; or

(c) after his receipt of a non-negotiable document of title or other written direction to deliver, as provided in subsection (4)(b) of Section 2—503.

(3) In any case not within subsection (1) or (2), the risk of loss passes to the buyer on his receipt of the goods if the seller is a merchant; otherwise the risk passes to the buyer on tender of delivery.

(4) The provisions of this section are subject to contrary agreement of the parties and to the provisions of this Article on sale on approval (Section 2—327) and on effect of breach on risk of loss (Section 2—510).

§ 2—510. Effect of Breach on Risk of Loss.

(1) Where a tender or delivery of goods so fails to conform to the contract as to give a right of rejection the risk of their loss remains on the seller until cure or acceptance.

(2) Where the buyer rightfully revokes acceptance he may to the extent of any deficiency in his effective insurance coverage treat the risk of loss as having rested on the seller from the beginning.

(3) Where the buyer as to conforming goods already identified to the contract for sale repudiates or is otherwise in breach before risk of their loss has passed to him, the seller may to the extent of any deficiency in his effective insurance coverage treat the risk of loss as resting on the buyer for a commercially reasonable time.

§ 2—511. Tender of Payment by Buyer; Payment by Check.

(1) Unless otherwise agreed tender of payment is a condition to the seller's duty to tender and complete any delivery.

(2) Tender of payment is sufficient when made by any means or in any manner current in the ordinary course of business unless the seller demands payment in legal tender and gives any extension of time reasonably necessary to procure it.

(3) Subject to the provisions of this Act on the effect of an instrument on an obligation (Section 3—310), payment by check is conditional and is defeated as between the parties by dishonor of the check on due presentment.

§ 2—512. Payment by Buyer Before Inspection.

(1) Where the contract requires payment before inspection non-conformity of the goods does not excuse the buyer from so making payment unless

(a) the non-conformity appears without inspection; or

(b) despite tender of the required documents the circumstances would justify injunction against honor under the provisions of this Act (Section 5—114).

(2) Payment pursuant to subsection (1) does not constitute an acceptance of goods or impair the buyer's right to inspect or any of his remedies.

§ 2—513. Buyer's Right to Inspection of Goods.

(1) Unless otherwise agreed and subject to subsection (3), where goods are tendered or delivered or identified to the contract for sale, the buyer has a right before payment or acceptance to inspect them at any reasonable place and time and in any reasonable manner. When the seller is required or authorized to send the goods to the buyer, the inspection may be after their arrival.

(2) Expenses of inspection must be borne by the buyer but may be recovered from the seller if the goods do not conform and are rejected.

(3) Unless otherwise agreed and subject to the provisions of this Article on C.I.F. contracts (subsection (3) of Section 2—321), the buyer is not entitled to inspect the goods before payment of the price when the contract provides

(a) for delivery "C.O.D." or on other like terms; or

(b) for payment against documents of title, except where such payment is due only after the goods are to become available for inspection.

(4) A place or method of inspection fixed by the parties is presumed to be exclusive but unless otherwise expressly agreed it does not postpone identification or shift the place for delivery or for passing the risk of loss. If compliance becomes impossible, inspection shall be as provided in this section unless the place or method fixed was clearly intended as an indispensable condition failure of which avoids the contract.

§ 2—514. **When Documents Deliverable on Acceptance; When on Payment.**

Unless otherwise agreed documents against which a draft is drawn are to be delivered to the drawee on acceptance of the draft if it is payable more than three days after presentment; otherwise, only on payment.

§ 2—515. **Preserving Evidence of Goods in Dispute.**

In furtherance of the adjustment of any claim or dispute

(a) either party on reasonable notification to the other and for the purpose of ascertaining the facts and preserving evidence has the right to inspect, test and sample the goods including such of them as may be in the possession or control of the other; and

(b) the parties may agree to a third party inspection or survey to determine the conformity or condition of the goods and may agree that the findings shall be binding upon them in any subsequent litigation or adjustment.

Part 6 Breach, Repudiation and Excuse

§ 2—601. **Buyer's Rights on Improper Delivery.**

Subject to the provisions of this Article on breach in installment contracts (Section 2—612) and unless otherwise agreed under the sections on contractual limitations of remedy (Sections 2—718 and 2—719), if the goods or the tender of delivery fail in any respect to conform to the contract, the buyer may

(a) reject the whole; or

(b) accept the whole; or

(c) accept any commercial unit or units and reject the rest.

§ 2—602. **Manner and Effect of Rightful Rejection.**

(1) Rejection of goods must be within a reasonable time after their delivery or tender. It is ineffective unless the buyer seasonably notifies the seller.

(2) Subject to the provisions of the two following sections on rejected goods (Sections 2—603 and 2—604),

(a) after rejection any exercise of ownership by the buyer with respect to any commercial unit is wrongful as against the seller; and

(b) if the buyer has before rejection taken physical possession of goods in which he does not have a security interest under the provisions of this Article (subsection (3) of Section 2—711), he is under a duty after rejection to hold them with reasonable care at the seller's disposition for a time sufficient to permit the seller to remove them; but

(c) the buyer has no further obligations with regard to goods rightfully rejected.

(3) The seller's rights with respect to goods wrongfully rejected are governed by the provisions of this Article on Seller's remedies in general (Section 2—703).

§ 2—603. **Merchant Buyer's Duties as to Rightfully Rejected Goods.**

(1) Subject to any security interest in the buyer (subsection (3) of Section 2—711), when the seller has no agent or place of business at the market of rejection a merchant buyer is under a duty after rejection of goods in his possession or control to follow any reasonable instructions received from the seller with respect to the goods and in the absence of such instructions to make reasonable efforts to sell them for the seller's account if they are perishable or threaten to decline in value speedily. Instructions are not reasonable if on demand indemnity for expenses is not forthcoming.

(2) When the buyer sells goods under subsection (1), he is entitled to reimbursement from the seller or out of the proceeds for reasonable expenses of caring for and selling them, and if the expenses include no selling commission then to such commission as is usual in the trade or if there is none to a reasonable sum not exceeding ten per cent on the gross proceeds.

(3) In complying with this section the buyer is held only to good faith and good faith conduct hereunder is neither acceptance nor conversion nor the basis of an action for damages.

§ 2—604. **Buyer's Options as to Salvage of Rightfully Rejected Goods.**

Subject to the provisions of the immediately preceding section on perishables if the seller gives no instructions within a reasonable time after notification of rejection the buyer may store the rejected goods for the seller's account or reship them to him or resell them for the seller's account with reimbursement as provided in the preceding section. Such action is not acceptance or conversion.

§ 2—605. **Waiver of Buyer's Objections by Failure to Particularize.**

(1) The buyer's failure to state in connection with rejection a particular defect which is ascertainable by reasonable inspection precludes him from relying on the unstated defect to justify rejection or to establish breach

(a) where the seller could have cured it if stated seasonably; or

(b) between merchants when the seller has after rejection made a request in writing for a full and final written statement of all defects on which the buyer proposes to rely.

(2) Payment against documents made without reservation of rights precludes recovery of the payment for defects apparent on the face of the documents.

§ 2—606. **What Constitutes Acceptance of Goods.**

(1) Acceptance of goods occurs when the buyer

(a) after a reasonable opportunity to inspect the goods signifies to the seller that the goods are conforming or that he will take or retain them in spite of their non-conformity; or

(b) fails to make an effective rejection (subsection (1) of Section 2—602), but such acceptance does not occur until the buyer has had a reasonable opportunity to inspect them; or

(c) does any act inconsistent with the seller's ownership; but if such act is wrongful as against the seller it is an acceptance only if ratified by him.

(2) Acceptance of a part of any commercial unit is acceptance of that entire unit.

§ 2—607. Effect of Acceptance; Notice of Breach; Burden of Establishing Breach After Acceptance; Notice of Claim or Litigation to Person Answerable Over.

(1) The buyer must pay at the contract rate for any goods accepted.

(2) Acceptance of goods by the buyer precludes rejection of the goods accepted and if made with knowledge of a non-conformity cannot be revoked because of it unless the acceptance was on the reasonable assumption that the non-conformity would be seasonably cured but acceptance does not of itself impair any other remedy provided by this Article for non-conformity.

(3) Where a tender has been accepted

(a) the buyer must within a reasonable time after he discovers or should have discovered any breach notify the seller of breach or be barred from any remedy; and

(b) if the claim is one for infringement or the like (subsection (3) of Section 2—312) and the buyer is sued as a result of such a breach he must so notify the seller within a reasonable time after he receives notice of the litigation or be barred from any remedy over for liability established by the litigation.

(4) The burden is on the buyer to establish any breach with respect to the goods accepted.

(5) Where the buyer is sued for breach of a warranty or other obligation for which his seller is answerable over

(a) he may give his seller written notice of the litigation. If the notice states that the seller may come in and defend and that if the seller does not do so he will be bound in any action against him by his buyer by any determination of fact common to the two litigations, then unless the seller after seasonable receipt of the notice does come in and defend he is so bound.

(b) if the claim is one for infringement or the like (subsection (3) of Section 2—312) the original seller may demand in writing that his buyer turn over to him control of the litigation including settlement or else be barred from any remedy over and if he also agrees to bear all expense and to satisfy any adverse judgment, then unless the buyer after seasonable receipt of the demand does turn over control the buyer is so barred.

(6) The provisions of subsections (3), (4) and (5) apply to any obligation of a buyer to hold the seller harmless against infringement or the like (subsection (3) of Section 2—312).

§ 2—608. Revocation of Acceptance in Whole or in Part.

(1) The buyer may revoke his acceptance of a lot or commercial unit whose non-conformity substantially impairs its value to him if he has accepted it

(a) on the reasonable assumption that its nonconformity would be cured and it has not been seasonably cured; or

(b) without discovery of such non-conformity if his acceptance was reasonably induced either by the difficulty of discovery before acceptance or by the seller's assurances.

(2) Revocation of acceptance must occur within a reasonable time after the buyer discovers or should have discovered the ground for it and before any substantial change in condition of the goods which is not caused by their own defects. It is not effective until the buyer notifies the seller of it.

(3) A buyer who so revokes has the same rights and duties with regard to the goods involved as if he had rejected them.

§ 2—609. Right to Adequate Assurance of Performance.

(1) A contract for sale imposes an obligation on each party that the other's expectation of receiving due performance will not be impaired. When reasonable grounds for insecurity arise with respect to the performance of either party the other may in writing demand adequate assurance of due performance and until he receives such assurance may if commercially reasonable suspend any performance for which he has not already received the agreed return.

(2) Between merchants the reasonableness of grounds for insecurity and the adequacy of any assurance offered shall be determined according to commercial standards.

(3) Acceptance of any improper delivery or payment does not prejudice the party's right to demand adequate assurance of future performance.

(4) After receipt of a justified demand failure to provide within a reasonable time not exceeding thirty days such assurance of due performance as is adequate under the circumstances of the particular case is a repudiation of the contract.

§ 2—610. Anticipatory Repudiation.

When either party repudiates the contract with respect to a performance not yet due the loss of which will substantially impair the value of the contract to the other, the aggrieved party may

(a) for a commercially reasonable time await performance by the repudiating party; or

(b) resort to any remedy for breach (Section 2—703 or Section 2—711), even though he has notified the repudiating party that he would await the latter's performance and has urged retraction; and

(c) in either case suspend his own performance or proceed in accordance with the provisions of this Article on the seller's right to identify goods to the contract notwithstanding breach or to salvage unfinished goods (Section 2—704).

§ 2—611. Retraction of Anticipatory Repudiation.

(1) Until the repudiating party's next performance is due he can retract his repudiation unless the aggrieved party has since the repudiation cancelled or materially changed his position or otherwise indicated that he considers the repudiation final.

(2) Retraction may be by any method which clearly indicates to the aggrieved party that the repudiating party intends to perform, but must include any assurance justifiably demanded under the provisions of this Article (Section 2—609).

(3) Retraction reinstates the repudiating party's rights under the contract with due excuse and allowance to the aggrieved party for any delay occasioned by the repudiation.

§ 2—612. "Installment Contract"; Breach.

(1) An "installment contract" is one which requires or authorizes the delivery of goods in separate lots to be separately accepted, even though the contract contains a clause "each delivery is a separate contract" or its equivalent.

(2) The buyer may reject any installment which is nonconforming if the non-conformity substantially impairs the value of that installment and cannot be cured or if the non-conformity is a defect in the required documents; but if the non-conformity does not fall within subsection (3) and the seller gives adequate assurance of its cure the buyer must accept that installment.

(3) Whenever non-conformity or default with respect to one or more installments substantially impairs the value of the whole contract there is a breach of the whole. But the aggrieved party reinstates the contract if he accepts a nonconforming installment without seasonably notifying of cancellation or if he brings an action with respect only to past installments or demands performance as to future installments.

§ 2—613. Casualty to Identified Goods.

Where the contract requires for its performance goods identified when the contract is made, and the goods suffer casualty without fault of either party before the risk of loss passes to the buyer, or in a proper case under a "no arrival, no sale" term (Section 2—324) then

(a) if the loss is total the contract is avoided; and

(b) if the loss is partial or the goods have so deteriorated as no longer to conform to the contract the buyer may nevertheless demand inspection and at his option either treat the contract as voided or accept the goods with due allowance from the contract price for the deterioration or the deficiency in quantity but without further right against the seller.

§ 2—614. Substituted Performance.

(1) Where without fault of either party the agreed berthing, loading, or unloading facilities fail or an agreed type of carrier becomes unavailable or the agreed manner of delivery otherwise becomes commercially impracticable but a commercially reasonable substitute is available, such substitute performance must be tendered and accepted.

(2) If the agreed means or manner of payment fails because of domestic or foreign governmental regulation, the seller may withhold or stop delivery unless the buyer provides a means or manner of payment which is commercially a substantial equivalent. If delivery has already been taken, payment by the means or in the manner provided by the regulation discharges the buyer's obligation unless the regulation is discriminatory, oppressive or predatory.

§ 2—615. Excuse by Failure of Presupposed Conditions.

Except so far as a seller may have assumed a greater obligation and subject to the preceding section on substituted performance:

(a) Delay in delivery or non-delivery in whole or in part by a seller who complies with paragraphs (b) and (c) is not a breach of his duty under a contract for sale if performance as agreed has been made impracticable by the occurrence of a contingency the nonoccurrence of which was a basic assumption on which the contract was made or by compliance in good faith with any applicable foreign or domestic governmental regulation or order whether or not it later proves to be invalid.

(b) Where the causes mentioned in paragraph (a) affect only a part of the seller's capacity to perform, he must allocate production and deliveries among his customers but may at his option include regular customers not then under contract as well as his own requirements for further manufacture. He may so allocate in any manner which is fair and reasonable.

(c) The seller must notify the buyer seasonably that there will be delay or non-delivery and, when allocation is required under paragraph (b), of the estimated quota thus made available for the buyer.

§ 2—616. Procedure on Notice Claiming Excuse.

(1) Where the buyer receives notification of a material or indefinite delay or an allocation justified under the preceding section he may by written notification to the seller as to any delivery concerned, and where the prospective deficiency substantially impairs the value of the whole contract under the provisions of this Article relating to breach of installment contracts (Section 2—612), then also as to the whole,

(a) terminate and thereby discharge any unexecuted portion of the contract; or

(b) modify the contract by agreeing to take his available quota in substitution.

(2) If after receipt of such notification from the seller the buyer fails so to modify the contract within a reasonable time not exceeding thirty days the contract lapses with respect to any deliveries affected.

(3) The provisions of this section may not be negated by agreement except in so far as the seller has assumed a greater obligation under the preceding section.

Part 7 Remedies

§ 2—701. Remedies for Breach of Collateral Contracts Not Impaired.

Remedies for breach of any obligation or promise collateral or ancillary to a contract for sale are not impaired by the provisions of this Article.

§ 2—702. Seller's Remedies on Discovery of Buyer's Insolvency.

(1) Where the seller discovers the buyer to be insolvent he may refuse delivery except for cash including payment for all goods theretofore delivered under the contract, and stop delivery under this Article (Section 2—705).

(2) Where the seller discovers that the buyer has received goods on credit while insolvent he may reclaim the goods upon demand made within ten days after the receipt, but if misrepresentation of solvency has been made to the particular seller in writing within three months before delivery the ten day limitation does not apply. Except as provided in this subsection the seller may not base a right to reclaim goods on the buyer's fraudulent or innocent misrepresentation of solvency or of intent to pay.

(3) The seller's right to reclaim under subsection (2) is subject to the rights of a buyer in ordinary course or other good faith purchaser under this Article (Section 2—403). Successful reclamation of goods excludes all other remedies with respect to them.

§ 2—703. Seller's Remedies in General.

Where the buyer wrongfully rejects or revokes acceptance of goods or fails to make a payment due on or before delivery or repudiates with respect to a part or the whole, then with respect to any goods directly affected and, if the breach is of the whole contract (Section 2—612), then also with respect to the whole undelivered balance, the aggrieved seller may

(a) withhold delivery of such goods;

(b) stop delivery by any bailee as hereafter provided (Section 2—705);

(c) proceed under the next section respecting goods still unidentified to the contract;

(d) resell and recover damages as hereafter provided (Section 2—706);

(e) recover damages for non-acceptance (Section 2—708) or in a proper case the price (Section 2—709);

(f) cancel.

§ 2—704. Seller's Right to Identify Goods to the Contract Notwithstanding Breach or to Salvage Unfinished Goods.

(1) An aggrieved seller under the preceding section may

(a) identify to the contract conforming goods not already identified if at the time he learned of the breach they are in his possession or control;

(b) treat as the subject of resale goods which have demonstrably been intended for the particular contract even though those goods are unfinished.

(2) Where the goods are unfinished an aggrieved seller may in the exercise of reasonable commercial judgment for the purposes of avoiding loss and of effective realization either complete the manufacture and wholly identify the goods to the contract or cease manufacture and resell for scrap or salvage value or proceed in any other reasonable manner.

§ 2—705. Seller's Stoppage of Delivery in Transit or Otherwise.

(1) The seller may stop delivery of goods in the possession of a carrier or other bailee when he discovers the buyer to be insolvent (Section 2—702) and may stop delivery of carload, truckload, planeload or larger shipments of express or freight when the buyer repudiates or fails to make a payment due before delivery or if for any other reason the seller has a right to withhold or reclaim the goods.

(2) As against such buyer the seller may stop delivery until

(a) receipt of the goods by the buyer; or

(b) acknowledgment to the buyer by any bailee of the goods except a carrier that the bailee holds the goods for the buyer; or

(c) such acknowledgment to the buyer by a carrier by reshipment or as warehouseman; or

(d) negotiation to the buyer of any negotiable document of title covering the goods.

(3) (a) To stop delivery the seller must so notify as to enable the bailee by reasonable diligence to prevent delivery of the goods.

(b) After such notification the bailee must hold and deliver the goods according to the directions of the seller but the seller is liable to the bailee for any ensuing charges or damages.

(c) If a negotiable document of title has been issued for goods the bailee is not obliged to obey a notification to stop until surrender of the document.

(d) A carrier who has issued a non-negotiable bill of lading is not obliged to obey a notification to stop received from a person other than the consignor.

§ 2—706. Seller's Resale Including Contract for Resale.

(1) Under the conditions stated in Section 2—703 on seller's remedies, the seller may resell the goods concerned or the undelivered balance thereof. Where the resale is made in good faith and in a commercially reasonable manner the seller may recover the difference between the resale price and the contract price together with any incidental damages allowed under the provisions of this Article (Section 2—710), but less expenses saved in consequence of the buyer's breach.

(2) Except as otherwise provided in subsection (3) or unless otherwise agreed resale may be at public or private sale including sale by way of one or more contracts to sell or of identification to an existing contract of the seller. Sale may be as a unit or in parcels and at any time and place and on any terms but every aspect of the sale including the method, manner, time, place and terms must be commercially reasonable. The resale must be reasonably identified as referring to the broken contract, but it is not necessary that the goods be in existence or that any or all of them have been identified to the contract before the breach.

(3) Where the resale is at private sale the seller must give the buyer reasonable notification of his intention to resell.

(4) Where the resale is at public sale

(a) only identified goods can be sold except where there is a recognized market for a public sale of futures in goods of the kind; and

(b) it must be made at a usual place or market for public sale if one is reasonably available and except in the case of goods which are perishable or threaten to decline in value speedily the seller must give the buyer reasonable notice of the time and place of the resale; and

(c) if the goods are not to be within the view of those attending the sale the notification of sale must state the place where the goods are located and provide for their reasonable inspection by prospective bidders; and

(d) the seller may buy.

(5) A purchaser who buys in good faith at a resale takes the goods free of any rights of the original buyer even though the seller fails to comply with one or more of the requirements of this section.

(6) The seller is not accountable to the buyer for any profit made on any resale. A person in the position of a seller (Section 2—707) or a buyer who has rightfully rejected or justifiably revoked acceptance must account for any excess over the amount of his security interest, as hereinafter defined (subsection (3) of Section 2—711).

§ 2—707. "Person in the Position of a Seller".

(1) A "person in the position of a seller" includes as against a principal an agent who has paid or become responsible for the price of goods on behalf of his principal or anyone who otherwise holds a security interest or other right in goods similar to that of a seller.

(2) A person in the position of a seller may as provided in this Article withhold or stop delivery (Section 2—705) and resell (Section 2—706) and recover incidental damages (Section 2—710).

§ 2—708. Seller's Damages for Non-Acceptance or Repudiation.

(1) Subject to subsection (2) and to the provisions of this Article with respect to proof of market price (Section 2—723), the measure of damages for non-acceptance or repudiation by the buyer is the difference between the market price at the time and place for tender and the unpaid contract price together with any incidental damages provided in this Article (Section 2—710), but less expenses saved in consequence of the buyer's breach.

(2) If the measure of damages provided in subsection (1) is inadequate to put the seller in as good a position as performance would have done then the measure of damages is the profit (including reasonable overhead) which the seller would have made from full performance by the buyer, together with any incidental damages provided in this Article (Section 2—710), due allowance for costs reasonably incurred and due credit for payments or proceeds of resale.

§ 2—709. Action for the Price.

(1) When the buyer fails to pay the price as it becomes due the seller may recover, together with any incidental damages under the next section, the price

(a) of goods accepted or of conforming goods lost or damaged within a commercially reasonable time after risk of their loss has passed to the buyer; and

(b) of goods identified to the contract if the seller is unable after reasonable effort to resell them at a reasonable price or the circumstances reasonably indicate that such effort will be unavailing.

(2) Where the seller sues for the price he must hold for the buyer any goods which have been identified to the contract and are still in his control except that if resale becomes possible he may resell them at any time prior to the collection of the judgment. The net proceeds of any such resale must be credited to the buyer and payment of the judgment entitles him to any goods not resold.

(3) After the buyer has wrongfully rejected or revoked acceptance of the goods or has failed to make a payment due or has repudiated (Section 2—610), a seller who is held not entitled to the price under this section shall nevertheless be awarded damages for non-acceptance under the preceding section.

§ 2—710. Seller's Incidental Damages.

Incidental damages to an aggrieved seller include any commercially reasonable charges, expenses or commissions incurred in stopping delivery, in the transportation, care and custody of goods after the buyer's breach, in connection with return or resale of the goods or otherwise resulting from the breach.

§ 2—711. Buyer's Remedies in General; Buyer's Security Interest in Rejected Goods.

(1) Where the seller fails to make delivery or repudiates or the buyer rightfully rejects or justifiably revokes acceptance then with respect to any goods involved, and with respect to the whole if the breach goes to the whole contract (Section 2—612), the buyer may cancel and whether or not he has done so may in addition to recovering so much of the price as has been paid

(a) "cover" and have damages under the next section as to all the goods affected whether or not they have been identified to the contract; or

(b) recover damages for non-delivery as provided in this Article (Section 2—713).

(2) Where the seller fails to deliver or repudiates the buyer may also

(a) if the goods have been identified recover them as provided in this Article (Section 2—502); or

(b) in a proper case obtain specific performance or replevy the goods as provided in this Article (Section 2—716).

(3) On rightful rejection or justifiable revocation of acceptance a buyer has a security interest in goods in his possession or control for any payments made on their price and any expenses reasonably incurred in their inspection, receipt, transportation, care and custody and may hold such goods and resell them in like manner as an aggrieved seller (Section 2—706).

§ 2—712. "Cover"; Buyer's Procurement of Substitute Goods.

(1) After a breach within the preceding section the buyer may "cover" by making in good faith and without unreasonable delay any reasonable purchase of or contract to purchase goods in substitution for those due from the seller.

(2) The buyer may recover from the seller as damages the difference between the cost of cover and the contract price together with any incidental or consequential damages as hereinafter defined (Section 2—715), but less expenses saved in consequence of the seller's breach.

(3) Failure of the buyer to effect cover within this section does not bar him from any other remedy.

§ 2—713. Buyer's Damages for Non-Delivery or Repudiation.

(1) Subject to the provisions of this Article with respect to proof of market price (Section 2—723), the measure of damages for non-delivery or repudiation by the seller is the difference between the market price at the time when the buyer learned of the breach and the contract price together

with any incidental and consequential damages provided in this Article (Section 2—715), but less expenses saved in consequence of the seller's breach.

(2) Market price is to be determined as of the place for tender or, in cases of rejection after arrival or revocation of acceptance, as of the place of arrival.

§ 2—714. Buyer's Damages for Breach in Regard to Accepted Goods.

(1) Where the buyer has accepted goods and given notification (subsection (3) of Section 2—607) he may recover as damages for any non-conformity of tender the loss resulting in the ordinary course of events from the seller's breach as determined in any manner which is reasonable.

(2) The measure of damages for breach of warranty is the difference at the time and place of acceptance between the value of the goods accepted and the value they would have had if they had been as warranted, unless special circumstances show proximate damages of a different amount.

(3) In a proper case any incidental and consequential damages under the next section may also be recovered.

§ 2—715. Buyer's Incidental and Consequential Damages.

(1) Incidental damages resulting from the seller's breach include expenses reasonably incurred in inspection, receipt, transportation and care and custody of goods rightfully rejected, any commercially reasonable charges, expenses or commissions in connection with effecting cover and any other reasonable expense incident to the delay or other breach.

(2) Consequential damages resulting from the seller's breach include

(a) any loss resulting from general or particular requirements and needs of which the seller at the time of contracting had reason to know and which could not reasonably be prevented by cover or otherwise; and

(b) injury to person or property proximately resulting from any breach of warranty.

§ 2—716. Buyer's Right to Specific Performance or Replevin.

(1) Specific performance may be decreed where the goods are unique or in other proper circumstances.

(2) The decree for specific performance may include such terms and conditions as to payment of the price, damages, or other relief as the court may deem just.

(3) The buyer has a right of replevin for goods identified to the contract if after reasonable effort he is unable to effect cover for such goods or the circumstances reasonably indicate that such effort will be unavailing or if the goods have been shipped under reservation and satisfaction of the security interest in them has been made or tendered.

§ 2—717. **Deduction of Damages From the Price.**

The buyer on notifying the seller of his intention to do so may deduct all or any part of the damages resulting from any breach of the contract from any part of the price still due under the same contract.

§ 2—718. **Liquidation or Limitation of Damages; Deposits.**

(1) Damages for breach by either party may be liquidated in the agreement but only at an amount which is reasonable in the light of the anticipated or actual harm caused by the breach, the difficulties of proof of loss, and the inconvenience or nonfeasibility of otherwise obtaining an adequate remedy. A term fixing unreasonably large liquidated damages is void as a penalty.

(2) Where the seller justifiably withholds delivery of goods because of the buyer's breach, the buyer is entitled to restitution of any amount by which the sum of his payments exceeds

    (a) the amount to which the seller is entitled by virtue of terms liquidating the seller's damages in accordance with subsection (1), or

    (b) in the absence of such terms, twenty per cent of the value of the total performance for which the buyer is obligated under the contract or $500, whichever is smaller.

(3) The buyer's right to restitution under subsection (2) is subject to offset to the extent that the seller establishes

    (a) a right to recover damages under the provisions of this Article other than subsection (1), and

    (b) the amount or value of any benefits received by the buyer directly or indirectly by reason of the contract.

(4) Where a seller has received payment in goods their reasonable value or the proceeds of their resale shall be treated as payments for the purposes of subsection (2); but if the seller has notice of the buyer's breach before reselling goods received in part performance, his resale is subject to the conditions laid down in this Article on resale by an aggrieved seller (Section 2—706).

§ 2—719. **Contractual Modification or Limitation of Remedy.**

(1) Subject to the provisions of subsections (2) and (3) of this section and of the preceding section on liquidation and limitation of damages,

    (a) the agreement may provide for remedies in addition to or in substitution for those provided in this Article and may limit or alter the measure of damages recoverable under this Article, as by limiting the buyer's remedies to return of the goods and repayment of the price or to repair and replacement of nonconforming goods or parts; and

    (b) resort to a remedy as provided is optional unless the remedy is expressly agreed to be exclusive, in which case it is the sole remedy.

(2) Where circumstances cause an exclusive or limited remedy to fail of its essential purpose, remedy may be had as provided in this Act.

(3) Consequential damages may be limited or excluded unless the limitation or exclusion is unconscionable. Limitation of consequential damages for injury to the person in the case of consumer goods is prima facie unconscionable but limitation of damages where the loss is commercial is not.

§ 2—720. **Effect of "Cancellation" or "Rescission" on Claims for Antecedent Breach.**

Unless the contrary intention clearly appears, expressions of "cancellation" or "rescission" of the contract or the like shall not be construed as a renunciation or discharge of any claim in damages for an antecedent breach.

§ 2—721. **Remedies for Fraud.**

Remedies for material misrepresentation or fraud include all remedies available under this Article for non-fraudulent breach. Neither rescission or a claim for rescission of the contract for sale nor rejection or return of the goods shall bar or be deemed inconsistent with a claim for damages or other remedy.

§ 2—722. **Who Can Sue Third Parties for Injury to Goods.**

Where a third party so deals with goods which have been identified to a contract for sale as to cause actionable injury to a party to that contract

(a) a right of action against the third party is in either party to the contract for sale who has title to or a security interest or a special property or an insurable interest in the goods; and if the goods have been destroyed or converted a right of action is also in the party who either bore the risk of loss under the contract for sale or has since the injury assumed that risk as against the other;

(b) if at the time of the injury the party plaintiff did not bear the risk of loss as against the other party to the contract for sale and there is no arrangement between them for disposition of the recovery, his suit or settlement is, subject to his own interest, as a fiduciary for the other party to the contract;

(c) either party may with the consent of the other sue for the benefit of whom it may concern.

§ 2—723. **Proof of Market Price: Time and Place.**

(1) If an action based on anticipatory repudiation comes to trial before the time for performance with respect to some or all of the goods, any damages based on market price (Section 2—708 or Section 2—713) shall be determined according to the price of such goods prevailing at the time when the aggrieved party learned of the repudiation.

(2) If evidence of a price prevailing at the times or places described in this Article is not readily available the price

prevailing within any reasonable time before or after the time described or at any other place which in commercial judgment or under usage of trade would serve as a reasonable substitute for the one described may be used, making any proper allowance for the cost of transporting the goods to or from such other place.

(3) Evidence of a relevant price prevailing at a time or place other than the one described in this Article offered by one party is not admissible unless and until he has given the other party such notice as the court finds sufficient to prevent unfair surprise.

§ 2–724. Admissibility of Market Quotations.

Whenever the prevailing price or value of any goods regularly bought and sold in any established commodity market is in issue, reports in official publications or trade journals or in newspapers or periodicals of general circulation published as the reports of such market shall be admissible in evidence. The circumstances of the preparation of such a report may be shown to affect its weight but not its admissibility.

§ 2–725. Statute of Limitations in Contracts for Sale.

(1) An action for breach of any contract for sale must be commenced within four years after the cause of action has accrued. By the original agreement the parties may reduce the period of limitation to not less than one year but may not extend it.

(2) A cause of action accrues when the breach occurs, regardless of the aggrieved party's lack of knowledge of the breach. A breach of warranty occurs when tender of delivery is made, except that where a warranty explicitly extends to future performance of the goods and discovery of the breach must await the time of such performance the cause of action accrues when the breach is or should have been discovered.

(3) Where an action commenced within the time limited by subsection (1) is so terminated as to leave available a remedy by another action for the same breach such other action may be commenced after the expiration of the time limited and within six months after the termination of the first action unless the termination resulted from voluntary discontinuance or from dismissal for failure or neglect to prosecute.

(4) This section does not alter the law on tolling of the statute of limitations nor does it apply to causes of action which have accrued before this Act becomes effective.

Article 2A
LEASES

Part 1 General Provisions

§ 2A–101. Short Title.

This Article shall be known and may be cited as the Uniform Commercial Code—Leases.

§ 2A–102. Scope.

This Article applies to any transaction, regardless of form, that creates a lease.

§ 2A–103. Definitions and Index of Definitions.

(1) In this Article unless the context otherwise requires:

(a) "Buyer in ordinary course of business" means a person who in good faith and without knowledge that the sale to him [or her] is in violation of the ownership rights or security interest or leasehold interest of a third party in the goods buys in ordinary course from a person in the business of selling goods of that kind but does not include a pawnbroker. "Buying" may be for cash or by exchange of other property or on secured or unsecured credit and includes receiving goods or documents of title under a pre-existing contract for sale but does not include a transfer in bulk or as security for or in total or partial satisfaction of a money debt.

(b) "Cancellation" occurs when either party puts an end to the lease contract for default by the other party.

(c) "Commercial unit" means such a unit of goods as by commercial usage is a single whole for purposes of lease and division of which materially impairs its character or value on the market or in use. A commercial unit may be a single article, as a machine, or a set of articles, as a suite of furniture or a line of machinery, or a quantity, as a gross or carload, or any other unit treated in use or in the relevant market as a single whole.

(d) "Conforming" goods or performance under a lease contract means goods or performance that are in accordance with the obligations under the lease contract.

(e) "Consumer lease" means a lease that a lessor regularly engaged in the business of leasing or selling makes to a lessee who is an individual and who takes under the lease primarily for a personal, family, or household "purpose [, if" the total payments to be made under the lease contract, excluding payments for options to renew or buy, do not exceed. . . .

(f) "Fault" means wrongful act, omission, breach, or default.

(g) "Finance lease" means a lease with respect to which:

(i) the lessor does not select, manufacture or supply the goods;

(ii) the lessor acquires the goods or the right to possession and use of the goods in connection with the lease; and

(iii) one of the following occurs:

(A) the lessee receives a copy of the contract by which the lessor acquired the goods or the right to possession and use of the goods before signing the lease contract;

(B) the lessee's approval of the contract by which the lessor acquired the goods or the right to possession and use of the goods is a condition to effectiveness of the lease contract;

(C) the lessee, before signing the lease contract, receives an accurate and complete statement designating the promises and warranties, and any disclaimers of warranties, limitations or modifications of remedies, or liquidated damages, including those of a third party, such as the manufacturer of the goods, provided to the lessor by the person supplying the goods in connection with or as part of the contract by which the lessor acquired the goods or the right to possession and use of the goods; or

(D) if the lease is not a consumer lease, the lessor, before the lessee signs the lease contract, informs the lessee in writing (a) of the identity of the person supplying the goods to the lessor, unless the lessee has selected that person and directed the lessor to acquire the goods or the right to possession and use of the goods from that person, (b) that the lessee is entitled under this Article to any promises and warranties, including those of any third party, provided to the lessor by the person supplying the goods in connection with or as part of the contract by which the lessor acquired the goods or the right to possession and use of the goods, and (c) that the lessee may communicate with the person supplying the goods to the lessor and receive an accurate and complete statement of those promises and warranties, including any disclaimers and limitations of them or of remedies.

(h) "Goods" means all things that are movable at the time of identification to the lease contract, or are fixtures (Section 2A—309), but the term does not include money, documents, instruments, accounts, chattel paper, general intangibles, or minerals or the like, including oil and gas, before extraction. The term also includes the unborn young of animals.

(i) "Installment lease contract" means a lease contract that authorizes or requires the delivery of goods in separate lots to be separately accepted, even though the lease contract contains a clause "each delivery is a separate lease" or its equivalent.

(j) "Lease" means a transfer of the right to possession and use of goods for a term in return for consideration, but a sale, including a sale on approval or a sale or return, or retention or creation of a security interest is not a lease. Unless the context clearly indicates otherwise, the term includes a sublease.

(k) "Lease agreement" means the bargain, with respect to the lease, of the lessor and the lessee in fact as found in their language or by implication from other circumstances including course of dealing or usage of trade or course of performance as provided in this Article. Unless the context clearly indicates otherwise, the term includes a sublease agreement.

(l) "Lease contract" means the total legal obligation that results from the lease agreement as affected by this Article and any other applicable rules of law. Unless the context clearly indicates otherwise, the term includes a sublease contract.

(m) "Leasehold interest" means the interest of the lessor or the lessee under a lease contract.

(n) "Lessee" means a person who acquires the right to possession and use of goods under a lease. Unless the context clearly indicates otherwise, the term includes a sublessee.

(o) "Lessee in ordinary course of business" means a person who in good faith and without knowledge that the lease to him [or her] is in violation of the ownership rights or security interest or leasehold interest of a third party in the goods, leases in ordinary course from a person in the business of selling or leasing goods of that kind but does not include a pawnbroker. "Leasing" may be for cash or by exchange of other property or on secured or unsecured credit and includes receiving goods or documents of title under a pre-existing lease contract but does not include a transfer in bulk or as security for or in total or partial satisfaction of a money debt.

(p) "Lessor" means a person who transfers the right to possession and use of goods under a lease. Unless the context clearly indicates otherwise, the term includes a sublessor.

(q) "Lessor's residual interest" means the lessor's interest in the goods after expiration, termination, or cancellation of the lease contract.

(r) "Lien" means a charge against or interest in goods to secure payment of a debt or performance of an obligation, but the term does not include a security interest.

(s) "Lot" means a parcel or a single article that is the subject matter of a separate lease or delivery, whether or not it is sufficient to perform the lease contract.

(t) "Merchant lessee" means a lessee that is a merchant with respect to goods of the kind subject to the lease.

(u) "Present value" means the amount as of a date certain of one or more sums payable in the future, discounted to the date certain. The discount is determined by the interest rate specified by the parties if the rate was not manifestly unreasonable at the time the transaction was entered into; otherwise, the discount is determined by a commercially reasonable rate that takes into account the facts and circumstances of each case at the time the transaction was entered into.

(v) "Purchase" includes taking by sale, lease, mortgage, security interest, pledge, gift, or any other voluntary transaction creating an interest in goods.

(w) "Sublease" means a lease of goods the right to possession and use of which was acquired by the lessor as a lessee under an existing lease.

(x) "Supplier" means a person from whom a lessor buys or leases goods to be leased under a finance lease.

(y) "Supply contract" means a contract under which a lessor buys or leases goods to be leased.

(z) "Termination" occurs when either party pursuant to a power created by agreement or law puts an end to the lease contract otherwise than for default.

(2) Other definitions applying to this Article and the sections in which they appear are:

"Accessions". Section 2A—310(1).
"Construction mortgage". Section 2A—309(1)(d).
"Encumbrance". Section 2A—309(1)(e).
"Fixtures". Section 2A—309(1)(a).
"Fixture filing". Section 2A—309(1)(b).
"Purchase money lease". Section 2A—309(1)(c).

(3) The following definitions in other Articles apply to this Article:

"Accounts". Section 9—106.
"Between merchants". Section 2—104(3).
"Buyer". Section 2—103(1)(a).
"Chattel paper". Section 9—105(1)(b).
"Consumer goods". Section 9—109(1).
"Document". Section 9—105(1)(f).
"Entrusting". Section 2—403(3).
"General intangibles". Section 9—106.
"Good faith". Section 2—103(1)(b).
"Instrument". Section 9—105(1)(i).
"Merchant". Section 2—104(1).
"Mortgage". Section 9—105(1)(j).
"Pursuant to commitment". Section 9—105(1)(k).
"Receipt". Section 2—103(1)(c).
"Sale". Section 2—106(1).
"Sale on approval". Section 2—326.
"Sale or return". Section 2—326.
"Seller". Section 2—103(1)(d).

(4) In addition Article 1 contains general definitions and principles of construction and interpretation applicable throughout this Article.

As amended in 1990.

§ 2A—104. Leases Subject to Other Law.

(1) A lease, although subject to this Article, is also subject to any applicable:

(a) certificate of title statute of this State: (list any certificate of title statutes covering automobiles, trailers, mobile homes, boats, farm tractors, and the like);

(b) certificate of title statute of another jurisdiction (Section 2A—105); or

(c) consumer protection statute of this State, or final consumer protection decision of a court of this State existing on the effective date of this Article.

(2) In case of conflict between this Article, other than Sections 2A—105, 2A—304(3), and 2A—305(3), and a statute or decision referred to in subsection (1), the statute or decision controls.

(3) Failure to comply with an applicable law has only the effect specified therein.

As amended in 1990.

§ 2A—105. Territorial Application of Article to Goods Covered by Certificate of Title.

Subject to the provisions of Sections 2A—304(3) and 2A—305(3), with respect to goods covered by a certificate of title issued under a statute of this State or of another jurisdiction, compliance and the effect of compliance or noncompliance with a certificate of title statute are governed by the law (including the conflict of laws rules) of the jurisdiction issuing the certificate until the earlier of (a) surrender of the certificate, or (b) four months after the goods are removed from that jurisdiction and thereafter until a new certificate of title is issued by another jurisdiction.

§ 2A—106. Limitation on Power of Parties to Consumer Lease to Choose Applicable Law and Judicial Forum.

(1) If the law chosen by the parties to a consumer lease is that of a jurisdiction other than a jurisdiction in which the lessee resides at the time the lease agreement becomes enforceable or within 30 days thereafter or in which the goods are to be used, the choice is not enforceable.

(2) If the judicial forum chosen by the parties to a consumer lease is a forum that would not otherwise have jurisdiction over the lessee, the choice is not enforceable.

§ 2A—107. Waiver or Renunciation of Claim or Right After Default.

Any claim or right arising out of an alleged default or breach of warranty may be discharged in whole or in part without consideration by a written waiver or renunciation signed and delivered by the aggrieved party.

§ 2A—108. Unconscionability.

(1) If the court as a matter of law finds a lease contract or any clause of a lease contract to have been unconscionable at the time it was made the court may refuse to enforce the lease contract, or it may enforce the remainder of the lease contract without the unconscionable clause, or it may so limit the application of any unconscionable clause as to avoid any unconscionable result.

(2) With respect to a consumer lease, if the court as a matter of law finds that a lease contract or any clause of a lease

contract has been induced by unconscionable conduct or that unconscionable conduct has occurred in the collection of a claim arising from a lease contract, the court may grant appropriate relief.

(3) Before making a finding of unconscionability under subsection (1) or (2), the court, on its own motion or that of a party, shall afford the parties a reasonable opportunity to present evidence as to the setting, purpose, and effect of the lease contract or clause thereof, or of the conduct.

(4) In an action in which the lessee claims unconscionability with respect to a consumer lease:

(a) If the court finds unconscionability under subsection (1) or (2), the court shall award reasonable attorney's fees to the lessee.

(b) If the court does not find unconscionability and the lessee claiming unconscionability has brought or maintained an action he [or she] knew to be groundless, the court shall award reasonable attorney's fees to the party against whom the claim is made.

(c) In determining attorney's fees, the amount of the recovery on behalf of the claimant under subsections (1) and (2) is not controlling.

§ 2A—109. Option to Accelerate at Will.

(1) A term providing that one party or his [or her] successor in interest may accelerate payment or performance or require collateral or additional collateral "at will" or "when he [or she] deems himself [or herself] insecure" or in words of similar import must be construed to mean that he [or she] has power to do so only if he [or she] in good faith believes that the prospect of payment or performance is impaired.

(2) With respect to a consumer lease, the burden of establishing good faith under subsection (1) is on the party who exercised the power; otherwise the burden of establishing lack of good faith is on the party against whom the power has been exercised.

Part 2 Formation and Construction of Lease Contract

§ 2A—201. Statute of Frauds.

(1) A lease contract is not enforceable by way of action or defense unless:

(a) the total payments to be made under the lease contract, excluding payments for options to renew or buy, are less than $1,000; or

(b) there is a writing, signed by the party against whom enforcement is sought or by that party's authorized agent, sufficient to indicate that a lease contract has been made between the parties and to describe the goods leased and the lease term.

(2) Any description of leased goods or of the lease term is sufficient and satisfies subsection (1)(b), whether or not it is specific, if it reasonably identifies what is described.

(3) A writing is not insufficient because it omits or incorrectly states a term agreed upon, but the lease contract is not enforceable under subsection (1)(b) beyond the lease term and the quantity of goods shown in the writing.

(4) A lease contract that does not satisfy the requirements of subsection (1), but which is valid in other respects, is enforceable:

(a) if the goods are to be specially manufactured or obtained for the lessee and are not suitable for lease or sale to others in the ordinary course of the lessor's business, and the lessor, before notice of repudiation is received and under circumstances that reasonably indicate that the goods are for the lessee, has made either a substantial beginning of their manufacture or commitments for their procurement;

(b) if the party against whom enforcement is sought admits in that party's pleading, testimony or otherwise in court that a lease contract was made, but the lease contract is not enforceable under this provision beyond the quantity of goods admitted; or

(c) with respect to goods that have been received and accepted by the lessee.

(5) The lease term under a lease contract referred to in subsection (4) is:

(a) if there is a writing signed by the party against whom enforcement is sought or by that party's authorized agent specifying the lease term, the term so specified;

(b) if the party against whom enforcement is sought admits in that party's pleading, testimony, or otherwise in court a lease term, the term so admitted; or

(c) a reasonable lease term.

§ 2A—202. Final Written Expression: Parol or Extrinsic Evidence.

Terms with respect to which the confirmatory memoranda of the parties agree or which are otherwise set forth in a writing intended by the parties as a final expression of their agreement with respect to such terms as are included therein may not be contradicted by evidence of any prior agreement or of a contemporaneous oral agreement but may be explained or supplemented:

(a) by course of dealing or usage of trade or by course of performance; and

(b) by evidence of consistent additional terms unless the court finds the writing to have been intended also as a complete and exclusive statement of the terms of the agreement.

§ 2A—203. Seals Inoperative.

The affixing of a seal to a writing evidencing a lease contract or an offer to enter into a lease contract does not render the writing a sealed instrument and the law with respect to sealed instruments does not apply to the lease contract or offer.

§ 2A–204. Formation in General.

(1) A lease contract may be made in any manner sufficient to show agreement, including conduct by both parties which recognizes the existence of a lease contract.

(2) An agreement sufficient to constitute a lease contract may be found although the moment of its making is undetermined.

(3) Although one or more terms are left open, a lease contract does not fail for indefiniteness if the parties have intended to make a lease contract and there is a reasonably certain basis for giving an appropriate remedy.

§ 2A–205. Firm Offers.

An offer by a merchant to lease goods to or from another person in a signed writing that by its terms gives assurance it will be held open is not revocable, for lack of consideration, during the time stated or, if no time is stated, for a reasonable time, but in no event may the period of irrevocability exceed 3 months. Any such term of assurance on a form supplied by the offeree must be separately signed by the offeror.

§ 2A–206. Offer and Acceptance in Formation of Lease Contract.

(1) Unless otherwise unambiguously indicated by the language or circumstances, an offer to make a lease contract must be construed as inviting acceptance in any manner and by any medium reasonable in the circumstances.

(2) If the beginning of a requested performance is a reasonable mode of acceptance, an offeror who is not notified of acceptance within a reasonable time may treat the offer as having lapsed before acceptance.

§ 2A–207. Course of Performance or Practical Construction.

(1) If a lease contract involves repeated occasions for performance by either party with knowledge of the nature of the performance and opportunity for objection to it by the other, any course of performance accepted or acquiesced in without objection is relevant to determine the meaning of the lease agreement.

(2) The express terms of a lease agreement and any course of performance, as well as any course of dealing and usage of trade, must be construed whenever reasonable as consistent with each other; but if that construction is unreasonable, express terms control course of performance, course of performance controls both course of dealing and usage of trade, and course of dealing controls usage of trade.

(3) Subject to the provisions of Section 2A–208 on modification and waiver, course of performance is relevant to show a waiver or modification of any term inconsistent with the course of performance.

§ 2A–208. Modification, Rescission and Waiver.

(1) An agreement modifying a lease contract needs no consideration to be binding.

(2) A signed lease agreement that excludes modification or rescission except by a signed writing may not be otherwise modified or rescinded, but, except as between merchants, such a requirement on a form supplied by a merchant must be separately signed by the other party.

(3) Although an attempt at modification or rescission does not satisfy the requirements of subsection (2), it may operate as a waiver.

(4) A party who has made a waiver affecting an executory portion of a lease contract may retract the waiver by reasonable notification received by the other party that strict performance will be required of any term waived, unless the retraction would be unjust in view of a material change of position in reliance on the waiver.

§ 2A–209. Lessee under Finance Lease as Beneficiary of Supply Contract.

(1) The benefit of the supplier's promises to the lessor under the supply contract and of all warranties, whether express or implied, including those of any third party provided in connection with or as part of the supply contract, extends to the lessee to the extent of the lessee's leasehold interest under a finance lease related to the supply contract, but is subject to the terms warranty and of the supply contract and all defenses or claims arising therefrom.

(2) The extension of the benefit of supplier's promises and of warranties to the lessee (Section 2A–209(1)) does not: (i) modify the rights and obligations of the parties to the supply contract, whether arising therefrom or otherwise, or (ii) impose any duty or liability under the supply contract on the lessee.

(3) Any modification or rescission of the supply contract by the supplier and the lessor is effective between the supplier and the lessee unless, before the modification or rescission, the supplier has received notice that the lessee has entered into a finance lease related to the supply contract. If the modification or rescission is effective between the supplier and the lessee, the lessor is deemed to have assumed, in addition to the obligations of the lessor to the lessee under the lease contract, promises of the supplier to the lessor and warranties that were so modified or rescinded as they existed and were available to the lessee before modification or rescission.

(4) In addition to the extension of the benefit of the supplier's promises and of warranties to the lessee under subsection (1), the lessee retains all rights that the lessee may have against the supplier which arise from an agreement between the lessee and the supplier or under other law.

As amended in 1990.

§ 2A–210. Express Warranties.

(1) Express warranties by the lessor are created as follows:

(a) Any affirmation of fact or promise made by the lessor to the lessee which relates to the goods and becomes part of the basis of the bargain creates an express warranty that the goods will conform to the affirmation or promise.

(b) Any description of the goods which is made part of the basis of the bargain creates an express warranty that the goods will conform to the description.

(c) Any sample or model that is made part of the basis of the bargain creates an express warranty that the whole of the goods will conform to the sample or model.

(2) It is not necessary to the creation of an express warranty that the lessor use formal words, such as "warrant" or "guarantee," or that the lessor have a specific intention to make a warranty, but an affirmation merely of the value of the goods or a statement purporting to be merely the lessor's opinion or commendation of the goods does not create a warranty.

§ 2A—211. Warranties Against Interference and Against Infringement; Lessee's Obligation Against Infringement.

(1) There is in a lease contract a warranty that for the lease term no person holds a claim to or interest in the goods that arose from an act or omission of the lessor, other than a claim by way of infringement or the like, which will interfere with the lessee's enjoyment of its leasehold interest.

(2) Except in a finance lease there is in a lease contract by a lessor who is a merchant regularly dealing in goods of the kind a warranty that the goods are delivered free of the rightful claim of any person by way of infringement or the like.

(3) A lessee who furnishes specifications to a lessor or a supplier shall hold the lessor and the supplier harmless against any claim by way of infringement or the like that arises out of compliance with the specifications.

§ 2A—212. Implied Warranty of Merchantability.

(1) Except in a finance lease, a warranty that the goods will be merchantable is implied in a lease contract if the lessor is a merchant with respect to goods of that kind.

(2) Goods to be merchantable must be at least such as

(a) pass without objection in the trade under the description in the lease agreement;

(b) in the case of fungible goods, are of fair average quality within the description;

(c) are fit for the ordinary purposes for which goods of that type are used;

(d) run, within the variation permitted by the lease agreement, of even kind, quality, and quantity within each unit and among all units involved;

(e) are adequately contained, packaged, and labeled as the lease agreement may require; and

(f) conform to any promises or affirmations of fact made on the container or label.

(3) Other implied warranties may arise from course of dealing or usage of trade.

§ 2A—213. Implied Warranty of Fitness for Particular Purpose.

Except in a finance of lease, if the lessor at the time the lease contract is made has reason to know of any particular purpose for which the goods are required and that the lessee is relying on the lessor's skill or judgment to select or furnish suitable goods, there is in the lease contract an implied warranty that the goods will be fit for that purpose.

§ 2A—214. Exclusion or Modification of Warranties.

(1) Words or conduct relevant to the creation of an express warranty and words or conduct tending to negate or limit a warranty must be construed wherever reasonable as consistent with each other; but, subject to the provisions of Section 2A—202 on parol or extrinsic evidence, negation or limitation is inoperative to the extent that the construction is unreasonable.

(2) Subject to subsection (3), to exclude or modify the implied warranty of merchantability or any part of it the language must mention "merchantability", be by a writing, and be conspicuous. Subject to subsection (3), to exclude or modify any implied warranty of fitness the exclusion must be by a writing and be conspicuous. Language to exclude all implied warranties of fitness is sufficient if it is in writing, is conspicuous and states, for example, "There is no warranty that the goods will be fit for a particular purpose".

(3) Notwithstanding subsection (2), but subject to subsection (4),

(a) unless the circumstances indicate otherwise, all implied warranties are excluded by expressions like "as is" or "with all faults" or by other language that in common understanding calls the lessee's attention to the exclusion of warranties and makes plain that there is no implied warranty, if in writing and conspicuous;

(b) if the lessee before entering into the lease contract has examined the goods or the sample or model as fully as desired or has refused to examine the goods, there is no implied warranty with regard to defects that an examination ought in the circumstances to have revealed; and

(c) an implied warranty may also be excluded or modified by course of dealing, course of performance, or usage of trade.

(4) To exclude or modify a warranty against interference or against infringement (Section 2A—211) or any part of it, the language must be specific, be by a writing, and be conspicuous, unless the circumstances, including course of performance, course of dealing, or usage of trade, give the lessee reason to know that the goods are being leased subject to a claim or interest of any person.

§ 2A—215. Cumulation and Conflict of Warranties Express or Implied.

Warranties, whether express or implied, must be construed as consistent with each other and as cumulative, but if that construction is unreasonable, the intention of the parties determines which warranty is dominant. In ascertaining that intention the following rules apply:

(a) Exact or technical specifications displace an inconsistent sample or model or general language of description.

(b) A sample from an existing bulk displaces inconsistent general language of description.

(c) Express warranties displace inconsistent implied warranties other than an implied warranty of fitness for a particular purpose.

§ 2A—216. Third-Party Beneficiaries of Express and Implied Warranties.

Alternative A

A warranty to or for the benefit of a lessee under this Article, whether express or implied, extends to any natural person who is in the family or household of the lessee or who is a guest in the lessee's home if it is reasonable to expect that such person may use, consume, or be affected by the goods and who is injured in person by breach of the warranty. This section does not displace principles of law and equity that extend a warranty to or for the benefit of a lessee to other persons. The operation of this section may not be excluded, modified, or limited, but an exclusion, modification, or limitation of the warranty, including any with respect to rights and remedies, effective against the lessee is also effective against any beneficiary designated under this section.

Alternative B

A warranty to or for the benefit of a lessee under this Article, whether express or implied, extends to any natural person who may reasonably be expected to use, consume, or be affected by the goods and who is injured in person by breach of the warranty. This section does not displace principles of law and equity that extend a warranty to or for the benefit of a lessee to other persons. The operation of this section may not be excluded, modified, or limited, but an exclusion, modification, or limitation of the warranty, including any with respect to rights and remedies, effective against the lessee is also effective against the beneficiary designated under this section.

Alternative C

A warranty to or for the benefit of a lessee under this Article, whether express or implied, extends to any person who may reasonably be expected to use, consume, or be affected by the goods and who is injured by breach of the warranty. The operation of this section may not be excluded, modified, or limited with respect to injury to the person of an individual to whom the warranty extends, but an exclusion, modification, or limitation of the warranty, including any with respect to rights and remedies, effective against the lessee is also effective against the beneficiary designated under this section.

§ 2A—217. Identification.

Identification of goods as goods to which a lease contract refers may be made at any time and in any manner explicitly agreed to by the parties. In the absence of explicit agreement, identification occurs:

(a) when the lease contract is made if the lease contract is for a lease of goods that are existing and identified;

(b) when the goods are shipped, marked, or otherwise designated by the lessor as goods to which the lease contract refers, if the lease contract is for a lease of goods that are not existing and identified; or

(c) when the young are conceived, if the lease contract is for a lease of unborn young of animals.

§ 2A—218. Insurance and Proceeds.

(1) A lessee obtains an insurable interest when existing goods are identified to the lease contract even though the goods identified are nonconforming and the lessee has an option to reject them.

(2) If a lessee has an insurable interest only by reason of the lessor's identification of the goods, the lessor, until default or insolvency or notification to the lessee that identification is final, may substitute other goods for those identified.

(3) Notwithstanding a lessee's insurable interest under subsections (1) and (2), the lessor retains an insurable interest until an option to buy has been exercised by the lessee and risk of loss has passed to the lessee.

(4) Nothing in this section impairs any insurable interest recognized under any other statute or rule of law.

(5) The parties by agreement may determine that one or more parties have an obligation to obtain and pay for insurance covering the goods and by agreement may determine the beneficiary of the proceeds of the insurance.

§ 2A—219. Risk of Loss.

(1) Except in the case of a finance lease, risk of loss is retained by the lessor and does not pass to the lessee. In the case of a finance lease, risk of loss passes to the lessee.

(2) Subject to the provisions of this Article on the effect of default on risk of loss (Section 2A—220), if risk of loss is to pass to the lessee and the time of passage is not stated, the following rules apply:

(a) If the lease contract requires or authorizes the goods to be shipped by carrier

(i) and it does not require delivery at a particular destination, the risk of loss passes to the lessee when the goods are duly delivered to the carrier; but

(ii) if it does require delivery at a particular destination and the goods are there duly tendered while in the possession of the carrier, the risk of loss passes to the lessee when the goods are there duly so tendered as to enable the lessee to take delivery.

(b) If the goods are held by a bailee to be delivered without being moved, the risk of loss passes to the lessee on acknowledgment by the bailee of the lessee's right to possession of the goods.

(c) In any case not within subsection (a) or (b), the risk of loss passes to the lessee on the lessee's receipt of the goods if the lessor, or, in the case of a finance lease, the supplier, is a merchant; otherwise the risk passes to the lessee on tender of delivery.

§ 2A—220. Effect of Default on Risk of Loss.

(1) Where risk of loss is to pass to the lessee and the time of passage is not stated:

(a) If a tender or delivery of goods so fails to conform to the lease contract as to give a right of rejection, the risk of their loss remains with the lessor, or, in the case of a finance lease, the supplier, until cure or acceptance.

(b) If the lessee rightfully revokes acceptance, he [or she], to the extent of any deficiency in his [or her] effective insurance coverage, may treat the risk of loss as having remained with the lessor from the beginning.

(2) Whether or not risk of loss is to pass to the lessee, if the lessee as to conforming goods already identified to a lease contract repudiates or is otherwise in default under the lease contract, the lessor, or, in the case of a finance lease, the supplier, to the extent of any deficiency in his [or her] effective insurance coverage may treat the risk of loss as resting on the lessee for a commercially reasonable time.

§ 2A—221. Casualty to Identified Goods.

If a lease contract requires goods identified when the lease contract is made, and the goods suffer casualty without fault of the lessee, the lessor or the supplier before delivery, or the goods suffer casualty before risk of loss passes to the lessee pursuant to the lease agreement or Section 2A—219, then:

(a) if the loss is total, the lease contract is avoided; and

(b) if the loss is partial or the goods have so deteriorated as to no longer conform to the lease contract, the lessee may nevertheless demand inspection and at his [or her] option either treat the lease contract as avoided or, except in a finance lease that is not a consumer lease, accept the goods with due allowance from the rent payable for the balance of the lease term for the deterioration or the deficiency in quantity but without further right against the lessor.

Part 3 Effect Of Lease Contract

§ 2A—301. Enforceability of Lease Contract.

Except as otherwise provided in this Article, a lease contract is effective and enforceable according to its terms between the parties, against purchasers of the goods and against creditors of the parties.

§ 2A—302. Title to and Possession of Goods.

Except as otherwise provided in this Article, each provision of this Article applies whether the lessor or a third party has title to the goods, and whether the lessor, the lessee, or a third party has possession of the goods, notwithstanding any statute or rule of law that possession or the absence of possession is fraudulent.

§ 2A—303. Alienability of Party's Interest Under Lease Contract or of Lessor's Residual Interest in Goods; Delegation of Performance; Transfer of Rights.

(1) As used in this section, "creation of a security interest" includes the sale of a lease contract that is subject to Article 9, Secured Transactions, by reason of Section 9—102(1)(b).

(2) Except as provided in subsections (3) and (4), a provision in a lease agreement which (i) prohibits the voluntary or involuntary transfer, including a transfer by sale, sublease, creation or enforcement of a security interest, or attachment, levy, or other judicial process, of an interest of a party under the lease contract or of the lessor's residual interest in the goods, or (ii) makes such a transfer an event of default, gives rise to the rights and remedies provided in subsection (5), but a transfer that is prohibited or is an event of default under the lease agreement is otherwise effective.

(3) A provision in a lease agreement which (i) prohibits the creation or enforcement of a security interest in an interest of a party under the lease contract or in the lessor's residual interest in the goods, or (ii) makes such a transfer an event of default, is not enforceable unless, and then only to the extent that, there is an actual transfer by the lessee of the lessee's right of possession or use of the goods in violation of the provision or an actual delegation of a material performance of either party to the lease contract in violation of the provision. Neither the granting nor the enforcement of a security interest in (i) the lessor's interest under the lease contract or (ii) the lessor's residual interest in the goods is a transfer that materially impairs the prospect of obtaining return performance by, materially changes the duty of, or materially increases the burden or risk imposed on, the lessee within the purview of subsection (5) unless, and then only to the extent that, there is an actual delegation of a material performance of the lessor.

(4) A provision in a lease agreement which (i) prohibits a transfer of a right to damages for default with respect to the whole lease contract or of a right to payment arising out of the transferor's due performance of the transferor's entire obligation, or (ii) makes such a transfer an event of default, is not enforceable, and such a transfer is not a transfer that materially impairs the prospect of obtaining return performance by, materially changes the duty of, or materially increases the burden or risk imposed on, the other party to the lease contract within the purview of subsection (5).

(5) Subject to subsections (3) and (4):

(a) if a transfer is made which is made an event of default under a lease agreement, the party to the lease contract not making the transfer, unless that party waives the default or otherwise agrees, has the rights and remedies described in Section 2A—501(2);

(b) if paragraph (a) is not applicable and if a transfer is made that (i) is prohibited under a lease agreement or (ii) materially impairs the prospect of obtaining return performance by, materially changes the duty of, or materially increases the burden or risk imposed on, the other party to the lease contract, unless the party not making the transfer agrees at any time to the transfer in the lease contract or otherwise, then, except as limited by contract, (i) the transferor is liable to the party not making the transfer for damages caused by the transfer to the extent that the damages could not reasonably be prevented by the party not making the transfer and (ii) a court having jurisdiction may grant other appropriate relief, including cancellation of the lease contract or an injunction against the transfer.

(6) A transfer of "the lease" or of "all my rights under the lease," or a transfer in similar general terms, is a transfer of rights and, unless the language or the circumstances, as in a transfer for security, indicate the contrary, the transfer is a delegation of duties by the transferor to the transferee. Acceptance by the transferee constitutes a promise by the transferee to perform those duties. The promise is enforceable by either the transferor or the other party to the lease contract.

(7) Unless otherwise agreed by the lessor and the lessee, a delegation of performance does not relieve the transferor as against the other party of any duty to perform or of any liability for default.

(8) In a consumer lease, to prohibit the transfer of an interest of a party under the lease contract or to make a transfer an event of default, the language must be specific, by a writing, and conspicuous.

As amended in 1990.

§ 2A—304. **Subsequent Lease of Goods by Lessor.**

(1) Subject to Section 2A—303, a subsequent lessee from a lessor of goods under an existing lease contract obtains, to the extent of the leasehold interest transferred, the leasehold interest in the goods that the lessor had or had power to transfer, and except as provided in subsection (2) and Section 2A—527(4), takes subject to the existing lease contract. A lessor with voidable title has power to transfer a good leasehold interest to a good faith subsequent lessee for value, but only to the extent set forth in the preceding sentence. If goods have been delivered under a transaction of purchase the lessor has that power even though:

(a) the lessor's transferor was deceived as to the identity of the lessor;

(b) the delivery was in exchange for a check which is later dishonored;

(c) it was agreed that the transaction was to be a "cash sale"; or

(d) the delivery was procured through fraud punishable as larcenous under the criminal law.

(2) A subsequent lessee in the ordinary course of business from a lessor who is a merchant dealing in goods of that kind to whom the goods were entrusted by the existing lessee of that lessor before the interest of the subsequent lessee became enforceable against that lessor obtains, to the extent of the leasehold interest transferred, all of that lessor's and the existing lessee's rights to the goods, and takes free of the existing lease contract.

(3) A subsequent lessee from the lessor of goods that are subject to an existing lease contract and are covered by a certificate of title issued under a statute of this State or of another jurisdiction takes no greater rights than those provided both by this section and by the certificate of title statute.

As amended in 1990.

§ 2A—305. **Sale or Sublease of Goods by Lessee.**

(1) Subject to the provisions of Section 2A—303, a buyer or sublessee from the lessee of goods under an existing lease contract obtains, to the extent of the interest transferred, the leasehold interest in the goods that the lessee had or had power to transfer, and except as provided in subsection (2) and Section 2A—511(4), takes subject to the existing lease contract. A lessee with a voidable leasehold interest has power to transfer a good leasehold interest to a good faith buyer for value or a good faith sublessee for value, but only to the extent set forth in the preceding sentence. When goods have been delivered under a transaction of lease the lessee has that power even though:

(a) the lessor was deceived as to the identity of the lessee;

(b) the delivery was in exchange for a check which is later dishonored; or

(c) the delivery was procured through fraud punishable as larcenous under the criminal law.

(2) A buyer in the ordinary course of business or a sublessee in the ordinary course of business from a lessee who is a merchant dealing in goods of that kind to whom the goods were entrusted by the lessor obtains, to the extent of the interest transferred, all of the lessor's and lessee's rights to the goods, and takes free of the existing lease contract.

(3) A buyer or sublessee from the lessee of goods that are subject to an existing lease contract and are covered by a certificate of title issued under a statute of this State or of another jurisdiction takes no greater rights than those provided both by this section and by the certificate of title statute.

§ 2A—306. **Priority of Certain Liens Arising by Operation of Law.**

If a person in the ordinary course of his [or her] business furnishes services or materials with respect to goods subject to a lease contract, a lien upon those goods in the possession of that person given by statute or rule of law for those materials or services takes priority over any interest of the lessor or lessee under the lease contract or this Article unless the lien is created by statute and the statute provides otherwise or unless the lien is created by rule of law and the rule of law provides otherwise.

§ 2A—307. Priority of Liens Arising by Attachment or Levy on, Security Interests in, and Other Claims to Goods.

(1) Except as otherwise provided in Section 2A—306, a creditor of a lessee takes subject to the lease contract.

(2) Except as otherwise provided in subsections (3) and (4) and in Sections 2A—306 and 2A—308, a creditor of a lessor takes subject to the lease contract unless:

(a) the creditor holds a lien that attached to the goods before the lease contract became enforceable,

(b) the creditor holds a security interest in the goods and the lessee did not give value and receive delivery of the goods without knowledge of the security interest; or

(c) the creditor holds a security interest in the goods which was perfected (Section 9—303) before the lease contract became enforceable.

(3) A lessee in the ordinary course of business takes the leasehold interest free of a security interest in the goods created by the lessor even though the security interest is perfected (Section 9—303) and the lessee knows of its existence.

(4) A lessee other than a lessee in the ordinary course of business takes the leasehold interest free of a security interest to the extent that it secures future advances made after the secured party acquires knowledge of the lease or more than 45 days after the lease contract becomes enforceable, whichever first occurs, unless the future advances are made pursuant to a commitment entered into without knowledge of the lease and before the expiration of the 45-day period.

§ 2A—308. Special Rights of Creditors.

(1) A creditor of a lessor in possession of goods subject to a lease contract may treat the lease contract as void if as against the creditor retention of possession by the lessor is fraudulent under any statute or rule of law, but retention of possession in good faith and current course of trade by the lessor for a commercially reasonable time after the lease contract becomes enforceable is not fraudulent.

(2) Nothing in this Article impairs the rights of creditors of a lessor if the lease contract (a) becomes enforceable, not in current course of trade but in satisfaction of or as security for a pre-existing claim for money, security, or the like, and (b) is made under circumstances which under any statute or rule of law apart from this Article would constitute the transaction a fraudulent transfer or voidable preference.

(3) A creditor of a seller may treat a sale or an identification of goods to a contract for sale as void if as against the creditor retention of possession by the seller is fraudulent under any statute or rule of law, but retention of possession of the goods pursuant to a lease contract entered into by the seller as lessee and the buyer as lessor in connection with the sale or identification of the goods is not fraudulent if the buyer bought for value and in good faith.

§ 2A—309. Lessor's and Lessee's Rights When Goods Become Fixtures.

(1) In this section:

(a) goods are "fixtures" when they become so related to particular real estate that an interest in them arises under real estate law;

(b) a "fixture filing" is the filing, in the office where a mortgage on the real estate would be filed or recorded, of a financing statement covering goods that are or are to become fixtures and conforming to the requirements of Section 9—402(5);

(c) a lease is a "purchase money lease" unless the lessee has possession or use of the goods or the right to possession or use of the goods before the lease agreement is enforceable;

(d) a mortgage is a "construction mortgage" to the extent it secures an obligation incurred for the construction of an improvement on land including the acquisition cost of the land, if the recorded writing so indicates; and

(e) "encumbrance" includes real estate mortgages and other liens on real estate and all other rights in real estate that are not ownership interests.

(2) Under this Article a lease may be of goods that are fixtures or may continue in goods that become fixtures, but no lease exists under this Article of ordinary building materials incorporated into an improvement on land.

(3) This Article does not prevent creation of a lease of fixtures pursuant to real estate law.

(4) The perfected interest of a lessor of fixtures has priority over a conflicting interest of an encumbrancer or owner of the real estate if:

(a) the lease is a purchase money lease, the conflicting interest of the encumbrancer or owner arises before the goods become fixtures, the interest of the lessor is perfected by a fixture filing before the goods become fixtures or within ten days thereafter, and the lessee has an interest of record in the real estate or is in possession of the real estate; or

(b) the interest of the lessor is perfected by a fixture filing before the interest of the encumbrancer or owner is of record, the lessor's interest has priority over any conflicting interest of a predecessor in title of the encumbrancer or owner, and the lessee has an interest of record in the real estate or is in possession of the real estate.

(5) The interest of a lessor of fixtures, whether or not perfected, has priority over the conflicting interest of an encumbrancer or owner of the real estate if:

(a) the fixtures are readily removable factory or office machines, readily removable equipment that is not primarily used or leased for use in the operation of the real estate, or readily removable replacements of domestic appliances that are goods subject to a consumer lease, and before the goods become fixtures the lease contract is enforceable; or

(b) the conflicting interest is a lien on the real estate obtained by legal or equitable proceedings after the lease contract is enforceable; or

(c) the encumbrancer or owner has consented in writing to the lease or has disclaimed an interest in the goods as fixtures; or

(d) the lessee has a right to remove the goods as against the encumbrancer or owner. If the lessee's right to remove terminates, the priority of the interest of the lessor continues for a reasonable time.

(6) Notwithstanding paragraph (4)(a) but otherwise subject to subsections (4) and (5), the interest of a lessor of fixtures, including the lessor's residual interest, is subordinate to the conflicting interest of an encumbrancer of the real estate under a construction mortgage recorded before the goods become fixtures if the goods become fixtures before the completion of the construction. To the extent given to refinance a construction mortgage, the conflicting interest of an encumbrancer of the real estate under a mortgage has this priority to the same extent as the encumbrancer of the real estate under the construction mortgage.

(7) In cases not within the preceding subsections, priority between the interest of a lessor of fixtures, including the lessor's residual interest, and the conflicting interest of an encumbrancer or owner of the real estate who is not the lessee is determined by the priority rules governing conflicting interests in real estate.

(8) If the interest of a lessor of fixtures, including the lessor's residual interest, has priority over all conflicting interests of all owners and encumbrancers of the real estate, the lessor or the lessee may (i) on default, expiration, termination, or cancellation of the lease agreement but subject to the agreement and this Article, or (ii) if necessary to enforce other rights and remedies of the lessor or lessee under this Article, remove the goods from the real estate, free and clear of all conflicting interests of all owners and encumbrancers of the real estate, but the lessor or lessee must reimburse any encumbrancer or owner of the real estate who is not the lessee and who has not otherwise agreed for the cost of repair of any physical injury, but not for any diminution in value of the real estate caused by the absence of the goods removed or by any necessity of replacing them. A person entitled to reimbursement may refuse

permission to remove until the party seeking removal gives adequate security for the performance of this obligation.

(9) Even though the lease agreement does not create a security interest, the interest of a lessor of fixtures, including the lessor's residual interest, is perfected by filing a financing statement as a fixture filing for leased goods that are or are to become fixtures in accordance with the relevant provisions of the Article on Secured Transactions (Article 9).

As amended in 1990.

§ 2A—310. Lessor's and Lessee's Rights When Goods Become Accessions.

(1) Goods are "accessions" when they are installed in or affixed to other goods.

(2) The interest of a lessor or a lessee under a lease contract entered into before the goods became accessions is superior to all interests in the whole except as stated in subsection (4).

(3) The interest of a lessor or a lessee under a lease contract entered into at the time or after the goods became accessions is superior to all subsequently acquired interests in the whole except as stated in subsection (4) but is subordinate to interests in the whole existing at the time the lease contract was made unless the holders of such interests in the whole have in writing consented to the lease or disclaimed an interest in the goods as part of the whole.

(4) The interest of a lessor or a lessee under a lease contract described in subsection (2) or (3) is subordinate to the interest of

(a) a buyer in the ordinary course of business or a lessee in the ordinary course of business of any interest in the whole acquired after the goods became accessions; or

(b) a creditor with a security interest in the whole perfected before the lease contract was made to the extent that the creditor makes subsequent advances without knowledge of the lease contract.

(5) When under subsections (2) or (3) and (4) a lessor or a lessee of accessions holds an interest that is superior to all interests in the whole, the lessor or the lessee may (a) on default, expiration, termination, or cancellation of the lease contract by the other party but subject to the provisions of the lease contract and this Article, or (b) if necessary to enforce his [or her] other rights and remedies under this Article, remove the goods from the whole, free and clear of all interests in the whole, but he [or she] must reimburse any holder of an interest in the whole who is not the lessee and who has not otherwise agreed for the cost of repair of any physical injury but not for any diminution in value of the whole caused by the absence of the goods removed or by any necessity for replacing them. A person entitled to reimbursement may refuse permission to remove until the party seeking removal gives adequate security for the performance of this obligation.

§ 2A—311. **Priority Subject to Subordination.**

Nothing in this Article prevents subordination by agreement by any person entitled to priority.

As added in 1990.

Part 4 Performance Of Lease Contract: Repudiated, Substituted And Excused

§ 2A—401. **Insecurity: Adequate Assurance of Performance.**

(1) A lease contract imposes an obligation on each party that the other's expectation of receiving due performance will not be impaired.

(2) If reasonable grounds for insecurity arise with respect to the performance of either party, the insecure party may demand in writing adequate assurance of due performance. Until the insecure party receives that assurance, if commercially reasonable the insecure party may suspend any performance for which he [or she] has not already received the agreed return.

(3) A repudiation of the lease contract occurs if assurance of due performance adequate under the circumstances of the particular case is not provided to the insecure party within a reasonable time, not to exceed 30 days after receipt of a demand by the other party.

(4) Between merchants, the reasonableness of grounds for insecurity and the adequacy of any assurance offered must be determined according to commercial standards.

(5) Acceptance of any nonconforming delivery or payment does not prejudice the aggrieved party's right to demand adequate assurance of future performance.

§ 2A—402. **Anticipatory Repudiation.**

If either party repudiates a lease contract with respect to a performance not yet due under the lease contract, the loss of which performance will substantially impair the value of the lease contract to the other, the aggrieved party may:

(a) for a commercially reasonable time, await retraction of repudiation and performance by the repudiating party;

(b) make demand pursuant to Section 2A—401 and await assurance of future performance adequate under the circumstances of the particular case; or

(c) resort to any right or remedy upon default under the lease contract or this Article, even though the aggrieved party has notified the repudiating party that the aggrieved party would await the repudiating party's performance and assurance and has urged retraction. In addition, whether or not the aggrieved party is pursuing one of the foregoing remedies, the aggrieved party may suspend performance or, if the aggrieved party is the lessor, proceed in accordance with the provisions of this Article on the lessor's right to identify goods to the lease contract notwithstanding default or to salvage unfinished goods (Section 2A—524).

§ 2A—403. **Retraction of Anticipatory Repudiation.**

(1) Until the repudiating party's next performance is due, the repudiating party can retract the repudiation unless, since the repudiation, the aggrieved party has cancelled the lease contract or materially changed the aggrieved party's position or otherwise indicated that the aggrieved party considers the repudiation final.

(2) Retraction may be by any method that clearly indicates to the aggrieved party that the repudiating party intends to perform under the lease contract and includes any assurance demanded under Section 2A—401.

(3) Retraction reinstates a repudiating party's rights under a lease contract with due excuse and allowance to the aggrieved party for any delay occasioned by the repudiation.

§ 2A—404. **Substituted Performance.**

(1) If without fault of the lessee, the lessor and the supplier, the agreed berthing, loading, or unloading facilities fail or the agreed type of carrier becomes unavailable or the agreed manner of delivery otherwise becomes commercially impracticable, but a commercially reasonable substitute is available, the substitute performance must be tendered and accepted.

(2) If the agreed means or manner of payment fails because of domestic or foreign governmental regulation:

(a) the lessor may withhold or stop delivery or cause the supplier to withhold or stop delivery unless the lessee provides a means or manner of payment that is commercially a substantial equivalent; and

(b) if delivery has already been taken, payment by the means or in the manner provided by the regulation discharges the lessee's obligation unless the regulation is discriminatory, oppressive, or predatory.

§ 2A—405. **Excused Performance.**

Subject to Section 2A—404 on substituted performance, the following rules apply:

(a) Delay in delivery or nondelivery in whole or in part by a lessor or a supplier who complies with paragraphs (b) and (c) is not a default under the lease contract if performance as agreed has been made impracticable by the occurrence of a contingency the nonoccurrence of which was a basic assumption on which the lease contract was made or by compliance in good faith with any applicable foreign or domestic governmental regulation or order, whether or not the regulation or order later proves to be invalid.

(b) If the causes mentioned in paragraph (a) affect only part of the lessor's or the supplier's capacity to perform, he [or she] shall allocate production and deliveries among his [or her] customers but at his [or her] option may include regular customers not then under contract for sale or lease as well as his [or her] own requirements for further manufacture. He [or she] may so allocate in any manner that is fair and reasonable.

(c) The lessor seasonably shall notify the lessee and in the case of a finance lease the supplier seasonably shall notify the lessor and the lessee, if known, that there will be delay or nondelivery and, if allocation is required under paragraph (b), of the estimated quota thus made available for the lessee.

§ 2A—406. Procedure on Excused Performance.

(1) If the lessee receives notification of a material or indefinite delay or an allocation justified under Section 2A—405, the lessee may by written notification to the lessor as to any goods involved, and with respect to all of the goods if under an installment lease contract the value of the whole lease contract is substantially impaired (Section 2A—510):

> (a) terminate the lease contract (Section 2A—505(2)); or

> (b) except in a finance lease that is not a consumer lease, modify the lease contract by accepting the available quota in substitution, with due allowance from the rent payable for the balance of the lease term for the deficiency but without further right against the lessor.

(2) If, after receipt of a notification from the lessor under Section 2A—405, the lessee fails so to modify the lease agreement within a reasonable time not exceeding 30 days, the lease contract lapses with respect to any deliveries affected.

§ 2A—407. Irrevocable Promises: Finance Leases.

(1) In the case of a finance lease that is not a consumer lease the lessee's promises under the lease contract become irrevocable and independent upon the lessee's acceptance of the goods.

(2) A promise that has become irrevocable and independent under subsection (1):

> (a) is effective and enforceable between the parties, and by or against third parties including assignees of the parties, and

> (b) is not subject to cancellation, termination, modification, repudiation, excuse, or substitution without the consent of the party to whom the promise runs.

(3) This section does not affect the validity under any other law of a covenant in any lease contract making the lessee's promises irrevocable and independent upon the lessee's acceptance of the goods.

As amended in 1990.

Part 5 Default

A. In General

§ 2A—501. Default: Procedure.

(1) Whether the lessor or the lessee is in default under a lease contract is determined by the lease agreement and this Article.

(2) If the lessor or the lessee is in default under the lease contract, the party seeking enforcement has rights and remedies as provided in this Article and, except as limited by this Article, as provided in the lease agreement.

(3) If the lessor or the lessee is in default under the lease contract, the party seeking enforcement may reduce the party's claim to judgment, or otherwise enforce the lease contract by self-help or any available judicial procedure or nonjudicial procedure, including administrative proceeding, arbitration, or the like, in accordance with this Article.

(4) Except as otherwise provided in Section 1–106(1) or this Article or the lease agreement, the rights and remedies referred to in subsections (2) and (3) are cumulative.

(5) If the lease agreement covers both real property and goods, the party seeking enforcement may proceed under this Part as to the goods, or under other applicable law as to both the real property and the goods in accordance with that party's rights and remedies in respect of the real property, in which case this Part does not apply.

As amended in 1990.

§ 2A—502. Notice After Default.

Except as otherwise provided in this Article or the lease agreement, the lessor or lessee in default under the lease contract is not entitled to notice of default or notice of enforcement from the other party to the lease agreement.

§ 2A—503. Modification or Impairment of Rights and Remedies.

(1) Except as otherwise provided in this Article, the lease agreement may include rights and remedies for default in addition to or in substitution for those provided in this Article and may limit or alter the measure of damages recoverable under this Article.

(2) Resort to a remedy provided under this Article or in the lease agreement is optional unless the remedy is expressly agreed to be exclusive. If circumstances cause an exclusive or limited remedy to fail of its essential purpose, or provision for an exclusive remedy is unconscionable, remedy may be had as provided in this Article.

(3) Consequential damages may be liquidated under Section 2A—504, or may otherwise be limited, altered, or excluded unless the limitation, alteration, or exclusion is unconscionable. Limitation, alteration, or exclusion of consequential damages for injury to the person in the case of consumer goods is prima facie unconscionable but limitation, alteration, or exclusion of damages where the loss is commercial is not prima facie unconscionable.

(4) Rights and remedies on default by the lessor or the lessee with respect to any obligation or promise collateral or ancillary to the lease contract are not impaired by this Article.

As amended in 1990.

§ 2A—504. **Liquidation of Damages.**

(1) Damages payable by either party for default, or any other act or omission, including indemnity for loss or diminution of anticipated tax benefits or loss or damage to lessor's residual interest, may be liquidated in the lease agreement but only at an amount or by a formula that is reasonable in light of the then anticipated harm caused by the default or other act or omission.

(2) If the lease agreement provides for liquidation of damages, and such provision does not comply with subsection (1), or such provision is an exclusive or limited remedy that circumstances cause to fail of its essential purpose, remedy may be had as provided in this Article.

(3) If the lessor justifiably withholds or stops delivery of goods because of the lessee's default or insolvency (Section 2A—525 or 2A—526), the lessee is entitled to restitution of any amount by which the sum of his [or her] payments exceeds:

> (a) the amount to which the lessor is entitled by virtue of terms liquidating the lessor's damages in accordance with subsection (1); or

> (b) in the absence of those terms, 20 percent of the then present value of the total rent the lessee was obligated to pay for the balance of the lease term, or, in the case of a consumer lease, the lesser of such amount or $500.

(4) A lessee's right to restitution under subsection (3) is subject to offset to the extent the lessor establishes:

> (a) a right to recover damages under the provisions of this Article other than subsection (1); and

> (b) the amount or value of any benefits received by the lessee directly or indirectly by reason of the lease contract.

§ 2A—505. **Cancellation and Termination and Effect of Cancellation, Termination, Rescission, or Fraud on Rights and Remedies.**

(1) On cancellation of the lease contract, all obligations that are still executory on both sides are discharged, but any right based on prior default or performance survives, and the cancelling party also retains any remedy for default of the whole lease contract or any unperformed balance.

(2) On termination of the lease contract, all obligations that are still executory on both sides are discharged but any right based on prior default or performance survives.

(3) Unless the contrary intention clearly appears, expressions of "cancellation," "rescission," or the like of the lease contract may not be construed as a renunciation or discharge of any claim in damages for an antecedent default.

(4) Rights and remedies for material misrepresentation or fraud include all rights and remedies available under this Article for default.

(5) Neither rescission nor a claim for rescission of the lease contract nor rejection or return of the goods may bar or be deemed inconsistent with a claim for damages or other right or remedy.

§ 2A—506. **Statute of Limitations.**

(1) An action for default under a lease contract, including breach of warranty or indemnity, must be commenced within 4 years after the cause of action accrued. By the original lease contract the parties may reduce the period of limitation to not less than one year.

(2) A cause of action for default accrues when the act or omission on which the default or breach of warranty is based is or should have been discovered by the aggrieved party, or when the default occurs, whichever is later. A cause of action for indemnity accrues when the act or omission on which the claim for indemnity is based is or should have been discovered by the indemnified party, whichever is later.

(3) If an action commenced within the time limited by subsection (1) is so terminated as to leave available a remedy by another action for the same default or breach of warranty or indemnity, the other action may be commenced after the expiration of the time limited and within 6 months after the termination of the first action unless the termination resulted from voluntary discontinuance or from dismissal for failure or neglect to prosecute.

(4) This section does not alter the law on tolling of the statute of limitations nor does it apply to causes of action that have accrued before this Article becomes effective.

§ 2A—507. **Proof of Market Rent: Time and Place.**

(1) Damages based on market rent (Section 2A—519 or 2A—528) are determined according to the rent for the use of the goods concerned for a lease term identical to the remaining lease term of the original lease agreement and prevailing at the times specified in Sections 2A–519 and 2A–528.

(2) If evidence of rent for the use of the goods concerned for a lease term identical to the remaining lease term of the original lease agreement and prevailing at the times or places described in this Article is not readily available, the rent prevailing within any reasonable time before or after the time described or at any other place or for a different lease term which in commercial judgment or under usage of trade would serve as a reasonable substitute for the one described may be used, making any proper allowance for the difference, including the cost of transporting the goods to or from the other place.

(3) Evidence of a relevant rent prevailing at a time or place or for a lease term other than the one described in this Article offered by one party is not admissible unless and until he [or she] has given the other party notice the court finds sufficient to prevent unfair surprise.

(4) If the prevailing rent or value of any goods regularly leased in any established market is in issue, reports in official

publications or trade journals or in newspapers or periodicals of general circulation published as the reports of that market are admissible in evidence. The circumstances of the preparation of the report may be shown to affect its weight but not its admissibility.

As amended in 1990.

B. Default by Lessor

§ 2A—508. Lessee's Remedies.

(1) If a lessor fails to deliver the goods in conformity to the lease contract (Section 2A—509) or repudiates the lease contract (Section 2A—402), or a lessee rightfully rejects the goods (Section 2A—509) or justifiably revokes acceptance of the goods (Section 2A—517), then with respect to any goods involved, and with respect to all of the goods if under an installment lease contract the value of the whole lease contract is substantially impaired (Section 2A—510), the lessor is in default under the lease contract and the lessee may:

(a) cancel the lease contract (Section 2A—505(1));

(b) recover so much of the rent and security as has been paid and is just under the circumstances;

(c) cover and recover damages as to all goods affected whether or not they have been identified to the lease contract (Sections 2A—518 and 2A—520), or recover damages for nondelivery (Sections 2A—519 and 2A—520);

(d) exercise any other rights or pursue any other remedies provided in the lease contract..

(2) If a lessor fails to deliver the goods in conformity to the lease contract or repudiates the lease contract, the lessee may also:

(a) if the goods have been identified, recover them (Section 2A—522); or

(b) in a proper case, obtain specific performance or replevy the goods (Section 2A—521).

(3) If a lessor is otherwise in default under a lease contract, the lessee may exercise the rights and pursue the remedies provided in the lease contract, which may include a right to cancel the lease, and in Section 2A–519(3).

(4) If a lessor has breached a warranty, whether express or implied, the lessee may recover damages (Section 2A—519(4)).

(5) On rightful rejection or justifiable revocation of acceptance, a lessee has a security interest in goods in the lessee's possession or control for any rent and security that has been paid and any expenses reasonably incurred in their inspection, receipt, transportation, and care and custody and may hold those goods and dispose of them in good faith and in a commercially reasonable manner, subject to Section 2A—527(5).

(6) Subject to the provisions of Section 2A—407, a lessee, on notifying the lessor of the lessee's intention to do so,

may deduct all or any part of the damages resulting from any default under the lease contract from any part of the rent still due under the same lease contract.

As amended in 1990.

§ 2A—509. Lessee's Rights on Improper Delivery; Rightful Rejection.

(1) Subject to the provisions of Section 2A—510 on default in installment lease contracts, if the goods or the tender or delivery fail in any respect to conform to the lease contract, the lessee may reject or accept the goods or accept any commercial unit or units and reject the rest of the goods.

(2) Rejection of goods is ineffective unless it is within a reasonable time after tender or delivery of the goods and the lessee seasonably notifies the lessor.

§ 2A—510. Installment Lease Contracts: Rejection and Default.

(1) Under an installment lease contract a lessee may reject any delivery that is nonconforming if the nonconformity substantially impairs the value of that delivery and cannot be cured or the nonconformity is a defect in the required documents; but if the nonconformity does not fall within subsection (2) and the lessor or the supplier gives adequate assurance of its cure, the lessee must accept that delivery.

(2) Whenever nonconformity or default with respect to one or more deliveries substantially impairs the value of the installment lease contract as a whole there is a default with respect to the whole. But, the aggrieved party reinstates the installment lease contract as a whole if the aggrieved party accepts a nonconforming delivery without seasonably notifying of cancellation or brings an action with respect only to past deliveries or demands performance as to future deliveries.

§ 2A—511. Merchant Lessee's Duties as to Rightfully Rejected Goods.

(1) Subject to any security interest of a lessee (Section 2A—508(5)), if a lessor or a supplier has no agent or place of business at the market of rejection, a merchant lessee, after rejection of goods in his [or her] possession or control, shall follow any reasonable instructions received from the lessor or the supplier with respect to the goods. In the absence of those instructions, a merchant lessee shall make reasonable efforts to sell, lease, or otherwise dispose of the goods for the lessor's account if they threaten to decline in value speedily. Instructions are not reasonable if on demand indemnity for expenses is not forthcoming.

(2) If a merchant lessee (subsection (1)) or any other lessee (Section 2A—512) disposes of goods, he [or she] is entitled to reimbursement either from the lessor or the supplier or out of the proceeds for reasonable expenses of caring for and disposing of the goods and, if the expenses include no disposition commission, to such commission as is usual in the trade, or if there is none, to a reasonable sum not exceeding 10 percent of the gross proceeds.

(3) In complying with this section or Section 2A—512, the lessee is held only to good faith. Good faith conduct hereunder is neither acceptance or conversion nor the basis of an action for damages.

(4) A purchaser who purchases in good faith from a lessee pursuant to this section or Section 2A—512 takes the goods free of any rights of the lessor and the supplier even though the lessee fails to comply with one or more of the requirements of this Article.

§ 2A—512. Lessee's Duties as to Rightfully Rejected Goods.

(1) Except as otherwise provided with respect to goods that threaten to decline in value speedily (Section 2A—511) and subject to any security interest of a lessee (Section 2A—508(5)):

(a) the lessee, after rejection of goods in the lessee's possession, shall hold them with reasonable care at the lessor's or the supplier's disposition for a reasonable time after the lessee's seasonable notification of rejection;

(b) if the lessor or the supplier gives no instructions within a reasonable time after notification of rejection, the lessee may store the rejected goods for the lessor's or the supplier's account or ship them to the lessor or the supplier or dispose of them for the lessor's or the supplier's account with reimbursement in the manner provided in Section 2A—511; but

(c) the lessee has no further obligations with regard to goods rightfully rejected.

(2) Action by the lessee pursuant to subsection (1) is not acceptance or conversion.

§ 2A—513. Cure by Lessor of Improper Tender or Delivery; Replacement.

(1) If any tender or delivery by the lessor or the supplier is rejected because nonconforming and the time for performance has not yet expired, the lessor or the supplier may seasonably notify the lessee of the lessor's or the supplier's intention to cure and may then make a conforming delivery within the time provided in the lease contract.

(2) If the lessee rejects a nonconforming tender that the lessor or the supplier had reasonable grounds to believe would be acceptable with or without money allowance, the lessor or the supplier may have a further reasonable time to substitute a conforming tender if he [or she] seasonably notifies the lessee.

§ 2A—514. Waiver of Lessee's Objections.

(1) In rejecting goods, a lessee's failure to state a particular defect that is ascertainable by reasonable inspection precludes the lessee from relying on the defect to justify rejection or to establish default:

(a) if, stated seasonably, the lessor or the supplier could have cured it (Section 2A—513); or

(b) between merchants if the lessor or the supplier after rejection has made a request in writing for a full and final written statement of all defects on which the lessee proposes to rely.

(2) A lessee's failure to reserve rights when paying rent or other consideration against documents precludes recovery of the payment for defects apparent on the face of the documents.

§ 2A—515. Acceptance of Goods.

(1) Acceptance of goods occurs after the lessee has had a reasonable opportunity to inspect the goods and

(a) the lessee signifies or acts with respect to the goods in a manner that signifies to the lessor or the supplier that the goods are conforming or that the lessee will take or retain them in spite of their nonconformity; or

(b) the lessee fails to make an effective rejection of the goods (Section 2A—509(2)).

(2) Acceptance of a part of any commercial unit is acceptance of that entire unit.

§ 2A—516. Effect of Acceptance of Goods; Notice of Default; Burden of Establishing Default after Acceptance; Notice of Claim or Litigation to Person Answerable Over.

(1) A lessee must pay rent for any goods accepted in accordance with the lease contract, with due allowance for goods rightfully rejected or not delivered.

(2) A lessee's acceptance of goods precludes rejection of the goods accepted. In the case of a finance lease, if made with knowledge of a nonconformity, acceptance cannot be revoked because of it. In any other case, if made with knowledge of a nonconformity, acceptance cannot be revoked because of it unless the acceptance was on the reasonable assumption that the nonconformity would be seasonably cured. Acceptance does not of itself impair any other remedy provided by this Article or the lease agreement for nonconformity.

(3) If a tender has been accepted:

(a) within a reasonable time after the lessee discovers or should have discovered any default, the lessee shall notify the lessor and the supplier, if any, or be barred from any remedy against the party notified;

(b) except in the case of a consumer lease, within a reasonable time after the lessee receives notice of litigation for infringement or the like (Section 2A—211) the lessee shall notify the lessor or be barred from any remedy over for liability established by the litigation; and

(c) the burden is on the lessee to establish any default.

(4) If a lessee is sued for breach of a warranty or other obligation for which a lessor or a supplier is answerable over the following apply:

(a) The lessee may give the lessor or the supplier, or both, written notice of the litigation. If the notice states that the person notified may come in and defend and that if the person notified does not do so that person will be bound in any action against that person by the lessee by any determination of fact common to the two litigations, then unless the person notified after seasonable receipt of the notice does come in and defend that person is so bound.

(b) The lessor or the supplier may demand in writing that the lessee turn over control of the litigation including settlement if the claim is one for infringement or the like (Section 2A—211) or else be barred from any remedy over. If the demand states that the lessor or the supplier agrees to bear all expense and to satisfy any adverse judgment, then unless the lessee after seasonable receipt of the demand does turn over control the lessee is so barred.

(5) Subsections (3) and (4) apply to any obligation of a lessee to hold the lessor or the supplier harmless against infringement or the like (Section 2A—211).

As amended in 1990.

§ 2A—517. **Revocation of Acceptance of Goods.**

(1) A lessee may revoke acceptance of a lot or commercial unit whose nonconformity substantially impairs its value to the lessee if the lessee has accepted it:

(a) except in the case of a finance lease, on the reasonable assumption that its nonconformity would be cured and it has not been seasonably cured; or

(b) without discovery of the nonconformity if the lessee's acceptance was reasonably induced either by the lessor's assurances or, except in the case of a finance lease, by the difficulty of discovery before acceptance.

(2) Except in the case of a finance lease that is not a consumer lease, a lessee may revoke acceptance of a lot or commercial unit if the lessor defaults under the lease contract and the default substantially impairs the value of that lot or commercial unit to the lessee.

(3) If the lease agreement so provides, the lessee may revoke acceptance of a lot or commercial unit because of other defaults by the lessor.

(4) Revocation of acceptance must occur within a reasonable time after the lessee discovers or should have discovered the ground for it and before any substantial change in condition of the goods which is not caused by the nonconformity. Revocation is not effective until the lessee notifies the lessor.

(5) A lessee who so revokes has the same rights and duties with regard to the goods involved as if the lessee had rejected them.

As amended in 1990.

§ 2A—518. **Cover; Substitute Goods.**

(1) After a default by a lessor under the lease contract of the type described in Section 2A—508(1), or, if agreed, after other default by the lessor, the lessee may cover by making any purchase or lease of or contract to purchase or lease goods in substitution for those due from the lessor.

(2) Except as otherwise provided with respect to damages liquidated in the lease agreement (Section 2A—504) or otherwise determined pursuant to agreement of the parties (Sections 1—102(3) and 2A—503), if a lessee's cover is by lease agreement substantially similar to the original lease agreement and the new lease agreement is made in good faith and in a commercially reasonable manner, the lessee may recover from the lessor as damages (i) the present value, as of the date of the commencement of the term of the new lease agreement, of the rent under the new lease agreement applicable to that period of the new lease term which is comparable to the then remaining term of the original lease agreement minus the present value as of the same date of the total rent for the then remaining lease term of the original lease agreement, and (ii) any incidental or consequential damages, less expenses saved in consequence of the lessor's default.

(3) If a lessee's cover is by lease agreement that for any reason does not qualify for treatment under subsection (2), or is by purchase or otherwise, the lessee may recover from the lessor as if the lessee had elected not to cover and Section 2A—519 governs.

As amended in 1990.

§ 2A—519. **Lessee's Damages for Non-Delivery, Repudiation, Default, and Breach of Warranty in Regard to Accepted Goods.**

(1) Except as otherwise provided with respect to damages liquidated in the lease agreement (Section 2A—504) or otherwise determined pursuant to agreement of the parties (Sections 1—102(3) and 2A—503), if a lessee elects not to cover or a lessee elects to cover and the cover is by lease agreement that for any reason does not qualify for treatment under Section 2A—518(2), or is by purchase or otherwise, the measure of damages for non-delivery or repudiation by the lessor or for rejection or revocation of acceptance by the lessee is the present value, as of the date of the default, of the then market rent minus the present value as of the same date of the original rent, computed for the remaining lease term of the original lease agreement, together with incidental and consequential damages, less expenses saved in consequence of the lessor's default.

(2) Market rent is to be determined as of the place for tender or, in cases of rejection after arrival or revocation of acceptance, as of the place of arrival.

(3) Except as otherwise agreed, if the lessee has accepted goods and given notification (Section 2A—516(3)), the measure of damages for non-conforming tender or delivery

or other default by a lessor is the loss resulting in the ordinary course of events from the lessor's default as determined in any manner that is reasonable together with incidental and consequential damages, less expenses saved in consequence of the lessor's default.

(4) Except as otherwise agreed, the measure of damages for breach of warranty is the present value at the time and place of acceptance of the difference between the value of the use of the goods accepted and the value if they had been as warranted for the lease term, unless special circumstances show proximate damages of a different amount, together with incidental and consequential damages, less expenses saved in consequence of the lessor's default or breach of warranty.

As amended in 1990.

§ 2A—520. Lessee's Incidental and Consequential Damages.

(1) Incidental damages resulting from a lessor's default include expenses reasonably incurred in inspection, receipt, transportation, and care and custody of goods rightfully rejected or goods the acceptance of which is justifiably revoked, any commercially reasonable charges, expenses or commissions in connection with effecting cover, and any other reasonable expense incident to the default.

(2) Consequential damages resulting from a lessor's default include:

> (a) any loss resulting from general or particular requirements and needs of which the lessor at the time of contracting had reason to know and which could not reasonably be prevented by cover or otherwise; and

> (b) injury to person or property proximately resulting from any breach of warranty.

§ 2A—521. Lessee's Right to Specific Performance or Replevin.

(1) Specific performance may be decreed if the goods are unique or in other proper circumstances.

(2) A decree for specific performance may include any terms and conditions as to payment of the rent, damages, or other relief that the court deems just.

(3) A lessee has a right of replevin, detinue, sequestration, claim and delivery, or the like for goods identified to the lease contract if after reasonable effort the lessee is unable to effect cover for those goods or the circumstances reasonably indicate that the effort will be unavailing.

§ 2A—522. Lessee's Right to Goods on Lessor's Insolvency.

(1) Subject to subsection (2) and even though the goods have not been shipped, a lessee who has paid a part or all of the rent and security for goods identified to a lease contract (Section 2A—217) on making and keeping good a tender of any unpaid portion of the rent and security due under the lease contract may recover the goods identified from the lessor if the lessor becomes insolvent within 10 days after receipt of the first installment of rent and security.

(2) A lessee acquires the right to recover goods identified to a lease contract only if they conform to the lease contract.

C. Default by Lessee

§ 2A—523. Lessor's Remedies.

(1) If a lessee wrongfully rejects or revokes acceptance of goods or fails to make a payment when due or repudiates with respect to a part or the whole, then, with respect to any goods involved, and with respect to all of the goods if under an installment lease contract the value of the whole lease contract is substantially impaired (Section 2A—510), the lessee is in default under the lease contract and the lessor may:

> (a) cancel the lease contract (Section 2A—505(1));

> (b) proceed respecting goods not identified to the lease contract (Section 2A—524);

> (c) withhold delivery of the goods and take possession of goods previously delivered (Section 2A—525);

> (d) stop delivery of the goods by any bailee (Section 2A—526);

> (e) dispose of the goods and recover damages (Section 2A—527), or retain the goods and recover damages (Section 2A—528), or in a proper case recover rent (Section 2A—529) (f) exercise any other rights or pursue any other remedies provided in the lease contract.

(2) If a lessor does not fully exercise a right or obtain a remedy to which the lessor is entitled under subsection (1), the lessor may recover the loss resulting in the ordinary course of events from the lessee's default as determined in any reasonable manner, together with incidental damages, less expenses saved in consequence of the lessee's default.

(3) If a lessee is otherwise in default under a lease contract, the lessor may exercise the rights and pursue the remedies provided in the lease contract, which may include a right to cancel the lease. In addition, unless otherwise provided in the lease contract:

> (a) if the default substantially impairs the value of the lease contract to the lessor, the lessor may exercise the rights and pursue the remedies provided in subsections (1) or (2); or

> (b) if the default does not substantially impair the value of the lease contract to the lessor, the lessor may recover as provided in subsection (2).

As amended in 1990.

§ 2A—524. Lessor's Right to Identify Goods to Lease Contract.

(1) After default by the lessee under the lease contract of the type described in Section 2A—523(1) or 2A—523(3)(a) or, if agreed, after other default by the lessee, the lessor may:

(a) identify to the lease contract conforming goods not already identified if at the time the lessor learned of the default they were in the lessor's or the supplier's possession or control; and

(b) dispose of goods (Section 2A—527(1)) that demonstrably have been intended for the particular lease contract even though those goods are unfinished.

(2) If the goods are unfinished, in the exercise of reasonable commercial judgment for the purposes of avoiding loss and of effective realization, an aggrieved lessor or the supplier may either complete manufacture and wholly identify the goods to the lease contract or cease manufacture and lease, sell, or otherwise dispose of the goods for scrap or salvage value or proceed in any other reasonable manner.

As amended in 1990.

§ 2A–525. Lessor's Right to Possession of Goods.

(1) If a lessor discovers the lessee to be insolvent, the lessor may refuse to deliver the goods.

(2) After a default by the lessee under the lease contract of the type described in Section 2A—523(1) or 2A—523(3)(a) or, if agreed, after other default by the lessee, the lessor has the right to take possession of the goods. If the lease contract so provides, the lessor may require the lessee to assemble the goods and make them available to the lessor at a place to be designated by the lessor which is reasonably convenient to both parties. Without removal, the lessor may render unusable any goods employed in trade or business, and may dispose of goods on the lessee's premises (Section 2A—527).

(3) The lessor may proceed under subsection (2) without judicial process if that can be done without breach of the peace or the lessor may proceed by action.

As amended in 1990.

§ 2A—526. Lessor's Stoppage of Delivery in Transit or Otherwise.

(1) A lessor may stop delivery of goods in the possession of a carrier or other bailee if the lessor discovers the lessee to be insolvent and may stop delivery of carload, truckload, planeload, or larger shipments of express or freight if the lessee repudiates or fails to make a payment due before delivery, whether for rent, security or otherwise under the lease contract, or for any other reason the lessor has a right to withhold or take possession of the goods.

(2) In pursuing its remedies under subsection (1), the lessor may stop delivery until

(a) receipt of the goods by the lessee;

(b) acknowledgment to the lessee by any bailee of the goods, except a carrier, that the bailee holds the goods for the lessee; or

(c) such an acknowledgment to the lessee by a carrier via reshipment or as warehouseman.

(3) (a) To stop delivery, a lessor shall so notify as to enable the bailee by reasonable diligence to prevent delivery of the goods.

(b) After notification, the bailee shall hold and deliver the goods according to the directions of the lessor, but the lessor is liable to the bailee for any ensuing charges or damages.

(c) A carrier who has issued a nonnegotiable bill of lading is not obliged to obey a notification to stop received from a person other than the consignor.

§ 2A—527. Lessor's Rights to Dispose of Goods.

(1) After a default by a lessee under the lease contract of the type described in Section 2A—523(1) or 2A–523(3)(a) or after the lessor refuses to deliver or takes possession of goods (Section 2A—525 or 2A—526), or, if agreed, after other default by a lessee, the lessor may dispose of the goods concerned or the undelivered balance thereof by lease, sale, or otherwise.

(2) Except as otherwise provided with respect to damages liquidated in the lease agreement (Section 2A—504) or otherwise determined pursuant to agreement of the parties (Sections 1—102(3) and 2A—503), if the disposition is by lease agreement substantially similar to the original lease agreement and the new lease agreement is made in good faith and in a commercially reasonable manner, the lessor may recover from the lessee as damages (i) accrued and unpaid rent as of the date of the commencement of the term of the new lease agreement, (ii) the present value, as of the same date, of the total rent for the then remaining lease term of the original lease agreement minus the present value, as of the same date, of the rent under the new lease agreement applicable to that period of the new lease term which is comparable to the then remaining term of the original lease agreement, and (iii) any incidental damages allowed under Section 2A—530, less expenses saved in consequence of the lessee's default.

(3) If the lessor's disposition is by lease agreement that for any reason does not qualify for treatment under subsection (2), or is by sale or otherwise, the lessor may recover from the lessee as if the lessor had elected not to dispose of the goods and Section 2A—528 governs.

(4) A subsequent buyer or lessee who buys or leases from the lessor in good faith for value as a result of a disposition under this section takes the goods free of the original lease contract and any rights of the original lessee even though the lessor fails to comply with one or more of the requirements of this Article.

(5) The lessor is not accountable to the lessee for any profit made on any disposition. A lessee who has rightfully rejected or justifiably revoked acceptance shall account to the lessor for any excess over the amount of the lessee's security interest (Section 2A—508(5)).

As amended in 1990.

§ 2A—528. Lessor's Damages for Non-acceptance, Failure to Pay, Repudiation, or Other Default.

(1) Except as otherwise provided with respect to damages liquidated in the lease agreement (Section 2A—504) or otherwise determined pursuant to agreement of the parties (Section 1—102(3) and 2A—503), if a lessor elects to retain the goods or a lessor elects to dispose of the goods and the disposition is by lease agreement that for any reason does not qualify for treatment under Section 2A—527(2), or is by sale or otherwise, the lessor may recover from the lessee as damages for a default of the type described in Section 2A—523(1) or 2A—523(3)(a), or if agreed, for other default of the lessee, (i) accrued and unpaid rent as of the date of the default if the lessee has never taken possession of the goods, or, if the lessee has taken possession of the goods, as of the date the lessor repossesses the goods or an earlier date on which the lessee makes a tender of the goods to the lessor, (ii) the present value as of the date determined under clause (i) of the total rent for the then remaining lease term of the original lease agreement minus the present value as of the same date of the market rent as the place where the goods are located computed for the same lease term, and (iii) any incidental damages allowed under Section 2A—530, less expenses saved in consequence of the lessee's default.

(2) If the measure of damages provided in subsection (1) is inadequate to put a lessor in as good a position as performance would have, the measure of damages is the present value of the profit, including reasonable overhead, the lessor would have made from full performance by the lessee, together with any incidental damages allowed under Section 2A—530, due allowance for costs reasonably incurred and due credit for payments or proceeds of disposition.

As amended in 1990.

§ 2A—529. Lessor's Action for the Rent.

(1) After default by the lessee under the lease contract of the type described in Section 2A—523(1) or 2A—523(3)(a) or, if agreed, after other default by the lessee, if the lessor complies with subsection (2), the lessor may recover from the lessee as damages:

> (a) for goods accepted by the lessee and not repossessed by or tendered to the lessor, and for conforming goods lost or damaged within a commercially reasonable time after risk of loss passes to the lessee (Section 2A—219), (i) accrued and unpaid rent as of the date of entry of judgment in favor of the lessor (ii) the present value as of the same date of the rent for the then remaining lease term of the lease agreement, and (iii) any incidental damages allowed under Section 2A—530, less expenses saved in consequence of the lessee's default; and

> (b) for goods identified to the lease contract if the lessor is unable after reasonable effort to dispose of

them at a reasonable price or the circumstances reasonably indicate that effort will be unavailing, (i) accrued and unpaid rent as of the date of entry of judgment in favor of the lessor, (ii) the present value as of the same date of the rent for the then remaining lease term of the lease agreement, and (iii) any incidental damages allowed under Section 2A—530, less expenses saved in consequence of the lessee's default.

(2) Except as provided in subsection (3), the lessor shall hold for the lessee for the remaining lease term of the lease agreement any goods that have been identified to the lease contract and are in the lessor's control.

(3) The lessor may dispose of the goods at any time before collection of the judgment for damages obtained pursuant to subsection (1). If the disposition is before the end of the remaining lease term of the lease agreement, the lessor's recovery against the lessee for damages is governed by Section 2A—527 or Section 2A—528, and the lessor will cause an appropriate credit to be provided against a judgment for damages to the extent that the amount of the judgment exceeds the recovery available pursuant to Section 2A—527 or 2A—528.

(4) Payment of the judgment for damages obtained pursuant to subsection (1) entitles the lessee to the use and possession of the goods not then disposed of for the remaining lease term of and in accordance with the lease agreement.

(5) After default by the lessee under the lease contract of the type described in Section 2A—523(1) or Section 2A—523(3)(a) or, if agreed, after other default by the lessee, a lessor who is held not entitled to rent under this section must nevertheless be awarded damages for non-acceptance under Sections 2A—527 and 2A—528.

As amended in 1990.

§ 2A—530. Lessor's Incidental Damages.

Incidental damages to an aggrieved lessor include any commercially reasonable charges, expenses, or commissions incurred in stopping delivery, in the transportation, care and custody of goods after the lessee's default, in connection with return or disposition of the goods, or otherwise resulting from the default.

§ 2A—531. Standing to Sue Third Parties for Injury to Goods.

(1) If a third party so deals with goods that have been identified to a lease contract as to cause actionable injury to a party to the lease contract (a) the lessor has a right of action against the third party, and (b) the lessee also has a right of action against the third party if the lessee:

> (i) has a security interest in the goods;

> (ii) has an insurable interest in the goods; or

> (iii) bears the risk of loss under the lease contract or has since the injury assumed that risk as against the lessor and the goods have been converted or destroyed.

(2) If at the time of the injury the party plaintiff did not bear the risk of loss as against the other party to the lease contract and there is no arrangement between them for disposition of the recovery, his [or her] suit or settlement, subject to his [or her] own interest, is as a fiduciary for the other party to the lease contract.

(3) Either party with the consent of the other may sue for the benefit of whom it may concern.

§ 2A—532. Lessor's Rights to Residual Interest.

In addition to any other recovery permitted by this Article or other law, the lessor may recover from the lessee an amount that will fully compensate the lessor for any loss of or damage to the lessor's residual interest in the goods caused by the default of the lessee.

As added in 1990.

Revised Article 3
NEGOTIABLE INSTRUMENTS

Part 1 General Provisions and Definitions

§ 3–101. Short Title.

This Article may be cited as Uniform Commercial Code— Negotiable Instruments.

§ 3–102. Subject Matter.

(a) This Article applies to negotiable instruments. It does not apply to money, to payment orders governed by Article 4A, or to securities governed by Article 8.

(b) If there is conflict between this Article and Article 4 or 9, Articles 4 and 9 govern.

(c) Regulations of the Board of Governors of the Federal Reserve System and operating circulars of the Federal Reserve Banks supersede any inconsistent provision of this Article to the extent of the inconsistency.

§ 3–103. Definitions.

(a) In this Article:

(1) "Acceptor" means a drawee who has accepted a draft.

(2) "Drawee" means a person ordered in a draft to make payment.

(3) "Drawer" means a person who signs or is identified in a draft as a person ordering payment.

(4) "Good faith" means honesty in fact and the observance of reasonable commercial standards of fair dealing.

(5) "Maker" means a person who signs or is identified in a note as a person undertaking to pay.

(6) "Order" means a written instruction to pay money signed by the person giving the instruction. The instruction may be addressed to any person, including the person giving the instruction, or to one or more persons jointly or in the alternative but not in succession. An authorization to pay is not an order unless the person authorized to pay is also instructed to pay.

(7) "Ordinary care" in the case of a person engaged in business means observance of reasonable commercial standards, prevailing in the area in which the person is located, with respect to the business in which the person is engaged. In the case of a bank that takes an instrument for processing for collection or payment by automated means, reasonable commercial standards do not require the bank to examine the instrument if the failure to examine does not violate the bank's prescribed procedures and the bank's procedures do not vary unreasonably from general banking usage not disapproved by this Article or Article 4.

(8) "Party" means a party to an instrument.

(9) "Promise" means a written undertaking to pay money signed by the person undertaking to pay. An acknowledgment of an obligation by the obligor is not a promise unless the obligor also undertakes to pay the obligation.

(10) "Prove" with respect to a fact means to meet the burden of establishing the fact (Section 1—201(8)).

(11) "Remitter" means a person who purchases an instrument from its issuer if the instrument is payable to an identified person other than the purchaser.

(b);(c) [Other definitions' section references deleted.]

(d) In addition, Article 1 contains general definitions and principles of construction and interpretation applicable throughout this Article.

§ 3—104. Negotiable Instrument.

(a) Except as provided in subsections (c) and (d), "negotiable instrument" means an unconditional promise or order to pay a fixed amount of money, with or without interest or other charges described in the promise or order, if it:

(1) is payable to bearer or to order at the time it is issued or first comes into possession of a holder;

(2) is payable on demand or at a definite time; and

(3) does not state any other undertaking or instruction by the person promising or ordering payment to do any act in addition to the payment of money, but the promise or order may contain (i) an undertaking or power to give, maintain, or protect collateral to secure payment, (ii) an authorization or power to the holder to confess judgment or realize on or dispose of collateral, or (iii) a waiver of the benefit of any law intended for the advantage or protection of an obligor.

(b) "Instrument" means a negotiable instrument.

(c) An order that meets all of the requirements of subsection (a), except paragraph (1), and otherwise falls within the definition of "check" in subsection (f) is a negotiable instrument and a check.

(d) A promise or order other than a check is not an instrument if, at the time it is issued or first comes into possession of a holder, it contains a conspicuous statement, however expressed, to the effect that the promise or order is not negotiable or is not an instrument governed by this Article.

(e) An instrument is a "note" if it is a promise and is a "draft" if it is an order. If an instrument falls within the definition of both "note" and "draft," a person entitled to enforce the instrument may treat it as either.

(f) "Check" means (i) a draft, other than a documentary draft, payable on demand and drawn on a bank or (ii) a cashier's check or teller's check. An instrument may be a check even though it is described on its face by another term, such as "money order."

(g) "Cashier's check" means a draft with respect to which the drawer and drawee are the same bank or branches of the same bank.

(h) "Teller's check" means a draft drawn by a bank (i) on another bank, or (ii) payable at or through a bank.

(i) "Traveler's check" means an instrument that (i) is payable on demand, (ii) is drawn on or payable at or through a bank, (iii) is designated by the term "traveler's check" or by a substantially similar term, and (iv) requires, as a condition to payment, a countersignature by a person whose specimen signature appears on the instrument.

(j) "Certificate of deposit" means an instrument containing an acknowledgment by a bank that a sum of money has been received by the bank and a promise by the bank to repay the sum of money. A certificate of deposit is a note of the bank.

§ 3–105. Issue of Instrument.

(a) "Issue" means the first delivery of an instrument by the maker or drawer, whether to a holder or nonholder, for the purpose of giving rights on the instrument to any person.

(b) An unissued instrument, or an unissued incomplete instrument that is completed, is binding on the maker or drawer, but nonissuance is a defense. An instrument that is conditionally issued or is issued for a special purpose is binding on the maker or drawer, but failure of the condition or special purpose to be fulfilled is a defense.

(c) "Issuer" applies to issued and unissued instruments and means a maker or drawer of an instrument.

§ 3–106. Unconditional Promise or Order.

(a) Except as provided in this section, for the purposes of Section 3–104(a), a promise or order is unconditional unless it states (i) an express condition to payment, (ii) that the promise or order is subject to or governed by another writing, or (iii) that rights or obligations with respect to the promise or order are stated in another writing. A reference to another writing does not of itself make the promise or order conditional.

(b) A promise or order is not made conditional (i) by a reference to another writing for a statement of rights with respect to collateral, prepayment, or acceleration, or (ii) because payment is limited to resort to a particular fund or source.

(c) If a promise or order requires, as a condition to payment, a countersignature by a person whose specimen signature appears on the promise or order, the condition does not make the promise or order conditional for the purposes of Section 3–104(a). If the person whose specimen signature appears on an instrument fails to countersign the instrument, the failure to countersign is a defense to the obligation of the issuer, but the failure does not prevent a transferee of the instrument from becoming a holder of the instrument.

(d) If a promise or order at the time it is issued or first comes into possession of a holder contains a statement, required by applicable statutory or administrative law, to the effect that the rights of a holder or transferee are subject to claims or defenses that the issuer could assert against the original payee, the promise or order is not thereby made conditional for the purposes of Section 3–104(a); but if the promise or order is an instrument, there cannot be a holder in due course of the instrument.

§ 3–107. Instrument Payable in Foreign Money.

Unless the instrument otherwise provides, an instrument that states the amount payable in foreign money may be paid in the foreign money or in an equivalent amount in dollars calculated by using the current bank-offered spot rate at the place of payment for the purchase of dollars on the day on which the instrument is paid.

§ 3–108. Payable on Demand or at Definite Time.

(a) A promise or order is "payable on demand" if it (i) states that it is payable on demand or at sight, or otherwise indicates that it is payable at the will of the holder, or (ii) does not state any time of payment.

(b) A promise or order is "payable at a definite time" if it is payable on elapse of a definite period of time after sight or acceptance or at a fixed date or dates or at a time or times readily ascertainable at the time the promise or order is issued, subject to rights of (i) prepayment, (ii) acceleration, (iii) extension at the option of the holder, or (iv) extension to a further definite time at the option of the maker or acceptor or automatically upon or after a specified act or event.

(c) If an instrument, payable at a fixed date, is also payable upon demand made before the fixed date, the instrument is payable on demand until the fixed date and, if demand for payment is not made before that date, becomes payable at a definite time on the fixed date.

§ 3–109. Payable to Bearer or to Order.

(a) A promise or order is payable to bearer if it:

(1) states that it is payable to bearer or to the order of bearer or otherwise indicates that the person in possession of the promise or order is entitled to payment;

(2) does not state a payee; or

(3) states that it is payable to or to the order of cash or otherwise indicates that it is not payable to an identified person.

(b) A promise or order that is not payable to bearer is payable to order if it is payable (i) to the order of an identified person or (ii) to an identified person or order. A promise or order that is payable to order is payable to the identified person.

(c) An instrument payable to bearer may become payable to an identified person if it is specially indorsed pursuant to Section 3—205(a). An instrument payable to an identified person may become payable to bearer if it is indorsed in blank pursuant to Section 3—205(b).

§ 3—110. Identification of Person to Whom Instrument Is Payable.

(a) The person to whom an instrument is initially payable is determined by the intent of the person, whether or not authorized, signing as, or in the name or behalf of, the issuer of the instrument. The instrument is payable to the person intended by the signer even if that person is identified in the instrument by a name or other identification that is not that of the intended person. If more than one person signs in the name or behalf of the issuer of an instrument and all the signers do not intend the same person as payee, the instrument is payable to any person intended by one or more of the signers.

(b) If the signature of the issuer of an instrument is made by automated means, such as a check-writing machine, the payee of the instrument is determined by the intent of the person who supplied the name or identification of the payee, whether or not authorized to do so.

(c) A person to whom an instrument is payable may be identified in any way, including by name, identifying number, office, or account number. For the purpose of determining the holder of an instrument, the following rules apply:

(1) If an instrument is payable to an account and the account is identified only by number, the instrument is payable to the person to whom the account is payable. If an instrument is payable to an account identified by number and by the name of a person, the instrument is payable to the named person, whether or not that person is the owner of the account identified by number.

(2) If an instrument is payable to:

(i) a trust, an estate, or a person described as trustee or representative of a trust or estate, the instrument is payable to the trustee, the representative, or a successor of either, whether or not the beneficiary or estate is also named;

(ii) a person described as agent or similar representative of a named or identified person, the instrument is payable to the represented person, the representative, or a successor of the representative;

(iii) a fund or organization that is not a legal entity, the instrument is payable to a representative of the members of the fund or organization; or

(iv) an office or to a person described as holding an office, the instrument is payable to the named person, the incumbent of the office, or a successor to the incumbent.

(d) If an instrument is payable to two or more persons alternatively, it is payable to any of them and may be negotiated, discharged, or enforced by any or all of them in possession of the instrument. If an instrument is payable to two or more persons not alternatively, it is payable to all of them and may be negotiated, discharged, or enforced only by all of them. If an instrument payable to two or more persons is ambiguous as to whether it is payable to the persons alternatively, the instrument is payable to the persons alternatively.

§ 3—111. Place of Payment.

Except as otherwise provided for items in Article 4, an instrument is payable at the place of payment stated in the instrument. If no place of payment is stated, an instrument is payable at the address of the drawee or maker stated in the instrument. If no address is stated, the place of payment is the place of business of the drawee or maker. If a drawee or maker has more than one place of business, the place of payment is any place of business of the drawee or maker chosen by the person entitled to enforce the instrument. If the drawee or maker has no place of business, the place of payment is the residence of the drawee or maker.

§ 3—112. Interest.

(a) Unless otherwise provided in the instrument, (i) an instrument is not payable with interest, and (ii) interest on an interest-bearing instrument is payable from the date of the instrument.

(b) Interest may be stated in an instrument as a fixed or variable amount of money or it may be expressed as a fixed or variable rate or rates. The amount or rate of interest may be stated or described in the instrument in any manner and may require reference to information not contained in the instrument. If an instrument provides for interest, but the amount of interest payable cannot be ascertained from the description, interest is payable at the judgment rate in effect at the place of payment of the instrument and at the time interest first accrues.

§ 3—113. Date of Instrument.

(a) An instrument may be antedated or postdated. The date stated determines the time of payment if the instrument is payable at a fixed period after date. Except as provided in Section 4—401(c), an instrument payable on demand is not payable before the date of the instrument.

(b) If an instrument is undated, its date is the date of its issue or, in the case of an unissued instrument, the date it first comes into possession of a holder.

§ 3—114. Contradictory Terms of Instrument.

If an instrument contains contradictory terms, typewritten terms prevail over printed terms, handwritten terms prevail over both, and words prevail over numbers.

§ 3—115. Incomplete Instrument.

(a) "Incomplete instrument" means a signed writing, whether or not issued by the signer, the contents of which show at the time of signing that it is incomplete but that the signer intended it to be completed by the addition of words or numbers.

(b) Subject to subsection (c), if an incomplete instrument is an instrument under Section 3—104, it may be enforced according to its terms if it is not completed, or according to its terms as augmented by completion. If an incomplete instrument is not an instrument under Section 3—104, but, after completion, the requirements of Section 3—104 are met, the instrument may be enforced according to its terms as augmented by completion.

(c) If words or numbers are added to an incomplete instrument without authority of the signer, there is an alteration of the incomplete instrument under Section 3—407.

(d) The burden of establishing that words or numbers were added to an incomplete instrument without authority of the signer is on the person asserting the lack of authority.

§ 3—116. Joint and Several Liability; Contribution.

(a) Except as otherwise provided in the instrument, two or more persons who have the same liability on an instrument as makers, drawers, acceptors, indorsers who indorse as joint payees, or anomalous indorsers are jointly and severally liable in the capacity in which they sign.

(b) Except as provided in Section 3—419(e) or by agreement of the affected parties, a party having joint and several liability who pays the instrument is entitled to receive from any party having the same joint and several liability contribution in accordance with applicable law.

(c) Discharge of one party having joint and several liability by a person entitled to enforce the instrument does not affect the right under subsection (b) of a party having the same joint and several liability to receive contribution from the party discharged.

§ 3—117. Other Agreements Affecting Instrument.

Subject to applicable law regarding exclusion of proof of contemporaneous or previous agreements, the obligation of a party to an instrument to pay the instrument may be modified, supplemented, or nullified by a separate agreement of the obligor and a person entitled to enforce the instrument, if the instrument is issued or the obligation is incurred in reliance on the agreement or as part of the same transaction giving rise to the agreement. To the extent an obligation is modified, supplemented, or nullified by an agreement under this section, the agreement is a defense to the obligation.

§ 3—118. Statute of Limitations.

(a) Except as provided in subsection (e), an action to enforce the obligation of a party to pay a note payable at a definite time must be commenced within six years after the due date or dates stated in the note or, if a due date is accelerated, within six years after the accelerated due date.

(b) Except as provided in subsection (d) or (e), if demand for payment is made to the maker of a note payable on demand, an action to enforce the obligation of a party to pay the note must be commenced within six years after the demand. If no demand for payment is made to the maker, an action to enforce the note is barred if neither principal nor interest on the note has been paid for a continuous period of 10 years.

(c) Except as provided in subsection (d), an action to enforce the obligation of a party to an unaccepted draft to pay the draft must be commenced within three years after dishonor of the draft or 10 years after the date of the draft, whichever period expires first.

(d) An action to enforce the obligation of the acceptor of a certified check or the issuer of a teller's check, cashier's check, or traveler's check must be commenced within three years after demand for payment is made to the acceptor or issuer, as the case may be.

(e) An action to enforce the obligation of a party to a certificate of deposit to pay the instrument must be commenced within six years after demand for payment is made to the maker, but if the instrument states a due date and the maker is not required to pay before that date, the six-year period begins when a demand for payment is in effect and the due date has passed.

(f) An action to enforce the obligation of a party to pay an accepted draft, other than a certified check, must be commenced (i) within six years after the due date or dates stated in the draft or acceptance if the obligation of the acceptor is payable at a definite time, or (ii) within six years after the date of the acceptance if the obligation of the acceptor is payable on demand.

(g) Unless governed by other law regarding claims for indemnity or contribution, an action (i) for conversion of an instrument, for money had and received, or like action based on conversion, (ii) for breach of warranty, or (iii) to enforce an obligation, duty, or right arising under this Article and not governed by this section must be commenced within three years after the [cause of action] accrues.

§ 3—119. Notice of Right to Defend Action.

In an action for breach of an obligation for which a third person is answerable over pursuant to this Article or Article 4, the defendant may give the third person written notice of the litigation, and the person notified may then give similar notice to any other person who is answerable over. If the notice states (i) that the person notified may come in and defend and (ii) that failure to do so will bind the person notified in an action later brought by the person giving the notice as to any determination of fact common to the two litigations, the person notified is so bound unless after seasonable receipt of the notice the person notified does come in and defend.

Part 2 Negotiation, Transfer, and Indorsement

§ 3–201. Negotiation.

(a) "Negotiation" means a transfer of possession, whether voluntary or involuntary, of an instrument by a person other than the issuer to a person who thereby becomes its holder.

(b) Except for negotiation by a remitter, if an instrument is payable to an identified person, negotiation requires transfer of possession of the instrument and its indorsement by the holder. If an instrument is payable to bearer, it may be negotiated by transfer of possession alone.

§ 3–202. Negotiation Subject to Rescission.

(a) Negotiation is effective even if obtained (i) from an infant, a corporation exceeding its powers, or a person without capacity, (ii) by fraud, duress, or mistake, or (iii) in breach of duty or as part of an illegal transaction.

(b) To the extent permitted by other law, negotiation may be rescinded or may be subject to other remedies, but those remedies may not be asserted against a subsequent holder in due course or a person paying the instrument in good faith and without knowledge of facts that are a basis for rescission or other remedy.

§ 3–203. Transfer of Instrument; Rights Acquired by Transfer.

(a) An instrument is transferred when it is delivered by a person other than its issuer for the purpose of giving to the person receiving delivery the right to enforce the instrument.

(b) Transfer of an instrument, whether or not the transfer is a negotiation, vests in the transferee any right of the transferor to enforce the instrument, including any right as a holder in due course, but the transferee cannot acquire rights of a holder in due course by a transfer, directly or indirectly, from a holder in due course if the transferee engaged in fraud or illegality affecting the instrument.

(c) Unless otherwise agreed, if an instrument is transferred for value and the transferee does not become a holder because of lack of indorsement by the transferor, the transferee has a specifically enforceable right to the unqualified indorsement of the transferor, but negotiation of the instrument does not occur until the indorsement is made.

(d) If a transferor purports to transfer less than the entire instrument, negotiation of the instrument does not occur. The transferee obtains no rights under this Article and has only the rights of a partial assignee.

§ 3–204. Indorsement.

(a) "Indorsement" means a signature, other than that of a signer as maker, drawer, or acceptor, that alone or accompanied by other words is made on an instrument for the purpose of (i) negotiating the instrument, (ii) restricting payment of the instrument, or (iii) incurring indorser's liability on the instrument, but regardless of the intent of the signer, a signature and its accompanying words is an indorsement unless the accompanying words, terms of the instrument, place of the signature, or other circumstances unambiguously indicate that the signature was made for a purpose other than indorsement. For the purpose of determining whether a signature is made on an instrument, a paper affixed to the instrument is a part of the instrument.

(b) "Indorser" means a person who makes an indorsement.

(c) For the purpose of determining whether the transferee of an instrument is a holder, an indorsement that transfers a security interest in the instrument is effective as an unqualified indorsement of the instrument.

(d) If an instrument is payable to a holder under a name that is not the name of the holder, indorsement may be made by the holder in the name stated in the instrument or in the holder's name or both, but signature in both names may be required by a person paying or taking the instrument for value or collection.

§ 3–205. Special Indorsement; Blank Indorsement; Anomalous Indorsement.

(a) If an indorsement is made by the holder of an instrument, whether payable to an identified person or payable to bearer, and the indorsement identifies a person to whom it makes the instrument payable, it is a "special indorsement." When specially indorsed, an instrument becomes payable to the identified person and may be negotiated only by the indorsement of that person. The principles stated in Section 3–110 apply to special indorsements.

(b) If an indorsement is made by the holder of an instrument and it is not a special indorsement, it is a "blank indorsement." When indorsed in blank, an instrument becomes payable to bearer and may be negotiated by transfer of possession alone until specially indorsed.

(c) The holder may convert a blank indorsement that consists only of a signature into a special indorsement by writing, above the signature of the indorser, words identifying the person to whom the instrument is made payable.

(d) "Anomalous indorsement" means an indorsement made by a person who is not the holder of the instrument. An anomalous indorsement does not affect the manner in which the instrument may be negotiated.

§ 3–206. Restrictive Indorsement.

(a) An indorsement limiting payment to a particular person or otherwise prohibiting further transfer or negotiation of the instrument is not effective to prevent further transfer or negotiation of the instrument.

(b) An indorsement stating a condition to the right of the indorsee to receive payment does not affect the right of the indorsee to enforce the instrument. A person paying the instrument or taking it for value or collection may disregard the condition, and the rights and liabilities of that person are not affected by whether the condition has been fulfilled.

(c) If an instrument bears an indorsement (i) described in Section 4—201(b), or (ii) in blank or to a particular bank using the words "for deposit," "for collection," or other words indicating a purpose of having the instrument collected by a bank for the indorser or for a particular account, the following rules apply:

> (1) A person, other than a bank, who purchases the instrument when so indorsed converts the instrument unless the amount paid for the instrument is received by the indorser or applied consistently with the indorsement.

> (2) A depositary bank that purchases the instrument or takes it for collection when so indorsed converts the instrument unless the amount paid by the bank with respect to the instrument is received by the indorser or applied consistently with the indorsement.

> (3) A payor bank that is also the depositary bank or that takes the instrument for immediate payment over the counter from a person other than a collecting bank converts the instrument unless the proceeds of the instrument are received by the indorser or applied consistently with the indorsement.

> (4) Except as otherwise provided in paragraph (3), a payor bank or intermediary bank may disregard the indorsement and is not liable if the proceeds of the instrument are not received by the indorser or applied consistently with the indorsement.

(d) Except for an indorsement covered by subsection (c), if an instrument bears an indorsement using words to the effect that payment is to be made to the indorsee as agent, trustee, or other fiduciary for the benefit of the indorser or another person, the following rules apply:

> (1) Unless there is notice of breach of fiduciary duty as provided in Section 3—307, a person who purchases the instrument from the indorsee or takes the instrument from the indorsee for collection or payment may pay the proceeds of payment or the value given for the instrument to the indorsee without regard to whether the indorsee violates a fiduciary duty to the indorser.

> (2) A subsequent transferee of the instrument or person who pays the instrument is neither given notice nor otherwise affected by the restriction in the indorsement unless the transferee or payor knows that the fiduciary dealt with the instrument or its proceeds in breach of fiduciary duty.

(e) The presence on an instrument of an indorsement to which this section applies does not prevent a purchaser of the instrument from becoming a holder in due course of the instrument unless the purchaser is a converter under subsection (c) or has notice or knowledge of breach of fiduciary duty as stated in subsection (d).

(f) In an action to enforce the obligation of a party to pay the instrument, the obligor has a defense if payment would violate an indorsement to which this section applies and the payment is not permitted by this section.

§ 3—207. Reacquisition.

Reacquisition of an instrument occurs if it is transferred to a former holder, by negotiation or otherwise. A former holder who reacquires the instrument may cancel indorsements made after the reacquirer first became a holder of the instrument. If the cancellation causes the instrument to be payable to the reacquirer or to bearer, the reacquirer may negotiate the instrument. An indorser whose indorsement is canceled is discharged, and the discharge is effective against any subsequent holder.

Part 3 Enforcement of Instruments

§ 3—301. Person Entitled to Enforce Instrument.

"Person entitled to enforce" an instrument means (i) the holder of the instrument, (ii) a nonholder in possession of the instrument who has the rights of a holder, or (iii) a person not in possession of the instrument who is entitled to enforce the instrument pursuant to Section 3—309 or 3—418(d). A person may be a person entitled to enforce the instrument even though the person is not the owner of the instrument or is in wrongful possession of the instrument.

§ 3—302. Holder in Due Course.

(a) Subject to subsection (c) and Section 3—106(d), "holder in due course" means the holder of an instrument if:

> (1) the instrument when issued or negotiated to the holder does not bear such apparent evidence of forgery or alteration or is not otherwise so irregular or incomplete as to call into question its authenticity; and

> (2) the holder took the instrument (i) for value, (ii) in good faith, (iii) without notice that the instrument is overdue or has been dishonored or that there is an uncured default with respect to payment of another instrument issued as part of the same series, (iv) without notice that the instrument contains an unauthorized signature or has been altered, (v) without notice of any claim to the instrument described in Section 3—306, and (vi) without notice that any party has a defense or claim in recoupment described in Section 3—305(a).

(b) Notice of discharge of a party, other than discharge in an insolvency proceeding, is not notice of a defense under subsection (a), but discharge is effective against a person who became a holder in due course with notice of the discharge. Public filing or recording of a document does not of itself constitute notice of a defense, claim in recoupment, or claim to the instrument.

(c) Except to the extent a transferor or predecessor in interest has rights as a holder in due course, a person does not acquire rights of a holder in due course of an instrument taken (i) by legal process or by purchase in an execution, bankruptcy, or creditor's sale or similar proceeding, (ii) by purchase as part of a bulk transaction not in ordinary course of business of the transferor, or (iii) as the successor in interest to an estate or other organization.

(d) If, under Section 3–303(a)(1), the promise of performance that is the consideration for an instrument has been partially performed, the holder may assert rights as a holder in due course of the instrument only to the fraction of the amount payable under the instrument equal to the value of the partial performance divided by the value of the promised performance.

(e) If (i) the person entitled to enforce an instrument has only a security interest in the instrument and (ii) the person obliged to pay the instrument has a defense, claim in recoupment, or claim to the instrument that may be asserted against the person who granted the security interest, the person entitled to enforce the instrument may assert rights as a holder in due course only to an amount payable under the instrument which, at the time of enforcement of the instrument, does not exceed the amount of the unpaid obligation secured.

(f) To be effective, notice must be received at a time and in a manner that gives a reasonable opportunity to act on it.

(g) This section is subject to any law limiting status as a holder in due course in particular classes of transactions.

§ 3–303. Value and Consideration.

(a) An instrument is issued or transferred for value if:

(1) the instrument is issued or transferred for a promise of performance, to the extent the promise has been performed;

(2) the transferee acquires a security interest or other lien in the instrument other than a lien obtained by judicial proceeding;

(3) the instrument is issued or transferred as payment of, or as security for, an antecedent claim against any person, whether or not the claim is due;

(4) the instrument is issued or transferred in exchange for a negotiable instrument; or

(5) the instrument is issued or transferred in exchange for the incurring of an irrevocable obligation to a third party by the person taking the instrument.

(b) "Consideration" means any consideration sufficient to support a simple contract. The drawer or maker of an instrument has a defense if the instrument is issued without consideration. If an instrument is issued for a promise of performance, the issuer has a defense to the extent performance of the promise is due and the promise has not been performed. If an instrument is issued for value as

stated in subsection (a), the instrument is also issued for consideration.

§ 3–304. Overdue Instrument.

(a) An instrument payable on demand becomes overdue at the earliest of the following times:

(1) on the day after the day demand for payment is duly made;

(2) if the instrument is a check, 90 days after its date; or

(3) if the instrument is not a check, when the instrument has been outstanding for a period of time after its date which is unreasonably long under the circumstances of the particular case in light of the nature of the instrument and usage of the trade.

(b) With respect to an instrument payable at a definite time the following rules apply:

(1) If the principal is payable in installments and a due date has not been accelerated, the instrument becomes overdue upon default under the instrument for nonpayment of an installment, and the instrument remains overdue until the default is cured.

(2) If the principal is not payable in installments and the due date has not been accelerated, the instrument becomes overdue on the day after the due date.

(3) If a due date with respect to principal has been accelerated, the instrument becomes overdue on the day after the accelerated due date.

(c) Unless the due date of principal has been accelerated, an instrument does not become overdue if there is default in payment of interest but no default in payment of principal.

§ 3–305. Defenses and Claims in Recoupment.

(a) Except as stated in subsection (b), the right to enforce the obligation of a party to pay an instrument is subject to the following:

(1) a defense of the obligor based on (i) infancy of the obligor to the extent it is a defense to a simple contract, (ii) duress, lack of legal capacity, or illegality of the transaction which, under other law, nullifies the obligation of the obligor, (iii) fraud that induced the obligor to sign the instrument with neither knowledge nor reasonable opportunity to learn of its character or its essential terms, or (iv) discharge of the obligor in insolvency proceedings;

(2) a defense of the obligor stated in another section of this Article or a defense of the obligor that would be available if the person entitled to enforce the instrument were enforcing a right to payment under a simple contract; and

(3) a claim in recoupment of the obligor against the original payee of the instrument if the claim arose from the transaction that gave rise to the instrument; but the claim of the obligor may be asserted against a transferee of the instrument only to reduce the amount

owing on the instrument at the time the action is brought.

(b) The right of a holder in due course to enforce the obligation of a party to pay the instrument is subject to defenses of the obligor stated in subsection (a)(1), but is not subject to defenses of the obligor stated in subsection (a)(2) or claims in recoupment stated in subsection (a)(3) against a person other than the holder.

(c) Except as stated in subsection (d), in an action to enforce the obligation of a party to pay the instrument, the obligor may not assert against the person entitled to enforce the instrument a defense, claim in recoupment, or claim to the instrument (Section 3—306) of another person, but the other person's claim to the instrument may be asserted by the obligor if the other person is joined in the action and personally asserts the claim against the person entitled to enforce the instrument. An obligor is not obliged to pay the instrument if the person seeking enforcement of the instrument does not have rights of a holder in due course and the obligor proves that the instrument is a lost or stolen instrument.

(d) In an action to enforce the obligation of an accommodation party to pay an instrument, the accommodation party may assert against the person entitled to enforce the instrument any defense or claim in recoupment under subsection (a) that the accommodated party could assert against the person entitled to enforce the instrument, except the defenses of discharge in insolvency proceedings, infancy, and lack of legal capacity.

§ 3—306. Claims to an Instrument.

A person taking an instrument, other than a person having rights of a holder in due course, is subject to a claim of a property or possessory right in the instrument or its proceeds, including a claim to rescind a negotiation and to recover the instrument or its proceeds. A person having rights of a holder in due course takes free of the claim to the instrument.

§ 3—307. Notice of Breach of Fiduciary Duty.

(a) In this section:

(1) "Fiduciary" means an agent, trustee, partner, corporate officer or director, or other representative owing a fiduciary duty with respect to an instrument.

(2) "Represented person" means the principal, beneficiary, partnership, corporation, or other person to whom the duty stated in paragraph (1) is owed.

(b) If (i) an instrument is taken from a fiduciary for payment or collection or for value, (ii) the taker has knowledge of the fiduciary status of the fiduciary, and (iii) the represented person makes a claim to the instrument or its proceeds on the basis that the transaction of the fiduciary is a breach of fiduciary duty, the following rules apply:

(1) Notice of breach of fiduciary duty by the fiduciary is notice of the claim of the represented person.

(2) In the case of an instrument payable to the represented person or the fiduciary as such, the taker has notice of the breach of fiduciary duty if the instrument is (i) taken in payment of or as security for a debt known by the taker to be the personal debt of the fiduciary, (ii) taken in a transaction known by the taker to be for the personal benefit of the fiduciary, or (iii) deposited to an account other than an account of the fiduciary, as such, or an account of the represented person.

(3) If an instrument is issued by the represented person or the fiduciary as such, and made payable to the fiduciary personally, the taker does not have notice of the breach of fiduciary duty unless the taker knows of the breach of fiduciary duty.

(4) If an instrument is issued by the represented person or the fiduciary as such, to the taker as payee, the taker has notice of the breach of fiduciary duty if the instrument is (i) taken in payment of or as security for a debt known by the taker to be the personal debt of the fiduciary, (ii) taken in a transaction known by the taker to be for the personal benefit of the fiduciary, or (iii) deposited to an account other than an account of the fiduciary, as such, or an account of the represented person.

§ 3—308. Proof of Signatures and Status as Holder in Due Course.

(a) In an action with respect to an instrument, the authenticity of, and authority to make, each signature on the instrument is admitted unless specifically denied in the pleadings. If the validity of a signature is denied in the pleadings, the burden of establishing validity is on the person claiming validity, but the signature is presumed to be authentic and authorized unless the action is to enforce the liability of the purported signer and the signer is dead or incompetent at the time of trial of the issue of validity of the signature. If an action to enforce the instrument is brought against a person as the undisclosed principal of a person who signed the instrument as a party to the instrument, the plaintiff has the burden of establishing that the defendant is liable on the instrument as a represented person under Section 3—402(a).

(b) If the validity of signatures is admitted or proved and there is compliance with subsection (a), a plaintiff producing the instrument is entitled to payment if the plaintiff proves entitlement to enforce the instrument under Section 3—301, unless the defendant proves a defense or claim in recoupment. If a defense or claim in recoupment is proved, the right to payment of the plaintiff is subject to the defense or claim, except to the extent the plaintiff proves that the plaintiff has rights of a holder in due course which are not subject to the defense or claim.

§ 3—309. Enforcement of Lost, Destroyed, or Stolen Instrument.

(a) A person not in possession of an instrument is entitled to enforce the instrument if (i) the person was in possession of the instrument and entitled to enforce it when loss of possession occurred, (ii) the loss of possession was not the result of a transfer by the person or a lawful seizure, and (iii) the person cannot reasonably obtain possession of the instrument because the instrument was destroyed, its whereabouts cannot be determined, or it is in the wrongful possession of an unknown person or a person that cannot be found or is not amenable to service of process.

(b) A person seeking enforcement of an instrument under subsection (a) must prove the terms of the instrument and the person's right to enforce the instrument. If that proof is made, Section 3—308 applies to the case as if the person seeking enforcement had produced the instrument. The court may not enter judgment in favor of the person seeking enforcement unless it finds that the person required to pay the instrument is adequately protected against loss that might occur by reason of a claim by another person to enforce the instrument. Adequate protection may be provided by any reasonable means.

§ 3—310. Effect of Instrument on Obligation for Which Taken.

(a) Unless otherwise agreed, if a certified check, cashier's check, or teller's check is taken for an obligation, the obligation is discharged to the same extent discharge would result if an amount of money equal to the amount of the instrument were taken in payment of the obligation. Discharge of the obligation does not affect any liability that the obligor may have as an indorser of the instrument.

(b) Unless otherwise agreed and except as provided in subsection (a), if a note or an uncertified check is taken for an obligation, the obligation is suspended to the same extent the obligation would be discharged if an amount of money equal to the amount of the instrument were taken, and the following rules apply:

(1) In the case of an uncertified check, suspension of the obligation continues until dishonor of the check or until it is paid or certified. Payment or certification of the check results in discharge of the obligation to the extent of the amount of the check.

(2) In the case of a note, suspension of the obligation continues until dishonor of the note or until it is paid. Payment of the note results in discharge of the obligation to the extent of the payment.

(3) Except as provided in paragraph (4), if the check or note is dishonored and the obligee of the obligation for which the instrument was taken is the person entitled to enforce the instrument, the obligee may enforce either the instrument or the obligation. In the case of an instrument of a third person which is negotiated to the obligee by the obligor, discharge of the obligor on the instrument also discharges the obligation.

(4) If the person entitled to enforce the instrument taken for an obligation is a person other than the obligee, the obligee may not enforce the obligation to the extent the obligation is suspended. If the obligee is the person entitled to enforce the instrument but no longer has possession of it because it was lost, stolen, or destroyed, the obligation may not be enforced to the extent of the amount payable on the instrument, and to that extent the obligee's rights against the obligor are limited to enforcement of the instrument.

(c) If an instrument other than one described in subsection (a) or (b) is taken for an obligation, the effect is (i) that stated in subsection (a) if the instrument is one on which a bank is liable as maker or acceptor, or (ii) that stated in subsection (b) in any other case.

§ 3—311. Accord and Satisfaction by Use of Instrument.

(a) If a person against whom a claim is asserted proves that (i) that person in good faith tendered an instrument to the claimant as full satisfaction of the claim, (ii) the amount of the claim was unliquidated or subject to a bona fide dispute, and (iii) the claimant obtained payment of the instrument, the following subsections apply.

(b) Unless subsection (c) applies, the claim is discharged if the person against whom the claim is asserted proves that the instrument or an accompanying written communication contained a conspicuous statement to the effect that the instrument was tendered as full satisfaction of the claim.

(c) Subject to subsection (d), a claim is not discharged under subsection (b) if either of the following applies:

(1) The claimant, if an organization, proves that (i) within a reasonable time before the tender, the claimant sent a conspicuous statement to the person against whom the claim is asserted that communications concerning disputed debts, including an instrument tendered as full satisfaction of a debt, are to be sent to a designated person, office, or place, and (ii) the instrument or accompanying communication was not received by that designated person, office, or place.

(2) The claimant, whether or not an organization, proves that within 90 days after payment of the instrument, the claimant tendered repayment of the amount of the instrument to the person against whom the claim is asserted. This paragraph does not apply if the claimant is an organization that sent a statement complying with paragraph (1)(i).

(d) A claim is discharged if the person against whom the claim is asserted proves that within a reasonable time before collection of the instrument was initiated, the claimant, or an agent of the claimant having direct responsibility with respect to the disputed obligation, knew that the instrument was tendered in full satisfaction of the claim.

§ 3—312. Lost, Destroyed, or Stolen Cashier's Check, Teller's Check, or Certified Check.

(a) In this section:

(1) "Check" means a cashier's check, teller's check, or certified check.

(2) "Claimant" means a person who claims the right to receive the amount of a cashier's check, teller's check, or certified check that was lost, destroyed, or stolen.

(3) "Declaration of loss" means a written statement, made under penalty of perjury, to the effect that (i) the declarer lost possession of a check, (ii) the declarer is the drawer or payee of the check, in the case of a certified check, or the remitter or payee of the check, in the case of a cashier's check or teller's check, (iii) the loss of possession was not the result of a transfer by the declarer or a lawful seizure, and (iv) the declarer cannot reasonably obtain possession of the check because the check was destroyed, its whereabouts cannot be determined, or it is in the wrongful possession of an unknown person or a person that cannot be found or is not amenable to service of process.

(4) "Obligated bank" means the issuer of a cashier's check or teller's check or the acceptor of a certified check.

(b) A claimant may assert a claim to the amount of a check by a communication to the obligated bank describing the check with reasonable certainty and requesting payment of the amount of the check, if (i) the claimant is the drawer or payee of a certified check or the remitter or payee of a cashier's check or teller's check, (ii) the communication contains or is accompanied by a declaration of loss of the claimant with respect to the check, (iii) the communication is received at a time and in a manner affording the bank a reasonable time to act on it before the check is paid, and (iv) the claimant provides reasonable identification if requested by the obligated bank. Delivery of a declaration of loss is a warranty of the truth of the statements made in the declaration. If a claim is asserted in compliance with this subsection, the following rules apply:

(1) The claim becomes enforceable at the later of (i) the time the claim is asserted, or (ii) the 90th day following the date of the check, in the case of a cashier's check or teller's check, or the 90th day following the date of the acceptance, in the case of a certified check.

(2) Until the claim becomes enforceable, it has no legal effect and the obligated bank may pay the check or, in the case of a teller's check, may permit the drawee to pay the check. Payment to a person entitled to enforce the check discharges all liability of the obligated bank with respect to the check.

(3) If the claim becomes enforceable before the check is presented for payment, the obligated bank is not obliged to pay the check.

(4) When the claim becomes enforceable, the obligated bank becomes obliged to pay the amount of the check to the claimant if payment of the check has not been made to a person entitled to enforce the check. Subject to Section 4—302(a)(1), payment to the claimant discharges all liability of the obligated bank with respect to the check.

(c) If the obligated bank pays the amount of a check to a claimant under subsection (b)(4) and the check is presented for payment by a person having rights of a holder in due course, the claimant is obliged to (i) refund the payment to the obligated bank if the check is paid, or (ii) pay the amount of the check to the person having rights of a holder in due course if the check is dishonored.

(d) If a claimant has the right to assert a claim under subsection (b) and is also a person entitled to enforce a cashier's check, teller's check, or certified check which is lost, destroyed, or stolen, the claimant may assert rights with respect to the check either under this section or Section 3—309.

Part 4 Liability of Parties

§ 3—401. Signature.

(a) A person is not liable on an instrument unless (i) the person signed the instrument, or (ii) the person is represented by an agent or representative who signed the instrument and the signature is binding on the represented person under Section 3—402.

(b) A signature may be made (i) manually or by means of a device or machine, and (ii) by the use of any name, including a trade or assumed name, or by a word, mark, or symbol executed or adopted by a person with present intention to authenticate a writing.

§ 3—402. Signature by Representative.

(a) If a person acting, or purporting to act, as a representative signs an instrument by signing either the name of the represented person or the name of the signer, the represented person is bound by the signature to the same extent the represented person would be bound if the signature were on a simple contract. If the represented person is bound, the signature of the representative is the "authorized signature of the represented person" and the represented person is liable on the instrument, whether or not identified in the instrument.

(b) If a representative signs the name of the representative to an instrument and the signature is an authorized signature of the represented person, the following rules apply:

(1) If the form of the signature shows unambiguously that the signature is made on behalf of the represented person who is identified in the instrument, the representative is not liable on the instrument.

(2) Subject to subsection (c), if (i) the form of the signature does not show unambiguously that the signature

is made in a representative capacity or (ii) the represented person is not identified in the instrument, the representative is liable on the instrument to a holder in due course that took the instrument without notice that the representative was not intended to be liable on the instrument. With respect to any other person, the representative is liable on the instrument unless the representative proves that the original parties did not intend the representative to be liable on the instrument.

(c) If a representative signs the name of the representative as drawer of a check without indication of the representative status and the check is payable from an account of the represented person who is identified on the check, the signer is not liable on the check if the signature is an authorized signature of the represented person.

§ 3—403. Unauthorized Signature.

(a) Unless otherwise provided in this Article or Article 4, an unauthorized signature is ineffective except as the signature of the unauthorized signer in favor of a person who in good faith pays the instrument or takes it for value. An unauthorized signature may be ratified for all purposes of this Article.

(b) If the signature of more than one person is required to constitute the authorized signature of an organization, the signature of the organization is unauthorized if one of the required signatures is lacking.

(c) The civil or criminal liability of a person who makes an unauthorized signature is not affected by any provision of this Article which makes the unauthorized signature effective for the purposes of this Article.

§ 3—404. Impostors; Fictitious Payees.

(a) If an impostor, by use of the mails or otherwise, induces the issuer of an instrument to issue the instrument to the impostor, or to a person acting in concert with the impostor, by impersonating the payee of the instrument or a person authorized to act for the payee, an indorsement of the instrument by any person in the name of the payee is effective as the indorsement of the payee in favor of a person who, in good faith, pays the instrument or takes it for value or for collection.

(b) If (i) a person whose intent determines to whom an instrument is payable (Section 3—110(a) or (b)) does not intend the person identified as payee to have any interest in the instrument, or (ii) the person identified as payee of an instrument is a fictitious person, the following rules apply until the instrument is negotiated by special indorsement:

(1) Any person in possession of the instrument is its holder.

(2) An indorsement by any person in the name of the payee stated in the instrument is effective as the indorsement of the payee in favor of a person who, in good faith, pays the instrument or takes it for value or for collection.

(c) Under subsection (a) or (b), an indorsement is made in the name of a payee if (i) it is made in a name substantially similar to that of the payee or (ii) the instrument, whether or not indorsed, is deposited in a depositary bank to an account in a name substantially similar to that of the payee.

(d) With respect to an instrument to which subsection (a) or (b) applies, if a person paying the instrument or taking it for value or for collection fails to exercise ordinary care in paying or taking the instrument and that failure substantially contributes to loss resulting from payment of the instrument, the person bearing the loss may recover from the person failing to exercise ordinary care to the extent the failure to exercise ordinary care contributed to the loss.

§ 3—405. Employer's Responsibility for Fraudulent Indorsement by Employee.

(a) In this section:

(1) "Employee" includes an independent contractor and employee of an independent contractor retained by the employer.

(2) "Fraudulent indorsement" means (i) in the case of an instrument payable to the employer, a forged indorsement purporting to be that of the employer, or (ii) in the case of an instrument with respect to which the employer is the issuer, a forged indorsement purporting to be that of the person identified as payee.

(3) "Responsibility" with respect to instruments means authority (i) to sign or indorse instruments on behalf of the employer, (ii) to process instruments received by the employer for bookkeeping purposes, for deposit to an account, or for other disposition, (iii) to prepare or process instruments for issue in the name of the employer, (iv) to supply information determining the names or addresses of payees of instruments to be issued in the name of the employer, (v) to control the disposition of instruments to be issued in the name of the employer, or (vi) to act otherwise with respect to instruments in a responsible capacity. "Responsibility" does not include authority that merely allows an employee to have access to instruments or blank or incomplete instrument forms that are being stored or transported or are part of incoming or outgoing mail, or similar access.

(b) For the purpose of determining the rights and liabilities of a person who, in good faith, pays an instrument or takes it for value or for collection, if an employer entrusted an employee with responsibility with respect to the instrument and the employee or a person acting in concert with the employee makes a fraudulent indorsement of the instrument, the indorsement is effective as the indorsement of the person to whom the instrument is payable if it is made in the name of that person. If the person paying the instrument or taking it for value or for collection fails to exercise ordinary care in paying or taking the instrument and that failure substantially contributes to loss resulting from the fraud, the person bearing the loss may recover from the person failing to exercise ordinary care to the extent the failure to exercise ordinary care contributed to the loss.

(c) Under subsection (b), an indorsement is made in the name of the person to whom an instrument is payable if (i) it is made in a name substantially similar to the name of that person or (ii) the instrument, whether or not indorsed, is deposited in a depositary bank to an account in a name substantially similar to the name of that person.

§ 3–406. Negligence Contributing to Forged Signature or Alteration of Instrument.

(a) A person whose failure to exercise ordinary care substantially contributes to an alteration of an instrument or to the making of a forged signature on an instrument is precluded from asserting the alteration or the forgery against a person who, in good faith, pays the instrument or takes it for value or for collection.

(b) Under subsection (a), if the person asserting the preclusion fails to exercise ordinary care in paying or taking the instrument and that failure substantially contributes to loss, the loss is allocated between the person precluded and the person asserting the preclusion according to the extent to which the failure of each to exercise ordinary care contributed to the loss.

(c) Under subsection (a), the burden of proving failure to exercise ordinary care is on the person asserting the preclusion. Under subsection (b), the burden of proving failure to exercise ordinary care is on the person precluded.

§ 3–407. Alteration.

(a) "Alteration" means (i) an unauthorized change in an instrument that purports to modify in any respect the obligation of a party, or (ii) an unauthorized addition of words or numbers or other change to an incomplete instrument relating to the obligation of a party.

(b) Except as provided in subsection (c), an alteration fraudulently made discharges a party whose obligation is affected by the alteration unless that party assents or is precluded from asserting the alteration. No other alteration discharges a party, and the instrument may be enforced according to its original terms.

(c) A payor bank or drawee paying a fraudulently altered instrument or a person taking it for value, in good faith and without notice of the alteration, may enforce rights with respect to the instrument (i) according to its original terms, or (ii) in the case of an incomplete instrument altered by unauthorized completion, according to its terms as completed.

§ 3–408. Drawee Not Liable on Unaccepted Draft.

A check or other draft does not of itself operate as an assignment of funds in the hands of the drawee available for its payment, and the drawee is not liable on the instrument until the drawee accepts it.

§ 3–409. Acceptance of Draft; Certified Check.

(a) "Acceptance" means the drawee's signed agreement to pay a draft as presented. It must be written on the draft and may consist of the drawee's signature alone. Acceptance may be made at any time and becomes effective when notification pursuant to instructions is given or the accepted draft is delivered for the purpose of giving rights on the acceptance to any person.

(b) A draft may be accepted although it has not been signed by the drawer, is otherwise incomplete, is overdue, or has been dishonored.

(c) If a draft is payable at a fixed period after sight and the acceptor fails to date the acceptance, the holder may complete the acceptance by supplying a date in good faith.

(d) "Certified check" means a check accepted by the bank on which it is drawn. Acceptance may be made as stated in subsection (a) or by a writing on the check which indicates that the check is certified. The drawee of a check has no obligation to certify the check, and refusal to certify is not dishonor of the check.

§ 3–410. Acceptance Varying Draft.

(a) If the terms of a drawee's acceptance vary from the terms of the draft as presented, the holder may refuse the acceptance and treat the draft as dishonored. In that case, the drawee may cancel the acceptance.

(b) The terms of a draft are not varied by an acceptance to pay at a particular bank or place in the United States, unless the acceptance states that the draft is to be paid only at that bank or place.

(c) If the holder assents to an acceptance varying the terms of a draft, the obligation of each drawer and indorser that does not expressly assent to the acceptance is discharged.

§ 3–411. Refusal to Pay Cashier's Checks, Teller's Checks, and Certified Checks.

(a) In this section, "obligated bank" means the acceptor of a certified check or the issuer of a cashier's check or teller's check bought from the issuer.

(b) If the obligated bank wrongfully (i) refuses to pay a cashier's check or certified check, (ii) stops payment of a teller's check, or (iii) refuses to pay a dishonored teller's check, the person asserting the right to enforce the check is entitled to compensation for expenses and loss of interest resulting from the nonpayment and may recover consequential damages if the obligated bank refuses to pay after receiving notice of particular circumstances giving rise to the damages.

(c) Expenses or consequential damages under subsection (b) are not recoverable if the refusal of the obligated bank to pay occurs because (i) the bank suspends payments,

(ii) the obligated bank asserts a claim or defense of the bank that it has reasonable grounds to believe is available against the person entitled to enforce the instrument, (iii) the obligated bank has a reasonable doubt whether the person demanding payment is the person entitled to enforce the instrument, or (iv) payment is prohibited by law.

§ 3—412. Obligation of Issuer of Note or Cashier's Check.

The issuer of a note or cashier's check or other draft drawn on the drawer is obliged to pay the instrument (i) according to its terms at the time it was issued or, if not issued, at the time it first came into possession of a holder, or (ii) if the issuer signed an incomplete instrument, according to its terms when completed, to the extent stated in Sections 3—115 and 3—407. The obligation is owed to a person entitled to enforce the instrument or to an indorser who paid the instrument under Section 3—415.

§ 3—413. Obligation of Acceptor.

(a) The acceptor of a draft is obliged to pay the draft (i) according to its terms at the time it was accepted, even though the acceptance states that the draft is payable "as originally drawn" or equivalent terms, (ii) if the acceptance varies the terms of the draft, according to the terms of the draft as varied, or (iii) if the acceptance is of a draft that is an incomplete instrument, according to its terms when completed, to the extent stated in Sections 3—115 and 3—407. The obligation is owed to a person entitled to enforce the draft or to the drawer or an indorser who paid the draft under Section 3—414 or 3—415.

(b) If the certification of a check or other acceptance of a draft states the amount certified or accepted, the obligation of the acceptor is that amount. If (i) the certification or acceptance does not state an amount, (ii) the amount of the instrument is subsequently raised, and (iii) the instrument is then negotiated to a holder in due course, the obligation of the acceptor is the amount of the instrument at the time it was taken by the holder in due course.

§ 3—414. Obligation of Drawer.

(a) This section does not apply to cashier's checks or other drafts drawn on the drawer.

(b) If an unaccepted draft is dishonored, the drawer is obliged to pay the draft (i) according to its terms at the time it was issued or, if not issued, at the time it first came into possession of a holder, or (ii) if the drawer signed an incomplete instrument, according to its terms when completed, to the extent stated in Sections 3—115 and 3—407. The obligation is owed to a person entitled to enforce the draft or to an indorser who paid the draft under Section 3—415.

(c) If a draft is accepted by a bank, the drawer is discharged, regardless of when or by whom acceptance was obtained.

(d) If a draft is accepted and the acceptor is not a bank, the obligation of the drawer to pay the draft if the draft is dishonored by the acceptor is the same as the obligation of an indorser under Section 3—415(a) and (c).

(e) If a draft states that it is drawn "without recourse" or otherwise disclaims liability of the drawer to pay the draft, the drawer is not liable under subsection (b) to pay the draft if the draft is not a check. A disclaimer of the liability stated in subsection (b) is not effective if the draft is a check.

(f) If (i) a check is not presented for payment or given to a depositary bank for collection within 30 days after its date, (ii) the drawee suspends payments after expiration of the 30-day period without paying the check, and (iii) because of the suspension of payments, the drawer is deprived of funds maintained with the drawee to cover payment of the check, the drawer to the extent deprived of funds may discharge its obligation to pay the check by assigning to the person entitled to enforce the check the rights of the drawer against the drawee with respect to the funds.

§ 3—415. Obligation of Indorser.

(a) Subject to subsections (b), (c), and (d) and to Section 3—419(d), if an instrument is dishonored, an indorser is obliged to pay the amount due on the instrument (i) according to the terms of the instrument at the time it was indorsed, or (ii) if the indorser indorsed an incomplete instrument, according to its terms when completed, to the extent stated in Sections 3—115 and 3—407. The obligation of the indorser is owed to a person entitled to enforce the instrument or to a subsequent indorser who paid the instrument under this section.

(b) If an indorsement states that it is made "without recourse" or otherwise disclaims liability of the indorser, the indorser is not liable under subsection (a) to pay the instrument.

(c) If notice of dishonor of an instrument is required by Section 3—503 and notice of dishonor complying with that section is not given to an indorser, the liability of the indorser under subsection (a) is discharged.

(d) If a draft is accepted by a bank after an indorsement is made, the liability of the indorser under subsection (a) is discharged.

(e) If an indorser of a check is liable under subsection (a) and the check is not presented for payment, or given to a depositary bank for collection, within 30 days after the day the indorsement was made, the liability of the indorser under subsection (a) is discharged.

§ 3—416. Transfer Warranties.

(a) A person who transfers an instrument for consideration warrants to the transferee and, if the transfer is by indorsement, to any subsequent transferee that:

(1) the warrantor is a person entitled to enforce the instrument;

(2) all signatures on the instrument are authentic and authorized;

(3) the instrument has not been altered;

(4) the instrument is not subject to a defense or claim in recoupment of any party which can be asserted against the warrantor; and

(5) the warrantor has no knowledge of any insolvency proceeding commenced with respect to the maker or acceptor or, in the case of an unaccepted draft, the drawer.

(b) A person to whom the warranties under subsection (a) are made and who took the instrument in good faith may recover from the warrantor as damages for breach of warranty an amount equal to the loss suffered as a result of the breach, but not more than the amount of the instrument plus expenses and loss of interest incurred as a result of the breach.

(c) The warranties stated in subsection (a) cannot be disclaimed with respect to checks. Unless notice of a claim for breach of warranty is given to the warrantor within 30 days after the claimant has reason to know of the breach and the identity of the warrantor, the liability of the warrantor under subsection (b) is discharged to the extent of any loss caused by the delay in giving notice of the claim.

(d) A [cause of action] for breach of warranty under this section accrues when the claimant has reason to know of the breach.

§ 3—417. Presentment Warranties.

(a) If an unaccepted draft is presented to the drawee for payment or acceptance and the drawee pays or accepts the draft, (i) the person obtaining payment or acceptance, at the time of presentment, and (ii) a previous transferor of the draft, at the time of transfer, warrant to the drawee making payment or accepting the draft in good faith that:

(1) the warrantor is, or was, at the time the warrantor transferred the draft, a person entitled to enforce the draft or authorized to obtain payment or acceptance of the draft on behalf of a person entitled to enforce the draft;

(2) the draft has not been altered; and

(3) the warrantor has no knowledge that the signature of the drawer of the draft is unauthorized.

(b) A drawee making payment may recover from any warrantor damages for breach of warranty equal to the amount paid by the drawee less the amount the drawee received or is entitled to receive from the drawer because of the payment. In addition, the drawee is entitled to compensation for expenses and loss of interest resulting from the breach. The right of the drawee to recover damages under this subsection is not affected by any failure of the drawee to exercise ordinary care in making payment. If the drawee accepts the draft, breach of warranty is a defense to the obligation of the acceptor. If the acceptor makes payment

with respect to the draft, the acceptor is entitled to recover from any warrantor for breach of warranty the amounts stated in this subsection.

(c) If a drawee asserts a claim for breach of warranty under subsection (a) based on an unauthorized indorsement of the draft or an alteration of the draft, the warrantor may defend by proving that the indorsement is effective under Section 3—404 or 3—405 or the drawer is precluded under Section 3—406 or 4—406 from asserting against the drawee the unauthorized indorsement or alteration.

(d) If (i) a dishonored draft is presented for payment to the drawer or an indorser or (ii) any other instrument is presented for payment to a party obliged to pay the instrument, and (iii) payment is received, the following rules apply:

(1) The person obtaining payment and a prior transferor of the instrument warrant to the person making payment in good faith that the warrantor is, or was, at the time the warrantor transferred the instrument, a person entitled to enforce the instrument or authorized to obtain payment on behalf of a person entitled to enforce the instrument.

(2) The person making payment may recover from any warrantor for breach of warranty an amount equal to the amount paid plus expenses and loss of interest resulting from the breach.

(e) The warranties stated in subsections (a) and (d) cannot be disclaimed with respect to checks. Unless notice of a claim for breach of warranty is given to the warrantor within 30 days after the claimant has reason to know of the breach and the identity of the warrantor, the liability of the warrantor under subsection (b) or (d) is discharged to the extent of any loss caused by the delay in giving notice of the claim.

(f) A [cause of action] for breach of warranty under this section accrues when the claimant has reason to know of the breach.

§ 3—418. Payment or Acceptance by Mistake.

(a) Except as provided in subsection (c), if the drawee of a draft pays or accepts the draft and the drawee acted on the mistaken belief that (i) payment of the draft had not been stopped pursuant to Section 4—403 or (ii) the signature of the drawer of the draft was authorized, the drawee may recover the amount of the draft from the person to whom or for whose benefit payment was made or, in the case of acceptance, may revoke the acceptance. Rights of the drawee under this subsection are not affected by failure of the drawee to exercise ordinary care in paying or accepting the draft.

(b) Except as provided in subsection (c), if an instrument has been paid or accepted by mistake and the case is not covered by subsection (a), the person paying or accepting may, to the extent permitted by the law governing mistake and restitution, (i) recover the payment from the person to whom or for whose benefit payment was made or (ii) in the case of acceptance, may revoke the acceptance.

(c) The remedies provided by subsection (a) or (b) may not be asserted against a person who took the instrument in good faith and for value or who in good faith changed position in reliance on the payment or acceptance. This subsection does not limit remedies provided by Section 3—417 or 4—407.

(d) Notwithstanding Section 4—215, if an instrument is paid or accepted by mistake and the payor or acceptor recovers payment or revokes acceptance under subsection (a) or (b), the instrument is deemed not to have been paid or accepted and is treated as dishonored, and the person from whom payment is recovered has rights as a person entitled to enforce the dishonored instrument.

§ 3—419. Instruments Signed for Accommodation.

(a) If an instrument is issued for value given for the benefit of a party to the instrument ("accommodated party") and another party to the instrument ("accommodation party") signs the instrument for the purpose of incurring liability on the instrument without being a direct beneficiary of the value given for the instrument, the instrument is signed by the accommodation party "for accommodation."

(b) An accommodation party may sign the instrument as maker, drawer, acceptor, or indorser and, subject to subsection (d), is obliged to pay the instrument in the capacity in which the accommodation party signs. The obligation of an accommodation party may be enforced notwithstanding any statute of frauds and whether or not the accommodation party receives consideration for the accommodation.

(c) A person signing an instrument is presumed to be an accommodation party and there is notice that the instrument is signed for accommodation if the signature is an anomalous indorsement or is accompanied by words indicating that the signer is acting as surety or guarantor with respect to the obligation of another party to the instrument. Except as provided in Section 3—605, the obligation of an accommodation party to pay the instrument is not affected by the fact that the person enforcing the obligation had notice when the instrument was taken by that person that the accommodation party signed the instrument for accommodation.

(d) If the signature of a party to an instrument is accompanied by words indicating unambiguously that the party is guaranteeing collection rather than payment of the obligation of another party to the instrument, the signer is obliged to pay the amount due on the instrument to a person entitled to enforce the instrument only if (i) execution of judgment against the other party has been returned unsatisfied, (ii) the other party is insolvent or in an insolvency proceeding, (iii) the other party cannot be served with process, or (iv) it is otherwise apparent that payment cannot be obtained from the other party.

(e) An accommodation party who pays the instrument is entitled to reimbursement from the accommodated party and is entitled to enforce the instrument against the accommodated party. An accommodated party who pays the instrument has no right of recourse against, and is not entitled to contribution from, an accommodation party.

§ 3—420. Conversion of Instrument.

(a) The law applicable to conversion of personal property applies to instruments. An instrument is also converted if it is taken by transfer, other than a negotiation, from a person not entitled to enforce the instrument or a bank makes or obtains payment with respect to the instrument for a person not entitled to enforce the instrument or receive payment. An action for conversion of an instrument may not be brought by (i) the issuer or acceptor of the instrument or (ii) a payee or indorsee who did not receive delivery of the instrument either directly or through delivery to an agent or a co-payee.

(b) In an action under subsection (a), the measure of liability is presumed to be the amount payable on the instrument, but recovery may not exceed the amount of the plaintiff's interest in the instrument.

(c) A representative, other than a depositary bank, who has in good faith dealt with an instrument or its proceeds on behalf of one who was not the person entitled to enforce the instrument is not liable in conversion to that person beyond the amount of any proceeds that it has not paid out.

Part 5 Dishonor

§ 3—501. Presentment.

(a) "Presentment" means a demand made by or on behalf of a person entitled to enforce an instrument (i) to pay the instrument made to the drawee or a party obliged to pay the instrument or, in the case of a note or accepted draft payable at a bank, to the bank, or (ii) to accept a draft made to the drawee.

(b) The following rules are subject to Article 4, agreement of the parties, and clearing-house rules and the like:

> (1) Presentment may be made at the place of payment of the instrument and must be made at the place of payment if the instrument is payable at a bank in the United States; may be made by any commercially reasonable means, including an oral, written, or electronic communication; is effective when the demand for payment or acceptance is received by the person to whom presentment is made; and is effective if made to any one of two or more makers, acceptors, drawees, or other payors.

> (2) Upon demand of the person to whom presentment is made, the person making presentment must

(i) exhibit the instrument, (ii) give reasonable identification and, if presentment is made on behalf of another person, reasonable evidence of authority to do so, and (. . .) sign a receipt on the instrument for any payment made or surrender the instrument if full payment is made.

(3) Without dishonoring the instrument, the party to whom presentment is made may (i) return the instrument for lack of a necessary indorsement, or (ii) refuse payment or acceptance for failure of the presentment to comply with the terms of the instrument, an agreement of the parties, or other applicable law or rule.

(4) The party to whom presentment is made may treat presentment as occurring on the next business day after the day of presentment if the party to whom presentment is made has established a cut-off hour not earlier than 2 P.M. for the receipt and processing of instruments presented for payment or acceptance and presentment is made after the cut-off hour.

§ 3—502. **Dishonor.**

(a) Dishonor of a note is governed by the following rules:

(1) If the note is payable on demand, the note is dishonored if presentment is duly made to the maker and the note is not paid on the day of presentment.

(2) If the note is not payable on demand and is payable at or through a bank or the terms of the note require presentment, the note is dishonored if presentment is duly made and the note is not paid on the day it becomes payable or the day of presentment, whichever is later.

(3) If the note is not payable on demand and paragraph (2) does not apply, the note is dishonored if it is not paid on the day it becomes payable.

(b) Dishonor of an unaccepted draft other than a documentary draft is governed by the following rules:

(1) If a check is duly presented for payment to the payor bank otherwise than for immediate payment over the counter, the check is dishonored if the payor bank makes timely return of the check or sends timely notice of dishonor or nonpayment under Section 4—301 or 4—302, or becomes accountable for the amount of the check under Section 4—302.

(2) If a draft is payable on demand and paragraph (1) does not apply, the draft is dishonored if presentment for payment is duly made to the drawee and the draft is not paid on the day of presentment.

(3) If a draft is payable on a date stated in the draft, the draft is dishonored if (i) presentment for payment is duly made to the drawee and payment is not made on the day the draft becomes payable or the day of presentment, whichever is later, or (ii) presentment for acceptance is duly made before the day the draft becomes payable and the draft is not accepted on the day of presentment.

(4) If a draft is payable on elapse of a period of time after sight or acceptance, the draft is dishonored if presentment for acceptance is duly made and the draft is not accepted on the day of presentment.

(c) Dishonor of an unaccepted documentary draft occurs according to the rules stated in subsection (b)(2), (3), and (4), except that payment or acceptance may be delayed without dishonor until no later than the close of the third business day of the drawee following the day on which payment or acceptance is required by those paragraphs.

(d) Dishonor of an accepted draft is governed by the following rules:

(1) If the draft is payable on demand, the draft is dishonored if presentment for payment is duly made to the acceptor and the draft is not paid on the day of presentment.

(2) If the draft is not payable on demand, the draft is dishonored if presentment for payment is duly made to the acceptor and payment is not made on the day it becomes payable or the day of presentment, whichever is later.

(e) In any case in which presentment is otherwise required for dishonor under this section and presentment is excused under Section 3—504, dishonor occurs without presentment if the instrument is not duly accepted or paid.

(f) If a draft is dishonored because timely acceptance of the draft was not made and the person entitled to demand acceptance consents to a late acceptance, from the time of acceptance the draft is treated as never having been dishonored.

§ 3—503. **Notice of Dishonor.**

(a) The obligation of an indorser stated in Section 3—415(a) and the obligation of a drawer stated in Section 3—414(d) may not be enforced unless (i) the indorser or drawer is given notice of dishonor of the instrument complying with this section or (ii) notice of dishonor is excused under Section 3—504(b).

(b) Notice of dishonor may be given by any person; may be given by any commercially reasonable means, including an oral, written, or electronic communication; and is sufficient if it reasonably identifies the instrument and indicates that the instrument has been dishonored or has not been paid or accepted. Return of an instrument given to a bank for collection is sufficient notice of dishonor.

(c) Subject to Section 3—504(c), with respect to an instrument taken for collection by a collecting bank, notice of dishonor must be given (i) by the bank before midnight of the next banking day following the banking day on which the bank receives notice of dishonor of the instrument, or (ii) by any other person within 30 days following the day on which the person receives notice of dishonor. With respect to any other instrument, notice of dishonor must be given within 30 days following the day on which dishonor occurs.

§ 3–504. Excused Presentment and Notice of Dishonor.

(a) Presentment for payment or acceptance of an instrument is excused if (i) the person entitled to present the instrument cannot with reasonable diligence make presentment, (ii) the maker or acceptor has repudiated an obligation to pay the instrument or is dead or in insolvency proceedings, (iii) by the terms of the instrument presentment is not necessary to enforce the obligation of indorsers or the drawer, (iv) the drawer or indorser whose obligation is being enforced has waived presentment or otherwise has no reason to expect or right to require that the instrument be paid or accepted, or (v) the drawer instructed the drawee not to pay or accept the draft or the drawee was not obligated to the drawer to pay the draft.

(b) Notice of dishonor is excused if (i) by the terms of the instrument notice of dishonor is not necessary to enforce the obligation of a party to pay the instrument, or (ii) the party whose obligation is being enforced waived notice of dishonor. A waiver of presentment is also a waiver of notice of dishonor.

(c) Delay in giving notice of dishonor is excused if the delay was caused by circumstances beyond the control of the person giving the notice and the person giving the notice exercised reasonable diligence after the cause of the delay ceased to operate.

§ 3–505. Evidence of Dishonor.

(a) The following are admissible as evidence and create a presumption of dishonor and of any notice of dishonor stated:

(1) a document regular in form as provided in subsection (b) which purports to be a protest;

(2) a purported stamp or writing of the drawee, payor bank, or presenting bank on or accompanying the instrument stating that acceptance or payment has been refused unless reasons for the refusal are stated and the reasons are not consistent with dishonor;

(3) a book or record of the drawee, payor bank, or collecting bank, kept in the usual course of business which shows dishonor, even if there is no evidence of who made the entry.

(b) A protest is a certificate of dishonor made by a United States consul or vice consul, or a notary public or other person authorized to administer oaths by the law of the place where dishonor occurs. It may be made upon information satisfactory to that person. The protest must identify the instrument and certify either that presentment has been made or, if not made, the reason why it was not made, and that the instrument has been dishonored by nonacceptance or nonpayment. The protest may also certify that notice of dishonor has been given to some or all parties.

Part 6 Discharge and Payment

§ 3–601. Discharge and Effect of Discharge.

(a) The obligation of a party to pay the instrument is discharged as stated in this Article or by an act or agreement with the party which would discharge an obligation to pay money under a simple contract.

(b) Discharge of the obligation of a party is not effective against a person acquiring rights of a holder in due course of the instrument without notice of the discharge.

§ 3–602. Payment.

(a) Subject to subsection (b), an instrument is paid to the extent payment is made (i) by or on behalf of a party obliged to pay the instrument, and (ii) to a person entitled to enforce the instrument. To the extent of the payment, the obligation of the party obliged to pay the instrument is discharged even though payment is made with knowledge of a claim to the instrument under Section 3–306 by another person.

(b) The obligation of a party to pay the instrument is not discharged under subsection (a) if:

(1) a claim to the instrument under Section 3–306 is enforceable against the party receiving payment and (i) payment is made with knowledge by the payor that payment is prohibited by injunction or similar process of a court of competent jurisdiction, or (ii) in the case of an instrument other than a cashier's check, teller's check, or certified check, the party making payment accepted, from the person having a claim to the instrument, indemnity against loss resulting from refusal to pay the person entitled to enforce the instrument; or

(2) the person making payment knows that the instrument is a stolen instrument and pays a person it knows is in wrongful possession of the instrument.

§ 3–603. Tender of Payment.

(a) If tender of payment of an obligation to pay an instrument is made to a person entitled to enforce the instrument, the effect of tender is governed by principles of law applicable to tender of payment under a simple contract.

(b) If tender of payment of an obligation to pay an instrument is made to a person entitled to enforce the instrument and the tender is refused, there is discharge, to the extent of the amount of the tender, of the obligation of an indorser or accommodation party having a right of recourse with respect to the obligation to which the tender relates.

(c) If tender of payment of an amount due on an instrument is made to a person entitled to enforce the instrument, the obligation of the obligor to pay interest after the due date on the amount tendered is discharged. If presentment is required with respect to an instrument and the obligor is able and ready to pay on the due date at every place of payment stated in the instrument, the obligor is deemed to have made tender of payment on the due date to the person entitled to enforce the instrument.

§ 3—604. Discharge by Cancellation or Renunciation.

(a) A person entitled to enforce an instrument, with or without consideration, may discharge the obligation of a party to pay the instrument (i) by an intentional voluntary act, such as surrender of the instrument to the party, destruction, mutilation, or cancellation of the instrument, cancellation or striking out of the party's signature, or the addition of words to the instrument indicating discharge, or (ii) by agreeing not to sue or otherwise renouncing rights against the party by a signed writing.

(b) Cancellation or striking out of an indorsement pursuant to subsection (a) does not affect the status and rights of a party derived from the indorsement.

§ 3—605. Discharge of Indorsers and Accommodation Parties.

(a) In this section, the term "indorser" includes a drawer having the obligation described in Section 3—414(d).

(b) Discharge, under Section 3—604, of the obligation of a party to pay an instrument does not discharge the obligation of an indorser or accommodation party having a right of recourse against the discharged party.

(c) If a person entitled to enforce an instrument agrees, with or without consideration, to an extension of the due date of the obligation of a party to pay the instrument, the extension discharges an indorser or accommodation party having a right of recourse against the party whose obligation is extended to the extent the indorser or accommodation party proves that the extension caused loss to the indorser or accommodation party with respect to the right of recourse.

(d) If a person entitled to enforce an instrument agrees, with or without consideration, to a material modification of the obligation of a party other than an extension of the due date, the modification discharges the obligation of an indorser or accommodation party having a right of recourse against the person whose obligation is modified to the extent the modification causes loss to the indorser or accommodation party with respect to the right of recourse. The loss suffered by the indorser or accommodation party as a result of the modification is equal to the amount of the right of recourse unless the person enforcing the instrument proves that no loss was caused by the modification or that the loss caused by the modification was an amount less than the amount of the right of recourse.

(e) If the obligation of a party to pay an instrument is secured by an interest in collateral and a person entitled to enforce the instrument impairs the value of the interest in collateral, the obligation of an indorser or accommodation party having a right of recourse against the obligor is discharged to the extent of the impairment. The value of an interest in collateral is impaired to the extent (i) the value of the interest is reduced to an amount less than the amount of the right of recourse of the party asserting discharge, or (ii) the reduction in value of the interest causes an increase in the amount by which the amount of the right of recourse exceeds the value of the interest. The burden of proving impairment is on the party asserting discharge.

(f) If the obligation of a party is secured by an interest in collateral not provided by an accommodation party and a person entitled to enforce the instrument impairs the value of the interest in collateral, the obligation of any party who is jointly and severally liable with respect to the secured obligation is discharged to the extent the impairment causes the party asserting discharge to pay more than that party would have been obliged to pay, taking into account rights of contribution, if impairment had not occurred. If the party asserting discharge is an accommodation party not entitled to discharge under subsection (e), the party is deemed to have a right to contribution based on joint and several liability rather than a right to reimbursement. The burden of proving impairment is on the party asserting discharge.

(g) Under subsection (e) or (f), impairing value of an interest in collateral includes (i) failure to obtain or maintain perfection or recordation of the interest in collateral, (ii) release of collateral without substitution of collateral of equal value, (iii) failure to perform a duty to preserve the value of collateral owed, under Article 9 or other law, to a debtor or surety or other person secondarily liable, or (iv) failure to comply with applicable law in disposing of collateral.

(h) An accommodation party is not discharged under subsection (c), (d), or (e) unless the person entitled to enforce the instrument knows of the accommodation or has notice under Section 3—419(c) that the instrument was signed for accommodation.

(i) A party is not discharged under this section if (i) the party asserting discharge consents to the event or conduct that is the basis of the discharge, or (ii) the instrument or a separate agreement of the party provides for waiver of discharge under this section either specifically or by general language indicating that parties waive defenses based on suretyship or impairment of collateral.

ADDENDUM TO REVISED ARTICLE 3
Notes to Legislative Counsel

1. If revised Article 3 is adopted in your state, the reference in Section 2—511 to Section 3—802 should be changed to Section 3—310.

2. If revised Article 3 is adopted in your state and the Uniform Fiduciaries Act is also in effect in your state, you may want to consider amending Uniform Fiduciaries Act § 9 to

conform to Section 3—307(b)(2)(iii) and (4)(iii). See Official Comment 3 to Section 3—307.

Revised Article 4
BANK DEPOSITS AND COLLECTIONS

Part 1 General Provisions and Definitions

§ 4—101. Short Title.

This Article may be cited as Uniform Commercial Code—Bank Deposits and Collections.

§ 4—102. Applicability.

(a) To the extent that items within this Article are also within Articles 3 and 8, they are subject to those Articles. If there is conflict, this Article governs Article 3, but Article 8 governs this Article.

(b) The liability of a bank for action or non-action with respect to an item handled by it for purposes of presentment, payment, or collection is governed by the law of the place where the bank is located. In the case of action or non-action by or at a branch or separate office of a bank, its liability is governed by the law of the place where the branch or separate office is located.

§ 4—103. Variation by Agreement; Measure of Damages; Action Constituting Ordinary Care.

(a) The effect of the provisions of this Article may be varied by agreement, but the parties to the agreement cannot disclaim a bank's responsibility for its lack of good faith or failure to exercise ordinary care or limit the measure of damages for the lack or failure. However, the parties may determine by agreement the standards by which the bank's responsibility is to be measured if those standards are not manifestly unreasonable.

(b) Federal Reserve regulations and operating circulars, clearing-house rules, and the like have the effect of agreements under subsection (a), whether or not specifically assented to by all parties interested in items handled.

(c) Action or non-action approved by this Article or pursuant to Federal Reserve regulations or operating circulars is the exercise of ordinary care and, in the absence of special instructions, action or non-action consistent with clearing-house rules and the like or with a general banking usage not disapproved by this Article, is prima facie the exercise of ordinary care.

(d) The specification or approval of certain procedures by this Article is not disapproval of other procedures that may be reasonable under the circumstances.

(e) The measure of damages for failure to exercise ordinary care in handling an item is the amount of the item reduced by an amount that could not have been realized by the exercise of ordinary care. If there is also bad faith it includes any other damages the party suffered as a proximate consequence.

§ 4—104. Definitions and Index of Definitions.

(a) In this Article, unless the context otherwise requires:

(1) "Account" means any deposit or credit account with a bank, including a demand, time, savings, passbook, share draft, or like account, other than an account evidenced by a certificate of deposit;

(2) "Afternoon" means the period of a day between noon and midnight;

(3) "Banking day" means the part of a day on which a bank is open to the public for carrying on substantially all of its banking functions;

(4) "Clearing house" means an association of banks or other payors regularly clearing items;

(5) "Customer" means a person having an account with a bank or for whom a bank has agreed to collect items, including a bank that maintains an account at another bank;

(6) "Documentary draft" means a draft to be presented for acceptance or payment if specified documents, certificated securities (Section 8—102) or instructions for uncertificated securities (Section 8—102), or other certificates, statements, or the like are to be received by the drawee or other payor before acceptance or payment of the draft;

(7) "Draft" means a draft as defined in Section 3—104 or an item, other than an instrument, that is an order;

(8) "Drawee" means a person ordered in a draft to make payment;

(9) "Item" means an instrument or a promise or order to pay money handled by a bank for collection or payment. The term does not include a payment order governed by Article 4A or a credit or debit card slip;

(10) "Midnight deadline" with respect to a bank is midnight on its next banking day following the banking day on which it receives the relevant item or notice or from which the time for taking action commences to run, whichever is later;

(11) "Settle" means to pay in cash, by clearing-house settlement, in a charge or credit or by remittance, or otherwise as agreed. A settlement may be either provisional or final;

(12) "Suspends payments" with respect to a bank means that it has been closed by order of the supervisory authorities, that a public officer has been appointed to take it over, or that it ceases or refuses to make payments in the ordinary course of business.

(b);(c) [Other definitions' section references deleted.]

(d) In addition, Article 1 contains general definitions and

principles of construction and interpretation applicable throughout this Article.

§ 4–105. "Bank"; "Depositary Bank"; "Payor Bank"; "Intermediary Bank"; "Collecting Bank"; "Presenting Bank".

In this Article:

(1) "Bank" means a person engaged in the business of banking, including a savings bank, savings and loan association, credit union, or trust company;

(2) "Depositary bank" means the first bank to take an item even though it is also the payor bank, unless the item is presented for immediate payment over the counter;

(3) "Payor bank" means a bank that is the drawee of a draft;

(4) "Intermediary bank" means a bank to which an item is transferred in course of collection except the depositary or payor bank;

(5) "Collecting bank" means a bank handling an item for collection except the payor bank;

(6) "Presenting bank" means a bank presenting an item except a payor bank.

§ 4–106. Payable Through or Payable at Bank: Collecting Bank.

(a) If an item states that it is "payable through" a bank identified in the item, (i) the item designates the bank as a collecting bank and does not by itself authorize the bank to pay the item, and (ii) the item may be presented for payment only by or through the bank.

Alternative A

(b) If an item states that it is "payable at" a bank identified in the item, the item is equivalent to a draft drawn on the bank.

Alternative B

(b) If an item states that it is "payable at" a bank identified in the item, (i) the item designates the bank as a collecting bank and does not by itself authorize the bank to pay the item, and (ii) the item may be presented for payment only by or through the bank.

(c) If a draft names a nonbank drawee and it is unclear whether a bank named in the draft is a co-drawee or a collecting bank, the bank is a collecting bank.

§ 4–107. Separate Office of Bank.

A branch or separate office of a bank is a separate bank for the purpose of computing the time within which and determining the place at or to which action may be taken or notices or orders shall be given under this Article and under Article 3.

§ 4–108. Time of Receipt of Items.

(a) For the purpose of allowing time to process items, prove balances, and make the necessary entries on its books to determine its position for the day, a bank may fix an afternoon hour of 2 P.M. or later as a cutoff hour for the handling of money and items and the making of entries on its books.

(b) An item or deposit of money received on any day after a cutoff hour so fixed or after the close of the banking day may be treated as being received at the opening of the next banking day.

§ 4–109. Delays.

(a) Unless otherwise instructed, a collecting bank in a good faith effort to secure payment of a specific item drawn on a payor other than a bank, and with or without the approval of any person involved, may waive, modify, or extend time limits imposed or permitted by this [act] for a period not exceeding two additional banking days without discharge of drawers or indorsers or liability to its transferor or a prior party.

(b) Delay by a collecting bank or payor bank beyond time limits prescribed or permitted by this [act] or by instructions is excused if (i) the delay is caused by interruption of communication or computer facilities, suspension of payments by another bank, war, emergency conditions, failure of equipment, or other circumstances beyond the control of the bank, and (ii) the bank exercises such diligence as the circumstances require.

§ 4–110. Electronic Presentment.

(a) "Agreement for electronic presentment" means an agreement, clearing-house rule, or Federal Reserve regulation or operating circular, providing that presentment of an item may be made by transmission of an image of an item or information describing the item ("presentment notice") rather than delivery of the item itself. The agreement may provide for procedures governing retention, presentment, payment, dishonor, and other matters concerning items subject to the agreement.

(b) Presentment of an item pursuant to an agreement for presentment is made when the presentment notice is received.

(c) If presentment is made by presentment notice, a reference to "item" or "check" in this Article means the presentment notice unless the context otherwise indicates.

§ 4–111. Statute of Limitations.

An action to enforce an obligation, duty, or right arising under this Article must be commenced within three years after the [cause of action] accrues.

Part 2 Collection of Items: Depositary and Collecting Banks

§ 4–201. Status of Collecting Bank As Agent and Provisional Status of Credits; Applicability of Article; Item Indorsed "Pay Any Bank".

(a) Unless a contrary intent clearly appears and before the time that a settlement given by a collecting bank for an item is or becomes final, the bank, with respect to an item, is an agent or sub-agent of the owner of the item and any settlement given for the item is provisional. This provision applies regardless of the form of indorsement or lack of indorsement and even though credit given for the item is subject to immediate withdrawal as of right or is in fact withdrawn; but the continuance of ownership of an item by its owner and any rights of the owner to proceeds of the item are subject to rights of a collecting bank, such as those resulting from outstanding advances on the item and rights of recoupment or setoff. If an item is handled by banks for purposes of presentment, payment, collection, or return, the relevant provisions of this Article apply even though action of the parties clearly establishes that a particular bank has purchased the item and is the owner of it.

(b) After an item has been indorsed with the words "pay any bank" or the like, only a bank may acquire the rights of a holder until the item has been:

(1) returned to the customer initiating collection; or

(2) specially indorsed by a bank to a person who is not a bank.

§ 4—202. Responsibility for Collection or Return; When Action Timely.

(a) A collecting bank must exercise ordinary care in:

(1) presenting an item or sending it for presentment;

(2) sending notice of dishonor or nonpayment or returning an item other than a documentary draft to the bank's transferor after learning that the item has not been paid or accepted, as the case may be;

(3) settling for an item when the bank receives final settlement; and

(4) notifying its transferor of any loss or delay in transit within a reasonable time after discovery thereof.

(b) A collecting bank exercises ordinary care under subsection (a) by taking proper action before its midnight deadline following receipt of an item, notice, or settlement. Taking proper action within a reasonably longer time may constitute the exercise of ordinary care, but the bank has the burden of establishing timeliness.

(c) Subject to subsection (a)(1), a bank is not liable for the insolvency, neglect, misconduct, mistake, or default of another bank or person or for loss or destruction of an item in the possession of others or in transit.

§ 4—203. Effect of Instructions.

Subject to Article 3 concerning conversion of instruments (Section 3—420) and restrictive indorsements (Section 3—206), only a collecting bank's transferor can give instructions that affect the bank or constitute notice to it, and a collecting bank is not liable to prior parties for any action taken pursuant to the instructions or in accordance with any agreement with its transferor.

§ 4—204. Methods of Sending and Presenting; Sending Directly to Payor Bank.

(a) A collecting bank shall send items by a reasonably prompt method, taking into consideration relevant instructions, the nature of the item, the number of those items on hand, the cost of collection involved, and the method generally used by it or others to present those items.

(b) A collecting bank may send:

(1) an item directly to the payor bank;

(2) an item to a nonbank payor if authorized by its transferor; and

(3) an item other than documentary drafts to a nonbank payor, if authorized by Federal Reserve regulation or operating circular, clearing-house rule, or the like.

(c) Presentment may be made by a presenting bank at a place where the payor bank or other payor has requested that presentment be made.

§ 4—205. Depositary Bank Holder of Unindorsed Item.

If a customer delivers an item to a depositary bank for collection:

(1) the depositary bank becomes a holder of the item at the time it receives the item for collection if the customer at the time of delivery was a holder of the item, whether or not the customer indorses the item, and, if the bank satisfies the other requirements of Section 3—302, it is a holder in due course; and

(2) the depositary bank warrants to collecting banks, the payor bank or other payor, and the drawer that the amount of the item was paid to the customer or deposited to the customer's account.

§ 4—206. Transfer Between Banks.

Any agreed method that identifies the transferor bank is sufficient for the item's further transfer to another bank.

§ 4—207. Transfer Warranties.

(a) A customer or collecting bank that transfers an item and receives a settlement or other consideration warrants to the transferee and to any subsequent collecting bank that:

(1) the warrantor is a person entitled to enforce the item;

(2) all signatures on the item are authentic and authorized;

(3) the item has not been altered;

(4) the item is not subject to a defense or claim in recoupment (Section 3—305(a)) of any party that can be asserted against the warrantor; and

(5) the warrantor has no knowledge of any insolvency proceeding commenced with respect to the maker or

acceptor or, in the case of an unaccepted draft, the drawer.

(b) If an item is dishonored, a customer or collecting bank transferring the item and receiving settlement or other consideration is obliged to pay the amount due on the item (i) according to the terms of the item at the time it was transferred, or (ii) if the transfer was of an incomplete item, according to its terms when completed as stated in Sections 3—115 and 3—407. The obligation of a transferor is owed to the transferee and to any subsequent collecting bank that takes the item in good faith. A transferor cannot disclaim its obligation under this subsection by an indorsement stating that it is made "without recourse" or otherwise disclaiming liability.

(c) A person to whom the warranties under subsection (a) are made and who took the item in good faith may recover from the warrantor as damages for breach of warranty an amount equal to the loss suffered as a result of the breach, but not more than the amount of the item plus expenses and loss of interest incurred as a result of the breach.

(d) The warranties stated in subsection (a) cannot be disclaimed with respect to checks. Unless notice of a claim for breach of warranty is given to the warrantor within 30 days after the claimant has reason to know of the breach and the identity of the warrantor, the warrantor is discharged to the extent of any loss caused by the delay in giving notice of the claim.

(e) A cause of action for breach of warranty under this section accrues when the claimant has reason to know of the breach.

§ 4—208. Presentment Warranties.

(a) If an unaccepted draft is presented to the drawee for payment or acceptance and the drawee pays or accepts the draft, (i) the person obtaining payment or acceptance, at the time of presentment, and (ii) a previous transferor of the draft, at the time of transfer, warrant to the drawee that pays or accepts the draft in good faith that:

(1) the warrantor is, or was, at the time the warrantor transferred the draft, a person entitled to enforce the draft or authorized to obtain payment or acceptance of the draft on behalf of a person entitled to enforce the draft;

(2) the draft has not been altered; and

(3) the warrantor has no knowledge that the signature of the purported drawer of the draft is unauthorized.

(b) A drawee making payment may recover from a warrantor damages for breach of warranty equal to the amount paid by the drawee less the amount the drawee received or is entitled to receive from the drawer because of the payment. In addition, the drawee is entitled to compensation for expenses and loss of interest resulting from the breach. The right of the drawee to recover damages under this subsection is not affected by any failure of the drawee to exercise ordinary care in making payment. If the drawee accepts the draft (i) breach of warranty is a defense to the

obligation of the acceptor, and (ii) if the acceptor makes payment with respect to the draft, the acceptor is entitled to recover from a warrantor for breach of warranty the amounts stated in this subsection.

(c) If a drawee asserts a claim for breach of warranty under subsection (a) based on an unauthorized indorsement of the draft or an alteration of the draft, the warrantor may defend by proving that the indorsement is effective under Section 3—404 or 3—405 or the drawer is precluded under Section 3—406 or 4—406 from asserting against the drawee the unauthorized indorsement or alteration.

(d) If (i) a dishonored draft is presented for payment to the drawer or an indorser or (ii) any other item is presented for payment to a party obliged to pay the item, and the item is paid, the person obtaining payment and a prior transferor of the item warrant to the person making payment in good faith that the warrantor is, or was, at the time the warrantor transferred the item, a person entitled to enforce the item or authorized to obtain payment on behalf of a person entitled to enforce the item. The person making payment may recover from any warrantor for breach of warranty an amount equal to the amount paid plus expenses and loss of interest resulting from the breach.

(e) The warranties stated in subsections (a) and (d) cannot be disclaimed with respect to checks. Unless notice of a claim for breach of warranty is given to the warrantor within 30 days after the claimant has reason to know of the breach and the identity of the warrantor, the warrantor is discharged to the extent of any loss caused by the delay in giving notice of the claim.

(f) A cause of action for breach of warranty under this section accrues when the claimant has reason to know of the breach.

§ 4—209. Encoding and Retention Warranties.

(a) A person who encodes information on or with respect to an item after issue warrants to any subsequent collecting bank and to the payor bank or other payor that the information is correctly encoded. If the customer of a depositary bank encodes, that bank also makes the warranty.

(b) A person who undertakes to retain an item pursuant to an agreement for electronic presentment warrants to any subsequent collecting bank and to the payor bank or other payor that retention and presentment of the item comply with the agreement. If a customer of a depositary bank undertakes to retain an item, that bank also makes this warranty.

(c) A person to whom warranties are made under this section and who took the item in good faith may recover from the warrantor as damages for breach of warranty an amount equal to the loss suffered as a result of the breach, plus expenses and loss of interest incurred as a result of the breach.

§ 4—210. Security Interest of Collecting Bank in Items, Accompanying Documents and Proceeds.

(a) A collecting bank has a security interest in an item and any accompanying documents or the proceeds of either:

(1) in case of an item deposited in an account, to the extent to which credit given for the item has been withdrawn or applied;

(2) in case of an item for which it has given credit available for withdrawal as of right, to the extent of the credit given, whether or not the credit is drawn upon or there is a right of charge-back; or

(3) if it makes an advance on or against the item.

(b) If credit given for several items received at one time or pursuant to a single agreement is withdrawn or applied in part, the security interest remains upon all the items, any accompanying documents or the proceeds of either. For the purpose of this section, credits first given are first withdrawn.

(c) Receipt by a collecting bank of a final settlement for an item is a realization on its security interest in the item, accompanying documents, and proceeds. So long as the bank does not receive final settlement for the item or give up possession of the item or accompanying documents for purposes other than collection, the security interest continues to that extent and is subject to Article 9, but:

(1) no security agreement is necessary to make the security interest enforceable (Section 9—203(1)(a));

(2) no filing is required to perfect the security interest; and

(3) the security interest has priority over conflicting perfected security interests in the item, accompanying documents, or proceeds.

§ 4—211. When Bank Gives Value for Purposes of Holder in Due Course.

For purposes of determining its status as a holder in due course, a bank has given value to the extent it has a security interest in an item, if the bank otherwise complies with the requirements of Section 3—302 on what constitutes a holder in due course.

§ 4—212. Presentment by Notice of Item Not Payable by, Through, or at Bank; Liability of Drawer or Indorser.

(a) Unless otherwise instructed, a collecting bank may present an item not payable by, through, or at a bank by sending to the party to accept or pay a written notice that the bank holds the item for acceptance or payment. The notice must be sent in time to be received on or before the day when presentment is due and the bank must meet any requirement of the party to accept or pay under Section 3—501 by the close of the bank's next banking day after it knows of the requirement.

(b) If presentment is made by notice and payment, acceptance, or request for compliance with a requirement under Section 3—501 is not received by the close of business on the day after maturity or, in the case of demand items, by

the close of business on the third banking day after notice was sent, the presenting bank may treat the item as dishonored and charge any drawer or indorser by sending it notice of the facts.

§ 4—213. Medium and Time of Settlement by Bank.

(a) With respect to settlement by a bank, the medium and time of settlement may be prescribed by Federal Reserve regulations or circulars, clearing-house rules, and the like, or agreement. In the absence of such prescription:

(1) the medium of settlement is cash or credit to an account in a Federal Reserve bank of or specified by the person to receive settlement; and

(2) the time of settlement is:

(i) with respect to tender of settlement by cash, a cashier's check, or teller's check, when the cash or check is sent or delivered;

(ii) with respect to tender of settlement by credit in an account in a Federal Reserve Bank, when the credit is made;

(iii) with respect to tender of settlement by a credit or debit to an account in a bank, when the credit or debit is made or, in the case of tender of settlement by authority to charge an account, when the authority is sent or delivered; or

(iv) with respect to tender of settlement by a funds transfer, when payment is made pursuant to Section 4A—406(a) to the person receiving settlement.

(b) If the tender of settlement is not by a medium authorized by subsection (a) or the time of settlement is not fixed by subsection (a), no settlement occurs until the tender of settlement is accepted by the person receiving settlement.

(c) If settlement for an item is made by cashier's check or teller's check and the person receiving settlement, before its midnight deadline:

(1) presents or forwards the check for collection, settlement is final when the check is finally paid; or

(2) fails to present or forward the check for collection, settlement is final at the midnight deadline of the person receiving settlement.

(d) If settlement for an item is made by giving authority to charge the account of the bank giving settlement in the bank receiving settlement, settlement is final when the charge is made by the bank receiving settlement if there are funds available in the account for the amount of the item.

§ 4—214. Right of Charge-Back or Refund; Liability of Collecting Bank: Return of Item.

(a) If a collecting bank has made provisional settlement with its customer for an item and fails by reason of dishonor, suspension of payments by a bank, or otherwise to receive settlement for the item which is or becomes final, the bank may revoke the settlement given by it, charge back the amount of any credit given for the item to its customer's account, or obtain refund from its customer, whether or not it is able to return the item, if by its midnight deadline or within a longer reasonable time after it learns the facts it returns the item or sends notification of the facts. If the return or notice is delayed beyond the bank's midnight deadline or a longer reasonable time after it learns the facts, the bank may revoke the settlement, charge back the credit, or obtain refund from its customer, but it is liable for any loss resulting from the delay. These rights to revoke, charge back, and obtain refund terminate if and when a settlement for the item received by the bank is or becomes final.

(b) A collecting bank returns an item when it is sent or delivered to the bank's customer or transferor or pursuant to its instructions.

(c) A depositary bank that is also the payor may charge back the amount of an item to its customer's account or obtain refund in accordance with the section governing return of an item received by a payor bank for credit on its books (Section 4—301).

(d) The right to charge back is not affected by:

(1) previous use of a credit given for the item; or

(2) failure by any bank to exercise ordinary care with respect to the item, but a bank so failing remains liable.

(e) A failure to charge back or claim refund does not affect other rights of the bank against the customer or any other party.

(f) If credit is given in dollars as the equivalent of the value of an item payable in foreign money, the dollar amount of any charge-back or refund must be calculated on the basis of the bank-offered spot rate for the foreign money prevailing on the day when the person entitled to the charge-back or refund learns that it will not receive payment in ordinary course.

§ 4—215. **Final Payment of Item by Payor Bank; When Provisional Debits and Credits Become Final; When Certain Credits Become Available for Withdrawal.**

(a) An item is finally paid by a payor bank when the bank has first done any of the following:

(1) paid the item in cash;

(2) settled for the item without having a right to revoke the settlement under statute, clearing-house rule, or agreement; or

(3) made a provisional settlement for the item and failed to revoke the settlement in the time and manner permitted by statute, clearing-house rule, or agreement.

(b) If provisional settlement for an item does not become final, the item is not finally paid.

(c) If provisional settlement for an item between the pre-senting and payor banks is made through a clearing house or by debits or credits in an account between them, then to the extent that provisional debits or credits for the item are entered in accounts between the presenting and payor banks or between the presenting and successive prior collecting banks seriatim, they become final upon final payment of the item by the payor bank.

(d) If a collecting bank receives a settlement for an item which is or becomes final, the bank is accountable to its customer for the amount of the item and any provisional credit given for the item in an account with its customer becomes final.

(e) Subject to (i) applicable law stating a time for availability of funds and (ii) any right of the bank to apply the credit to an obligation of the customer, credit given by a bank for an item in a customer's account becomes available for withdrawal as of right:

(1) if the bank has received a provisional settlement for the item, when the settlement becomes final and the bank has had a reasonable time to receive return of the item and the item has not been received within that time;

(2) if the bank is both the depositary bank and the payor bank, and the item is finally paid, at the opening of the bank's second banking day following receipt of the item.

(f) Subject to applicable law stating a time for availability of funds and any right of a bank to apply a deposit to an obligation of the depositor, a deposit of money becomes available for withdrawal as of right at the opening of the bank's next banking day after receipt of the deposit.

§ 4—216. **Insolvency and Preference.**

(a) If an item is in or comes into the possession of a payor or collecting bank that suspends payment and the item has not been finally paid, the item must be returned by the receiver, trustee, or agent in charge of the closed bank to the presenting bank or the closed bank's customer.

(b) If a payor bank finally pays an item and suspends payments without making a settlement for the item with its customer or the presenting bank which settlement is or becomes final, the owner of the item has a preferred claim against the payor bank.

(c) If a payor bank gives or a collecting bank gives or receives a provisional settlement for an item and thereafter suspends payments, the suspension does not prevent or interfere with the settlement's becoming final if the finality occurs automatically upon the lapse of certain time or the happening of certain events.

(d) If a collecting bank receives from subsequent parties settlement for an item, which settlement is or becomes final and the bank suspends payments without making a settlement for the item with its customer which settlement is or becomes final, the owner of the item has a preferred claim against the collecting bank.

Part 3 Collection of Items: Payor Banks

§ 4–301. Deferred Posting; Recovery of Payment by Return of Items; Time of Dishonor; Return of Items by Payor Bank.

(a) If a payor bank settles for a demand item other than a documentary draft presented otherwise than for immediate payment over the counter before midnight of the banking day of receipt, the payor bank may revoke the settlement and recover the settlement if, before it has made final payment and before its midnight deadline, it

(1) returns the item; or

(2) sends written notice of dishonor or nonpayment if the item is unavailable for return.

(b) If a demand item is received by a payor bank for credit on its books, it may return the item or send notice of dishonor and may revoke any credit given or recover the amount thereof withdrawn by its customer, if it acts within the time limit and in the manner specified in subsection (a).

(c) Unless previous notice of dishonor has been sent, an item is dishonored at the time when for purposes of dishonor it is returned or notice sent in accordance with this section.

(d) An item is returned:

(1) as to an item presented through a clearing house, when it is delivered to the presenting or last collecting bank or to the clearing house or is sent or delivered in accordance with clearing-house rules; or

(2) in all other cases, when it is sent or delivered to the bank's customer or transferor or pursuant to instructions.

§ 4–302. Payor Bank's Responsibility for Late Return of Item.

(a) If an item is presented to and received by a payor bank, the bank is accountable for the amount of:

(1) a demand item, other than a documentary draft, whether properly payable or not, if the bank, in any case in which it is not also the depositary bank, retains the item beyond midnight of the banking day of receipt without settling for it or, whether or not it is also the depositary bank, does not pay or return the item or send notice of dishonor until after its midnight deadline; or

(2) any other properly payable item unless, within the time allowed for acceptance or payment of that item, the bank either accepts or pays the item or returns it and accompanying documents.

(b) The liability of a payor bank to pay an item pursuant to subsection (a) is subject to defenses based on breach of a presentment warranty (Section 4–208) or proof that the person seeking enforcement of the liability presented or transferred the item for the purpose of defrauding the payor bank.

§ 4–303. When Items Subject to Notice, Stop-Payment Order, Legal Process, or Setoff; Order in Which Items May Be Charged or Certified.

(a) Any knowledge, notice, or stop-payment order received by, legal process served upon, or setoff exercised by a payor bank comes too late to terminate, suspend, or modify the bank's right or duty to pay an item or to charge its customer's account for the item if the knowledge, notice, stop-payment order, or legal process is received or served and a reasonable time for the bank to act thereon expires or the setoff is exercised after the earliest of the following:

(1) the bank accepts or certifies the item;

(2) the bank pays the item in cash;

(3) the bank settles for the item without having a right to revoke the settlement under statute, clearing-house rule, or agreement;

(4) the bank becomes accountable for the amount of the item under Section 4–302 dealing with the payor bank's responsibility for late return of items; or

(5) with respect to checks, a cutoff hour no earlier than one hour after the opening of the next banking day after the banking day on which the bank received the check and no later than the close of that next banking day or, if no cutoff hour is fixed, the close of the next banking day after the banking day on which the bank received the check.

(b) Subject to subsection (a), items may be accepted, paid, certified, or charged to the indicated account of its customer in any order.

Part 4 Relationship Between Payor Bank and its Customer

§ 4–401. When Bank May Charge Customer's Account.

(a) A bank may charge against the account of a customer an item that is properly payable from the account even though the charge creates an overdraft. An item is properly payable if it is authorized by the customer and is in accordance with any agreement between the customer and bank.

(b) A customer is not liable for the amount of an overdraft if the customer neither signed the item nor benefited from the proceeds of the item.

(c) A bank may charge against the account of a customer a check that is otherwise properly payable from the account, even though payment was made before the date of the check, unless the customer has given notice to the bank of the postdating describing the check with reasonable certainty. The notice is effective for the period stated in Section 4–403(b) for stop-payment orders, and must be received at such time and in such manner as to afford the bank a reasonable opportunity to act on it before the bank takes any action with respect to the check described in Section 4–303. If a bank charges against the account of a customer a check before the date stated in the notice of post-dating, the bank is liable for damages for the loss resulting from its act. The loss may include damages for dishonor of subsequent items under Section 4—402.

(d) A bank that in good faith makes payment to a holder may charge the indicated account of its customer according to:

(1) the original terms of the altered item; or

(2) the terms of the completed item, even though the bank knows the item has been completed unless the bank has notice that the completion was improper.

§ 4—402. Bank's Liability to Customer for Wrongful Dishonor; Time of Determining Insufficiency of Account.

(a) Except as otherwise provided in this Article, a payor bank wrongfully dishonors an item if it dishonors an item that is properly payable, but a bank may dishonor an item that would create an overdraft unless it has agreed to pay the overdraft.

(b) A payor bank is liable to its customer for damages proximately caused by the wrongful dishonor of an item. Liability is limited to actual damages proved and may include damages for an arrest or prosecution of the customer or other consequential damages. Whether any consequential damages are proximately caused by the wrongful dishonor is a question of fact to be determined in each case.

(c) A payor bank's determination of the customer's account balance on which a decision to dishonor for insufficiency of available funds is based may be made at any time between the time the item is received by the payor bank and the time that the payor bank returns the item or gives notice in lieu of return, and no more than one determination need be made. If, at the election of the payor bank, a subsequent balance determination is made for the purpose of reevaluating the bank's decision to dishonor the item, the account balance at that time is determinative of whether a dishonor for insufficiency of available funds is wrongful.

§ 4—403. Customer's Right to Stop Payment; Burden of Proof of Loss.

(a) A customer or any person authorized to draw on the account if there is more than one person may stop payment of any item drawn on the customer's account or close the account by an order to the bank describing the item or account with reasonable certainty received at a time and in a manner that affords the bank a reasonable opportunity to act on it before any action by the bank with respect to the item described in Section 4—303. If the signature of more than one person is required to draw on an account, any of these persons may stop payment or close the account.

(b) A stop-payment order is effective for six months, but it lapses after 14 calendar days if the original order was oral and was not confirmed in writing within that period. A stop-payment order may be renewed for additional six-month periods by a writing given to the bank within a period during which the stop-payment order is effective.

(c) The burden of establishing the fact and amount of loss resulting from the payment of an item contrary to a stop-payment order or order to close an account is on the customer. The loss from payment of an item contrary to a stop-payment order may include damages for dishonor of subsequent items under Section 4—402.

§ 4—404. Bank Not Obliged to Pay Check More Than Six Months Old.

A bank is under no obligation to a customer having a checking account to pay a check, other than a certified check, which is presented more than six months after its date, but it may charge its customer's account for a payment made thereafter in good faith.

§ 4—405. Death or Incompetence of Customer.

(a) A payor or collecting bank's authority to accept, pay, or collect an item or to account for proceeds of its collection, if otherwise effective, is not rendered ineffective by incompetence of a customer of either bank existing at the time the item is issued or its collection is undertaken if the bank does not know of an adjudication of incompetence. Neither death nor incompetence of a customer revokes the authority to accept, pay, collect, or account until the bank knows of the fact of death or of an adjudication of incompetence and has reasonable opportunity to act on it.

(b) Even with knowledge, a bank may for 10 days after the date of death pay or certify checks drawn on or before the date unless ordered to stop payment by a person claiming an interest in the account.

§ 4—406. Customer's Duty to Discover and Report Unauthorized Signature or Alteration.

(a) A bank that sends or makes available to a customer a statement of account showing payment of items for the account shall either return or make available to the customer the items paid or provide information in the statement of account sufficient to allow the customer reasonably to identify the items paid. The statement of account provides sufficient information if the item is described by item number, amount, and date of payment.

(b) If the items are not returned to the customer, the person retaining the items shall either retain the items or, if the items are destroyed, maintain the capacity to furnish legible copies of the items until the expiration of seven years after receipt of the items. A customer may request an item from the bank that paid the item, and that bank must provide in a reasonable time either the item or, if the item has been destroyed or is not otherwise obtainable, a legible copy of the item.

(c) If a bank sends or makes available a statement of account or items pursuant to subsection (a), the customer must exercise reasonable promptness in examining the statement or the items to determine whether any payment was not authorized because of an alteration of an item or because a purported signature by or on behalf of the customer was not authorized. If, based on the statement or items provided, the customer should reasonably have discovered the unauthorized payment, the customer must promptly notify the bank of the relevant facts.

(d) If the bank proves that the customer failed, with respect to an item, to comply with the duties imposed on the customer by subsection (c), the customer is precluded from asserting against the bank:

> (1) the customer's unauthorized signature or any alteration on the item, if the bank also proves that it suffered a loss by reason of the failure; and

> (2) the customer's unauthorized signature or alteration by the same wrongdoer on any other item paid in good faith by the bank if the payment was made before the bank received notice from the customer of the unauthorized signature or alteration and after the customer had been afforded a reasonable period of time, not exceeding 30 days, in which to examine the item or statement of account and notify the bank.

(e) If subsection (d) applies and the customer proves that the bank failed to exercise ordinary care in paying the item and that the failure substantially contributed to loss, the loss is allocated between the customer precluded and the bank asserting the preclusion according to the extent to which the failure of the customer to comply with subsection (c) and the failure of the bank to exercise ordinary care contributed to the loss. If the customer proves that the bank did not pay the item in good faith, the preclusion under subsection (d) does not apply.

(f) Without regard to care or lack of care of either the customer or the bank, a customer who does not within one year after the statement or items are made available to the customer (subsection (a)) discover and report the customer's unauthorized signature on or any alteration on the item is precluded from asserting against the bank the unauthorized signature or alteration. If there is a preclusion under this subsection, the payor bank may not recover for breach or warranty under Section 4—208 with respect to the unauthorized signature or alteration to which the preclusion applies.

§ 4—407. Payor Bank's Right to Subrogation on Improper Payment.

If a payor has paid an item over the order of the drawer or maker to stop payment, or after an account has been closed, or otherwise under circumstances giving a basis for objection by the drawer or maker, to prevent unjust enrichment and only to the extent necessary to prevent loss to the bank by reason of its payment of the item, the payor bank is subrogated to the rights

> (1) of any holder in due course on the item against the

drawer or maker;

> (2) of the payee or any other holder of the item against the drawer or maker either on the item or under the transaction out of which the item arose; and

> (3) of the drawer or maker against the payee or any other holder of the item with respect to the transaction out of which the item arose.

Part 5 Collection of Documentary Drafts

§ 4—501. Handling of Documentary Drafts; Duty to Send for Presentment and to Notify Customer of Dishonor.

A bank that takes a documentary draft for collection shall present or send the draft and accompanying documents for presentment and, upon learning that the draft has not been paid or accepted in due course, shall seasonably notify its customer of the fact even though it may have discounted or bought the draft or extended credit available for withdrawal as of right.

§ 4—502. Presentment of "On Arrival" Drafts.

If a draft or the relevant instructions require presentment "on arrival", "when goods arrive" or the like, the collecting bank need not present until in its judgment a reasonable time for arrival of the goods has expired. Refusal to pay or accept because the goods have not arrived is not dishonor; the bank must notify its transferor of the refusal but need not present the draft again until it is instructed to do so or learns of the arrival of the goods.

§ 4—503. Responsibility of Presenting Bank for Documents and Goods; Report of Reasons for Dishonor; Referee in Case of Need.

Unless otherwise instructed and except as provided in Article 5, a bank presenting a documentary draft:

> (1) must deliver the documents to the drawee on acceptance of the draft if it is payable more than three days after presentment, otherwise, only on payment; and

> (2) upon dishonor, either in the case of presentment for acceptance or presentment for payment, may seek and follow instructions from any referee in case of need designated in the draft or, if the presenting bank does not choose to utilize the referee's services, it must use diligence and good faith to ascertain the reason for dishonor, must notify its transferor of the dishonor and of the results of its effort to ascertain the reasons therefor, and must request instructions.

However, the presenting bank is under no obligation with respect to goods represented by the documents except to follow any reasonable instructions seasonably received; it has a right to reimbursement for any expense incurred in following instructions and to prepayment of or indemnity for those expenses.

§ 4–504. Privilege of Presenting Bank to Deal With Goods; Security Interest for Expenses.

(a) A presenting bank that, following the dishonor of a documentary draft, has seasonably requested instructions but does not receive them within a reasonable time may store, sell, or otherwise deal with the goods in any reasonable manner.

(b) For its reasonable expenses incurred by action under subsection (a) the presenting bank has a lien upon the goods or their proceeds, which may be foreclosed in the same manner as an unpaid seller's lien.

Article 4A
FUNDS TRANSFERS

Part 1 Subject Matter and Definitions

§ 4A–101. Short Title.
This Article may be cited as Uniform Commercial Code—Funds Transfers.

§ 4A–102. Subject Matter.
Except as otherwise provided in Section 4A–108, this Article applies to funds transfers defined in Section 4A–104.

§ 4A–103. Payment Order—Definitions.
(a) In this Article:

(1) "Payment order" means an instruction of a sender to a receiving bank, transmitted orally, electronically, or in writing, to pay, or to cause another bank to pay, a fixed or determinable amount of money to a beneficiary if:

   (i) the instruction does not state a condition to payment to the beneficiary other than time of payment,

   (ii) the receiving bank is to be reimbursed by debiting an account of, or otherwise receiving payment from, the sender, and

   (iii) the instruction is transmitted by the sender directly to the receiving bank or to an agent, funds-transfer system, or communication system for transmittal to the receiving bank.

(2) "Beneficiary" means the person to be paid by the beneficiary's bank.

(3) "Beneficiary's bank" means the bank identified in a payment order in which an account of the beneficiary is to be credited pursuant to the order or which otherwise is to make payment to the beneficiary if the order does not provide for payment to an account.

(4) "Receiving bank" means the bank to which the sender's instruction is addressed.

(5) "Sender" means the person giving the instruction to the receiving bank.

(b) If an instruction complying with subsection (a)(1) is

to make more than one payment to a beneficiary, the instruction is a separate payment order with respect to each payment.

(c) A payment order is issued when it is sent to the receiving bank.

§ 4A–104. Funds Transfer—Definitions.
In this Article:

(a) "Funds transfer" means the series of transactions, beginning with the originator's payment order, made for the purpose of making payment to the beneficiary of the order. The term includes any payment order issued by the originator's bank or an intermediary bank intended to carry out the originator's payment order. A funds transfer is completed by acceptance by the beneficiary's bank of a payment order for the benefit of the beneficiary of the originator's payment order.

(b) "Intermediary bank" means a receiving bank other than the originator's bank or the beneficiary's bank.

(c) "Originator" means the sender of the first payment order in a funds transfer.

(d) "Originator's bank" means (i) the receiving bank to which the payment order of the originator is issued if the originator is not a bank, or (ii) the originator if the originator is a bank.

§ 4A–105. Other Definitions.
(a) In this Article:

(1) "Authorized account" means a deposit account of a customer in a bank designated by the customer as a source of payment of payment orders issued by the customer to the bank. If a customer does not so designate an account, any account of the customer is an authorized account if payment of a payment order from that account is not inconsistent with a restriction on the use of that account.

(2) "Bank" means a person engaged in the business of banking and includes a savings bank, savings and loan association, credit union, and trust company. A branch or separate office of a bank is a separate bank for purposes of this Article.

(3) "Customer" means a person, including a bank, having an account with a bank or from whom a bank has agreed to receive payment orders.

(4) "Funds-transfer business day" of a receiving bank means the part of a day during which the receiving bank is open for the receipt, processing, and transmittal of payment orders and cancellations and amendments of payment orders.

(5) "Funds-transfer system" means a wire transfer network, automated clearing house, or other communication system of a clearing house or other association of banks through which a payment order by a bank may be transmitted to the bank to which the order is addressed.

(6) "Good faith" means honesty in fact and the observance of reasonable commercial standards of fair dealing.

(7) "Prove" with respect to a fact means to meet the burden of establishing the fact (Section 1—201(8)).

(b) Other definitions applying to this Article and the sections in which they appear are:

"Acceptance"	Section 4A—209
"Beneficiary"	Section 4A—103
"Beneficiary's bank"	Section 4A—103
"Executed"	Section 4A—301
"Execution date"	Section 4A—301
"Funds transfer"	Section 4A—104
"Funds-transfer system rule"	Section 4A—501
"Intermediary bank"	Section 4A—104
"Originator"	Section 4A—104
"Originator's bank"	Section 4A—104
"Payment by beneficiary's bank to beneficiary"	Section 4A—405
"Payment by originator to beneficiary"	Section 4A—406
"Payment by sender to receiving bank"	Section 4A—403
"Payment date"	Section 4A—401
"Payment order"	Section 4A—103
"Receiving bank"	Section 4A—103
"Security procedure"	Section 4A—201
"Sender"	Section 4A—103

(c) The following definitions in Article 4 apply to this Article:

"Clearing house"	Section 4—104
"Item"	Section 4—104
"Suspends payments"	Section 4—104

(d) In addition, Article 1 contains general definitions and principles of construction and interpretation applicable throughout this Article.

§ 4A—106. **Time Payment Order Is Received.**

(a) The time of receipt of a payment order or communication cancelling or amending a payment order is determined by the rules applicable to receipt of a notice stated in Section 1—201(27). A receiving bank may fix a cut-off time or times on a funds-transfer business day for the receipt and processing of payment orders and communications cancelling or amending payment orders. Different cut-off times may apply to payment orders, cancellations, or amendments, or to different categories of payment orders, cancellations, or amendments. A cut-off time may apply to senders generally or different cut-off times may apply to different senders or categories of payment orders. If a payment order or communication cancelling or amending a payment order is received after the close of a funds-transfer business day or after the appropriate cut-off time on a funds-transfer business day, the receiving bank may treat the payment order or communication as received at the opening of the next funds-transfer business day.

(b) If this Article refers to an execution date or payment date or states a day on which a receiving bank is required to take action, and the date or day does not fall on a funds-transfer business day, the next day that is a funds-transfer business day is treated as the date or day stated, unless the contrary is stated in this Article.

§ 4A—107. **Federal Reserve Regulations and Operating Circulars.**

Regulations of the Board of Governors of the Federal Reserve System and operating circulars of the Federal Reserve Banks supersede any inconsistent provision of this Article to the extent of the inconsistency.

§ 4A—108. **Exclusion of Consumer Transactions Governed by Federal Law.**

This Article does not apply to a funds transfer any part of which is governed by the Electronic Fund Transfer Act of 1978 (Title XX, Public Law 95—630, 92 Stat. 3728, 15 U.S.C. § 1693 et seq.) as amended from time to time.

Part 2 **Issue and Acceptance of Payment Order**

§ 4A—201. **Security Procedure.**

"Security procedure" means a procedure established by agreement of a customer and a receiving bank for the purpose of (i) verifying that a payment order or communication amending or cancelling a payment order is that of the customer, or (ii) detecting error in the transmission or the content of the payment order or communication. A security procedure may require the use of algorithms or other codes, identifying words or numbers, encryption, callback procedures, or similar security devices. Comparison of a signature on a payment order or communication with an authorized specimen signature of the customer is not by itself a security procedure.

§ 4A—202. **Authorized and Verified Payment Orders.**

(a) A payment order received by the receiving bank is the authorized order of the person identified as sender if that person authorized the order or is otherwise bound by it under the law of agency.

(b) If a bank and its customer have agreed that the authenticity of payment orders issued to the bank in the name of the customer as sender will be verified pursuant to a security procedure, a payment order received by the receiving bank is effective as the order of the customer, whether or not authorized, if (i) the security procedure is a commercially reasonable method of providing security against unauthorized payment orders, and (ii) the bank proves that it accepted the payment order in good faith and in compliance with the security procedure and any written agreement or instruction of the customer restricting acceptance of payment orders issued in the name of the customer. The bank is not required to follow an instruction that violates a written agreement with the customer or notice of which is not received at a time and in a manner affording the bank a reasonable opportunity to act on it before the payment order is accepted.

(c) Commercial reasonableness of a security procedure is a question of law to be determined by considering the wishes of the customer expressed to the bank, the circumstances of the customer known to the bank, including the size, type, and frequency of payment orders normally issued by the customer to the bank, alternative security procedures offered to the customer, and security procedures in general use by customers and receiving banks similarly situated. A security procedure is deemed to be commercially reasonable if (i) the security procedure was chosen by the customer after the bank offered, and the customer refused, a security procedure that was commercially reasonable for that customer, and (ii) the customer expressly agreed in writing to be bound by any payment order, whether or not authorized, issued in its name and accepted by the bank in compliance with the security procedure chosen by the customer.

(d) The term "sender" in this Article includes the customer in whose name a payment order is issued if the order is the authorized order of the customer under subsection (a), or it is effective as the order of the customer under subsection (b).

(e) This section applies to amendments and cancellations of payment orders to the same extent it applies to payment orders.

(f) Except as provided in this section and in Section 4A—203(a)(1), rights and obligations arising under this section or Section 4A—203 may not be varied by agreement.

§ 4A—203. Unenforceability of Certain Verified Payment Orders.

(a) If an accepted payment order is not, under Section 4A—202(a), an authorized order of a customer identified as sender, but is effective as an order of the customer pursuant to Section 4A—202(b), the following rules apply:

(1) By express written agreement, the receiving bank may limit the extent to which it is entitled to enforce or retain payment of the payment order.

(2) The receiving bank is not entitled to enforce or retain payment of the payment order if the customer proves that the order was not caused, directly or indirectly, by a person (i) entrusted at any time with duties to act for the customer with respect to payment orders or the security procedure, or (ii) who obtained access to transmitting facilities of the customer or who obtained, from a source controlled by the customer and without authority of the receiving bank, information facilitating breach of the security procedure, regardless of how the information was obtained or whether the customer was

at fault. Information includes any access device, computer software, or the like.

(b) This section applies to amendments of payment orders to the same extent it applies to payment orders.

§ 4A—204. Refund of Payment and Duty of Customer to Report with Respect to Unauthorized Payment Order.

(a) If a receiving bank accepts a payment order issued in the name of its customer as sender which is (i) not authorized and not effective as the order of the customer under Section 4A—202, or (ii) not enforceable, in whole or in part, against the customer under Section 4A—203, the bank shall refund any payment of the payment order received from the customer to the extent the bank is not entitled to enforce payment and shall pay interest on the refundable amount calculated from the date the bank received payment to the date of the refund. However, the customer is not entitled to interest from the bank on the amount to be refunded if the customer fails to exercise ordinary care to determine that the order was not authorized by the customer and to notify the bank of the relevant facts within a reasonable time not exceeding 90 days after the date the customer received notification from the bank that the order was accepted or that the customer's account was debited with respect to the order. The bank is not entitled to any recovery from the customer on account of a failure by the customer to give notification as stated in this section.

(b) Reasonable time under subsection (a) may be fixed by agreement as stated in Section 1—204(1), but the obligation of a receiving bank to refund payment as stated in subsection (a) may not otherwise be varied by agreement.

§ 4A—205. Erroneous Payment Orders.

(a) If an accepted payment order was transmitted pursuant to a security procedure for the detection of error and the payment order (i) erroneously instructed payment to a beneficiary not intended by the sender, (ii) erroneously instructed payment in an amount greater than the amount intended by the sender, or (iii) was an erroneously transmitted duplicate of a payment order previously sent by the sender, the following rules apply:

(1) If the sender proves that the sender or a person acting on behalf of the sender pursuant to Section 4A—206 complied with the security procedure and that the error would have been detected if the receiving bank had also complied, the sender is not obliged to pay the order to the extent stated in paragraphs (2) and (3).

(2) If the funds transfer is completed on the basis of an erroneous payment order described in clause (i) or (iii) of subsection (a), the sender is not obliged to pay the order and the receiving bank is entitled to recover from the beneficiary any amount paid to the beneficiary to the extent allowed by the law governing mistake and restitution.

(3) If the funds transfer is completed on the basis of a payment order described in clause (ii) of subsection (a), the sender is not obliged to pay the order to the extent the amount received by the beneficiary is greater than the amount intended by the sender. In that case, the receiving bank is entitled to recover from the beneficiary the excess amount received to the extent allowed by the law governing mistake and restitution.

(b) If (i) the sender of an erroneous payment order described in subsection (a) is not obliged to pay all or part of the order, and (ii) the sender receives notification from the receiving bank that the order was accepted by the bank or that the sender's account was debited with respect to the order, the sender has a duty to exercise ordinary care, on the basis of information available to the sender, to discover the error with respect to the order and to advise the bank of the relevant facts within a reasonable time, not exceeding 90 days, after the bank's notification was received by the sender. If the bank proves that the sender failed to perform that duty, the sender is liable to the bank for the loss the bank proves it incurred as a result of the failure, but the liability of the sender may not exceed the amount of the sender's order.

(c) This section applies to amendments to payment orders to the same extent it applies to payment orders.

§ 4A–206. Transmission of Payment Order through Funds-Transfer or Other Communication System.

(a) If a payment order addressed to a receiving bank is transmitted to a funds-transfer system or other third party communication system for transmittal to the bank, the system is deemed to be an agent of the sender for the purpose of transmitting the payment order to the bank. If there is a discrepancy between the terms of the payment order transmitted to the system and the terms of the payment order transmitted by the system to the bank, the terms of the payment order of the sender are those transmitted by the system. This section does not apply to a funds-transfer system of the Federal Reserve Banks.

(b) This section applies to cancellations and amendments to payment orders to the same extent it applies to payment orders.

§ 4A–207. Misdescription of Beneficiary.

(a) Subject to subsection (b), if, in a payment order received by the beneficiary's bank, the name, bank account number, or other identification of the beneficiary refers to a nonexistent or unidentifiable person or account, no person has rights as a beneficiary of the order and acceptance of the order cannot occur.

(b) If a payment order received by the beneficiary's bank identifies the beneficiary both by name and by an identifying or bank account number and the name and number identify different persons, the following rules apply:

(1) Except as otherwise provided in subsection (c), if the beneficiary's bank does not know that the name and number refer to different persons, it may rely on the number as the proper identification of the beneficiary of the order. The beneficiary's bank need not determine whether the name and number refer to the same person.

(2) If the beneficiary's bank pays the person identified by name or knows that the name and number identify different persons, no person has rights as beneficiary except the person paid by the beneficiary's bank if that person was entitled to receive payment from the originator of the funds transfer. If no person has rights as beneficiary, acceptance of the order cannot occur.

(c) If (i) a payment order described in subsection (b) is accepted, (ii) the originator's payment order described the beneficiary inconsistently by name and number, and (iii) the beneficiary's bank pays the person identified by number as permitted by subsection (b)(1), the following rules apply:

(1) If the originator is a bank, the originator is obliged to pay its order.

(2) If the originator is not a bank and proves that the person identified by number was not entitled to receive payment from the originator, the originator is not obliged to pay its order unless the originator's bank proves that the originator, before acceptance of the originator's order, had notice that payment of a payment order issued by the originator might be made by the beneficiary's bank on the basis of an identifying or bank account number even if it identifies a person different from the named beneficiary. Proof of notice may be made by any admissible evidence. The originator's bank satisfies the burden of proof if it proves that the originator, before the payment order was accepted, signed a writing stating the information to which the notice relates.

(d) In a case governed by subsection (b)(1), if the beneficiary's bank rightfully pays the person identified by number and that person was not entitled to receive payment from the originator, the amount paid may be recovered from that person to the extent allowed by the law governing mistake and restitution as follows:

(1) If the originator is obliged to pay its payment order as stated in subsection (c), the originator has the right to recover.

(2) If the originator is not a bank and is not obliged to pay its payment order, the originator's bank has the right to recover.

§ 4A–208. Misdescription of Intermediary Bank or Beneficiary's Bank.

(a) This subsection applies to a payment order identifying an intermediary bank or the beneficiary's bank only by an identifying number.

(1) The receiving bank may rely on the number as the proper identification of the intermediary or benefi-

ciary's bank and need not determine whether the number identifies a bank.

(2) The sender is obliged to compensate the receiving bank for any loss and expenses incurred by the receiving bank as a result of its reliance on the number in executing or attempting to execute the order.

(b) This subsection applies to a payment order identifying an intermediary bank or the beneficiary's bank both by name and an identifying number if the name and number identify different persons.

(1) If the sender is a bank, the receiving bank may rely on the number as the proper identification of the intermediary or beneficiary's bank if the receiving bank, when it executes the sender's order, does not know that the name and number identify different persons. The receiving bank need not determine whether the name and number refer to the same person or whether the number refers to a bank. The sender is obliged to compensate the receiving bank for any loss and expenses incurred by the receiving bank as a result of its reliance on the number in executing or attempting to execute the order.

(2) If the sender is not a bank and the receiving bank proves that the sender, before the payment order was accepted, had notice that the receiving bank might rely on the number as the proper identification of the intermediary or beneficiary's bank even if it identifies a person different from the bank identified by name, the rights and obligations of the sender and the receiving bank are governed by subsection (b)(1), as though the sender were a bank. Proof of notice may be made by any admissible evidence. The receiving bank satisfies the burden of proof if it proves that the sender, before the payment order was accepted, signed a writing stating the information to which the notice relates.

(3) Regardless of whether the sender is a bank, the receiving bank may rely on the name as the proper identification of the intermediary or beneficiary's bank if the receiving bank, at the time it executes the sender's order, does not know that the name and number identify different persons. The receiving bank need not determine whether the name and number refer to the same person.

(4) If the receiving bank knows that the name and number identify different persons, reliance on either the name or the number in executing the sender's payment order is a breach of the obligation stated in Section 4A—302(a)(1).

§ 4A—209. Acceptance of Payment Order.

(a) Subject to subsection (d), a receiving bank other than the beneficiary's bank accepts a payment order when it executes the order.

(b) Subject to subsections (c) and (d), a beneficiary's bank accepts a payment order at the earliest of the following times:

(1) When the bank (i) pays the beneficiary as stated in Section 4A—405(a) or 4A—405(b), or (ii) notifies the beneficiary of receipt of the order or that the account of the beneficiary has been credited with respect to the order unless the notice indicates that the bank is rejecting the order or that funds with respect to the order may not be withdrawn or used until receipt of payment from the sender of the order;

(2) When the bank receives payment of the entire amount of the sender's order pursuant to Section 4A—403(a)(1) or 4A—403(a)(2); or

(3) The opening of the next funds-transfer business day of the bank following the payment date of the order if, at that time, the amount of the sender's order is fully covered by a withdrawable credit balance in an authorized account of the sender or the bank has otherwise received full payment from the sender, unless the order was rejected before that time or is rejected within (i) one hour after that time, or (ii) one hour after the opening of the next business day of the sender following the payment date if that time is later. If notice of rejection is received by the sender after the payment date and the authorized account of the sender does not bear interest, the bank is obliged to pay interest to the sender on the amount of the order for the number of days elapsing after the payment date to the day the sender receives notice or learns that the order was not accepted, counting that day as an elapsed day. If the withdrawable credit balance during that period falls below the amount of the order, the amount of interest payable is reduced accordingly.

(c) Acceptance of a payment order cannot occur before the order is received by the receiving bank. Acceptance does not occur under subsection (b)(2) or (b)(3) if the beneficiary of the payment order does not have an account with the receiving bank, the account has been closed, or the receiving bank is not permitted by law to receive credits for the beneficiary's account.

(d) A payment order issued to the originator's bank cannot be accepted until the payment date if the bank is the beneficiary's bank, or the execution date if the bank is not the beneficiary's bank. If the originator's bank executes the originator's payment order before the execution date or pays the beneficiary of the originator's payment order before the payment date and the payment order is subsequently cancelled pursuant to Section 4A—211(b), the bank may recover from the beneficiary any payment received to the extent allowed by the law governing mistake and restitution.

§ 4A—210. Rejection of Payment Order.

(a) A payment order is rejected by the receiving bank by a notice of rejection transmitted to the sender orally, electronically, or in writing. A notice of rejection need not use any particular words and is sufficient if it indicates that the receiving bank is rejecting the order or will not execute or pay the order. Rejection is effective when the notice is given if transmission is by a means that is reasonable in the circumstances. If notice of rejection is given by a means that is not reasonable, rejection is effective when the notice is received. If an agreement of the sender and receiving bank establishes the means to be used to reject a payment order, (i) any means complying with the agreement is reasonable and (ii) any means not complying is not reasonable unless no significant delay in receipt of the notice resulted from the use of the noncomplying means.

(b) This subsection applies if a receiving bank other than the beneficiary's bank fails to execute a payment order despite the existence on the execution date of a withdrawable credit balance in an authorized account of the sender sufficient to cover the order. If the sender does not receive notice of rejection of the order on the execution date and the authorized account of the sender does not bear interest, the bank is obliged to pay interest to the sender on the amount of the order for the number of days elapsing after the execution date to the earlier of the day the order is cancelled pursuant to Section 4A—211(d) or the day the sender receives notice or learns that the order was not executed, counting the final day of the period as an elapsed day. If the withdrawable credit balance during that period falls below the amount of the order, the amount of interest is reduced accordingly.

(c) If a receiving bank suspends payments, all unaccepted payment orders issued to it are are deemed rejected at the time the bank suspends payments.

(d) Acceptance of a payment order precludes a later rejection of the order. Rejection of a payment order precludes a later acceptance of the order.

§ 4A—211. Cancellation and Amendment of Payment Order.

(a) A communication of the sender of a payment order cancelling or amending the order may be transmitted to the receiving bank orally, electronically, or in writing. If a security procedure is in effect between the sender and the receiving bank, the communication is not effective to cancel or amend the order unless the communication is verified pursuant to the security procedure or the bank agrees to the cancellation or amendment.

(b) Subject to subsection (a), a communication by the sender cancelling or amending a payment order is effective to cancel or amend the order if notice of the communication is received at a time and in a manner affording the receiving bank a reasonable opportunity to act on the communication before the bank accepts the payment order.

(c) After a payment order has been accepted, cancellation or amendment of the order is not effective unless the receiving bank agrees or a funds-transfer system rule allows cancellation or amendment without agreement of the bank.

(1) With respect to a payment order accepted by a receiving bank other than the beneficiary's bank, cancellation or amendment is not effective unless a conforming cancellation or amendment of the payment order issued by the receiving bank is also made.

(2) With respect to a payment order accepted by the beneficiary's bank, cancellation or amendment is not effective unless the order was issued in execution of an unauthorized payment order, or because of a mistake by a sender in the funds transfer which resulted in the issuance of a payment order (i) that is a duplicate of a payment order previously issued by the sender, (ii) that orders payment to a beneficiary not entitled to receive payment from the originator, or (iii) that orders payment in an amount greater than the amount the beneficiary was entitled to receive from the originator. If the payment order is cancelled or amended, the beneficiary's bank is entitled to recover from the beneficiary any amount paid to the beneficiary to the extent allowed by the law governing mistake and restitution.

(d) An unaccepted payment order is cancelled by operation of law at the close of the fifth funds-transfer business day of the receiving bank after the execution date or payment date of the order.

(e) A cancelled payment order cannot be accepted. If an accepted payment order is cancelled, the acceptance is nullified and no person has any right or obligation based on the acceptance. Amendment of a payment order is deemed to be cancellation of the original order at the time of amendment and issue of a new payment order in the amended form at the same time.

(f) Unless otherwise provided in an agreement of the parties or in a funds-transfer system rule, if the receiving bank, after accepting a payment order, agrees to cancellation or amendment of the order by the sender or is bound by a funds-transfer system rule allowing cancellation or amendment without the bank's agreement, the sender, whether or not cancellation or amendment is effective, is liable to the bank for any loss and expenses, including reasonable attorney's fees, incurred by the bank as a result of the cancellation or amendment or attempted cancellation or amendment.

(g) A payment order is not revoked by the death or legal incapacity of the sender unless the receiving bank knows of the death or of an adjudication of incapacity by a court of competent jurisdiction and has reasonable opportunity to act before acceptance of the order.

(h) A funds-transfer system rule is not effective to the extent it conflicts with subsection (c)(2).

§ 4A—212. Liability and Duty of Receiving Bank Regarding Unaccepted Payment Order.

If a receiving bank fails to accept a payment order that it is obliged by express agreement to accept, the bank is liable for breach of the agreement to the extent provided in the agreement or in this Article, but does not otherwise have any duty to accept a payment order or, before acceptance, to take any action, or refrain from taking action, with respect to the order except as provided in this Article or by express agreement. Liability based on acceptance arises only when acceptance occurs as stated in Section 4A—209, and liability is limited to that provided in this Article. A receiving bank is not the agent of the sender or beneficiary of the payment order it accepts, or of any other party to the funds transfer, and the bank owes no duty to any party to the funds transfer except as provided in this Article or by express agreement.

Part 3 Execution of Sender's Payment Order by Receiving Bank

§ 4A—301. Execution and Execution Date.

(a) A payment order is "executed" by the receiving bank when it issues a payment order intended to carry out the payment order received by the bank. A payment order received by the beneficiary's bank can be accepted but cannot be executed.

(b) "Execution date" of a payment order means the day on which the receiving bank may properly issue a payment order in execution of the sender's order. The execution date may be determined by instruction of the sender but cannot be earlier than the day the order is received and, unless otherwise determined, is the day the order is received. If the sender's instruction states a payment date, the execution date is the payment date or an earlier date on which execution is reasonably necessary to allow payment to the beneficiary on the payment date.

§ 4A—302. Obligations of Receiving Bank in Execution of Payment Order.

(a) Except as provided in subsections (b) through (d), if the receiving bank accepts a payment order pursuant to Section 4A—209(a), the bank has the following obligations in executing the order:

(1) The receiving bank is obliged to issue, on the execution date, a payment order complying with the sender's order and to follow the sender's instructions concerning (i) any intermediary bank or funds-transfer system to be used in carrying out the funds transfer, or (ii) the means by which payment orders are to be transmitted in the funds transfer. If the originator's bank issues a payment order to an intermediary bank, the originator's bank is obliged to instruct the intermediary bank according to the instruction of the originator. An intermediary bank in the funds transfer is similarly bound by an instruction given to it by the sender of the payment order it accepts.

(2) If the sender's instruction states that the funds transfer is to be carried out telephonically or by wire transfer or otherwise indicates that the funds transfer is to be carried out by the most expeditious means, the receiving bank is obliged to transmit its payment order by the most expeditious available means, and to instruct any intermediary bank accordingly. If a sender's instruction states a payment date, the receiving bank is obliged to transmit its payment order at a time and by means reasonably necessary to allow payment to the beneficiary on the payment date or as soon thereafter as is feasible.

(b) Unless otherwise instructed, a receiving bank executing a payment order may (i) use any funds-transfer system if use of that system is reasonable in the circumstances, and (ii) issue a payment order to the beneficiary's bank or to an intermediary bank through which a payment order conforming to the sender's order can expeditiously be issued to the beneficiary's bank if the receiving bank exercises ordinary care in the selection of the intermediary bank. A receiving bank is not required to follow an instruction of the sender designating a funds-transfer system to be used in carrying out the funds transfer if the receiving bank, in good faith, determines that it is not feasible to follow the instruction or that following the instruction would unduly delay completion of the funds transfer.

(c) Unless subsection (a)(2) applies or the receiving bank is otherwise instructed, the bank may execute a payment order by transmitting its payment order by first class mail or by any means reasonable in the circumstances. If the receiving bank is instructed to execute the sender's order by transmitting its payment order by a particular means, the receiving bank may issue its payment order by the means stated or by any means as expeditious as the means stated.

(d) Unless instructed by the sender, (i) the receiving bank may not obtain payment of its charges for services and expenses in connection with the execution of the sender's order by issuing a payment order in an amount equal to the amount of the sender's order less the amount of the charges, and (ii) may not instruct a subsequent receiving bank to obtain payment of its charges in the same manner.

§ 4A—303. Erroneous Execution of Payment Order.

(a) A receiving bank that (i) executes the payment order of the sender by issuing a payment order in an amount greater than the amount of the sender's order, or (ii) issues a payment order in execution of the sender's order and then issues a duplicate order, is entitled to payment of the amount of the sender's order under Section 4A—402(c) if that subsection is otherwise satisfied. The bank is entitled to recover from the beneficiary of the erroneous order the excess payment received to the extent allowed by the law governing mistake and restitution.

(b) A receiving bank that executes the payment order of the sender by issuing a payment order in an amount less than the amount of the sender's order is entitled to payment of the amount of the sender's order under Section 4A—402(c) if (i) that subsection is otherwise satisfied and (ii) the bank corrects its mistake by issuing an additional payment order for the benefit of the beneficiary of the sender's order. If the error is not corrected, the issuer of the erroneous order is entitled to receive or retain payment from the sender of the order it accepted only to the extent of the amount of the erroneous order. This subsection does not apply if the receiving bank executes the sender's payment order by issuing a payment order in an amount less than the amount of the sender's order for the purpose of obtaining payment of its charges for services and expenses pursuant to instruction of the sender.

(c) If a receiving bank executes the payment order of the sender by issuing a payment order to a beneficiary different from the beneficiary of the sender's order and the funds transfer is completed on the basis of that error, the sender of the payment order that was erroneously executed and all previous senders in the funds transfer are not obliged to pay the payment orders they issued. The issuer of the erroneous order is entitled to recover from the beneficiary of the order the payment received to the extent allowed by the law governing mistake and restitution.

§ 4A–304. Duty of Sender to Report Erroneously Executed Payment Order.

If the sender of a payment order that is erroneously executed as stated in Section 4A–303 receives notification from the receiving bank that the order was executed or that the sender's account was debited with respect to the order, the sender has a duty to exercise ordinary care to determine, on the basis of information available to the sender, that the order was erroneously executed and to notify the bank of the relevant facts within a reasonable time not exceeding 90 days after the notification from the bank was received by the sender. If the sender fails to perform that duty, the bank is not obliged to pay interest on any amount refundable to the sender under Section 4A–402(d) for the period before the bank learns of the execution error. The bank is not entitled to any recovery from the sender on account of a failure by the sender to perform the duty stated in this section.

§ 4A–305. Liability for Late or Improper Execution or Failure to Execute Payment Order.

(a) If a funds transfer is completed but execution of a payment order by the receiving bank in breach of Section 4A–302 results in delay in payment to the beneficiary, the bank is obliged to pay interest to either the originator or the beneficiary of the funds transfer for the period of delay caused by the improper execution. Except as provided in subsection (c), additional damages are not recoverable.

(b) If execution of a payment order by a receiving bank in breach of Section 4A–302 results in (i) noncompletion of the funds transfer, (ii) failure to use an intermediary bank designated by the originator, or (iii) issuance of a payment order that does not comply with the terms of the payment order of the originator, the bank is liable to the originator for its expenses in the funds transfer and for incidental expenses and interest losses, to the extent not covered by subsection (a), resulting from the improper execution. Except as provided in subsection (c), additional damages

are not recoverable.

(c) In addition to the amounts payable under subsections (a) and (b), damages, including consequential damages, are recoverable to the extent provided in an express written agreement of the receiving bank.

(d) If a receiving bank fails to execute a payment order it was obliged by express agreement to execute, the receiving bank is liable to the sender for its expenses in the transaction and for incidental expenses and interest losses resulting from the failure to execute. Additional damages, including consequential damages, are recoverable to the extent provided in an express written agreement of the receiving bank, but are not otherwise recoverable.

(e) Reasonable attorney's fees are recoverable if demand for compensation under subsection (a) or (b) is made and refused before an action is brought on the claim. If a claim is made for breach of an agreement under subsection (d) and the agreement does not provide for damages, reasonable attorney's fees are recoverable if demand for compensation under subsection (d) is made and refused before an action is brought on the claim.

(f) Except as stated in this section, the liability of a receiving bank under subsections (a) and (b) may not be varied by agreement.

Part 4 Payment

§ 4A–401. Payment Date.

"Payment date" of a payment order means the day on which the amount of the order is payable to the beneficiary by the beneficiary's bank. The payment date may be determined by instruction of the sender but cannot be earlier than the day the order is received by the beneficiary's bank and, unless otherwise determined, is the day the order is received by the beneficiary's bank.

§ 4A–402. Obligation of Sender to Pay Receiving Bank.

(a) This section is subject to Sections 4A–205 and 4A–207.

(b) With respect to a payment order issued to the beneficiary's bank, acceptance of the order by the bank obliges the sender to pay the bank the amount of the order, but payment is not due until the payment date of the order.

(c) This subsection is subject to subsection (e) and to Section 4A–303. With respect to a payment order issued to a receiving bank other than the beneficiary's bank, acceptance of the order by the receiving bank obliges the sender to pay the bank the amount of the sender's order. Payment by the sender is not due until the execution date of the sender's order. The obligation of that sender to pay its payment order is excused if the funds transfer is not completed by acceptance by the beneficiary's bank of a payment order instructing payment to the beneficiary of that sender's payment order.

(d) If the sender of a payment order pays the order and was not obliged to pay all or part of the amount paid, the bank receiving payment is obliged to refund payment to the extent the sender was not obliged to pay. Except as provided in Sections 4A—204 and 4A—304, interest is payable on the refundable amount from the date of payment.

(e) If a funds transfer is not completed as stated in subsection (c) and an intermediary bank is obliged to refund payment as stated in subsection (d) but is unable to do so because not permitted by applicable law or because the bank suspends payments, a sender in the funds transfer that executed a payment order in compliance with an instruction, as stated in Section 4A—302(a)(1), to route the funds transfer through that intermediary bank is entitled to receive or retain payment from the sender of the payment order that it accepted. The first sender in the funds transfer that issued an instruction requiring routing through that intermediary bank is subrogated to the right of the bank that paid the intermediary bank to refund as stated in subsection (d).

(f) The right of the sender of a payment order to be excused from the obligation to pay the order as stated in subsection (c) or to receive refund under subsection (d) may not be varied by agreement.

§ 4A—403. Payment by Sender to Receiving Bank.

(a) Payment of the sender's obligation under Section 4A—402 to pay the receiving bank occurs as follows:

(1) If the sender is a bank, payment occurs when the receiving bank receives final settlement of the obligation through a Federal Reserve Bank or through a funds-transfer system.

(2) If the sender is a bank and the sender (i) credited an account of the receiving bank with the sender, or (ii) caused an account of the receiving bank in another bank to be credited, payment occurs when the credit is withdrawn or, if not withdrawn, at midnight of the day on which the credit is withdrawable and the receiving bank learns of that fact.

(3) If the receiving bank debits an account of the sender with the receiving bank, payment occurs when the debit is made to the extent the debit is covered by a withdrawable credit balance in the account.

(b) If the sender and receiving bank are members of a funds-transfer system that nets obligations multilaterally among participants, the receiving bank receives final settlement when settlement is complete in accordance with the rules of the system. The obligation of the sender to pay the amount of a payment order transmitted through the funds-transfer system may be satisfied, to the extent permitted by the rules of the system, by setting off and applying against the sender's obligation the right of the sender to receive payment from the receiving bank of the amount of any other payment order transmitted to the sender by the receiving bank through the funds-transfer system. The aggregate balance of obligations owed by each sender to each receiving bank in the funds-transfer system may be satisfied, to the extent permitted by the rules of the system, by setting off and applying against that balance the aggregate balance of obligations owed to the sender by other members of the system. The aggregate balance is determined after the right of setoff stated in the second sentence of this subsection has been exercised.

(c) If two banks transmit payment orders to each other under an agreement that settlement of the obligations of each bank to the other under Section 4A—402 will be made at the end of the day or other period, the total amount owed with respect to all orders transmitted by one bank shall be set off against the total amount owed with respect to all orders transmitted by the other bank. To the extent of the setoff, each bank has made payment to the other.

(d) In a case not covered by subsection (a), the time when payment of the sender's obligation under Section 4A—402(b) or 4A—402(c) occurs is governed by applicable principles of law that determine when an obligation is satisfied.

§ 4A—404. Obligation of Beneficiary's Bank to Pay and Give Notice to Beneficiary.

(a) Subject to Sections 4A—211(e), 4A—405(d), and 4A—405(e), if a beneficiary's bank accepts a payment order, the bank is obliged to pay the amount of the order to the beneficiary of the order. Payment is due on the payment date of the order, but if acceptance occurs on the payment date after the close of the funds-transfer business day of the bank, payment is due on the next funds-transfer business day. If the bank refuses to pay after demand by the beneficiary and receipt of notice of particular circumstances that will give rise to consequential damages as a result of nonpayment, the beneficiary may recover damages resulting from the refusal to pay to the extent the bank had notice of the damages, unless the bank proves that it did not pay because of a reasonable doubt concerning the right of the beneficiary to payment.

(b) If a payment order accepted by the beneficiary's bank instructs payment to an account of the beneficiary, the bank is obliged to notify the beneficiary of receipt of the order before midnight of the next funds-transfer business day following the payment date. If the payment order does not instruct payment to an account of the beneficiary, the bank is required to notify the beneficiary only if notice is required by the order. Notice may be given by first class mail or any other means reasonable in the circumstances. If the bank fails to give the required notice, the bank is obliged to pay interest to the beneficiary on the amount of the payment order from the day notice should have been given until the day the beneficiary learned of receipt of the payment order by the bank. No other damages are recoverable. Reasonable attorney's fees are also recoverable if demand for interest is made and refused before an action is brought on the claim.

(c) The right of a beneficiary to receive payment and damages as stated in subsection (a) may not be varied by agreement or a funds-transfer system rule. The right of a beneficiary to be notified as stated in subsection (b) may be varied by agreement of the beneficiary or by a funds-transfer system rule if the beneficiary is notified of the rule before initiation of the funds transfer.

§ 4A–405. Payment by Beneficiary's Bank to Beneficiary.

(a) If the beneficiary's bank credits an account of the beneficiary of a payment order, payment of the bank's obligation under Section 4A–404(a) occurs when and to the extent (i) the beneficiary is notified of the right to withdraw the credit, (ii) the bank lawfully applies the credit to a debt of the beneficiary, or (iii) funds with respect to the order are otherwise made available to the beneficiary by the bank.

(b) If the beneficiary's bank does not credit an account of the beneficiary of a payment order, the time when payment of the bank's obligation under Section 4A–404(a) occurs is governed by principles of law that determine when an obligation is satisfied.

(c) Except as stated in subsections (d) and (e), if the beneficiary's bank pays the beneficiary of a payment order under a condition to payment or agreement of the beneficiary giving the bank the right to recover payment from the beneficiary if the bank does not receive payment of the order, the condition to payment or agreement is not enforceable.

(d) A funds-transfer system rule may provide that payments made to beneficiaries of funds transfers made through the system are provisional until receipt of payment by the beneficiary's bank of the payment order it accepted. A beneficiary's bank that makes a payment that is provisional under the rule is entitled to refund from the beneficiary if (i) the rule requires that both the beneficiary and the originator be given notice of the provisional nature of the payment before the funds transfer is initiated, (ii) the beneficiary, the beneficiary's bank, and the originator's bank agreed to be bound by the rule, and (iii) the beneficiary's bank did not receive payment of the payment order that it accepted. If the beneficiary is obliged to refund payment to the beneficiary's bank, acceptance of the payment order by the beneficiary's bank is nullified and no payment by the originator of the funds transfer to the beneficiary occurs under Section 4A–406.

(e) This subsection applies to a funds transfer that includes a payment order transmitted over a funds-transfer system that (i) nets obligations multilaterally among participants, and (ii) has in effect a loss-sharing agreement among participants for the purpose of providing funds necessary to complete settlement of the obligations of one or more participants that do not meet their settlement obligations. If the beneficiary's bank in the funds transfer accepts a payment order and the system fails to complete settlement pursuant to its rules with respect to any payment order in the funds transfer, (i) the acceptance by the beneficiary's bank is nullified and no person has any right or obligation based on the acceptance, (ii) the beneficiary's bank is entitled to recover payment from the beneficiary, (iii) no payment by the originator to the beneficiary occurs under Section 4A–406, and (iv) subject to Section 4A–402(e), each sender in the funds transfer is excused from its obligation to pay its payment order under Section 4A–402(c) because the funds transfer has not been completed.

§ 4A–406. Payment by Originator to Beneficiary; Discharge of Underlying Obligation.

(a) Subject to Sections 4A–211(e), 4A–405(d), and 4A–405(e), the originator of a funds transfer pays the beneficiary of the originator's payment order (i) at the time a payment order for the benefit of the beneficiary is accepted by the beneficiary's bank in the funds transfer and (ii) in an amount equal to the amount of the order accepted by the beneficiary's bank, but not more than the amount of the originator's order.

(b) If payment under subsection (a) is made to satisfy an obligation, the obligation is discharged to the same extent discharge would result from payment to the beneficiary of the same amount in money, unless (i) the payment under subsection (a) was made by a means prohibited by the contract of the beneficiary with respect to the obligation, (ii) the beneficiary, within a reasonable time after receiving notice of receipt of the order by the beneficiary's bank, notified the originator of the beneficiary's refusal of the payment, (iii) funds with respect to the order were not withdrawn by the beneficiary or applied to a debt of the beneficiary, and (iv) the beneficiary would suffer a loss that could reasonably have been avoided if payment had been made by a means complying with the contract. If payment by the originator does not result in discharge under this section, the originator is subrogated to the rights of the beneficiary to receive payment from the beneficiary's bank under Section 4A–404(a).

(c) For the purpose of determining whether discharge of an obligation occurs under subsection (b), if the beneficiary's bank accepts a payment order in an amount equal to the amount of the originator's payment order less charges of one or more receiving banks in the funds transfer, payment to the beneficiary is deemed to be in the amount of the originator's order unless upon demand by the beneficiary the originator does not pay the beneficiary the amount of the deducted charges.

(d) Rights of the originator or of the beneficiary of a funds transfer under this section may be varied only by agreement of the originator and the beneficiary.

Part 5 Miscellaneous Provisions

§ 4A–501. Variation by Agreement and Effect of Funds-Transfer System Rule.

(a) Except as otherwise provided in this Article, the rights and obligations of a party to a funds transfer may be varied by agreement of the affected party.

(b) "Funds-transfer system rule" means a rule of an association of banks (i) governing transmission of payment orders by means of a funds-transfer system of the association or rights and obligations with respect to those orders, or (ii) to the extent the rule governs rights and obligations between banks that are parties to a funds transfer in which a Federal Reserve Bank, acting as an intermediary bank, sends a payment order to the beneficiary's bank. Except as otherwise provided in this Article, a funds-transfer system rule governing rights and obligations between participating banks using the system may be effective even if the rule conflicts with this Article and indirectly affects another party to the funds transfer who does not consent to the rule. A funds-transfer system rule may also govern rights and obligations of parties other than participating banks using the system to the extent stated in Sections 4A—404(c), 4A—405(d), and 4A—507(c).

§ 4A—502. Creditor Process Served on Receiving Bank; Setoff by Beneficiary's Bank.

(a) As used in this section, "creditor process" means levy, attachment, garnishment, notice of lien, sequestration, or similar process issued by or on behalf of a creditor or other claimant with respect to an account.

(b) This subsection applies to creditor process with respect to an authorized account of the sender of a payment order if the creditor process is served on the receiving bank. For the purpose of determining rights with respect to the creditor process, if the receiving bank accepts the payment order the balance in the authorized account is deemed to be reduced by the amount of the payment order to the extent the bank did not otherwise receive payment of the order, unless the creditor process is served at a time and in a manner affording the bank a reasonable opportunity to act on it before the bank accepts the payment order.

(c) If a beneficiary's bank has received a payment order for payment to the beneficiary's account in the bank, the following rules apply:

(1) The bank may credit the beneficiary's account. The amount credited may be set off against an obligation owed by the beneficiary to the bank or may be applied to satisfy creditor process served on the bank with respect to the account.

(2) The bank may credit the beneficiary's account and allow withdrawal of the amount credited unless creditor process with respect to the account is served at a time and in a manner affording the bank a reasonable opportunity to act to prevent withdrawal.

(3) If creditor process with respect to the beneficiary's account has been served and the bank has had a reasonable opportunity to act on it, the bank may not reject the payment order except for a reason unrelated to the service of process.

(d) Creditor process with respect to a payment by the originator to the beneficiary pursuant to a funds transfer may be served only on the beneficiary's bank with respect to the debt owed by that bank to the beneficiary. Any other bank served with the creditor process is not obliged to act with respect to the process.

§ 4A—503. Injunction or Restraining Order with Respect to Funds Transfer.

For proper cause and in compliance with applicable law, a court may restrain (i) a person from issuing a payment order to initiate a funds transfer, (ii) an originator's bank from executing the payment order of the originator, or (iii) the beneficiary's bank from releasing funds to the beneficiary or the beneficiary from withdrawing the funds. A court may not otherwise restrain a person from issuing a payment order, paying or receiving payment of a payment order, or otherwise acting with respect to a funds transfer.

§ 4A—504. Order in Which Items and Payment Orders May Be Charged to Account; Order of Withdrawals from Account.

(a) If a receiving bank has received more than one payment order of the sender or one or more payment orders and other items that are payable from the sender's account, the bank may charge the sender's account with respect to the various orders and items in any sequence.

(b) In determining whether a credit to an account has been withdrawn by the holder of the account or applied to a debt of the holder of the account, credits first made to the account are first withdrawn or applied.

§ 4A—505. Preclusion of Objection to Debit of Customer's Account.

If a receiving bank has received payment from its customer with respect to a payment order issued in the name of the customer as sender and accepted by the bank, and the customer received notification reasonably identifying the order, the customer is precluded from asserting that the bank is not entitled to retain the payment unless the customer notifies the bank of the customer's objection to the payment within one year after the notification was received by the customer.

§ 4A—506. Rate of Interest.

(a) If, under this Article, a receiving bank is obliged to pay interest with respect to a payment order issued to the bank, the amount payable may be determined (i) by agreement of the sender and receiving bank, or (ii) by a funds-transfer system rule if the payment order is transmitted through a funds-transfer system.

(b) If the amount of interest is not determined by an agreement or rule as stated in subsection (a), the amount is calculated by multiplying the applicable Federal Funds rate by the amount on which interest is payable, and then multiplying the product by the number of days for which interest is payable. The applicable Federal Funds rate is the average of the Federal Funds rates published by the Federal Reserve Bank of New York for each of the days for which interest is payable divided by 360. The Federal Funds rate for any day on which a published rate is not available is the same as the published rate for the next preceding day for which there is a published rate. If a receiving bank that accepted a payment order is required to refund payment to the sender of the order because the funds transfer was not completed, but the failure to complete was not due to any fault by the bank, the interest payable is reduced by a percentage equal to the reserve requirement on deposits of the receiving bank.

§ 4A—507. **Choice of Law.**

(a) The following rules apply unless the affected parties otherwise agree or subsection (c) applies:

> (1) The rights and obligations between the sender of a payment order and the receiving bank are governed by the law of the jurisdiction in which the receiving bank is located.

> (2) The rights and obligations between the beneficiary's bank and the beneficiary are governed by the law of the jurisdiction in which the beneficiary's bank is located.

> (3) The issue of when payment is made pursuant to a funds transfer by the originator to the beneficiary is governed by the law of the jurisdiction in which the beneficiary's bank is located.

(b) If the parties described in each paragraph of subsection (a) have made an agreement selecting the law of a particular jurisdiction to govern rights and obligations between each other, the law of that jurisdiction governs those rights and obligations, whether or not the payment order or the funds transfer bears a reasonable relation to that jurisdiction.

(c) A funds-transfer system rule may select the law of a particular jurisdiction to govern (i) rights and obligations between participating banks with respect to payment orders transmitted or processed through the system, or (ii) the rights and obligations of some or all parties to a funds transfer any part of which is carried out by means of the system. A choice of law made pursuant to clause (i) is binding on participating banks. A choice of law made pursuant to clause (ii) is binding on the originator, other sender, or a receiving bank having notice that the funds-transfer system might be used in the funds transfer and of the choice of law by the system when the originator, other sender, or receiving bank issued or accepted a payment order. The beneficiary of a funds transfer is bound by the choice of law if, when the funds transfer is initiated, the beneficiary has notice that the funds-transfer system might be used in the funds transfer and of the choice of law by the system. The law of a jurisdiction selected pursuant to this subsection may govern, whether or not that law bears a reasonable relation to the matter in issue.

(d) In the event of inconsistency between an agreement under subsection (b) and a choice-of-law rule under sub-

section (c), the agreement under subsection (b) prevails.

(e) If a funds transfer is made by use of more than one funds-transfer system and there is inconsistency between choice-of-law rules of the systems, the matter in issue is governed by the law of the selected jurisdiction that has the most significant relationship to the matter in issue.

[Articles 5, 6, 7, and 8 are not included here.]

Article 9

SECURED TRANSACTIONS; SALES OF ACCOUNTS AND CHATTEL PAPER

Note: *The adoption of this Article should be accompanied by the repeal of existing statutes dealing with conditional sales, trust receipts, factor's liens where the factor is given a nonpossessory lien, chattel mortgages, crop mortgages, mortgages on railroad equipment, assignment of accounts and generally statutes regulating security interests in personal property.*

Where the state has a retail installment selling act or small loan act, that legislation should be carefully examined to determine what changes in those acts are needed to conform them to this Article. This Article primarily sets out rules defining rights of a secured party against persons dealing with the debtor; it does not prescribe regulations and controls which may be necessary to curb abuses arising in the small loan business or in the financing of consumer purchases on credit. Accordingly there is no intention to repeal existing regulatory acts in those fields by enactment or re-enactment of Article 9. See Section 9—203(4) and the Note thereto.

Part 1 Short Title, Applicability and Definitions

§ 9—101. **Short Title.**

This Article shall be known and may be cited as Uniform Commercial Code—Secured Transactions.

§ 9—102. **Policy and Subject Matter of Article.**

(1) Except as otherwise provided in Section 9—104 on excluded transactions, this Article applies

> (a) to any transaction (regardless of its form) which is intended to create a security interest in personal property or fixtures including goods, documents, instruments, general intangibles, chattel paper or accounts; and also

> (b) to any sale of accounts or chattel paper.

(2) This Article applies to security interests created by contract including pledge, assignment, chattel mortgage, chattel trust, trust deed, factor's lien, equipment trust, conditional sale, trust receipt, other lien or title retention contract and lease or consignment intended as security. This Article does not apply to statutory liens except as provided in Section 9—310.

(3) The application of this Article to a security interest in a secured obligation is not affected by the fact that the obligation is itself secured by a transaction or interest to which this Article does not apply.

§ 9—103. **Perfection of Security Interest in Multiple State Transactions.**

(1) Documents, instruments and ordinary goods.

(a) This subsection applies to documents, instruments, rights to proceeds of written letters of credit, and goods other than those covered by a certificate of title described in subsection (2), mobile goods described in subsection (3), and minerals described in subsection (5).

(b) Except as otherwise provided in this subsection, perfection and the effect of perfection or non-perfection of a security interest in collateral are governed by the law of the jurisdiction where the collateral is when the last event occurs on which is based the assertion that the security interest is perfected or unperfected.

(c) If the parties to a transaction creating a purchase money security interest in goods in one jurisdiction understand at the time that the security interest attaches that the goods will be kept in another jurisdiction, then the law of the other jurisdiction governs the perfection and the effect of perfection or non-perfection of the security interest from the time it attaches until thirty days after the debtor receives possession of the goods and thereafter if the goods are taken to the other jurisdiction before the end of the thirty-day period.

(d) When collateral is brought into and kept in this state while subject to a security interest perfected under the law of the jurisdiction from which the collateral was removed, the security interest remains perfected, but if action is required by Part 3 of this Article to perfect the security interest,

(i) if the action is not taken before the expiration of the period of perfection in the other jurisdiction or the end of four months after the collateral is brought into this state, whichever period first expires, the security interest becomes unperfected at the end of that period and is thereafter deemed to have been unperfected as against a person who became a purchaser after removal;

(ii) if the action is taken before the expiration of the period specified in subparagraph (i), the security interest continues perfected thereafter;

(iii) for the purpose of priority over a buyer of consumer goods (subsection (2) of Section 9—307), the period of the effectiveness of a filing in the jurisdiction from which the collateral is removed is governed by the rules with respect to perfection in subparagraphs (i) and (ii).

(2) Certificate of title.

(a) This subsection applies to goods covered by a certificate of title issued under a statute of this state or of another jurisdiction under the law of which indication of a security interest on the certificate is required as a condition of perfection.

(b) Except as otherwise provided in this subsection, perfection and the effect of perfection or non-perfection

of the security interest are governed by the law (including the conflict of laws rules) of the jurisdiction issuing the certificate until four months after the goods are removed from that jurisdiction and thereafter until the goods are registered in another jurisdiction, but in any event not beyond surrender of the certificate. After the expiration of that period, the goods are not covered by the certificate of title within the meaning of this section.

(c) Except with respect to the rights of a buyer described in the next paragraph, a security interest, perfected in another jurisdiction otherwise than by notation on a certificate of title, in goods brought into this state and thereafter covered by a certificate of title issued by this state is subject to the rules stated in paragraph (d) of subsection (1).

(d) If goods are brought into this state while a security interest therein is perfected in any manner under the law of the jurisdiction from which the goods are removed and a certificate of title is issued by this state and the certificate does not show that the goods are subject to the security interest or that they may be subject to security interests not shown on the certificate, the security interest is subordinate to the rights of a buyer of the goods who is not in the business of selling goods of that kind to the extent that he gives value and receives delivery of the goods after issuance of the certificate and without knowledge of the security interest.

(3) Accounts, general intangibles and mobile goods.

(a) This subsection applies to accounts (other than an account described in subsection (5) on minerals) and general intangibles (other than uncertificated securities) and to goods which are mobile and which are of a type normally used in more than one jurisdiction, such as motor vehicles, trailers, rolling stock, airplanes, shipping containers, road building and construction machinery and commercial harvesting machinery and the like, if the goods are equipment or are inventory leased or held for lease by the debtor to others, and are not covered by a certificate of title described in subsection (2).

(b) The law (including the conflict of laws rules) of the jurisdiction in which the debtor is located governs the perfection and the effect of perfection or non-perfection of the security interest.

(c) If, however, the debtor is located in a jurisdiction which is not a part of the United States, and which does not provide for perfection of the security interest by filing or recording in that jurisdiction, the law of the jurisdiction in the United States in which the debtor has its major executive office in the United States governs the perfection and the effect of perfection or non-perfection of the security interest through filing. In the alternative, if the debtor is located in a jurisdiction which is not a part of the United States or Canada and the collateral is accounts or general intangibles for money due or to become due, the security interest may be perfected by notification to the account debtor. As used in this paragraph, "United States" includes its territories and possessions and the Commonwealth of Puerto Rico.

(d) A debtor shall be deemed located at his place of business if he has one, at his chief executive office if he has more than one place of business, otherwise at his residence. If, however, the debtor is a foreign air carrier under the Federal Aviation Act of 1958, as amended, it shall be deemed located at the designated office of the agent upon whom service of process may be made on behalf of the foreign air carrier.

(e) A security interest perfected under the law of the jurisdiction of the location of the debtor is perfected until the expiration of four months after a change of the debtor's location to another jurisdiction, or until perfection would have ceased by the law of the first jurisdiction, whichever period first expires. Unless perfected in the new jurisdiction before the end of that period, it becomes unperfected thereafter and is deemed to have been unperfected as against a person who became a purchaser after the change.

(4) Chattel paper.

The rules stated for goods in subsection (1) apply to a possessory security interest in chattel paper. The rules stated for accounts in subsection (3) apply to a nonpossessory security interest in chattel paper, but the security interest may not be perfected by notification to the account debtor.

(5) Minerals.

Perfection and the effect of perfection or non-perfection of a security interest which is created by a debtor who has an interest in minerals or the like (including oil and gas) before extraction and which attaches thereto as extracted, or which attaches to an account resulting from the sale thereof at the wellhead or minehead are governed by the law (including the conflict of laws rules) of the jurisdiction wherein the wellhead or minehead is located.

(6) Investment property.

(a) This subsection applies to investment property.

(b) Except as otherwise provided in paragraph (f), during the time that a security certificate is located in a jurisdiction, perfection of a security interest, the effect of perfection or non-perfection, and the priority of a security interest in the certificated security represented thereby are governed by the local law of that jurisdiction.

(c) Except as otherwise provided in paragraph (f), perfection of a security interest, the effect of perfection or non-perfection, and the priority of a security interest in an uncertificated security are governed by the local law of the issuer's jurisdiction as specified in Section 8—110(d).

(d) Except as otherwise provided in paragraph (f), perfection of a security interest, the effect of perfection or non-perfection, and the priority of a security interest in a security entitlement or securities account are governed by the local law of the securities intermediary's jurisdiction as specified in Section 8—110(e).

(e) Except as otherwise provided in paragraph (f), perfection of a security interest, the effect of perfection or non-perfection, and the priority of a security interest in a commodity contract or commodity account are governed by the local law of the commodity intermediary's jurisdiction. The following rules determine a "commodity intermediary's jurisdiction" for purposes of this paragraph:

(i) If an agreement between the commodity intermediary and commodity customer specifies that it is governed by the law of a particular jurisdiction, that jurisdiction is the commodity intermediary's jurisdiction.

(ii) If an agreement between the commodity intermediary and commodity customer does not specify the governing law as provided in subparagraph (i), but expressly specifies that the commodity account is maintained at an office in a particular jurisdiction, that jurisdiction is the commodity intermediary's jurisdiction.

(iii) If an agreement between the commodity intermediary and commodity customer does not specify a jurisdiction as provided in subparagraphs (i) or (ii), the commodity intermediary's jurisdiction is the jurisdiction in which is located the office identified in an account statement as the office serving the commodity customer's account.

(iv) If an agreement between the commodity intermediary and commodity customer does not specify a jurisdiction as provided in subparagraphs (i) or (ii) and an account statement does not identify an office serving the commodity customer's account as provided in subparagraph (iii), the commodity intermediary's jurisdiction is the jurisdiction in which is located the chief executive office of the commodity intermediary.

(f) Perfection of a security interest by filing, automatic perfection of a security interest in investment property granted by a broker or securities intermediary, and automatic perfection of a security interest in a commodity contract or commodity account granted by a commodity intermediary are governed by the local law of the jurisdiction in which the debtor is located.

§ 9—104. **Transactions Excluded From Article.**

This Article does not apply

(a) to a security interest subject to any statute of the United States, to the extent that such statute governs the rights of parties to and third parties affected by transactions in particular types of prperty; or

(b) to a landlord's lien; or

(c) to a lien given by statute or other rule of law for services or materials except as provided in Section 9—310 on priority of such liens; or

(d) to a transfer of a claim for wages, salary or other compensation of an employee; or

(e) to a transfer by a government or governmental subdivision or agency; or

(f) to a sale of accounts or chattel paper as part of a sale of the business out of which they arose, or an assignment of accounts or chattel paper which is for the purpose of collection only, or a transfer of a right to payment under a contract to an assignee who is also to do the performance under the contract or a transfer of a single account to an assignee in whole or partial satisfaction of a preexisting indebtedness; or

(g) to a transfer of an interest in or claim in or under any policy of insurance, except as provided with respect to proceeds (Section 9—306) and priorities in proceeds (Section 9—312); or

(h) to a right represented by a judgment (other than a judgment taken on a right to payment which was collateral); or

(i) to any right of set-off; or

(j) except to the extent that provision is made for fixtures in Section 9—313, to the creation or transfer of an interest in or lien on real estate, including a lease or rents thereunder; or

(k) to a transfer in whole or in part of any claim arising out of tort; or

(*l*) to a transfer of an interest in any deposit account (subsection (1) of Section 9—105), except as provided with respect to proceeds (Section 9—306) and priorities in proceeds (Section 9—312).

(m) to a transfer of an interest in a letter of credit other than the rights to proceeds of a written letter of credit.

§ 9—105. Definitions and Index of Definitions.

(1) In this Article unless the context otherwise requires:

(a) "Account debtor" means the person who is obligated on an account, chattel paper or general intangible;

(b) "Chattel paper" means a writing or writings which evidence both a monetary obligation and a security interest in or a lease of specific goods, but a charter or other contract involving the use or hire of a vessel is not chattel paper. When a transaction is evidenced both by such a security agreement or a lease and by an instrument or a series of instruments, the group of writings taken together constitutes chattel paper;

(c) "Collateral" means the property subject to a security interest, and includes accounts and chattel paper which have been sold;

(d) "Debtor" means the person who owes payment or other performance of the obligation secured, whether or not he owns or has rights in the collateral, and includes the seller of accounts or chattel paper. Where the debtor and the owner of the collateral are not the same person, the term "debtor" means the owner of the collateral in any provision of the Article dealing with the collateral, the obligor in any provision dealing with the obligation, and may include both where the context so requires;

(e) "Deposit account" means a demand, time, savings, passbook or like account maintained with a bank, savings and loan association, credit union or like organization, other than an account evidenced by a certificate of deposit;

(f) "Document" means document of title as defined in the general definitions of Article 1 (Section 1—201), and a receipt of the kind described in subsection (2) of Section 7—201;

(g) "Encumbrance" includes real estate mortgages and other liens on real estate and all other rights in real estate that are not ownership interests;

(h) "Goods" includes all things which are movable at the time the security interest attaches or which are fixtures (Section 9—313), but does not include money, documents, instruments, investment property, commodity contracts accounts, chattel paper, general intangibles, or minerals or the like (including oil and gas) before extraction. "Goods" also includes standing timber which is to be cut and removed under a conveyance or contract for sale, the unborn young of animals, and growing crops;

(i) "Instrument" means a negotiable instrument (defined in Section 3—104), or any other writing which evidences a right to the payment of money and is not itself a security agreement or lease and is of a type which is in ordinary course of business transferred by delivery with any necessary indorsement or assignment. The term does not include investment property.

(j) "Mortgage" means a consensual interest created by a real estate mortgage, a trust deed on real estate, or the like;

(k) An advance is made "pursuant to commitment" if the secured party has bound himself to make it, whether or not a subsequent event of default or other event not within his control has relieved or may relieve him from his obligation;

(*l*) "Security agreement" means an agreement which creates or provides for a security interest;

(m) "Secured party" means a lender, seller or other person in whose favor there is a security interest, including a person to whom accounts or chattel paper have been sold. When the holders of obligations issued under an indenture of trust, equipment trust agreement or the like are represented by a trustee or other person, the representative is the secured party;

(n) "Transmitting utility" means any person primarily engaged in the railroad, street railway or trolley bus business, the electric or electronics communications transmission business, the transmission of goods by pipeline, or the transmission or the production and transmission of electricity, steam, gas or water, or the provision of sewer service.

(2) Other definitions applying to this Article and the sections in which they appear are:

"Account". Section 9—106.

"Attach". Section 9—203.

"Commodity contract". Section 9—115.

"Commodity customer". Section 9—115.

"Commodity intermediary". Section 9—115.

"Construction mortgage". Section 9—313(1).

"Consumer goods". Section 9—109(1).

"Control". Section 9—115.

"Equipment". Section 9—109(2).

"Farm products". Section 9—109(3).

"Fixture". Section 9—313(1).

"Fixture filing". Section 9—313(1).

"General intangibles". Section 9—106.

"Inventory". Section 9—109(4).

"Investment property". Section 9—115.

"Lien creditor". Section 9—301(3).

"Proceeds". Section 9—306(1).

"Purchase money security interest". Section 9—107.

"United States". Section 9—103.

(3) The following definitions in other Articles apply to this Article:

"Broker". Section. 8—102.

"Certified security". Section 8—102.

"Check". Section 3—104.

"Clearing corporation". Section 8—102.

"Contract for sale". Section 2—106.

"Control". Section 8—106.

"Delivery". Section 8—301.

"Entitlement holder". Section 8—102.

"Financial asset". Section 8—102.

"Holder in due course". Section 3—302.

"Letter of credit". Section 5—102.

"Note". Section 3—104.

"Proceeds of a letter of credit". Section 5—114(a).

"Sale". Section 2—106.

"Securities intermediary". Section 8—102.

"Security". Section 8—102.

"Security certificate". Section 8—102.

"Security entitlement". Section 8—102.

"Uncertertificated security". Section 8—102.

(4) In addition Article 1 contains general definitions and principles of construction and interpretation applicable throughout this Article.

§ 9—106. **Definitions: "Account"; "General Intangibles".**

"Account" means any right to payment for goods sold or leased or for services rendered which is not evidenced by an instrument or chattel paper, whether or not it has been earned by performance. "General intangibles" means any personal property (including things in action) other than goods, accounts, chattel paper, documents, instruments, investment property, rights to proceeds of written letters of credit, and money. All rights to payment earned or unearned under a charter or other contract involving the use or hire of a vessel and all rights incident to the charter or contract are accounts.

§ 9—107. **Definitions: "Purchase Money Security Interest".**

A security interest is a "purchase money security interest" to the extent that it is

(a) taken or retained by the seller of the collateral to secure all or part of its price; or

(b) taken by a person who by making advances or incurring an obligation gives value to enable the debtor to acquire rights in or the use of collateral if such value is in fact so used.

§ 9—108. **When After-Acquired Collateral Not Security for Antecedent Debt.**

Where a secured party makes an advance, incurs an obligation, releases a perfected security interest, or otherwise gives new value which is to be secured in whole or in part by after-acquired property his security interest in the after-acquired collateral shall be deemed to be taken for new value and not as security for an antecedent debt if the debtor acquires his rights in such collateral either in the ordinary course of his business or under a contract of purchase made pursuant to the security agreement within a reasonable time after new value is given.

§ 9—109. **Classification of Goods; "Consumer Goods"; "Equipment"; "Farm Products"; "Inventory".**

Goods are

(1) "consumer goods" if they are used or bought for use primarily for personal, family or household purposes;

(2) "equipment" if they are used or bought for use primarily in business (including farming or a profession) or by a debtor who is a non-profit organization or a governmental subdivision or agency or if the goods are not included in the definitions of inventory, farm products or consumer goods;

(3) "farm products" if they are crops or livestock or supplies used or produced in farming operations or if they are products of crops or livestock in their unmanufactured states (such as ginned cotton, wool-clip, maple syrup, milk and eggs), and if they are in the possession of a debtor engaged in raising, fattening, grazing or other farming operations. If goods are farm products they are neither equipment nor inventory;

(4) "inventory" if they are held by a person who holds them for sale or lease or to be furnished under contracts of service or if he has so furnished them, or if they are raw materials, work in process or materials used or consumed in a business. Inventory of a person is not to be classified as his equipment.

§ 9—110. Sufficiency of Description.

For purposes of this Article any description of personal property or real estate is sufficient whether or not it is specific if it reasonably identifies what is described.

§ 9—111. Applicability of Bulk Transfer Laws.

The creation of a security interest is not a bulk transfer under Article 6 (see Section 6—103).

§ 9—112. Where Collateral Is Not Owned by Debtor.

Unless otherwise agreed, when a secured party knows that collateral is owned by a person who is not the debtor, the owner of the collateral is entitled to receive from the secured party any surplus under Section 9—502(2) or under Section 9—504(1), and is not liable for the debt or for any deficiency after resale, and he has the same right as the debtor

(a) to receive statements under Section 9—208;

(b) to receive notice of and to object to a secured party's proposal to retain the collateral in satisfaction of the indebtedness under Section 9—505;

(c) to redeem the collateral under Section 9—506;

(d) to obtain injunctive or other relief under Section 9—507(1); and

(e) to recover losses caused to him under Section 9—208(2).

§ 9—113. Security Interests Arising Under Article on Sales or Under Article on Leases.

A security interest arising solely under the Article on Sales (Article 2) or the Article on Leases is subject to the provisions of this Article except that to the extent that and so long as the debtor does not have or does not lawfully obtain possession of the goods

(a) no security agreement is necessary to make the security interest enforceable; and

(b) no filing is required to perfect the security interest; and

(c) the rights of the secured party on default by the debtor are governed (i) by the Article on Sales (Article 2) in the case of a security interest arising solely under such Article or (ii) by the Article on Leases (Article 2A) in the case of a security interest arising solely under such Article.

§ 9—114. Consignment.

(1) A person who delivers goods under a consignment which is not a security interest and who would be required to file under this Article by paragraph (3)(c) of Section 2—326 has priority over a secured party who is or becomes a creditor of the consignee and who would have a perfected security interest in the goods if they were the property of the consignee, and also has priority with respect to identifiable cash proceeds received on or before delivery of the goods to a buyer, if

(a) the consignor complies with the filing provision of the Article on Sales with respect to consignments (paragraph (3)(c) of Section 2—326) before the consignee receives possession of the goods; and

(b) the consignor gives notification in writing to the holder of the security interest if the holder has filed a financing statement covering the same types of goods before the date of the filing made by the consignor; and

(c) the holder of the security interest receives the notification within five years before the consignee receives possession of the goods; and

(d) the notification states that the consignor expects to deliver goods on consignment to the consignee, describing the goods by item or type.

(2) In the case of a consignment which is not a security interest and in which the requirements of the preceding subsection have not been met, a person who delivers goods to another is subordinate to a person who would have a perfected security interest in the goods if they were the property of the debtor.

§ 9—115. Investment Property.

(1) In this Article:

(a) "Commodity account" means an account maintained by a commodity intermediary in which a commodity contract is carried for a commodity customer.

(b) "Commodity contract" means a commodity futures contract, an option on a commodity futures contract, a commodity option, or other contract that, in each case, is:

(i) traded on or subject to the rules of a board of trade that has been designated as a contract market for such a contract pursuant to the federal commodities laws; or

(ii) traded on a foreign commodity board of trade, exchange, or market, and is carried on the books of a commodity intermediary for a commodity customer.

(c) "Commodity customer" means a person for whom a commodity intermediary carries a commodity contract on its books.

(d) "Commodity intermediary" means:

(i) a person who is registered as a futures commission merchant under the federal commodities laws; or

(ii) a person who in the ordinary course of its business provides clearance or settlement services for a board of trade that has been designated as a contract market pursuant to the federal commodities laws.

(e) "Control" with respect to a certificated security, uncertificated security, or security entitlement has the meaning specified in Section 8—106. A secured party has control over a commodity contract if by agreement among the commodity customer, the commodity intermediary, and the secured party, the commodity intermediary has agreed that it will apply any value distributed on account of the commodity contract as directed by the secured party without further consent by the commodity customer. If a commodity customer grants a security interest in a commodity contract to its own commodity intermediary, the commodity intermediary as secured party has control. A secured party has control over a securities account or commodity account if the secured party has control over all security entitlements or commodity contracts carried in the securities account or commodity account.

(f) "Investment property" means:

(i) a security, whether certificated or uncertificated;

(ii) a security entitlement;

(iii) a securities account;

(iv) a commodity contract; or

(v) a commodity account.

(2) Attachment or perfection of a security interest in a securities account is also attachment or perfection of a security interest in all security entitlements carried in the securities account. Attachment or perfection of a security interest in a commodity account is also attachment or perfection of a security interest in all commodity contracts carried in the commodity account.

(3) A description of collateral in a security agreement or financing statement is sufficient to create or perfect a security interest in a certificated security, uncertificated security, security entitlement, securities account, commodity contract, or commodity account whether it describes the collateral by those terms, or as investment property, or by description of the underlying security, financial asset, or commodity contract. A description of investment property collateral in a security agreement or financing statement is sufficient if it identifies the collateral by specific listing, by category, by quantity, by a computational or allocational formula or procedure, or by any other method, if the iden-

tity of the collateral is objectively determinable.

(4) Perfection of a security interest in investment property is governed by the following rules:

(a) A security interest in investment property may be perfected by control.

(b) Except as otherwise provided in paragraphs (c) and (d), a security interest in investment property may be perfected by filing.

(c) If the debtor is a broker or securities intermediary a security interest in investment property is perfected when it attaches. The filing of a financing statement with respect to a security interest in investment property granted by a broker or securities intermediary has no effect for purposes of perfection or priority with respect to that security interest.

(d) If a debtor is a commodity, intermediary, a security interest in a commodity contract or a commodity account is perfected when it attaches. The filing of a financing statement with respect to a security interest in a commodity contract or a commodity account granted by a commodity intermediary has no effect for purposes of perfection or priority with respect to that security interest.

(5) Priority between conflicting security interests in the same investment property is governed by the following rules:

(a) A security interest of a secured party who has control over investment property has priority over a security interest of a secured party who does not have control over the investment property.

(b) Except as otherwise provided in paragraphs (c) and (d), conflicting security interests of secured parties each of whom has control rank equally.

(c) Except as otherwise agreed by the securities intermediary, a security interest in a security entitlement or a securities account granted to the debtor's own securities intermediary has priority over any security interest granted by the debtor to another secured party.

(d) Except as otherwise agreed by the commodity intermediary, a security interest in a commodity contract or a commodity account granted to the debtor's own commodity intermediary has priority over any security interest granted by the debtor to another secured party.

(e) Conflicting security interests granted by a broker, a securities intermediary, or a commodity intermediary which are perfected without control rank equally.

(f) In all other cases, priority between conflicting security interests in investment property is governed by Section 9—312(5), (6), and (7). Section 9—312(4) does not apply to investment property.

(6) If a security certificate in registered form is delivered to a secured party pursuant to agreement, a written security agreement is not required for attachment or enforceability of the security interest, delivery suffices for perfection of the

security interest, and the security interest has priority over a conflicting security interest perfected by means other than control, even if a necessary indorsement is lacking.

§ 9—116. Security Interest Arising in Purchase or Delivery of Financial Asset.

(1) If a person buys a financial asset through a securities intermediary in a transaction in which the buyer is obligated to pay the purchase price to the securities intermediary at the time of the purchase, and the securities intermediary credits the financial asset to the buyer's securities account before the buyer pays the securities intermediary, the securities intermediary has a security interest in the buyer's security entitlement securing the buyer's obligation to pay. A security agreement is not required for attachment or enforceability of the security interest, and the security interest is automatically perfected.

(2) If a certificated security, or other financial asset represented by a writing which in the ordinary course of business is transferred by delivery with any necessary indorsement or assignment is delivered pursuant to an agreement between persons in the business of dealing with such securities or financial assets and the agreement calls for delivery versus payment, the person delivering the certificate or other financial asset has a security interest in the certificated security or other financial asset securing the seller's right to receive payment. A security agreement is not required for attachment or enforceability of the security interest, and the security interest is automatically perfected.

Part 2 Validity of Security Agreement and Rights of Parties Thereto

§ 9—201. General Validity of Security Agreement.

Except as otherwise provided by this Act a security agreement is effective according to its terms between the parties, against purchasers of the collateral and against creditors. Nothing in this Article validates any charge or practice illegal under any statute or regulation thereunder governing usury, small loans, retail installment sales, or the like, or extends the application of any such statute or regulation to any transaction not otherwise subject thereto.

§ 9—202. Title to Collateral Immaterial.

Each provision of this Article with regard to rights, obligations and remedies applies whether title to collateral is in the secured party or in the debtor.

§ 9—203. Attachment and Enforceability of Security Interest; Proceeds; Formal Requisites.

(1) Subject to the provisions of Section 4—210 on the security interest of a collecting bank, Sections 9—115 and 9—116 on security interests in investment property, and Section 9—113 on a security interest arising under the Articles on Sales and Leases, a security interest is not enforceable against the debtor or third parties with respect

to the collateral and does not attach unless:

 (a) the collateral is in the possession of the secured party pursuant to agreement, the collateral is investment property and the secured party has control pursuant to agreement, or the debtor has signed a security agreement which contains a description of the collateral and in addition, when the security interest covers crops growing or to be grown or timber to be cut, a description of the land concerned;

 (b) value has been given; and

 (c) the debtor has rights in the collateral.

(2) A security interest attaches when it becomes enforceable against the debtor with respect to the collateral. Attachment occurs as soon as all of the events specified in subsection (1) have taken place unless explicit agreement postpones the time of attaching.

(3) Unless otherwise agreed a security agreement gives the secured party the rights to proceeds provided by Section 9—306.

(4) A transaction, although subject to this Article, is also subject to . . . .*, and in the case of conflict between the provisions of this Article and any such statute, the provisions of such statute control. Failure to comply with any applicable statute has only the effect which is specified therein.

Note: At * in subsection (4) insert reference to any local statute regulating small loans, retail installment sales and the like.

 The foregoing subsection (4) is designed to make it clear that certain transactions, although subject to this Article, must also comply with other applicable legislation.

 This Article is designed to regulate all the "security" aspects of transactions within its scope. There is, however, much regulatory legislation, particularly in the consumer field, which supplements this Article and should not be repealed by its enactment. Examples are small loan acts, retail installment selling acts and the like. Such acts may provide for licensing and rate regulation and may prescribe particular forms of contract. Such provisions should remain in force despite the enactment of this Article. On the other hand if a retail installment selling act contains provisions on filing, rights on default, etc., such provisions should be repealed as inconsistent with this Article except that inconsistent provisions as to deficiencies, penalties, etc., in the Uniform Consumer Credit Code and other recent related legislation should remain because those statutes were drafted after the substantial enactment of the Article and with the intention of modifying certain provisions of this Article as to consumer credit.

§ 9—204. After-Acquired Property; Future Advances.

(1) Except as provided in subsection (2), a security agreement may provide that any or all obligations covered by the security agreement are to be secured by after-acquired collateral.

(2) No security interest attaches under an after-acquired property clause to consumer goods other than accessions (Section 9—314) when given as additional security unless

the debtor acquires rights in them within ten days after the secured party gives value.

(3) Obligations covered by a security agreement may include future advances or other value whether or not the advances or value are given pursuant to commitment (subsection (1) of Section 9—105).

§ 9—205. Use or Disposition of Collateral Without Accounting Permissible.

A security interest is not invalid or fraudulent against creditors by reason of liberty in the debtor to use, commingle or dispose of all or part of the collateral (including returned or repossessed goods) or to collect or compromise accounts or chattel paper, or to accept the return of goods or make repossessions, or to use, commingle or dispose of proceeds, or by reason of the failure of the secured party to require the debtor to account for proceeds or replace collateral. This section does not relax the requirements of possession where perfection of a security interest depends upon possession of the collateral by the secured party or by a bailee.

§ 9—206. Agreement Not to Assert Defenses Against Assignee; Modification of Sales Warranties Where Security Agreement Exists.

(1) Subject to any statute or decision which establishes a different rule for buyers or lessees of consumer goods, an agreement by a buyer or lessee that he will not assert against an assignee any claim or defense which he may have against the seller or lessor is enforceable by an assignee who takes his assignment for value, in good faith and without notice of a claim or defense, except as to defenses of a type which may be asserted against a holder in due course of a negotiable instrument under the Article on Negotiable Instruments (Article 3). A buyer who as part of one transaction signs both a negotiable instrument and a security agreement makes such an agreement.

(2) When a seller retains a purchase money security interest in goods the Article on Sales (Article 2) governs the sale and any disclaimer, limitation or modification of the seller's warranties.

§ 9—207. Rights and Duties When Collateral is in Secured Party's Possession

(1) A secured party must use reasonable care in the custody and preservation of collateral in his possession. In the case of an instrument or chattel paper reasonable care includes taking necessary steps to preserve rights against prior parties unless otherwise agreed.

(2) Unless otherwise agreed, when collateral is in the secured party's possession

(a) reasonable expenses (including the cost of any insurance and payment of taxes or other charges) incurred in the custody, preservation, use or operation of the collateral are chargeable to the debtor and are secured by the collateral;

(b) the risk of accidental loss or damage is on the debtor to the extent of any deficiency in any effective insurance coverage;

(c) the secured party may hold as additional security any increase or profits (except money) received from the collateral, but money so received, unless remitted to the debtor, shall be applied in reduction of the secured obligation;

(d) the secured party must keep the collateral identifiable but fungible collateral may be commingled;

(e) the secured party may repledge the collateral upon terms which do not impair the debtor's right to redeem it.

(3) A secured party is liable for any loss caused by his failure to meet any obligation imposed by the preceding subsections but does not lose his security interest.

(4) A secured party may use or operate the collateral for the purpose of preserving the collateral or its value or pursuant to the order of a court of appropriate jurisdiction or, except in the case of consumer goods, in the manner and to the extent provided in the security agreement.

§ 9—208. Request for Statement of Account or List of Collateral.

(1) A debtor may sign a statement indicating what he believes to be the aggregate amount of unpaid indebtedness as of a specified date and may send it to the secured party with a request that the statement be approved or corrected and returned to the debtor. When the security agreement or any other record kept by the secured party identifies the collateral a debtor may similarly request the secured party to approve or correct a list of the collateral.

(2) The secured party must comply with such a request within two weeks after receipt by sending a written correction or approval. If the secured party claims a security interest in all of a particular type of collateral owned by the debtor he may indicate that fact in his reply and need not approve or correct an itemized list of such collateral. If the secured party without reasonable excuse fails to comply he is liable for any loss caused to the debtor thereby; and if the debtor has properly included in his request a good faith statement of the obligation or a list of the collateral or both the secured party may claim a security interest only as shown in the statement against persons misled by his failure to comply. If he no longer has an interest in the obligation or collateral at the time the request is received he must disclose the name and address of any successor in interest known to him and he is liable for any loss caused to the debtor as a result of failure to disclose. A successor in interest is not subject to this section until a request is received by him.

(3) A debtor is entitled to such a statement once every six months without charge. The secured party may require payment of a charge not exceeding $10 for each additional statement furnished.

Part 3 Rights of Third Parties; Perfected and Unperfected Security Interests; Rules of Priority

§ 9—301. **Persons Who Take Priority Over Unperfected Security Interests; Rights of "Lien Creditor".**

(1) Except as otherwise provided in subsection (2), an unperfected security interest is subordinate to the rights of

(a) persons entitled to priority under Section 9—312;

(b) a person who becomes a lien creditor before the security interest is perfected;

(c) in the case of goods, instruments, documents, and chattel paper, a person who is not a secured party and who is a transferee in bulk or other buyer not in ordinary course of business or is a buyer of farm products in ordinary course of business, to the extent that he gives value and receives delivery of the collateral without knowledge of the security interest and before it is perfected;

(d) in the case of accounts, general intangibles, and investment property a person who is not a secured party and who is a transferee to the extent that he gives value without knowledge of the security interest and before it is perfected.

(2) If the secured party files with respect to a purchase money security interest before or within ten days after the debtor receives possession of the collateral, he takes priority over the rights of a transferee in bulk or of a lien creditor which arise between the time the security interest attaches and the time of filing.

(3) A "lien creditor" means a creditor who has acquired a lien on the property involved by attachment, levy or the like and includes an assignee for benefit of creditors from the time of assignment, and a trustee in bankruptcy from the date of the filing of the petition or a receiver in equity from the time of appointment.

(4) A person who becomes a lien creditor while a security interest is perfected takes subject to the security interest only to the extent that it secures advances made before he becomes a lien creditor or within 45 days thereafter or made without knowledge of the lien or pursuant to a commitment entered into without knowledge of the lien.

§ 9—302. **When Filing Is Required to Perfect Security Interest; Security Interests to Which Filing Provisions of This Article Do Not Apply.**

(1) A financing statement must be filed to perfect all security interests except the following:

(a) a security interest in collateral in possession of the secured party under Section 9—305;

(b) a security interest temporarily perfected in instruments, certificated securities, or documents without delivery under Section 9—304 or in proceeds for a 10 day period under Section 9—306;

(c) a security interest created by an assignment of a beneficial interest in a trust or a decedent's estate;

(d) a purchase money security interest in consumer goods; but filing is required for a motor vehicle required to be registered; and fixture filing is required for priority over conflicting interests in fixtures to the extent provided in Section 9—313;

(e) an assignment of accounts which does not alone or in conjunction with other assignments to the same assignee transfer a significant part of the outstanding accounts of the assignor;

(f) a security interest of a collecting bank (Section 4—210) or arising under the Articles on Sales and Leases (see Section 9—113) or covered in subsection (3) of this section;

(g) an assignment for the benefit of all the creditors of the transferor, and subsequent transfers by the assignee thereunder.

(h) a security interest in investment property which is perfected without filing under Section 9—115 or Section 9—116.

(2) If a secured party assigns a perfected security interest, no filing under this Article is required in order to continue the perfected status of the security interest against creditors of and transferees from the original debtor.

(3) The filing of a financing statement otherwise required by this Article is not necessary or effective to perfect a security interest in property subject to

(a) a statute or treaty of the United States which provides for a national or international registration or a national or international certificate of title or which specifies a place of filing different from that specified in this Article for filing of the security interest; or

(b) the following statutes of this state; [list any certificate of title statute covering automobiles, trailers, mobile homes, boats, farm tractors, or the like, and any central filing statute.]; but during any period in which collateral is inventory held for sale by a person who is in the business of selling goods of that kind, the filing provisions of this Article (Part 4) apply to a security interest in that collateral created by him as debtor; or

(c) a certificate of title statute of another jurisdiction under the law of which indication of a security interest on the certificate is required as a condition of perfection (subsection (2) of Section 9—103).

(4) Compliance with a statute or treaty described in subsection (3) is equivalent to the filing of a financing statement under this Article, and a security interest in property subject to the statute or treaty can be perfected only by compliance therewith except as provided in Section 9—103 on multiple state transactions. Duration and renewal of perfection of a security interest perfected by compliance with the statute or treaty are governed by the provisions of

the statute or treaty; in other respects the security interest is subject to this Article.

§ 9—303. When Security Interest Is Perfected; Continuity of Perfection.

(1) A security interest is perfected when it has attached and when all of the applicable steps required for perfection have been taken. Such steps are specified in Sections 9—115, 9—302, 9—304, 9—305 and 9—306. If such steps are taken before the security interest attaches, it is perfected at the time when it attaches.

(2) If a security interest is originally perfected in any way permitted under this Article and is subsequently perfected in some other way under this Article, without an intermediate period when it was unperfected, the security interest shall be deemed to be perfected continuously for the purposes of this Article.

§ 9—304. Perfection of Security Interest in Instruments, Documents, Proceeds of a Written Letter of Credit, and Goods Covered by Documents; Perfection by Permissive Filing; Temporary Perfection Without Filing or Transfer of Possession.

(1) A security interest in chattel paper or negotiable documents may be perfected by filing. A security interest in the rights to proceeds of a written letter of credit can be perfected only by the secured party's taking possession of the letter of credit. A security interest in money or instruments (other than instruments which constitute part of chattel paper) can be perfected only by the secured party's taking possession, except as provided in subsections (4) and (5) of this section and subsections (2) and (3) of Section 9—306 on proceeds.

(2) During the period that goods are in the possession of the issuer of a negotiable document therefor, a security interest in the goods is perfected by perfecting a security interest in the document, and any security interest in the goods otherwise perfected during such period is subject thereto.

(3) A security interest in goods in the possession of a bailee other than one who has issued a negotiable document therefor is perfected by issuance of a document in the name of the secured party or by the bailee's receipt of notification of the secured party's interest or by filing as to the goods.

(4) A security interest in instruments, certificated securities, or negotiable documents is perfected without filing or the taking of possession for a period of 21 days from the time it attaches to the extent that it arises for new value given under a written security agreement.

(5) A security interest remains perfected for a period of 21 days without filing where a secured party having a perfected security interest in an instrument, a certificated security, a negotiable document or goods in possession of a bailee other than one who has issued a negotiable document therefor

(a) makes available to the debtor the goods or documents representing the goods for the purpose of ultimate sale or exchange or for the purpose of loading, unloading, storing, shipping, transshipping, manufacturing, processing or otherwise dealing with them in a manner preliminary to their sale or exchange, but priority between conflicting security interests in the goods is subject to subsection (3) of Section 9—312; or

(b) delivers the instrument or certificated security to the debtor for the purpose of ultimate sale or exchange or of presentation, collection, renewal or registration of transfer.

(6) After the 21 day period in subsections (4) and (5) perfection depends upon compliance with applicable provisions of this Article.

§ 9—305. When Possession by Secured Party Perfects Security Interest Without Filing.

A security interest in goods, instruments, money, negotiable documents, or chattel paper may be perfected by the secured party's taking possession of the collateral. A security interest in the right to proceeds of a written letter of credit may be perfected by the secured party's taking possession of the letter of credit. If such collateral other than goods covered by a negotiable document is held by a bailee, the secured party is deemed to have possession from the time the bailee receives notification of the secured party's interest. A security interest is perfected by possession from the time possession is taken without a relation back and continues only so long as possession is retained, unless otherwise specified in this Article. The security interest may be otherwise perfected as provided in this Article before or after the period of possession by the secured party.

§ 9—306. "Proceeds"; Secured Party's Rights on Disposition of Collateral.

(1) "Proceeds" includes whatever is received upon the sale, exchange, collection or other disposition of collateral or proceeds. Insurance payable by reason of loss or damage to the collateral is proceeds, except to the extent that it is payable to a person other than a party to the security agreement. Any payments or distributions made with respect to investment property collateral are proceeds. Money, checks, deposit accounts, and the like are "cash proceeds". All other proceeds are "noncash proceeds".

(2) Except where this Article otherwise provides, a security interest continues in collateral notwithstanding sale, exchange or other disposition thereof unless the disposition was authorized by the secured party in the security agreement or otherwise, and also continues in any identifiable proceeds including collections received by the debtor.

(3) The security interest in proceeds is a continuously perfected security interest if the interest in the original collateral was perfected but it ceases to be a perfected security

interest and becomes unperfected ten days after receipt of the proceeds by the debtor unless

(a) a filed financing statement covers the original collateral and the proceeds are collateral in which a security interest may be perfected by filing in the office or offices where the financing statement has been filed and, if the proceeds are acquired with cash proceeds, the description of collateral in the financing statement indicates the types of property constituting the proceeds; or

(b) a filed financing statement covers the original collateral and the proceeds are identifiable cash proceeds; or

(c) the original collateral was investment property and the proceeds are identifiable cash proceeds; or

(d) the security interest in the proceeds is perfected before the expiration of the ten day period.

Except as provided in this section, a security interest in proceeds can be perfected only by the methods or under the circumstances permitted in this Article for original collateral of the same type.

(4) In the event of insolvency proceedings instituted by or against a debtor, a secured party with a perfected security interest in proceeds has a perfected security interest only in the following proceeds:

(a) in identifiable noncash proceeds and in separate deposit accounts containing only proceeds;

(b) in identifiable cash proceeds in the form of money which is neither commingled with other money nor deposited in a deposit account prior to the insolvency proceedings;

(c) in identifiable cash proceeds in the form of checks and the like which are not deposited in a deposit account prior to the insolvency proceedings; and

(d) in all cash and deposit accounts of the debtor in which proceeds have been commingled with other funds, but the perfected security interest under this paragraph (d) is

(i) subject to any right to set-off; and

(ii) limited to an amount not greater than the amount of any cash proceeds received by the debtor within ten days before the institution of the insolvency proceedings less the sum of (I) the payments to the secured party on account of cash proceeds received by the debtor during such period and (II) the cash proceeds received by the debtor during such period to which the secured party is entitled under paragraphs (a) through (c) of this subsection (4).

(5) If a sale of goods results in an account or chattel paper which is transferred by the seller to a secured party, and if the goods are returned to or are repossessed by the seller or the secured party, the following rules determine priorities:

(a) If the goods were collateral at the time of sale, for an indebtedness of the seller which is still unpaid, the original security interest attaches again to the goods and continues as a perfected security interest if it was perfected at the time when the goods were sold. If the security interest was originally perfected by a filing which is still effective, nothing further is required to continue the perfected status; in any other case, the secured party must take possession of the returned or repossessed goods or must file.

(b) An unpaid transferee of the chattel paper has a security interest in the goods against the transferor. Such security interest is prior to a security interest asserted under paragraph (a) to the extent that the transferee of the chattel paper was entitled to priority under Section 9—308.

(c) An unpaid transferee of the account has a security interest in the goods against the transferor. Such security interest is subordinate to a security interest asserted under paragraph (a).

(d) A security interest of an unpaid transferee asserted under paragraph (b) or (c) must be perfected for protection against creditors of the transferor and purchasers of the returned or repossessed goods.

§ 9—307. **Protection of Buyers of Goods.**

(1) A buyer in ordinary course of business (subsection (9) of Section 1—201) other than a person buying farm products from a person engaged in farming operations takes free of a security interest created by his seller even though the security interest is perfected and even though the buyer knows of its existence [subject to the Food Security Act of 1985 (7 U.S.C. Section 1631)].

(2) In the case of consumer goods, a buyer takes free of a security interest even though perfected if he buys without knowledge of the security interest, for value and for his own personal, family or household purposes unless prior to the purchase the secured party has filed a financing statement covering such goods.

(3) A buyer other than a buyer in ordinary course of business (subsection (1) of this section) takes free of a security interest to the extent that it secures future advances made after the secured party acquires knowledge of the purchase, or more than 45 days after the purchase, whichever first occurs, unless made pursuant to a commitment entered into without knowledge of the purchase and before the expiration of the 45 day period.

§ 9—308. **Purchase of Chattel Paper and Instruments.**

A purchaser of chattel paper or an instrument who gives new value and takes possession of it in the ordinary course of his business has priority over a security interest in the chattel paper or instrument

(a) which is perfected under Section 9—304 (permissive filing and temporary perfection) or under Section 9—306 (perfection as to proceeds) if he acts without knowledge that the specific paper or instrument is subject to a security interest; or

(b) which is claimed merely as proceeds of inventory subject to a security interest (Section 9—306) even though he knows that the specific paper or instrument is subject to the security interest.

§ 9—309. Protection of Purchasers of Instruments, Documents and Securities.

Nothing in this Article limits the rights of a holder in due course of a negotiable instrument (Section 3—302) or a holder to whom a negotiable document of title has been duly negotiated (Section 7—501) or a bona fide purchaser of a security (Section 8—302) and the holders or purchasers take priority over an earlier security interest even though perfected. Filing under this Article does not constitute notice of the security interest to such holders or purchasers.

§ 9—310. Priority of Certain Liens Arising by Operation of Law.

When a person in the ordinary course of his business furnishes services or materials with respect to goods subject to a security interest, a lien upon goods in the possession of such person given by statute or rule of law for such materials or services takes priority over a perfected security interest unless the lien is statutory and the statute expressly provides otherwise.

§ 9—311. Alienability of Debtor's Rights: Judicial Process.

The debtor's rights in collateral may be voluntarily or involuntarily transferred (by way of sale, creation of a security interest, attachment, levy, garnishment or other judicial process) notwithstanding a provision in the security agreement prohibiting any transfer or making the transfer constitute a default.

§ 9—312. Priorities Among Conflicting Security Interests in the Same Collateral.

(1) The rules of priority stated in other sections of this Part and in the following sections shall govern when applicable: Section 4—208 with respect to the security interests of collecting banks in items being collected, accompanying documents and proceeds; Section 9—103 on security interests related to other jurisdictions; Section 9—114 on consignments.

(2) A perfected security interest in crops for new value given to enable the debtor to produce the crops during the production season and given not more than three months before the crops become growing crops by planting or otherwise takes priority over an earlier perfected security interest to the extent that such earlier interest secures obligations due more than six months before the crops become growing crops by planting or otherwise, even though the person giving new value had knowledge of the earlier security interest.

(3) A perfected purchase money security interest in inventory has priority over a conflicting security interest in the same inventory and also has priority in identifiable cash proceeds received on or before the delivery of the inventory to a buyer if

(a) the purchase money security interest is perfected at the time the debtor receives possession of the inventory; and

(b) the purchase money secured party gives notification in writing to the holder of the conflicting security interest if the holder had filed a financing statement covering the same types of inventory (i) before the date of the filing made by the purchase money secured party, or (ii) before the beginning of the 21 day period where the purchase money security interest is temporarily perfected without filing or possession (subsection (5) of Section 9—304); and

(c) the holder of the conflicting security interest receives the notification within five years before the debtor receives possession of the inventory; and

(d) the notification states that the person giving the notice has or expects to acquire a purchase money security interest in inventory of the debtor, describing such inventory by item or type.

(4) A purchase money security interest in collateral other than inventory has priority over a conflicting security interest in the same collateral or its proceeds if the purchase money security interest is perfected at the time the debtor receives possession of the collateral or within ten days thereafter.

(5) In all cases not governed by other rules stated in this section (including cases of purchase money security interests which do not qualify for the special priorities set forth in subsections (3) and (4) of this section), priority between conflicting security interests in the same collateral shall be determined according to the following rules:

(a) Conflicting security interests rank according to priority in time of filing or perfection. Priority dates from the time a filing is first made covering the collateral or the time the security interest is first perfected, whichever is earlier, provided that there is no period thereafter when there is neither filing nor perfection.

(b) So long as conflicting security interests are unperfected, the first to attach has priority.

(6) For the purposes of subsection (5) a date of filing or perfection as to collateral is also a date of filing or perfection as to proceeds.

(7) If future advances are made while a security interest is perfected by filing, the taking of possession, or under Section 8—321 on securities, the security interest has the same priority for the purposes of subsection (5) with respect to the future advances as it does with respect to the first advance. If a commitment is made before or while the security interest is so perfected, the security interest has the same priority with respect to advances made pursuant

thereto. In other cases a perfected security interest has priority from the date the advance is made.

§ 9—313. **Priority of Security Interests in Fixtures.**

(1) In this section and in the provisions of Part 4 of this Article referring to fixture filing, unless the context otherwise requires

(a) goods are "fixtures" when they become so related to particular real estate that an interest in them arises under real estate law

(b) a "fixture filing" is the filing in the office where a mortgage on the real estate would be filed or recorded of a financing statement covering goods which are or are to become fixtures and conforming to the requirements of subsection (5) of Section 9—402

(c) a mortgage is a "construction mortgage" to the extent that it secures an obligation incurred for the construction of an improvement on land including the acquisition cost of the land, if the recorded writing so indicates.

(2) A security interest under this Article may be created in goods which are fixtures or may continue in goods which become fixtures, but no security interest exists under this Article in ordinary building materials incorporated into an improvement on land.

(3) This Article does not prevent creation of an encumbrance upon fixtures pursuant to real estate law.

(4) A perfected security interest in fixtures has priority over the conflicting interest of an encumbrancer or owner of the real estate where

(a) the security interest is a purchase money security interest, the interest of the encumbrancer or owner arises before the goods become fixtures, the security interest is perfected by a fixture filing before the goods become fixtures or within ten days thereafter, and the debtor has an interest of record in the real estate or is in possession of the real estate; or

(b) the security interest is perfected by a fixture filing before the interest of the encumbrancer or owner is of record, the security interest has priority over any conflicting interest of a predecessor in title of the encumbrancer or owner, and the debtor has an interest of record in the real estate or is in possession of the real estate; or

(c) the fixtures are readily removable factory or office machines or readily removable replacements of domestic appliances which are consumer goods, and before the goods become fixtures the security interest is perfected by any method permitted by this Article; or

(d) the conflicting interest is a lien on the real estate obtained by legal or equitable proceedings after the security interest was perfected by any method permitted by this Article.

(5) A security interest in fixtures, whether or not perfected, has priority over the conflicting interest of an encumbrancer or owner of the real estate where

(a) the encumbrancer or owner has consented in writing to the security interest or has disclaimed an interest in the goods as fixtures; or

(b) the debtor has a right to remove the goods as against the encumbrancer or owner. If the debtor's right terminates, the priority of the security interest continues for a reasonable time.

(6) Notwithstanding paragraph (a) of subsection (4) but otherwise subject to subsections (4) and (5), a security interest in fixtures is subordinate to a construction mortgage recorded before the goods become fixtures if the goods become fixtures before the completion of the construction. To the extent that it is given to refinance a construction mortgage, a mortgage has this priority to the same extent as the construction mortgage.

(7) In cases not within the preceding subsections, a security interest in fixtures is subordinate to the conflicting interest of an encumbrancer or owner of the related real estate who is not the debtor.

(8) When the secured party has priority over all owners and encumbrancers of the real estate, he may, on default, subject to the provisions of Part 5, remove his collateral from the real estate but he must reimburse any encumbrancer or owner of the real estate who is not the debtor and who has not otherwise agreed for the cost of repair of any physical injury, but not for any diminution in value of the real estate caused by the absence of the goods removed or by any necessity of replacing them. A person entitled to reimbursement may refuse permission to remove until the secured party gives adequate security for the performance of this obligation.

§ 9—314. **Accessions.**

(1) A security interest in goods which attaches before they are installed in or affixed to other goods takes priority as to the goods installed or affixed (called in this section "accessions") over the claims of all persons to the whole except as stated in subsection (3) and subject to Section 9—315(1).

(2) A security interest which attaches to goods after they become part of a whole is valid against all persons subsequently acquiring interests in the whole except as stated in subsection (3) but is invalid against any person with an interest in the whole at the time the security interest attaches to the goods who has not in writing consented to the security interest or disclaimed an interest in the goods as part of the whole.

(3) The security interests described in subsections (1) and (2) do not take priority over

(a) a subsequent purchaser for value of any interest in the whole; or

(b) a creditor with a lien on the whole subsequently obtained by judicial proceedings; or

(c) a creditor with a prior perfected security interest in the whole to the extent that he makes subsequent advances

if the subsequent purchase is made, the lien by judicial proceedings obtained or the subsequent advance under the prior perfected security interest is made or contracted for without knowledge of the security interest and before it is perfected. A purchaser of the whole at a foreclosure sale other than the holder of a perfected security interest purchasing at his own foreclosure sale is a subsequent purchaser within this section.

(4) When under subsections (1) or (2) and (3) a secured party has an interest in accessions which has priority over the claims of all persons who have interests in the whole, he may on default subject to the provisions of Part 5 remove his collateral from the whole but he must reimburse any encumbrancer or owner of the whole who is not the debtor and who has not otherwise agreed for the cost of repair of any physical injury but not for any diminution in value of the whole caused by the absence of the goods removed or by any necessity for replacing them. A person entitled to reimbursement may refuse permission to remove until the secured party gives adequate security for the performance of this obligation.

§ 9—315. Priority When Goods Are Commingled or Processed.

(1) If a security interest in goods was perfected and subsequently the goods or a part thereof have become part of a product or mass, the security interest continues in the product or mass if

(a) the goods are so manufactured, processed, assembled or commingled that their identity is lost in the product or mass; or

(b) a financing statement covering the original goods also covers the product into which the goods have been manufactured, processed or assembled.

In a case to which paragraph (b) applies, no separate security interest in that part of the original goods which has been manufactured, processed or assembled into the product may be claimed under Section 9—314.

(2) When under subsection (1) more than one security interest attaches to the product or mass, they rank equally according to the ratio that the cost of the goods to which each interest originally attached bears to the cost of the total product or mass.

§ 9—316. Priority Subject to Subordination.

Nothing in this Article prevents subordination by agreement by any person entitled to priority.

§ 9—317. Secured Party Not Obligated on Contract of Debtor.

The mere existence of a security interest or authority given to the debtor to dispose of or use collateral does not impose contract or tort liability upon the secured party for the debtor's acts or omissions.

§ 9—318. Defenses Against Assignee; Modification of Contract After Notification of Assignment; Term Prohibiting Assignment Ineffective; Identification and Proof of Assignment.

(1) Unless an account debtor has made an enforceable agreement not to assert defenses or claims arising out of a sale as provided in Section 9—206 the rights of an assignee are subject to

(a) all the terms of the contract between the account debtor and assignor and any defense or claim arising therefrom; and

(b) any other defense or claim of the account debtor against the assignor which accrues before the account debtor receives notification of the assignment.

(2) So far as the right to payment or a part thereof under an assigned contract has not been fully earned by performance, and notwithstanding notification of the assignment, any modification of or substitution for the contract made in good faith and in accordance with reasonable commercial standards is effective against an assignee unless the account debtor has otherwise agreed but the assignee acquires corresponding rights under the modified or substituted contract. The assignment may provide that such modification or substitution is a breach by the assignor.

(3) The account debtor is authorized to pay the assignor until the account debtor receives notification that the amount due or to become due has been assigned and that payment is to be made to the assignee. A notification which does not reasonably identify the rights assigned is ineffective. If requested by the account debtor, the assignee must seasonably furnish reasonable proof that the assignment has been made and unless he does so the account debtor may pay the assignor.

(4) A term in any contract between an account debtor and an assignor is ineffective if it prohibits assignment of an account or prohibits creation of a security interest in a general intangible for money due or to become due or requires the account debtor's consent to such assignment or security interest.

Part 4 Filing

§ 9—401. Place of Filing; Erroneous Filing; Removal of Collateral.

First Alternative Subsection (1)

(1) The proper place to file in order to perfect a security interest is as follows:

(a) when the collateral is timber to be cut or is minerals or the like (including oil and gas) or accounts subject to subsection (5) of Section 9—103, or when the financing statement is filed as a fixture filing (Section 9—313) and the collateral is goods which are or are to become fixtures, then in the office where a mortgage on the real estate would be filed or recorded;

(b) in all other cases, in the office of the [Secretary of State].

Second Alternative Subsection (1)

(1) The proper place to file in order to perfect a security interest is as follows:

(a) when the collateral is equipment used in farming operations, or farm products, or accounts or general intangibles arising from or relating to the sale of farm products by a farmer, or consumer goods, then in the office of the . . . . in the county of the debtor's residence or if the debtor is not a resident of this state then in the office of the . . . . in the county where the goods are kept, and in addition when the collateral is crops growing or to be grown in the office of the . . . . in the county where the land is located;

(b) when the collateral is timber to be cut or is minerals or the like (including oil and gas) or accounts subject to subsection (5) of Section 9—103, or when the financing statement is filed as a fixture filing (Section 9—313) and the collateral is goods which are or are to become fixtures, then in the office where a mortgage on the real estate would be filed or recorded;

(c) in all other cases, in the office of the [Secretary of State].

Third Alternative Subsection (1)

(1) The proper place to file in order to perfect a security interest is as follows:

(a) when the collateral is equipment used in farming operations, or farm products, or accounts or general intangibles arising from or relating to the sale of farm products by a farmer, or consumer goods, then in the office of the . . . . in the county of the debtor's residence or if the debtor is not a resident of this state then in the office of the . . . . in the county where the goods are kept, and in addition when the collateral is crops growing or to be grown in the office of the . . . . in the county where the land is located;

(b) when the collateral is timber to be cut or is minerals or the like (including oil and gas) or accounts subject to subsection (5) of Section 9—103, or when the financing statement is filed as a fixture filing (Section 9—313) and the collateral is goods which are or are to become fixtures, then in the office where a mortgage on the real estate would be filed or recorded;

(c) in all other cases, in the office of the [Secretary of State] and in addition, if the debtor has a place of business in only one county of this state, also in the office of . . . . of such county, or, if the debtor has no

place of business in this state, but resides in the state, also in the office of . . . . of the county in which he resides.

Note: *One of the three alternatives should be selected as subsection (1).*

(2) A filing which is made in good faith in an improper place or not in all of the places required by this section is nevertheless effective with regard to any collateral as to which the filing complied with the requirements of this Article and is also effective with regard to collateral covered by the financing statement against any person who has knowledge of the contents of such financing statement.

(3) A filing which is made in the proper place in this state continues effective even though the debtor's residence or place of business or the location of the collateral or its use, whichever controlled the original filing, is thereafter changed.

Alternative Subsection (3)

[(3) A filing which is made in the proper county continues effective for four months after a change to another county of the debtor's residence or place of business or the location of the collateral, whichever controlled the original filing. It becomes ineffective thereafter unless a copy of the financing statement signed by the secured party is filed in the new county within said period. The security interest may also be perfected in the new county after the expiration of the four-month period; in such case perfection dates from the time of perfection in the new county. A change in the use of the collateral does not impair the effectiveness of the original filing.]

(4) The rules stated in Section 9—103 determine whether filing is necessary in this state.

(5) Notwithstanding the preceding subsections, and subject to subsection (3) of Section 9—302, the proper place to file in order to perfect a security interest in collateral, including fixtures, of a transmitting utility is the office of the [Secretary of State]. This filing constitutes a fixture filing (Section 9—313) as to the collateral described therein which is or is to become fixtures.

(6) For the purposes of this section, the residence of an organization is its place of business if it has one or its chief executive office if it has more than one place of business.

Note: *Subsection (6) should be used only if the state chooses the Second or Third Alternative Subsection (1).*

§ 9—402. Formal Requisites of Financing Statement; Amendments; Mortgage as Financing Statement.

(1) A financing statement is sufficient if it gives the names of the debtor and the secured party, is signed by the debtor, gives an address of the secured party from which information concerning the security interest may be obtained, gives a mailing address of the debtor and contains a statement indicating the types, or describing the items, of collateral. A financing statement may be filed before a

security agreement is made or a security interest otherwise attaches. When the financing statement covers crops growing or to be grown, the statement must also contain a description of the real estate concerned. When the financing statement covers timber to be cut or covers minerals or the like (including oil and gas) or accounts subject to subsection (5) of Section 9—103, or when the financing statement is filed as a fixture filing (Section 9—313) and the collateral is goods which are or are to become fixtures, the statement must also comply with subsection (5). A copy of the security agreement is sufficient as a financing statement if it contains the above information and is signed by the debtor. A carbon, photographic or other reproduction of a security agreement or a financing statement is sufficient as a financing statement if the security agreement so provides or if the original has been filed in this state.

(2) A financing statement which otherwise complies with subsection (1) is sufficient when it is signed by the secured party instead of the debtor if it is filed to perfect a security interest in

(a) collateral already subject to a security interest in another jurisdiction when it is brought into this state, or when the debtor's location is changed to this state. Such a financing statement must state that the collateral was brought into this state or that the debtor's location was changed to this state under such circumstances; or

(b) proceeds under Section 9—306 if the security interest in the original collateral was perfected. Such a financing statement must describe the original collateral; or

(c) collateral as to which the filing has lapsed; or

(d) collateral acquired after a change of name, identity or corporate structure of the debtor (subsection (7)).

(3) A form substantially as follows is sufficient to comply with subsection (1):

Name of debtor (or assignor) . . . .
Address . . . .
Name of secured party (or assignee) . . . .
Address . . . .
1. This financing statement covers the following types (or items) of property:
    (Describe) . . . .
    . . . .
2. (If collateral is crops) The above described crops are growing or are to be grown on:
    (Describe Real Estate) . . . .
3. (If applicable) The above goods are to become fixtures on *
*Where appropriate substitute either "The above timber is standing on . . . ." or "The above minerals or the like (including oil and gas) or accounts will be financed at the wellhead or minehead of the well or mine located on . . . ."
    (Describe Real Estate) . . . .

and this financing statement is to be filed [for record] in the real estate records. (If the debtor does not have an interest of record) The name of a record owner is

. . . .

4. (If products of collateral are claimed) Products of the collateral are also covered.

(use
whichever

. . . .
Signature of Debtor (or Assignor)

is
applicable)

. . . .
Signature of Secured Party
(or Assignee)

(4) A financing statement may be amended by filing a writing signed by both the debtor and the secured party. An amendment does not extend the period of effectiveness of a financing statement. If any amendment adds collateral, it is effective as to the added collateral only from the filing date of the amendment. In this Article, unless the context otherwise requires, the term "financing statement" means the original financing statement and any amendments.

(5) A financing statement covering timber to be cut or covering minerals or the like (including oil and gas) or accounts subject to subsection (5) of Section 9—103, or a financing statement filed as a fixture filing (Section 9—313) where the debtor is not a transmitting utility, must show that it covers this type of collateral, must recite that it is to be filed [for record] in the real estate records, and the financing statement must contain a description of the real estate [sufficient if it were contained in a mortgage of the real estate to give constructive notice of the mortgage under the law of this state]. If the debtor does not have an interest of record in the real estate, the financing statement must show the name of a record owner.

(6) A mortgage is effective as a financing statement filed as a fixture filing from the date of its recording if

(a) the goods are described in the mortgage by item or type; and

(b) the goods are or are to become fixtures related to the real estate described in the mortgage; and

(c) the mortgage complies with the requirements for a financing statement in this section other than a recital that it is to be filed in the real estate records; and

(d) the mortgage is duly recorded.

No fee with reference to the financing statement is required other than the regular recording and satisfaction fees with respect to the mortgage.

(7) A financing statement sufficiently shows the name of the debtor if it gives the individual, partnership or corporate name of the debtor, whether or not it adds other trade names or names of partners. Where the debtor so changes his name or in the case of an organization its name, identity or corporate structure that a filed financing statement becomes seri-

ously misleading, the filing is not effective to perfect a security interest in collateral acquired by the debtor more than four months after the change, unless a new appropriate financing statement is filed before the expiration of that time. A filed financing statement remains effective with respect to collateral transferred by the debtor even though the secured party knows of or consents to the transfer.

(8) A financing statement substantially complying with the requirements of this section is effective even though it contains minor errors which are not seriously misleading.

Note: *Language in brackets is optional.*

Note: *Where the state has any special recording system for real estate other than the usual grantor-grantee index (as, for instance, a tract system or a title registration or Torrens system) local adaptations of subsection (5) and Section 9—403(7) may be necessary. See Mass.Gen.Laws Chapter 106, Section 9—409.*

§ 9—403. What Constitutes Filing; Duration of Filing; Effect of Lapsed Filing; Duties of Filing Officer.

(1) Presentation for filing of a financing statement and tender of the filing fee or acceptance of the statement by the filing officer constitutes filing under this Article.

(2) Except as provided in subsection (6) a filed financing statement is effective for a period of five years from the date of filing. The effectiveness of a filed financing statement lapses on the expiration of the five year period unless a continuation statement is filed prior to the lapse. If a security interest perfected by filing exists at the time insolvency proceedings are commenced by or against the debtor, the security interest remains perfected until termination of the insolvency proceedings and thereafter for a period of sixty days or until expiration of the five year period, whichever occurs later. Upon lapse the security interest becomes unperfected, unless it is perfected without filing. If the security interest becomes unperfected upon lapse, it is deemed to have been unperfected as against a person who became a purchaser or lien creditor before lapse.

(3) A continuation statement may be filed by the secured party within six months prior to the expiration of the five year period specified in subsection (2). Any such continuation statement must be signed by the secured party, identify the original statement by file number and state that the original statement is still effective. A continuation statement signed by a person other than the secured party of record must be accompanied by a separate written statement of assignment signed by the secured party of record and complying with subsection (2) of Section 9—405, including payment of the required fee. Upon timely filing of the continuation statement, the effectiveness of the original statement is continued for five years after the last date to which the filing was effective whereupon it lapses in the same manner as provided in subsection (2) unless another continuation statement is filed prior to such lapse. Succeeding continuation statements may be filed in the same manner to continue the effectiveness of the original statement. Unless a statute on disposition of public records pro-

vides otherwise, the filing officer may remove a lapsed statement from the files and destroy it immediately if he has retained a microfilm or other photographic record, or in other cases after one year after the lapse. The filing officer shall so arrange matters by physical annexation of financing statements to continuation statements or other related filings, or by other means, that if he physically destroys the financing statements of a period more than five years past, those which have been continued by a continuation statement or which are still effective under subsection (6) shall be retained.

(4) Except as provided in subsection (7) a filing officer shall mark each statement with a file number and with the date and hour of filing and shall hold the statement or a microfilm or other photographic copy thereof for public inspection. In addition the filing officer shall index the statement according to the name of the debtor and shall note in the index the file number and the address of the debtor given in the statement.

(5) The uniform fee for filing and indexing and for stamping a copy furnished by the secured party to show the date and place of filing for an original financing statement or for a continuation statement shall be $. . . . . if the statement is in the standard form prescribed by the [Secretary of State] and otherwise shall be $. . . . ., plus in each case, if the financing statement is subject to subsection (5) of Section 9—402, $. . . . . . . The uniform fee for each name more than one required to be indexed shall be $. . . . . . . The secured party may at his option show a trade name for any person and an extra uniform indexing fee of $. . . . . . . shall be paid with respect thereto.

(6) If the debtor is a transmitting utility (subsection (5) of Section 9—401) and a filed financing statement so states, it is effective until a termination statement is filed. A real estate mortgage which is effective as a fixture filing under subsection (6) of Section 9—402 remains effective as a fixture filing until the mortgage is released or satisfied of record or its effectiveness otherwise terminates as to the real estate.

(7) When a financing statement covers timber to be cut or covers minerals or the like (including oil and gas) or accounts subject to subsection (5) of Section 9—103, or is filed as a fixture filing, [it shall be filed for record and] the filing officer shall index it under the names of the debtor and any owner of record shown on the financing statement in the same fashion as if they were the mortgagors in a mortgage of the real estate described, and, to the extent that the law of this state provides for indexing of mortgages under the name of the mortgagee, under the name of the secured party as if he were the mortgagee thereunder, or where indexing is by description in the same fashion as if the financing statement were a mortgage of the real estate described.

Note: *In states in which writings will not appear in the real estate records and indices unless actually recorded the bracketed language in subsection (7) should be used.*

§ 9—404. Termination Statement.

(1) If a financing statement covering consumer goods is filed on or after . . . ., then within one month or within ten days following written demand by the debtor after there is no outstanding secured obligation and no commitment to make advances, incur obligations or otherwise give value, the secured party must file with each filing officer with whom the financing statement was filed, a termination statement to the effect that he no longer claims a security interest under the financing statement, which shall be identified by file number. In other cases whenever there is no outstanding secured obligation and no commitment to make advances, incur obligations or otherwise give value, the secured party must on written demand by the debtor send the debtor, for each filing officer with whom the financing statement was filed, a termination statement to the effect that he no longer claims a security interest under the financing statement, which shall be identified by file number. A termination statement signed by a person other than the secured party of record must be accompanied by a separate written statement of assignment signed by the secured party of record complying with subsection (2) of Section 9—405, including payment of the required fee. If the affected secured party fails to file such a termination statement as required by this subsection, or to send such a termination statement within ten days after proper demand therefor, he shall be liable to the debtor for one hundred dollars, and in addition for any loss caused to the debtor by such failure.

(2) On presentation to the filing officer of such a termination statement he must note it in the index. If he has received the termination statement in duplicate, he shall return one copy of the termination statement to the secured party stamped to show the time of receipt thereof. If the filing officer has a microfilm or other photographic record of the financing statement, and of any related continuation statement, statement of assignment and statement of release, he may remove the originals from the files at any time after receipt of the termination statement, or if he has no such record, he may remove them from the files at any time after one year after receipt of the termination statement.

(3) If the termination statement is in the standard form prescribed by the [Secretary of State], the uniform fee for filing and indexing the termination statement shall be $. . . . . . ., and otherwise shall be $. . . . . . ., plus in each case an additional fee of $. . . . . . . for each name more than one against which the termination statement is required to be indexed.

Note: *The date to be inserted should be the effective date of the revised Article 9.*

§ 9—405. Assignment of Security Interest; Duties of Filing Officer; Fees.

(1) A financing statement may disclose an assignment of a security interest in the collateral described in the financing statement by indication in the financing statement of the name and address of the assignee or by an assignment itself or a copy thereof on the face or back of the statement. On presentation to the filing officer of such a financing statement the filing officer shall mark the same as provided in Section 9—403(4). The uniform fee for filing, indexing and furnishing filing data for a financing statement so indicating an assignment shall be $. . . . . . . if the statement is in the standard form prescribed by the [Secretary of State] and otherwise shall be $. . . . . . ., plus in each case an additional fee of $. . . . . . . for each name more than one against which the financing statement is required to be indexed.

(2) A secured party may assign of record all or part of his rights under a financing statement by the filing in the place where the original financing statement was filed of a separate written statement of assignment signed by the secured party of record and setting forth the name of the secured party of record and the debtor, the file number and the date of filing of the financing statement and the name and address of the assignee and containing a description of the collateral assigned. A copy of the assignment is sufficient as a separate statement if it complies with the preceding sentence. On presentation to the filing officer of such a separate statement, the filing officer shall mark such separate statement with the date and hour of the filing. He shall note the assignment on the index of the financing statement, or in the case of a fixture filing, or a filing covering timber to be cut, or covering minerals or the like (including oil and gas) or accounts subject to subsection (5) of Section 9—103, he shall index the assignment under the name of the assignor as grantor and, to the extent that the law of this state provides for indexing the assignment of a mortgage under the name of the assignee, he shall index the assignment of the financing statement under the name of the assignee. The uniform fee for filing, indexing and furnishing filing data about such a separate statement of assignment shall be $. . . . . if the statement is in the standard form prescribed by the [Secretary of State] and otherwise shall be $. . . . ., plus in each case an additional fee of $. . . . . for each name more than one against which the statement of assignment is required to be indexed. Notwithstanding the provisions of this subsection, an assignment of record of a security interest in a fixture contained in a mortgage effective as a fixture filing (subsection (6) of Section 9—402) may be made only by an assignment of the mortgage in the manner provided by the law of this state other than this Act.

(3) After the disclosure or filing of an assignment under this section, the assignee is the secured party of record.

§ 9—406. Release of Collateral; Duties of Filing Officer; Fees.

A secured party of record may by his signed statement release all or a part of any collateral described in a filed financing statement. The statement of release is sufficient if it contains a description of the collateral being released, the name and address of the debtor, the name and address of the secured party, and the file number of the financing statement. A statement of release signed by a person other than the secured party of record must be accompanied by a separate written statement of assignment signed by the secured party of record and complying with subsection (2) of Section 9—405, including payment of the required fee. Upon presentation of such a statement of release to the filing officer he shall mark the statement with the hour and date of filing and shall note the same upon the margin of the index of the filing of the financing statement. The uniform fee for filing and noting such a statement of release shall be $. . . . . . if the statement is in the standard form prescribed by the [Secretary of State] and otherwise shall be $. . . . . ., plus in each case an additional fee of $. . . . . for each name more than one against which the statement of release is required to be indexed.

§ 9—407. Information From Filing Officer.

[(1) If the person filing any financing statement, termination statement, statement of assignment, or statement of release, furnishes the filing officer a copy thereof, the filing officer shall upon request note upon the copy the file number and date and hour of the filing of the original and deliver or send the copy to such person.]

[(2) Upon request of any person, the filing officer shall issue his certificate showing whether there is on file on the date and hour stated therein, any presently effective financing statement naming a particular debtor and any statement of assignment thereof and if there is, giving the date and hour of filing of each such statement and the names and addresses of each secured party therein. The uniform fee for such a certificate shall be $. . . . . . if the request for the certificate is in the standard form prescribed by the [Secretary of State] and otherwise shall be $. . . . . . . Upon request the filing officer shall furnish a copy of any filed financing statement or statement of assignment for a uniform fee of $. . . . . . per page.]

Note: *This section is proposed as an optional provision to require filing officers to furnish certificates. Local law and practices should be consulted with regard to the advisability of adoption.*

§ 9—408. Financing Statements Covering Consigned or Leased Goods.

A consignor or lessor of goods may file a financing statement using the terms "consignor," "consignee," "lessor," "lessee" or the like instead of the terms specified in Section 9—402. The provisions of this Part shall apply as appropriate to such a financing statement but its filing shall not of itself be a factor in determining whether or not the consignment or lease is intended as security (Section 1—201(37)). However, if it is determined for other reasons that the consignment or lease is so intended, a security interest of the consignor or lessor which attaches to the consigned or leased goods is perfected by such filing.

Part 5 Default

§ 9—501. Default; Procedure When Security Agreement Covers Both Real and Personal Property.

(1) When a debtor is in default under a security agreement, a secured party has the rights and remedies provided in this Part and except as limited by subsection (3) those provided in the security agreement. He may reduce his claim to judgment, foreclose or otherwise enforce the security interest by any available judicial procedure. If the collateral is documents the secured party may proceed either as to the documents or as to the goods covered thereby. A secured party in possession has the rights, remedies and duties provided in Section 9—207. The rights and remedies referred to in this subsection are cumulative.

(2) After default, the debtor has the rights and remedies provided in this Part, those provided in the security agreement and those provided in Section 9—207.

(3) To the extent that they give rights to the debtor and impose duties on the secured party, the rules stated in the subsections referred to below may not be waived or varied except as provided with respect to compulsory disposition of collateral (subsection (3) of Section 9—504 and Section 9—505) and with respect to redemption of collateral (Section 9—506) but the parties may by agreement determine the standards by which the fulfillment of these rights and duties is to be measured if such standards are not manifestly unreasonable:

(a) subsection (2) of Section 9—502 and subsection (2) of Section 9—504 insofar as they require accounting for surplus proceeds of collateral;

(b) subsection (3) of Section 9—504 and subsection (1) of Section 9—505 which deal with disposition of collateral;

(c) subsection (2) of Section 9—505 which deals with acceptance of collateral as discharge of obligation;

(d) Section 9—506 which deals with redemption of collateral; and

(e) subsection (1) of Section 9—507 which deals with the secured party's liability for failure to comply with this Part.

(4) If the security agreement covers both real and personal property, the secured party may proceed under this Part as to the personal property or he may proceed as to both the real and the personal property in accordance with his rights and remedies in respect of the real property in which case the provisions of this Part do not apply.

(5) When a secured party has reduced his claim to judgment the lien of any levy which may be made upon his collateral by virtue of any execution based upon the judgment shall relate back to the date of the perfection of the security interest in such collateral. A judicial sale, pursuant to such execution, is a foreclosure of the security interest by judicial procedure within the meaning of this section, and

the secured party may purchase at the sale and thereafter hold the collateral free of any other requirements of this Article.

§ 9—502. Collection Rights of Secured Party.

(1) When so agreed and in any event on default the secured party is entitled to notify an account debtor or the obligor on an instrument to make payment to him whether or not the assignor was theretofore making collections on the collateral, and also to take control of any proceeds to which he is entitled under Section 9—306.

(2) A secured party who by agreement is entitled to charge back uncollected collateral or otherwise to full or limited recourse against the debtor and who undertakes to collect from the account debtors or obligors must proceed in a commercially reasonable manner and may deduct his reasonable expenses of realization from the collections. If the security agreement secures an indebtedness, the secured party must account to the debtor for any surplus, and unless otherwise agreed, the debtor is liable for any deficiency. But, if the underlying transaction was a sale of accounts or chattel paper, the debtor is entitled to any surplus or is liable for any deficiency only if the security agreement so provides.

§ 9—503. Secured Party's Right to Take Possession After Default.

Unless otherwise agreed a secured party has on default the right to take possession of the collateral. In taking possession a secured party may proceed without judicial process if this can be done without breach of the peace or may proceed by action. If the security agreement so provides the secured party may require the debtor to assemble the collateral and make it available to the secured party at a place to be designated by the secured party which is reasonably convenient to both parties. Without removal a secured party may render equipment unusable, and may dispose of collateral on the debtor's premises under Section 9—504.

§ 9—504. Secured Party's Right to Dispose of Collateral After Default; Effect of Disposition.

(1) A secured party after default may sell, lease or otherwise dispose of any or all of the collateral in its then condition or following any commercially reasonable preparation or processing. Any sale of goods is subject to the Article on Sales (Article 2). The proceeds of disposition shall be applied in the order following to

(a) the reasonable expenses of retaking, holding, preparing for sale or lease, selling, leasing and the like and, to the extent provided for in the agreement and not prohibited by law, the reasonable attorneys' fees and legal expenses incurred by the secured party;

(b) the satisfaction of indebtedness secured by the security interest under which the disposition is made;

(c) the satisfaction of indebtedness secured by any

subordinate security interest in the collateral if written notification of demand therefor is received before distribution of the proceeds is completed. If requested by the secured party, the holder of a subordinate security interest must seasonably furnish reasonable proof of his interest, and unless he does so, the secured party need not comply with his demand.

(2) If the security interest secures an indebtedness, the secured party must account to the debtor for any surplus, and, unless otherwise agreed, the debtor is liable for any deficiency. But if the underlying transaction was a sale of accounts or chattel paper, the debtor is entitled to any surplus or is liable for any deficiency only if the security agreement so provides.

(3) Disposition of the collateral may be by public or private proceedings and may be made by way of one or more contracts. Sale or other disposition may be as a unit or in parcels and at any time and place and on any terms but every aspect of the disposition including the method, manner, time, place and terms must be commercially reasonable. Unless collateral is perishable or threatens to decline speedily in value or is of a type customarily sold on a recognized market, reasonable notification of the time and place of any public sale or reasonable notification of the time after which any private sale or other intended disposition is to be made shall be sent by the secured party to the debtor, if he has not signed after default a statement renouncing or modifying his right to notification of sale. In the case of consumer goods no other notification need be sent. In other cases notification shall be sent to any other secured party from whom the secured party has received (before sending his notification to the debtor or before the debtor's renunciation of his rights) written notice of a claim of an interest in the collateral. The secured party may buy at any public sale and if the collateral is of a type customarily sold in a recognized market or is of a type which is the subject of widely distributed standard price quotations he may buy at private sale.

(4) When collateral is disposed of by a secured party after default, the disposition transfers to a purchaser for value all of the debtor's rights therein, discharges the security interest under which it is made and any security interest or lien subordinate thereto. The purchaser takes free of all such rights and interests even though the secured party fails to comply with the requirements of this Part or of any judicial proceedings

(a) in the case of a public sale, if the purchaser has no knowledge of any defects in the sale and if he does not buy in collusion with the secured party, other bidders or the person conducting the sale; or

(b) in any other case, if the purchaser acts in good faith.

(5) A person who is liable to a secured party under a guaranty, indorsement, repurchase agreement or the like and who receives a transfer of collateral from the secured party

or is subrogated to his rights has thereafter the rights and duties of the secured party. Such a transfer of collateral is not a sale or disposition of the collateral under this Article.

§ 9—505. Compulsory Disposition of Collateral; Acceptance of the Collateral as Discharge of Obligation.

(1) If the debtor has paid sixty per cent of the cash price in the case of a purchase money security interest in consumer goods or sixty per cent of the loan in the case of another security interest in consumer goods, and has not signed after default a statement renouncing or modifying his rights under this Part a secured party who has taken possession of collateral must dispose of it under Section 9—504 and if he fails to do so within ninety days after he takes possession the debtor at his option may recover in conversion or under Section 9—507(1) on secured party's liability.

(2) In any other case involving consumer goods or any other collateral a secured party in possession may, after default, propose to retain the collateral in satisfaction of the obligation. Written notice of such proposal shall be sent to the debtor if he has not signed after default a statement renouncing or modifying his rights under this subsection. In the case of consumer goods no other notice need be given. In other cases notice shall be sent to any other secured party from whom the secured party has received (before sending his notice to the debtor or before the debtor's renunciation of his rights) written notice of a claim of an interest in the collateral. If the secured party receives objection in writing from a person entitled to receive notification within twenty-one days after the notice was sent, the secured party must dispose of the collateral under Section 9—504. In the absence of such written objection the secured party may retain the collateral in satisfaction of the debtor's obligation. Amended in 1972.

§ 9—506. Debtor's Right to Redeem Collateral.

At any time before the secured party has disposed of collateral or entered into a contract for its disposition under Section 9—504 or before the obligation has been discharged under Section 9—505(2) the debtor or any other secured party may unless otherwise agreed in writing after default redeem the collateral by tendering fulfillment of all obligations secured by the collateral as well as the expenses reasonably incurred by the secured party in retaking, holding and preparing the collateral for disposition, in arranging for the sale, and to the extent provided in the agreement and not prohibited by law, his reasonable attorneys' fees and legal expenses.

§ 9—507. Secured Party's Liability for Failure to Comply With This Part.

(1) If it is established that the secured party is not proceeding in accordance with the provisions of this Part disposition may be ordered or restrained on appropriate terms and conditions. If the disposition has occurred the debtor or any person entitled to notification or whose security interest has been made known to the secured party prior to the disposition has a right to recover from the secured party any loss caused by a failure to comply with the provisions of this Part. If the collateral is consumer goods, the debtor has a right to recover in any event an amount not less than the credit service charge plus ten per cent of the principal amount of the debt or the time price differential plus 10 per cent of the cash price.

(2) The fact that a better price could have been obtained by a sale at a different time or in a different method from that selected by the secured party is not of itself sufficient to establish that the sale was not made in a commercially reasonable manner. If the secured party either sells the collateral in the usual manner in any recognized market therefor or if he sells at the price current in such market at the time of his sale or if he has otherwise sold in conformity with reasonable commercial practices among dealers in the type of property sold he has sold in a commercially reasonable manner. The principles stated in the two preceding sentences with respect to sales also apply as may be appropriate to other types of disposition. A disposition which has been approved in any judicial proceeding or by any bona fide creditors' committee or representative of creditors shall conclusively be deemed to be commercially reasonable, but this sentence does not indicate that any such approval must be obtained in any case nor does it indicate that any disposition not so approved is not commercially reasonable.

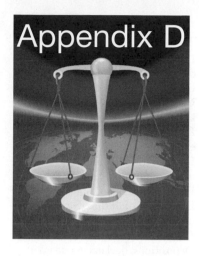

Appendix D

Spanish Equivalents for Important Legal Terms in English

Abandoned property: bienes abandonados

Acceptance: aceptación; consentimiento; acuerdo

Acceptor: aceptante

Accession: toma de posesión; aumento; accesión

Accommodation indorser: avalista de favor

Accommodation party: firmante de favor

Accord: acuerdo; convenio; arregio

Accord and satisfaction: transacción ejecutada

Act of state doctrine: doctrina de acto de gobierno

Administrative law: derecho administrativo

Administrative process: procedimiento o metódo administrativo

Administrator: administrador (-a)

Adverse possession: posesión de hecho susceptible de proscripción adquisitiva

Affirmative action: acción afirmativa

Affirmative defense: defensa afirmativa

After-acquired property: bienes adquiridos con posterioridad a un hecho dado

Agency: mandato; agencia

Agent: mandatorio; agente; representante

Agreement: convenio; acuerdo; contrato

Alien corporation: empresa extranjera

Allonge: hojas adicionales de endosos

Answer: contestación de la demande; alegato

Anticipatory repudiation: anuncio previo de las partes de su imposibilidad de cumplir con el contrato

Appeal: apelación; recurso de apelación

Appellate jurisdiction: jurisdicción de apelaciones

Appraisal right: derecho de valuación

Arbitration: arbitraje

Arson: incendio intencional

Articles of partnership: contrato social

Artisan's lien: derecho de retención que ejerce al artesano

Assault: asalto; ataque; agresión

Assignment of rights: transmisión; transferencia; cesión

Assumption of risk: no resarcimiento por exposición voluntaria al peligro

Attachment: auto judicial que autoriza el embargo; embargo

Bailee: depositario

Bailment: depósito; constitución en depósito

Bailor: depositante

Bankruptcy trustee: síndico de la quiebra

Battery: agresión; física

Bearer: portador; tenedor

Bearer instrument: documento al portador

Bequest or legacy: legado (de bienes muebles)

Bilateral contract: contrato bilateral

Bill of lading: conocimiento de embarque; carta de porte

Bill of Rights: declaración de derechos

Binder: póliza de seguro provisoria; recibo de pago a cuenta del precio

Blank indorsement: endoso en blanco

Blue sky laws: leyes reguladoras del comercio bursátil

Bond: título de crédito; garantía; caución

Bond indenture: contrato de emisión de bonos; contrato del ampréstito

Breach of contract: incumplimiento de contrato

Brief: escrito; resumen; informe

Burglary: violación de domicilio

Business judgment rule: regla de juicio comercial
Business tort: agravio comercial

Case law: ley de casos; derecho casuístico
Cashier's check: cheque de caja
Causation in fact: causalidad en realidad
Cease-and-desist order: orden para cesar y desistir
Certificate of deposit: certificado de depósito
Certified check: cheque certificado
Charitable trust: fideicomiso para fines benéficos
Chattel: bien mueble
Check: cheque
Chose in action: derecho inmaterial; derecho de acción
Civil law: derecho civil
Close corporation: sociedad de un solo accionista o de un grupo restringido de accionistas
Closed shop: taller agremiado (emplea solamente a miembros de un gremio)
Closing argument: argumento al final
Codicil: codicilo
Collateral: guarantía; bien objeto de la guarantía real
Comity: cortesía; cortesía entre naciones
Commercial paper: instrumentos negociables; documentos a valores commerciales
Common law: derecho consuetudinario; derecho común; ley común
Common stock: acción ordinaria
Comparative negligence: negligencia comparada
Compensatory damages: daños y perjuicios reales o compensatorios
Concurrent conditions: condiciones concurrentes
Concurrent jurisdiction: competencia concurrente de varios tribunales para entender en una misma causa
Concurring opinion: opinión concurrente
Condition: condición
Condition precedent: condición suspensiva

Condition subsequent: condición resolutoria
Confiscation: confiscación
Confusion: confusión; fusión
Conglomerate merger: fusión de firmas que operan en distintos mercados
Consent decree: acuerdo entre las partes aprobado por un tribunal
Consequential damages: daños y perjuicios indirectos
Consideration: consideración; motivo; contraprestación
Consolidation: consolidación
Constructive delivery: entrega simbólica
Constructive trust: fideicomiso creado por aplicación de la ley
Consumer protection law: ley para proteger el consumidor
Contract: contrato
Contract under seal: contrato formal o sellado
Contributory negligence: negligencia de la parte actora
Conversion: usurpación; conversión de valores
Copyright: derecho de autor
Corporation: sociedad anómina; corporación; persona jurídica
Co-sureties: cogarantes
Counterclaim: reconvención; contrademanda
Counteroffer: contraoferta
Course of dealing: curso de transacciones
Course of performance: curso de cumplimiento
Covenant: pacto; garantía; contrato
Covenant not to sue: pacto or contrato a no demandar
Covenant of quiet enjoyment: garantía del uso y goce pacífico del inmueble
Creditors' composition agreement: concordato preventivo
Crime: crimen; delito; contravención
Criminal law: derecho penal
Cross-examination: contrainterrogatorio
Cure: cura; cuidado; derecho de remediar un vicio contractual
Customs receipts: recibos de derechos aduaneros

Damages: daños; indemnización por daños y perjuicios
Debit card: tarjeta de dé bito
Debtor: deudor
Debt securities: seguridades de deuda
Deceptive advertising: publicidad engañosa
Deed: escritura; título; acta translativa de domino
Defamation: difamación
Delegation of duties: delegación de obligaciones
Demand deposit: depósito a la vista
Depositions: declaración de un testigo fuera del tribunal
Devise: legado; deposición testamentaria (bienes inmuebles)
Directed verdict: veredicto según orden del juez y sin participación activa del jurado
Direct examination: interrogatorio directo; primer interrogatorio
Disaffirmance: repudiación; renuncia; anulación
Discharge: descargo; liberación; cumplimiento
Disclosed principal: mandante revelado
Discovery: descubrimiento; producción de la prueba
Dissenting opinion: opinión disidente
Dissolution: disolución; terminación
Diversity of citizenship: competencia de los tribunales federales para entender en causas cuyas partes intervinientes son cuidadanos de distintos estados
Divestiture: extinción premature de derechos reales
Dividend: dividendo
Docket: orden del día; lista de causas pendientes
Domestic corporation: sociedad local
Draft: orden de pago; letrade cambio
Drawee: girado; beneficiario
Drawer: librador
Duress: coacción; violencia

Easement: servidumbre
Embezzlement: desfalco; malversación
Eminent domain: poder de expropiación

Employment discrimination: discriminación en el empleo
Entrepreneur: empresario
Environmental law: ley ambiental
Equal dignity rule: regla de dignidad egual
Equity security: tipo de participación en una sociedad
Estate: propiedad; patrimonio; derecho
Estop: impedir; prevenir
Ethical issue: cuestión ética
Exclusive jurisdiction: competencia exclusiva
Exculpatory clause: cláusula eximente
Executed contract: contrato ejecutado
Execution: ejecución; cumplimiento
Executor: albacea
Executory contract: contrato aún no completamente consumado
Executory interest: derecho futuro
Express contract: contrato expreso
Expropriation: expropriación

Federal question: caso federal
Fee simple: pleno dominio; dominio absoluto
Fee simple absolute: dominio absoluto
Fee simple defeasible: dominio sujeta a una condición resolutoria
Felony: crimen; delito grave
Fictitious payee: beneficiario ficticio
Fiduciary: fiduciaro
Firm offer: oferta en firme
Fixture: inmueble por destino, incorporación a anexación
Floating lien: gravamen continuado
Foreign corporation: sociedad extranjera; U.S. sociedad constituída en otro estado
Forgery: falso; falsificación
Formal contract: contrato formal
Franchise: privilegio; franquicia; concesión
Franchisee: persona que recibe una concesión
Franchisor: persona que vende una concesión
Fraud: fraude; dolo; engaño
Future interest: bien futuro

Garnishment: embargo de derechos
General partner: socio comanditario

General warranty deed: escritura translativa de domino con garantía de título
Gift: donación
Gift *causa mortis*: donación por causa de muerte
Gift *inter vivos*: donación entre vivos
Good faith: buena fe
Good faith purchaser: comprador de buena fe

Holder: tenedor por contraprestación
Holder in due course: tenedor legítimo
Holographic will: testamento olográfico
Homestead exemption laws: leyes que exceptúan las casas de familia de ejecución por duedas generales
Horizontal merger: fusión horizontal

Identification: identificación
Implied-in-fact contract: contrato implícito en realidad
Implied warranty: guarantía implícita
Implied warranty of merchantability: garantía implícita de vendibilidad
Impossibility of performance: imposibilidad de cumplir un contrato
Imposter: imposter
Incidental beneficiary: beneficiario incidental; beneficiario secundario
Incidental damages: daños incidentales
Indictment: auto de acusación; acusación
Indorsee: endorsatario
Indorsement: endoso
Indorser: endosante
Informal contract: contrato no formal; contrato verbal
Information: acusación hecha por el ministerio público
Injunction: mandamiento; orden de no innovar
Innkeeper's lien: derecho de retención que ejerce el posadero
Installment contract: contrato de pago en cuotas
Insurable interest: interés asegurable
Intended beneficiary: beneficiario destinado

Intentional tort: agravio; cuasi-delito intencional
International law: derecho internacional
Interrogatories: preguntas escritas sometidas por una parte a la otra o a un testigo
Inter vivos trust: fideicomiso entre vivos
Intestacy laws: leyes de la condición de morir intestado
Intestate: intestado
Investment company: compañia de inversiones
Issue: emisión

Joint tenancy: derechos conjuntos en un bien inmueble en favor del beneficiario sobreviviente
Judgment *n.o.v.*: juicio no obstante veredicto
Judgment rate of interest: interés de juicio
Judicial process: acto de procedimiento; proceso jurídico
Judicial review: revisión judicial
Jurisdiction: jurisdicción

Larceny: robo; hurto
Law: derecho; ley; jurisprudencia
Lease: contrato de locación; contrato de alquiler
Leasehold estate: bienes forales
Legal rate of interest: interés legal
Legatee: legatario
Letter of credit: carta de crédito
Levy: embargo; comiso
Libel: libelo; difamación escrita
Life estate: usufructo
Limited partner: comanditario
Limited partnership: sociedad en comandita
Liquidation: liquidación; realización
Lost property: objetos perdidos

Majority opinion: opinión de la mayoría
Maker: persona que realiza u ordena; librador
Mechanic's lien: gravamen de constructor
Mediation: mediación; intervención
Merger: fusión
Mirror image rule: fallo de reflejo
Misdemeanor: infracción; contravención

Mislaid property: bienes extraviados
Mitigation of damages: reducción de daños
Mortgage: hypoteca
Motion to dismiss: excepción parentoria
Mutual fund: fondo mutual

Negotiable instrument: instrumento negociable
Negotiation: negociación
Nominal damages: daños y perjuicios nominales
Novation: novación
Nuncupative will: testamento nuncupativo

Objective theory of contracts: teoria objetiva de contratos
Offer: oferta
Offeree: persona que recibe una oferta
Offeror: oferente
Order instrument: instrumento o documento a la orden
Original jurisdiction: jurisdicción de primera instancia
Output contract: contrato de producción

Parol evidence rule: regla relativa a la prueba oral
Partially disclosed principal: mandante revelado en parte
Partnership: sociedad colectiva; asociación; asociación de participación
Past consideration: causa o contraprestación anterior
Patent: patente; privilegio
Pattern or practice: muestra o práctica
Payee: beneficiario de un pago
Penalty: pena; penalidad
Per capita: por cabeza
Perfection: perfeción
Performance: cumplimiento; ejecución
Personal defenses: excepciones personales
Personal property: bienes muebles
Per stirpes: por estirpe
Plea bargaining: regateo por un alegato
Pleadings: alegatos
Pledge: prenda

Police powers: poderes de policia y de prevención del crimen
Policy: póliza
Positive law: derecho positivo; ley positiva
Possibility of reverter: posibilidad de reversión
Precedent: precedente
Preemptive right: derecho de prelación
Preferred stock: acciones preferidas
Premium: recompensa; prima
Presentment warranty: garantía de presentación
Price discrimination: discriminación en los precios
Principal: mandante; principal
Privity: nexo jurídico
Privity of contract: relación contractual
Probable cause: causa probable
Probate: verificación; verificación del testamento
Probate court: tribunal de sucesiones y tutelas
Proceeds: resultados; ingresos
Profit: beneficio; utilidad; lucro
Promise: promesa
Promisee: beneficiario de una promesa
Promisor: promtente
Promissory estoppel: impedimento promisorio
Promissory note: pagaré; nota de pago
Promoter: promotor; fundador
Proximate cause: causa inmediata o próxima
Proxy: apoderado; poder
Punitive, or exemplary, damages: daños y perjuicios punitivos o ejemplares

Qualified indorsement: endoso con reservas
Quasi contract: contrato tácito o implícito
Quitclaim deed: acto de transferencia de una propiedad por finiquito, pero sin ninguna garantía sobre la validez del título transferido

Ratification: ratificación
Real property: bienes inmuebles
Reasonable doubt: duda razonable
Rebuttal: refutación

Recognizance: promesa; compromiso; reconocimiento
Recording statutes: leyes estatales sobre registros oficiales
Redress: reporación
Reformation: rectificación; reforma; corrección
Rejoinder: dúplica; contrarréplica
Release: liberación; renuncia a un derecho
Remainder: substitución; reversión
Remedy: recurso; remedio; reparación
Replevin: acción reivindicatoria; reivindicación
Reply: réplica
Requirements contract: contrato de suministro
Rescission: rescisión
Res judicata: cosa juzgada; res judicata
Respondeat superior: responsabilidad del mandante o del maestro
Restitution: restitución
Restrictive indorsement: endoso restrictivo
Resulting trust: fideicomiso implícito
Reversion: reversión; sustitución
Revocation: revocación; derogación
Right of contribution: derecho de contribución
Right of reimbursement: derecho de reembolso
Right of subrogation: derecho de subrogación
Right-to-work law: ley de libertad de trabajo
Robbery: robo
Rule 10b-5: Regla 10b-5

Sale: venta; contrato de compreventa
Sale on approval: venta a ensayo; venta sujeta a la aprobación del comprador
Sale or return: venta con derecho de devolución
Sales contract: contrato de compraventa; boleto de compraventa
Satisfaction: satisfacción; pago
Scienter: a sabiendas
S corporation: S corporación
Secured party: acreedor garantizado
Secured transaction: transacción garantizada
Securities: volares; titulos; seguridades

Security agreement: convenio de seguridad

Security interest: interés en un bien dado en garantía que permite a quien lo detenta venderlo en caso de incumplimiento

Service mark: marca de identificación de servicios

Shareholder's derivative suit: acción judicial entablada por un accionista en nombre de la sociedad

Signature: firma; rúbrica

Slander: difamación oral; calumnia

Sovereign immunity: immunidad soberana

Special indorsement: endoso especial; endoso a la orden de una person en particular

Specific performance: ejecución precisa, según los términos del contrato

Spendthrift trust: fideicomiso para pródigos

Stale check: cheque vencido

Stare decisis: acatar las decisiones, observar los precedentes

Statutory law: derecho estatutario; derecho legislado; derecho escrito

Stock: acciones

Stock warrant: certificado para la compra de acciones

Stop-payment order: orden de suspensión del pago de un cheque dada por el librador del mismo

Strict liability: responsabilidad unconditional

Summary judgment: fallo sumario

Tangible property: bienes corpóreos

Tenancy at will: inguilino por tiempo indeterminado (según la voluntad del propietario)

Tenancy by sufferance: posesión por tolerancia

Tenancy by the entirety: locación conyugal conjunta

Tenancy for years: inguilino por un término fijo

Tenancy in common: specie de copropiedad indivisa

Tender: oferta de pago; oferta de ejecución

Testamentary trust: fideicomiso testamentario

Testator: testador (-a)

Third party beneficiary contract: contrato para el beneficio del tercero-beneficiario

Tort: agravio; cuasi-delito

Totten trust: fideicomiso creado por un depósito bancario

Trade acceptance: letra de cambio aceptada

Trademark: marca registrada

Trade name: nombre comercial; razón social

Traveler's check: cheque del viajero

Trespass to land: ingreso no authorizado a las tierras de otro

Trespass to personal property: violación de los derechos posesorios de un tercero con respecto a bienes muebles

Trust: fideicomiso; trust

Ultra vires: ultra vires; fuera de la facultad (de una sociedad anónima)

Unanimous opinion: opinión unámine

Unconscionable contract or clause: contrato leonino; cláusula leonino

Underwriter: subscriptor; asegurador

Unenforceable contract: contrato que no se puede hacer cumplir

Unilateral contract: contrato unilateral

Union shop: taller agremiado; empresa en la que todos los empleados son miembros del gremio o sindicato

Universal defenses: defensas legitimas o legales

Usage of trade: uso comercial

Usury: usura

Valid contract: contrato válido

Venue: lugar; sede del proceso

Vertical merger: fusión vertical de empresas

Voidable contract: contrato anulable

Void contract: contrato nulo; contrato inválido, sin fuerza legal

Voir dire: examen preliminar de un testigo a jurado por el tribunal para determinar su competencia

Voting trust: fideicomiso para ejercer el derecho de voto

Waiver: renuncia; abandono

Warranty of habitability: garantía de habitabilidad

Watered stock: acciones diluídos; capital inflado

White-collar crime: crimen administrativo

Writ of attachment: mandamiento de ejecución; mandamiento de embargo

Writ of *certiorari*: auto de avocación; auto de certiorari

Writ of execution: auto ejecutivo; mandamiento de ejecutión

Writ of mandamus: auto de mandamus; mandamiento; orden judicial

Glossary

A

Abandoned property Property with which the owner has voluntarily parted, with no intention of recovering it.

Acceleration clause A clause that allows a payee or other holder of a time instrument to demand payment of the entire amount due, with interest, if a certain event occurs, such as a default in the payment of an installment when due.

Acceptance A voluntary act by the offeree that shows assent, or agreement, to the terms of an offer; may consist of words or conduct.

Acceptor A drawee that promises to pay an instrument when the instrument is presented later for payment.

Accession Occurs when an individual adds value to personal property by either labor or materials. In some situations, a person may acquire ownership rights in another's property through accession.

Accommodation party A person who signs an instrument for the purpose of lending his or her name as credit to another party on the instrument.

Accord and satisfaction An agreement for payment (or other performance) between two parties, one of whom has a right of action against the other. After the payment has been accepted or other performance has been made, the "accord and satisfaction" is complete and the obligation is discharged.

Accredited investors In the context of securities offerings, "sophisticated" investors, such as banks, insurance companies, investment companies, the issuer's executive officers and directors, and persons whose income or net worth exceeds certain limits.

Act of state doctrine A doctrine that provides that the judicial branch of one country will not examine the validity of public acts committed by a recognized foreign government within its own territory.

Actionable Capable of serving as the basis of a lawsuit.

Actual malice Real and demonstrable evil intent. In a defamation suit, a statement made about a public figure normally must be made with actual malice (with either knowledge of its falsity or a reckless disregard of the truth) for liability to be incurred.

Adhesion contract A "standard form" contract, such as that between a large retailer and a consumer, in which the stronger party dictates the terms.

Adjudicate To render a judicial decision. In the administrative process, the proceeding in which an administrative law judge hears and decides on issues that arise when an administrative agency charges a person or a firm with violating a law or regulation enforced by the agency.

Administrative agency A federal or state government agency established to perform a specific function. Administrative agencies are authorized by legislative acts to make and enforce rules to administer and enforce the acts.

Administrative law The body of law created by administrative agencies (in the form of rules, regulations, orders, and decisions) in order to carry out their duties and responsibilities.

Administrative law judge (ALJ) One who presides over an administrative agency hearing and who has the power to administer oaths, take testimony, rule on questions of evidence, and make determinations of fact.

Administrative process The procedure used by administrative agencies in the administration of law.

Administrator One who is appointed by a court to handle the probate (disposition) of a person's estate if that person dies intestate (without a valid will) or if the executor named in the will cannot serve.

Adverse possession The acquisition of title to real property by occupying it openly, without the consent of the owner, for a period of time specified by a state statute. The occupation must be actual, open, notorious, exclusive, and in opposition to all others, including the owner.

Affirmative action Job-hiring policies that give special consideration to members of protected classes in an effort to overcome present effects of past discrimination.

After-acquired property Property of the debtor that is acquired after the execution of a security agreement.

Agency A relationship between two parties in which one party (the agent) agrees to represent or act for the other (the principal).

Agent A person who agrees to represent or act for another, called the principal.

Agreement A meeting of two or more minds in regard to the terms of a contract; usually broken down into two events—an offer by one party to form a contract, and an acceptance of the offer by the person to whom the offer is made.

Alien corporation A designation in the United States for a corporation formed in another country but doing business in the United States.

Alienation In real property law, a term used to define the process of transferring land out of one's possession (thus "alienating" the land from oneself).

Alternative dispute resolution (ADR) The resolution of disputes in ways other than those involved in the traditional judicial process. Negotiation, mediation, and arbitration are forms of ADR.

Answer Procedurally, a defendant's response to the plaintiff's complaint.

Anticipatory repudiation An assertion or action by a party indicating that he or she will not perform an obligation that the party is contractually obligated to perform at a future time.

Antitrust laws Laws protecting commerce from unlawful restraints.

Appraisal right The right of a dissenting shareholder, if he or she objects to an extraordinary transaction of the corporation (such as a merger or consolidation), to have his or her shares appraised and to be paid the fair value of his or her shares by the corporation.

Appropriation In tort law, the use by one person of another person's name, likeness, or other identifying characteristic without permission and for the benefit of the user.

Arbitration The settling of a dispute by submitting it to a disinterested third party (other than a court), who renders a decision that is (usually) legally binding.

Arbitration clause A clause in a contract that provides that, in case of a dispute, the parties will submit the dispute to arbitration rather than litigate the dispute in court.

Arson The malicious burning of another's dwelling. Some statutes have expanded this to include any real property regardless of ownership and the destruction of property by other means—for example, by explosion.

Articles of incorporation The document filed with the appropriate governmental agency, usually the secretary of state, when a business is incorporated; state statutes usually prescribe what kind of information must be contained in the articles of incorporation.

Articles of partnership A written agreement that sets forth each partner's rights and obligations with respect to the partnership.

Artisan's lien A possessory lien given to a person who has made improvements and added value to another person's personal property as security for payment for services performed.

Assault Any word or action intended to make another person fearful of immediate physical harm; a reasonably believable threat.

Assignment The act of transferring to another all or part of one's rights arising under a contract.

Assumption of risk A defense against negligence that can be used when the plaintiff is aware of a danger and voluntarily assumes the risk of injury from that danger.

Attachment In the context of secured transactions, the process by which a security interest in the property of another becomes enforceable. In the context of judicial liens, a court-ordered seizure and taking into custody of property prior to the securing of a judgment for a past-due debt.

Automatic stay In bankruptcy proceedings, the suspension of virtually all litigation and other action by creditors against the debtor or the debtor's property; the stay is effective the moment the debtor files a petition in bankruptcy.

Award   In the context of litigation, the amount of money awarded to a plaintiff in a civil lawsuit as damages. In the context of arbitration, the arbitrator's decision.

B

Bailee   One to whom goods are entrusted by a bailor. Under the UCC, a party who, by a bill of lading, warehouse receipt, or other document of title, acknowledges possession of goods and contracts.

Bailment   A situation in which the personal property of one person (a bailor) is entrusted to another (a bailee), who is obligated to return the bailed property to the bailor or dispose of it as directed.

Bailor   One who entrusts goods to a bailee.

Bankruptcy court   A federal court of limited jurisdiction that handles only bankruptcy proceedings. Bankruptcy proceedings are governed by federal bankruptcy law.

Battery   The unprivileged, intentional touching of another.

Bearer   A person in the possession of an instrument payable to bearer or indorsed in blank.

Bearer instrument   Any instrument that is not payable to a specific person, including instruments payable to the bearer or to "cash."

Bequest   A gift by will of personal property (from the verb—to bequeath).

Beyond a reasonable doubt   The standard of proof used in criminal cases. If there is any reasonable doubt that a criminal defendant did not commit the crime with which he or she has been charged, then the verdict must be "not guilty."

Bilateral contract   A type of contract that arises when a promise is given in exchange for a return promise.

Bill of Rights   The first ten amendments to the U.S. Constitution.

Binder   A written, temporary insurance policy.

Binding authority   Any source of law that a court must follow when deciding a case. Binding authorities include constitutions, statutes, and regulations that govern the issue being decided, as well as court decisions that are controlling precedents within the jurisdiction.

Blank indorsement   An indorsement that specifies no particular indorsee and that can consist of a mere signature. An order instrument that is indorsed in blank becomes a bearer instrument.

Blue laws   State or local laws that prohibit the performance of certain types of commercial activities on Sunday.

Blue sky laws   State laws that regulate the offer and sale of securities.

Bona fide occupational qualification (BFOQ)   Identifiable characteristics reasonably necessary to the normal operation of a particular business. These characteristics can include gender, national origin, and religion, but not race.

Bond   A certificate that evidences a corporate (or government) debt. It is a security that involves no ownership interest in the issuing entity.

Bond indenture   A contract between the issuer of a bond and the bondholder.

Bounty payment   A reward (payment) given to a person or persons who perform a certain service—such as informing legal authorities of illegal actions.

Breach of contract   The failure, without legal excuse, of a promisor to perform the obligations of a contract.

Brief   A formal legal document submitted by the attorney for the appellant or the appellee (in answer to the appellant's brief) to an appellate court when a case is appealed. The appellant's brief outlines the facts and issues of the case, the judge's rulings or jury's findings that should be reversed or modified, the applicable law, and the arguments on the client's behalf.

Burglary   The unlawful entry into a building with the intent to commit a felony. (Some state statutes expand this to include the intent to commit any crime.)

Business ethics   Ethics in a business context; a consensus of what constitutes right or wrong behavior in the world of business and the application of moral principles to situations that arise in a business setting.

Business invitees   Those people, such as customers or clients, who are invited onto business premises by the owner of those premises for business purposes.

Business judgment rule   A rule that immunizes corporate management from liability for actions that result in corporate losses or damages if the actions are undertaken in good faith and are within both the power of the corporation and the authority of management to make.

Business necessity   A defense to allegations of employment discrimination in which the employer demonstrates that an employment practice that discriminates against members of a protected class is related to job performance.

Business tort The wrongful interference with another's business rights.

Bylaws A set of governing rules adopted by a corporation or other association.

C

Case law The rules of law announced in court decisions. Case law includes the aggregate of reported cases that interpret judicial precedents, statutes, regulations, and constitutional provisions.

Cashier's check A check drawn by a bank on itself.

Categorical imperative A concept developed by the philosopher Immanuel Kant as an ethical guideline for behavior. In deciding whether an action is right or wrong, or desirable or undesirable, a person should evaluate the action in terms of what would happen if everybody else in the same situation, or category, acted the same way.

Causation in fact An act or omission without which an event would not have occurred.

Cease-and-desist order An administrative or judicial order prohibiting a person or business firm from conducting activities that an agency or court has deemed illegal.

Certificate of deposit (CD) A note of a bank in which a bank acknowledges a receipt of money from a party and promises to repay the money, with interest, to the party on a certain date.

Certificate of incorporation The primary document that evidences corporate existence (referred to as articles of incorporation in some states).

Certificate of limited partnership The basic document filed with a designated state official by which a limited partnership is formed.

Certified check A check that has been accepted by the bank on which it is drawn. Essentially, the bank, by certifying (accepting) the check, promises to pay the check at the time the check is presented.

Charitable trust A trust in which the property held by a trustee must be used for a charitable purpose, such as the advancement of health, education, or religion.

Chattel All forms of personal property.

Check A draft drawn by a drawer ordering the drawee bank or financial institution to pay a certain amount of money to the holder on demand.

Checks and balances The national government is composed of three separate branches: the executive, the legislative, and the judicial branches. Each branch of the government exercises a check upon the actions of the others.

Choice-of-language clause A clause in a contract designating the official language by which the contract will be interpreted in the event of a future disagreement over the contract's terms.

Choice-of-law clause A clause in a contract designating the law (such as the law of a particular state or nation) that will govern the contract.

Chose in action A right that can be enforced in court to recover a debt or to obtain damages.

Citation A reference to a publication in which a legal authority—such as a statute or a court decision—or other source can be found.

Civil law The branch of law dealing with the definition and enforcement of all private or public rights, as opposed to criminal matters.

Civil law system A system of law derived from that of the Roman Empire and based on a code rather than case law; the predominant system of law in the nations of continental Europe and the nations that were once their colonies. In the United States, Louisiana is the only state that has a civil law system.

Clearinghouse A system or place where banks exchange checks and drafts drawn on each other and settle daily balances.

Close corporation A corporation whose shareholders are limited to a small group of persons, often including only family members. The rights of shareholders of a close corporation usually are restricted regarding the transfer of shares to others.

Closed shop A firm that requires union membership by its workers as a condition of employment. The closed shop was made illegal by the Labor-Management Relations Act of 1947.

Codicil A written supplement or modification to a will. A codicil must be executed with the same formalities as a will.

Collateral Under Article 9 of the UCC, the property subject to a security interest, including accounts and chattel paper that have been sold.

Collateral promise A secondary promise that is ancillary (subsidiary) to a principal transaction or primary contractual relationship, such as a promise made by one person to pay the debts of another if the latter fails to perform. A collateral promise normally must be in writing to be enforceable.

Collecting bank Any bank handling an item for collection, except the payor bank.

Commerce clause The provision in Article I, Section 8, of the U.S. Constitution that gives Congress the power to regulate interstate commerce.

Commingle To mix together. In corporate law, if personal and corporate interests are commingled to the extent that the corporation has no separate identity, a court may "pierce the corporate veil" and expose the shareholders to personal liability.

Common carrier An owner of a truck, railroad, airline, ship, or other vehicle who is licensed to offer transportation services to the public, generally in return for compensation or a payment.

Common law That body of law developed from custom or judicial decisions in English and U.S. courts, not attributable to a legislature.

Common stock Shares of ownership in a corporation that give the owner of the stock a proportionate interest in the corporation with regard to control, earnings, and net assets; shares of common stock are lowest in priority with respect to payment of dividends and distribution of the corporation's assets upon dissolution.

Community property A form of concurrent ownership of property in which each spouse technically owns an undivided one-half interest in property acquired during the marriage. This form of joint ownership occurs in only nine states and Puerto Rico.

Comparative negligence A theory in tort law under which the liability for injuries resulting from negligent acts is shared by all parties who were negligent (including the injured party), on the basis of each person's proportionate negligence.

Compensatory damages A money award equivalent to the actual value of injuries or damages sustained by the aggrieved party.

Complaint The pleading made by a plaintiff alleging wrongdoing on the part of the defendant; the document that, when filed with a court, initiates a lawsuit.

Computer crime Any act that is directed against computers and computer parts, that uses computers as instruments of crime, or that involves computers and constitutes abuse.

Concurrent conditions Conditions in a contract that must occur or be performed at the same time; they are mutually dependent. No obligations arise until these conditions are simultaneously performed.

Concurrent jurisdiction Jurisdiction that exists when two different courts have the power to hear a case. For example, some cases can be heard in a federal or a state court.

Condition A qualification, provision, or clause in a contractual agreement, the occurrence of which creates, suspends, or terminates the obligations of the contracting parties.

Condition precedent A condition in a contract that must be met before a party's promise becomes absolute.

Condition subsequent A condition in a contract that operates to terminate a party's absolute promise to perform.

Confession of judgment The act of a debtor in permitting a judgment to be entered against him or her by a creditor, for an agreed sum, without the institution of legal proceedings.

Confiscation A government's taking of privately owned business or personal property without a proper public purpose or an award of just compensation.

Confusion The mixing together of goods belonging to two or more owners so that the separately owned goods cannot be identified.

Consent Voluntary agreement to a proposition or an act of another. A concurrence of wills.

Consequential damages Special damages that compensate for a loss that is not direct or immediate (for example, lost profits). The special damages must have been reasonably foreseeable at the time the breach or injury occurred in order for the plaintiff to collect them.

Consideration Generally, the value given in return for a promise. The consideration, which must be present to make the contract legally binding, must be something of legally sufficient value and bargained for and must result in a detriment to the promisee or a benefit to the promisor.

Consignment A transaction in which an owner of goods (the consignor) delivers the goods to another (the consignee) for the consignee to sell. The consignee pays the consignor for the goods when they are sold by the consignee.

Consolidation A contractual and statutory process in which two or more corporations join to become a completely new corporation. The original corporations cease to exist, and the new corporation acquires all their assets and liabilities.

Constitutional law Law based on the U.S. Constitution and the constitutions of the various states.

Constructive delivery An act equivalent to the actual, physical delivery of property that cannot be physically delivered because of difficulty or impossibility; for example, the transfer of a key to a safe constructively delivers the contents of the safe.

Constructive eviction A form of eviction that occurs when a landlord fails to perform adequately any of the undertakings (such as providing heat in the winter) required by the lease, thereby making the tenant's further use and enjoyment of the property exceedingly difficult or impossible.

Constructive trust An equitable trust that is imposed in the interests of fairness and justice when someone wrongfully holds legal title to property. A court may require the owner to hold the property in trust for the person or persons who rightfully should own the property.

Consumer-debtor An individual whose debts are primarily consumer debts (debts for purchases made primarily for personal or household use).

Continuation statement A statement that, if filed within six months prior to the expiration date of the original financing statement, continues the perfection of the original security interest for another five years. The perfection of a security interest can be continued in the same manner indefinitely.

Contract An agreement that can be enforced in court; formed by two or more parties who agree to perform or to refrain from performing some act now or in the future.

Contractual capacity The threshold mental capacity required by the law for a party who enters into a contract to be bound by that contract.

Contributory negligence A theory in tort law under which a complaining party's own negligence contributed to or caused his or her injuries. Contributory negligence is an absolute bar to recovery in a minority of jurisdictions.

Conversion The wrongful taking, using, or retaining possession of personal property that belongs to another.

Conveyance The transfer of a title to land from one person to another by deed; a document (such as a deed) by which an interest in land is transferred from one person to another.

"Cooling off" laws Laws that allow buyers a period of time, such as two to three days, in which to cancel door-to-door sales contracts.

Copyright The exclusive right of "authors" to publish, print, or sell an intellectual production for a statutory period of time. A copyright has the same monopolistic nature as a patent or trademark, but it differs in that it applies exclusively to works of art, literature, and other works of authorship (including computer programs).

Corporate social responsibility The concept that corporations can and should act ethically and be accountable to society for their actions.

Corporate charter The document issued by a state agency or authority (usually the secretary of state) that grants a corporation legal existence and the right to function.

Corporation A legal entity formed in compliance with statutory requirements. The entity is distinct from its shareholders-owners.

Cost-benefit analysis A decision-making technique that involves weighing the costs of a given action against the benefits of the action.

Co-surety A joint surety; a person who assumes liability jointly with another surety for the payment of an obligation.

Counterclaim A claim made by a defendant in a civil lawsuit that in effect sues the plaintiff.

Counteroffer An offeree's response to an offer in which the offeree rejects the original offer and at the same time makes a new offer.

Course of dealing Prior conduct between parties to a contract that establishes a common basis for their understanding.

Course of performance The conduct that occurs under the terms of a particular agreement; such conduct indicates what the parties to an agreement intended it to mean.

Covenant not to sue An agreement to substitute a contractual obligation for some other type of legal action based on a valid claim.

Cover Under the UCC, a remedy of the buyer that allows the buyer or lessee, on the seller's or lessor's breach, to purchase the goods from another seller or lessor and substitute them for the goods due under the contract. If the cost of cover exceeds the cost of the contract goods, the breaching seller or lessor will be liable to the buyer or lessee for the difference. In obtaining cover, the buyer or lessee must act in good faith and without unreasonable delay.

Cram-down provision A provision of the Bankruptcy Code that allows a court to confirm a debtor's Chapter 11 reorganization plan even though only one class of creditors has accepted it. To exercise the court's right under this provision, the court must demonstrate that the plan does not discriminate unfairly against any creditors and is fair and equitable.

Creditors' composition agreement An agreement formed between a debtor and his or her creditors in which the creditors agree to accept a lesser sum than that owed by the debtor in full satisfaction of the debt.

Crime A wrong against society proclaimed in a statute and, if committed, punishable by society through fines and/or imprisonment—and, in some cases, death.

Criminal law Law that defines and governs actions that constitute crimes. Generally, criminal law has to do with wrongful actions committed against society for which society demands redress.

Cure The right of a party who tenders nonconforming performance to correct his or her performance within the contract period [UCC 3–508].

D

Damages Money sought as a remedy for a breach of contract or for a tortious act.

Debtor Under Article 9 of the UCC, a debtor is any party who owes payment or performance of a secured obligation, whether or not the party actually owns or has rights in the collateral.

Debtor in possession (DIP) In Chapter 11 bankruptcy proceedings, a debtor who is allowed to continue in possession of the estate in property (the business) and to continue business operations.

Deed A document by which title to property (usually real property) is passed.

Defalcation The misuse of funds.

Defamation Anything published or publicly spoken that causes injury to another's good name, reputation, or character.

Default The failure to observe a promise or discharge an obligation. The term is commonly used to mean the failure to pay a debt when it is due.

Default judgment A judgment entered by a court against a defendant who has failed to appear in court to answer or defend against the plaintiff's claim.

Defendant One against whom a lawsuit is brought; the accused person in a criminal proceeding.

Defense That which a defendant offers and alleges in an action or suit as a reason why the plaintiff should not recover or establish what he or she seeks.

Deficiency judgment A judgment against a debtor for the amount of a debt remaining unpaid after collateral has been repossessed and sold.

Delegation of duties The act of transferring to another all or part of one's duties arising under a contract.

Depositary bank The first bank to receive a check for payment.

Deposition The testimony of a party to a lawsuit or a witness taken under oath before a trial.

Destination contract A contract for the sale of goods in which the seller is required or authorized to ship the goods by carrier and deliver them at a particular destination. The seller assumes liability for any losses or damage to the goods until they are tendered at the destination specified in the contract.

Devise To make a gift of real property by will.

Devisee One designated in a will to receive a gift of real property.

Disaffirmance The legal avoidance, or setting aside, of a contractual obligation.

Discharge The termination of an obligation. In contract law, discharge occurs when the parties have fully performed their contractual obligations or when events, conduct of the parties, or operation of the law releases the parties from performance. In bankruptcy proceedings, the extinction of the debtor's dischargeable debts.

Disclosed principal A principal whose identity is known to a third party at the time the agent makes a contract with the third party.

Discovery A phase in the litigation process during which the opposing parties may obtain information from each other and from third parties prior to trial.

Disparagement of property An economically injurious falsehood made about another's product or property. A general term for torts that are more specifically referred to as slander of quality or slander of title.

Disparate-impact discrimination A form of employment discrimination that results from certain employer practices or procedures that, although not discriminatory on their face, have a discriminatory effect.

Disparate-treatment discrimination A form of employment discrimination that results when an employer intentionally discriminates against employees who are members of protected classes.

Dissolution The formal disbanding of a partnership or a corporation. It can take place by (1) acts of the partners or, in a corporation, of the shareholders and board of directors; (2) the death of a partner; (3) the expiration of a time period stated in a partnership agreement or a certificate of incorporation; or (4) judicial decree.

Diversity of citizenship   Under Article III, Section 2, of the Constitution, a basis for federal court jurisdiction over a lawsuit between (1) citizens of different states, (2) a foreign country and citizens of a state or of different states, or (3) citizens of a state and citizens or subjects of a foreign country. The amount in controversy must be more than $75,000 before a federal court can take jurisdiction in such cases.

Dividend   A distribution to corporate shareholders of corporate profits or income, disbursed in proportion to the number of shares held.

Docket   The list of cases entered on a court's calendar and thus scheduled to be heard by the court.

Document of title   Paper exchanged in the regular course of business that evidences the right to possession of goods (for example, a bill of lading or a warehouse receipt).

Domestic corporation   In a given state, a corporation that does business in, and is organized under the law of, that state.

Dominion   Ownership rights in property, including the right to possess and control the property.

Double jeopardy   A situation occurring when a person is tried twice for the same criminal offense; prohibited by the Fifth Amendment to the Constitution.

Draft   Any instrument drawn on a drawee (such as a bank) that orders the drawee to pay a certain sum of money, usually to a third party (the payee), on demand or at a definite future time.

Dram shop act   A state statute that imposes liability on the owners of bars and taverns, as well as those who serve alcoholic drinks to the public, for injuries resulting from accidents caused by intoxicated persons when the sellers or servers of alcoholic drinks contributed to the intoxication.

Drawee   The party that is ordered to pay a draft or check. With a check, a financial institution is always the drawee.

Drawer   The party that initiates a draft (such as a check), thereby ordering the drawee to pay.

Due diligence   A required standard of care that certain professionals, such as accountants, must meet to avoid liability for securities violations. Under securities law, an accountant will be deemed to have exercised due diligence if he or she followed generally accepted accounting principles and generally accepted auditing standards and had, "after reasonable investigation, reasonable grounds to believe and did believe, at the time such part of the registration statement became effective, that the statements therein were true and that there was no omission of a material fact required to be stated therein or necessary to make the statements therein not misleading."

Due process clause   The provisions of the Fifth and Fourteenth Amendments to the Constitution that guarantee that no person shall be deprived of life, liberty, or property without due process of law. Similar clauses are found in most state constitutions.

Dumping   The selling of goods in a foreign country at a price below the price charged for the same goods in the domestic market.

Duress   Unlawful pressure brought to bear on a person, causing the person to perform an act that he or she would not otherwise perform.

Duty of care   The duty of all persons, as established by tort law, to exercise a reasonable amount of care in their dealings with others. Failure to exercise due care, which is normally determined by the "reasonable person standard," constitutes the tort of negligence.

E

Early neutral case evaluation   A form of alternative dispute resolution in which a neutral third party evaluates the strengths and weakness of the disputing parties' positions; the evaluator's opinion forms the basis for negotiating a settlement.

Easement   A nonpossessory right to use another's property in a manner established by either express or implied agreement.

Electronic fund transfer (EFT)   A transfer of funds with the use of an electronic terminal, a telephone, a computer, or magnetic tape.

Emancipation   In regard to minors, the act of being freed from parental control; occurs when a child's parent or legal guardian relinquishes the legal right to exercise control over the child. Normally, a minor who leaves home to support himself or herself is considered emancipated.

Embezzlement   The fraudulent appropriation of money or other property by a person to whom the money or property has been entrusted.

Eminent domain   The power of a government to take land for public use from private citizens for just compensation.

Employment at will   A common law doctrine under which either party may terminate an employment relationship at any time for any reason, unless a contract specifies otherwise.

Employment discrimination Treating employees or job applicants unequally on the basis of race, color, national origin, religion, gender, age, or disability; prohibited by federal statutes.

Enabling legislation A statute enacted by Congress that authorizes the creation of an administrative agency and specifies the name, composition, purpose, and powers of the agency being created.

Entrapment In criminal law, a defense in which the defendant claims that he or she was induced by a public official—usually an undercover agent or police officer—to commit a crime that he or she would otherwise not have committed.

Equal dignity rule In most states, a rule stating that express authority given to an agent must be in writing if the contract to be made on behalf of the principal is required to be in writing.

Equal protection clause The provision in the Fourteenth Amendment to the Constitution that guarantees that no state will "deny to any person within its jurisdiction the equal protection of the laws." This clause mandates that the state governments treat similarly situated individuals in a similar manner.

Equitable principles and maxims General propositions or principles of law that have to do with fairness (equity).

Establishment clause The provision in the First Amendment to the Constitution that prohibits Congress from creating any law "respecting an establishment of religion."

Estate in property In bankruptcy proceedings, all of the debtor's legal and equitable interests in property presently held, wherever located, together with certain jointly owned property, property transferred in transactions voidable by the trustee, proceeds and profits from the property of the estate, and certain property interests to which the debtor becomes entitled within 180 days after filing for bankruptcy.

Estopped Barred, impeded, or precluded.

Estray statute A statute defining finders' rights in property when the true owners are unknown.

Ethics Moral principles and values applied to social behavior.

Eviction A landlord's act of depriving a tenant of possession of the leased premises.

Exclusionary rule In criminal procedure, a rule under which any evidence that is obtained in violation of the accused's constitutional rights guaranteed by the Fourth, Fifth, and Sixth Amendments, as well as any evidence derived from illegally obtained evidence, will not be admissible in court.

Exclusive jurisdiction Jurisdiction that exists when a case can be heard only in a particular court or type of court.

Exclusive-dealing contract An agreement under which a seller forbids a buyer to purchase products from the seller's competitors.

Exculpatory clause A clause that releases a contractual party from liability in the event of monetary or physical injury, no matter who is at fault.

Executed contract A contract that has been completely performed by both parties.

Execution An action to carry into effect the directions in a court decree or judgment.

Executor A person appointed by a testator to see that his or her will is administered appropriately.

Executory contract A contract that has not as yet been fully performed.

Executory interest A future interest, held by a person other than the grantor, that or begins some time after the termination of the preceding estate.

Express contract A contract in which the terms of the agreement are fully and explicitly stated in words, oral or written.

Express warranty A seller's or lessor's oral or written promise, ancillary to an underlying sales or lease agreement, as to the quality, description, or performance of the goods being sold or leased.

Extension clause A clause in a time instrument that allows the instrument's date of maturity to be extended into the future.

F

Federal form of government A system of government in which the states form a union and the sovereign power is divided between a central government and the member states.

Federal question A question that pertains to the U.S. Constitution, acts of Congress, or treaties. A federal question provides a basis for federal jurisdiction.

Federal Reserve System A network of twelve central banks, located around the country and headed by the Federal Reserve Board of Governors. Most banks in the United States have Federal Reserve accounts.

Fee simple An absolute form of property ownership entitling the property owner to use, possess, or dispose of the property as he or she chooses during his or her lifetime. Upon death, the interest in the property descends to the owner's heirs; a fee simple absolute.

Fee simple absolute An ownership interest in land in which the owner has the greatest possible aggregation of rights, privileges, and power. Ownership in fee simple absolute is limited absolutely to a person and his or her heirs; a fee simple absolute.

Fee simple defeasible An ownership interest in real property that can be taken away (by the prior grantor) upon the occurrence or nonoccurrence of a specified event.

Felony A crime—such as arson, murder, rape, or robbery—that carries the most severe sanctions, usually ranging from one year in a state or federal prison to the forfeiture of one's life.

Fictitious payee A payee on a negotiable instrument whom the maker or drawer does not intend to have an interest in the instrument. Indorsements by fictitious payees are not treated as unauthorized under Article 3 of the UCC.

Fiduciary As a noun, a person having a duty created by his or her undertaking to act primarily for another's benefit in matters connected with the undertaking. As an adjective, a relationship founded upon trust and confidence.

Financing statement A document prepared by a secured creditor and filed with the appropriate state or local official to give notice to the public that the creditor claims an interest in collateral belonging to the debtor named in the statement. The financing statement must be signed by the debtor, contain the addresses of both the debtor and the creditor, and describe the collateral by type or item.

Firm offer An offer (by a merchant) that is irrevocable without consideration for a period of time (not longer than three months). A firm offer by a merchant must be in writing and must be signed by the offeror.

Fixture A thing that was once personal property but that has become attached to real property in such a way that it takes on the characteristics of real property and becomes part of that real property.

Floating lien A security interest in proceeds, after-acquired property, or property purchased under a line of credit (or all three); a security interest in collateral that is retained even when the collateral changes in character, classification, or location.

Foreign corporation In a given state, a corporation that does business in the state without being incorporated therein.

Foreign exchange market A worldwide system in which foreign currencies are bought and sold.

Forgery The fraudulent making or altering of any writing in a way that changes the legal rights and liabilities of another.

Formal contract A contract that by law requires for its validity a specific form, such as executed under seal.

Forum-selection clause A provision in a contract designating the court, jurisdiction, or tribunal that will decide any disputes arising under the contract.

Franchise Any arrangement in which the owner of a trademark, trade name, or copyright licenses another to use that trademark, trade name, or copyright, under specified conditions or limitations, in the selling of goods and services.

Franchisee One receiving a license to use another's (the franchisor's) trademark, trade name, or copyright in the sale of goods and services.

Franchisor One licensing another (the franchisee) to use his or her trademark, trade name, or copyright in the sale of goods or services.

Fraudulent misrepresentation (fraud) Any misrepresentation, either by misstatement or omission of a material fact, knowingly made with the intention of deceiving another and on which a reasonable person would and does rely to his or her detriment.

Free exercise clause The provision in the First Amendment to the Constitution that prohibits Congress from making any law "prohibiting the free exercise" of religion.

Fungible goods Goods that are alike by physical nature, by agreement, or by trade usage. Examples of fungible goods are wheat, oil, and wine that are identical in type and quality.

Future interest An interest in real property that is not at present possessory but will or may become possessory in the future.

G

Garnishment A legal process used by a creditor to collect a debt by seizing property of the debtor (such as wages) that is being held by a third party (such as the debtor's employer).

General partner In a limited partnership, a partner who assumes responsibility for the management of the partnership and liability for all partnership debts.

Generally accepted accounting principles (GAAP) The conventions, rules, and procedures necessary to define accepted accounting practices at a particular time. The source of the principles is the Federal Accounting Standards Board.

Generally accepted auditing standards (GAAS) Standards concerning an auditor's professional qualities and the judgment exercised by him or her in the performance of an examination and report. The source of the standards is the American Institute of Certified Public Accountants.

Gift Any voluntary transfer of property made without consideration, past or present.

Gift *causa mortis* A gift made in contemplation of death. If the donor does not die of that ailment, the gift is revoked.

Gift *inter vivos* A gift made during one's lifetime and not in contemplation of imminent death, in contrast to a gift *causa mortis*.

Good faith purchaser A purchaser who buys without notice of any circumstance that would put a person of ordinary prudence on inquiry as to whether the seller has valid title to the goods being sold.

Good Samaritan statute A state statute that provides that persons who rescue or provide emergency services to others in peril—unless they do so recklessly, thus causing further harm—cannot be sued for negligence.

Grand jury A group of citizens called to decide, after hearing the state's evidence, whether a reasonable basis (probable cause) exists for believing that a crime has been committed and whether a trial ought to be held.

Guarantor A person who agrees to satisfy the debt of another (the debtor) only after the principal debtor defaults; a guarantor's liability is thus secondary.

H

Holder Any person in the possession of an instrument drawn, issued, or indorsed to him or her, to his or her order, to bearer, or in blank.

Holder in due course (HDC) A holder who acquires a negotiable instrument for value; in good faith; and without notice that the instrument is overdue, that it has been dishonored, that any person has a defense against it or a claim to it, or that the instrument contains unauthorized signatures, alterations, or is so irregular or incomplete as to call into question its authenticity.

Holographic will A will written entirely in the signer's handwriting and usually not witnessed.

Homestead exemption A law permitting a debtor to retain the family home, either in its entirety or up to a specified dollar amount, free from the claims of unsecured creditors or trustees in bankruptcy.

Hot-cargo agreement An agreement in which employers voluntarily agree with unions not to handle, use, or deal in nonunion-produced goods of other employers; a type of secondary boycott explicitly prohibited by the Labor-Management Reporting and Disclosure Act of 1959.

I

Identification In a sale of goods, the express designation of the goods provided for in the contract.

Implied warranty A warranty that the law derives by implication or inference from the nature of the transaction or the relative situation or circumstances of the parties.

Implied warranty of fitness for a particular purpose A warranty that goods sold or leased are fit for a particular purpose. The warranty arises when any seller or lessor knows the particular purpose for which a buyer or lessee will use the goods and knows that the buyer or lessee is relying on the skill and judgment of the seller or lessor to select suitable goods.

Implied warranty of habitability An implied promise by a landlord that rented residential premises are fit for human habitation—that is, in a condition that is safe and suitable for people to live in.

Implied warranty of merchantability A warranty that goods being sold or leased are reasonably fit for the general puposc for which thcy arc sold or leased, are properly packaged and labeled, and are of proper quality. The warranty automatically arises in every sale or lease of goods made by a merchant who deals in goods of the kind sold or leased.

Implied-in-fact contract A contract formed in whole or in part from the conduct of the parties (as opposed to an express contract).

Impossibility of performance A doctrine under which a party to a contract is relieved of his or her duty to perform when performance becomes impossible or totally impracticable (through no fault of either party).

Imposter One who, by use of the mails, telephone, or personal appearance, induces a maker or drawer to issue an instrument in the name of an impersonated payee. Indorsements by imposters are not treated as unauthorized under Article 3 of the UCC.

Incidental beneficiary A third party who incidentally benefits from a contract but whose benefit was not the reason the contract was formed; an incidental beneficiary has no rights in a contract and cannot sue to have the contract enforced.

Incidental damages Damages resulting from a breach of contract, including all reasonable expenses incurred because of the breach.

Independent contractor One who works for, and receives payment from, an employer but whose working conditions and methods are not controlled by the employer. An independent contractor is not an employee but may be an agent.

Indictment (pronounced in-*dyte*-ment) A charge by a grand jury that a named person has committed a crime.

Indorsee The person to whom a negotiable instrument is transferred by indorsement.

Indorsement A signature placed on an instrument for the purpose of transferring one's ownership rights in the instrument.

Indorser A person who transfers an instrument by signing (indorsing) it and delivering it to another person.

Informal contract A contract that does not require a specified form or formality in order to be valid.

Information A formal accusation or complaint (without an indictment) issued in certain types of actions (usually criminal actions involving lesser crimes) by a law officer, such as a magistrate.

Innkeeper's lien A possessory lien placed on the luggage of hotel guests for hotel charges that remain unpaid.

Insider trading The purchase or sale of securities on the basis of "inside information" (information that has not been made available to the public) in violation of a duty owed to the company whose stock is being traded.

Insolvent Under the UCC, a term describing a person who ceases to pay "his debts in the ordinary course of business or cannot pay his debts as they become due or is insolvent within the meaning of federal bankruptcy law" [UCC 1–201(23)].

Installment contract Under the UCC, a contract that requires or authorizes delivery in two or more separate lots to be accepted and paid for separately.

Insurable interest An interest either in a person's life or well-being or in property that is sufficiently substantial that insuring against injury to (or the

death of) the person or against damage to the property does not amount to a mere wagering (betting) contract.

Insurance A contract in which, for a stipulated consideration, one party agrees to compensate the other for loss on a specific subject by a specified peril.

Integrated contract A written contract that constitutes the final expression of the parties' agreement. If a contract is integrated, evidence extraneous to the contract that contradicts or alters the meaning of the contract in any way is inadmissible.

Intellectual property Property resulting from intellectual, creative processes. Patents, trademarks, and copyrights are examples of intellectual property.

Intended beneficiary A third party for whose benefit a contract is formed; an intended beneficiary can sue the promisor if such a contract is breached.

Intentional tort A wrongful act knowingly committed.

Inter vivos **trust** A trust created by the grantor (settlor) and effective during the grantor's lifetime; a trust not established by a will.

Intermediary bank Any bank to which an item is transferred in the course of collection, except the depositary or payor bank.

International law The law that governs relations among nations. National laws, customs, treaties, and international conferences and organizations are generally considered to be the most important sources of international law.

Interrogatories A series of written questions for which written answers are prepared and then signed under oath by a party to a lawsuit, usually with the assistance of the party's attorney.

Intestacy laws State statutes that specify how property will be distributed when a person dies intestate (without a valid will); also called statutes of descent and distribution.

Intestate As a noun, one who has died without having created a valid will; as an adjective, the state of having died without a will.

Investment company A company that acts on behalf of many smaller shareholders-owners by buying a large portfolio of securities and professionally managing that portfolio.

J

Joint tenancy The joint ownership of property by two or more co-owners of property in which each co-owner owns an undivided portion of the property. Upon the death of one of the joint tenants, his or her interest automatically passes to the surviving joint tenants.

Joint and several liability   In partnership law, a doctrine under which a plaintiff may sue, and collect a judgment from, one or more of the partners separately (severally, or individually) or all of the partners together (jointly). This is true even if one of the partners sued did not participate in, ratify, or know about whatever it was that gave rise to the cause of action.

Joint liability   Shared liability. In partnership law, partners incur joint liability for partnership obligations and debts. For example, if a third party sues a partner on a partnership debt, the partner has the right to insist that the other partners be sued with him or her.

Judicial review   The process by which a court decides on the constitutionality of legislative enactments and actions of the executive branch.

Jurisdiction   The authority of a court to hear and decide a specific action.

Jurisprudence   The science or philosophy of law.

Justiciable (pronounced jus-*tish*-a-bul) controversy   A controversy that is not hypothetical or academic but real and substantial; a requirement that must be satisfied before a court will hear a case.

L

Larceny   The wrongful taking and carrying away of another person's personal property with the intent to permanently deprive the owner of the property. Some states classify larceny as either grand or petit, depending on the property's value.

Law   A body of enforceable rules governing relationships among individuals and between individuals and their society.

Lease   In real property law, a contract by which the owner of real property (the landlord, or lessor) grants to a person (the tenant, or lessee) an exclusive right to use and possess the property, usually for a specified period of time, in return for rent or some other form of payment.

Lease agreement   In regard to the lease of goods, an agreement in which one person (the lessor) agrees to transfer the right to the possession and use of property to another person (the lessee) in exchange for rental payments.

Leasehold estate   An estate in realty held by a tenant under a lease. In every leasehold estate, the tenant has a qualified right to possess and/or use the land.

Legacy   A gift of personal property under a will.

Legatee   One designated in a will to receive a gift of personal property.

Lessee   A person who acquires the right to the possession and use of another's property in exchange for rental payments.

Lessor   A person who sells the right to the possession and use of property to another in exchange for rental payments.

Levy   The obtaining of money by legal process through the seizure and sale of property, usually done after a writ of execution has been issued.

Libel   Defamation in written form.

License   A revocable right or privilege of a person to come on another person's land.

Lien (pronounced *leen*)   An encumbrance upon a property to satisfy a debt or protect a claim for payment of a debt.

Life estate   An interest in land that exists only for the duration of the life of some person, usually the holder of the estate.

Limited liability company (LLC)   A hybrid form of business enterprise that offers the limited liability of the coporation but the tax advantages of a partnership.

Limited liability partnership (LLP)   A form of partnership that allows professionals to enjoy the tax benefits of a partnership while avoiding personal liability for the malpractice of other partners.

Limited partner   In a limited partnership, a partner who contributes capital to the partnership but has no right to participate in the management and operation of the business. The limited partner assumes no liability for partnership debts beyond the capital contributed.

Limited partnership   A partnership consisting of one or more general partners (who manage the business and are liable to the full extent of their personal assets for debts of the partnership) and one or more limited partners (who contribute only assets and are liable only to the extent of their contributions).

Liquidated damages   An amount, stipulated in the contract, that the parties to a contract believe to be a reasonable estimation of the damages that will occur in the event of a breach.

Liquidation   In regard to corporations, the process by which corporate assets are converted into cash and distributed among creditors and shareholders according to specific rules of preference. In regard to bankruptcy, the sale of all of the nonexempt assets of a debtor and the distribution of the proceeds to the debtor's creditors. Chapter 7 of the Bankruptcy Code provides for liquidation bankruptcy proceedings.

Litigation   The process of resolving a dispute through the court system.

Long arm statute   A state statute that permits a state to obtain personal jurisdiction over nonresident defendants. A defendant must have certain "minimum contacts" with that state for the statute to apply.

Lost property   Property with which the owner has involuntarily parted and then cannot find or recover.

M

Mailbox rule   A rule providing that an acceptance of an offer becomes effective upon dispatch (upon being placed in a mailbox), if mail is, expressly or impliedly, an authorized means of communication of acceptance to the offeror.

Maker   One who promises to pay a certain sum to the holder of a promissory note or certificate of deposit (CD).

Malpractice   Professional misconduct or the lack of the requisite degree of skill as a professional. Negligence—the failure to exercise due care—on the part of a professional, such as a physician or an attorney, is commonly referred to as malpractice.

Mechanic's lien   A statutory lien upon the real property of another, created to ensure payment for work performed and materials furnished in the repair or improvement of real property, such as a building.

Mediation   A method of settling disputes outside of court by using the services of a neutral third party, who acts as a communicating agent between the parties and assists the parties in negotiating a settlement.

Merchant   A person who is engaged in the purchase and sale of goods. Under the UCC, a person who deals in goods of the kind involved in the sales contract; for further definitions, see UCC 2–104.

Merger   A contractual and statutory process in which one corporation (the surviving corporation) acquires all of the assets and liabilities of another corporation (the merged corporation). The shareholders of the merged corporation receive either payment for their shares or shares in the surviving corporation.

Mini-trial   A private proceeding in which each party to a dispute argues its position before the other side and vice versa. A neutral third party may be present and act as an adviser if the parties fail to reach an agreement.

Minimum wage   The lowest wage, either by government regulation or union contract, that an employer may pay an hourly worker.

Mirror image rule   A common law rule that requires, for a valid contractual agreement, that the terms of the offeree's acceptance adhere exactly to the terms of the offeror's offer.

Misdemeanor   A lesser crime than a felony, punishable by a fine or imprisonment for up to one year in other than a state or federal penitentiary.

Mislaid property   Property with which the owner has voluntarily parted and then cannot find or recover.

Mitigation of damages   A rule requiring a plaintiff to have done whatever was reasonable to minimize the damages caused by the defendant.

Money laundering   Falsely reporting income that has been obtained through criminal activity as income obtained through a legitimate business enterprise—in effect, "laundering" the "dirty money."

Mortgagee   Under a mortgage agreement, the creditor who takes a security interest in the debtor's property.

Mortgagor   Under a mortgage agreement, the debtor who gives the creditor a security interest in the debtor's property in return for a mortgage loan.

Motion for a directed verdict   In a jury trial, a motion for the judge to take the decision out of the hands of the jury and direct a verdict for the moving party on the ground that the other party has not produced sufficient evidence to support his or her claim.

Motion for a new trial   A motion asserting that the trial was so fundamentally flawed (because of error, newly discovered evidence, prejudice, or other reason) that a new trial is necessary to prevent a miscarriage of justice.

Motion for judgment N.O.V.   A motion requesting the court to grant judgment in favor of the party making the motion on the ground that the jury verdict against him or her was unreasonable and erroneous.

Motion for judgment on the pleadings   A motion by either party to a lawsuit at the close of the pleadings requesting the court to decide the issue solely on the pleadings without proceeding to trial. The motion will be granted only if no facts are in dispute.

Motion for summary judgment A motion requesting the court to enter a judgment without proceeding to trial. The motion can be based on evidence outside the pleadings and will be granted only if no facts are in dispute.

Motion to dismiss A pleading in which a defendant asserts that the plaintiff's claim fails to state a cause of action (that is, has no basis in law) or that there are other grounds on which a suit should be dismissed.

Mutual fund A specific type of investment company that continually buys or sells to investors shares of ownership in a portfolio.

N

National law Law that pertains to a particular nation (as opposed to international law).

Natural law The belief that government and the legal system should reflect universal moral and ethical principles that are inherent in human nature. The natural law school is the oldest and one of the most significant schools of legal thought.

Necessaries Necessities required for life, such as food, shelter, clothing, and medical attention; may include whatever is believed to be necessary to maintain a person's standard of living or financial and social status.

Negligence The failure to exercise the standard of care that a reasonable person would exercise in similar circumstances.

Negligence *per se* An act (or failure to act) in violation of a statutory requirement.

Negotiable instrument A signed writing that contains an unconditional promise or order to pay an exact sum of money, on demand or at an exact future time, to a specific person or order, or to bearer.

Negotiation In regard to dispute settlement, a process in which parties attempt to settle their dispute informally, with or without attorneys to represent them. In regard to instruments, the transfer of an instrument in such a way that the transferee (the person to whom the instrument is transferred) becomes a holder.

No-par shares Corporate shares that have no face value—that is, no specific dollar amount is printed on their face.

Nominal damages A small monetary award (often one dollar) granted to a plaintiff when no actual damage was suffered.

Notary public A public official authorized to attest to the authenticity of signatures.

Novation The substitution, by agreement, of a new contract for an old one, with the rights under the old one being terminated. Typically, there is a substitution of a new person who is responsible for the contract and the removal of an original party's rights and duties under the contract.

Nuisance A common law doctrine under which persons may be held liable for using their property in a manner that unreasonably interferes with others' rights to use or enjoy their own property.

Nuncupative will An oral will (often called a deathbed will) made before witnesses; usually limited to transfers of personal property.

O

Objective theory of contracts A theory under which the intent to form a contract will be judged by outward, objective facts (what the party said when entering into the contract, how the party acted or appeared, and the circumstances surrounding the transaction) as interpreted by a reasonable person, rather than by the party's own secret, subjective intentions.

Offer A promise or commitment to perform or refrain from performing some specified act in the future.

Offeree A person to whom an offer is made.

Offeror A person who makes an offer.

Option contract A contract under which the offeror cannot revoke his or her offer for a stipulated time period, and the offeree can accept or reject the offer during this period without fear that the offer will be made to another person. The offeree must give consideration for the option (the irrevocable offer) to be enforceable.

Order for relief A court's grant of assistance to a complainant. In bankruptcy proceedings, the order relieves the debtor of the immediate obligation to pay the debts listed in the bankruptcy petition.

Order instrument A negotiable instrument that is payable "to the order of an identified person" or "to an identified person or order."

Output contract An agreement in which a seller agrees to sell and a buyer agrees to buy all or up to a stated amount of what the seller produces.

Overdraft A check written on a checking account in which there are insufficient funds to cover the amount of the check.

P

Par-value shares Corporate shares that have a specific face value, or formal cash-in value, written on them, such as one dollar.

Parol evidence rule A substantive rule of contracts under which a court will not receive into evidence the parties' prior negotiations, prior agreements, or contemporaneous oral agreements if that evidence contradicts or varies the terms of the parties' written contract.

Partially disclosed principal A principal whose identity is unknown by a third person, but the third person knows that the agent is or may be acting for a principal at the time the agent and the third person form a contract.

Partnership An agreement by two or more persons to carry on, as co-owners, a business for profit.

Past consideration An act done before the contract is made, which ordinarily, by itself, cannot be consideration for a later promise to pay for the act.

Patent A government grant that gives an inventor the exclusive right or privilege to make, use, or sell his or her invention for a limited time period. The word patent usually refers to some invention and designates either the instrument by which patent rights are evidenced or the patent itself.

Payee A person to whom an instrument is made payable.

Payor bank The bank on which a check is drawn (the drawee bank).

Penalty A sum inserted into a contract, not as a measure of compensation for its breach but rather as punishment for a default. The agreement as to the amount will not be enforced, and recovery will be limited to actual damages.

Per capita A Latin term meaning "per person." In the law governing estate distribution, a method of distributing the property of an intestate's estate in which each heir in a certain class (such as grandchildren) receives an equal share.

Per stirpes A Latin term meaning "by the roots." In the law governing estate distribution, a method of distributing an intestate's estate in which each heir in a certain class (such as grandchildren) takes the share to which his or her deceased ancestor (such as a mother or father) would have been entitled.

Perfection The legal process by which secured parties protect themselves against the claims of third parties who may wish to have their debts satisfied out of the same collateral; usually accomplished by the filing of a financing statement with the appropriate government official.

Performance In contract law, the fulfillment of one's duties arising under a contract with another; the normal way of discharging one's contractual obligations.

Periodic tenancy A lease interest in land for an indefinite period involving payment of rent at fixed intervals, such as week to week, month to month, or year to year.

Personal defenses Defenses that can be used to avoid payment to an ordinary holder of a negotiable instrument but not a holder in due course (HDC) or a holder with the rights of an HDC.

Personal property Property that is movable; any property that is not real property.

Persuasive authority Any legal authority or source of law that a court may look to for guidance but on which it need not rely in making its decision. Persuasive authorities include cases from other jurisdictions and secondary sources of law.

Petition in bankruptcy The document that is filed with a bankruptcy court to initiate bankruptcy proceedings. The official forms required for a petition in bankruptcy must be completed accurately, sworn to under oath, and signed by the debtor.

Petty offense In criminal law, the least serious kind of criminal offense, such as a traffic or building-code violation.

Plaintiff One who initiates a lawsuit.

Plea bargaining The process by which a criminal defendant and the prosecutor in a criminal case work out a mutually satisfactory disposition of the case, subject to court approval; usually involves the defendant's pleading guilty to a lesser offense in return for a lighter sentence.

Pleadings Statements made by the plaintiff and the defendant in a lawsuit that detail the facts, charges, and defenses involved in the litigation; the complaint and answer are part of the pleadings.

Pledge A common law security device (retained in Article 9 of the UCC) in which personal property is turned over to the creditor as security for the payment of a debt and retained by the creditor until the debt is paid.

Police powers Powers possessed by states as part of their inherent sovereignty. These powers may be exercised to protect or promote the public order, health, safety, morals, and general welfare.

Policy In insurance law, a contract between the insurer and the insured in which, for a stipulated consideration, the insurer agrees to compensate the insured for loss on a specific subject by a specified peril.

Positive law The body of conventional, or written, law of a particular society at a particular point in time.

Power of attorney A written document, which is usually notarized, authorizing another to act as one's agent; can be special (permitting the agent to do specified acts only) or general (permitting the agent to transact all business for the principal).

Precedent A court decision that furnishes an example or authority for deciding subsequent cases involving identical or similar facts.

Preemption A doctrine under which certain federal laws preempt, or take precedence over, conflicting state or local laws.

Preemptive rights Rights held by shareholders that entitle them to purchase newly issued shares of a corporation's stock, equal in percentage to shares presently held, before the stock is offered to any outside buyers. Preemptive rights enable shareholders to maintain their proportionate ownership and voice in the corporation.

Preference In bankruptcy proceedings, property transfers or payments made by the debtor that favor (give preference to) one creditor over others. The bankruptcy trustee is allowed to recover payments made both voluntarily and involuntarily to one creditor in preference over another.

Preferred stock Classes of stock that have priority over common stock both as to payment of dividends and distribution of assets upon the corporation's dissolution.

Premium In insurance law, the price paid by the insured for insurance protection for a specified period of time.

Prenuptial agreement An agreement made before marriage that defines each partner's ownership rights in the other partner's property. Prenuptial agreements must be in writing to be enforceable.

Presentment The act of presenting an instrument to the party liable on the instrument to collect payment; presentment also occurs when a person presents an instrument to a drawee for acceptance.

Presentment warranties Implied warranties, made by any person who presents an instrument for payment or acceptance, that (1) the person obtaining payment or acceptance is entitled to enforce the instrument or is authorized to obtain payment or acceptance on behalf of a person who is entitled to enforce the instrument, (2) the instrument has not been altered, and (3) the person obtaining payment or acceptance has no knowledge that the signature of the drawer of the instrument is unauthorized.

Prima facie **case** A case in which the plaintiff has produced sufficient evidence of his or her conclusion that the case can go to to a jury; a case in which the evidence compels the plaintiff's conclusion if the defendant produces no evidence to disprove it.

Primary source of law A document that establishes the law on a particular issue, such as a constitution, a statute, an administrative rule, or a court decision.

Principal In agency law, a person who agrees to have another, called the agent, act on his or her behalf.

Privilege In tort law, the ability to act contrary to another person's right without that person's having legal redress for such acts. Privilege may be raised as a defense to defamation.

Privity of contract The relationship that exists between the promisor and the promisee of a contract.

Probable cause Reasonable grounds to believe the existence of facts warranting certain actions, such as the search or arrest of a person.

Probate court A state court of limited jurisdiction that conducts proceedings relating to the settlement of a deceased person's estate.

Procedural law Law that establishes the methods of enforcing the rights established by substantive law.

Proceeds Under Article 9 of the UCC, whatever is received when the collateral is sold or otherwise disposed of, such as by exchange.

Product liability The legal liability of manufacturers, sellers, and lessors of goods to consumers, users, and bystanders for injuries or damages that are caused by the goods.

Profit In real property law, the right to enter upon and remove things from the property of another (for example, the right to enter onto a person's land and remove sand and gravel therefrom).

Promise A declaration that something either will or will not happen in the future.

Promisee A person to whom a promise is made.

Promisor A person who makes a promise.

Promissory estoppel A doctrine that applies when a promisor makes a clear and definite promise on which the promisee justifiably relies; such a promise is binding if justice will be better served by the enforcement of the promise.

Promissory note A written promise made by one person (the maker) to pay a fixed sum of money to another person (the payee or a subsequent holder) on demand or on a specified date.

Promoter A person who takes the preliminary steps in organizing a corporation, including (usually) issuing a prospectus, procuring stock subscriptions, making contract purchases, securing a corporate charter, and the like.

Property Legally protected rights and interests in anything with an ascertainable value that is subject to ownership.

Prospectus A document required by federal or state securities laws that describes the financial operations of the corporation, thus allowing investors to make informed decisions.

Proximate cause Legal cause; exists when the connection between an act and an injury is strong enough to justify imposing liability.

Proxy In corporation law, a written agreement between a stockholder and another under which the stockholder authorizes the other to vote the stockholder's shares in a certain manner.

Puffery A salesperson's often exaggerated claims concerning the quality of property offered for sale. Such claims involve opinions rather than facts and are not considered to be legally binding promises or warranties.

Punitive damages Money damages that may be awarded to a plaintiff to punish the defendant and deter future similar conduct.

Purchase-money security interest (PMSI) A security interest that arises when a seller or lender extends credit for part or all of the purchase price of goods purchased by a buyer.

Q

Qualified indorsement An indorsement on a negotiable instrument in which the indorser disclaims any contract liability on the instrument; the notation "without recourse" is commonly used to create a qualified indorsement.

Quasi contract A fictional contract imposed on parties by a court in the interests of fairness and justice; usually, quasi contracts are imposed to avoid the unjust enrichment of one party at the expense of another.

Quitclaim deed A deed intended to pass any title, interest, or claim that the grantor may have in the property but not warranting that such title is valid. A quitclaim deed offers the least amount of protection against defects in the title.

Quorum The number of members of a decision-making body that must be present before business may be transacted.

R

Ratification The act of accepting and giving legal force to an obligation that previously was not enforceable.

Real property Land and everything attached to it, such as foliage and buildings.

Reasonable person standard The standard of behavior expected of a hypothetical "reasonable person." The standard against which negligence is measured and that must be observed to avoid liability for negligence.

Receiver In a corporate dissolution, a court-appointed person who winds up corporate affairs and liquidates corporate assets.

Recording statutes Statutes that allow deeds, mortgages, and other real property transactions be recorded so as to provide notice to future purchasers or creditors of an existing claim on the property.

Red herring A preliminary prospectus that can be distributed to potential investors after the registration statement (for a securities offering) has been filed with the Securities and Exchange Commission. The name derives from the red legend printed across the prospectus stating that the registration has been filed but has not become effective.

Reformation A court-ordered correction of a written contract so that it reflects the true intentions of the parties.

Regulation Z A set of rules promulgated by the Federal Reserve Board to implement the provisions of the Truth-in-Lending Act.

Release A contract in which one party forfeits the right to pursue a legal claim against the other party.

Remainder A future interest in property held by a person other than the original owner.

Remedy The relief given to an innocent party to enforce a right or compensate for the violation of a right.

Replevin (pronounced ruh-*pleh*-vin) An action to recover specific goods in the hands of a party who is wrongfully withholding them from the other party.

Reply Procedurally, a plaintiff's response to a defendant's answer.

Requirements contract An agreement in which a buyer agrees to purchase and the seller agrees to sell all or up to a stated amount of what the buyer needs or requires.

Res ipsa loquitur A doctrine under which negligence may be inferred simply because an event occurred, if it is the type of event that would not occur in the absence of negligence. Literally, the term means "the facts speak for themselves."

Rescission (pronounced reh-*sih*-zhen) A remedy whereby a contract is canceled and the parties are returned to the positions they occupied before the contract was made; may be effected through the mutual consent of the parties, by their conduct, or by court decree.

Respondeat superior (**pronounced ree-*spahn*-dee-uht soo-*peer*-ee-your**) In Latin, "Let the master respond." A doctrine under which a principal or an employer is held liable for the wrongful acts committed by agents or employees while acting within the scope of their agency or employment.

Restitution An equitable remedy under which a person is restored to his or her original position prior to loss or injury, or placed in the position he or she would have been in had the breach not occurred.

Restrictive indorsement Any indorsement on a negotiable instrument that requires the indorsee to comply with certain instructions regarding the funds involved. A restrictive indorsement does not prohibit the further negotiation of the instrument.

Resulting trust An implied trust arising from the conduct of the parties. A trust in which a party holds the actual legal title to another's property but only for that person's benefit.

Retained earnings The portion of a corporation's profits that has not been paid out as dividends to shareholders.

Reversionary interest A future interest in property retained by the original owner.

Revocation In contract law, the withdrawal of an offer by an offeror; unless the offer is irrevocable, it can be revoked at any time prior to acceptance without liability.

Right of first refusal The right to purchase personal or real property—such as corporate shares or real estate—before the property is offered for sale to others.

Right of contribution The right of a co-surety who pays more than his or her proportionate share upon a debtor's default to recover the excess paid from other co-sureties.

Right of reimbursement The legal right of a person to be restored, repaid, or indemnified for costs, expenses, or losses incurred or expended on behalf of another.

Right of subrogation The right of a person to stand in the place of (be substituted for) another, giving the substituted party the same legal rights that the original party had.

Right-to-work law A state law providing that employees are not to be required to join a union as a condition of obtaining or retaining employment.

Risk A prediction concerning potential loss based on known and unknown factors.

Risk management Planning that is undertaken to protect one's interest should some event threaten to undermine its security. In the context of insurance, risk management involves transferring certain risks from the insured to the insurance company.

Robbery The act of forcefully and unlawfully taking personal property of any value from another; force or intimidation is usually necessary for an act of theft to be considered a robbery.

Rule of four A rule of the United States Supreme Court under which the Court will not issue a writ of *certiorari* unless at least four justices approve of the decision to issue the writ.

Rulemaking The process undertaken by an administrative agency when formally adopting a new regulation or amending an old one. Rulemaking involves notifying the public of a proposed rule or change and receiving and considering the public's comments.

S

S corporation A close business corporation that has met certain requirements as set out by the Internal Revenue Code and thus qualifies for special income-tax treatment. Essentially, an S corporation is taxed the same as a partnership, but its owners enjoy the privilege of limited liability.

Sale The passing of title from the seller to the buyer for a price.

Sale on approval A type of conditional sale in which the buyer may take the goods on a trial basis. The sale becomes absolute only when the buyer approves of (or is satisfied with) the goods being sold.

Sale or return A type of conditional sale in which title and possession pass from the seller to the buyer; however, the buyer retains the option to return the goods during a specified period even though the goods conform to the contract.

Sales contract   A contract for the sale of goods under which the ownership of goods is transferred from a seller to a buyer for a price.

Scienter (pronounced sy-*en*-ter)   Knowledge by the misrepresenting party that material facts have been falsely represented or omitted with an intent to deceive.

Search warrant   An order granted by a public authority, such as a judge, that authorizes law-enforcement personnel to search particular premises or property.

Seasonably   Within a specified time period, or, if no period is specified, within a reasonable time.

SEC Rule 10b-5   A rule of the Securities and Exchange Commission that makes it unlawful, in connection with the purchase or sale of any security, to make any untrue statement of a material fact or to omit a material fact if such omission causes the statement to be misleading.

Secondary boycott   A union's refusal to work for, purchase from, or handle the products of a secondary employer, with whom the union has no dispute, for the purpose of forcing that employer to stop doing business with the primary employer, with whom the union has a labor dispute.

Secondary source of law   A publication that summarizes or interprets the law, such as a legal encyclopedia, a legal treatise, or an article in a law review.

Secured party   A lender, seller, or any other person in whose favor there is a security interest, including a person to whom accounts or chattel paper has been sold.

Secured transaction   Any transaction in which the payment of a debt is guaranteed, or secured, by personal property owned by the debtor or in which the debtor has a legal interest.

Security   Generally, a stock certificate, bond, note, debenture, warrant, or other document given as evidence of an ownership interest in a corporation or as a promise of repayment by a corporation.

Security agreement   An agreement that creates or provides for a security interest between the debtor and a secured party.

Security interest   Any interest "in personal property or fixtures which secures payment or performance of an obligation" [UCC 1–201(37)].

Self-defense   The legally recognized privilege to protect one's self or property against injury by another. The privilege of self-defense protects only

acts that are reasonably necessary to protect one's self or property.

Seniority system   In regard to employment relationships, a system in which those who have worked longest for the company are first in line for promotions, salary increases, and other benefits; they are also the last to be laid off if the work force must be reduced.

Service mark   A mark used in the sale or the advertising of services, such as to distinguish the services of one person from the services of others. Titles, character names, and other distinctive features of radio and television programs may be registered as service marks.

Sexual harassment   In the employment context, the granting of job promotions or other benefits in return for sexual favors or language or conduct that is so sexually offensive that it creates a hostile working environment.

Shareholder's derivative suit   A suit brought by a shareholder to enforce a corporate cause of action against a third person.

Shelter principle   The principle that the holder of a negotiable instrument who cannot qualify as a holder in due course (HDC), but who derives his or her title through an HDC, acquires the rights of an HDC.

Shipment contract   A contract for the sale of goods in which the seller is required or authorized to ship the goods by carrier. The buyer assumes liability for any losses or damage to the goods after they are delivered to the carrier.

Short-form merger   A merger between a subsidiary corporation and a parent corporation that owns at least 90 percent of the outstanding shares of each class of stock issued by the subsidiary corporation. Short-form mergers can be accomplished without the approval of the shareholders of either corporation.

Signature   Under the UCC, "any symbol executed or adopted by a party with a present intention to authenticate a writing."

Slander   Defamation in oral form.

Slander of quality (trade libel)   The publication of false information about another's product, alleging that it is not what its seller claims.

Slander of title   The publication of a statement that denies or casts doubt upon another's legal ownership of any property, causing financial loss to that property's owner.

Small claims courts   Special courts in which parties may litigate small claims (usually, claims involving $2,500 or less). Attorneys are not required in small claims courts, and in many states attorneys are not allowed to represent the parties.

Sole proprietorship The simplest form of business, in which the owner is the business; the owner reports business income on his or her personal income tax return and is legally responsible for all debts and obligations incurred by the business.

Special indorsement An indorsement on an instrument that indicates the specific person to whom the indorser intends to make the instrument payable; that is, it names the indorsee.

Specific performance An equitable remedy requiring exactly the performance that was specified in a contract; usually granted only when money damages would be an inadequate remedy and the subject matter of the contract is unique (for example, real property).

Spendthrift trust A trust created to protect the beneficiary from spending all the money to which he or she is entitled. Only a certain portion of the total amount is given to the beneficiary at any one time, and most states prohibit creditors from attaching assets of the trust.

Stale check A check, other than a certified check, that is presented for payment more than six months after its date.

Standing to sue The requirement that an individual must have a sufficient stake in a controversy before he or she can bring a lawsuit. The plaintiff must demonstrate that he or she either has been injured or threatened with injury.

Stare decisis (pronounced *ster*-ay dih-*si*-ses) A common law doctrine under which judges are obligated to follow the precedents established in prior decisions.

Statute of Frauds A state statute under which certain types of contracts must be in writing to be enforceable.

Statute of limitations A federal or state statute setting the maximum time period during which a certain action can be brought or certain rights enforced.

Statutory law The body of law enacted by legislative bodies (as opposed to constitutional law, administrative law, or case law).

Stock An equity (ownership) interest in a corporation, measured in units of shares.

Stock certificate A certificate issued by a corporation evidencing the ownership of a specified number of shares in the corporation.

Stock warrant A certificate that grants the owner the option to buy a given number of shares of stock, usually within a set time period.

Stop-payment order An order by a bank customer to his or her bank not to pay or certify a certain check.

Strict liability Liability regardless of fault. In tort law, strict liability may be imposed on defendants in cases involving abnormally dangerous activities, dangerous animals, or defective products.

Sublease A lease executed by the lessee of real estate to a third person, conveying the same interest that the lessee enjoys but for a shorter term than that held by the lessee.

Substantive law Law that defines, describes, regulates, and creates legal rights and obligations.

Summary jury trial (SJT) A method of settling disputes in which a trial is held, but the jury's verdict is not binding. The verdict acts only as a guide to both sides in reaching an agreement during the mandatory negotiations that immediately follow the summary jury trial.

Summons A document informing a defendant that a legal action has been commenced against him or her and that the defendant must appear in court on a certain date to answer the plaintiff's complaint. The document is delivered by a sheriff or any other person so authorized.

Supremacy clause The provision in Article VI of the Constitution that provides that the Constitution, laws, and treaties of the United States are "the supreme Law of the Land." Under this clause, state and local laws that directly conflict with federal law will be rendered invalid.

Surety A person, such as a cosigner on a note, who agrees to be primarily responsible for the debt of another.

Suretyship An express contract in which a third party to a debtor-creditor relationship (the surety) promises to be primarily responsible for the debtor's obligation.

T

Taking The taking of private property by the government for public use. Under the Fifth Amendment to the Constitution, the government may not take private property for public use without "just compensation."

Tangible property Property that has physical existence and can be distinguished by the senses of touch, sight, and so on. A car is tangible property; a patent right is intangible property.

Target corporation The corporation to be acquired in a corporate takeover; a corporation to whose shareholders a tender offer is submitted.

Tenancy at sufferance A type of tenancy under which one who, after rightfully being in possession of leased premises, continues (wrongfully) to occupy the property after the lease has been terminated. The tenant has no rights to possess the property and occupies it only because the person entitled to evict the tenant has not done so.

Tenancy at will A type of tenancy under which either party can terminate the tenancy without notice; usually arises when a tenant who has been under a tenancy for years retains possession, with the landlord's consent, after the tenancy for years has terminated.

Tenancy by the entirety The joint ownership of property by a husband and wife. Neither party can transfer his or her interest in the property without the consent of the other.

Tenancy for years A type of tenancy under which property is leased for a specified period of time, such as a month, a year, or a period of years.

Tenancy in common Co-ownership of property in which each party owns an undivided interest that passes to his or her heirs at death.

Tender An unconditional offer to perform an obligation by a person who is ready, willing, and able to do so.

Tender offer An offer to purchase made by one company directly to the shareholders of another (target) company; often referred to as a "takeover bid."

Testamentary trust A trust that is created by will and therefore does not take effect until the death of the testator.

Testator One who makes and executes a will.

Third party beneficiary One for whose benefit a promise is made in a contract but who is not a party to the contract.

Tippee A person who receives inside information.

Tombstone ad An advertisement, historically in a format resembling a tombstone, of a securities offering. The ad informs potential investors of where and how they may obtain a prospectus.

Tort A civil wrong not arising from a breach of contract. A breach of a legal duty that proximately causes harm or injury to another.

Tortfeasor One who commits a tort.

Totten trust A trust created by the deposit of a person's own money in his or her own name as a trustee for another. It is a tentative trust, revocable at will until the depositor dies or completes the gift in his or her lifetime by some unequivocal act or declaration.

Trade acceptance A draft that is drawn by a seller of goods ordering the buyer to pay a specified sum of money to the seller, usually at a stated time in the future. The buyer accepts the draft by signing the face of the draft, thus creating an enforceable obligation to pay the draft when it comes due. On a trade acceptance, the seller is both the drawer and the payee.

Trade name A term that is used to indicate part or all of a business's name and that is directly related to the business's reputation and goodwill. Trade names are protected under the common law (and under trademark law, if the name is the same as the firm's trademarked property).

Trade secrets Information or processes that give a business an advantage over competitors who do not know the information or processes.

Trademark A distinctive mark, motto, device, or implement that a manufacturer stamps, prints, or otherwise affixes to the goods it produces so that they may be identified on the market and their origins made known. Once a trademark is established (under the common law or through registration), the owner is entitled to its exclusive use.

Transfer warranties Implied warranties, made by any person who transfers an instrument for consideration to subsequent transferees and holders who take the instrument in good faith, that (1) the transferor is entitled to enforce the instrument, (2) all signatures are authentic and authorized, (3) the instrument has not been altered, (4) the instrument is not subject to a defense or claim of any party that can be asserted against the transferor, and (5) the transferor has no knowledge of any insolvency proceedings against the maker, the acceptor, or the drawer of the instrument.

Traveler's check A check that is payable on demand, drawn on or payable through a bank, and designated as a traveler's check.

Treaty An agreement formed between two or more independent nations.

Trespass to land The entry onto, above, or below the surface of land owned by another without the owner's permission or legal authorization.

Trespass to personal property The unlawful taking or harming of another's personal property; interference with another's right to the exclusive possession of his or her personal property.

Trust An arrangement in which title to property is held by one person (a trustee) for the benefit of another (a beneficiary).

Trust indorsement An indorsement for the benefit of the indorser or a third person; also known as an agency indorsement. The indorsement results in legal title vesting in the original indorsee.

U

U.S. trustee A government official who performs certain administrative tasks that a bankruptcy judge would otherwise have to perform.

Ultra vires (pronounced *uhl*-trah *vye*-reez) A Latin term meaning "beyond the powers"; in corporate law, acts of a corporation that are beyond its express and implied powers to undertake.

Unconscionable (pronounced un-*kon*-shun-uh-bul) contract (or unconscionable clause) A contract or clause that is void on the basis of public policy because one party, as a result of his or her disproportionate bargaining power, is forced to accept terms that are unfairly burdensome and that unfairly benefit the dominating party.

Underwriter In insurance law, the insurer, or the one assuming a risk in return for the payment of a premium.

Undisclosed principal A principal whose identity is unknown by a third person, and the third person has no knowledge that the agent is acting for a principal at the time the agent and the third person form a contract.

Unenforceable contract A valid contract rendered unenforceable by some statute or law.

Unilateral contract A contract that results when an offer can only be accepted by the offeree's performance.

Union shop A place of employment in which all workers, once employed, must become union members within a specified period of time as a condition of their continued employment.

Universal defenses Defenses that are valid against all holders of a negotiable instrument, including holders in due course (HDCs) and holders with the rights of HDCs.

Unreasonably dangerous product In product liability, a product that is defective to the point of threatening a consumer's health and safety. A product will be considered unreasonably dangerous if it is dangerous beyond the expectation of the ordinary consumer or if a less dangerous alternative was economically feasible for the manufacturer, but the manufacturer failed to produce it.

Usage of trade Any practice or method of dealing having such regularity of observance in a place, vocation, or trade as to justify an expectation that it will be observed with respect to the transaction in question.

Usury Charging an illegal rate of interest.

Utilitarianism An approach to ethical reasoning in which ethically correct behavior is not related to any absolute ethical or moral values but to an evaluation of the consequences of a given action on those who will be affected by it. In utilitarian reasoning, a "good" decision is one that results in the greatest good for the greatest number of people affected by the decision.

V

Valid contract A contract that results when elements necessary for contract formation (agreement, consideration, legal purpose, and contractual capacity) are present.

Venue (pronounced *ven*-yoo) The geographical district in which an action is tried and from which the jury is selected.

Vesting The creation of an absolute or unconditional right or power.

Void contract A contract having no legal force or binding effect.

Voidable contract A contract that may be legally avoided (canceled, or annulled) at the option of one of the parties.

Voir dire (pronounced vwahr-*deehr*) A French phrase meaning "to speak the truth." In jury trials, the phrase refers to the process in which the attorneys question prospective jurors to determine whether they are biased or have any connection with a party of the action or with a prospective witness.

Voting trust An agreement (trust contract) under which legal title to shares of corporate stock is transferred to a trustee who is authorized by the shareholders to vote the shares on their behalf.

W

Warranty deed A deed in which the grantor guarantees to the grantee that the grantor has title to the property conveyed in the deed, that there are no encumbrances on the property other than what the grantor has represented, and that the grantee will enjoy quiet possession of the property; a deed that provides the greatest amount of protection for the grantee.

Watered stock Shares of stock issued by a corporation for which the corporation receives, as payment, less than the stated value of the shares.

Whistleblowing An employee's disclosure to government, the press, or upper-management authorities that the employer is engaged in unsafe or illegal activities.

White-collar crime Nonviolent crime committed by individuals or corporations to obtain a personal or business advantage.

Will An instrument directing what is to be done with the testator's property upon his or her death, made by the testator and revocable during his or her lifetime. No interests in the testator's property pass until the testator dies.

Winding up The second of two stages involved in the termination of a partnership or corporation. Once the firm is dissolved, it continues to exist legally until the process of winding up all business affairs (collecting and distributing the firm's assets) is complete.

Workers' compensation laws State statutes establishing an administrative procedure for compensating workers' injuries that arise out of—or in the course of—their employment, regardless of fault.

Working papers The various documents used and developed by an accountant during an audit.

Working papers include notes, computations, memoranda, copies, and other papers that make up the work product of an accountant's services to a client.

Workout An out-of-court agreement between a debtor and his or her creditors in which the parties work out a payment plan or schedule under which the debtor's debts can be discharged.

Writ of attachment A court's order, prior to a trial to collect a debt, directing the sheriff or other officer to seize nonexempt property of the debtor; if the creditor prevails at trial, the seized property can be sold to satisfy the judgment.

Writ of *certiorari* (pronounced sur-shee-uh-*rah-ree*) A writ from a higher court asking the lower court for the record of a case.

Writ of execution A court's order, after a judgment has been entered against the debtor, directing the sheriff to seize (levy) and sell any of the debtor's nonexempt real or personal property. The proceeds of the sale are used to pay off the judgment, accrued interest, and costs of the sale; any surplus is paid to the debtor.

Wrongful discharge An employer's termination of an employee's employment in violation of an employment contract or laws that protect employees.

Table of Cases

Index